THE BOOK OF GENESIS

SUPPLEMENTS TO VETUS TESTAMENTUM

Editor in Chief
Christl M. Maier

Editorial Board

R. P. Gordon – J. Joosten – G. N. Knoppers – A. van der Kooij –
A. Lemaire – S. L. Mckenzie – C. A. Newsom – H. Spieckermann –
J. Trebolle Barrera – N. Wazana – S. D. Weeks – H. G. M. Williamson

Formation and Interpretation of Old Testament Literature
Editors
Craig A. Evans and Peter W. Flint

Number 152

THE BOOK OF GENESIS

Composition, Reception, and Interpretation

Edited by
Craig A. Evans, Joel N. Lohr, and David L. Petersen

SBL PRESS

Atlanta

Copyright © 2012 by Koninklijke Brill NV, Leiden, The Netherlands

This edition is published under license from Koninklijke Brill NV, Leiden, The Netherlands, by SBL Press.

All rights reserved. No part of this work may be reproduced or transmitted in any form or by any means, electronic or mechanical, including photocopying and recording, or by means of any information storage or retrieval system, except as may be expressly permitted by the 1976 Copyright Act or in writing from the publisher. Requests for permission should be addressed in writing to the Rights and Permissions Department, Koninklijke Brill NV, Leiden, The Netherlands.

Authorization to photocopy items for internal or personal use is granted by Brill provided that the appropriate fees are paid directly to The Copyright Clearance Center, 222 Rosewood Drive, Suite 910, Danvers, MA 01923, USA. Fees are subject to change.

Library of Congress Control Number: 2017931598

Printed on acid-free paper.

CONTENTS

Preface IX
Abbreviations XI
List of Contributors XXI

PART ONE

GENERAL TOPICS

The Study of the Book of Genesis: The Beginning of Critical Reading .. 3
   Jean-Louis Ska

Genesis in the Pentateuch 27
   Konrad Schmid

Historical Context 51
   Ronald Hendel

Literary Analysis 83
   Robert S. Kawashima

PART TWO

ISSUES IN INTERPRETATION

The Formation of the Primeval History 107
   Jan Christian Gertz

Food and the First Family: A Socioeconomic Perspective 137
   Carol Meyers

Abraham Traditions in the Hebrew Bible outside the Book of Genesis 159
   Thomas Römer

The Jacob Tradition 181
   Erhard Blum

Genesis 37–50: Joseph Story or Jacob Story? 213
   Richard J. Clifford

Joseph and Wisdom 231
    Michael V. Fox

How the Compiler of the Pentateuch Worked: The Composition of
    Genesis 37 263
    Baruch J. Schwartz

The World of the Family in Genesis 279
    Naomi A. Steinberg

PART THREE

TEXTUAL TRANSMISSION AND RECEPTION HISTORY

Genesis in Josephus... 303
    Christopher T. Begg

Cain and Abel in Second Temple Literature and Beyond 331
    John Byron

Genesis in the Dead Sea Scrolls 353
    Sidnie White Crawford

Genesis and Its Reception in Jubilees 375
    C.T.R. Hayward

Textual and Translation Issues in Greek Genesis 405
    Robert J.V. Hiebert

When the Beginning Is the End: The Place of Genesis in the
    Commentaries of Philo 427
    Gregory E. Sterling

The Reception of Genesis in Pseudo-Philo's *Liber Antiquitatum
    Biblicarum* 447
    Rhonda J. Burnette-Bletsch

Genesis in the New Testament 469
    Craig A. Evans

Genesis in Aramaic: The Example of Chapter 22 495
    Bruce Chilton

The *Vetus Latina* and the Vulgate of the Book of Genesis 519
    David L. Everson

Genesis in Syriac 537
  Jerome A. Lund

The Fathers on Genesis 561
  Andrew Louth

Genesis in Rabbinic Interpretation 579
  Burton L. Visotzky

Genesis, the Qur'ān and Islamic Interpretation 607
  Carol Bakhos

PART FOUR

GENESIS AND THEOLOGY

The Theology of Genesis 635
  Joel S. Kaminsky

Genesis in the Context of Jewish Thought 657
  Marvin A. Sweeney

Genesis and Ecology 683
  Terence E. Fretheim

INDICES

Scripture and Other Ancient Writings 709
Modern Authors 751

PREFACE

The Book of Genesis: Composition, Reception, and Interpretation contains twenty-nine essays on a range of topics in four main sections: (a) General Topics; (b) Issues in Interpretation; (c) Textual Transmission and Reception History; and (d) Genesis and Theology. The contributors were invited with a view to representing the spectrum of opinion in the current interpretation of the Book of Genesis, on the topics just mentioned.

This is the sixth volume in the series The Formation and Interpretation of Old Testament Literature (FIOTL), which appears in the Vetus Testament Supplements (VTSup). The purpose of the FIOTL volumes is to examine and explore the prehistory, contents, and themes of the books of the Old Testament/Hebrew Bible as well as their reception and interpretation in later Jewish and Christian literature. The volumes that have appeared to date have treated Isaiah (1997), Daniel (2001), Leviticus (2002), Psalms (2004), and Kings (2010). More volumes are in preparation.

The editors would like to extend thanks to various people. First, to all the contributors for meeting various deadlines and working hard and harmoniously to render the editing process smooth and effective. Second, to a number of graduate assistants who helped with indexing and other matters, especially Tyler Bennicke, Brian LePort, Greg Monette, and Tyler Vandergaag. Third, to Prof. Dr. Christl M. Maier and the VTSup Board for their support of the FIOTL volumes as part of the VTSup series. Fourth, and finally, we are most grateful to the team at Brill Academic Publishers, especially Liesbeth Hugenholtz and Gera van Bedaf for their guidance and encouragement in the production of this book.

November 1, 2011

Craig A. Evans
Acadia Divinity College

Joel N. Lohr
Trinity Western University

David L. Petersen
Emory University

ABBREVIATIONS

For most terms, sigla, and abbreviations of journals and other secondary sources, see Patrick H. Alexander et al., eds., *The SBL Handbook of Style for Ancient Near Eastern, Biblical, and Early Christian Studies* (Peabody, Mass.: Hendrickson, 1999). For Qumran sigla, see also Joseph A. Fitzmyer, *The Dead Sea Scrolls: Major Publications and Tools for Study* (rev. ed.; SBLRBS 20; Atlanta: Scholars Press, 1990), 1–8.

AASF	Annales Academiae Scientiarum Fennicae
ÄAT	Ägypten und Altes Testament
AAWG.PH	Abhandlungen der Akademie der Wissenschaften in Göttingen. Philologisch-Historische Klasse
AB	Anchor Bible (Commentary Series)
ABD	David N. Freedman, ed., *The Anchor Bible Dictionary* (6 vols.; New York: Doubleday, 1992)
ABP	Michael V. Fox, *Proverbs 1–9* (Anchor Bible 18A; New York: Doubleday, 2000) and *Proverbs 10–31* (Anchor Bible 18B; New Haven: Yale University Press, 2009)
AbrN	*Abr-Nahrain*
AbrNSup	Abr-Nahrain Supplement Series
AcOr	*Acta orientalia*
Aeg	*Aegyptus*
AEL	Miriam Lichtheim, ed., *Ancient Egyptian Literature* (3 vols.; Berkeley: University of California Press, 1973–1980)
AGJU	Arbeiten zur Geschichte des antiken Judentums und des Urchristentums
AHR	*American Historical Review*
AJP	*American Journal of Philology*
AJSR	*Association for Jewish Studies Review*
ALGHJ	Arbeiten zur Literatur und Geschichte des hellenistischen Judentums
AnBib	Analecta biblica
ANEP	J.B. Pritchard, ed., *The Ancient Near East in Pictures Relating to the Old Testament* (Princeton: Princeton University Press, 1954)
ANET	J.B. Pritchard, ed., *Ancient Near Eastern Texts Relating to the Old Testament* (3rd ed.; Princeton, Princeton University Press, 1969)
ANF	*Ante-Nicene Fathers*
ANRW	Wolfgang Haase and Hildegard Temporini, eds., *Aufstieg und Niedergang der römischen Welt* (Berlin: de Gruyter, 1979–)
AOS	American Oriental Series

APOT	R.H. Charles, ed., *Apocrypha and Pseudepigrapha of the Old Testament* (2 vols.; Oxford: Clarendon, 1913)
ArBib	The Aramaic Bible
AS	*Aramaic Studies*
ASBF	Analecta Studium Biblicum Franciscanum
ATANT	Abhandlungen zur Theologie des Alten und Neuen Testaments
ATAT	Arbeiten zu Text und Sprache im Alten Testament
ATD	Das Alte Testament Deutsch
ATM	Altes Testament und Moderne
b.	born
BA	*Biblical Archaeologist*
BAG	W. Bauer, W.F. Arndt, and F.W. Gingrich, *A Greek-English Lexicon of the New Testament* (Chicago: University of Chicago Press, 1957)
BAGD	W. Bauer, W.F. Arndt, F.W. Gingrich, and F.W. Danker, *A Greek-English Lexicon of the New Testament* (2nd ed.; Chicago: University of Chicago Press, 1979)
BAR	*Biblical Archaeology Review*
BASOR	*Bulletin of the American Schools of Oriental Research*
BBET	Beiträge zur biblischen Exegese und Theologie
BDAG	W. Bauer, F.W. Danker, W.F. Arndt, and F.W. Gingrich, *Greek-English Lexicon of the New Testament and Other Early Christian Literature* (3rd ed.; Chicago: University of Chicago Press, 1999)
BDB	F. Brown, S.R. Driver, and C.A. Briggs, *A Hebrew and English Lexicon of the Old Testament* (Oxford: Clarendon, 1907)
BEAT	Beiträge zur Einleitung ins Alte Testament
BETL	Bibliotheca ephemeridum theologicarum lovaniensium
BHK	R. Kittel, *Biblia hebraica*
BHS	*Biblia hebraica stuttgartensia*
BHT	Beiträge zur historischen Theologie
BI	*Biblical Illustrator*
Bib	*Biblica*
BibOr	Biblica et orientalia
BibSem	The Biblical Seminar
BIOSCS	*Bulletin of the International Organization for Septuagint and Cognate Studies*
BIS	Biblical Interpretation Series
BJS	Brown Judaic Studies
BK	*Bibel und Kirche*
BKAT	Biblischer Kommentar Altes Testament
BN	*Biblische Notizen*
BO	*Bibliotheca orientalis*
BR	*Biblical Research*
BSac	*Bibliotheca Sacra*
BSt	Biblische Studien
BThSt	Biblisch-Theologische Studien
BTM	Benjamin R. Foster, *Before the Muses: An Anthology of Akkadian Literature* (2 vols.; Bethesda, Md.: CDL Press, 1993)

BWANT	Beiträge zur Wissenschaft vom Alten und Neuen Testament
BZ	*Biblische Zeitschrift*
BZABR	Beihefte zur Zeitschrift für altorientalische und biblische Rechtsgeschichte
BZAW	Beihefte zur Zeitschrift für die alttestamentliche Wissenschaft
BZNW	Beihefte zur Zeitschrift für die neutestamentliche Wissenschaft
CAT	Manfried Dietrich, Oswald Loretz, and Joaquín Sanmartín, eds., *The Cuneiform Alphabetic Texts from Ugarit, Ras Ibn Hani and Other Places* (Münster: Ugarit-Verlag, 1995)
CBC	Cambridge Bible Commentary
CBIII	Papyrus Chester Beatty III. Alan H. Gardiner, ed., *Hieratic Papyri in the British Museum. Third Series: Chester Beatty Gift* (London: British Museum, 1935)
CBET	Contributions to Biblical Exegesis and Theology
CBQ	*Catholic Biblical Quarterly*
CBQMS	Catholic Biblical Quarterly Monograph Series
CC	Continental Commentaries
CCSL	Corpus Christianorum Series Latina
CD	Damascus Document
CEJL	Commentaries on Early Jewish Literature
CJA	Christianity and Judaism in Antiquity
col(s).	column(s)
COS	William W. Hallo and K. Lawson Younger Jr., eds., *Context of Scripture* (3 vols.; Leiden: Brill, 1997–2002)
CQS	Companion to the Qumran Scrolls
CR	*Critical Review of Books in Religion*
CRINT	Compendia rerum iudaicarum ad novum testamentum
CSCD	Cambridge Studies in Christian Doctrine
CSCO	Corpus scriptorum christianorum orientalium
CSJH	Chicago Studies in the History of Judaism
CSR	*Christian Scholars Review*
CSS	Collected Studies Series
CSSH	*Comparative Studies in Society and History*
CurBS	*Currents in Research: Biblical Studies*
C-XIII, C-XIV	Papyri Carlsberg XIII and XIV. Aksel Volten, ed., *Demotische Traumdeutung (Pap. Carlsberg XIII und XIV verso)* (Kopenhagen: Munksgaard, 1942)
d.	died
DBAT	*Dielheimer Blätter zum Alten Testament und seiner Rezeption in der Alten Kirche*
DDD	Karel van der Toorn, Bob Becking and Pieter W. van der Horst, eds., *Dictionary of Deities and Demons in the Bible* (2nd ed.; Leiden: Brill, 1999)
DJD	Discoveries in the Judaean Desert
DSD	*Dead Sea Discoveries*
dtr	deuteronomistic

DVLG	*Deutsche Vierteljahrsschrift für Literaturwissenschaft und Geistesgeschichte*
Ebib	Études bibliques
EHAT	Exegetisches Handbuch zum Alten Testament
EHS	Europäische Hochschulschriften
EI	P.J. Bearman, Th. Bianquis, C.E. Bosworth, E. van Donzel, and W.P. Heinrichs, eds., *Encyclopaedia of Islam* (2nd ed.; 12 vols. Leiden: Brill, 2002).
EML	Encyclopaedia Miqra'it Library
EncJud	C. Roth and G. Wigoder, eds., *Encyclopaedia Judaica* (16 vols.; Jerusalem: Keter, 1971–1972)
ErFor	Erträge der Forschung
ESV	English Standard Version (Bible)
ETR	*Études théologiques et religieuses*
FAT	Forschungen zum Alten Testament
FB	Forschung zur Bibel
FF	*Forschungen und Fortschritte*
FGrH	F. Jacoby, *Die Fragmente der griechischen Historiker* (Berlin: Weidmann, 1923–1930; Leiden: Brill, 1940–1958)
FIOTL	Formation and Interpretation of Old Testament Literature
FJTC	Flavius Josephus Translation and Commentary
FRC	Family, Religion, and Culture Series
FRLANT	Forschungen zur Religion und Literatur des Alten und Neuen Testaments
GA	Gesammelte Aufsätze
GDNES	Gorgias Dissertations Near Eastern Studies
GH	Gorgias Handbooks
GKC	*Gesenius' Hebrew Grammar* (ed. E. Kautzsch; trans. A.E. Cowley; 2nd ed.; Oxford: Clarendon, 1910)
GP	Gospel Perspectives
GTA	Göttinger theologische Arbeiter
HALOT	L. Koehler, W. Baumgartner, and J.J. Stamm, eds., *The Hebrew and Aramaic Lexicon of the Old Testament* (ed. and trans. under the supervision of M.E.J. Richardson; 4 vols.; Leiden: Brill, 1994–1999)
HAR	*Hebrew Annual Review*
HAT	Handbuch zum Alten Testament
HB	Hebrew Bible
HBS	Herders biblischen Studien
HBT	*Horizons in Biblical Theology*
HDR	Harvard Dissertations in Religion
Hermeneia	Hermeneia: A Critical and Historical Commentary on the Bible
HKAT	Handkommentar zum Alten Testament
HNT	Handbuch zum Neuen Testament
HOS	Handbook of Oriental Studies
HR	*History of Religions*
HS	*Hebrew Studies*
HSM	Harvard Semitic Monographs

HSS	Harvard Semitic Studies
HTKAT	Herders theologischer Kommentar zum Alten Testament
HTR	*Harvard Theological Review*
HUCA	*Hebrew Union College Annual*
IBHS	Bruce K. Waltke and M. O'Connor, *An Introduction to Biblical Hebrew Syntax* (Winona Lake, Ind.: Eisenbrauns, 1990)
IBR	Institute for Biblical Research
ICC	International Critical Commentary
IEJ	*Israel Exploration Journal*
IHC	Islamic History and Civilization: Studies and Texts
Int	*Interpretation*
IOS	*Israel Oriental Society*
IPTS	Islamic Philosophy, Theology, and Science
IRT	Issues in Religion and Theology
JAAR	*Journal of the American Academy of Religion*
JANES	*Journal of the Ancient Near Eastern*
JAOS	*Journal of the American Oriental Society*
JBL	*Journal of Biblical Literature*
JBT	Jahrbuch für biblische Theologie (Monograph Series)
JCP	Jewish and Christian Perspectives
JE	*Jüdische Enzyklopädie*
JECS	*Journal of Early Christian Studies*
JEOL	*Jaarbericht van het Vooraziatisch-Egyptisch Gezelschap (Genootschap) Ex oriente lux*
JES	*Journal of Ecumenical Studies*
JJS	*Journal of Jewish Studies*
JLCRS	Jordan Lectures in Comparative Religion Series
JNES	*Journal of Near Eastern Studies*
JNSL	*Journal of Northwest Semitic Languages*
JPS	Jewish Publication Society
JQR	*Jewish Quarterly Review*
JR	*Journal of Religion*
JRS	*Journal of Roman Studies*
JSJ	*Journal for the Study of Judaism in the Persian, Hellenistic and Roman Period*
JSJSup	Journal for the Study of Judaism in the Persian, Hellenistic and Roman Period Supplement Series
JSNT	*Journal for the Study of the New Testament*
JSNTSup	Journal for the Study of the New Testament Supplement Series
JSOT	*Journal for the Study of the Old Testament*
JSOTSup	Journal for the Study of the Old Testament Supplement Series
JSP	*Journal for the Study of the Pseudepigrapha*
JSPSup	Journal for the Study of the Pseudepigrapha Supplement Series
JSQ	*Jewish Studies Quarterly*
JSS	*Journal of Semitic Studies*
JTS	*Journal of Theological Studies*
KAT	Kommentar zum Alten Testament

KD	*Kerygma und Dogma*
KEHAT	Kurzgefasstes exegetisches Handbuch zum Alten Testament
LBH	Late Biblical Hebrew
LCL	Loeb Classical Library
LD	Lectio divina
LHBOTS	Library of Hebrew Bible/Old Testament Studies
LSJ	Liddell, Scott, Jones, *Greek-English Lexicon*
LSTS	Library of Second Temple Studies
LXX	Septuagint
MdB	Le Monde de la Bible
MGWJ	*Monatschrift für Geschichte und Wissenschaft des Judentums*
MM	J.H. Moulton and G. Milligan, eds., *The Vocabulary of the Greek New Testament* (London: Hodder and Stoughton, 1930; repr., Grand Rapids: Eerdmans, 1974)
MPIL	Monographs of the Peshitta Institute, Leiden
MS(S).	manuscript(s)
MSU	Mitteilungen des Septuaginta-Unternehmens
MT	Masoretic Text
NAB	New American Bible
NASB	New American Standard Bible
n.d.	no date (cited)
NEchtB	Neue Echter Bibel
NETS	Albert Pietersma and Benjamin G. Wright, eds., *A New English Translation of the Septuagint and the Other Greek Translations Traditionally Included under That Title* (New York: Oxford University Press, 2007)
NICNT	New International Commentary on the New Testament
NICOT	New International Commentary on the Old Testament
NIGTC	New International Greek Testament Commentary
NIV	New International Version (Bible)
NJB	New Jerusalem Bible
NJPS	*Tanakh: The Holy Scriptures: The New JPS Translation According to the Traditional Hebrew Text*
NovTSup	Novum Testamentum Supplements
n.p.	no publisher (cited)
NRSV	New Revised Standard Version (Bible)
NSKAT	Neuer Stuttgarter Kommentar Altes Testament
NTG	New Testament Guides
NTM	New Testament Message
NTS	*New Testament Studies*
OBO	Orbis biblicus et orientalis
OBT	Overtures to Biblical Theology
OCM	Oxford Classical Monographs
OPA	Les Œuvres de Philon d'Alexandrie
Or	*Orientalia*
OrChr	*Oriens christianus*
OrChrAn	Orientalia christiana analecta

OT	Old Testament
OTL	Old Testament Library
OTM	Oxford Theological Monographs
OTP	James H. Charlesworth, ed., *Old Testament Pseudepigrapha* (2 vols.; Garden City, N.Y.: Doubleday, 1983–1985)
OTS	*Oudtestamentische Studiën* (Journal)
OTS	Oudtestamentische Studiën (Monograph Series)
OtSt	*Oudtestamentische Studiën*
OTT	Old Testament Theology
PAAJR	*Proceedings of the American Academy of Jewish Research*
PACS	Philo of Alexandria Commentary Series
PAM	Palestine Archaeological Museum (in reference to the accession numbers of the photographs of the Dead Sea Scrolls)
PCW	Leopold Cohn, Paul Wendland, Sigofred Reiter, and Ioannes Leisegang, eds., *Philonis Alexandrini opera quae supersunt* (7 vols.; Berlin: Georg Reimer, 1896–1930; 2nd ed.; Berlin: de Gruyter, 1962)
PEQ	*Palestine Exploration Quarterly*
PG	J. Migne, ed., *Patrologia graeca*
PGL	G.W.H. Lampe, ed., *Patristic Greek Lexicon* (Oxford: Oxford University Press, 1968)
PHSC	Perspectives on Hebrew Scriptures and its Contexts
PL	J. Migne, ed., *Patrologia latina*
PL.	plural, plate
PLCL	Francis Henry Colson, George Herbert Whitaker, and Ralph Marcus, eds., *Philo* (10 vols. and 2 supplementary vols.; Loeb Classical Library; Cambridge: Harvard University Press, 1929–1962).
Proof	*Prooftexts: A Journal of Jewish Literary History*
PRSt	*Perspectives in Religious Studies*
PTSDSSP	Princeton Theological Seminary Dead Sea Scrolls Project
R.	Rabbi
RA	*Revue d'assyriologie et d'archéologie orientale*
RB	*Revue biblique*
REB	Revised English Bible
repr.	reprint(ed)
RestQ	*Restoration Quarterly*
rev.	revised
RevQ	*Revue de Qumran*
RHPR	*Revue d'histoire et de philosophie religieuses*
RM	Rowohlts Monographien
RPT	Religion in Philosophy and Theology
RSB	*Religious Studies Bulletin*
RSPT	*Revue des sciences philosophiques et théologiques*
RTP	*Revue de théologie et de philosophie*
SAC	Studies in Antiquity & Christianity
SAHL	Studies in the Archaeology and History of the Levant
SAIS	Studies in the Aramaic Interpretation of Scripture
SAL	Studies in Arabic Literature

SamP	Samaritan Pentateuch
SANT	Studien zum Alten und Neuen Testament
SB	F. Preisigke et al., eds., *Sammelbuch Griechischer Urkunde aus Ägypten*
SAPERE	Scripta Antiquitatis Posterioris ad Ethicam REligionemque pertinentia
SB	Sources bibliques
SBAB	Stuttgarter biblische Aufsatzbände
SBB	Stuttgarter biblische Beiträge
SBG	Studies in Biblical Greek
SBL	Society of Biblical Literature
SBLBMI	Society of Biblical Literature The Bible and its Modern Interpreters
SBLDS	Society of Biblical Literature Dissertation Series
SBLEJL	Society of Biblical Literature Early Judaism and Its Literature
SBLit	Studies in Biblical Literature Series
SBLRBS	Society of Biblical Literature Resources for Biblical Study
SBLSCS	Society of Biblical Literature Septuagint and Cognate Studies
SBLSP	Society of Biblical Literature Seminar Papers
SBLSymS	Society of Biblical Literature Symposium Series
SBLTT	Society of Biblical Literature Texts and Translations
SBS	Stuttgarter Bibelstudien
SBTS	Sources for Biblical and Theological Study
SC	Sources chrétiennes (Paris: Cerf, 1943–)
ScrHier	Scripta hierosolymitana
SCS	Septuagint Commentary Series
SDSSRL	Studies in the Dead Sea Scrolls and Related Literature
SE	*Studia Evangelica*
SFSHJ	South Florida Studies in the History of Judaism
SH	*Studia Heirosolymitana*
SHANE	Studies in the History of the Ancient Near East
SHBC	Smyth & Helwys Bible Commentary
SHCANE	Studies in the History and Culture of the Ancient Near East
SHR	Studies in the History of Religions
SHT	Studies in Historical Theology
SJ	Studia Judaica
SJLA	Studies in Judaism in Late Antiquity
SJOT	*Scandinavian Journal of the Old Testament*
SO	*Symbolae osloenses*
Sound	*Soundings*
SP	Sacra Pagina
SPAMA	Studies in Philo of Alexandria and Mediterranean Antiquity
SPhA	*Studia Philonica Annual: Studies in Hellenistic Judaism*
SPhilo	*Studia Philonica*
SRB	Studies in Rewritten Bible
SSH	*Social Science History*
SSL	Studies in Semitic Languages and Linguistics
SSN	Studia semitica neerlandica

ST	*Studia theologica*
STDJ	Studies on the Texts of the Desert of Judah
STLI	*Studies and Texts*. Philip W. Lown Institute of Advanced Judaic Studies, Brandeis University.
StOr	Studia orientalia
StPB	Studia post-biblica
StZ	*Stimmen der Zeit*
SUNT	Studien zum Umwelt des Neuen Testaments
SUNY	State University of New York
SVTP	Studia in veteris testamenti pseudepigrapha
SWBA	Social World of Biblical Antiquity
SWR	Studies in Women and Religion
TAD	Bezalel Porten and Ada Yardeni, eds., *Textbook of Aramaic Documents from Ancient Egypt* (4 vols.; Jerusalem: Hebrew University, 1986–1999)
TAPS	Transactions of the American Philosophical Society
TB	Theologische Bücherei
TBN	Themes in Biblical Narrative
TCH	The Transformation of the Classical Heritage (Series)
TDOT	G.J. Botterweck and H. Ringgren, eds., *Theological Dictionary of the Old Testament* (Grand Rapids: Eerdmans, 1974–)
Th	*Theology*
THAT	E. Jenni and C. Westermann, eds., *Theologisches Handwörterbuch zum Alten Testament* (2 vols.; Munich: Kaiser, 1971–1976)
ThH	Théologie historique
THKNT	Theologischer Handkommentar zum Neuen Testament
THL	Theory and History of Literature (Series)
TLG	*Thesaurus linguae graecae: Canon of Greek Authors and Works* (ed. L. Berkowitz and K.A. Squitier; 3rd ed.; Oxford: Oxford University Press, 1990)
TQ	*Theologische Quartalschrift*
TRE	*Theologische Realenzyklopädie*
TrinJ	*Trinity Journal*
TRu	*Theologische Rundschau*
TS	*Theological Studies*
TS	Texts and Studies
TSAJ	Texte und Studien zum antiken Judentum
TSK	*Theologische Studien und Kritiken*
TSQ	Texts and Studies on the Qurʾān
TTZ	*Trierer theologische Zeitschrift*
TU	Texte und Untersuchungen
TUGAL	Texte und Untersuchungen zur Geschichte der altchristlichen Literatur
TW	Theologische Wissenschaft
TZ	*Theologische Zeitschrift*
UCOP	University of Cambridge Oriental Publications
UTB	Uni-Taschenbücher

VC	*Vigiliae christianae*
VF	*Verkündigung und Forschung*
Vg.	Vulgate
VT	*Vetus Testamentum*
VTSup	Vetus Testamentum Supplements
WBC	Word Biblical Commentary
WMANT	Wissenschaftliche Monographien zum Alten und Neuen Testament
WO	*Die Welt des Orients*
WUNT	Wissenschaftliche Untersuchungen zum Neuen Testament
WWSup	Word and World Supplement Series
YJS	Yale Judaica Series
ZA	*Zeitschrift für Assyriologie*
ZABR	*Zeitschrift für altorientalische und biblische Rechtgeschichte*
ZAW	*Zeitschrift für die alttestamentliche Wissenschaft*
ZBK	Zürcher Bibelkommentare
ZDPV	*Zeitschrift des deutschen Palästina-Vereins*
ZNW	*Zeitschrift für die neutestamentliche Wissenschaft*
ZPE	*Zeitschrift für Papyrologie und Epigraphik*
ZTK	*Zeitschrift für Theologie und Kirche*

LIST OF CONTRIBUTORS

Carol Bakhos
University of California, Los Angeles

Christopher T. Begg
Catholic University of America, Washington, D.C.

Erhard Blum
Universität Tübingen

Rhonda J. Burnette-Bletsch
Greensboro College

John Byron
Ashland Seminary

Bruce Chilton
Bard College, Annandale-on-Hudson

Richard J. Clifford
Boston College

Sidnie White Crawford
University of Nebraska-Lincoln

Craig A. Evans (Editor)
Acadia Divinity College, Wolfville, Nova Scotia

David L. Everson
Xavier University, Cincinnati

Michael V. Fox
University of Wisconsin-Madison

Terence E. Fretheim
Luther Seminary, St. Paul

Jan Christian Gertz
Universität Heidelberg

C.T.R. Hayward
Durham University

Ronald Hendel
University of California, Berkeley

Robert J. V. Hiebert
Trinity Western University, Langley, British Columbia

Joel S. Kaminsky
Smith College, Northampton

Robert S. Kawashima
University of Florida, Gainesville

Joel N. Lohr (Editor)
Trinity Western University, Langley, British Columbia

Andrew Louth
Durham University

Jerome A. Lund
Temple Baptist College, Cincinnati

Carol Meyers
Duke University, Durham, North Carolina

David L. Petersen (Editor)
Emory University, Atlanta

Thomas Römer
Collège de France, Paris and Université de Lausanne

Konrad Schmid
Universität Zürich

Baruch J. Schwartz
The Hebrew University of Jerusalem

Jean-Louis Ska
Pontifical Biblical Institute, Rome

Naomi A. Steinberg
DePaul University, Chicago

Gregory E. Sterling
University of Notre Dame

Marvin A. Sweeney
Claremont Lincoln University and Claremont School of Theology

Burton L. Visotzky
Jewish Theological Seminary, New York

PART ONE

GENERAL TOPICS

THE STUDY OF THE BOOK OF GENESIS: THE BEGINNING OF CRITICAL READING

Jean-Louis Ska

INTRODUCTION

"Genesis ist eine Sammlung von Sagen"—"Genesis is a collection of popular tales." Everyone knows Gunkel's motto at the beginning of his commentary on the Book of Genesis.[1] Gunkel's commentary is a milestone in the study of Genesis for many reasons. Two of them seem to me to be of special importance. First, Gunkel affirms very clearly that the book of Genesis is not unified—it is a "collection" of texts rather than a coherent literary work, or "book" in the modern sense of the word. Second, it contains "popular tales," or "legends"—the German word *Sage* has been translated in different ways and has been the object of several discussions.[2] One thing is clear, however: for Gunkel the book of Genesis does not belong to the literary genre of historiography.

Gunkel's motto is familiar, but what is much less familiar is the terrible battle that took place over this affirmation, and similar affirmations, before Gunkel's commentary and even for a long time afterwards. Another commentary on Genesis published not long before Gunkel's bears the significant title *The Unity of the Book of Genesis*, by William Henry Green (1895).[3]

---

[1] Hermann Gunkel, *Genesis übersetzt und erklärt* (8th ed.; HKAT 1/1; Göttingen: Vandenhoeck & Ruprecht, 1969), vii; translated as *Genesis* (trans. Mark E. Biddle; Macon, Ga.: Mercer University Press, 1997).

[2] See, for instance, John J. Scullion, "*Märchen, Sage, Legende*: Towards a Clarification of Some Literary Terms Used by Old Testament Scholars," *VT* 34 (1984): 321–336.

[3] William Henry Green, *The Unity of the Book of Genesis* (New York: Charles Scribner's Sons, 1895). See other similar titles such as Moritz Drechsler, *Die Einheit und Ächtheit der Genesis oder Erklärung derjenigen Erscheinungen in der Genesis, welche wider den Mosaischen Ursprung derselben geltend gemacht werden* (Hamburg: Perthes, 1838); Johannes Heinrich Kurtz, *Beiträge zur Vertheidigung und Begründung der Einheit des Pentateuchs* (Königsberg:

Historicity is another topic that has agitated spirits for a long time. Let me mention only one title that everyone will recall since it provoked innumerable reactions and upheavals, and is still discussed today: *The Historicity of the Patriarchal Narratives*, by Thomas L. Thompson.[4]

"Unity," "historicity": with these two words we come to grips with some of the main problems raised by the Book of Genesis. To be sure, there are many problems, and in this short article I will not be able to mention them all. There have been and there are still many—some would say too many—theories about the Book of Genesis. Let me bring up three series of problems at least. First, there is the question as to whether we find in Genesis a combination of different sources, or of original fragments put together at a later stage, or of an original kernel to which several supplements were added at different moments, or—possibly—a combination of these models.[5] Second, there is an ongoing discussion on the possible presence, in Genesis, of several redactions and traces of different editions, or the hand of real "authors."[6] Third, from the point of view of methodology, there is a debate about the respective value of synchronic and/or diachronic exegesis.[7]

My contention is, however, that a large number of discussions about the Book of Genesis originate in a fundamental difference of point of view. Some stress from the start that the Book of Genesis is a human work of literature that can be studied "as any other book" or any other piece of literature. Others, on the contrary, insist on the peculiar character of this book, its

---

Gräfe, 1844); and Kurtz, *Die Einheit der Genesis: Ein Beitrag zur Kritik und Exegese der Genesis* (Berlin: Wohlgemuth, 1846).

[4] Thomas L. Thompson, *The Historicity of the Patriarchal Narratives: The Quest for the Historical Abraham* (BZAW 133; Berlin: de Gruyter, 1974).

[5] See, for instance, Bill T. Arnold, "Pentateuchal Criticism, History of," in *Dictionary of the Old Testament: Pentateuch* (ed. T. Desmond Alexander and David W. Baker; Leicester: InterVarsity, 2003), 622–631.

[6] For a summary of the debate and a very personal position on this issue, see John Van Seters, *The Edited Bible: The Curious History of the 'Editor' in Biblical Criticism* (Winona Lake, Ind.: Eisenbrauns, 2006).

[7] See, for instance, Johan C. de Moor, ed., *Synchronic or Diachronic? A Debate on Method in Old Testament Exegesis* (OTS 35; Leiden: Brill, 1995); Erhard Blum, "Von Sinn und Nutzen der Kategorie 'Synchronie' in der Exegese," in *David und Saul im Widerstreit—Diachronie und Synchronie im Wettstreit: Beiträge zur Auslegung des ersten Sanuelbuches* (ed. Walter Dietrich; OBO 206; Göttingen: Vandenhoeck & Ruprecht, 2004), 16–29; and Alphonso Groenewald, "Synchrony and/or Diachrony: Is there a Way out of the Methodological Labyrinth?" in *A Critical Study of the Pentateuch: An Encounter between Europe and Africa* (ed. Eckart Otto and J. Le Roux; ATM 20; Münster: Lit Verlag, 2005), 50–61.

claim to truth, its theological aspect, and its religious content that prevent the reader from treating the book as other works of "profane" or secular literature. On the one side, we find Hermann Gunkel; on the other, we find Ernst Wilhelm Hengstenberg (1802–1869)[8] or, to a lesser extent, Franz Delitzsch (1813–1890).[9]

I will try to show that this is an old question, as old as Ibn Ezra at least, and that it caused a number of storms in the academic waters of the eighteenth and the nineteenth centuries. This will enable us, I think, to understand better what is at stake today in our discussion on the same topic. I will start with Ibn Ezra, although it would be possible to go back to earlier periods and mention some related discussions among the rabbis or the fathers of the Church.[10] The reason I chose to begin with Ibn Ezra is simple: he has been particularly influential, especially when we consider Spinoza's use of his insights. The next step in my inquiry will take us to the eighteenth and the nineteenth centuries, where we will look at Richard Simon, Astruc, Eichhorn, and Ilgen. I will try to examine how each of these authors endeavored to read Genesis from a critical and "human" point of view. I will also endeavor to show that real progress in the exegesis of Genesis depends, to a large extent, on the answer given to the question of whether Genesis can be read "as any other book" or not. I hope that the lessons of the past will be useful for the present and the near future.

---

[8] See especially, *Die Authentie des Pentateuchs*. Erwiesen von Ernst Wilhelm Hengstenberg (BEAT 1; Berlin: Ludwig Oehmigke, 1836).

[9] Franz Julius Delitzsch, *Commentar über die Genesis* (4th ed.; Leipzig: Dörffling und Franke, 1872 [1st ed. 1852]). Delitzsch, however, was not completely opposed to higher criticism and recognized the existence of sources in the Pentateuch. But they were all very ancient, older than Moses.

[10] See, for instance, Solomon Schechter, "Geniza Specimens: The Oldest Collection of Bible Difficulties, by a Jew," *JQR* 13 (1901): 345–374. The author of the fragments in question seems to be a Qaraite. The problems raised by this writer are, for the most part, of a juridical nature, and about differences between pentateuchal laws and regulations found elsewhere in the Scriptures, especially in Ezechiel. Origen is probably one of the first Fathers of the Church who asked some critical questions. On Origen's exegesis, see Henri de Lubac, *Histoire et esprit: L'intelligence de l'Écriture d'après Origène* (Théologie 16; Paris: Aubier, 1950); Origène, *Philocalie 1–20 sur les Écritures: La lettre à Africanus sur l'histoire de Suzanne* (ed. and trans. Marguerite Harl and Nicolas de Lange; SC 302; Paris: Le Cerf, 1983), 90–100; and Origène, *De principiis: Traité des Principes* (ed. and trans. Henri Crouzel and Manlio Simonetti; SC 252–253, 268–269, 312; Paris: Le Cerf, 1978–1984).

Ibn Ezra and the Literal Interpretation of Genesis

"It appears to me that we are to interpret the account of the serpent literally."[11] Abraham Ibn Ezra,[12] the great Spanish rabbi, comes to this conclusion after discussing the positions of several authorities on whether the snake in Gen 3 could really speak. Ibn Ezra lists the interpretations proposed by his predecessors.[13] Some contend that the serpent spoke not through words, but through signs. Others assert that the serpent was in reality Satan. Rabbi Saadiah Gaon,[14] in his reading, argues that only humans are able to speak. Therefore neither the snake in Gen 3 nor Balaam's donkey in Num 24 really spoke: an angel spoke for them. Rabbi Samuel ben Hofni,[15] however, contradicts Rabbi Saadiah Gaon on this point. In his turn, Rabbi Solomon ibn Gabirol[16] takes issue with Rabbi Samuel ben Hofni and ends up siding with Rabbi Saadiah Gaon.

Eventually, Ibn Ezra opts for a literal understanding of the passage. According to Ibn Ezra, we have to understand that the serpent was able to speak. His reasons are two. First, God who bestowed intelligence on man could bestow intelligence on the serpent as well. In other words, there is no reason to limit God's power. Second, it is not possible to imagine that an angel of God could speak to the woman as the snake does in Gen 3. If an angel speaks these words instead of the serpent, then the angel is guilty of the sin committed and not the serpent. Moreover, an angel is God's messenger and cannot rebel against God. How can God send an angel to deceive the first couple? Further, Ibn Ezra states, an angel cannot act on his own accord, against God's will.

This example of early exegesis of the Book of Genesis is very instructive. Centuries later Hermann Gunkel would come to a simpler solution and resort to "literary genres."[17] According to Gunkel, it is normal for animals to speak—and nobody is surprised by it—in *Märchen* and *Sagen*. Ibn Ezra argues from the logic of the narrative and opens the way that would lead to Gunkel's method. For Ibn Ezra, God is almighty. We would say that the divinity represented in the narrative is almighty. Therefore we must

---

[11] *Ibn Ezra's Commentary on the Pentateuch: Genesis (Bereshit)* (ed. and trans. H. Norman Strickman and Arthur M. Silver; New York: Menorah, 1988), 66.
[12] B. Tudela [Spain], 1089—d. London or Calahorra [Spain], 1164.
[13] Ibn Ezra, *Genesis*, 66–67.
[14] Sa'adiah ben Yosef Gaon, b. Egypt, 882/892—d. Baghdad, 942.
[15] Samuel ben Hofni (d. 1034) was the last gaon of Sura, in Babylonia.
[16] Solomon ibn Gabirol, b. in Malaga, about 1021; d. about 1058 in Valencia.
[17] Gunkel, *Genesis*, ix–xiii.

suppose that the God who created an intelligent human being is also able to create an intelligent animal. This is confirmed by Gen 3:1, which affirms that "the serpent was more subtle than any beast of the field." The second reason adduced by Ibn Ezra is also logical and theological. It is not possible to reconcile the role of the serpent in Gen 3 with the function of an angel of God, at least as that function is usually represented in the Bible. Therefore, it was the serpent that spoke, not an angel.

Ibn Ezra is not only looking for "meaning" in the account in Genesis. He is looking for logic and inner coherency. As we will see, Ibn Ezra is surely one of the first exegetes of the Book of Genesis in the modern sense of the word. He seriously takes into account the rabbinic saying according to which "the Torah speaks in the language of men."[18] Whatever is said in the Torah, therefore, must be understandable according to the general rules of human language.

Two main aspects of Ibn Ezra's method deserve special attention. The first is what I would call his sense of history. The second is his way of solving problems through harmonization, quite common among rabbis, but with a real feel for the difficulties of the text.

Ibn Ezra and Chronology

"The general rule thus is that the Bible does not always list events in chronological order."[19] This principle is enunciated by Ibn Ezra when dealing with a problem of the logical sequence between Gen 11:32 and 12:4. According to Gen 11:26, Terah was 70 when Abraham is born. According to Gen 12:4, Abraham is 75 when he leaves Haran for the land of Canaan. Hence Terah at that time would have been 145. Genesis 11:32 states that Terah dies at the age of 205, which means that he lived 60 more years after his son Abraham left Haran for Canaan.[20] The problem is that narrative sequence (see 11:32–12:1) suggests that Abraham left Haran after Terah's death.

Ibn Ezra contends that the command found in Gen 12:1, "Leave your country ...," was actually given before Gen 11:31, which records Terah's and his household's journey from Ur of the Chaldeans to Haran, on the way to the land of Canaan. In this way, the text appears more logical and its

---

[18] *Sifre Numbers*, 112: דברה תורה כלשון בני אדם.
[19] Ibn Ezra, *Genesis*, 148. For the rabbinical principle, אין מקדם ומאוחר בתורה, "There is no earlier and later in the Torah," see, for example, *Pesahim* 6b; *Mekhilta D'Rabbi Yishmael Beshallah* 7; *Sifrei Bemidbar* 64; *Ecc. Rabbah* 1:12, and several other places.
[20] Ibn Ezra, *Genesis*, 149.

chronology is respected, at least according to Ibn Ezra.[21] Ibn Ezra points to another chronological difficulty, that of the clash between Num 1:1 and Num 9:1. Num 1:1 states that YHWH spoke to Moses on the first day of the *second* month of the second year after Israel had come out of Egypt. The second text says that God gave instruction to the same people of Israel in the desert on the first day of the *first* month after they had come out of Egypt. The Talmud comments on this passage by saying, "there is no before and no afterwards in the Torah" (*b. Pesah* 6b).

The important point, however, is that Ibn Ezra noticed the problem because he was looking for logic and coherency in reading the Torah. He was not only looking for theological meaning and moral application. His approach and attention to chronological details reveal a new mindset and mark Ibn Ezra out.

The great Rashi[22] comes to the same conclusion, but the explanation he gives reveals a very different spirit. For Rashi the Torah does not want to publicize Abraham's departure because, according to Jewish custom, he would have had to remain with his aged father and take care of him.[23] Where Ibn Ezra looks for critical insights, Rashi is more attentive to justify the moral behaviour of the patriarchs who must be edifying figures for his readers.[24]

The same kind of problem arises again on at least three other occasions, which we will discuss in turn. In our first example, Ibn Ezra notes that the message contained in Gen 25:23—where God announces to Rebecca that she is about to give birth to twins—came through a prophet or through Abraham himself who was a prophet (Gen 20:7). Important here is that Ibn Ezra explains that Abraham could be the author of the prophecy since "[he] did not pass away until her [Rebecca's] sons were fifteen years of age."[25]

---

[21] Ibn Ezra, *Genesis*, 147.
[22] Rashi (Rabbi Shlomo ben Yitzhak), b. Troyes (France), 1040—d. Troyes (France), 1105.
[23] Rashi, *The Torah: With Rashi's Commentary Translated, Annotated, and Elucidated* (ed. Yisrael Isser Zvi Herczeg; 5 vols.; Brooklyn: Mesorah, 1994–1998), 1:112.
[24] Ramban (Rabbi Moshe ben Nachman or Nachmanides; b. Gerona, 1194—d. Land of Israel, 1270) criticizes both Rashi and the Midrash and comes back to an interpretation similar to that of Ibn Ezra: "[...] I wonder about their words for this is the customary way for Scripture to relate the life of a father, his begetting a son, and his death, and afterwards to begin the narration of the son in all generations." See Ramban, *Commentary on the Torah: Genesis* (ed. and trans. Charles B. Chavel; New York: Shilo, 1971), 162. Ramban also notes that Noah was still alive when Abraham was born and "that Shem lived throughout Abraham's life span." According to the Babylonian Talmud, *Baba Bathra* 121b, "Jacob saw Shem."
[25] Ibn Ezra, *Genesis*, 249.

Since Abraham was 100 years old when Isaac was born (Gen 21:5) and Isaac was 60 years old when Esau and Jacob were born (Gen 25:26), Esau and Jacob would be 15 years old when Abraham died at the age of 175 (Gen 25:7). But, in the chronology of the narrative, the report of Abraham's death precedes that of Esau and Jacob's birth and the reader is given the impression that Abraham is already dead when the twins are born.

A comparison with Rashi is again enlightening. The latter introduces a more human or pious explanation. For Rashi, Abraham dies when Esau and Jacob were 15 and so he "did not see Esau going bad ways." This would have prevented him from dying "in a good old age." This is thus the reason why Abraham died at the age of 175 (Gen 25:7)—five years less than Isaac who dies at the age of 180 (Gen 35:28).[26]

In another example, Ibn Ezra uses Gen 37:35 to point out that Isaac was still alive when Joseph was sold by his brothers and lived twelve years more. The calculation is rather complicated. Isaac was 60 when Esau and Jacob were born (Gen 25:26). Jacob was 91 when Joseph was born. This can be deduced from Gen 41:46—Joseph is 30 when he is appointed vizier over Egypt—and nine years later Jacob arrives in Egypt, after seven years of abundance (Gen 41:29, 47) and two years of famine (Gen 45:6). At that time Jacob is 130 (Gen 47:9) and Joseph 39. Thus Joseph is 91 years younger than his father. Isaac dies at the age of 180 (Gen 35:28), which means that at that time Jacob was 120 and Joseph 29. Joseph was sold at the age of 17 (Gen 37:2), which means that Isaac died 12 years after Joseph was sold. Again the narrative sequence does not follow the chronological order.[27]

The last important example is found in Gen 38:1 and will be taken up later by Spinoza in his argumentation against the Mosaic authorship of the Pentateuch. In his comment on the first sentence in Gen 38, the story of Judah and Tamar, Ibn Ezra asserts that the expression "And it came to pass at that time" cannot refer to the time Joseph was sold. The events recounted in Gen 38 must precede the events in Gen 37. Again a little computation is necessary. We saw that Joseph was sold at the age of 17 (Gen 37:2), that he

---

[26] Rashi, *The Torah*, 1:279.
[27] The same phenomenon is noted by Rashi, *The Torah*, 1:397–398, who quotes the Talmudic principle "There is no earlier and later in the Torah" (see n. 19). Ramban, *Genesis*, 451, quotes Ibn Ezra regarding Gen 37:3, "[Joseph] was the son of [Jacob's] old age." But Ramban disagrees with Ibn Ezra since all of Jacob's sons were born when their father was old. Hence he prefers a slightly different interpretation: "The correct interpretation appears to me that it was the custom of the elders to take one of their younger sons to be with them to attend them."

became vizier over Egypt at the age of 30 (Gen 41:46), and that Jacob and his sons came down to Egypt after seven years of abundance and two year of famine (Gen 45:6). Joseph was thus 39 years old. The span of time between Gen 37 and Gen 47 is 22 years. It is impossible that all the events recounted in Gen 38 could have occurred in such a short span of time. Actually, in Gen 38, Judah marries and begets three sons. The three grow up and two of them are married to Tamar. Judah then has intercourse with his daughter-in-law who bears twins. One of them already has two sons when coming down to Egypt with his grandfather Jacob (Gen 46:12).

Ibn Ezra once again sees a discrepancy between the narrative and the chronological order and solves the problem by re-establishing a more logical chronological order. Without quoting his source, Spinoza will use Ibn Ezra's argument to show that the Pentateuch cannot have been written by one and the same author, namely Moses, but by somebody that compiled different documents at a later time. For Spinoza, this compiler is Ezra.[28]

Needless to say, in more modern times, these problems are solved in recognizing the hand of different writers at work in the Book of Genesis. Ibn Ezra had already pinpointed some of the problems that led modern exegesis to elaborate new theories such as source and redaction criticism.

Some Important Exegetical Insights

A good example of Ibn Ezra's critical exegesis is to be found in a discussion on Gen 22:1–2.[29] The problem is that the narrative seems to imply that God puts Abraham to the test and, therefore, did not know in advance what Abraham's response would be. Some have proposed to solve this theological problem by reading the verb *nś'* (נשא), "to lift up," "to exalt," instead of *nsh* (נסה), "to prove," "to put to the test." This is, for instance, the exegesis proposed by the Midrash which suggests that God did not put Abraham to the test, but "exalted" him by showing his absolute obedience to his Lord.[30] Ibn Ezra's reaction is categorical: "However, the plain meaning of the entire chapter contradicts this interpretation. The word *nissah* is thus to be taken literally."[31] In other words, Ibn Ezra introduces a very simple

---

[28] Baruch Spinoza, *Tractatus theologico-politicus* (Amsterdam: Jan Rieuwertsz, 1663, 1670, 1677), ch. 8.
[29] Ibn Ezra, *Genesis*, 222–223.
[30] *Bereshit Rabbah*, 80:55.
[31] Ibn Ezra, *Genesis*, 222.

rule of exegesis. The meaning of a word or a sentence is always to be interpreted in agreement with its context. Moreover, if a sentence or a narrative contradicts a theological idea, for instance divine omniscience as in Genesis 22, one should not tamper with the text to make it fit that idea.

For the same reasons, Ibn Ezra rejects a similar attempt to alter the plain meaning of the text and thus to take the edge off God's dreadful command to Abraham in 22:2. The text there says, "Take your son, your only son, the one whom you love, Isaac, [...] and offer him as a burnt offering on one of the mountains that I shall show you."[32] The Midrash reads the verb *'lh* (עלה) in this sentence in the sense of "going up." The meaning would be: "bring him up to one of the mountains that I shall show you." Ibn Ezra shows that the narrative does not support this interpretation since Abraham actually decided to sacrifice his son and did everything accordingly. When there is a conflict between the plain meaning of a text and certain theological views, Ibn Ezra always opts for the plain meaning of the text.

Another case is to be found in his commentary on the same text, Gen 22:1–19, this time on the last verse of the chapter. Genesis 22:19 says: "So Abraham returned to his young men, and they arose and went together to Beer-Sheba; and Abraham lived at Beer-Sheba." Since Isaac is not mentioned in the verse, some Jewish commentators inferred that Abraham actually slaughtered his son on the mountain.[33] Ibn Ezra again opposes this view because it contradicts the plain sense of the text, in which the angel of YHWH clearly forbids Abraham to slay his son (22:12).

Ibn Ezra's main critical insights pertain to Gen 12:6 and 22:14, as is well known. These texts are among the five passages pinpointed by Ibn Ezra as very problematic. With respect to Gen 12:6, "And the Canaanite was then in the land," he writes: "It is possible that the Canaanites seized the land of Canaan from some other tribe at that time. Should this interpretation be incorrect, there is a secret meaning to the text. Let the one who understands it remain silent."[34] Clearly, Ibn Ezra felt that this text could not have been written by Moses, especially because of the adverb "then" (Hebrew אז). At the time of Moses, the Canaanites were still in the land. Regarding the idea

---

[32] The translations are taken from the *NRSV*, sometimes with slight changes for the sake of clarity.
[33] On this line of interpretation, see George W. Coats, "A Journey into Oblivion: A Structural Analysis of Gen. 22:1–19," *Sound* 58 (1975): 243–256.
[34] Ibn Ezra, *Genesis*, 151.

that Gen 22:14 must refer to the temple of Jerusalem, Ibn Ezra tells his reader to check what he says at the beginning of his commentary on the Book of Deuteronomy.[35]

As we saw earlier, Ibn Ezra often pleads in favour of a literal interpretation of the biblical text.[36] In one case his reflections anticipate very recent discoveries. A case in point is Gen 28:10 where the narrator simply states that "Jacob went out from Beer-Sheba and went to Haran."[37] *Prima facie*, the verse summarizes Jacob's whole journey from Beer-Sheba to Haran and the following narrative should tell us what happened in Haran after the patriarch's arrival. This is not the case, however, since Gen 28:10–22 is about Jacob's vision at Bethel.

Ibn Ezra reports Saadiah Gaon's opinion which alleges that the preterite *wayyēlek* has, in this case, the same value as the infinitive *talēket*; he thus translates: "Jacob went out from Beer-Sheba to go to Haran."[38] The Midrash opts for a similar solution because it asserts that Jacob arrived in Haran on the very day he left Beer-Sheba.[39]

Ibn Ezra understands the text in a different way and prefers to interpret the second part of the verse *literally*: "After telling us that Jacob left Beersheba and went to Haran, Scripture returns and tells us what he encountered on the way to Haran."[40] This means that Gen 28:10 contains a general statement followed by details given afterwards, according to one of Hillel's rules, *kᵉlal upᵉrat*, that could be translated by this simple formula: "The general first, the particular afterwards."[41]

---

[35] In his commentary on Deut 1:1, Ibn Ezra gives a list of the texts that, as he understands things, could not have been written by Moses. The five texts are: (a) The final twelve verses of Deuteronomy (34:1–12); (b) "Moses wrote" (Deut 31:22); (c) "At that time the Canaanites dwelt in the land" (Gen 12:6); (d) "In the mountain of God, He will appear" (Gen 22:14); and (e) "Behold his bed is a bed of iron" (Deut 3:11). One should add Deut 1:1: "These are the words that Moses spoke [...] *on the other side of the Jordan.*"

[36] Other cases in point are, for instance, Gen 29:17 (the word *rakkôt* means "weak"); and Gen 31:50 ("If you shall afflict my daughters").

[37] Ibn Ezra, *Genesis*, 275.

[38] Ibn Ezra, *Genesis*, 275, n. 6.

[39] *Bereshit Rabbah*, 68:9.

[40] Ibn Ezra, *Genesis*, 275.

[41] This is a phenomenon that I proposed to call "proleptic summary." Cf. Jean Louis Ska, "Sommaires proleptiques en Gn 27 et dans l'histoire de Joseph," *Bib* 73 (1992): 518–527; Ska, "Quelques exemples de sommaires proleptiques dans les récits bibliques," in *Congress Volume Paris 1992* (ed. J.A. Emerton; VTSup 61; Leiden: Brill, 1995), 315–326; and Klaus Koenen, "Prolepsen im alttestamentlichen Erzählungen: Eine Skizze," *VT* 47 (1997): 456–477.

Summary

It was worthwhile, I think, spending some time with Ibn Ezra and rediscovering some of his important critical insights. To sum up in one sentence his hermeneutics, I would again quote one of his favorite sayings: "A verse never departs from its literal meaning."[42] As we will see, this will be the object of further discussions.

"Nothing New under the Sun"—Some Key Figures of the Seventeenth and the Eighteenth Centuries

Richard Simon: Prophets or Scribes?

"J'aime mieux dire qu'un autre écrivain a ajouté quelque chose aux livres de Moïse, que de le faire passer toujours pour un prophète"—"I prefer to say that another writer added something to Moses' books than to pass him [Moses] off always for a prophet".[43] This reflection by Jacques Bonfrère (1625) clearly shows that Ibn Ezra's spirit was very much alive in the exegetical world during the Renaissance. Bonfrère is not isolated at all. His reflections reveal, on the contrary, that the mentality of many radically changed and that exegetes react very differently to difficulties in the biblical text. They no longer look for supernatural or theological explanations, for example the spirit of prophecy. They look for rational and historical explanations. A case in point is a text found in Esau's genealogy (Gen 36:31): "These are the kings who reigned in the land of Edom, before any king reigned over the Israelites." It is of course very difficult to attribute this verse to Moses unless one affirms that he foresaw the future thanks to a supernatural gift of a prophetic insight. Bonfrère opts—significantly—for a different solution, one that opens the way to new kinds of readings. If this verse cannot be attributed to Moses as author, it means that exegetes can now study the Book of Genesis in a different way and ask questions about its authors and the history of its composition.

Bonfrère is quoted by Richard Simon in his *Histoire Critique du Vieux Testament* (1678) who uses this example to buttress his view that Moses did not write the whole of the Pentateuch.[44] The shift from a more theological and

---

[42] *Shabbat* 63a; *Yevamot* 11b, 24a. See Ibn Ezra, *Genesis*, 15.

[43] Jacques Bonfrère (1573–1642), *Pentateuchus Moysis commentario illustratus* (Antwerp: Ex Officina Plantiniana, 1625).

[44] Richard Simon, *Histoire critique du Vieux Testament* (Paris: Billaine, 1678; repr.,

theocentric to a more anthropocentric, humanistic, and historical reading of Genesis is manifest in the following sentence by the same Richard Simon: "Premièrement il est impossible d'entendre parfaitement les livres sacrés à moins qu'on ne sache auparavant les différents états où le texte de ces livres s'est trouvé selon les différents temps et les différents lieux, et si l'on n'est instruit exactement de tous les changements qui lui sont survenus"—"First it is impossible to understand wholly the sacred books unless one knows beforehand the different stages these books went through in different periods and different places, and unless one is informed with precision about all the changes they underwent."[45] The key word in this sentence is "changes." The biblical books were not composed at once by one author, and they were not transmitted intact through the ages. The biblical books, in other words, have a history and they bear the scars of that history. Richard Simon immediately draws a conclusion from this first affirmation:

> De plus, comme ces mêmes prophètes, qu'on peut appeler scribes publics, pour les distinguer des autres écrivains particuliers, avaient la liberté de faire des recueils des anciens actes qui étaient conservés dans les archives de la République [des Hébreux], et de donner à ces mêmes actes une nouvelle forme, en y ajoutant ou diminuant ce qu'ils jugeaient à propos, on donnera par ce principe une raison solide des additions et changements qui se trouvent dans les livres sacrés, sans que pour cela leur autorité soit diminuée, puisque les auteurs de ces additions ou changements ont été de véritables prophètes dirigés par l'Esprit de Dieu. C'est pourquoi les changements qu'ils ont pu introduire dans les anciens actes auront la même autorité que le reste du texte de la Bible.[46]

> Moreover, those same prophets that one can call public scribes to distinguish them from the other private writers, had the freedom to create compilations of ancient documents that were preserved in the archives of the Republic [of the Hebrews], and to give these same documents a new shape, adding or taking away what they judged necessary to be treated in this way. Thanks to this principle, one will find solid grounds to justify the additions and changes that are found in these sacred books, without diminishing their authority for this reason since the authors of these additions or changes were true

---

Rotterdam: Reenier Leers, 1685; repr., nouvelle édition annotée et introduite par Pierre Gibert; Paris: Bayard, 2008), 132. I here quote the new edition by Gibert. For a summary of Richard Simon's work, see John W. Rogerson, "Richard Simon," in *Hebrew Bible/Old Testament: The History of Its Interpretation, Volume 2: From the Renaissance to the Enlightenment* (ed. Magne Sæbø; Göttingen: Vandenhoeck & Ruprecht, 2008), 838–843.

[45] Simon, *Histoire critique*, 75.
[46] All the translations from French and German are mine unless otherwise stated.

prophets lead by the Spirit of God. Therefore the changes that they may have introduced into the ancient documents will have the same authority as the rest of the text of the Bible.

This text is important and therefore I have quoted it at length. Two major points must be underlined. First, Richard Simon is aware that a serious question will inescapably arise from his theory of "public scribes," namely, the question of the Scriptures' authority. Simon solves the problem by extending "inspiration" to all the scribes, and not only to Moses or the "prophets" who, according to ancient Jewish and Christian tradition, had written the biblical books. *All* the writers or scribes were inspired by the same spirit.

The second point is more interesting for modern exegesis. Richard Simon calls the "prophets" of religious tradition "public scribes." We pass from the world of religious and theological hermeneutics to that of historical inquiry regarding the origin of the biblical books, in particular of Genesis. Simon of course attributes "inspiration" to these scribes, but he calls them henceforth "public scribes" and will explain many difficulties of the text by resorting to their interventions.[47] An explanation of the text requires this shift in mentality. Only when the text loses its sacred aura—which does not mean that it loses its theological value—and is no longer "untouchable," does exegesis such as that of Richard Simon and his followers become possible. New avenues for biblical interpretation are opened to scholars.

As for the Book of Genesis, Richard Simon is aware of a serious problem raised by the temporal distance that separates the events recounted, for instance the creation of the world, and Moses, the supposed author of the whole Pentateuch.[48] Simon excludes two possible explanations. First, nowhere is it written that God dictated to Moses everything we find in Genesis and which happened centuries before Moses. Second, nowhere is it said either that Moses wrote these matters thanks to a special spirit of prophecy. There are two other possible explanations—and we will find them again and again in biblical research: "Moïse a eu sans doute d'autres

---

[47] Norbert Lohfink, "Über die Irrtumlosigkeit und die Einheit der Schrift," *StZ* 174 (1964): 161–181; reprinted in *Das Siegeslied am Schilfmeer: Christliche Auseinandersetzung mit dem Alten Testament* (Frankfurt: Knecht, 1965), 44–80, solves the problem in a different way. For him, inspiration is primarily a quality of the books, not of the writers. Moreover, "inspiration" is a quality of the Scriptures as a whole rather than of each single book or of each single part of a book.

[48] Simon, *Histoire critique*, 150–156, ch. VII: *De quelle manière les livres de la Loi ont été écrits. Livres attribués aux patriarches qui ont vécu avant Moïse* [...]—(*How the books of the Law have been written. Books attributed to the patriarchs who lived before Moses* [...]).

mémoires, soit qu'ils fussent écrits ou qu'ils fussent conservés de vive voix jusqu'à lui dans les familles que Dieu avait choisies pour lui être fidèles dans le véritable culte de la religion"—"Moses probably had other memoirs, either written or preserved orally until his time in families that God had chosen to be faithful to him in the true cult of religion."[49] Simon again substitues supernatural with historical means to explain the composition of Genesis. No direct dictation by God, no prophetic spirit. Rather, either written or oral traditions are appealed to.

Of course such affirmations had to provoke strong reactions. Between the 18th, 20th, and 22nd of July, 1678, some 1,300 copies of Simon's book were burnt in Paris by order of king Louis the XIV and the Royal Council. The whole affair had been instigated by the famous orator, bishop Bossuet.[50] Thanks goodness, however, some copies were saved and Simon's ideas survived this *auto-da-fé*. He will be quoted and used by Astruc, Eichhorn, Ilgen, and many others, as we will see.

Jean Astruc: Moses' Book or Documents Used by Moses?[51]

Il n'est donc pas possible que Moïse ait pu savoir par lui-même ce qu'il rapporte dans la Genèse, et par conséquent il faut ou qu'il ait été instruit par révélation ou qu'il l'ait appris par le rapport de ceux qui en avaient été eux-mêmes les témoins. Je ne connais personne qui ait avancé la première opinion, et je crois que personne ne s'avisera jamais de l'avancer. Moïse parle toujours, dans la Genèse, comme un simple historien; il ne dit nulle part que ce qu'il raconte lui ait été inspiré.[52]

Hence it is not possible that Moses may have known by himself everything he recounts in Genesis and, therefore he must have been instructed through revelation or that he heard it through the reports of those that had been themselves eyewitnesses. I do not know anyone who advanced the first opinion

---

[49] Simon, *Histoire critique*, 151. See, on this problem, Pierre Gibert, *L'invention critique de la Bible: XVe–XVIIIe siècle* (Bibliothèque des Histoires; Paris: Gallimard, 2010), 262–269 (*De la qualité des prophètes*).

[50] For a summary of these events, see Gibert, "Introduction," in *Histoire critique*, 11–13.

[51] The title of the original edition is *Conjectures sur les mémoires originaux dont il paroît que Moyse s'est servi pour composer le Livre de la Genèse* (Bruxelles: Fricx, 1753). This edition was anonymous. On Jean Astruc, see the introduction by Pierre Gibert, *Jean Astruc—Conjectures sur la Genèse: Introductions et notes* (Paris: Noêsis, 1999), 15–119; John Jarick, ed., *Sacred Conjectures: The Context and Legacy of Robert Lowth and Jean Astruc* (LHBOTS 457; London: T&T Clark, 2007); and John W. Rogerson, "Jean Astruc," in *Hebrew Bible/Old Testament: The History of Its Interpretation, Volume 2: From the Renaissance to the Enlightenment* (ed. Magne Sæbø; Göttingen: Vandenhoeck & Ruprecht, 2008), 846–847. I quote from Gibert's edition.

[52] Astruc, *Mémoires*, 132.

and I do not think that anyone will dare to advance it. Moses always speaks, in the book of Genesis, as a mere historian, and he does not say anywhere that what he says has been revealed to him by inspiration.

Astruc repeats in this statement what had been affirmed before him, among others, by Bonfrère and Simon, but this is now—almost—taken for granted. The author of Genesis, who Astruc still believes to be Moses, cannot be the eyewitness of all that is recounted in his work. His source of information, however, cannot be supernatural, that is, divine inspiration. The consequence he draws is different, however, and this marks a progress in the study of Genesis:

> Ce premier point une fois établi, le reste souffre peu de difficulté. Il n'y a que deux moyens par où la connaissance des faits antérieurs ait pu être transmise à Moïse, ou par une tradition purement orale, c'est-à-dire de bouche à bouche; ou par une tradition écrite, c'est-à-dire par des relations ou Mémoires laissés par écrit.[53]

> This first point once established, the rest does not create many difficulties. There are only two means through which knowledge of previous facts may have been transmitted to Moses, either through a merely oral tradition, which means from mouth to mouth; or through a written tradition, i.e. through reports or Memoirs put in writing.

Two main points must be underscored. Astruc distinguishes two ways of handing knowledge down from generation to generation, either through oral tradition or through written documents. Richard Simon had already spoken of "oral tradition" and is perhaps the first one to have used this terminology in biblical exegesis.[54] Astruc, however, adds the possibility of having in the Pentateuch, in particular in Genesis, different written documents, and not only additions by later scribes, as in the case of Simon. For the first time, Genesis and Exodus 1–2 are divided into several independent literary works written by different authors. Two of these documents will have a long destiny, the one characterized by the use of the divine appellative ʾĕlōhîm, and the other one that uses the divine name yhwh. But one should not forget that Astruc found many other documents in Genesis, up to thirteen which he labeled using different letters, from A to M. In category C he classified some of the repetitions and to his category D belonged the rest, namely material foreign to Hebrew history, such as, for instance, Gen 14 or Esau's genealogy in Gen 36. Moreover, he suggested that there were some

---

[53] Astuc, *Mémoires*, 133.
[54] Simon, *Histoire critique*, 81–82; 150–151.

glosses and a few late additions by the last compiler. He proposed that the authors of these documents were Amram, Moses' father (who had received ancient traditions from his ancestors, perhaps Levi, for instance), the patriarch Joseph, the Midianites (for some genealogies), and the Moabites and the Ammonites for Gen 19:29–38. All of these documents precede Moses, of course, since he made use of them.

The main merit of Astruc's work, however, is the discovery of possible written documents in Genesis.[55] We should be clear that it would be premature to classify Astruc among the inventors of a "documentary hypothesis" since he accounted for the existence of many separate documents, those we find in his D column, subdivided into eight columns (E–M). We find in Genesis, according to Astruc's hypothesis, and to use a more common vocabulary, "documents" and "fragments" side by side. It is possible, however, to distinguish them thanks to the use of different divine appellations or to the presence of doublets. We may perhaps stumble upon some glosses or later additions inserted by the compiler. With this we have the main categories that future exegetes will use in their study of Genesis. More important, however, is the question asked by Jean Astruc, a question specifically about *written documents* that were put together in Genesis to achieve its present form.

Johann Gottfried Eichhorn and the Pre-Mosaic Documents

Johann Gottfried Eichhorn is often presented as one of the pioneers of biblical scholarship in Pentateuchal studies. In my opinion, however, his contribution is perhaps less important than often claimed. The main insight regarding the existence of "sources" or documents in Genesis is clearly due to Astruc, as Eichhorn honestly acknowledges.[56] He applied Astruc's prin-

---

[55] This is underlined by several authors. Karl David Ilgen, for instance, explicitly speaks of a "discovery" ("Entdeckung"): "[...] denn was andere vor ihm dunkel ahneten, verdient den Nahmen Entdeckung nicht"—"[...] since what others obscurely guessed does not deserve the name 'discovery'" (*Die Urkunden des ersten Buchs von Moses in ihrer Urgestalt zum bessern Verständniß und richtigern Gebrauch derselben in ihrer gegenwärtigen Form aus dem hebräischen mit kritischen Anmerkungen und Nachweisungen auch einer Abhandlung über die Trennung der Urkunden* [Halle: Hemmerde und Schwetschke, 1798], x). See also Hermann Hupfeld, *Die Quellen der Genesis und die Art ihrer Zusammensetzung von neuem untersucht* (Berlin: Verlag von Wiegandt und Grieken, 1853), 1, n. 1: "ein feiner Kopf von wirklich kritischer Begabung"—"a fine head with real critical talent."

[56] Johannes Gottfried Eichhorn, *Einleitung in das Alte Testament* (3 vols.; Leipzig: Weidmann, 1780–1783, ²1787, ³1795–1803, ⁴1823), 3:22: "Endlich hat Astrük [*sic*], ein berühmter Arzt, das gethan, woran sich kein Kritikus von Profession wagen wollte, und die ganze Genesis in

ciples systematically and he studied the whole of the Pentateuch, which Astruc did not do. His main contribution, however, is in the field of methodology. Eichhorn used a clearly defined set of criteria to distinguish the original documents called "articles" ("Aufsätze") or, sometimes, "documents" ("Urkunden").⁵⁷ His three main criteria are: (a) the repetitions (to illustrate this criterion Eichhorn chooses the flood narrative of Gen 6–9; see 42–51); (b) the style ("die Schreibart"—Eichhorn mentions here, among other things, the use of different divine appellations, "Elohim" [*'ĕlōhîm*] and "Jehovah" [*yhwh*], but also some favorite expressions [e.g. "Lieblingsausdrücke"]; see 51–59 and 57–59); and (c) some characteristics in content ("Charakter"—for instance, the genealogies in the Jehovah document are of cosmographic or geographic nature, whereas those in the Elohim document of a chronological nature; see 60–64).

In addition to this, Eichhorn elaborates a theory about the origin of Genesis. According to his model we have at the beginning oral traditions, an element that dates back to Richard Simon (19, 24, 65–66). In a second phase, these traditions were put into writing, first in the form of single short units. In the third phase these short units were integrated into larger written documents, as he states (6):

> Die ältesten Geisteswerke bestanden daher immer aus einer Sammlung kürzer Aufsätze, die lange einzeln vorhanden waren, ehe sie mittels einer vieles zugleich fassenden Schreibmaterie, auf einem Stück Leinenwand oder auf an einander gefügten Häuten, mit einander in Verbindung gebracht wurden.

> The oldest intellectual works consisted therefore of collections of smaller accounts that remained for a long time isolated before they were put together thanks to some material that could contain [larger texts], for instance a piece of linen or several animal skins assembled together.⁵⁸

---

einzelne Fragmente zerlegt"—"Finally Astruc, a famous physician, did what no professional critic wanted to venture doing, and divided the whole of Genesis into single fragments." This quotation is from the third volume of the fourth edition (1823), where Eichhorn justifies several of his positions, especially after the publication of Ilgen's work. Subsequent unidentified page references in the main text and notes refer to this volume.

⁵⁷ See Eichhorn, *Einleitung*, 39, where he justifies the use of the term "Urkunde." Eichhorn speaks of Gen 2:4–3:19 as an independent "document."

⁵⁸ See also 37: "Endlich auch die schriftliche Verzeichnung der Begebenheiten selbst fängt vom Einzelnen an, und beschäftigt sich lange mit einzelnen Arten von Merkwürdigkeiten, ehe man das Ganze zu umfassen, und die einzeln nieder geschriebenen Sagen an einander zu reihen unternimmt."—"Eventually the redaction of the events themselves begins with the single units too and remains interested for a long time in single sorts of remarkable facts before one undertakes the composition of the whole and the arrangement of the single popular stories in a certain order."

Eventually, these documents were compiled to form the present text of Genesis (93–94). The two main documents are named after the divine appellation that each uses: the Elohim document and the Jehovah document. These were combined into one literary work at the time of Moses or right afterwards (93–94). Some texts, however, do not belong to those two main documents, such as, for instance, Gen 2:4–3:19; 14; 33:18–34:31; 36:1–43; 49:1–27 (see 39–42, 91). All these texts—but one—are well-known riddles of biblical exegesis: Gen 14, the campaign of the four great kings against the five kings of the cities around the Dead Sea; 36:1–43, the genealogy of Esau/Edom; 33:18–34:31, the story of Dinah and Sichem; and 49:1–27, Jacob's blessing of his twelve sons. The unexpected text in this list is Gen 2:4–3:19, the Eden narrative. But Eichhorn insists on the peculiar style of the two chapters—he speaks of its "childish tone" ("Kinderton"), and of the unusual use of both divine names together, Jehovah and Elohim (39–41).

Regarding the dating of the texts, Eichhorn mentions a principle that was to have much success and would be used by generations of exegetes. The simpler a text is, the more ancient it is too: "[…] je älter ein Schriftsteller sey […], desto einfacher, kürzer, deutlicher und begreiflicher sey die Darstellung, und je später, desto dunkler, verworrener, rätselhafter sey ihr Inhalt." (70–71)—"The more ancient a writer is, the simpler, the shorter, the clearer and the more understandable the presentation is, and the later [the writer is], the more obscure, the more complicated and the more puzzling the content is." This principle is of course sometimes misleading. Eichhorn himself uses it to demonstrate the antiquity of Gen 1, a text that most exegetes consider today to be post-exilic.

As we saw, Eichhorn believes that the documents we find in Genesis predate Moses. He argues that neither the Old nor the New Testament speak of Moses as the author of Genesis. The Book of Genesis itself never hints at Moses as its possible author. The first to affirm this were Philo, Josephus, and the Talmud. Moreover, texts from Genesis are quoted in the rest of the Pentateuch. For instance, Moses' blessing (Deut 33) echoes and re-uses that of Jacob (Gen 49); Joseph's last will (Gen 50:25) is quoted in Exod 13:19; the commandment of the Sabbath in Exod 20:11 refers to Gen 2:1–3. For Eichhorn, Genesis was therefore known at the time of Moses. Eichhorn adds that the name of the personality that united the sources does not matter, though fidelity to the sources he used does (93–94). This means that Eichhorn does not defend Moses' authorship of Genesis outright, but believes in the early composition of the book since it was composed at the time of Moses or earlier (94).

Lastly, let us mention a basic reflection about the nature of the book of Genesis that will bring us back to Ibn Ezra (18):

> Nirgends, weder in einer deutlichen Stelle, noch in einem entfernten Winke, gibt die Genesis ihre Nachrichten für unmittelbare Eröffnungen Gottes aus. Sie will also nicht den bloßen Gedanken einer näheren Prüfung durch ein untrügliches αὐτὸς ἔφα nieder schlagen—sie selbst will menschlich gelesen und geprüft sein.
>
> Nowhere, neither in a clear place nor in a remote corner, does Genesis present its content as immediate divine revelations. It does not want therefore to knock down the mere idea of a closer examination through an unmistakable αὐτὸς ἔφα—[the book itself] wants to be read and tested in a human way.

Genesis, according to Eichhorn, is a human work and should be read as such. For this reason, the exegete is entitled to use in his or her reading of the biblical book all the methods used in reading and studying any ancient literary documents. This is of course what Eichhorn did.

Karl-David Ilgen

Karl David Ilgen is often identified as the inventor of the distinction between two "Elohists": the first being the ancestor of the Priestly Writer (P) of the classical documentary hypothesis, and the other being the Elohist of the same hypothesis. But this description, often found in classical introductions to the Pentateuch, does not stand up to closer scrutiny. To be sure, Ilgen introduced the appellations "Jehovist" and "Elohist" into our exegetical vocabulary. He also definitely distinguished between two Elohists; however, he did this above all because of the presence of doublets in the Joseph Story from which the divine name YHWH is almost entirely absent except in Gen 39.[59] The two Elohists of Ilgen therefore have little to do with the classical Elohist (E) and Priestly Writer (P). Hermann Hupfeld is a better candidate for the prize reserved to the one who first distinguished the future E and P.

Another idea often held about Ilgen is that he distinguishes as many as seventeen "documents" in Genesis. These "documents," however, should rather be called "pieces" or "parts" ("Stücke," "Theile") of the three main "documents" ("Urkunden") that Ilgen distinguishes in the Book of Genesis (341–346). An "organizer" or "compiler" ("Zusammensteller," "Zusammenordner," "Sammler")[60] divided up the three original documents and

---

[59] Ilgen, *Urkunden*, 393–394. Subsequent unidentified page references refer to this work.
[60] 344. Ilgen purposely avoids calling this activity that of an "author" ("Verfasser").

rearranged the pieces according to a (mostly) chronological order. The work of the critic is to identify the different "parts" and to recompose the three original documents, namely the Jehovist and the two Elohists.

Ilgen uses four criteria to recognize and classify the different "pieces": (a) the misplaced "titles," namely the so-called *toledot* formulae (351–362); (b) the repetitions (cf. Astruc) (362–376);[61] (c) the different styles ("Schreibarten")—Ilgen mentions here the use of different divine appellations (יהוה and אלהים), and he takes, among other examples, the flood story as representative (376–400; flood story: 382–384);[62] and (d) the difference in "characters" of the sources, i.e. the differences in content and theology (400–409).

The main contributions of Ilgen are, besides his clear methodology, two basic affirmations. First, the study of Genesis can proceed only when scholars are convinced that critical study is not a lack of respect towards sacred books. In other words, respect for the content of the sacred books should not prevent scholars from examining its form and seeing possible errors, differences, tensions, and even contradictions within texts (viii–ix). Second, it is obvious, according to Ilgen, that Christian theology does not thwart historical inquiries. Some of his statements may sound sacrilegious, even today, but he is clearly convinced that progress in biblical studies depends on a critical viewpoint that should not be hampered by an all too strong (and wrong) sense of reverence towards the form of the Holy Scriptures.[63] But let us quote Ilgen himself (xii–xiii):

---

[61] Ilgen adds an important remark, saying that Homer, for instance, often describes the same scenes in the same way. Repetition is a normal stylistic feature in antiquity (362–366) and can be used for distinguishing sources only when it can be demonstrated that repetition cannot be justified in any other way. Ilgen quotes the grammarian Macrobius, *Sat.*, 5.15: "Nescio, quomodo Homerum repetitio illa unice decet, et est genio antiqui poetae digna"— "But I do not know in which way [this] repetition is suitable to Homer in a unique way and is worthy of the genius of the ancient poet." Ilgen taught classical literature, in particular Homer and Cicero. See Bodo Seidel, *Karl David Ilgen und die Pentateuchforschung im Umkreis der sogenannten Älteren Urkundenhypothese. Studien zur Geschichte der exegetischen Hermeneutik in der Späten Aufklärung* (BZAW 213; Berlin: de Gruyter, 1993), 70–78.

[62] Ilgen is very cautious and says, for instance, that one must distinguish between "style" and "vocabulary." The typical construction of the sentence is more important than the use of particular words.

[63] We find a similar idea expressed by Hupfeld, *Die Quellen*, xi–xiv; he invites his readers to recognize the "volle Menschlichkeit der Schrift [...], um darin zugleich ihre wahre Göttlichkeit, ihre volle Gottmenschlichkeit zu erkennen."—"[We must recognize] the full humanity of the Scripture, in order to recognize at the same time its true divinity, its full divine-humanity" (xiv). On Hupfeld, consult Otto Kaiser, "An Heir of Astruc in a Remote German University: Hermann Hupfeld and the 'New Documentary Hypothesis'," in Jarick, *Sacred Conjectures*, 220–248.

Man unterscheidet immer noch nicht genug das dokumentirte Faktum von der ungewissen Tradition, und kann es aus den angeführten Umständen noch nicht unterscheiden; man weiß immer noch nicht den Gränzpunkt zu bestimmen, wo die Sage aufhört, und die Geschichte anhebt. Man redet noch von einem Vater Abraham, den man will gesehen haben, da man doch keinen gesehenen Abraham, sondern nur einen gedachten, und eingebildeten, und nach der Einbildung dargestellten Abraham hat.

One does not yet distinguish the documented fact from the vague tradition, and one cannot separate it [the documented fact] from the given circumstances. One does not yet know how to identify the point where popular legend finishes and history begins. One still speaks of a Father Abraham whom one wants to have seen, although the Abraham one has is not seen, but only thought of, and imagined, and represented according to that imagination.[64]

Ilgen adds to this first example other difficulties. He proceeds by speaking of Moses who must have promulgated a law that was never changed or adapted according to new situations.[65] Israel's ancestors offer sacrifices exactly as Aaron did long afterwards. They honor the creator of the world who was known only much later. They must live according to principles that were enforced several generations afterwards (xiii). This is affirmed, let us notice, not by a recent member of any "minimalist" school of exegesis. This is affirmed by Ilgen, in 1798. "There is nothing new under the sun" (Qoh 1:9), one is tempted to say. These difficulties, especially the anachronisms and contradictions in the book of Genesis, can be solved, according to Ilgen, only when one separates the elements belonging to the different sources ("Quellen") or documents ("Urkunden"), and then recomposes or reconstructs these documents. What is noteworthy here is Ilgen's distinguished sense of history. The results of his research will be criticized and, for the

---

[64] Wilhelm Martin Leberecht de Wette is of the same opinion: "Was man vielleicht für zu kühn erkennen wird, daß ich den ganzen Pentateuch von Anfang bis Ende in mythischer Bedeutung nehme, ist doch weiter nichts als Consequenz: denn wie das Einzelne, so auch das Ganze."—"One may perhaps take this [affirmation] as too bold, namely that I interpret the whole Pentateuch, from the beginning till the end, in a mythological key. This is however nothing but a [logical] consequence [of the observation that we have poetry and not history in the Old Testament]: just as [one explains] the detail, so [one has to explain] the whole too" (*Beiträge zur Einleitung in das Alte Testament* [2 vols. Halle: Schimmelpfennig, 1806–1807; repr., Hildesheim: Georg Olms, 1971], 2:iii–iv).

[65] Ilgen, *Urkunden*, xiii, proposes to compare Moses, the supposed author of the whole Pentateuch, to a "Cramer unserer Zeiten," a retailer, a monger, that can sell (almost) everything, especially civil and cultic laws.

most part, forgotten—at least today. Hupfeld, however, recognizes his debt towards Ilgen[66] and his research is surely a landmark in the exegesis of the Book of Genesis.

To sum up, the study of Genesis owes much to Ilgen. His main contribution, let us repeat, is not the "discovery" of a second Elohist, but rather the proposal of a clear exegetical and historical methodology.

Conclusion

In a few words, this short stroll through the history of exegesis shows that by the year 1800 we had almost all the ingredients that were needed for the critical interpretation of the Book of Genesis: (a) scholars were convinced that it was possible to look for sources in Genesis; (b) they had developed some instruments to discover and identify these sources; and (c) they had established some criteria for dating the texts, although none of them dared to propose a precise date for the sources they identified. Colenso, Kuenen, Reuss, Graf, and Wellhausen were to refine the studies of their predecessors; they were to change the order and dating of the sources, and there were long discussions about the attribution of verses and even parts of verses to the different sources and redactions yet to come.[67] But one will have to wait until Gunkel to see something like a truly new plant grow in the exegetical garden of Genesis. Gunkel introduced new insights and new methods. I am not speaking here only of "literary genres" and "Sitz im Leben." I am speaking of "Die Kunstform der Sagen der Genesis"—"The artistic form of the popular stories in Genesis."[68] With Gunkel, the exegete is not only a scientist, he or she also has to be an artist.[69] But that is another story.

---

[66] Hupfeld, *Die Quellen*, viii–ix.

[67] There are, of course, many excellent publications on this. See, for instance, Cornelis Houtman, *Der Pentateuch: Die Geschichte seiner Erforschung neben einer Auswertung* (CBET 9; Kampen: Kok Pharos, 1994), 98–183.

[68] Gunkel, *Genesis*, xxvi–xlvi.

[69] As Gunkel states: "Denn Exegese im höchsten Sinne ist mehr eine Kunst als eine Wissenschaft"—"Exegesis in the highest sense of the word is more an art than a science"; see his "Ziele und Methoden der Erklärung des Alten Testaments," in *Reden und Aufsätze* (Göttingen: Vandenhoek & Ruprecht, 1913), 11–29, here 14.

Select Bibliography

Arnold, Bill T. "Pentateuchal Criticism, History of." Pages 622–631 in *Dictionary of the Old Testament: Pentateuch*. Edited by T. Desmond Alexander and David W. Baker. Leicester: InterVarsity, 2003.

Astruc, Jean. *Conjectures sur les mémoires originaux dont il paroît que Moyse s'est servi pour composer le Livre de la Genèse*. Bruxelles: Fricx, 1753. Repr., *Conjectures sur la Genèse: Introductions et notes par Pierre Gibert*. Paris: Noêsis, 1999.

Bonfrère, Jacques. *Pentateuchus Moysis commentario illustratus*. Antwerp: Ex Officina Plantiniana, 1625.

De Moor, Johan C., ed. *Synchronic or Diachronic? A Debate on Method in Old Testament Exegesis*. Oudtestamentische Studiën 35. Leiden: Brill, 1995.

De Wette, Wilhelm Martin Leberecht. *Beiträge zur Einleitung in das Alte Testament*. 2 vols. Halle: Schimmelpfennig, 1806–1807. Repr., Hildesheim: Georg Olms, 1971.

Delitzsch, Franz Julius. *Commentar über die Genesis*. 4th ed. Leipzig: Dörffling und Franke, 1872. 1st ed. 1852.

Drechsler, Moritz. *Die Einheit und Ächtheit der Genesis oder Erklärung derjenigen Erscheinungen in der Genesis, welche wider den Mosaischen Ursprung derselben geltend gemacht werden*. Hamburg: Perthes, 1838.

Eichhorn, Johannes Gottfried. *Einleitung in das Alte Testament*. 3 vols. Leipzig: Weidmann, 1780–1783 (1st ed.), 1787–1790 (2nd ed.), 1795–1803 (3rd ed.), 1823–1824 (4th ed.; 5 vols.).

Gibert, Pierre. *L'invention critique de la Bible: XVe–XVIIIe siècle*. Bibliothèque des Histoires. Paris: Gallimard, 2010.

Green, William Henry. *The Unity of the Book of Genesis*. New York: Charles Scribner's Sons, 1895.

Gunkel, Hermann. *Genesis*. 6th ed. Handkommentar zum Alten Testament 1/1. Göttingen: Vandenhoeck & Ruprecht, 1964. Reprint of 3rd ed. (1910). Translated by Mark E. Biddle. Macon, Ga.: Mercer University Press, 1997.

———. *Reden und Aufsätze*. Göttingen: Vandenhoek & Ruprecht, 1913.

Hengstenberg, Ernst Wilhelm. *Die Authentie des Pentateuchs*. Beiträge zur Einleitung ins Alte Testament 1. Berlin: Ludwig Oehmigke, 1836.

Houtman, Cornelis. *Der Pentateuch: Die Geschichte seiner Erforschung neben einer Auswertung*. Contributions to Biblical Exegesis and Theology 9. Kampen: Kok Pharos, 1994.

Hupfeld, Hermann. *Die Quellen der Genesis und die Art ihrer Zusammensetzung von neuem untersucht*. Berlin: Verlag von Wiegandt und Grieken, 1853.

Ibn Ezra, Abraham. *Ibn Ezra's Commentary on the Pentateuch: Genesis (Bereshit)*. Edited and translated by H. Norman Strickman and Arthur M. Silver. New York: Menorah, 1988.

Ilgen, Karl David. *Die Urkunden des ersten Buchs von Moses in ihrer Urgestalt zum bessern Verständniß und richtigern Gebrauch derselben in ihrer gegenwärtigen Form aus dem hebräischen mit kritischen Anmerkungen und Nachweisungen auch einer Abhandlung über die Trennung der Urkunden*. Halle: Hemmerde und Schwetschke, 1798.

Jarick, John, ed. *Sacred Conjectures: The Context and Legacy of Robert Lowth and Jean Astruc*. Library of Hebrew Bible/Old Testament Studies 457. London: T&T Clark, 2007.
Kurtz, Johannes Heinrich. *Beiträge zur Vertheidigung und Begründung der Einheit des Pentateuchs*. Königsberg: Gräfe, 1844.
——. *Die Einheit der Genesis: Ein Beitrag zur Kritik und Exegese der Genesis*. Berlin: Wohlgemuth, 1846.
Ramban (Nachmanides). *Commentary on the Torah: Genesis*. Edited and translated by Charles B. Chavel. New York: Shilo Publishing House, 1971.
Rashi. *The Torah: With Rashi's Commentary Translated, Annotated, and Elucidated*. Edited by Yisrael Isser Zvi Herczeg. 5 vols. Brooklyn: Mesorah Publications, 1994–1998.
Sæbø, Magne, ed. *Hebrew Bible/Old Testament: The History of Its Interpretation, Volume 2: From the Renaissance to the Enlightenment*. Göttingen: Vandenhoeck & Ruprecht, 2008.
Schechter, Solomon. "Geniza Specimens: The Oldest Collection of Bible Difficulties, by a Jew." *Jewish Quarterly Review* 13 (1901): 345–374.
Seidel, Bodo. *Karl David Ilgen und die Pentateuchforschung im Umkreis der sogenannten Älteren Urkundenhypothese: Studien zur Geschichte der exegetischen Hermeneutik in der Späten Aufklärung*. Beihefte zur Zeitschrift für die alttestamentliche Wissenschaft 213. Berlin: de Gruyter, 1993.
Simon, Richard. *Histoire critique du Vieux Testament*. Paris: Billaine, 1678. Repr., Rotterdam: Reenier Leers, 1685. Repr., nouvelle édition annotée et introduite par Pierre Gibert; Paris: Bayard, 2008.
Spinoza, Baruch. *Tractatus theologico-politicus*. Amsterdam: Jan Rieuwertsz, 1663, 1670, 1677.
Thompson, Thomas L. *The Historicity of the Patriarchal Narratives: The Quest for the Historical Abraham*. Beihefte zur Zeitschrift für die alttestamentliche Wissenschaft 133. Berlin: de Gruyter, 1974.
Van Seters, John. *The Edited Bible: The Curious History of the 'Editor' in Biblical Criticism*. Winona Lake, Ind.: Eisenbrauns, 2006.

GENESIS IN THE PENTATEUCH

Konrad Schmid

INTRODUCTION

In the heyday of the Documentary Hypothesis it was a common assumption that most texts in Genesis were to be interpreted as elements of narrative threads that extended beyond the book of Genesis and at least had a pentateuchal or hexateuchal scope (J, E, and P). To a certain degree, exegesis of the book of Genesis was therefore tantamount to exegesis of the book of Genesis in the Pentateuch or Hexateuch. The *Theologische Realenzyklopädie*, one of the major lexica in the German-speaking realm, has for example no entry for "Genesis" but only for the "Pentateuch" and its alleged sources. At the same time, it was also recognized that the material—oral or written—which was processed and reworked by the authors of the sources J, E, and P originated within a more modest narrative perspective that was limited to the single stories or story cycles, a view emphasized especially by Julius Wellhausen, Hermann Gunkel, Kurt Galling, and Martin Noth:[1] J and E were not authors, but collectors.[2] Gunkel even went a step further: "'J' and 'E' are not individual writers, but schools of narrators."[3] But with the successful reception of Gerhard von Rad's 1938 hypothesis of a traditional matrix now accessible through the "historical creeds" like Deut 26:5–9, which was assumed to have also been the intellectual background of the older oral material, biblical scholarship began to lose sight of the view taken by Wellhausen, Gunkel, Galling, and Noth. In addition, von Rad saw J and

---

[1] Julius Wellhausen, *Die Composition des Hexateuchs und der historischen Bücher des Alten Testaments* (3rd ed.; Berlin: Reimer, 1899); Hermann Gunkel, *Genesis* (6th ed.; HKAT 1/1; Göttingen: Vandenhoeck & Ruprecht, 1964 [repr. of the 1910 ed.]), translated as *Genesis* (trans. Mark E. Biddle; Macon, Ga.: Mercer University Press, 1997); Kurt Galling, *Die Erwählungstraditionen Israels* (Giessen: Töpelmann, 1928); and Martin Noth, *A History of Pentateuchal Traditions* (trans. with an Introduction by Bernhard W. Anderson; Chico, Calif.: Scholars Press, 1981 [German original 1948]).

[2] See also Ronald S. Hendel, "Book of Genesis," in *ABD* 2:933–941.

[3] Gunkel, *Genesis*, LXXXV (English translation mine; the original states: "'J' und 'E' sind also nicht Einzelschriftsteller, sondern Erzählerschulen").

E as "theologians," rather than the collectors proposed by Gunkel, and von Rad's view had an enormous impact on subsequent scholarship.[4] His position dominated pentateuchal research in the mid-twentieth century, and it was also predominately his view of the Documentary Hypothesis that was received in the English-speaking world.

The mid-seventies of the last century provided a caesura: scholars like Rolf Rendtorff[5] and Erhard Blum drew attention to the pre-pentateuchal orientations of the texts now contained within the book of Genesis.[6] However, Blum, for example, still holds that the concept of the pentateuchal history is much older than its first literary formations, thereby seeming to overcome Gerhard von Rad's conception on a literary, but not necessarily tradition-historical, level.[7]

Pentateuchal scholarship has changed dramatically in the last three decades, at least when seen in a global perspective. The confidence of earlier assumptions about the formation of the Pentateuch no longer exists, a situation that might be lamented but that also opens up new and—at least in the view of some scholars—potentially more adequate paths to understand its composition.[8] One of the main results of the new situation is that neither

---

[4] Gerhard von Rad, "Das formgeschichtliche Problem des Hexateuchs," in *Gesammelte Studien zum Alten Testament* (TB 8; Munich: Kaiser, 1958), 9–86; translated as "The Form Critical Problem of the Hexateuch," in *The Problem of the Hexateuch and Other Essays* (trans. E.W. Trueman Dickens; London: SCM Press, 1984), 1–78.

[5] Rolf Rendtorff, *Das überlieferungsgeschichtliche Problem des Pentateuch* (BZAW 147; Berlin: de Gruyter, 1977). See also his "Der 'Jahwist' als Theologe? Zum Dilemma der Pentateuchkritik," in *Congress Volume Edinburgh 1974* (ed. G.W. Anderson, et al.; VTSup 28; Leiden: Brill, 1975), 158–166; translated as "The 'Yahwist' as Theologian? The Dilemma of Pentateuchal Criticism," *JSOT* 3 (1977): 2–10, which is in direct conversation with von Rad's notion of J as "theologian."

[6] For a more detailed treatment of these processes, see Konrad Schmid, *Genesis and the Moses Story: Israel's Dual Origins in the Hebrew Bible* (Siphrut 3; Winona Lake, Ind.: Eisenbrauns, 2010), 7–16, 334–347; and Schmid, "Has European Pentateuchal Scholarship Abandoned the Documentary Hypothesis? Some Reminders on Its History and Remarks on Its Current Status," in *The Pentateuch: International Perspectives on Current Research* (ed. Thomas B. Dozeman, Konrad Schmid, and Baruch J. Schwartz; FAT 78; Tübingen: Mohr Siebeck, 2011), 17–30.

[7] Erhard Blum, *Die Komposition der Vätergeschichte* (WMANT 57; Neukirchen-Vluyn: Neukirchener, 1984), 360–361; and David M. Carr, *Reading the Fractures of Genesis: Historical and Literary Approaches* (Louisville: Westminster John Knox, 1996), 217–218.

[8] See, e.g., Georg Fischer, "Zur Lage der Pentateuchforschung," *ZAW* 115 (2003): 608–616; Thomas Römer, "Hauptprobleme der gegenwärtigen Pentateuchforschung," *TZ* 60 (2004): 289–307; Römer, "La formation du Pentateuque: histoire de la recherche," in *Introduction à l'Ancien Testament* (ed. Thomas Römer, Jean-Daniel Macchi, and Christophe Nihan; MdB 49; Geneva: Labor et Fides, 2004), 67–84; Thomas B. Dozeman and Konrad Schmid, eds., *A Farewell to the Yahwist? The Composition of the Pentateuch in Recent European Scholarship*

traditional nor newer theories can be taken as the accepted starting point of analysis; rather, they are, at most, possible ends. The following discussion therefore strives to base itself on textual observations and not on a specific theory of the formation of the Pentateuch.

The Book of Genesis as a Prologue to the Moses Story

On the level of the final shape of the Pentateuch,[9] it is fairly obvious that the book of Genesis serves as a kind of introduction or prologue to what follows in Exodus through Deuteronomy.[10] It narrates the pre-history in terms of the global beginnings (Gen 1–11) and the ancestry of Israel (Gen 12–50), whose story under the leadership of Moses until before the entry in the promised land is then told in the four latter books of the Pentateuch. Exodus begins and continues where Genesis ends; there is some connecting overlap between the fringes of the two books.

The narrative from Exodus through Deuteronomy is bound together as a presentation of the life of Moses, framed by the reports of his birth (Exod 2) and his death (Deut 34), covering the 120 years of his life. In addition, Exodus through Deuteronomy offer all the law collections of the Torah. The book of Genesis introduces this *vita Mosis* including the biblical law corpora by contextualizing it in the framework of global history, world chronology,[11] and the pre-history of Moses' people.

(SBLSymS 34; Atlanta: Society of Biblical Literature, 2006); Eckart Otto, *Das Gesetz des Mose* (Darmstadt: Wissenschaftliche Buchgesellschaft, 2007); Otto, "Kritik der Pentateuchkomposition: Eine Diskussion neuerer Entwürfe," in *Die Tora: Studien zum Pentateuch: Gesammelte Aufsätze* (ed. Eckart Otto; BZABR 9; Wiesbaden: Harrassowitz, 2009), 143–167; Otto, "Die Tora im Alten Testament: Entstehung und Bedeutung für den Pentateuch," *BK* 65 (2010): 19–23; and Konrad Schmid, *Literaturgeschichte des Alten Testaments* (Darmstadt: Wissenschaftliche Buchgesellschaft, 2008), 37–41. The current situation is evaluated very critically by Joel S. Baden, *J, E, and the Redaction of the Pentateuch* (FAT 68; Tübingen: Mohr Siebeck, 2009), who defends the basic tenets of the traditional Documentary Hypothesis while specifically emphasizing the separateness of J and E before D.

[9] For a differentiated view on this notion see Erhard Blum, "Gibt es die Endgestalt des Pentateuch?" in *Congress Volume Leuven 1989* (ed. J.A. Emerton; VTSup 43; Leiden: Brill, 1991), 46–57.

[10] Matthias Millard, *Die Genesis als Eröffnung der Tora: Kompositions- und auslegungsgeschichtliche Annäherungen an das erste Buch Mose* (WMANT 90; Neukirchen-Vluyn: Neukirchener, 2001). See also John Van Seters, *Prologue to History: The Yahwist as Historian in Genesis* (Louisville: Westminster John Knox, 1992) for his understanding of J.

[11] For the details of the chronology, also regarding the different textual versions, see Jeremy Hughes, *Secrets of the Times: Myth and History in Biblical Chronology* (JSOTSup 66; Sheffield: Sheffield Academic Press, 1990).

Nevertheless, the function of Genesis in the Pentateuch is apparently not exhausted by describing it as introduction to the Moses story. It is fairly obvious that Genesis introduces and discusses themes and topics which do not have a counterpart later on in Exodus-Deuteronomy and which cannot be described as merely introductory elements. This is for example true for the cosmological and the anthropological arguments of the Primeval History, although they also relate to some extent to the sanctuary and law texts in Exodus-Deuteronomy.[12] On a theological level, it needs to be noted that the promises to the ancestors in Genesis, concerning offspring and land possession, are fulfilled in the context of Exodus-Deuteronomy only with respect to offspring (see explicitly Exod 1:7 on the literary level of P). The land promise remains unfulfilled until the conquest of Canaan narrated in the book of Joshua (see Josh 21:43–45), and it becomes unfulfilled again after the loss of the land described at the end of the book of Kings (see 2 Kgs 25:11–12, 21–22, 26).[13] The promise theme is probably the most prominent element in Genesis that has a significance of its own.[14] In this respect,

---

[12] For example, this is discernible in the theological design of the sanctuary in Exod 25–40 (see especially the interconnections between Gen 1:31; 2:1–3 and Exod 39:32, 43; 40:33) as a "creation within creation" (see Erhard Blum, *Studien zur Komposition des Pentateuch* [BZAW 189; Berlin: de Gruyter, 1990], 306–311; Peter Weimar, "Sinai und Schöpfung: Komposition und Theologie der priesterlichen Sinaigeschichte," *RB* 95 [1988]: 337–385; and Bernd Janowski, "Tempel und Schöpfung: Schöpfungstheologische Aspekte der priesterschriftlichen Heiligtumskonzeption," in *Schöpfung und Neuschöpfung* [ed. Ingo Baldermann et al.; JBT 5; Neukirchen-Vluyn: Neukirchener, 1990], 37–69; reprinted in *Gottes Gegenwart in Israel: Beiträge zur Theologie des Alten Testaments* [Neukirchen-Vluyn: Neukirchener, 1993], 214–246). On the logical interconnection between Gen 6:5, 8:21, and Deut 30:6, see Thomas Krüger, "Das menschliche Herz und die Weisung Gottes: Elemente einer Diskussion über Möglichkeiten und Grenzen der Tora-Rezeption im Alten Testament," in *Das menschliche Herz und die Weisung Gottes: Studien zur alttestamentlichen Anthropologie und Ethik* (ATANT 96; Zürich: TVZ, 2009), 107–136; and Konrad Schmid, "Die Unteilbarkeit der Weisheit: Überlegungen zur sogenannten Paradieserzählung Gen 2f. und ihrer theologischen Tendenz," *ZAW* 114 (2002): 21–39.

[13] See on these texts Christoph Levin, "The Empty Land in Kings," in *The Concept of Exile in Ancient Israel and its Historical Contexts* (ed. Ehud Ben Zvi and Christoph Levin; BZAW 404; Berlin: de Gruyter, 2010), 61–89.

[14] In terms of redaction history, the promises in Genesis have to be seen on very different levels: there are probably quite ancient promises like the promise of a son in Gen 18:10, which belongs to the substance of that narrative. However, most of the promises obviously have redactional origins that seek to connect the stories and story cycles in Gen 12–50 to a larger whole. Examples can be found in Gen 12:1–3; 13:14–17; 28:13–15; Gen 31:3, 13; and Gen 46:2–4. Rendtorff in particular has pointed to the fact that the promises usually are not integral parts of the narratives they are found in. Still, they have to be differentiated in terms of their literary genesis. Some of the earlier redactional promises might have originated after 722 BCE, compensating theologically for the fall of the northern kingdom, even while the bulk of them

Genesis counterbalances the Moses story in Exodus-Deuteronomy, which takes place completely outside of Israel's land (except for the tribes settling east of Jordan in Num 32): the narrative scenery of Gen 12–50 is mostly in Canaan itself, and the promise of the land (Gen 12:7; 13:17; 15:18–21; 17:8; 28:13; 35:12; etc.) is a motif that compensates for Israel's landless existence in Exodus-Deuteronomy within the overall context of the Pentateuch. It is therefore no surprise that this Genesis theme is taken up subsequently and regularly in the following books (Gen 50:24; Exod 32:13; 33:1; Num 32:11; Deut 34:4; see below for discussion on these texts).

Diachronic Perspectives

Although the transition from Genesis to Exodus is quite smooth and narratively plausible, it is apparent when viewed historically that neither was Genesis originally written in order to be continued in Exodus nor did Exodus necessarily presuppose Genesis as its introduction.[15] The Joseph story in particular, which in the present shape of the Pentateuch serves as a bridge between Genesis and Exodus, contains different aims than simply telling how Israel came to Egypt.[16] In Gen 50, after already having moved *in toto* to Egypt, Israel returns to Canaan again; by means of only one verse (Gen 50:14), the people is transferred back to Egypt again.[17] In addition, the image

---

also presuppose the destruction of Jerusalem and Judah in 587 BCE; see Matthias Köckert, *Vätergott und Väterverheißungen: Eine Auseinandersetzung mit Albrecht Alt und seinen Erben* (FRLANT 142; Göttingen: Vandenhoeck & Ruprecht, 1988); and Köckert, "Verheißung," *TRE* 34:697–704. Reinhard G. Kratz, *The Composition of the Historical Books of the Old Testament* (trans. John Bowden; London: T&T Clark, 2005), 262–265, still opts for a preexilic setting for Gen 12:1–3 and 28:13–15, but after 722 BCE. Gen 12:1–3 and 28:13–15 bind the Abraham and the Jacob cycles together.

[15] For Exod 2 as the original opening of the exodus story, see Eckart Otto, "Mose und das Gesetz: Die Mose-Figur als Gegenentwurf Politischer Theologie zur neuassyrischen Königsideologie im 7. Jh. v. Chr.," in *Mose: Ägypten und das Alte Testament* (SBS 189; Stuttgart: Katholisches Bibelwerk, 2000), 43–83; David M. Carr, "Genesis in Relation to the Moses Story," in *Studies in the Book of Genesis: Literature, Redaction and History* (ed. A. Wénin; BETL 155; Leuven: Peeters, 2001), 293–295; and Schmid, *Genesis and the Moses Story*, 122–144.

[16] See Kratz, *The Composition of the Historical Books of the Old Testament*, 274–279; and Konrad Schmid, "Die Josephsgeschichte im Pentateuch," in *Abschied vom Jahwisten: Die Komposition des Hexateuch in der jüngsten Diskussion* (ed. Jan Christian Gertz, Konrad Schmid, and Markus Witte; BZAW 315; Berlin: de Gruyter, 2002), 83–118.

[17] On Gen 50:14, see especially Jan Christian Gertz, "The Transition between the Books of Genesis and Exodus," in Dozeman and Schmid, *A Farewell to the Yahwist?*, 73–87, who attributes this verse to P.

of the cruel and ignorant Pharaoh in Exod 1–15 is not well prepared by the Joseph story, which itself offers a completely different image of the Egyptian king. Neither is Israel's plight as forced laborers explained. The Israelites arrived as peaceful peasants in Egypt: how did they become slaves? Finally, the chronological adjustment between Genesis and Exodus is also spotty: According to Exod 12:40, Israel is said to have served for 430 years in Egypt; on the other hand, according to Exod 2:1, Moses seems to be Levi's grandson on his maternal side, which hardly allows for more than 100 years between Genesis and Exodus.[18] These differences in chronology also provide a hint that the transition from Genesis to Exodus does not belong to the core narrative of either of those books.

Despite some important introductory functions for the following books, Genesis also shows, as we have already seen, clear signs of having existed as a stand-alone literary unit for some portion of its literary growth. Genesis is a special book within the Pentateuch: it is the most self-sufficient one.[19] This is also corroborated by a comparison of its closing words to those of the other pentateuchal books, revealing the special status of Genesis within the Pentateuch. Exodus-Deuteronomy seem to be construed redactionally as a four-book series by their last verses, while the book of Genesis is not an integral part of that series (see the formulations "before the eyes of all [the house of] Israel" in Exod 40:38 and Deut 34:12, and "these are the commandments ... that YHWH commanded ..." in Lev 27:34 and Num 36:13, which form an *inclusio*).[20]

Consequently, it is not far fetched to conclude that the origins and the earlier formative stages of the book of Genesis do not yet show the awareness of neighboring texts and books, hinting at their original literary independence. It is a quite common and well-established assumption even within the Documentary Hypothesis that, e.g., the Abraham-Lot stories, the Jacob cycle, and the Joseph story were separate literary units before being worked together into a proto-Genesis book and then incorporated into the "sources."[21]

---

[18] See Schmid, *Genesis and the Moses Story*, 5.

[19] See David L. Petersen, "The Genesis of Genesis," in *Congress Volume Ljubljana 2007* (ed. André Lemaire; VTSup 133; Leiden: Brill, 2010), 28: "Hence, I maintain that Genesis is not simply one portion of the larger Pentateuch; Genesis is a book of its own right."

[20] See Ehud Ben Zvi, "The Closing Words of the Pentateuchal Books: A Clue for the Historical Status of the Book of Genesis within the Pentateuch," *BN* 62 (1992): 7–11.

[21] See e.g. Werner H. Schmidt, *Einführung in das Alte Testament* (5th ed.; Berlin: de Gruyter, 1995), 63–75; and John J. Collins, *Introduction to the Hebrew Bible* (Minneapolis: Fortress, 2004), 86–88.

Therefore, the question arises: At what point in their literary history were the traditions now contained in the book of Genesis linked to the still growing Pentateuch? Put this way, the question opens up many possibilities for speculation. When dealing with the literary history of a biblical book, the danger of leaving the ground of safe assumptions cannot always be avoided. There are no copies of the book of Genesis of the sixth or fourth century BCE by which some theories about its composition could be empirically verified or falsified. Only the final versions of the book—extant in the different textual witnesses of Genesis—are known. Nevertheless, it is possible to identify and discuss some more or less clear textual elements in the book of Genesis that establish such links and that allow some conclusions. According to a quite common methodological consensus in diachronic biblical studies, it makes sense to begin with the (allegedly) later texts and then to proceed gradually to earlier ones.[22] This methodological principle applies with particular importance for my section on "Further Links from Genesis to the Other Books of the Pentateuch" below; meanwhile, the Priestly texts form a well-defined literary corpus of their own, a topic to which we now turn.

The Priestly Layer in Genesis and the Following Pentateuchal Books

There is one set of texts in Genesis belonging to a prominent textual layer that runs at least through Genesis and Exodus—traditionally known as the "Priestly Code" (P)—which are very well connected among each other.[23] Nineteenth-century scholarship believed P to be the foundational layer of

---

[22] See e.g. Rudolf Smend, *Die Entstehung des Alten Testaments* (4th ed.; TW 1; Stuttgart: Kohlhammer, 1991), 9–12.

[23] See the standard text assignments by Karl Elliger, "Sinn und Ursprung der priesterlichen Geschichtserzählung," *ZTK* 49 (1952): 121–143; reprinted in *Kleine Schriften zum Alten Testament: Zu seinem 65. Geburtstag am 7. März 1966* (ed. Hartmut Gese and Otto Kaiser; TB 32; Munich: Kaiser, 1966), 174–198; Norbert Lohfink, "Die Priesterschrift und die Geschichte" in *Congress Volume Göttingen 1977* (ed. J.A. Emerton; VTSup 29; Leiden: Brill, 1978), 183–225; reprinted in *Studien zum Pentateuch* (SBAB 4; Stuttgart: Katholisches Bibelwerk, 1988), 213–253; and Eckart Otto, "Forschungen zur Priesterschrift," *TRu* 62 (1997): 1–50. P probably originally ended in the Sinai pericope; for more, see Thomas Pola, *Die ursprüngliche Priesterschrift: Beobachtungen zur Literarkritik und Traditionsgeschichte von P^g* (WMANT 70; Neukirchen-Vluyn: Neukirchener, 1995); and Petersen, "Genesis of Genesis," 38. The traditional solution (P ends in Deut 34) is defended by Christian Frevel, *Mit dem Blick auf das Land die Schöpfung erinnern: Zum Ende der Priestergrundschrift* (HBS 23; Freiburg: Herder, 2000).

the Pentateuch, which in some sense holds still true: P apparently established the main thread along which older, formerly independent text materials have also been arranged.[24]

Despite all the uncertainties of pentateuchal research, P still remains a sufficiently safe assumption.[25] Its texts probably formed a once independent literary entity that might have been written at the end of the sixth century BCE.[26]

In terms of P, Genesis is therefore very well linked to the rest of the Pentateuch,[27] which of course also accords with P's basic theological perspective, one which views the patriarchal period as the theological basis of Israel—not the Sinai events.[28]

Nevertheless, the tight coherence between Genesis and Exodus in P still betrays the binding together of two divergent narrative blocks, as can be seen especially in Exod 6:3: in the commissioning of Moses, God introduces himself as YHWH despite the fact that he appeared to Abraham, Isaac, and Jacob as *El Shadday*.[29] This gradual revelation of God has, of course, some function within P, but it also reflects the different theological profiles of Genesis and Exodus that result from their particular literary-historical backgrounds.

---

[24] Theodor Nöldeke, "Die s.g. Grundschrift des Pentateuch," in *Untersuchungen zur Kritik des Alten Testaments* (Kiel: Schwers, 1886), 1–144.

[25] See, e.g., Blum, *Studien zur Komposition des Pentateuch*, 221; and Carr, *Fractures*, 43.

[26] P's political theology presupposes Persian imperial ideology, which sets 539 BCE as a *terminus a quo* (see Konrad Schmid, "Gibt es eine 'abrahamitische Ökumene' im Alten Testament? Überlegungen zur religionspolitischen Theologie der Priesterschrift in Genesis 17," in *Die Erzväter in der biblischen Tradition: Festschrift für Matthias Köckert* [ed. Anselm C. Hagedorn and Henrik Pfeiffer; BZAW 400; Berlin: de Gruyter, 2009], 67–92). A *terminus ad quem* might be seen in the conquest of Egypt by Cambyses in 525 BCE, which is probably not reflected in P because Egypt seems to be excluded from P's vision of a peaceful world under God's rule (see Exod 7–11 and 12:12 as well as, in particular, Albert de Pury, "P^g as the Absolute Beginning," in *Les dernières rédactions du Pentateuque, de l'Hexateuque et de l'Ennéateuque* [ed. Thomas Römer and Konrad Schmid; BETL 203; Leuven: Peeters, 2007], 99–128, especially 123–128).

[27] To my mind, P is also the first author in the Pentateuch to have established a literary link between Gen and Exod and thereby also to have created the basic narrative outline of the Pentateuch. For details, see my *Genesis and the Moses Story* and below nn. 73 and 76; for opposing views, see n. 74 below.

[28] See the (still) groundbreaking study of Walther Zimmerli, "Sinaibund und Abrahambund: Ein Beitrag zum Verständnis der Priesterschrift," *TZ* 16 (1960): 268–280, reprinted in Zimmerli, *Gottes Offenbarung: Gesammelte Aufsätze zum Alten Testament* (TB 19; Munich: Kaiser, 1963), 205–217; see also Schmid, *Genesis and the Moses Story*, 238–248.

[29] For more on this, see W. Randall Garr, "The Grammar and Interpretation of Exodus 6:3," *JBL* 111 (1992): 385–408.

Furthermore, the Genesis portions of P show some signs of being self contained. This results partly from the history of the material, partly from the theological focus of P on the covenant with Abraham (Gen 17), but in addition, notice should be take of the incorporation of the "toledot"-book in P, which covers the primeval and the patriarchal periods of Genesis in two series of five "toledot." Its redactional reception within P can best be observed in Gen 5:1–3: The original superscription of the "toledot"-book is still discernible (5:1a, 3), but was adjusted in light of Gen 1:1–2:4a, especially with respect to "Adam" as a designation for the species of human beings and as a proper noun of its first representative, which triggered the insertion of 5:1b, 2.[30]

Further Links from Genesis to the Other Books of the Pentateuch

Some of the strongest links from Genesis to the following books are provided by the Priestly layer. But it seems that in the non-P material, especially in the post-P material, such connections can be discerned as well.[31] Against the tenets of the Documentary Hypothesis it needs to be stressed that there is no reason to assume that "non-P" always equals "pre-P." The following discussion begins with those texts that have in view the widest literary horizon and at the same time are allegedly the youngest ones. We will then proceed backwards in time to alleged older layers that, however, probably still all belong to the post-P history of Genesis.

Redactional Portions in Genesis Embedding the Book in the Hexateuch (Gen 50:25)

As is well known, there is one set of texts in the sequence of Genesis through Joshua that explicitly belongs together. No element makes sense without the others, therefore they must be part of one and the same literary layer:

---

[30] Schmid, *Genesis and the Moses Story*, 236–237; see also David M. Carr, "Βίβλος γενέσεως Revisitited: A Synchronic Analysis of Genesis as Part of the Torah," *ZAW* 110 (1998): 159–172, 327–347, especially 169–170. A different explanation is offered by Christoph Levin, "Die Redaktion R^P in der Urgeschichte," in *Auf dem Weg zur Endgestalt von Genesis bis II Regum: Festschrift Hans-Christoph Schmitt zum 65. Geburtstag* (ed. Martin Beck and Ulrike Schorn; BZAW 370; Berlin: de Gruyter, 2006), 27–28; cf. Claus Westermann, *Genesis, 1. Teilband: Genesis 1–11* (BKAT 1/1; Neukirchen-Vluyn: Neukirchener, 1974), 481–482.

[31] Eckart Otto, "Forschungen zum nachpriesterschriftlichen Pentateuch," *TRu* 67 (2002): 125–155.

the transfer of Joseph's bones from Egypt back to Canaan in Gen 50:25, Exod 13:19, and Josh 24:32.[32] This is sufficient evidence to claim that at least at the stage of this series of statements, represented in Genesis by (at least[33]) Gen 50:25, the book of Genesis was subject to a redaction comprising the Hexateuch (Genesis-Joshua). In addition, Josh 24:2–4 looks back to Gen 11–12, introducing, however, a new idea contrary to the presentation of Abraham in Genesis with the reference to his and his father's idolatry in Mesopotamia. The location of Josh 24 in Shechem probably also refers back to Gen 12:6, 8 where Abraham is said to have erected the first altar in the land of Canaan.[34] Finally, Joseph and Joshua are paralleled by their ages of 110 years (Gen 50:22; Josh 24:29). However, neither Gen 12:6, 8, nor Gen 11:27–32, nor Gen 50:26 show any awareness of Josh 24. Therefore, it is rather implausible to assign these statements to the same layer: they are probably earlier texts that were taken up later by Josh 24.

It is disputed whether this redaction aimed at establishing a stand-alone Hexateuch or whether this is a literary device to constitute only a "literary" Hexateuch[35] within an Enneateuch (Genesis-Kings).[36] A decision in this question is dependent upon how one understands Josh 24, which will not be discussed here.[37]

---

[32] See Markus Witte, "Die Gebeine Josefs," in Beck and Schorn, *Auf dem Weg zur Endgestalt von Genesis bis II Regum*, 139–156.

[33] As Erhard Blum, *Vätergeschichte*, 44–45, convincingly argues, the motif of Jacob's purchase of the plot (Gen 33:19) also belongs to the same layer of texts.

[34] The LXX places Josh 24 in Shiloh (Josh 24:1, 25), which is probably the result of an anti-Samaritan tendency in its *Vorlage*; see Christophe Nihan, "The Torah between Samaria and Judah: Shechem and Gerizim in Deuteronomy and Joshua," in *The Pentateuch as Torah: New Models for Understanding its Promulgence and its Acceptance* (ed. Bernard M. Levinson and Gary N. Knoppers; Winona Lake, Ind.: Eisenbrauns, 2007), 187–223, esp. 197, n. 31.

[35] Erhard Blum, "Der kompositionelle Knoten am Übergang von Josua zu Richter: Ein Entflechtungsvorschlag," in *Deuteronomy and Deuteronomic Literature: Festschrift C.H.W. Brekelmans* (ed. Marc Vervenne and Johan Lust; BETL 133; Leuven: Leuven University Press, 1997), 181–212; Eckart Otto, *Das Deuteronomium im Pentateuch und im Hexateuch: Studien zur Literaturgeschichte von Pentateuch und Hexateuch im Lichte des Deuteronomiumrahmens* (FAT 30; Tübingen: Mohr 2000), 175–211; Reinhard Achenbach, "Pentateuch, Hexateuch, und Enneateuch: Eine Verhältnisbestimmung," *ZABR* 11 (2005): 122–154; Thomas Römer and Marc Zvi Brettler, "Deuteronomy 34 and the Case for a Persian Hexateuch," *JBL* 119 (2000): 401–419; and Thomas Römer, "Das doppelte Ende des Josuabuches: Einige Anmerkungen zur aktuellen Diskussion um 'deuteronomistisches Geschichtswerk' und 'Hexateuch,'" *ZAW* 118 (2006): 523–548.

[36] Schmid, *Genesis and the Moses Story*, 208–213; 342; and Reinhard Gregor Kratz, "Der vor- und der nachpriesterschriftliche Hexateuch," in Gertz, Schmid, and Witte, *Abschied vom Jahwisten*, 295–323.

[37] See the contributions in Römer and Schmid, *Les dernières rédactions du Pentateuque, de l'Hexateuque et de l'Enneateuque*.

Redactional Portions in Genesis Embedding the Book in the Pentateuch (Gen 50:24; Gen 6:1–4; Gen 22:15–18; 26:3b–5)

Besides the Josh 24 network, there are also texts in Genesis that hint to redactional interests that strive to bind the five books of the Pentateuch together. In particular, David Clines[38] and Thomas Römer[39] have pointed out that the notion of the promise of the land to Abraham, Isaac, and Jacob as oath—without the apposition אבות "fathers"—in Gen 50:24, Exod 32:13, 33:1, Num 32:11, and Deut 34:4 runs through the Pentateuch as a whole. It is especially noteworthy that this motif cannot be found in the subsequent books of Joshua – 2 Kings.[40] Apparently, the promise of land to Abraham, Isaac, and Jacob as an oath is indeed a topic binding the Pentateuch together.

This point can be buttressed in literary-historical terms by the observation that the five texts putting forward the notion of the land promise to Abraham, Isaac, and Jacob as an oath seem to presuppose P and D. Thus, they probably belong to the latest literary developments of the Torah. It seems that they have combined the motif of the land promise as oath that is prominent in the Deuteronomistic parts of Deuteronomy (see Deut 1:8, 35; 6:10, 18, 23; 7:13; 8:1; 9:5; 10:11; 11:9, 21; 19:8; 26:3, 15; 28:11; 30:20; 31:7, 20–21; 34:4) with the Priestly conviction that God's acting towards Israel is rooted in the covenant with the ancestors (cf. Gen 17). The result is the notion of the promise of the land to Abraham, Isaac, and Jacob as an oath.[41] Consequently, Gen 50:24 can be interpreted as an element of a redaction establishing the Pentateuch as a literary unit.[42]

---

[38] David J.A. Clines, *The Theme of the Pentateuch* (rev. ed.; JSOTSup 10; Sheffield: Sheffield Academic Press, 1997).

[39] Thomas Römer, *Israels Väter: Untersuchungen zur Väterthematik im Deuteronomium und in der deuteronomistischen Tradition* (OBO 99; Freiburg, Switz. and Göttingen: Universitätsverlag and Vandenhoeck & Ruprecht, 1990), 566.

[40] Schmid, *Genesis and the Moses Story*, 271–279.

[41] For detailed analysis, see Römer, *Israels Väter*.

[42] For a discussion of the literary-historical relationship between Gen 50:24 and 50:25 see Erhard Blum, "Die literarische Verbindung von Erzvätern und Exodus: Ein Gespräch mit neueren Endredaktionshypothesen," in Gertz, Schmid, and Witte, *Abschied vom Jahwisten*, 145–146; and Schmid, *Genesis and the Moses Story*, 99–100, 214–215, 274–278. Vice versa, Deut 34:4 refers back to the beginning of the Pentateuch, to Gen 12:7 and 13:15 and thus forms an *inclusio*. First, Deut 34:4 quotes the promise of the land given in Gen 12:7. Second, there are clear interconnections between Deut 34:1–4 and Gen 13:10–15. The cross references between Deut 34:1–4 and Gen 12:7, 13:10–15 are especially remarkable, as Gen 12:1–3, 7 and 13:10–17 belong closely together and might be part of one and the same narrative arc, as Matthias Köckert has suggested in *Vätergott und Väterverheißungen*, 250–255; cf. Blum, *Studien zur*

A second element needs to be taken into account when discussing literary elements in Genesis that might be elements of a Pentateuch redaction. Genesis 6:1–4 narrates the somewhat difficult story about the intermarriage between the בני אלהים and the daughters of humankind.[43] Within this text the limitation of human age to 120 years is mentioned (Gen 6:3). It has often been observed,[44] starting as early as Josephus,[45] that this motif is recurrent in Deut 34:7, where Moses is said to have died at the age of 120 years. This life span is not unique in the ancient world,[46] so there is no need to postulate a specific link between Gen 6:3 and Deut 34:7 merely on the basis of that number. Nevertheless, there is a good argument within Deut 34 that shows that Deut 34:7 is alluding to Gen 6:3. Moses death' notice is followed by the amazing statement that he died in the best of health: "His sight was unimpaired and his vigor had not abated."[47] This is especially striking because this statement also creates a contradiction to the text in Deut 31:1–2, where Moses complaints he is no longer at his prime: he is no longer able to go forth and come home—i.e., he is likely no longer capable of military leadership. The emphasis on Moses' health in Deut 34:7 tells the reader that Moses dies for no other reason than that his life span has reached the limit set by God in Gen 6:3. If Deut 34:7 takes up Gen 6:3, the opposite question may be asked: was Gen 6:3 written to prepare for Deut 34:7? This seems indeed to be the case because Gen 6:3 and Deut 34:7 share the same theological

---

Komposition des Pentateuch, 214, n. 35. Deut 34:1–4 seems to take up the promise network of Gen 12–13 as a whole and stresses the fact that the land promised to Abraham is still promised to Israel. But unlike the case of Gen 50:24, there is no indication that Deut 34:1–4 belongs to the same layer as the promise network in Gen 12–13.

[43] See Mirjam and Ruben Zimmermann, "'Heilige Hochzeit' der Göttersöhne und Menschentöchter," *ZAW* 111 (1999): 327–352; Helge Kvanvig, "Gen 6,1–4 as an Antediluvian Event," *SJOT* 16 (2002): 79–112; Kvanvig, "The Watcher Story and Genesis: An Intertextual Reading," *SJOT* 18 (2004): 163–183; and Andreas Schüle, "The Divine-Human Marriages (Genesis 6:1–4) and the Greek Framing of the Primeval History," *TZ* 65 (2009): 116–128.

[44] See e.g. Benno Jacob, *Das erste Buch der Tora: Genesis* (New York: Schocken, 1934), 176–177.

[45] Cf. Josephus, *Ant.* 2.152; 3.95; 4.176–193; see Klaus Haacker and Peter Schäfer, "Nachbiblische Traditionen vom Tod des Mose," in *Josephus-Studien: Untersuchungen zu Josephus, dem antiken Judentum und dem Neuen Testament, Otto Michel zum 70. Geburtstag gewidmet* (ed. Otto Betz, Klaus Haacker, and Martin Hengel; Göttingen: Vandenhoeck & Ruprecht, 1974), 147–174, esp. 148.

[46] See Kvanvig, "Gen 6,1–4 as an Antediluvian Event," 99. Gunkel, *Genesis*, 58 points to Herodotus, *Histories* 3.23 as a parallel to the life span of "120 years" (in this case of Ethiopians).

[47] Otto, *Deuteronomium im Pentateuch*, 226, points to the antithetical composition of Isaac (Gen 27:1) and Moses (Deut 34:7), both connected by the term ההכ, used only here.

profile. Deuteronomy 34:7 states that Moses is not allowed to enter the promised land simply because his life span has run out—not because of any sort of wrongdoing—which is a third alternative explanation of why Moses may not enter the promised land in contrast to the "D" tradition on the one hand (e.g., Deut 1:34–37; 3:25–27)[48] and the P tradition on the other (e.g., Num 20:12). The "Priestly" tradition (probably not "P^g", but rather "P^s") in Num 20:12 assumes that Moses went against God by *striking* the rock when God had ordered a *verbal* miracle ("speak with the rock"; Num 20:8) and possibly even doubted that striking the rock would bring forth water;[49] thus Moses became guilty of faithlessness. The "Deuteronomistic" tradition, on the other hand, includes Moses in the collective guilt of the people: "Even with me YHWH was angry *on your account.*"[50] Both "explanations" reckon with Moses' guilt, be it on a personal level (as in accordance with Priestly thought), be it on a collective level (following Deuteronomistic thinking). In contrast, Deut 34:7 agrees with neither positions.[51] It instead offers its own interpretation: Moses is not allowed to enter the promised land because his life span of 120 years has just run out. Moses' death east of the Jordan is not caused by personal or collective debt, but by fate, i.e. by the divinely ordained limitation of human life.

Interestingly, this theological profile of Deut 34:7—where Moses' death has nothing to do with personal guilt, but rather with fate—matches the thematic thrust of Gen 6:3 within the framework of Gen 6:1–4.[52] In its current literary position, the heavenly interference of divine sons with human daughters offers a (additional) reason for the flood.[53] The flood is not

---

[48] For its placement within redaction history see Otto, *Deuteronomium im Pentateuch*, 22–23; as well as Christian Frevel, "Ein vielsagender Abschied: Exegetische Blicke auf den Tod des Mose," *BZ* 45 (2001): 220–221, n. 37.

[49] The statement in Num 20:10—kept vague probably out of respect for Moses—would then be interpreted as follows: "Should we really be able to produce water from this rock?"

[50] See Deut 1:37 and 3:26 ("YHWH got angry with me because of you").

[51] Thomas Römer, "Deuteronomium 34 zwischen Pentateuch, Hexateuch und deuteronomistischem Geschichtswerk," *ZABR* 5 (1999): 167–178; and Römer and Brettler, "Deuteronomy 34 and the case for a Persian Hexateuch," 408.

[52] See especially Manfred Oeming, "Sünde als Verhängnis: Gen 6,1–4 im Rahmen der Urgeschichte des Jahwisten," *TTZ* 102 (1993): 34–50.

[53] David J.A. Clines, "The Significance of the 'Son of God' Episode (Genesis 6:1–4) in the Context of the 'Primeval History' (Genesis 1–11)" *JSOT* 13 (1979): 33–46; Ronald S. Hendel, "Of Demigods and the Deluge: Towards an Interpretation of Genesis 6:1–4," *JBL* 106 (1987): 13–26; and Andreas Schüle, "The Divine-Human Marriages (Genesis 6:1–4) and the Greek Framing of the Primeval History," *TZ* 65 (2009): 116–128.

only solicited by human guilt (as Gen 6:5–8 states), but also by transcendent fate. Responsibility for the mixing of the human and divine sphere, caused by the בני אלהים, does not fall on the shoulders of humankind. Rather, it just happens to them. Therefore, the literary *inclusio* between Gen 6:3 and Deut 34:7 seems to go back to one and the same hand: Gen 6:3 looks forward to Deut 34:7, and Deut 34:7 refers back to Gen 6:3.

Finally, mention should be made of the passages in Genesis that portray Abraham as a pious observer of the Torah (Gen 22:18b and 26:5b within their contexts of Gen 22:15–18 and Gen 26:3b–5).[54] It is obvious that they reflect the inclusion of the book of Genesis in the Torah and therefore portray the ancestors in the book of Genesis as followers of the Torah.[55] Nevertheless, they are unable to hide the fact that the law was only given later on by Moses, giving rise to the explanation of the book of Jubilees, which deals with the question how Israel's ancestors before Moses could be observant without the law. Its solution was a metaphysical one: by means of heavenly tablets the ancestors who came before Moses were already informed of the law.[56] Genesis 22:18b stands within 22:15–18, which is an addition to Gen 22:1–14, 19, a text probably of post-P origin.[57] Genesis 26:5b is closely interconnected with Gen 22:15–18 and is to be attributed to the same redactional layer.[58]

It cannot be taken for granted that Gen 50:24; 6:1–4; 22:15–18; and 26:3b–5 all stem from one and the same hand. They share the common interest to anchor the book of Genesis within the Pentateuch, but they might also have been inserted at different times.

---

[54] Beate Ego, "Abraham als Urbild der Toratreue Israels: Traditionsgeschichtliche Überlegungen zu einem Aspekt des biblischen Abrahambildes," in *Bund und Tora: Zur theologischen Begriffsgeschichte in alttestamentlicher, frühjüdischer und urchristlicher Tradition* (ed. Friedrich Avemarie and Hermann Lichtenberger; WUNT 92; Tübingen: Mohr, 1996), 25–40.

[55] Blum, *Vätergeschichte*, 363–365, counted these texts among the D-redaction of Genesis, which he now dates post-P; see his "Die literarische Verbindungen," 140–145.

[56] On this motif see Florentino García Martínez, "The Heavenly Tablets in the Book of Jubilees," in *Studies in the Book of Jubilees* (ed. Matthias Albani, Jörg Frey, and Armin Lange; TSAJ 65; Tübingen: Mohr Siebeck, 1997), 243–260.

[57] See the discussion in Konrad Schmid "Die Rückgabe der Verheißungsgabe: Der 'heilsgeschichtliche' Sinn von Genesis 22 im Horizont innerbiblischer Exegese," in *Gott und Mensch im Dialog: Festschrift für Otto Kaiser zum 80. Geburtstag* (ed. Markus Witte; BZAW 345; Berlin: de Gruyter, 2004), 1:271–300.

[58] See the detailed argumentation of Blum, *Vätergeschichte*, 362–364.

Redactional Portions in Genesis
Linking the Book to the Exodus Story (Gen 15)

Genesis 15 involves the most prominent bridge text in Genesis that serves as a literary connection between Genesis to Exodus: Gen 15:13–16 contains a preview that explicitly speaks of a four hundred year sojourn (גור) of Israel as slaves (עבד) and oppressed (ענה) people in Egypt (15:13), of the judgment (דין) of Egypt (15:14a), and of the departure (יצא) of Israel (15:14b, 16) lasting four generations.

It is unclear, however, how this piece fits within the literary history of the book of Genesis. Within the framework of the Documentary Hypothesis, Gen 15 has never been classified convincingly. The frequently presented idea that Gen 15 solemnly introduces "E" was never fully accepted. Today it has been largely abandoned, even among the advocates of "E," especially since Gen 15 only uses the Tetragrammaton, while אלהים never appears. But even the segmentation of "J" and "E" that was often attempted did not succeed convincingly. Thus, it was not possible to classify Gen 15 within the framework of the Documentary Hypothesis.[59] As an alternative, scholars sought to explain Gen 15 "as a Deuteronomistic *corpus separatum*."[60] However, for various reasons, this option proved unsuccessful as well, especially because the specific notion of covenant in Gen 15 hardly fits Deuteronomistic ideas. Recent proposals include those of Römer and Ha who theorize that Gen 15 represents a re-reading of Genesis 17 (P) so that Genesis 15 should therefore be dated after "P."[61] At least for the verses 15:13–16, this option has been accepted also among traditional scholarship, especially because v. 14 (רכוש) and v. 15 (שיבה וטבה) use language otherwise known especially from P texts.[62]

The overall post-Priestly dating of Gen 15 depends on how the literary integrity of the chapter is seen. This need not be decided here[63] but, at

---

[59] For a full discussion, see Schmid, *Genesis and the Moses Story*, 158–161.

[60] Shemaryahu Talmon, "'400 Jahre' oder 'vier Generationen' (Gen 15,13–15): Geschichtliche Zeitangaben oder literarische Motive," in *Die Hebräische Bibel und ihre zweifache Nachgeschichte: Festschrift für Rolf Rendtorff zum 65. Geburtstag* (ed. Erhard Blum, Christian Macholz, and Ekkehard W. Stegemann; Neukirchen-Vluyn: Neukirchener, 1990), 13.

[61] See Thomas Römer, "Gen 15 und Gen 17: Beobachtungen und Anfragen zu einem Dogma der 'neueren' und 'neuesten' Pentateuchkritik," *DBAT* 26 (1989/90): 32–47; and John Ha, *Genesis 15: A Theological Compendium of Pentateuchal History* (BZAW 181; Berlin: de Gruyter, 1989).

[62] See Schmid, *Genesis and the Moses Story*, 166–167 and 166, n. 5.

[63] For a recent proposal, see Jan Christian Gertz, "Abraham, Mose und der Exodus: Beobachtungen zur Redaktionsgeschichte von Gen 15," in Gertz, Schmid, and Witte, *Abschied*

any rate, it seems more or less obvious that the explicit links in Gen 15 presuppose P.

Other portions of Genesis have also been discussed as links to the book of Exodus. Genesis 12:10–20 offers clear associations to the exodus story. The wording of this passage shows that these associations seem to be intended. Pharaoh is struck (נגע) with plagues, as in Exod 11:1. In 12:20, he sends (שלח) Abraham and his entourage forth thereby echoing the leading word of Exod 5–11.[64] Even the commands to let Abraham and Moses go correspond to one another (קח ולך in Gen 12:19 and קחו ולכו in Exod 12:32). "In many respects, the episode is accordingly shaped as a prefiguration of the later exodus, as a piece of salvation history at the beginning of the history of Israel."[65] How one should evaluate this prefiguration is by no means clear at first glance. It might be considered that this anticipation is suited to a critical note; Abraham does not prefigure Moses, but Moses is an epigone of Abraham. However one sees it, Gen 12:10–20 is not exactly a literary bridge between Genesis and Exodus that would connect the flow of events in these two books. The typological correspondence between Abraham and Moses is also quite conceivable between two literarily independent narrative works. The echoes of the exodus do not persuasively signify a presumed literary connection from Genesis to Exodus.[66]

Yet another text often seen as a literary connection between Genesis and Exodus is Gen 46:1–5a.[67] God appears to Jacob and allows him to migrate to Egypt. A promise of fertility and a promise of a return then follow, along with the affirmation that Joseph will close Jacob's eyes (Gen 46:4). The Joseph story does not otherwise reckon with such direct revelations of God, and Gen 46:1–5a strongly recalls the language and content of the preceding ancestral narratives. Blum has worked out the connections from Gen 46:1–5a to the promises in Gen 31:11, 13; Gen 26:2–3; and Gen 12:1–2.[68] According to him, Gen 46:1–5 thus includes the Joseph story in the complex of ancestral transmissions and establishes 12–50 as a large "ancestral story."

---

vom Jahwisten, 63–81; see also Konrad Schmid, "The So-Called Yahwist and the Literary Gap between Genesis and Exodus," in Dozeman and Schmid, *A Farewell to the Yahwist?*, 38, n. 34.

[64] See Blum, *Vätergeschichte*, 309; Schmid, *Genesis and the Moses Story*, 57–58; see also Wolfgang Oswald, "Die Erzeltern als Schutzbürger: Überlegungen zum Thema von Gen 12,10–20 mit Ausblick auf Gen 20; 21,22–34 und Gen 26," *BN* 106 (2001): 79–89.

[65] Blum, *Vätergeschichte*, 309 (my translation). See also the references to the predecessors in Blum, *Vätergeschichte*, 309, n. 14 and Ha, *Genesis 15*, 199–200.

[66] Carr, "Genesis in Relation to the Moses Story," 273–295.

[67] See Blum, *Vätergeschichte*, 246.

[68] See Blum, *Vätergeschichte*, 246–249, 297–301.

Genesis 46:4a (because of the usage of עלה) is often specified as a "anticipatory reference to Exodus."[69] However, this understanding is neither required nor suggested by the text. The explicit horizon of Gen 46:1–5a does not extend beyond Gen 50. The sequence of events that verses 3–4 delineate is as follows: YHWH will move with Jacob to Egypt (3b, 4a), in order to make him into a great people there (גוי גדול in 3b), in order to lead him out again (4a),[70] and Joseph will close his eyes (4b). If one arranges this anticipatory sequence to the subsequent events, then one does not see beyond the Joseph story. Jacob moves to Egypt in Gen 46:5–7. Genesis 47:27b notes the multiplication of Israel (רבה; פרה), and Gen 50:7–13 specifies the return to Canaan as well as the burial of Jacob by Joseph.

Gen 46:3–4	Themes	Genesis 46–50
v. 3b, 4a	trek to Egypt	46:5–7
v. 3b	becoming a nation	47:27b
v. 4a	return	50:7–10
v. 4b	Jacob's burial	50:13

Genesis 46:1–5a only looks forward to the return of Jacob to Canaan in Gen 50, but not to the return of Israel in Exodus-Joshua. However, that means that Gen 46:1–5a has been formulated precisely for the ancestral story encompassing Gen 12–50.[71]

It might be helpful to corroborate this proposal of a late redactional connection between Genesis and Exodus by looking at the very beginning of the book Exodus. It is striking that the statement about Israel becoming a great people does not refer back to the prominent non-Priestly promises of increase at the beginning of the patriarchal narrative (e.g. Gen 12:2; 13:13).

---

[69] See Blum, *Vätergeschichte*, 247.

[70] That the second person singular suffix should "relate collectively to Israel" (Rainer Kessler, "Die Querverweise im Pentateuch: Überlieferungsgeschichtliche Untersuchung der expliziten Querverbindungen innerhalb des vorpriesterlichen Pentateuchs" [Ph.D. diss., University of Heidelberg, 1972], 164, n. 4; 317, in connection with Gerhard von Rad, *Das erste Buch Mose: Genesis* [12th ed.; ATD 2/4; Göttingen: Vandenhoek & Ruprecht, 1987], 352) has little support. Rather, Gunkel correctly noted, "'I will bring you back' in a coffin. This announces Jacob's burial in Canaan" (Gunkel, *Genesis*, 440 [Biddle's translation]; Westermann, *Genesis 37–50*, 156, sees it differently).

[71] This is also assumed in Blum's conception (see *Vätergeschichte*, 360). Blum, however, differentiates. He believes that "the hearer/reader … [i.e., for the understanding of Gen 46:1–5a] does not (require) a literary context, but knowledge of the salvation historical outline to the conquest." Blum has now modified his opinion; see his "Die literarische Verbindung," 132–133, n. 63.

The comparison of the promise of descendants to Abraham in Gen 12:2 and the statement of Pharaoh in Exod 1:9 illustrates the absence of a clear relationship between the two bodies of literature.

Gen 12:2
And I will make you to a great people (גוי גדול).

Exod 1:9
And he [Pharaoh] spoke to his people: Behold, the people (עם) of the children of Israel are more (רב) and mightier (ועצום) than we.

On the other hand it is all the more remarkable that the connections on the P-level are very tight.

Gen 1:28
Be fruitful (פרו), and multiply (ורבו), and fill (ומלאו) the earth (את הארץ)

Gen 9:7
And you, be fruitful (פרו), and multiply (ורבו); increase abundantly (שרצו) in the earth, and multiply (ורבו) therein.

Gen 17:2
And I will multiply (וארבה) you exceedingly (במאד מאד).

Exod 1:7
And the children of Israel were fruitful (פרו), and increased abundantly (וישרצו), and multiplied (וירבו), and waxed (ויעצמו) exceeding mighty (במאד מאד); and the land (והארץ) was filled (ותמלא) with them.

If the non-Priestly substance of the patriarchal and exodus narratives was really written by the same author, telling parts of one and the same story in Genesis and Exodus, it would be very difficult to explain why he did not correlate the promise to become a great people with its fulfillment, as it is done in P. Therefore, it is much more likely that Gen 12:2 and Exod 1:9 belong to different text layers rather than to assume that we have here a J bridge between Genesis and Exodus.

Beside Exod 1 and the P-links, explicit references back to Genesis are found especially in the report on the commissioning of Moses in Exod 3 (see Exod 3:6, 13–16). Again, recent discussions have proposed that either the whole chapter[72] or at least these references are post-P,[73] although others

---

[72] Eckart Otto, "Die nachpriesterschriftliche Pentateuchredaktion im Buch Exodus," in *Studies in the Book of Exodus: Redaction—Reception—Interpretation* (ed. Marc Vervenne; BETL 126; Leuven: Peeters, 1996), 61–111; and Schmid, *Genesis and the Moses Story*, 172–193.

[73] See Jan Christian Gertz, *Tradition und Redaktion in der Exoduserzählung: Untersuchungen zur Endredaktion des Pentateuch* (FRLANT 189; Göttingen: Vandenhoeck & Ruprecht,

have argued to the contrary.[74] A comparison of Exod 3 with its P counterpart in Exod 6:2–8 shows some striking features which might support the case for a post-P setting of Exod 3:1–4:17. Firstly, Exod 6:2–8 plays out in Egypt whereas Exod 3 is located on the mountain of God, i.e., holy territory. It is improbable that P would have secondarily profaned the place of Moses' commissioning. Secondly, Exod 3–4 seems to integrate secondarily the problems that arise later with Moses' mandate into the call of Moses itself in the context of P. Exodus 6:9 tells of Israel's unwillingness to listen to Moses after he has spoken with the people, and then Moses is to perform the signs before Pharaoh. In Exod 4:1, Moses complains about Israel's disobedience without ever having talked to the people. As a result, Moses receives the power to perform signs in front of his people (4:2–9) already at this point in the narrative, which anticipates the plagues of Egypt. Thirdly, there are some allusions in the wording of Exod 3:7, 9 to P passages (see in particular the use of the root צעק), especially Exod 2:24–25, which are difficult to explain in a pre-P setting of Exod 3–4.

To err on the side of caution, Exod 3–4 does not, therefore, rule out the possibility that the literary connection between Genesis and the Moses story is a rather late phenomenon in the redaction history of the Pentateuch. To my mind, this took place in the wake of P, who was the first to formulate the basic narrative blueprint of the Pentateuch.[75]

Conclusions

In current scholarship, it is no longer possible to explain the composition of the book of Genesis from the outset within the framework of the Documentary Hypothesis. While the composite character of the book as such

---

2000), 233–348; Blum, "Die literarische Verbindung"; and Thomas Römer, "Exodus 3–4 und die aktuelle Pentateuchdiskussion," in *The Interpretation of Exodus: Studies in Honour of Cornelis Houtman* (ed. Riemer Roukema; CBET 44; Leuven: Peeters, 2006), 65–79.

[74] See Thomas B. Dozeman, "The Commission of Moses and the Book of Genesis," in Dozeman and Schmid, *A Farewell to the Yahwist?*, 107–129; John Van Seters, "The Patriarchs and the Exodus: Bridging the Gap between Two Origin Traditions," in Roukema, *The Interpretation of Exodus*, 1–15; Hans-Christoph Schmitt, "Erzvätergeschichte und Exodusgeschichte als konkurrierende Ursprungslegenden Israels—ein Irrweg der Pentateuchforschung," in Hagedorn and Pfeiffer, *Die Erzväter in der biblischen Tradition*, 241–266; and Graham I. Davies, "The Transition from Genesis to Exodus," in *Genesis, Isaiah and Psalms: A Festscrift to Honour Professor John Emerton for His Eightieth Birthday* (ed. Katherine J. Dell, Graham I. Davies, and Yee Von Koh; VTSup 135; Leiden: Brill, 2010), 59–78.

[75] See on this especially de Pury, "P^g as the Absolute Beginning."

is undeniable, it is by no means clear or even probable that its literary history is to be described by the merger of layers that already extended in their earliest forms beyond the boundaries of Genesis, as was supposed for J and E. Rather, the opposite seems to be true. As Hermann Gunkel and Martin Noth noted, the legends in Genesis and also their collections into different cycles did not yet include a horizon of events reaching into the book of Exodus or even beyond.

If P should not have been the first author to combine Genesis and the Moses story, then, at any rate, such a connection seems not to have been established much earlier than P.[76] In Exod 6:2–3, an undisputed literary cornerstone of P,[77] it is still possible to observe the fact that the sequence of Genesis and Exodus was not an obvious or self-evident concept. The same seems to be true for the inclusion of themes of the books of Genesis and Exodus in the prophetic books (see especially Ezek 33:24) or the Psalms.[78] At least in the older portions of these literary works, there is little evidence suggesting that a literary link between Genesis and Exodus is already in place, as Albert de Pury, Thomas Römer, Reinhard G. Kratz, Jan C. Gertz, Matthias Köckert, Eckart Otto, Jean-Louis Ska, and others have suggested[79] following some basic observations made especially by Kurt Galling and Martin Noth.[80]

---

[76] Kratz, *The Composition of the Historical Books of the Old Testament*, 276, 79; and Blum, "Die literarische Verbindung."

[77] Schmid, *Genesis and the Moses Story*, 241–242.

[78] Schmid, *Genesis and the Moses Story*, 70–80; contrast, however, Schmitt, "Erzvätergeschichte und Exodusgeschichte als konkurrierende Ursprungslegenden Israels," 242–245. For Hos 12, which is especially important for Albert de Pury, "Erwägungen zu einem vorexilischen Stämmejahwismus: Hos 12 und die Auseinandersetzung um die Identität Israels und seines Gottes," in *Ein Gott allein? JHWH-Verehrung und biblischer Monotheismus im Kontext der israelitischen und altorientalischen Religionsgeschichte* (ed. Walter Dietrich and Martin A. Klopfenstein; OBO 139; Freiburg, Switz. and Göttingen: Universitätsverlag and Vandenhoeck & Ruprecht, 1994), 413–439, see now the thorough treatment of Erhard Blum, "Hosea 12 und die Pentateuchüberlieferungen" in Hagedorn and Pfeiffer, *Die Erzväter in der biblischen Tradition*, 318–319, who concludes that Hos 12 presupposes a Jacob story and a Moses story that conceptually belong into a sequence, but of which it is not possible to determine whether or not they are connected in terms of a literary unit.

[79] See Römer, *Israels Väter*; Albert de Pury, "Le cycle de Jacob comme légende autonome des origines d'Israël," in *Congress Volume Leuven 1989* (ed. J.A. Emerton; VTSup 43; Leiden: Brill, 1991), 78–96; Gertz, *Tradition und Redaktion in der Exoduserzählung*, 381–388; Otto, "Mose und das Gesetz," 43–83; Otto, *Das Deuteronomium im Pentateuch und im Hexateuch*; Eckart Otto, *Mose: Geschichte und Legende* (Munich: Beck, 2006); Otto, *Das Gesetz des Mose*; Kratz, *The Composition of the Historical Books of the Old Testament*; Jean-Louis-Ska, *Introduction to Reading the Pentateuch* (trans. Pascale Dominique; Winona Lake, Ind.: Eisenbrauns, 2006), 196–202; and Petersen, "Genesis of Genesis," 28–30.

[80] See n. 1 above.

The redaction-historical separation of Genesis and Exodus and the following books before P has wide-reaching consequences for the understanding of the history of religion and theology of the Hebrew Bible that can only be touched on in a very preliminary way here. Firstly, it is obvious that this new perspective abandons the thesis so popular in the twentieth century that the religion of ancient Israel is based on salvation history (*Heilsgeschichte*). That such a view can no longer be maintained has become more and more clear by recent results of literary analyses of the Pentateuch on the one hand and the numerous archaeological finds published in recent years on the other.[81] The historical religion of Israel looked quite different than the biblical picture suggests. The polemics of the Deuteronomists are probably closer to the preexilic reality in ancient Israel than the normative-orthodox statements in the Bible that promulgate a salvation-history based monotheism. Therefore, the paradigm of a clear discontinuity between ancient Israel, who believed in its God revealing himself in history, and its neighbors, who venerated the cyclically returning phenomena of nature, can no longer be maintained. This paradigm of discontinuity was developed in the wake of Karl Barth's dialectical theology and can be explained as an extrapolation of its basic tenets into the history of ancient Israel's religion. It presupposes that Israel occupies a very special place in the ancient Near East from its very beginning. But if Genesis and the Moses story were not interconnected until the late exilic or early Persian period, if there was no early (i.e. Solomonic) or at least monarchic (Josiah) conception of a salvation history that begins with the creation and ends with the conquest of the land, Israel must be seen in religion-historical continuity rather than discontinuity with its neighbors. The paradigm of discontinuity is not a peculiarity of ancient Israel but rather a characteristic feature of the Judaism of the Persian period, which projected its ideals back into the Hebrew Bible.

Over against the assumptions of the Documentary Hypothesis, Genesis and the Moses story in Exodus through Numbers and Deuteronomy stood next to each other as two *competing* concepts containing two traditions of the origin of Israel with different theological profiles. The different conceptions still remain visible behind the carefully crafted final form of the Pentateuch. Genesis is mainly autochthonous and inclusive, while the Moses story in the following books is allochthonous and exclusive. Of course

---

[81] For an overview, see Friedhelm Hartenstein, "Religionsgeschichte Israels—ein Überblick über die Forschung seit 1990," *VF* 48 (2003): 2–28.

such a polar opposition can only serve as a model, but it points nevertheless to a basic difference between the two blocks of tradition. To be more precise, the patriarchal narrative constructs a picture of the origin of Israel in its own land—a fact that is especially prominent in the specific formulations of the promises of the land, which do not presuppose that there will be several centuries between promise and fulfillment. At the same time the patriarchal story is both theologically and politically inclusive: the gods of Canaan can—without any problems—be identified with YHWH, and the Patriarchs dwell together with the inhabitants of the land and make treaties with them. In contrast, the story of the exodus stresses Israel's origin abroad in Egypt and puts forward an exclusive theological argument: YHWH is a jealous god that does not tolerate any other gods besides himself (Exod 20:3–5; 34:14; Deut 5:7–9); further, the Israelites shall not make peace with the inhabitants of the land (cf. Exod 23:32–33; 34:12, 15; Deut 12:29–31; 16:21; 20:16–17; 25:19).

The Pentateuch therefore contains both concepts that also serve as arguments in modern discussions: inclusiveness and exclusiveness. However, this important inner-biblical difference regarding how Genesis and the Moses story determine both Israel's origins and its relation to its land and to other nations only becomes fully apparent by means of historical reconstruction. Seen from this perspective, it becomes evident that the Pentateuch is a document of agreement between different positions. Although the debate over this issue continues, its formation seems to be interpreted within the context of Persian imperial policy.[82] Genesis is mainly a dissenting but a most prominent voice in the Pentateuch that has been included in it, and now constitutes an integral part of it, bearing specific theological importance.

---

[82] See the discussion in James W. Watts, ed., *Persia and Torah: The Theory of Imperial Authorization of the Pentateuch* (SBLSymS 17; Atlanta: Scholars Press, 2001); and Konrad Schmid, "The Persian Imperial Authorization as Historical Problem and as Biblical Construct: A Plea for Differentiations in the Current Debate," in Knoppers and Levinson, *The Pentateuch as Torah*, 22–38. For the redactional logic of the formation of the Pentateuch see Ernst Axel Knauf, "Audiatur et altera pars: Zur Logik der Pentateuch-Redaktion," *BK* 53 (1998): 118–126.

Select Bibliography

Blum, Erhard. *Die Komposition der Vätergeschichte.* Wissenschaftliche Monographien zum Alten und Neuen Testament 57. Neukirchen-Vluyn: Neukirchener, 1984.

———. "Die literarische Verbindung von Erzvätern und Exodus: Ein Gespräch mit neueren Endredaktionshypothesen." Pages 199–156 in *Abschied vom Jahwisten: die Komposition des Hexateuch in der jüngsten Diskussion.* Edited by Jan Christian Gertz, Konrad Schmid and Markus Witte. Beihefte zur Zeitschrift für die alttestamentliche Wissenschaft 315. Berlin: de Gruyter, 2002.

Carr, David M. *Reading the Fractures of Genesis: Historical and Literary Approaches.* Louisville: Westminster John Knox, 1996.

———. "Βίβλος γενέσεως Revisited: A Synchronic Analysis of Genesis as Part of the Torah." *Zeitschrift für die alttestamentliche Wissenschaft* 110 (1998): 159–172, 327–347.

———. "Genesis in Relation to the Moses Story." Pages 293–295 in *Studies in the Book of Genesis: Literature, Redaction and History.* Edited by André Wénin. Bibliotheca ephemeridum theologicarum Lovaniensium 155. Leuven: Peeters, 2001.

Clines, David J.A. *The Theme of the Pentateuch.* 2nd ed. Journal for the Study of the Old Testament Supplement Series 10. Sheffield: Sheffield Academic Press, 1997.

Davies, Graham I. "The Transition from Genesis to Exodus." Pages 59–78 in *Genesis, Isaiah and Psalms: A Festschrift to Honour Professor John Emerton for His Eightieth Birthday.* Edited by Katherine J. Dell, Graham I. Davies, and Yee Von Koh. Supplements to Vetus Testamentum 135. Leiden: Brill, 2010.

Dozeman, Thomas B. and Konrad Schmid, eds. *A Farewell to the Yahwist? The Composition of the Pentateuch in Recent European Scholarship.* Soctiey of Biblical Literature Symposium Series 34. Atlanta: Society of Biblical Literature, 2006.

Gertz, Jan Christian. *Tradition und Redaktion in der Exoduserzählung.* Forschungen zur Religion und Literatur des Alten Testaments 189. Göttingen: Vandenhoeck & Ruprecht, 2000.

Ha, John. *Genesis 15: A Theological Compendium of Pentateuchal History.* Beihefte zur Zeitschrift für die alttestamentliche Wissenschaft 181; Berlin: de Gruyter, 1989.

Kratz, Reinhard G. *The Composition of the Historical Books of the Old Testament.* Translated by J. Bowden. London: T&T Clark, 2005. Translation of *Die Komposition der erzählenden Bücher des Alten Testaments: Grundwissen der Bibelkritik.* Göttingen: Vandenhoeck & Ruprecht, 2000.

Millard, Matthias. *Die Genesis als Eröffnung der Tora: Kompositions- und auslegungsgeschichtliche Annäherungen an das erste Buch Mose.* Wissenschaftliche Monographien zum Alten und Neuen Testament 90. Neukirchen-Vluyn: Neukirchener, 2001.

Noth, Martin. *A History of Pentateuchal Traditions.* Translated with an Introduction by Bernhard W. Anderson. Chico, Cailf.: Scholars Press, 1981. Translation of *Überlieferungsgeschichte des Pentateuch.* 2nd ed. Stuttgart: Kohlhammer, 1948.

Otto, Eckart. "Forschungen zum nachpriesterschriftlichen Pentateuch." *Theologische Rundschau* 67 (2002): 125–155.

Petersen, David L. "The Genesis of Genesis." Pages 27–40 in *Congress Volume Ljubljana 2007*. Edited by André Lemaire. Supplements to Vetus Testamentum 133. Leiden: Brill, 2010.

Pury, Albert de. "Le cycle de Jacob comme légende autonome des origines d'Israël." Pages 78–96 in *Congress Volume Leuven 1989*. Edited by J.A. Emerton. Supplements to Vetus Testamentum 43. Leiden: Brill, 1991.

———. "Pg as the Absolute Beginning." Pages 99–128 in *Les dernières rédactions du Pentateuque, de l'Hexateuque et de l'Ennéateuque*. Edited by Thomas Römer and Konrad Schmid. Bibliotheca ephemeridum theologicarum lovaniensium 203. Leuven: Peeters, 2007.

Römer, Thomas. *Israels Väter: Untersuchungen zur Väterthematik im Deuteronomium und in der deuteronomistischen Tradition*. Orbis Biblicus et Orientalis 99. Freiburg, Switz. and Göttingen: Universitätsverlag and Vandenhoeck & Ruprecht, 1990.

Schmid, Konrad. *Genesis and the Moses Story: Israel's Dual Origins in the Hebrew Bible*. Siphrut 3. Translated by James D. Nogalski. Winona Lake, Ind.: Eisenbrauns, 2010. Revised and updated translation of *Erzväter und Exodus: Untersuchungen zur doppelten Begründung der Ursprünge Israels in den Geschichtsbüchern des Alten Testaments*. Wissenschaftliche Monographien zum Alten und zum Neuen Testament 81. Neukirchen-Vluyn: Neukirchener, 1999.

Schmitt, Hans-Christoph. "Erzvätergeschichte und Exodusgeschichte als konkurrierende Ursprungslegenden Israels—ein Irrweg der Pentateuchforschung." Pages 241–266 in *Die Erzväter in der biblischen Tradition: Festschrift für Matthias Köckert*. Edited by Anselm C. Hagedorn and Henrik Pfeiffer. Beihefte zur Zeitschrift für die alttestamentliche Wissenschaft 400. Berlin: de Gruyter, 2009.

Ska, Jean-Louis. *Introduction to Reading the Pentateuch*. Translated by Pascale Dominique. Winona Lake, Ind.: Eisenbrauns, 2006.

Van Seters, John. "The Patriarchs and the Exodus: Bridging the Gap between Two Origin Traditions." Pages 1–15 in *The Interpretation of Exodus: Studies in Honour of Cornelis Houtman*. Edited by Riemer Roukema. Contributions to Biblical Exegesis and Theology 44. Leuven: Peeters, 2006.

HISTORICAL CONTEXT

Ronald Hendel

Inquiry into the historical context of the book of Genesis has been a leitmotif of modern biblical scholarship, and it remains a highly contested topic. Such inquiry has multiple facets, each of which has implications for the others, and this complexity contributes to the diversity of scholarly positions. The weak connective tissue of many recent arguments about the historical context of Genesis is a reflection of the paucity of historical data, which is—alas—the condition of historians of Levantine antiquity. Cognizance of the limits of our evidence should constrain our historical speculations. These preliminary caveats are important because recent scholarship in this area is too often colored by arguments that are more akin to sectarian polemic than reasoned historiography.[1]

The interrelated facets of the historical context of the book of Genesis may be loosely resolved into three categories: setting, cultural memory, and form. By setting I mean the time, place, and culture when the various strata of the book were written—this is literary history, which involves the results of historical linguistics, ancient Near Eastern history, and source and redaction criticism. By cultural memory I mean the relationship between the representations of the past in Genesis and actual prior events or circumstances—this involves the history of tradition and the assessment of the historicity of these traditions. By form I mean the kinds and genres of discourse in the book and the varieties of historical consciousness that they represent—this involves form criticism and the history of historiography. I will address each of these facets in turn, with the caveat that my discussions are far from comprehensive. I will refrain from full engagement with the extensive bibliography and current debates in each area, which would make a synthetic foray impossible.

---

[1] I am referring to so-called "maximalist" and "minimalist" scholarship relating to Genesis, e.g., respectively, Kenneth A. Kitchen, *On the Reliability of the Old Testament* (Grand Rapids: Eerdmans, 2003); and Thomas L. Thompson, *The Mythic Past: Archaeology and the Myth of Israel* (New York: Basic Books, 2000). On the historiographical issues, see, e.g., V. Philips Long, ed., *Israel's Past in Present Research: Essays on Ancient Israelite Historiography* (SBTS 7; Winona Lake, Ind.: Eisenbrauns, 1999).

Setting

The time, place, and culture in which the various strata of Genesis were written constitute the first historical context that I will consider. For ancient texts that lack a colophon, we must rely in the first instance on the evidence of language. Genesis was written in Hebrew (with one Aramaic sequence, יגר שהדותא, spoken in Gen 31:47 by Laban "the Aramean," giving a touch of local color). Following the standard periodization of ancient Hebrew—Archaic Biblical Hebrew, Classical Biblical Hebrew, and Late Biblical Hebrew—it is relatively clear that there are texts of all three periods in the book. In addition to the evidence of language, occasional internal references to international events or circumstances can help further specify the time, place, and context of textual composition.

The Evidence of Language

The one Genesis text written in Archaic Biblical Hebrew is the poetic "Blessing of Jacob" in Gen 49.[2] Verse 11, which describes Judah, provides a good illustration of the linguistic features of archaic Hebrew poetry.

אסרי לגפן עירה	He ties his ass to a vine,
ולשרקה בני אתנו	to a noble vine the son of his she-ass.
כבס ביין לבשו	He washes his clothes in wine,
ובדם ענבים סותה	in the blood of grapes his tunic.

In this verse of twelve words, five—אסרי, עירה, שרקה, בני (in construct), and סותה—are *hapax legomena*. This is a remarkable concentration of rare words and constructions.

The word אסרי, pointed as a participle in MT, is best read as an infinitive absolute (*'ĕsōrî) functioning as a finite verb, parallel to כבס.[3] The usage

---

[2] See Frank M. Cross and David Noel Freedman, *Studies in Ancient Yahwistic Poetry* (SBLDS 21; Missoula, Mont.; Scholars Press, 1975; repr. Grand Rapids: Eerdmans, 1997), 46–63; and generally Angel Sáenz-Badillos, "The Language of Archaic Biblical Poetry," in Sáenz-Badillos, *A History of the Hebrew Language* (trans. John Elwolde; Cambridge: Cambridge University Press, 1993), 56–62, and references. The recent monographs of Raymond de Hoop, *Genesis 49 in its Literary and Historical Context* (OTS 39; Leiden: Brill, 1999), 74–77, and Jean-Daniel Macchi, *Israël et ses tribus selon Genèse 49* (OBO 171; Fribourg, Suisse: Éditions universitaires, 1999) are agnostic about the linguistic data in the text and tentatively prefer a United Monarchy and post-exilic date, respectively.

[3] William L. Moran, "The Hebrew Language in Its Northwest Semitic Background," in Moran, *Amarna Studies: Collected Writings* (ed. John Huehnergard and Shlomo Izre'el; HSS 54; Winona Lake, Ind.; Eisenbrauns, 2003), 207.

of the infinitive absolute with final *i* (usually called a *ḥiriq compaganis*) is known from the fourteenth century Amarna letters from Jerusalem and Byblos. It is probably also identifiable in the archaic poem "The Song of the Sea," נאדרי (**neʾdōrî*, Exod 15:6), which is also pointed as a participle in MT. William Moran hypothesizes that this old ending on infinitives absolute is an "adverbial -*i*," with the sense of "surely X," similar to the semantics of the infinitive absolute in the paranomastic construction.[4] Under this proposal, the sense of our verse would be "He surely ties his ass to a vine." Reading this form as an infinitive absolute is preferable to the traditional reading as a participle ("tying" or "he who ties"), which would make this poetic line a subordinate clause. Since participles with a *ḥiriq compaganis* are attested in the Bible, and since the use of the infinitive absolute was rare in Late Biblical Hebrew, the two unusual forms in Gen 49:11 and Exod 15:6 were reanalyzed as participles in the reading tradition inherited by the Masoretes (Gen 49:11 was read this way already in the LXX). The Samaritan Pentateuch reinterprets the form in Gen 49:11 as a passive participle (אסורי).

The form בני in the construct chain בני אתנו is also archaic. A final *i* on a noun in construct form is attested in Akkadian (usually to break up a consonant cluster) and in Northwest Semitic and Hebrew place names and personal names (e.g. עבדיאל, "servant of God").[5] A comparable instance in old biblical poetry is found in "The Blessing of Moses," שכני סנה ("dweller of the bush," Deut 33:16). Of the hundreds of construct phrases consisting of בן-X in Hebrew, only in Gen 49:11 do we find the form בני-X with this archaic morpheme.[6]

The other three *hapaxes*—עירה, שרקה, and סותה—are less useful as diagnostic data for chronology. They are either rare biforms of well-attested Hebrew words (עיר, שרק) or identifiable by cognates (סות is known from Phoenician). Interestingly, the forms עירה and סותה preserve the older spelling of *matres lectionis* (word-final ה for ō), whereas the spelling of the better-known words in this verse has been revised to the conventions of Second Temple scribes (word-final ו for ō in אתנו and לבשו). The incomplete revision

---

[4] William L. Moran, "The Use of the Canaanite Infinitive Absolute," *Amarna Studies*, 157. Note that the final **i > ī* is not an old case ending, since the Amarna letters have a fully functioning case system, and the case of these forms is not genitive.

[5] Scott C. Layton, *Archaic Features of Canaanite Personal Names in the Hebrew Bible* (HSM 47; Atlanta: Scholars Press, 1990), 107–122.

[6] Compare the form בנו-PN, with the old nominative case ending, in the patronymic of Balak son of Ṣippor, בנו צפר (Num 23:18) in the poetry of "The Oracles of Balaam," in contrast to the ordinary spelling, בן צפור, in the prose context (Num 22:2, 4, etc.).

of spelling, in which the odd words were unrevised, indicates that this text was composed relatively early.

The metaphor or kenning, דם ענבים ("blood of grapes"), which is an intensifying parallel to יין ("wine") also occurs only here, although a similar phrase (דם הענב, with a definite article preceding "grapes" in the singular) occurs in "The Song of Moses" (Deut 32:14). The closest analogue is found in Ugaritic poetry, where the kenning, dm ʿṣm ("blood of trees") is parallel to yn ("wine").[7] The continuity of this poetic diction with older Canaanite poetry and the disuse of this diction in classical Hebrew poetry are plausible indicators of antiquity.

The density of rare words and archaic features argues for a relatively early historical context for this poem. The previous verse refers to the royal ideology of the Davidic king (v. 10: "The scepter shall never depart from Judah"), which indicates that the text is not earlier than the late eleventh century BCE. A date in the early monarchy would suit these data.

Within this historical setting, the meaning of the verse is evident. The people of Judah, personified both by the eponymous ancestor and the Davidic king, have such great wealth and fertility that they can be profligate about precious wine and vineyards. As Abraham Ibn Ezra observed, "The yield of his vineyards will be so abundant that his ass can turn aside to the vine and he won't care if it eats the grapes."[8] Similarly, because of the superabundance of wine, Ibn Ezra continues, "he will wash his clothes in wine rather than water." This is an image of a great wealth and prestige, where precious agricultural commodities can be used like water and fodder. Note that washing in red wine ("the blood of grapes") would turn Judah's clothes into a royal color, like the famous Phoenician purple that colored royal garb throughout antiquity.[9] Through these vivid viticultural images, a simple tribe becomes a royal house.

There are a few traces of Late Biblical Hebrew in Genesis. Alexander Rofé has isolated several late linguistic features in "The Betrothal of Rebekah" (Genesis 24).[10] Consider the following verse, spoken by Abraham to his servant:

---

[7] *CAT* 1.4.iv.38, etc.

[8] Quoted in Robert Alter, *Genesis: Translation and Commentary* (New York: Norton, 1996), 296.

[9] Hebrew ארגמן is "wool dyed reddish-purple," which is roughly the color of wine. If סות has a Phoenician semantic resonance, this may contribute to the royal imagery.

[10] Alexander Rofé, "An Enquiry into the Betrothal of Rebekah," in *Die hebräische Bibel und ihre zweifache Nachgeschichte: Festschrift für Rolf Rendtorff zum 65. Geburtstag* (ed. Erhard

Put your hand beneath my thigh, that I may make you swear by YHWH, God of the heavens and God of the earth, that you shall not take a wife for my son from the daughters of the Canaanites in whose midst I live. (Gen 24:2–3)

There are two late features in this verse. The divine epithet אלהי השמים ("God of the heavens") is characteristic of Second Temple diction, and probably derives from Aramaic אלה שמיא. The Aramaic is found in Ezra 5:12, 6:9, 10; 7:12, 21; Dan 2:18, 19, 37, 44 and several times in the Elephantine papyri (fifth century BCE). In Hebrew this epithet occurs in Gen 24:3, 7; Jonah 1:9; Ezra 1:2 = 2 Chr 36:23; and Neh 1:4, 5; 2:4, 20, and the variant אל השמים in Ps 136:26. The epithet may a Jewish adaptation of the older Aramaic divine name בעל שמין.[11] Another late feature, also derived from Aramaic, is the use of the relative pronoun אשר in the phrase, אשר לא תקח, "that you shall not take." In Classical Biblical Hebrew, the oath formula is אם תקח. The phrase with אשר is a calque on the Aramaic phrase with דלא (which is the wording of Targum Onqelos of Gen 24:3). The use of אשר in this syntax is characteristic of Late Biblical Hebrew (Esth 2:10; 6:2; Dan 1:8; Neh 8:14, 15; 10:31; 13:1, 16).

This passage in Gen 24 echoes two other Genesis texts. The command, "put your hand beneath my thigh," is identical to Gen 47:29 (E). The prohibition, "you shall not take a wife for my son from the daughters of the Canaanites," is nearly identical to Gen 38:1,6 (P): "you shall not take a wife from the daughters of Canaan." It is possible that the expansion in 24:2 of the divine epithet "God of the heavens" (cf. 24:7) with "and God of the earth" is an echo of God who created "the heavens and the earth" in Gen 1:1 (P). (Compare Gen 14:19, from another relatively late text, which expands the old title "El creator of earth" into "El most high, creator of heaven and earth," probably also an echo of the pairing of heaven and earth in Gen 1:1.) This weighty command by Abraham seems to be a pastiche of phrases and ideas from other texts, focused on the anathema of marrying Canaanite women, which is characteristic of P and postexilic books.

The late features in Gen 24 may indicate a later overwriting or expansion of the text in Second Temple times, or may suggest that the entire chapter is late. There are other occasional late linguistic features in other Genesis

---

Blum, Christian Macholz, and Ekkehard W. Stegemann; Neukirchen-Vluyn: Neukirchener, 1990), 27–39; cf. Gary A. Rendsburg, "Some False Leads in the Identification of Late Biblical Hebrew Texts: The Cases of Genesis 24 and 1 Samuel 2:27–36," *JBL* 121 (2002): 23–35, who concurs that these features are Aramaisms.

[11] See Herbert Niehr, "God of Heaven," *DDD*, 370–372.

texts, such as ויאמן ("and he believed," simple *waw* + perfect) at the head of a clause in Gen 15:6, a chapter that is also arguably late or overwritten in the late period.[12]

Outside of these few texts with features of Archaic Biblical Hebrew or Late Biblical Hebrew, the language of Genesis belongs to the period of Classical Biblical Hebrew, which ranges roughly from the ninth-sixth centuries BCE.[13] This is the language of Hebrew inscriptions from this period and is very close to the contemporary language of Moabite and other Northwest Semitic inscriptions.[14]

There are some linguistic features that allow us to discern chronological changes within Classical Biblical Hebrew, which enable us to establish a relative chronology among the major sources of Genesis. For instance, the usage of the short and long forms of first-person pronoun, אני and אנכי, differs distinctively between J/E and P. (To set the backdrop, both forms are used in earlier Northwest Semitic [e.g., Ugaritic], and the short form is used almost exclusively in Late Biblical Hebrew.) In J and E both forms are used, with the long form more frequent: the short form occurs 48 times, the long form 81 times.[15] In P the short form is used almost exclusively (ca. 130 times) and the long form used only once (Gen 23:4). This pattern in P is almost exactly the same as the book of Ezekiel. As scholars have long noted, these data indicate that J and E are prior to P.[16]

---

[12] See S.R. Driver, *A Treatise on the Use of the Tenses in Hebrew and Some Other Syntactical Questions* (London: Oxford University Press, 1892; repr., Grand Rapids: Eerdmans, 1998), 161; Alexander Rofé, *Introduction to the Composition of the Pentateuch* (BibSem 58; Sheffield: Sheffield Academic Press, 1999), 92.

[13] On the features of Classical Biblical Hebrew, see recently Jan Joosten, "The Distinction between Classical and Late Biblical Hebrew as Reflected in Syntax," *HS* 46 (2005): 327–339. Since we lack lengthy tenth-century Northwest Semitic prose for comparison, I tentatively indicate the upper limit at the ninth century; see further Seth L. Sanders, *The Invention of Hebrew* (Urbana, Ill.: University of Illinois Press, 2009).

[14] Gad B. Sarfatti, "Hebrew Inscriptions of the First Temple Period: A Survey and Some Linguistic Comments," *Maarav* 3 (1982): 55–83, esp. 58: "At first glance the language of these documents appears to be identical with the Biblical Hebrew of the First Temple Period. Passages from the Lachish Letters could be interpolated into the Book of Jeremiah with no noticeable difference."

[15] BDB, 59b.

[16] S.R. Driver, "On Some Alleged Linguistic Affinities of the Elohist," *Journal of Philology* 11 (1882): 222–223; Julius Wellhausen, *Prolegomena to the History of Israel* (Edinburgh: Black, 1885), 389; and recently Robert Polzin, *Late Biblical Hebrew: Toward a Historical Typology of Biblical Hebrew Prose* (Missoula, Mont.; Scholars Press, 1976), 126–127; Mark F. Rooker, *Biblical Hebrew in Transition: The Language of the Book of Ezekiel* (JSOTSup 90; Sheffield: Sheffield Academic Press, 1990), 72–74.

This arrow of relative chronology is corroborated by the distribution of the Qal passive, which was replaced by the Niphal in the latter part of the Classical period.[17] The Qal passive is still used in J and E, but in the same constructions P uses the Niphal. Compare the following:

> As for Seth, a son was born (*yullad*) to him, and he named him Enosh. He was the first to worship in YHWH's name.[18] (Gen 4:26; J)
>
> Also the children of Machir son of Manasseh were born (*yull^edû*) on Joseph's knees.[19] (Gen 50:23; E)
>
> Abraham named his son who was born (*nôlad*) to him, whom Sarah had borne him, Isaac.... Abraham was one hundred years old when Isaac, his son, was born (*b^ehiwwaled*) to him.[20] (Gen 21:3, 5; P)

The language of P reflects a period when the Qal passive has become obsolete in this construction, in contrast to the earlier language of J and E. Interestingly, some of P's source documents still use the Qal passive.[21] The change from Qal passive to Niphal illustrates the changes that occurred within the period of Classical Biblical Hebrew, and corroborate the chronological implications of the use of the first-person pronoun. Other linguistic features further corroborate this relative chronology.[22]

Foreign Affairs

Allusions to details of international relations can also serve to specify the historical horizons of the compositional strata of Genesis. There are no clear references to known historical persons or events, but there are some details that arguably preserve historical memories that have a specifiable chronological range. The most perspicuous of these details—which were already identified by Julius Wellhausen—refer to Aram, Edom, and Mesopotamia.[23]

---

[17] Ronald Hendel, "'Begetting' and 'Being Born' in the Pentateuch: Notes on Historical Linguistics and Source Criticism," *VT* 50 (2000): 42–45. The discussion below slightly revises my characterization of the P source in this article.

[18] So also Gen 6:1; 10:21, 25. Note that 4:18 (ויולד) has been modernized as a Niphal.

[19] So also Gen 41:50.

[20] So also Gen 10:1; 17:17; 48:5.

[21] Gen 35:26; 36:5; 46:22, 27.

[22] E.g., the construal of singular collectives as plural and the decreased use of the infinitive absolute in P and LBH; see Polzin, *Late Biblical Hebrew*, 98–99; Rooker, *Hebrew in Transition*, 94–96.

[23] See Wellhausen, *Prolegomena*, 322 (Edom), 323 (Aram), 338 and 342 (Mesopotamia); and recently John A. Emerton, "The Date of the Yahwist," in *In Search of Pre-exilic Israel: Proceedings of the Oxford Old Testament Seminar* (ed. John Day; JSOTSup 406; London: T&T Clark, 2004), 107–129.

Aram. Jacob's flight from Laban and their treaty in "the mountain(s) of Gilead" (הר הגלעד) in Genesis 31 resonates with the historical relations between Israel and Aram in the ninth to early eighth centuries BCE. This chapter is primarily E, with a doublet of the treaty that combines details of J and E. The historical allusion is indicated in the twofold reference to "Laban the Aramean" (Gen 31:20, 24) during the scene of Jacob's flight and Laban's pursuit. These are the only references to Laban as "the Aramean" in J and E. When Laban catches up with Jacob, the ethnic and territorial horizons are foregrounded in the narrative:

> [Laban] took his kinsmen with him and pursued after him for seven days, and overtook him in the mountain(s) of Gilead. And God came to Laban the Aramean in a dream, saying "Watch yourself, lest you speak to Jacob either good or evil." (31:23–24)

Laban "the Aramean" is in league with "his kinsmen" (אחיו) in martial pursuit of Jacob and his family, who are the ancestors of the twelve tribes of Israel. God's timely intervention prevents a violent confrontation and yields a negotiated peace at a new boundary in the mountain(s) of Gilead. At this place, Jacob and Laban enter into a treaty (ברית), which is marked by a mound of stones and a stone pillar. Laban says to Jacob:

> This mound is a witness and the pillar is a witness, that I shall not cross over to you past this mound and that you shall not cross over to me past this mound and this pillar for evil. (Gen 31:51–52)

Notably, Laban and Jacob each use their native language to name the mound as a "mound of witness" (יגר שהדותא in Aramaic and גל עד in Hebrew, 31:47)—the only time that Aramaic is used in Genesis. This joint speech-act foregrounds the distinctive ethnic and linguistic identities of Jacob and Laban, and expresses the significance of this ritual scene as the establishment of a territorial boundary, marked by boundary stones, between Israel and Aram.

As many scholars have observed, this scene resonates with the boundary wars between the Omride kings of Israel and the Aramean kings of Damascus in Gilead during the ninth – early eighth centuries BCE.[24] Twice the book of Kings relates battles at Ramoth-Gilead (lit. "high places of Gilead," 1 Kgs 22; 2 Kgs 8:28–29). This location corresponds semantically to "the mountain(s) of Gilead" (הר הגלעד) in Gen 31. In 1 Kgs 20:34 we are told of a treaty (ברית) between King Ahab and Ben-Hadad of Aram at Aphek, north of

---

[24] See Emerton, "Date of the Yahwist," 116–117, and references.

Gilead. Interestingly, the ninth century Aramaic royal inscription from Tel Dan also mentions a treaty (indicated by the lexeme גזר, "to cut [a treaty]") between Aram and Israel, plausibly in the time of Ahab.[25] This inscription refers to a battle in which the Aramean king (presumably Hazael of Damascus) defeated and killed Kings Joram of Israel and Ahaziah of Judah. The parallel account in 2 Kgs 8:28 places this battle at Ramoth-Gilead. This battle, attested in biblical and extrabiblical texts, can be dated to around 840 BCE. (We need not adjudicate whether Joram and Ahaziah were killed during this battle—on this point the Bible and the Tel Dan inscription disagree.)[26]

In sum, military confrontations and treaties in and around Gilead between Israel and Aram were historical realities during the ninth and early eighth centuries BCE. These provide the obvious context for the confrontation and treaty between Jacob and Laban "the Aramean" in Gen 31. These historical details are projected backward into patriarchal times, such that their reflex in recent memory is given a historical genealogy, as the famous events of the ancestral past authorize and foreshadow the events of the more recent past.

Edom. A similar historical context obtains for Isaac's equivocal blessing of Esau, from the J source, which predicts the future liberation of Esau's descendants, the people of Edom:[27]

> By your sword you shall live,
>   and your brother you shall serve.
> But when you rebel,
>   you shall break his yoke from your neck.   (Gen 27:40)

According to the book of Kings (which has, of course, varying degrees of historical accuracy), Edom successfully rebelled against Judah during the reign of the same King Joram, ca. 850–840 BCE:

> In his days Edom rebelled against the hand of Judah and enthroned a king to rule over it. Joram crossed over to Zair with all his chariots. He arose by night

---

[25] Shmuel Aḥituv, *Echoes from the Past: Hebrew and Cognate Inscriptions from the Biblical Period* (Jerusalem: Carta, 2008), 467–469; see the discussion of Nadav Na'aman, "The Contribution of Royal Inscriptions for a Re-evaluation of the Book of Kings as a Historical Sources," in Na'aman, *Ancient Israel's History and Historiography: The First Temple Period* (Winona Lake, Ind.: Eisenbrauns, 2006), 202–203, and references.

[26] See Na'aman's discussion in the previous note.

[27] On Edom in J, see further Emerton, "Date of the Yahwist," 114–116; and Ernest W. Nicholson, *The Pentateuch in the Twentieth Century: The Legacy of Julius Wellhausen* (Oxford: Oxford University Press, 1998), 159–160.

and attacked Edom and its chariot officers who had surrounded him, but the troops fled to their tents. So Edom has been in rebellion against the hand of Judah until this day. (2 Kgs 8:20–22)

This brief notice may be an excerpt from an annalistic account.[28] In any case, since it relates a Judean defeat and lacks any theological or political *Tendenz*, it has a reasonable claim to historical credibility. This notice of Edomite rebellion may, as Thomas Levy has argued, correlate with the archaeological evidence for intensified copper production beginning in the mid-ninth century at the Edomite metallurgical site of Khirbet en-Nahas (lit. "Ruin of Copper").[29] The broken Judean yoke may be a cause or a consequence of Edomite economic expansion.

I would emphasize that the Genesis passage provides what the Kings passage lacks—a justification for Edom's rebellion, stemming from Isaac's prophetic blessing. After his years of servitude, Esau will finally have autonomy from his younger brother. Such is Esau's (Edom's) political fate according to old father Isaac. As in the case of Aram, the events of the recent past take on a deeper resonance by their genealogical descent from the foundational events of patriarchal times.

Mesopotamia. The historical contexts of the relations with Aram and Edom in these Genesis passages from J and E belong roughly to the horizons of the ninth – early eighth centuries BCE. The cultural memory of these conflicts would naturally have persisted for some time. The same general chronological horizon obtains for the allusions to Mesopotamian history in the J source. As Wellhausen observed, in J "we are told that Babylon is the great world-city, [and] that the Assyrian Empire is in existence, with the cities of Nineveh and Calah and Resen."[30] Babylon is the great world-city in the Tower of Babel story, which reflects broadly the historical context of the first half of the first millennium BCE, when Babylon was a great cultural center.[31] The references to Assyrian Empire gives us a

---

[28] Mordechai Cogan and Hayim Tadmor, *II Kings: A New Translation with Introduction and Commentary* (AB 11; New York: Doubleday, 1988), 96.

[29] Thomas E. Levy, "'You Shall Make for Yourself No Molten Gods': Some Thoughts on Archaeology and Edomite Ethnic Identity," in *Sacred History, Sacred Literature: Essays on Ancient Israel, the Bible and Religion in Honor of R.E. Friedman on his Sixtieth Birthday* (ed. Shawna Dolansky; Winona Lake, Ind.: Eisenbrauns, 2008), 244–251.

[30] Wellhausen, *Prolegomena*, 338.

[31] From the time of Nebuchadnezzar I (eleventh century BCE) to Nabonidus (sixth century BCE). Christoph Uehlinger (*Weltreich und 'eine Rede': Eine neue Deutung der sogenannten Turmbauerzählung (Gen 11,1–9)* [OBO 101; Freiburg: Universitätsverlag Freiburg, 1990],

narrower horizon—again, the ninth-eighth centuries BCE. The brief narrative of Nimrod in J relates:

> The chief cities of his kingdom were Babel and Erech and Akkad and Calneh, in the land of Sumer. From that land he went up to Asshur and built Nineveh and Rehovot Ir and Calah and Resen, between Nineveh and Calah, the great city. (Gen 10:10–12)

This is a stylized resumé of Babylonian and Assyrian history.[32] The description of Assyrian civilization describes Calah as העיר הגדלה, "the great city." This gives us a particular horizon. Calah became "the great city" of the Assyrian Empire ca. 880 BCE, when Assurnasirpal II made it his imperial capital. Kirk Grayson writes: "Assurnasirpal totally transformed the insignificant village into a metropolis which was suitable to the center of the empire he created."[33] Notably, the city god of Calah was Ninurta, whose name probably lies behind the biblical Nimrod. Calah remained the administrative center of Assyria until ca. 704 BCE, when Sennacherib moved the imperial capital to Nineveh and greatly expanded that city. Subsequently, Nineveh (not Calah) would be the natural reference of "the great city," as it is in Jonah 1:2. In sum, the Nimrod narrative in J has as its historical horizon the Assyrian Empire of the ninth-eighth centuries BCE.

A final reference to Mesopotamia will give us a historical horizon for the P source in the seventh-sixth centuries BCE. Twice in Gen 11 the land of Abram's birth is identified as אור כשדים, "Ur of the Chaldeans." As scholars have long recognized, the use of the ethnic term "Chaldeans" to denote southern Mesopotamia can only refer to the period after the eighth century, when the Chaldeans gained political and economic power in the region. "Chaldeans" is used as a synonym for "Babylon" in biblical writings during the Neo-Babylonian period (late seventh – early sixth century, e.g., in Jeremiah, Second Isaiah, and the latter chapters of 2 Kings) and thereafter. The use of "Chaldeans" in Gen 11 most plausibly reflects the horizon of the Neo-Babylonian period or after:

> Terah took his son Abram, and Haran's son Lot, his grandson, and his daughter-in-law Sarai, his son Abram's wife, and he sent them from Ur of the Chaldeans to go the land of Canaan. (Gen 11:31)

514–536) has argued that the story originally referred to the abandoned construction of the city of Dur-Šarrukin ("Fort of Sargon") in 705 BCE after the death of Sargon II, but this seems overly specific and requires that the "Tower of Babel" motif is secondary in the narrative.

[32] See Karel van der Toorn and Pieter W. van der Horst, "Nimrod Before and After the Bible," *HTR* 83 (1990): 1–16; Peter Machinist, "Nimrod," *ABD* 4:1116–1118.

[33] A. Kirk Grayson, "Calah," *ABD* 1:808.

The P designation of Ur of the Chaldeans as the patriarchal homeland contrasts with the J source, where the patriarchal homeland is Haran (see below). However, in the J verse of Gen 11:28, Terah's death is located "in the land of his birth, in Ur of the Chaldeans." Most scholars have recognized the awkward apposition of the second phrase as a secondary gloss, which a redactor has added to harmonize "his homeland" with "Ur of the Chaldees" three verses later (11:31).[34] In other words, Ur of the Chaldeans in 11:28 is most plausibly a harmonizing gloss, dependent on the P specification of the place name in v. 31.

A Neo-Babylonian horizon of the P reference to "Ur of the Chaldeans" holds a particular poignancy. Abram's homeland in Babylonia overwrites the older homeland in Haran, which becomes a second home ("They came to Haran and dwelled there," 11:31, P). The revised homeland in the Babylonian heartland is the area where the Judean exiles were forced to dwell after the Babylonian conquests and deportations of 597 and 586 BCE. If this is Abram's birthplace, then it is by definition the exiled Judeans' ancestral home. The exile is, in this sense, a homecoming. At the same time, it is a home that Abram left, on God's command, in his journey to the Promised Land. In sum, the "updating" of the patriarchal homeland in P is not a scholastic detail, but a way of making intelligible the present situation of the Babylonian exile in the light of Abraham's ancient migration from Babylonia to Zion. This compressed reference is comparable to Second Isaiah's explicit invocation of Abraham in the context of his prophecy of the return to Zion (Isa 51:2).[35] The present, once again, has its genealogy in the foundational events of the patriarchal past. In this case the genealogy may suggest a future redemption.

The patriarchal homeland in P has its natural historical horizons in the Babylonian exile. As Wellhausen observed, "consider[ing] that Abraham is said to have migrated into Palestine from Ur, from Chaldea, it is hardly possible to reject the idea that the circumstances of the exile had some influence in molding the priestly form of the patriarchal legends."[36]

---

[34] See John A. Emerton, "The Source Analysis of Genesis XI 27–32," *VT* 42 (1992): 37–46.

[35] The question of why Ur is the homeland, rather than Babylon for example, is more obscure—perhaps it is premised on a wordplay with אור ("light"), which has a positive and often redemptive nuance (cf. Gen 1:3; Isa 42:6).

[36] Wellhausen, *Prolegomena*, 342; and recently, Ranier Albertz, *Israel in Exile: The History and Literature of the Sixth Century B.C.E.* (SBLit 3; Atlanta: Society of Biblical Literature, 2003), 257.

I should note that much recent scholarship on the historical setting of Genesis has tended toward a later dating of the Pentateuchal sources, often dating them wholly to the Persian or even Hellenistic periods. In light of the recent critiques of these late datings by Ernest Nicholson and John Emerton, I find that the older analyses of the historical setting of Genesis, as refurbished above, remain credible and provide the most cogent explanation of the linguistic and historical data.[37] There are no data in Genesis that compel later dates for J and E than the ninth-eighth centuries or for P later than the seventh-sixth centuries.[38] As Nicholson and Emerton aptly emphasize, the positive portrait of Esau/Edom in J (see Gen 33) argues against a post-exilic date, when Edom was widely vilified in biblical writings.[39] With regard to literary style, as John Barton has observed of the "Succession Narrative" in Samuel-Kings, the J and E sources belong to the *floruit* of biblical narrative prose in the pre-exilic—and more precisely, pre-Deuteronomistic—period, and have little in common with postexilic prose works.[40]

Cultural Memory

The term "cultural memory" refers to the collective representation of the past in the present.[41] We have already addressed several representations of

---

[37] See further on the continental model, Ronald Hendel, "Is the 'J' Primeval Narrative an Independent Composition? A Critique of Crüsemann's 'Die Eigenständigkeit der Urgeschichte,'" in *The Pentateuch: International Perspectives on Current Research* (ed. Thomas B. Dozeman, Konrad Schmid, and Baruch J. Schwartz; FAT; Tübingen: Mohr Siebeck, 2011), 181–205.

[38] A few qualifiers: there are arguably some Persian loanwords in portions of P, which suggest that the P work was composed and revised over many years; see Baruch A. Levine, *Numbers 1–20: A New Translation with Introduction and Commentary* (AB 4; New York: Doubleday, 1993), 107–108. Genesis 14, 15, and 24 are, as noted above, arguably independent of the major sources; see Rofé, *Introduction*, 91–93. Finally, some of the promises to the patriarchs embedded in J and E may be redactional expansions; see John A. Emerton, "The Origin of the Promises to the Patriarchs in the Older Sources of the Book of Genesis," *VT* 32 (1982): 14–32; Alexander Rofé, "Promise and Covenant: The Promise to the Patriarchs in Late Biblical Literature," in *Divine Promises to the Fathers in the Three Monotheistic Religions: Proceedings of a Symposium Held in Jerusalem, March 24–25th, 1993* (ed. Alviero Niccacci; ASBF 40; Jerusalem: Franciscan Press, 1995), 52–59; but see the cautions of Joel S. Baden, *J, E, and the Redaction of the Pentateuch* (FAT 68; Tübingen: Mohr Siebeck, 2009), 243–247, where he argues that only Gen 22:15–18 is clearly secondary.

[39] See above, n. 27.

[40] John Barton, "Dating the 'Succession Narrative,'" in *In Search of Pre-exilic Israel: Proceedings of the Oxford Old Testament Seminar* (ed. John Day; JSOTSup 406; London: T&T Clark, 2004), 102–105.

[41] Ronald Hendel, "Cultural Memory," in *Reading Genesis: Ten Methods* (ed. Ronald Hen-

events and situations relating to Aram, Edom, and Mesopotamia—these are examples of how the recent past was reconfigured in biblical narrative and retrojected to the era of the ancestors, thereby creating an ancient warrant for recent history. Cultural memory tends to sift the remembered past for elements that are relevant for the present, and recombines those memories with other narrative lore into authoritative traditions. The mix of myth, legend, and history in cultural memory is difficult to untangle, but the close examination of these tangled skeins is the task of the historian of memory.

Biblical scholars have long sought to identify authentic historical memories from the pre-Israelite period (i.e., prior to the Israelite settlement, ca. 1200 BCE) within the narratives of Genesis, but the plausible results are very meager. The optimism of William F. Albright's generation, that archaeology could pinpoint the historical context of particular Genesis stories in a particular "patriarchal period," turns out to have been misplaced. Textual and archaeological evidence from Mari, Nuzi, and other second millennium sites were interpreted very loosely to yield correspondences with Genesis, or were taken as local customs when in fact they represented widespread Near Eastern norms that lasted for a millennium or more.[42] The current consensus is that there is little or no historical memory of pre-Israelite events or circumstances in Genesis.

A problem with both the Albrightian and the current consensus is a lack of distinction between different scales and qualities of historical time. Fernand Braudel makes an important set of distinctions here, addressing "the distinction, within historical time, of a geographical time, a social time, and an individual time."[43] Geographical time is the slowest scale of change, which concerns climate, topology, and other aspects of the historical *longue durée*. Social time is the middle scale, "a history of gentle rhythms, of groups and groupings," regarding economies, societies, and civilizations, which change over generations and centuries. Individual time is the most

---

del; Cambridge: Cambridge University Press, 2010), 28–46; and Hendel, *Remembering Abraham: Culture, Memory, and History in the Hebrew Bible* (New York: Oxford University Press, 2005).

[42] See John Van Seters, *Abraham in History and Tradition* (New Haven: Yale University Press, 1975); Thomas L. Thompson, *The Historicity of the Patriarchal Narratives: The Quest for the Historical Abraham* (BZAW 133; New York: de Gruyter, 1974); and more recently, P. Kyle McCarter and Ronald Hendel, "The Patriarchal Age: Abraham, Isaac and Jacob," in *Ancient Israel: From Abraham to the Roman Destruction of the Temple* (ed. Hershel Shanks; 2nd ed.; Washington, D.C.: Biblical Archaeology Society, 1999), 1–31.

[43] Fernand Braudel, *On History* (trans. Sarah Matthews; Chicago: University of Chicago Press, 1980), 4.

local scale, "a history of short, sharp, nervous vibrations." This is the history of events, *l'histoire événementielle*, which is the conventional focus of historians. By distinguishing among these different timescales of history, Braudel enables us to characterize more clearly the ways that cultural memory relates to the various phenomena of the past.

Biblical scholars tend to be attuned to the history of events—concerning kings and prophets, military campaigns, and so on. As a consequence, inquiry into historical memory in Genesis tends to focus on this narrow scale of time. Did Abraham battle a coalition of eastern kings (Gen 14)? Did he visit a Philistine king (Gen 20)? Did Joseph become a high official in Egypt (Gen 41)? Was he sold into slavery for twenty shekels (Gen 37)?[44] These historical questions relate to the time of individual events, the smallest scale of history. Cultural memory is liable to forget particular events within a few generations. The exceptions tend to be historical traumas, such as a major battle (e.g. the battle of Kosovo in Serbian epic) or other disruptive events (e.g. the first encounter with Spaniards in Hopi tradition). When one looks beyond a few generations, cultural memory tends to forget or blur these small time scales and relates instead to larger scales of historical time, particularly to the scale of "social time." This timescale does not pertain to small, punctuated events, but to the longer rhythms of society, religion, ethnicity, and economy. For the distant past, this is the scale of time for which we should expect to find memory traces in Genesis.

Amid the proposals of Albright's generation of historians, there are at least two items that plausibly preserve genuine memories of pre-Israelite history on the scale of social time. The first concerns memories of the ancestral homeland; the second concerns the religion of El.[45]

The Ancestral Homeland

There are several explicit and implicit memories in Genesis concerning the ancestral homeland in the region of Haran, a well-known city in the

---

[44] For instance, Kitchen (*Reliability*, 344–345) dates the sale of Joseph to the eighteenth century BCE, when the price of slaves in Mesopotamia was roughly 20 shekels. He overlooks, however, the notice that Joseph is 17 years old when he is sold into slavery (Gen 37:2), for which 20 shekels was arguably a normal price in monarchic Israel, as argued by Gordon J. Wenham, "Leviticus 27:2–8 and the Price of Slaves," *ZAW* 90 (1978): 264–265. Leviticus 27 lists 20 shekels as the "vow of the value of a human being" for a male from 5 to 25 years old, and 50 shekels for a male between twenty and sixty years old. The standard slave price of ca. 50–60 shekels in Neo-Assyrian texts, which is adduced by Kitchen for the eighth century price of slaves, also supports Wenham's proposal.

[45] The following refines my treatment in *Remembering Abraham*, 50–54.

Balikh River basin of upper Mesopotamia.[46] According to J, E, and later sources, this is the patriarchal homeland, where Abram was born and where Abram's brother Nahor continued to dwell after Abram's journey to Canaan. It is where daughters from Nahor's lineage were found as proper wives for Isaac and Jacob, and where the eponymous ancestors of eleven of the twelve tribes were born.[47] As noted above, the P sources have overwritten the memory of the ancestral homeland of Haran with a previous home in Ur of the Chaldeans (Gen 11:31), but P retains the notice that Abram's family dwelled in Haran prior to Abram's journey to Canaan (Gen 11:31–32). This tradition is also mentioned in Joshua's oration at Shechem: "Your fathers dwelled across the [Euphrates] River in olden times—Terah, father of Abraham and Nahor" (Josh 24:2). The ancestral locale, "across the River" (עבר הנהר), refers to northern Syria and upper Mesopotamia, the region of Haran (cf. 2 Sam 10:16). This geographical term was probably understood as the source of the ethnic name "Hebrew" (עברי), meaning roughly, "one from across (the River)."

The cultural memory in Genesis that the region of Haran was the ancestral homeland is attested not only by these textual references, but also by the implicit testimony of Abraham's genealogy. As scholars have noted, the personal names in the genealogical segment from Serug to Abraham and his brothers (Gen 11:20–27) have particular affinities to place names in and around Haran.

Serug
|
Nahor
|
Terah
|
Abram, Nahor, Haran

The personal name Serug ($S^e r\hat{u}g$) corresponds to a place-name from this region known from Neo-Assyrian texts. The Assyrian form, $Sar\bar{u}gi$, is precisely equivalent, by normal phonological and morphological rules, to Hebrew $S^e r\hat{u}g$. The personal name Nahor ($N\bar{a}h\hat{o}r$) occurs twice in Abram's genealogy as the name of his grandfather and his brother (the custom of papponymy). The city of $Nahur$ is well-known in Old Babylonian, Old Assyrian, and Middle Assyrian texts as a major center in the Ḫabur River Basin,

---

[46] See esp. Daniel E. Fleming, "Mari and the Possibilities of Biblical Memory," *RA* 92 (1998): 65–71.

[47] Genesis 24, 27–30; Benjamin is the only son born in Canaan (Gen 35:18).

east of Haran. Akkadian *Naḫur*, is precisely equivalent to Hebrew *Nāḥôr*. The personal name Terah (*Teraḥ*) corresponds consonantally to the place-name *Til-Turāḫi* ("Hill of the Ibex") in the region of Haran, known from Neo-Assyrian texts, but the Hebrew name has a different vocalic pattern. The name of Abram's brother Haran (*Hārān*) seems to be a weakened form (with initial *he* rather than *ḥet*) of the place-name Haran (Hebrew *Ḥārān*, Akkadian *Ḥarrānu*). In sum, this sequence of four generations in Abram's genealogy appears to preserve a frozen memory of locales in the ancestral homeland in upper Mesopotamia. It is a sequence of implicit memory traces, which corroborates the explicit memory of the ancestral homeland in the narrative itself.

We know from the archives of Mari that this region was the homeland of two major tribal confederacies during the Old Babylonian period (ca. 1800–1600 BCE), the Binu Yamina ("Sons of the South") and the Binu Sim'al ("Sons of the North"), who in aggregate were called Amorites (*amurrû*, "Westerners"). In a recent study of these texts, Daniel Fleming describes the character and geographical spread of these tribal confederations:

> The Sim'alite and Yaminite confederacies of the Amorrite tribal peoples shared in broad terms the same framework of pastoralist existence. Both had highly integrated town-dwelling and mobile herdsman components of their own, and both encroached on the larger regional towns and took them over where possible, while still prizing their own tribal identities. ... [T]here were broad regional patterns in the distribution of Yaminite and Sim'alite populations. The Sim'alites considered their primary grazing lands to lie in the Ḫabur River Basin, especially in Ida-Maraṣ, with the Yaminites oriented more to the south and west, all the way to the Mediterranean and southern Syria.[48]

The city of Haran was a tribal center of the Yaminites, where in one text they celebrate a ritual treaty with a coalition of local kings.[49] Nahor was a major city in Ida-Maraṣ, in the heart of Sim'alite territory. As Fleming notes, the Yaminites dwelled westward all the way to the Mediterranean coast, north of Israel. These geographical details make a genetic connection between the Israelite memory of the tribal homeland and the ancient Amorite tribes a distinct possibility.[50]

---

[48] Daniel E. Fleming, *Democracy's Ancient Ancestors: Mari and Early Collective Governance* (Cambridge: Cambridge University Press, 2004), 93.

[49] Fleming, *Democracy's Ancient Ancestors*, 200.

[50] Fleming, "Mari," 41–78; and Jean-Marie Durand, "Réalités amorrites et traditions bibliques," *RA* 92 (1998): 3–39.

The cultural memories in Genesis of the tribal homeland in and around Haran seem to cohere in a broad sense with the general picture of Amorite tribal life in the first half of the second millennium BCE. During the Late Bronze Age (ca. 1500–1200) the major sites in the region of Haran became largely depopulated,[51] and politics and culture were dominated by Hurrian and Hittite kingdoms.[52] Toward the end of the Late Bronze Age, the region saw the rise of Aramean tribal culture, which in the Iron Age led to the rivalry between Israel and Aram (see above). But in the biblical texts, at the same time that the Arameans are seen as rivals and enemies, they are also relatives—Laban and his family live in Haran, the patriarchal homeland. This is a curious twist. Our foreign rival is also our kin, and he dwells in our ancestral home.

The overlay of Aramean ethnicity on top of older memory traces of the ancestral homeland accounts for this curious paradox. It explains why the rival Arameans are at the same time the patriarchal ancestors. It explains why in Genesis the ancestral homeland is home to "Laban the Aramean." The old Amorite memories have been updated to reflect current ethnic and tribal realities. It is not likely that the Israelites would have identified their origins as Aramean without prior ancestral traditions linked to this locale. Moreover, Hebrew is relatively distantly related to Aramean among the Northwest Semitic languages.[53] An Amorite ancestry of these memories suits the historical facts, accounting for the significance of the Haran region. As Fleming observes:

> The Genesis tradition of a north Syrian origin for Abraham and his family is both central to the narrative and difficult to explain in terms of peoples and regional political relations during the lives of the Israelites states, the exiles, or early Judaism ... These are not the Areameans known to the writers' direct experience.[54]

By the process of cultural memory, which conflates antique details into a picture of the past with present relevance, the second millennium homeland takes on a first millennium ethnic coloring. Hence the Israelite worshiper at the festival of the first-fruits proclaims, "My father was a perishing (?) Aramean." In Hebrew this ritual formula has assonance and rhythm:

---

[51] T.J. Wilkinson, "Water and Human Settlement in the Balikh Valley, Syria: Investigations from 1992–1995," *Journal of Field Archaeology* 25 (1998): 63–87.

[52] Durand, "Réalités," 7–8.

[53] See W. Randall Garr, *Dialect Geography of Syria-Palestine, 1000–586 B.C.E.* (Philadelphia: University of Pennsylvania Press, 1985).

[54] Fleming, "Mari," 67–68.

'*arammi 'oved 'avi*. Each word links with the sounds of the next, as the chain of memories draws the cultural identity of Israel into a contemporary model of the past. In the remembered past, the patriarchal homeland must—in the Iron Age—become an Aramean land. The cultural memory of the ancestral homeland is a palimpsest, in which traces of second millennium memories are still visible behind first millennium realities.

These old memories are not accounts of individual historical events, *l'histoire événementielle*. Rather, they pertain to social time, the long rhythms of ethnic and social phenomena. Some early Israelites must have traced their ancestry to these old tent-dwelling tribes, and, as the patriarchal traditions crystallized, the patriarchs and matriarchs were amalgamated with the old memories of an ancient homeland across the River.[55]

El Religion

The portrait of the religion of the patriarchs also arguably holds memory traces of pre-Israelite religion. As scholars have noted, there are many continuities between the El religion of the patriarchs and the religion of the Late Bronze Age Canaan known primarily from the Ugaritic texts.[56] In these texts, El is the high god of the Canaanite pantheon. Some of his titles are "Bull El," "Creator of Creatures," "Father of Humans," and "Father of Years" (idiomatically, "Ancient One"). A title known from a Hittite text, "El, Creator of Earth," is also known from later Phoenician and Aramaic inscriptions and, notably, a Hebrew inscription from late eighth or early seventh century Jerusalem.[57] The continuities between Bronze Age Canaanite and Iron Age Israelite religion are indisputable, and they persist throughout Israelite history.

---

[55] Compare the Turkish memory of ancient Central Asian origins (see Anthony D. Smith, *Myths and Memories of the Nation* [Oxford: Oxford University Press, 1999], 76–78); the North African bedouin memory of migration from the Arabian peninsula in the thirteenth century, as recounted in the oral epic, *Sirat Bani Hilal* (see Bridget Connelly, *Arab Epic and Identity* [Berkeley: University of California Press, 1986]); and, closer to home, the memory of Philistine origins in the Aegean (e.g., Amos 9:7; Jer 47:4) and the name of the seventh century king of Ekron, *'kyš*, "the Achaean" (see Seymour Gitin, "Philistines in the Books of Kings," in *The Book of Kings: Sources, Composition, Historiography and Reception* [ed. Andre Lemaire and Baruch Halpern; VTSup 139; Leiden: Brill, 2010], 301–364, esp. 343).

[56] Frank M. Cross, *Canaanite Myth and Hebrew Epic: Essays on the History of the Religion of Israel* (Cambridge: Harvard University Press, 1973); Mark S. Smith, *The Early History of God: Yahweh and the Other Deities in Ancient Israel* (San Francisco: Harper & Row, 1990); and John Day, *Yahweh and the Gods and Goddesses of Canaan* (JSOTSup 265; Sheffield: Sheffield Academic Press, 2000).

[57] Aḥituv, *Echoes from the Past*, 40–42.

Is it possible to isolate pre-Israelite memories of El religion in Genesis? Since El was a bi-name of YHWH throughout Israelite history (as already in the archaic poetry), we need not see El in Genesis as a different god than YHWH. As Frank Cross notes, "El is rarely if ever used in the Bible as the proper name of a non-Israelite, Canaanite deity in the full consciousness of a distinction between El and YHWH, god of Israel."[58] Yet there is a conscious memory in at least two strands of Genesis—E and P—that the worship of El is earlier than the worship of YHWH. This is made explicit with the revelation of the name YHWH to Moses in Exod 3 (E) and 6 (P):

> I am the God of your father, the God of Abraham, the God of Isaac, and the God of Jacob .... Thus you shall say to the children of Israel, YHWH, the God of your fathers, the god of Abraham, the God of Isaac, and the God of Jacob sent me to you. (Exod 3:6, 15, E)

> I am YHWH. I appeared to Abraham, to Isaac, and to Jacob as El Shaddai, but my name YHWH I did not make known to them. (Exod 6:2–3, P)

Corresponding to these statements, in the E and P sources God is never called YHWH prior to Exod 3 and 6, respectively. This is a native model of religious history in which God was known to the pre-Mosaic ancestors as El, Elohim, or other El compounds (El Shadday, El the God of Israel, El of Bethel, etc.) until he revealed his most authentic name, YHWH, to Moses. The sequence of divine names in this native theory coheres roughly with the historical record, in which worship of El preceded worship of YHWH in the region of Canaan and Israel. (Note that two prominent cultic sites in the patriarchal narratives, Bethel and Penuel, are compounded with El, as is the name Israel.)

This explicit native theory in E and P is implicitly corroborated in the J source. While J places the beginnings of worship of YHWH in the generation of Enosh (Gen 4:26), it is notable that, as Albrecht Alt observed, there are no names compounded with YHWH until the era of Moses (Jochebed and Joshua are the first). That is to say, J implicitly agrees with the schema of E and P in that the ancestors had El-names, not YHWH-names, prior to the Mosaic period. In Genesis there are seventeen names compounded with El and none with YHWH.[59] (Interestingly, there is one name compounded with Hadad and one with Syrian Baal—Ishmael's son Hadad and Benjamin's son Ashbel.) In other words, the memory of patriarchal religion in the J source is also a palimpsest. The older worship of El, as visible implicitly in

---

[58] Cross, *Canaanite Myth*, 44.
[59] See Hendel, *Remembering Abraham*, 50.

the theophoric element of names, is overwritten with the explicit worship of YHWH beginning in primeval generations. The early worship of YHWH is arguably a feature of J's universalism, in which YHWH is the God of the whole world. But through this universalism we may glimpse the memory traces of pre-Yahwistic El worship, and of the view that YHWH is solely the God of Israel, as is explicitly the case in E and P.

This universalism of J is evident in YHWH's promise to Abram: "All the families of the earth shall be blessed through you" (Gen 12:3). The memory of Abraham has global relevance. In the Assyrian period—the immediate historical context for the J source (see above)—this universalism has a particular nuance. At a time when a foreign empire had established hegemony over Israel, it is remarkable to claim that the subject people's God and their peculiar destiny have universal relevance. In other words, as Baruch Levine has observed, there are political resonances to the global exaltation of YHWH in J and other texts from the Assyrian period.[60]

This proud assertion of universalism at a time of foreign rule can also be seen in two Hebrew inscriptions, one from the Assyrian period and one from the Neo-Babylonian period. From a cave inscription near En-Gedi of the late eighth or early seventh century, perhaps carved by a refugee during an Assyrian invasion:[61]

ברך יהו[ה] ... ברך בגי[ם אדני ה]מלך ברך אדני

Blessed be YHW[H] ... Blessed among the nation[s be my lord?] the king. Blessed be my lord.

And from a cave inscription near Lachish of the early sixth century, perhaps carved by a refugee from a Babylonian invasion:[62]

YHWH is God of all the earth.   יהוה אלהי כל הארץ

To assert the universalism of YHWH and (perhaps) his king at a time of Assyrian and Babylonian hegemony is a message of hope and resistance, and provides compensation for the ills of history. It is also, as Levine observes, the birth of unqualified monotheism.

The claim in J that YHWH was God of all the earth already in Enosh's generation is an expression of a new theological-political claim that overwrites the older cultural memory of the El religion of the patriarchs. This older memory is, again, memory on the scale of social time, not a memory

---

[60] Baruch Levine, "Assyrian Ideology and Biblical Monotheism," *Iraq* 67 (2005): 411–427.
[61] Aḥituv, *Echoes from the Past*, 236–239.
[62] Aḥituv, *Echoes from the Past*, 233–235.

of particular, punctual events. The old memory is partially effaced and reinterpreted in Genesis, which is to say that it is a cultural memory of the past, and so is refashioned to express current sensibilities.

FORM

The genres and discursive forms of Genesis are a part of its historical context.[63] They belong to the cultural repertoire of ancient Israel and as such had ready-made horizons of expectations built into them. A genealogy, a blessing, or an ancestral story were familiar forms of speech, which evoked and expressed particular features of Israelite knowledge. These forms provided a variety of representational possibilities for recounting the past in the present, and they featured particular styles of historical consciousness. The past is mediated to the present through such discursive forms; they are the lexicon and syntax of collective memory.

These genres and forms had two interrelated modes of production—one in the family and tribal setting of oral tradition, and the other in the institutions and practices of scribal literacy. The following texts provide a glimpse of these two social contexts:

> Remember the days of old,
>   Consider the years of antiquity
> Ask your father, and he will tell you
>   Your elders, and they will recount to you.   (Deut 32:8)
>
> This is the scroll (ספר) of the genealogy of Adam.   (Gen 5:1)

The first passage, from "The Song of Moses," evokes the family and tribal setting of oral traditions of the collective past. These are narratives handed down through the generations, recounted by fathers and elders, which acculturate young Israelites by initiating them into the ancestral stories. The fathers and elders speak with the authority of tradition, since they are vested with power and are the patriarchal agents for the preservation and flourishing of the lineage. The collective memories of the past are part of the vital "social motor" that sustains and renews the group's identity and practices. This generational motor ensures the present relevance of the events of the remembered past.

---

[63] See John Barton, *Reading the Old Testament: Method in Biblical Study* (2nd ed.; Louisville: Westminster John Knox, 1996), 8–18, 30–43.

The second passage, which introduces the primeval genealogy from Adam to Noah, evokes the scribal context of the literary composition of Genesis. Even as the stories and lore are in various degrees derived from the oral traditions of family, tribe, and other social contexts, the texts as we have them were composed by literate individuals who had access to the scribal training necessary to become proficient in literary production. These were the educated elite, comprised of various social groups, including scribes, priests, royal courtiers, military officers, and wealthy landowners. As Karel van der Toorn has recently emphasized, we cannot understand the biblical texts properly without taking into account the scribal practices and institutions of ancient Israel.[64]

Van der Toorn observes that ancient scribes produced writings that were less like "books" in the modern (or even Late Antique and Medieval) sense and more like anthologies:

> The patriarchal stories in Genesis, just as the Epic of Gilgamesh in Babylonian literature, consist of a string of episodes owing their unity to the principal protagonists of the various stories. Their disposition is paratactic rather than hypotactic; the style is "additive rather than subordinative."[65]

Literary, religious, and historical texts were, to borrow Aby Warburg's expression, "archives of memory." The form of Genesis as a whole illustrates this scribal style. Each of the major sources (J, E, P) is an anthology of traditions, and the additive literary practice allowed other scribes and editors to insert more texts. In the J primeval narrative of Gen 2–11, the J source collects and recomposes a series of stories of primeval times, sets them into a chronological order, and provides a web of echoing key-words and phrases to produce a thematic continuity.[66] When a scribal editor combined the J, E, and P texts, he inserted various (usually brief) redactional transitions, clarifications, and harmonizations.[67] Other texts were later added or overwritten

---

[64] Karel van der Toorn, *Scribal Culture and the Making of the Hebrew Bible* (Cambridge: Harvard University Press, 2007).

[65] Van der Toorn, *Scribal Culture*, 15; the quote is from Walter Ong.

[66] Ronald Hendel, "*Leitwort* Style and Literary Structure in the J Primeval Narrative," in *Sacred History, Sacred Literature: Essays on Ancient Israel, the Bible and Religion in Honor of R.E. Friedman on his Sixtieth Birthday* (ed. Shawna Dolansky; Winona Lake, Ind.: Eisenbrauns, 2008), 93–109.

[67] E.g., Gen 2:4a; 5:1b–2; 7:3a, 8–9, 23b; see Bernard M. Levinson, "The Right Chorale: From the Poetics to the Hermeneutics of the Hebrew Bible," in *'Not in Heaven': Coherence and Complexity in Biblical Narrative* (ed. Jason P. Rosenblatt and Joseph C. Sitterson; Bloomington: Indiana University Press, 1991), 139–141; Baden, *Redaction of the Pentateuch*, 263–285.

(Gen 14, 15, 24), and other scribal revisions appear in the various textual traditions.[68] The additive, anthological scribal art is evident at every stage in the composition of Genesis.

The interplay of the scribal-literary art of the Genesis writers with their inherited forms and genres is a fundamental aspect of the innovative prose style of Genesis. As Robert Alter observes, drawing on the insights of Russian Formalism:

> The process of literary creation ... is an unceasing dialectic between the necessity to use established forms in order to be able to communicate coherently and the necessity to break and remake these forms because they are arbitrary restrictions and because what is merely repeated automatically no longer conveys a message.[69]

In other words, literature always refashions inherited forms in order to communicate afresh. Continuity and innovation are always in dialogue, within the bounds of cultural expectations and literary imagination.

Transformations of the Flood

A brief glance at the Flood narrative will illustrate some of these dynamics of form and historical context. In the wider narrative background of Gen 6–9 are the Mesopotamian flood traditions, known from the Old Babylonian myth of *Atraḫasis*, the Middle Babylonian Flood tablet at Ugarit, the Flood narrative in the Standard Babylonian *Gilgamesh Epic* (tablet XI), and other sources.[70] As scholars have long observed, there are clear continuities between the older Mesopotamian Flood traditions and the biblical traditions. Stories of the Flood arguably traveled from Mesopotamian to Israelite culture via oral and written traditions, mediated by multilingual traders, travelers, and scribes. Once the traditions became native to Israel, the J and P writers independently reshaped the story through their scribal-literary art. I will briefly sketch two instances of the reshaping of tradition in the J version.

---

[68] E.g., the variant chronologies of Gen 5 and 11 in MT, SamP, and LXX; see Ronald Hendel, *The Text of Genesis 1–11: Textual Studies and Critical Edition* (New York: Oxford University Press, 1998), 61–80.

[69] Robert Alter, *The Art of Biblical Narrative* (New York: Basic Books, 1981), 62.

[70] See Jeffrey H. Tigay, *The Evolution of the Gilgamesh Epic* (Philadelphia: University of Pennsylvania Press, 1982), 214–240; and A.R. George, *The Babylonian Gilgamesh Epic: Introduction, Critical Edition and Cuneiform Texts* (Oxford: Oxford University Press, 2003), 1:508–528.

The J source relates the Flood story after the strange tale of the Sons of God and the Daughters of Men (Gen 6:1–4). The writer created a transition and counterpoint by the use of what Martin Buber called the *"Leitwort* style":[71]

When man began to multiply (לרב) ... the Sons of God (בני האלהים) saw (ויראו) that the daughters of men (בנות האדם) were beautiful (טבת).   (Gen 6:1–2)

YHWH saw (וירא) how great (רבה) was the evil of man (רעת האדם)   (Gen 6:5)

In this echo-chamber of words, note the contrasting acts of "seeing" (וירא) by the two sets of divine protagonists, the Sons of God and YHWH. The former see the טבת ("goodness, beauty") of the בנות האדם ("daughters of men") when humans were רב ("multiplied, abundant") on earth, whereupon they lust after the women and take them as wives. In contrast, YHWH sees how רבה ("great, abundant") was רעת האדם ("the evil of man"), whereupon he concocts the Flood to destroy humans because of their moral state. The sexual perception of human beauty by the lesser gods contrasts with YHWH's ethical perception of human evil. Note the contrasting nuances of "seeing"—the lesser gods see the goodness of the female body, whereas YHWH sees the evil of the human heart, a deeper and more tragic vision. This juxtaposition of vision and sensibility through the artful manipulation of words creates a new resonance for the onset of the Flood and an evocative backdrop for YHWH's harsh decision. It also creates a literary bridge between two distinct stories.

A further way in which the J writer—or the older Israelite oral tradition—transforms the inherited form involves the tension within YHWH's complicated motives.[72] According to the *Atraḥasis* myth, the god Enlil sends the Flood to eliminate the noise caused by the teeming population of humans. The Flood is his countermeasure to the noisy consequence of humans multiplying. In Gen 6:1, "When man began to multiply" creates a different problem, that of the abundance of beautiful women who catch the eyes of the Sons of God. It is not clear whether this different consequence of human population growth is a deliberate reshaping of the Mesopotamian motif—perhaps an ironic twist—but it clearly reconfigures the dynamics of plot and

---

[71] See Hendel, "*Leitwort* Style."

[72] I am building on the observations of William L. Moran, "A Mesopotamian Myth and Its Biblical Transformation," in Moran, *The Most Magic Word: Essays on Babylonian and Biblical Literature* (ed. Ronald Hendel; CBQMS 35; Washington, D.C.: Catholic Biblical Association, 2002), 59–74.

motive between the Mesopotamian and biblical traditions. More importantly, in contrast to Enlil, YHWH has an ethical motive to send the Flood, and yet he also decides—like the wise Enki, the creator of humans in *Atraḥasis*—to save humans from annihilation. YHWH's motivations draw together the destructive force of Enlil and the compassion of Enki. This conjunction yields a portrait of a seemingly conflicted God, bent on destruction and salvation concurrently. At the end of the J Flood story, YHWH seems to admit that it was unwise to destroy all life because of human evil, and he seems to reconcile himself to the irredeemably flawed humans (Gen 8:21). By this monotheistic revision of the older story, where one God now plays the roles of cosmic destroyer and wise savior, the J story yields a complex concept of God, who balances, sometimes precariously, the competing imperatives of justice and compassion.

In all of these ways we see how the J version of the Flood story transforms the inherited forms. The scribal-literary art of the writer and the transformative variability—what Paul Zumthor calls "mouvance"[73]—of Israelite oral traditions play complementary roles in these transformations.

Genealogy

The transformation of literary forms and traditions in Genesis highlights the primacy of interpretation in the biblical memories of the past. As I have argued previously, "To the biblical writers, the traditional stories of the collective past are true, though these stories are subject to revision in order to maintain or revive their purchase on the truth."[74] The forms of the past in Genesis are interpretations of older forms, and do not represent a depiction of the past that is wholly new or discontinuous with prior versions. The parallels with Mesopotamian and Canaanite myth and epic are sufficient to establish this point. Genesis is an anthology of cultural memories that relate not to events themselves but to prior representations of the past. It is a memory archive that has its ancestry in prior memories.

In this respect I submit that modern terms such as myth, legend, epic, and the like, while valuable analytically, are inexact categories to denote the genres and forms of Genesis. In my view a more revealing term is the one used in Genesis, תלדות, which means "begettings, descendants, genealogy." Genesis 2:4, a redactional bridge between the creation stories, says, "These

---

[73] Paul Zumthor, *Oral Poetry: An Introduction* (trans. Kathryn Murphy-Judy; THL 70; Minneapolis: University of Minnesota Press, 1990), 202–208.

[74] Hendel, *Remembering Abraham*, 97.

are the descendants of heaven and earth," meaning roughly, this is the genealogy or offshoot of creation. The genealogical formula, "these are the descendants of X," occurs ten times in Genesis, five times in the primeval narrative and five times in the patriarchal narratives, forming an internal structuring frame for the book.[75] More importantly, it describes what the anthology of Genesis does—it articulates a genealogical narrative from the birth of the cosmos to the birth and lives of the eponymous ancestors of the twelve tribes of Israel. It is a genealogy of the world, which moves toward the teleological focus of the genealogy, the people Israel.

This native designation for the Genesis narrative clarifies the prominence of genealogical lists and the stories of threats to the continuity of the lineage, including fratricide and exile (Gen 4, 27, 37), descents to Egypt (e.g. Gen 12:10–20, which foreshadows the Exodus story), barren wives, endangered sons (Gen 21–22) and dead husbands (Gen 38, in which Tamar's ruse rescues Judah's lineage). Moreover, it sheds light on the large-scale form of Genesis as a genealogical narrative. As a genealogy, which is a form that attracts new information, it accommodates the additive nature of scribal composition. Moreover, a genealogy has a limit and a goal. It must depict Israel's genealogical structure in the era for which it is an ethnic mirror, that is, the historical context of the composition of Genesis.

To this end, certain genealogical elements are required. The relationships with other peoples must be represented in genealogical form, with neighboring nations represented as relatives of varying propinquity to Israel. Hence the following links are embedded in the stories and genealogies during the patriarchal period:

generation of Jacob/Israel	—	Esau (Edom)
generation of Isaac	—	Ishmael (North Arabian peoples)
generation of Abraham	—	Nahor (Arameans), Lot (Moab and Ammon), Qeturah (South Arabian peoples)

These are Israel's neighbors, with whom Israel felt historical and ethnic affinity. More distant genealogical ties are provided in "The Table of Nations" in Gen 10. (Note that the Phoenicians—sons of Canaan—were felt to

---

[75] Genesis 2:4 (heaven and earth); 5:1 (Adam); 6:9 (Noah); 10:1 (sons of Noah); 11:10 (Shem); 11:27 (Terah); 25:12 (Ishmael); 25:19 (Isaac); 36:1 (Esau); 37:2 (Jacob); note that 36:9 (Esau) is secondary; see Cross, *Canaanite Myth*, 301–305; David M. Carr, *Reading the Fractures of Genesis: Historical and Literary Approaches* (Louisville: Westminster John Knox Press, 1996), 70–75; and Carr, "Βιβλος γενεσεως Revisited: A Synchronic Analysis of Patterns in Genesis as Part of the Torah," *ZAW* 110 (1998): 159–172, 327–347.

be more distantly related than the above peoples; see Gen 10:15–19, J.) With the exception of the Qeturah tribes, each of these neighbors has ancestral stories associated with them, delineating their relationships and rivalries with the ancestors of Israel.

These neighboring people are at the same time historical *Others*, with their own distinctive cultural traits, but are related to the collective *Self*, as close branches of the patriarchal lineage. In particular, Esau and Ishmael are depicted as peoples with patriarchal blessings, which, while ambivalent, warrant admiration. God says of Ishmael, "I will make him into a great nation" (Gen 21:18, E), and Esau is ultimately depicted as a noble and generous figure, whom Jacob addresses as "My lord" (Gen 33, J). There is a dialectic of inclusion and estrangement between Israel and its neighbors in these texts.[76]

A further condition of this genealogical structure is worth noting. As Ernest Nicholson has emphasized, the individual stories and the genealogical sequence of Abraham—Isaac—Jacob have many connections and complementary features, including the genealogical origins of Israel's neighbors. These continuities "cannot plausibly be accounted for in terms of a secondary editorial linking together of independent narratives composed in isolation from one another."[77] In other words, a wholly atomistic compositional history of Genesis is not credible. The additive quality of scribal technique is counterbalanced by the ethnological requirements of the genealogical form. The large-scale genealogy is like the gravitational field into which the individual stories are set, many of which themselves concern genealogical issues. The small-scale and the large-scale features of Genesis must have coexisted in a dialectic relationship in the compositional history of this cultural genealogy.

The generic self-definition of Genesis as a genealogical text helps to illuminate the resonance of the text as an ancestral archive of memory, as an engine for cultural self-fashioning, as a position towards the formative past, and as a scribal-literary production. The historical consciousness that animates this native genre operates by structuring the past as a vast genealogy, with an initial point—the creation of an ordered cosmos—and a teleological end-point, the current and future well-being of the people Israel. This generic form shapes the sense of the past in Genesis, from the תלדות of heaven and earth to the תלדות of Jacob-Israel.

---

[76] Hendel, *Remembering Abraham*, 3–30.
[77] Nicholson, *Pentateuch*, 120.

Conclusions

To draw the threads of my discussion together, I return to some problems involved in inquiry into the historical context of Genesis. Three related problems are pertinent. First, because of the paucity of relevant historical data, scholars tend to compensate by filling in the gaps with dubious or impressionistic arguments. On the extremes are the maximalists and minimalists, who are ardent about their convictions and tend to produce decidedly partial arguments—partial in both senses, as addressing only part of the data and as taking a partisan line. As we have noted, there are various categories of data germane to the historical context of Genesis. An approach that focuses on one group of data to the exclusion of the others will inevitably yield a flawed result.

A second problem is the general decline of interest in historical inquiry among biblical scholars. This derives, at least in part, from the acrimonious tone of many recent historical debates. The minimal yield of such debates generates an understandable desire to move on to more productive topics. As a consequence, many scholars now believe that literary and cultural studies of the Hebrew Bible need not be rooted in or supplemented by historical inquiry. This has created a proliferation of intellectual divides within the field, which in my view yields an impoverishment of biblical studies generally. History is a necessary dimension—but not a sufficient one—in the study of an ancient religious text.

A third and clearly related problem is the generally narrow construal of historical inquiry in the field. The main focus is on the history of events, which, as noted above, is only one level of historical time. The intermediate scale of time that Braudel calls "social time" is the more fruitful historical context for the narrative representations of the past in Genesis. There are precious few historical events—perhaps none—to which the narratives of Genesis correspond, but there are traces of cultural memories—of ethnic origins, religious practices, and tribal customs—that belong to this larger scale of history. A richer concept of the scope of historical inquiry and the scales of historical time may help to break down some of the current impasses.

The results of my discussion can be summarized as follows. First, the history of the composition of Genesis can be ascertained to a reasonable degree by attending to the evidence of language and to the occasional references to foreign affairs. The most basic linguistic indicators are the distinctions of archaic, classical, and late Biblical Hebrew in various texts of Genesis. Within classical Biblical Hebrew there are smaller categories of linguistic change, such as the demise of the Qal passive and its replacement by the Niphal, and the change in the distribution of the 1cs pronouns, אני and אנכי (and the demise of the latter in late Biblical Hebrew). On the basis of these and related linguistic distinctions, one can ascertain a relative chronology in which the Blessing of Jacob in Gen 49 is archaic, the J and E sources are classical, the P source is late classical, and a few chapters (esp. Gen 24) have traces of late Biblical Hebrew. The chronological range for these periods is ca. eleventh-tenth century (archaic), ca. tenth/ninth-sixth centuries (classical), and post-sixth century (late), with gradual transitions and regional "waves" throughout.

From the occasional references to foreign nations, we can specify a more precise chronological range for the major sources. The border treaty between Jacob and Laban, who pointedly bears the ethnonym "the Aramean" (Gen 31, J and E), arguably correlates with the Aramean wars of the ninth – early eighth centuries BCE. The prophecy of Esau's liberation from Jacob's rule (Gen 27:40, J) correlates with Edomite history of the ninth century. The schematic history of Nimrod (Gen 10:10–12, J) describe the configuration of cities in the Assyrian empire of the ninth-eighth century. The reference to "Ur of the Chaldeans" (Gen 11:31, P) correlates with the Neo-Babylonian period. The designation of this city as Abram's homeland arguably alludes to the situation of Judean exiles after 597. On the basis of these references to foreign affairs, we may specify the range of dates as follows: J and E belong to the horizon of the ninth-eighth centuries BCE, and P belongs to the horizon of the sixth century BCE.

Another kind of historical context refers to the possibility of pre-Israelite historical memories that have been preserved in the chain of oral and written traditions. In my view there are strong cases for two such historical memories, one pertaining to the location of the patriarchal homeland in the region of Haran, and the second pertaining to the worship of the high god El prior to his self-identification as YHWH. Both of these cultural memories arguably derive from historical situations of the pre-Israelite period, which have been overlaid with contemporary dress (the old Amorite homeland is now Aramean, and El is now YHWH). In this process, the remembered past is inevitably refashioned to retain present relevance, but a kernel of historical memory in these cases persists.

A third category of historical context pertains to the forms and genres of discourse about the past in Genesis. These genres are historical conventions with their own embedded sets of cultural expectations. The individual stories also have a historical context in their relationships to older stories and traditions. The Flood story is a perspicuous example of how narrative forms and traditions that derive from older Near Eastern cultures have distinctive revisions in Israelite culture. These processes of continuity and change are well-illustrated by the assemblage of stories in Gen 6–9 when compared to their older Mesopotamian congeners. Features of literary design and character development (particularly in the complex character of YHWH) can be delineated richly within this historical context.

Finally, the native genre-term in Genesis for these stories, תלדות, "generations" (in P), allows us to trace the multiple implications of the genealogical form of Genesis: the large-scale literary structure of the book, the genealogical concerns of the individual stories, and the dialectical relationships between Israel and its neighboring "kin." The self-designation of the stories as תלדות allows us to perceive the book as operating in genealogical time, which begins in the beginning and has its *telos* in the "becoming" of the tribal ancestors of Israel.

Select Bibliography

Baden, Joel S. *J, E, and the Redaction of the Pentateuch*. Forschungen zum Alten Testament 68. Tübingen: Mohr Siebeck, 2009.

Carr, David M. *Reading the Fractures of Genesis: Historical and Literary Approaches*. Louisville: Westminster John Knox Press, 1996.

Emerton, John A. "The Date of the Yahwist." Pages 107–129 in *In Search of Pre-exilic Israel: Proceedings of the Oxford Old Testament Seminar*. Edited by John Day. Journal for the Study of the Old Testament Supplement Series 406. London: T&T Clark, 2004.

Fleming, Daniel E. "Mari and the Possibilities of Biblical Memory." *Revue d'assyriologie et d'archéologie orientale* 92 (1998): 41–78.

Hendel, Ronald. *Remembering Abraham: Culture, Memory, and History in the Hebrew Bible*. New York: Oxford University Press, 2005.

Hendel, Ronald, ed. *Reading Genesis: Ten Methods*. Cambridge: Cambridge University Press, 2010.

Joosten, Jan. "The Distinction between Classical and Late Biblical Hebrew as Reflected in Syntax." *Hebrew Studies* 46 (2005): 327–339.

Nicholson, Ernest W. *The Pentateuch in the Twentieth Century: The Legacy of Julius Wellhausen*. Oxford: Oxford University Press, 1998.

Rofé, Alexander. *Introduction to the Composition of the Pentateuch*. Biblical Seminar 58. Sheffield: Sheffield Academic Press, 1999.

Ska, Jean-Louis. *Introduction to Reading the Pentateuch*. Translated by Pascale Dominique. Winona Lake, Ind.: Eisenbrauns, 2006.

Wénin, A., ed. *Studies in the Book of Genesis: Literature, Redaction and History*. Bibliotheca ephemeridum theologicarum lovaniensium 155. Leuven: Leuven University Press, 2001.

LITERARY ANALYSIS[1]

Robert S. Kawashima

In order to understand what literary analysis of the Bible is (and should yet become), we must first understand its uneasy relationship to biblical criticism proper. In spite of their common descent from modern philology, literary studies and biblical studies are at best distant relatives.[2] Their reunion took place fairly recently, for it entailed crossing the great historical divide that had opened up between the Bible and the idea of Literature in the eighteenth century, when hermeneutics came to equate the meaning of biblical narrative with its reference, whether historical or ideal, to the exclusion of its realistic or "history-like" literary sense—that event Hans Frei called the "eclipse of biblical narrative."[3] The fullest, most coherent version of the literary approach to the Bible, that of Robert Alter—who came to the Bible, one should recall, via the discipline of comparative literature, not biblical studies per se—only began to be articulated in the 1970s, and it did not reach its fully developed form until the publication of *The Art*

---

[1] I have presented different versions of this chapter on various occasions, most recently in May 2010 at *Alterations: A Celebration in Honor of Robert Alter on his 75th Birthday*. Of those present that day, I am particularly grateful to Robert Alter, Ron Hendel, Chana Kronfeld, and Herb Marks for their supportive responses. Special thanks are due to Hayden White, since it was in his graduate seminar on "The Rhetoric of History," taught for Berkeley's Rhetoric Department some 15 years ago, that I first started thinking about the "figural" meaning of Genesis.

[2] See my related remarks on the "genealogy" shared by these two disciplines in "Sources and Redaction," in *Reading Genesis: Ten Methods* (ed. Ronald Hendel; New York: Cambridge University Press, 2010), 47–70.

[3] Hans W. Frei, *The Eclipse of Biblical Narrative: A Study in Eighteenth and Nineteenth Century Hermeneutics* (New Haven: Yale University Press, 1974). According to Frei, biblical interpreters were virtually unanimous in equating the meaning of the Bible with its supposed reference to some "subject matter" extrinsic to the text itself, whether this was thought to be "historical events, the general consciousness or form of life of an era, a system of ideas, the author's intention, the inward moral experience of individuals, the structure of human existence, or some combination of them; in any case, the meaning of the text is not identical with the text" (278). This perspective created a blind spot, namely, no one could conceive of a specifically literary interpretation of biblical narrative as realistic or "history-like" *fiction*, whose meaning would be intrinsic to the text and therefore independent of reference.

of Biblical Narrative in 1981.[4] Upon finally arriving at the shores of the Bible, literary analysis, with its foreign critical idiom and exotic scholarly customs, met with an uneven reception from the locals, who were not always sure what to make of this academic newcomer. Thirty years later, it is still far from clear that it has been fully accepted by the field, which continues to be predominantly historical in orientation.[5]

This orientation can be traced back, again, to biblical narrative's "eclipse" in the eighteenth century. For as soon as the Bible was credited with possibly historical reference—rather than simply being equated with history—"biblical history" was transformed from an axiom to a conjecture, defended by some, challenged by others, confronted by all. Criticism ever since of the Book of Genesis (and of the Bible in general) has been largely defined in terms of the discipline of history.[6] What could one know about Abraham and the "patriarchal age," Joseph and the Hebrews' sojourn in Egypt? What historical information, that is, can one hope to recover from Genesis? The answer, it turns out, is almost entirely negative: we can know very little about the history of Bronze-Age Canaan as it relates to Genesis.[7] Faced with this impasse, some scholars have recently begun arguing that, even if Genesis is not a history in the narrow sense, it still conserves a form of

---

[4] Robert Alter, *The Art of Biblical Narrative* (New York: Basic Books, 1981). I do not mean to deny the existence and importance of earlier literary studies of the Bible. The publication of *The Art of Biblical Narrative*, however, constitutes part of a watershed in the history of biblical interpretation. In 1978–1979, Frank Kermode delivered his Norton Lectures at Harvard on the Gospel of Mark, published as *The Genesis of Secrecy: On the Interpretation of Narrative* (Cambridge: Harvard University Press, 1979). And a few years later, Northrop Frye would publish his important if problematic study of the Bible: *The Great Code: The Bible and Literature* (New York: Harcourt Brace Jovanovich, 1982). One could, no doubt, expand the list of examples. This constellation of books marks a shift in the status of the Bible within the humanities, perhaps visible as well in Gene M. Tucker and Douglas A. Knight, eds., *Humanizing America's Iconic Book* (Chico, Calif.: Scholars Press, 1982).

[5] For this reason, important biblical scholars continue to disparage the literary approach to the Bible. The list of detractors is impressive and thus disheartening: Frank Moore Cross; James Kugel; Simon B. Parker; Karel van der Toorn. The charge usually has to do with an alleged "anachronism" intrinsic to literary analysis of an ancient religious text such as the Bible. See my arguments against this allegation in "Comparative Literature and Biblical Studies: The Case of Allusion," *Proof* 27 (2007): 324–344. The tradition of theological exegesis constitutes a partial exception to this historical orientation, though as Frei demonstrates, biblical theology has had to negotiate its relationship to history as well.

[6] Frei describes the hermeneutical shift in *Eclipse of Biblical Narrative*, 51–65.

[7] This is not to denigrate the ongoing and fascinating efforts to reconstruct the history of bronze-age Canaan: see, e.g., Hershel Shanks, et al., *The Rise of Ancient Israel* (Washington, D.C.: Biblical Archaeology Society, 1992).

historical information, namely, "cultural memory."[8] But if this search for memory incorporates insights drawn from anthropology, literary studies and other disciplines, it is still fundamentally historical in orientation, inasmuch as it treats the Bible as a source of information about the past, extrinsic to the text.

Literary analysis, conversely, seeks knowledge of biblical literature as such, as an end in itself, irrespective of its possible historical reference. I do not mean to divorce literature from history. In fact, literary and historical methods can and should operate in a type of symbiosis: literary analysis should inform historical reconstruction; historical reconstruction should inform literary interpretation. As Alter's programmatic definition of his literary approach indicates, however, literature contains an autonomous non-referential dimension, namely, its intrinsic form and content: "By literary analysis I mean the manifold varieties of minutely discriminating attention to the artful use of language, to the shifting play of ideas, conventions, tone, sound, imagery, syntax, narrative viewpoint, compositional units, and much else; the kind of disciplined attention, in other words, which through a whole spectrum of critical approaches has illuminated, for example, the poetry of Dante, the plays of Shakespeare, the novels of Tolstoy."[9] In the eyes of an historically oriented field, the literary critic's engagement in the merely "imaginary" realm of art has often seemed eccentric, trivial even, in comparison to the historian's enterprise, which derives a certain *gravitas* from its heroic attempt to reconstruct historical "reality" out of faint traces of the past.[10] Regardless of one's perspective on the relative merits of historical and literary studies, one should not obscure the distinction between them.

As Alter thus implies, literary analysis includes everything from formal theoretical accounts of biblical narrative and poetry to practical interpretive readings of individual passages. But it does not necessarily involve aesthetic evaluation. It may be the case, as Alter has consistently maintained, that the

---

[8] See Ronald Hendel's chapter in this volume see also his *Remembering Abraham: Culture, Memory, and History in the Hebrew Bible* (New York: Oxford University Press, 2005); and "Cultural Memories," in *Reading Genesis*, 28–46; see also Mark S. Smith, *The Memoirs of God: History, Memory, and the Experience of the Divine in Ancient Israel* (Minneapolis: Fortress Press, 2004).

[9] Alter, *Art of Biblical Narrative*, 12–13.

[10] The field of literary studies itself, it should be added, has of late seemed hesitant to study literature for its own sake—many literary scholars undertaking what are, in essence, instrumental readings of literature, under various "interdisciplinary" guises, intended to make literary art seem more relevant or useful to a philistine world.

Bible contains some exquisite examples of literary art: the JE narratives of the Pentateuch; the David Story in Samuel; the poetry of Job. But a piece of writing need not be an artistic masterpiece to repay careful literary analysis. The Priestly source, for example—which, after all, constitutes the longest Pentateuchal source—can hardly be classified as literary art, but this does not mean that it cannot be profitably studied in broadly literary fashion. In fact, as a carefully constructed theological and legal edifice, P richly rewards "disciplined attention" to the sorts of literary and linguistic features mentioned by Alter.[11] An aesthetically and intellectually poorer composition, however, will not. Consider, for example, the bowdlerized version of the David Story found in Chronicles. Chronicles may be of immense scholarly value, but great literature it is not. And inasmuch as literary analysis should only be able to find what is actually already there in the text, its findings in the case of Chronicles should be correspondingly meager.

Literary study of the narratives of Genesis has taken numerous forms,[12] but these devolve, broadly speaking, to three basic approaches: poetics, rhetoric, and style. The "poetic" approach, of which Alter is the principle representative, consists of reconstructing the literary principles or "conventions" employed by the biblical writers in rendering their received and/or invented stories: type-scenes, the interplay between narration and dialogue, characterization, and so on.[13] For a time, scholars also devoted a fair amount of attention to the "rhetorical" structures and related features shaping various episodes in Genesis—*chiasmus*, etc. Here J.P. Fokkelman's "structural and stylistic analyses" come foremost to mind.[14] If this approach

---

[11] See, e.g., Robert S. Kawashima, "The Priestly Tent of Meeting and the Problem of Divine Transcendence: An 'Archaeology' of the Sacred," *JR* 86 (2006): 226–257; and "The Jubilee Year and the Return of Cosmic Purity," *CBQ* 65 (2003): 370–389. While I applaud Chaya Halberstam's recent literary analysis of certain legal passages in the Bible, it does not follow that one should, as she suggests, blur the distinction between law and literature; see her "The Art of Biblical Law," *Proof* 27 (2007): 345–364.

[12] I leave biblical poetry to the side. Verse is incidental to Genesis as a whole, and its analysis would raise a distinct set of literary issues beyond the scope of this chapter.

[13] Alter himself does not define his approach in terms of "poetics," but the conventions he brings to light are in essence the poetic principles underlying the creation (*poiēsis*) of biblical literature. In spite of significant differences, then, there is a family resemblance between his work and explicitly poetics-oriented studies: e.g., Adele Berlin, *Poetics and Interpretation of Biblical Narrative* (Sheffield: Almond Press, 1983); and Meir Sternberg, *The Poetics of Biblical Narrative: Ideological Literature and the Drama of Reading* (Bloomington: Indiana University Press, 1985).

[14] J.P. Fokkelman, *Narrative Art in Genesis: Specimens of Stylistic and Structural Analysis* (SSN 17; Assen: Van Gorcum, 1975). He soon went on to produce a massive study of the Books

has seemingly run its course, due to its inherent limitations,[15] one cannot deny that it occasionally leads to valuable insights—and it may well be the case that more work remains to be done in this area, though perhaps at a broader cultural level.[16] Third, some have analyzed biblical narrative in terms of its verbal medium—language, grammar, style, and so on. This was the great contribution of Erich Auerbach's landmark study, "Odysseus' Scar," in which he elucidated the literary consequences following from the radically different narrative "styles" of Homer's *Odyssey* and Genesis.[17] As I have argued elsewhere—based on linguistic and stylistic analyses of Homeric and Ugaritic epic and of biblical narrative—what Auerbach actually discovered was the distinct aesthetic qualities intrinsic, respectively, to the verbal media of oral-traditional poetry and literary (written) prose.[18] Of course, these various levels of analysis necessarily interact with each other.[19] Alter made it clear from the start that the art of biblical narrative was essentially related to the medium of written prose.[20] Similarly, Fokkelman's "analyses" were not just "structural" but also "stylistic," albeit in his limited use of this term.

I would finally make special mention here of source criticism, which, one should recall, used to be known as "literary criticism." It is true that biblicists (of both literary and historical persuasions) generally classify it as an historically oriented method—perhaps in part because Julius Wellhausen, the principle spokesman for the Documentary Hypothesis, presented it as part

---

of Samuel: *Narrative Art and Poetry in the Books of Samuel: A Full Interpretation Based on Stylistic and Structural Analyses* (4 vols.; Assen: Van Gorcum, 1980–1993).

[15] For further discussion of the problems and limitations of this approach, see my review of Jerome T. Walsh, *Style and Structure in Biblical Hebrew Narrative* (Collegeville, Minn.: The Liturgical Press, 2001), in *HS* 44 (2003): 243–245.

[16] It is noteworthy, e.g., that the final book by Mary Douglas (at least of those published during her lifetime) should be dedicated to "ring composition": *Thinking in Circles: An Essay on Ring Composition* (New Haven: Yale University Press, 2007).

[17] Erich Auerbach, *Mimesis: The Representation of Reality in Western Literature* (trans. Willard R. Trask; Princeton: Princeton University Press, 1953), 3–23.

[18] Robert S. Kawashima, *Biblical Narrative and the Death of the Rhapsode* (Indiana Studies in Biblical Literature; Bloomington: Indiana University Press, 2004); see also my summary overview of this approach in "The Syntax of Narrative Forms," in *Narratives of Egypt and the Ancient Near East: Literary and Linguistic Approaches* (ed. F. Hagen, J. Johnston, W. Monkhouse, K. Piquette, J. Tait, and M. Worthington; Leuven: Peters, 2011), 341–369.

[19] Style may be relevant to both rhetoric and poetics; it is less clear how to relate rhetorical structure to poetic convention. Chiasms, e.g., have no intrinsic literary significance.

[20] See in particular Alter's discussion of biblical Hebrew prose style in his *Genesis: Translation and Commentary* (New York: W.W. Norton, 1996), xxvi–xxxix.

of his *Geschichte Israels*.²¹ But in fact, source analysis in and of itself has nothing to do with historical analysis, the former playing a purely preparatory role to the latter—its "prolegomena," as Wellhausen put it. In this regard, source criticism is analogous to textual criticism: just as textual criticism must establish the text before its provenance can be studied, so source criticism must determine the text's provenance—i.e., isolate its underlying sources—before these individual documents can be analyzed further, whether as historical sources or literary works. Thus, far from being inimical to literary analysis, source criticism (no less than textual criticism) is neutral in regard to the distinction between historical and literary studies. Indeed, inasmuch as the modern study of literature generally conceptualizes works in relation to authors—"the poetry of Dante, the plays of Shakespeare, the novels of Tolstoy," in Alter's words—I would go so far as to say that source criticism can and should play an integral role in literary interpretation, for it and it alone is able to restore to the literary critic the discrete authorial compositions contained within the biblical books.

If I thus advocate for a literary approach that interprets each source individually, the question still remains: What does the Book of Genesis, in its final redacted form, mean? Here, literary analysis might contribute still more to biblical studies. In fact, one of the early promises of the literary approach to the Bible was precisely that it would draw scholarly attention back to the final text as we have it.²² Unfortunately, apart from the occasional suggestive remark,²³ literary analysis has generally dismissed or neglected source criticism, typically under the banner of that infelicitously named false dichotomy between "synchronic" and "diachronic" analysis.²⁴

---

²¹ Wellhausen's *magnum opus* was originally published as *Geschichte Israels* (Berlin: G. Reimer, 1878); later as *Prolegomena zur Geshichte Israels* (1882); in English as *Prolegomena to the History of Israel* (1885).

²² Canonical criticism, too, privileges the biblical text in its final form, but I do not think it is compatible with the literary approach I espouse here: the former grounds the text in the community that grants it canonical status, viz., in its reception; the latter conceptualizes the text in relation to its authors and editors, i.e., its composition or point(s) of origin. See my further remarks on authorial and editorial intention in "Sources and Redaction," 49–51, 61–64.

²³ See for example the brief exchange between Alter and David Damrosch in Alter, *Art of Biblical Narrative*, 131–154; David Damrosch, *The Narrative Covenant: Transformations of Genre in the Growth of Biblical Literature* (San Francisco: Harper & Row, 1987), 298–326; and Robert Alter, *The World of Biblical Literature* (New York: Basic Books, 1992), 1–24. Compare Berlin, *Poetics*, 111–134.

²⁴ The dichotomy is false because, not only is source criticism wholly compatible with literary analysis, but literary analysis itself should be no more or less "diachronic" or "syn-

The complex composition of Genesis does indeed present a major obstacle to any reading of the final text, for it renders the text we have before us unsuitable for a purely linear reading. Namely, the temptation is to read each verse of Genesis as if it seamlessly continued the previous verse, whereas the Documentary Hypothesis has crucially taught us that this is simply not the case at numerous junctures in the text. However, the inconvenience of this truth does not provide sufficient grounds for its dismissal. Appeals to "intertextuality" and the "implied author" notwithstanding, then, a fully developed and coherent literary reading of Genesis as a whole requires a complex interpretive process that focuses on each of the sources individually and then on their redaction.[25]

Since such a reading is beyond the scope of this chapter, I will offer here instead an approach to interpreting Genesis as a whole that will allow us to bracket, at least temporarily, the problems posed by its redaction: viz., a "figural" reading of its "thematic structure." And I will simplify this reading even further by restricting it to the Patriarchal History. The underlying thematic logic of Genesis, having shaped each of the sources as well as their redaction, endows Genesis with a certain type of "unity," and this thematic unity makes possible an episodic reading of Genesis that avoids the pitfalls of a linear and continuous reading for its plot.[26] This approach is not meant to ward off source criticism in the name, yet again, of literary analysis. It is only as a concession to the limits of this chapter that I offer this merely preliminary interpretation of Genesis, the full version of which would incorporate its compositional history.

What does the Patriarchal History mean? Genesis 12–36 consists of an assortment of ancestral tales, in the course of which three generations of nomadic Hebrews get married, have children, and encounter various

---

chronic" than the text it studies. In other words, literary analysis of Genesis should incorporate the findings of source criticism, not reject them. The dichotomy is infelicitously named because its terms imply that the individual literary work is analogous to *langue* (a language as a system)—the latter constituting the object of both diachronic and synchronic linguistics, as defined by Saussure. Finally, framing these issues in this way implies that one is free to "apply" one or the other mode of reading to any text, whereas modern critical reading should dutifully adapt itself to the nature and demands of a given text.

[25] See Kawashima, "Sources and Redaction," esp. 61–70.

[26] Similarly, Alter, in his earlier work, tended to offer strictly local interpretations, which in general allowed him, quite successfully in my view, to avoid source-critical problems—though I do not claim this was a conscious strategy on his part. His more recent work, namely his ongoing series of translations with commentary, raises more complicated methodological problems, but I cannot address these here.

foreigners, wandering all the while through a land destined to be, but not yet, theirs. At the literal level, then, these stories simply recount a version—not particularly reliable, as we now know—of Israel's "historical" past, namely, the people, places, and events ostensibly involved in Israel's national origins. But these ancestors happen to bear the very names of Israel and its twelve tribes. At a second figural level, then, these personae do not merely precede Israel in time as ancestral cause to national effect, but in some non-historical, non-causal way symbolize or, better, prefigure the nation itself.[27] To the extent that the Patriarchal History reflects certain historical realities of, say, preexilic Israel, one might loosely compare it to political allegory, or at least discern within it a number of vaguely allegorical elements.[28] It would be a mistake, however, to attempt to correlate every detail of Genesis with an historical entity or event—the fallacy of allegorizing—for these stories have clearly taken on a fictive, literary life of their own, quite independent of any grounding the tradition may once have had in historical facts. Conversely, even if Genesis turned out to be a pure fiction with no relation to Israelite history, the specifically literary interpretation offered below would still stand, since literary meaning is, as I noted earlier, logically distinct from historical reference.

It is at this figural level that Genesis as a whole makes sense. If its plot appears on the surface to be rather directionless, not unlike the wanderings of the patriarchs themselves, there is beneath their peregrinations a coherent thematic logic: the construction of Israelite identity, particularly through and against the surrounding nations. Almost every single episode in Gen 12–36 involves an interaction between the emerging Self of Israel and one of its paradigmatic Others. These episodes take one of two forms, which I refer to as "discriminations" and "encounters," depending on whether the Other takes the form, respectively, of a kinsman who could potentially supplant Israel as God's elect, or of a foreigner whose presence measures the efficacy of Israel's blessing. On the one hand, God *discriminates*, in each generation, between a patriarch and a rival kinsman, singling out the one for divine favor, while relegating the other to a footnote of covenantal history:

---

[27] "Figural" here refers to a literary trope, not the theological (specifically apocalyptic) concept described by Auerbach in his important essay, "Figura," in *Scenes from the Drama of European Literature* (Minneapolis: University of Minnesota Press, 1984), 11–76.

[28] Ilana Pardes provides an analogous sort of interpretation of the exodus and wilderness narratives in *The Biography of Ancient Israel: National Narratives in the Bible* (Berkeley: University of California Press, 2000).

Abraham rather than Lot, Isaac rather than Ishmael, Jacob rather than Esau. In each case, the patriarch bears signs of culture, the rival, marks of nature.[29] On the other hand, Israel's ancestors *encounter* various foreign rivals: Egyptians, Philistines, Arameans, et al.[30] In each case, the chosen patriarch prospers, usually at the expense of his rival, whether through divine intervention, apparent luck, and/or unscrupulous trickery. But if these traditions thus denigrate the Other as uncultured, unblessed, unchosen, they do not celebrate the moral triumph of the Self. Abraham, Isaac, and Jacob are not uniformly more righteous than their counterparts. Divine election, then, does not coincide with merit, but rather contains an element of the arbitrary. For the God of Israel remained, in the end, inscrutable.[31]

Discriminations

I begin by examining the figural opposition between nature and culture underlying the series of discriminations in the Patriarchal History. The first to take place is that between Abraham and Lot, the first generation of the descendants of Terah to settle in Canaan (11:27–32). Lot may not rival Abraham as a peer, but as long as the uncle remains without an heir, the nephew cannot but threaten, by his mere existence, the uncle's legacy with an horizontal displacement.[32] Due to their prosperity, moreover, a rivalry over grazing rights quickly develops between the two (Gen 13:8–12). Abraham

---

[29] See Hayden White, "The Forms of Wildness: Archaeology of an Idea," in *Tropics of Discourse: Essays in Cultural Criticism* (Baltimore: Johns Hopkins University Press, 1978), 150–182.

[30] Robert L. Cohn takes a similar approach to these "encounters," but arrives at substantially different interpretations in "Before Israel: The Canaanites as Other in Biblical Tradition," in *The Other in Jewish Thought and History: Constructions of Jewish Culture and Identity* (ed. Laurence J. Silberstein and Robert L. Cohn; New York: New York University Press, 1994), 74–90.

[31] For recent studies of this central biblical idea, see: Seock-Tae Sohn, *The Divine Election of Israel* (Grand Rapids: Eerdmans, 1991); David Novak, *The Election of Israel: The Idea of the Chosen People* (Cambridge: Cambridge University Press, 1995); Joel S. Kaminsky, *Yet I Loved Jacob: Reclaiming the Biblical Concept of Election* (Nashville: Abingdon Press, 2007); and Joel N. Lohr, *Chosen and Unchosen: Conceptions of Election in the Pentateuch and Jewish-Christian Interpretation* (Siphrut 2; Winona Lake, Ind.: Eisenbrauns, 2009).

[32] Or, one might arguably see here a rivalry between Abraham and his brother Haran (Lot's father): see Kaminsky, *Yet I Loved Jacob*, 29–30. According to P, Terah for some unstated reason (perhaps stated in the tradition) heads for Canaan, but gets waylaid at Haran (11:27–32). Abraham and Lot thus complete Terah's unfinished quest, opening the question of which of Terah's son will prove to be his successor in Canaan.

suggests that they part company in peace rather remain together in conflict, and, in spite of being the elder, magnanimously offers his nephew first pick of the lands lying before them. This parting of ways, which will recur in the lives of Isaac and Jacob, figurally enacts the discrimination between chosen and unchosen, as each patriarch marches toward his respective future. Lot, seeing that the Jordan plain is "well-watered like the garden of YHWH, like the land of Egypt" (13:10), decides to settle in Sodom. While it is perfectly logical for Lot to want to settle in this Edenic locale, he not only becomes "guilty by association," but his decision itself is subtly condemned by J. The human condition as decreed by God in Gen 3 is to be banished from the garden—i.e., from God's immediate providential care—and to live rather in a state of toil and uncertainty as befits mere mortals.[33] Any attempt to return to that prelapsarian bliss enjoyed for a time by Adam and Eve thus constitutes an act of *hubris*, a bid to escape humankind's designated existential plight. And for J, it is precisely the perennial river that provides this escape. Its unfailing waters and the material security they provide lead inevitably to a life of careless decadent ease, whereas the sporadic nature of rain forces one to be ever mindful of one's creatural status (cf. Deut 11:10–17). Precisely for this reason, the two earthly sites compared to YHWH's garden—namely, Egypt and the Dead Sea—come under God's wrath for outrages committed against the divine order.

Lot's sojourn in Sodom (Gen 19) further develops this theme. In terms of the opposition of nature versus culture, Sodom and Gomorrah do not fall under the category of nature so much as anti-civilization, the monstrous inversion of culture.[34] The entire episode centers on the theme of hospitality, the very foundation of civilization, which, one might say, begins the moment one can seek food and shelter in a stranger's home. Lot in effect wins his family's salvation by protecting the strangers who have come under his roof, even at grave risk to his household—arguably outdoing his uncle's hospitality in the previous scene (Gen 18). If Lot thus maintains the sanctity of the guest-host relationship, the men of Sodom subvert it instead, seeking to rape the strangers who have entered their city's gates. One might compare this incident with Odysseus' encounter with the cyclops in Book 9 of the *Odyssey*. The latter is not merely an uncultured barbarian, but an

---

[33] For further discussion, see my *"Homo Faber* in J's Primeval History," *ZAW* 116 (2004): 483–501.

[34] See especially Robert Alter, "Sodom as Nexus," in *The Book and the Text: The Bible and Literary Theory* (ed. Regina M. Schwartz; Oxford: Blackwwell, 1990), 146–160.

impious perversion of civilized man, who seeks to devour those who have entered the shelter of his cave. Odysseus and a few lucky companions escape thanks only to the wiles of culture, overcoming their fearsome "host" specifically with wine—an emblematic achievement of culture (see, e.g., Gen 5:29; 9:20–21). In the aftermath of divine judgment, Lot and his two daughters, living uneasily at the edge of "ground zero," decide to flee to the hills and live in a cave—reminiscent, again, of Homer's cyclops. Lot's daughters, desperate for offspring, ply their father with wine on two successive nights, in order to lie with him, each in turn. Having just relocated from a prosperous city to a primitive cave, Abraham's would-be rival is finally thrust by this transgression of the incest taboo altogether beyond the pale of civilization. Not coincidentally, the sons so conceived are the ancestors of Moab and Ammon. And at the very moment that Lot sires his incestuous brood, Abraham receives at long last the son of the promise, Isaac (Gen 21:1–2).[35]

The next generation brings a second rivalry, this time between Isaac and Ishmael. It is important to remember that it is the latter who is Abraham's eldest son. True, he is born to a mere "handmaid" (16:1), but the same domestic arrangement will not later prevent Bilhah and Zilpah from begetting four of Israel's tribes: Dan, Naphtali, Gad, and Asher (Gen 30). Ishmael's low birth, however, does come into play when Sarah demands, in effect, that Abraham disown his firstborn son and divorce his second wife: "And Sarah saw the son of Hagar the Egyptian, whom she had born to Abraham, playing. And she said to Abraham, 'Cast out that slave woman and her son, for the son of that slave woman shall not inherit with my son, with Isaac'" (Gen 21:9–10). What Sarah sees is the son of an Egyptian. What she insists on expelling from her house is the son of a slave, a subhuman beast of burden. In terms of what would now be called his "race" and "class," Ishmael is to be despised as the Other, inferior as such to her own son.

In fact, Ishmael is relegated to this secondary status while yet in his mother's womb. Hagar, while fleeing from Sarah's abuse, encounters the Angel of YHWH and takes part in a variation of the "annunciation typescene," a narrative convention typically reserved for the birth of important figures, not only in the Bible—Isaac, Jacob and Esau, Samson, and Samuel—

---

[35] The annunciation of Isaac's birth (18:10) places the blessed event about a year into the future, during which interval Lot's story unfolds. The pluperfect construction which reintroduces Sarah into the narrative—"And YHWH had visited [*wayhwh pāqad*] Sarah as he had said" (21:1)—thus carefully synchronizes these parallel births, a literary effect more marked in J, before the insertion of Gen 20.

but also in the Ugaritic epics *Aqhat* and *Kirta*.³⁶ It is significant, then, that Ishmael's birth should be given this formal literary treatment: "I will greatly increase your seed so that it will be too numerous to count. ... Look, you are pregnant, and you will give birth to a son, and you will call him Ishmael. For YHWH has listened to your distress. And he will be a wild ass of a man, his hand against all, and the hand of all against him, and he will dwell in the face of all his kin" (Gen 16:11–12). A rather mixed blessing. He is destined to multiply—unchosen perhaps, but a son of Abraham nonetheless. But the oracle figuratively describes him as an animal, more precisely, a "wild" (i.e., undomesticated) beast, which is to say, he will lead an antisocial existence, in the face, but beyond the reach, of the bonds of human fellowship. The prophecy comes true. Ishmael and his mother move to the wilderness (21:14, 20–21). What is more, he becomes an archer, that is, a human predator, living off the flesh of wild game, as opposed to domesticated livestock (21:20). One should finally note that Hagar, having been cast out of Abraham's household, finds an Egyptian wife for her son. In modern parlance, Ishmael returns to his "ethnic roots." Although God is with him—out of respect, again, for his father Abraham—his status as Other is nonetheless confirmed. He thus begets the tribe of Ishmaelites, whose full and permanent nomadism corresponds to the wild, anti-social nature of their eponymous ancestor.

The rivalry between Jacob and Esau develops the figural opposition of nature versus culture most explicitly and elaborately.³⁷ It too begins *in utero*. Suffering terribly from a difficult pregnancy, Rebekah, ever the forceful and decisive matriarch, seeks out an explanation from God, thus initiating her own "annunciation" type-scene: a prenatal fraternal struggle, she discovers, has begun in her womb between diametrically opposed twins (25:22–23). This struggle continues in the birth canal itself, as Jacob stubbornly holds onto Esau's heel during their delivery. Their opposition is immediately and visibly apparent at birth, for already as a newborn infant, Esau is like a "hairy

---

³⁶ See Robert Alter, "How Convention Helps us Read: The Case of the Bible's Annunciation Type-Scene," *Proof* 3 (1983): 115–130; and Simon B. Parker, *The Pre-Biblical Narrative Tradition: Essays on the Ugaritic Poems Keret and Aqhat* (SBLRBS 24; Atlanta: Scholars Press, 1989). I distinguish furthermore between the literary and oral-traditional techniques underlying type-scenes, respectively, in the Bible and in Homeric and Ugaritic epic; see my "Verbal Medium and Narrative Art in Homer and the Bible," *Philosophy and Literature* 28 (2004): 103–117; and *Biblical Narrative and the Death of the Rhapsode*, 161–189.

³⁷ See Ronald Hendel, *The Epic of the Patriarch: The Jacob Cycle and the Narrative Traditions of Canaan and Israel* (HSM 42; Atlanta: Scholars Press, 1987), 111–131; and Hendel, *Remembering Abraham*, 9–13.

cloak" (25:25)—literally as furry as a beast, it later becomes clear, in contrast to his markedly smooth younger brother (27:11). Esau's distinctive reddish coloring (*'admônî*) reinforces his inhuman otherness, or at least functions as an eponymous ethnic marker for Edom. I do not mean to suggest that the Edomites actually had a ruddy complexion, merely that Esau's "barbaric" appearance (and later behavior) constitutes a figural projection of his descendants' otherness. Similar to Ishmael—not coincidentally, his future father-in-law—Esau is a "skilled hunter, a man of the field" (25:27); Jacob, in stark contrast, is "a retiring [*tam*] man, living in tents."[38] Inasmuch as the spatial opposition between field and tent is gendered—outdoor-nature-male versus indoor-culture-female—the distribution of parental favoritism reinforces the brothers' figural opposition: Isaac, we are told, "loved Esau because he had a taste for game, but Rebekah loved Jacob" (25:28). In this case, the male half of the equation is linked specifically to animal desire.

Jacob and Esau's rivalry comes to a head when the former buys the latter's birthright. Each brother is occupied, respectively, in what has just been established as a typical day's work: Jacob cooks at home while Esau returns from the field, perhaps from hunting, but if so, apparently without success. This particular afternoon, however, Esau, a slave (like his father) to his bodily appetites, effectively sells his future for the immediate gratification of a hot meal. His use of language further corroborates his emerging characterization: "Feed me, please, some of this red red" (25:30). On the one hand, he decorously employs the particle "please" (*nā'*). On the other, he brutishly refers to Jacob's stew as "this red red" (*hā'ādōm hā'ādōm hazzeh*)—another pun on Edom, this time in connection with Esau's ravenous hunger. As has been plausibly suggested, one should probably understand Esau's verb choice "feed me" (*hal'îtēnî*), which occurs only this one time in the Bible, in light of rabbinic Hebrew, where it refers specifically to the feeding of animals—cf. German *füttern*.[39] Jacob, conversely, behaves like a classic trickster, outwitting his barely older but much stronger brother through his cunning—brain versus brawn. If Esau thinks with his stomach, even to the point of "despising" his birthright (25:34), Jacob thinks only of material gain, even to the point of ruthlessly exploiting his twin brother. If Esau is a willing victim here, Jacob's proposal is hardly one of brotherly love.

---

[38] In light of the almost archetypal opposition between these brothers, I take the ambiguous Hebrew term *tam*—variously translated as "quiet" or "mild" or "innocent"—to describe Jacob's general demeanor as the precise opposite of Esau's predatory nature.

[39] See especially Abba Ben-David, *Biblical Hebrew and Mishnaic Hebrew* (2 vols.; Tel Aviv: Dvir, 1967–1971) [Hebrew].

Esau may willingly sell his birthright, but he in no way consents to the theft of his blessing (Gen 27). In this tightly crafted scene, the whole family contributes to the realization of the struggle first conceived in Rebekah's womb. The axis of culture will defeat the axis of nature. Isaac, now old and blind, asks Esau to hunt and cook wild game in order to stimulate the bestowal of patriarchal blessing—thus persisting in his long established preference for his firstborn son. Rebekah, having overheard this request, instructs her favorite to trick the blessing out her husband. She has domesticated meat ready at hand and is thus able to prepare a suitable meal before Esau. The woman in the tent beats the hunter in the field. Even Isaac marvels at what he mistakes for his elder son's speed. The quick-witted Jacob improvises a satisfactory explanation: "Because YHWH your God brought success upon me" (27:20). Rebekah, furthermore, disguises Jacob under animal skins and her other son's clothing. Culture can imitate nature, but not vice versa. It is worth noting that Isaac's blessing, intended for Esau, evokes the richness of nature, here appropriated by culture: "See, the smell of my son is like the smell of a field that YHWH has blessed. May God give you of the dew of heaven and of the fat of the earth, and abundance of grain and wine" (27:28). Like the disenfranchised Ishmael, Esau is relegated to a secondary status and associated with anti-social violence: "Look, away from the fat of the earth will your home be, and away from the dew of heaven above. By your sword will you live, and your brother will you serve. When you break free, you will shake loose his yoke from off your neck" (27:39–40). He will eventually break free from his younger brother's dominion, but in the meantime he has been metaphorically reduced to a beast of burden.

One should also consider P's account of Jacob and Esau's respective choice of wives. Esau has already married Canaanite women, specifically Hittites, a source of "bitterness" for his parents (26:34–35). Jacob, however, must go back to Mesopotamia to find his wife, for Isaac and Rebekah, at least according to P, expressly send him there for this very purpose (27:46–28:2). Esau, finally realizing the error of his ways, tries at last to please his parents by marrying the "right sort of girl," but it is too little, too late. He marries a daughter of Ishmael—a son of Abraham, it is true, but the wrong son, the unchosen son. P may not inflect these marriages with the opposition between nature and culture, but through Esau's latter marriage, P in a sense establishes an ontological identity between two generations of the nonelect. And Esau's earlier marriages to local Hittite women further if indirectly contribute to the construction of Self, since all the sources deny the possibility that Israel is native to Canaan—a point we return to below.

In fact, P, too, recounts a series of discriminations. As various scholars have noted, P divides history into four distinct dispensations, which one might designate in terms of four emblematic figures: Adam, Noah, Abraham, Moses. Frank Cross demonstrated in particular that the latter three periods are marked by three covenants, each more exclusive than the last, and each associated with a particular name of God and a specific covenantal "sign" (ʾôt): the Noahic covenant between Elohim and "all flesh" (humans and animals), signified by the rainbow (9:1–17); the Abrahamic covenant between El Shadday and Abraham and his "seed" (Ishmael as well as Isaac), signified by circumcision (17:1–14); the Mosaic covenant between YHWH and Israel (Exod 6:2–8), signified by the Sabbath (31:12–17).[40] If the Noahic covenant is universal—approximating the idea of "natural" religion—the two succeeding covenants discriminate between those within and those without. According to P's schema, interestingly enough, Ishmael and (implicitly) Esau—but not Lot—have a portion in the Abrahamic covenant. At the same time, however, P discriminates between Isaac and the other sons of Abraham by making him the first male to be born into the Abrahamic covenant and thus circumcised on the eighth day in full observance of the law (21:4). And ultimately, only the children of Jacob-Israel will be selected for the Mosaic covenant. One should note in particular the careful progression of the signs themselves: from the natural and public sign of the rainbow to the cultural and private sign of circumcision to the esoteric religious sign of the Sabbath, which subsists not in concrete substance but abstract ritual. Circumcision thus inscribes the Abrahamic covenant onto the Abrahamite body, transforming a natural object into a cultural one. Similarly, the Sabbath inscribes the Israelite's very life (viz., time) with a religious (i.e., cultural) observance, transferring it from the realm of the profane to that of the sacred. For P as well, then, divine election consists in a type of elevated culture.

Through these discriminations, the patriarchal traditions contemplate the nature of chosen-ness: Why did YHWH prefer Israel to their rival kin? In doing so, they actually acknowledge a certain kinship with various neighboring tribes—Moab and Ammon through Lot, the Ishmaelites through Abraham's firstborn, and Edom through Esau. Indeed, they go so far as to

---

[40] Frank Moore Cross, *Canaanite Myth and Hebrew Epic: Essays in the History of the Religion of Israel* (Cambridge: Harvard University Press, 1973), 295–300; see also Kawashima, "Sources and Redaction," 56–58.

suggest that God had or perhaps even still has a relationship with these Others. In the patently related tradition preserved in Deut 2, for example, YHWH explicitly warns Israel not to "contend" with the children of Lot and of Esau. Nonetheless, for reasons not entirely correlated to merit or virtue, it is Abraham, Isaac, and Jacob who are chosen. The biblical writers thus refrain from providing a triumphalist explanation, contenting themselves instead with subtly differentiating Israel from these Others through the figural opposition of culture versus nature.

ENCOUNTERS

I turn next to the so-called "wife-sister" stories, in effect, three related "encounters" between a patriarch and a foreign rival: Abraham and Pharaoh (J); Abraham and Abimelech (E); Isaac and Abimelech (J).[41] As David L. Petersen has demonstrated, albeit in different terms, it is useful to analyze them together as a type-scene.[42] In each, the husband introduces his wife to a foreign populace as his unmarried sister, which is to say, as a sexually available female;[43] the lie is eventually exposed; while the patriarch, in spite of his misdeed, prospers. What these encounters actually accomplish is to present the ancestral matriarch with two rival husbands. One might compare them, then, to the stories of rival wives: Sarah and Hagar, Rachel and Leah (and Bilhah and Zilpah). If the latter stories set up and resolve a rivalry between wives in terms of the son(s) each gives birth to, the former set up and resolve a rivalry between husbands in terms of the metaphysical potency of each as expressed in his propensity to succeed.[44] Needless to say, the divine blessing resting upon the patriarchs overwhelms that of their rivals.

---

[41] For a brief recent discussion of these scenes and the issues involved, see Tikva Frymer-Kensky, *Reading the Women of the Bible: A New Interpretation of Their Stories* (New York: Schocken, 2002), 93–98, with further references there.

[42] Petersen, rejecting form-criticism's crude understanding of "genre," speaks instead of "theme" and "motif," in an analysis that anticipates in striking ways Alter's approach to biblical "type-scenes"; see his "A Thrice-Told Tale: Genre, Theme, and Motif," *BR* 18 (1973) 30–43.

[43] On the troubling lack of legal status granted to women in these stories and the biblical world in general, see Robert S. Kawashima, "Could a Woman Say 'No' in Biblical Israel? On the Genealogy of Legal Status in Biblical Law and Literature," *AJSR* 35 (2011): 1–22.

[44] Contrast Mark E. Biddle's different analysis in "The 'Endangered Ancestress' and Blessing for the Nations," *JBL* 109 (1990): 599–611; followed by Kaminsky, *Yet I Loved Jacob*, 30; and by Lohr, *Chosen and Unchosen*, 109–110.

Not long after Abraham embarks on his semi-nomadic life in Canaan, a famine ravages the land (Gen 12:10), forcing Abraham and his family to migrate to Egypt, which is, thanks to the Nile, generally impervious to drought and famine. Fearing for his life on account of his lovely wife—can these foreigners be trusted to respect his marriage?, he wonders—Abraham sojourns with Sarah in Egypt as brother and sister. Pharaoh, hearing of Sarah's beauty, procures her for his "house" (v. 15), that is, takes her for his "wife" (v. 19), and "for her sake [deals] well with" Abraham (v. 16). In spite of various attempts to justify and/or explain away his bad behavior, the fact remains that Abraham makes his wife sexually available to another man and profits thereby. Formally, this sequence of events closely resembles that transaction known as prostitution.[45] In other words, the fault clearly lies with Abraham, and yet, we are told, "YHWH afflicted Pharaoh and his house with great plagues" (v. 17)—foreshadowing the later conflict between Israel and Egypt. Understandably upset by Abraham's subterfuge, Pharaoh "sends" him, his wife, and his possessions out of Egypt under escort (v. 20)—again foreshadowing the exodus. What are we to make of this injustice? Just a few verses earlier (also in J), God promised to bless Abraham, moreover, to bless those who bless him and curse those who curse him (12:2–3). Apparently, the divine blessing resting upon Abraham, conceptualized as a type of quasi-material possession, operates regardless of the ethical particulars of any given situation. In the present case, Pharaoh, although unwitting and thus innocent, comes to harm because he has taken Abraham's wife for himself. By the same logic, when Isaac, old, blind and feeble, discovers that he has been tricked into blessing the wrong son, he cannot simply take it back, for it is a *fait accompli*. As he bitterly admits: "I have blessed him. Indeed, blessed he will be" (27:33). One might compare the principle governing the patriarch to that governing Odysseus throughout his adventures, a type of epic tautology: Odysseus succeeds because Athena causes him to succeed.

Abraham uses the same ploy some time later—in a different source—while sojourning in Gerar. This time King Abimelech "takes" Sarah into his household (20:2). In contrast to the incident with Pharaoh, this story is at pains to maintain Sarah's marital purity: God himself prevented Abimelech from sinning, from consummating his marriage with Abraham's wife. This is crucial, since in both the E source in which this story originates and in the final redacted version of Genesis, she gives birth to Isaac just afterward.

---

[45] See the striking parallel in Middle Assyrian Laws A ¶ 24, according to which Sarah (and presumably Abraham) would be guilty of a serious crime.

But if Sarah is above reproach in this encounter, the silence maintained in Gen 12 regarding her marriage to Pharaoh seems all the more pregnant in comparison. At any rate, to return to Gen 20, Abimelech, speaking to God in a dream, maintains his innocence: "Lord, will you actually kill a righteous nation? Didn't he say to me, 'She is my sister,' and she herself said, 'He is my brother'? I did this with innocent heart and clean hands" (vv. 4–5). God in fact agrees (v. 6). In other words, if one can speak of guilt here, it falls again to Abraham and Sarah, but this does not prevent God from striking Abimelech's household with barrenness (v. 18) or from threatening Abimelech himself with death (v. 3). Moreover, it is the victim Abimelech who must approach the perpetrator Abraham—who is even said to be a prophet in this episode—in an act of contrition, and make restitution for the uncommitted crime. Not only does he restore Sarah to her husband and pay a fine to publicly vindicate her as a virtuous wife, but he also allows Abraham to settle in his land (vv. 14–16). Again, the patriarch profits through his deception. The moral of the story comes in its denouement in Gen 21. Taking note of Abraham's prosperity, Abimelech shrewdly initiates, as a matter of national security, a covenant of non-aggression with his rival (v. 23), incredulously declaring "God is with you in all that you do" (v. 22).

In the third and final instance of this type-scene (Gen 26), it is Isaac who sojourns in Gerar, now explicitly if anachronistically identified as Philistine. There is a famine in the land as in the days of his father (Gen 12), but rather than go down to Egypt, which would have been the more logical choice, he remains in Canaan, as per God's instructions (26:1–6). Tradition thus conspicuously hedges Isaac in. Just as he is the first to fulfill completely the Abrahamic covenant of circumcision, so he is the first to live out his life entirely within the promised land. For unlike Abraham and Jacob, he neither comes from nor returns to Mesopotamia; neither does he wander as far south as Egypt, whether temporarily like his father, or permanently like his son. The reason Isaac's life is so poor in narrative interest, then, is that he is little more than a plot function. He is merely the link—missing for many years, then nearly broken (Gen 22)—between the covenant (Abraham) and the nation (Jacob). Evoking in his very name the "laughter" ($ṣḥq$) brought by the son of old age into the patriarchal household—just as the annunciation of Aqhat's birth brings laughter ($yṣḥq$) to the aged Danel—Isaac stands for the promise as such, born to Abraham for the sake of begetting Israel.

As a reward for his obedience, God promises Isaac: "I will be with you and bless you, for to you and your seed I will give all these lands, and I will fulfill the oath that I swore to Abraham your father" (26:3). In effect, Isaac inherits his father's divine election. He thus ends up in Gerar, where he, like his father, presents his wife as his sister. In this case, the lie is discovered by Abimelech before any marital violation can take place, the mere possibility of which angers the foreign king: "What's this you've done to us? One of the people might easily have lain with your wife, and you would have brought guilt upon us" (v. 10). In this particular encounter, then, the rivalry between Self and Other is deflected from wife to wealth. In spite of the famine, Isaac reaps a hundredfold and prospers to such an extent that he provokes fear and envy in the Philistines (vv. 12–14), leading Abimelech to banish Isaac from Gerar: "for you have become much too powerful for us" (v. 16). There follows a series of disputes over water rights between Isaac and the Philistine shepherds (vv. 17–22). While these are never resolved, the Philistines eventually recognize that it behooves them to initiate a covenant of non-aggression with this patriarch, who lives such a preternaturally charmed life: "You are now the blessed of YHWH," they grudgingly acknowledge (v. 29). It is finally worth noting that since Gerar lies within what will eventually become Philistine territory, the covenants Abimelech establishes with the patriarchs are meant to condemn, however anachronistically, the Philistines' later hostility towards Israel.

P, too, recounts an encounter, namely, Abraham's negotiation with the "sons of Heth" in Gen 23—the same Canaanite tribe Esau will later marry into (cf. 27:46–28:9). Perhaps coincidentally, Sarah once again is involved in her husband's negotiations: she has just died, and so Abraham wishes to purchase the cave of Machpelah as a family burial site. In stark contrast to the JE encounters, however, P's unfolds with dignified restraint. Once again, the foreign rival recognizes the patriarch's divine blessing: "You are a prince of God in our midst" (23:6). This time, however, Abraham, far from prospering at the expense of this Other, insists on paying for the cave and its field at the full asking price, in spite of their first being offered to him as a gift (cf. Gen 14:22–24). If the encounters with the Philistines result in treaties of non-aggression, this encounter provides a legal foothold in the land itself.

Whereas the "discriminations" analyzed earlier contemplate the nature of Israel's chosen-ness, these "encounters" in complementary fashion meditate on the nature of Israel's blessing. If three different men will lay claim to Sarah, it is the power of Abraham's blessing that will resolve the marital conflicts that he himself created. If Isaac recklessly exposes his Philistine neighbors to the dangerous possibility of an adulterous liaison with his supposed sister, it is he nonetheless who prospers at the very gates of Gerar. If all three of these wife-sister episodes are premised on a profound distrust of the Other, it is these foreigners who, ironically, express a genuine sense of horror at the mere idea of a married woman having relations with a man not her husband. In fact, the Egyptians and the Philistines arguably occupy the moral high ground over their Hebrew rivals, who bring about what the narratives unanimously presuppose to be morally reprehensible situations. For reasons lying beyond the norms of human justice, however, Abraham and Isaac prosper at the expense of the Other, who in most of these encounters feels compelled by force of circumstance to acknowledge the special blessing of this chosen people. Through these admissions, the biblical writers effectively appropriate the foreigner's voice in order to define the Israelite Self. God has blessed them; indeed, blessed they will be.

Conclusion

What does the Patriarchal History mean? At a figural level, Gen 12–36, starting from the premise that YHWH has chosen and blessed Israel, projects this theological reality onto a legendary past, which we now know as the "patriarchal age." The patriarchs and their rivals thus function as narrative concepts for thinking about Israel's identity. How did they come to be chosen? What does it mean to be blessed by God? What is interesting is that these traditions refuse to idealize the past—and they are richer for doing so. The concept of blessing, for example, is more meaningful for not being identified with ethical superiority. On the one hand, Abraham comes dangerously close to murdering his son, which—if we set aside the troubling moral dimension—at least demonstrates his absolute willingness to obey God. This story is meant to indicate, among other things, that he somehow "earned" his blessing. But Jacob, on the other hand, "earns" his blessing by tricking a dying, blind old man, namely, his father. Similarly, these traditions have greater literary impact for daring to give voice to the Other. There is genuine pathos in Esau's outcry against the theft of his blessing by his ostensibly more civilized twin brother: "Is he not indeed named Jacob? For he has supplanted me these two times. My birthright has he taken, and look, now he has taken my blessing" (27:36). Similarly, there is justified anger in Abimelech's outburst against the treachery of his foreign guest: "What have you done to us, and how have I sinned against you, that you have brought upon us and upon my kingdom such great guilt? Things that are not done [$l\bar{o}$' $y\bar{e}$'$\bar{a}\acute{s}\hat{u}$] have you done with me" (20:9). Note the appeal to an implicit norm of civilized behavior, which will recur at crucial points in Genesis.

This interpretive schema can be extended to account for the whole of Genesis. The Primeval History (Gen 1–11) not only sets the stage of world history upon which Israel's family drama will play itself out, but also establishes the thematic backdrop for the patriarchs' discriminations and encounters: blessing and curse; chosen and unchosen. If the Primeval History thus functions as the book's introduction, the story of Joseph in Egypt (Gen 37–50) serves as its conclusion. It comprises discriminations—the fraternal strife besetting Jacob's sons—as well as encounters—Joseph's fall and rise among the Egyptians. And within the larger narrative structure of the Pentateuch, it also provides the crucial transition from figural to literal Israel. At the end of Genesis, Jacob's household goes down to Egypt (46:8–27); there in Egypt, these seventy souls—having left the affliction of barrenness behind in Canaan—are "fruitful" and "multiply" (Gen 47:27), eventually becoming a "people" that will terrify the king of Egypt himself (Exod 1:7–9).

In keeping with this chapter's focus on the Patriarchal History, however, I conclude with a few observations about Jacob's prolonged visit with his uncle, Laban the Aramean. If Pharaoh and Abimelech constitute figures of early Israel's two archenemies, Egypt and Philistia, Laban stands for Israel's pre-Yahwistic, Mesopotamian past. Their story is, in a sense, a hybrid of discrimination and encounter. Jacob, effectively retracing the steps of his immigrant grandfather, returns to "the old country," where he both confronts the foreignness of his family's past and is called by YHWH out of it. This time it is the rival who tricks the patriarch, giving him the wrong wife-cousin in marriage—marrying off the younger before the elder "is not done" (*loʾ yēʿāśeh*), Laban explains to his irate nephew (Gen 29:26; cf. 20:9). But it is the patriarch, once again, who prospers at the expense of the Other—whose sons accuse their cousin and brother-in-law, Jacob, of having "taken everything that was our father's" (Gen 31:1; cf. 27:36). If the discrimination between Abraham and Lot effectively dismisses Haran's lineage, here, the descendants of Abraham's other brother, Nahor, are disqualified. This time, God calls Jacob to return to Canaan, while warning Laban, in a dream, not to interfere (31:24). The boundary marker set up between the two distinguishes Self from Other, present from past (31:44–53).

Finally, whether Jacob makes this journey in order to flee from his brother's wrath or to search for a suitable wife, the sources agree that it was there in Mesopotamia that he married Laban's two daughters and their two handmaids, there that he fathered eleven of twelve sons along with one daughter. What does this mean? Above all, that Israel is not native to Israel. Not only does Abraham come from abroad; Jacob must also go abroad before being renamed—i.e., figurally becoming—Israel. Not only Jacob, but Abraham and Isaac all marry women from Mesopotamia. It is only in the generation of the tribes, that is, Jacob's children, that intermarriage with the local population is allowed, and the first attempt at it, namely, Dinah's, ends in murder and mayhem—for Shechem had done something that "is not done" (*lō'yēʿāśeh*) in Israel (Gen 34:7; cf. 29:26). For this very reason, however, Jacob's family is, for all intents and purposes, Mesopotamian. Thus, as they approach Bethel, where they will soon build an altar to Elohim, Jacob must prepare his family for its new life: they are to put away their foreign gods, purify themselves, and change their clothes (Gen 35). They discard their old identity like so much baggage—which they leave buried under an oak near Shechem. Here, the redactor chooses to insert a Priestly text recounting how Jacob is (once again) renamed Israel, as El Shaddai bestows upon Jacob-Israel the promises originally made to Abraham and Isaac: "Be fruitful and multiply. ... And the land that I gave to Abraham and to Isaac, to you will I give it, and to your offspring after you I will give the land" (Gen 35:11–12; cf. 47:27). Only then is Benjamin, the twelfth and final son and the tribe of the first king of Israel, born on the way to Ephrath. With this sequence of events, Genesis completes its figural representation of the nation of Israel.

SELECT BIBLIOGRAPHY

Alter, Robert. *The Art of Biblical Narrative*. New York: Basic Books, 1981.
———. *Genesis: Translation and Commentary*. New York: W.W. Norton & Co., 1996.
Auerbach, Erich. "Odysseus' Scar." Pages 3–23 in *Mimesis: The Representation of Reality in Western Literature*. Translated by Willard Trask. Princeton: Princeton University Press, 1953.
Barthes, Roland. "The Struggle With the Angel: Textual Analysis of Genesis 32:22–32." Pages 125–141 in *Image, Music, Text*. Translated by Stephen Heath. New York: Hill and Wang, 1977.
Berlin, Adele. *Poetics and Interpretation of Biblical Narrative*. Sheffield: Almond Press, 1983.
Damrosch, David. *The Narrative Covenant: Transformations of Genre in the Growth of Biblical Literature*. San Francisco: Harper & Row, 1987.
Fokkelman, J.P. *Narrative Art in Genesis: Specimens of Stylistic and Structural Analysis*. Studia Semitica Neerlandica 17. Assen: Van Gorcum, 1975.
Josipovici, Gabriel. *The Book of God: A Response to the Bible*. New Haven: Yale University Press, 1988.
Kawashima, Robert S. *Biblical Narrative and the Death of the Rhapsode*. Bloomington: Indiana University Press, 2004.
———. "Comparative Literature and Biblical Studies: The Case of Allusion." *Prooftexts: A Journal of Jewish Literary History* 27 (2007): 324–344.
Pardes, Ilana. *Countertraditions in the Bible: A Feminist Approach*. Cambridge: Harvard University Press, 1992.
Sternberg, Meir. *The Poetics of Biblical Narrative: Ideological Literature and the Drama of Reading*. Bloomington: Indiana University Press, 1985.

PART TWO

ISSUES IN INTERPRETATION

THE FORMATION OF THE PRIMEVAL HISTORY[*]

Jan Christian Gertz

Introduction:
The General Characteristics of the Primeval History

The Primeval History in the Hebrew Bible uses exemplary narratives to engage questions about the genesis of the world as well as about the origin of humankind and the beginning of culture. This is not a naïve form of historiography that somehow replaces historical and scientific inquiry with beautiful narratives. Rather, these narratives constitute a statement of basic belief, fairly widespread in ancient cultures, emphasizing that everything (present and future) received its essence at the beginning. The corresponding linguistic form of expression might be 'mythical relation.' That humanity is at the centre of such an essential definition is derived from mythical reason (*Wesenbestimmung aus mythischem Grunde*).[1] Humanity thus exists in manifold relations to each other as well as to the non-human creation and to God. From the beginning the report of the genesis of the world and of its chronological and spatial order is focused on the cosmos of human experience and on humanity's destiny in such a world. Accordingly, any statements regarding the world before creation, the heaven above the visible sky, or the abyss of the sea are reduced to include only that which is absolutely necessary for the story to progress. In contrast, humanity's commissioning and its ability to rule the world (as well as the non-human creation) are placed prominently at the end of the works of creation, a high point that occupies a fair amount of space (Gen 1:1–2:3). That focus is intensified in the Eden narrative (Gen 2:4–3:24), in the story of the fratricide of Cain (Gen 4:1–16), and in the notes about Cain's offspring. Here we find an even clearer etiological focus on the basic conditions of human existence. By using the

---

[*] My sincere thanks to my colleagues Anselm C. Hagedorn and Joel N. Lohr for their help in preparing the English version of this article.
[1] Lothar Perlitt, "Die Urgeschichte im Werk Gottfried Benns," in *Werden und Wirken des Alten Testaments: Festschrift für Claus Westermann zum 70. Geburtstag* (ed. Rainer Albertz et al., Göttingen: Vandenhoeck & Ruprecht, 1980), 9–37, 11, with reference to Franz Overbeck and the late eighteenth and early nineteenth century debate on 'myth.'

contrasting background of Eden as a place of effortless and safe existence as well as of a naïve and unspoilt relationship between man and woman on the one hand, and to God on the other, these stories describe what we might call the "ambivalence" of human existence: the essential bond of the אדם (man) with the אדמה (earth), that from which the man is taken (Gen 2:7), from where he derives his sustenance by arduous work, and to where he returns in death (Gen 3:17–19); the relationship as well as the simultaneous enmity between humanity and animals (Gen 2:18–19; 3:15); bearing children through painful means (Gen 3:16); the exchange of human closeness for a hierarchy within humanity (Gen 3:16); the experience of being elevated or demoted, independent of human accomplishment, which leads to deadly violence amongst brothers (Gen 4:1–16); and finally, the advancement of humankind (Gen 3:22) and humanity's cultural progress (Gen 3:21; 4:17, 20–22) through discovering practical knowledge (Gen 3:7), while at the same time alienating itself from God (Gen 3:24; 4:11, 14) and experiencing a rise in violence (Gen 4:8, 14–15, 23–24). The episode about the sons of God and human women (Gen 6:1–4) combines the topics already mentioned in the Eden narrative, i.e. humanity's decrepitude and the (sexual) delineation of the human from the divine realm, a topic picked up again later in the story of the Tower of Babel (Gen 11:1–9). Finally, categorical statements about the predominance of violence as well as about human nature serve as a frame for the extensive narrative of the flood (Gen 6:5–9:17). The irreversible disposition of humankind towards evil and the excess of violence provoke God's decision to undo his creation (Gen 6:5–7, 11–13) and—after the end of the flood—will evoke the weary statement of God regarding the post-diluvian world (Gen 8:21). At the same time, God's different reaction in regard to the unchanging evaluation of humanity before and after the flood represent a deep break within the Primeval History. The near complete extinction of all life is pitted against a new beginning that includes a promise ensuring the sustainability of creation (Gen 8:21–22; 9:9–17). The price for such a promise is the introduction of regulated controls that stand in contrast to the original will of the creator (Gen 9:1–7; cf. Gen 1:28–31a). The story of the flood thus serves as a counter-myth to the story of the creation in that it demonstrates the consequences that result from the vitiation of the creation. As a prelude to an epoch that stretches as far into the future as the time of the reader, the story of the flood stands as an explanation of how the challenges of creation were overcome.[2]

---

[2] Cf. Erhard Blum, "Urgeschichte," *TRE* 34 (2002): 436–445, esp. 437.

In the sense of a description of a truly primeval period—one that precedes every history—the Primeval History of the Hebrew Bible is a closed, or we might say complete entity and was subsequently understood as such. But even though the chapters appear to address general topics of humanity and want to narrate the origins of the *conditio humana*, one has to note that the narrative does not want simply to relate general topics such as 'world' or 'humankind.' Rather, these chapters aim at the reification of these general terms, addressing the existing world as well as existing humanity. As far as the Primeval History is concerned, this means the perspective of an entity called Israel—no matter how one wants to define it. Such a reading is quite obvious from the text itself. Shem, Ham, and Japheth are the sons of Noah, who—together with their father Noah and their anonymous mother—survive the flood. Later it is said of them: "These three were the sons of Noah, and from these the whole world branched out" (Gen 9:19). The following Table of Nations explicates this idea (Gen 10:1–32) and closes with the genealogy of Shem that ends with Terah and Abram (Gen 11:10–32). At the end of the Primeval History we find the specific history of the departure of the ancestors of Israel from Ur of the Chaldeans. The primeval period thus paves the way for the subsequent history of the origins of Israel.

The coexistence of the Primeval History in Gen 1–9 and the ethnically and geographically differentiated world in Gen 10–11 has again and again resulted in attempts to find the end of the Primeval History in the note about Noah's death in Gen 9:29; Gen 10–11 is then seen as material leading towards the Patriarchal narratives.[3] As far as the final form of the text is concerned, several observations make such a disposition difficult to accept: the colophon to the table of nations as well as the beginning of the genealogy of Shem both refer to the flood as their point of departure (Gen 10:32; 11:10). The table of nations as well as the story of the Tower of Babel are primeval in character as they refer to humanity as a whole and in Gen 11:1 humanity is even the acting subject. Finally, and most importantly, the current context connects the primeval events with the history of Abraham by offering a genealogy (תולדת) without gaps starting with the first human couple (Gen 5:1; 6:9; 10:1; 11:10, 27). These observations suggest that on the level of the final form of the text we have to assume a close topical and structural relationship

---

[3] Cf. Norbert Clemens Baumgart, "Das Ende der biblischen Urgeschichte in Gen 9,29," *BN* 82 (1996): 27–58; Baumgart, "Gen 5,29—ein Brückenvers in der Urgeschichte und zugleich ein Erzählerkommentar," *BN* 92 (1998): 21–37; and Baumgart, *Die Umkehr des Schöpfergottes: Zu Komposition und religionsgeschichtlichem Hintergrund von Gen 5–9* (HBS 22; Freiburg: Herder, 1999), 34–37.

between the Primeval History and the following history of the origins of Israel. At the same time, however, such observations do not preclude the possibility that literary boundaries were moved during the long history that gave rise to the Primeval History.

Perspectives on the History of Scholarship

Historical critical research on the biblical tradition began with the analysis of the Primeval History.[4] While it was still possible to provide an answer to the fundamental question of how Moses, in the book of Genesis, was able to relay events that happened before his time by reference to traditional documents, several observations—such as the coexisting accounts of the creation (Gen 1:1–2:3) and of the Eden narrative (Gen 2:4–3:24)—led to the distinction of two groups of texts within the Primeval History and beyond. The arguments for such a distinction were first collected by Henning Bernhard Witter (1683–1715) and have been repeated numerous times since then.[5] These include the alteration of the divine name in both groups of texts, the major stylistic differences between Gen 1:1–2:3 and the following chapters, the factual discrepancies between the two accounts of the creation, as well as the restatement of the creation account after it was said that "the heaven and earth were finished and all their array" (Gen 2:1). Witter's observations were soon forgotten but restated in more detail by Jean Astruc (1684–1766), who for the first time expanded the basis of his inquiry to include the book of Genesis (as well as Exod 1–2) as a whole. As far as the Primeval History was concerned, he noted the repetitions in the flood narrative and in the table of nations.[6] Forgotten once again, Witter's and

---

[4] See Christoph Bultmann, *Die biblische Urgeschichte in der Aufklärung* (BHT 110; Tübingen: Mohr Siebeck, 1999), esp. 49–85.

[5] Henning Bernhard Witter, *Jura Israelitarum in Palaestinam terram Chananaeam, Commentatione in Genesin perpetua sic demonstrata, ut idiomatis authentici nativus sensus fideliter detegatur, Mosis autoris primaeva intentio sollicite definiatur adeoque corpus doctrinae et juris cum antiquissimum, tum consummatissimum tandem eruatur; accedit in paginarum fronte ipse textus Hebraeus cum versione Latina* (Hildesheim: Schröder, 1711). Concerning Witter, cf. Hans Bardtke, "Henning Bernhard Witter: Zur 250: Wiederkehr seiner Promotion zum Philosophiae Doctor am 6. November 1704 zu Helmstedt," *ZAW* 66 (1954): 153–181; and Pierre Gibert, "De l'intuition à l'évidence: la multiplicité documentaire dans la Genèse chez H.B. Witter et Jean Astruc," in *Sacred Conjectures: The Context and Legacy of Robert Lowth and Jean Astruc* (ed. John Jarick; LHBOTS 457; New York: T&T Clark, 2007), 174–189.

[6] Jean Astruc, *Conjectures sur la Genèse: Introduction et notes de Pierre Gibert* (Paris: Noêsis, 1999). The original version, which was anonymously published in 1753 at Brussels, was titled: "*Conjectures sur les Mémoires originaux dont il paroit que Moyse s'est servi pour*

Astruc's observations were finally disseminated more widely by Johann Gottfried Eichhorn (1752–1827) and henceforth generally accepted as the 'older documentary hypothesis.'[7]

There is no need to survey the subsequent course of scholarship here.[8] As far as our topic is concerned it must suffice to note that the predominant (but never undisputed) idea that two originally independent sources were brought together, a model that was then applied to the Pentateuch as a whole, has come under attack in recent years.[9] As it is well known, in the Primeval History the (classic) *newer documentary hypothesis* assumes an older Yahwistic source (which is sometimes further differentiated) and a younger source P. Despite the fact that some voices dispute the character of P as a source, and consequently interpret the priestly texts as a layer of editing (*Bearbeitungsschicht*),[10] it is the non-P—i.e. the Yahwistic text—that is controversial. The problem of why these texts do not form a coherent narrative was explained by the *classic documentary hypothesis* by arguing that P served as the basis for the redactors.[11] When the documents were joined, the non-P texts functioned as additions to P. Nowadays it is frequently argued that the non-P texts were composed as an addition to P from the

---

composer le Livre de la Genèse. Avec des remarques, qui appuient ou qui éclaircissent ces conjectures." On Astruc and his predecessors, cf. Jan Christian Gertz, "Jean Astruc and Source Criticism in the Book of Genesis," in Jarick, *Sacred Conjectures*, 190–203; as well as Jean-Louis Ska's essay in the present volume.

[7] Johann Gottfried Eichhorn, *Einleitung in das Alte Testament* (3 vols.; 2nd ed.; Reutlingen: Grözinger, 1787–1790), 2:245–348 (1st ed. = 1780–1783, 2:294–409). The often quoted reference to Astruc can be found in the 2nd ed. at 2:246 or in the 1st ed. at 2:297. For more on Eichhorn, see Rudolf Smend, *Deutsche Alttestamentler in drei Jahrhunderten* (Göttingen: Vandenhoeck & Ruprecht, 1989), 25–37.

[8] On the history of pentateuchal scholarship, see Cornelis Houtman, *Der Pentateuch: Die Geschichte seiner Erforschung neben einer Auswertung* (CBET 9; Kampen: Pharos, 1994), as well as the review of previous scholarship (focused on the question of the combination of both groups of texts) in Markus Witte, *Die biblische Urgeschichte: Redaktions- und theologiegeschichtliche Beobachtungen zu Genesis 1,1–11,26* (BZAW 265; Berlin: de Gruyter, 1998), 1–43.

[9] Cf. Jan Christian Gertz, Konrad Schmid, and Markus Witte, eds., *Abschied vom Jahwisten: Die Komposition des Hexateuch in der jüngsten Diskussion* (BZAW 315; Berlin: de Gruyter, 2002); Thomas B. Dozeman and Konrad Schmid, eds., *A Farewell to the Yahwist? The Composition of the Pentateuch in Recent European Interpretation* (SBLSymS 34; Atlanta: SBL, 2006); and Jean-Louis Ska, *Introduction to Reading the Pentateuch* (trans. Pascale Dominique; Winona Lake, Ind.: Eisenbrauns, 2006).

[10] With regard to P in Gen 1–11, see Erhard Blum, *Studien zur Komposition des Pentateuch* (BZAW 189; Berlin: de Gruyter, 1990), 278–285.

[11] Cf. Martin Noth, *Überlieferungsgeschichte des Pentateuch* (1st ed.; Stuttgart: Kohlhammer, 1948; 3rd ed.; Darmstadt: Wissenschaftliche Buchgesellschaft, 1960).

beginning. This post-exilic reworking also used pre-P traditions[12] and was constructed as a programmatic front end to Gen 12 ff.[13] If the hypothesis of a non-P version of the Primeval History is maintained, the question of the original literary horizon of such a work arises. A widespread but by no means undisputed opinion regards the non-P version as an independent narrative about the creation and the initial existence of humanity on earth.[14] Such a view is linked to the question of the original extent of the non-P narrative. Again, several options have been put forward. Some scholars argue that such an independent Primeval History contained all major non-P texts of Gen 1–11,[15] while others limit it—following the structure of P and in analogy to the Mesopotamian narratives—to the suspense/tension of creation and flood (Gen *2–4; *6–9). Here, the story of Noah and his sons (Gen *9:18–29), the table of nations (Gen *10), and the story of the Tower of Babel (Gen 11:1–9) are seen as later additions that aim to bridge the earlier material with Gen 12 ff.[16] The non-P narrative of the flood poses a special problem and it has been questioned whether this text originally belonged to the basic layer

---

[12] See Joseph Blenkinsopp, "A Post-Exilic Lay Source in Genesis 1–11," in Gertz, Schmid, and Witte, *Abschied vom Jahwisten*, 49–61; Andreas Schüle, *Der Prolog der hebräischen Bibel: Der literar- und theologiegeschichtliche Diskurs der Urgeschichte (Gen 1–11)* (ATANT 86; Zürich: Theologischer Verlag, 2006); and Martin Arneth, *Durch Adams Fall ist ganz verderbt ...: Studien zur Entstehung der alttestamentlichen Urgeschichte* (FRLANT 217; Göttingen: Vandenhoeck & Ruprecht, 2007). Concerning Gen 2:4–3:24, see also Eckart Otto, "Die Paradieserzählung Genesis 2–3: Eine nachpriesterschriftliche Lehrerzählung in ihrem religionshistorischen Kontext," in *'Jedes Ding hat seine Zeit ...' Studien zur israelitischen und altorientalischen Weisheit: Diethelm Michel zum 65. Geburtstag* (ed. Anja A. Diesel et al.; BZAW 241; Berlin: de Gruyter, 1996), 167–192; for Gen 6:5–8:22*, see Jean-Louis Ska, "The Story of the Flood: A Priestly Writer and Some Later Editorial Fragments (1994)," in *The Exegesis of the Pentateuch: Exegetical Studies and Basic Questions* (FAT 66; Tübingen: Mohr Siebeck, 2009), 1–22; and Erich Bosshard-Nepustil, *Vor uns die Sintflut: Studien zu Text, Kontexten und Rezeption der Fluterzählung Genesis 6–9* (BWANT 165; Stuttgart: Kohlhammer, 2005).

[13] Schüle, *Prolog*.

[14] Frank Crüsemann, "Die Eigenständigkeit der Urgeschichte: Ein Beitrag zur Diskussion um den 'Jahwisten'," in *Die Botschaft und die Boten: Festschrift für Hans Walter Wolff zum 70. Geburtstag* (ed. Jörg Jeremias and Lothar Perlitt; Neukirchen-Vluyn: Neukirchener, 1981), 11–29; Witte, *Urgeschichte*; Baumgart, *Umkehr*; and Jan Christian Gertz, "Babel im Rücken und das Land vor Augen: Anmerkungen zum Abschluß der Urgeschichte und zum Anfang der Erzählungen von den Erzeltern Israels," in *Die Erzväter in der biblischen Tradition: Festschrift für Matthias Köckert* (ed. Anselm C. Hagedorn and Henrik Pfeiffer; BZAW 400, Berlin: de Gruyter, 2009), 9–34.

[15] David M. Carr, *Reading the Fractures of Genesis: Historical and Literary Approaches* (Louisville: Westminster John Knox, 1996), 235–240; and Blum, "Urgeschichte," 439–440.

[16] Witte, *Urgeschichte*; and Gertz, "Babel."

of the non-P texts. In addition to these options, the *classic documentary hypothesis*, with major or minor modifications, can still be found as well.[17]

Despite the rather confusing current state of research, our short overview can conclude on a somewhat comforting note: historical-critical scholarship agrees that we can distinguish and differentiate two groups of texts in Gen 1–11, which can be delineated because of their linguistic profile and content and that are internally linked by several cross-references. Following the ground-breaking analyses of Hermann Hupfeld, Eberhard Schrader, Karl Budde, and Hermann Gunkel, the texts are distributed as follows:[18] the texts belonging to the priestly layer and starting with the creation account (Gen 1:1–2:3) are the genealogy of Adam (Gen 5:1–27, 28*, 30–32), one version of the flood (Gen 6:9–9:17 [18a, 19]*; 9:28), one table of nations (Gen 10:1–7, 20, 22–23, 31–32), and lastly the genealogy of Shem (Gen 11:10–26). Non-P texts are the Eden narrative (Gen 2:4b–3:24), the story of Cain's fratricide as well as the genealogy of Cain and Seth (Gen 4:1–26; 5:28–29*), the illicit marriages of the sons of God (Gen 6:1–4), the second version of the flood (Gen 6:5–8:22*), Noah the winegrower (Gen 9:[18–19]20–27), a further table of nations (Gen 10:8–19, 21, 24–30), and finally the Tower of Babel story (Gen 11:1–9). As far as the basic distribution is concerned, dissent is limited to some small details such as several verses in the flood story (Gen 7:7, 17a, 22*, 23a; 8:3a) and some marginal verses (Gen 2:4a; 9:18a, 19). In this sense the consensus formed by Witter, Astruc, and Eichhorn during the eighteenth century remains valid.

Redaction-Historical Case Studies

As mentioned above, the original literary character of the non-P texts of the Primeval History (independent version of the Primeval History versus late post-exilic reworking of P), as well as the delimitation of the non-P texts (with regard to the following Patriarchal narratives in Gen 12 ff. and their

---

[17] See, *inter alia*, Christoph Levin, *Der Jahwist* (FRLANT 157; Göttingen: Vandenhoeck & Ruprecht, 1993); Horst Seebaß, *Genesis I: Urgeschichte (1,1–11,26)* (Neukirchen-Vluyn: Neukirchener, 1996); and André LaCocque, *The Trial of Innocence: Adam, Eve, and the Yahwist* (Eugene, Ore.: Cascade, 2006).

[18] Herrmann Hupfeld, *Die Quellen der Genesis und die Art ihrer Zusammensetzung von neuem untersucht* (Berlin: Wiegandt & Grieben, 1853); Eberhard Schrader, *Studien zur Kritik und Erklärung der biblischen Urgeschichte: Gen Cap. I–XI* (Zürich: Meyer & Zeller, 1863); Karl Budde, *Die Biblische Urgeschichte (Gen 1–12,5)* (Gießen: Ricker'sche Buchhandlung, 1883); and Hermann Gunkel, *Genesis übersetzt und erklärt* (3rd ed.; HKAT 1/1; Göttingen: Vandenhoeck & Ruprecht, 1910).

literary unity), is very controversial. The following cursory reading of the material explores aspects of this debate.

The Redactional Bridge between the Priestly Creation Account and the Non-P Eden Narrative (Gen 2:4a)

It is common to regard Gen 2:4 as the colophon to the priestly account of the creation. This assumption has percolated into the layout of the *Biblia Hebraica Stuttgartensia*, which deviates from Codex Leningradensis on this point.[19] This way of structuring the text was first proposed by Werner Carl Ludwig Ziegler. The reasoning behind such a view is as follows: the Toledot-formula is an integral part of P and Gen 2:4a refers back to the preceding text (cf. Gen 1:1), while the text following the verse is definitely of non-P origin.[20] However, in all other instances the Toledot-formula is only used as a heading (cf. Gen 5:1; 6:9; 10:1; 11:10, 27; 25:12, 19; 36:1, 9; 37:2; outside Genesis cf. Num 3:1; Ruth 4:18; 1 Chr 1:29),[21] and since the priestly account of the creation has its own summary in Gen 2:3 that corresponds to Gen 1:1, Gen 2:4a has to be regarded as the heading of the following Eden narrative. As such, the verse establishes literary ties between the priestly creation account and the Eden narrative by referring to the content of the preceding passage, by using some of its formulas, and by anticipating what follows. Here the direct sequence of the temporal identification in Gen 2:4a (בהבראם), and the anacrusis of the Gen 2:4b (ביום עשׂות)—which also has a temporal aspect and again mentions the creation of 'earth and heaven,'—is remarkable. In the current context, this repetition of the time measurement has to be understood as a carefully placed fermata in the narrative. Having done so, the following material will appear to be an explication of the already reported creation in the sense of a later realization that seems to 'catch up' (*'nachholende Vergegenwärtigung'*). The differences between the priestly creation account and the non-P Eden narrative, those probably

---

[19] Codex Leningradensis leaves a blank line between Gen 2:3 and Gen 2:4.
[20] Werner Carl Ludwig Ziegler, "Kritik über den Artikel von der Schöpfung nach unserer gewöhnlichen Dogmatik," in *Magazin für Religionsphilosophie, Exegese und Kirchengeschichte* (ed. Heinrich P.C. Henke; Helmstedt: Fleckeisen, 1794), 2:1–113, esp. 13, 50.
[21] See also the LXX, which adds ἡ βίβλος to match Gen 5:1 and thus stresses that Gen 2:4a is to be understood as a heading; on the Toledot-formula see David M. Carr, "βίβλος γενέσεως Revisited: A Synchronic Analysis of Patterns in Genesis as Part of the Torah," *ZAW* 110 (1998): 159–172 and 327–347, esp. 164–165.

already recognized by ancient readers, can thus be explained as different perspectives on the same event. The most important part, the creation of humankind, is then considered separately and in more detail.

How can we evaluate such findings as far as a redaction-history is concerned? It is widely assumed that Gen 2:4a was—as part of a once independent priestly Primeval History—originally placed before Gen 1:1. Only after the connection of P with the non-P narrative by a redactor was the position of the verse changed so that it now serves as a redactional transition and superscription to the Eden narrative.[22] But this is hardly plausible because Gen 1:1 is a perfectly valid superscription. Additionally, the singular mentioning of the "Book of the Toledot" (ספר תולדת) in Gen 5:1 is a strong indication that within the independent priestly Primeval History the series of Toledot formulae opened with Adam in Gen 5:1 and that the report of the creation served (as is now the case!) as a prologue to the history of the Toledot of Israel. On the basis of such observations it seems clear that Gen 2:4a was from the outset composed as a redactional bridge linking the priestly and non-P account of creation.

Generally it is assumed that Gen 2:4a, together with several further minor additions,[23] joins two originally independent versions of the Primeval History (two source hypothesis). However, a number of voices have recently joined the debate, voices that do not want to limit redactional activity to Gen 2:4a and several additional words. Rather, these scholars argue that the Eden narrative itself should be seen as Midrash-like exegesis of, or correction to, Gen 1.[24] In this view, the Eden narrative criticizes the rather optimistic presentation of the priestly creation account. Such criticism takes place from a sapiential (sometimes also described as 'wisdom-sceptic') position because of the experiences of the post-exilic period. The main aim of the Eden narrative is thus to explain how a creation that was labeled 'very

---

[22] Thus most recently Witte, *Urgeschichte*, 55 with n. 14 (bibliography).

[23] The additions are as follows: Gen 2:7b; the supplementation of the bipartite list in Gen 2:20 and 3:14 by the clause "to all the cattle" (לכל הבהמה ו); as well as (possibly) the expansion of the Tetragrammaton to YHWH-God and the unclear phrase "living creature" (נפש היה) in Gen 2:19.

[24] Cf. Blenkinsopp, "Post-Exilic Lay Source"; Otto, "Paradieserzählung"; Andreas Schüle, "Made in the 'Image of God': The Concepts of Divine Images in Gen 1–3," *ZAW* 117 (2005): 1–20; Schüle, *Prolog*; Arneth, *Adam*; Tryggve N.D. Mettinger, *The Eden Narrative: A Literary and Religio-Historical Study of Genesis 2–3* (Winona Lake, Ind.: Eisenbrauns, 2007); and Jean-Louis Ska, "Genesis 2–3: Some Fundamental Questions," in *Beyond Eden: The Biblical Story of Paradise (Genesis 2–3) and Its Reception History* (ed. Konrad Schmid and Christoph Riedweg; FAT 2/34; Tübingen: Mohr Siebeck, 2008), 1–27.

good' (cf. Gen 1:31) could become corrupted in such a way that God thought it necessary to throw creation back into primeval chaos. In addition to the 'gap' in the narrative structure of P,[25] in particular it is the conviction that Gen 2:4 is a literary device that leads to such an assumption. In this case the Eden narrative as a whole is linked to the Toledot-formula—inspired by P— of Gen 2:4a.[26] Andreas Schüle goes further and adds a redaction-historical argument to the debate. In Gen 2:7 he detects—in the breathing of man, made from earth—a corrective to Gen 1:26–27 and its idea that humans were made in the divine-likeness. In the course of the composition, Schüle suggests, the text utilized insights gained from the Mesopotamian mouth-opening and mouth-washing ritual *pīt/mīs pî* but changed this ritual in significant ways. Since the 'image' in Gen 2 is in need of a companion and will be expelled from Eden in Gen 3, the breathing ritual of 2:7 provides a needed, critical dissociation from Gen 1:26–27 that will demonstrate to what extent man is the image of God and to what extent he is unable to be thus.[27]

It remains questionable whether the concept of breathing life into man in Gen 2:7 is dependent upon specific knowledge of the aforementioned ritual. It might suffice to refer to the natural condition of human breathing simply as a sign of life (and respiratory arrest as a sign of death; see Ps 104:29–30; Job 34:14–15), especially because the ritual mentioned above was part of elite knowledge and its details were thus not known widely. If we cannot find a direct dependence upon such a ritual, it would seem that any arguments made to suggest that the ritual has been changed and used in order to augment Gen 1:26–27 and nuance its concept of the divine likeness are futile.[28]

A close reading unveils a series of reasons that speak in favor of the old view whereupon Gen 2:4a and Gen 2:4b are the product of different auctorial hands.[29] In looking at the differences in language and terminology of

---

[25] Previously this "gap" was used as the reason to describe P as an addition that was placed around the non-P texts; see Frank Moore Cross, *Canaanite Myth and Hebrew Epic: Essays in the History of the Religion of Israel* (Cambridge: Harvard University Press, 1973), 306–307.

[26] See especially Otto, "Paradieserzählung," 185–188, who follows Terje Stordalen, "Genesis 2,4: Restudying a *locus classicus*," *ZAW* 104 (1992): 163–177.

[27] Schüle, "Image"; and Schüle, *Prolog*, 161–165.

[28] Cf. Walter Bührer, "Der Baum in der Mitte des Gartens: Prägende Traditionen hinter der biblischen Paradieserzählung" (Magisterarbeit/M.A. thesis, Universität Heidelberg, 2008), 78–82.

[29] Out of the plethora of secondary literature, see Witte, *Urgeschichte*, 55–56; Henrik Pfeiffer, "Der Baum in der Mitte des Gartens: Zum überlieferungsgeschichtlichen Ursprung der Paradieserzählung (Gen 2,4b–3,24)," *ZAW* 112 (2000): 487–500 (Part I), esp. 495; and *ZAW* 113 (2001): 2–16 (Part II); as well as Jan Christian Gertz, "Von Adam zu Enosch: Überlegungen

the two hemistichs that transmit the information regarding the creation of 'heaven and earth,' it is noteworthy that both entities are undetermined (or anarthrous) in Gen 2:4b while they are used determinately in Gen 2:4a. Their inverted order could still be explained as a chiastic inclusion of v. 4a (השמים והארץ) in v. 4b (ארץ ושמים). Further, the change from a passive voice in v. 4a (בהבראם) to an active one in v. 4b (עשות יהוה אלהים), as well as the different verbs describing the act of creation (ברא in v. 4a and עשה in v. 4b), could be seen as a stylistic variant.[30] But the indeterminate use of earth and heaven in v. 4b and the simultaneous change of the order to 'heaven and earth' cannot be explained on purely stylistic grounds. The indeterminate use of 'earth and heaven' in Ps 148:13, often quoted in the debates surrounding this verse, cannot come into play here as that verse does not contain a change from determined to indeterminate speech within a syntactic unity.[31] Similarly, the use of the Toledot-formula in Gen 5:1 and Num 3:1 does not prove that Gen 2:4a was originally part of Gen 2:4b–7.[32] To argue for the literary unity of the verse, it is often stated that in all three instances the Toledot-formula is followed by an expression introduced by ביום. Here, however, Gen 2:4 differs characteristically from Gen 5:1 and Num 3:1: in contrast to the postulated parallels, the context is interrupted by the temporal specification dependent upon the Toledot-formula. This specification in turn competes with Gen 2:4b.[33] Furthermore, the Toledot-formula—understood as a superscription—competes in content and function with the fairly complex superscription of the Eden narrative in vv. 4b–7.[34] All this seems to point to the fact that Gen 2:4a and Gen 2:4b were not written by the same author. For a redaction-historical evaluation we have to note the following: the missing

---

zur Entstehungsgeschichte von Genesis 2–4," in *Gott und Mensch im Dialog: Festschrift für Otto Kaiser zum 80. Geburtstag* (ed. Markus Witte; BZAW 345.1: Berlin: de Gruyter, 2004), 215–236, esp. 218–220.

[30] Cf. Gordon J. Wenham, *Genesis 1–15* (WBC 1; Waco, Tex.: Word, 1987), 46; Stordalen, "Genesis 2,4," 174–175; and Otto, "Paradieserzählung," 187.

[31] See Witte, *Urgeschichte*, 55–56; and Pfeiffer, "Baum I," 495 with n. 34. Contrast Stordalen, "Genesis 2,4," 175; and Otto, "Paradieserzählung," 187, who both refer to Jer 10:11a and 10:11b but in that case 'heaven and earth,' and 'earth and heaven' are determined and thus part of a true chiasm.

[32] Stordalen, "Genesis 2,4," 171–173; and Otto, "Paradieserzählung," 187.

[33] Cf. Witte, *Urgeschichte*, 54; Pfeiffer, "Baum I," 495 n. 34; and Gertz, "Adam," 219.

[34] Gen 2:4b–7 is a pendens construction; here ביום refers to the *imperfectum consecutivum* וייצר in v. 7 and vv. 5 and 6 form a parenthesis; see Walter Groß, *Die Pendenskonstruktion im biblischen Hebräisch: Studien zum althebräischen Satz I* (ATAT 27; Sankt Ottilien: EOS-Verlag, 1987), 49–55.

determination of 'earth and heaven' makes it difficult to understand Gen 2:4b–7 as a continuation (*Fortschreibung*) of Gen 2:4a. On the other hand, it is quite possible that a redactor, influenced by Gen 1, also used the determination when he formulated Gen 2:4a (see Gen 1:1, 15, 17, 20, 26, 28, 30; 2:1).

Further observations offer proof for the argument that Gen 2:4b–3:24* was not written as a supplement to the priestly creation account and was probably also unaware of it. The priestly verb ברא used to describe the act of creation (cf. בהבראם in Gen 2:4a) is not picked up either in a positive sense or with regard to the striking theological idea of a creation by divine word alone as proposed in Gen 1. Above all, however, it is important to remind ourselves of the often-noted differences between the priestly creation account and the non-P Eden narrative as far as the presentation of the primeval condition of the world, as well as the creation of humankind and its environment are concerned. These differences can also be noticed apart from the overall literary progression and one gets the impression that they are not formulated by a sloppy redactor or in the light of a certain theological or literary thrust. All this points to the thesis that in Gen 1–3 two, originally independent, texts were joined together by a redactor. If one understands the non-P narrative as a reworking that corrects the optimism of the priestly creation account, one recognizes the intention of the redactor who placed the texts in their current order. Traces of this redaction can be found in the texts themselves and we can separate them—as was shown for Gen 2:4a— quite clearly from the basic layer (*Grundbestand*) as secondary additions.

The Two Versions of the Descendants of Adam (Gen 4:1–2, 17–26; 5:28–29 and Gen 5:3–28*, 30–32)

There is a broad consensus that the genealogical notes regarding the descendants of Cain and Seth in Gen 4 are not part of P, while the 'Toledot Adam' in Gen 5 are part of the priestly source. Similarly, the position first stated by Philipp Buttman in 1828 that both texts represent two version of the same genealogy is generally accepted.[35] Although Gen 4 differentiates between the genealogical lines of the Cainites and the Sethites, all parts of both lineages—with the exception of the descendants of Lamech— return in the Toledot Adam. There are only some small differences such as

---

[35] Philipp Carl Buttmann, *Mythologus oder gesammelte Abhandlungen über die Sagen des Alterthums* (2 vols.; Berlin: Mylius'sche Buchhandlung, 1828–1929), 1:171.

distinct orthography and placement. If one further takes into account the differences in the chronological system in Gen 5—as displayed by the significant traditions of the Masoretic Text, the Septuagint, and the Samaritan Pentateuch—a fresh look at the genealogies might provide some information regarding the origin of the Primeval History. This is especially so when we remember that the formation of a genealogical tradition follows laws different from those that determine narratives.

Before we offer a redaction-historical evaluation of the parallels and differences in the genealogies in Gen 4 and Gen 5, we have to look at the context of these genealogies. The segment introduced by the Toledot of Heaven and Earth in Gen 2:4a contains the generation of the first human couple (Gen 2:4b–3:24) and their first descendants, Cain, Abel, and Seth as well as their children (Gen 4:1–26). In some ways, one would expect the Toledot Adam to be given in Gen 4:1 and not at Gen 5:1–2. Its current position is caused by the fact that the present context is the product of a redaction that was bound by a predetermined narrative sequence. Leaving this aside for the moment, we note that the current order displays a coherent design.[36] As it is the case elsewhere, the Toledot-formula—as a superscription with its variable elements—refers back to the events that preceded it. Already on the level of the priestly stratum, Gen 5:1b–2 takes up the statements regarding the creation of humankind in Gen 1:27–28: here the statement regarding the likeness serves as the model for the transition from creation to procreation in Gen 5:3 (בדמותו כצלמו).[37] Accordingly, the notes on Seth and the fathering of Enosh have to be understood in the current context, i.e. in neglecting the literary development of the structure of the current text, they point back to the final passage from Gen 4 (compare Gen 5:3 with Gen 4:25

---

[36] Cf. Thomas Hieke, *Die Genealogien der Genesis* (HBS 39, Freiburg: Herder, 2003), 80–90.

[37] Within the priestly stratum, Gen 5:1b–2(3*) immediately follows the creation account. Thus, it is often described as a redactional resumption of Gen 1:27–28 and 2:4a including Gen 2:4b–3:24 into the priestly context. Cf. Levin, *Jahwist*, 99–100; and (as an argument against an originally independent priestly document) Blum, *Studien*, 280. The problem can be avoided if one recognizes (a) the redactional character of Gen 2:4a (see above), and (b) the fact that the Toledot-formula always refers to the preceding text. Additionally, the transition to the individuation of Adam, which is hard to describe *per se*, is explained by recourse to the idea of likeness and as a first fulfillment of the promise of fruitfulness in Gen 1:28. Thus, the recourse to Gen 1:27–28 is appropriate. If P used an already existing "book of the Toledot," Gen 5:1a, 3*, and 4–5 probably belong to the older document, while 5:1b–2, and 3* date from P (cf. Carr, *Fractures*, 72–73). However, those who argue against a source-critical distinction within Gen 5:1–3 include Gunkel, *Genesis*, 134–135 and more recently e.g. Witte, *Urgeschichte*, 126–127 as well as Arneth, *Adam*, 34–39.

and Gen 5:6 with Gen 4:26). Thus, the Toledot from Adam to Noah are tied directly to the lineage of 'Adam—Seth—Enosh' in Gen 4:25-26, which leads to the subsequent overview of the lineages of the descendants of the first couple. The descendants of Cain, however, are painted negatively because of his act of violence and Lamech's blatant inclination towards aggression. In the current context, their lineage (Gen 4:17-24) is not continued. Instead, Gen 4:25 initiates a new genealogy with Seth, the third son born to Adam as a replacement for Abel who was killed. The total absence of any violent acts gives this genealogy a positive connotation. The Toledot Adam in Gen 5 clearly include the earlier genealogy 'Adam—Seth—Enosh' of Gen 4:25-26; irrespective of the well-known overlaps of Gen 5 with Gen 4:17-24 they represent a genealogy that excludes the descendants of Cain. In this picture, Noah, the hero of the flood, is no descendant of Cain who killed his brother. Rather, he is placed amongst the descendants of Seth—who replaces Abel whose offering was pleasing to YHWH (Gen 4:4)—and Enosh, during whose time the worship of YHWH began (Gen. 4:26). Such an understanding of the Toledot Adam in Gen 5, which is a parallel version to Gen 4:17-24, and 25-26 according to the perspective of literary history, is triggered by the sequence of Gen 4:25-26 and Gen 5:1-32 in the current context alone. Such an understanding is further made possible by variants in the spelling and the order of some names, as well as by the absence of a fratricide story in Gen 5.

When looking at the Toledot Adam in Gen 5 in more detail we have to investigate first the chronological differences of the Samaritan Pentateuch (SamP) and the Masoretic Text (MT).[38] While the years and dates of the first five generations from Adam to Mahalalel are identical, they begin to differ for the next five generations from Jared to Noah as well as for the date of the flood calculated from them.[39] According to the MT, the flood begins in the year 1656; the chronological dates of the SamP, however, result in the year 1307. The reference point for the longer chronology in the MT is

---

[38] See the groundbreaking treatment of Budde, *Urgeschichte*, 89–116; Alfred Jepsen, "Zur Chronologie des Priesterkodex," *ZAW* 47 (1929): 251–255; and more recently esp. Martin Rösel, *Übersetzung als Vollendung der Auslegung: Studien zur Genesis-Septuaginta* (BZAW 223, Berlin: de Gruyter, 1994), 129–144 (the following owes much to this latter study). Rösel also discusses the chronology of the Septuagint, which offers a new calculation based upon 5000 *anno mundi* as the date of the dedication of the Temple. For our purposes we can safely sidestep the issue of numbers in the Septuagint here as well as the varying chronologies of Jubilees and Josephus.

[39] For a synopsis, see Rösel, *Übersetzung*, 131.

probably the rededication of the Second Temple by the Maccabees in the year 4000 *anno mundi*.[40] The SamP, in contrast, dates the flood according to the establishment of the sanctuary on Mt. Gerizim in the year 2800 *anno mundi*.[41] The different chronology is connected to differing views on the destiny and evaluation of the patriarchs. According to the MT, only Methuselah, well advanced in years, lived to see the year of the flood in his 956th year while all other patriarchs die peacefully before its beginning. In contrast, the SamP clearly distinguishes between the first five generations and the five that follow. While the dates of the deaths of the first five generations are unambiguously placed before the flood according to the SamP, the now much younger Methuselah as well as Jared and Lamech all die in the year of the flood. From among the patriarchs of the second half of the genealogy, only Noah and Enoch (who was taken by God in the year 887 according to the SamP) survive. The message of the SamP is clear: with the exception of Enoch and Noah, the lives of the patriarchs of the sixth to tenth generation come to an end in the year of the flood. Since the genealogy assumes an average life-span of 900 years, they die at 847 (Jared), 720 (Methuselah), and 656 (Lamech) years old, i.e., before their time. This characterizes them—in contrast to Noah, Enoch, and the patriarchs of the first five generations—as sinners. Here Enoch is an especially interesting case. He would have only celebrated his 780th birthday in the year of the flood but since he walked with God (ויתהלך חנוך את־האלהים) his removal from the face of the earth saves him from death. The significance of the fate of Enoch is further stressed by the fact, that—in the SamP—all the patriarchs witnessed his removal, while in the MT Adam was already dead (930 MT) when Enoch was removed (987 MT) and Noah was not even born (1556 MT). Since the life-span of the patriarchs who die in the year of the flood decreases according to the SamP, the reverse is possible that sin amongst Noah's contemporaries increased from generation to generation (cf. Gen 6:9). As such, the genealogy thereby displays a steep incline in sin that prepares for the coming divine assessment that all flesh had corrupted its ways on earth (cf. Gen

---

[40] Cf. Rösel, *Übersetzung*, 135, with reference to Aimo E. Murtonen, "On the Chronology of the Old Testament," *ST* 8 (1955): 133–137; as well as Klaus Koch, "Sabbatstruktur der Geschichte: Die sogenannte Zehn-Wochen-Apokalypse (I Hen 93,1–10; 91,11–17) und das Ringen um die alttestamentlichen Chronologien im späten Israelitentum," *ZAW* 95 (1983): 403–430; and (similarly) Jeremy Hughes, *Secrets of the Times: Myth and History in Biblical Chronology* (JSOTSup 66; Sheffield: JSOT Press, 1990), 237–238.

[41] Jepsen, "Chronologie," 253.

6:12). Thus the SamP solves a conceptual puzzle within the originally independent version of P, which moves rather suddenly (i.e. in only ten generations) from a very good creation (Gen 1:31) to the scathing condemnation of creation by God (Gen 6:11–12). On the other hand, the readings of the MT are in agreement with the concept of the current context: here the lineage of the sons of Cain does not survive the flood and the descendants of Seth are evaluated positively throughout. This feature could be an indication that the shorter chronology found in the SamP preserved the older version of the once independent Priestly Source while the MT used the possibilities offered by the current context for its longer chronology.[42] Naturally such *external* evidence for the existence of an immediate sequence of Gen 1:1–2:3 and 5:1–32 in P contains several exegetical insecurities. It becomes clear, however, that the alignment in the course of the connection of P with non-P material cannot be limited to the moment of combination (*documentary hypothesis*) or to the expansion of P with the non-P texts (as in the *supplementary model*). As far as Gen 5 is concerned, the process of alignment—the so called final redaction—extends into the formation of the (proto-)MT. Independent of such considerations there are good reasons to regard the MT of Gen 5 as the younger version of the chronology. This can be shown by the fact that the MT significantly raises the age of fathering by hundred (or less) years from Jared onwards,[43] i.e. the age that the MT in accordance with Samaritanus also mentions for Enoch's fathering of Methuselah (Gen 5:21—65 years in the MT and SamP) and the age that is presupposed throughout Gen 11. Also, the acquaintance of Noah and Enoch—only possible according to the SamP—corresponds to the intention of the text and the names of the patriarchs Jared ('Decline') and Methuselah ('Man of the Javelin') display a violent connotation, something that fits well—like the violence associated with Lamech—with their death in the year of the flood according to the SamP.[44]

In comparing Gen 5 and Gen 4 one inevitably gets the impression that the family tree of the descendants of Seth in Gen 5, as preserved in P, was divided in Gen 4 after Enosh (Gen 5:9–11) to accommodate the story of Cain (= Kenan) and Abel, which is missing in P. In so doing, the ten generations

---

[42] Samaritanus modifies the text where necessary for its chronological schema (e.g. Gen 11), while the MT preserved the older date in Gen 11.

[43] Cf. Rösel, *Übersetzung*, 130. The exception is Shem in Gen 11:10–26 (MT) as in the SamP and the LXX he is 100 years old.

[44] Budde, *Urgeschichte*, 96, 99–100.

of the priestly Toledot of Adam are allocated to two genealogies in the non-P text; here, Cain and Seth are counted as one generation because they are brothers. To understand these two genealogies it is important to note that within the priestly Toledot of Adam a fragment of the non-P text was preserved—Gen 5:29*. This note on the naming of Noah deviates in several ways from the regular form of such genealogical notes within that context. Particularly striking is the use of the Tetragrammaton within a priestly context and the obvious reference (מן־האדמה אשר אררה יהוה) to Gen 3:17 and Gen 4:11 as well as the pointer to Gen 6:5–8 and Gen 8:21–22. These texts are part of the non-P stratum of the Primeval History. For this reason it makes perfect sense to find here a dispersed note of the non-P narrative reporting the birth of Noah—especially as this event would otherwise have remained unmentioned.[45] In the context of the non-P narrative the verse would have been spoken by Enosh. That Enosh was eliminated when the non-P text was combined with the priestly genealogy can be explained by the natural limits that even the most creative inner-biblical exegesis of the Hebrew Bible has to recognize: according to Gen 5 and according to the current context it is now *Lamech* (the descendant of Seth!) who is the father of Noah. Thus, the non-P text offers two alternative family trees: the descendants of Cain in Gen 4:17–22 (Cain, Enoch, Irad, Mehujael, Methushael, Lamech and his four children) and the line of the descendants of Seth in Gen 4:25–26; 5:29* (Seth, Enosh, and Noah). According to the course of the narrative, the family tree of the descendants of the fratricidal Cain ends in the flood, while the other line, Noah and his household, survives. Since the grandfather Seth and his grandson Kenan were transformed into brothers when the family of Seth was split, there was room for a tenth generation. These are the children of Lamech whose mentioning provided space for several cultural-historical details. They are important because the ambivalent attitude towards the progress of culture (all cultural innovators are descendants of the murderer Cain) and the diminishing of divine proximity are significant motifs of the non-P texts of the Primeval History. Additionally, Lamech could not remain childless because of his boasting song (Gen 4:23–24), something that underlines his and his descendants' inclination towards violence, which will lead to disaster.

---

[45] See Levin, *Jahwist*, 99; and Carr, *Fractures*, 70. In contrast see Witte, *Urgeschichte*, 207–217, who attributes the verse, like the notes on Seth and Enosh in Gen 4:25–26, to the final redaction. That the notes are in some way related to the final redaction is without question but the expulsion of Gen 4:25–26 from the non-P stratum of Gen 4 cannot be substantiated; see Gertz, "Adam," 221–222, 233–235.

How can we evaluate the relationship between Gen 4 and Gen 5 redaction-historically? One could argue that a post-P editor in Gen 4 used the Toledot Adam from Gen 5, transformed them, and placed them before the priestly text. Against such a supplementary model, however, it has to be said that the current context does not give the impression that an editor was able to act freely in that way. Also, such a solution does not explain the survival of Gen 5:29*. Additionally, the transformation of Cain into the son of Adam and brother of Seth became necessary because the Cain and Abel story was added later—Genesis 4 represents the secondary version here. On the other hand, the succession 'Mehalalel—Jared—Enoch' in Gen 5, as opposed to the order 'Enoch—Irad—Mehujael,' in Gen 4 can be explained best by the priestly concept in which Enoch becomes the counterexample to the patriarchs who will die in the flood, those in the second part of the genealogy. This is further underlined by the fact that Enoch and Noah form the closure of the second triad and of the third triad of the descendants of Seth. Regarding the position of Enoch, P offers a secondary version. These observations, as well as the minor deviations in orthography, support the view that Gen 4 and Gen 5 are based on a common *Vorlage* that was used in two independent versions. Only the redactional alignment of the two versions created a coexistence of the genealogies of the descendants of Cain and Seth.

The Two Versions of the Flood (Gen 6:5–9:17)

Again, there is a broad consensus regarding the differentiation of non-P and P material in the flood narrative. Also, it is undisputed that the non-P text contains a gap since the building of the ark is missing. Today, this observation is explained by arguing that the non-P text is a late reworking of the priestly narrative of the flood.[46] In contrast to such an explanation, the standard explanation of the documentary hypothesis—that the building report of the non-P text dropped out when both sources were brought together—appears awkward, *prima facie* at least. However, one should not dismiss this solution too prematurely. Methodologically speaking, one cannot exclude

---

[46] The arguments for and against such a view are collected in Jan Christian Gertz, "Beobachtungen zum literarischen Charakter und zum geistesgeschichtlichen Ort der nichtpriesterschriftlichen Sintfluterzählung," in *Auf dem Weg zur Endgestalt von Genesis bis II Regum: Festschrift Hans-Christoph Schmitt zum 65. Geburtstag* (ed. Martin Beck and Ulrike Schorn; BZAW 370; Berlin: de Gruyter, 2006), 41–57.

the possibility that a text was omitted. Empirically speaking, in a secondary text a document that can be completely reconstructed remains the exception. When investigating the missing building report of the ark in the non-P text, one can provide good reasons for why it was omitted (when both versions were combined) on conceptual grounds. For example, the priestly instruction to build the ark in Gen 6:9–22 corresponds to the instructions regarding the building of the tent of meeting in Exod 25–40*.[47] If such an association was to be maintained, one could not avoid omitting the non-P report of the building of the ark.[48] This assumption is supported by the fact that the missing non-P report left traces in the current literary context. The non-P note which mentions the opening of "the window of the ark that Noah had made" (את־חלון התבה אשר עשה) in Gen 8:6 clearly presupposes such a report. In the current context, the cross reference אשר עשה has no reference since P does not mention a חלון. Therefore, the building report, presupposed in Gen 8:6, cannot be found in Gen 6:9–22 (P). The same can be said about the 'roof' (מכסה) spoken of in Gen 8:13b, which is also not mentioned by P. An explicit cross-reference is missing here. Of course in the current context the priestly צהר in Gen 6:16 and the non-P חלון in Gen 8:6b, as well as the priestly פתח in Gen 6:16 and the non-P מכסה in Gen 8:13b, are identified; however, the use of such rather complicated identifications shows that they were probably not original.

The question remains regarding why a redactor who combined the P and non-P versions of the flood decided to omit the non-P report of the building of the ark but forgot to eliminate the non-P note about the opening of the window. First of all, we need to be clear that the note does not interrupt the intended pairing of, or correspondence between, the building of the ark with the tent of meeting. Much more important, however, is the observation that the minuscule scene introduces the following bird-scene. This scene does not have a counterpart in the priestly text and the redactor apparently did not want to omit it. Here the non-P text actually serves as an addition to P. In contrast to the proponents of a supplementary model, we have to observe that the function of a text for a redactor does not provide us with any information regarding its original literary character. This can be shown by the texts themselves. The motif of the birds is taken from the

---

[47] Benno Jacob, *Das Buch Genesis* (Berlin: Schocken, 1934; repr., Stuttgart: Calwer, 2000), 187; Thomas Pola, *Die ursprüngliche Priesterschrift: Beobachtungen zur Literarkritik und Traditionsgeschichte von Pg* (WMANT 70; Neukirchen-Vluyn: Neukirchener, 1995), 286–290, 367; and Baumgart, *Umkehr*, 531–559.

[48] Baumgart, *Umkehr*, 415–416.

11th tablet of the Gilgamesh-Epos (XI 145–154), a text to which the non-P narratives of the flood and in the rest of the Primeval History display a remarkable affinity. This observation confirms the old view that redactors tend to use knowledge in written or oral form. How did that happen in our case? It is highly unlikely that a redactor, interested in religion-historical topics, chose selected scenes from his copy of the Akkadian original and inserted them into his version of the flood and the Primeval History. The selection, as well as several changes that can be observed when compared to the original (like the order of the birds), seems instead to point to a variant of the flood narrative in Hebrew. Since the allusions to the Gilgamesh-Epos are not confined to the 11th tablet and to the flood narrative, one may assume the existence of a non-P Primeval History influenced by the Gilgamesh-Epos (and other Mesopotamian myths), one used by the redactor of our text to supplement P.

Finally we have to look at the structure of the text as a whole. The most striking feature of the text is the double outer frame of the flood narrative: the non-P texts of Gen 6:5–8 and Gen 8:20–22 on the one hand, and Gen 6:9–22 and 9:1–17 on the other. Thus, the prominent opening and closing passages of the flood narrative are distributed to P and non-P texts. If anything, such an observation seems to point to a two-source hypothesis. Here we can add the following: normally a Toledot-formula opens a new section. In the flood narrative, however, the priestly Toledot-formula in Gen 6:9 is pushed aside by the non-P opening. As a result, the Toledot-formula signals a break in the bipartite prologue. Apparently the structure of the current context interferes with an older priestly structure. Similar things can be said of the closure of the flood narrative. In Gen 8:21–22 (non-P), YHWH promises never again to doom the earth; YHWH will endure the evil of humankind from now on and will safeguard the rhythms of nature that bless the earth. Unmistakably, this promise refers to the first prologue in Gen 6:5–8 and is composed rhythmically. Thus, Gen 8:21–22 is the climax and last point of a flood narrative that begins with Gen 6:5–8. In the current context, however, the momentous passage Gen 9:1–17 follows. The close connections to Gen 6:9–22 make it impossible to separate these verses from the flood narrative. In the current context, blessing and covenant form the closing act of the flood narrative. As a result, Gen 8:20–22 is pushed aside and thus transformed into an inner caesura of the flood narrative. Again, the structure of the current context interferes with the older boundaries of the text. This time it is the structure of the non-P text. The conclusion is obvious: the current context is based on two older *Vorlagen*, each of which has its own structural principles.

The Problem of the Literary Unity of the Non-P Text
(Gen 2:4–3:24; Gen 9:18–29 and 11:1–9)

Ever since Karl Budde's groundbreaking study, the literary unity of the non-P text of the Primeval History has been hotly debated.[49] As far as the current scholarly debate is concerned, two questions are of general interest: (1) the internal differentiation of the non-P text, and (2) its literary horizon.

1. Following Budde, scholars prefer to distinguish between a basic layer (*Grundschicht*) or source and its later reworking. The point of departure for such a differentiation is the oft-noted ambivalence that is present between an optimistic affirmation of the world and a pessimistic cultural critique within the Eden narrative. This observation—together with the evaluation that the naming of the woman in Gen 3:20–21 represents an inadequate reaction to the curses in Gen 3:17–19—generally leads to a source-critical distinction between an original anthropogony in Gen 2:4b–24* and 3:20–21 and a secondary reworking of the text by the author of Gen 3* (with additional supplements in Gen 2)—who introduces the idea of sin.[50] The story of Cain and Abel in Gen 4:2–16 along with the non-P passages of the flood narrative are also often attributed to this reworking which further explores the motif of sin.[51] Against such a source-critical differentiation, convincing arguments were mounted that demonstrate the literary unity of the text.[52] We do not have to repeat these arguments here. It will suffice to say the following: as is often the case, a reconstructed base text cannot eliminate all of the problems involved. Thus, the designation of the woman

---

[49] Budde, *Urgeschichte*.

[50] The current debate owes a great deal to the seminal study of Levin, *Jahwist*, 82–92, who himself is dependent on the tradition-historical differentiations of Paul Humbert, *Études sur le récit du paradis et de la chute dans la Genèse* (Mémoires de l'Université de Neuchâtel 14; Neuchâtel: Université, 1940). For a different application of this proposal see Witte, *Urgeschichte*, 53–61, 77–78, 79–87, 116–117, 151–166, 184–192, 333–334; and Reinhard G. Kratz, *Die Komposition der erzählenden Bücher des Alten Testaments: Grundwissen der Bibelkritik* (UTB 2157; Göttingen: Vandenhoeck & Ruprecht, 2000), 254–256. David M. Carr, "The Politics of Textual Subversion: A Diachronic Perspective on the Garden of Eden Story," *JBL* 112 (1993): 577–595, finds an anti-sapiential reworking of the "Early Creation Narrative" here.

[51] Cf. Levin, *Jahwist*, 103–104; and Kratz, *Komposition*, 255–256, 259–262. Julius Wellhausen had already argued that the flood narrative cannot be part of the (Yahwistic) base text since a series of texts appear not to know it; see his *Die Composition des Hexateuchs und der historischen Bücher des Alten Testaments* (Berlin: Reimer, 1885), 7–12.

[52] Cf. Pfeiffer, "Baum I+II"; Konrad Schmid, "Die Unteilbarkeit der Weisheit: Überlegungen zur sogenannten Paradieserzählung Gen 2f. und ihrer theologischen Tendenz," *ZAW* 114 (2002): 21–39; Blenkinsopp, "A Post-exilic lay source"; Erhard Blum, "Von Gottesunmittelbarkeit zu Gottähnlichkeit: Überlegungen zur theologischen Anthropologie der

by the man using the kinship formula in Gen 2:23, and as *Chawwa* in view of her following function as a mother in Gen 3:20, is hardly original or more fitting than the position of Gen 3:20 in the current context. As a result, scholars have sometimes eliminated Gen 2:23 and suggested that Gen 3:20 immediately followed Gen 2:22. But this seems impossible since the building of the woman from a rib (Gen 2:22)—a motif not known elsewhere in the ancient Near East—is spun out of the kinship formula (Gen 2:23).[53] The coexistence of Gen 2:23 and 3:20 in one text can only be explained if one assumes that the woman and man underwent a fundamental change between the two naming episodes of the woman. It is precisely that change that is explicated by the fall narrative of Gen 3. Only the fall unlocks the mystery of sexual differentiation for humankind and introduces the man and woman to their destinations with respect to life on earth, i.e. to the cultivation of the soil and to procreation.[54] Accordingly, the curses mention sexual differentiation, the pain of childbearing (Gen 3:16), and the tilling of the ground (Gen 3:17–19a)—topics that are realized in the naming of the woman as *Chawwa* and in the man's dismissal from the garden to work the ground. In short, a source-critical differentiation into an older anthropogony and a younger reworking, which introduces the aspect and theological dimension of sin, creates more problems than it will solve. Rather, the Eden narrative is a sophisticated composition. The ambivalent prevailing mood is intentional, as is the case in other ancient literary works. The ambivalent experience of human existence is the real subject matter of the Eden narrative and the noted change in the prevailing mood is a stylistic instrument to account for such experience.

2. It was Gerhard von Rad who speculated that the original connection of the primeval material with the stories of the patriarchs was the genuine work of the Yahwist whose Primeval History reached its destination in the call of Abraham in Gen 12:1–3.[55] According to his widely received thesis, the

---

Paradieserzählung," in *Textgestalt und Komposition: Exegetische Beiträge zu Tora und Vordere Propheten* (ed. Wolfgang Oswald; FAT 69; Tübingen: Mohr Siebeck, 2010), 1–19; Gertz, "Adam"; Schüle, *Prolog*, 149–156; Arneth, *Adam*, 97–147, 230–236; and Bührer, *Baum*, 7–58.

[53] I here follow Schmid, "Unteilbarkeit," 25 with n. 29; and Blum, "Gottesunmittelbarkeit," 4–5. Contrast Christoph Uehlinger, "Eva als 'lebendiges Kunstwerk': Traditionsgeschichtliches zu Gen 2,21–22(23.24) und 3,20," *BN* 43 (1988): 90–99.

[54] Blum, "Gottesunmittelbarkeit," 5.

[55] Gerhard von Rad, *Das formgeschichtliche Problem des Hexateuch* (BWANT 4/26, Stuttgart: Kohlhammer, 1938), 58–62, and (esp.) his *Das erste Buch Mose: Genesis* (9th ed.; ATD 2/4; Göttingen: Vandenhoeck & Ruprecht, 1972), 9–10, 116–118, 121–123; translated as *Genesis: A*

theological conception of such a combination is determined by the interplay of two antidromic movements: on the one hand there is an "increase in sin to avalanche proportions" ("lawinenartigen Anwachsen der Sünde"),[56] and on the other there is a "secret increasing power of grace" ("heimliches Mächtigwerden der Gnade").[57] Only the Tower of Babel episode is *prima facie* out of line here. This alleged final catastrophe, however, simply marks the transition to the salvation history beginning in Gen 12. That is, the call of Abraham provides an answer to the open question regarding God's relationship to his indignant and scattered humanity and at the same time it introduces an individual history of grace to a universal outlook.[58]

Von Rad's characterization of the non-P texts in Gen 1–11 as a history of continuing disaster provoked considerable protest.[59] These voices noted that it is especially difficult to fit the non-P story of the flood into such an overall composition.[60] The totality of sin, stated in the prologue to the flood, the severity of the judgment that leads to the near total destruction of humanity, as well as the divine decision towards the end of the flood story not to punish sin in the same way despite its prevalence make it difficult to reconcile the flood with von Rad's assumed logic of escalation.[61] Furthermore, in comparison to the flood narrative it is difficult to see the story of the Tower of Babel as the final instance of merciless divine judgment upon humanity.[62] As result of the debate surrounding von Rad's model,

---

Commentary (2nd ed.; OTL; London: SCM, 1963), 22–23, 148–150, 153–156. Previous indications of such a view are already found in Budde, *Urgeschichte*, 409; and Willy Staerk, "Zur alttestamentlichen Literarkritik: Grundsätzliches und Methodisches," *ZAW* 42 (1924): 34–74, 38, 56, 64. See also Odil Hannes Steck, "Genesis 12,1–3 und die Urgeschichte des Jahwisten," in *Probleme biblischer Theologie: Gerhard von Rad zum 70. Geburtstag* (ed. Hans Walter Wolff; München: Kaiser, 1971), 525–554.

[56] Von Rad, *Genesis*, 116 (ET 148).
[57] Von Rad, *Genesis*, 10 (ET 23).
[58] Von Rad, *Genesis*, 116 (ET 148).
[59] See especially Claus Westermann, *Genesis 1–11* (BKAT 1/1; Neukirchen-Vluyn: Neukirchener, 1974), 73–74, 85–86; and Crüsemann, "Eigenständigkeit."
[60] See the clear presentation of Kratz, *Komposition*, 252, who proposes—following Wellhausen, *Composition*, 7–14—that the story of the Tower of Babel be attributed to a non-P version of the Primeval History that did not yet know the story of the flood. As in Wellhausen, Kratz's proposal hinges on a differentiation between an older anthropogony and a younger reworking in Gen 2–3 introducing sin. Others argue that the non-P parts of the flood narrative are a redactional addition to P. As shown above, I find both proposals unconvincing.
[61] See Jan Christian Gertz, "Noah und die Propheten: Rezeption und Reformulierung eines altorientalischen Mythos," *DVLG* 81 (2007): 503–522.
[62] Von Rad, *Genesis*, 117 (ET 149).

scholars began to argue for a diachronic independence of non-P's Primeval History.⁶³ The reasons for such an independence are simple: the fragility of the assumed link to the Patriarchal narratives (on the level of the non-P text), and the significant conceptual differences between both bodies of text. On the positive side, we can point to the thematic and conceptual unity of the non-P Primeval History. The non-P narrative contains a finely woven network of cross-references but these references do not expand beyond it. On the other hand, the non-P Patriarchal history never refers to the Primeval History. In particular, Gen 12:1–3, the purported destination and vanishing point of the non-P Primeval History, shows no signs of cross-references to the previous chapters.⁶⁴ As far as the content is concerned, the etiologies of these sections are quite different in that the Patriarchal material seems to esteem the semi-nomadic lifestyles of the patriarchs and their families, which according to the Primeval History must be regarded as unsettled and cursed (Gen 4:1–16). In short, it is easier to understand the non-P Primeval History as a previously independent composition than as a dependent front end to the Patriarchal narratives. This opinion is shared by a number of scholars; what is debated, however, is the extent and end point of such an independent non-P Primeval History.

Focusing on the final form of the text is fairly widespread; as a result, the story of the Tower of Babel (Gen 11:1–9) is often seen as the end of the non-P Primeval History.⁶⁵ However, when we consider the importance of an ending, or stern (*Achtergewicht*), within biblical narratives, it is difficult to imagine that a narrative cycle that originated in Judah, Israel, or even in the circles of the Babylonian Diaspora ended on the following note: "Therefore it was called Babel; because there YHWH confused the language of all the earth; and from there YHWH scattered them abroad over the face of all the earth" (Gen 11:9). It seems entirely implausible that a *biblical* etiology that seeks to explain the basic conditions of life in the way the non-P Primeval History does would end this way. Our evaluation is supported by the fact that it is difficult to find ancient Near Eastern parallels that assume a similar

---

⁶³ Cf. Crüsemann, "Eigenständigkeit"; Erhard Blum, *Die Komposition der Vätergeschichte* (WMANT 57; Neukirchen-Vluyn: Neukirchener, 1984), 359–360; Blum, "Urgeschichte," 438–439; Carr, *Fractures*, 234–248; and Witte, *Urgeschichte*, 192–205.

⁶⁴ See Crüsemann, "Eigenständigkeit," 18–22; Blum, *Komposition*, 349–361; and Witte, *Urgeschichte*, 192–200.

⁶⁵ Detailed arguments for such a view can be found in Carr, *Fractures*, 235–240; and Blum, "Urgeschichte," 439–440.

(supposed) order of creation, flood, and Tower of Babel.[66] In particular, the *Babyloniaca* of Berossus, a work written in Hellenistic times to demonstrate the importance of Babylon and one often cited in support of the 'Creation—Flood—Babel' model by older literature, actually shows how difficult it is to assume that a biblical narrative work would end with Gen 11:9. The final note of Berossus' work, a work probably written without using an older Mesopotamian *Vorlage*, reports the rebuilding of his hometown destroyed by the flood at the behest of the gods!

The above-mentioned reasons suggest the need for skepticism regarding any attempt to find the end of the independent non-P Primeval History in the story of the Tower of Babel. On the other hand, there are a number of reasons to suggest that the Primeval History ends after the flood.[67] The basic progression of such a Primeval History can be quickly sketched out. It is fundamentally a history of crises and decline. It begins with humanity's ability to choose between things destructive and conducive to life, an ability gained against the will of the creator God (Gen 2:4b–3:24). The following fratricide serves as an example to illustrate a poor choice (Gen 4:1–16). The crisis reaches its climax in the prologue to the flood when God passes judgment on humanity, which contains a reflection questioning the creation of all life more generally (Gen 6:5–8). The crisis is solved by YHWH's promise not to destroy creation again: the survival of creation is now separated from human acts. The ambivalence of human life we outlined earlier is not abolished but from now on accepted and understood as part of the order of creation (see Gen 8:21–22 with reference to Gen 3:17; 4:10–11). If the story of the flood is seen as a story of a resolved crisis and of a principal challenge to creation, it serves as the ideal closure to a narrative work that begins with the creation of human life and the ambivalence associated with the human condition. Furthermore, the promise to maintain creation would have been spoken into the realities of life for the story's authors and readers. Finally, we need to remember that a story which begins with creation and ends with a flood is analogous to other ancient Near Eastern literature such as the Atrahasis-Epos and the Sumerian narrative of the flood. In the light of the obvious familiarity the non-P narrative authors had with such traditions, this argument becomes very important.[68]

---

[66] See Witte, *Urgeschichte*, 190–191, with further bibliography.
[67] See Witte, *Urgeschichte*, 184–205; Baumgart, *Umkehr*, 385–398; and already Rolf Rendtorff, "Genesis 8,21 und die Urgeschichte des Jahwisten," *KD* 7 (1961): 69–78.
[68] See in detail Baumgart, *Umkehr*, 419–495; and Gertz, "Noah," 514–522.

If the non-P Primeval History originally ended with the flood, this implies that all of the following non-P stories were added at a later stage. This probably happened in the context of a Primeval Narrative that already consisted of the P and non-P texts. Whether these texts were written for such a context is a different question. As far as Gen 9:18–29 is concerned, I am fairly confident that they were. The story of Noah and his sons belongs to the non-P back-story of the genealogical material of the priestly Primeval History in Gen 9:18a, 19, and 28–29.[69] As far as Gen 11:1–9 is concerned, one could argue that we here have an older tradition; however, the literarily homogenous story of the Tower of Babel seems to be handed down in a such a way that it has to be understood as an unfolding of the priestly note regarding the dispersion of humanity in Gen 9:19.[70] It is hardly a literary-historical accident that both stories fit much better into the current context, shaped by the structure of the P Primeval History rather than into an independent non-P Primeval History. Finally, the miraculous episode of the 'angel marriages' (Gen 6:1–4) is a further candidate for a similarly late (post-P) addition.[71]

The Formation of the Primeval History

The two-source-hypothesis appears to remain a valid model to explain the origins of the biblical Primeval History, albeit with some modifications. There is little need to correct the literary-historical data for the priestly texts that we only mentioned in passing. Concerning the identification of priestly—and thus also non-priestly—texts, the consensus remains well founded. The same can be said of dating P to the end of the Exilic period or to the beginning of the Second Temple period. Equally undeniable is the fact that P is a source that begins in Gen 1 and moves beyond the Primeval History.[72] If we are to maintain loyalty to the two-source-hypothesis, however,

---

[69] See Jan Christian Gertz, "Hams Sündenfall und Kanaans Erbfluch: Anmerkungen zur kompositionsgeschichtlichen Stellung von Gen 9,18–29," in *'Gerechtigkeit und Recht zu üben' (Gen 18,19): Studien zur altorientalischen und biblischen Rechtsgeschichte, zur Religionsgeschichte Israels und zur Religionssoziologie: Festschrift für Eckart Otto zum 65. Geburtstag* (ed. Reinhard Achenbach and Martin Arneth; BZABR 13; Wiesbaden: Harrassowitz, 2009), 81–95.

[70] Gertz, "Babel."

[71] Cf. Marc Vervenne, "All They Need Is Love: Once More Genesis 6.1–4," in *Words Remembered, Texts Renewed: Essays in Honour of John F.A. Sawyer* (ed. Jon Davies, Graham Harvey, and Wilfred G.E. Watson; JSOTSup 195; Sheffield: JSOT Press, 1995), 19–40.

[72] The question of the extent of P is deliberately left open here since it moves beyond the focus of this article. I am convinced, however, that P extends at least into the Sinai-Pericope.

we have to re-evaluate the relationship between P and non-P texts. I would be hesitant to exclude *a priori* the possibility that P did know—minimally as hearsay—the older non-P texts. Further, it is undeniable that there was some knowledge of other traditions from elsewhere in the ancient Near East. Much remains open regarding the identification of such traditions—something we could not explore here—and their modes of reception. Here we should at least mention that models that explain the priestly reception of such traditions by participation in, rather than dissociation from, a common scientific culture should be favored.[73]

Our findings regarding the non-P texts within the Primeval History were heterogeneous: they are neither part of an overall source nor in total a reworking (*Bearbeitunsgschicht*) of the priestly text. As far as the non-P context of Gen 2:4b–8:22 is concerned, there are good reasons to argue for an independent Primeval History. The non-P texts following Gen 8:22, similar to Gen 6:1–4, are probably additions that already presuppose a connection between the P and non-P material or—at least—have to be seen in the context of such a connection. Ancient authors and redactors tend to be guided by tradition. In this respect it may be possible that a post-P reworking of the material introduced traditions and additions that were formulated *ad hoc*, as well as an older narrative that involved creation, the formation of culture, and a flood, into the context of P. Proposing a date for such an independent non-P Primeval History is difficult. The following seems certain, however: Mesopotamian traditions of the flood were known and these traditions were absorbed in the light of the prophecy of doom.[74] This points to a dating not earlier than the seventh century.

Select Bibliography

Arneth, Martin. *Durch Adams Fall ist ganz verderbt …: Studien zur Entstehung der alttestamentlichen Urgeschichte*. Forschungen zur Religion und Literatur des Alten und Neuen Testaments 217. Göttingen: Vandenhoeck & Ruprecht, 2007.

Baumgart, Norbert Clemens. *Die Umkehr des Schöpfergottes: Zu Komposition und religionsgeschichtlichem Hintergrund von Gen 5–9*. Herders Biblische Studien 22. Freiburg: Herder, 1999.

Blenkinsopp, Joseph. "A Post-exilic lay source in Genesis 1–11." Pages 49–61 in

---

[73] Jan Christian Gertz, "Antibabylonische Polemik im priesterlichen Schöpfungsbericht?" *ZTK* 106 (2009): 137–155.

[74] Gertz, "Noah."

Abschied vom Jahwisten: Die Komposition des Hexateuch in der jüngsten Diskussion. Edited by Jan Christian Gertz, Konrad Schmid, and Markus Witte. Beihefte zur Zeitschrift für die alttestamentliche Wissenschaft 315. Berlin: de Gruyter, 2002.

Blum, Erhard. "Urgeschichte." *Theologische Realenzyklopädie* 34 (2002): 436–445.

———. "Von Gottesunmittelbarkeit zu Gottähnlichkeit. Überlegungen zur theologischen Anthropologie der Paradieserzählung." Pages 1–19 in *Textgestalt und Komposition: Exegetische Beiträge zu Tora und Vordere Propheten*. Edited by Wolfgang Oswald. Forschungen zum Alten Testament 69. Tübingen: Mohr Siebeck, 2010.

Budde, Karl. *Die Biblische Urgeschichte (Gen 1–12,5)*. Gießen: Ricker'sche Buchhandlung, 1883.

Carr, David M. *Reading the Fractures of Genesis: Historical and Literary Approaches*. Louisville: Westminster John Knox, 1996.

———. "The Politics of Textual Subversion: A Diachronic Perspective on the Garden of the Eden Story." *Journal of Biblical Literature* 112 (1993): 577–595.

Dietrich, Walter. "'Wo ist dein Bruder?' Zu Tradition und Intention von Genesis 4." Pages 159–172 in *Theopolitik: Studien zur Theologie und Ethik des Alten Testaments*. Neukirchen-Vluyn: Neukirchener, 2002.

Gertz, Jan Christian. "Antibabylonische Polemik im priesterlichen Schöpfungsbericht?" *Zeitschrift für Theologie und Kirche* 106 (2009): 137–155.

———. "Babel im Rücken und das Land vor Augen: Anmerkungen zum Abschluß der Urgeschichte und zum Anfang der Erzählungen von den Erzeltern Israels." Pages 9–34 in *Die Erzväter in der biblischen Tradition: Festschrift für Matthias Köckert*. Edited by Anselm C. Hagedorn and Henrik Pfeiffer. Beihefte zur Zeitschrift für die alttestamentliche Wissenschaft 400. Berlin: de Gruyter, 2009.

———. "Noah und die Propheten: Rezeption und Reformulierung eines altorientalischen Mythos." *Deutsche Vierteljahrsschrift für Literaturwissenschaft und Geistesgeschichte* 81 (2007): 503–522.

Levin, Christoph. *Der Jahwist*. Forschungen zur Religion und Literatur des Alten und Neuen Testaments 157. Göttingen: Vandenhoeck & Ruprecht, 1993.

Mettinger, Tryggve N.D. *The Eden Narrative: A Literary and Religio-Historical Study of Genesis 2–3*. Winona Lake, Ind.: Eisenbrauns, 2007.

Otto, Eckart. "Die Paradieserzählung Genesis 2–3: Eine nachpriesterschriftliche Lehrerzählung in ihrem religionshistorischen Kontext." Pages 167–192 in *'Jedes Ding hat seine Zeit ...' Studien zur israelitischen und altorientalischen Weisheit: Diethelm Michel zum 65. Geburtstag*. Edited by Anja A. Diesel, Reinhard G. Lehmann, Eckart Otto, and Andreas Wagner. Beihefte zur Zeitschrift für die alttestamentliche Wissenschaft 241. Berlin: de Gruyter, 1996.

Pfeiffer, Henrik. "Der Baum in der Mitte des Gartens. Zum überlieferungsgeschichtlichen Ursprung der Paradieserzählung (Gen 2,4b–3,24)." *Zeitschrift für die alttestamentliche Wissenschaft* 112 (2000): 487–500; 113 (2001): 2–16.

Rendtorff, Rolf. "L'histoire biblique des origines (Gen 1–11) dans le contexte de la rédaction "sacerdotale" du Pentateuque." Pages 83–94 in *Le Pentateuque en question: Les origines et la composition des cinq premiers livres de la Bible a la lumiere de recherches recentes*. 2nd ed. Edited by Albert de Pury. Le Monde de la Bible 19. Geneva: Labor et Fides, 1989.

Schüle, Andreas. *Der Prolog der hebräischen Bibel: Der literar- und theologiegeschichtliche Diskurs der Urgeschichte (Gen 1–11)*. Abhandlungen zur Theologie des Alten und Neuen Testaments 86. Zürich: Theologischer Verlag, 2006.

Schmidt, Werner H. *Die Schöpfungsgeschichte der Priesterschrift: Zur Überlieferungsgeschichte von Genesis 1,1–2,4a und 2,4b–3,24*. 3rd ed. Wissenschaftliche Monographien zum Alten und Neuen Testament 17. Neukirchen-Vluyn: Neukirchener, 1973.

Ska, Jean-Louis. "The Story of the Flood: A Priestly Writer and Some Later Editorial Fragments." Pages 1–22 in *The Exegesis of the Pentateuch: Exegetical Studies and Basic Questions*. Forschungen zum Alten Testament 66. Tübingen: Mohr Siebeck, 2009.

Steck, Odil Hannes. *Der Schöpfungsbericht der Priesterschrift: Studien zur literarkritischen und überlieferungsgeschichtlichen Problematik von Genesis 1,1–2,4a*. 2nd ed. Forschungen zur Religion und Literatur des Alten und Neuen Testaments 115. Göttingen: Vandenhoeck & Ruprecht, 1981.

Uehlinger, Christoph. *Weltreich und 'eine Rede': Eine neue Deutung der sogenannten Turmbauerzählung (Gen 11,1–9)*. Orbis biblicus et orientalis 101. Freiburg: Universitätsverlag, 1990.

Vermeylen, Jacques. "La descendance de Caïn et la descendance d'Abel (Gen 4,17–26 + 5,28b–29)." *Zeitschrift für die alttestamentliche Wissenschaft* 103 (1991): 175–193.

Witte, Markus. *Die biblische Urgeschichte: Redaktions- und theologiegeschichtliche Beobachtungen zu Genesis 1,1–11,26*. Beihefte zur Zeitschrift für die alttestamentliche Wissenschaft 265. Berlin: de Gruyter, 1998.

FOOD AND THE FIRST FAMILY:
A SOCIOECONOMIC PERSPECTIVE

Carol Meyers

Introduction

Food and humanity are intertwined—in the biblical creation stories as well as in biological reality. It is no accident that the food sources for humanity are announced in Gen 1 as soon as human beings are created (Gen 1:29) and that food-producing plants are mentioned in Gen 2 before the creation of humankind is described (Gen 2:5–7). Without sources of nutrition, human life is inconceivable. Yet the role and significance of food is rarely contemplated in biblical studies, and food as a biocultural phenomenon seldom if ever figures in our thinking about the opening chapters of the Hebrew Bible.

Perhaps the best example of inattention to food as a thematic aspect of the beginning of Genesis is that the recurrence of ’*kl* ("to eat") is virtually ignored. In reference to human consumption, the root appears twenty-one times—a multiple of seven contributing to symbolic emphasis, in Gen 2–3.[1] This strikingly frequent usage gives ’*kl* the status of a "word-motif," rhetorically drawing attention to an important theme.[2] The abstract notion—that food is an intrinsic human concern—is given concrete form and dramatic emphasis by the abundant repetition of ’*kl*. This word-motif denotes a primary Israelite existential issue while also advancing the narrative plot. That YHWH God's first words to the first human concerns what they can eat (Gen 2:16) also signals food's importance.

Why are these signs of food as a theme overlooked? Several factors come to mind:

1. Food is not the same kind of issue for us in the developed world as it was for the ancient Israelites. We have too much; and, as will become clear, they often had too little. And few of us have a direct connection

---

[1] In contrast, the word "sin" never appears in Gen 2–3 but often figures prominently in interpretations of these chapters.
[2] See Robert Alter, *The Art of Biblical Narrative* (New York: Basic Books, 1981), 92, 95.

with our food sources. Yet we tend to interpret ancient texts as if the world was the same in essential ways for the ancients as for us.

2. The interpretive trajectory examining the misdeeds of the first family has dominated the study of Gen 2–4 since antiquity even though the Hebrew Bible itself, despite its concern about disobedience, never references their problematic deeds. In fact, the archetypal humans are barely mentioned after chapter 4.[3] In contrast, they appear frequently in Jewish and Christian interpretive traditions. Adam, for example, is mentioned more often in the New Testament than in the Hebrew Bible. This post-Hebrew Bible prominence stems from the interests of early Judaism and Christianity in sin, evil, disobedience, punishment, human responsibility, and related matters; and the focus on these issues in the earliest references to Gen 2–4 (e.g., Sir 25:24; Wis 10:1–3; 1 Tim 2:13–15; 1 John 3:12) has influenced virtually all subsequent scholarship.[4]

3. Because they present two episodes, the narratives about the first couple (Gen 2–3) and the first offspring (Gen 4) tend to be examined independently of each other.[5] Yet the human characters in all three chapters are part of the same first family, and subsistence issues inextricably link them. They may have originally been separate literary units; but in their canonical form, one is an essential and complementary sequel to the other. In fact, they are distinct from Gen 1 but part of a longer beginnings tradition that continues to Gen 11:26. That is, the story of the first family is the opening section of a longer story that precedes the ancestor narratives of Gen 12–50.[6]

---

[3] Only Adam and Seth appear elsewhere: in the genealogies of Gen 5 and 1 Chron 1.

[4] This scholarship is voluminous, and the reader is referred to the analyses and exhaustive bibliographies of two recent monographs for further information about the words and passages discussed in this essay: Terje Stordalen, *Echoes of Eden: Genesis 2–3 and Symbolism of the Eden Garden in Biblical Hebrew Literature* (CBET 25; Leuven: Peeters, 2000); and Tryggve N.D. Mettinger, *The Eden Narrative: A Literary and Religio-Historical Study of Genesis 2–3* (Winona Lake, Ind.: Eisenbrauns, 2007). Claus Westermann's classic work (*Genesis 1–11: A Commentary* [trans. John J. Scullion; CC; Minneapolis: Augsburg, 1984]) is still valuable for its extensive bibliography, lexical observations, and general comments.

[5] Note that the first two monographs mentioned in the preceding note analyze Gen 2–3 but not Gen 4; and many textbooks and commentaries treat the two episodes independently. A notable exception is Ilana Pardes (*Countertraditions in the Bible: A Feminist Approach* [Cambridge: Harvard University Press, 1992], 40), who insists that Gen 4 is an "immediate continuation" of Gen 2–3.

[6] Richard J. Clifford, *Creation Accounts in the Ancient Near East and in the Bible* (CBQMS 26; Washington, D.C.: Catholic Biblical Association, 1994), 144–145.

Taken together, these factors have obviated understanding Gen 2–4 in relation to subsistence concerns. Thus a fresh look at the first family—the first children as well as their parents—using the lens of food, that essential component of human life, is warranted.

The first family episodes are arguably among Israel's early narrative traditions.[7] Perhaps their most important characteristic, at least for the purposes of this essay, is their etiological character. As part of ancient Israel's beginnings stories, these tales and those that follow (Gen 5–11) "explain" various existing, and sometimes troubling or puzzling aspects of the cosmos or society. They provide mythic—and therefore non-provable—causes for what people may observe or confront in daily life. In so doing, they function to help people "understand" and thus accept the inevitable status quo, the reality of the world as they know it.

Several comments about terminology are in order before proceeding. First, "Israelite" and "Israel" are used as general cultural designations rather than specifically political ones. Second, Gen 2–4 refers to the first family episodes beginning in 2:4b (not 2:1) and ending in 4:16 (although some comments on 4:17–25 are included). Third, "food" in the title represents subsistence systems. Fourth, "socioeconomic" in the subtitle indicates that the first family narratives are considered in relation to the economic basis of highland life and to the human (social) responses to environmental potential and problems. Finally, "peasant" is used as a descriptor of Israelite agrarians.[8] Peasants are best understood as small, rural agriculturalists who produce for their own consumption and not for profit. Their immediate context is the household, which is a unit of consumption as well as production. Unlike more primitive cultivators, who are isolated from larger social or political structures, peasants are part of a more complex society in which elites typically appropriate a portion of what peasants produce (as in sacrifices offered at local, regional, or state shrines; or in some form of tribute or taxation). Whether they own their land or farm it as tenants, peasants typically feel closely connected to their land holdings, which are their

---

[7] These chapters are generally attributed to the Yahwist (J) and dated to the early monarchic period. Despite the problems in the traditional understanding of a composite Pentateuch, the literary integrity and Iron IIA or B date of Gen 2–4 remain tenable and are accepted here. However, a later date, as supported *inter alia* by Mettinger (*Eden Narrative*, 11, 134) and Stordalen (*Echoes of Eden*, 206–213), would not significantly affect the perspectives of this essay.

[8] For social science definitions of "peasant," see John R. Jackson, "Enjoying the Fruit of One's Labor: Attitudes toward Male Work and Workers in the Hebrew Bible" (Ph.D. diss., Duke University, 2005), 62–66.

means of subsistence and their way of life. The biblical concept of *naḥălâ*—whether implying ownership by a patrimonial household (*bêt 'āb*) or YHWH or both—surely reflects the strong attachment of Israelite peasants to their immoveable property.

In considering the first family episodes of Gen 2–4 as complementary responses to the highland environment in which Israelites lived throughout the Iron Age, this paper will first review relevant aspects of that environment with respect to the production and consumption of food and then turn to a close look at the narratives themselves.

Israelite Food Issues Relating to the First Family

This section discusses two major features of the Israelite food supply: the subsistence system of the highlands, and the dietary regime supported by that subsistence system.

Highland Subsistence System

The Israelite food system is best characterized as the agrarian mode of production in which sustenance is acquired by exploiting cultivable land using plow technology.[9] More specifically, in the southern Levant and in the Mediterranean world in general, this mode of production involved dry-farming—also called dryland farming or rainfall agriculture—which means that moisture for crops comes mainly from seasonal rainfall rather than from springs, rivers, or irrigation. In addition, animal husbandry was an important but subsidiary component of the dry-farming regime.[10]

This combination of dry-farming and small-animal herding has three basic requirements. One is soil quality that will support the growth of food crops in the valleys (and, through the construction of terraces, on some of the slopes) and the growth of natural pasturage for animal grazing on the non-arable slopes. Another is rainfall as the chief water source, hence the term rainfall agriculture. The third is sufficient human labor to meet the ebb and flow of seasonal tasks, with periods of intensive work interspersed with periods of less arduous toil. A single farmer was not

---

[9] Gerhard Lenski, *Ecological-Evolutionary Theory: Principles and Applications* (Boulder, Colo.: Paradigm, 2004), 84, Fig. 5.1, 96–97.

[10] See Aharon Sasson, *Animal Husbandry in Ancient Israel: A Zooarchaeological Perspective on Livestock Exploitation, Herd Management and Economic Strategies* (Approaches to Anthropological Archaeology; London: Equinox, 2010).

adequate for this labor pattern; a farm family, with spouse and offspring contributing to subsistence tasks, was essential.[11]

These three requirements were not always met, and there were consequences. The biggest challenge was the periodic insufficiency of rainfall and the concomitant shortfall of crops.[12] Annual rainfall is seasonal and highly variable; and the productivity of arable land is vulnerable to fluctuations in both the timing and the amounts of rain. A twenty-five percent deviation from the mean annual rainfall occurs in as many as four years in twenty.[13] Years with above average precipitation do not translate into the storage of surpluses for years with scant rain, nor does an adequate absolute amount of rainfall always mean enough water for crop development. The results of the inevitable and recurrent shortages of rainfall are periodic agricultural shortfalls often exacerbated by damage from insects, hail, or blight and by political factors such as warfare and taxes.

These recurrent environmental and political factors meant that food supplies were frequently inadequate, and continual if not chronic hunger and malnutrition affected much of the peasant population.[14] Strategies for coping with food shortages may have fended off starvation and death but rarely eliminated endemic hunger and malnutrition.[15] Studies of the ancient Aegean, with its similar ecosystems, show an even direr picture.[16] And ethnographic data, as in this poignant description of life in a Greek mountain town, provide a similar grim assessment:

> Of all the villager's crops wheat is the most vital, and the phrase 'to eat bread' is still a typical way in the village of saying 'to eat'; but the winning of bread from the rocky fields is, as the villagers say, 'an agonizing struggle' (ἀγωνία). For

---

[11] David C. Hopkins, "Life on the Land: The Subsistence Struggles of Early Israel," *BA* 50 (1987): 178–191. Hopkins focuses on Iron I Israel, but many of his observations pertain to agrarians throughout the biblical period.

[12] The constraints on agriculture are described in detail in David C. Hopkins, *The Highlands of Canaan: Agricultural Life in the Early Iron Age* (SWBA 3; Sheffield: Almond, 1985), 77–108.

[13] Hopkins, *Highlands*, 89.

[14] Chronic hunger and malnutrition are not the same as periodic famines, which are widespread and catastrophic food shortages. Famines surely affected the Israelites; they figure prominently in the ancestor narratives of Genesis, in several episodes of the Former Prophets, and, along with warfare and pestilence, in prophetic warnings about the consequences of disobedience (e.g., Jer 14:12).

[15] Hopkins (*Highlands*, 211–252) discusses these strategies; cf. Peter Garnsey, *Food and Society in Classical Antiquity* (Key Themes in Ancient History; Cambridge: Cambridge University Press, 1999), 35–41.

[16] Garnsey, *Food and Society*, 2, 30, 34–35.

the greater part of the year nature, if not actually hostile to man, is at least relatively intractable. Day after day the farmer wears himself out in clearing, burning, ploughing, double-ploughing, sowing, hoeing, weeding; all through the year there are risks from hail, floods, drought, locusts, diseases, any one of which could, particularly in the past, reduce him to debt and hunger.[17]

The economic basis for human life in the highlands of Palestine allowed for survival, but the cost in energy and worry was often considerable. "Eating with difficulty is a condition of life outside Eden."[18]

Dietary Regime[19]

The Palestinian agrarian system supported the so-called Mediterranean triad mentioned frequently in the Hebrew Bible: bread (grains), wine (grapes), and oil (olives). Of these three commodities, grains were by far the most important. In contemporary developing countries cereals comprise fifty-seven percent of the daily caloric intake.[20] The percentage in ancient Israel was likely higher—as much as seventy-five percent.[21] So important were grains that the word for bread, *leḥem*, sometimes designates "food" in the Hebrew Bible.[22] Pulses were also essential foods, although they contributed proportionally fewer calories than did grains.

Other foodstuffs supplemented this basic pattern but probably did not often provide enough essential nutrients.[23] Eggs and maybe poultry, more likely from wild than domestic birds, were occasionally consumed. Other than pulses few vegetables could be grown without irrigation and even then were available only seasonally. Several tree fruits—figs, pomegranates, and dates—are prominent in biblical imagery and are among the seven species

---

[17] Juliet du Boulay, *Portrait of a Greek Mountain Village* (Oxford: Clarendon, 1974), 56. The use of "bread" to designate food more generally is similar to the use of *leḥem* in the Hebrew Bible (as in Gen 3:19); see n. 20.

[18] Ellen Davis, *Scripture, Culture, and Agriculture: An Agrarian Reading of the Bible* (Cambridge: Cambridge University Press, 2009), 141.

[19] This discussion draws mainly on two recent studies: Oded Borowski, "Eat, Drink, and Be Merry: The Mediterranean Diet," *Near Eastern Archaeology* 67 (2004): 96–107; and Nathan MacDonald, *What Did the Ancient Israelites Eat?: Diet in Biblical Times* (Grand Rapids: Eerdmans, 2008). Note, however, that Borowski is probably too optimistic in considering the Israelite diet balanced, as is MacDonald in suggesting increased meat consumption in Iron II.

[20] David Grigg, "The Geography of Food Consumption: A Review," *Progress in Human Geography* 19 (1995), 346, Table 3.

[21] MacDonald, *What Did the Ancient Israelites Eat?*, 19.

[22] Werner Dommershausen, "*leḥem*," *TDOT* 7: 523–524.

[23] MacDonald, *What Did the Israelites Eat?*, 59–59, 80–87. The current acclaim for the so-called Mediterranean diet is based on relatively recent dietary patterns, not ancient reality.

characterizing the land's idealized fertility (Deut 8:8). Only the fig, however, was regularly consumed, mainly in its dried form; fresh figs were considered a "delicacy."[24] Most products of fruit trees were "prestige foods" not available to the peasant majority.[25]

The herd animals that were the complement to food crops in the Israelite dry-farming system provided some dairy products but only at certain seasons. Meat itself was not a dietary staple. Animal protein usually occupies a large portion of the dinner plate in the developed world but is absent or nearly so in developing countries, where traditional plant-based diets dominate.[26] Animal consumption patterns in the southern Levant and Mediterranean basin in antiquity were similar.[27] Growing enough fodder for large herds or flocks was not an economical way to use the limited arable land, which was needed for food crops for humans; and the natural pasturage on hillsides has limited capability for sustaining animals. Consequently, people consumed meat only occasionally, at special meals or feasts.[28]

Nevertheless, small groups of domesticated animals were an important component of the agrarian regime.[29] The relatively few cattle served mainly as draft animals. The more numerous sheep and goats provided wool and hair for textiles and for seasonal dairy products. Just as important, animals were a fall-back resource for coping with crop shortfalls. Because they can survive on marginal lands when plant-food yields are low, they are the "classic stored food" that can be slaughtered and eaten in times of extreme food crises.[30] Animals were "a mobile resource subject to a different set of environmental constraints than fixed fields of crops."[31]

Peasants thus ate little meat, for good economic reasons; but the same was not true for elites. References to meat consumption in the Hebrew Bible and in classical and ancient Near Eastern texts are related to affluence,

---

[24] Oded Borowski, *Agriculture in Iron Age Israel* (Winona Lake, Ind.: Eisenbrauns, 1987), 115–116; see Jer 24:1–5.
[25] Borowski, *Agriculture*, 93. This was also true in the ancient Aegean; so Garnsey, *Food and Society*, 127.
[26] According to 1980s data, less than five percent of daily calories in those countries comes from meat; see Grigg, "Geography of Food Consumption," 346, Table 3.
[27] Borowski, "Eat, Drink, and Be Merry," 100; Garnsey, *Food and Society*, 16.
[28] Carol Meyers, "The Function of Feasts: An Anthropological Perspective on Israelite Religious Festivals," in *Social Theory and the Study of Israelite Religion: Retrospect and Prospect* (ed. Saul M. Olyan; Resources for Biblical Study; Atlanta: Society of Biblical Literature, forthcoming).
[29] Hopkins, *Highlands*, 245–250.
[30] Hopkins, *Highlands*, 248; Garnsey, *Food and Society*, 40.
[31] Hopkins, "Life on the Land," 188.

especially that of royalty. Meat, like most fruits, was a prestige food. For example, the hyperbolic list of extravagant daily provisions for Solomon's household includes cattle, sheep, goats, several game animals, and poultry (1 Kgs 4:22–23 [Heb. 1 Kgs 5:2–3]). The way to impress special guests was with choice cuts of meat (e.g., Gen 18:7–8; Judg 13:15).[32] Mesopotamian records show that the largest amounts of meat were allocated to kings and deities, with soldiers and palace personnel also receiving an ample supply.[33] The choicest human fare typically models foods offered to deities, and meat was a major part of the sacrificial regimens of ancient Israel as well as of ancient Near Eastern and classical societies.[34] It is no accident that the general term for "sacrifice" in the Hebrew Bible is *zābaḥ*, meaning "to slaughter."[35] Meat is the food of the gods *par excellence*.

Food and the First Family

The First Couple

The Eden narrative begins with a description of the economic basis for life outside the garden, which is where the episode will end. The dry-farming economy, supplemented by livestock, that characterizes the central highlands of Palestine is implicit in the opening words of the story in Gen 2:5. The three requirements for this subsistence pattern—vegetation for both pasturage and food, rainfall, and human labor—are all mentioned:

> Before any pasturage (*śîaḥ haśśādeh*) was on the earth (*'ereṣ*),
> And before any field crops (*'eśeb haśśādeh*) had sprung up,
> Since YHWH God had not sent rain upon the earth (*'ereṣ*)
> And there was no man (*'ādām*) to cultivate (*'ăbōd*) the arable land (*'ădāmâ*).[36]

---

[32] Feasts were part of the dynamics of political change; see Nathan MacDonald, *Not Bread Alone: The Uses of Food in the Old Testament* (Oxford: Oxford University Press, 2008), 134–165.

[33] Karen Rhea Nemet-Nejat, *Daily Life in Ancient Mesopotamia* (Daily Life Through History; Westport, Conn.: Greenwood, 1998), 159; Henri Limet, "The Cuisine of Ancient Sumer," *BA* 50 (1987): 136–137. Limet (140) calls the diet of most others "frugal."

[34] Thus priestly officials, who received a portion of many of the animal offerings, were also among the elites who had frequent access to meat.

[35] The root *zbḥ* similarly indicates bloody sacrifice in all Semitic languages; so Jan Bergman, Helmer Ringgren, and Bernhard Lang, "*zābhach; zebhach*" *TDOT* 4: 8–11, 17.

[36] This translation is by Theodore Hiebert, *The Yahwist's Landscape: Nature and Religion in Early Israel* (New York: Oxford University Press, 1996), 32–33. I would contest only his

The pre-creation world lacks the three elements needed for the Israelite agrarian system.

The first element—the pair "pasturage" and "field crops"—are specific terms for the two basic kinds of plant life in the Israelite subsistence strategy. "Pasturage" refers to the natural vegetation on hillsides too rocky or steep for cultivation, that is, the non-cultivable "earth" (*'ereṣ*) on which small herd animals could graze; and "field crops" denotes the plant foods, grown on arable *'ādāmâ*, that were the mainstay of the Israelite diet.[37] The second essential element—one too often overlooked—is rainfall. The productivity of the soil and thus human survival were dependent upon rainfall, making it a "central feature" of this narrative.[38] The water (*'ēd*) mentioned in the next verse (2:6) is a loan-word attested in Akkadian and Sumerian; it denotes the sub-surface flow understood to be the source of all waters and is background information.[39]

The third element, humanity, is portrayed as inextricably linked to the land by virtue of the wordplay in which the human (*'ādām*) will work the arable land (*'ādāmâ*) and also will be formed from it (2:7). Indeed, when the verb *'bd* ("to work") takes the object *'ādāmâ*, it denotes a specific kind of work: agriculture. The phrase "cultivate (work) the arable land" (2:5) signals that the archetypal humans are to be agriculturalists (who engage in limited animal husbandry) and not pastoralists. This phrase appears again in 3:23 when life outside the garden begins. The anticipated and actualized reality of agrarian life forms an *inclusio*, framing the Eden episode of the first family tale. Humans were intended all along to be cultivators. But cultivating was neither easy nor always successful, as YHWH's stinging words to the first man, the archetypal farmer, make abundantly clear (Gen 3:18–19). The fertility of the arable soil (*'ādāmâ*) is compromised by YHWH's curse, and only through grueling toil can field crops (*'eśeb haśśśādeh*) yield food (*leḥem*).[40]

---

using "man" to translate *'ādām*, which might be better rendered "human" or "human being"; see David E.S. Stein, *The Contemporary Torah: A Gender-Sensitive Adaptation of the JPS Translation* (New York: Jewish Publication Society, 2006), 3. Other translations are the author's unless otherwise noted.

[37] Hiebert, *Yahwist's Landscape*, 37–38. Pasturage probably precedes field crops in this passage because it grows naturally on non-cultivable hillsides, whereas field crops require human intervention, which has not yet been mentioned.

[38] So Bill T. Arnold, *Genesis* (New Cambridge Bible Commentary; New York: Cambridge University Press, 2009), 57.

[39] Arnold, *Genesis*, 57.

[40] See nn. 15 and 20 above.

The need for intense labor is so great that women must contribute substantially to agrarian tasks and also bear many offspring, as mandated in YHWH's words to the woman.[41]

Within the *inclusio* denoting the role of humans as agrarians lies a fleeting glimpse of a different world, a garden (*gan*). Another word-motif appearing repeatedly in the Eden tale,[42] "garden" is especially important because of its imagery. The English word garden usually evokes images of ornamental flowers and trees growing in a profusion of blooms and scents, or of vegetable gardens with plants and herbs in neat rows. The ancient Israelite concept of gardens fits neither of these images. The word *gan* occurs forty-one times in the Hebrew Bible, and the feminine *gannah* appears sixteen times. Both are derived from *gnn*, "to protect, surround," which is found eight times. The greatest concentration of occurrences, as might be expected, is in the Eden episode. Examining its use elsewhere in the Hebrew Bible provides evidence of the salient features of gardens, all of which have resonance with features of the garden of Gen 2–3:

1. Gardens are safe, enclosed spaces with limited access. The verb *gnn* always occurs with YHWH as the subject and with Jerusalem or the people as the object of God's encircling protection (e.g., 2 Kgs 20:6; Isa 31:5; Zech 12:8). Indeed, walls are mentioned several times in relation to royal gardens (see item 7). No enclosure is mentioned for the Gen 2–3 garden; but the Eden imagery in Ezekiel is suggestive in depicting a "fence" of precious stones surrounding the garden (Ezek 28:13), just as a hedge surrounds a vineyard in Isa 5:5 and a wall of precious stones will protect Jerusalem in Isa 54:11–12.[43] A cherub and "fire-stones" are part of the garden imagery in Ezek 28:14 and 16; and cherubim and a fiery sword guard the garden in Gen 3:24. Eden is thus a protected space not accessible to all.

---

[41] Gen 3:16a should be translated "I will make great your toil and your pregnancies"; see Carol Meyers, "Eve," in *Women in Scripture: A Dictionary of Named and Unnamed Women in the Hebrew Bible, the Apocryphal/Deuterocanonical Books, and the New Testament* (ed. Carol Meyers, Toni Craven, and Ross S. Kraemer; Boston: Houghton Mifflin, 2000), 81.

[42] It occurs thirteen times, which may be a symbolic combination of three and ten, each indicating completeness.

[43] Moshe Greenberg, *Ezekiel 21–37: A New Translation with Introduction and Commentary* (AB 22A; New York: Doubleday, 1887), 581–582. The Edens of Ezekiel and Genesis differ in some ways but also have attributes in common. Mettinger (*Eden Narrative*, 85–98) usefully compares and contrasts them, although his supposition that Gen 2–3 is based on Ezekiel's Eden may be questioned.

2. Gardens are places in which trees, not vines or other horticultural specimens, flourish.[44] Some texts refer generically to a garden's "trees" (e.g., Ezek 31:9) or "fruit trees" (Qoh 2:5). Others refer to specific trees: aloes (Num 24:6), cedars (Num 24:6; Ezek 31:8), cypresses (Ezek 31:8), oaks (Isa 1:29, 30), palm trees (Num 24:6), and plane trees (Ezek 31:8). Similarly, trees—and not pasturage or field crops—are the only kind of plant life said to be in the Eden garden and also in Ezekiel's Eden (31:8; 31:9). These trees are both ornamental and fruitful: "every tree that was pleasant to the sight and good for eating" (Gen 2:9). The aspect of pleasure precedes that of consumption when God plants the garden; the food itself is not an essential nutrient (see item 6).[45]
3. The trees of a garden are not individual specimens spread out in meadows or fields; they are plentiful and close together. The word "forest" appears with garden in Qoh 2:5–6, and Ezek 31:9 refers to a "profusion" of branches. An enclosed place, dense with trees, is suggested by the imagery of Song 8:13, where the male lover is listening for the sound of his beloved—presumably he will hear her before he can see her. In the Eden garden, the first couple hears "the sound of YHWH God walking around in the garden" (Gen 3:8); they hear but do not see the deity because of the densely wooded character of the garden.
4. Gardens are places with water supplies that are both permanent and copious, and rain is never the source. The water can come from fountains (Song 4:12, 15), pools (Neh 3:15; Qoh 2:5–6), rivers (Gen 13:10;[46] Num 24:6), springs (Isa 58:11), streams (Song 4:15), or wells (Song 4:15). The presence of abundant water in an eschatological passage in Isaiah signifies that plentiful and unending water is the *sine qua non* of gardens: "and you shall be like a saturated garden, like a spring of water, whose waters never fail" (Isa 58:11).[47] The water in Eden is exemplary in

---

[44] Two passages (Deut 11:10; 1 Kgs 21:2) mention "vegetable gardens" and seem to be exceptions. In both cases the word *gan* is paired with *yārāq*; otherwise, *gan* alone is a tree-filled place.

[45] When the tree qualities of 2:9 are echoed in 3:6, the tree's appeal as food is mentioned first; perhaps, now that humans are on the scene and about to eat, gustatory qualities take precedence, adumbrating post-Eden reality.

[46] This verse word does not actually have the word "river," but it gives examples of places (Egypt and the Jordan valley) that are well watered by ever-flowing rivers.

[47] "Saturated garden" also appears in Jer 31:12 to describe life in the eschatological future: like a very wet garden, people will never "languish," i.e., never experience the fatigue and weakness of hunger, which was all too often present in peasant life.

its abundance—the river made to water Eden (Gen 2:10) has sufficient water to divide into four branches, all extensive water sources themselves. The Eden river would be the equivalent of four great waterways combined, and rain is never mentioned.[48]

5. None of the biblical passages referring to gardens suggests that toil is necessary to maintain them. Gardens are said to be planted (Jer 29:5, 28; cf. Qoh 2:5), as is the Eden garden, or "made" (Amos 9:14; Qoh 2:5). However, they are never said to be worked (cultivated); in fact, they have a self-sustaining quality. In depicting the false prosperity of the wicked, Bildad refers to the way plant life regenerates in a garden (Job 8:16). And, according to a verse in Isaiah (61:11), "a garden makes its seeds sprout forth."[49] These passages present gardens as low-maintenance spaces; they can sustain growth with little or no human intervention. As such, they are similar to the contemporary concept of "permaculture," in which systems are meant to be as self-sustaining as possible by following their internal mechanisms for productivity in relation to their natural habitats.[50]

The language used for the role of the humans in the garden likewise implies minimal intervention. YHWH God's directive (Gen 2:15) to the primeval person consists of two verbs (*'bd; šmr*) joined by *waw* and typically translated as separate terms. For example, the NRSV has "to till it and keep it"; the NJPS reads "to till it and tend it"; and the NAB has "to cultivate it and care for it." These translations, like many others, understand *'bd* to involve agricultural labor of the sort appearing in 2:5 in reference to cultivation, outside the garden, by working (tilling) the ground.[51] But the situation in Eden is different, for gardens do

---

[48] Two of these waterways—the Tigris and the Euphrates—are well known. The identity of the other two—Pishon and Gihon—is uncertain; but their names perhaps mean "springing" and "gushing" and thus indicate a similar bounty of water.

[49] In the preceding, parallel line the "earth" brings forth its shoots; the word for earth is *'ereṣ* not *'ādāmâ*, land that has to be cultivated (cf. Gen 2:5).

[50] Permaculture is a contraction of "permanent agriculture" or "permanent culture"; see Steve Diver, *Introduction to Permaculture: Concepts and Resources* (ATTRA Publication #CT083; Fayetteville, Ariz.: National Sustainable Agriculture Information Service), n.p. Cited 6 August 2010. Online: http://attra.ncat.org/attra-pub/perma.html. Its similarity to Eden is suggested by Carol A. Newsom, "Common Ground: An Ecological Reading of Genesis 2–3," in *The Earth Story in Genesis* (ed. Norman C. Habel and Shirley Wurst; The Earth Bible 2; Sheffield: Sheffield Academic Press, 2000), 65.

[51] Some (e.g., Phyllis Trible, *God and the Rhetoric of Sexuality* [OBT; Philadelphia: Fortress, 1979], 85) propose that *'bd* suggests "serving" God, since the verb can mean "to serve." But that hardly fits the syntax of the verse.

not require that kind of arduous labor. The two verbs should perhaps be understood as an example of verbal hendiadys, where two verbs joined by a conjunction express a single concept.[52] The kind of work envisioned in the Edenic garden is simply to maintain or guard it, as in the reference to the "guards" of fields in Jer 4:17 or the "guardian" or "keeper" of the royal forest in Neh 2:8. In these two instances and in other similar ones, the participle (*šōmēr*) of *šmr* is used. Thus the "work" in the Eden garden is simply the task of watching over it, not cultivating it.[53] Whatever the humans were to do in the garden, it was not the toil of cultivators.

6. Fertility and plenty are important features of gardens. In the Song of Songs, where *gan* and *gannah* words are found almost as often as is *gan* in Gen 2–3, they evoke fertility and plenty. In fact, their prominence in the Song has prompted the suggestion that it is a midrash on the Eden tale.[54] But the fruitfulness of gardens, in the Song and elsewhere in the Hebrew Bible, is not the same as the fertility of the crop-bearing soil (*'ădāmâ*); rather, it produces luxury edibles (as in Qoh 2:5; Song 4:16) and not basic subsistence crops.[55] The Eden trees are said to bear an unspecified kind of "fruit," unlikely to have been one of ancient Israel's dietary staples. The only tree product important for nutrition in ancient Israel was the olive; but the primal couple eat the fruit directly from the tree (Gen 3:6), and olives are too bitter to be eaten raw, without curing or sun-drying.[56] The Eden fruits thus should be considered prestige foods, or exotica—foodstuffs available to the elite but not to the average peasant. These fruit flourish in the special

---

[52] See Bill T. Arnold and John H. Choi, *A Guide to Biblical Hebrew Syntax* (New York: Cambridge University Press, 2003), 148–149.

[53] Neither the traditional translations nor the suggestion here that the verbs form a hendiadys accounts for the fact that the verbs have the feminine object ending. Because "garden" is not feminine, it does not seem to be the antecedent. Since feminine *'ădāmâ*, is the usual object of "work" (as in 2:5 and 3:23), it may residually be the reference of the suffix; so Jackson (*Work*, 179). More likely, the antecedent is the feminine toponym Eden; see Westermann, *Genesis 1–11*, 184.

[54] Trible (*God and the Rhetoric of Sexuality*, 44–65) sees the motifs of a garden and plentiful water as parallels to Eden, which becomes her hermeneutical lens for analyzing the Song.

[55] Jeremiah's instruction to the exiles in Babylon to build houses there and "to plant gardens and eat their fruit" (Jer 29:5, 28) may be an exception. However, because the exiles were elites, not peasant farmers, and because they lived near ever-flowing rivers, the fruit of these gardens may well have been the luxurious extras, available in addition to the foods of their daily diet.

[56] In antiquity, virtually all olives were pressed to extract the oil, the major source of fat in the Israelite diet, rather than being cured or dried for eating; Borowski, *Agriculture*, 124–125.

conditions of a garden, with unfailing supplies of water. We are not told about the basic sustenance, if any, of the primal couple; but we see that the trees of Eden produce pleasurable extras, not essential staples.
7. Gardens are the domain of elites. Nine biblical passages mention royal gardens, which surrounded or were adjacent to the palace (as in Esth 1:5; 7:8) and which provided luxury fruits as well as a shady repose or a place for leisurely strolls or elaborate banquets. The presence and symbolic significance of royal gardens in Mesopotamian texts is well known;[57] and a prominent example of monumental art from Mesopotamia shows King Ashurbanipal and his queen feasting in their luxuriant garden near their palace in Nineveh.[58] Just as royal palaces are the model for God's heavenly abode, royal gardens are no doubt the exemplar for God's garden, referred to by the phrases "garden of God" (Ezek 28:13; 31:8, 8, 9) and "garden of YHWH" (Gen 13:10; Isa 51:3).[59] God's dwelling place on high was in the midst of a luxuriant garden with a border of precious stones (Ezek 28:13).[60] The Eden of Genesis is not explicitly called the "garden of God."[61] However, in one eschatological passage "Eden" and "garden of YHWH" appear in parallel lines:

> For YHWH comforts Zion,
> comforts all her ruined places;
> he will make her wilderness like Eden,
> her desert like the garden of YHWH.... (Isa 51:3)

In the aggregate, the occurrences of gardens in biblical texts other than Gen 2–3 depict special spaces that are fundamentally different from and spatially separate from the areas around them, the areas where most people live and work. In addition, many of the features of gardens—especially plentiful water and luxuriant growth—resonate with the imagery conveyed

---

[57] Summarized in Stordalen, *Echoes of Eden*, 84–88.

[58] *ANEP*, no. 451.

[59] The biblical idea of God's garden may originate in Canaanite language describing Baal's territory as a place with natural springs and abundant trees; see B. Jacobs-Hornig, "*gan*," *TDOT* 3:37–38.

[60] Mesopotamian literature is also replete with mythic gardens, some—such as the "border" garden, a numinous place between the divine and human realms—have features similar to Eden; see Stordalen, *Echoes of Eden*, 139–155, 160–161.

[61] That phrase may have a separate origin; yet Gen 3:8, where YHWH God walks in the Eden garden in the evening, implies that it is indeed God's garden. The complicated use of "Eden" is summarized in Benjamin Kedar-Kopfstein, "*ēden; ʿādan; ʿădînâ; ʿădānîm; ʿednâ; maʿădannîm; maʿădannôt*," *TDOT* 10: 486–490.

by the term Eden (*'ēden*). God plants "a garden in Eden" (Gen 2:8), and "Eden" (in Ezekiel) elliptically represents this primeval "garden of (= which is in) Eden."[62] In its verbal form, the root *'dn* means "luxuriate, feast, live luxuriously"; and as an appellative it "refers to that which is associated with a luxurious life."[63] Eden thus designates a well-watered, fertile area epitomized by the gardens of a deity, the ultimate sovereign.[64] A Sumero-Akkadian word meaning "steppe" had long been proposed as the origin of biblical Eden, but that idea has lost credibility because of the evidence of the Tell Fekheriye bilingual in which old Aramaic *m'dn* is equivalent to an Assyrian verb meaning "to enrich, make abundant."[65] That abundance is the result of plentiful water.[66] The term *m'dn* appears in the inscription as an epithet of Hadad, the life-giving water-god; and it directly follows an epithet calling the god "water-controller of all rivers." This imagery is surely relevant to the designation of Eden as a well-watered, luxuriant garden, a place for elites—gods and kings—and off-limits to humans except for its caretakers. The Eden imagery, like that of gardens, bears no resemblance to the circumstances of daily life for most Israelites. It is not a place for the production of essential foodstuffs. It is the pleasure realm of the elites of agrarian societies.

Food and the First Offspring

The Cain and Abel episode of the first family story presents a conflict arising from the two components of the dry-farming subsistence strategy of the highlands—field crops and supplemental animal husbandry. In the language that precedes (Gen 2:5) and concludes (Gen 3:17–19, 23) the Eden tale, the primal couple are agrarians; and their offspring follow in their parental footsteps, each playing a role in the agrarian household envisioned as the fundamental way of life since the beginning of time.[67] In Gen 4:2, Cain does the cultivation—"works the arable ground"—and Abel tends the "small livestock" (*ṣō'n*).[68] Abel is the herder because, in the division of labor

---

[62] Greenberg, *Ezekiel*, 581.
[63] Kedar-Kopfstein, "*'ēden*," 483–484.
[64] Kedar-Kopfstein, "*'ēden*," 487–488.
[65] See, *inter alia*, Alan R. Millard, "The Etymology of Eden," *VT* 34 (1984): 103–106.
[66] Jonas C. Greenfield, "A Touch of Eden," in *Orientalia J. Duchesne-Guillemin Emerito Oblata* (Acta Iranica 23; Leiden: Brill, 1984), 221–224.
[67] See the discussion above of Gen 2:5.
[68] This translation of *ṣō'n*, rather than the usual "sheep," is that of G. Waschke ("*ṣō'n*," *TDOT* 12:200), who recognizes that *ṣō'n* designates the small herd animals, both sheep and

typical of agrarian households comprising farming and herding regimes, the task of tending to the animals usually falls to the youngest son (or perhaps to daughters).[69] The brothers together are carrying out the tasks of an agrarian food system. Moreover, the sibling rivalry and conflict that are also part of this episode (and other Genesis narratives) is rooted in agrarian territorial issues. Older son-younger son tension is rooted in Israelite patrilineality, in which the older son is the primary heir and thus has more prestige and power. When kinship groups share limited resources of arable land, sibling conflict arises and has potentially dire results if not resolved by negotiation.[70]

In short, the Cain-Abel episode is rooted in tension between brothers working in the same socio-economic system, not between a farmer and a nomad representing discrete systems.[71] The long-held notion of a settled-nomadic dichotomy as the underlying socio-economic pattern of this narrative is no longer tenable—at least not in the way usually supposed, as will become clear in the Discussion section below.

The tragic clash between the first children arises because of what they each bring to YHWH: field crops and animals. Food for the deity is the issue. Their sacrifices are called *minḥâ* (in 4:3–5), which is a general term for an offering as a gift to the deity. But what they offer differs according to their responsibilities in the mixed agrarian economy of the highlands. Cain's offering corresponds to his role as a cultivator in the household of the first family. His offering is called *pĕrî hā'ădāmâ*, a phrase representing all the food crops of the highland agrarian regime.[72] But are they suitable offerings? Biblical texts mentioning food crops as offerings call them *bikkurim*, sometimes with *rē'šît*, meaning "first products" or "choice prod-

---

goats, typically herded together in the Palestinian highlands because they required the same type of pasturage.

[69] E.g., David, as youngest son, takes the family flocks out to pasture (1 Sam 17:14–15, 34; 2 Sam 7:8). Herding is virtually always the task of children rather than adults; see Candice Bradley, "Women's Power, Children's Labor," *Cross-Cultural Research* 27 (1993): 77, 92, Table 19.

[70] Hiebert, *Yahwist's Landscape*, 40. The negative example of the Cain-and-Abel conflict contrasts strongly with the less violent resolutions of other family conflicts in Genesis: Abraham and Lot, Jacob and Esau, Joseph and his brothers.

[71] Hiebert, *Yahwist's Landscape*, 38–39.

[72] Cf. Deut 28:51, where that phrase is paired with animal offspring to denote the two parts of the subsistence system; and it is equated with "grain, wine, and oil" in the second part of the verse. The semantic scope of *pĕrî* is thus different from its use in the Eden tale, where it denotes tree fruit as opposed to field crops. See Benjamin Kedar-Kopfstein and Heinz-Josef Fabry, "*pārâ; pĕrî*," *TDOT* 12:86.

ucts" (e.g., Exod 23:19; Num 18:13). Thus Cain apparently did not bring proper foodstuffs. Abel's offering is presented in greater detail. He brings a first-born animal, a gift that has higher status than do field crops, at least in the biblical taxonomy of sacrificial substances.[73] Pentateuchal texts, for example, insist that first-born clean beasts belong to YHWH (e.g., Exod 13:2; 34:19; Lev 27:26), and no such special selectivity is mentioned for first fruits. In addition, Abel's offering is the fatty portion, which is the best part of the animal and considered a special delicacy (cf. Ps 63:5 [Heb. 63:6]).

Just as an ancient Israelite, whether peasant or king, would prefer a gift of fatty, tender (young) meat instead of mundane field crops, so too does YHWH favor Abel's gift. As noted in the Dietary Regime section, meat in the ancient Near East was the food for deities and elites but was only occasionally consumed by peasant farmers. If the text is not explicit in giving YHWH's reason for favoring the animal sacrifice, it is because the reason would be so obvious to the ancient audience. In relation to the subsistence economy and the attendant cultural value of animal foods in ancient Israel, of course Abel's offering would be favored. Familiarity with the food system that is the context for the Cain-Abel episode makes YHWH's response comprehensible.

The ensuing murder of Abel leads to the banishment of Cain. The theme of expulsion following wrong-doing plays out in this episode as in the preceding Eden one. Cain's parents had to leave the idyllic garden and begin their difficult lives as farmers; now Cain must depart from that agrarian life. YHWH sends him away with the ringing words *nāʾ wānād tihyeh bāʾāreṣ* (Gen 4:12; cf. 4:14). The two verbs (*nûaʿ* and *nûd*) each indicate a back-and-forth motion such as the swaying of a reed in the water (1 Kgs 14:15) or tree branches in the wind (Isa 7:2); but when the latter denotes wandering, it portrays it as a miserable plight (Ps 56:8 [Heb. 56:9]). Together, the two verbs perhaps serve as a hendiadys, indicating that Cain will be "wandering unhappily on the earth." Rather than denoting the status of a fugitive, as is often assumed, the verbs portrays Cain's entry into another subsistence mode, that of the pastoralist or semi-pastoralist. Two other features of Cain's dismissal from his parents' household support this understanding. First is that he will be moving about on the *ʾereṣ* "earth," not on the agrarian's *ʾădāmâ*, "arable land." Second, Cain is told explicitly that the *ʾădāmâ* will "no longer be productive for you" (Gen 4:12). Sometimes translated "strength,"

---

[73] Matitiahu Tsevat, "*běkhôr, bkr, běhkōrâh, bikûrrîm*," *TDOT* 2:122.

kōaḥ in this verse means "produce" or "bounty," that is, the yield of the vital energy or strength of the cultivable ground (cf. Job 31:39).

Abel is dead, and Cain's life as a farmer has come tragically to an end. Yet the agrarian life of the first family is not doomed. Rather, it is sustained when the first parents have a third son, Seth (Gen 4:25), who replaces Abel as the younger son. But, as elsewhere in Genesis, the younger displaces the elder; and later-born Seth also replaces the banished Cain as heir to the family's agrarian life.[74] The genealogical traditions that follow provide appropriate lineages for both Seth and Cain.[75] In Gen 5, Seth is the fitting ascendant of the lineage leading from Adam through Lamech to Noah, who is called "a man of arable ground" (Gen 9:20). The Cainite lineage of Gen 4 stops with Lamech, whose sons eponymously represent animal husbandry (pastoralism) and the closely related "arts" of music and metallurgy, whose practitioners are often itinerants.[76] Cain the wanderer is thus the ascendant of those three migratory groups.[77]

Discussion

Two socio-economic patterns, settled (agrarian) and migratory, form the socio-economic background for the first-family episodes in Genesis. Israelite agrarian life—a dry-farming system (rainfall agriculture) in which humans are dependant mainly on crops, with small herd animals playing an important but subsidiary role—appears as the norm in YHWH God's announcement of the three elements of existence in Gen 2:5. However, as agrarians in the Iron Age highlands would have known all too well, agrarian subsistence was fraught with difficulty. Peasants in such situations typically imagine what the effortless life of the elites might be like. Eden is thus a garden in which the three elements of agrarian reality are problem free: tall and fruitful trees for pleasure eating rather than field crops and pasturage for survival; constantly flowing water sources rather than unreliable rainfall; and humans guarding the luxuriant growth rather than laboriously

---

[74] See Joel N. Lohr, "Righteous Abel, Wicked Cain: Genesis 4:1–16 in the Masoretic Text, the Septuagint, and the New Testament," *CBQ* 71 (2009): 486, 495.

[75] For a comparison of the Gen 4 and 5 genealogies, see Arnold, *Genesis*, 84–87.

[76] These "professions" are linked in classical mythology; so Nahum M. Sarna, *The JPS Torah Commentary: Genesis* (Philadelphia: Jewish Publication Society, 1989), 37.

[77] The etymology of his name (*qayin*) may also connect him with itinerant groups and even to the Kenites; see Baruch Halpern, "Kenites," *ABD* 4:17–19, and Richard S. Hess, "Cain," *ABD* 1:806.

cultivating the soil. Both in time and space, Eden is far removed from the agrarian economy, with its persistent crop failures and concomitant hunger and malnutrition. The blissful and fleeting experience of the first couple in the Eden garden is the exemplar for the eschatological hope of an altogether different world in biblical prophecy (e.g., Isa 58:11; Jer 31:12; Ezek 36:35; Amos 9:14). These texts depict an *Endzeit* Eden that would give everyone access to the luxuriant plenty of *Urzeit* Eden.[78] As in many cultural imaginings of an idyllic place of effortless existence, the Eden (or garden) concept is an expression of hope for relief from the anxieties and labors of daily life.[79]

As different as peasant reality is from Eden, the true polar opposite of Eden in relation to the three elements of agrarian life lies in the subsistence mode of migratory peoples: they have little water; their territories support pasturage but not crops; and they do not primarily cultivate. Moreover, the livestock-based livelihood of ancient pastoralists was not fully self-sufficient but rather typically depended to some extent on adjacent agrarians, often in unwelcome ways. Pastoralists in the arid and semi-arid areas of the Near East to this day graze their flocks on the fringes of settled lands, or, in the dry season, on the stubble in the fields of agrarians, competing with agrarians for pasturage and at times stealing the animals of peasant farmers to enlarge their own herds.[80] In the social hierarchy of areas where pastoralists and agrarians overlap, the latter consider the former inferior.[81] Consequently, these groups were considered a threat to cultivators and are often presented negatively in Near Eastern literature, including the Hebrew Bible. The banished Cain of Gen 4 represents the migratory groups who frequently menaced the highland agrarians and are generally portrayed as enemies in the Hebrew Bible.[82] And prophetic texts present Eden and the wilderness environment of pastoralists as opposite realms. In the Isaiah passage already cited (51:3) the destruction of Zion makes her a "wilderness" and a "desert,"

---

[78] Its *Urzeit* quality is signaled by the use of *miqqedem* (2:8), which likely has a temporal sense meaning "from the beginning" rather than "in the east"; see Stordalen, *Echoes of Eden*, 261–270.

[79] Kedar-Kopfstein, "*ēden*," 488.

[80] Norman K. Gottwald, *The Tribes of Yahweh: A Sociology of the Religion of Liberated Israel* (Maryknoll, N.Y.: Orbis, 1979), 437–439. Pastoralists sometimes also engage in limited agriculture for a few months of the year.

[81] Harold A. Koster and Joan Bouza Koster, "Competition or Symbiosis?: Pastoral Adaptive Strategies in the Southern Argolid, Greece," in *Regional Variation in Modern Greece and Cyprus* (ed. Muriel Dimen and Ernestine Friedl; Annals of the New York Academy of Sciences 268; New York: Annals of the New York Academy of Sciences, 1976), 283.

[82] E.g., the Midianites and Amalekites in Judg 6:3–6.

but the restored land will be like Eden. Similarly, in Ezek 36:35 the "desolate" destroyed land will become like Eden; and in Joel 2:3 "desolate" wilderness is the opposite of the Eden garden. In both instances the root *šmm* ("desolate") denotes an uninhabited wasteland, lacking cultivable land and suitable only for wanderers.

The narratives of Gen 2–4, with the two first-family episodes read together, are etiologies for the contrasting subsistence modes—the agrarian norm and the migratory other. Peasants who sense that the product of their work is not entirely under their control and is not always sufficient to meet their needs inevitably seek to comprehend how that could be. Their difficult life is typically understood to be the result of a misdeed. In the Hebrew Bible, human disobedience in the Eden episode explains the hardships of agrarian life. The Cain episode then introduces another subsistence mode. Migratory life, etiologically explained as punishment for the heinous crime of fratricide, is the truly unacceptable way of life.[83] The reality of peasant life may be dramatically different from idyllic Eden, but it is a less onerous fate than that of itinerant peoples. A strikingly similar contrast between hard-working, "good" farmers and pastoralists who are bandits or barbarians, permeates classical literature.[84]

Both episodes in Gen 2–4 portray the negative consequences of human wrongdoing. Elsewhere in the Pentateuch, conversely, proper behavior—individually and collectively, in human interactions and in religious life—is related to the hope for agrarian prosperity. Rather than Edenic bliss, obedience to God means that abundant rains will come at the right seasons (Lev 26:3–4; Deut 28:12) and that both crops and livestock, requiring cultivating and shepherding, will flourish (Deut 28:4, 11). Agrarian labor is assumed and accepted as part of achieving that prosperity.[85] People would still work, but the problems of agrarian life would come to an end. Complying with God's commandments would mean that the storehouses of heaven—that is, rainfall—would be available to the peasantry (Deut 28:12), whose own storehouses would thus be filled. The socio-economic environment is a powerful

---

[83] The word "brother" occurs seven times Gen 4:1–17, thus emphasizing that Cain's death is fratricide; and the word "sin" first appears in the Bible in Gen 4:7 in relation to Cain's horrific act.

[84] Garnsey, *Food and Society*, 61–71.

[85] Although there are instances in the Hebrew Bible—such as the oppressive servitude in Egypt, or the forced work of day-laborers or slaves—of negative views about work, agricultural labor is generally viewed positively, despite its uncertainties and difficulties, as is typical of peasant societies; so Jackson ("Enjoying the Fruit"), who has looked at attitudes to work in similar peasant cultures.

factor shaping biblical themes and language; food is thus a major thematic presence not only in the episodes of the first family at the beginning of time but also in images of future time.

SELECT BIBLIOGRAPHY

Borowski, Oded. "Eat, Drink, and Be Merry: The Mediterranean Diet." *Near Eastern Archaeology* 67 (2004): 96–107.
Hiebert, Theodore. *The Yahwist's Landscape: Nature and Religion in Early Israel*. New York: Oxford University Press, 1996.
Hopkins, David C. *The Highlands of Canaan: Agricultural Life in the Early Iron Age*. Social World of Biblical Antiquity Series, 3. Sheffield: Almond, 1985.
———. "Life on the Land: The Subsistence Struggles of Early Israel." *Biblical Archaeologist* 50 (1987): 178–191.
———. "'All Sorts of Field Work': Agricultural Labor in Ancient Palestine." Pages 149–172 in *To Break Every Yoke: Essays in Honor of Marvin L. Chaney*. Edited by Robert B. Coote and Norman K. Gottwald. Social World of Biblical Antiquity. Second Series 2. Sheffield: Sheffield Phoenix Press, 2007.
Jacobs-Hornig, B. "*gan*." *TDOT* 3:34–39.
Kedar-Kopfstein, Benjamin. "'ēden; 'ādan; 'ădînâ; 'ădānîm; 'ednâ; ma'ădannîm; ma'ădannôt." *TDOT* 10: 481–490.
MacDonald, Nathan. *Not Bread Alone: The Uses of Food in the Old Testament*. Oxford: Oxford University Press, 2008.
———. *What Did the Ancient Israelites Eat?: Diet in Biblical Times*. Grand Rapids, Mich.: Eerdmans, 2008.
Mettinger, Tryggve, N.D. *The Eden Narrative: A Literary and Religio-Historical Study of Genesis 2–3*. Winona Lake, Ind.: Eisenbrauns, 2007.
Meyers, Carol. "The Function of Feasts: An Anthropological Perspective on Israelite Religious Festivals." In *Social Theory and the Study of Israelite Religion: Retrospect and Prospect*. Edited by Saul M. Olyan. Resources for Biblical Study. Atlanta: Society of Biblical Literature, **forthcoming**.
Millard, Alan R. "The Etymology of Eden." *Vetus Testamentum* 34 (1984): 103–106.
Newsom, Carol A. "Common Ground: An Ecological Reading of Genesis 2–3." Pages 60–72 in *The Earth Story in Genesis*. Edited by Norman C. Habel and Shirley Wurst. The Earth Bible 2. Sheffield: Sheffield Academic Press, 2000.
Stordalen, Terje. *Echoes of Eden: Genesis 2–3 and Symbolism of the Eden Garden in Biblical Hebrew Literature*. Contributions to Biblical Exegesis and Theology 25. Leuven: Peeters, 2000.

ABRAHAM TRADITIONS IN THE HEBREW BIBLE OUTSIDE THE BOOK OF GENESIS

Thomas Römer

Introduction

When archeology of Israel/Palestine ceased to be "Biblical Archaeology" and liberated itself from the control of biblical scholars, the status of the Bible for the interpretation of archeological discoveries was significantly revised. The reconstruction of the history of Israel and Judah in the Bronze and Iron Ages needs no longer to start with the biblical accounts but rather with the interpretation of "archaeological evidence." Only then, after this initial step, can and should biblical texts be used as secondary sources among others.[1]

In what follows, I will apply a similar methodology to the question of the origins and composition of the Abraham traditions in the Hebrew Bible. Recent scholarship regarding the Abraham cycle can be divided in two groups. The first approach argues that the formation of Gen 12–36 has to be explained in the context of a global model applied to the entire Pentateuch, namely the documentary hypothesis. Some scholars have adopted quite a late date for the Yahwist (in the exilic period) and abandoned or radically modified the Elohistic document,[2] whereas others reaffirm,

---

[1] For the debate about the use of archaeology and biblical sources for the construction of a history of Israel and Judah see, among others, Ernst Axel Knauf, "From History to Interpretation," in *The Fabric of History: Text, Artifact and Israel's Past* (ed. Diana Vikander Edelman; JSOTSup 127; Sheffield: Sheffield Academic Press, 1991), 26–64; Thomas L. Thompson, *Early History of the Israelite People: From the Written and Archaeological Sources* (SHANE 4; Leiden: Brill, 1992); Jean-Daniel Macchi, "Histoire d'Israël ou Histoire de la Palestine?," *ETR* 70 (1995): 85–97; Hans M. Barstad, "History and the Hebrew Bible" in *Can a 'History of Israel' Be Written?* (ed. Lester L. Grabbe; JSOTSup 245; Sheffield: Sheffield Academic Press, 1997), 37–64; and Israel Finkelstein and Neil Asher Silberman, *The Bible Unearthed: Archeology's New Vision of Ancient Israel and the Origin of its Sacred Texts* (New York: Free Press, 2001).

[2] Christoph Levin, *Der Jahwist* (FRLANT 157; Göttingen: Vandenhoeck & Ruprecht, 1993); John Van Seters, *The Pentateuch: A Social Science Commentary* (Trajectories; Sheffield: Sheffield Academic Press, 1999); Hans-Christoph Schmitt, *Arbeitsbuch zum Alten Testament* (UTB 2146; Göttingen: Vandenhoeck & Ruprecht, 2005).

sometimes quite dogmatically, the value of the classical hypothesis as elaborated by Kuenen and Wellhausen.[3] Yet, it seems that all scholars working with a documentary hypothesis agree that the (literary) formation of the Abraham traditions is simply part of the first edition of a narrative spanning the whole Pentateuch and undertaken by J (or E).

The second approach suggests that the (literary) link between the Patriarchs and Exodus was made at a fairly late point, and that the first stages of the formation of the Abraham traditions took place in the context of the elaboration of a Patriarchal narrative, unrelated at that point to the composition of other pentateuchal traditions.[4] These scholars, who favor a "fragmentary hypothesis," present various diachronic schemas,[5] but they agree that a specific model for the understanding of Gen 12–36 is more appropriate than the documentary hypothesis.

Can an investigation of Abraham outside of Genesis provide some clarification in this debate? Or to put the question differently: what would we know about the Abraham traditions (and the formation of the Abraham cycle) if all that we possessed were the books of the Hebrew Bible apart from Genesis?

A First Overview

The various references to Abraham in the Hebrew Bible outside of the Book of Genesis can be classified depending on whether Abraham appears alone or is mentioned together with other figures from the Ancestral Narratives.

---

[3] Horst Seebass, "Pentateuch," *TRE* 26 (1996): 185–209; Ludwig Schmidt, "Im Dickicht der Pentateuchforschung: Ein Plädoyer für die umstrittene Neuere Urkundenhypothese," *VT* 60 (2010): 400–420. See, somewhat differently, Joel S. Baden, *J, E, and the Redaction of the Pentateuch* (FAT 68; Tübingen: Mohr Siebeck, 2009).

[4] Rolf Rendtorff, *The Problem of the Process of Transmission in the Pentateuch* (JSOTSup 89; Sheffield: JSOT Press, 1990 [German original 1976]); Erhard Blum, *Die Komposition der Vätergeschichte* (WMANT 57; Neukirchen-Vluyn: Neukirchener, 1984); David M. Carr, *Reading the Fractures of Genesis: Historical and Literary Approaches* (Louisville: Westminster John Knox Press, 1996); and Matthias Köckert, "Die Geschichte der Abrahamüberlieferung," in *Congress Volume Leiden 2004* (ed. André Lemaire; VTSup 109; Leiden: Brill, 2006), 103–128.

[5] For on overview of the different positions see Jan Christian Gertz, Konrad Schmid, and Markus Witte, eds., *Abschied vom Jahwisten: die Komposition des Hexateuch in der jüngsten Diskussion* (BZAW 315; Berlin: de Gruyter, 2002); and Thomas B. Dozeman and Konrad Schmid, eds., *A Farewell to the Yahwist? The Composition of the Pentateuch in Recent European Interpretation* (SBLSymS 34; Atlanta: Society of Biblical Literature, 2006).

Abraham	Ezek 33:24; Ps 47:10;[6] 2 Chr 20:7; Neh 9:7–8; Ps 105:42
Abraham + Isaac	
Abraham + Sarah	Isa 51:2
Abraham + Jacob (* = Israel)	Isa 29:22; 41:8; 63:16*; Mic 7:20; Ps 105:6
Abraham + Isaac + Jacob (* = Israel)	Exod 2:24; 3:6, 15, 16; 4:5; 6:3, 8; 32:13*; 33:1; Lev 26:42; Num 32:11; Deut 1:8; 6:10; 9:5, 27; 29:12; 30:20; 34:4; Josh 24:2–5; 1 Kgs 18:36*; 2 Kgs 13:23; Jer 33:26 (MT[7]); 1 Chr 1:27–34*; 1 Chr 29:18*; 2 Chr 30:6*; Ps 105:9–10 (= 1 Chr 16:16–17)

The above list warrants a number of observations. In some texts, Abraham appears alone without the other patriarchs. Outside the Torah, he is most often mentioned in the books of Isaiah and in Chronicles. He is never mentioned with Isaac alone, but several times with Jacob (or Israel). Most often he appears in a triad with Isaac and Jacob (Israel) and those texts do generally not contain much specific information. They speak of the "God of Abraham, Isaac and Jacob" (Exod 3:6, 15,16; 4:5; 1 Kgs 18:36; 1 Chr 29:18; 2 Chr 30:6), of the covenant that YHWH made with the Patriarchs (Exod 2:24; 6:8; Lev 26:42; Deut 29:12; 2 Kgs 23,23), or of the land that he swore to give to them or to their offspring (Exod 6:8; 33:1; Num 32:11; Deut 1:8; 6:10; 9:5; 30:20; 34:4). Sometimes, all three are simply called "YHWH's servants" (Exod 32:13; Deut 9:27). These texts are probably quite late and presuppose the Patriarchal traditions of Genesis. Generally speaking, none of the texts that mention Abraham outside of Genesis can be dated before the sixth century BCE. That essentially means that Abraham's (literary) career probably starts much later than Jacob's.

In those passages where Abraham appears alone, Ezek 33:24 is most interesting and we will start our inquiry with that passage.

Ezekiel 33:24: Abraham and the Land

The passage Ezek 33:23–29 contains a *disputatio*[8] against the inhabitants of the land (Jerusalem?) who were not in exile and who claimed possession of the land. It begins by quoting a claim of the population:

> The word of YHWH came to me: "Son of man, the inhabitants of these ruins (ישבי החרבות) in the land of Israel are saying, 'Abraham was only one (אחד),

---

[6] V. 5 mentions Jacob.
[7] Lacking in the LXX.
[8] Walter Zimmerli, *Ezechiel* (BK 13; Neukirchen-Vluyn: Neukirchener, 1969), 817.

yet he possessed the land (וַיִּירַשׁ אֶת־הָאָרֶץ), but we are many; to us the land has been given (לָנוּ נִתְּנָה) for a possession (לְמוֹרָשָׁה).'" (vv. 23–24)

This claim is heavily rejected by the prophet and further destruction is announced:

> This is what you must say to them, "This is what the Lord YHWH says: 'As surely as I live, those living in the ruins (אֲשֶׁר בֶּחֳרָבוֹת) will die by the sword, those in the open field I will give (נְתַתִּיו) to the wild beasts for food, and those who are in the strongholds and caves will die of disease. I will turn the land into a desolate ruin (וְנָתַתִּי אֶת־הָאָרֶץ שְׁמָמָה) ... Then they will know that I am YHWH when I turn the land into a desolate ruin (בְּתִתִּי אֶת־הָאָרֶץ שְׁמָמָה) because of all the abominable deeds they have committed.'" (vv. 27–29)

This rejection uses a play on words through the root נתן: Instead of the land, YHWH will "give" its inhabitants to death and their land to desolation. This might point to a conflict between the deportees of 597 and those who remained in the land.

Verses 25–26, which mention cultic reasons for the divine judgment against the inhabitants of the land, are missing in the LXX*[9] and are therefore probably a very late addition.[10] It is disputed whether this oracle should be attributed to the prophet Ezekiel himself[11] or a "golah-oriented" redaction[12] revising the original message of the prophet in order to strengthen the claim that the first Babylonian golah represented the true Israel. Even if the passage is the work of a later redaction it is very plausible that Ezek 33:24 quotes an existing saying of the non-deported Judean population. Their claim about the land is probably directed against the exiles; this is clearly the case in a parallel passage in 11:14–18.[13] Another possibility would be that the adage refers to Edomite occupation of the land after the fall of Judah (see the root ירש in Ezek 35:10 and the substantive מוֹרָשָׁה in 36:2–3, 5).[14] But the polemical context makes it more plausible that here we witness an inner Judean conflict between the Babylonian golah and the 'people of the land.'

---

[9] In the LXX the messenger formula at the beginning of v. 25 introduces the oracle of vv. 27–29. There is also a change between the second person singular in vv. 25–26 to the 3rd person plural in v. 27.

[10] Against Zimmerli, *Ezechiel*, 815.

[11] See Zimmerli, *Ezechiel*, 818, and most commentaries.

[12] So especially Karl-Friedrich Pohlmann, *Das Buch des Propheten Hesekiel (Ezechiel): Kapitel 20–48* (ATD 22.2; Göttingen: Vandenhoeck & Ruprecht, 2001), 454–456. Similarly Jörg Garscha, *Studien zum Ezechielbuch: Eine redaktionskritische Untersuchung* (EHS 23/23; Bern: Peter Lang, 1974), 298–302.

[13] Ezek 11:15 contains a parallel formulation: לָנוּ [הִיא] נִתְּנָה הָאָרֶץ לְמוֹרָשָׁה but without reference to Abraham.

[14] So Pohlmann, *Hesekiel*, 454–456.

The reference to Abraham is particularly interesting. Firstly, it is assumed that he is a known figure, which clearly indicates that the oldest Abraham traditions are not an invention from the Babylonian period. Secondly, he is presented as אחד, as "one." This adverb creates an opposition with the רבים. It is also noteworthy that the link with Jacob or a land promised to Jacob is apparently unimportant (or unknown?). Thirdly, the text says that Abraham possessed or took possession of the land, which indicates that the saying of the non-deportees is based upon an Abraham tradition—one that told how the patriarch came to possess the land. Interestingly, there is no allusion to a divine gift or the promise of the land. Furthermore there is no indication of a "Mesopotamian" origin of the patriarch. Abraham appears as an autochthonous figure. A tradition about Abraham's immigration from Mesopotamia would have been seen as contrary to the claims of the people who remained in the land.[15] Without knowing the Genesis account, one could imagine the existence of a "profane" settlement of the Patriarch. The verb ירש is very rare in the Abraham traditions;[16] however, it occurs five times in Gen 15, probably the latest text of the Abraham cycle.[17] Therefore it seems plausible that Gen 15 presupposes the saying or the tradition of Ezek 33:24 and reinterprets it as a divine promise for "all Israel"—those in the land, and those whom YHWH will bring back to the land.[18] Outside of Ezekiel, the term occurs only in Deut 33:4 and Exod 6:8. The latter may also depend on Ezek 33:24. Exod 6:8 would then also be a new reading of the claim of Ezek 33:24, since Exod 6:8 announces the possession, by the Exodus generation, of the land that YHWH had promised by oath to the Patriarchs.[19]

---

[15] This supports the hypothesis that the idea of Abraham's origin in Mesopotamia only occurs in the latest layers of the Abraham tradition; see also Köckert, "Abrahamüberlieferung," 106.

[16] It is much more frequent in Deuteronomy and in dtr texts. Outside Gen 15 it occurs only in 21:10 (in the sense of "be an heir"), 22:17 and 24:60 ("possess the gates of the enemies"). In the Jacob story see the P-text 28:4 ("to possess the land of sojourning").

[17] John Ha, *Genesis 15: A Theological Compendium of Pentateuchal History* (BZAW 181; Berlin New York: 1989); Thomas Römer, "Gen 15 und Gen 17: Beobachtungen und Anfragen zu einem Dogma der 'neueren' und 'neuesten' Pentateuchkritik," *DBAT* 26 (1990): 32–47; and Konrad Schmid, *Erzväter und Exodus: Untersuchungen zur doppelten Begründung der Ursprünge Israels innerhalb der Geschichtsbücher des Alten Testaments* (WMANT 81; Neukirchen-Vluyn: Neukirchener, 1999), 172–185.

[18] Thomas Römer, *Israels Väter: Untersuchungen zur Väterthematik im Deuteronomium und in der deuteronomistischen Tradition* (OBO 99; Göttingen: Vandenhoeck & Ruprecht, 1990), 515–516.

[19] Peter Weimar, *Untersuchungen zur priesterschriftlichen Exodusgeschichte* (FB 9; Würzburg: Echter Verlag, 1973), 150; and Bernard Gosse, "Exode 6,8 comme réponse à Ezéchiel 33,24," *RHPR* 74 (1994): 241–247.

To sum up: Ezek 33:24 is probably the oldest attestation of Abraham outside of the book of Genesis. It shows that he is a known figure and that his tradition is related to the possession of the land.

The other texts in which we find Abraham mentioned in relation to the land are much more recent. In 2 Chr 20:7 a prayer of Jehoshaphat, which has no parallel in the books of Kings, mentions the land that YHWH gave to Abraham's offspring: "Did you not, O our God, drive out (הורשת) the inhabitants of this land (את־ישבי הארץ) before your people Israel, and give it to the offspring of your friend Abraham for ever?" Interestingly, the root ירש occurs again, but this time in the *hiphil* and in a military sense, as is the case also especially in the books of Numbers, Deuteronomy, Joshua and Judges. And, in keeping with the dtr tradition, the 'inhabitants of the land' are the autochthonous people that must be expelled from the land. Apparently the Chronicler wants to combine the tradition of the conquest of the land with the Abraham land tradition. An additional text speaking of the gift of the land to Abraham alone is Neh 9:7–8, to which we will return later. This passage obviously summarizes Gen 15, but in contrast to this text, it quotes the standard list of the nations with six names.[20] Therefore, we have here a strategy similar to 2 Chr 20:7. The list of the people belongs to the dtr tradition of the land and is now linked to Abraham. In both texts, Abraham has apparently become the most important Patriarch. This is also the case in Ps 105, a text that apparently presupposes (a first edition of) the Pentateuch.[21] This Psalm mentions the Patriarchs in detail (vv. 9–10), including Joseph (vv. 17–22). But, like Neh 9, Abraham receives a privileged position, since he appears at the end of the summary in 105:42 in a statement indicating that YHWH's beneficent interventions for Israel took place because of his word to Abraham (v. 42), which also includes the gift of the land (v. 44: the lands of the nations).[22]

---

[20] The standard form has six or seven names; cf. Tomoo Ishida, "The Structure and Historical Implications of the Lists of Pre-Israelite Nations," *Bib* 60 (1979): 461–490. The author of Gen 15:19–21 adds three unusual names of groups that have very positive relations with Israel, transforming the bellicose character of the list. For more details see Thomas Römer, "Abraham and the 'Law and the Prophets'," in *The Reception and Remembrance of Abraham* (ed. Pernille Carstens and Niels Peter Lemche; PHSC 13; Piscataway, N.J.: Gorgias Press, 2011), 87–102.

[21] Hans-Joachim Kraus, *Psalmen* (BKAT 15.2; Neukirchen-Vluyn: Neukirchener, 1978), 719.

[22] The astonishing and singular expression ארצות גוים does not really fit the conquest of Canaan; on this expression see my comments on Ps 105.

Isaiah 51:2: Abraham and His Descendants

The saying about Abraham and his possession of the land quoted in Ezek 33:24 seems presupposed by the author of Isa 51:1–3:

> Listen to me, you that pursue righteousness, you that seek YHWH. Look to the rock from which you were hewn, and to the cavity, the cistern[23] from which you were dug.
>
> Look to Abraham your father and to Sarah who bore you; for he was one (אחד) when I called him (קראתיו), I blessed him (ואברכהו)[24] and made him many (וארבהו).
>
> For YHWH will comfort Zion; he will comfort all her ruins (כל־חרבתיה), and will make her wilderness like Eden, her desert like the garden of YHWH ...

These verses open a section, which ends in Isa 51:11[25] and whose theme is the restoration of Zion: vv. 1–3 mention Sarah, Abraham, and their offspring and Zion's consolation; vv. 9–11 allude to YHWH's battle against the Sea as an image for the (new) exodus, which allows for the return of the exiles (v. 3 and v. 11 contain the same expression "joy and gladness"); and the middle section (vv. 4–8) deals with YHWH's justice and law.[26]

One finds rather divergent opinions about the literary unity and the date of this passage. Against the traditional attribution to Second Isaiah,[27] a number of scholars postulate different redactional layers.[28] According to

---

[23] בור (lacking in Syr) may be a gloss to explain the *hapax legomenon* מקבת.

[24] For the vocalization of the MT, and the rendering as a past tense in the versions, see John Goldingay and David F. Payne, *A Critical and Exegetical Commentary on Isaiah 40–55* (ICC; 2 vols.; London: T&T Clark, 2006), 2:224. 1 Q Isa reads "I made/make him fruitful" (ואפרהו) which fits the context very well. The couple פרה and רבה appears especially in priestly or later texts of Genesis, Exod 1:7, and Lev 26:9 (in *hiphil* only Gen 17:20; 28:3; 48:4; Lev 26:9). It is difficult to decide whether this was the original text. One could argue that the MT altered the text in order to make it fit with Gen 12:2. On the other hand, the Qumran reading may also be understood as an attempt to parallel the text with a standard expression of Genesis (see Edward Y. Kutscher, *The Language and Linguistic Background of the Isaiah Scroll* [STDJ 6; Leiden: Brill, 1974], 275–276). פרה in the *hiphil* is used in relation to Abraham (and Ishmael) in the P text Gen 17:6 and 20 (against Hans-Jürgen Hermisson, *Deuterojesaja 49,14–52,12* [BKAT 11/12–14; Neukirchen-Vluyn: Neukirchener, 2010], 153).

[25] Many commentators argue that the passage ends in 51:8, but the parallel between v. 11 and v. 3 seems to favor a delimitation 51:1–11. The correspondence between Abraham at the beginning (v. 2) and the new exodus at the end (v. 10) further support this idea.

[26] For a more detailed structure see Frederick Holmgren, "Chiastic Structure in Isaiah LI 1–11," *VT* 19 (1969): 196–201.

[27] See, for instance (with regard to 51:1–10), Georg Fohrer, *Jesaja 40–66* (ZBK 19.3; 2nd ed.; Zürich: Theologischer Verlag, 1986), 143–148.

[28] See the summary of the different positions in Goldingay and Payne, *Isaiah 40–55* 2:221.

Steck, 51:1–8 belong to a global Isaiah redaction from the Hellenistic period, which already had the entire book in view, and reworked an older oracle in vv. 4–5 followed originally by vv. 9–10a.[29] Other commentators, like van Oorschot or Hermisson, consider that the different layers of 51:1–8 (9–11) were edited in the context of a still independent 'second Isaiah scroll.'[30] If, as is often argued, Isa 51:1–11 takes up and reinterprets themes from other passages of Second Isaiah (and not so much from the other parts of the book),[31] then it seems plausible to adopt the idea that 51:1–11 constitute a homogenous text created by a redactor who revises the older material from the very beginning of the Persian period.[32] The exact date of Isa 51:1–3 is difficult to assess. What is clear, however, is that the evocation of Sarah and Abraham seems to presuppose and to "correct" the passage of Ezek 33:23–29.

Ezek 33:23–24

Son of man, the inhabitants of these ruins (ישבי החרבות) in the land of Israel are saying, 'Abraham was one (אחד), yet he possessed the land, but we are many (רבים); to us the land has been given for a possession'

Isa 51:2–3

Look to <u>Abraham your father</u> and to Sarah who bore you; for <u>he was one</u> (אחד) when I called him, I blessed him <u>and made him many</u> (וארבהו). For YHWH will comfort Zion; he will comfort all her <u>ruins</u> (כל־חרבתיה)

Both texts share common features. They present Abraham as "one" and contrast him to his "many" descendants. Both texts mention the "ruins," even if with a different purpose. Whereas Ezek 33:24–29 is extremely hostile to the inhabitants of the "ruins," Isa 51:3 announces the consolation of Zion's

---

[29] Odil Hannes Steck, "Zions Tröstung: Beobachtungen und Fragen zu Jesaja 51,1–11" in *Die hebräische Bibel und ihre zweifache Nachgeschichte: Festschrift für Rolf Rendtorff zum 65. Geburtstag* (ed. Erhard Blum, Christian Macholz and Ekkehard W. Stegemann; Neukirchen-Vluyn: Neukirchener, 1990), 257–276 (reprinted in Steck, *Gottesknecht und Zion: Gesammelte Aufsätze zu Deuterojesaja* [FAT 4; Tübingen: Mohr, 1992], 73–91).

[30] Jürgen van Oorschot, *Von Babel zum Zion: Eine literarkritische und redaktionsgeschichtliche Untersuchung* (BZAW 206; Berlin: de Gruyter, 1993), 250–253 and *passim*; he argues that 51:9–10 belong to a "first Jerusalem redaction," 51:4–5 to an "imminent expectation" layer, and 51:1–2 and 7–8 to a "secondary Zion strand," which is the last redaction in the context of an independent scroll containing Isa 40–55*. Compare Hermisson, *Deuterojesaja 49,14–52,12*, 156–160.

[31] Karl Elliger, *Deuterojesaja in seinem Verhältnis zu Tritojesaja* (BWANT 63; Stuttgart: Kohlhammer, 1933), 200–204.

[32] See Hermisson, *Deuterojesaja 49,14–52,12*, 160, who speaks of a "redactional unity" (*redaktionelle Einheit*) of 51:1–8, with the possible exception of v. 6.

ruins. It looks as if the author of Isa 51:1–3[33] wanted to overcome the conflict between the inhabitants of the land and the exiles. Therefore he promises consolation for the ruins of Zion (v. 3) as well as the return of the exiles (v. 11), emphasizing the unity of "all Israel." In contrast to Ezek 33:23–29, the theme associated with Abraham is not land, but offspring. This is probably also the reason for the (only) mention of Sarah (outside the book of Genesis). Does this text presuppose a written Abraham story[34] and if so, in which form? According to Köckert, 51:2 presupposes the priestly text Gen 11:27–32 about Sarah's barrenness.[35] However, this theme also appears in the older story of Gen 16, and the root חיל is not related to sterility, but generally describes labor pains at birth. This root does not occur in Gen 12–25. The verb ברך occurs several times in the Abraham narrative,[36] but it is a very frequent verb for denoting God's favorable actions towards human beings; the verb רבה is however used in the P-text of Gen 17, but again we have to ask whether this really denotes a literary dependency. The rare expression "garden of YHWH" (Isa 51:3) appears in the Lot story (Gen 13:10), but in a different context, since there it designates the former regions of Sodom and Gomorrah.[37] And finally, the root קרא is not used in the Abraham story to describe God calling Abraham,[38] it seems more anchored in the context of Second Isaiah, where it appears frequently to express God's call of his people or servants.[39] Methodologically one can therefore explain the occurrence of this root in 51:2 as part of Second Isaiah's theology of "divine call," or as a *relecture* of this call, now applied to Abraham.[40]

Isa 51:2 suggests that the theme of offspring was an important part of the Abraham traditions, probably from the beginning. Therefore, the best solution is to consider 51:2 as an allusion to this motif, which does not depend on

---

[33] The parallels between Ezek 33:24 and Isa 51:2–3 invalidate van Oorschot's assertion (*Babel*, 248) that v. 3 has nothing to do with v. 2.

[34] Steck, *Gottesknecht und Zion*, 90.

[35] Köckert, "Abrahamüberlieferung," 110.

[36] See, however, the text-critical problem discussed above.

[37] This is the only other place it occurs in the Hebrew Bible; however, see "garden of god" in Ezek 28:13 and 31:8–9.

[38] In Gen 22:11 and 15 it is YHWH's angel that calls Abraham in order to stop his sacrifice. The only text where the deity calls someone directly is Gen 20:9, where the object is Abimelech. In most of the other cases, it simply means "to name" or describes a human invocation of God.

[39] See especially Isa 41:9; 42:6; 43:1,7; 45:1–3; 48:12–15; 49:1; 51:2.

[40] There is a close connection between Isa 51:2 and 41:8–9. This parallel will be discussed below.

a written text from the Genesis story.⁴¹ This is also supported by the somewhat strange 51:1, which has no parallel in Genesis: "Look to the rock (צור) from which you were hewn, and to the cavity, the cistern (מקבת בור) from which you were dug." It is often argued that these metaphors apply to Abraham (and Sarah) and are based on the archaic conception of people born out of earth or stones.⁴² This explanation supports the notion that Abraham was originally an autochthonous figure. The rock metaphor however is often applied to YHWH (see especially Deut 32:18, where the divine rock also gives birth [ילד and חיל] to the people or to Zion). The latter would fit well with the use of בור, which reminds one of Zion as a place of abundant water.⁴³ According to Steck, the "cutting off" refers to the exile from Zion,⁴⁴ but this does not fit very well with the parallel construction of v. 1 and v. 2. This structure suggests that the Zion metaphor is now transferred to Abraham and Sarah. In Isa 54:1 Zion is presented as a barren woman who has not been in labor (לא־חלה) and who will have many (רבים) children. If the author of Isa 51:1 already knows Isa 54:1, his aim would be to apply the traditional metaphor of Zion/Jerusalem as a wife (with YHWH as her 'husband')⁴⁵ to Abraham and Sarah. In 51:1–3 Zion is no longer the mother, rather it becomes the place where YHWH's beneficent intervention will happen. The new parents of Israel are now Abraham, who receives the title 'father,' and Sarah. This shift denotes an attempt to demythologize the Jerusalem/Zion tradition and to construct Abraham as the ancestor of 'all Israel.'⁴⁶

It should be noted, however, that elsewhere in the book of Isaiah this transfer of the title "father" to Abraham triggered a very sharp reaction. We will explore this issue more fully in the following section.

To summarize quickly the results of our analysis thus far, Ezek 33:24 and Isa 51:2 present the two main themes of the Abraham narrative in Genesis: land and offspring. Both texts probably do not depend on specific texts of Gen 12–26.⁴⁷ As such, they are the oldest references to Abraham outside the book of Genesis, and they lend support to the notion

---

[41] Hermann Vorländer, *Die Entstehungszeit des jehowistischen Geschichtswerkes* (EHS 32/109; Frankfurt: Peter Lang, 1978), 54–55.
[42] Fohrer, *Jesaja 40–66*, 143.
[43] Steck, *Gottesknecht und Zion*, 85. Interestingly the *hapax legomenon* מקבת ('cavity') occurs with other terms from Isa 51:1 in the Siloam Tunnel inscription; see J. Gerald Janzen, "Rivers in the Desert of Abraham and Sarah and Zion (Isaiah 51:1–3)," *HAR* 10 (1986): 139–155.
[44] Steck, *Gottesknecht und Zion*, 84–85.
[45] Van Oorschot, *Babel*, 260.
[46] Interestingly, Sarah is not explicitly called "mother."
[47] Again, note that the case is more disputed with regard to Isa 51:2.

that the oldest Abraham traditions already contained stories about the land and about Abraham's offspring.

Abraham in the Book of Isaiah

Abraham appears in all three parts of the book: besides 51:2, he is mentioned in 29:22; 41:8 and 63:16. He may therefore belong to a "book-redaction", which tries (probably in several steps) to unify the book by introducing traversing themes and recurring expressions, as shown by Rendtorff and others.[48]

In Isa 29:22–23 Abraham appears in a passage that announces Jacob's consolation:

> Therefore thus says YHWH to[49] the house of Jacob, who redeemed Abraham: No longer shall Jacob be ashamed, no longer shall his face grow pale. For when he sees his children, the work of my hands, in his midst, they will sanctify my name; they will sanctify the Holy One of Jacob, and will stand in awe of the God of Israel.

It is quite possible that the apposition אשר פדה את־אברהם is a later addition.[50] It interrupts the oracle, which is addressed to the house of Jacob. The root פדה seems to presuppose a tradition about Abraham's liberation from his idolatrous family, which is attested in Jubilees 12.[51] It is likely that an older oracle, originally addressed to Jacob, was revised by a redactor who, in the context of a later edition of the book Isaiah, wanted to transform Jacob's children into Abraham's children, in accordance with Isa 51:1–3. The evocation of Abraham in this verse may therefore belong to a late redaction of the Isaiah scroll.

---

[48] Rolf Rendtorff, "Zur Komposition des Buches Jesaja," *VT* 34 (1984): 295–320 (reprinted in his *Kanon und Theologie: Vorarbeiten zu einer Theologie des Alten Testaments* [Neukirchen-Vluyn: Neukirchener, 1991], 141–161).

[49] The Masoretic אֶל is often changed into אֵל (El, god; for instance, see Hans Wildberger, *Jesaja 28–39* [BKAT 10.3; Neukirchen-Vluyn: Neukirchener, 1982], 1134–1135), but this is unnecessary, especially if the apposition is to be considered as a gloss or a late insert. See also אלהים in v. 23.

[50] August Dillmann and Rudolf Kittel, *Der Prophet Jesaja* (KEHAT 5; 6th ed.; Leipzig: Hirzel, 1898), 266; cf. Willem A. Beuken, *Jesaja 28–39* (HTKAT; Freiburg: Herder, 2010), 147, who argues that the same redactor has added (in v. 23) "they will sanctify my name" and the following plural.

[51] Dillmann and Kittel, *Jesaja*, 266. Wildberger (*Jesaja 28–39*, 1143–1144) thinks that the dtr term פדה had been transferred here to Abraham. Beuken (*Jesaja 28–39*, 148) argues that Jub 12:20 cannot be the source of this addition. However, one might ask whether the redactor already knows a similar tradition.

The oracle of salvation in Isa 41:8–13, which takes up the Assyrian and Babylonian royal oracles,[52] opens with the following call:

> and you Israel, my servant, Jacob, whom I have chosen, offspring of Abraham, my friend, you whom I have seized from the extremities of the earth and called from its remote regions. I told you: You are my servant, I have chosen you and not rejected you. (41:1–8)

The triad "Israel, Jacob, Abraham" is somewhat astonishing and has no other parallels in the Hebrew Bible. Therefore one may ask whether the original text contained only the traditional *parallelismus membrorum*, "Israel // Jacob," very common in Second Isaiah,[53] and whether a later redactor added the second part of the verse.[54] This "Abraham redactor" could be the same one who redacted Isa 29 and the author of Isa 51:1–3. He would have added the two references to Abraham in Isa 29 and 41 in order to prepare the way for the transfer from Jacob to Abraham. However, most commentators consider that the mention of YHWH's friend Abraham was part of the original oracle. In this case it would be possible to understand v. 9—even though it is addressed to "Israel," a name which represents the Diaspora (?) community—as an allusion to Abraham's call out from Mesopotamia (Gen 12:1–3; 15:7).[55] Yet, the wording of v. 9 does not contain clear allusions to texts from Genesis, but reflects classical Second Isaiah terminology (Isa 40:28; 41:5; 43:6; 49:6, etc.). Hence, it seems more plausible to understand the reference to Abraham as a late insertion in order to reinterpret an older oracle[56] about the gathering of "Israel" by giving it a new foundation in YHWH's friendship[57] with Abraham. The friendship language used to describe the relationship between YHWH and Abraham does not occur in the Genesis account. The only parallel is in 2 Chr 20:7, a text that may depend on Isa 41:8.[58] This title, which expresses a close relationship between

---

[52] Claus Westermann, *Das Buch Jesaja: Kapitel 40–66* (ATD 19; 3rd ed.; Göttingen: Vandenhoeck & Ruprecht, 1966), 60–62.

[53] See for instance Ulrich Berges, *Jesaja 40–48* (HTKAT; Freiburg: Herder, 2008), 189.

[54] Fohrer, *Jesaja 40–66*, 36 and van Oorschot, *Babel*, 54, n. 162.

[55] See, among others, Westermann, *Jesaja 40–66*, 60; and Berges, *Jesaja 40–48*, 191.

[56] In later Jewish and Christian understanding this reinterpretation also affects 41:1–7. The rise and call of the unnamed Cyrus in 41:2 is related to Abraham's call; see Berges, *Jesaja 40–48*, 179.

[57] According to the MT the "lover" (or the "one-loving-me") is Abraham; in the LXX, Abraham is the object of YHWH's love ("whom-I-have-loved"). See further Moshe H. Goshen-Gottstein, "Abraham—Lover or Beloved of God," in *Love and Death in the Ancient Near East: Essays in Honor of Marvin H. Pope* (ed. John H. Marks and Robert McClive Good; Guilford, Conn.: Four Quarters Publishing, 1987), 101–104.

[58] Berges, *Jesaja 40–48*, 176 and 190. Outside the Hebrew Bible see CD 3:2; Jas 2:23; Sura 4:124.

Abraham and his God, may presuppose texts or traditions like Gen 18 or 22, where Abraham's loyalty vis-à-vis YHWH is depicted. This text thus prepares the reader for the "father" title given to Abraham in Isa 52:2, a title also criticized in the same book of Isaiah.

The last mention of Abraham occurs in the third part of the book in Isa 63:16:

> For you are our father. Abraham does not know us, and Israel does not recognize us. You, YHWH, are our father, 'our-deliverer-from-ancient-times (מעולם)' is your name.

The verse is part of the lamentation of 63:7–64:11[59] though its date is disputed.[60] It clearly reacts against Isa 52:3 (and probably also against Isa 58:13–14,[61] in which Jacob is mentioned as "father") claiming that only YHWH is the father of his people. This shows that, even if the passage 63:7–64:11 looks like an independent "psalm," it presupposes texts from Second and perhaps also First Isaiah[62] and was possibly created as a conclusion to the whole book of Isaiah.[63] Apparently there was some debate about the importance of Abraham (and Jacob?) as Israel's "father." The author of Isa 63:7–64:11 is aware of the other occurrences of Abraham (and Jacob) in Isaiah and, at the end of the book, he wants to downplay his function as an identity marker by rejecting a genealogical claim and perhaps also the entire Abraham traditions. Interestingly, the "historical summary" in v. 11 starts with remembering the "ancient days" (יְמֵי־עוֹלָם, cf. מֵעוֹלָם in v. 16) of YHWH's history with his people.

---

[59] Willem A.M. Beuken, 'Abraham weet van ons niet' (Jesaja 63:16): De grond van Israëls vertrouwen tijdens de ballingschap (Nijkerk: Callenbach, 1986); and Irmtraud Fischer, Wo ist Jahwe? Das Volksklagelied Jes 63,7–64,11 als Ausdruck des Ringens um eine gebrochene Beziehung (SBB 19; Stuttgart: Katholisches Bibelwerk, 1989).

[60] Traditionally this poem or prayer was thought to reflect the situation between 587 and 525. A redactor would thus have inserted this originally independent piece; see Westermann, Jesaja 40–66, 306–307; Jacques Vermeylen, Du prophète Isaïe à l'apocalyptique: Isaïe, I–XXXV, miroir d'un demi-millénaire d'expérience religieuse en Israël (EBib; Paris: Gabalda, 1978), 491–492; and John D.W. Watts, Isaiah 34–66 (WBC 25; Dallas: Word, 1987), 331. More recent publications suggest a date at the end of the Persian or beginning of the Hellenistic period; see Odil Hannes Steck, Studien zu Tritojesaja (BZAW 203; Berlin: de Gruyter, 1991), 241–242; and Johannes Goldenstein, Das Gebet der Gottesknechte: Jesaja 63,7–64,11 im Jesajabuch (WMANT 92; Neukirchen-Vluyn: Neukirchener, 2001), 228–235.

[61] H.A. Brongers, "Einige Bemerkungen zu Jes 58,13–14," ZAW 87 (1975): 212–216. The exhortation to keep the sabbath in this passage ends with a promise that the addressees will be given "Jacob's inheritance." The images used are not taken over from the Jacob tradition but from Deut 32:13.

[62] See the texts mentioned by Steck, Studien, 238–241.

[63] This is a relatively common view in continental European research; see the presentation in Peter Höffken, Jesaja: der Stand der theologischen Diskussion (Darmstadt: Wissenschaftliche Buchgeschaft), 2004, 99–100.

These "ancient days" do not start with Abraham, but with Moses ("They remembered the ancient days: Moses his 'kinsmen.'[64] Where is the one who brought them up out of the sea with the shepherd of his flock?[65] Where is the one who put within him his holy spirit, who caused his glorious arm to march at Moses' right who divided the waters before them to make for himself an everlasting [עולם] name, who caused them to march in the primeval waters [בתהמות]?" vv. 11–13a). This beginning with the evocations of Moses and the Exodus shows traces of a conflict between the patriarchs and the Exodus traditions. The author of 63:7–64:11 apparently rejected the Abraham and Jacob traditions and was opposed to those who claimed Abraham as their father (אָב); YHWH's "kinsmen" (עַם) is Moses. There are not many texts in the Hebrew Bible which apply the term "father" to YHWH (see also 64:7); in the context of the book of Isaiah the transfer of the title from Abraham to YHWH is however prepared through a number of texts, which use paternal and maternal metaphors to express YHWH's care for Israel (42:14; 43:6–7; 45:11; 49:15 and others). The denial of the father title for Abraham taints the last mention of the Patriarch in the Isaiah scroll with a polemical note, which is later taken up in the New Testament.[66] The opinion presented in Isa 63:10–16 stands in contrast to a passage in Mic 7:20: "You will show faithfulness to Jacob and loyalty to Abraham, as you have sworn to our fathers from the days of old (מימי קדם)." Here the beginnings include Jacob and Abraham, who represent the addressees of the oracle. Such a collective understanding of Abraham is rare in the Hebrew Bible and presupposes Isa 51:2–3.[67] The term אבות may either refer to Abraham and Jacob or to the Exodus generation.[68] Be this as it may, the conclusion of the Micah scroll, which, according to Utzschneider was added in the third century BCE[69] and may be therefore contemporary with Isa 63:7–

---

[64] In the MT, v. 11 is quite obscure. The reference to מֹשֶׁה עַמּוֹ is lacking in the LXX, but is present in the Qumran scroll as well as in the Vg. Instead of עמו some Syriac MSS have "his servant." This is certainly an attempt to make the Hebrew text more comprehensive and cannot be original. The word עם should be understood as expressing a very close relationship between Moses and YHWH as for instance in Deut 34:10–12. The following verse also reminds one of Deut 34:10–12.

[65] Contrary to the MT, one should read not "shepherds" but "shepherd," in agreement with the LXX. The "shepherd" probably refers to Moses (see Exod 3:1).

[66] See Matt 3:9 and John 8:31–59.

[67] Helmut Utzschneider, *Micha* (ZBK 24.1; Zürich: Theologischer Verlag, 2005), 169; and Jörg Jeremias, *Die Propheten Joel, Obadja, Jona, Micha* (ATD 24.3; Göttingen: Vandenhoeck & Ruprecht, 2007), 232.

[68] See for the latter solution Römer, *Väter*, 538–539.

[69] Utzschneider, *Micha*, 27.

64:11, clearly represents Abraham as a figure to which the addressees can identify—which is the dominant concept in the other late references to the Patriarch in the Hebrew Bible.

Abraham and the "Exodus" from Mesopotamia (Josh 24:2–5; Neh 9:7–8 and Ps 105)

In the Abraham narrative only one text declares that YHWH brought Abraham out of Egypt: Gen 15:7, which belongs to the latest layers of the entire Pentateuch.[70] According to Gen 11:27–12:5, it is Abraham's father, Terah, who takes the initiative to leave Ur with his family in order to settle down in Harran. And, according to 12:1–4, Abram receives the divine call in Harran (see 11:31). Genesis 15:7 antedates the relation between Abraham and YHWH into its very beginnings in Ur. This idea also occurs in Josh 24 and Nehemiah. In Josh 24, "Ur of the Chaldeans" is not mentioned but clearly presupposed:

> Your fathers—Terah the father of Abraham and the father of Nahor[71]—lived beyond the River (בעבר הנהר) since the ancient times (מעולם) and served other gods. Then I took your father Abraham from beyond the River led him through all the land of Canaan and made his offspring many. I gave him Isaac; and to Isaac I gave Jacob and Esau. (Josh 24:2–4)

The expression בעבר הנהר parallels the Assyrian designation *eber nāri*, which was also used by the Babylonians and Persians,[72] here in order to designate Mesopotamia.[73] According to Josh 24, and in contrast to Isa 63:11 as well as many other biblical texts, Israel's origins are not located in Egypt, but in Mesopotamia. Contrary to the beginning of the Abraham narrative, Josh 24:2 gives a reason for Abraham's "exodus" out of Mesopotamia. The idea that the "fathers" worshipped other gods there can be explained in three

---

[70] The post-priestly character of Gen 15 (or its original version) is often asserted in recent European research; see Römer, "Gen 15 und Gen 17," 32–47; Schmid, *Erzväter*, 172–185; Christoph Levin, "Jahwe und Abraham im Dialog: Genesis 15," in *Gott und Mensch im Dialog: Festschrift für Otto Kaiser zum 80. Geburtstag* (ed. Markus Witte; BZAW 345; Berlin: de Gruyter, 2004), 237–257; Ludwig Schmidt, "Genesis XV," *VT* 56 (2006): 251–267; and Erhard Blum, "The Literary Connection Between the Books of Genesis and Exodus and the End of the Book of Joshua," in Dozeman and Schmid, *A Farewell to the Yahwist?*, 89–106.

[71] The insertion about Terah is unanimously understood to be a later gloss, since it does not fit with the foregoing plural. It seems the glossator wanted to create a link with Gen 11:27 and avoid the idea that Abraham is part of the idolatrous "fathers."

[72] Oded Lipschitz, *The Fall and Rise of Jerusalem: Judah under Babylonian Rule* (Winona Lake, Ind.: Eisenbrauns, 2005), 2–3.

[73] In the Hebrew Bible the expression can carry two different meanings. The use in Josh 24:2 implies a Judean (or Samaritan) location of the author; see Moshé Anbar, *Josué et l'alliance de Sichem (Josué 24:1–28)* (BET 25; Frankfurt: Peter Lang, 1992), 121.

different manners: (a) it could be understood as the retro-projection of the Deuteronomistic theme that the Babylonian exiles had to serve the gods of the land into which they were deported (Deut 4:27–28; 28:36 and 64; Jer 16:13);[74] (b) Josh 24:2 already presupposes a tradition which appears two or three centuries later in the Book of Jubilees (chapters 11–12);[75] or (c) this text is a midrashic rereading of the Genesis account, trying to explain why Abraham left his home.[76] (This rereading would have been the starting point for the story in Jubilees and later Jewish legends about the idolatrous behavior of Abraham's people in Mesopotamia.) In any case, Josh 24:2–3 presupposes the priestly parts and later elements of the Abraham narrative (e.g. Gen 15:7)[77] and presents Abraham as the most important of the three patriarchs. He is the only one who is called "father" (in opposition to the "fathers" in Mesopotamia), and he receives much more attention than Isaac and Jacob. The two major themes of the Abraham narrative are mentioned: land[78] and a numerous (רבה) offspring (see Isa 52:2). A similar picture of Abraham is found in Neh 9

> You are YHWH, the God who chose Abram and brought him out of Ur of the Chaldeans (והוצאתו מאור כשדים) and gave him the name Abraham; and you found his heart faithful (נאמן) before you and made with him a covenant (וכרות עמו הברית) to give the land of the Canaanite, the Hittite, the Amorite, the Perizzite, the Jebusite, and the Girgashite to his descendants (לזרעו); and you have fulfilled your promise, for you are righteous (צדיק).   (Neh 9:7–8)

This text resembles the written text of the Genesis narrative to a closer level, especially Gen 17 and Gen 15, which the author seems to quote.[79] The focus here is on Abraham's faithfulness (see Gen 15:6: והאמן), YHWH's justice (see Gen 15:6: צדקה),[80] and the gift of the land to Abraham's

---

[74] Anbar, *Josué*, 121–122. The choice that is offered to the people in 24:15 (to serve the gods of their fathers beyond the river, or the gods of the land, or YHWH) could favor such an understanding.

[75] Johannes Hollenberg, "Die deuteronomistischen Bestandtheile des Buches Josua," *TSK* 47 (1874): 462–506, 486.

[76] Similarly Ernst Axel Knauf, *Josua* (ZBK 6; Zürich: Theologischer Verlag, 2008), 195.

[77] Josh 24 was written in the middle of the Persian period and reflects the attempt to add the scroll of Joshua to the Pentateuch; see, among others, Thomas Römer and Marc Z. Brettler, "Deuteronomy 34 and the Case for a Persian Hexateuch," *JBL* 119 (2000): 401–419.

[78] Interestingly, YHWH does not "give" the land to Abraham (YHWH makes him go into the whole land of Canaan), Isaac, nor Jacob, but to Esau he gives Seir. According to the author of Josh 24, the Edomite territory is also a gift of YHWH, and Israel receives the land only after Joshua's conquest (24:13).

[79] All roots or expressions in brackets occur in Gen 15.

[80] The author of Neh 9 understands Gen 15:6 to be referring to YHWH's (not Abraham's)

offspring.[81] Abraham's superiority is evident since this "historical summary," which starts with creation (v. 6), only mentions Abraham and then jumps directly to the fathers in Egypt without any transition. This is an indication that the original autonomy of the Abraham and the exodus traditions can still be perceived even in very late texts.[82]

Josh 24 and Neh 9 share several themes and expressions.[83] They both insist on the fact that YHWH brought Abraham out of Mesopotamia and they reflect a transformation of the original autochthonous Patriarch into an identity marker for Jews from the Babylonian Diaspora, who are invited to follow in the footsteps of their ancestor. They also indicate the growing popularity of Abraham at the expense of Isaac and Jacob in the late Persian and early Hellenistic period (which is later reflected for instance in Sir 44:19–23).[84]

In the Hebrew Bible this trend is also perceptible in Ps 105. As in Neh 9, YHWH's promise to Abraham functions in Ps 105 as the trajectory for the entire, subsequent history. For example, references to the divine promise to (or covenant with) Abraham[85] frame the historical summary in vv. 8 and 42–43. Following the evocation of Isaac and Jacob (who receive the same promise of the land as Abraham: vv. 9b–11), which contain the themes of their status as גרים (vv. 12–15),[86] the summary shifts to the Joseph story (vv. 16–23), which is explained in a rather detailed way. This may be an indication that the Joseph story was less well known than the other traditions

---

justice; for discussion on Gen 15:6, see Lloyd Gaston, "Abraham and the Righteousness of God," *HBT* 2 (1980): 39–68; Manfred Oeming, "Ist Genesis 15,6 ein Beleg für die Anrechnung des Glaubens zur Gerechtigkeit?," *ZAW* 95 (1983): 182–197; and Sascha Flüchter and Lars Schnor, "Die Anrechnung des Glaubens zur Gerechtigkeit: Ein rezeptionsgeschichtlicher Versuch zum Verständnis von Gen 15,6 MT," *BN* 109 (2001): 27–44.

[81] Contrary to Gen 15, which ends with an unusual list of 10 nations of the land, Neh 9:8 returns to the classical six.

[82] Römer, *Väter*, 540; and Köckert, "Abrahamüberlieferung," 115. According to Antonius H.J. Gunneweg (*Nehemia* [KAT 19,2; Gütersloh: Mohn, 1987], 129), Neh 9 belongs "zweifellos zu den jüngsten Stücken des AT."

[83] For a comparison of both texts see Römer, *Väter*, 326–327.

[84] The praise of Abraham is much longer than that of Isaac and Jacob, of whom it is only said that they benefit from Abraham's behavior and God's promises to him.

[85] Abraham is already mentioned in parallel with Jacob in v. 6 where addressees are described, in the manner of Deutero-Isaiah, as offspring of Abraham and Jacob.

[86] The root גור may allude to Gen 17:8 or 12:10; 20:1; 21:23, 34. According to Kraus (*Psalmen*, 105) and Köckert ("Abrahamüberlieferung," 116–117), vv. 13–15 refer to the three versions of "the patriarch's wife in danger." This may well be the case. The designation of the Patriarchs as "prophets" may stem from Gen 20:7, where Abraham is called a נביא. The astonishing title משיחים is without parallel in the Ancestral Narratives.

of the Pentateuch—an argument supporting the theory of a late insertion of the Joseph story into the narrative framework of the Pentateuch.[87] The Abraham-frame followed by the recalling of Israel's joyful exodus (vv. 42–43) gives the impression that the exodus and the gift of the land both depend on YHWH's remembering (זכר) his "holy word" to Abraham. The root may allude to the P-text Exod 2:24, but, contrary to that text, Ps 105:42 excludes Isaac and Jacob from the divine remembrance. The astonishing and singular expression ארצות גוים in v. 44 does not really fit the conquest of Canaan; rather, it evokes a situation of Diaspora (see the expressions in Ezek 12:15; 20:32, 41 and also Gen 26:3). Ps 105 therefore concludes with "an open end" which may be understood either as the possibility of a new entry into the land or as a valorizing of a Diaspora situation.[88] In Ps 105 Abraham is not called "father" but receives another honorific title: עבד (v. 42), a term otherwise attributed in the dtr tradition to Moses[89] and David.

The growing importance of Abraham also appears in Ps 47:10: "The volunteers[90] of the peoples gather as the people of the God of Abraham.[91] For the shields of the earth (מגני ארץ)[92] belong to God; he is highly exalted." In this Psalm from the Persian or even Hellenistic times,[93] Abraham appears as the "father" of all those who recognize that the God of Israel is the one

---

[87] Ps 105 is the only text in the Hebrew Bible outside the Hexateuch that mentions the Joseph story. For more on the current debate regarding the composition of the Joseph story and its insertion in the Pentateuch, see Christoph Uehlinger, "Fratrie, filiations et paternités dans l' histoire de Joseph (Genèse 37–50*)," in *Jacob: Commentaire à plusieurs voix de Gen. 25–36* (ed. Jean-Daniel Macchi and Thomas Römer; MdB 44; Geneva: Labor et Fides, 2001), 303–328; Konrad Schmid, "Die Josephsgeschichte im Pentateuch," in Gertz, Schmid, and Witte, *Abschied vom Jahwisten*, 83–118; as well as the essay by Baruch Schwartz in this volume.

[88] In the latter case, Ps 105 would have a different position than Neh 9.

[89] Cf. Ps 105:26.

[90] The traditional translation of "princes" is derived from the LXX; the Hebrew word indicates someone who does something voluntarily, and it becomes a "technical term for a member of a community" (HALOT).

[91] Some commentators and translations construct a mixture from the MT and LXX and translate: "gather along with the people of the God of Abraham." This is a theological correction, which is unjustified; see rightly Frank-Lothar Hossfeld and Erich Zenger, *Die Psalmen: Psalm 1–50* (NEchtB 29; Würzburg: Echter Verlag, 1993), 291.

[92] This may be a title for the kings of the nations (see Hossfeld and Zenger, *Psalmen*, 293). If the Psalm presupposes the Abraham narrative, one may also ask if this is an allusion to Gen 15:1, where YHWH presents himself as a "shield" for Abraham.

[93] It is often argued that an older "nationalistic" psalm in vv. 2–5* has been revised towards a universalistic perspective. But both parts can be also read as a passage from the nationalistic to the universalistic perspective; see Manfred Oeming and Joachim Vette, *Das Buch der Psalmen: Psalm 42–89* (NSKAT 13.2; Stuttgart: Katholisches Bibelwerk, 2010), 40–41.

true God (see Isa 2:3–5; Zech 8:20–23, etc.). This astonishing description of Abraham as an identity figure for all people who adhere to YHWH[94] can be understood as an exegesis of Josh 24:2–3 or of a similar tradition according to which Abraham broke with the gods of his fathers in order to serve YHWH.[95] Here we see something of a first step towards making Abraham into the father of all monotheists.

Abraham in the Patriarchal Triad

In two thirds of the texts that mention Abraham in the Hebrew Bible outside of the book of Genesis, he appears first in the triad "Abraham, Isaac and Jacob (Israel)"; in many cases the triad is used to characterize YHWH as the "God of Abraham, Isaac and Jacob (Israel)." Another frequent use is the allusion to the divine land promise (sometimes also covenant) made to the Patriarchs. It is difficult to decide what kind of Abraham and other patriarchal traditions are presupposed by these texts. They clearly know the genealogical system of Gen 12–35, and outside the book of Genesis the "oldest" attestation of this triad can be found in the P-texts: Exod 2:24; 6:3; and 6:8, which create a literary connection between the Patriarchs and the Exodus. All the other occurrences of the triad in the books of Exodus to Deuteronomy may well belong to one (or more) Pentateuch-redaction(s),[96] which aim to make the Patriarchs and YHWH's promises to them the mortar of the Torah.[97] The two uses of the Patriarchal triad in 1 Kgs 18:36 and 2 Kgs 13:23 also occur in redactional inserts that are probably not older than the "Pentateuch redaction."[98] The occurrences in Jer 33:26, which belong to a

---

[94] Interestingly "Jacob" in v. 5 represents Israel (see Deut 32:9).
[95] Hossfeld and Zenger, *Psalmen*, 293.
[96] Römer, *Väter*, 548–549, 553, 561–566; and Konrad Schmid, "Der Pentateuchredaktor: Beobachtungen zum theologischen Profil des Toraschlusses in Dtn 34," in *Les dernières rédactions du Pentateuque, de l'Hexateuque et de l'Ennéateuque* (ed. Thomas Römer and Konrad Schmid; BETL 203; Leuven: Peeters, 2007), 183–197.
[97] This redaction is clearly limited to the Pentateuch. The mention of the Patriarchal triad in Deut 34:4 introduces a quotation of Gen 12:7 and reveals itself as a "frame."
[98] For 1 Kgs 18:36 see, among others, Winfried Thiel, "Deuteronomistische Redaktionsarbeit in den Elia-Erzählungen," in *Congress Volume Leuven 1989* (ed. John A. Emerton; VTSup 43; Leiden: Brill, 1991), 148–171, 167; and Susanne Otto, *Jehu, Elia und Elisa: Die Erzählung von der Jehu-Revolution und die Komposition der Elia-Elisa-Erzählungen* (BWANT 152; Stuttgart: Kohlhammer, 2001), 157. 2 Kgs 13:23 clearly interrupts the sequence 13:22 and 24 (in the LXX the verse has been transferred after 13:7) and probably depends on the Priestly texts Exod 2:24 and Lev 26:42 (see Martin Rehm, *Das zweite Buch der Könige: Ein Kommentar*

passage that is lacking in the LXX, and in Chronicles are, at the earliest, from the end of the Persian or more probably from the Hellenistic period. That confirms the idea that the formulaic usage of the Patriarchal triad only started at the beginning of the Persian period,[99] probably with P.

Concluding Remarks

The investigation of the passages mentioning Abraham in the Hebrew Bible outside the book of Genesis has confirmed a current position in continental Abraham research: namely, Abraham started his literary career not much before the exilic period. That does not exclude the possibility that there were older oral traditions about this ancestor but these are very difficult to reconstruct. These traditions were probably about an autochthonous figure, as might still be reflected in the oldest mention of Abraham outside Genesis, Ezek 33:24. Here Abraham is used by the non-exiled population in order to claim its possession of the land, and this claim only makes sense if Abraham is understood as having been in the land forever. Ezek 33:24 emphasizes a strong tie between Abraham and the land but not with the other Patriarchs; on the contrary, Abraham is called "one alone" (אחד). In some passages, Abraham appears together with Jacob, yet Isaac is only linked to him in the late triadic formula. The parallels between Abraham and Jacob suggest that the link between these two ancestors could have been the first step to combine a Northern (Jacob) and Southern tradition.[100] In any case, these passages use the two names in parallel in a postexilic context in order to express the unity of YHWH's people.

In the book of Isaiah, Abraham plays quite an important role. He appears in the three parts of the book, and, with many other themes and terms, strengthens the scroll's redactional coherence. The most important text is Isa 51:1–3, which takes up and modifies the claim of Ezek 33:24. Abraham being compared to a rock could also be understood in an autochthonous

---

[Würzburg: Echter Verlag, 1982], 135; for a late Persian or early Hellenistic period redactor, consult A. Šanda, *Die Bücher der Könige* [EHAT 9; Münster: Aschendorffsche Verlagsbuchhandlung, 1912], 138).

[99] Raymond Jacques Tournay, "Genèse de la triade 'Abraham-Isaac-Jacob'," *RB* 103 (1996): 321–336.

[100] A trace of this is perhaps still perceptible in Gen 28:13 where YHWH presents himself to Jacob as the "God of Abraham, your father." The descriptor "and the god of Isaac" looks very much like a gloss.

sense, but more importantly Abraham here appears together with Sarah and becomes Israel's "father." This father-title is, however, contested in Isa 63:16 and the polemic shows that, during the Persian period, Abraham did not yet appeal to all groups of nascent Judaism. Nonetheless, texts like Josh 24 and Neh 9 indicate that Abraham comes to be more and more an important identity marker. Like P and later texts in Genesis, these two passages present him as an "exodical" figure whom God brought out of Mesopotamia. Abraham's growing importance is also reflected in Pss 105 and 47 in which Abraham (as opposed to Jacob) becomes the father of all people willing to worship the God of Israel.

SELECT BIBLIOGRAPHY

Bautch, Richard J. "An Appraisal of Abraham's Role in Postexilic Covenants." *Catholic Biblical Quarterly* 71 (2009): 42–63.

Biberger, Bernd. *Unsere Väter und wir: Unterteilung von Geschichtsdarstellungen in Generationen und das Verhältnis der Generationen im Alten Testament.* Bonner biblische Beiträge 145. Berlin: Philo Verlagsgesellschaft, 2003.

Blenkinsopp, Joseph. "Abraham as Paradigm in the Priestly History in Genesis." *Journal of Biblical Literature* 128 (2009): 225–241.

Blum, Erhard. *Die Komposition der Vätergeschichte.* Wissenschaftliche Monographien zum Alten und Neuen Testament 57. Neukirchen-Vluyn: Neukirchener, 1984.

Diebner, B. "'Isaak' und 'Abraham' außerhalb Gen 12–50: Eine Sammlung literaturgeschichtlicher Beobachtungen nebst einigen überlieferungsgeschichtlichen Spekulationen." *Dielheimer Blätter zum Alten Testament und seiner Rezeption in der Alten Kirche* 7 (1974): 38–50.

Dozeman, Thomas B., and Konrad Schmid, eds. *A Farewell to the Yahwist? The Composition of the Pentateuch in Recent European Interpretation.* Society of Biblical Literature Symposium Series 34. Atlanta: Society of Biblical Literature, 2006.

Fischer, Irmtraud. *Wo ist Jahwe? Das Volksklagelied Jes 63,7–64,11 als Ausdruck des Ringens um eine gebrochene Beziehung.* Stuttgarter biblische Beiträge 19. Stuttgart: Katholisches Bibelwerk, 1989.

———. *Die Erzeltern Israels: Feministisch-theologische Studien zu Genesis 12–36.* Beihefte zur Zeitschrift für die alttestamentliche Wissenschaft 222. Berlin: de Gruyter, 1994.

Garscha, Jörg. *Studien zum Ezechielbuch: Eine redaktionskritische Untersuchung.* Europäische Hochschulschriften Reihe 23, Theologie 23. Bern: Peter Lang, 1974.

Goldenstein, Johannes. *Das Gebet der Gottesknechte: Jesaja 63,7–64,11 im Jesajabuch.* Wissenschaftliche Monographien zum Alten und Neuen Testament 92. Neukirchen-Vluyn: Neukirchener, 2001.

Hagedorn, Anselm C., and Henrik Pfeiffer, eds. *Die Erzväter in der biblischen Tradition: Festschrift für Matthias Köckert.* Beihefte zur Zeitschrift für die alttestamentliche Wissenschaft 400. Berlin: de Gruyter, 2009.

Hardmeier, Christof. "Erzählen—Erzählung—Erzählgemeinschaft: Zur Rezeption von Abrahamserzählungen in der Exilsprophetie." Pages 35–55 in *Erzähldiskurs und Redepragmatik im Alten Testament: Unterwegs zu einer performativen Theologie der Bibel.* Forschungen zum Alten Testament 46. Tübingen: Mohr Siebeck, 2005.

Köckert, Matthias. "Die Geschichte der Abrahamüberlieferung." Pages 103–128 in *Congress Volume Leiden 2004.* Edited by André Lemaire. Vetus Testamentum Supplements 109. Leiden: Brill, 2006.

Kühlewein, Johannes. *Geschichte in den Psalmen.* Calwer theologische Monographien. Reihe A, Bibelwissenschaft 2. Stuttgart: Calwer Verlag, 1973.

Pury, Albert de. "Abraham: The Priestly Writer's 'Ecumenical' Ancestor." Pages 163–181 in *Rethinking the Foundations: Historiography in the Ancient World and in the Bible. Essays in Honour of John Van Seters.* Edited by Steven L. McKenzie and Thomas Römer. Beihefte zur Zeitschrift für die alttestamentliche Wissenschaft 294; Berlin: de Gruyter, 2000.

Römer, Thomas. *Israels Väter: Untersuchungen zur Väterthematik im Deuteronomium und in der deuteronomistischen Tradition.* Orbis biblicus et orientalis 99. Göttingen: Vandenhoeck & Ruprecht, 1990.

———. "The Exodus in the Book of Genesis." *Svensk Exegetisk Årsbok* 75 (2010): 1–20.

Tournay, Raymond Jacques. "Genèse de la triade 'Abraham-Isaac-Jacob'." *Revue biblique* 103 (1996): 321–336.

Schmid, Konrad. *Erzväter und Exodus: Untersuchungen zur doppelten Begründung der Ursprünge Israels innerhalb der Geschichtsbücher des Alten Testaments.* Wissenschaftliche Monographien zum Alten und Neuen Testament 81. Neukirchen-Vluyn: Neukirchener, 1999. Translated into English as *Genesis and the Moses Story: Israel's Dual Origins in the Hebrew Bible.* Siphrut 3. Winona Lake, Ind.: Eisenbrauns, 2010.

Merwe, Barend Jacobus van der. *Pentateuchtradisies in die prediking van Deutero-Jesaja.* Groningen: J.B. Wolters, 1956.

Steck, Odil Hannes. *Gottesknecht und Zion: Gesammelte Aufsätze zu Deuterojesaja.* Forschungen zum Alten Testament 4. Tübingen: Mohr Siebeck, 1992.

———. *Studien zu Tritojesaja.* Beihefte zur Zeitschrift für die alttestamentliche Wissenschaft 203. Berlin: de Gruyter, 1991.

Tiemeyer, Lena-Sofia. "Abraham—A Judahite Prerogative." *Zeitschrift für die alttestamentliche Wissenschaft* 120 (2008): 49–66.

Oorschot, Jürgen van. *Von Babel zum Zion: Eine literarkritische und redaktionsgeschichtliche Untersuchung.* Beihefte zur Zeitschrift für die alttestamentliche Wissenschaft 206. Berlin: de Gruyter, 1993.

Van Seters, John. *Abraham in History and Tradition.* New Haven: Yale University Press, 1975.

Vorländer, Hermann. *Die Entstehungszeit des jehowistischen Geschichtswerkes.* Europäische Hochschulschriften Reihe 23, Theologie 109. Frankfurt: Peter Lang, 1978.

THE JACOB TRADITION

Erhard Blum

I. Boundaries and Themes of the Story of Jacob in Genesis

From a canonical perspective, the stories of Jacob (and Esau) represent the *toledot* (= [story of] descendants) of his (/their) father which begin with the *toledot*-formula for Isaac in Gen 25:19 and end with Isaac's death and burial by his two sons at Mamre in 35:27–29. They are followed immediately by the *toledot* of Esau (36:1) and then by the *toledot* of Jacob (cf. 37:2 and 50:12–13), which comprise the Story of Joseph and his brothers.[1] At the same time, that well 'delimited' tradition of Isaac's sons shows some diversity in terms of narrative coherence: while ch. 25B[2] to 33 (without ch. 26!) form a remarkably integrated story with regard to plot, theme(s) and narrative art, the subsequent chs. 34 and 35 cover Jacob's way from Shechem to Hebron with rather loosely connected episodes and notes.

Gen 26, comprising a small cycle of narratives about Isaac and the Philistines, does not form an integral part of the Story of Jacob.[3] Isaac and Rebekah do not seemingly have children here as could be expected after ch. 25B. Moreover, a household with children would contradict Isaac's pretense presenting Rebekah as his sister (26:7–11) from the start. Nevertheless, some tradent apparently found it appropriate to fill the time-gap between the young family of Isaac in 25B and the episode expecting his death in 27 with narratives about Isaac and his wife[4]

---

[1] For a detailed description of the structure built by the *toledot*-formulae and by stereotyped notes of death and burial throughout the story of the ancestors cf. Erhard Blum, *Die Komposition der Vätergeschichte* (WMANT 57; Neukirchen-Vluyn: Neukirchener, 1984), 432–446.

[2] In this contribution, "Gen 25B" will serve as an abbreviation for "Gen 25:19–34."

[3] For a canonical reading of Gen 25–35, including ch. 26, see Michael A. Fishbane, "Composition and Structure in the Jacob Cycle (Gen. 25:19–35:22)," *JJS* 26 (1975): 15–38.

[4] Another aspect supporting this juxtaposition might have been the theme of blessing elaborated so much—though in different ways—in both ch. 26 and 27; cf. J.P. Fokkelman, *Narrative Art in Genesis: Specimens of Stylistic and Structural Analysis* (SSN 17; Amsterdam: van Gorcum, 1975), 113–115.

that originated in their own place and time⁵ different from the cycle about Jacob.⁶

Therefore, the main Story of Jacob is to be found in Gen 25B*; *27–33. With regard to its main characters and places, its plot has a clear tripartite structure, which is only slightly extended by two (or three) scenes of an unexpected encounter of the main protagonist with God (or divine beings) which mark major turning points in the story:

  A. Jacob and Esau—in Canaan: 25B+27
    C. Jacob's encounter with God at Bethel: 28:10–22
  B. Jacob and Laban—in Aram: 29–31(32:1)
    C'. Jacob's encounter with God(/gods) at (Mahanaim and) Penuel: 32:(2–3) 23–33
  A'. Jacob and Esau—in Canaan: 32–33.

This story is built out of smaller episodes and scenes which are mostly characterized by the unity of characters and place, as well as by an individual line of tension. On the basis of this episodic narration Hermann Gunkel spoke of a "Jakob-Esau-Laban-Sagenkranz" ("Jacob-Laban-Esau cycle of tales"), a description which was in line with his general assumption that the narrative tradition in the Bible started with small, rather simple units, which were later intertwined into larger 'cycles.' Nevertheless Gunkel himself already recognized that at least the last part (A') of our story presupposes basic components of both, A and B.⁷ One should go further: part A' functions as a real finale leading to a climax that throws new light on the story as a whole. We have reason, therefore, to speak not merely of a "cycle of tales," but of a major integrated story with themes of its own.

Two of its main themes are 'strife' and 'blessing.' Often, though not always, both themes are actually combined into one: 'struggle for blessing,' especially with regard to the twins, Jacob and Esau. Their struggle begins in

---

⁵ In general terms, Gen 26 clearly has a southern-Judahite context in contrast with the northern setting of the Jacob-tradition (see section IV), showing well-known affinities with the Abraham traditions.

⁶ According to Reinhard G. Kratz, *Die Komposition der erzählenden Bücher des Alten Testaments: Grundwissen der Bibelkritik* (UTB 2157; Göttingen: Vandenhoeck & Ruprecht, 2000), 272, the nucleus of Gen 27 (vv. 1–4, 5b, 18a, 24–27bα, 28) knew only Esau as eldest son of Isaac, continuing several Isaac episodes from ch. 26. However, one might ask whether the supposed nucleus forms a coherent unit with a narrative purpose.

⁷ Hermann Gunkel, *Genesis übersetzt und erklärt* (3rd ed.; HKAT 1/1; Göttingen: Vandenhoeck & Ruprecht, 1910), 292.

their mother's womb (25:22), and the birth reveals Jacob's ambition to be the first one by grasping Esau's heel (25:25–26). This ambition seems to belong to his nature, for in the first scene narrated after their birth he seizes an opportunity to correct his disadvantage and makes Esau sell his birthright for a lentil stew (25:29–34). At the same time, the note about Isaac's love for Esau, the hunter, and Rebekah's love for Jacob (25:28) indicates an involvement of the parents into their sons' rivalry. This sets the stage for the decisive act in Gen 27, in which the old father wishes to give his blessing before his death to the beloved son Esau, but it is Jacob who, instructed by his mother, actually gets this blessing through cunning actions and trickery. Now, in his pain after the imposture, Esau declares that Jacob's very name reveals his real nature, hearing it with a second meaning, "deceiver"; high emotions seem to enable the coarse man to express this in impressively designed sentences, somewhere between prose and poetry (27:36):

הכי קרא שמו יעקב ויעקבני זה פעמים
את־בכרתי לקח והנה עתה לקח בכרתי

Perceiving the artfully narrated drama of the father's growing distress and Esau's despair (27:30–36), the reader cannot but identify with the betrayed father and with Esau who fell victim to his brother. It does not come as a surprise that this conflict, initially treated on Esau's side with a dull lack of interest, now bursts into open hatred; accordingly Jacob must flee from his father's house (27:42–45; 28:10). Nevertheless, the situation is not drawn in a black and white manner altogether, for the reader will not forget the oracle in which YHWH predicted the supremacy of the younger son from the outset which was granted later through the paternal blessings (cf. 25:23 with 27:29, 40). For the time being the question remains: how do Jacob's trickster character and the divine intervention in his favor correlate?[8]

Jacob's encounter with YHWH and his celestial staff on his way to Rebekah's brother Laban (Gen 28) continues the narrative line of divine assistance for Jacob who connects this assistance with the hope for his return *be-šalom* to his paternal family (*bet ʾabi*) (28:21). In Aram, however, Jacob is reminded of his past as a trickster when Laban gives him Leah after he has worked seven years for Rachel. In answer to his reproach: "Why have

---

[8] See further below pp. 185–186.

you deceived me?" Laban holds up a mirror to Jacob: "This is not done in our country—giving the younger before the firstborn."[9] Jacob's exposition as *le trompeur trompé*, however, appears to be the start of a new chain of cheating with Laban as the main victim. Thus it is his daughter Rachel who steals the household gods during Jacob's secret departure from Laban and hides them from her father—showing a bit of cunning worthy of both, her father and her husband (31:19, 33–35).

In return, it fits the pattern of God's recurrent care for people who are in an unfavorable position that YHWH "opened the womb of Leah," because she was unloved, whereas Rachel remained "barren" (29:30–31). This causes a bitter strife within Jacob's own family, a continued struggle between the two women for their husband's love and for children as a criterion for their relative standing in the family. Both make use of their maids for that purpose. Leah, however, will not find Jacob's love, and Rachel will be heard by God and conceive only in the very end (30:22–24).

The other conflict between Laban and Jacob is again about the blessing (30:25–43): Being aware that Jacob's work in service to him is blessed by YHWH, he does not want let him go home. Instead, he accepts a deal offered by Jacob which looks highly profitable for Laban, because Jacob's share should consist only of rare kinds of sheep and goats. Using cunning tricks, however, Jacob manages to increase his own flock immensely at Laban's expense. The implied logic seems clear: Laban is falling victim to the trickster Jacob in the very same field in which he had succeeded to exploit his nephew, i.e. in Jacob's work for him. In the following chapter, however, a pointed flashback in the speech given by Jacob to his wives brings a different reality to light: Jacob's skills as shepherd are not the reason for his wealth but rather God's hidden intervention, revealed by a divine messenger (31:9–12). Divine speeches in dreams, one addressed to Jacob (31:13), the other to Laban (31:24, 29), also initiate Jacob's 'escape' from Aram and prevent an outraged Laban from using force against Jacob's camp. Instead, both parties come to an agreement after a lengthy, but pointed dispute. They make a treaty in Gilead at a place called Mizpah, in which Jacob promises to treat Laban's daughters well, and both make a commitment not to go beyond that place into the territory of the other to do harm. The gods of the Father of each side will be guarantors of the treaty (31:53–54).

---

[9] The use of *hṣʿyrh* (instead of *hqṭnh*) calls to mind Gen 25:23b where—in turn—*bkwr* seems to be consciously avoided.

Following this reconciliation and in pointed contrast to it, the unsolved conflict with his brother immediately catches up with Jacob, anticipated by still another encounter with a 'camp of divine beings.' Facing the imminent meeting with Esau and his 400 men (32:7), he takes two preventive measures. At first he divides his camp (*mḥnh*) into two in order to save a remnant in case Esau will attack (32:8–9). Then[10] he transforms parts of his company (*mḥnh*) into a present/tribute (*mnḥh*), split into several herds, and sends them ahead in an attempt to appease Esau's 'face' (*panim*) (32:14–21). On that night at the ford of the Jabbok, however, he has to prevail 'face to face' against another opponent whose divine identity is only gradually revealed, both to Jacob and to the reader (32:23–33).[11] In wrestling with God[12] Jacob wins the blessing all over again—just before the meeting with Esau. Moreover, the new name he receives[13] marks his change: He is a 'new man,' not "the trickster" (*yʿqb*) anymore, as Esau had rightly called him, but "he who was in strife with God (about his blessing)" (*yśr'l*)! The initial tension between the divine oracle to Rebekah in 25:23 and Jacob's unambiguous presentation as a deceiver is solved here. But the divine solution comprises both, the blessed one and the unblessed one, as the finale of the finale shows: Seeing Esau in the morning light of the next day near Penuel, Jacob "bows down to the ground seven times" before his brother (33:4). This suggests an almost *verbatim* reversal of the blessing that Isaac had given to Jacob in 27:29. In other words: the blessed one, as he bows to the unblessed one, gives up any triumphant claim on his superior status. At the same time,

---

[10] With regard to the supposed structure of time in 32:14a, 22 see below note 72.

[11] The narrative refinement of the Penuel episode exceeds that of any other part of the Story of Jacob. It marks the center of the last part (C') between Jacob's preparation and his meeting with Esau, but has a meaningful prelude in the short note about Jacob's encounter with the divine messengers at Mahanaim (32:2b–3), which in turn mirrors the Bethel-episode in 28:11–19 in several aspects. See the fine exegesis of the Penuel story in its context by Hermann Spieckermann, *Der Gotteskampf. Der Gotteskampf: Jakob und der Engel in der Bibel und Kunst* (Zürich: TVZ, 1997).

[12] It is possible that the narrator understood *'lhym* in 32:31 in the sense of "a god/divine being," identifying the anonymous fighter with one of the "divine camp," who met Jacob already in 32:2. Even in this case the "man" is thought of as acting as God's representative and Jacob's fright (v. 31) would be justified. It is not clear to me why such an understanding should require a direct sequence of 32:2–3 and 32:24–30; pace Tzemah Yoreh, "Jacob's Struggle," *ZAW* 117 (2004): 95–97.

[13] The wording "You shall no longer be called …" does not function as a formula used in a registry office, but is used here to introduce a second name emphasizing the 'sense' of the new name. In a similar, even more emphatic manner the name "Israel" is introduced in the P-layer (35:10); nevertheless P continues, constantly using "Jacob."

however, Esau shows—by embracing and kissing his brother—that he, on his part, has given up the old strife (33:4; cf. also 33:9b). As Jacob/Israel himself sums up, he cannot but interpret the happy end, hinting gratefully at his nocturnal encounter at Penuel, through this parallel wording:

32:31   ותנצל נפשי   כי־ראיתי אלהים פנים אל־פנים ...
33:10   ותרצני   כי על־כן ראיתי פניך כראת פני אלהים ...

The major lines of the whole story come here to an end. The drama of the brothers is wound up by a narrative 'formula of separation' in 33:16–17a which mirrors a parallel formula in 32:1b, 2a (Laban and Jacob).[14] In 33:17 the formula introduces a few etiological notes marking Jacob's way through Sukkot and Shechem (33:18*, 20), probably also Bethel (35:6*-7*),[15] and up to the place of Benjamin's birth and Rachel's tomb on the way to Efrat (35:16–20). By the time of this epilogue, Jacob/Israel has returned to Cisjordan, and with Benjamin the number of the *bne yiśra'el* is full (cf. 30:24!).

Last, but not least, the story has a dimension which is fundamental to all the outlined aspects of meaning when read in the perspective of the narrator and his addressees: it is part of their own—collective—'biography.' From the beginning, readers know that the child described at his birth as *'admoni*, *kᵉ'aderet śeʿar* represents Edom, and that Jacob is Israel. It is the story about the origin of peoples (*goyim*) and their environment. According to the genealogical conception of all groups in which socials structures are based primarily on relations of kinship, the (hi)story of tribes or nations begins with individual families. Thus stories of origins (*Ursprungsgeschichten*) tell family stories with which the hearers/readers see themselves in a continuity of descent. In addition, the narrated world and the addressees' world are *etiologically* correlated. In this correlation it is essential that the ancestors as characters in a plot do not "stand for" ancient tribes or peoples, but they *are* those tribes or peoples. Therefore the popular attempts in modern research to 'decode' these stories like allegories in order to reconstruct ancient histories are projections which miss the semantics inherent to those traditions.

---

[14] See Isac Leo Seeligmann, "Hebräische Erzählung und biblische Geschichtsschreibung," in *Gesammelte Studien zur Hebräischen Bibel* (FAT 41; Tübingen: Mohr Siebeck, 2004), 121–123 (repr. of *TZ* 18 [1962]: 305–325).

[15] With regard to these etiological notes see further below before n. 49.

II. Redundancy as a Stylistic Device in the Story of Jacob

The eminent skill of the storyteller(s) in the Story of Jacob—the narrative art in select episodes as well as in its whole—has drawn considerable attention in scholarly work. Suffice it to mention here the sensitive 'classic' commentators (like Gunkel or Gerhard von Rad within a historical-critical framework, or Benno Jacob with a more traditional-apologetical approach) or the pioneering literary readings of J.P. Fokkelman.[16] In the present context the narrative shape of our story in its whole range cannot be discussed adequately. Some stylistic phenomena, however, should be pointed out because of their fundamental significance concerning the narrative 'logic' of our texts which seems to be significantly different from modern textual concepts. These stylistic features might be subsumed under an 'intentional redundancy' which covers several phenomena on different textual levels.

Especially in the realm of discourse with longer speeches, there are structures quite similar to the *parallelismus membrorum* in poetic verses. The clearest examples can be found in the dispute between Laban and Jacob in Gen 31:36–44. Reading sentence for sentence reveals semantically paired structures almost throughout. There is, of course, no regular rhythm or meter, but instead the structures are quite often underscored by alliteration, rhyme, and so on.[17] It seems to be a rhetorically elaborated prose that aims to express the speaker's emotions and to heighten its persuasive force. In 31:45–54, such parallel structures are motivated by factual complexity: the episode plays etiologically with a compound toponym ("Mizpah [in] Gilead") intertwining the introduction of two cultic installations (heap/*gal* and pillar/*maṣṣeba*) and two material aspects of the agreement (Laban's daughters / good neighborly relations) between the partners of the treaty.

Another, less formal device for enriching the complexity of the narrated world is to connect different elements in that world through their linguistic signs. Common means are variations, allusions, puns, and so forth between words, phrases, sentences, etc., on the levels of sound/orthography, syntax

---

[16] Fokkelman, *Narrative Art*, 48–81, 86–241. Cf. also Martin Buber, "Leitwortstil in der Erzählung des Pentateuchs," in Martin Buber and Franz Rosenzweig, *Die Schrift und ihre Verdeutschung* (Berlin: Schocken, 1936), 211–238, here 223–226; Johannes Taschner, *Verheißung und Erfüllung in der Jakoberzählung (Gen 25,19–33,17): Eine Analyse ihres Spannungsbogens* (HBS 27; Freiburg: Herder, 2000).

[17] See also Gen 27:44b, 45a. Such features are, of course, not restricted to our story; see for instance Amos 7:10–17 or Combination I of the Deir ʿAlla Plaster Texts.

or meaning. These features belong to what Isac Seeligmann called the *Spielelement* in the Hebrew Bible.[18] Certainly, such "plays" function in our stories not just as *l'art pour l'art* but as a means of pointing to the nature of things/persons or to a deeper connection between them. In this sense, most onomastic etiologies are based on (often creative) word-plays. In our story, however, we have Esau's emphatic interpretation of Jacob's name as "deceiver" (27:36) besides the explicit derivation of "Jacob" in 25:26 (from ʿaqeb—heel). Esau's own name is derived from śeʿar—"hair" (25:25); apparently this somewhat imprecise pun is chosen because it enables an implied, but clear play with śeʿir, one of the names of Esau's future land. His second name "Edom" is explained in the scene with the lentil stew (25:30), but already alluded to at his birth (25:25). Redundant allusions or interpretations like these should not be seen as odd or contradicting features but as intentional representations of a multifaceted reality, as indications of an integrating 'deep structure' behind. Thus the meaningful connection of Jacob's encounters with the divine messengers and with his brother Esau is indicated by the reiteration of the messenger and camp motifs. The latter provides a *Leitwort* (*mḥnh*) that is taken up by a recurrent word field built through paronomasia: *mḥnh—mnḥa—ḥnn—ḥn*.[19] Together with other key words like *ra'ah*, *panim*, *šalaḥ*, *ʿabar*, *šem*, *brk* these expressions build a tightly intertwined texture that lends a highly elaborated shape to the narrative finale of the whole story. The texture has its culmination in the episode of Jacob's fight at the Jabbok which is shaped in multiple, dense paronomasia around the names "Jacob" (*ybq*, *kp*, √*yqʿ*, √*'bq*), "Israel" (√*śrh*, *'elohim*), "Jabbok" (see "Jacob"), and "Peniel" (*ra'iti 'elohim panim 'el panim*). Obviously, the author had some ambition to form his narrative in a most com-

---

[18] Isac Leo Seeligmann, "Voraussetzungen der Midraschexegese," in *Congress Volume: Copenhagen 1953* (VTSup 1; Leiden: Brill 1953), 150–181 (repr. in *Gesammelte Studien*, 1–30); and Buber and Rosenzweig, *Schrift*. With regard to the midrashic play with names, rich material is discussed by Yair Zakovitch in his unpublished M.A. Thesis (*kefel midrᵉše šem*, Jerusalem 1971) and in several publications, for instance "Explicit and Implicit Name-Derivatons," *HAR* 4 (1980): 167–181, and recently, "Implied Synonyms and Antonyms: Textual Criticism vs. the Literary Approach," in *Emanuel: Studies in Hebrew Bible, Septuagint and Dead Sea Scrolls in Honor of Emanuel Tov* (ed. Shalom M. Paul et al.; VTSup 94; Leiden: Brill, 2003), 833–849. For a systematic treatment of "midrashic name derivations" in the HB see Moshe Garsiel, *Biblical Names: A Literary Study of Midrashic Derivations and Puns* (trans. Phyllis Hackett; Ramat Gan: Bar-Ilan University Press, 1991).

[19] Cf. Erhard Blum, "Die Komplexität der Überlieferung. Zur diachronen und synchronen Auslegung von Gen 32,23–33," in *Textgestalt und Komposition: Exegetische Beiträge zu Tora und Vordere Propheten* (ed. Wolfgang Oswald; FAT 69; Tübingen: Mohr Siebeck, 2010), 43–84 (repr. of *DBAT* 15 [1980]: 2–55); and Garsiel, *Names*, 241–242.

plex and artistic way which challenges and—at the same time—guides the reader to reveal its concealed meanings, or as Erich Auerbach would have called it: *die Hintergründlichkeit*.[20]

With regard to the macro-level we find intentional redundancy in structures of thematic or episodic parallelisms/repetitions. Thus Gen 25B, though doubling in some sense the struggle for the blessing, functions as a prelude to Gen 27[21] which intensifies the story about the twins' strife. As has long been observed, Jacob's encounter with God in Gen 28 has its meaningful narrative counterpart in the Jabbok episode. Moreover, the latter's prelude, the meeting with the divine camp in 32:2b–3, appears to be built consciously as a 'duplicate' of essential parts of the Bethel episode mirroring the transitional position of ch. 28 in Jacob's *vita*. In terms of plot, the antagonism between the sisters Leah and Rachel echoes the strife between Jacob and his brother, whereas its narrative elaboration shows parallel structures only to a limited extent. In contrast, the story of Jacob's wealth at Laban's expense is told twice (30:28–43; 31:4–12, 41–42)—in great detail and out of two divergent perspectives (see above), recalling the 'stereometric' dimension of some *parallelismus membrorum* in OT poetics. In this case, however, there remain some inconsistencies between the parallel accounts that demand further explanation (see below).

The narrative elaboration in parallel structures reaches its climax in Gen 32–33. We already mentioned the meaningful duplication of the Jacob-Esau encounter in the realm of the divine. In addition, the meeting in the human sphere is anticipated by Jacob's doubled but complementary preparations already outlined. Both actions are taken up successively in the actual meeting with his brother;[22] nevertheless they are smoothly intertwined here into one thread: the 'splitting' of the family according to the children's mothers (33:1–7) mirrors the preventive action in 32:8–9, both marked by *wyḥṣ* (32:8b and 33:1b). The account, however, also recalls in some respects the sending of the *minḥah* (32:14–22).[23] Conversely, the brother's talk about that present

---

[20] Erich Auerbach, *Mimesis: Dargestellte Wirklichkeit in der abendländischen Literatur* (Francke: Bern 1946), 5–27, with his famous comparison of Homer's *Odyssey* (Book 19) with Gen 22.

[21] Evidently, Gen 27 can not be read without 25B.

[22] Gen 33:1–7 basically corresponds to 32:1–9; 33:8–11 refers mainly to the 'tribute' of 32:14–21.

[23] Cf. the sending/presentation in stages; the formulation *'br lpny* in 33:3 as in 32:17 together with the factual reversal: Jacob not coming "behind" (32:19b, 21a) but "in front" (33:3a); the expression *ḥnn 'lhym* (33:5b // 33:11!) as part of the key word cluster with *mnḥh* etc.

refers back not only to 32:14–22 but also to the sending of the messengers in 32:6.[24] Obviously one major aim of such a 'prolonging' narration is the creation of a dramatic effect; from 32:4 on, an increasing suspense is built up. Moreover, it is due only to the bold narration of Jacob's encounter with Esau that an overall balance with the first part of the story and its heavy episodes in Gen 25B; 27 and 28 is reached. Last, but not least, it provides the material for a subtle theology of blessing. The manifold poetic *Bauformen* in this prose are the necessary precondition for those achievements.

III. The Issue of Diachronic (Dis)Unity

The Story of Jacob as it has been treated so far in a synchronic perspective is different from the canonical Jacob tradition in Genesis. Several texts like Gen 26 or 34 have been excluded on the basis of such aspects as the narrative (in)coherence of the plot, style, and so on. The necessary interaction between synchronic and diachronic approaches becomes evident here: insofar as the synchronic reading attempts to understand the text in question as a whole, it necessarily presupposes the diachronic unity and intentional independence of that text. Thus literary connections transcending the supposed unity falsify that supposition unless they belong diachronically to a different context. If so, how can we avoid the obvious danger of creating our own imaginary text units through circular arguments? It all depends on a careful procedure relying on the convergence of different mutually independent data. Though the full inquiry which would be needed cannot be offered in this context, some crucial distinctions shall be explicated. Fortunately, we can start with diachronic positions which are widely accepted in modern exegesis.

The Priestly Layer

The identification of the Priestly layer ("P") in Genesis is almost undisputed (in the main lines) since the basic study of Theodor Nöldeke (1869).[25] In Gen 25–35, there are about 29 Priestly verses: Gen 25:19–20, 26b; 26:34–35; 27:46–

---

[24] Gen 32:6: "... and I have sent to tell my lord, in order that I may find favor in your sight." // 33:8: "He said, 'What do you mean by all this company that I met?' He answered, 'In order that I may find favor in my lord's sight.'"

[25] Theodor Nöldeke, "Die s.g. Grundschrift des Pentateuchs," in *Untersuchungen zur Kritik des Alten Testaments* (Kiel: Schwers, 1869), 1–144.

28:9; 31:17–18;[26] 33:18aα‏א‎.β; 35:(6?) 9–15,[27] 22b–29. As indicated above, 25:19–20[28] and 35:27–29 provide a seamless frame constituting the *toledot* of Isaac which include Priestly and non-Priestly material on Isaac's descendants. At the same time the major P-pericopes (27:46–28:9; 35:9–15) clearly duplicate and contradict important non-P-episodes (Isaac's blessing in ch. 27; Jacob in Bethel, 28:11–22), an observation which seems to support the conception of an independent P-source. Nevertheless, the data in the Jacob tradition raise serious questions with regard to this widely accepted understanding of P.

First, it is obvious that the Priestly texts listed above are far from constituting a complete narrative strand. The gaps are substantial, and not only concerning Jacob's sojourn at Paddan Aram. The omission of major parts of the Priestly strand can, of course, not be excluded, though it does not fit the common view that the redactors generally preferred the P-texts to the non-P-tradition. Second, a closer examination reveals that the major P-pericopes show odd references to the pre-Priestly parallels with interesting diachronic implications. The best example is probably the Bethel text in Gen 35 and its counterpart in Gen 28. These two episodes provide a textbook example of a literary doublet indeed. The same event is described twice: after a divine revelation (including promises to the Patriarch), Jacob erects a *Massebah* in Gen 35 (exactly as in ch. 28), pours oil over it (as in 28), and names the place "Bethel" (as in 28). There is not even an attempt to harmonize the traditions. How is this juxtaposition of the pericopes in our Genesis to be understood? The key for an answer lies in the different *skopoi* of the passages: As *hieros logos*, Gen 28 deals mainly with the place whose holiness Jacob discovers, and with the stone that he dedicates as a *Massebah*. Genesis 35 employs exactly these two elements, in part in identical language. At the same time, however, the message is inverted: Bethel is no longer the place at which YHWH *dwells*—the "house of God" or the "gate of heaven" (as in Gen 28)—but is now described three times, redundantly, as "the place at which he (God) *spoke* with him" (vv. 13, 14, 15) and from which God "*ascended*" (v. 13). Accordingly, the cult stele in Gen 28 now

---

[26] Martin Noth, *Überlieferungsgeschichte des Pentateuch* (Stuttgart: Kohlhammer, 1948; repr., Darmstadt: Wissenschaftliche Buchgesellschaft, 1960), 17–18, assigns (as many others) only v. 18αβb to P. Cf., however, Gen 12:5; 35:27; 36:6; and 46:5–6.

[27] See Nöldeke, "Grundschrift," 27. Since Julius Wellhausen, *Die Composition des Hexateuchs und der historischen Bücher des Alten Testaments* (3rd ed.; Berlin: Reimer, 1899), 322, v. 14 is mostly assigned to a non-Priestly source; but then the explanation of the given text remains a riddle; cf. Blum, *Komposition*, 266–267 with n. 22.

[28] As in other cases, the introduction with the *toledot*-formula has replaced an older narrative opening.

functions as a memorial to the divine speech (v. 14a) and the anointing of the *massebah* appears transformed into an *ad-hoc* libation (v. 14b). This means that Gen 35 employs the narrative framework of the *hieros logos* in order to negate its etiological point! In other words, the Priestly tradent of Gen 35 has revised the old Bethel story by juxtaposing his "contra-version" to it. Still one might ask if the proposed reading of 35:9–15 necessarily requires the juxtaposition of both episodes in the same context. It is possible that the P-author not only knew the older tradition himself but could rely on his addressee's knowledge as well. Such a reasoning, however, cannot explain all the data: given the meaning of 35:9–15 as an intentional 'retelling' of Gen 28:11–19, its proper place in an independent literary work would not be at Jacob's return from Paddan Aram but at the very position of the older Bethel episode. Such a possibility, however, must be excluded from the outset for any P-context because of the proximity of Isaac's blessing (28:1–9).[29] In other words, the given structure of two extended blessings for Jacob, one before his departure to Laban (28:1–9) and the other at his return (35:9–15), offers the optimal condition for an intertwining of these pericopes with the non-P-narrative. Should this be considered a pure coincidence?

Based on these data and similar ones in other parts of "P" on the one hand and on the well known features indicating an occasionally high degree of 'independence' of the P-strand on the other hand, I propose that the P-tradition be seen as a literary layer that was conceived separately (in its main parts) but with the intention of a combined 'edition' including the non-Priestly '*Vorlage*.' "P" can then neither be defined as 'source' nor as 'redaction'; rather one should speak of a 'composition' or 'edition' showing a peculiar history of production.[30]

Non-Priestly Expansions

The major non-Priestly Jacob episodes which are not part of the primary Story of Jacob, Gen 34 and 35:1–5(6–7), belong to quite different contexts. *Genesis 34* shows the sons of Jacob no more as the "tender" children of

---

[29] Albert de Pury, "The Jacob Story and the Beginning of the Formation of the Pentateuch," in *A Farewell to the Yahwist? The Composition of the Pentateuch in Recent European Scholarship* (ed. Thomas B. Dozeman and Konrad Schmid; SBLSymS 34, Atlanta: Society of Biblical Literature, 2006), 64–65, suggests that 35:9–15 be split in order to place 35:6aα, 11–15 before Jacob's stay with Laban and 35:9–10 at his return. Consequently, he drops the undisputed Priestly blessing in 27:46–28:9; perhaps by mistake? But see the paraphrase (on p. 64).

[30] For a detailed discussion see Erhard Blum, *Studien zur Komposition des Pentateuch* (BZAW 189; Berlin: de Gruyter, 1990), 229–285.

33:11, but as revenging their sister's rape by murdering the men of Shechem and plundering the city. Guided by the implicit evaluations the readers expect a negative judgment on the main protagonists Simeon and Levi. This judgment, however, will be heard only in the poem called the "Blessing of Jacob" spoken before his death (49:5–7). The short report about Reuben's intercourse with his father's concubine in 35:21–22a shows the very same structure: its open ending[31] builds up a suspense that will be maintained until 49:3–4. Read in this perspective, both Gen 34 and 35:21–22 represent etiological traditions explaining the peculiar status of the tribes in question, in this case that of Simeon and Levi and their being "divided" and "scattered" in Israel. At the same time, the curses against the first three sons prepare for the exaltation of Judah who actually gains the blessing of the firstborn in 49:8–12. Whatever the case, we are dealing here with a rather late pro-Judahite (pro-Davidic) thread of traditions in the stories of the ancestors.

Genesis 35:1–7 in its present form clearly builds upon ch. 34 (cf. 34:30–31; 35:5), and most probably also upon an older note about Jacob building an altar at Bethel called *'el bet'el* in 35:6*, 7.

In the given text, the name *'el bet-'el* refers to the place, i.e. Bethel; the resulting semantics, however, seem odd. The nearby note in 33:20 shows with *wyṣb ... mzbḥ* an unexpected construction as well. Here, the altar gets the name *'el 'elohe yisra'el*. Wellhausen already suggested that an original *mṣbh* has been substituted with *mzbḥ*.[32] The possibility that the strange *mqwm* in 35:7 was inserted in order to replace an older *mzbḥ* (v 7aα!) suggests itself even more. Probably, some later tradent did not like such a bold authorization of an altar at Bethel by the Patriarch. Nevertheless, the names of the cultic objects still form valuable sources for early religion in Israel: *'el 'elohe yisra'el*, i.e. "El is the god of Israel/El, the god of Israel," points to a pre-Yahwistic 'Israel' in the Shechem-area worshipping the high god El. Likewise, *'el bet-'el* can be interpreted as "El is in Beth-El/El of Bethel" reflecting the non-Yahwistic pre-history of that Israelite cult-place. As part of the Story of Jacob, however, the component *'el* does not function as a proper name but as the appellative with the connotation "strong," "powerful," "mighty," etc. This is confirmed by the intra-textual correspondence between 35:7 and the divine self-introduction in 31:13: *'anoki ha'el bet-'el* meaning "I am the god [who is in] Bethel."[33] Moreover, according to the narrative logic Jacob comes full circle in 35:7, referring to his departures to and from Aram, both marked by the 'god dwelling in

---

[31] See already August Dillmann, *Die Genesis* (6th ed.; KEHAT 11; Leipzig: Hirzel, 1892), 380.

[32] Wellhausen, *Composition*, 48 n. 1.

[33] The phrase is linguistically correct; see Blum, *Komposition*, 63 n. 11, 189; pace Axel Graupner, *Der Elohist: Gegenwart und Wirksamkeit des transzendenten Gottes in der Geschichte* (WMANT 97; Neukirchen-Vluyn: Neukirchener, 2002), 254–245; his presumption that an irregular construction was chosen in order to avoid the Tetragrammaton ignores the resumption of an 'idiomatic' phrase (35:7).

Beth-el.' At Shechem in 33:20, Jacob is closing a narrower circle: the use of Jacob's new name "Israel" points back to the encounter at Penuel. Thus the naming of the presumed *maṣṣeba* sounds like a summarizing confession: "(Indeed,) a mighty god is Israel's god!"

At the same time, Gen 35:1–5 stands in a frame of reference which is wider than the contexts of Gen 34 and the older Story of Jacob: the verses show strong connections to Josh 24, constituting a kind of typological correspondence between the acts of Jacob/Israel in Shechem under the *'lh* and of Joshua at that same place. This connection is tightened further by an explicit reference back to Gen 33:19 in Josh 24:32, which is mediated by the short notes about Joseph's bones (50:25–26; Exod 13:19); this implies that we are here dealing with references within one and the same literary work. Such an idea is supported by the peculiar statement in Josh 24:2 that "your ancestors—Terah and his sons Abraham and Nahor—lived beyond the Euphrates and served other gods" (NRSV), which has been derived from our Jacob tradition in a classic inner-biblical midrash. That is, those "foreign gods" among Jacob's household which he put away were none other than the "gods" of Laban (Gen 31:30, 32), the son of Nahor (29:5), i.e. the *teraphim* that Rachel had stolen from her father's house (31:20) beyond "the river" (31:21). Whereas these *teraphim* play merely a folkloristic role in the ancient story, the tradent-exegete of Gen 35:1–5//Josh 24 has transformed them into a fundamental theological issue, i.e. the "foreign gods" worshiped beyond the Euphrates.

With regard to the place of the Gen 35*/Josh 24-stratum in the literary history of the Pentateuch and the Former Prophets, there are strong indications that these texts belong to a late compositional stratum which aimed to constitute a hexateuchal "Book of the Torah" (Josh 24:26).[34]

Finally, we shall discuss a third group of non-Priestly passages skipped over in the synchronic description above: the *divine promises* given to the ancestor or cited by him. In the realm of the Jacob tradition, the divine speech addressed to Jacob at Bethel in Gen 28:13a*-15 forms the most prominent example of this genre. After God's self-introduction "I am YHWH, the god of your father Abraham and the god of Isaac," the piece begins in v. 13b with the promise to Jacob to give him and his descendants the land on which

---

[34] For a more detailed discussion see Blum, *Komposition*, 35–61, and more recently Blum, "The Literary Connection between the Books of Genesis and Exodus and the End of the Book of Joshua," in *A Farewell to the Yahwist? The Composition of the Pentateuch in Recent European Scholarship* (ed. Thomas B. Dozeman and Konrad Schmid; SBLSymS 34, Atlanta: Society of Biblical Literature, 2006), 96–104.

he is sleeping. Verse 14 comprises the promises to multiply his descendants like the dust of the earth and that all the families of the earth will bless themselves/one another by Jacob/Israel as the example of a blessed one.[35] Finally, the promise in v. 15 refers to Jacob's actual situation: God will preserve him on the way and bring him home. Apart from the last one all the promises have parallels in the other ancestor traditions. Most significant are the apparent connections to divine speeches at the beginning of the stories of Abraham (12:3b; 13:14–17). In our context, this evidence raises the question of how the relationship between these promises and the main narrative about Jacob should be diachronically defined.[36] Fortunately, this can be discussed without having come to firm conclusions about literary-critical issues in Gen 28. It is sufficient at this stage to compare how both the promises on the one hand, and the narrative on the other, treat the topics of land and people.

In the narrative the idea that the brothers Esau and Jacob will have a land to live in appears to be taken for granted; it is a natural matter. The question of which land is destined for each one is settled by way of etiological allusions or implications. Thus the intended readers know right from Esau's birth where the home of the "hairy red" boy will be. His father's prediction in 27:39b makes a further allusion to this and 32:4 and 33:14 can presuppose the *fait accompli* without further explanation. Jacob's/Israel's land is implicitly and *pars pro toto* marked by several places, mostly named by Jacob himself on his way (Beersheba, Bethel, Gilead, etc.). The 'frontier' treaty in the mountains of Gilead at Mizpa (31:23–53) with Laban, the Aramean (31:20, 24), implies the fact that Jacob has reached here his 'own land' as well. Isaac's blessing also assumes this line of thought: its theme is not the assurance of land to his son, but the land's abundant fecundity and its rich fruits (27:28).

---

[35] For this understanding of *brk* (nif.) *b-* see, inter alios, Blum, *Komposition*, 350–353, and recently Zakovitch, "Implied Synonyms," 837–838; for a different view, see Keith N. Grüneberg, *Abraham, Blessing and the Nations: A Philological and Exegetical Study of Genesis 12:3 in its Narrative Context* (BZAW 332; Berlin: de Gruyter, 2003).

[36] With regard to the patriarchal promises in general this issue has been bothering scholars for a long time; cf. Gunkel, *Genesis, passim*; Jan Hoftijzer, *Die Verheissungen an die drei Erzväter* (Leiden: Brill, 1956), 28–30; Claus Westermann, *Die Verheißungen an die Väter: Studien zur Vätergeschichte* (FRLANT 116; Göttingen: Vandenhoeck & Ruprecht, 1976); Rolf Rendtorff, *Das überlieferungsgeschichtliche Problem des Pentateuch* (BZAW 147; Berlin: de Gruyter, 1977), 37–40, 57–65; George W. Coats, "Strife without Reconciliation: A Narrative Theme in the Jacob Traditions," in *Werden und Wirken des Alten Testaments: Festschrift für Claus Westermann zum 70. Geburtstag* (ed. Rainer Albertz et al., Göttingen: Vandenhoeck & Ruprecht, 1980), 82–106; and J.A. Emerton, "The Origin of the Promises to the Patriarchs in the Older Sources of the Book of Genesis," *VT* 32 (1982): 14–32.

In contrast, in the divine speech of 28:13 the focus has shifted significantly. Now, the possession of the land itself has become the subject. What was formerly the unquestioned presupposition now forms the explicit assertion. A similar shift occurs in the ensuing promise in v. 14a: the promise of countless descendants transcends the narrated world by anchoring the great future of the people in God's word. Regarding the theme of blessing (v. 14b) one might *prima facie* see a correspondence between the promise in 28:14b and Laban's statement in 30:27b: "YHWH has blessed me because of you." The context, however, shows that Laban benefits from the blessed Jacob's *work* with his flock. That is not the proper meaning of 28:14b, regardless of whether one sees here a promise that Israel will be the *universal* paradigm for a blessed one or—according to the Christian tradition—the mediator of a universal blessing.

What is then the *raison d'être* of these promises which relate to the fundamental conditions of Israel's existence? Jan Hoftijzer has introduced an important idea concerning this issue some decades ago.[37] According to him the patriarchal promises reflect the experience of national catastrophes since the destruction of the northern kingdom by the Assyrians, which shook the unquestioned confidence in Israel's/Judah's existence in their land.[38] Prophetical texts like Ezek 33:24 or Isa 51:2 indicate, in fact, the major significance of the ancestor traditions in the exilic discourse on Israel's future. It was probably in this period that greater compositions of the ancestor stories were formed with the divine promises as constitutive elements. At any rate, it seems compelling that the main narrative in Gen 25B;*27–33 did not yet comprise the promises in 28:13b–14.[39]

The prayer of Jacob in Gen 32:10–14 contains two references to previous revelations of YHWH: v. 10b alludes to 31:3, v. 13 to the promise in 28:14a.[40] The prayer as a whole has been recognized as a later insertion by Gunkel et al.[41] Apparently, this

---

[37] Hoftijzer, *Verheissungen*. This work did not get the attention it deserved among his fellow scholars until the 1970s.

[38] This is in contrast to the dating in the Davidic-Solomonic era, which was dominant in earlier research.

[39] In my view it is conceivable that 28:13a*, 15* formed the nucleus of the divine speech in this episode; cf. Hos 12:7; *pace* Blum, *Komposition*, but with my later, "Noch einmal: Jakobs Traum in Bethel—Genesis 28,10–22," in *Rethinking the Foundations: Historiography in the Ancient World and in the Bible. Essays in Honour of John Van Seters* (ed. Steven L. McKenzie and Thomas Römer; BZAW 294; Berlin: de Gruyter, 2000), 43–44.

[40] Gunkel, *Genesis*, 357. For a detailed discussion see Blum, *Komposition*, 155–157 (with reference to older literature).

[41] See Gunkel, *Genesis*. John Skinner, *A Critical and Exegetical Commentary on Genesis* (ICC; Edinburgh: T&T Clark, 1910), 406, gives a concise summary: vv. 10–13 "can be removed

THE JACOB TRADITION   197

relatively late *Einschreibung* intends to show the patriarch as an exemplary pious man (already before the Jabbok episode), adding a further theological dimension to the final act. Gen 31:3 has a similar tendency: Jacob's initiative to return to his home is governed completely by an explicit divine order.

Source-Criticism in the Jacob Story

The foregoing analysis did not adhere to any variant of the documentary hypothesis, which had been prevalent in Pentateuchal criticism since the nineteenth century, but has lost its predominance in the last decades, at least in German-speaking research. Since the distinction between "J" and "E" still plays an important part in the international discourse, it seems appropriate to discuss its performance in the Story of Jacob more in detail. 'Spot checks' of three representative passages—Gen 28:10–22; Gen 31, and Gen 32–33[42]—shall serve this purpose.

(a) Gen 28:10–22 is one of the few episodes in the Pentateuch in which the separation of supposedly interwoven threads of J and E is defined almost unanimously by different source critics. For methodological reasons, however, we shall begin with a look at the literary shape and structure with as little bias as possible. Starting from the narrative center, one finds Jacob's dream (vv. 12–15) presented as a carefully described scenery:

a12	ויחלם
b/c	והנה סלם מצב ארצה / וראשו מגיע השמימה
d	והנה מלאכי אלהים עלים וירדים בו
a13	והנה יהוה נצב עליו

The scene comprises three elements or agents: a ramp (*slm*), divine messengers (*ml'ky 'lhym*), and YHWH. Each one is introduced by an opening *weʰinneh* ("and behold") and an impressive syntactical *ostinato*: each sentence is built following the basic pattern subject—participle—locative adjunct/complement. The first *weʰinneh* governs two sentences describing the ramp; the second *weʰinneh* introduces one sentence with two participles; and the third one gives the basic pattern with YHWH as focus. The

---

without loss of continuity, 14a being a natural continuation of 9. The insertion gives an interpretation of the 'two camps' at variance with the primary motive of the division (v. 9); and its spirit is different from that of the narrative in which it is embedded."

[42] According to Noth, *Überlieferungsgeschichte*, 30–31, 38, the E-source is restricted to the Bethel episode (in Gen 28), the birth of Jacob's children (in 29–30), the departure from Laban (31) and to the finale in chs. 32–33. In all of these passages two parallel threads of E and J are allegedly intertwined.

resultant "stepped structure" not only mirrors—so to speak—the imagined ramp/stairway, but also the *conceptual* climax leading from the heavenly ramp to the divine messengers and, finally, to the Deity himself. At the same time, the sentences in the first line rhyme with the antonyms "earth" and "heaven" suffixed with a *heh locale*, and the second and third lines both end with a preposition with a suffix in the third person (sing. masc.). Last, but not least, the first and the last sentence are bracketed by participles of the same root *nṣb*: *muṣṣab—niṣṣab*, a word-play which is taken up later with *maṣṣeba*. It would be difficult to find in biblical prose a passage surpassing the density of our scene description.

Moreover, after the divine speech and his awakening, Jacob relates the divine world seen in his dream with the place (*hmqwm*) he came upon by chance in two speeches which take up the three main components of our dream scene—as is common in biblical style, in reversed order: firstly YHWH himself: *'aken yeš yhwh bammaqom hazze*; secondly the *mal'ake 'elohim* as part of the divine 'household': *'en ze ki im bet 'lohim*; and finally the heavenly rampart: *weze šaʿar haššamayim*.[43] Formally reversing the climax in vv. 12–13a*, Jacob starts his own conclusions, appropriately, with God himself. In contrast, his two speeches show a climax in terms of his involvement: the first speech (v. 16) gives expression to his insight and surprise ("and I did not know it!"); the second (v. 17), explicitly marked by *wyr'*, gives expression to his fear in the face of the place's holiness.

Thus shaping Jacob's verbal reaction in two speeches proves meaningful in several respects: it highlights not only the cognitive and the affective consequences of Jacob's experience (again, in the appropriate sequence), but, even more significantly, it also enables the narration to give the suitable space to both, YHWH, the most important actor in any terms, and the holy place, the most important matter in terms of pragmatics with respect to the world of the addressees.[44]

The factual consequences of Jacob's insights and affects are sharply presented in the report of Jacob's actions before and after his nighttime experience. By means of verbal reiteration another frame is built (v. 11 paralleling

---

[43] These references are, of course, not only based on the recurrence of the terms אלהים and שמים, but also on the conceptual relationship between 'God's household' and "God's house," and between the 'ramp leading to heaven' and "the gate of heaven" respectively. Sean McEvenue, "A Return to Sources in Genesis 28,10–22?," *ZAW* 106 (1994): 381, calls in question these relations, though even the alleged Elohistic layer would not work without them. For a more differentiated exposition see Blum, *Komposition*, 9–16.

[44] For a more general perspective cf. also E.J. Revell, "The Repetition of Introductions to Speech as a Feature of Biblical Hebrew," *VT* 47 (1987): 91–110.

v. 18),⁴⁵ now enclosing the dream and the verbal response. It shows the fundamental transformation of the place and the stone in Jacob's perception, which is summed up in his naming the anonymous place as *bet 'el* in v. 19a.

According to a lasting source-critical consensus,⁴⁶ our episode emerged from the combination of two previously independent narrative threads: J in vv. 10, 13–16, 19a(b) and E in vv. 11–12, 17–18, 20, 21a(b), 22. Thus, source critics suggest cutting the vision at the third line and Jacob's verbal response between vv. 16 and 17. However, one has to ask if explaining the highly styled structure, especially of vv. 12–13a*, as the accidental result of the combination of two sources would not go far beyond a sound diachronic reasoning.⁴⁷ At best, the option of a redactional expansion would be conceivable, assuming that an author has fitted his additions meticulously to his 'Vorlage' to create an artful whole.⁴⁸ Still, the arguments for such a diachronic explanation would have to be weighty.

Two main arguments have been made since the classical critics.⁴⁹ The first is the alleged tension caused by the juxtaposition of the so-called "names of God" *yhwh* and *'elohim*. The second is the claim that vv. 16 and 17 form a doublet, both stating the "holiness of the place."⁵⁰ This second argument, however, misses the individuality of the two speeches outlined above; they simply do not have the same propositional meaning,⁵¹ and v. 16 does not constitute an expression of fear nor v. 17 an expression of surprise.

---

⁴⁵ Blum, *Komposition*, 9. Pointing to such correspondences does not imply the claim of an overall "chiasmus" covering the whole pericope; pace McEvenue, "Sources," 378–380.

⁴⁶ There is in this case some dissent as well, with regard to 'minor' questions (the unity of v. 11, the source-critical identifications of vv. 19, 21b, 22b), which must not deter us in this context, however.

⁴⁷ Unfortunately, McEvenue, "Sources," has not grasped this point in his discussion.

⁴⁸ This option has been suggested by David M. Carr, *Reading the Fractures of Genesis: Historical and Literary Approaches* (Louisville: Westminster John Knox, 1996), 206–207, esp. n. 57, who sees vv. 13–16 as an expansion by the author of his Proto-Genesis-Composition. See also John Van Seters, *Prologue to History: The Yahwist as Historian in Genesis* (Louisville: Westminster John Knox, 1992), 292–295 (earlier tradition in vv. 11–12, 16aα, 17–19a); and Kratz, *Komposition*, 270–274, 280.

⁴⁹ Additionally, Wellhausen, *Composition*, 30–31, argues that (a) the suffix in *'lyw* cannot refer to *slm*, stating that *niṣṣab 'al* means only "stand before," and that (b) YHWH speaking "from heaven upon the ramp" (?) would require *qr'* as *verbum dicendi*. But not only are the statements (a) and (b) inaccurate (cf. Amos 7:7 and the language in 28:13 [just *'lyw*] and in Isa 6), but also the given context does not exclude the understanding that YHWH stood before/over Jacob (the matter depends on the conception the readers had concerning YHWH's presence at Bethel).

⁵⁰ Gunkel, *Genesis*, 316, et al. Carr, *Reading*, 207, argues for a "doubling of Jacob's surprised response."

⁵¹ The reader would probably agree that both propositions include the idea of the holiness of the place, but that is not what the utterances are stating.

The predominant argument, however, involves the name of God in vv. 13 and 16, applying the *Hauptkriterium*[52] of Pentateuchal criticism since at least the nineteenth century. It presupposes that any juxtaposition of the divine name YHWH and the Hebrew common noun for "God"—*'elohim*—suffices to suspect different authors. Despite its lasting reputation, this criterion is philologically unfounded, however.[53] In fact, we are dealing here with an astonishing *idée fixe* in OT research. Interestingly enough, this holds true only for Pentateuchal criticism; there are plenty of interchanges of *elohim* and the Tetragrammaton in the former Prophets and beyond without anyone claiming different sources or redactions in those cases.[54] And indeed, the linguistic data are fundamentally clear. There are no "two names of God" in Hebrew: The Israelite God has but *one* name (the Tetragrammaton), whereas *'elohim*, *'el*, and so on constitute appellatives, sometimes used like titles. Therefore, *YHWH* and *'elohim* stand in the same linguistic relationship to each other as *David* and *hmlk* or as *Necho* and *par'oh*.[55] There is nothing strange about these nouns being used interchangeably in the same text. They can be combined as well: *pr'h nkh* is "Pharaoh Necho" (Jer 46:2), so *yhwh 'lhym* (Gen 2–3 *passim*; Exod 9:30; 2 Sam 7:25, 26 etc.) just means "God Yahwe." There might be, of course, authors who prefer either the proper name "David" or the title "the king," but stylistic criteria should never function as an *a-priori* argument! That is, however, the way in which the so-called argument of the "names of God" has often been used in Pentateuchal source criticism. The reasons for that peculiar approach to the Pentateuch seem to be deeply rooted in the history of the discipline: the beginnings of the historical approach to the Bible were primarily connected

---

[52] Wellhausen, *Composition*, 32.

[53] For a detailed linguistic discussion of the issue see Erhard Blum, "Der vermeintliche Gottesname 'Elohim'," in *Gott Nennen: Gottes Namen und Gott als Name* (ed. Ingolf U. Dalferth and Philipp Stoellger; RPT 35; Tübingen: Mohr Siebeck, 2008), 97–119.

[54] A few random examples include: 1 Sam 3:3 (*wnr 'lhym trm ykbh wšmw'l škb bhkl yhwh 'šr šm 'rwn 'lhym*); 11:6–7 (*rwḥ 'lhym/pḥd yhwh*); 2 Sam 3:9 (*'lhym/yhwh*); 2 Sam 6:7–9 (*yhwh/ h'lhym/'rwn h'lhjm/yhwh/'rwn yhwh*); 2 Sam 14:16–17 (*nḥlt 'lhym/ml'k h'lhym/yhwh*); 15:31–32 (*yhwh/'lhjm*); 1 Chr 21:30–22:1 (*'lhym/yhwh/byt yhwh h'lhym*); 2 Chr 18:31 (... *wyhwh 'zrw wysytm 'lhym mmnw*).

[55] Though determined in general, פרעה is used without the article. This is analogous to the use of אלהים (as "God"). Another interesting analogy includes the use of βασιλευς without the article referring to the Great King of Persia (in Herodotus). Common to these titles is that their reference is definite in the speaker's world. In such cases, one may speak of an "absolute title." With regard to אלהים this condition is given in a henotheistic or monotheistic context. Additionally, the Hebrew writer/speaker has the choice between אלהים and האלהים, seemingly without any semantic difference (cf. for instance Gen 6:9–12; 22:1, 8, 9 and the examples in n. 54 above).

with the Primeval History (Gen 1–11), in which the preference for the divine name or for the common noun/absolute title in different layers is indeed apparent. Given, furthermore, the theological system in P concerning the revelation of God's name (Exod 6), it was tempting to generalize this criterion at least in the realm of the Pentateuch[56] and almost to lend it an *a priori* authority.

An unbiased reading, in fact, reveals that we have, in the Pentateuch as in other parts of the canon, texts using either the divine name or other Hebrew divine designations (common nouns/titles) as well as texts which show both side by side. In the latter, the interchange of designations seems to occur only rarely for the sake of some 'deeper' meaning.[57] In most cases it appears arbitrarily or induced by slight nuances or seemingly superficial reasons or conditioned by idiomatic language. The phenomenon cannot be restricted to early or late literature either; one only needs to compare the designations of God in the speech of the wise woman from Tekoa (2 Sam 14) with the Chronicler's version of David's census in 1 Chr 21. Here and there the designations change randomly.

Consequently, varying divine designations in the Jacob story do not require an explanation *per se*. Nevertheless, some remarks (limited to the main story) may be added here in order to illustrate the options just mentioned above: the first three verses of the opening episode (25:21–23) use the name *yhwh*. This way the narrative identifies the god of Isaac's/Jacob's family who will play the decisive role. Genesis 27 has the name three times, apart from v. 20 twice directly connected with the blessing (vv. 7, 27). In phrases with *brk* the divine name seems to be idiomatic: in the Hebrew epigraphic sources the evidence is clear-cut. The same can be observed in the biblical traditions, where God, when introduced as the giver of a blessing, is referred to almost exclusively by the Tetragrammaton; major exceptions are, to my knowledge, only the introductions to Priestly blessings in Genesis (according to the theological scheme of P) and the so-called "Elohistic Psalter."[58] The corpus of Isaac's blessing has *ha'elohim* in 27:28; I do not see a special reason for this.

---

[56] Neither Gen 4:26 nor Exod 3:13–16 speaks about the revelation of a previously unknown name; pace McEvenue, "Sources," 386. Regarding Exod 3, see Christopher R. Seitz, "The Call of Moses and the 'Revelation' of the Divine Name: Source-Critical Logic and its Legacy," in *Theological Exegesis: Essays in Honor of Brevard S. Childs* (ed. Christopher R. Seitz and Kathryn Greene-McCreight; Grand Rapids: Eerdmans, 1999), 150–154; see already Benno Jacob, *Das Buch Exodus* (ed. Shlomo Mayer; Stuttgart: Calwer, 1997 [written in 1935–1943]), 59–71.

[57] As is probably the case in Gen 22; cf. Blum, *Komposition*, 323.

[58] For an isolated example, see the blessing of the non-Israelite Melchizedek in Gen 14:19–20 using *'l 'lyn*.

In Gen 28:10–19 God himself is called by his name; the etiological derivation of the place name "Bethel" is introduced by *bet 'elohim* in Jacob's speech, which is prepared itself by *mal'ake 'elohim* in the dream (see above). In the apodosis of Jacob's vow (vv. 20, 21*, 22), the functional term *bet 'elohim* constitutes another pun with *bet 'el*, and it has no better correspondence in the protasis than *'elohim*.[59]

The next cluster of divine designations starts with the divine name in 29:31–35.[60] The switch to *'elohim* occurs with Jacob's argument against a desperate Rachel that he (as a human) is not in God's place (30:2). Thereafter we have the common noun eight times until Joseph, whose name is—with deliberate redundancy[61]— interpreted twice using *'elohim* as well as *yhwh* for a double alliteration.

The Tetragrammaton in 30:27, 30 continues the thread of v. 24, being simply idiomatic here (as subject of *wybrk*). The next switch to *'elohim* occurs in Jacob's speech to his wives, when he speaks about the 'god of his father' (31:5). Moreover, the whole passage narrating the process of separation between Laban's and Jacob's families (ch. 31) is about children, fathers, and their gods like a *tema con variazioni*. Therefore it should not be surprising that the common noun prevails in 31:5–53. There are only two exceptions: The reference in 31:13 to the revelation at Bethel uses neither *yhwh* nor *elohim* but *hael bet-el* alluding simultaneously to another cultic name at the sanctuary, i.e. *'l bet-el* (35:7), with which the addressees were most probably familiar. An occasional occurrence of *yhwh* can be found in the etiological derivation of "Mizpah" in 31:49, probably induced by a slight alliteration.

The even more consistent use of *'elohim* in Gen 32–33 (seven times) does not come as a surprise either. The encounter with the messengers at Mahanaim forms a deliberate reminder of the Bethel-encounter, picking up the *mal'ake 'elohim* and substituting *bet 'elohim* with *mahane 'elohim*. In the Penuel-episode there is actually no alternative because of the puns (a) with "Israel," (b) with "Penuel," and (c) because of the meaningful vagueness of the opponent's identity. The report on the brothers' encounter continues using the same language (three times), once (33:10) in a clear reference to 32:31.

---

[59] Verse 21b probably did not belong to the older story, unless one prefers to read the sentence as part of the *protasis* ("if YHWH will behave towards me as [my] god"[?]); *yhwh* would then be a suitable anaphora to *'elohim* in v. 20. If, however, the sentence represents a variant of the 'covenant-formula' and should be read as the beginning of the apodosis ("then YHWH shall be my God") then we have a logical as well as conceptual incoherence between the *protasis* and the *apodosis*. At any rate, the formulation with the indirect object in the first person is unique to 28:21b and implies a conception peculiar to Josh 24 (see v. 22). This might suggest connecting 28:21b with the redaction of Gen 35:1–5 and Josh 24 outlined previously; cf. Blum, *Komposition*, 89–91.

[60] This provides an alliteration with "Yehuda" in v. 35.

[61] Rachel's first statement (in 30:23) closes the theme of her dramatic conflict with her sister/fellow-wife, the second one (v. 24) points to the future and functions as a narrative 'place marker' for the last son still to be born. This 'redundancy' fits perfectly with the narration underscoring the birth of Rachel's firstborn as the apex of the whole passage.

At any rate, the overall conclusion with regard to the Bethel episode in Gen 28 seems quite clear: there is actually no compelling evidence one way or the other, be it for the common source-critical analysis or for recent redaction-critical variations severing vv. 12 and 13a.

(b) A detailed analysis of the complex ch. 31 would go beyond the scope of this contribution. Instead, we shall focus on the more or less unanimously agreed upon separated versions of how Jacob received his wealth according to Gen 30:25–43 on the one hand and according to *31:1–16 on the other hand. Under the premises of the documentary hypothesis the first piece is assigned to J, the other to E. Some major contradictions between the pieces have been pointed out already.[62] Although one might consider the possibility of two complementary versions, one as the narrator's report focusing on Jacob as a trickster, the other as Jacob's narration focusing on divine causality, the differences stand out here in the extreme. Moreover, at least one contradiction remains unsettled: whereas Jacob obviously makes his wealth at Laban's expense in 30:41–43, this aspect remains completely hidden from the hearer/reader in ch. 31. There are thus good reasons to look for a diachronic explanation of the tensions just mentioned.

The popular presumption of parallel sources, however, raises questions. First, it seems evident that Jacob's speech in 31:4–12 presupposes a previously narrated report on Jacob's success with the flock that caused the anger of Laban.[63] Consequently, one has to assume the loss of a substantial narration of the alleged E-strand. But what could have been the plot line of that lost part? Certainly Jacob's success would be based on an agreement with Laban concerning sheep and goats with a peculiar pattern, quite similar to the narrative in ch. 30, though more complicated (31:7!). Assuming such a possibility, the next question arises with regard to the divine revelation reported extensively in Jacob's speech to his wives: on the one hand, a straight record by the narrator forming a bold doublet to 31:10–13 can be ruled out. On the other hand, however, is it conceivable that the scene with the divine messenger providing the decisive clue to Jacob's situation would be given in a flashback from the outset?

This brings us back to the crucial issue concerning the given story in Gen 30–31: it is the peculiar way in which the plot-elements of 31:7–13

---

[62] See above p. 184.
[63] See Gen 31:2, 4. A source-critical approach tends to see 31:1, 2 as a doublet. Nothing, however, prevents us from reading the verses as complementary information building a slight climax ("to hear—to see," "Laban's sons—Laban himself").

(including the divine message) are integrated into the greater narrative that requires an explanation. In other words, what is the *raison d'être* for such a narration using a flashback? The most reasonable answer seems to be that it was designed in order to re-tell an existing story by expanding it with an additional perspective. This way, Jacob's speech can function as a theological corrective to the story of his successful 'skill,' providing a *doppelte Kausalität* (Seeligmann).

This conclusion has interesting implications. Based on 'old' literary-critical observations, we have strong indications of a redactional/compositional (pre-)history of the Story of Jacob. Obviously, the layer of 31:4-16 has also left its marks on other parts of Gen 31 (see below). At the same time it is strongly connected with the Bethel episode in Gen 28 as evidenced by 31:13. Given the cross-relationship of the Bethel story with Gen 32-33 (Mahanaim, Penuel), this points to the probability that the layer under discussion in Gen 31 played a constitutive role in the shaping of our 'Story of Jacob.' For that reason I have suggested that it be called a "compositional layer (*Kompositionsschicht*)."[64] Under such circumstances the ability to reconstruct the tradition used cannot necessarily be expected. Nevertheless, such an attempt does not seem futile from the outset, at least in the portion beginning with 31:19,[65] since we find significant literary techniques here like resumptive repetitions (*Wiederaufnahmen*) or anticipating repetitions (*Vorwegnahmen*) that can be used as devices for a diachronic *Fortschreibung*.[66]

---

[64] Blum, *Komposition*, 168-171.

[65] It seems impossible to reconstruct a coherent narrative line without the Teraphim-episode. This is why the diverse proposals to separate extensive J/E-threads fail. Thus in Noth's J (31:1, 3, 17, 18aα, 19a, 20, 21aαb, 22-23, 25bα, [25bβ], 26aα, 27, 30a, 31 ... 36a, 38-40, 46*, [(47), 48], [49], 51*-52*, 53a; see Noth, *Überlieferungsgeschichte*, 30-31) Laban's speech breaks off with v. 30a and Jacob's anger in v. 36 is thus unfounded, both because the Teraphim incident is taken out. In contrast, Graupner, *Elohist*, 262, leaves the Teraphim in J, but now has Laban's speech breaking off with 31:30a (continuing with Jacob's answer in vv. 31, 41-42) in E. Consequently, assuming that the note about Rachel's theft of the Teraphim (31:19b) belongs to the pre-compositional stratum, the conclusion is inevitable that the scene in 31:5-16 has replaced some earlier version of Jacob's conversation with his wives.

[66] As is known, such techniques may serve as redactional as well as authorial devices. In this case it seems that they coincide with diachronically significant cross-references (see already Blum, *Komposition*, 124-126). So we have a clear *Wiederaufnahme* in 31:23b//25a framing a divine nocturnal revelation to Laban, which is referred to by him in v. 29 (see Blum, *Komposition*, 126) and by Jacob in v. 42b. Verses 41-44 as a whole show parallels to 31:5-16 in several aspects; their opening line marks a new part in Jacob's answer to Laban by resuming the preceding opening in v. 38. As a result, it seems reasonable to consider 31:24-25a, 29, 41-44 as part of our compositional layer founded on the earlier narrative in 31:19-23, 25bα, 26-28, 30-40 (except for some glosses).

Especially in the concluding pact-scene, however, any such attempt will be nothing but tentative.⁶⁷

(c) Source-critical analysis of Gen 32–33 generally ascribes 32:4–9, (10–13), 14a to J, 32:1–3, 14b–22 to E, 33:1–17 to J and E (in divergent attributions), and 32:23–33 either to J,⁶⁸ E,⁶⁹ or both.⁷⁰ Such divisions in Gen 32–33 are due to a systemic compulsion to find parallel accounts rather than cogent textual evidence; to see 32:4–9, 14a and 32:14b–22 as doublets is to ignore that only vv. 4–9 provide information necessary for vv. 14b–22, i.e. Esau is coming to meet his brother!⁷¹ This implies that 32:14b–22 does not constitute a narrative strand standing on its own feet but the continuation of vv. 4–9, the alleged doublet 32:14a//22b forming an integrating element.⁷²

---

⁶⁷ Under the assumptions that (a) the etiological line of Mizpa: צפה—המצבה—המצפה connected with the care of Laban's daughters (vv. 49–50), and the line of Gilead: עד—גל—גלעד connected primarily with the border pact (vv. 51–52) should be distinguished diachronically, and that (b) v. 48a forms an 'anticipatory repetition' of vv. 51*-52a* allowing the insertion of the explicit name derivations and of the familial issue in vv. 48b–50, the following literary stratigraphy might be considered: (I) 31:46, 51–54 continuing 31:40 as basic narrative; (II) 31:45, 48–50 and the references to the Masseba in vv. 51b, 52 as a compositional layer; (III) later scribal alterations in vv. 45–46 ("Jacob" instead of "Laban") and the 'learned' insertion of v. 47.

⁶⁸ This is the majority position; see for instance Wellhausen, *Composition*, 44; Noth, *Überlieferungsgeschichte*, 31; and recently Jochen Nentel, *Die Jakobserzählungen: Ein literar- und redaktionskritischer Vergleich der Theorien zu Entstehung des Pentateuch* (München: AVM, 2009), 286–293 and n. 813 (with literature).

⁶⁹ Dillmann, *Genesis*, 360, 363–365 (*et passim*); recently Horst Seebass, *Genesis II/2: Väter- geschichte II (23,1–36,43)* (Neukirchen-Vluyn: Neukirchener, 1999), 398–399; Yoreh, "Struggle"; Jeremy M. Hutton, "Jacob's 'Two Camps' and Transjordanian Geography: Wrestling with Order in Genesis 32," *ZAW* 122 (2010): 20–32; and cf. also Hans-Christoph Schmitt, "Der Kampf Jakobs mit Gott in Hos 12:3 ff. und in Gen 32,23 ff.: Das Verständnis der Verborgenheit Gottes im Hoseabuch und im Elohistischen Geschichtswerk," in *Ich bewirke das Heil und erschaffe das Unheil (Jesaja 45,7): Studien zur Botschaft der Propheten. Festschrift für Lothar Ruppert zum 65. Geburtstag* (ed. F. Diedrich and B. Willmes; FB 88; Würzburg: Echter, 1998), 397–430; note that E forms a redactional layer according to Schmitt.

⁷⁰ For instance Gunkel, *Genesis*, 359–363.

⁷¹ This expectation in 32:14b–22 is evidenced by Jacob's instructions to his servant in v. 18 ("When Esau my brother meets you …") and by the narrative logic; otherwise Jacob would have no reason to start sending herds at the Jabbok (!) in the direction of Edom.

⁷² The understanding of the parallel time-markers depends on the readers' presuppositions. If they think it natural that five herds will be sent ahead in the night, they will see the two verses as references to the same night. Pace the argument of Wellhausen, *Composition*, 43, often echoed: in this case "the narrative does not come [viz. with 32:22a] to the point it had reached already" [translation mine] in 32:14a. Instead we have a deliberate contrast: While a part of his flock moved ahead, Jacob himself did not move from the "camp," a note which, of course, forms a preparation to v. 23. If the readers, however, do not reckon with such an action at night, they will naturally understand the events of 32:14b–22 as taking place on the next day.

Recently introduced arguments regarding the "Transjordan geography" do not support a source-critical analysis either. Jeremy Hutton presumes for Jacob's route in J "a north-south movement, in which ... Seir is the destination (32,4; 33,14.16)," and for E "an east-west movement beginning in the land of the 'children of the east' (Gen 29,1) ...."[73] In addition, presuming that "E"—now—"presents the etiology of Mahanaim (32,2b–3) before that of Penuel (32,31) and both occur before Jacob crosses the river" he concludes that according to J "Penuel is located on the southern bank of the Jabbok, and Mahanaim on the north," whereas E implies the location of Mahanaim on the south as well. He then suggests transferring the Mahanaim etiology in 32:2b–3 at the end of the Penuel episode after *32:25–32a (!) in the *original* E-strand. It was, then, the JE-redactor who transposed 32:2b–3 to its present context. The alleged problem, however, is built on questionable suppositions: neither do 32:3; 33:14, 16 imply an intention of Jacob to go from Aram to Edom,[74] nor do 32:24–25 *per se* indicate clearly on which side of the river Jacob "was left alone."[75] Further, there is no need to break up the extended exposition in 32:23–25a literarily,[76] because v. 23 gives the main information with regard to the (other) protagonists, while v. 24 unfolds the process of transferring in order to prepare v. 25a.

At the same time, the source divisions here tear apart the dense network of allusions and word-plays outlined above. Thus the partially redundant fivefold *panim* in 32:21–22a just before the Penuel-scene might be enough to call into question the attribution of 32:14b–22 and 32:23–33 to different sources. The same holds true with regard to the parallelism between 33:10 and 32:31 cited above (p. 186) which is ignored or denied among proponents of source analysis;[77] it is not only Jacob's hint of the encounter with the divine being that builds the bridge but the semantic and syntactic correspondence as well.[78]

---

[73] Hutton, "Geography," 26.

[74] Jacob's own destination is revealed neither by his sending messengers nor by his keeping Esau in suspense.

[75] Note that '*br hifil* does not mean "send across" in the strict sense.

[76] Pace Blum, *Komposition*, 144. Rightly Graupner, *Elohist*, 278.

[77] The only exception I could find so far is Otto Procksch, *Die Genesis übersetzt und erklärt* (3rd ed.; KAT 1; Leipzig: Deichert 1924), 198, who assigns both texts to J—at a price: the splitting of 32:23–33 into two literary threads.

[78] See again Procksch, *Genesis*. Benno Jacob, *Das Buch Genesis* (Berlin: Schocken, 1934; repr., Stuttgart: Calwer Verlag, 2000), 646–647, points rightly to the cultic language used here by Jacob including the idea that one should not come "with empty hands" to the Deity (Exod 23:15, 17, etc.) and the hope for divine acceptance (*raṣon*); he also highlights the Penuel-encounter (32:31) as the context enabling this language. Graupner's attempt to escape this nexus includes the proposal to read the last word in 33:10 as an *imperfectum copulativum* of the 2nd person with modal meaning (*Elohist*, 281 with n. 563); such a form, however, does not exist in the Old Hebrew verbal system (see Erhard Blum, "Das althebräische Verbsystem— eine synchrone Analyse," in *Sprachliche Tiefe—Theologische Weite* [ed. Oliver Dyma and Andreas Michel; BThSt 91; Neukirchen-Vluyn: Neukirchener, 2008], 91–142).

In sum, the great finale of our Story of Jacob shows in its narrative substance both: an impressive complexity and literary unity. In contrast to ch. 31 there are no traces of the integration of an earlier *literary* tradition. The earlier material included in ch. 31 by the 'compositional layer' comprised apparently some story of Jacob and Laban, presumably as part of a bipartite Jacob-Esau-Laban-narrative (in Gen 25B*; 27*; *29–31). Our tripartite composition, however, was shaped by an author who created—possibly relying on oral traditions—especially the finale and the corresponding Bethel story as well as the compositional elements in Gen 31. Presumably, he also rewrote the episode about the birth of Jacob's children.[79] Moreover, since we received the story as a whole from this narrator's hand, any attempt at reconstructing the presumed earlier tradition word-for-word would remain conjectural. For this reason, the following discussion of the probable historical setting of our tradition will focus upon the Story of Jacob described so far.

IV. The Historical Setting of the Story of Jacob

Knowing the historical context of a biblical narrative is essential for a full understanding of its purpose—and *vice versa*, peculiar pragmatic textual features often deliver the most reliable criteria for defining the intended addressees and the historical conditions. In this respect etiological traditions have a significant advantage in that they are anchored in a more or less specific historical constellation, i.e. the conditions under which the question, answered by the etiology, makes sense.

The Story of Jacob as a narrative of origins (*Ursprungsgeschichte*) implies a fundamental etiology of Israel (and some of its neighbors), which prima facie might fit constellations lasting for a long time. It includes, however, more specific etiological components too, first and foremost the *hieros logos* of the sanctuary at Bethel (Gen 28). Admittedly, there have been several proposals in recent decades to reckon with a flourishing sanctuary at Bethel even in the seventh and sixth centuries BCE,[80] but such claims

---

[79] The main indicators are the exact correspondences with the structuring of Jacob's family in ch. 33 and the eminent role of Joseph (30:22–25; 33:7). The obviously secondary introduction of the maids in 29:24, 29; 31:33* is not so clear as evidence; pace Blum, *Komposition*, 170.

[80] See for instance Timo Veijola, *Verheissung in der Krise: Studien zur Literatur und Theologie der Exilszeit anhand des 89. Psalms* (AASF B/22; Helsinki: Suomalainen Tiedeakatemia,

have lacked any evidence from the outset.[81] Gen 28:11–22 and the references to cultic installations in Bethel in 31:13; 35:7 therefore point strongly to the destruction of the Northern Kingdom by the Assyrians (722–720) as *terminus ante quem* for our narrative.[82] Further considerations actually limit its possible original context to the relatively short period of the northern state.[83]

This northern setting is confirmed and highlighted in the story by all other places embedded into the story and introduced by name in an etiological manner: Mizpa/Gilead, Mahanaim, Penuel, Sukkot, Shechem. Remarkably, Penuel, which appears, narratively speaking, as the counterpart of Bethel, had some importance in the early years of the northern kingdom, functioning as one of the residences of Jeroboam I (1 Kgs 12:25). The extraordinary introduction of Joseph in the birth story of Jacob's sons (29:31–30:24) and in the dramatic climax in ch. 33 (v. 7) also points to the north. As is well known, Joseph represented by far the greatest and strongest tribal group in the northern kingdom. Last, but not least, the story introduces the one ancestor's name that served—*inter alia*—as the 'constitutional' name of the Northern Kingdom: "Israel."

At first glance two elements of the Jacob story are seemingly not fully compatible with such a setting: southern Esau/Edom as a twin-brother of Jacob/Israel and their father Isaac at Beersheba (28:10). In the first case geography seems to stand in the way of connecting Edom with a northern Israelite tradition. However, mere geography is not always enough to explain social reality (of which ancestor traditions are a part). The chance finding of epigraphic texts at Kuntillet ʿAjrud (probably early eighth century BCE) throws some light on a complicated historical reality: although lying in the northern Sinai-peninsula on the route to Elath/Edom, all Hebrew personal names (comprising the Israelite divine name) are of northern origin. Moreover, the inscriptions repeatedly communicate blessings "by YHWH

1982), 194–197; and Ernst Axel Knauf, "Bethel: The Israelite Impact on Judean Language and Literature," in *Judah and the Judeans in the Persian Period* (ed. Oded Lipschits and Manfred Oeming; Winona Lake, Ind.: Eisenbrauns 2006), 291–349.

[81] From an archaeological point of view, not even one wall of Bethel's sanctuary has been found so far. Moreover, a recent examination of the excavated pottery has shown the lack of evidence for any significant settlement activity in Iron Age IIC and in the Babylonian/Persian period at the site of Bethel; see Israel Finkelstein and Lily Singer-Avitz, "Reevaluating Bethel," *ZDPV* 125 (2009): 33–48. The adduced exegetical evidence (Jer 41:5–6; Zech 7:2) does not stand up to closer examination.

[82] According to OT records some cultic activities continued at Bethel under Assyrian rule until King Josiah. There is, however, no hint of such a peculiar situation in the Jacob material.

[83] Pre-royal times can be excluded because of the pan-Israelite orientation of the story as well as the Davidic-Solomonic era because of the narrative's negligence of Jerusalem.

of Samaria" as well as "by YHWH of Teman/YHWH of the south."[84] These northern traders apparently acknowledged a special connection of their 'state' god with the region of Teman which is associated with Edom (cf. Amos 1:11–12), a connection that recalls the opening of the Song of Deborah in Judg 5:4–5: "YHWH, when you went out from Seir,/when you marched from the field of Edom ... The mountains quaked before YHWH,/the One of Sinai,/before YHWH, the God of Israel." Whichever way the tradition of a close relationship with Edom/Seir was received in northern Israel, apparently they could feel a kinship with those distant, 'wild' relatives in several respects. Whatever the case, the remarkably sympathetic introduction of the deceived Esau in Gen 27 as well as in Gen 33 is more conceivable in the North than in Judah with its bloody neighbor strife.

The role of the Isaac tradition including Beersheba in the Story of Jacob is part of its inclusive conception of Israel which is reflected, of course, in the integration of Judah as Jacob's fourth son, but no less in his ancestors Abraham and Isaac (cf. 31:42, 53; 28:13a). Apparently, however, the figure of Isaac was of peculiar significance for the northerners, at least in the later eighth century BCE. This is evidenced by the Book of Amos in which Israel is not only called *yiṣḥaq* (Amos 7:9) or *bet yiṣḥaq* (7:16), but is warned not to go on pilgrimage to Beersheba (5:5; cf. also 8:14a).

Finally, Israelite interests in Beersheba (Isaac) and in Teman (Edom) could reinforce each other insofar as Isaac was the ancestor of both Jacob/Israel *and* Edom and insofar as Israelite travelers to Sinai/Teman went through Beersheba (cf. 1 Kgs 19:3, 8).

All things considered, it appears to be beyond reasonable doubt that the primary home of our Story of Jacob was the kingdom of Israel. Further, so-to-speak 'external' evidence is given by the reception of the Jacob tradition in Hos 12. The way in which the prophet alludes to almost all parts of the story we have in Genesis proves that he can presuppose quite naturally his addressees' familiarity with a story like this.[85] Can its composition be dated even more exactly? In 1984 I suggested the very beginning of the Northern Kingdom as the most appropriate date, mainly on the basis of the correspondence between political actions of the founding king Jeroboam I in Bethel and Penuel (as reported in 1 Kgs 12:25–33) and several major plot lines in the Story of Jacob.[86] Undoubtedly, the story has an enormous legitimating force with regard to fundamental aspects of Israelite identity and religion. This holds true, however, not only for the era of Jeroboam.

---

[84] See for instance Shmuel Ahituv, *Handbook of Ancient Hebrew Inscriptions* (2nd ed.; EML 21; Jerusalem: Mosad Bialik, 2005 [Hebrew]), 232–245.

[85] Cf. the analysis in Erhard Blum, "Hosea 12 und die Pentateuchüberlieferungen," in *Die Erzväter in der biblischen Tradition: Festschrift für Matthias Köckert* (ed. Anselm C. Hagedorn and Henrik Pfeiffer; BZAW 400, Berlin: de Gruyter, 2009), 291–321.

[86] See Blum, *Komposition*, 175–186.

Moreover, assuming such an early date for our main composition would make it hard to find a conceivable context for the presumed earlier bipartite narrative (in Gen 25B*; 27*; *29–31). Although it probably did not include traditions like Gen 28 and 32, its northern outlook seems clear as well. Thus the time of the kingdom of Israel up to the last third of the eighth century BCE might be considered for the formation of the Story of Jacob and its *Vorstufe*—but probably excluding the era of the fierce Aramean wars (second half of the ninth century BCE) because in the narration on the relations between the Aramean Laban and Jacob/Israel there is no reflection at all of the horror and hatred experienced in that time. Tentatively, one might conjecture a literary formation of the earlier Jacob-Esau-Laban-story before those wars (i.e. in the Omride era) and the composition of the tripartite Story of Jacob in the eighth century,[87] perhaps under the second Jeroboam, probably in the realm of the sanctuary at Bethel. If we were to imagine what could have belonged to the curriculum for the education of Israelite scribes, our Story of Jacob would certainly be a first-rank candidate. After the end of the northern state, it became the core of a broader story of Israel's ancestors.[88]

Select Bibliography

Blum, Erhard. *Die Komposition der Vätergeschichte*. Wissenschaftliche Monographien zum Alten und Neuen Testament 57. Neukirchen-Vluyn: Neukirchener, 1984.

Carr, David M. *Reading the Fractures of Genesis: Historical and Literary Approaches*. Louisville: Westminster John Knox, 1996.

Coats, George W. "Strife without Reconciliation: A Narrative Theme in the Jacob Traditions." Pages 82–106 in *Werden und Wirken des Alten Testaments: Festschrift für Claus Westermann zum 70. Geburtstag*. Edited by Rainer Albertz, Hans-Peter Muller, Hans Walter Wolff and Walther Zimmerli. Göttingen: Vandenhoeck & Ruprecht, 1980.

Fishbane, Michael A. "Composition and Structure in the Jacob Cycle (Gen. 25:19–35:22)." *Journal of Jewish Studies* 26 (1975): 15–38.

---

[87] Assuming such a differentiation, another tension will perhaps find an explanation: whereas 31:22–23 and the frontier-treaty in 31:51–53* (i.e. the earlier tradition) presuppose Laban living in the realm of Damascus (see also 29:1), his location at Haran (27:43; 28:10; 29:5) seems to imply a shift of the supposed origin of the Arameans to northern Syria. This 'knowledge' might have been taken up by the author of the full Jacob story. For somewhat divergent conjectures see Blum, *Komposition*, 164–167, 343–344 n. 11.

[88] I am most grateful to Mr. David Cloutier for improving the English of an earlier draft of this paper.

Fokkelman, J.P. *Narrative Art in Genesis: Specimens of Stylistic and Structural Analysis.* Studia Semitica Neerlandica 17. Amsterdam: van Gorcum, 1975.
Gunkel, Hermann. *Genesis.* 3rd ed. Handkommentar zum Alten Testament 1/1. Göttingen: Vandenhoeck & Ruprecht, 1910.
Hendel, Ronald S. *The Epic of the Patriarch: The Jacob Cycle and the Narrative Traditions of Canaan and Israel.* Harvard Semitic Monographs 42. Atlanta: Scholars Press, 1987.
Hoftijzer, Jacob. *Die Verheissungen an die drei Erzväter.* Leiden: Brill, 1956.
Kugel, James L. *The Ladder of Jacob: Ancient Interpretations of the Biblical Story of Jacob and his Children.* Princeton: University Press, 2006.
Macchi, Jean-Daniel, and Thomas Römer, eds. *Jacob: Commentaire à plusieurs voix de Gen. 25 36—Mélanges offert à Albert de Pury.* Le Monde de la Bible 44. Genève: Labor et Fides, 2001.
Rad, Gerhard von. *Genesis: A Commentary.* Translated by John H. Marks. Old Testament Library. Philadelphia: Westminster, 1961.
Spieckermann, Hermann. *Der Gotteskampf: Jakob und der Engel in der Bibel und Kunst.* Zürich: Theologischer Verlag, 1997.
Van Seters, John. *Prologue to History: The Yahwist as Historian in Genesis.* Louisville: Westminster John Knox, 1992.

GENESIS 37–50:
JOSEPH STORY OR JACOB STORY?

Richard J. Clifford

Genesis 37–50, almost universally known as the Joseph Story, fascinates ordinary readers even as it leaves scholars with question about its boundaries and unity. Many scholars question whether ch. 38 (about Judah's family) and ch. 49 (the Testament of Jacob) belong in "a story about Joseph." Before examining these questions, it should be recalled that modern scholarly analysis stands in the long shadow of Hermann Gunkel (1910) on the one hand, and Gerhard von Rad (1954; 1972) on the other.[1] To Gunkel, the story was a "novella" with folkloric elements, the chapters were intended as a bridge to the book of Exodus, and chs. 38 and 49 "stand completely outside the framework of the Joseph narrative."[2] Von Rad argued that chs. 37–50 (especially the J source) were covertly dealing with issues of monarchy and its officialdom, and "Wisdom" themes characteristic of his "Solomonic Enlightenment" were reflected in Joseph's management of Egyptian affairs and enlightening of his brothers. Subsequent interpreters have taken some of these positions as starting points, though not always in agreement with them.[3] Most commentators on Genesis, nonetheless, persist in the

---

[1] Gunkel, *Genesis* (trans. Mark E. Biddle; Macon, Ga.: Mercer University Press, 1997 [German original 1910]); the quotation is from p. 380; von Rad, *Genesis* (OTL; trans. John H. Marks; Philadelphia: Westminster, 1972 [1st German ed. 1961]). All translations of biblical texts are my own except where noted.

[2] Gunkel, *Genesis*, 380.

[3] Among several recent articles dissenting from the consensus are Friedemann W. Golka, "Genesis 37–50—Joseph Story or *Israel*-Joseph Story?" *CurBS* 2 (2004): 153–177, and Bryan Smith, "The Central Role of Judah in Genesis 37–50," *BSac* 162 (April–June 2005): 158–174. Gordon J. Wenham is one of the few dissenting commentators. In *Genesis 16–50* (WBC 2; Dallas: Word, 1994), he states that omitting chs. 38 and 48–50 "represents a failure to grasp the author's understanding of his material" (244); and "The 'Joseph Story' is somewhat of a misnomer for these chapters" (245). Accepting the fact that Jacob also plays a major role, Horst Seebass entitles chs. 37–50 "Der Jacob/Israel Zyklus," in his *Genesis III: Josephsgeschichte (37,1–50,26)* (Neukirchen-Vluyn: Neukirchener Verlag, 2000); he is followed by Lothar Ruppert, *Genesis* (FB; Würzburg: Echter Verlag, 2008), 4:18. Michael V. Fox has criticized von Rad's highlighting of wisdom themes in "Wisdom in the Joseph Story," *VT* 51 (2001): 26–41; see also his essay in the present volume.

judgments that Joseph is the dominant character, chs. 38 and 49 are marginal, and ch. 45, Joseph's revelation of himself to his brothers, is the climax of the story.[4]

There are, however, solid reasons for questioning whether "The Joseph Story" accurately describes chs. 37–50. The heading in 37:2, אלה תלדות יעקב, "This is the line of Jacob," refers to the entire family of Isaac, not to one son only, in accord with the usage of the formula elsewhere in Genesis; Judah plays an important role as do the other primary Leah sons Reuben, Simeon, and Levi (especially if one includes chs. 34–35; see below); Jacob is present actually or virtually throughout the story; focus on Joseph alone obscures the powerful Genesis theme of rivalry for firstborn privilege that one expects to find in the twelve brothers no less than in Cain and Abel, Ishmael and Isaac, and Esau and Jacob; viewing Joseph as the central character eviscerates the drama, for it inevitably makes Joseph's "reconciliation" with his brothers in ch. 45 the climax of the story, relegating chs. 46–50 (one third of the text!) to an anticlimactic appendix. Bryan Smith perceptively notes the irony of scholars who "begin by praising Genesis 37–50 for its high literary quality, but then they contradict that praise by denying that the narrative possesses one of the most basic characteristics of high literary quality, namely, unity."[5] A re-examination is called for.

My re-examination will bring to the fore two neglected aspects of the story: the powerful rivalry between the brothers for firstborn status, and the brothers' recognition of a divine plan trumping their own plans. My analysis will proceed in three parts. Part I will argue that the Genesis theme of fraternal striving for firstborn status provides the major dramatic tension. The tension actually begins in chs. 34–35 rather than in ch. 37, and so it will be necessary to consider these earlier chapters. The rivalry among the sons sets up the expectation that their father Jacob will ultimately

---

[4] Among the scholars who omit ch. 38 from their "Joseph Story" or downgrade its importance are Donald B. Redford, *A Study of the Biblical Story of Joseph (Genesis 37–50)* (VTSup 20; Leiden: Brill, 1970), 16; George W. Coats, *From Canaan to Egypt: Structural and Theological Context for the Joseph Story* (CBQMS 4; Washington, D.C.: Catholic Biblical Association, 1976); Robert E. Longacre, *Joseph: A Story of Divine Providence: A Text Theoretical and Textlinguistic Analysis of Genesis 37 and 39–48* (2nd ed.; Winona Lake, Ind.: Eisenbrauns, 2003), esp. ch. 1; Claus Westermann, *Genesis 37–50: A Commentary* (trans. John J. Scullion; CC; Minneapolis: Augsburg, 1986), 24; and Ruppert, *Genesis*, 4:17–18.

[5] Smith, "The Central Role of Judah," 159. One might also add that many analyses leave key dramatic issues unexplained such as Judah's profound change from instigator of the plan to sell Joseph into slavery (ch. 37) and scorner of marriage customs (ch. 38) to noble spokesman of family unity in ch. 44; many also do not give a convincing explanation for the brothers' request for forgiveness in 50:15–21.

have to declare which of them will enjoy firstborn privilege; he does so in his Testament in ch. 49. Part II builds on my earlier study of ch. 38.[6] That study explored the parallel between Joseph's and Judah's going down from their brothers and reached the conclusion that Judah's confession in 38:26 ("She [Tamar] is the righteous one, not I"[7]) was nothing less than his recognition of the divine force increasing his family in spite of his own sinful choices. The present essay develops the conclusion by arguing that Judah's recognition was followed by two more such recognitions: Joseph's in 45:1–13 and the brothers' (as a group) in 50:15–21. Part III elaborates the dramatic necessity of Jacob's Testament (ch. 49): Jacob regains his paternal authority by adjudicating his sons' status, declaring that firstborn privilege will be shared by Rachel's son Joseph and Leah's son Judah. Thus the controversial chs. 38 and 49 not only belong to the story, they are essential to its plausibility.

I. Sibling Rivalry in Genesis 34–50

It hardly needs stating how important firstborn status was in a traditional agrarian society. The oldest son inherited the largest share of the family plot (a double portion according to Deut 21:15–17) and he gained honor and family leadership in a culture where such recognition was dearly prized. In Gen 37–50, or as I shall argue, in Gen 34–50, firstborn status plays an especially significant role, for Jacob's twelve sons are the eponymous ancestors of the twelve tribes, and the sons' standing in the family foreshadows the relationships of the later tribes. It should be noted that in the Genesis stories firstborn status was not primarily a matter of biological birth, but involved the father's preference and, of course, divine choice operating with subtle hints and paradoxical means.

To understand the full scope of the brothers' rivalry we must begin at ch. 34, though nearly all scholars begin "The Joseph Story" in ch. 37 on the basis of the introductory heading in 37:2: "This is the line of Jacob."[8] It should

---

[6] "Genesis 38: Its Contribution to the Joseph Story," *CBQ* 66 (2004): 519–532.

[7] For the translation, see Bruce K. Waltke and M. O'Connor, *IBHS*, 265: "In a comparison of exclusion, the subject alone possesses the quality connoted by the adjective or stative verb, to the exclusion of the thing compared." Waltke and O'Connor correctly render the phrase, "She is in the right, *not* I," and adduce as the closest analogue Hos 6:6, "For ... I desire ... acknowledgment of God, *not ʿōlôt*."

[8] The *tōlĕdôt* formula occurs five times in the "Primordial History" (Gen 2:4a; 5:1; 6:9; 10:1;

be remembered, however, that the headings in Genesis are an editor's devices for arranging venerable traditions for a new audience.[9] That an editor inserted the *tōlĕdōt* heading into the *middle* of the story he inherited is made likely by the fact that ch. 34, not ch. 37, is the actual turning point in the family narrative.[10] By the end of ch. 33, Jacob has brought his large family safely back to Canaan. He has successfully resolved the chief obstacle to his return—the enmity of Esau—by reconciling with his brother. Now he is ready for a new chapter in his life and will prepare for the next generation of the family. His sons have reached adulthood, and ch. 34 describes their first independent actions and his response. The relationship of father to sons, and of the sons to each other in Canaan, will prove to be problematic. The rivalry between the sisters Leah and Rachel that characterized family life in Paddan-Aram develops in Canaan into rivalry between their sons. And Jacob will be no more successful at moderating his sons' rivalry than he was at moderating their mothers' rivalry (30:1–2). His failure takes its toll on him. As Wenham notes,

> There [in chs. 32–33] we learned how the fearful and alienated Jacob was changed into the new Israel, who boldly returned to Canaan and made peace with his brother Esau. ... But this story [ch. 34] shows Jacob's old nature reasserting itself, a man whose moral principles are weak, who is fearful of standing up for right when it may cost him dearly, who doubts God's power to protect, and who allows hatred to divide him from his children just as it had divided him from his brother.[11]

In numerous passages—Gen 34; 35:22; 37; 42:1–4, 35–38; and 43:1–14—Jacob's sons spurn his authority and jockey for self-advantage. As the family prepares for the next generation, divisive discord looms ominously over it—between wives, father and sons, and brothers. Yet just as Jacob was able, over time, to surmount the first set of crises in Paddan-Aram caused by Esau's

---

11:10) and five times in the "Ancestral History" (11:27; 25:12; 25:19; [36:1], 9; 37:2). Gen 36:9 is often reckoned as "secondary."

[9] The scholarly consensus is that the target audience for the final version of the Pentateuch was the post-Babylonian-destruction generation(s). The old traditions were interpreted afresh, but were not invented for this audience. In times of crisis, authors retrieve and interpret their past rather than invent traditions. Such an approach was particularly true in cultures in which new things were suspect unless venerable traditions.

[10] Wenham, *Genesis 16–50*, 300, assesses in detail scholarly opinion on whether or not 33:18–20 close off the Paddan-Aram segment of the Jacob story. He finds, correctly in my view, that vv. 18–20 bring the segment to a close with the entire family safely settled in Canaan. A new phase, with new issues, begins in ch. 34.

[11] *Genesis 16–50*, 318.

hostility, Laban's conniving, and his wives' quarrels, so he will, in the course of the story, surmount the second set of crises in Canaan and Egypt caused by his rebellious sons, his own folly, and the worldwide famine.

Father-son conflict emerges soon after the family's arrival in Canaan. In Gen 34:30–31, when Jacob rebuked Simeon and Levi for recklessly endangering the family by their brutal avenging of their sister, his sons openly contemned his authority: "Should our sister be treated like a whore?"[12] Jacob took no action against them. In 35:22, when Reuben publicly usurped his father's authority by sleeping with his father's concubine Bilhah, "Israel heard of it" but did nothing. Even prior to ch. 37, then, the three oldest of the four primary sons of Leah—Reuben, Simeon, and Levi—have attempted to wrest family leadership from their father. One has to assume that the fourth son of Leah, Judah, was fully aware that he was the only unsullied candidate left among the primary Leah sons. Hence, Judah's persuading his brothers to sell Joseph into slavery in 37:25–27 and foiling Reuben's plan to restore Joseph to his father should be viewed as, respectively, eliminating the most likely candidate for firstborn status, and frustrating Reuben's attempt to repair his relationship with his father by saving Joseph.[13] Judah's attempt to advance his cause in ch. 37 is the third and climactic rebellion by a Leah son.[14]

But why would an editor have inserted 37:2 if, as I argue, the original story of Jacob's adult sons actually began with ch. 34? Possibly, the editor wanted to underscore the parallel between the blessings given to Esau in ch. 36 and the greater blessings given to Jacob in chs. 37–50. Genesis 36:1, ואלה תלדות עשו ("This is the line of Esau"), is clearly meant to parallel 37:2, אלה תלדות יעקב ("This is the line of Jacob"), in accord with the Genesis custom of mentioning first the blessings given to the non-elect son and second, the blessings given to the elect son. Whatever the precise reason, the editorial insertion of 37:2

---

[12] The two brothers have good reason to assume that Jacob is not very concerned about the dishonoring of the Leah daughter Dinah, their full sister (Wenham, *Genesis 16–50*, 317). In Gen 33:2, Jacob, fearing the worst as Esau and his 400 men approach his family, puts his two concubines and their children in the front line to absorb any attack and Leah and her children in the next line of defense. In the rear, the safest position, he places Rachel and Joseph.

[13] So also Joel S. Kaminsky, "Reclaiming a Theology of Election: Favoritism in the Joseph Story," *PRSt* 2 (2004): 138.

[14] Series of three are common in the story: three trips by the family to Egypt (chs. 42; 43–45; 46–47), three stages in Joseph's rise to power in Egypt (39:1–20; 39:21–40:23; 41:1–57), and, as I argue in this essay, three acknowledgments by the sons of divine interventions.

had the unintended consequence of disconnecting Judah's action from the actions of his three brothers in chs. 34–35. The ultimate effect was to obscure the theme of sibling rivalry.

Chapter 37 swings the spotlight from Leah's sons to Rachel's son Joseph (vv. 2–17). The shift is not unexpected, given the alternation of attention to their mothers Leah and Rachel in chs. 29–30. In view of the plot so far, one should interpret Joseph's dreams in ch. 37 as his preemptive claim on family leadership, analogous to the actions of the Leah sons. And as Jacob did with Leah's sons, so he does with Rachel's son—he fails at family leadership. Though he does rebuke Joseph for his second dream, he otherwise so favors Joseph that he provokes his other sons to murderous rage. A further indication of his inept leadership is his using Joseph to spy on his sons, first on the sons of Bilhah and Zilpah (37:2) and then on all of them (37:14).

To summarize, sibling rivalry has influenced the sons' behavior since ch. 34. By ch. 37, the rivalry has narrowed down to two—the Leah son Judah and the Rachel son Joseph. The three oldest Leah sons have disqualified themselves (34; 35:22). Reuben, to be sure, is still competing for family leadership with Judah in 37:18–36 and 42:37–42, but those two occasions only demonstrate that Judah's prospects are increasing at his expense.

The rivalry between Reuben and Judah in ch. 37 brings another Genesis theme to the surface: a son's evil acts are turned into means of family salvation. In ch. 37, both Reuben and Judah try to dissuade their brothers from killing Joseph outright, reminding them that slaying him (Reuben in v. 21) or shedding his blood (Judah in v. 26) would put the brothers in danger of divine retribution. The intentions of the two brothers differ radically, however. Reuben's intent is to rescue Joseph from the pit and restore him to his father (v. 22), whereas Judah's is to sell him to a passing caravan and be rid of him forever (v. 27). If we disregard for the moment the source-critical issues of 37:18–36 with its putative Reuben and Judah sources, and simply look at the effects of the two brothers' proposals, we see that one plan is righteous (Reuben's) and the other wicked (Judah's). But consider what would have happened if the brothers had heeded Reuben rather than Judah. The family would have perished in the famine, for it would have had no patron in Egypt to ensure its survival. Judah's immoral counsel, then, adopted by the brothers, paradoxically becomes the means of family survival. Sounded here, though not for the first time in the story,[15] is the

---

[15] The first reference to divine intervention to send Joseph to Egypt seems to be the mysterious "man" (אִישׁ) in 37:15–17 who steers Joseph to his brothers in Dothan, which just

important theme that the brothers will later come to publicly acknowledge: malicious acts are turned into means of salvation for the family.

II. The Three Recognition Scenes

1. *Recognition of the Divine Plan by Judah the Son of Leah (38:26)*

As traditional Jewish exegesis has noticed and a number of modern scholars accept,[16] chs. 38 and 39–41 invite the reader to view the stories of Joseph and Judah as complementary. Both men "went down" (ירד) from their brothers (38:1 and 39:1), were involved in deceptions involving a kid from the flock and an article of clothing (37:31–33; 38:15), married foreign women (38:2; 41:45), and fathered two sons who competed for firstborn status (38:27–30; 48:17–21). There are, furthermore, striking linguistic similarities between Tamar's returning Judah's seal, cord, and staff to him in 38:25–26 for his recognition, and the brothers returning Joseph's bloodied coat to their father for his recognition in 37:32–33:

> (Tamar) sent ... and said ... recognize, pray ... and (Judah) recognized and said ...;
>
> [the brothers] sent ... and said ... recognize, pray ... and [Jacob] recognized it and said ...

Moreover, Israelites in the monarchic period would be disposed to regard the tribes of Joseph and Judah as connected yet competing and would not have been surprised to learn that what happened to Judah in ch. 38 would happen in an analogous way to Joseph in chs. 39–41.

In ch. 38, Judah went down from his brothers and settled near an Adullamite named Hirah (38:1). Attempting to begin a family, he continued unabated the immoral course he embarked on in ch. 37.[17] Marrying a Canaanite

---

happens to be on the caravan route to Egypt. It should also be noted that all of Judah's interventions in Genesis—whether well intentioned (42:37–38; 44:18–34) or ill intentioned (37:26–28; 38:1–34)—result in the salvation of the family.

[16] See n. 6 above, as well as Jon D. Levenson, *The Death and Resurrection of the Beloved Son: The Transformation of Child Sacrifice in Judaism and Christianity* (New Haven: Yale University Press, 1993), 157–164.

[17] Westermann believes Judah's conduct simply reflects a primitive period when exogamous marriage would have been accepted as normal (*Genesis 37–50*, 51). Yet the narrator is not an anthropologist recording primitive customs, but an author in full control of his material, fully conscious of the deviant behavior of Judah in the context of Genesis customs.

woman, he had three sons by her: Er, Onan, and Shelah. To Er he gave Tamar as a wife. When Er and then Onan were killed by YHWH for their wicked conduct, Judah, wrongly blaming Tamar for their deaths, refused to follow the Levirate law that required his sole remaining son Shelah to have a child by Tamar. Instead, he sent Tamar home to her father. Tamar, however, biding her time, disguised herself as a prostitute and, during the sheepshearing festivities, had sexual relations with the unknowing Judah, receiving as a pledge for later payment Judah's seal, cord, and staff. When Judah tried to send payment to the "prostitute" and get back his pledge, she could not be found and Judah wrote off his pledge as lost. A few months later, Judah discovered that Tamar was pregnant and decreed that she should be burned alive (an excessive penalty). As she was led out to the pyre, Tamar showed him the pledges proving he was the father of her child. Stunned, Judah recognized that his own self-willed attempts to found a family had failed and that Tamar's bizarre act had in effect enlarged his family. He declared, "She is the righteous one, not I!" "Righteous" here means what it meant in the case of Noah (Gen 6:9; 7:1)—doing the will of God. Tamar had done the will of God, albeit unwittingly. Judah's recognition in Gen 38:26 is the denouement of the chapter. After his recognition, Judah rises to a level of moral behavior from which he will never deviate. Gone forever is the Judah who conspired against his brother, scorned endogamous marriage, disregarded Levirate law, consorted with a prostitute, and recklessly condemned a family member. The transformed Judah will say to Jacob in 43:8–9: "Let the boy go with me ... I myself will stand surety for him," and will speak for the brothers in 44:18–34, offering to be detained in order to send his brother Benjamin home to Jacob. In short, in 38:26 Judah recognizes a divine power enlarging and healing the family, subverting stupid and selfish acts, and enabling small men to become heroes—and he embraces it.

The style of ch. 38 reinforces the story. Verses 1–11 introduce the characters and set up the dramatic tension. The divine slaying of Judah's two sons and his unwillingness to give Tamar to Shelah imperil the family line. Against those scholars who regard vv. 1–11 as mere background for the real narrative of vv. 12–30, one must insist that the entire chapter is dramatic. The breathless pace and absence of dialogue in vv. 1–11 are narratively significant. Judah is a one-man show, making all the decisions with little regard for others and for family traditions. Even the divine slaying of his children does not slow him down. The rapid pace and terse descriptions evoke Judah's brusque and imperious style. By the end of v. 11, his unilateral actions have generated powerful dramatic tensions that will only be resolved by Tamar's act, Judah's recognition (v. 26), and the birth of new sons (vv. 27–30). It is precisely outlandish actions—YHWH's unelaborated slaying of the sons, Tamar's and Judah's transgressions, and their final actions (Tamar's display of the pledges, and Judah's acknowledgment of divine intervention)—that makes this chapter distinctive and unforgettable.

The above review is at least a partial rebuttal of the scholarly consensus that ch. 38 is marginal to the main narrative. But another powerful argument can be made: without ch. 38, the extraordinary change in Judah's character is inexplicable. In 37:26–27, he successfully persuaded his brothers to sell Joseph to slave traders. Yet in 43:8–10, the one-time pitiless schemer offers to stand surety for Benjamin, which persuades Jacob to let Benjamin go to Egypt; in 44:14–34, he offers to take Benjamin's place so that the boy could return to his father, which persuades Joseph to release Benjamin and bring Jacob to Egypt; in 46:28, he is selected as the family representative to meet with Joseph; and in 49:8–12, Jacob again recognizes his sterling qualities by choosing him to share firstborn status with Joseph (49:22–26). How could a literary masterpiece not provide readers with an explanation for a main character's radical change from heel to hero?[18]

Further proof for the brothers' recognition of divine intervention is the recurrence of word pairs noted by Joel Kaminsky: "recognition/non-recognition (נכר/לא נכר); remembering/forgetting (נשה or זכר/שכח), and knowing/not knowing (ידע/ לא ידע). Not only do Jacob and Judah recognize the clothing accoutrements presented before them in chapters 37 and 38, but Joseph recognizes his brothers and they fail to recognize him in Genesis 42:7–8."[19] Kaminsky concludes "that there is a connection between the ubiquity of these three word pairs and the fact that God is rarely overtly active in this story. ... these key word pairs hint to the reader that one should look back on the events in one's memory and recognize how God's providential hand has been guiding life's events, acknowledging God as the source of one's blessing—as Joseph himself eventually does (Gen 45:4–11)."[20]

---

[18] The same can be said about the character of Joseph. There has to be a believable dramatic explanation of how a spoiled and clueless boy became a loving brother. The answer given below is that when he heard Judah's speech in 44:14:34, he experienced his own plans crumbling and a new and brilliant plan emerging.

[19] "Reclaiming a Theology of Election," 145.

[20] "Reclaiming a Theology of Election," 146.

2. Recognition of the Divine Plan by Joseph the Son of Rachel (45:1–13)

It was perhaps inevitable that the artful story-telling and rich Egyptian coloring of chs. 39–41 would push Joseph to the forefront of the narrative. God-fearing, charming, and divinely gifted in interpreting dreams, he differs radically from the arrogant Judah. The charm that won over Potiphar and the Pharaoh seems to have also won over most commentators who view him as a saintly sage guiding his brothers to repentance. The scholarly consensus, however, is without textual support. What little the text tells about Joseph's state of mind at this point reveals something quite different: a man deeply angry at his brothers. He is worried about how they are treating his father[21] and Benjamin. In 43:29–34 Joseph expresses love for only one brother—his full brother Benjamin. When he first sees Benjamin, "Joseph hurried out, for he was overcome with feeling toward his brother and was on the verge of tears; he went into a room and wept there. Then he washed his face, reappeared, and—now in control of himself—gave the order, 'Serve the meal'" (v. 31, NJPS). Another textual clue to Joseph's feelings is the names he gave his two sons (41:51–52): Manasseh, for "God has made me forget (נשה) all my trouble and my father's house," and Ephraim, for "God has made me fruitful (פרה) in the land of my affliction." The first name tells us that Joseph thanks God for erasing the memory of his family, and the second that he thanks God for enabling him to have a family and perhaps also to feed the surrounding nations. Joseph refers to Canaan as a land of "affliction," the word used of the sufferings of Israel in hostile Egypt in Exod 3:7. In Joseph's eyes, his brothers belong to a past he has erased. Now he is an Egyptian, a son of Pharaoh, not of Israel. And Pharaoh has given him a name, Zaphenath-paneah, which has replaced his old name, and an Egyptian wife, Asenath, daughter of a priest of On.

That Joseph is angry at his brothers seems to account for his words and actions in ch. 42 better than assuming he is a compassionate sage leading his brothers to repentance.[22] His bullying accusations that they are spies

---

[21] Joseph's concern for his father's safety and well-being is well expressed in 45:3: אני יוסף העוד אבי חי, "Is *my* father still in good health?" How to render translate *ḥay* has challenged translators. It cannot be rendered, "Is my father *still alive*?", for Judah has just said Jacob is still living. "Is my father *well*?" makes better sense, for Joseph suspects that the brothers have been abusing the old man as they did many years before when they sold his favorite son into slavery.

[22] Gunkel's comment (*Genesis*, 424) on Joseph's rough treatments of his brothers is on the mark: "It has been said that he wants to 'test' or even 'reform' them and that he acts as the 'tool of providence,' 'under the impulse of a higher necessity,' contrary to his natural inclinations (so Dillmann, even more complicated and modern according to Franz Delitzsch).

(vv. 9–14) puts the confused and frightened brothers on the defensive, pushing them to blurt out the details he wants to know. His beloved father and younger brother are still living and well. It is Joseph's exclusive concern for Jacob and Benjamin that best explains his sudden change of strategy in 42:18–26. Initially, Joseph had decided to take all of the brothers hostage and send back only one to fetch Benjamin (42:16–17); instead, he suddenly changed his mind and detained only one (Simeon), sending all the others back. Why? The most obvious answer is that Joseph suddenly realizes that nine men can carry more grain back to Jacob's family than one.[23] The change, however, triggers a reaction in his brothers that Joseph may not have foreseen. Sending back *all* the brothers except *one* to the father recreates in a single stroke the brothers' long-ago crime. It signals to them that their present distress is *divine* vengeance because of the perfect symmetry between crime and punishment: one brother who does not return to his father for one brother who does not return to his father. That is the most likely reason the brothers say to each other, "Alas, we are being punished on account of our brother (אבל אשמים אנחנו על־אחינו), because we looked on his anguish (ראינו צרת נפשו), yet paid no heed as he pleaded with us. This is why this distress (הצרה הזאת) has come upon us" (42:21 NJPS). In 42:24, Joseph then turned away from them and wept. One should not, however, conclude that Joseph weeps because his brothers are repenting of their sin against him. They are not asking for God's forgiveness, but simply acknowledging the condign punishment that in the Bible betokens *divine* vengeance. They are expressing fear that punishment is about to be loosed upon them. In 50:15, the brothers will acknowledge the same principle—evil deeds come back upon their perpetrators (והשב ישיב לנו את כל־הרעה אשר גמלנו אתו). Joseph responds tearfully to an emotional scene (cf. Gen 27:38; 1 Sam 24:17; 2 Sam 13:36). Furthermore, assuming that Joseph is suspicious of his brothers' motives best explains why he insists that they bring Benjamin if they want more grain in the future. The most natural explanation is that Joseph wants to rescue Benjamin from their clutches, believing (as he has every right to do) that the brothers are mistreating Rachel's younger son as they mistreated him.

The ancient narrator thinks much more simply: Joseph wants to punish his brothers—in the understanding of antiquity—base 'revenge' because they deserve punishment indeed. ... One should not import Christian ideas here." Mark A. O'Brien likewise questions the consensus on Joseph's kindly wisdom, in "The Contribution of Judah's Speech, Genesis 44:18–34, to the Characterization of Joseph," *CBQ* 59 (1997): 427–447.

[23] So also Wenham, *Genesis 16–50*, 408.

A straightforward reading of the text thus suggests that Joseph detests the brothers whom he believes have not changed and that he cares only for his father and his full brother Benjamin. Love for those two makes him control his anger and send back grain to Jacob's family. In short, Joseph has as much need for enlightenment as Judah had in ch. 38, and his recognition in 45:1–13 is as essential to the story as Judah's in 38:26.

Joseph will soon be shocked into enlightenment as Judah was—by the abrupt overturning of his carefully laid plan. As already noted, Joseph's plan had two goals: to ship back as much grain as possible to his father on the backs of his ten brothers, and to rescue Benjamin from their clutches. His tactic to achieve both goals is described in 44:1–17: plant his silver cup in Benjamin's sack, send officers to search the brothers' bags and find the cup in Benjamin's bag, detain Benjamin and send the others home with the grain. Thus, in one stroke Joseph would convey food to his father and rescue his full brother. On the basis of his past knowledge, Joseph assumed that the brothers would give up Benjamin as readily as they gave him up many years before.

But Joseph sees his plan fall to pieces when he hears Judah's speech in 44:18–34. Judah tells him that the brothers refuse to leave Benjamin behind because they realize his detention will mean their father's death, and that he himself will take Benjamin's place. If Joseph persists in his own plan, he will cause the death of his father and end up not with his full brother, but with the very brother who engineered his sale into slavery! At this point Joseph, like Judah in ch. 38, recognizes his own plan crumbling and a better one replacing it.

What effect does this interpretation have on the so called reconciliation of the brothers in 45:1–13 which is generally regarded as the climax of the story? The passage must be regarded not as Joseph's reconciliation with his brothers but his *recognition* that his own plan of rescue and revenge has been trumped by another plan. Though Joseph recognizes the divine plan, the text does not say that the brothers do.[24] In 45:1–15a, only Joseph speaks and acts. He treats Benjamin differently from the others. Only in the last three words of the text (45:15b) do we learn that his brothers "spoke to him" (reversing 37:4). But do the brothers understand what Joseph does? The text

---

[24] Commentators have noticed that the brothers do not apologize and that Joseph does not express forgiveness; e.g., George W. Coats, *From Canaan to Egypt: Structural and Theological Content for the Joseph Story* (CBQMS 4; Washington, D.C.: Catholic Biblical Association, 1976), 83–84, and Peter Miscall, "The Jacob and Joseph Stories as Analogies," *JSOT* 6 (1978): 28–40, esp. 38.

does not say so, and their post-funeral ploy in 50:15–21 demonstrates they do not. At this stage in the story, only Judah and Joseph know from personal experience that a powerful force is undoing human plans and operating to bring the family together.

3. *Recognition of the Divine Plan by the Brothers as a Group (50:15–21)*

After coming together to bury their father in 50:1–14, the brothers convey to Joseph their father's "deathbed instruction" that Joseph forgive them. The stratagem makes clear that they assumed Joseph had refrained from taking vengeance on them only to please Jacob; with Jacob dead, Joseph will most probably take revenge. Though the reason for Joseph's weeping at their message (50:17) is not stated, one can plausibly see it as motivated by the same reasons as his earlier weeping: his response to the emotional events affecting the family. When he receives the brothers' message, he can only repeat verbatim what he had said earlier: "Though you intended evil against me, God intended it for good so that the entire family could survive, as it has now." But Joseph adds an important sentence to what he said in ch. 45: "Am I in the place of God?" (v. 19). As Gunkel has perceptively noted, the phrase "does not mean that judgment and punishment are God's alone. Instead, it means, 'I am not in a position to thwart God's plans; God's plans now are salvation and deliverance.'"[25] Having seen from personal experience (45:1–13) how God turned around the crime to benefit the entire family, Joseph has decided not to interfere with the process. In this third and climactic recognition scene, the brothers (treated here as a single dramatic character) similarly acknowledge the divine plan.

A modern reader might suppose that Judah would surely have been able to persuade his brothers that God had turned their sin into a means for increasing his family. Indeed Joseph explicitly told his brothers that very thing in 45:5–8. But the story proceeds as if they were not persuaded. The story-teller evidently assumes that each brother or group of brothers had to come to that conclusion for themselves through a deep personal experience. First Judah, then Joseph, and lastly the other brothers had to arrive at this insight by seeing the collapse of their plans and a new plan suddenly unfolding.

---

[25] Gunkel, *Genesis*, 464.

III. Jacob Acts as Patriarch and Adjudicates Firstborn Status for His Son

To say that all the brothers came to recognize that God has turned their self-centered plans into means of family survival is to tell only half the story. Something more is needed: the patriarch Jacob has to announce God's will regarding who is firstborn. There must be a leader for the next generation, indeed for the generations far in the future, for the twelve sons are the eponymous ancestors of Israel. But before any son can be appointed, the father must be restored. Jacob has lost control of his family and his decisions have been disregarded. Simeon and Levi defied him and Reuben tried to usurp his position, and he did nothing. He foolishly favored one son to the near-destruction of the family. Depressed and self-absorbed, he has been defied and manipulated by his sons since they reached adulthood. No less than his sons, Jacob needs rescue.

It must be admitted that his personal history does not give much hope of a satisfactory adjudication of his sons' status, since Jacob's father Isaac on *his* deathbed was manipulated outrageously by his wife and son.[26] But the return of Joseph, the son of his beloved Rachel, has brought him back to life (Gen 45:26–28). Rising majestically to his full stature as family head, he adopts Joseph's two sons as his own in ch. 48, and pronounces the destinies of his twelve sons in ch. 49. He rejects Reuben, Simeon, and Levi as firstborn (vv. 3–7), choosing instead Joseph (vv. 22–26) and Judah (vv. 8–12) as co-firstborn. The two sons are singled out, but the blessings given to each differ subtly. Judah is given political power:[27]

---

[26] I am indebted to Meir Steinberg, *The Poetics of Biblical Narrative: Ideological Literature and the Drama of Reading* (Bloomington: Indiana University Press, 1985), 349–354, for his comments about Jacob's unexpected rise to grandeur and responsibility. I am grateful to Professor Gary Anderson for pointing out the reference.

[27] For this excerpt and the one that follows, see the indispensable study of Raymond de Hoop, *Genesis 49 in Its Literary and Historical Context* (OtSt 29; Leiden: Brill, 1999). MT *yābō' šîlōh* in v. 10c is the most controverted passage in Genesis. There are five main opinions: (1) MT *šîlōh* is the northern shrine "Shiloh," interpreted in two different ways: (a) as the name of the messiah, hence KJV "until Shiloh comes," or (b) as the old northern shrine, "until he comes to Shiloh," that is, the Davidic king once again extends his authority to the northern kingdom, symbolized by Shiloh (see Isa 11:13); (2) Correct the vowels of MT *šîlōh* to *šellô*, "to whom [it] belongs," with several ancient versions and NIV and REB; (3) *šîlōh* is an Akkadian loanword *šēlu*, "ruler"; (4) Emend MT *šîlōh* to *mšîlōh*, "his ruler" (cf. Mic 5:1); (5) *šîlōh* is actually two words, *šay*, "tribute," and *lōh*, "to him," i.e., "tribute (is brought/they bring) to him," with some Jewish traditions, several modern scholars, and the translations NAB, NJPS, NRSV, and NJB. I adopt it because it requires no emendation of consonants, *šay* is well attested (Isa 18:17; Pss 68:30 and 76:12), and, most important, the proposal preserves the parallelism.

> ⁸Judah, your brothers shall praise you:
> your hand will be on the neck of your enemies,
> and your father's sons will bow before you ...
> ¹⁰The scepter shall not pass away from Judah,
> the mace from between his feet,
> so that tribute is brought to him,
> to him the obedience of the peoples.

Joseph is given a blessing on his fertile fields. The northern kingdom was indeed the most fertile area in Israel. But nothing is said about Joseph ruling his brothers:

> ²²A colt of a wild she-ass is Joseph,²⁸
> a colt of a wild she-ass by a spring,
> (a colt of) wild asses in Shur.
> ²³Archers attacked him fiercely, shot arrows,
> they pressed him hard with their weapons,
> ²⁴but each man's bow was suddenly shattered,
> the forearms, the arms, of each fell slack,
> from the hand of the Mighty One of Jacob,
> from the Shepherd, the Stone of Israel,
> ²⁵from the God of your father who helps you.
> May El Shaddai bless you,
> with the blessings of the heavens above,
> the blessings of the abyss resting below,

---

²⁸ Like his brothers Judah, Issachar, Dan, Naphtali, and Benjamin, Joseph is compared to an animal, in this case a wild ass (v. 22). Unlike the ass of modern Europe and the Americas, which is proverbial for being stupid and stubborn, the wild ass in the ancient East (probably *equus hemionus or equus hemippus*) was renowned for its large size, beauty, and speed. Job 39:5–8 celebrates the animal's ability to live free in the wilderness, "Who let the wild ass go free, loosed the swift ass from bonds? I made the steppe its home, the salt land its dwelling. It scorns the tumult of the city; never hears the shouts of the driver. It ranges the mountains for pasture, and searches after any green thing." In Gen 49:23–24, hunters pursue this magnificent desert creature, but a divine intervention shatters their bows and enfeebles their arms. Though hunting the wild ass is not elsewhere mentioned in the Bible and Israelites apparently did not eat its meat, Assyrian reliefs show them being hunted (*ANEP* §186) and several texts mention the hunt. The sudden turning of the tables on the hunters makes clear that God has intervened. Protection from attack is the first of the seven blessings mentioned in vv. 25–26.

Interpretations of בן פרת (v. 22a, a unique phrase) have gone in two contrary directions. LXX, *Tg. Onq.*, and most commentators until recently related to Heb. *prh* and assumed Joseph is compared to a fruitful plant (e.g., NRSV, "Joseph is a fruitful bough"). The translation is problematic, however: (1) All other comparisons in the poem (vv. 9, 14, 17, 21, 27) are from the animal kingdom as is the variant in Deut 33:17; (2) בנות, "daughters," nowhere else means branches or roots, and (c) צעד, "to stride," is improbable for creeping roots or branches. Following NAB and NJPS, I assume an animal comparison.

the blessings of breasts and womb;
²⁶the blessings of bud and blossom,
the blessings of the eternal mountains,
the favor of the everlasting hills.
May they be on the head of Joseph,
on the forehead of the prince among his brothers.

Joseph's fertility is celebrated, but no reference is made to his political power. And indeed, this was the northern tribes great gift—to be the breadbasket of Israel. Jacob's Testament takes a distinctly Judahite view of the divided monarchy.

The story of Jacob's line thus ends where it ought to end, not at ch. 45, but at chs. 49–50 with Jacob's Testament and burial by all twelve sons. The Genesis theme of sibling rivalry has played itself out and been resolved. The story ends with wholeness (the brothers are twelve again and the family seventy), reconciliation (brother with brothers, father with sons), and appropriate leadership for the next generation (Judah and Joseph will share it). God has been revealed as the One who turns vicious stratagems into means of survival. The family is now positioned for the next stage of God's plan, but thanks to the divine healing, the new threat will be external, not internal.

SELECT BIBLIOGRAPHY

Alter, Robert. *Genesis: Translation and Commentary*. New York: W.W. Norton, 1996.
Clifford, Richard J. "Genesis 38: Its Contribution to the Joseph Story." *Catholic Biblical Quarterly* 66 (2004): 519–532.
Coats, George W. *From Canaan to Egypt: Structural and Theological Context for the Joseph Story*. Catholic Biblical Quarterly Monograph Series 4. Washington, D.C.: Catholic Biblical Association, 1976.
Golka, Friedemann W. "Genesis 37–50—Joseph Story or *Israel*-Joseph Story?" *Currents in Research: Biblical Studies* 2 (2004): 153–177.
Greenspahn, Frederick E. *When Brothers Dwell Together: The Preeminence of Younger Siblings in the Hebrew Bible*. New York: Oxford University Press, 1994.
Kaminsky, Joel S. *Yet I Loved Jacob: Reclaiming the Biblical Concept of Election*. Nashville: Abingdon, 2007.
Kugel, James L. *In Potiphar's House: The Interpretive Life of Biblical Texts*. Cambridge: Harvard University Press, 1990.
———. *Traditions of the Bible: A Guide to the Bible As It Was at the Start of the Common Era*. Cambridge: Harvard University Press, 1998.
Levenson, Jon D. *The Death and Resurrection of the Beloved Son: The Transformation of Child Sacrifice in Judaism and Christianity*. New Haven: Yale University Press, 1995.

Longacre, Robert E. *Joseph: A Story of Divine Providence: A Text Theoretical and Textlinguistic Analysis of Genesis 37 and 39–48*. 2nd ed. Winona Lake, Ind.: Eisenbrauns, 2003.

Redford, Donald B. *A Study of the Biblical Story of Joseph (Genesis 37–50)*. Vetus Testamentum Supplements 20. Leiden: Brill, 1970.

Smith, Bryan. "The Central Role of Judah in Genesis 37–50." *Bibliotheca Sacra* 162 (April–June 2005): 158–174.

Wenham, Gordon J. *Genesis 16–50*. Word Biblical Commentary 2. Dallas: Word, 1994.

Westermann, Claus. *Genesis 37–50: A Commentary*. Translated by John J. Scullion. Continental Commentaries. Minneapolis: Augsburg, 1986.

JOSEPH AND WISDOM

Michael V. Fox

Gerhard von Rad's thesis that Joseph is a Wisdom Tale energized the study of the Joseph Story.[1] Scholars began looking seriously at the signal features of the narrative and finding—or denying—parallels in Wisdom Literature. This story, von Rad argued, was written to provide an exemplar of wisdom virtues to young men aspiring to a career in the Solomonic court. In his view, "The narrative of *Gen.* XXXIX reads as if it had been devised expressly to illustrate the warnings of the wisdom writers;"[2] and further: "We can only say that the Joseph Story, with its strong didactic motive, belongs to the category of early wisdom writing."[3] In an earlier study, I discussed this thesis and argued against it.[4] The present study revisits this issue, looking at other facets of the relation between the Joseph Story and wisdom. I begin by surveying the meaning of the terms for "wisdom" (Part I). I then undertake a more nuanced assessment of the relation of the role of wisdom in the Joseph Story (Part II). Next I reexamine the relation of the story to Wisdom Literature (Part III). Finally I situate the story with respect to another wisdom-related genre, "The Disgrace and Rehabilitation of a Minister" (Part IV).

I. Terminology

It is first necessary to be clear on what we mean by "wisdom." We must distinguish (1) "wisdom" as a human faculty or knowledge from (2) "Wisdom" in the sense of Wisdom Literature with its characteristic ideas and literary forms.

---

[1] Gerhard von Rad, "The Joseph Narrative and Ancient Wisdom," in *The Problem of the Hexateuch and other Essays* (New York: McGraw-Hill, 1966), 292–300. For practical purposes, "Joseph Story" refers to Gen 37–50, though only the narrative segments that involve Joseph are relevant.
[2] Von Rad, "Joseph Narrative," 295.
[3] Von Rad, "Joseph Narrative," 299.
[4] Michael V. Fox, "Wisdom in the Joseph Story," *VT* 51 (2001): 26–41.

(1) The faculty of wisdom is designated by a number of synonyms in the Bible and Ben Sira, most prominently חכמה.[5] The criterial feature for חכמה in all its uses is a high degree of knowledge and skill in any domain, in other words, "expertise," though I will continue using the traditional translation, "wisdom." The concept of wisdom in the Bible does not inherently imply moral virtue, and indeed wisdom in the biblical sense can be used wrongfully (e.g., 2 Sam 13:13; Isa 3:3; 19:11; 29:14; Ezek 38:13). Wisdom may be manifest in the following interrelated forms: (a) Learned knowledge and skills, including craftsmanship (e.g., Exod 35:31; 36:4; Isa 40:20), business acumen (e.g. Ezek 28:5), and intellectual learning (e.g., Jer 8:8; 9:22; Qoh 1:16; Dan 1:4; Sir 14:20; 51:15, ms B). (b) The ability to understand the implications of situations and interpret signs, and texts ("perceptiveness," "astuteness," "reasoning ability") (e.g., 2 Sam 14:20; Jer 9:11; Hos 14:10; Ps 107:43; Job 34:34; Qoh 8:1; Sir 3:29). (c) Skill in devising stratagems and plans (e.g., 2 Sam 14:2; 20:16; Jer 4:22; Job 5:13; Qoh 4:13). (d) Good judgment in practical and interpersonal matters (e.g., 1 Kgs 5:9; Job 39:17; Prov 10:14; 11:30; Qoh 2:3; 7:10; Sir 11:1). (e) Moral wisdom, the knowledge of what is right and the *desire* to do it (e.g., Prov 1:7; 4:6, 11; 10:31; 13:14; this is probably its usual sense in Proverbs, in combination with [d]). Wisdom Literature seeks to instill wisdom of types b-e. The biblical concept of wisdom is not a holistic one; wisdom is not an indivisible power. Someone who has the wisdom of learning or magic may lack moral wisdom or the skills that succeed in business.

(2) "Wisdom Literature." This is one meaning that חכמה does not have in the Bible. The notion of Wisdom Literature is a scholarly construct. Such constructs are entirely legitimate and necessary insofar as they bracket a species of texts that share salient features. Such constructs allow for sharper comparisons and studies of literary history.[6] Contrary to the common practice, I

---

[5] The most important synonyms are תבונה, בינה, and דעת. There are distinctions among them, but for practical purposes anything designated by one of these terms can be called חכמה. I describe the semantic field of wisdom in ABP 1:29–38 (see the abbreviation list at the end of this essay) and, in greater detail, in my "Words for Wisdom," ZA 6 (1993): 149–169.

[6] The concept of Wisdom Literature would, nevertheless, have been recognizable to the sages. The prologue of Proverbs promises that the book will help the wise man to "understand proverbs and epigrams, the words of the wise and their enigmas" (1:6). In other words, the book holds forms of literature appropriate for study and contemplation. Egyptian does have a term for "Wisdom Instruction." This is not, as sometimes thought, sb'yt ("instruction"), for this can designate any kind of teaching, but rather sb'yt mtrt ("instruction in rectitude"). This term is used in the titles of the New Kingdom instructions of Amenemope, Anii, and Hori (see ABP 1:21). Still, the concept of a genre of "Wisdom Literature" embracing similar texts in different cultures and periods is a modern construct.

would confine the term to didactic Wisdom—counsels in the art of right living like Proverbs, Ben Sira, Ptahhotep, Amenemope, Ahiqar, Shupeʾawilum, and others whose family characteristics are quite clear.[7] If we include texts with a significantly different form and message, like Job, The Egyptian Dialogue of Pessimism, and "Ludlul" (the "Babylonian Job"), the genre becomes amorphous and has less value for comparisons. Not all wisdom—think of the mercantile wisdom of Tyre in Ezek 28 or the magical wisdom of the Chaldeans in Daniel—is in the domain of Wisdom Literature. Similarly Joseph is wise in ways not promoted in Wisdom Literature.

II. Joseph Is Wise

Almost all scholars have considered Joseph wise.[8] Lindsay Wilson has carefully and accurately combed the Joseph Story for indications of what he calls "'wisdom-like elements'" (his scare-quotes).[9] By this he means "themes, characters and motifs ... typical of wisdom books."[10] Finding a substantial number of such elements, he believes, constitutes an argument for wisdom influence but is not a criterion for genre identification.[11] My purpose in Part I is different from Wilson's insofar as I am looking not only for the qualities praised in Proverbs, but also for the faculty of wisdom in all its richness, and occasional dubiousness, as is known from many genres of biblical literature.

Master of Dreams

An Egyptian would have recognized Joseph as a wise man even for his skills in dream interpretation alone. When he proves able to surpass the native magicians, he does so by operating in their arena and applying a recognizable hermeneutics of oneirocriticism known from Egyptian sources.

The Bible takes the magic of the Egyptians seriously (Exod 7:11–12a, 22; 8:3), though the magic of the Hebrew heroes is more powerful (Exod 7:12b; 8:14; 9:11).[12] Egyptian magicians laid claim to a great array of skills, all of

---

[7] ABP 1:17–19.
[8] An exception is Donald B. Redford, *A Study of the Biblical Story of Joseph (Genesis 37–50)* (VTSup 20; Leiden: Brill, 1970), 103–105, who says that Joseph does not fit the wisdom ideal of the "long-suffering, 'silent,' modest man who controls his spirit" (104).
[9] Lindsay Wilson, *Joseph, Wise and Otherwise: The Intersection of Wisdom and Covenant in Genesis 37–50* (Milton Keynes: Paternoster, 2004), 35–37 and *passim*.
[10] Wilson, *Joseph*, 35.
[11] Wilson, *Joseph*, 37, 297–302 and *passim*.
[12] The same functionaries are called "magicians" in Exod 7:22; 8:3, 14, 15; 9:11. Respect for

them in the range of wisdom, called *rḫt*, the precise equivalent of חכמה. One important form of wisdom was magic, which was closely allied with other kinds of learning and intellectual strengths. Magic (a power that could be applied to ancient "sciences" such as medicine and divination) was considered a gift of the gods for humanity's welfare.[13] Indeed, a wise man might combine magical and divinatory skills with moral wisdom. In Papyrus Westcar (from the early Middle Kingdom), one Djedi, who is explicitly called "wise," is brought before the king to display his magical prowess.[14] He performs some tricks but also shows moral courage, eloquently remonstrating with the king who has proposed using a human in a potentially deadly experiment. The sage then, respectfully but boldly, prophesies the birth of the children who will replace the king's own dynasty. The magic Djedi performs is a side-attraction. What is important is the (*ex eventu*) prophecy of a tidal change in Egyptian affairs.

Much later, in the Ptolemaic story now designated Setne II, a scribe by the name of Si-Osire excels in wisdom, meaning that he is learned in books and proverbs, in reciting spells, and in performing magic (*AEL* 3:142). A tale within the tale relates how another, more ancient, wise man, Horus son of Paneshe, defeats a Nubian sorceress (*AEL* 3:144–150).[15] He sleeps in the temple and has a dream in which he is told how to get a book of magic that will protect the Pharaoh. When he wakes up, "He understood that what had happened was the doing of the god. He acted according to every word that had been said to him in the dream" (*AEL* 3:147). Horus's realization that the dream was God's doing is very much like Joseph's insistence that *God* was showing his intentions to Pharaoh (Gen 41:48). After Horus banishes the sorceress, Pharaoh lauds him as a superlatively "good scribe and a learned

---

foreign learning in magic and divination is shown also in the book of Daniel, for Daniel's learning in the "wisdom" of the Chaldeans (1:17, 20) is an object of esteem, though only a greater type of wisdom proves adequate to the mantic challenges facing Daniel.

[13] Phibis says, "[God] created the dream to show the way to the dreamer in his blindness" (Pap. Insinger 32.13; *AEL* 3:210–211). The Instruction to Merikare (lines 136–137) apparently says, "He made for them magic as weapons to ward off what may happen, and dreams by night as well as by day" (thus Nili Shupak, "A Fresh Look at the Dreams of the Officials and of the Pharaoh in the Story of Joseph (Genesis 40–41) in Light of Egyptian Dreams," *JANES* 30 [2006]: 103–138, at 106). However, the text is uncertain.

[14] *AEL* 1:215–222.

[15] Another tale about Horus son of Paneshe (= Ḥor son of Punesh) is preserved in fragmentary form in an Aramaic document from Elephantine (TAD 1.C1.2). This shows that the Demotic version has its roots in an earlier period, perhaps the fifth century, and shows that some tales of this sort were possibly accessible to an international audience.

man" (*AEL* 3:151). It is not the dream itself that draws Pharaoh's praise, but rather the wise man's ability to use it for the good of the kingdom.

The wisdom of the instructions and the wisdom of divination (such as exhibited by Djedi) were not two incompatible areas of learning in Egypt. A Late Egyptian encomium on the ancient scribes calls several sages, most of whom are known as authors of Wisdom books, "the wise scribes, since the time that came after the gods [the primordial age], those who foretold what would come."[16] The encomium further says: "The wise men who foretold what would come: what came forth from their mouths has come to pass; it is found in their utterances, written in their scrolls."[17] They foretold the future not as prophets communicating a god's will but as scholars who applied their learning to divination of various sorts.

Joseph is not learned in the scribal arts, but his explication of dreams is an act of the wisdom of oneiromancy. Though Joseph is not called a diviner, his servant seems to assume that a "man such as him" practices divination with his cup (44:15).

The greatest affinities of the treatment of dreams in the Joseph Story are with Egyptian practices, known to the author at least in general form.[18] In the Joseph Story, as in the Egyptian dream books (and unlike the rest of the Bible, apart from the Joseph-influenced book of Daniel [chs. 2, 4, and 7][19] and the incident in Judg 7:13–14), divine communication comes via visual symbols rather than plain verbal statements. No god or angel interprets the dreams; rather (in spite of Joseph's protestations in 40:8 and 41:16, on which see below), the interpreter is a human, not God.

---

[16] Pap. Chester Beatty IV, verso 2.5–6. My translation.

[17] Pap. Chester Beatty IV, verso 3.7–8. Since the extant Wisdom instructions of these authors do not actually foretell the future, the named sages apparently wrote texts, or were remembered as having written texts, that did so. This shows that the authors of Wisdom did not constitute a distinct "Wisdom school" dedicated to the production of Wisdom instructions.

[18] Shupak, "Fresh Look," 105–110. Symbol dreams are relatively rare in Mesopotamian sources, where they are confined to Sumero-Babylonian literary works, with several in Gilgamesh. The interpretation of symbol dreams was more extensively developed in Egypt and is documented in practical oneiromancy.

Still, it is likely that the Joseph author's ideas about Egyptian oneiromancy came also from other sources, foreign and Israelite. Fishbane describes a uniform biblical style of dream and vision explication, with the citation and atomization of the content. Typically there is a presentation of the entire content, then a selected repetition of its lemmata plus interpretation. See Michael A. Fishbane, *Biblical Interpretation in Ancient Israel* (Oxford: Clarendon, 1985), 447–452. Similar structures are used in Mesopotamia and Egypt (452–454).

[19] On the use of the Joseph Story in Daniel, see Ludwig A. Rosenthal, "Die Josephgeschichte mit den Buchern Ester und Daniel Verglichen," *ZAW* 15 (1895): 278–284; *ZAW* 17 (1897): 125–138.

Our sources offer no information about the procedures used by an Egyptian wise man in interpreting dreams. There is no suggestion of any ritual or ecstatic state to facilitate the decipherment (though incubation was used to invite dreams), and no technical devices are employed. Nor do we know just how the art of interpretation was taught and learned. The type of texts that remain, the dream books, suggest that the Egyptians taught dream interpretation as they taught reading and arithmetic: by repetition of examples, with no higher level of methodological abstraction. The dream books are collections of dreams and their interpretations. The most important exemplars are Papyrus Chester Beatty III (CBIII), from the thirteenth century BCE (or possibly earlier),[20] and Papyri Carlsberg XIII and XIV (C-XIII, C-XIV), from the second century CE.[21] In CBIII, all entries share the same main protasis, written once: "(If a man sees himself in a dream)." Then each one has its own subordinate protasis and its own apodosis; for example:[22] (1) "(If a man sees himself in a dream), seizing wood belonging to the god in his hand. Bad: finding misdeed in him by his god" (CBIII, 9.26). (2) "(If a man sees himself in a dream) being given white bread [$ḥd$]. Good: It means something (at which his face) will light up [$ḥdi$]" (CBIII 3.4). (3) "(If a man sees himself in a dream) binding malefic people at night. Good: taking away the speech of his enemies" (CBIII 4.5). (4) "(If a man sees himself in a dream) seeing his penis hard [$nḫt$]. Bad: victory [$nḫtw$] to his enemies." (5) "Wenn er süsses Bier trinkt, wird er sich freuen" (C-XIVa, 2[23]). (6) "Wenn sie eine Katze gebiert, wird sie viele Kinder gebären" (C-XIVf, 1). (7) "Ein kupfernes Messer (?): Er wird froh sein im Herzen" (Berlin P 15683[24]).

---

[20] Alan H. Gardiner, *Hieratic Papyri in the British Museum. Third Series: Chester Beatty Gift* (London: British Museum, 1935). Kasia Szpakowska, *Behind Closed Eyes: Dreams and Nightmares in Ancient Egypt* (Swansea, Wales: Classical Press of Wales, 2003), 61–122, surveys the contents and analytical techniques of this text and provides a translation with comments.

[21] Transcribed and translated in Aksel Volten, *Demotische Traumdeutung (Pap. Carlsberg XIII und XIV verso)* (Kopenhagen: Munksgaard, 1942). The papyri have demonstrably earlier origins and are dependent on earlier dream collections, including CBIII (Volten, *Demotische Traumdeutung*, 4–16). There are other second century CE dream texts with affinities with the Carlsberg papyri; for example William J. Tait, *Papyri from Tebtunis in Egyptian and in Greek* (3rd Memoir; London: Egypt Exploration Society, 1977), texts 16 and 17; and Karl-Theodor Zauzich, "Aus zwei demotischen Traumbüchern," *Archiv für Papyrusforschung* 27 (1980): 91–98. Other texts, both in Late Period hieratic and Demotic, are as yet unpublished; see the remark in Szpakowska, *Behind Closed Eyes*, 114 and Zauzich, *Aus zwei demotische Traumbüchern*, 91.

[22] The translations from Chester Beatty III are by Robert K. Ritner, *COS* 1:53–54.

[23] From Volten, *Demotische Traumdeutung*, 91, 99.

[24] Zauzich, *Aus zwei demotische Traumbüchern*, 93. This text condenses the protasis into a simple noun or noun-clause.

The apodoses are not fully predictable—there would be no need for dream books or expertise if they were—but there is usually some sort of congruency between image and meaning that shows the associative logic generating the interpretation. Types of congruencies are thematic (the same topic on both sides of the equation), psychological (the affective aspect of the dream experience testifies to an external reality;[25] examples 4, 5); analogical (the structure of the dream event reflects the structure of the external event—or its reverse; examples 1, 3, 5); and paronomastic (a word in the apodosis resembles one in the protasis by sound or writing; example 2); gapped (a word that is present in the protasis resembles one that is absent but implied by congruity in the apodosis[26]). Very often, however, the logic of the connection, if any, remains obscure (examples 6 and 7).

It is wisdom that allowed an Egyptian interpreter to bridge symbol and meaning, and this is present in just the same way in the Joseph Story. The dream episodes were intended to make sense to a readership at least vaguely familiar with the way Egyptians understood dreams. Such a familiarity is not unlikely. Although the technicians of interpretation were learned scribes and their arts esoteric, the interest in interpretations was widespread, and manuals, such as those mentioned above, were written to help the literate serve ordinary clients. In Ptolemaic times, fascination with dreams was extensive. People kept dream diaries and dream interpreters would hawk their services on the pilgrimage route of the Serapeum in Memphis.[27]

Genesis 37: Joseph's Dreams
Joseph's own dreams (Gen 37:5–7, 9) are apparently easy to understand. Still, the interpretive process is the same as for more difficult dreams.

---

[25] Shupak observes that dreams were thought to be caused by external forces, not psychological realities (Shupak, "Fresh Look," 106). However, the Egyptians believed that psychological states *are* caused by gods. In a love song, a girl who wants her mother to go inside so that her beloved can come to her prays, "O Golden One, put that in her heart!" (See Michael V. Fox, *The Song of Songs and the Ancient Egyptian Love Songs* [Madison: University of Wisconsin, 1985], 55.) Numerous love spells attempt to impose an emotion on another's heart. There was also the idea of "the God in the Heart," a divine force propelling people to do certain things. The application of psychological categories to our analysis of interpretation is certainly valid.

[26] Christian Leitz describes a type of dream with a concealed word play, in which a word in the protasis calls to mind one that is only implied in the apodosis ("Traumdeutung im alten Ägypten nach einem Papyrus des Neuen Reiches," in *Heilkunde und Hochkultur I: Geburt, Seuche und Traumdeutung in den antiken Zivilisationen des Mittelmeerraumes* [ed. Axel Karenberg and Christian Leitz; Münster: Lit, 2000], 221–246, at 229–230).

[27] Robert K. Ritner, "Dream Books," in *Oxford Encyclopedia of Ancient Egypt* (ed. Donald B. Redford; Oxford: Oxford University Press, 2001), 1:410–411.

It would be worthwhile considering another "easy" symbol dream first, a dream received by one foreigner and interpreted by another, in Judg 7:13–14. A Midianite soldier dreams of a round loaf of bread rolling into the camp and knocking down the tent. Oppenheim says that for such dreams "interpretations can be dispensed with,"[28] but interpretation is *not* dispensed with. The Midianite dreamer's companion explains that the loaf must be the sword of Gideon and that God has given the Midianite camp into his hand. Neither the Midianite nor Joseph's father and brothers are wise, but anyone can have a degree of wisdom or a moment of wisdom.[29] In Judg 7, part of the dream is a symbol—the spinning loaf—and part is a metonymy—the destruction of the tent for the devastation of the Moabite army. The other soldier decodes by analogy (the loaf rolls or spins like a sword; cf. Gen 3:24), but he also sees his own fear mirrored in the dream. When Gideon overhears the exchange he knows that his enemy's morale is shaken.

Joseph's father and brothers quickly interpret Joseph's dreams by psychological analogy, taking both dreams together as Joseph's expectation or wish for future dominion over his family (37:8, 10). These dreams are apparently so transparent that von Rad concludes that they "contain no profound, possibly mythological symbolism or anything of the sort ... they are quite simple, pictorial prefigurations of coming events and conditions. They present only silent pictures, without any explanatory word, to say nothing then of a divine address."[30] But this simplicity is an illusion. Sheaves and stars do not bow; in fact, luminaries *cannot* bow. The family feels that Joseph's dreams are symptomatic of his attitudes. Gideon understands the dream *and* its interpretation as psychological symptoms (Judg 7:15). The symbols in Joseph's and the soldier's dreams cloak the future; the butler's, baker's, and Pharaoh's dreams will do the same. There is no fundamental difference in the way they are understood, only that more wisdom is needed for the decoding of the second group.

Moreover, the brothers do not fully understand what Joseph's dreams signify. They assume that the images reveal Joseph's state of mind, his current arrogance and wish for power. This is not necessarily so; Joseph

---

[28] A. Leo Oppenheim, *The Interpretation of Dreams in the Ancient Near East* (TAPS 46/3; Philadelphia: American Philosophical Society, 1956), 179–373, at 207.

[29] For example, Haman's wife and "wise men" realize that his fall before Mordecai is inevitable (Esth 6:13).

[30] Gerhard von Rad, *Genesis: A Commentary* (rev. ed.; OTL; Philadelphia: Westminster, 1972), 351.

may simply be naively reporting his dreams. The brothers are projecting their own attitudes, for they feel marginalized by their father's partialities. We do not really know what Joseph feels at this stage. Possibly he makes sense of his dreams only years later, when his brothers bow before him (Gen 42:9). In any case, they do not grasp a theological implication that Joseph himself realizes only retrospectively, in 45:5–8, when the dreams prefigure not just his preeminence but his future responsibility as provider for his family, for he sees himself as a ruler, and a ruler's duty is to provide for the hungry.[31] By the time of the brothers' second visit (in 45:5–8), Joseph has matured to the point of being able to understand what Lanckau (adopting a Sumerian usage) identifies as the "kernel," or the latent meaning of the early dreams: "Die verborgen göttliche Führung erkennend, begreift Josef auch seine Function für das Haus Israel in Ägypten," which is to say that "[n]ur als Segensträger ist Josef auch der Herrscher."[32] Joseph has grown into moral and religious wisdom, a greater achievement than being a "master of dreams."

The ability of ordinary persons to interpret dreams without inspiration or even particular wisdom shows that the principle that "interpretations belong to God" (40:8) does not mean that interpreters necessarily receive divine communications.[33]

Genesis 40: The Butler's and Baker's Dreams
The symbolism in the chief butler's and baker's dreams is not entirely transparent but it is far from arbitrary, as commentators have regularly shown by offering convincing explanations for most components.[34] The

---

[31] Jörg Lanckau, *Der Herr der Träume: Eine Studie zur Funktion des Traumes in der Josefsgeschichte der hebräischen Bible* (ATANT 85; Zurich: TVZ, 2006), 325–328.
[32] Lanckau, *Herr der Träume*, 327, 28.
[33] Daniel, however, does not use his own wisdom in the decoding, but a greater power's. To show this, the author has the king in ch. 2 withhold the narrative of the dream. Daniel must learn both the dream and its meaning from an inspired communication. In chs. 7–10, the explanatory communication comes in lengthy disquisitions from angels, after Daniel confesses his inability to make sense of what he has seen.
[34] Insights into the logic of Joseph's interpretations in Gen 40 are provided by, among others, Shupak, "Fresh Look," 118–120; Wilson, *Joseph*, 115–119; Lanckau, *Herr der Träume*, 210–212; 225–230; and Scott B. Noegel, *Nocturnal Ciphers: The Allusive Language of Dreams in the Ancient Near East* (AOS 89; New Haven: American Oriental Society, 2007), 208–232. Lanckau observes that the divine "inspiration" Joseph claims does not mean that the interpretation lacks an inner logic. There is one, and "Hörer und Leser sind eingeladen, sie zu entdecken. In dieser Erzählung ist Traumdeutung nicht einfach als übernatürliche

fact that the butler sees himself fulfilling his former role while the baker is frustrated in his attempt is a clear indicator that the two men expect success and failure respectively. The birds' devouring the bread adumbrates the devouring of the baker's flesh by carrion fowl. The verb "lift up" allows for the two-pronged word play, though this is ambiguous and can only reinforce what Joseph already realizes.[35] As for the number three signifying three days, perhaps the rapidity of the sequence of events in the dreams indicates the briefest relevant time unit, namely days.[36] More likely—or perhaps also likely—is that Joseph and the prisoners (the latter two undoubtedly well-versed in court protocol) are well aware that Pharaoh's birthday is three days off, and that amnesties and other public announcements are pending.[37]

Crucial to Joseph's success is his sensitivity to psychology. Like the Midianite soldier, Gideon, and Joseph's father and brothers, Joseph perceives a correspondence between the dreams and the dreamers' states of mind. The butler's dream conveys a confidence that bespeaks an innocent conscience; the baker's dream is redolent with a despondency that betrays guilt. Without much of a stretch, Joseph's reasoning—as reconstructed from its results—can be compared to Freudian dream theory that attempts to disclose the desires and fears of the subconscious that are latent in the symbolism of the dream. (An Egyptian would have had no problem with the idea of the subconscious if it were called the "heart."[38]) Uncomfortable ("displaced") thoughts and drives may arise from the subconsciousness in dreams, and

---

Einsicht, sondern als menschliche Interpretation dargestellt. Es ist allerdings ein Mensch, der beispielhaft eine intensive Gottesbeziehung lebt. Inspiration ist in Autorperspecktive wesentlich 'Personalinspiration'" (211).

[35] Dreams and their components are multivalent. In the Carlsberg papyri, the same dream can have different meanings for different people, depending on whether they are "followers of Horus" or "followers of Seth"; see Volten, *Demotische Traumdeutung*, 15.

[36] "Joseph examined the dream and saw that this event happened very quickly, for at once (the vine) blossomed and bloomed, and the grapes ripened and it made wine. Therefore (Joseph) chose the minimal time (unit) and said 'days' and not 'months' or 'years'" (David Qimḥi, in the Rabbinic Bible; similarly Lanckau, *Der Herr der Träume*, 211).

[37] That this would happen on Pharaoh's birthday is a premise of the story. There is no other evidence for this practice in Egypt. However, in the preface to Anchsheshonqy (4.8; *AEL* 3:163), the king's ascension-day was the occasion for amnesties, and this reflects a practice known from the reign of Ramesses IV (1166–1160 BCE) and reminiscences elsewhere; see H.S. Smith, "A Note on Amnesty," *JEA* 54 (1968): 209–214, at 212–213.

[38] The heart knows things that its possessor might like to keep repressed. Ch. 30B in the Book of the Dead implores the heart not to rise up as witness and betray the dead person's secrets in his final judgment. A lovesick girl implores her heart not to make a fool of her, but her heart goes its own way; see Fox, *Song of Songs*, 53.

many entries in the dream books show exactly this happening. The Egyptian wise men were magicians, and good magicians must be good psychologists.³⁹

Genesis 41:1–46a: Pharaoh's Dreams

"At the end of two years, Pharaoh dreamed, and he saw himself standing next to the Nile" (41:1) (lit., "and behold, he was standing ..."; והנה marks participant perspective). This opening has a significant resemblance to CBIII, in which the dream events are not described directly (as in the Demotic dream texts) but are introduced as something seen in a dream: "If a man sees himself in a dream [doing this or that]." Pharaoh's dreams in Gen 41 resembles Egyptian royal dreams in three components not found elsewhere, namely the mention of the time of the dream (41:1a), the location envisioned (41:1b), and the dreamer's awakening (41:4b).⁴⁰

The professional oneirocritics fail to decode Pharaoh's dreams.⁴¹ Then, alerted by the butler to the skilled interpreter still in prison, Pharaoh summons Joseph. Pharaoh's dreams and Joseph's interpretations can easily be transposed into the oneirocritic form of CBIII: "If a man sees himself in a dream seeing seven fat cows coming up from the Nile: good. It means seven years of plenty. If a man sees himself in a dream seeing seven emaciated cows coming up from the Nile: bad. It means seven years of famine." Cows and grain are the main food resources of Egypt, and it is clear that they are just alternative symbols, because harvests would prosper and decline in the same years as livestock. Pharaoh himself seems to recognize that they are the same dream, because he calls them "my dream" in the singular (41:17, 22, cf. 15), and an interpreter (whether oneirocritic or psychoanalyst) must be alert to cues from the dreamer. Then without pause, in a way that allows

---

³⁹ Joseph's sensitivity to psychology is shown also in the way he tests his brothers in order to elicit their true attitude toward their crime and in the way he tells them not to be agitated or squabble during the journey back to Canaan (45:24). Joseph realizes that they were likely to fall into mutual incriminations (as they had already begun to do).

⁴⁰ Shupak, "Fresh Look," 113. The dream of the Ethiopian pharaoh Tanutamun (seventh century) includes a symbol—two serpents—and its interpretation. Upon awakening, the king asks "Why has this happened to me?" and is told that the two serpents signify that he will be given Upper and Lower Egypt. Whereupon he exclaims "True indeed is the dream; it is beneficial to him who places it in his heart but evil for him who does not know it." See Oppenheim, *Interpretation of Dreams*, 251.

⁴¹ The clause ואין פותר אותם suggests that they tried unsuccessfully. To indicate that they were dumbfounded would call for a verb referring to an earlier stage in the attempt—"they could not open their mouths," "and no one spoke a word," or the like—rather than a verb that designates successful interpretation.

Pharaoh to think that the interpretation is continuing, Joseph presents a plan for dealing with the famine. Pharaoh is immediately convinced both by the interpretation and the plan, and says to his servants: "Does there exist another man like this, in whom there is the spirit of God?" (v. 38).[42] And to Joseph he says, "Since God has informed you of all this, there is no one as perceptive and wise [נבון וחכם] as you" (v. 39). But what makes Pharaoh so sure that Joseph is right? After all, not even the fat years have begun.

Here, as often, Thomas Mann is a keen reader of the silent spaces in the Joseph Story. His Joseph says:

> I will reveal to you the mystery of dreaming: the interpretation is earlier than the dream, and when we dream, the dream proceeds from the interpretation. How otherwise could it happen that a man knows perfectly when an interpretation is false, and cries: "Away with you, ignoramus!"[43]

Pharaoh knows that Joseph's interpretation is right because it *feels* right; it clicks into place, in the way an erudite decipherment of arcane symbols would not do.[44] Thus it may be said that "Pharaoh Prophesies," as Mann aptly titles the chapter. It is Pharaoh who has penetrated (though without comprehension) the secret of the future.[45] Pharaoh's sense that he is participating in the revelation—encouraged by Joseph's statement, "What God is about to do he is telling Pharaoh" (41:25)—gives the king the momentum to carry out the duty implicit in the divine message by immediately appointing Joseph as executor of the plan.

Joseph's interpretation clicks into place because, at least in retrospect, the dream (to adopt Joseph's singular) does not seem that abstruse.[46] The

---

[42] Lit., "Is there found [הנמצא] ...?" Also possible is "Can we find ...?"

[43] Thomas Mann, *Joseph and his Brothers* (trans. H.T. Lowe-Porter; New York: A.A. Knopf, 1948), 893.

[44] It does so in Dan 2 because there Daniel first demonstrates amazing insight by revealing the hidden content of the royal dreams and showing access to the royal subconscious.

[45] The same may be said of Tanutamun's response to his dream's interpretation; see n. 40.

[46] Two intriguing clues have been mentioned but not accepted. (1) A Ptolemaic ideogram for *rnpt* "year" is the cow (see Redford, *Biblical Story of Joseph*, 205). However, this usage is not found prior to the Ptolemaic period. (2) An anagram of *rnpt* is *npr(t)*. *Npri*, the god of grain, is pictured with seven ears of grain on his head or body as early as the Pyramid Texts (J.M.A. Janssen, "Egyptological Remarks on the Story of Joseph in Genesis," *JEOL* 14 [1955–1956]: 63–72, at 66). This connection is quite remarkable, but the anagram is never actually used for "year." In any case, to unravel these clues would require an expert and intimate acquaintance with Hieroglyphic writing. This could be gained only through extensive education in the scribal schools, which the author of the Joseph Story does not otherwise display. The author has some real knowledge of Egyptian culture but is

cows and grain are hardly even symbols; they are the thing itself, the main food staples of Egypt. Starving cows and blasted grain are facts of famine and plainly depict this disaster, so that the fat, healthy food sources must represent the opposite. As for seven of each kind signifying seven years, there aren't many meaningful alternatives. Or, if alternatives can be imagined, once the identification with years is made, it seems right, for famine comes in years (with the failure of the annual rise of the Nile), not in smaller segments of time. Moreover, if the cows and ears stand for something else, why do they come in succession rather than stand in some sort of array? As Mann's Joseph says to Amenhotep IV (as Mann identifies this Pharaoh):

> "What are they that come up out of the casket of eternity, one after the other, not together but in succession, and no break is between the going and the coming and no interruption in their line?" "The years," cried Amenhotep, snapping his fingers as he held them up."[47]

Of course Joseph's interpretation is correct because the author made it correct. But if the point were to exalt Joseph's divine inspiration, the author could have provided a more obscure communication, one harder to decode, something more like the dreams in Dan 2 and 7 and Daniel's visions in chs. 8, 9, and 10–11, for example. These symbols are not comprehensible, even to Daniel's wisdom. Daniel must receive special revelations. In Dan 2, the king believes the interpretation because Daniel first shows himself able to reveal the dream's secret content.[48] (Dan 4 is more like Gen 40–41.) In Dan 2, though the wise men are allowed to hear the dream, they cannot explain it. Daniel, like Joseph, can quickly interpret the dream (which is not terribly

---

unclear or erroneous in several regards. See the surveys in Janssen (see above) and Redford, *Biblical Story of Joseph*, 187–243.

Noegel, *Nocturnal Ciphers*, 133–140 is especially alert to paronomasia in dreams. The ones he mentions include פרות ("cows") and (the unused) פרה ("be fruitful"); שבע ("seven") and שבע ("abundance"); בשר ("flesh"), calling to mind the (unused) בשר ("give good news"); and ותבאנה אל קרבנה ("and they came into their midst"), suggesting immediacy and evoking (the unused) קרוב ("near," "soon"). But since word-plays like these do not distinguish between the good and bad phases of each dream or identify specific components they do not further the decipherment. They may, however, have rhetorical value.

[47] Mann, *Joseph and his Brothers*, 947.

[48] Dan 5, the writing on the wall, is patterned on the dream-tale form in ch. 2. The king accepts Daniel's interpretation of the writing immediately, because Daniel can first read the inscription, which the magicians failed to do. (Apparently the writing is not in ordinary Aramaic script, but a cryptic writing, since they cannot read it, let alone decode it, in Dan 5:8.)

enigmatic[49]) right away. But, unlike in Gen 41, the interpretation itself does not impress the king. He knows it is right only when he has undergone the predicted punishment.

The dream Joseph interprets is accessible to human wisdom, and the scene with Pharaoh (as well as 41:45b–57; 47:13–26) seems designed to demonstrate that the wisdom of Jewish courtiers can aid their monarchs. Joseph is divinely inspired, not divinely informed. Pharaoh does believe that Joseph received the information from God (41:39a), but this need not mean a sudden verbal revelation in the moment between the time Joseph hears dreams and interprets them. That is not the way that symbol-dream interpretations worked in Egypt or this story. Pharaoh regards Joseph's brilliant interpretation as evidence that the spirit of God is *already* in him, not that he received the explication whole in a moment of revelation. When he says, "Since God has informed (הודיע) you of all this" (41:39b), הודיע means that God gave Joseph the knowledge to make the accurate deduction. The successful application of the human mind, which is to say, wisdom, is what does the job in the Joseph Story.

What then does Joseph mean when he says "Not I. It is God who will give Pharaoh a favorable answer" (41:16b) and, earlier, "Do not interpretations belong to God?" (40:8b)? And what does the author intend when he has Pharaoh recognize that Joseph possesses the spirit of God and that no one is as perceptive and wise as Joseph (41:38–39)? For Redford, "Divine inspiration takes us out of the practical world of the Wisdom school and into the realm of the story teller. By its very nature it is miraculous, a gift of god, not a cultivated virtue."[50] But can't wisdom be a gift from God, and can't a gift be cultivated?

The faculty of wisdom is a divine gift. Proverbs 2 describes the synergy of endowment and development. Education commences with the father's teaching and its rote incorporation by the child, complemented by the learner's own thought and inquiry. *Then* God steps into the picture and grants wisdom.[51] Elihu voices a verity when he says of wisdom, "Indeed it is a spirit in man, and the breath of Shadday (which) gives them understanding" (Job 32:8). In other words, it is God's spirit/breath that infuses humans with wisdom. (Hence a person—Elihu has himself in mind—can have wisdom

---

[49] Trees are symbols of royalty in Ezek 17 and 31; note especially Dan 2:7. A stone is a symbol of Israel in Ps 118:22.
[50] Redford, *Biblical Story of Joseph*, 103.
[51] ABP 1:131–134.

even when young). Bezalel and other artists are filled with "the spirit of wisdom"—which manifests itself as artistic skill in this case (Exod 28:3; 31:6). The plans Bezalel is to execute are handed to him, but the skill—wisdom—to carry them out is his own. According to Isa 11:2, there will rest upon the ideal king "the spirit of YHWH ... the spirit of wisdom, the spirit of understanding, the spirit of planning and might, the spirit of knowledge and the fear of YHWH." (The spirit of YHWH is thus called because it comes from him. It is defined in a series of appositions as "the spirit of wisdom and understanding, etc."[52]) That the ruler is "inspired" or inspirited does not mean that God imparts to him the particulars of his wisdom (such as what he will decide in judgment), but only that the ruler will have the faculty ("spirit") that will enable him to think and act effectively. The ruler has charisma but is not a prophet, because the spirit of YHWH alone does not make him one.

Hence von Rad is mistaken to claim that "Joseph means to say that the interpretation of dreams is not a human art but a *charisma* which God can grant."[53] Joseph believes that his human art is a charisma *and* God-given.[54] "Do not interpretations belong to God?" (40:8b; similarly 41:16b) is a pious disclaimer but not exactly a modest one, for even as Joseph denies that he has special skills he is claiming to possess a very significant power: divine guidance. This is the source of Joseph's self-confidence, but the disclaimer has tactical value too. Joseph cannot be too self-effacing if he wants Pharaoh to recognize in *him* the man who is "wise and perceptive" (41:33) who should be appointed to oversee the preparations for the years of famine.

Planner

Joseph's possession of the spirit of God gives him a wisdom that manifests itself in his ability to think ahead, to plan for exigencies, and to find ways to protect against dangers. Joseph is wise in possessing the faculty of עצה (though this word is not used here). עצה (best translated "plan" or "planning ability" rather than "counsel," since it is not always communicated to others) is a power much esteemed in Wisdom Literature (see Prov 8:14). But Joseph's

---

[52] The absence of the conjunction before the other "spirits" shows that they are in apposition to "the spirit of YHWH." Thus Samuel David Luzzatto, *Sefer Yesha'yahu* (1855; repr. Tel Aviv: Dvir, 1970), 110. Similarly David Qimḥi in the *Rabbinic Bible*.

[53] Von Rad, *Genesis*, 366.

[54] See the remark of Lanckau quoted in n. 34.

competency is not perfect, and he is aware that he needs God's help to achieve his goals. He may be confident of receiving this because they are God's goals too.

Joseph shows that he is always thinking ahead and preparing for the future when he immediately follows up his interpretation of the butler's dream with a request, asking him to remember him to Pharaoh and get him out of "this pit" (40:15). The request pays off: not immediately, as Joseph had hoped, but two years later, when it is most valuable. Joseph's request shows that he had expected the butler to request his release from prison. But if he had done so, that probably would not have worked, since Pharaoh had just spared the butler's life and would have no motive to grant him another request, and if he had, Joseph would not be in a position to step in at the crucial juncture. Given God's favor toward Joseph, we are to understand the butler's negligence as an unforeseeable divine benefit to Joseph and all Israel. By the violation of his wish, Joseph was in effect held in place for the moment of need. Only when he could interpret Pharaoh's dream could Joseph put Pharaoh in his debt and win his good will on his own merit. On the principle that "Many designs are in a man's heart, but it is the Lord's plan that comes to pass" (Prov 19:21), the frustration of human plans may work for the better. It certainly did so when the brothers sold Joseph into slavery. As Joseph later explains to them, "You planned evil against me, but God planned it for good, so that he could act this very day (למען עשׂה כיום הזה) to save the lives of many people" (Gen 50:20). God's action "this very day" must refer to Joseph's instructions to his brothers to bring the family to Egypt. Joseph has reason to believe that God is working through him.

When Joseph stands before Pharaoh he is called wise for the only time in the story, when Pharaoh says, "there is no one as perceptive and wise [נבון וחכם] as you" (41:39b). Joseph is here praised for two feats: his interpretation of the dreams and the plan that he immediately appends to his interpretation. Pharaoh must recognize the interpretation as wise or he would not have accepted the suggested plan.[55] But the plan is esteemed no less. After all, Pharaoh appoints Joseph vizier, not chief dream interpreter.[56] Of course,

---

[55] Stuart Weeks (*Early Israelite Wisdom* [OTM; Oxford: Clarendon, 1994], 104) says that 41:39 praises only the revelation that Joseph has received, not Joseph's interpretive ability. But without the validity of the interpretation, the plan is meaningless, and as for "wise and understanding" implying "just government with divine aid" (104), the words themselves do not have that implication, and in any case that is not the quality that Pharaoh is concerned with at this point.

[56] Lanckau, *Herr der Träume*, 358.

Pharaoh can "know" that Joseph's counsels are astute only in the way he can already affirm his interpretation: they are coherent and seem to be just good sense, even before they have been put to the test. The alacrity, clarity, and confidence of Joseph's statements make them convincing and "demonstrate that he himself is the model of the official he describes."[57] And, in fact, Joseph had put the words in Pharaoh's mouth, by telling him to seek out "a man perceptive and wise" (41:33). The pieces of the puzzle were there—the interpretation, the plan, and the wise man to carry it out. Joseph made it easy for Pharaoh to put them together and "solve" the problem for himself. This Pharaoh is eager for easy solutions, as will immediately become evident when he delivers his country into the power of a stranger just now taken from prison, making him ruler in all regards but the ceremonial—the "throne" (41:40).[58]

Immediately upon his investiture, Joseph undertakes the execution of his plan on the largest possible scale. The account of this undertaking begins in 41:45b–49, 53–57 and resumes (with some chronological overlap) in 47:13–26. Joseph saves the Egyptians by selling them the grain he had appropriated earlier and, in three stages, turns them into slaves or (in terms of their economic function) sharecroppers. Joseph's actions display חכמה (though not what we usually call "wisdom"), more specifically the aspect of wisdom called עצה and תחבולות, which are goal-oriented, morally neutral stratagems.

Joseph earns the desperate population's gratitude ("you have kept us alive," they say in 47:25[59]), but his first loyalty is to the king. Joseph also has the good sense to placate the priesthood by sparing temple property (47:22, 26b). The author clearly regards Joseph's actions with admiration, not only the taxation and reallocation of resources (which are needed to save the people from starvation) but also their exploitation to subjugate the peasantry to the crown. Joseph is the king's man and beholden to him

---

[57] W. Lee Humphreys, *Joseph and his Family: A Literary Study* (SPOT; Columbia, S.C.: University of South Carolina, 1988), 143.

[58] Ahasuerus resembles Joseph's pharaoh in this regard. He hands over power to Mordecai and Esther and lets them deal with the crisis (Esth 8:2, 8). In both cases this trait may be introduced as a sly comment on gentile rulers, though Pharaoh is portrayed more positively.

[59] Victor Hurowitz has pointed to Mesopotamian parallels to the enslavement formula ("Joseph's Enslavement of the Egyptians (Genesis 47.13–26) in Light of Famine Texts from Mesopotamia," *RB* 101 [1994]: 355–362). It is not certain that Joseph's action derives from Mesopotamian sources, because pentateuchal laws reflect the same stages of debt enslavement and may be the source of the steps Joseph undertakes; see Gordon J. Wenham, *Genesis 16–50* (WBC 2; Dallas: Word, 1994), 448.

alone.[60] In summarizing Mordecai's achievements, the book of Esther says that "King Ahasuerus placed a tax on the land and the coastlands" (Esth 10:1), an act relevant only if understood as Mordecai's doing. The point of Esth 10:1 and Gen 47:13–26 is that highly placed Jewish officials use their wisdom to benefit their employers as well as their own people. This message would be particularly suitable to a Diaspora audience.[61]

Less clear is whether Joseph is applying strategic wisdom in his interaction with his brothers in chapters 42–45 and whether the author wants us to admire this behavior as especially wise. In these episodes alone Joseph is taken aback by events. He guides the course of events, but it is not clear that he has an overall plan. I disagree that he is "a brow-beating tyrant who plays with his victims like a cat with a mouse"[62] and with other negative assessments of his behavior at this stage.

Joseph's anger when he first recognizes his brothers is well justified and not something alien to the wise, who can certainly be angry with fools (like his brothers!) and speak to them "harshly" (Gen 42:8–9).[63] But Joseph is not merely vindictive. If he were, he could have had the brothers imprisoned

---

[60] Indeed (as suggested to me by my wife Jane Fox), one of the motives for Pharaoh's alacrity in appointing a recently imprisoned foreigner as virtual ruler may be that in the hard decisions of taxation and reallocation of resources that lay ahead, an outsider could act more effectively on Pharaoh's behalf. An outsider would have no complicating political, local, or familial allegiances that might bias him or make him suspect of biases toward a particular group. Awareness of such possible motives could make Pharaoh's decision more plausible to the readers.

[61] Several scholars have placed the Joseph Story in the Diaspora. Harald M. Wahl, "Das Motiv des 'Aufstiegs' in der Hofgeschichte: Am Beispiel von Joseph, Esther und Daniel," *ZAW* 112 (2000): 59–74, for example, identifies the Joseph Story as an Aufstiegsberichte, in which the promotion of the protagonist symbolizes Israel's self-assertion in the Diaspora. The point of the Joseph Story, however, is not the rise of Joseph but the responsibility of the Jewish official to his ethnic group. Also holding to a Diaspora setting is Arndt Meinhold, "Die Gattung der Josephgeschichte und des Estherbuches: Diaporanovelle I," *ZAW* 87 (1975): 306–324. The Diaspora novella, according to Meinhold, seeks to rationalize Diaspora existence and provide a model for Jewish life there. Thomas Römer sets the story in the Egyptian Diaspora ("La Narration, une Subversion: L'histoire de Joseph (Gn 37–50) et les Romans de la Diaspora," in *Narrativity in Biblical and Related Texts* [ed. George J. Brooke and Jean-Daniel Kaestli; Leuven: Leuven University Press, 2000], 17–29). However, the Egyptian Diaspora does not seem to have cultivated classical Hebrew as their language of expression rather than Aramaic, nor do I see any critique of the Jerusalem establishment in the story, as Römer claims. This does not argue against a Diaspora origin in itself. Joseph could serve as a model Jewish official in a foreign court. Redford (*Biblical Story of Joseph*, 47–65) points to linguistic features in the story that support a postexilic dating.

[62] Redford, *Biblical Story of Joseph*, 104.

[63] Observe how Lady Wisdom chastises fools in Prov 1:24–27.

or executed without further ado.⁶⁴ But he is also quick-witted and shrewd enough not to reveal himself too soon. If he had, they would have responded with a profusion of meaningless apologies and contemptible appeals for mercies and beneficences on familial grounds. To achieve a meaningful reconciliation, he must probe their souls and see how they would act in crisis, a crisis he creates in stages.

Already in the first visit, Joseph learns that the brothers know their guilt and have been agonizing about their deed over the years (42:21–22). The turning point comes in Judah's speech. Judah proved in 38:26 that he can take responsibility for his folly, and he does so again in 44:18–34.⁶⁵ Joseph now knows that Judah will place his brother and father before his own freedom. Joseph can no longer contain himself, and in a rush of emotions reveals himself. It is not clear why he was trying to restrain himself and what he would have done if he had been able to maintain a stony exterior. Did he have plans for further testing? Punishment? In any case, Joseph has acted reasonably and thoughtfully, but not with the cool calculation that brought him to power and saved Egypt. Wisdom does not seem to be the most obvious quality of his interaction with his brothers, until he reassures them that what they did was God's plan.

---

[64] However, it may be noted that harshness in a ruler is consistent with wisdom in the treatment of the wicked. Ptahhotep advises severe repression of crime to serve as an example (§ 36; *AEL* 1:73). Merikare's father (the teacher in this instruction) demands stern repression of rebellion, including capital punishment for rebels (*AEL* 1:99, 100). Prov 20:26 apparently advocates a brutal form of torture or execution for the wicked, and Prov 19:12a seems to admire royal wrath.

[65] The rhetoric of Judah's long speech has been well appreciated; see in particular Robert Alter, *The Art of Biblical Narrative* (New York: Basic Books, 1981), 163–177 and Humphreys, *Joseph and his Family*, 81–92. Three factors in particular are striking for their subtlety. First, Judah knows that the Egyptian is interested in their youngest brother (42:16; 43:34) and their father (43:27), and he builds his plea on concern for them. Second, Judah is assertive, almost accusatory, in his appeal. He reminds Joseph that he told the brothers to bring him their youngest brother and (as Judah rephrases Joseph's orders) ואשימה עיני עליו ("and I will set my eye on him") (44:21). "Setting the eye on" need not indicate a beneficent intention, but it can. In Jer 39:12 it means watching over and caring for someone, and that is the natural implication of Judah's rephrasing. Joseph, Judah implies, promised to safeguard Benjamin. Third, Joseph's logic is faulty, for the brothers' ability to produce Benjamin will not prove that they are not spies. The slippage in logic is a symptom of emotional intensity behind Joseph's words. Judah seems to sense this, for he plays on the stranger's personal interest in their brother and hints that the Egyptian shares responsibility for what happens to the boy and his father.

God-Fearer

Joseph declares that he fears God (42:18). The fear of God is the starting point of wisdom (Prov 1:7; 9:10; Sir 1:11–2:18), but it is not a distinctively sapiential virtue, being frequently praised elsewhere (e.g. Gen 22:12; Exod 18:21; Deut 25:18; Ps 115:13, and often). The fear of God is genuine fear, not, as often claimed, just a placid reverence,[66] but the nature of the emotion varies with the possessor. At root, it is the fear of God's displeasure. For a child, fear of God may be simply dread of punishment. At a more advanced stage, following upon the development of one's wisdom, fear of God is also a cognitive awareness of God's will (Prov 2:5). It becomes "a form of conscience that calls for an intellectual adhesion to a principle, the divine order, the concept of goodness of life, and this is a guarantee of 'success.' "[67] As conscience, the fear of God motivates right behavior even in the absence of socially enforced sanctions when the deeds are clandestine.[68] When Joseph tells his brothers that he fears God, he is reassuring them that he will act with ethical constraints rather than bringing unchecked power to bear against them. Though the term "fear of God" is not used in Gen 39, we are to understand that this is what fortifies Joseph's refusal to succumb to severe sexual harassment at the hands of his master's wife when he refuses to sin against God and his human master (39:8–9), even in secret, even to his own detriment.

Fear of God is coupled with awareness of divine control of human events. This awareness comes to the fore in two crucial passages, 45:5–8 and 50:20. In both, Joseph reassures his brothers: He is not in God's stead to seek vengeance, which is to say, to attempt to right wrongs by violence outside a judicial setting (a recourse warned against in Prov 20:22 and forbidden in Lev 19:18). Humans lack the breadth of perspective to understand the long-term consequences of actions. Only after many years did Joseph come to realize that his brothers' attack and his own suffering was part of God's plan

---

[66] In Prov 14:27, fear of God is parallel to avoidance of lethal snares, which is motivated by dread not reverence. The emotion in Prov 24:21, "Fear the Lord, my son, and the king" is anxiety before superior powers, occasioned by the fact that both can cause sudden harm (v. 22).

[67] Dermot Cox, "Fear or Conscience? *Yir'at YHWH* in Proverbs 1–9," *SH* 3 (1982): 83–90, at 89. Similarly Joachim Becker speaks of the "intellectualizing tendency [Zug]" of the fear of God in Proverbs (*Gottesfurcht im Alten Testament* [Rome: Pontifical Biblical Institute, 1965], 217). For further discussion see ABP 1:69–71.

[68] Thus, if there were fear of God in Gerar, Abraham would not have worried about being killed there (Gen 20:11). The Hebrew midwives (or the midwives of the Hebrews) in Egypt spare the Hebrew males because, and only because, they feared God (Exod 1:17).

to save lives. Human wisdom has its limits because of both human ignorance and God's sometimes mysterious will. True wisdom is to recognize these limits.[69] Divine control of human events is a frequent theme in Wisdom Literature throughout the ancient Near East,[70] including the Bible. In fact, it is inevitably an assumption of almost any theism.

For all his humble recognition of God as the real source of his success, Joseph in effect interprets his own actions and decisions as an extension of God's will. When Joseph reassures his brothers that it was God who put the money in their sacks (43:23), he is not lying, for he sees his own action as carrying out God's plan. He also sees his own unintended experience as a step in God's plan, for, as he tells his brothers, "it was not you who sent me here but God" (45:5b). Everything in his life serves God's purposes. But Joseph does not rely on God to make the decisions. He immediately and rather verbosely instructs his brothers to hasten to bring his father to him and informs them where they shall dwell (45:9–13). "We do not suddenly discover at the end that we have been an audience in some grand puppet show staged by a divine puppeteer," W. Lee Humphreys says.[71] Joseph's sense of power lies in his assurance that he is serving God's purposes.

Joseph's belief that divine control makes even suffering and evil work for the better is not determinism but confidence in God's support, a sense that God is working on his side, promoting *Joseph's* purposes even beyond where his own wisdom takes them. We see this belief on several occasions. He tells the butler, "Do not interpretations belong to God?" then immediately urges him: "Please tell me (your dreams)" (40:8b). Joseph sees himself as God's intermediary, but as an interpreter and executor rather than a prophet. He does not relay God's words, as a prophet would, but interprets signs of God's will that he sees before him, as in Pharaoh's dreams, the brothers' criminal actions, and his own suffering. And he carries out what he believes are God's plans, though he has not stood in God's counsel. As interpreter of earthly events and executor of good plans he is a wise man, not a "weisheitlicher Prophet."[72]

---

[69] Note the antithesis between "he who trusts in his own heart" and "one who goes in wisdom" in Prov 28:26.

[70] See the discussion in ABP on Prov 16:1–9, with citations from other Wisdom literatures. For example, Ptahhotep §6 (*AEL* 1:65); Amenemope §18 (*AEL* 2:157); Prov 16:1–9; 20:24, 27; 21:3; Ahiqar 1.1C.169–170, esp. "for it is not in a man's power to lift [his] feet or set them down apart from the gods" (170).

[71] Humphreys, *Joseph and his Family*, 128.

[72] "Vielleicht kann Josef so als ein 'weisheitlicher Prophet' verstanden werden, dessen Offenbarungsmedium der Traum ist" (Lanckau, *Herr der Träume*, 359). In ch. 37 Joseph may

The commentators emphasize Joseph's humility and submission to divine plans. But Joseph also radiates confidence. At the start, it is hard to tell if his disclosing his dreams to his brothers shows cockiness or just naivety. At age seventeen he was certainly not wise but did show a self-possession that would mature into a wise confidence. Later, he displays a surer confidence when he lectures Potiphar's wife at length about his ethical duties to his master and his God when he could just have kept his distance. Even as a prisoner serving the butler and baker, he offers to interpret their dreams with aplomb and does so with assurance. With a sense of his own potential importance he asks the butler to intervene on his behalf with Pharaoh himself instead of a lesser official. After interpreting Pharaoh's dreams as ordered, he immediately offers precise advice unbidden, to Pharaoh no less. The confidence that enabled him to do so was surely part of what led Pharaoh to place complete trust in this Semitic ex-prisoner. Set second to the king, Joseph immediately takes charge and levies heavy taxes on the Egyptians, who cannot yet grasp his ends. Later, he buys their property, then their freedom, from them, reducing them to serfdom and paying them with grain that they had themselves produced, even while managing to evoke their appreciation for saving their lives. If his youthful dreams served a purpose other than to enrage his brothers and get himself shipped off to Egypt, it was to imbue him with a certainty that he was destined for great things, and this may have helped him achieve them.

The sages of Wisdom Literature too radiate confidence. This feeling is not a smug notion that assumes that the righteous always prosper, and, conversely, that the prosperous must be righteous. They do, however, believe that one who does the right and wise thing may be confident of having a good life, though not necessarily material wealth. Though, in principle, God's plans are hidden, the wise give advice on the assumption that they know well what God wants and rejects, and that one who conforms to God's will can expect his help and protection.[73] This, and not a helpless fatalism, is the message of Prov 16:1–9.[74] Wisdom Literature promises בטחון,

---

be said to prophesy, since he receives the dreams, but the most important dreams in the story are Pharaoh's, in Gen 41.

[73] Proverbs expresses a confidence in the viability of good planning in 8:14; 11:14; 15:22; 24:6 and elsewhere. In fact, assurances like Prov 4:26 may sound overconfident; hence cautions like Prov 16:9 are provided as a counterweight, to insist on the limitations of human calculations.

[74] ABP 2:606–607 discusses the confidence of the wise, with quotations from cognate literatures.

which means both (external) security and (inner) confidence; see Prov 1:33; 3:23; 10:9; 11:15. Among the Egyptian sages, Ptahhotep, who speaks about the uncertainty of the one's fortunes (§§ 6, 10), is convinced that following his wisdom will lead to security and success. Even Amenemope, who is keenly aware of the frailty of human foresight and control of destiny (§§ 7, 18), believes that the "silent man" is secure and confident and will prosper (§§ 4, 5, 7, 15). He defines his book as "instructions for well-being" (Prologue, 1.1–2). In fact, the silence of "the truly silent man," Amenemope's ideal, is not simply keeping quiet so much as inner tranquility, a confidence that things will work out to benefit oneself. God's will is ultimately inscrutable, but the "way of life," including material success, can be achieved by moral and personal virtues.

Confidence and tranquility are not foreign to other genres, of course. Isaiah demands confidence—meaning trust in God—during a political crisis (Isa 7:4, 9), though he does not feel it was achieved. The gift of security together with the confidence that comes with it (אל תירא שלי, בטי, חי) is a covenantal promise (Deut 12:10; 33:28). It is foreseen as a future, eschatological, blessing (Jer 30:10), though not described as a historical fact, except for 1 Kgs 5:5. It is impossible to quantify the following observation, but it seems to me that confidence in the abilities of the individual mind to prepare for the future and respond to a present crisis is far more prominent in didactic Wisdom Literature than in most biblical genres, where the atmosphere is typically an edgy expectation of oncoming disaster or a sense of loss due to past ones. The Joseph Story is aligned with Wisdom Literature in this regard. What von Rad says about the tone of 47:13–26 applies to the entire narrative: "[T]here pervades the narrative a naïve pleasure in the possibilities of human wisdom, which can conquer economic difficulties by a venturesome shift of values ...."[75] But does that make the Joseph Story a Wisdom Tale?

III. Is the Joseph Story a Wisdom Tale?

Von Rad's classification of the Joseph Story as a Wisdom Tale provoked an ongoing debate about the relation of the story to Wisdom Literature.[76] Some scholars affirm this classification. Thus, essentially, R.N. Whybray,[77]

---

[75] Von Rad, *Genesis*, 405.
[76] Von Rad, "Joseph Narrative," 292–300.
[77] R.N. Whybray, "The Joseph Story and Pentateuchal Criticism," *VT* 18 (1968): 522–528.

J.P.H. Wessels,[78] Hans-Peter Müller,[79] Hans Straus,[80] and Jörg Lanckau.[81] Others (e.g., James Crenshaw,[82] Donald Redford,[83] Claus Westermann,[84] Lothar Ruppert,[85] Stuart Weeks,[86] and Michael Fox[87]) have insisted on the story's distance from Wisdom Literature. Most scholars speak more vaguely of "wisdom influence" on the story (thus George Coats,[88] Humphreys,[89] and Wilson[90]). See the critical surveys by Fox[91] and Wilson.[92]

The hypothesis of influence from Wisdom Literature (written or oral) is plausible; but the commonalities between the Joseph Story and didactic Wisdom could as well reflect values drawn from the cultures from which they were derived, not from a particular school of thought.[93] In any case,

---

[78] J.P.H. Wessels, "The Joseph Story as a Wisdom Novelette," in *Old Testament Essays* (ed. J.A. Loader and J.H. le Roux; Pretoria: University of South Africa, 1984), 2:39–60.

[79] Hans-Peter Müller, "Die weisheitliche Lehrerzählung im Alten Testament und seiner Umwelt," *WO* 9 (1977): 77–98.

[80] Hans Strauss, "Weisheitliche Lehrerzählungen im und um das Alte Testament," *ZAW* 116 (2004): 379–395.

[81] Lanckau, *Herr der Träume*, 355.

[82] James L. Crenshaw, "Method in Determining Wisdom Influence upon 'Historical' Literature," *JBL* 88 (1969): 129–142.

[83] Redford, *Biblical Story of Joseph*, esp. 100–105. Redford argues that many of Joseph's characteristics *contradict* the wisdom ideal.

[84] Claus Westermann, *Genesis 37–50: A Commentary* (trans. John J. Scullion; CC; Minneapolis: Augsburg, 1986), 26–27, 247–248.

[85] Lothar Ruppert, *Die Josepherzählung der Genesis* (SANT 11; Munich: Kösel-Verlag, 1965).

[86] Stuart Weeks, *Early Israelite Wisdom*, 92–109.

[87] Fox, "Joseph Story," 26–41.

[88] George W. Coats, "Joseph Story and Ancient Wisdom: A Reappraisal," *CBQ* 35 (1973): 285–297, at 290. Coats restricts the didactic function to what he regards as the "kernel" of the Joseph Story, Gen 39–41. Its purpose is to teach "future administrators the proper procedure for using power," rather than how to rise to power (290).

[89] Humphreys, *Joseph and his Family*, 150.

[90] Wilson, *Joseph*, 300–302.

[91] Fox, "Joseph Story," 26–29.

[92] Wilson, *Joseph*, 7–27.

[93] I argue against the hypothesis of a "Wisdom school" in ABP 1:8–9 (and, more extensively, in "The Social Location of the Book of Proverbs," in *Texts, Temples, and Traditions: A Tribute to Menahem Haran* [ed. Michael V. Fox et al.; Winona Lake, Ind.: Eisenbrauns, 1996], 227–239). I observe that the same persons could write works of very different genres. One Egyptian scribe, Amennakht, a known historical personage, wrote at least six works of different genres: a Wisdom instruction, a poem of nostalgia for Thebes, a satirical poem, two hymns to Ramses IV, and a hymn to a god (ABP 1:8, with references). Mark Sneed's recent refutation of the idea that the authors of Wisdom Literature belonged to a separate "tradition" with its own worldview and traditions ("Is the 'Wisdom Tradition' a Tradition?," *CBQ* 73 [2011]: 50–71) is basically justified, though I think that didactic Wisdom Literature is a well-defined genre, with a characteristic set of forms, assumptions, and teachings that are distinct from, though not opposed to, what we see elsewhere in the Bible.

von Rad's hypothesis that Joseph is a Wisdom Tale is stronger and more interesting because it potentially says more about the Joseph Story—its Sitz im Leben, its character, and its purposes.

Von Rad understands a Wisdom Tale (of which he mentions no other exemplars) to be a story portraying a paragon of the virtues inculcated by Wisdom Literature and serving as an example to young men, in particular those hoping to rise in the royal court. Von Rad's assumption that the story originated in the Solomonic court assumes the historical accuracy of the Deuteronomic portrayal of Solomon, something few scholars would accept today. But the Solomonic setting is secondary to von Rad's thesis and can be set aside. What is essential is his conception of the Joseph narrative and his belief that the narrative echoes Wisdom Literature and is meant to reinforce it.

Wisdom books, according to von Rad, "depict a man who by his upbringing, his modesty, his learning, his courtesy and his self-discipline has acquired true nobility of character."[94] Joseph "is the very picture of just such a young man at his best, well-bred and finely educated, steadfast in faith and versed in the ways of the world."[95] Joseph, von Rad argues, displays the virtues taught in Proverbs: He avoids strange woman (cf. Prov 7 and elsewhere); he is "cool of spirit" and slow to anger (cf. Prov 14:29); he restrains his lips (cf. Prov 17:28); he keeps silence and conceals his knowledge (cf. Prov 10:19; 12:23); he controls his spirit (cf. Prov 14:30); he refuses to seek revenge (cf. Prov 24:29); he is humble (cf. Prov 15:33; 18:12; 22:4); and, above all, he fears God (cf. Prov 1:7; 9:10). This is a good description of the ideal man projected by Proverbs.[96] It largely fits Joseph—as it would any wise person—though we must note that Joseph's upbringing was terrible and he was neither "well-bred" nor "finely educated." It seems to me that von Rad is describing a different epitome, one taken from the nineteenth century German ideal of *Bildung*.[97]

---

[94] Von Rad, "Joseph Narrative," 294.

[95] Von Rad, "Joseph Narrative," 295.

[96] However, there is no "prohibition of any display of emotion" (as von Rad, "Joseph Narrative," 296, believes). The wise man was not a robot. He certainly could show anger against fools. What sayings like Prov 12:16; 14:17, 29; and 15:30 warn against is uncontrolled anger.

[97] "B[ildung] bedeutet Anregung aller Kräfte, damit dies sich über die Aneignung der Welt in wechselhafter Ver- und Beschränkung harmonisch-proportionierlich entfalten und zu einer sich selbst bestimmenden Individualität führen, die in ihrer Idealität u[nd] Einzigartigkeit der Menschheit bereichert" (*Brockhaus Enzyklopädie*, 1987, 3:314).

Joseph does embody many of the virtues advocated by Wisdom Literature. Wisdom teaches a man to shun sexual advances by another man's wife (Prov 2:16–22; 5:1–23; 6:20–35; 7:1–27; 22:14; 23:27). And, it should be noted, Joseph's scolding of Potiphar's wife (Gen 39:8–9) does have the tone of a sage's lecture in Proverbs. But Gen 39 does not work as a paradigm of wise behavior. In Proverbs, ethical behavior brings its reward. Joseph's behavior brings no direct benefit. He is punished for a crime he tried to avoid. When he finally prospers it is not because of his virtue but *in spite of it*. It may be—though this is not said—that God's future favor was a reward for Joseph's virtue in Potiphar's house, but Wisdom Literature emphasizes tangible and comprehensible connections between deed and consequence.

As for Joseph's practical wisdom, he was undoubtedly a good steward for Potiphar (39:2, 5), and this paid off—but only in the short run. Whatever Joseph achieved in Potiphar's house was left behind him. In prison, his wisdom, with God's help, certainly made life easier for him, but he is brought to the fore only by a confluence of fortuitous (that is, divinely guided but unpredictable) events. First, the prisoners he is tending have dreams he can interpret. Then the butler forgets Joseph's request only to recall it at just the right moment. Joseph's wisdom is ready to be applied when the occasion arises, but there is little in this that can be emulated, except perhaps a readiness to deploy one's talents when the occasion arises.

Joseph does rise to power and serve a king, an achievement promised to diligent scribes and scholars in Amenemope § 30; Prov 22:29; and Sir 8:8. Wisdom Literature does not directly teach how to rise in status but rather how to do well in one's current situation. There is little in Joseph's rise that could be used as an example to future administrators, except for his taxation policy in 47:13–26. Proverbs mentions grain distribution in 11:26: "(a) He who withholds grain—the nation will curse him; (b) but he who distributes grain will have blessings on his head." Joseph would be a rather puzzling model for this advice, since he both withholds grain and distributes it. Moreover, since Joseph's planning required extraordinary information about the future it would not be a useful example for other officials.

As noted earlier, Joseph's foremost display of wisdom is in his dream interpretations. Here I must disagree with what I said in my 2001 article, that "There is no hint that Joseph uses his intellectual powers to figure out the meaning of the dreams."[98] There I maintained that the interpretations came from God, and revelation is not in the realm of wisdom and in any case

---

[98] Fox, "Joseph Story," 32–33.

cannot be emulated.[99] In Part II of the present essay I argued that Joseph's interpretations are very much a matter of wisdom, not verbal revelation. But this kind of wisdom, oneirocriticism, is of no interest to Israelite or other ancient Near Eastern Wisdom Literature. In fact, Ben Sira warns against taking dreams seriously (Sir 34 [31]:1–7; similarly Qoh 5:2), though he rather ambiguously allows that a dream from God may have significance (34 [31]:6). Joseph's successful application of wisdom in this case is not an exemplar of anything taught in Wisdom Literature (or mentioned by von Rad among the sapiential virtues that Joseph exhibits). Also wise in Egyptian terms is Joseph's care to embalm his father and give him a grand burial (in accordance with several Egyptian exhortations[100]). But this would be of no interest to Israelite sages and would not invite emulation.

As for Joseph's theology, his insistence that human knowledge can be overridden by God's will (Gen 45:5–8 and 50:20) is certainly wise and is found in a number of Wisdom passages, such as Prov 16:9; 20:24; 19:21; Ptahhotep §6; Amenemope §18; and more. But this principle permeates the entire Bible and does not point to a specifically Wisdom origin. Jeremiah 10:23 states the principle exactly, and Isa 55:8 makes it a declaration of God.[101] What Wisdom Literature does is to cast this widely-accepted principle in memorable apothegmatic form, which Joseph does not do.

Although Joseph's wisdom is not an infusion of information such as Daniel receives, Joseph does have his wisdom as a divine endowment— the spirit of God (Gen 41:38). This gift was not achieved by experience, investigation, or learning.

The Joseph Story has many motifs found in Wisdom Literature; but works of other types share many of them, such as the spurned wife, the wise man as savior, and the wise official dealing with famine.[102] If one isolates in the Joseph Story motifs that are found in Wisdom Literature, then of course the story resembles that genre. But if one casts a wider net, the picture looks different. The story both overlaps Wisdom Literature—since both speak about wise men—and stands at a certain distance from it, because there are aspects of Joseph's wisdom that are of no interest in the didactic Wisdom Literature of Israel.

---

[99] Fox, "Joseph Story," 32–33.
[100] Hardjedef (*AEL* 1:58–59); Anii (*AEL* 2:138), and Anchsheshonqy (*AEL* 3:168). Hardjedef's counsel is often repeated in school texts.
[101] See Fox, "Joseph Story," 36.
[102] Redford (*Biblical Story of Joseph*, 90–102) lists several such motifs.

IV. The Disgrace and Rehabilitation of a Minister

There is one type of narrative that deserves to be called a Wisdom Tale because it occurs several times in conjunction with Wisdom books and its protagonists are called wise. The formula underlying this narrative may be called The Disgrace and Rehabilitation of a Minister.[103] A wise man suffers an injustice, usually imprisonment, at the hands of the king. He is later exonerated and restored. The latter component may be lost, in the case of fragmentary texts, or absent, as in Anchsheshonqy, making the label only partly applicable. The following exemplars of this tale survive:

Ahiqar (the counsels are eighth-seventh century BCE, in Aramaic; the frame narrative is later[104]). Ahiqar, a wise and exalted Assyrian official under Sennacherib and Esarhaddon, is accused by his adopted son of sedition and is condemned to death. However, Ahiqar persuades the noble in charge of his execution to spare his life. Ahiqar goes into hiding, where he complains of his betrayal and declaims counsels of wisdom. The Aramaic text lacks the ending, but later versions have the Assyrian king remembering Ahiqar in a moment when his wisdom is needed and regretting his disposal. When informed by somebody that Ahiqar is still alive, the king gladly restores him to his position as vizier and counselor and makes use of his wisdom.

Earlier than Ahiqar, and perhaps lying at its source, is a Sumero-Babylonian proverb that reads:

> The wise vizier, whose wisdom his king [Akkadian: his lord] has not heeded, and any valuable (person) forgotten by his master, when a need arises for him (i.e., for his wisdom), he will be reinstated.[105]

Ramesseum Papyrus I (Egyptian, Middle Kingdom).[106] This fragmentary instruction has a narrative about a scribe, Sisobek, who was imprisoned and

---

[103] This term is used by Alexander H. Krappe, "Is the story of Ahiqar the Wise of Indian Origin?," *JAOS* 61 (1941): 280–284. (The answer is no.) Krappe shows this motif to be present in a great variety of sources from world literature. Redford (*Biblical Story of Joseph*, 97) points to the appearance of this motif in a variety of ancient Near Eastern and Hellenistic tales. I define the corpus somewhat differently from Redford. I would not include Dan 3 and 6, because Daniel's qualifications as a wise man are not relevant to his endangerment and rescue.

[104] See ABP 2:769, with references. The fifth century Aramaic manuscript was found at Elephantine, as were fragments of a later Demotic translation. The latter has affinities to two Syriac versions. In one of them (S₂), Ahiqar is tricked into going with an army to a valley, which gives the king the impression that he is trying to subvert him. The rewriting of the frame narrative shows an ongoing interest in the Wise Man Disgraced and Redeemed motif.

[105] Erica Reiner, "The Etiological Myth of the Seven Sages," *Or* 30 (1961): 1–11, at 8.

[106] John W.B. Barns, *Five Ramesseum Papyri* (Oxford: Griffith Institute, 1956), 1–14.

placed in danger. After his release, he declaims on the unpredictability of human fortunes and the futility of passion and loquacity. He offers various counsels, particularly on proper demeanor in speech.

Anchsheshonqy (Demotic; Ptolemaic, perhaps earlier). Anchsheshonqy accidently comes upon a scheme against Pharaoh. He tries to dissuade the schemer, his friend, but is overheard and accused of treason for failing to report the plot and is sent to prison. There he is allowed writing implements and composes a lament on injustice and writes counsels to his son. The instruction (which is complete) ends with Anchsheshonqy still in prison. The absence of the expected redemption may be a bitter comment on the uncertainties of fate.

A Demotic tale on a jar (Jar A, Letter I; Demotic; Late Ptolemaic[107]). In a (fictitious) letter, the magician and chief scribe Ḥi-ḥor writes to Pharaoh. Ḥi-ḥor was sitting in the prison at Elephantine when two birds appeared to him and told him to write his story on two papyrus rolls, which they will take to the forecourt of Pharaoh. Ḥi-ḥor does so and gives one scroll to each bird, and they do as promised. The text is very fragmentary, but we may assume that the birds' mission was successful, for otherwise there would be no point in their appearance. Letter II,[108] of uncertain relation to the first, is very fragmentary. It seems to deny the legitimacy of a putative son (he was only "eine Pflegekind" [l. 11; translation uncertain], recalling Ahiqar's treacherous adopted son Nadin). The writer also says, "Möge man mir meine Freiheit geben" (l. 13), pointing to the motif of the imprisoned scribe.

Joseph, like the other wise men in this genre, is unjustly imprisoned and subsequently released, whereupon he can serve the king with his wisdom. Joseph does not offer apothegmatic counsels of wisdom, but he does give wise advice to Pharaoh (41:33–36). Another version of the Joseph Story fits the formula even better: Ps 105:17–24.

In this retelling of the Joseph Story, Joseph's experience is included among God's "wonders" (Ps 105:5) in a recounting of *Heilsgeschichte*. Joseph's suffering in prison becomes his central experience (vv. 18–19), which is not the case in the Joseph Story proper. The psalmist understands this suffering as a trial, a period of purgation that readies Joseph for his future role. The hero's purity rather than his wisdom is the redeeming virtue, and the dreams go unmentioned. The king becomes a savior sent by God: "[God] sent a king, who released him, a ruler of peoples, who

---

[107] Wilhelm Spiegelberg, *Demotische Texte auf Krügen* (Leipzig: J.C. Hinrichs, 1912), 14–15.
[108] Spiegelberg, *Demotische Texte*, 15–17.

let him go" (v. 20).¹⁰⁹ There is no explanation for the king's intervention or Joseph's appointment other than the fulfillment of God's word. In this telling, Joseph's power is used for *instruction*. The king gives Joseph power "to discipline¹¹⁰ his princes at his desire and instruct his elders" (v. 22). The discipline/instruction presumably takes the form of orders on how to carry out the famine preparations. Still, Joseph's actions remain vague. In v. 23, Israel simply "comes" to Egypt, with no mention of Joseph's initiative or guidance. The psalm theologizes the story, making it a recounting of God's saving action and eliding human factors other than spiritual readiness.

The theme of the Disgrace and Rehabilitation of a Minister and its association with wise men and their words insists on something that didactic Wisdom Literature notes but does not usually dwell on: that wisdom does not fully protect a man from the vicissitudes of fortune.¹¹¹ Most of these tales (insofar as they are intact) have the wise man ultimately redeemed from his travails, but they do not show him achieving his own redemption. The role of chance or (indistinguishably) fate is the main factor. The Joseph Story is a partial exception insofar as Joseph uses his own skills to exploit the opportunities that open before him, but he could not determine what and when these would be. The retelling in Ps 105 eliminates even this degree of initiative. Joseph simply endures his tribulations until "the time [God's] word came to pass" (v. 19).

The wisdom in this genre is not what von Rad had in mind when he assigned the Joseph Story to Wisdom, and it certainly does not provide a useful example for a man wishing to succeed at court. But it does show an awareness of the vulnerability of the human condition, a vulnerability to which even the wise are subject. It brings to light the dangers presented by a ruler's or master's moods and mistakes (noted also in Prov 16:14; TAD 1.C1.84–86); and the frame narratives of Ahiqar and Ankhsheshonqy (*AEL* 3:162–163), and it reminds the reader that he controls his fate only to a

---

¹⁰⁹ I take the subject of שלח in v. 20 as God (as in v. 17) rather than "a king," since the king has not yet been mentioned.

¹¹⁰ The MT has לֶאְסֹר, whose expected meaning is "to bind." This does not fit the context well, because Joseph's ability to imprison nobles is not directly related to his deeds in the story; *instruction*, however, is. In the light of the parallel, we should understand this verb as a by-form of ליסר; thus LXX παιδεῦσαι. In Hos 10:10, אסר (in באסרם) seems to mean "discipline"; cf. LXX ἐν τῷ παιδεύεσθαι αὐτούς; see HALOT 75b.

¹¹¹ This becomes important in the book of Qohelet (see, e.g., 2:14–23, 24–25; 7:13–14; 8:9–14; and constantly) and its contemporary Phibis (Pap. Insinger), which ends every chapter by emphasizing that man cannot secure his just rewards, for "The fate and the fortune that come, it is the god who determines them."

limited extent—more limited, perhaps, than the Wisdom books themselves assume, in spite of their caveats about divine control. At the same time, the tales of the Wise Man Disgraced and Redeemed (except for Anchsheshonqy) do hold out hope to one who finds himself suffering unjustly at the hands of an uncomprehending ruler or master.

V. Conclusion

Wisdom is central to the Joseph Story. Joseph's wisdom is evident in his ability to interpret dreams, in his practical shrewdness and planning ability, and in his fear of God. Nevertheless, it is unlikely that the story was intended as a paradigm for the teachings of the genre we call Wisdom Literature, though Joseph's behavior usually accords with the ideals of that genre. The Joseph Story does have affinities to a type of story often appearing in conjunction with Wisdom texts, namely the genre now called "The Disgrace and Rehabilitation of a Minister," which teaches that the wise too are subject to the vicissitudes of the "time of misfortune" (Qoh 9:11).

Select Bibliography

Foreign Sources

For publication data and bibliography on the texts cited, see ABP 2:1119–1120 and the relevant entries in *AEL* and *BTM*. Translations:

Egyptian: Anchsheshonqy: *AEL* 3:159–184; Anii: *AEL* 2:135–146; Amenemope: *AEL* 2:146–163; Hardjedef: see *AEL* 1:58–59; Merikare: *AEL* 1:97–109; Phibis (Pap. Insinger): *AEL* 3:184–217; Ptahhotep: *AEL* 1:61–80.
Mesopotamian: Dialogue of Pessimism: *BTM* 2:815–818; "Ludlul" ("Let Me Praise the Lord of Wisdom"): *BTM* 1:308–325; Shupe'awilum: *BTM* 1:332–335.
Syrian: Ahiqar: TAD C1.1–2= vol. 3, pp. 25–53.

Modern Scholarship on the Joseph Story

Coats, George W. "The Joseph Story and Ancient Wisdom: A Reappraisal." *Catholic Biblical Quarterly* 35 (1973): 285–297.
Fox, Michael V. "Wisdom in the Joseph Story." *Vetus Testamentum* 51 (2001): 26–41.
Humphreys, W. Lee. *Joseph and his Family: A Literary Study*. Studies on Personalities of the Old Testament. Columbia, S.C.: University of South Carolina, 1988.
Lanckau, Jörg. *Der Herr der Träume: Eine Studie zur Funktion des Traumes in der Josefsgeschichte der hebräischen Bible*. Abhandlungen zur Theologie des Alten und Neuen Testaments 85. Zurich: TVZ, 2006.

Mann, Thomas. *Joseph and his Brothers*. Translated by H.T. Lowe-Porter. New York: A.A. Knopf, 1948.

Rad, Gerhard von. "The Joseph Narrative and Ancient Wisdom." Pages 292–300 in *The Problem of the Hexateuch and other Essays*. Translated by E.W. Trueman Dicken. New York: McGraw-Hill, 1966. Translation of "Josephgeschichte und ältere Chokma." *Supplements to Vetus Testamentum* 1 (1953): 120–127.

Redford, Donald B. *A Study of the Biblical Story of Joseph (Genesis 37–50)*. Supplements to Vetus Testamentum 20. Leiden: Brill, 1970.

Shupak, Nili. "A Fresh Look at the Dreams of the Officials and of the Pharaoh in the Story of Joseph (Genesis 40–41) in Light of Egyptian Deams." *Journal of the Ancient Near Eastern Society* 30 (2006): 103–138.

Wilson, Lindsay. *Joseph, Wise and Otherwise: The Intersection of Wisdom and Covenant in Genesis 37–50*. Paternoster Biblical Monographs. Milton Keynes: Paternoster, 2004.

HOW THE COMPILER OF THE PENTATEUCH WORKED: THE COMPOSITION OF GENESIS 37[*]

Baruch J. Schwartz

The story of Joseph's descent to Egypt in Gen 37 is intended to explain how the chain of events that ultimately led to Israel's arrival in Egypt and eventual enslavement there was set into motion. A close reading of the text reveals that the account contains no fewer than four functionally equivalent, competing doublets,[1] six irreconcilable contradictions,[2] and eight inexplicable disruptions in the narrative,[3] rendering it unintelligible in its canonical form.[4]

---

[*] This essay is a portion of a comprehensive source-critical study of the Joseph story now in preparation. For the present, see also Baruch J. Schwartz, "Joseph's Descent into Egypt: The Composition of Genesis 37," in *The Joseph Story in the Bible and Throughout the Ages*, special issue of *Beth Mikra* 55 (ed. Lea Mazor; 2010 [Hebrew]), 1–30. Sincere thanks to Mr. Marshall Cunningham and to Dr. Sarah Shectman for their assistance in preparing this article for publication. It is a privilege to acknowledge the Israel Science Foundation for its continued generous support of my source-critical study of the Pentateuch.

[1] (1) The reason for the brothers' enmity: Jacob's favoritism and Joseph's resultant dreams of grandeur, or Joseph's intolerable, slanderous tale-bearing; (2) the two notifications of the brothers' decision to murder Joseph: to put him to death (*lahămîtô*, v. 18) on the one hand, and to kill (*wĕnahargēhû*, vv. 19–20) and throw him into a cistern on the other; (3) Reuben's plan to save Joseph on the one hand, and Judah's suggestion to sell him to the Ishmaelites on the other; and (4) the chance arrival of the Ishmaelites on the one hand, and the equally fortuitous appearance of the Midianites on the other.

[2] (1) Jacob's family as agrarian as opposed to sheepherders; (2) Jacob's silence as opposed to his reprimand; (3) Jacob's full awareness of the ill will his other sons bear toward Joseph on the one hand; on the other, his dispatch of Joseph to a clear and present danger of death by their hand; (4) Joseph's being sold by his brothers (v. 27a) as opposed to his being sold by the Midianites, to the Ishmaelites, while still in Canaan, or by the Ishmaelites to Potiphar; (5) the brothers' assumption that Joseph has died by drowning on the one hand and their consent to pulling him out of the cistern and selling him on the other; and (6) Reuben's dismay at Joseph's disappearance, despite his having participated fully in the plot to sell him to the Ishmaelites.

[3] (1) Following v. 2a1α, "These are the descendants of Jacob"; (2) at the beginning of v. 3; (3) in the middle of v. 11; (4) at the beginning of v. 19; (5) following v. 25a1, "Then they sat down to a meal"; (6) at the beginning of v. 28; (7) in the middle of v. 28; and (8) at the beginning of v. 29.

[4] Classical source criticism addresses the unintelligibility of the canonical form by resolving the text into its constituent strands, J, E, and P. This method dominated the critical commentaries and introductions from the nineteenth to the mid-twentieth century; see, for

Alongside the discrepancies are numerous points at which the text flows smoothly and displays neither contradiction, duplication nor disruption.[5] Further, the disruptions are all temporary; each broken thread resumes later in the chapter precisely where it was abandoned earlier. Once these inconsistencies have been acknowledged, the literarily contiguous portions of text may be identified, after which it emerges that the segments of text bearing a clear mutual affinity readily align along two distinct axes.[6] Along one of them (see Figure 1), we find Jacob's favoritism and the special garment he provides for Joseph, Joseph's dreams,[7] the plot to murder him in cold blood, Judah's successful attempt to prevent the murder (as a result of which Joseph is not cast into a cistern at all), and the sale of Joseph to

---

instance: William E. Addis, *The Documents of the Hexateuch* (2 vols.; London: David Nutt, 1892–1898); John Skinner, *A Critical and Exegetical Commentary on the Book of Genesis* (2nd ed.; ICC; Edinburgh: T&T Clark, 1930), 442–520; S.R. Driver, *The Book of Genesis* (10th ed.; WC; London: Methuen, 1916), 319–401; and Ephraim A. Speiser, *Genesis: A New Translation with Introduction and Commentary* (AB 1; Garden City, N.Y.: Doubleday, 1964), 287–378. Much additional literature on the Joseph cycle can be found in Claus Westermann, *Genesis 37–50* (trans. John J. Scullion; Minneapolis: Fortress, 1986); trans. of *Genesis 37–50* (BKAT 3; Neukirchen-Vluyn: Neukirchener, 1982), 15–18.

[5] (a) Vv. 3–11a; (b) vv. 11b–18; (c) vv. 19–20; (d) vv. 21–22; (e) vv. 25a2–27; (f) vv. 29–30; and (g) vv. 31–35.

[6] Verses 1–2a1α belong to a third narrative. Scholarly consensus correctly recognizes this as a segment of P and indeed as P's sole contribution to Gen 37. The role of this brief notice within the original Priestly document was apparently to serve as a subscript to what precedes it, the account of the life of Jacob until his return from Paddan Aram to Canaan, while at the same time providing the transition to the next episode in P, namely, the descent of Jacob and his sons to Egypt in Joseph's footsteps. The original sequel to the Priestly passage in our chapter was therefore some sort of notice to the effect that Joseph went to settle in Egypt, which was followed in P by the brief account of Joseph's entry into Pharaoh's service, the Egyptian name bestowed upon him by Pharaoh, his marriage, and finally the journey of Jacob and his family to Egypt, where Joseph had already settled, in the wake of a famine that did not affect Egypt. Since all of these events must have occurred after the events in our chapter, there was no need for any further portion of P's text to be included in the compiled version at this point. The remaining segments of the once-continuous Priestly text of the Torah were incorporated at the appropriate points in the sequence of events as reconstructed by the compiler in the chapters that follow (37:1–2a1α + ≈ 39:1a; 41:45–46a, 54b; 46:6–27). On the Priestly portions of the Joseph cycle, see for the present Schwartz, "Joseph's Descent," and compare P. Weimar, "Aufbau und Struktur der priesterschriftlichen Jakobsgeschichte," *ZAW* 86 (1974): 174–203, esp. 195 n. 86.

[7] The cause of Joseph's brothers' enmity has been an impediment to scholars in their attempts to disentangle the sources in ch. 37. Gunkel, Skinner, Westermann, and others see here three separate causes: Joseph's tale-bearing, his father's favoritism, and his arrogance and dreams. They naturally assign these "distinct" causes to the three sources of the Torah: the tale-bearing to P, the favoritism to J, and Joseph's arrogance and dreams to E. However, this line of inquiry fails to recognize that the dreams and the preferential treatment—made manifest in the distinctive garments that Jacob would give Joseph—are a single motif.

the Ishmaelites. Along the other axis (see Figure 2), we find the brothers tending flocks of sheep, Joseph's tale-bearing and its consequences, the journey to the wilderness, Reuben's failed attempt to fool his brothers and rescue Joseph, Joseph in the cistern and his abduction by Midianites.

Each set of passages, taken in isolation and in its given form and order, constitutes an independent and virtually complete narrative text. The two texts are thoroughly incompatible with each other, but each one is an internally consistent section of one of the two documents that comprise the non-Priestly portion of the Pentateuch.[8] The former (Figure 1) is a section of J; the latter (Figure 2) is a segment of E.[9]

Figure 1: J

³Now Israel loved Joseph best of all his sons, for he was the child of his old age; and he made him an ornamented tunic. ⁴When his brothers saw that their father loved him more than any of his brothers, they hated him so that they could not speak a friendly word to him. ⁵Once Joseph had a dream which he told to his brothers, and they hated him even more. ⁶He said to them, "Hear

---

[8] Noteworthy among the attempts made by the documentarians to isolate these documents are the following: Hermann Gunkel, *Genesis* (trans. Mark E. Biddle; Macon, Ga.: Mercer University Press, 1997 [German original 1910]), 466, who assigns vv. 3–4, 13a, 14b, 18b, 21, 23, 25–27, 28a2 ("They sold Joseph to the Ishmaelites for twenty pieces of silver"), 31, 32 (excluding "they had the ornamented tunic taken to their father"), 33 (excluding "a savage beast devoured him"), 34b, 35a to J and vv. 5–11, 13b, 14a, 15–17, 18a, 19–20, 22, 24, 28 (excluding "They sold ... silver"), 29–30, 32a2, 33a2, 34a, 35b–36 to E; Driver, *Book of Genesis*, 319–401, who assigns vv. 2b–4, 12–18, 21, 25–27, 28a2 ("They sold ... silver"), 31–35 to J and vv. 5–11, 19–20, 22–24, 28 (excluding "They sold ... silver"), 30, 36 to E; Martin Noth, *A History of Pentateuchal Traditions* (trans. Bernhard W. Anderson; Chico, Calif.: Scholars Press, 1981 [German original 1948]), 30–35, who attributes vv. 3a, 4–5a, 6–21, 25–27, 28a2–28b to J and vv. 3b, 22–24, 28a1, 29–31, (32a1) 32a2–36 to E; and Richard E. Friedman, "Torah (Pentateuch)," *ABD* 6:609, who claims that J consists of vv. 2b, 3b, 5–11, 19–20, 23, 25b–27, 28b, 31–35 and E of vv. 3a, 4, 12–18, 21–22, 24, 25a, 28a, 29–30.

[9] The translation is essentially that of *Tanakh: A New Translation of the Holy Scriptures According to the Traditional Hebrew Text* (Philadelphia: Jewish Publication Society, 1985), with occasional stylistic changes made for clarity. The points at which the originally separate J and E accounts have been combined in the canonical Torah are indicated in Figures 1 and 2 by the scissors (✂); at these points, the source documents show every sign of having been originally continuous. On the precise markers of J and E in this chapter, see Schwartz, "Joseph's Descent," 18 and *passim*. For the technique of differentiating among the documents by employing multiple typefaces, see, e.g., the never-completed Polychrome Bible (Paul Haupt, *The Sacred Books of the Old Testament: A Critical Edition of the Hebrew Text, Printed in Colors* [Baltimore: Johns Hopkins, 1893–1904]) and, more recently, in Richard E. Friedman's edition of the Torah (*The Bible with Sources Revealed: A New View into the Five Books of Moses* [San Francisco: Harper, 2003]). Adopting this graphically useful method of representing the text does not imply acceptance of the source divisions suggested by these or other earlier scholars.

this dream which I have dreamed: ⁷There we were binding sheaves in the field, when suddenly my sheaf stood up and remained upright; then your sheaves gathered around and bowed low to my sheaf." ⁸His brothers answered, "Do you mean to reign over us? Do you mean to rule over us?" And they hated him even more for his talk about his dreams. ⁹He dreamed another dream and told it to his brothers, saying, "Look, I have had another dream: And this time, the sun, the moon and eleven stars were bowing down to me." ¹⁰And when he told it to his father and brothers, his father berated him. "What," he said to him, "is this dream you have dreamed? Are we to come, I and your mother and your brothers, and bow low to you to the ground?" ¹¹His brothers were wrought up at him, ✂ ¹⁹and they said to one another, "Here comes that dreamer! ²⁰Come now, let us kill him and throw him into one of the cisterns; and we can say, 'A savage beast devoured him.' We shall see what comes of his dreams!" ✂ ²³When Joseph came up to his brothers, they stripped Joseph of his tunic, the ornamented tunic that he was wearing. ✂ ²⁵ᵇThey looked up and saw a caravan of Ishmaelites coming from Gilead, their camels bearing gum, balm, and ladanum to be taken to Egypt. ²⁶Then Judah said to his brothers, "What do we gain by killing our brother and covering up his blood? ²⁷Come, let us sell him to the Ishmaelites, but let us not do away with him ourselves. After all, he is our brother, our own flesh." His brothers agreed. ✂ ²⁸ᵃ²⁻ᵇThey sold Joseph for twenty pieces of silver to the Ishmaelites, who brought Joseph to Egypt. ✂ ³¹Then they took Joseph's tunic, slaughtered a kid, and dipped the tunic in the blood. ³²They had the ornamented tunic taken to their father, and they said, "We found this. Please examine it; is it your son's tunic or not?" ³³He recognized it, and said, "My son's tunic! A savage beast devoured him! Joseph was torn by a beast!" ³⁴Jacob rent his clothes, put sackcloth on his loins, and observed mourning for his son many days. ³⁵All his sons and daughters sought to comfort him; but he refused to be comforted, saying, "No, I will go down mourning to my son in Sheol." Thus his father bewailed him.

Figure 2: E

²ᵃ¹ᵝ⁻ᵇ*At seventeen years of age, Joseph tended the flocks with his brothers, as a lad among the sons of his father's wives Bilhah and Zilpah. Joseph brought bad reports of them to their father,* ✂ ¹¹ᵇ*but his father kept the matter to himself.* ¹²*One time, when his brothers had gone to pasture their father's flock at Shechem,* ¹³*Israel said to Joseph, "Your brothers are pasturing at Shechem. Come, I will send you to them." He answered, "I am ready."* ¹⁴*So he said to him, "Go and see how your brothers are and how the flocks are faring, and bring me back word." So he sent him from the valley of [...],*¹⁰ *and when he reached*

---

¹⁰ The word *ḥebrôn* in the compiled text of the chapter is apparently not E's. In the E narrative, not only is Jacob's arrival in Hebron never mentioned; it seems quite clear that E imagines a northern setting for all of the events connected with Jacob. E must have originally contained a different toponym at this point, and the compiler has apparently replaced it in

Shechem, ¹⁵*a man came upon him wandering in the fields. The man asked him, "What are you looking for?"* ¹⁶*He answered, "I am looking for my brothers. Could you tell me where they are pasturing?"* ¹⁷*The man said, "They have gone from here, for I heard them say: Let us go to Dothan." So Joseph followed his brothers and found them at Dothan.* ¹⁸*They saw him from afar, and before he came close to them they conspired to kill him.* ✕ ²¹*But when Reuben heard it, he tried to save him from them. He said, "Let us not take his life."* ²²*And Reuben went on, "Shed no blood! Cast him into that cistern out in the wilderness, but do not touch him yourselves"—intending to save him from them and restore him to his father.* ✕ ²⁴*So they took him and cast him into the cistern. The cistern was empty; there was no water in it.* ^{25a1}*Then they sat down to a meal.* ✕ ^{28a1}*Some Midianite traders passed by and pulled Joseph up out of the cistern.* ✕ ²⁹*When Reuben returned to the cistern and saw that Joseph was not in the cistern, he rent his clothes.* ³⁰*Returning to his brothers, he said, "The boy is gone! Now, what am I to do?"* ✕ ³⁶*The Midianites, meanwhile, had sold him in Egypt to Potiphar, a courtier of Pharaoh and his chief steward.*

The purpose of the following discussion is to account for the text in its present form. How was the canonical text of Gen 37 produced? Can the critic detect the procedure to which the compiler[11] adhered in the process of combining the two segments from J and E into a single text so as to arrive at the result we have before us?[12]

---

order to harmonize this portion of the account of Joseph's disappearance with P's explicit—and therefore decisive—notice that Jacob and his sons have settled in Hebron (Gen 35:27). Furthermore, as noted by ancient and medieval interpreters (see *Gen. Rab.* 84:13, adduced as well by Rashi on this verse), Hebron is situated high in the hills and no valley bears its name. Most probably, then, E read, "So he sent him from *the valley of* [supply: the name of some other place], and he reached Shechem," and the compiler, in his attempt to harmonize, created the meaningless expression "valley of Hebron." For the views of those scholars who treat the phrase either as a gloss or as a scribal error, see Gunkel, *Genesis*, 391 (and the further literature cited there); and Donald B. Redford, *A Study of the Biblical Story of Joseph* (*Genesis 37–50*) (VTSup 20; Leiden: Brill, 1970), 28–29.

[11] The terms "composition" and "compiler" are preferable to the more common terms "redaction," "redactor," and "editor"; on this point and the ramifications of the approach it represents, see Menahem Haran, *The Biblical Collection: Its Consolidation to the End of the Second Temple Times and Changes of Form to the End of the Middle Ages* (3 vols.; Jerusalem: Bialik Institute, 2003 [Hebrew]), 2:5 and *passim*.

[12] In the section that follows I delineate this process on the assumption that the composition of the Torah from its four sources was carried out in its entirety at one time and by a single compiler, and this indeed seems to be the case; see Joel S. Baden. *J, E, and the Redaction of the Pentateuch* (FAT 68; Tübingen: Mohr Siebeck, 2009), esp. 255–286. But even if it is assumed, along with the majority of classical source critics, that only after J and E were fused into one text (the supposed "JE" document) was the latter then combined with P, the absence of any Priestly material in vv. 2a1β-36 makes this controversy irrelevant to the issue of how J and E were combined in this case.

The first question to address is why it was deemed necessary to merge these two texts in the first place. Having arrived in both sources at similar stories occurring at approximately the same point in the larger chain of events, the compiler first needed to determine whether these were the accounts of two separate *events*, each one to be included in its own appropriate point along the continuum of the intertwined documents, or two *reports* of a single occurrence and consequently to be merged into a single, composite textual unit. In this case, the decision seems to have been a simple one. Though each of the sources gave a unique and independent account of Joseph's descent into Egypt, the compiler rightly reasoned that the descent itself could not have occurred more than once. The narratives must therefore be separate accounts of it, and the only way to incorporate them in the Torah was to fuse them into a single text.

Once this determination was made, the compiler proceeded as he did throughout the Pentateuch. Two principles guided him: maximal preservation of each of the source texts, in their precise, verbal form and given order, if possible in their entirety and without addition;[13] and alternating from one source to another as required by strictly chronological criteria, placing what must have occurred first before what must logically have come next. This reflects neither the compiler's preferences nor his ideology but is rather the inevitable and logical result of purely literary considerations. The following analysis will demonstrate just how this procedure was carried out.

Of the two narratives, only E begins with background information (37:2a1β-2); J does not.[14] Realizing this, the compiler has begun his composi-

---

[13] This is not to imply that the documents have everywhere been preserved in their entirety, but rather that deletion or truncation should not automatically be assumed to have occurred whenever one of the sources fails to display all of the components present in the others. Only when one of the threads clearly exhibits an inexplicable gap in the storyline or narrative logic should the critic raise the possibility that something has been omitted from the source document—either in the process of composition or prior to it, either intentionally or through scribal error.

[14] For the purposes of the discussion here, I avoid being drawn into the question of whether the beginnings of the two original stories have been preserved in the canonical version, or whether one or both of them were perhaps deleted when the documents were combined. This issue is inseparable from such other questions as the completeness of each of the sources that lay before the compiler, the extent and character of the chronological continuity present in each of them, and the precise identification of the passages that directly preceded and followed the segments of the three threads present in our chapter. It is also closely related to the question of whether the search for beginnings and conclusions to each narrative episode is justified at all, and whether perhaps scholars have been overly influenced

tion with this preliminary material, which originally served to set the stage for E's tale of Joseph's disappearance. Placing this, as he had to, immediately after the Priestly segment that originally served as the subscription to the account of Jacob's life in Canaan (vv. 1–2a1α),[15] the compiler has thus composed vv. 1–2 of the chapter.

Both J and E now turn to the reason for Joseph's brothers' animosity toward him. There being no reason to imagine that the tale-bearing described in E preceded the favoritism and the dreams recounted in J or vice versa, how was the compiler to proceed? Here he has adhered to another rule that guides him throughout the Torah: to continue the thread of each source as long as possible, moving to one of the others only at the precise point at which, in order for the chronological progression to be maintained, a segment of one of the other sources must be incorporated so as not to be omitted. Thus, the compiler has remained with E, incorporating E's account of Joseph's behavior (v. 2b), which is, after all, directly connected to what precedes it, namely, the description of Jacob's sons as sheepherders.

At this point, however, before he could proceed to the specific events that resulted in Joseph's sad fate, the compiler moved to J's account, beginning as it does with its own version of Joseph's "crime": the preferential treatment he received from Jacob (vv. 3–4) and his annoying dreams (vv. 5–11a). In this manner, the two competing explanations for Joseph's brothers' hatred toward him became vv. 2b–11a.

The two sources now proceed to tell of Joseph's brothers' resolve to do away with him. However, only E tells of what preceded the brothers' conspiracy, namely, the journey to Shechem and Dothan (vv. 12–17). This is in no way surprising; only in E did the plot to murder Joseph take place far away from the family homestead, because only in E are Jacob's sons imagined to have been sheepherders, and only in E is Joseph dispatched to find them and bring his father word of their welfare. In J, on the other hand, the entire affair took place close to home, most likely in one of the fields in which Joseph and his brothers routinely gathered sheaves—as may be inferred from Joseph's first dream. The plot to kill Joseph in J, rather than being brought about by some specific occurrence, is the direct result of the

---

by the internal divisions of the canonical text—often, perhaps primarily, identified according to the internal divisions of P—and assuming that the source documents must all have had similar internal divisions, instead of considering the possibility that in one or another of the sources the passage at hand may simply have been presented as the immediate and direct continuation of whatever preceded, without any need for a new opening.

[15] See n. 6, above.

brothers' rising hatred (vv. 4, 5, 8)—hatred that finally fermented into rage (v. 11).[16] The compiler thus placed E's account of the brothers' travel and Joseph's journey to seek them before J's tale of the conspiracy.

Intuiting that E's notice of Jacob's silence at Joseph's tale-bearing (note the pluperfect[17] in the words *wĕ'ābîw šāmar 'et haddābār* in v. 11b) serves as the immediate background to his decision to dispatch Joseph to Shechem, the compiler has placed it right before the account of the two journeys. Thus these two portions of E were incorporated in the compiled text as vv. 11b–17.

Logic dictates that the brothers could not have come up with the novel idea of killing Joseph twice. The compiler's next task was thus to combine the two accounts of the actual conspiracy to commit the murder—E's (v. 18) and J's (vv. 19–20). He has followed the same procedure as before, first continuing the preceding thread: E. Moreover, of the two, the E segment is also the only one that includes introductory words ("They saw him from afar …"); clearly this must have preceded the actual act of resolving to embark upon fratricide. Thus E's report came first, and only after incorporating it did the compiler move on to the corresponding segment of J. Since E's report of the conspiracy is extremely concise ("they conspired to kill him"), while J's is far more detailed ("and they said to one another, 'Here comes that dreamer! Come now, let us kill him and throw him into one of the cisterns; and we can say, A savage beast devoured him. We shall see what comes of his dreams!'"), the resulting composite text creates the illusion of having been designed with generalization preceding elaboration—though this was certainly not an intentional, or even conscious, act on the part of the compiler.[18] In this way, the two reports of the conspiracy to murder Joseph became vv. 18–20 of the chapter.

---

[16] On the precise meanings of *śn'*, "hate," and *qn'*, "rage," see Arnold B. Ehrlich, *Mikra Kiphesuto* (3 vols.; Berlin: Pappelauer, 1899; repr., New York: Ktav, 1969), 1:101; compare Gordon J. Wenham, *Genesis 16–50* (WBC 2; Dallas: Word, 1994), 352. The prose formulation here may be compared to the poetic phrase, "There is the cruelty of wrath (*ḥēmâ*, lit. 'venom'), the overflowing of anger (*ap*, lit. '[flaring of] nostrils'), but who can withstand fury (*qin'â*)?" (Prov 27:4). The traditional rendering "jealousy" is not apposite in these contexts.

[17] See GKC § 106f–g.

[18] For another possibility, namely, that according to J the brothers did indeed intend to kill Joseph in cold blood but not to throw his body into a cistern and that the words "and throw him into one of the pits" are not those of J at all, but are rather the invention of the compiler, according to which Reuben emerges not as disagreeing with his brothers' idea but merely improving on it, and for the reasons to prefer the suggestion given here, see at length Schwartz, "Joseph's Descent," 22–23 n. 43.

J, the source from which the last segment was inserted, next goes on to relate that the brothers promptly began to perpetrate their crime precisely as planned (v. 23). The next words of E, however, tell of Reuben's plea to abandon the original plan and to replace it with one that would not entail killing their brother with their bare hands (vv. 21–22). The compiler thus reverted here to E, particularly since the very first words of this segment of E, *wayyišmaʿ rĕʾûbēn* ("But when Reuben heard ..."), must follow directly upon the discussion in which the murder was planned.

Reuben's plea follows naturally upon the conspiracy for another reason: it too involves the idea of casting Joseph into a cistern. Thus, only after incorporating it was the compiler able to return to the commission of the crime, beginning with the notice that Joseph's brothers stripped him of his tunic (v. 23) and proceeding next to relate that they cast him into a cistern (v. 24), since obviously they could not have first thrown him into the cistern and then snatched his tunic. In this way, the accounts of Reuben's proposal, of the forcible removal of Joseph's tunic and of his being cast into the cistern became vv. 21–24 of the chapter. This in turn gave rise to an eminently implausible set of circumstances, for in the composite text, the idea of casting Joseph into a cistern is suggested twice, first as a way of disposing of his corpse after killing him in cold blood, and then as a method of bringing about his death by drowning (or, for Reuben, a ruse actually designed to save his life).

J tells next of the arrival of the Ishmaelites (vv. 25a2–b), while the E narration continues with the arrival of the Midianites (vv. 25a1 + 28a1). Both begin with introductory phrases: "Then they sat down to a meal" in E; "They looked up" in J. The last segment inserted having been from E (v. 24), the compiler remained with the E thread and placed E's introductory phrase before J's—reasoning plausibly that the brothers first sat down to eat and only then looked up and saw travelers approaching; if they had noticed the travelers' arrival first, they would not have begun their meal. Then, after J's introductory phrase, he remained with the J thread, including the remainder of the account of the Ishmaelites' arrival (v. 25a2–b), the report of Judah's new initiative that it inspires (vv. 26–27a), and the notice of the brothers' acquiescence (v. 27b). He could not have done otherwise; if he had picked up the E thread instead, relating first the arrival of the Midianites, he would have had no place to insert the notice of the arrival of the Ishmaelites and of Judah's initiative. Joseph would already have been fished out of the cistern and would be well on the way to Egypt before the Ishmaelites ever arrived on the scene. Only after completing J's account of the arrival of the Ishmaelites and Judah's plan was he able to revert to the remainder of E (v. 28a1). Thus, in the only order possible, these segments of the two sources came to be vv. 25–28a1 of the chapter.

Arriving at the conclusion of the account of Joseph's rescue/abduction by the Midianites as told in E, the compiler would have realized that if he were to proceed immediately to the next section of E, namely, to Reuben's return to the cistern and his dismay at discovering that Joseph has vanished (vv. 29–30), this would prevent him from including the next segment of J: the report of the sale of Joseph to the Ishmaelites (v. 28a2). For following this, both sources speak at length of the reaction of the parties to Joseph's unexplained disappearance; the compiler could hardly have backtracked to convey a few more details regarding Joseph's fate. He therefore inserted J's notice that "They sold Joseph for twenty pieces of silver to the Ishmaelites," along with the direct continuation of this sentence in J, "who brought Joseph to Egypt" (v. 28b), only afterward proceeding to Reuben's dismay at finding that Joseph has disappeared. In this way J's report of the sale of Joseph, J's notice that Joseph was brought to Egypt, and E's account of Reuben's return to the cistern were combined to constitute vv. 28a2–30.

In its authentic context, of course, the report of the sale of Joseph to the Ishmaelites was the direct sequel to the account of the brothers' acceptance of Judah's initiative. J read: "His brothers agreed, so they sold Joseph for twenty pieces of silver to the Ishmaelites, who brought Joseph to Egypt"; obviously the sale was performed by the brothers. Whether the compiler was conscious of having distorted—at least, obscured—this fact by creating a clause in which the only syntactically possible subject of the verb *wayyimkĕrû* "sold" is "some Midianite traders" is difficult to say with certainty. Such matters are inseparable from the larger and far more complex issue of the compiler's awareness, or lack thereof, of the exegetical inconsistencies rampant in his own work, a question to which no unequivocal reply can be offered. The compiler's thoughts aside, the canonical text definitely relates, in direct contradistinction to the original intent of the words "they sold Joseph for twenty pieces of silver to the Ishmaelites," that before the brothers managed to make their way back to the cistern to retrieve Joseph and sell him to the Ishmaelites, some Midianites appeared out of nowhere and did precisely what the brothers had intended to do themselves.[19]

---

[19] The utter implausibility of this sequence of events is quite evident, and is confirmed by Joseph's comforting words to his brothers at 45:5: "Do not be distressed, or angry with yourselves, for selling me here." This notice indicates that it was the brothers who sold Joseph—in total contradiction to the simple sense of v. 28. See also Rashbam's telling comment: "The plain sense of the words 'Some Midianite men, merchants, passed by' is that

The compiler was now left with only two more segments of text: J's report of the tragic news and the bloodied tunic being presented to Jacob along with the latter's agonized response (vv. 31–35) on the one hand, in which the action leaves the scene of the crime behind and returns to the house of Jacob and his sons; and the continuation of E's narration, which has by now moved to Egypt, in which we are informed that meanwhile, the Midianites[20] made off with Joseph and sold him to an Egyptian (v. 36), on the other. The E segment is phrased in the pluperfect (*wĕhammĕdānîm mākrû*), indicating that in the context of E's narrative it served as a narrative transition to the next act of the drama, Joseph's adventures in Egypt.[21] Fully aware of this, the compiler quite logically deemed it most appropriate to lower the curtain on Jacob and his sons in Canaan before proceeding to raise it on Joseph and his life in Egypt. Thus the tragic scene of the bloodied tunic and the report of Joseph being sold to Potiphar, in this precise order, became the concluding verses of the chapter, vv. 31–36.

Of course, the unambiguous notice that the Midianites sold Joseph to Potiphar (v. 36) is irreconcilable with the equally unambiguous statement that it was none other than the Ishmaelites who brought Joseph to Egypt (v. 28b, confirmed in 39:1). Once again, the question of whether the compiler imagined that the Ishmaelites, after purchasing Joseph from the Midianites (!) for 20 pieces of silver and bringing him to Egypt, proceeded to re-sell him there to some other Midianites whom they conveniently happened to find on hand and that the latter in turn sold him to Potiphar, or whether he perhaps thought that the *mĕdānîm* mentioned in v. 36 were distinct from the Midianites,[22] or that the Ishmaelites and the Midianites were one and the same people, cannot be answered with anything more than arbitrary speculation. It may in fact be unwise to raise this question in the first place, since we have no way of ascertaining whether the compiler was even aware of the inconsistencies that he created by interweaving the texts as he did, and if he was aware of them, whether he gave any thought at all to the presumed need to resolve them or to how one might go about doing

---

they just happened to pass by and to sell him to Ishmaelites. Even if it were posited, for the sake of argument, that 'and they sold Joseph to the Ishmaelites' refers to the brothers, one would have to presume that they then instructed the Midianites to pull him out, after which they sold him" (my translation).

[20] Following the view of most scholars, *mĕdānîm* in v. 36 is either a linguistic variant of, or a scribal error for, *midyānîm*; see for example Westermann, *Genesis*, 34; and Ernst A. Knauf, "Medan," *ABD* 4:656.

[21] E's story of Joseph's life in Egypt appears in Gen 40:1 ff.

[22] See *Gen Rab.* 84 (end); compare also Gen 25:2.

so. What is certain is that by taking upon himself, along with the task of merging the source documents into a single continuous text, the maximal preservation of the documents in their given form, the compiler of the Torah demonstrated that he attached far greater importance to the verbal inviolability of the sources than he attached to the plausibility, consistency of content and exegetical clarity of the final product.

It should now be clear that the interweaving of the relevant portions of J, E and P[23] at this point in the Torah thus resulted in the only possible text that could have been produced from these three narrative threads. Constrained by the method he took upon himself, the compiler had no alternative but to arrive at this arrangement of his sources, in precisely this order:

> [1]Now Jacob was settled in the land where his father had sojourned, the land of Canaan. [2]This, then, is the line of Jacob. *At seventeen years of age, Joseph tended the flocks with his brothers, as a lad among the sons of his father's wives Bilhah and Zilpah. Joseph brought bad reports of them to their father.* [3]Now Israel loved Joseph best of all his sons, for he was the child of his old age; and he had made him an ornamented tunic. [4]When his brothers saw that their father loved him more than any of his brothers, they hated him so that they could not speak a friendly word to him. [5]Once Joseph had a dream which he told to his brothers; and they hated him even more. [6]He said to them, "Hear this dream which I have dreamed: [7]There we were binding sheaves in the field, when suddenly my sheaf stood up and remained upright; then your sheaves gathered around and bowed low to my sheaf." [8]His brothers answered, "Do you mean to reign over us? Do you mean to rule over us?" And they hated him even more for his talk about his dreams. [9]He dreamed another dream and told it to his brothers, saying, "Look, I have had another dream: And this time, the sun, the moon and eleven stars were bowing down to me." [10]And when he told it to his father and brothers, his father berated him. "What," he said to him, "is this dream you have dreamed? Are we to come, I and your mother and your brothers, and bow low to you to the ground?" [11]His brothers were enraged at him. *His father kept the matter to himself.* [12]*One time, when his brothers had gone to pasture their father's flock at Shechem,* [13]*Israel said to Joseph, "Your brothers are pasturing at Shechem. Come, I will send you to them." He answered, "I am ready."* [14]*And he said to him, "Go and see how your brothers are and how the flocks are faring, and bring me back word." So he sent him from the valley of Hebron.*[24] *When he reached Shechem,* [15]*a man came upon him wandering in the fields. The man asked him, "What are you looking for?"* [16]*He answered, "I am looking for my brothers. Could you tell me where they are pasturing?"* [17]*The man said, "They have gone from here, for I heard them say: Let us go to Dothan." So Joseph followed his brothers and found them at Dothan.*

---

[23] See above, n. 6.
[24] See above, n. 10.

¹⁸*They saw him from afar, and before he came close to them they conspired to kill him.* ¹⁹And they said to one another, "Here comes that dreamer! ²⁰Come now, let us kill him and throw him into one of the pits; and we can say, 'A savage beast devoured him.' We shall see what comes of his dreams!" ²¹*When Reuben heard it, he tried to save him from them. He said, "Let us not take his life."* ²²*And Reuben said, "Shed no blood! Cast him into that pit out in the wilderness, but do not touch him yourselves"—intending to save him from them and restore him to his father.* ²³When Joseph came up to his brothers, they stripped Joseph of his tunic, the ornamented tunic that he was wearing. ²⁴*They took him and cast him into the pit. The pit was empty; there was no water in it.* ²⁵*Then they sat down to a meal.* Looking up, they saw a caravan of Ishmaelites coming from Gilead, their camels bearing gum, balm, and ladanum to be taken to Egypt. ²⁶Then Judah said to his brothers, "What do we gain by killing our brother and covering up his blood? ²⁷Come, let us sell him to the Ishmaelites, but let us not do away with him ourselves. After all, he is our brother, our own flesh." His brothers agreed. ²⁸*Some Midianite traders passed by, and they pulled Joseph up out of the pit.* They sold Joseph for twenty pieces of silver to the Ishmaelites, who brought Joseph to Egypt. ²⁹*When Reuben returned to the pit and saw that Joseph was not in the pit, he rent his clothes.* ³⁰*Returning to his brothers, he said, "The boy is gone! Now, what am I to do?"* ³¹Then they took Joseph's tunic, slaughtered a kid, and dipped the tunic in the blood. ³²They had the ornamented tunic taken to their father, and they said, "We found this. Please examine it; is it your son's tunic or not?" ³³He recognized it, and said, "My son's tunic! A savage beast devoured him! Joseph was torn by a beast!" ³⁴Jacob rent his clothes, put sackcloth on his loins, and observed mourning for his son many days. ³⁵All his sons and daughters sought to comfort him; but he refused to be comforted, saying, "No, I will go down mourning to my son in Sheol." Thus his father bewailed him. ³⁶*The Midianites, meanwhile, had sold him in Egypt to Potiphar, a courtier of Pharaoh and his chief steward.*

Our analysis demonstrates, first and foremost, that the process of composition of Gen 37 was essentially a *canonical* one, aimed at collecting, collating and preserving literary works already in existence. The outcome of the compilation process was determined—to the letter—by the pre-existing sources themselves. These were received by the compiler in the form of fully shaped, continuous and internally consistent written narratives, and the compiler viewed them as possessing a measure of sanctity that rendered it desirable, indeed obligatory, to refrain as much as possible from altering, detracting from or adding to them.

Genesis 37 in its canonical form shows no signs of being the result of creative narrative art, nor does it appear to be the work of ideologically or theologically motivated redactors who, having selected freely those sources and traditions that were best suited to their purposes, molded them into a new whole precisely as they wished. The compiler of Gen 37 had no say in determining either its content or its form; he was responsible neither for its themes and motifs nor for its religious teachings; he was not even at liberty to decide what to include and what to exclude.[25] All of these aspects of literary license and creativity belong to the earlier stages in the formation of the Torah. They most certainly played a major role in the creation of the sources themselves, and they were, without a doubt, decisive factors in the gradual development and crystallization of the traditions that preceded the sources and upon which the authors of the sources did indeed draw with considerable freedom. However, they have no role whatsoever in the composition, i.e., the compilation, of the canonical Torah.[26]

The analysis of Gen 37 reveals further that no single source served as the underlying text to which the compiler added what he deemed appropriate from the other documents. The compiler did not use E as his Vorlage, adding to it whatever portions of J and P he felt that he needed, nor did he use J as his primary text, adding to it whatever he chose from E and P.[27] He did not stratify, superimposing portions of a later document upon an earlier one or portions of an earlier one upon a later one. The unmistakable impression one receives is that the compiler attached equal weight to the two narratives—as well as to the opening segment from P, which he placed precisely where he was obligated to place it—and so he combined them by alternating between them, adhering meticulously to the principles of composition we have identified: maximal preservation of each source, strict chronological progression, avoidance of addition and deletion and continuing the thread of each narrative as long as possible, moving to the other thread at exactly the point when it becomes necessary to do so, not a single word earlier or later.

Finally and most crucially, our analysis reveals that the result arrived at by the compiler, the composite chapter in its canonical form, is, given the method that he evidently employed, the only possible result that could have been obtained. The final form of the chapter is not a function of the

---

[25] It is therefore impossible to accept Alter's view that the editor included both versions of the story because of his "desire to hint at a kind of moral equivalence between kidnapping and murder," and that the "overlap," as Alter puts it, "of the apparently fatal disappearance of Joseph with the deliberate selling of Joseph suggests that selling him into slavery is a virtual murder." See Robert Alter, *The Art of Biblical Narrative* (New York: Basic Books, 1981), 167.

[26] That is, what is usually referred to as the "redaction" of the Pentateuch; see above, n. 11.

[27] Nor can it be argued that the compiler was using P as his frame-narrative, inserting portions of J and of E as needed; though this notion is a commonplace in scholarship, it is not borne out by the detailed analysis of the Torah narrative.

compiler's ideological agenda, theological tendencies, aesthetic tastes, or artistic abilities. His role was confined entirely to the painstaking arrangement of the existing texts in combined form. The case of Gen 37 is in no way atypical; the composite narratives throughout the remainder of the Pentateuch all yield similar results.[28]

Select Bibliography

Addis, William E. *The Documents of the Hexateuch*. 2 vols. London: David Nutt, 1892–1898.
Baden, Joel S. *J, E, and the Redaction of the Pentateuch*. Forschungen zum Alten Testament 68. Tübingen: Mohr Siebeck, 2009.
Driver, S.R. *The Book of Genesis*. 10th ed. Westminster Commentaries. London: Methuen, 1916.
Friedman, Richard E. "Torah (Pentateuch)." Pages 605–622 in vol. 6 of *Anchor Bible Dictionary*. Edited by David Noel Freedman. 6 vols. New York: Doubleday, 1992.
———. *The Bible with Sources Revealed* (San Francisco: Harper, 2003).
Gunkel, Hermann. *Genesis*. 6th ed. Handkommentar zum Alten Testament 1/1. Göttingen: Vandenhoeck & Ruprecht, 1964. Reprint of 3rd ed. (1910). Translated by Mark E. Biddle. Macon, Ga.: Mercer University Press, 1997.
Loewenstamm, Samuel. E. "Reuben and Judah in the Cycle of Joseph-Stories." Pages 35–41 in *From Babylon to Canaan: Studies in the Bible and its Oriental Background*. Jerusalem: Magnes, 1992.
Lowenthal, Eric I. *The Joseph Narrative in Genesis: An Interpretation*. New York: Ktav, 1973.
Neufeld, Ernest. "The Anatomy of the Joseph Cycle." *Jewish Bible Quarterly* 22 (1994): 38–46.
Redford, Donald B. *A Study of the Biblical Story of Joseph (Genesis 37–50)*. Vetus Testamentum Supplements 20. Leiden: Brill, 1970.
Rendsburg, Gary A. "Redactional Structuring in the Joseph Story: Genesis 37–50." Pages 215–232 in *Mappings of the Biblical Terrain: The Bible as Text*. Edited by Vincent L. Trollers and John Maier. London: Associated University Presses, 1990.
Schmid, Konrad. *Genesis and the Moses Story: Israel's Dual Origins in the Hebrew Bible*. Siphrut 3. Translated by James D. Nogalski. Winona Lake, Ind.: Eisenbrauns, 2010. Revised and updated translation of *Erzväter und Exodus: Untersuchungen zur doppelten Begründung der Ursprünge Israels in den Geschichtsbüchern des Alten Testaments*. Wissenschaftliche Monographien zum Alten und Neuen Testament 81. Neukirchen-Vluyn: Neukirchener, 1999.

---

[28] Note that this discussion has been careful to avoid making any assumptions about the date or background of the sources J, E, or P. These matters should be treated only within the context of the historical study of each of the sources *in its entirety*, and within the framework of the composition of the entire Torah. The strictly literary discussion of any particular composite text is independent of these questions.

Schmitt, Hans-Christoph. "Die Hintergründe der 'neusten Pentateuchkritik' und der literarische Befund der Josephsgeschichte Gen 37–50." *Zeitschrift für die alttestamentliche Wissenschaft* 97 (1985): 161–179.

Schwartz, Baruch J. "Joseph's Descent into Egypt: The Composition of Genesis 37." Pages 1–30 in *The Joseph Story in the Bible and Throughout the Ages*. Edited by Lea Mazor. Special issue of *Beth Mikra* 55 (2010). In Hebrew.

———. "The Torah: Its Five Books and Four Documents." Pages 161–226 in vol. 1 of *The Literature of the Hebrew Bible: Introductions and Studies*. Edited by Zipora Talshir. 2 vols. Jerusalem: Yad Ben-Zvi, 2011. In Hebrew.

Skinner, John. *A Critical and Exegetical Commentary on Genesis*. 2nd ed. International Critical Commentary. Edinburgh: T&T Clark, 1930.

Speiser, Ephraim A. *Genesis: A New Translation with Introduction and Commentary*. Anchor Bible 1. Garden City, N.Y.: Doubleday, 1964.

Van Seters, John. "The Joseph Story: Some Basic Observations." Pages 361–388 in *Egypt, Israel and the Ancient Mediterranean World: Studies in Honor of Donald B. Redford*. Edited by Gary N. Knoppers and Antoine Hirsch. Probleme der Ägyptologie 20. Leiden: Brill, 2004.

Weimar, P. "Aufbau und Struktur der priesterschriftlichen Jakobsgeschichte." *Zeitschrift für die alttestamentliche Wissenschaft* 86 (1974): 174–203.

Wenham, Gordon J. *Genesis 16–50*. Word Biblical Commentary 2. Dallas: Word, 1994.

Westermann, Claus. *Genesis 37–50*. Translated by John J. Scullion. Minneapolis: Fortress, 1986. Translation of *Genesis 37–50*. Biblischer Kommentar Altes Testament 3. Neukirchen-Vluyn: Neukirchener, 1982.

Whybray, R.N. "The Joseph Story and Pentateuchal Criticism." *Vetus Testamentum* 18 (1968): 522–528.

THE WORLD OF THE FAMILY IN GENESIS

Naomi A. Steinberg

INTRODUCTION

Genesis functions as the prologue to how ancient Israel chose to recount her beginnings and to represent her identify. On the significance of this, Westermann remarks:

> The whole arrangement shows that at the time when a people was coming into being and a state was being formed, the perspective was based cn the memory of origin from families and ancestors. Thus is expressed the basic meaning of the family for all further forms of community, and thus is acknowledged that whatever happens in these more developed communities and their spheres of endeavor, be it in politics, economics, civilization, education, art, and religion, goes back to what has happened in the family. No other form of community can ever completely replace the family.[1]

In other words, the texts of Genesis describe the roots of ancient Israel in the first families of humanity, leading up to the stories surrounding Abraham, Isaac, and Jacob and their families. Amazingly, although the memories of family recounted in Genesis may be fictional, these stories of family life still find echoes in contemporary family institutions and family values.

The systematic historical study of the family—both modern and ancient—belies the assumption that the family was ever a static entity with one definition fixed for all times.[2] Genesis, also, does not provide a static

---

[1] Claus Westermann, *Genesis 12–36: A Commentary* (CC; Minneapolis: Augsburg, 1984), 23.

[2] A review of past research on the family cross-culturally suggests that the subject of the history of the family came into its own with the publication of Philippe Ariès's *Centuries of Childhood* (New York: Vintage, 1962). Although scholars have rejected Ariès's thesis that childhood was the invention of Europe in the Middles Age, the scholarship generated to refute this argument gave birth to systematic and nuanced attention to the history of the family and to the processes that have bearing on social change in family life over time and place. For a critique of Ariès, see, e.g., Linda Pollack, *Forgotten Children: Parent-Child Relations from 1500–1900* (New York: Cambridge University Press, 1983). Recent research on the history of the family is too extensive to cite here. For further discussion of the development of historical study of the family and the issues raised in this research, see, e.g.,

definition of the family. The biblical material is complicated because of the uncertain dates of biblical and related data and the diverse terms and the different translations of Hebrew terminology for family units. But progress can be made. In addition to a close reading of the text, many tools are available for understanding the families in Genesis: anthropological, ethnographic, cross-cultural analogies, literary analysis, and so on. Dutcher-Walls in her recent survey of the past five decades of scholarly investigation of families in the Bible,[3] describes the range of methodological approaches that have emerged in past research on the family in ancient Israel. However, a brief example of the range of interpretations may be useful.

Genesis 16 sets in motion the dynamics between Sarah, Abraham, and Hagar in the quest for an heir to continue the lineage of Abraham when his wife Sarah is barren. A theological reading of Gen 16, such as the one offered by Westermann, emphasizes God's role in this narrative: "God has closed Sarah's womb and has announced to Hagar the birth of a son. He grants new life; he denies new life."[4] However, a social world interpretation of the same text focuses on the social reality of a barren woman, Sarah, in a society where the expectation was that a wife must bear a son to carry on her husband's lineage. From this perspective, Sarah's actions are interpreted as the behavior of a barren wife, and not as reflective of her particular personality. They expose the necessity for a woman to bear an heir to her husband in order to fulfill her role in her marriage. The desperation is so great that Sarah is willing to use her servant Hagar as her replacement. Sarah tells Abraham, "Go in to my slave girl; it may be that I shall obtain children by her" (16:2b). Human biology may be a rather ineffective arrangement for perpetuation of the family due to the various potential obstacles that may interfere with reproduction, so it is no wonder that Genesis exhibits a variety of "solutions" to family continuity.

John Demos, "Reflections on the History of the Family: A Review Essay," *SCCH* 15 (1973): 493–503; Louise A. Tilly and Miriam Cohen, "Does the Family Have A History?" *SSH* 6 (1982): 181–199; Tamara K. Hareven, "The History of the Family and the Complexity of Social Change," *AHR* 96 (1991): 95–124; and the essays in *The History of the Family: An International Quarterly* which began publication in 1996.

[3] For a discussion of the past fifty years of social world research on the family, see Patricia Dutcher-Walls, "The Clarity of Double Vision: Seeing the Family in Sociological and Anthropological Perspective," in *The Family in Life and In Death—The Family in Ancient Israel: Sociological and Archaeological Perspectives* (ed. Patricia Dutcher-Walls; New York: T&T Clark, 2009), 1–15.

[4] Westermann, *Genesis 12–36*, 250.

The systematic study of the family in Genesis requires attention to many topics related to the family and the many individuals who comprise the family. It is no easy task to offer grand theories about the world of the family in Genesis. Genesis recounts the origins of the cosmos (Gen 1–3), primeval history, i.e., the families of the first human beings on earth (3:1–11:26), followed by stories of the call for a unique relationship with God (11:27–50:26) and the generations of the family line chosen to answer that call. Across its fifty chapters and its themes of creation, disobedience, and divine selection, Genesis focuses on a variety of families and family structures. These narratives present a picture of family life that at times appears familiar to the modern reader and at other times is quite puzzling. We should not assume that the narratives mirror the reality of everyday life in ancient Israel because we cannot be certain if the texts are an accurate rendition of everyday life in the founding generations of Israelite history. In their final canonical form, the texts are shaped by a point of view that may not reflect the perspective of the time when the text was originally written. We are, however, able to extrapolate from Genesis something about the world of the family without being positive that Genesis reflects how things "really" were. Genesis may reflect the ideology of how family life should be rather than the reality of how it actually was.

Themes

In this section we cover several themes or motifs that are threaded through family life in Genesis. In the next section I consider the families in Genesis in greater detail. Following that, we will address issues regarding children in Genesis, and in the final section I offer some concluding observations on the world of the family in Genesis.

Names and Genealogies

"Genesis is a book whose plot is genealogy."[5] The structure of Genesis constructs the family through genealogies that move the plot of Genesis forward. Genesis is divided into ten sections organized by the heading "these are the generations," i.e., the so-called *tôlēdôt* formulae. These sections are arranged into two groups of five: one group for the early ancestors (2:4a; 5:1;

---

[5] Naomi A. Steinberg, "The Genealogical Framework of the Family Stories in Genesis," *Semeia* 46 (1989): 41–50.

6:9; 10:1; 11:10) and the second group of five for the ancestors of Israel (11:27; 25:12, 19; 36:1; 37:2). This structure is a literary device intended to give structure to the narratives that surround it and to anchor them in a story line; yet, it reveals an implicit concern for the generation of family over time—beginning with the family of humanity. Within these genealogies the family line is traced as father begets son, and so forth. Explicit is the pervasive interest in kinship and family intended to carry through the divine command "to be fruitful, and multiply, and fill the earth" (1:28). Analysis of structure and theme in Genesis in its final form reveals a focus on kinship and family as a divine concern from creation through the sojourn of Jacob's family in Egypt.

The genealogies, regardless of their accuracy, provide a lens into Israel's self-understanding as a family of individuals in a world where everyone is basically directly or indirectly related to everyone else. These genealogies bring order by breaking groups of people down into what sociologists today would label as house of the father (בית אב), the clan (משפחה), and the tribe (שבט). At the same time, research on the social function of genealogy helps us to see that biblical genealogies—as they relate one group to the next—are not only biologically determined but are social constructions of kinship. Genesis constructs the world of the family as individuals who come from a common ancestor and who marry within that kinship group. The genealogies construct the line of Israel through males descended from Terah and his sons, and therefore show little concern for including the names of the women of the Terahite lineage in the Genesis genealogies. However, as the ancestral stories reveal, the family line depends on key actions of women in addition to their bearing sons to guarantee patrilineal descent.

Monogamy and Polygamy

In the so-called Yahwistic account of creation, the bond between the man and woman in Gen 2:24[6] suggests a monogamous family in contrast with the polygamous families of Abraham (two wives, one slave, Hagar, belonging to Sarah), Esau (six wives), and Jacob (two wives, two slaves belonging to his wives) later in Genesis. These polygamous types of family structures appear as legitimate alternatives to monogamy. Indeed, of the major couples, only Adam and Eve, Isaac and Rebekah, and Joseph and Asenath seem to be monogamous. Noah is also in a monogamous marriage (6:18) but his wife is not named.

---

[6] Gen 2:24–25 (NRSV): "Therefore a man leaves his father and his mother and clings to his wife, and they become one flesh."

Help in understanding these patterns of marriage in Genesis comes from cross-cultural studies of marriage and kinship. The social scientific labels given to the diverse marriage arrangements joining men and women reflect the male point of view regarding the legal status of the women in the marriage. Polycoity—a form of marriage in which a man takes other women, who are of lower status than his primary wife, as his secondary wife—reflects the circumstances of Abraham, married to one legal wife, Sarah, and to one slave/concubine, Hagar. Polygyny—a form of marriage in which a man may have more than one wife at a time, but the women are of equal status—occurs in the marriage of Jacob to the two sisters Rachel and Leah; the precise label for this marriage is sororal polygyny. However, ultimately Bilhah and Zilpah become secondary wives of Jacob, rendering the household arrangement one of polycoity. The term serial monogamy applies in cases of marriage with only one spouse at a time. Genesis 25:1–6 suggests that Abraham married Keturah after Sarah died. That being the case, the marriage would be categorized as serial monogamy.

Together these examples provide evidence of the competing models of the social structures of marriage and family life in the ancestral stories of Genesis.[7]

Heirs

In order for a man to continue his patrilineage, he must become the father of a son. However, the wives of Abraham, Isaac, and Jacob are barren when they are introduced in the texts. An important motif in Genesis is that barrenness can be cured by God: Sarah is cured (18:9–5; 21:1–3), Rebecca is cured (25:21), and Rachel is cured (30:22).

The relevant questions for understanding family and heirship in Genesis include: How does a wife's infertility to produce an heir to her husband's lineage affect the social status of a married woman in ancient Israel? What alternative options are available for providing her husband with a male heir in order to carry on his patrilineage? These questions are tied to the diverse marriage arrangements discussed above, whereby women are brought into a marriage for procreative purposes in order that there is a male heir to perpetuate the family line into the future. Moreover, the marriage arrangements expose issues of determining which son is an appropriate heir to his father's descent line in the case of the birth of multiple

---

[7] There are also extreme examples of family life that are very far from typical: Lot and his daughters (18:30–38) and Judah and Tamar (38:12–30).

sons, e.g., Abraham expels Ishmael, son of Hagar (Gen 21) in order to secure Isaac, son of Sarah, as his heir. The emphasis is on lineal/vertical heirship. There is tension between single and multiple heirship because division of inheritance yields smaller shares of property (both moveable and immovable goods), leading to reduced economic productivity for each heir. The patrilineal heir not only carries on the descent line going back to Terah; the heir is the recipient of family land. For example, problems of heirship and inheritance which were so carefully worked out in favor of Isaac must not be tampered with when Abraham takes another wife, Keturah, after the death of Sarah (25:1–11). Only Isaac can be recognized as heir to Abraham. So Abraham gives his entire inheritance to his heir Isaac (v. 5) but recognized his paternal responsibility to his children by Keturah and gave them gifts (v. 6).

Conflict

Family organization and dynamics are also the subject matter in the stories of primeval history, with the exception of the Tower of Babel narrative in Gen 11:1–10. When the narratives of early humanity (1–11) are compared with those of the ancestors (12–50), a pattern emerges that ties the stories together. Both the stories of primeval history and the ancestral stories that make up the remaining chapters of Genesis focus on the conflicts that pit men against men and women against women. Rarely do individuals of the same gender cooperate with each other; more often than not, they quarrel and exhibit jealousy and anger. The behavior of woman against woman, and man against man leads to highly disruptive patterns of family life throughout Genesis.

First we consider the conflict between women. The example of the continual conflict between Sarah and Hagar in Gen 16 and 21 stands alongside the case of competition between Rachel and Leah to produce offspring for Jacob (30:1–24) and indicates that conflict over childbearing pits woman and woman. The stories of Sarah, Hagar, and Abraham, and Jacob and his wives make clear that in the world of the family in Genesis women have little control over their bodies; they must use their bodies as a tool for legitimating their place in their husband's household by bearing sons to their husband. In these examples, the competition is occasioned by a social world in which women's self-definition and worth come through their ability to bear sons to their husbands. Rachel and Leah, although sisters, as co-wives compete against each other as child bearers because motherhood in Genesis appears to establish the socioeconomic worth of a woman and to secure her place in her husband's household. A woman's role is to build up the lineage in order for the family to continue into the next generation and maintain family stability.

There are many examples of competition between men. Cain murders Abel (4:8), Noah curses Ham (9:25–27), Abraham expels Ishmael (21:8–14), Jacob cheats Esau out of his birthright (25:29–34) and then tricks Isaac into giving him a blessing (27), Laban cheats Jacob out of his wages (31:7), and Joseph's brothers sell him into slavery (37:12–28). The pattern is that of one man displacing another—and even going so far as to commit fratricide in the example of Cain and Abel—out of self-interest in an attempt by one man (or a group of brothers) to gain power over another man within the kinship unit. Conflict appears to reflect a desire to be rid of competitors for positions of authority and for rights to inherit whatever economic goods are available. One man must deprive another man of something in order for the first man to succeed. The rights that accompany the status of heir shape the strategies used to achieve this position. In some of the examples, the tension between siblings can be explained as an attempt to establish the priority of one male over another for family leadership. The issue of succession is one that brings conflict between men.[8]

Thus, stability does not appear to be a feature of typical family life. Rather, conflict—and sometimes violence—characterize family life even as the members of the family work for continuity from one generation to the next.

Altars and Sacrifices and Meals

A common practice of family life in both primeval and ancestral history is the building of altars. Cain and Abel (4:3–4), Noah (8:20), and the patriarchs—with the exception of Isaac—engage in this ritual behavior. Abraham builds multiple altars (12:7–8; 13:8), which are sometimes linked with sacrificial offerings (including the case of the near sacrifice of Isaac, who is bound to an altar in 22:9–14). On some occasions there is just a sacrifice, e.g., Gen 15:9–21. Sometimes the ritual of altar building is accompanied by

---

[8] For detailed discussion of the conflict between Abraham and Lot (Gen 13), Jacob and Laban (Gen 31), and Jacob and Esau (Gen 32), see David L. Petersen, "Genesis and Family Values," *JBL* 124 (2005): 18–22. Regarding conflict in the ancestral stories, he concludes: "Members of the family, on occasion, harbored murderous intent. However, by using one or another strategy—distancing, oaths, contracts, legal separation, verbal combat, gifting, battles of wit—they were able to resolve that conflict without physical violence" (23). However, outside the ancestral stories, in the case of Cain and Abel, the conflict results in fratricide.

a sacrifice, and a meal is also eaten, as in the example of Gen 31:54, when Jacob and Laban separate. These practices together are interpreted as evidence of family religion revolving around an ancestor cult and local deities in the world of the ancestors of Genesis.[9]

Meal preparation—without an accompanying sacrifice—is also recounted as a feature of the world of the family. Jacob feeds Esau (25:29–34) and later Esau makes food for Isaac (27:31). Meals are sometimes for the purpose of hospitality (18:1–8), although they can be celebratory, as at the time of the weaning of Isaac (21:8).[10] Although women prepare meals, they do not eat with the recipients (18:6–8; 27:5–17).

The Families of Genesis

Anthropological Models

As I have argued elsewhere, anthropological models of family organization emphasize the importance of the following issues in Genesis: marriage choice, heirship, offspring (particularly males), first born males, and division of inheritance.[11] A pattern of marriage and family life based on patrilineal, patrilocal endogamy (with regard to males and only partly for females) whose aim is economic, i.e., intended to guarantee production and reproduction of the family from one generation to the next, emerges from the text and explains recurring behavior from one generation to the next. The focus on patrilineal, patrilocal endogamy means that from the male perspective, a man from the lineage of Terah has as his preferred spouse a woman who is descended from the Terahite line, and that after marriage the couple lives with the husband's family in order to live on the land, i.e., the inheritance, that will sustain the family as they work to reproduce a primary male heir to move the family forward into the next generation.

The family is both a descent group and a residential unit in ancient Israel. It is a multi-generational unit and consists of "a conjugal couple and their unmarried children, together with their married sons and their wives and children, as well as other unmarried or dependent paternal kinfolk and

---

[9] Karel van der Toorn, *Family Religion in Babylon, Ugarit, and Syria: Continuity and Change in the Forms of Religious Life* (SHCANE 7; Leiden: Brill, 1996), 181–265.

[10] In one example, Gen 13:17–24, a sacrificial meal is prepared by Melchizedek—someone outside the family unit—for Abraham.

[11] Naomi A. Steinberg, *Marriage and Kinship in Genesis: A Household Economics Perspective* (Minneapolis: Fortress Press, 1993), 137–138.

slaves."¹² There are, of course, slaves, some of whom bear children for the patrilineage. The family is the smallest unit of social organization; it is a socioeconomic unit. In Genesis, the family is represented by the Hebrew term בית אב: the house of the father, or ancestral household. Another term for this domestic group is the consanguineal family, or the joint family household.

As others have noted, an individual lived daily life within the sphere of the circle of the בית אב, the house of the father, the smallest unit of society and the residential and lineage group translated as the joint family household. The kinship unit immediately above the family household was the משפחה, the clan, an enlargement of the kinship circle to include lineages related by marriage. Finally, the שבט, the tribe, refers to the so-called tribal level of organization of later Israel which brings together clans related by descent from a common ancestor—whether related by blood or fictitious.¹³ These concentric circles of kinship organization structured the society. In Genesis, the focus of family life is on the level of the family household. The kinship network focuses on the extended family network of Gen 11:27, a genealogy that on the horizontal level links Terah and his sons and on the

---

¹² J. David Schloen, *The House of the Father as Fact and Symbol: Patrimonialism in Ugarit and the Ancient Near East* (SAHL 2; Winona Lake, Ind.: Eisenbrauns, 2001), 108. As Schloen shows, the biblical data on family structure is corroborated by archaeological evidence (135–183). For purposes of this essay, I rely primarily on the biblical texts in order to reconstruct the world of the family in Genesis. For further discussion of the realities of the family in ancient Israel—as opposed to a literary reading of family traditions—the basic resources are: Lawrence E. Stager, "The Archaeology of the Family in Ancient Israel," *BASOR* 260 (1985): 1–35; Leo G. Perdue et al., eds., *Families in Ancient Israel* (FRC; Louisville: Westminster John Knox, 1997). One of the problems to consider in discussing the world of the family in Genesis is the historical context to which these stories belong—a different issue than the time when the texts were redacted and put into their final canonical form. Although it is impossible to determine the date of the period of the ancestors, the world of the family reflected through the patterns that emerge from the text conform to Iron I archaeological data analyzed by Stager and Schloen. All the same, the stories of Gen 12–50 cannot be utilized as an historical resource for data on early Israel.

¹³ Archaeological evidence, too, has changed how we interpret the family and its significance in ancient Israel. As Meyers states, "We have been concerned with ethnicities and kingdoms, not with individual family groups. The 'state' or 'city-state' or 'tribe' has been reckoned the primary social structure, when in reality the *household*, as the basic unit of production and reproduction, is the primary socio-economic unit of society should be acknowledged as the social and economic center of any settlement." See Carol Meyers, "Material Remains and Social Relations: Women's Culture in Agrarian Household of the Iron Age," in *Symbiosis, Symbolism, and the Power of the Past: Canaan, Ancient Israel and Their Neighbors from the Late Bronze Age through Roman Palaestina* (ed. William G. Dever and Seymour Gittin; Winona Lake, Ind.: Eisenbrauns, 2003), 427.

lineal level traces the Israelite line through Abram. The family story texts do not address the kinship connections that obligate the family household to the clan and the tribe; the focus is on fathers and sons, uncles and nephews, and cousins within the kinship unit centered on Terah.[14]

Although some have argued that marriage in the family stories functioned to establish alliances,[15] I have argued elsewhere that the data supports the thesis for the interconnection between marriage and patrilineal descent. The preferred marriage pattern for establishing the line of Terah is for a man—whose parents are both from this lineage—to marry a woman within the patrilineage of Terah. Thus, a man marries within the lineage—endogamy—and establishes the descent line rather than marrying outside—exogamy—and forming an alliance. The line of Abraham (entitled to the land of Israel: Gen 12:1–3) is determined by socially constructed patterns of kinship, i.e., a culturally determined emphasis on both blood and marriage as the preferred method for constructing the lineage, rather than on descent which is an absolute determined solely by blood line.[16]

In ancient Israel, the family was the basic social and economic unit of society. Identity for individuals was tied to this corporate unit, rather than to separate concerns. A person's identity was determined by her/his relationships to others, rather than autonomy. The emphasis in the family stories is on how individuals go through their lives in order to fulfill the relational roles expected of them, rather than on how they relate emotionally.

Patrilineal, patrilocal endogamy serves as the basis for the world of the family in Genesis as grounded in values of production and reproduction. Family continuity was predicated on the transmission of lineal heirship and the transmission of property to this lineal heir. These issues govern the marriage patterns and family life in the ancestral stories of Genesis.

---

[14] However, in Gen 12:3 when God calls Abraham and promises him that "through you all the families of the earth will be blessed," the term used is מִשְׁפְּחֹת. The family household of Terah, traced through Abraham, interrelates with the larger kinship group of the clan.

[15] Mara E. Donaldson, "Kinship Theory in the Patriarchal Narratives: The Case of the Barren Wife," *JAAR* 49 (1981): 77–87; Terry J. Prewitt, "Kinship Structures and the Genesis Genealogies," *JNES* 40 (1981): 87–98; Robert A. Oden, "Jacob as Father, Husband, and Nephew: Kinship Studies and the Patriarchal Narratives," *JBL* 102 (1983): 189–205; and Oden, "The Patriarchal Narratives as Myth: The Case of Jacob," in *The Bible without Theology: The Theological Tradition and Alternatives to It* (San Francisco: Harper & Row, 1987), 106–130, 183–187.

[16] Naomi A. Steinberg, "Alliance or Descent? The Function of Marriage in Genesis," *JSOT* 51 (1991): 45–55.

Abraham

On the surface, the introduction of Abram as one of three sons to Terah (11:26–27) appears to be in traditional genealogical format, linking a father to his sons in the descending generation. The part of Abraham's household that will become the families of Israel derives from the lineage of Terah. However, biology intervenes: Sarah, the wife of Abram, is barren (11:30). All societies that emphasize patrilineal descent must have strategies for overcoming this possibility. Although in recent times it is known that barrenness can be caused by infertility in either the male or the female, in biblical Israel the female was blamed.

The narratives of Gen 12–25 explore multiple options for establishing heirship through Abraham, in light of the fact that his wife Sarah is barren. Analysis of the narrative from the perspective of issues of establishing patrilineal descent reveals that one option for heirship focuses on Abram's nephew Lot, the son of his deceased brother Haran. The possibility of adoption, i.e., creating heirship, through Abram's closest male relative in the descending generation, provides the rationale for Lot to travel with Abram when the latter leaves his homeland and moves to the land of Canaan (12:4–5). However, if Lot is to be designated the heir to his paternal uncle Abraham, he must reside on the land that will be inherited as his patrimony. Ultimately arguments over land (because they both need more space—Abraham saves Lot, indicating they are not angry with each other) bring about a separation between Abraham and Lot, with the result that Lot moves outside the boundaries of the designated landed inheritance (13:2–18). Later, after the departure of Lot, Abraham states that his heir will be Eliezer of Damascus (15:2–3).

Genesis 16 introduces the subject of an heir for Abram, but this time from the perspective of his barren wife Sarah. Sarah's actions not only serve to help the reader appreciate the importance of production and reproduction in the world of the family in Genesis, but introduce them from the point of view of a woman—and barren wife—whose social validation and future in the family are determined by her reproductive capabilities.

Genesis 16 also introduces Hagar, the Egyptian handmaid, into the family household of Abraham and Sarah. In this chapter, Sarah comes up with a plan, to which Abram agrees, whereby he will impregnate Sarah's Egyptian handmaid Hagar, who will then bear a son that will be counted as the offspring of Sarah and Abram. The story assumes the existence of polycoity, a form of marriage, mentioned earlier, in which a woman other than a man's primary wife functions as a secondary wife of lower status.

Hagar remains a slave belonging to Sarah and serves as a substitute/surrogate mother for Sarah.[17]

Hagar is not consulted about this plan; she is not asked whether she is willing to be a party to it. Hagar is forced to become a surrogate mother in order to produce a child for the barren Sarah. Similar dynamics operate in the cases of Bilhah and Zilpah, servants to Rachel and Leah, who are given to Jacob for procreative purposes (see below). As slaves these women do not have control of their bodies in these circumstances.

The household position of Sarah as primary wife is very different than Hagar's position as a slave, i.e., Hagar is both a secondary wife and a concubine. A primary wife is a woman bringing property into the marriage (through direct and/or indirect dowry) and who has legal and economic rights not available to a woman who does not bring in property. Her status is elevated if she is descended through the patrilineage of Terah, as is Sarah (20:12). By contrast, a slave has a lower status—economically and legally. Her marriage can easily be dissolved by the husband whereas the primary wife has protection against divorce through the property she brings to the marriage union. Hagar's status is separated from the status of her child, who is considered a legitimate heir to its biological father, Abram, and to Sarah, Abram's primary wife.[18]

We see through these family dynamics that it is not individuals who shape family goals and identity but community identity that shapes individual behavior and interests. One's duty is to the family, rather than to fulfill personal ambitions. Sarah acts based on societal expectations that a woman will bear her husband a son to perpetuate his lineage into the descending generation. Her failure to fulfill this expectation may help to explain the reason Abraham gives her away twice to foreign leaders (12:10–20; 20) before she finally bears a son to him and secures her position in the family. The case of the so-called wife-sister story in Gen 12:10–20 exemplifies a daughter/sister's lack of control over her fate in matters pertaining to

---

[17] Some scholars argue that Sarah's plan can best be explained in light of parallels with second millennium documents from Nuzi recounting Hurrian custom. Based on a Nuzi marriage contract, it would appear that a barren wife was expected to provide her husband with a slave woman to bear children to him. For more on the parallels between the biblical text and the Nuzi texts, see Ephraim A. Speiser, *Genesis: A New Translation with Introduction and Commentary* (AB 1; Garden City, N.Y.: Doubleday, 1964), 120–121.

[18] The code of Hammurabi §146 legislates for conflict between a barren wife and a slave who has been brought in to bear children with the husband of the barren woman, indicating that the use of a surrogate to resolve the problem of barrenness was a common one. See also Prov 30:21–23.

the socioeconomic survival of her family unit; just as Sarah has no choice in Abraham's plan to give her to the Egyptians, later Rebekah has no real choice concerning her marriage to Isaac (Gen 24). Furthermore, Abraham reaps significant financial gains[19] in exchange for Sarah, as does Rebekah's family in negotiations for her marriage to Isaac (24:10, 22, 30, 35, 47, 53).

The birth of Ishmael to his father Abram seemingly resolves the problem of the continuance of the patrilineage of Terah through his son Abram in lieu of Eliezer (15:2–3), until the time that a son is borne by Sarah to Abram. Although it might seem that the birth of Isaac would be interpreted as Abram is twice blessed, the pattern in Genesis is that only one son is singled out to continue the patrilineage, i.e., the pattern is one of a lineal— as opposed to a segmented—genealogy in order to preserve family land (that is, not dividing it into smaller and smaller tracts). In Gen 21, a choice is made for Isaac over Ishmael as heir to the patrilineage of Terah. The choice appears to be an unexpected one because Ishmael is, after all, the first born son of Abraham. The motif in Genesis is that a rationale is implied when the first born does not inherit.

Sarah is the agent who presses for the expulsion of Hagar and Ishmael in order that her son Isaac will be designated heir to Abraham. Our analysis yields the following sense of event in the life cycle of a woman in ancient Israel: "Being a woman is not enough; one has to become a wife. Being a wife is not enough; one has to become a mother."[20] To this we might add: Being a mother is not enough, one must be the mother of her husband's heir. Yet, the story upholds Sarah's perspective that Isaac is preferred over Ishmael as heir to Abraham, although both are biological sons of Abraham. However, the choice between the two sons brings us to the importance of the mothers, Hagar and Sarah, in the narrative and to ancient Israelite perspectives on marriage and family. The pattern that emerges is that the preferred spouse for a son of the Terahite lineage is a woman descended from the same lineage and the preferred mother of the heir to this same lineage is a woman from the lineage. Sarah is from the lineage of Terah (20:12), whereas Hagar is of Egyptian origins and thus outside the boundaries of the line of Terah.

---

[19] When Abraham and Sarah travel to Gerar in the second so-called wife-sister story, Abimelech gives Abraham livestock and servants despite the fact that Abimelech never takes Sarah from Abraham. Together, the texts suggests that Abraham is in fact a wealthy man; see his exchange with Melchizedek, King of Salem on accepting gifts (Gen 14:17–21) and his purchase of the cave of Machpelah (Gen 23).

[20] Karin R. Andriolo, "Myth and History: A General Model and Its Application to the Bible," *American Anthropologist* 83 (1981): 261–284, here 272.

Moreover, the course of events is determined by Sarah's insistence on the expulsion of Hagar and Ishmael. Abraham acts in both Gen 16 and 21 based on Sarah's demands. Sarah's status as primary wife and mother through her Terahite patrilineal links allows her to control the determination of the heir to her husband and to secure her status in the family. Her behavior throughout Gen 12–21 make clear that for an Israelite woman, biology is destiny.

Sarah's choice of her own son Isaac—over Ishmael—not only secures her son as heir to his father, but, using cross-cultural analogues, binds Isaac to her as a source of physical and economic security in her old age. Although the inflated ages of biblical characters makes it difficult to be precise about life spans, the age differential in extra-biblical marriage contracts between a groom and bride suggests that a wife would be expected to outlive her husband because the relative difference between the spouses' ages was typically over a decade.[21] Although we are unable to consider the inflated ages of individuals in Genesis as reliable indicator of life expectancy in ancient Israel, the age difference between Sarah and Abraham is in basic conformity with the data from ancient Near Eastern marriage contracts. According to Gen 17:17, Abraham is ten years old than Sarah. Thus, Sarah's strategy in Gen 21 is to focus on securing security for her old age through her son Isaac. Without a son, she could not do this. Yet, in both Gen 16 and 21 Sarah must work through the agency of Abraham in order to accomplish her goals to finally legitimate her position through the birth of Isaac.

Isaac

Thus, due to Abraham's acceptance of Sarah's demands in Gen 21, issues of heirship and inheritance through the lineage of Terah now focus on Isaac. Isaac will be Abraham's lineal heir. However, before Isaac can assume this status, he will need a wife to provide him with a son who will then move the patrilineage forward into the descending generation.

The genealogical plot shifts in Gen 22:20–24 to a brief genealogical notice that provides further data on patterns of marriage for the descendants of Terah. In Gen 22:23 we learn of the birth of Rebekah, who is from the second generation descended through Nahor, brother of Abraham. In other words, Rebekah is from the patrilineage of Terah and, from the point of view of the biblical text, an appropriate spouse for Isaac, who is also from the same

---

[21] Martha T. Roth, "Age at Marriage and the Household: A Study of Neo-Babylonian and Neo-Assyrian Forms," *CSSH* 28 (1987): 715–747.

patrilineage. Their marriage provides a further example of the endogamous marriages that characterize the kinship unit constructed as the Terahite genealogy. Thus, in Gen 24 when Abraham's servant goes searching for an appropriate wife for his master's son, we are aware that Rebekah has the "correct" kinship credentials to become Isaac's bride: Rebekah is the daughter of Bethuel, who is a son of Nahor, who is a son of Terah.

The resulting marriage between Isaac and Rebekah serves as an example upholding the claim that the world of the family of Terah in Genesis was characterized by patrilineal endogamy. Moreover, the marriage also exemplifies the claim that such marriages were patrilocal, i.e., upon marriage the bride came to reside with the family of her husband. Thus, we note that although the servant returns to the original homeland of Abraham's family, Haran, to find a bride for Isaac (11:31), he is explicitly told that the bride must return with him to Canaan where Isaac lives; under no circumstances can Isaac move to Aram-naharaim to live with his bride. The specification that Abraham's heir must live on his land ties back to Gen 13 and the removal of Lot as potential heir to Abram after Lot moves outside of Canaan. The pattern is one of patrilocal residence for the lineal heir to Terah through Abraham.

The argument above for the economic basis of a marriage between a man and his primary wife receives confirmation from the details of the gifts Rebekah receives from the servant on behalf of Abraham in the marriage negotiations for a bride for Isaac (24:10, 22, 30, 35, 47, 53). These gifts communicate to Rebekah and her family that Rebekah's future husband will be able to provide well for her; these gifts are an indirect dowry that serves to solidify the economic basis of the marriage between Rebekah and Isaac. Marriage is grounded in the economics that control patrilineal, patrilocal endogamy. Romantic love does not play a role at this point in contracting the marriage.[22]

No sooner than the marriage is arranged and Rebekah is living with Isaac, Rebekah's barrenness is overcome through Isaac's prayers to God (25:21). Rebekah bears Isaac two sons, Jacob and Esau, a situation that provides the reader with information about the resolution of descent and inheritance when a monogamous marriage yields more than one potential lineal heir.

---

[22] However, the text is clear that Abraham mourns Sarah's death (23:2), Isaac loved Rebekah after she became his wife (24:67), and Jacob loved Rachel (29:18). On the rise of romantic love—rather than economic success—in the nineteenth century as the basis for family relationships, see Tamara K. Hareven, "Modernization and Family History: Perspectives on Social Change," *Signs* 2 (1976): 190–206.

Isaac, the patriarch of the family, is deceived by Rebekah and Jacob and manipulated into blessing Jacob instead of Esau (Gen 27). All the same, Isaac is clear regarding his role and his duty as head of the family: it is his responsibility to designate the son who will get the blessing needed to become heir to the Israelite family line. Isaac does not know that Esau, the first born son, has sold his birthright to Jacob in a moment of weakness occasioned by hunger (25:29–34). In addition, Esau violates the sine qua non for being reckoned his father's lineal heir through his marriage to Hittite women (26:34). Through his marriages Esau further distances himself from the possibility of being primary heir to his father Isaac. Esau losses his birthright, his father's blessing, and he makes the wrong marriage choices from the perspective of the Terahite lineage.

Based on Gen 27:5–17, Rebekah's love for her son Jacob and her favoritism towards him appear to be determined by her knowledge (25:23) that he will bring her personal security in the future as the lineal heir to his father Isaac. Hence, Jacob lies twice to his father in order to receive the blessing passed on from him.

Jacob's marriages to Rachel and Leah, daughters of Laban, descended from the lineage of Nahor (29:5), brother to Terah, secure his position as heir to Isaac. The world of the family of Terah is built up from sons whose mothers are of the patrilineage and who marry woman from the patrilineage. The marriage of a man to two sisters, i.e., women of equal social standing, is an example of sororal polygyny. Moreover, Jacob's wives have maids, Bilhah and Zilpah, who also bear sons to Jacob; the arrangement uniting Jacob to both his primary wives and their maids is best characterized as polycoity with the addition of the two maidservants to the list of Jacob's wives.

Jacob

Jacob's wives Rachel, Leah, Bilhah, and Zilpah bear him twelve sons and one daughter.[23] Gen 36–50 recounts events in their lives and provides further data to reconstruct the world of the biblical family. However, these texts are distinct from those of the generations of Abraham and Isaac. The life of the family in the generation of Jacob's children does not directly relate to the marriage choices, inheritance, and heirship issues discussed above. Yet

---

[23] Dinah is the only named daughter of Leah and Jacob (Gen 30:21). Other unnamed daughters are referred to in Gen 46:15. The story of Dinah (Gen 34) addresses issues of endogamy and exogamy from the perspective of an Israelite woman.

the emphasis on production and reproduction characteristic of the world of the Genesis family continues in the generation of Jacob's children.

Instead, the focus shifts from a lineal/vertical genealogy, focused on the choice of only one son, to a segmented/horizontal genealogy, where all of Jacob's sons become his heirs. The lack of interest in exclusivity of heirship is clear when Jacob blesses his twelve sons in Gen 49. No one son is singled out as lineal heir to Jacob. Instead the lineage clearly shifts from vertical to horizontal reckoning. Heirship has become decentralized.

Thus, we see that all of Jacob's wives sons are counted as his direct descendants. When the family moves down to Egypt (Gen 46), the emphasis on family fusion stems not from property and inheritance decisions but concern with social survival as a distinct unit in a new land. Without residence in the land promised to Abraham in Gen 12:1–3 as an indicator of descent from the Terahite lineage, the sons are legitimated as members of the lineage through their father Jacob.

In conclusion, because no son is excluded all the sons of Jacob are his direct heirs. By default, outside the land promised to Abraham, the patrilineage of Terah shifts from vertical to horizontal listing in the generation of the sons of Jacob. From a literary perspective, the story loses interest in choosing a lineal heir. Moreover, from an anthropological perspective on genealogy and family life, we may understand this shift by noting that the combination of vertical and horizontal genealogies in Genesis results in the structural creation of a family tree. The shift from a lineal to a segmented genealogy yields genealogical depth in the world of the family in Genesis and allows us to trace multiple descent lines for the Terahite patrilineage at the time when they no longer reside inside the land promised to them through Abraham.

Children

The preceding analysis has primarily focused on the dynamics of adults. The texts in Genesis do not specifically identify a particular age or rite at which a boy becomes a man or a girl a woman. There are no "child" marriages in Genesis. Indeed, there are no life stage markers described in Genesis, other than the birth rite of circumcision (17:12–13) and weaning (21:8).[24]

---

[24] Outside Genesis one finds the important gender segregated ritual performed by Jephthah's daughter (Judg 11:37–40).

Our attempt to grasp the perspective of Genesis on the meaning of childhood begins with the societal concern for the preservation of the patrilineage. At least a first born son was valued. Yet, we do know that although the births of both Ishmael and Isaac were sources of joy to their father Abraham, Abraham ultimately expels Ishmael (21:8–21) and then prepares to kill Isaac (Gen 22). Abraham's sons, like his wives, are objects of patriarchal control—both of child abandonment and near child sacrifice. Parental interests take priority over the survival of a child.[25] Further, Judah can choose wives for his sons (Gen 38) without consulting them. A child is a placeholder in the patrilineage, whose value depends not on individual personality traits but because he is defined by his ability to move the patrilineage forward to the next generation both through reproduction and through economic survival.

Less information is available about the childhood of daughters than of sons. However, just as Abraham had rights over his sons Isaac and Ishmael, Lot has rights over his daughters and offers to turn them over to angry men for sexual intercourse (19:1–11). Jacob and his sons turn the circumstances of the dishonoring of Dinah into an occasion to plunder the Shechemites; the men gain at the expense of Dinah (34:27–29). And, Judah can choose that his daughter-in-law Tamar not be given in levirate marriage to his son Shelah (38:11). On the other hand, Gen 24 recounts details of how Rebekah came to be the wife of Isaac and offers further data on the construction of childhood for a daughter in Genesis. We can supplement this information with the details of Rachel and Leah in later chapters. Together they support the construction of childhood for daughters, as well as for sons, as the property of parental control and valued for their contributions to the production of the family as an economic unit.[26] Notwithstanding occasional mention of emotional ties between parents and child, the meaning of childhood was determined by the group interests that controlled all members of the family unit. The world of the family in the biblical period does not place a premium on individual autonomy.

---

[25] In Gen 21:8–21, the story of the expulsion of Ishmael, Ishmael is never identified by name. The impersonal means of identifying him in the text—e.g., "the son of Hagar the Egyptian, whom she had borne to Abraham" (v. 9), "the son of this slave woman" (v. 10), "the boy" (v. 12), etc.—may reflect the narrator's discomfort with the course of events at this point in the story.

[26] Thus, when Laban agreed to the marriage between Rebekah and Isaac, he was showered with gifts by Abraham's servant (Gen 24:53).

The family interest was, as stated earlier, in production and reproduction. Thus, the importance of daughters for contracting endogamous marriages that served to continue the patrilineage requires further exploration. The three daughters, Rebekah, Rachel, and Leah are brought into the narratives at precisely the point in the family life cycle when their roles in the process of maintaining family structure become important. Rebekah is first introduced as an individual who participates in the socioeconomic survival of the family through her work of watering the animals. Her behavior is important not as an indicator of this one individual but as data contributing to the pattern of family life for a daughter whose behavior serves the economic interests of the family.

The patrilocal custom is enforced by Abraham when instructs his servant that the prospective wife he finds for Isaac in the land of Abraham's birth must come to Isaac in Canaan to live. The endogamous custom is enforced by Abraham when instructs his servant to find a wife from the patrilineage of Terah. Rebekah has little choice in the matter of whether or not she will leave with the servant and marry Isaac, despite the text of Gen 24:58 where she gives her consent. The decision is ultimately not in her hands but she must comply with the group interests in furthering the continuance of the Terahite patrilineage in a social world where marriage was the only option available to a woman, and where marriage, descent, and inheritance are tightly interconnected. Significantly, Rebekah's mother and the slaves that go with her are unnamed in the story.

Genesis 29:9 continues the pattern of a daughter working for family economic interests; here Rachel is introduced as the daughter of Laban who shepherds her father's sheep. The next verse establishes the kinship unit that controls the story and the genealogical plot: Rachel is the daughter of Laban, who is the brother of Jacob's mother Rebekah, i.e., a marriage between Jacob and Rachel conforms to the pattern of endogamous marriage that the narratives uphold. Of course, the intervention of Laban in the course of events results in Jacob ultimately marrying both of Laban's daughters. Jacob's marriage is characterized as sororal polygamy, a type of marriage in which a man has more than one wife and the wives are of equal status in the marriage because they are sisters. The competition between the two sisters/wives later to produce children for Jacob serves as a reminder that a woman's worth in her husband's family was determined by her ability to contribute to the patrilineage. Biology was destiny. The status of a woman was intimately tied to her reproductive capabilities. A woman's power and authority in the family and her security for the future depend on her ability to displace any other child bearing women in the domestic group and to establish her reproductive success as the mother of the heir to the patrilineage. Yet, as the case of Sarah and Hagar has made clear, the more wives a man has (whatever their status) the more chances there are for genealogical continuity.

Conclusions

There is no single or simple definition of the family in Genesis. Yet, the Genesis stories make it clear that the family is the basic unit of social organization. The family is hierarchically structured and all members of the family are bound by the group interest in production and reproduction of the בית אב from one generation to the next. Individual behavior aims at family survival both on a daily basis and from one generation to the next. Men and women relate to each other within the family based on their roles that sustain and maintain family order and survival and guarantee their security within this family structure. In this kinship system, generational continuity is governed by principles of patrilineal, patrilocal endogamy.

The narratives of Gen 11:10–35:29 establish strict boundaries of exclusivity for the family of the Terahite lineage through a pattern of endogamous marriage. Marriage to one's patrilineal kin functions to keep property within this group. Thus, the world of the family in Genesis recognizes neighbors of Israel as members of the family, e.g., Ishmael's descendants are named and their land claims acknowledged (25:12–18) but they are not direct descendants of the privileged lineage traced through Terah. Nonetheless, God keeps his promise to Abraham regarding Ishmael (20:12); Ishmael prospers, has twelve sons (20:13–16) and a daughter (28:9), just like Jacob, and both Ishmael and Isaac bury Abraham (20:9).

We see that women are important to the family not as individuals in their own right but to guarantee generational progression and as primary wives whose Terahite pedigree legitimates their husbands as appropriate heirs to the lineage. Analyses of the narratives reveal that in the social world of the ancestral stories children—whether sons or daughters—are valued for their ability to contribute to the socioeconomic development of the בית אב. This pattern upholds the family values of production and reproduction and maintains patrilineal, patrilocal endogamy. The narratives only seriously explore the social roles of sons and daughters when they are of marriageable age; for daughters this would undoubtedly meant being of childbearing age. Neither sons nor daughters have a serious voice in their choice of a spouse—despite Gen 24:58. Once they were married, the burden falls on daughters—now wives—to prove their worth to the family through their reproductive successes.

Finally, in the world of the family in primeval history, we discover conflict between woman and man (Gen 2–3), between brother and brother, i.e., between Cain and Abel (4:2–16), and between father and sons, i.e., Noah, Ham, Shem, and Japheth (9:20–27). The same relationship conflicts continue in the ancestral stories and can all be found in, e.g., Gen 27, where husband competes with wife, brother competes against brother, and father is in conflict with son regarding the choice of an heir to continue the patrilineage into the next generation.

Thus, patterns emerge of how men and women operate with the family world in Gen 1–50. These patterns are linked to the formation and development of the family unit over the life cycle of the בית אב in Gen 12–50. Neither men nor women appear to have peaceful ties with same sex individuals within the family. The world of the family is characterized by conflict and competition. The rivalry between individuals emerges throughout the generations of humankind from the beginning to the end of Genesis.

Select Bibliography

Donaldson, Mara E. "Kinship Theory in the Patriarchal Narratives: The Case of the Barren Wife." *Journal of the American Academy of Religion* 49 (1981): 77–87.
Dutcher-Walls, Patricia, ed. *The Family in Life and In Death—The Family in Ancient Israel: Sociological and Archaeological Perspectives*. New York: T&T Clark, 2009.
Jay, Nancy. *Throughout Your Generations Forever: Sacrifice, Religion, and Paternity*. Chicago: University of Chicago Press, 1992.
Oden, Robert A. "Jacob as Father, Husband, and Nephew: Kinship Studies and the Patriarchal Narratives." *Journal of Biblical Literature* 102 (1983): 189–205.
Perdue, Leo G., Joseph Blenkinsopp, John J. Collins, and Carol Meyers, eds. *Families in Ancient Israel*. Family, Religion, and Culture Series. Louisville: Westminster John Knox, 1997.
Petersen, David L. "Genesis and Family Values." *Journal of Biblical Literature* 124 (2005): 5–23.
Prewitt, Terry J. "Kinship Structures and Genesis Genealogies." *Journal of Near Eastern Studies* 40 (1981): 87–98.
Schloen, David. *The House of the Father as Fact and Symbol: Patrimonialism in Ugarit and the Ancient Near East*. Studies in the Archaeology and History of the Levant 2. Winona Lake, Ind.: Eisenbrauns, 2001.
Stager, Lawrence E. "The Archaeology of the Family in Ancient Israel." *Bulletin of the American Schools of Oriental Research* 260 (1985): 1–35.
Steinberg, Naomi A. "The Genealogical Framework of the Family Stories in Genesis." *Semeia* 46 (1989): 41–50.

———. *Kinship and Marriage in Genesis: A Household Economics Perspective.* Minneapolis: Fortress, 1993.

———. "Sociological Approaches: Toward a Sociology of Childhood in the Hebrew Bible." Pages 251–269 in *Method Matters: Essays on the Interpretation of the Hebrew Bible in Honor of David L. Petersen.* Edited by Joel M. LeMon and Kent Harold Richards. Atlanta: Society of Biblical Literature, 2009.

Steinmetz, Devorah. *From Father to Son: Kinship, Conflict, and Continuity in Genesis.* Literary Currents in Biblical Interpretation. Louisville: Westminster John Knox, 1991.

Wilson, Robert. *Genealogy and History in the Biblical World.* New Haven: Yale University Press, 1977.

PART THREE

TEXTUAL TRANSMISSION AND RECEPTION HISTORY

GENESIS IN JOSEPHUS

Christopher T. Begg

The long series of books making up the Old Testament begins with the one called Genesis in Christian tradition. Josephus' voluminous retelling of biblical and postbiblical history in his *Jewish Antiquities* (*Ant.*) begins, after a prologue (*Ant.* 1.1–26), with a rendition of Genesis that comprises *Ant.* 1.27–2.200.[1] Given the division between books 1 and 2 that occurs within this segment, one might divide it up into three main content units: *Ant.* 1.27–160 (from creation to the introduction of Abraham = Gen 1–11); 1.161–346 (from the call of Abraham through the death of Isaac = Gen 12–35); and 2.1–200 (the subsequent careers of Esau, Jacob, and the latter's sons = Gen 36–50). In this essay, I propose to do three things. Firstly, I shall consider the various kinds of sources that Josephus (may have) used for his presentation in *Ant.* 1.27–2.200. Secondly, I shall attempt to catalogue (and provide) examples of the different kinds of rewriting techniques Josephus applied to the source materials available to him. Finally, I shall highlight the distinctive features of Josephus' version of Genesis vis-à-vis both the biblical book itself and several other early Jewish rewritings of the latter.

Josephus' Sources

Josephus' primary source for what he tells in *Ant.* 1.27–2.200 was obviously the Book of Genesis itself, as indicated by the fact that all but one of Genesis' fifty chapters has a content parallel—however compressed or otherwise

---

[1] For the Greek text and English translation of *Ant.* 1.27–2.200, I use Henry St. John Thackeray, *Josephus Jewish Antiquities Books I–IV* (LCL 242; Cambridge: Harvard University Press, 1930), 14–251. I have likewise consulted the annotated translations of the segment by Julien Weill, *Oeuvres complètes de Flavius Josèphe, Antiquités Judaïques Livres I–IV* (Paris: Leroux, 1900), 1:7–14; Étienne Nodet, *Flavius Josèphe Les Antiquités Juives: Livres I à III traduction et notes* (vol. 1B; Paris: Cerf, 1990), 8–104; and Louis H. Feldman, *Judean Antiquities 1–4* (ed. Steve Mason; FJTC 3; Leiden: Brill, 1999), 10–186. I have profited as well from the treatments of Josephus' version of Genesis in the monographs of Salomo Rappaport, *Agada und Exegese bei Flavius Josephus* (Vienna: Alexander Kohut Memorial Foundation, 1930) and Thomas W. Franxman, *Genesis and the 'Jewish Antiquities' of Flavius Josephus* (BibOr 35; Rome: Biblical Institute Press, 1979).

modified—in his version.² The further—and much more difficult—question is however: which text-form(s) of the biblical book did he employ? This question arises given the fact that the historian's version evidences agreements with distinctive readings now of one, now of another of the ancient textual witnesses for Genesis, even as in still other instances it diverges from all these. Thus, e.g., in *Ant.* 1.176 Josephus specifies, in accordance with MT Gen 46:27, seventy as the number of descendants who accompanied Jacob to Egypt, whereas the LXX speaks of seventy-five. Conversely, he agrees with LXX Gen 5:3-4 in having Adam beget Seth at age two-hundred and thirty and then living to eight-hundred *contra* the MT's figures of one-hundred and thirty and seven-hundred, respectively.³ Elsewhere, Josephus shares items, absent in both MT and LXX Genesis, with one or more of the targums: in *Ant.* 1.50, e.g., he represents God depriving the tempter snake of its feet and endowing it with poison, as does *Tg. Ps.-J.* Gen 3:15, while in 1.58 he speaks, in a way reminiscent of *Tg. Onq.* and *Tg. Ps.-J.* Gen 4:14, of Cain's sacrifice and penitence in response to God's denunciation of his murder of Abel. Over against such cases of agreement with a given Genesis witness stand those instances where Josephus' data diverge from all of these. In *Ant.* 1.149, e.g., he records Shem's begetting Arphaxad twelve years after the flood, as opposed to the two years cited in MT, LXX and the targums' Gen 11:11.

Still further complicating the situation surrounding the question of the text-form(s) of Genesis used by Josephus are various additional, more general considerations/factors. Above all there is the fact that even when reproducing biblical content, Josephus consistently does so by way of paraphrase, thereby obscuring the underlying biblical text he is using. It also needs to be kept in mind that the MT, LXX, and targums manuscripts on the one hand, and those of *Antiquities* itself on the other, frequently differ among themselves, with the resultant uncertainty about which text of both the latter and the former is to be taken as the basis of a comparison between them.⁴

---

² The sole exception is Gen 38, the unedifying story of the patriarch Judah's impregnating his daughter in law Tamar whom he takes to be a prostitute.

³ More generally, Josephus' chronological indications for both the antediluvian and postdiluvian generations generally agree, in cases of divergence between the MT and the LXX, with those of the latter; see the charts in Thackeray, *Josephus Jewish Antiquities*, 39, 73.

⁴ In *Ant.* 1.346, e.g., Josephus states that Isaac died at age 185. This figure is five years higher than that cited in the MT, the targums, and the LXX of Gen 35:28 according to the Göttingen edition. In the critical apparatus of that edition, one notes, however, that one LXX witness, i.e. the Old Latin (LA¹), has the same higher figure as does Josephus. In this case, then, should one suppose that Josephus was utilizing some prior text form of the Old Latin's reading, or rather, e.g., that he is citing from (faulty) memory?

The many instances of Josephus' giving names and figures divergent from those in any extant witness further raise the question of whether he may in such instances have misread the biblical text before him or relied on his (faulty) memory of this. Finally, as to the relationship between Josephus and the targums, the literary fixation of the latter is generally dated centuries after Josephus' time. How then are the parallels between the two corpora to be accounted for? Given the unlikelihood that the redactors of the targums knew the writings of Josephus, did Josephus have access to some earlier written form of the targums, or do their commonalities reflect rather a shared use of preexisting (oral) tradition?

The above remarks point up the uncertainties surrounding the question of Josephus' text(s) of Genesis. I agree, however, with Louis H. Feldman that there is sufficient evidence for positing that Josephus did utilize Genesis—and the Pentateuch in general—in varying text-forms and in the three languages known to him, i.e. Hebrew, Greek, and Aramaic.[5]

Whatever text(s) of it he may have employed, Josephus clearly did make large-scale use of the biblical Book of Genesis. There are, however, indications that his version of Genesis in *Ant.* 1.27–2.200 has been influenced by his knowledge of other biblical books as well. In 2.199, e.g., he anticipates the notice of Exod 1:6 about the death of Joseph's brothers, while his reference (2.75)—unparalleled in Exod 41 itself—to Pharaoh's "forgetting" the interpretation of the two dreams he had received seems inspired by the experience of King Nebuchadnezzar recounted in Dan 2:1 (and *Ant.* 10.195).

Beyond the Bible itself, what other sources did Josephus use in composing our segment? Several categories of such extrabiblical sources may be distinguished, each of which raises uncertainties of its own. Among these, the series of (presumably) non-Jewish writers (e.g., Berossus, Nicolas of Damascus, the Sibyl) whom Josephus cites by name (and in some instances actually quotes) in four distinct connections in *Ant.* 1.27–2.200—i.e. 1.93–94 + 107–108, 118–119, 158–160, and 240[6]—stands out, since here Josephus calls explicit

---

[5] See the detailed argumentation in Louis H. Feldman, *Josephus's Interpretation of the Bible* (Berkeley: University of California Press, 1998), 23–31. By contrast, Étienne Nodet holds that Josephus made (exclusive) use of a Hebrew text of the Pentateuch that had significant affinities with the *Vorlage* of Codex B of the LXX (*Flavius Josèphe Les Antiquités juives, I. Livres I à III, A. Introduction et texte* [Paris: Cerf, 1991], xxvii–xxix).

[6] For a listing of the authors in question and the topics concerning which Josephus adduces them, see James E. Bowley, "Josephus's Use of Greek Sources for Biblical History," in *Pursuing the Text: Studies in Honor of Ben Zion Wacholder on the Occasion of his Seventieth Birthday* (ed. John C. Reeves and John Kampen; JSOTSup 184; Sheffield: Sheffield Academic Press, 1994), 202–215, at 205.

attention to his use of nonbiblical material. Questions arise, however, as to which of these authors, many of whose writings have either not come down to us or survive only in the excerpts cited by later compilers, Josephus actually had read for himself. That he did not do so for all of them is clear in the case of "Cleodemus the prophet, also called Malchos" whose testimony about Abraham's children by Keturah he acknowledges having derived from Alexander Polyhistor in 1.240. That same encylopedist is likely also Josephus' source for his quotation of "the Sibyl" regarding the confusion of languages in 1.118, since the wording of that quotation stands closer to Alexander's paraphrase (as preserved in Eusebius, *Praep. ev.* 9.17–18) than to the actual text of *Sib. Or.* 3.97–104. In the above instances, Josephus actually names Greek authors whose works he knew—at whatever remove. There remains, however, the further question of what other Greek authors, be these poets (e.g., Homer), historians (Thucydides), playwrights (Sophocles, Euripides) or philosophers (e.g., Plato), Josephus may be utilizing in our segment though without naming them. This question arises given the numerous terminological and motival contacts between Josephus' presentation in *Ant.* 1.27–2.200 (and more generally throughout *Ant.*) that have been highlighted especially by Henry St. John Thackeray[7] and Louis H. Feldman.[8] E.g., in *Ant.* 2.108, Josephus uses the same (rare) word μετάμελος ("contrition") as does Thucydides (7.55),[9] while his portrayal of Isaac in Gen 22 evidences numerous reminiscences of the figure of Iphigenia in various plays of Euripides.[10] Such contacts lead one to ask: are these sufficiently close and distinctive that one should conclude to a literary dependence of *Ant.* on these other Greek writings? And if so, was it Josephus himself who drew on them (so Feldman) or rather the "assistants" whose collaboration in polishing the Greek of the *J.W.* he acknowledges in *Ag. Ap.* 1.50 (as posited by Thackeray)? In my view, utilization of the Greek classics, whether by Josephus himself or his assistants, cannot be excluded in principle. In any particular instance, however, one needs to consider just how compelling is the case for such utilization, as opposed to a more diffused cultural awareness of stock formulations, motifs, plot lines, and so on, by him or them (see further below).

Similar questions arise regarding another body of possible source material for Josephus' rendition of Genesis, i.e. such (likely) earlier retellings of

---

[7] Henry St. John Thackeray, *Josephus: The Man and the Historian* (New York: Jewish Institute of Religion Press, 1929; repr., New York: Ktav Publishing House, 1967), 100–124.
[8] Feldman, *Josephus's Interpretation*, 171–179.
[9] See Feldman, *Judean Antiquities 1–4*, 164, n. 315.
[10] On these, see Feldman, *Josephus's Interpretation*, 266–285.

biblical history as Artapanus, Eupolemus, *Jubilees*,[11] Philo,[12] the *Genesis Apocryphon*, and the *Testament of the Twelve Patriarchs* (the *Testament of Joseph* in particular). Scholars cited above (see n. 1) have called attention to the many, often striking similarities between Josephus' expansions/modifications of the biblical account and what one reads in these other writings (e.g., in both *Ant.* 2.126 and *Ios.* 36.211 the brothers on their second departure from Egypt are pursued not just by Joseph's steward, as in Gen 44:6, but by a whole group whom Joseph sends out after them). How though are such commonalities to be accounted for? Do they, e.g., require one to suppose that Josephus had perused the above-mentioned works and selectively incorporated extrabiblical items from them into his own presentation? Or, alternatively, should one think of a shared dependence of Josephus and these other writings on a pre-existing tradition—as would seem more likely to be the case both where a given parabiblical item is common to Josephus and more than one of the above works as well as in that of the numerous affinities between Josephus' amplifications of the Bible's content and those met in Jewish writings that are either contemporaneous with Josephus (e.g., Pseudo-Philo's *L.A.B.*)[13] or later than his writings (e.g., such rabbinic-midrashic documents as *Pirqe Rabbi Eliezer* and *Midrash Genesis Rabbah*)?[14] Or yet again, might Josephus and his various predecessors in the rewriting of the Bible have independently hit upon a particular "solution" to some perceived difficulty of the biblical account that they have in common?[15] Given these various potential explanations of their shared features, one should be cautious about positing Josephus' direct dependence on the works of earlier, postbiblical Jewish writers, works of which—in contrast

---

[11] On the parallels between *Ant.* and *Jubilees* (2nd century BCE), see Betsy Halpern-Amaru, "Flavius Josephus and *The Book of Jubilees*: A Question of Source," *HUCA* 72 (2001): 15–44. Halpern-Amaru posits a direct dependence of the former on the latter.

[12] On the Josephus-Philo relationship, see Feldman, *Josephus's Interpretation*, 51–52. The Philonic works with which *Ant.* 1.27–2.200 has the most sustained commonalities are *Opif.*, *Abr.*, and above all *Ios.*

[13] Both *Ant.* and *L.A.B.* are generally dated towards the end of the first century CE. On their similarities (and differences) vis-à-vis the Bible itself, see Louis H. Feldman, "Prolegomenon," in *The Biblical Antiquities of Philo, Now First Translated from the Old Latin Version* by M.R. James (reissued ed.; New York: Ktav, 1971), lviii–lxvi.

[14] On the relationship (via shared tradition) between Josephus and the later rabbinic corpus, see Feldman, *Josephus's Interpretation*, 65–73.

[15] One might, e.g., posit such an explanation for the above-mentioned fact of both Josephus and Philo's having the brothers pursued by a whole body of Egyptians rather than Joseph's steward alone as in Genesis; independently of each other, both authors concluded that it would have been difficult for a single pursuer to compel the eleven brothers to return with him.

to his handling of pagan authors—he generally makes no mention[16] and whose many differences with Josephus' presentation also need to kept in mind.

The final "source" for Josephus' rendering of Genesis is one that is still more resistant to being "pinned down" than are the literary productions discussed above. And yet, this last source would seem to have had a significant role in the historian's adaptation of the biblical data. Under this head, I have in view the historian's knowledge—gained more by "osmosis" than by consultation of particular writings—of practices (e.g., crucifixion, adoption, kosher observances), geographical names, mythological tales, cultural values, etc. that were current among Gentiles and/or Jews of his time and which he, consciously or unconsciously, frequently "retrojects" into the Genesis story. To this category of Josephus' unwritten "sources" further pertain his own background (e.g., as a proud scion of the Jerusalem priesthood) and life experiences (e.g., his going over to the Roman side in the Jewish War) and the resultant interests, preoccupations, and so on that left their imprint on his reworking of Genesis as well.[17]

In summary, Josephus appears to have had a variety of sources, biblical and extra-biblical, written and unwritten, available to him for his rewriting of Genesis. In many cases, however, the precise form in which he knew these sources eludes any confident determination. And that uncertainty, in its turn, affects what can be said about our next topic: his various ways of handling sources. Where, e.g., Josephus diverges from Genesis' own presentation on any given point is the divergence the result of the historian's own exegetical creativity or rather due to his following an existing extrabiblical tradition (of whatever sort)? Moreover, to posit the latter explanation for the peculiarity of Josephus' account still leaves one with the question: what was it about this tradition that Josephus found congenial to his purposes and so prompted him to incorporate it when, on the other hand, he does not utilize many other traditions that had developed around the biblical Genesis narrative?

---

[16] Josephus names Philo only once in his corpus (*Ant.* 18.259–260), and there simply as the leader of the Alexandrian Jewish delegation to the Emperor Caligula (Gaius).

[17] In, e.g., his version of the Joseph story (as well as in many other contexts of *Ant.*), Josephus highlights the "envy" of which biblical figures were the object. That emphasis corresponds to the recurrent references to the envy that his own success provoked among his compatriots in the *Life* (see 424–425, 429); cf. Feldman, *Josephus's Interpretation*, 198–203.

Josephus' Rewriting Techniques in *Ant.* 1.27–2.200

Within the range of rewriting techniques that Josephus applies to the data of Genesis one might distinguish four main categories: amplifications, omissions, rearrangements, and (other) modifications, each of which can be further subdivided. It likewise should be noted that Josephus frequently applies several rewriting techniques in conjunction (e.g., he omits certain biblical material even as he interjects other matter in its place), the result being that it is often difficult to sharply distinguish one technique from another or to precisely characterize Josephus' handling of a particular Genesis passage. Keeping these complicating factors in view, I shall now provide examples of each of the above four categories of rewriting techniques and their assorted variants that, collectively, endow *Ant.* 1.27–2.200 with its distinctiveness vis-à-vis Genesis itself.

1. *Amplifications*

Throughout our segment, Josephus amplifies the Genesis narrative with other material. These amplifications differ markedly among themselves in terms of, e.g., their extent, source, character, and purpose(s). As examples of the various sorts of amplifications exhibited by *Ant.* 1.27–2.220, I note the following:

(a) As pointed out above, in four distinct contexts Josephus interrupts the flow of his Genesis-based presentation in order to interject mention (and in some instances to provide brief excerpts from their works) of authors writing in Greek, who, purportedly, had something to say about a given biblical happening or figure. The four contexts are *Ant.* 1.93–94 (the Flood), 107–108 (the high ages attributed to the early human generations), 118–119 (the Tower of Babel), and 158–160, 240 (the career of Abraham). In the first three of these instances, the event recorded in the Bible might be thought to strain the credulity of Greco-Roman readers and so call for "confirmation" from the side of those readers' own literary "authorities," while in the case of Abraham, the fact of his being mentioned or alluded to by Gentile authors would enhance the patriarch's status in the eyes of the non-Jewish audience for which *Ant.* is primarily intended.[18]

---

[18] On the intended audience of *Ant.* (primarily cultivated Gentiles, but secondarily also fellow Jews), see Feldman, *Josephus's Interpretation*, 46–50.

(b) Another recurrent added element within Josephus' presentation is his interjection—to which Genesis itself has no equivalent—of (mostly first person) editorial remarks. These, in turn, have a variety of contents: they announce Josephus' intention of treating a given topic in a subsequent, separate work (see, e.g., 1.29 [the rationale for Moses' speaking in Gen 1:5 of "one day" rather than "a first day"])[19] or at a later point within *Ant.* itself (see 1.136 [a look ahead to the account of Moses' Ethiopian war he will relate in 2.338–353]); point back to what he has already related, whether in the *J.W.* (e.g., 1.203 [Josephus alludes to his previous description of the desolate situation of the Sodom site in *J.W.* 4.483–485]) or earlier in *Ant.* (e.g., 1.135 [cross reference to Nimrod's arrogation of power as cited in 1.113–115]). Still other such remarks inform readers of his *modus operandi* (see, e.g., 1.129 [his Hellenizing of Hebrew proper names] and 2.176–177 [his decision, contrary to his usual practice in such instances, to reproduce the lengthy list of Jacob's descendants from Gen 46:8–20]).

(c) In the same line, Josephus repeatedly adduces the figure of Moses—nowhere mentioned in Genesis itself—as the authority behind the biblical account he is reproducing; see 1.26, 29, 33, 34 (the creation story).

(d) He attaches brief encomia for the four patriarchs Abraham (1.256), Isaac (1.346), Jacob (2.196), and Joseph (2.198) to the Bible's death and burial notices for them. Similarly, he supplies (1.53) contrasting moral evaluations of the brothers Abel and Cain (compare Gen 4:2), just as he expatiates, without biblical warrant, on the latter's depravity even after his sparing by God in 1.60–61.

(e) He provides biblical episodes with an explicit moral or draws lessons therefrom about human nature: see 1.178 (Abraham's victory over the invader kings [Gen 14] makes clear that the size of an army matters less than its fighting spirit) and 2.10 (people, as the case of Joseph's brothers demonstrates, are envious of the successes even of near relatives).

(f) Josephus regularly informs readers of the current Greek names for biblical places (e.g., "Idoumaia" for Edom, 2.3) and months (the second month of the Hebrew calendar is equivalent to the Macedonian "Dios," 1.80).

---

[19] In *Ant.* 1.193 and 214 Josephus promises a fuller discussion of circumcision elsewhere.

(g) Similarly, he calls attention to the fact that some phenomenon cited in Genesis currently exists: 1.92 (the remains of the Ark);[20] 1.203 (the pillar of salt into which Lot's wife was transformed); and 1.212 (the name "Beer-sheba").

(h) In many instances, Josephus fills "gaps" left in the Genesis account concerning characters' emotional states, motivations, purposes in doing as they do, and the effects of others' initiatives upon them. Examples of this kind of amplification include: Noah cursed not Ham, but rather Canaan (so Gen 9:24) given the former's status as his son (1.142); Isaac and Abraham "embrace" following the latter's escape from sacrifice by his father (1.236); Rachel carries off her father's image (Gen 31:19) as a means of securing pardon should Laban pursue the fugitives (1.311); Joseph, in relating his second dream to his brothers (Gen 37.9), does so with no suspicion of their animosity towards him (2.13); and Pharaoh's cupbearer rejoices (2.69) over Joseph's favorable interpretation of his dream (Gen 41:15). Beyond such psychologizing "gap-fillers," Josephus also satisfies readers' curiosity about other matters where the Genesis narratives leave one with unanswered questions. Thus, in 1.52 he not only supplies meanings for the names "Cain" and "Abel" but also mentions the daughters born to Adam and Eve, figures whose existence the continuation of the biblical narrative simply presupposes. Thereafter, in 1.54, he resolves another source of perplexity for Bible readers: why did God "regard" Abel's offering but not that of Cain? (Gen 4:4–5),[21] while in 1.55 he informs us, as Gen 4 itself does not, of what became of Abel's corpse once Cain kills him (Cain hid this, "thinking to escape detection"). Nor are readers of Josephus' version of Gen 22 left to wonder how old Isaac was at the time of his near sacrifice: 1.227 supplies the (biblically) missing figure, i.e. 25 years old.

(i) Another significant category of Josephan amplifications in *Ant.* 1.27–2.200 involves Genesis' "speech element." On occasion, Josephus provides characters with discourses that lack all basis in the Bible itself. The most notable instance in this regard is the extended exchange he attributes to

---

[20] Josephus' insertion of this detail is likely inspired by the text of Berossus that he proceeds to quote in 1.93, the wording of which is quite reminiscent of Josephus' own in 1.92.

[21] Josephus' response to the question is that God "... is honoured by things that grow spontaneously and in accordance with natural laws [Abel's milk and firstlings of the flock], and not by products forced from nature by the ingenuity of grasping men [Cain's first fruits]."

Abraham and Isaac at the moment when all has been prepared for the latter's sacrifice in 1.228–232.[22] More often, however, the historian markedly elaborates the words attributed to characters by the Bible itself. Particularly conspicuous examples of his doing so are Reuben's words to his brothers about what is to be done with Joseph (compare Gen 37:21–22 and 2.21–31), the verbal duet between Joseph and Potiphar's wife (compare Gen 39:7–12 and 2.42–53), and above all, Judah's plea to Joseph on behalf of Benjamin (compare Gen 44:18–34 and 2.140–158).

(j) Finally, in several instances, Josephus introduces new characters into his rendition of biblical narratives, e.g., the "shepherds," unmentioned in Gen 21:8–21, who come to Hagar's assistance in 1.219 and the "horsemen" who accompany Joseph's "steward" in pursuit of the brothers (compare 2.126–136 and Gen 44:6–13 [where only the former figure is cited]).

2. Omissions

Over against Josephus' numerous and various amplifications of Genesis data stand his equally frequent and diverse omissions of the book's material. Only exceptionally, it might be noted initially, does he omit a Genesis passage *tout court*. The two instances of his doing so both involve unedifying sexual behavior within the direct line of Abraham, i.e. the marital problems of Tamar that culminate in her father in law Judah's (unwittingly) having sexual relations with her (Gen 38) and Reuben's intercourse with his father's concubine Bilhah (Gen 35:22).[23] At the same time, it should also be pointed out that Josephus does significantly compress the content of the following chapters/segments of Genesis: 15, 17, 23, 24, 30:21–31:16, 35, 47–50.

As to the specific kinds of omissions found in 1.27–2.200, the following may be distinguished:

---

[22] This inserted exchange takes the place of the notices on Abraham's binding Isaac and laying him upon the wood on the altar in Gen 22:9. Here then, as so often, Josephus' application of one rewriting technique (addition) goes together with his utilization of another one (omission).

[23] On the other hand, Josephus does provide a version of an equally salacious Genesis episode, i.e., Lot's incest with his daughters (Gen 19:30–38; see *Ant.* 1.204–206). Here, however, the characters pertain to a collateral line, i.e. that of Abraham's nephew Lot. Elsewhere, Josephus simply eliminates certain biblical happenings that convey a negative image of his people, e.g., the Golden Calf affair (Exod 32–34) and the idolatrous origins of the Danite priesthood (Judg 17–18).

(a) In general, Josephus' version (somewhat) diminishes the role assigned the Deity in Genesis, in line with what Louis H. Feldman has called *Ant.*'s "detheologizing tendency."[24] This tendency expresses itself, first of all, in his passing over multiple (theologically unproblematic) mentions of God by the narrator or characters of Genesis. So, e.g., in his rendering of Gen 41 (Joseph's elucidation of Pharaoh's dream and his resultant ascendancy) in 2.75–94, the multiple biblical invocations of God's role in the process (see 41:16,25,32,38,49,51,52) all disappear.[25] In other cases, however, Josephus omits numerous Genesis references to God that raise theological difficulties due to their, e.g., anthropomorphic/anthropathetic or polytheistic *Gottesbild*. In particular, he jettisons the divine speech of Gen 1:26 where the Deity uses the plural form ("let us make") and proposes to make humans "in our image, after our likeness." In the continuation of the creation account, he passes over both the mention of God's "walking in the garden" (Gen 2:8) and his making garments for the first couple (Gen 2:20). Similarly, his version of the Tower of Babel episode (1.114–119) dispenses with the double reference to the Lord's "coming down" (Gen 11:5,7) to deal with humanity's construction, while in the Josephan flood narrative (1.75–103) one does not hear either of God's "regret" over making man (Gen 6:6,7b), nor of his "smelling" the fragrance of Noah's sacrifice and "saying in his heart" (8:20).

(b) The same concern that prompts Josephus to omit (certain of) Genesis' problematic notices about God also shows itself in his excision of a number of the source's depictions of the failings of the ancestors. Abraham does not laugh in response to God's promise of a son through Sarah (Gen 17:17), nor does he address God with the presumptuous question attributed to him in Gen 18:25 ("shall not the Judge of all the earth do right?"). Isaac's lying about the status of Rebekah and his being confronted about this by Abimelech (Gen 26:7–11) remains without a Josephan counterpart, as does Jacob's double, mendacious identification of himself as Esau in response to his father's questions (see Gen 27:18,24).[26] When retelling the story of

---

[24] On this tendency, see Feldman, *Josephus's Interpretation*, 202–212.
[25] On the other hand, however, Josephus does introduce his version of Gen 41 in *Ant.* 2.74 with a biblically unparalleled reference to God's acting through the following events to effect Joseph's release.
[26] *Jub.* 36:13,19 likewise avoids having Jacob respond to Isaac's queries about his identity with the lies ascribed to him in Gen 27; in the *Jubilees* version of both 27:19 and 24, Jacob simply asserts "I am your son." This may well be an instance where Josephus and *Jubilees* "corrected" the presentation of Genesis independently of each other.

Dinah's rape (Gen 34) in 1.337–340, Josephus omits the fraudulent demand made by Jacob's sons that the Shechemites be circumcised if they are to intermarry with them and Simeon and Levi's later taking advantage of the Shechemites' incapacity for resistance following their circumcision (see 34:13–25).[27] Joseph too comes off better in Josephus' presentation due to his omission of the youth's giving Jacob an "ill report" about his brothers (Gen 37:2), and the mentions of his "speaking roughly" to them on their first appearance before him in Egypt (Gen 42:7,30).

(c) Josephus also uses omission in 1.27–2.220 for more strictly narrative purposes, i.e. to dispose of Genesis' duplications and apparent incoherences. The double notice on Adam's begetting Seth in Gen 4:25 and 5:3 is reduced to one in 1.68. In Gen 37:25–28,36; 39:1, there is the well-known confusion concerning the identity of the people who buy Joseph and take him to Egypt—is it the Ishmaelites or the Midianites? Such confusion disappears in Josephus' account of the transaction (2.32–33), where only the Ishmaelites/Arabs are mentioned. Again, Gen 42 recounts a double finding by the brothers of the money that Josephus had ordered to be put back in their sacks, first by one of them at a lodging place on their return journey (v. 28) and then by all of them once back in Jacob's house (v. 35); in 43:16, however, the brothers report to Joseph's steward that they collectively found their money upon coming to "the lodging place." Such a presentation raises questions about why the other brothers do not forthwith examine their own sacks following the initial discovery by one of them and immediately return to Joseph to report the matter but rather proceed with their journey, and why their subsequent statement to the steward "misrepresents" the place of their collective discovery. Josephus eliminates these difficulties by passing over the discovery cited in Gen 42:28, and simply having all the brothers find their money once back home (2.113) and then accurately report this to the steward in 2.120. A final example of this particular procedure is Josephus' "discarding" of God's second communication to Jacob at Bethel (Gen 35:9–15), given that its content had already been (largely) dealt with in two previous episodes that are used by him, i.e. Gen 28:10–22 (// 1.278–284) and 32:22–32 (// 1.331–334).

---

[27] In Josephus' version of Gen 34, the Shechemites, who have become intoxicated in their celebration of a festival, are slaughtered by Simeon and Levi.

(d) In the interests of greater concision, Josephus also conflates into one what in Genesis are distinct speeches by characters. Gen 22:11–12 and 22:15–18, e.g., record two separate addresses to Abraham by "the angel of the Lord," with Abraham's sacrifice of the ram and naming of the site (22:13–14) intervening. *Ant.* 1.233–235, by contrast, has God himself speak a single time to Abraham at the sacrificial locale, after which he discloses the ram to the patriarch (1.236). Similarly, Josephus conflates Joseph's twofold self-disclosure to his brothers (Gen 45:3a,4–13), separated by mention of the latter's "dismay" (45:3b), into a single one (2.161–165), only after which he cites the brothers' response (2.166).

(e) More generally, often, though not invariably (see "i" under amplifications above), Josephus reduces characters' speechifying and the exchanges between them so as to move things more quickly to the outcome of a given episode. The prolonged negotiations between Abraham and the natives regarding a burial place for Sarah in Gen 23:3–15 are compacted by him (1.237) into an allusion to the Canaanites' "offering burial ground for her [Sarah] at the public expense," after which he immediately recounts Abraham's actual purchase of the site (// Gen 23:16). Much reduced are likewise the series of declarations the Lord makes to Abraham in Gen 15:13–16,18–21, these getting a single short paragraph allotted to them in 1.185, even as the lengthy dialogue between the Lord and Abraham concerning the fate of Sodom in Gen 18:16–33 is drastically abbreviated in 1.199b–200.

(f) Josephus also omits source items that detract from the movement of the narrative towards a climactic moment. Gen 29:1–11, e.g., features multiple references to a stone covering the mouth of the well at Haran and when and by whom it is to be removed. These references appear to lack a function in their context, the focus of which is the bringing together of Jacob and Rachel. Hence it is not surprising that in his rendering of the episode in 1.285–293, Josephus omits all reference to the well-stone. Again, in recounting Joseph's encounters with his brothers in Egypt, Genesis (see 42:6; 43:26,28) repeatedly mentions their prostrating themselves before him. Josephus has no equivalent to these notices. Rather, he portrays a single obeisance before Joseph, first by Judah and then by the other brothers, that comes at a narrative high point (2.159), just after Judah has concluded his impassioned appeal for Benjamin.[28] Likewise material that appears to

---

[28] See Feldman, *Judean Antiquities 1–4*, 174–175, n. 416.

run counter to the mood Josephus is trying to create around a given episode is eliminated by him; e.g., the protracted scene in which the dying Jacob insists on blessing Joseph's sons in a way contrary to their father's wishes (Gen 48:8–20) lacks a parallel in 2.194–195.[29]

(g) Finally, certain of Josephus' omissions in 1.27–2.220 seem designed to keep his (uninitiated Gentile) readers from losing interest by sparing such readers elements of Genesis that they would find boring (e.g., the long lists of Edomite figures in Gen 36:15–42),[30] not readily intelligible (e.g., the apparently minuscule name changes of "Abram" [LXX Ἀβράμ] to "Abraham" [LXX Ἀβραάμ] and of "Sarai" [LXX Σάρα] to "Sarah" [LXX Σάρρα] in Gen 17:5 and 17:15 respectively),[31] not in accord with their notions of proper decorum (Jacob's kissing Rachel [Gen 29:11] immediately upon first meeting her),[32] or likely to offend their sensitivities on the inflammatory subject of "ownership" of the land of Palestine (e.g., the Lord's bestowing all the land that Abram will see and walk upon to "you and your descendants forever" in Gen 13:14–17).[33] At the same time, Josephus also, on occasion, omits components of Genesis that might "scandalize" readers of his own people given their divergence from (likely) Jewish practice of his time, e.g., Abraham's serving his angelic visitors both meat and dairy products (Gen 18:8)[34] or the embalming of Jacob (Gen 50:3) and Joseph (Gen 50:25 MT) in Egypt.[35]

---

[29] See Feldman, *Judean Antiquities 1–4*, 185, n. 549.

[30] Josephus does reproduce the list of the descendants of Jacob who go down to Egypt of Gen 46:8–27 in 2.177b–183. He prefaces his doing so, however, with a quasi-apology (2.176–177a) to his readers in which he informs them that the listing of the names is necessary to make a point, i.e. that his people are of Mesopotamian, not Egyptian, origin.

[31] See Feldman, *Judean Antiquities 1–4*, 72, n. 594. Josephus does follow Gen 32:28 in recording Jacob's change of name to "Israel" (*Ant.* 1.333). Here, however, the two names are more clearly distinct from each and the latter helps explain the familiar designation used for the patriarch's descendants, i.e. "Israelites." It should also be noted that Josephus, having cited the name change, thereafter continues invariably to use the name "Jacob" rather than alternating between "Jacob" and "Israel" as does the remainder of Genesis, thereby leaving readers with the question of why one name rather than the other is employed in a particular context.

[32] See Feldman, *Judean Antiquities 1–4*, 111–112, n. 847.

[33] On Josephus' omission of this sequence, see Feldman, *Judean Antiquities 1–4*, 64, n. 541. Elsewhere, the historian reformulates such Genesis passages, turning divine land promises to the patriarchs and their descendants into announcements by the Deity that the latter will occupy the land by their military initiatives—a matter of (distant) historical fact that need not entail a contemporary Jewish claim to the land over which the Romans had recently reasserted their dominion.

[34] See Feldman, *Judean Antiquities 1–4*, 174–175, n. 612.

[35] See Feldman, *Judean Antiquities 1–4*, 185, n. 554; 186, n. 560.

3. Rearrangements

Another noteworthy rewriting technique employed by Josephus repeatedly in 1.27–2.200 is his rearrangements, i.e. departures from the sequence in which Genesis presents its material. Josephus takes such liberties both with regard to the placement of entire segments and of the internal order of a given episode. In all such instances, the question arises as to what might have prompted Josephus to have recourse to rearrangement when he usually does adhere to Genesis' (and more generally the Bible's) order.

(a) The most conspicuous instances of the above technique are those involving entire passages. In 1.110–147, e.g., Josephus reserves the sequence of Gen 10:1–32 (the table of the nations) and 11:1–9 (the tower of Babel), making the emergence of the different peoples spoken of in the former passage the outcome of the dispersal of the tower builders recounted in the latter. Having traced the line running from Peleg through Terah father of Abram in accordance with Gen 11:18–32 in 1.148–152, Josephus proceeds in 1.153 to append the content of a much later Genesis passage, i.e. Gen 22:20–23, which supplies information concerning Abram's brother "Nahor" cited in Gen 11:27,29. Another such instance concerns the continuation of 1.207–212a, Josephus' version of Gen 20:1–18 (Abraham's quasi-deception of Abimelech concerning the status of Sarah) to which Josephus "tacks on" a (much abbreviated) rendition of Gen 21:22–34, given that this (earlier) passage features the same two main characters. Also noteworthy is Josephus' shifting of the incident of Esau's selling of his birthright to Jacob (Gen 25:29–33) from its biblical context, i.e. as the conclusion to a sequence (25:19–34) dealing with the beginnings of the siblings' rivalry; in his presentation this becomes the lead-in (2.1–4) to his parallel (2.5–6) to Gen 36 (the descendants of Esau).

(b) Also, however, Josephus not infrequently rearranges Genesis' sequence within a given episode. As examples of his doing so, I note the following: in Gen 2:23 ("woman") and 3:20 ("Eve") the two designations for the first female human stand at some distance apart; Josephus' equivalents to the two items occur together in a single paragraph (1.36). Further on in his version of the "fall story" of Gen 3, Josephus reorders God's words of condemnation in vv. 14–19 (serpent, woman, man), making the Deity pronounce judgment first on the man, then the woman, and finally the serpent (1.49–50), thereby highlighting the punishment imposed on Adam. Much later, Josephus has Jacob challenge Laban to make a search for his stolen property (1.322) only after he has remonstrated at length with his father-in-law (1.317–321), whereas in Gen 31:32–42 he does the reverse.[36] Again, whereas Gen 47:8–27 lists Jacob's sons by Leah, Zilpah, Rachel, and Bilhah, in 2.177–183 Josephus enumerates the patriarch's progeny first by Leah, then Rachel, next Bilhah and finally Zilpah, in this way keeping together the two sets of mothers (wives and concubines) and giving literary priority to the former.

4. Other Modifications

My final category of Josephus' rewriting techniques in 1.27–2.200 is a "catch-all" one; to it I assign still other kinds of adaptations of the Genesis material beyond the three discussed above. Under it I shall provide examples of stylistic, terminological, and content modifications made by him of the biblical data.

(a) Josephus introduces a variety of *stylistic-type* modifications of Genesis' presentation, these concerning its manner of formulation, tense of verbs, and so on. The most noteworthy instance of this phenomenon is his regular substitution of hypotaxis for the prevailing parataxis of MT and LXX Genesis; compare, e.g., the series of sentences strung together by "and" concerning the Lord's interaction with Kain in LXX Gen 4:13–15 ("And Kain said to the Lord ... And the Lord God said to him ... And the Lord allocated a sign to Kain ..." NETS) and the extended period with its multiple subordinate clauses with which Josephus reports their exchange in 1.59. Frequently as well, Josephus substitutes indirect for Genesis' standardized use of direct discourse (compare, e.g., Gen 15:4–5 "the word of the Lord came to him ... 'your own son shall be your heir ...' and he [the Lord said] 'Look towards heaven and number the stars ... so shall your descendants be'" and 1.183b "God announced that a son would be born to him, whose posterity would be so great as to be comparable in number to the stars").[37] In the case of verbal forms, Josephus on occasion replaces a MT/LXX past form with the

---

[36] In this instance, Josephus' rearrangement highlights Jacob's self-confidence and assertiveness vis-à-vis Laban whom he proceeds to reproach for his mistreatment of himself even before Laban has been thrown on the defensive by the failure of his search for his "stolen" gods that Jacob invites him to make.

[37] On occasion, Josephus does retain the direct discourse of his source, e.g., in his immediately preceding version (*Ant.* 1.183a) of the exchange between Abram and the Lord (Gen 15:1–3). On his preference for indirect over direct discourse as reflective of the contemporary Atticizing revival, see Christopher T. Begg, *Josephus' Account of the Early Divided Monarchy (AJ 8,212–420): Rewriting the Bible* (BETL 108; Leuven: Leuven University Press, 1993), 12–13, n. 38.

historic present (compare, e.g., Gen 21:4 "Abraham circumcised [περιέτεμειν] his son Isaac when he was eight days old" and 1.214 "eight days later they [Abraham and Sarah] promptly circumcise [περιτέμενουσι] him [Isaac]").[38] In other instances, Josephus replaces the "momentary" past forms of the MT/LXX with an imperfect that highlights the repeated performance of the action in question (compare Gen 42:21 "each man said [εἶπεν] to his brother ..." and 2.107 "they [Joseph's brothers] continued to deplore [ἀνωλοφύροντο] to each other the unfortunate fate of Joseph ..."). More generally, Josephus tends to recast Genesis' hyperbolic formulations (compare Gen 22:17, where the angel declares to Abraham "I will multiply your descendants as the stars of heaven and as the sand which is on the sea shore," and 1.235 "he moreover told that their race would swell into a multitude of nations ..."), just as he rewords Genesis' poetry in prosaic terms (compare Jacob's blessing of his sons in Gen 49:1–27, with its characteristic parallelism, and Josephus' rendition in 2.194 "he foretold to them in prophetic words how each of their descendants was destined to find a habitation in Canaan ...").

Under the stylistic modification heading we might also mention Josephus' handling of Genesis' etymological indications. In Genesis, these indications are generally allusive and implicit in nature, being conveyed by a character's remark about a given name. Josephus, by contrast, presents the Bible's etymological information by way of an editorial statement that a word/name has a particular meaning in Hebrew. Compare in this regard, e.g., the "man's" word to Jacob in Gen 32:28: "Your name shall ... be called ... Israel for you have striven with God and men ..." versus "He ... bade him take the name of Israel, which in the Hebrew tongue denotes the opponent of an angel of God" (1.333).[39] Compare as well in the same context "So Jacob called the name of the place Peniel, saying, 'For I have seen God face to face ...'" (Gen 32:30) and "Jacob ... named the place Phanuel, that is to say 'the face of God'" (1.334).

Another stylistic modification which Josephus explicitly acknowledges making for the sake of Gentile readers is his "Hellenization" of Hebrew names; see 1.129.

---

[38] On Josephus' use of the historic present as reflective of an Atticizing tendency also operative among other contemporary Greek writers, see Begg, *Josephus' Account*, 10–11, n. 32 (and the literature cited there).

[39] In this instance, Josephus' recasting of Genesis' etymological indication goes together with his giving a meaning of his own to the name "Israel," one which coheres better with his explicit designation—absent in Genesis itself—of Jacob's opponent as an "angel of God" in *Ant.* 1.332, 334.

Josephus' stylistic modification of Genesis is evident as well in those instances where he opts to present matters in a different manner than does the Bible. In Gen 31:38–42, e.g., Jacob upbraids Laban for his mistreatment of him over the course of their time together. Josephus turns the patriarch's discourse into an editorial comment: "and indeed Laban had used Jacob exceedingly ill" (*Ant.* 1.320–321).[40] Another such case concerns the interactions between Josephus and the two Egyptian officials imprisoned along with him. In Gen 41, the two latter figures are introduced simultaneously (v. 2), and both together are urged by Joseph to tell their dreams to him (v. 8), as they proceed to do (vv. 9–19). In 2.63–73a, by contrast, we hear of the second official (the baker) only after the first (the cupbearer) has been presented, related his dream, and had this interpreted by Joseph; thereby, Josephus enables readers to focus on each official for himself.

(b) Josephus also modifies his Genesis material *terminologically*. On the one hand, he more or less systematically avoids certain of Genesis' key words. Two particularly striking examples in this regard are Genesis's alternative name for God, i.e. YHWH (LXX κύριος),[41] and διαθήκη (= ברית) in the sense of "covenant."[42] In addition, he tends not to utilize such other key terms of Genesis as "bless" (with God as subject; see, e.g., Gen 1:22,28) and the designation of humans as God's "image and likeness" (Gen 1:26–27; 5:1; 9:6).[43] Conversely, the historian introduces a series of *Leitworte* of his own, these drawn particularly from the Greek philosophical and literary corpus. Instances include: ὕβρις (five times in 1.27–2.20) and its related forms (ὑβρίζω [six times], ὑβριστής [two times], ἐχυβρίζω [two times]),[44] the abstract neuter form τὸ θεῖον

---

[40] For the content of this notice, Josephus draws, in first place, on the account of Laban's machinations regarding the flocks to the detriment of Jacob in Gen 30:25–36 previously passed over by him. Here then, Josephus brings several rewriting techniques (rearrangement, reformulation) to bear on the Genesis material.

[41] On Josephus' virtually total avoidance of κύριος as a divine designation throughout his writings—due, it would appear, to the non-currency of that designation (in an absolute sense, i.e. simply "[the] Lord") in Greek literature apart from the LXX—see Begg, *Josephus' Account*, 45, n. 218 (and the literature cited there).

[42] On Josephus' invariable replacement of the LXX's usages of διαθήκη in the specialized biblical sense of "covenant"—a usage not current in secular Greek—see Begg, *Josephus' Account*, 100–101, n. 69 and the literature cited there.

[43] In this instance, a concern with maintaining divine transcendence—evident elsewhere in Josephus' reworking of Genesis—may be operative.

[44] On Josephus' recurrent utilization of "hubris" terminology, so prominent in Greek tragedy, and of the complex of ideas associated with this ("satiety," "nemesis"), see Feldman, *Josephus's Interpretation*, 180–181.

(six times) πρόνοια ("providence," nine times),[45] and εὐδαιμονία ("happiness," fifteen times),[46] along with its cognates εὐδαιμονέω (nine times) and εὐδαίμων (twelve times).

(c) Finally, Josephus' modifications of Genesis data extend also to its *content*. Such content modifications take a variety of forms in 1.27–2.200. Sometimes, e.g., what Genesis ascribes to one character is attributed to another figure by Josephus. Thus, while in Gen 22:11–12 and 22:15–18, an "angel of the Lord" (twice) addresses Abraham regarding his sacrifice of Isaac, in 1.233–235 God himself speaks to the patriarch.[47] Analogously, the angels' smiting of the Sodomites with blindness in Gen 19:11 becomes the Deity's own action in 1.202.[48] Josephus effects similar "transfers" with regard to the human characters of the Genesis story: According to Gen 25:22 Rebekah "inquires of the Lord" concerning her problem pregnancy; 1.257 represents Isaac as making the inquiry. Similarly, Joseph "weeps" in Gen 45:14–15, but in 2.166 it is his brothers who do this.

Related instances of Josephus' content modifications in 1.27–2.200 are his using different designations for Genesis' personages: in Gen 20:8 Abimelech speaks to his "servants" about God's message to him; 1.208b uses rather the Hellenistic/Roman court title "friends" for the group, while previously (1.202) Josephus replaces the reference to the "sons in law" of Lot (Gen 19:14) with a reference to them as the "suitors" of his "virgin daughters."[49]

---

[45] On Josephus' utilization of this key Stoic term, see Harold W. Attridge, *The Interpretation of Biblical History in the* Antiquitates Judaicae *of Flavius Josephus* (HDR 7; Missoula, Mont.: Scholars Press, 1976), 71–106.

[46] This key word of Greek ethics is not found in the LXX. On Josephus' use of it, see Steve Mason, *Flavius Josephus on the Pharisees: A Composition-Critical Study* (StPB 39; Leiden: Brill, 1991), 185.

[47] Josephus' modification here is perhaps motivated by the desire to highlight the authority/importance of the declarations made to Abraham at this moment as also by a concern for "symmetry": God who issued the order for Abraham to sacrifice Isaac (so Gen 22:2 // 1.223–225) is also the one to prevent the sacrifice.

[48] On Josephus' "angelology"—which exhibits considerable variety in its handling of the biblical "angel material," sometimes replacing the Bible's reference to angels, but at others introducing them into contexts where the Bible does not mention them—see Christopher T. Begg, "Angels in the Work of Josephus," in *Deuterocanonical and Cognate Literature Yearbook 2007: Angels: The Concept of Celestial Beings—Origins, Development and Reception* (ed. Friedrich Vinzenz Reiterer, Tobias Nicklas, and Karin Schöpflin; Berlin: de Gruyter, 2007), 525–536.

[49] Here Josephus' nomenclature modification serves to resolve the apparent contradiction between Gen 19:8 (the virginal status of Lot's daughters) and 19:14 (Lot warns his "sons in law who had married his daughters"); see Feldman, *Judean Antiquities 1–4*, 76, n. 625.

In still other cases, what is modified by Josephus are the words and actions attributed to the biblical characters. So, e.g., in Gen 40:19,22 the fate of Pharaoh's chief baker is beheading following by hanging on a tree; 2.73 "updates" the procedure, having him undergo crucifixion *more Romano*. Earlier (Gen 19:24), the Lord "rains down brimstone and fire" upon Sodom and Gomorrah, in contrast to 1.203 where, in a fashion reminiscent of Zeus/Jupiter, he "hurls his bolt from the sky."[50] The Josephan Jacob, for his part, does not ask his angelic wrestling opponent to tell him his name (so Gen 32:29a), but rather (1.333) "to declare what destiny was in store for him."[51] Another noteworthy instance of Josephus' modifying the content of a biblical character's words concerns the blessing Isaac imparts to Jacob (supposing him to be Esau) of Gen 27:27b–29 in 1.272. As Thackeray[52] points out, Josephus' version of the blessing is "wholly independent" of its biblical "parallel," for whose iussive formulation and poetically concrete evocations of, e.g., "the dew of heaven" and "fatness of the earth" it substitutes a direct address to God with a much more abstract tenor.

Josephus further modifies Genesis' content so as to harmonize divergences between one context and another of the book. A notorious instance of such divergence in Genesis concerns the three wives of Esau and their respective fathers in Gen 26:24; 28:9 (Judith, daughter of Beeri; Basemeth, daughter of Elon; and Mahalath, daughter of Ishmael) and 36:2 (Adah, daughter of Elon; Oholibamah, daughter of Anah, daughter [MT/LXX son] of Zibeon; and Basemath, daughter of Ishmael). Josephus' (largely) resolves the discordances between these two listings in his own double enumeration of Esau's spouses in 1.265, 267 (Ada, daughter of Helon; Alibame, daughter of Eusebeon;[53] Basemathe, daughter of Ishmael) and 2.4 where the three wives are listed without mentions of their fathers as Alibame, Adasa (compare Ada, 1.265), and Basemathe.

Finally, Josephus uses content modifications to "improve" the biblical image of certain characters. A first instance of this category relates to the circumstances of Esau's marriage of the daughter of Ishmael (see above).

---

[50] On this feature, see Feldman, *Judean Antiquities 1–4*, 77, n. 627.

[51] Josephus' modification here might be inspired by the consideration that the man in Gen 32:29b seems to view Jacob's question as an inappropriate one and, in fact, never answers it. Josephus disposes of this depiction of Jacob as one whose wrongful questions are rebuffed by his interlocutor by having him pose a question to which the latter is ready to respond.

[52] *Josephus Jewish Antiquities*, 133, n. a.

[53] In making "Alibame" (Oholibamah, Gen 36:2) the daughter of "Eusebeon" (Zibeon, Gen 36:2), Josephus leaves aside the intervening figure of Anah (Gen 36:2).

According to Gen 28:6–9, he does this after perceiving Jacob's good example in not seeking a wife among the "Canaanite women" and his parents' disapproval of such women. In Josephus' version (1.277) of the affair, Ishmael had already married "Basemath" prior to Jacob's initiative, doing this precisely in order to "gratify" his parents, and further showing himself "deeply devoted" to his new, more suitable wife. Also the Josephan Joseph benefits from a modification of the biblical account of him. In Gen 47:20–26, Joseph, in his capacity as the king's viceroy, acquires, in return for the food he gives them, all the lands of the Egyptians (the priests excepted) as a permanent possession for Pharaoh, for whom the Egyptians are henceforth to work as sharecroppers, retaining four-fifths of what they produce. Josephus' rendition of this happening (2.190–193) presents a more generous, magnanimous Joseph who returns the Egyptians' land to them, once the famine is over.[54]

CONCLUSION

How, given the application by Josephus of the above rewriting techniques, does his rendering of Genesis compare with the biblical book itself? Overall, it might be said that *Ant.* 1.27–2.200 is meant to be a revised and improved version of the Genesis story which, as such, will make that story—and the Jewish people whose story it is—more accessible, appealing, and easier to relate to for *Ant.*'s primary intended audience, i.e. cultivated Gentile readers of Greek (see n. 18). More specifically, Josephus rewrites Genesis in a smoother, more flowing, and connected fashion (hypotaxis rather than parataxis), taking care as well to provide more in the way of transitions between and closing notices for narrative units, as well as reminders of what has been said earlier and foreshadowings of what is to come. He frequently interjects himself into the narrative itself—as the Genesis author(s) does not—explaining how he intends to proceed and why (see, e.g., his statement concerning his rationale for citing the names of the seventy members of Jacob's household who go down to Egypt in 2.176–177a); in so doing he gives readers the assurance that they are in the hand of a literary guide who "knows what he is doing." Lest those readers' eyes and ears be jarred by strange-sounding Hebrew names, he regularly "Hellenizes" the biblical names he does cite—even as he simply passes many others and avoids reproducing changes of characters' names that could well seem minimal

---

[54] See Feldman, *Judean Antiquities 1–4*, 184, n. 543.

and unclear in their import (Abram/Abraham; Sarai/Sarah). In the same line, Josephus, as pointed out above, avoids using Greek terms with LXX meanings that were not generally current, while also incorporating into his version various key words of the Greek literary and philosophical tradition. At various junctures, he adduces an array extra-biblical authorities whose mentions of a given Genesis happening would serve to enhance the credibility of Josephus' version in the eyes of Gentile readers. To that same end he likewise presents an extended reflection (1.105–106) designed to lend a certain plausibility to the high ages for the early generations that he takes over from Genesis. To keep readers from feeling confused, he obviates discrepancies present in the biblical record (see, e.g., Esau's wives and their respective fathers) and fills gaps left in Genesis' account (e.g., where did Adam and Eve's sons find their mates?; why did God approve Abel's offering but disregard Cain's?).[55] To sustain reader interest, Josephus frequently "streamlines" Genesis material, both narrative and discourse, particularly when the amount of attention devoted to a given item might appear out of proportion to its significance for the wider story line (e.g., the negotiations between Abraham and the Lord [Gen 18] or those between the former and the Hittites [Gen 23]). Conversely, Josephus is not adverse to amplifying the biblical account where this concerns matters that Gentile readers would presumably find more congenial, particularly moments of high pathos and tension (the near sacrifice of Isaac; Reuben and Judah's pleas on behalf of an endangered brother; and the exchange between the amorous wife of Potiphar and Joseph) that had their analogues in Greek literature. Cultivated readers could also be expected to appreciate the added elements of irony Josephus works into his presentation; a noteworthy instance of this feature is the recurrent use, for a total of five times, of words of the ευδαιμον-stem (see above) throughout his version of the Gen 22 story with its chilling depiction of a near case of a son's death at his father's hands.[56]

---

[55] Whereas Josephus does dispose of many of Genesis' problems/questions, it should be recognized that his presentation itself is not lacking in problems of its own. Thus, e.g., in 1.343 he connects the name "Benjamin," which Jacob gives to his youngest son, with "the suffering he had caused his mother" Rachel, who dies giving birth to him. In fact, however, this meaning fits the name, not mentioned by Josephus, which Rachel herself gives her son in Gen 35:18a, i.e. "Ben-oni," rather than the name "Benjamin" ("son of the right hand") awarded him by Jacob in Gen 35:18b. Again, his statements in 2.186 (*in fine*) ("the Egyptians were forbidden to occupy themselves with pasturage") and 2.188 ("it was there [in Heliopolis] that his own [Pharaoh's] shepherds had their pasturage") seem difficult to harmonize.

[56] On the above terminological irony, see Feldman, *Judean Antiquities 1–4*, 85, n. 683.

The just cited distinctive features of Josephus' version primarily concern stylistic and terminological procedures that aim to make this more appealing reading for a cultivated Gentile audience than Genesis itself would have been. In addition, however, Josephus' version evidences tendencies[57] having more to do with matters of content which, in their various ways, would also serve to enhance the palatability of his work for fastidious non-Jewish readers who would be approaching it in light of their own literary and philosophical traditions as well as of their prejudices and suspicions regarding the Jewish people themselves. To such readers, Josephus offers, in 1.27–2.200, a (somewhat) "de-theologized" version of the Genesis events, in which many source mentions of God are omitted or diminished, in favor of greater attention to human initiatives and the motivations that inform these, with "psychologizing" comments being accorded a much larger place than they have in the Bible's account. Moreover, where Josephus does retain biblical references to God's role in events, he attenuates those features of Genesis' divinity (anthropomorphism, anthropathetism, arbitrariness, ignorance, excessive immanence, ambiguities on the subject of monotheism) that would prove off-putting to philosophically-minded readers, while also utilizing a "non-biblical" theological vocabulary (e.g., "the Deity," "providence") that those readers would find familiar.

Josephus likewise deals with the human characters of Genesis and their stories in ways designed to convey a more attractive and engaging image of his people's earliest history to non-Jewish readers. The weaknesses and failings that Genesis ascribes to the ancestors are regularly played down by him, as are their conflictual interactions with other peoples. With regard to the latter point, Josephus' attenuation of the Jacob-Esau conflict (and of the negative characteristics of both brothers) is especially noteworthy. His doing this would make particularly good sense if, as Feldman has argued, already by Josephus' time the rabbinically well-attested association of Esau-Edom with Rome had gained a certain currency and so would have been known also to Roman readers.[58] In any case, Josephus also endeavors to stimulate and maintain his Gentile readers' interest in the Genesis material by accentuating its romantic/erotic dimension, as seen, e.g., in his handling of Sarah *chez* Pharaoh and Abimelech, the Sodomites and Lot's angelic

---

[57] It should be emphasized that Josephus' "tendencies" are just that: they are ways of dealing with the biblical data that he often, but by no means invariably, adopts. Josephus is not rigidly constrained by his "tendencies," any one of which can be overruled in a given case by other considerations (or even by a certain caprice/arbitrariness on his part).

[58] See Feldman, *Judean Antiquities 1–4*, 104–106, n. 805.

visitors, Jacob and Rachel, and above all Joseph and the wife of Potiphar, where, in each case, he goes beyond the Bible itself in underscoring the physical appeal of one character(s) and the love/lust this engenders on the part of the other(s).[59]

Josephus' rewriting of Genesis also serves to counter still other current Gentile negative stereotypes about his people. It was alleged, e.g., that the Jews were a people without significant cultural achievements to their credit who concerned themselves only with their own kind. Josephus's distinctive portrayal of Abraham as a font of mathematical, astronomical, and theological knowledge who is eager to dialogue with the Egyptians about this (see 1.154–155, 161, 166–168) serves to refute both allegations.[60] Jews were also accused by their Gentile detractors of being an impecunious people, a charge which Josephus essays to contravene by further elaborating Genesis' own references to the wealth of the patriarchs; see, e.g., the divine promise—unparalleled in Gen 22—made to Abraham after the near sacrifice of Isaac of "increasing wealth" for his race (1.235).[61] In the same context of his rendering of the *Aqedah* incident, Josephus contrives to address both the charge that the Jews were militarily undistinguished cowards[62] and Roman sensitivities about claims to the land of Palestine as something eternally awarded them by God, claims which the Jews had recently reasserted in so violent a fashion. The historian does this by reformulating the angel's promise "your descendants shall possess the gate of their enemies" (Gen 22:17b) as a prediction by God that "they would subdue Canaan by their arms" (1.235b), this putting the emphasis on the people's own military valor rather than on a divine "land grant" to them. One further charge leveled against the Jews in Josephus' time was that they were ambitious schemers out to wrest power for themselves. To counteract such an charge, Josephus repeatedly retouches the biblical portrait of Joseph's viceroyship in Egypt so as to make clear that the hero always "knew his place" vis-à-vis Pharaoh. Thus, e.g., in 2.193 he appends the comment concerning Joseph's economic measures (Gen 47:20–26): "By these means Joseph increased at once his own reputation with the Egyptians and their loyalty to the king."

---

[59] On "eroticization" as a hallmark of Josephus' rewriting of the Bible as a whole, see Feldman, *Josephus's Interpretation*, 185–188 ("romantic motifs").

[60] On the above passages and their apologetic thrust, see Feldman, *Judean Antiquities 1–4*, 56, nn. 496, 501; 57–58, n. 504; 60–61, n. 518; 63, n. 536; and 64, n. 538.

[61] On the above charge and Josephus' response to it throughout his presentation of biblical history, see Feldman, *Josephus's Interpretation*, 93.

[62] On this charge, and Josephus' implicit refutation of it via his retelling of biblical history, see Feldman, *Josephus's Interpretation*, 106–109.

In terms then of the distinctiveness of both its form and content Josephus' version of Genesis might be seen as a sustained, multifaceted effort to make the biblical story of his people's beginnings a more pleasurable and instructive reading experience for a Gentile audience, one from which they were intended to come away with an enhanced appreciation for Jews, their history, and their God.[63]

In concluding the foregoing discussion on the distinctive features of Josephus' version of Genesis, I would like to add a summary remark of comparison between that version and those found in three other ancient Jewish reworkings of Genesis (or portions thereof), i.e. Pseudo-Philo, *Jubilees*, and Philo's *De Iosepho*. What distinguishes Josephus' rendition of Genesis from that of Pseudo-Philo are, on the one hand, the latter's penchant for using the very words of the biblical book (as opposed to Josephus' paraphrasing tendency) and, on the other, its extreme compression of the segment Gen 12–50, whose content Pseudo-Philo reduces to a single chapter (*L.A.B.* 8) of 14 "verses" (compare Josephus' more much extensive reproduction of the segment in *Ant.* 1.154–2.200). As for *Jubilees*, it, like Josephus, does offer a quite expansive retelling of the Genesis material. At the same time, however, it also diverges from his presentation in its frequently very close adherence to the scriptural wording, its preoccupation with precise datings of events, and its interjection of lengthy passages that have no basis in the biblical record itself (see, e.g., *Jubilees* 37–39, the violent confrontation between the families of Jacob and Esau after Isaac's death that results in the slaying of Esau). Finally, whereas Philo's treatise *De Iosepho* exhibits numerous striking commonalities with Josephus in its embellishment of the Genesis Joseph story (see above), it also, notwithstanding its relatively literal approach to the Bible's story line, does nonetheless not refrain from interjecting philosophical/allegorical reflections (see e.g., Philo's remarks [*Ios.* 22.125–26.156] inspired by Joseph's interpretation of Pharaoh's dreams on the nature and significance of dreams) to which Josephus' more action-oriented account lacks a parallel. Thus, the Josephan version of Genesis stands out as something distinctive not only from its source text, but also from other earlier (*Jubilees* and Philo) and contemporary (Pseudo-Philo) attempts at reworking the biblical story in the interest of later audiences.[64]

---

[63] On occasion, Josephus' reworking of the Genesis material seems to have concerns of his "secondary" audience, i.e. fellow Jews, in view; see above on his handling of Abraham's "kosher" transgression in Gen 18.

[64] With regard to the differences between Josephus' version and those of the other three Genesis renditions touched on above, it should be kept in mind that while Josephus' account

Select Bibliography

Attridge, Harold W. *The Interpretation of Biblical History in the* Antiquitates Judaicae *of Flavius Josephus*. Harvard Dissertations in Religion 7. Missoula, Mont.: Scholars Press, 1976.

Begg, Christopher T. *Josephus' Account of the Early Divided Monarchy (AJ 8,212–420): Rewriting the Bible*. Bibliotheca ephemeridum theologicarum lovaniensium 108. Leuven: Leuven University Press, 1993.

———. *Josephus' Story of the Later Monarchy (AJ 9,1–10,185)*. Bibliotheca ephemeridum theologicarum lovaniensium 145. Leuven: Leuven University Press, 2000.

———. *Flavius Josephus Judean Antiquities 5–7*. Edited by Steve Mason. Flavius Josephus Translation and Commentary 4. Leiden: Brill, 2005.

———. "Angels in the Work of Josephus." Pages 525–536 in *Deuterocanonical and Cognate Literature Yearbook 2007: Angels: The Concept of Celestial Beings—Origins, Development and Reception*. Edited by Friedrich Vinzenz Reiterer, Tobias Nicklas, and Karin Schöpflin. Berlin: de Gruyter, 2007.

Bloch, Heinrich. *Die Quellen des Flavius Josephus in seiner Archäologie*. Leipzig: Teubner, 1879. Repr., Wiesbaden: Sändig, 1968.

Bowley, James E. "Josephus's Use of Greek Sources for Biblical History." Pages 202–215 in *Pursuing the Text: Studies in Honor of Ben Zion Wacholder on the Occasion of His Seventieth Birthday*. Edited by John C. Reeves and John Kampen. Journal for the Study of the Old Testament Supplement Series 184. Sheffield: Sheffield Academic Press, 1994.

Feldman, Louis H. *Josephus's Interpretation of the Bible*. Berkeley: University of California Press, 1998.

———. *Studies in Josephus' Rewritten Bible*. Journal for the Study of Judaism in the Persian, Hellenistic and Roman Period Supplement Series 58. Leiden: Brill, 1998.

———. *Judean Antiquities 1–4*. Edited by Steve Mason. Flavius Josephus Translation and Commentary 3. Leiden: Brill, 1999.

Franxman, Thomas W. *Genesis and the 'Jewish Antiquities' of Flavius Josephus*. Biblica et orientalia 35. Rome: Biblical Institute Press, 1979.

Halpern-Amaru, Betsy. "Flavius Josephus and *The Book of Jubilees*: A Question of Source." *Hebrew Union College Annual* 72 (2001): 15–44.

Hölscher, Gustav. "Josephus." Pages 1934–2000 in vol. 9 of *Paulys Realencyclopädie der classischen Altertumswissenschaft*. Edited by August F. Pauly. New edition edited by Georg Wissowa. 49 vols. Stuttgart: Metzler, 1893–1978.

Nodet, Étienne, *Flavius Josèphe Les Antiquités juives: Livres I à III, A. Introduction et texte*. Paris: Cerf, 1990.

———. *Flavius Josèphe Les Antiquités juives I: Livres I à III, B. Traduction et notes*. Paris: Cerf, 1990.

Rappaport, Salomo. *Agada und Exegese bei Flavius Josephus*. Vienna: Alexander Kohut Memorial Foundation, 1930.

---

is addressed primarily to a Gentile audience, the others are directed—in first place if not exclusively—to a Jewish readership. This underlying distinction would help explain many of the detailed divergences among them.

Schalit, Abraham. *Josephus, Antiquities of the Jews.* 3 vols. Jerusalem: Mosad Bialik, 1944–1963 (Hebrew).
Stern, Menachem, ed. *Greek and Latin Authors on Jews and Judaism.* 3 vols. Jerusalem: Israel Academy of Arts and Sciences, 1974–1984.
Thackeray, Henry St. John. *Josephus Jewish Antiquities Books I–IV.* Loeb Classical Library 242. Cambridge: Harvard University Press, 1930.
———. *Josephus: The Man and the Historian.* New York: Jewish Institute of Religion Press, 1929. Repr., New York: Ktav Publishing House, 1967.
Weill, Julien. *Oeuvres complètes de Flavius Josèphe, Antiquités Judaïques Livres I–IV.* Paris: Leroux, 1900.

CAIN AND ABEL IN SECOND TEMPLE LITERATURE AND BEYOND

John Byron

Genesis 4 is short on details. In 4:1–2 we are told the names of Eve's two sons and their respective occupations. The story then immediately shifts to a description of their sacrificial practices. Genesis does not provide any details about the brothers apart from their names and occupations. We are not told, for instance, anything about their personalities, their relationship with their parents or how they may have interacted with God prior to their presentation of sacrifices. In fact, Abel does not even get a speaking part in this drama. But in spite of the paucity of detail, later interpreters found little difficulty with expanding the details of the story and attributing characteristics to them not found in Gen 4.

The purpose of the following essay is to highlight two of the many ways in which later exegetes interpreted and embellished Gen 4 so as to transform the two brothers into representative types of humanity. In the case of Abel, the fact that his sacrifice was the first to be accepted by God established him as an ideal figure, which in turn led some to label him as the first righteous individual. For Cain, his infamy as the first murderer resulted in his identification as the archetype of all wicked people. These new roles provided the brothers a new lease on life beyond Gen 4. As the first righteous person, Abel was sometimes seen as the archetype for the oppressed poor. Cain, on the other hand, became the archetype of the wicked rich.

Righteous Abel

It is not clear when the classification of Abel as a righteous individual first began. The LXX, for instance, mirrors the Hebrew version of Gen 4:2 closely and does not expand the text in any way that hints at Abel's righteousness. There is a Greek fragment of *Jub.* 4:1 that calls Abel righteous (τὸν δίκαιον Ἄβελ), but there is no evidence for this reading in any of the extant Hebrew and Ethiopic copies of *Jubilees* suggesting that it is probably a later interpolation made by a Christian copyist.[1]

---

[1] Albert-Marie Denis, *Concordance grecque des Pseudépigraphes d'Ancien Testament* (Louvain-la-Neuve: Université catholique de Louvain, Institut orienta, 1987), 89, 902.

The Wisdom of Solomon may provide one of the earliest indications that Abel was considered to be among the righteous. Wisdom 10:1–21 contains a list of seven righteous heroes each of whom is paired with a wicked counterpart. The list begins with Adam in the garden and ends with the Israelite Exodus from Egypt. Each of the contrasting pairs demonstrates how Wisdom benefited the Israelite people throughout their history.[2] Wisdom saves those who embrace her and punishes those who reject her. Heading these seven pairs is a contrast between Adam and his firstborn son, Cain.[3] Wisdom is said to have sustained Adam in spite of his blunder (10:1). Cain, on the other hand, is said to have rejected Wisdom, committed fratricide (10:3) and, as a result of his crime, died in the flood (10:4). Interestingly, this is the only pair of the seven in this chapter that does *not* designate an individual as 'righteous.' While Noah (10:4), Abraham (10:5), Lot (10:6), Jacob (10:10), Joseph (10:13), and Israel (10:20) are all labeled as righteous, Adam is not. Instead we have the only instance in this chapter in which an individual is designated as unrighteous rather than righteous. Cain is called an unrighteous man (ἄδικος) when he rejects wisdom and kills his brother (10:3). While this is inconsistent with the format of the subsequent pairs in the chapter, the reader could conclude that Adam was a righteous individual even though he is not designated as such.

But what of Abel? In 10:3 Abel functions as the evidence for Cain's unrighteousness. Even more so than in the Genesis account, his role here is minor. But since Adam is contrasted with the actions of his firstborn son, readers might inquire about the status of Adam's second son. The fact that Cain committed a crime and Abel did not suggests that Abel was innocent.[4] Thus, although the author of the Wisdom of Solomon does not list Abel as one of the righteous individuals, readers could easily surmise that since Cain was unrighteous, Abel was righteous.[5]

---

[2] David Winston, *The Wisdom of Solomon: A New Translation with Introduction and Commentary* (AB 43; Garden City, N.Y.: Doubleday, 1979), 211; John R. Levison, *Portraits of Adam in Early Judaism: From Sirach to 2 Baruch* (JSPSup 1; Sheffield: Sheffield Academic Press, 1988), 57.

[3] In keeping with the custom of the book, *Wisdom* does not mention any historical character by name. Since the book presupposes familiarity with the Jewish Scriptures, it is assumed that the reader would recognize the stories of Adam and Cain (John Allen Fitzgerald Gregg, ed., *The Wisdom of Solomon: In the Revised Version with Introduction and Notes* [Cambridge: Cambridge University Press, 1922], 95).

[4] Levison, *Portraits of Adam*, 51.

[5] Paul Ellingworth, *The Epistle to the Hebrews: A Commentary on the Greek Text* (NIGTC; Grand Rapids: Eerdmans, 1993), 572; Karina Martin Hogan, "The Exegetical Background of the 'Ambiguity of Death' in the Wisdom of Solomon," *JSJ* 30 (1999): 1–24, esp. 22.

Fourth Maccabees provides some insight as to how Abel came to be considered an ideal figure. In the closing chapter of the book, the mother of the seven martyred brothers is given a chance to address her sons.[6] In the speech the mother recalls for her sons the lessons taught by their father (18:10–19). The father is presented as one who fulfilled the injunctions of Deut 6 by teaching his children the commandments of God, the meaningfulness of the covenant, and by teaching them through paradigm.[7] The catalog of the father's lessons is presented in two parts. The first part highlights the stories of eight ideal figures in Israelite history who suffered unjustly. Abel, Isaac, Joseph, Phinehas, the three young men and Daniel are all presented as a paradigm of those who remained obedient to God to the point of death (18:11–13).[8] Part two is a chain of five scriptural quotations, each of which contains promises of rescue and/or reward for those suffering unjustly. In the context of the brutal torture scenes in 4 Maccabees during which the seven brothers embrace death rather than disobey God, the paradigmatic figures and the scriptural promises become applicable to their situation. Particularly relevant here is the recitation of the first five words of Ps 34:20 (33:20 LXX) which declares "Many are the tribulations of the righteous" (18:15). This quotation supplies a dictum for the reader of 4 Maccabees that has already been reflected in the stories of Abel, Joseph, the three young men, and Daniel. These stories prepare the reader, as a righteous person, to expect affliction.[9] Abel's place at the head of the list reflects not only the chronological order in which Israel's ideal figure lived; it also positions him as the initial paradigm for those righteous individuals who suffer death. Unlike Wis 10:3, Abel is not merely a prop to demonstrate Cain's unrighteousness. Instead, it is Cain who moves to the background and Abel is brought forward as the first example of a righteous figure who was unjustly murdered. By recalling Abel's fate the author of 4 Macc 18 demonstrates

---

[6] As it presently stands, ch. 18 is probably a later insertion since the mother has already addressed her sons in 16:6–25 and then committed suicide in 17:1. The second speech in ch. 18 is an expanded version of the first, but this does not deny it rhetorical value particularly in the way that it catalogs the lives of ideal figures in Israel's history (David A. deSilva, *4 Maccabees: Introduction and Commentary on the Greek Text in Codex Sinaiticus* [SCS; Leiden: Brill, 2006], 256–257).

[7] DeSilva, *4 Maccabees*, 259.

[8] In the case of Isaac, the source of the trial is God's testing of Abraham. Phinehas represents those whose vigilance stems the tide of lawlessness among the Israelites (deSilva, *4 Maccabees*, 260).

[9] Jan Willem van Henten, *The Maccabean Martyrs as Saviours of the Jewish People: A Study of 2 and 4 Maccabees* (JSJSup 57; Leiden: Brill, 1997), 240; deSilva, *4 Maccabees*, 262.

that the righteous have suffered since the beginning of creation and, as the other ideal figures in 18:11–13 reveal, this is the fate that all righteous individuals can expect. Thus, even though no declaration of righteousness is pronounced over Abel in Gen 4, it is awarded to him posthumously by later interpreters who perceive him as the first example of righteous suffering.

Philo, of course, has much to say about Cain and Abel and often interprets the two brothers according to Greek Stoic ideas. He describes the younger son as the embodiment of virtue (ἀρετή) and holiness (ὁσιότης), one who refers all things to God and represents all those who love God (*Sacr.* 10, 14; *Det.* 32).[10] Cain, on the other hand, is representative of evil (κακία) and one who refers all things to himself (*Sacr.* 14; *Det.* 32).

In spite of the large amount of space that Philo dedicates to the interpretation of the two brothers' story, there is only one possible reference to Abel's status as righteous. In his commentary on Genesis, Philo explains why Moses details the occupation of the younger brother, Abel, before that of Cain, the older brother. It is as a part of this commentary that, for the first and only time, Philo contrasts the two brothers by labeling specifically the one as righteous and the other as evil.

> Even though the righteous man (ὁ δίκαιος) was younger in time than the wicked one (τοῦ φαύλου), still he was older in activity. Wherefore now, when their activities are appraised, he is placed first in order. (*QG* 1.59)

Ralph Marcus notes that the word he translates here as righteous is supported by Procopius of Gaza.[11] The difficulty, of course, is that extant Greek versions of Philo's *Questions in Genesis* are fragmentary and the bulk of the work is preserved in Armenian. When Marcus rendered his translation he was confident that "the Armenian language is singularly well designed to reproduce the word-order, word compound and many of the idioms of the Greek."[12] However, the appeal to Procopius notwithstanding, caution should be exercised when referring to this portion of Philo's works. Without an actual Greek text to consult, it is difficult to determine whether Philo used ὁ δίκαιος to describe Abel or whether the Armenian text and Procopius are anachronistically conditioned by an awareness of the Abel traditions. The fact that this seems to be the only occurrence in which Philo describes

---

[10] Georg Strecker, *The Johannine Letters: A Commentary on 1, 2, and 3 John* (trans. Linda M. Maloney; Hermeneia; Minneapolis: Fortress, 1996), 109; Flavius Josephus, *Judean Antiquities 1–4* (trans and commentary by Louis H. Feldman; repr., Leiden: Brill, 2004), 19 n. 112.

[11] Ralph Marcus, trans., *Philo, Supplement I: Questions and Answers on Genesis* (LCL 380; Cambridge: Harvard University Press, 1953), 36.

[12] Marcus, *Philo, Supplement I*, vii.

Abel as righteous, weakens the evidence that he is working within this part of the Abel traditions. Thus while Philo attributes many qualities of virtue to Abel, it is not clear that righteousness is one of them.

Josephus may be among the first of those who unambiguously associates the concept of righteousness with Abel. In *Antiquities* Josephus provides a description of the two brothers:

> Now the brothers rejoiced in different pursuits. For Abel, the youngest, had regard for righteousness (δικαιοσύνης) and, believing that God was present with him in all which he did, gave consideration to virtue (ἀρετή); and his life was that of a shepherd. Cain on the other hand, was completely evil (πονηρότατος) and only interested in what he could gain. He was the first to think of plowing the earth.[13]   (*Ant.* 1.53)

The description of Abel as one who "had regard for righteousness" is part of Josephus's moralizing tendency in *Antiquities*. On a number of occasions he makes brief additions or alterations to the biblical narrative in order to stress that the biblical characters are examples of virtue from which moral lessons may be drawn.[14] As a part of these expansions, Josephus explicitly elaborates on the virtues and/or vices of a biblical character in order to demonstrate their paradigmatic qualities.[15] Characteristics worthy of emulation include: courage, godliness, wisdom, and moderation. But the most common virtue to be applied to a character is righteousness (δικαιοσύνης). Attridge notes that in *Antiquities* righteousness "is so common as to be virtually without content. Δίκαιος is applied by Josephus to almost every positively evaluated figure in the biblical history. The term thus functions as the most inclusive designation for virtue in general."[16]

In addition to Abel, other major biblical characters who receive this designation in *Antiquities* include: Noah (1.99), Abraham (1.158), Jacob (2:149), Samuel (6.294), Abigail (6.308), David (7.110), Solomon (8.21), and Jehoshaphat (8.394). Similar to 4 Macc 18:11, however, is Abel's designation as the first righteous person. In 4 Maccabees the list of righteous individuals begins with Abel not Adam. In Wis 10 Adam is the only positive character *not* designated as righteous, although one could imply as much. In *Antiquities* 'righteousness' is never used in conjunction with Adam. Abel is the first biblical

---

[13] Translation mine.
[14] Harold W. Attridge, *The Interpretation of Biblical History in the* Antiquitates Judaicae *of Flavius Josephus* (HDR 7; Missoula, Mont.: Scholars Press, 1976), 68. See also the essay by Begg in this volume.
[15] Attridge, *Interpretation of Biblical History*, 109.
[16] Attridge, *Interpretation of Biblical History*, 115.

character with which this quality is associated. Thus, while righteousness in *Antiquities* is a virtue that is applied widely to positively evaluated figures in the biblical history, Abel stands at the head of all of these. This suggests, then, that the developing traditions surrounding the figure of Abel understood him to be the first human being who possessed qualities that could and should be emulated. Adam's status as the first created being and his previous experiences with God may have disqualified him as an unsuitable paradigm. But Abel's status as the first human to obey God outside of the garden made him a role model that could be emulated by all who lived in the Post-Edenic world.

The NT exhibits a similar interpretative trajectory. For instance, at the conclusion of the seven woes against the scribes and Pharisees, Jesus' condemnation of the religious leadership is interpreted through the figure of Abel. In Matt 23:35 the Matthean Jesus explicitly refers to Abel as righteous ("Αβελ τοῦ δικαίου). Luke's version of this saying in 11:51 does not refer to Abel as 'righteous' which may suggest that it is a Matthean addition to the Q source.[17] If it is an addition it demonstrates the degree of familiarity that Matthew had with the Abel tradition so that describing Abel as righteous was a natural expansion of the Q source.

1John 3:12 declares that Abel was righteous because of his deeds. While Matthew turns Abel's righteousness into an epithet, the author of 1John connects Abel's status as righteous to the deeds he performed prior to his murder. In 3:12 the writer asks why Cain killed Abel and then answers: "because his deeds were evil but his brother's righteous" (ἔργα αὐτοῦ πονηρὰ ἦν τὰ δὲ τοῦ ἀδελφοῦ αὐτοῦ δίκαια). Whether Abel's 'righteous deeds' refer back to his divinely sanctioned sacrificial practices or something else is not explicated.[18] But the author is clearly working within the righteous Abel tradition as evidenced by his use of terminology similar to that of Philo (*QG* 1.59) and Josephus (*Ant.* 1.53).[19] What is noteworthy here is the use of the Cain and Abel story once again as a paradigm for the readers. 1John 3:12 exhorts readers *not* to be like Cain (οὐ καθὼς) who murdered his righteous brother. Moreover, they should not be shocked if the world hates them

---

[17] James M. Robinson, Paul Hoffman, and John S. Kloppenborg, eds., *The Critical Edition of Q: Synopsis Including the Gospels of Matthew and Luke, Mark and Thomas with English, German, and French Translations of Q and Thomas* (Leuven: Peeters, 2000), 288; Dale C. Allison Jr., *The Intertextual Jesus: Scripture in Q* (Harrisburg: Trinity, 2000), 85.

[18] Strecker, *Johannine Letters*, 109.

[19] Judith Lieu, "What Was From The Beginning: Scripture and Tradition in the Johannine Epistles," *NTS* 39 (1993): 458–477, esp. 467.

(3:13). Just as Cain hated Abel and eventually killed him, so too followers of Jesus should, like Abel, expect to be persecuted by those who hate them.[20] As in 4 Maccabees and Josephus, Abel becomes a paradigm for positive, righteous behavior.

In Heb 11:4 Abel is presented as a paradigmatic figure who is extolled for both his righteousness and faith. In this chapter the author provides a definition of faith (vv. 1–3) followed by a list of characters from biblical history whose faith earned them God's approval. Heading the list, once more, is Abel, who, because of his faith, was determined by God to be righteous (ἐμαρτυρήθη εἶναι δίκαιος). Whether Abel was declared righteous because of his sacrificial technique or his faith is a matter for discussion.[21] But it is perhaps the common tradition of Abel as a righteous individual that leads the author of Hebrews to conclude that Abel also possessed faith. Earlier in 10:38, the author provided a quotation of Hab 2:4, "My righteous one will live by faith." This quotation, in turn, becomes the basis for the faith of Abel and the rest of the paradigmatic figures listed in ch. 11 since faith and righteousness were linked together directly.[22] For the author of Hebrews, then, Abel becomes the first example of faith and righteousness that should be modeled by readers of the epistle.

In addition to the above, there is an abundance of examples in which Abel is referred to as 'righteous' and only a sampling of them can be offered here. For instance, in the *Mart. Ascen. Isa.* 9:7–10 the seer is taken into the seventh heaven where he describes seeing "all of the righteous from the time of Adam onwards" including "holy Abel and all the righteous" who together worship the Lord (9:28). Reference to Abel's righteousness is also found among the *Hellenistic Synagogal Prayers* (6:4; 12:53), *Tg. Neof.* Gen 4:8, the Epistles of Cyprian (55.5; 80.2), the *Celementine Homilies* (2.16), the *Gospel of Pseudo-Matthew*[23] and the *Chronographia* of George Synkellos.[24]

---

[20] Raymond E. Brown, *The Epistles of John: A New Translation with Introduction and Commentary* (AB 30; Garden City, N.Y.: Doubleday, 1982), 444.

[21] James Moffatt, *Epistle to the Hebrews* (ICC; Edinburgh: T&T Clark, 1924), 163–164; Harold W. Attridge, *The Epistle to the Hebrews: A Commentary on the Epistle to the Hebrews* (Hermeneia; Philadelphia: Fortress, 1989), 316–317; and William L. Lane, *Hebrews 9–13* (WBC 47b; Dallas: Word, 1991), 334–335.

[22] Ellingworth, *Epistle to the Hebrews*, 572; David A. deSilva, *Perseverance in Gratitude: A Socio-rhetorical Commentary on the Epistle to the Hebrews* (Grand Rapids: Eerdmans, 2000), 388.

[23] *Ps.-Mt.* 7 contains an interesting statement put into the mouth of Mary in which she claims that there was no one righteous in the world before Abel.

[24] George Synkellos, *Chronographia*, 9.

When specific 'righteousness' terminology is missing, Abel is portrayed in variously different ways as the embodiment of virtue. Thus, the *T. Iss.* 5:4 refers to Abel as 'holy' and as such places him in the position of being the first saint (καθὼς εὐλόγησε πάντας τοὺς ἁγίους ἀπὸ Αβελ ἕως τοῦ νῦν). Augustine too lists Abel as the first saint at the head of a list of saints that culminates with John the Baptist (*C. du. ep. Pelag.* 3.24). And the *Apocalypse of Sederach* says that the divine virtue of love dwelt in the heart of Abel (1.18). A survey of the literature reveals that those authors who label Abel as 'righteous' are usually Christians heavily influenced by the NT. Many times these authors include material about Abel as a part of a quotation of Matt 23:35 through which they are reading Gen 4.

What we can observe, then, is that Abel's status as a righteous person is an exegetical development probably associated with the acceptable sacrifice he offered to God and his unjust death. The fact that Abel was the first person in the Bible to actively please God and be accepted by God outside of the garden positioned him as the first paradigmatic figure. While this status was equally the result of his position in biblical chronology as well as his demonstration of virtue, it nonetheless earned him the honor of being placed at the head of paradigmatic lists like those found in 4 Macc 18 and Heb 4. A noticeable aspect of this tradition is that Abel is declared to be the first righteous person while Adam is not. This is not to suggest that Adam was not righteous as is hinted in Wis 10:1–3 and the *Martyrdom and Ascension of Isaiah*. It was probably taken for granted that Adam was righteous by virtue of his relationship with God in the garden. But Abel is the first person to demonstrate righteousness when it really matters. In contrast to his father, Abel lived in a world that forced one to choose righteousness. As the tragic story of the two brothers reveals, Abel was the first in this new world to choose righteousness while Cain chose unrighteousness. As such, Abel became an ideal figure, the first example among many to follow who were to be emulated by those who, like Abel, suffered unjustly.

WICKED CAIN

As with Abel, Cain was saddled by interpreters with titles and character traits that do not appear explicitly in the Gen 4 story. A survey of the literature demonstrates that exegetes were just as happy to employ any number and type of descriptions to identify Cain as the first murderer, but, as would be expected, in a much more negative light.

Once again, among the earliest documents to attach a descriptive to Cain is the Wisdom of Solomon. As noted above, Cain is presented in 10:3 as the first person to reject Wisdom and to be labeled 'unrighteous' (ἄδικος). The significance of this presentation is that he has the notoriety of being the only person in this list to be referred to in this way. Even the collective enemies of the 'righteous' are not called ἄδικοι. It seems that as the first one to commit murder, and to head the list of the enemies of the righteous ones, Cain became the archetype of all wrongdoers and thus earned him an extraordinary name.[25] Furthermore, in 10:4 Cain is regarded as the reason for the flood thereby making his responsibility for evil far greater than is communicated in Gen 4.[26] The result is that the author of Wisdom enhances the evil of Cain so that he is responsible for three crimes, each related to and more serious than the first. He rejects Wisdom, murders his brother and brings destruction upon the world.

In *Ant.* 1.53, Josephus contrasts the dispositions of Cain and Abel. Following the order in Gen 4:2, he describes Abel's occupation first, but then adds an interpretive gloss stating that Abel was "one who had regard for righteousness." Similar to the author of Wisdom, however, Josephus enhances the depiction of Cain's evil by the way he uses the adjective πονηρός. In 1.53 Josephus portrays Cain as 'wholly evil' (πονηρότατος) using the superlative form of the adjective which seems to be a calculated move to present a totally depraved Cain. In 1.61 Cain is described as advancing evil to the extent that not only does he increase his own wickedness, but he even becomes a teacher of evil activities to others (διδάσκαλος αὐτοῖς ὑπῆρχε πονηρῶν). Lastly, in 1.66, using the superlative form of πονηρός again, Josephus claims that Cain's descendants became even more evil than him and that each one, in succession, surpassed the other in their evil exploits (Κάιος τοὺς ἐγγόνους πονηροτάτους συνέβη γενέσθαι). As in Wisdom, no longer is Cain only the first to commit murder. According to Josephus, Cain is the institutor, teacher and progenitor of all evil. Cain and his children are responsible for the decline of humanity.[27]

Among the numerous negative descriptions that Philo uses for Cain he says that Cain is an atheist (*Det.* 103, 119) and those who think like him are a part of the race of Cain (*Post.* 42). Elsewhere he calls Cain wicked

---

[25] Hogan, "Exegetical Background," 22.
[26] Levison, *Portraits of Adam*, 60–61.
[27] Attridge, *Interpretation of Biblical History*, 123; Feldman, *Judean Antiquities 1–4*, 21–22.

(*QG* 1.59), the representative of evil doctrine (*Sacr.* 1.5) and the ultimate symbol of wickedness (*Fug.* 64).

Christian authors also followed this interpretive trajectory. 1 John 3:12 describes Cain as unrighteous and a murderer (πονηροῦ ἦν καὶ ἔσφαξεν τὸν ἀδελφὸν αὐτοῦ). In Jude 11 those who walk in the way of Cain are condemned (τῇ ὁδῷ τοῦ Κάιν), a statement which resonates with the claim made by Josephus that not only was Cain evil, but that he also instructed others how to perform evil deeds.[28] *1 Clement* 4:7 views Cain as the prototype of hatred and envy towards one's brother that leads to murder. In an epistle attributed to Ignatius Cain is called the successor to the devil (*Hero* 5) and in the *Apocryphon of John* he is called 'unrighteous' (*Ap. John* II, 24, 16–25, 118–119).

Rabbinic interpreters were not always as critical of Cain as their predecessors, but they were not above making some sharp comments about him. In *Gen. Rab.* 2:3, we find a parallel to the claim in Wisdom and Josephus that Cain's evil actions had repercussions on creation. Rabbi Judah interpreted the description of the earth as 'void' in Gen 1:2 as a reference to Cain. Connecting Cain's act of lawlessness with the chaos of the pre-creation world, he said: "And void refers to Cain, who desired to return the world back to formlessness and emptiness." Other interpreters referred to Cain as an 'empty pot' (*Gen. Rab.* 19:11) or a 'vessel full of urine' (*Num. Rab.* 20:6).

Another title commonly applied to Cain is the label of 'fratricide' (ἀδελφοκτόνος). It seems that the first murderer was sometimes branded for the specific type of murder he committed. Thus, in Wis 10:3 we read that an unrighteous man perished because he committed fratricide (ἀδελφοκτόνοις) in a fit of anger. Philo refers to Cain as a fratricide no less than ten times and sometimes uses the label as a way to talk about Cain without mentioning his name.[29] The same branding of Cain is found in Josephus's *Ant.* 1.65, a fragment of *Jub.* 4:15,[30] and in *1 Clem.* 4:7.[31]

In the NT, specific 'fratricide' terminology (i.e. ἀδελφοκτόνος) does not appear in conjunction with Cain. But there is one instance that strongly suggests that some authors were aware of the tradition. 1 John 3:15 states that everyone who hates his brother is an ἀνθρωποκτόνος. This word is usually

---

[28] Richard J. Bauckham, *Jude, 2 Peter* (WBC 50; Waco, Tex.: Word, 1983), 79.
[29] *Det.* 96; *Post.* 49; *Agr.* 21; *Virt.* 199; *Cher.* 52; *Fug.* 60; and *Praem.* 72, 74.
[30] Denis, *Concordance*, 902.
[31] See also Tertullian, *Pat.* 5; and *Hel. Syn. Pr.* 12:54.

translated as 'murderer' or 'manslayer' and is rarely used in classical Greek.³² In 1John there is no explicit connection between Cain and ἀνθρωποκτόνος, but since the brothers are used as an illustration the implications are understood. Cain hated and killed his brother and as the first murderer serves as the chief representative for all brother haters who are labeled an ἀνθρωποκτόνος.³³ The familial language that permeates 1John 3 suggests that in spite of the terminology used, the author has a particular type of murder in mind: fratricide. The author presents a contrast between those who are children of God and those who are not and condemns all who hate their brothers.³⁴ Although the terminology in 3:15 can be more accurately translated as 'murderer' or 'manslayer,' using familial language and the Cain and Abel illustration would have made it easy to identify the act as a specific type of murder: fratricide.³⁵

---

³² The only other appearance of the term in the NT is in John 8:44 where Jesus uses it to label the devil as one who was a murderer from the beginning. Rather than tackle the more complicated questions surrounding the relationship between the Gospel and the Epistle, it seems more prudent to agree with those who suggest that the similarities between the two documents are the result of being heirs to the same set of interpretive traditions (Brown, *The Epistles of John*, 447; Lieu, "What Was From The Beginning," 476–477; Ruth B. Edwards, *The Johannine Epistles* [NTG; Sheffield: Sheffield Academic Press, 1996], 55; and John Painter, *1, 2, and 3John* [SP 18; Collegeville, Minn.: Liturgical Press, 2002], 23).

³³ It is striking that both times the term is used in the NT there is a connection to the devil. In John 8:44 the devil is the father of 'the Jews' and in 1John 3:12 Cain is said to be from the evil one. The depiction of Cain as the son of the devil was a well established tradition in Jewish and Christian literature and the tradition's probable influence on the Gospel and 1John can be acknowledged without rehearsing it in detail here. For a full discussion of the tradition, see Jan Dochhorn, "Mit Kain kam der Tod in die Welt: Zur Auslegung von SapSal 2,24 in 1Clem 3, 4; 4, 1–7, mit einem Seitenblick auf Polykarp, Phil. 7,1 und Theophilus, Ad Autol. II, 29, 3–4," *ZNW* 98 (2007): 105–159; James L. Kugel, *Traditions of the Bible: A Guide to the Bible as it was at the Start of the Common Era* (Cambridge: Harvard University Press, 1998),147, 157; Lieu, "What Was From The Beginning," 467–468; and N.A. Dahl, "Der Erstgeborene Satans und der Vater des Teufels (Polyk. 7,1 und Joh 8,44)," in *Apophoreta: Festschrift für Ernst Haenchen zu seinem 70. Geburtstag* (ed. W. Eltester and F.H. Kettler; BZNW 30; Berlin: Töpelmann, 1964), 70–84.

³⁴ There may be some connection to Jesus tradition here with anger towards one's brother being connected to murder in Matt 5:21–24 (Alan E. Brooke, *The Johannine Epistles* [ICC; Edinburgh: T&T Clark 1912], 94; Stephen S. Smalley, *1, 2, 3John*. [WBC 51; Waco, Tex.: Word, 1984], 191; and Dale C. Allison Jr., *Studies in Matthew: Interpretation Past and Present* [Grand Rapids: Baker Academic, 2005], 65–78). A similar theme is found later in the Jewish work *Der. Er. Rab.* 11:13 (57b), which attributes the following saying to Rabbi Eliezer ben Hyrcanus, a contemporary of the Johannine authors: "He who hates his neighbor is among the shedders of blood" (Brown, *The Epistles of John*, 447).

³⁵ For a more thorough treatment of the Cain and Abel traditions in 1John see my "Slaughter, Fratricide and Sacrilege: Cain and Abel Traditions in 1John 3," *Biblica* 88 (2007): 526–535.

The branding of Cain is a development of his crime. Ancient exegetes were not satisfied with merely calling him 'unrighteous' or 'wicked.' Instead they magnified his crime in ways that cannot be found in Gen 4. Not only was Cain the first to commit murder, he was also the first to reject Wisdom, promote evil, and bring about the destruction of the world. He is, in many ways, the prototype of the wicked: the first to bring evil into the world and to multiply it. While his crime earned him a certain level of notoriety, it was the specific type of murder that attracted the attention of some exegetes. Cain committed fratricide, which in the minds of some authors was very serious indeed. So serious, in fact, that the author of 1John could appeal to the story as part of his warning to the brother haters.

Cain and Abel beyond the Grave

In addition to character traits that identified the brothers as either righteous or evil, some later interpreters expanded Gen 4 to give the brothers a new lease on life. Rather than end their story in Genesis, ancient interpreters made the brothers representatives of the oppressed and the oppressors. They did this through the way that they interpreted Abel's crying blood in Gen 4:10 and the meaning of Cain's name in Gen 4:1.

In Gen 4:10 Abel's blood cries out from the ground and attracts God's attention to the scene. When later interpreters approached this passage, however, they were faced with an interpretive conundrum. In the Hebrew version the term for 'blood' (דם) is in the plural rather than singular construct. This results in a reading which, if literally translated, means the "voice of your brother's *bloods* are crying out" (קול דמי אחיך צעקים). How should this wrinkle in the text be understood?

Some interpreters chose not to contend with the problem. Josephus, for instance, completely avoids mentioning the talking blood by not including it in his version of the Cain and Abel story. Instead the reader is left to guess how God knew that Abel was dead (*Ant.* 1.55–56).[36] Philo employs a similar approach when he overlooks the blood and only concerns himself with

---

[36] This may be an attempt to gloss over the way Genesis seems to present God as ignorant of Abel's location and current condition. Rather than try to explain the situation Josephus simply expunges that aspect of the story. Philo asks a similar question in *QG* 1.68. Feldman, *Judean Antiquities 1–4*, 20 n. 119.

Abel's 'voice' which he understands as God continuing to hear the prayers of the worthy even though they are dead (*QG* 1.70).³⁷

Such an interpretive strategy may be behind Heb 11:4 where Abel, although dead, is still speaking (ἀποθανὼν ἔτι λαλεῖ). Here the author is not concerned with Abel's blood, but the ongoing effects of the crying voice.³⁸ The overshadowing of the blood by the 'voice' is what Serge Ruzer identifies as the spiritual existence of Abel. There is no need for blood, only the ongoing cry of the innocent before God.³⁹ Righteous Abel continues to speak even after his death.

For the compilers of the Mishnah, the fact that the blood was in the plural indicated that it was not only Abel who was murdered, but also any potential children (*m. Sanh.* 4:40).⁴⁰ However, these are not merely potential children, but, as some ancient interpreters suggested, children who would have been righteous as Abel was righteous.⁴¹ This interpretation is also found in some targums and midrashim where God accuses Cain of killing a "great multitude of righteous."⁴²

One of the more interesting examples of this motif is *1 En.* 22.5–7 where the blood is replaced by the spirit and voice of Abel which continues to cry out to God.⁴³ In the vision Enoch sees Abel and other spirits who were killed. Together they appeal to God that Cain's seed be exterminated from the earth. Although it is difficult to determine if the spirits crying out

---

³⁷ Serge Ruzer, "The Cave of Treasures On Swearing by Abel's Blood and Expulsion from Paradise: Two Exegetical Motifs in Context," *JECS* 9 (2001): 251–271, esp. 264.

³⁸ Some commentators dispute that Heb 11:4 is referring to Abel's blood speaking (e.g., William L. Lane, *Hebrews 9–13* [WBC 47b; Dallas: Word, 1991], 335–336) but Ton Hilhorst has argued that Heb 12:24 strengthens this claim by demonstrating that Abel's blood speaks of justice while Christ's of Grace ("Abel's Speaking in Hebrews 11.4 and 12.24," in *Eve's Children: The Biblical Stories Retold and Interpreted in Jewish and Christian Traditions* [ed. Gerard P. Luttikhuizen; TBN 5; Leiden: Brill, 2003], 119–127, esp. 126). See also deSilva, *Perseverance in Gratitude*, 388–389.

³⁹ Ruzer, "Cave of Treasures," 267.

⁴⁰ James L. Kugel, "Cain and Abel in Fact and Fable: Genesis 4:1–16," in *Hebrew Bible or Old Testament: Studying the Bible in Judaism and Christianity* (ed. Roger Brooks and John J. Collins; Notre Dame, Ind.: University of Note Dame Press, 1990), 167–190, esp. 180.

⁴¹ Lieu, "What Was From The Beginning," 468–469.

⁴² *Tg. Onq.* also accuses Cain of killing Abel's potential seed but does not attribute any quality of righteousness to them. For a comparison of the Targumic Versions of this verse see Geza Vermes, "The Targumic Versions of Genesis 4:3–16," in *Post-Biblical Jewish Studies* (SJLA 8; Leiden: Brill, 1975), 92–126.

⁴³ George W.E. Nickelsburg notes the parallels between *1 En.* 9:2 and that of 22:7 and suggests that the crying spirits in both of these passages may have been deduced through an exegetical connection between Gen 4:10 and Gen 9:4 where the blood דם is the נפש of man (*1 Enoch 1* [Hermeneia; Minneapolis: Fortress, 2001], 208).

with Abel are meant to indicate his own potential righteous offspring, it is likely that the passage is working to some degree within that interpretive understanding of the plural blood found in Gen 4.10. What is clear is that the purpose of crying out by Abel and the righteous multitudes is to ask God to either remove Cain's ancestors or those who have murdered the righteous from the earth.[44]

In addition to the above there is also a tradition in Jewish and Christian literature of vengeance prayers offered by those persecuted to the point of death. Often they are influenced, as in *1 Enoch*, by the cry of Abel's blood in Gen 4:10 and combined with a request for retaliation for the murder of the righteous. Examples of such prayers can be found in 2 Macc 8:2–4, Rev 6:9–11, the *Sib. Or.* 3:307–313, and the *T. Mos.* 9:6–7. Common to these prayers is the mention of either shed blood or blood crying out and the demand that God avenge the death of the righteous.[45]

Abel's status as the first righteous murder victim transformed him into a representative of the oppressed. The grammatical anomaly in Gen 4:10 meant that Abel's tragic story did not have to end with his murder. Although he has no speaking part in Gen 4, Abel went on to have a major role in requesting that God bring vengeance upon all those who had unjustly killed the righteous. The once silent Abel became the spokesman for oppressed.[46]

Since Abel came to represent the oppressed to ancient interpreters it was only a short walk to make Cain the representative of those who do the oppressing. Helping this interpretive trajectory was the meaning of Cain's name. Names in the Bible are often imbued with particular significance. People are named based on events surrounding their birth or future roles they will play. Cain's name was often interpreted to mean 'possession.' In Gen 4:2 Cain's name is part of a word play in Eve's cryptic statement made at her first son's birth. This word play is created by her claim to have 'gained' (קנה) a man which has a poetic similarity to the name Cain (קין).[47] When Eve's statement was translated into Greek the word play was lost.[48] But in spite of this, some interpreters seem to have been aware of the assonance

---

[44] Nickelsburg, *1 Enoch 1*, 305–306.
[45] Loren T. Stuckenbruck, *1 Enoch 91–108* (CEJL; Berlin: de Gruyter, 2007), 312.
[46] For a more thorough treatment of Abel as a figure of vengeance see my "Abel's Blood and the Ongoing Cry for Vengeance," *CBQ* 23 (2011): 743–756.
[47] Unlike Cain, no meaning is given to Abel's name by Eve. Outside of the Bible Abel's name was sometimes interpreted as meaning 'breath,' 'nothing' or 'sorrow' (Josephus, *Ant.* 1.52; Philo, *Migr.* 13.74).
[48] John William Wevers, *Notes on the Greek Text of Genesis* (SBLSCS 35; Atlanta: Scholars Press, 1993), 51.

between Cain's name and his mother's statement. Although working in Greek, they used their knowledge of this word play in Hebrew to develop traditions about Cain. The result is that Cain was portrayed as a greedy individual who oppressed others in order to gain riches.

In his rendition of Gen 4 Josephus notes that Cain's name signifies 'possession,' (κτῆσιν) which he interprets to mean that Cain was greedy (πρὸς τὸ κερδαίνειν μόνον [*Ant.* 1.52–53]). This is evidenced by Cain's choice of occupation. Abel became a shepherd, a choice representing his acknowledgement of God and nature (*Ant.* 1.53–54). Cain, on the other hand, was the first to think of plowing the land, an act that Josephus interprets as forcing the ground to yield in an unnatural way. But Josephus does not end his attack on Cain's character here. After recounting Abel's murder and Cain's punishment, Josephus goes on to claim that Cain continued to become even more wicked (*Ant.* 1.60). He increased his property and possessions through robbery and force and become a teacher of wickedness to others. And as if this was not enough, Josephus credits Cain with the invention of weights and measures which led humanity away from a simple life based on trust into one steeped in deception, dishonesty, and the continued pursuit to increase possessions and property (*Ant.* 1.61).[49]

Although Philo does not credit Cain with the invention of weights and measures, he does emphasize the notion that Cain was driven to gain more property and possessions. As with Josephus, this too is predicated on Philo's understanding of Cain's name meaning 'possession' (*Cher.* 52). The central flaw in Cain's character, according to Philo, was his failure to recognize that all possessions belonged to God rather than him (*Cher.* 52, 65).[50] For Philo, Cain is the ultimate narcissist. He represents self-love and those who are willing to go to any lengths in order to secure riches, honor, glory and authority. According to Philo, Cain's partisans are those in society who are

---

[49] Plato notes that in primitive humanity people were neither rich nor poor and thus free from envy and strife (*Leg.* 3.679B3–C2). This may be what has influenced Josephus' description as he attempts to establish Cain as the proto-deceiver. See Feldman, *Judean Antiquities 1–4*, 22 n. 133.

[50] This was why God rejected Cain's offering and Philo accuses Cain of being deficient in two areas: (1) he was late in bringing an offering to God; and (2) he did not offer God the first fruits of his harvest. This is the tragic result of individuals, like Cain, who either think they are the source of all the good things they enjoy or, even worse, they acknowledge God as the source but somehow think they deserve them (*Sacr.* 52–56). See Hindy Najman, "Cain and Abel as Character Traits," in *Eve's Children: The Biblical Stories Retold and Interpreted in Jewish and Christian Traditions* (ed. Gerard P. Luttikhuizen; TBN 5; Leiden: Brill, 2003), 107–118, esp. 113, 115.

rich, live a life of luxury, are strangers to labor and are constantly in the company of those people or things that bring them pleasure (*Det.* 32–34). In his efforts to portray Cain as an archetype he labels anyone who is a lover of self as a 'Cain' and therefore a murderer (*Det.* 78). Noting that Genesis never discusses how or when Cain died, Philo concludes that his wickedness lives on and thus, like Cain, never dies (*Conf.* 122; *Fug.* 60, 64). In this way, Philo is able to attribute the presence of evil in the world and the pursuit of possessions to the ongoing influence of Cain and those who follow in his footsteps.

The sentiments found in Philo and Josephus is in the midrash as well. In *Gen. Rab.* 22:9 we find Cain associated with Ps 37:14:

> R. Joshua said in R. Levi's name: "It is written, *The wicked have drawn out their sword*—this refers to Cain; *to cast down the poor and needy* refers to Abel."[51]

A similar connection is made to Prov 28:3 which says "a ruler who oppresses the poor is like a beating rain that leaves no food." This proverb is referenced in *Exod. Rab.* 31:17 and applied to Cain of whom it is said he was impatient to possess the whole earth and that his desire for property and possessions motivated him to kill Abel. Finally, in *Eccl. Rab.* 6:2.1 we find that the person described in Eccl 6:3 who lives many years, but does not have satisfaction of soul is alluding to Cain because he was not satisfied with his money and his possessions.[52]

Even when Cain is not mentioned by name, echoes of the tradition linking him to the oppression of the poor can be detected. One such example is found in Sir 34:19–22:

> The Most High is not pleased with the offerings of the ungodly; and he is not propitiated for sins by a multitude of sacrifices. Like one who kills a son before his father's eyes is the man who offers a sacrifice from the property of the poor. The bread of the needy is the life of the poor; whoever deprives them of it is a man of blood. To take away a neighbor's living is to murder him; to deprive an employee of his wages is to shed blood.[53]

---

[51] Translation taken from Harry Freedman and Maurice Simons, *Midrash Rabbah* (London: Soncino, 1961).

[52] The author, like Philo, is aware of Genesis' failure to mention Cain's death. The author suggests that Ecclesiastes' statement that the unsatisfied individual has no burial is a description of how Cain lived until the time of Noah and was then swept away by the flood, thus denying Cain a proper burial. The claim that the passage alludes to Abel as one who suffers an untimely death is predicated on a Hebrew word play. The word for untimely death is *nefel* from the root *nafal*, 'to fall', which is how Abel died as a result of his brother's violence.

[53] Translation mine.

Although Cain is not mentioned by name in this passage there are several traits listed here that is part of an interpretive trajectory concerning Cain: (1) a rejected offering; (2) the crime of murder; (3) depriving the poor of their property and wages; and (4) the claim that the oppression of the poor is analogous to shedding innocent blood.

What we observe then is the existence of two parallel traditions that sometimes interconnect. On the one hand there is a strong tradition that condemns those who oppress the poor.[54] On the other hand, there is yet another tradition that also condemns the oppression of the poor, but identifies the oppressors with wicked Cain and the oppressed with righteous Abel. Because of the considerable thematic overlaps between the two traditions, one could easily move between them without the need to mention Cain and Abel by name. As the traditions developed, Cain and Abel became archetypes for the wicked oppressors and the righteous poor and it was not necessary to differentiate between the two traditions. Other examples of these overlapping traditions may include Sir 21:5 where, like the cry of Abel's blood, the prayer of the poor reaches up to the ears of God. This is followed by a warning against the rich building houses with other people's money (21:8). Similarly, in *1 En.* 99:11–16 the wicked are described, as in Josephus and Sirach, as those who use deceitful weights and measures and build homes through the labor of others. Although Cain is not mentioned by name in these texts, the parallels between the two traditions concerning the oppression of the poor are notable.

Echoes of this overlapping tradition are found in the NT as well. James 5:1–6 contains a condemnation of wealthy individuals who persecute the poor.

> Come now, rich people, weep, wailing over your miseries that are coming. Your riches have rotted, and your garments have become moth-eaten. Your gold and silver have become rusted, and their corrosion will be a testimony against you, and will consume your flesh like fire. You have stored up treasure for the last days. Behold, the wages of the workers who harvest your fields, which you kept back by fraud, they cry out, and the cries of the harvesters have reached the ears of the Lord of hosts. You have lived on the earth in luxury and in pleasure; you have nourished your hearts for the day of slaughter. You condemned and murdered the righteous one. Does he not resist you?[55]

---

[54] Greed for money, power, and position was one of the most significant vices to be warned against in Jewish literature (Prov 1:11; Eccl 4:1–4; Wis 2:18–20; *1 En.* 94 ff. [Attridge, *Interpretation of Biblical History*, 122]).

[55] Translation mine.

As one listens to the statements found in 5:1–6 it is possible to hear an echo of the Cain and Abel story. Indeed, this would not be the first time such an echo has been heard. A number of scholars have noted that the cry of the harvesters reaching the ears of the Lord of hosts in Jas 5:4 is similar to Abel's blood crying out to the Lord from the ground in Gen 4:10.[56] The setting for the passage in James is the condemnation of the rich who have abused the poor.[57] However, the eschatological tone of the passage changes to one of encouragement in 5:7 when James shifts his remarks to the oppressed by calling for patience and promising them that God will act on their behalf in the future.[58] This is similar to what we have already seen in relation to Abel's cry for vengeance in *1 En.* 22:5–7 and the vengeance prayer tradition. If, as seems possible, James's readers were familiar with the way that the tradition incorporated the condemnation of the rich as part of the Cain and Abel story, then it would not be impossible for them to hear the echoes of Gen 4 in James's statements. Thus their conclusion would have been that those who oppress the poor and withhold their wages are guilty of the same crimes committed by Cain.

The meaning of Cain's name led to an exegetical development whereby the first murderer also became the archetype for those who oppress the poor. Josephus, Philo and the rabbis accused Cain of being a greedy, scheming individual whose motivation for murdering Abel was so that he could gain more wealth and possessions. At the same time, there existed a parallel tradition in Judaism and Christianity that was concerned with how the righteous poor were oppressed by the wicked rich. This tradition included a broad condemnation of the practices of those rich individuals who oppressed these righteous poor in order to further enrich themselves. The cries of the poor were portrayed as continually ascending to God requesting vengeance even if they had been murdered. The Cain tradition followed the same trajectory as the first, but rather than describe the situation in

---

[56] Bo Reicke, *The Epistles of James, Peter, and Jude: Introduction, Translation, and Notes* (AB 37; Garden City, N.Y.: Doubleday, 1963), 51; Martin Dibelius, *A Commentary on the Epistle of James* (trans. Michael A. Williams; Hermeneia; Philadelphia: Fortress, 1976), 238; Ralph P. Martin, *James* (WBC 48; Waco, Tex.: Word, 1988), 179; and James H. Ropes, *An Exegetical and Critical Commentary on the Epistle of Saint James* (New York: Charles Scribner's Sons, 1916), 289.

[57] James has a consistently negative portrayal of the rich (1:10–11; 2:6–7; 5:1–6). For a discussion of James' attitude towards the rich see David Hutchinson Edgar, *Has God Not Chosen the Poor?: The Social Setting of the Epistle of James* (JSNTSup 206; Sheffield: Sheffield Academic Press, 2001).

[58] Edgar, *Has God Not Chosen?*, 188, 198.

general terms, those working in this tradition borrowed imagery from the Cain and Abel story in order to establish archetypes of the wicked rich and the righteous poor. Because the traditions were both focused on the same goal, condemnation of the rich, one did not have to choose between them. Both traditions were equally useful and overlapped to such a degree that one could easily read the one and still hear echoes of the other.

Conclusion

The Cain and Abel story provided ancient interpreters with a seemingly unending source of exegetical expansions. Missing details, unusual syntax, and unexplained aspects led to developments that transformed the two brothers into archetypical figures for Jewish and Christian readers.

Abel's death meant, in many ways, a new life for him. Although his appearance in Genesis was brief and tragic, the subsequent incarnations given to him in interpretive traditions made him into an ideal figure. The fact that he was the first to offer an acceptable sacrifice in a post-Edenic world made him the first righteous individual. As such, he topped the list of ideal figures from Israel's history that were to be emulated. The result is a number of traditions in Jewish and Christian literature that identify him as 'Abel the righteous.'

Closely related to Abel's status as 'righteous' are the exegetical developments surrounding the crying blood in Gen 4:10. Rather than merely interpret the shed blood as evidence of Cain's crime, exegetes understood it as a cry for vengeance. Reflecting this perception of Abel's blood is the tradition of vengeance prayers. These prayers demanding justice from God for the shed blood of the innocent often echoed the language and imagery of Gen 4:10. As such Abel became a perpetual voice for the righteous demanding vengeance from God for the death of the innocent.

Cain's infamy extended far beyond his act of violence. Ancient exegetes were not satisfied with merely calling him 'unrighteous' or 'wicked.' Instead they magnified his crime in ways that cannot be found in Gen 4. Not only was Cain the first to commit murder, he was also the first to reject Wisdom, promote evil, and bring about the destruction of the world. The pens of interpreters turned him into the prototype of the wicked. He was listed as the first to bring evil into the world and to multiply it. Not only was he the first murderer he was also the archetypical oppressor of the poor. Interpreters accused Cain of being a greedy, scheming individual whose motivation for murdering Abel was so that he could gain more wealth and possessions. The result was that Cain's multiplying of evil was motivated by his greed. He not only sought gain for himself, but taught others how to commit evil acts in the pursuit for riches. Cain's imprint can be found upon a number of texts that lament the oppression of the poor.

SELECT BIBLIOGRAPHY

Allison, Dale C., Jr. "Murder and Anger, Cain and Abel." Pages 65–78 in *Studies in Matthew: Interpretation Past and Present*. Grand Rapids: Baker Academic, 2005.

Aptowitzer, Victor. *Kain und Abel in der Agada: den Apokryphen, der hellenistischen, christlichen und muhammedanischen Literatur*. Vienna: R. Verlag Löewitt, 1922.

Bassler, Jouette M. "Cain and Abel in the Palestinian Targums." *Journal for the Study of Judaism* 17 (1986): 56–64.

Brock, Sebastian P. "A Syriac Life of Abel." *Muséon: Revue d'études orientales* 87 (1974): 467–492.

Byron, John. *Cain and Abel in Text and tradition: Jewish and Christian Interpretations of the First Sibling Rivalry*. Themes in Biblical Narrative 14. Leiden: Brill, 2011.

———. "Cain's Rejected Offering: Interpretive Approaches to a Theological Problem." *Journal for the Study of the Pseudepigrapha* 18 (2008): 3–23.

———. "Living in the Shadow of Cain: Echoes of a Developing Tradition in James 5:1–6." *Novum Testamentum* 48 (2006): 261–274.

———. "Righteous Abel and the Cry for Vengeance." *Catholic Biblical Quarterly* 73 (2011): 743–756.

———. "Slaughter, Fratricide and Sacrilege: Cain and Abel Traditions in 1 John 3." *Biblica* 88 (2007): 526–535.

Chilton, Bruce. "A Comparative Study of Synoptic Development: The Dispute between Cain and Abel in the Palestinian Targums and the Beelzebub Controversy in the Gospels." *Journal of Biblical Literature* 101 (1982): 533–562.

Dochhorn, Jan. "Mit Kain kam der Tod in die Welt: Zur Auslegung vun SapSal 2,24 in 1 Clem 3, 4; 4, 1–7, mit einem Seitenblick auf Polykarp, Phil. 7,1 und Theophilus, Ad Autol. II, 29, 3–4." Zeitschrift für die neutestamentliche Wissenschaft 98 (2007): 105–159.

Glenthøj, Johannes Bartholdy. *Cain and Abel in Syriac and Greek Writers (4th–6th Centuries)*. Corpus Scriptorium Christiamorum Orientalium 567. Lovanii: Peeters, 1997.

Hayward, C.T.R. "What Did Cain Do Wrong? Jewish and Christian Exegesis of Genesis 4:3–6." Pages 101–123 in *The Exegetical Encounter between Jews and Christians in Late Antiquity*. Edited by Emmanouela Grypeou and Helen Spurling. Jewish and Christian Perspective Series 18. Leiden: Brill, 2009.

Kim, Anglea Y. "Cain and Abel in the Light of Envy: A study in the History of Interpretation of Envy in Genesis 4:1–16." *Journal for the Study of the Pseudepigrapha* (2001): 65–84.

Kugel, James L. "Cain and Abel in Fact and Fable: Genesis 4:1–16." Pages 167–190 in *Hebrew Bible or Old Testament: Studying the Bible in Judaism and Christianity*.

Edited by Roger Brooks and John J. Collins. Notre Dame, Ind.: University of Note Dame Press, 1990.

Luttikhuizen, Gerard P., ed. *Eve's Children: The Biblical Stories Retold and interpreted in Jewish and Christian Traditions*. Themes in Biblical Narrative 5. Leiden: Brill, 2003.

Quinones, Ricardo, J. *The Changes of Cain: Violence and the Lost Brother in Cain and Abel Literature*. Princeton: Princeton University Press, 1991.

Ruzer, Serge. "The Cave of Treasures On Swearing by Abel's Blood and Expulsion from Paradise: Two Exegetical Motifs in Context." *Journal of Early Christian Studies* 9 (2001): 251–271.

Springer, A.J. "Proof of Identification: Patristic and Rabbinic Exegesis of the Cain and Abel Narrative." *Studia Patristica* 39 (2006): 259–271.

Tromp, Johannes. "Cain and Abel in the Greek and Armenian/Georgian Recensions of the *Life of Adam and Eve*." Pages 278–282 in *Literature on Adam and Eve: Collected Essays*. Edited by Gary A. Anderson, Michael E. Stone, and Johannes Tromp. Studia in Veteris Testamenti pseudepigrapha 15. Leiden: Brill, 2000.

Vermes, Geza. "The Targumic Versions of Genesis 4:3–16." Pages 92–126 in *Post-Biblical Jewish Studies*. Studies in Judaism in Late Antiquity 8. Leiden: Brill, 1975.

GENESIS IN THE DEAD SEA SCROLLS

Sidnie White Crawford

The book of Genesis occupies a prominent place in the Qumran collection of the Dead Sea Scrolls.[1] This is true for Genesis as simply a scriptural text, but also as Genesis is reworked, rewritten, and interpreted in other Second Temple Jewish works found at Qumran. This article will by necessity proceed through the various texts individually, discussing each one separately. I will then tie the texts and their themes together at the end of the article.

Genesis Manuscripts

Nineteen fragmentary manuscripts of Genesis itself were found in caves 1, 2, 4, 6 and 8 at Qumran.[2] The oldest, 6QpaleoGen, written in paleo-Hebrew script, dates paleographically between 250–150 BCE, while the latest, 4QGen^b, dates between 30–100 CE.[3] The nineteen manuscripts between them cover parts of almost all the chapters of Genesis, beginning with 1:1–28 (4QGen^b) and ending with 50:26(?) (4QpaleoGen-Exod^l). In addition, four other fragmentary manuscripts of Genesis were found in other find sites in

---

[1] This article will refer almost entirely to the collection of manuscripts found in the eleven caves near the ruins of Qumran. Other Judean Desert find sites will be referred to occasionally.

[2] D. Barthélemy, "Genèse," in *Qumran Cave I* (ed. D. Barthélemy and J.T. Milik; DJD 1; Oxford: Clarendon, 1955), 49–50; M. Baillet, "Genèse," in *Les 'Petites Grottes' de Qumran* (ed. M. Baillet, J.T. Milik, and R. de Vaux; DJD 3; Oxford: Clarendon, 1962), 48–49; James R. Davila, "4QGen-Exod^a-4QGen^k," in *Qumran Cave 4, VII, Genesis to Numbers* (ed. Eugene Ulrich et al.; DJD 12; Oxford: Clarendon, 1994), 7–78; Patrick W. Skehan, Eugene Ulrich, and Judith E. Sanderson, "4QpaleoGenesis-Exodus^l – 4QpaleoGenesis^m," in *Qumran Cave 4, IV, Palaeo-Hebrew and Greek Biblical Manuscripts* (DJD 9; Oxford: Clarendon, 1992), 17–52; Émile Puech, "4QGenèse^n," in *Qumrân Grotte 4, XVIII, Textes Hébreux (4Q521–4Q528, 4Q576–4Q579)* (ed. Émile Puech; DJD 25; Oxford: Clarendon, 1998), 195–204; M. Baillet, "Genèse en écriture paleo-hébraïque," in *Les 'Petites Grottes' de Qumran* (ed. M. Baillet, J.T. Milik, and R. de Vaux; DJD 3; Oxford: Clarendon, 1962), 105–106; and M. Baillet, "Genèse," in *Les 'Petites Grottes' de Qumran* (ed. M. Baillet, J.T. Milik, and R. de Vaux; DJD 3; Oxford: Clarendon, 1962), 147–148.

[3] Brian Webster, "Chronological Index of the Texts from the Judaean Desert," in *The Texts from the Judaean Desert: Indices and an Introduction to the Discoveries in the Judaean Desert Series* (ed. Emanuel Tov; DJD 39; Oxford: Clarendon, 2002), 351–446, esp. 378, 434.

the Judean Desert (two from Wadi Murabbaʿat, one from Wadi Sdeir, and one from Masada).[4] These manuscripts all date paleographically to the late first – early second century CE.[5] All of these manuscripts conform to the proto-Masoretic text-type in Genesis.[6]

The relatively large number of manuscripts of Genesis preserved in the Judean Desert caves speaks to its importance as a scriptural text in the Second Temple period. We now turn to the use of Genesis in other compositions discovered in the Qumran caves, a use so extensive that it establishes Genesis as a seminal text for the sect that preserved the Qumran scrolls.

Rewritten Bible

Reworked Pentateuch

The first group of text reusing the book of Genesis for exegetical purposes is the group known as Reworked Pentateuch. The five manuscripts in this group, 4Q158[7] and 4Q364–367,[8] are not copies of one another, but differ in extent and purpose.[9] 4Q364 and 4Q365 self-present as complete manuscripts of the Pentateuch, albeit with a hyperexpanded text, while 4Q158, 4Q366 and 4Q367 are collections of Pentateuchal passages, some-

---

[4] J.T. Milik, "Genèse, Exode, Nombres," in *Les Grottes de Murabbaʿat* (ed. P. Benoit, J.T. Milik, and R. de Vaux; DJD 2; Oxford: Clarendon, 1961), 75–78; Émile Puech, "Fragment d'un rouleau de la Genese provenant du desert de Juda (Gen. 33,18–34,3)," *RevQ* 10 (1979–1981): 163–166; Catherine Murphy, "Sdeir Genesis," in *Miscellaneous Texts from the Judaean Desert* (ed. James Charlesworth et al.; DJD 38; Oxford: Clarendon, 2000), 117–124; Shemaryahu Talmon, "Hebrew Fragments from Masada," in *Masada VI: Yigael Yadin Excavations 1963–1965, Final Reports* (ed. Shemaryahu Talmon and Yigael Yadin; Jerusalem: Israel Exploration Society, 1999), 31–35.

[5] Webster, "Chronological Index," 438, 440.

[6] James R. Davila, "Genesis, Book of," in *The Encyclopedia of the Dead Sea Scrolls* (ed. Lawrence H. Schiffman and James C. VanderKam; 2 vols.; New York: Oxford, 2000), 1:299–300.

[7] John M. Allegro, "Biblical Paraphrase: Genesis, Exodus," in *Qumrân Cave 4, I (4Q158–4Q186)* (DJD 5; Oxford: Clarendon, 1968), 1–6. See also John Strugnell, "Notes en marge du volume V des 'Discoveries in the Judaean Desert of Jordan'," *RevQ* 7 (1970): 163–276.

[8] Emanuel Tov and Sidnie White, "Reworked Pentateuch," in *Qumran Cave 4, VIII, Parabiblical Texts, Part I* (ed. Harold Attridge et al.; DJD 13; Oxford: Clarendon, 1995), 187–352.

[9] For a more in-depth discussion, see George J. Brooke, "4Q158: Reworked Pentateuchᵃ or Reworked Pentateuch A?" *DSD* 8 (2001): 219–241; Sidnie White Crawford, *Rewriting Scripture in Second Temple Times* (Grand Rapids: Eerdmans, 2008); Michael H. Segal, "4QReworked Pentateuch or 4QPentateuch?" in *The Dead Sea Scrolls Fifty Years After Their Discovery* (ed. Lawrence H. Schiffman, Emanuel Tov, and James C. VanderKam; Jerusalem: Israel Exploration Society, 2000), 391–399.

times reworked for exegetical purposes. 4Q158 and 4Q364 rework passages from Genesis most extensively, and so will be treated at length.

4Q158. Fragments 1–2 present Gen 32:25–32 followed by Exod 4:27–28. The fragments do not contain a running text of Genesis; lines 1–2 contain fragmentary words not identifiable as text from Genesis, followed immediately by Gen 32:25–32, the story of Jacob wrestling with the angel at Penuel (lines 3–13). Exod 4:27–28, Aaron's meeting with Moses at Sinai, follows in the next line (lines 14–15). The reason for the juxtaposition of these two passages is not entirely clear. The best suggestion is that the passage in Exodus immediately preceding Exod 4:27 narrates the story of God's attack on Moses at night on the road to Egypt (Exod 4:24–26), so that the two passages portray important figures in a dangerous physical encounter with a night demon/divine being.[10] However, since there are no remains of Exod 4:24–26 preserved on the fragments, the connection remains uncertain.

The text of Gen 32:25–32 in 4Q158 has been expanded beyond other witnesses. It contains several small additions:

Line 3 (Gen 32:25) adds the word שמה, "there."
Line 4 adds the work ו[י]אחזהו, "and he clung to him," at the end of v. 26.
Line 5 contains the word אל[י?, "to me [?]" at the end of v. 27.
Line 6 adds the phrase לי מה to v. 30.

More importantly, 4Q158 adds, in lines 7–10, the words of the angel's blessing over Jacob, at the end of their encounter:

7. [And he bless]ed him [there], saying, 'May the Lo[rd] make you fruitful, [and multiply] you [
8. [know]ledge and insight. May he preserve you from all wrongdoing, and [
9. until this day and forever more[
10. Then the man went on his way, having blessed Jacob there.

This short addition fills an exegetical gap in the received text of Genesis: did the angel bless Jacob, and if so, what did he say?

Finally, in lines 12–13, 4Q158 reworks the received text of Genesis so that the avoidance of eating the thigh muscle on the hip socket is not merely a matter of custom, but a legal matter: ויאמר אל תואנכל ...]על שתי כפות הירך ה[יום הזה. "And he said, 'You shall not ea[t ...]on the hip sockets to t[his day.'" This subtle change elevates the alimentary prohibition to the status of a commandment.

---

[10] Michael H. Segal, "Biblical Exegesis in 4Q158: Techniques and Genre," *Textus* 29 (1998): 45–62, esp. 48.

Another small fragment, frg. 3, may contain a rewritten passage of Genesis, for it mentions Jacob by name. The editor identified it with Gen 32:31. However, this placement is uncertain, since the preserved words on the fragment do not correspond exactly to this verse. Rather, the fragment seems to contain some sort of discourse by Jacob, the exact location of which in Genesis is unclear.[11]

4Q364. 4Q364, an extensively preserved manuscript of an expanded Pentateuch copied in the first century BCE, includes twelve fragments containing passages from Genesis, beginning in ch. 25 and concluding in ch. 48.[12] Most of these fragments preserve simply a running text of Genesis according to other ancient witnesses, with variants. There are, however, five fragments with indications of expansion (frgs. 1a–b, 3 col. ii, 4b–e cols. i and ii, 5b col. ii, and frg. 10).[13] I will discuss those expansions for which the evidence is straightforward.

Frg. 4b–e col. ii preserves Gen 30:26–36, and shares a harmonization with the SamP, found in lines 21–26.

21. And [the angel of God spo]ke [to Jacob in a dream and said, 'Jacob,' and he said,]
22. 'He[re am I.' He said, 'Lift up] your [eyes and see that all the male goats which are mounting]
23. [the flock are ring-streaked and spe]ckled [and grizzled, for I have seen what Laban has done]
24. [to you. I am the God of Bethel wh]ere [you anointed a pillar and where you vowed]
25. [a vow to me there. And now, arise, go out] fr[om this land and return to the land]
26. [of your] fa[thers and I will deal well with you.']

This harmonization looks ahead to Gen 31:11–13, where Jacob tells Rachel and Leah that he has had a dream in which God instructs him to return to Canaan. However, the received text of Genesis never reports Jacob actually having the dream. This harmonization, shared with the SamP, remedies the gap in the text by supplying the dream sequence.

Frg. 3 col. ii contains an expansion of six lines before Gen 28:6.

1. him you shall see[
2. you shall see (him) in good health[
3. your death, and unto your eyes [lest I be deprived of even]

---

[11] Segal, "Biblical Exegesis in 4Q158," 53–54.
[12] Tov and White, "Reworked Pentateuch," 201, 204.
[13] Tov and White, "Reworked Pentateuch," 205–211, 213–214, 216–217.

4. the two of you. And [Isaac] called [Rebekah his wife and he told]
5. her all [these] things [
6. after Jacob her son [and she wept
7. ²⁸:⁶Now Esau saw that [Isaac had blessed Jacob and sent him away]
8. to Pa[dan] Aram to find from [there a wife] for him[

This expansion appears to contain Rebekah's words to the departing Jacob, and Isaac's attempt to console her. The expansion adds pathos to what is otherwise a rather dry report in Genesis. Jubliees 27 contains parallel text: "The spirit of Rebecca was grieved after Jacob her son" (27:14), and "And we shall see him in peace" (27:17). It is not easy to determine whether 4Q364 or its predecessors served as a source for Jubilees or vice versa, but if the passage in 4Q364 was a source for Jubilees, it would indicate that this version of the Pentateuch was given the same authority as other versions.

Interestingly, the same type of scene also appears in Tobit, where Tobit and his wife Anna bid farewell to their departing son Tobias (Tob 5:18–22). Anna weeps, and Tobit attempts to comfort her. This similarity may point to a common type scene in the Jewish tradition.

The other fragments listed above contain short embellishments, seemingly to clarify what might be considered obscurities in the received text. Some of these expansions may have been longer, but certainty is lacking (frgs. 4b–e col. ii, line 3, 5b col. ii, and frg. 10). It is possible that 4Q364, frg. 5b col. ii, line 13 contained the same expansion as 4Q158, frgs. 1–2 (discussed above), since both texts contain ויאמר against ויקרא of the other witnesses, but unfortunately the 4Q364 fragment breaks off at this point, so we cannot be sure.

The Genesis Apocryphon

The Genesis Apocryphon was discovered in Cave 1, Qumran, in a single, badly decayed copy. When it was first unrolled, only cols. 2 and 19–22 were decipherable.[14] In the 1990s, with the use of advanced imaging techniques, much more of the early columns were revealed, giving a more complete picture of the contents of the scroll.[15] The scroll is written in Aramaic and

---

[14] Nahman Avigad and Yigael Yadin, *A Genesis Apocryphon: A Scroll from the Wilderness of Judaea* (Jerusalem: Magnes, 1956). Several fragments that had been peeled off the outside of the scroll were published by J.T. Milik, "Apocalypse de Lamech," in *Qumran Cave I* (ed. D. Barthélemy and J.T. Milik; DJD 1; Oxford: Clarendon, 1955), 86–87.

[15] Jonas C. Greenfield and Elisha Qimron, "The Genesis Apocryphon col. xii," *AbrNSup* 3 (1992): 70–77; Matthew Morgenstern, Elisha Qimron, and Daniel Sivan, "The Hitherto Unpublished Columns of the Genesis Apocryphon," *AbrN* 33 (1995): 30–54; and Daniel

its paleographic date lies between 25 BCE and 50 CE. Fitzmyer, following Kutscher, has characterized the language of the scroll as "Middle Aramaic," falling between the Aramaic of Daniel and later Western Aramaic.[16] This places the date of the language of the scroll from some time in the first century BCE to the first century CE. Since the date of the language of the scroll and its paleographic date adhere so closely, it is possible that the scroll is an autograph. However, given the decayed condition of the scroll, it is impossible to be certain.[17] If the scroll is not an autograph, then its date of composition becomes an open question. Some scholars place its composition in the first century BCE, close to the date of its language and paleography.[18] Others date it much earlier in the Second Temple period, to the second or even the third centuries BCE.[19] The arguments for the date of composition center around the Genesis Apocryphon's relationship to the books of Enoch and Jubilees, with which it shares significant overlaps.

The Genesis Apocryphon, as its name implies, retells selected stories from the book of Genesis. It is divided into two parts. The first, narratives concerning Noah, is found in cols. 0–17, while the second part, centered around Abraham, is found in cols. 19–22 (col. 18 remains undecipherable).[20] The Apocryphon begins in Gen 5, evidently entirely omitting any mention of the creation or Garden of Eden narratives, and proceeds in order (though with extensive omissions) through Gen 15:1–4. At this point the manuscript breaks off; we do not possess the ending.

A. Machiela, *The Dead Sea Genesis Apocryphon: A New Text and Translation with Introduction and Special Treatment of Columns 13–17* (STDJ 79; Leiden: Brill, 2009).

[16] Joseph A. Fitzmyer, *The Genesis Apocryphon of Qumran Cave 1 (1Q20): A Commentary* (3rd ed.; BibOr 18B; Rome: Pontifical Biblical Institute, 2004), 29–37, 302. Fitzmyer's commentary on the Genesis Apocryphon is the most complete, and his translations will be followed here.

[17] See Joseph A. Fitzmyer, "Genesis Apocryphon," in *The Encyclopedia of the Dead Sea Scrolls* (ed. Lawrence H. Schiffman and James C. VanderKam; 2 vols.; New York: Oxford, 2000), 1:302–304, esp. 302; and Fitzmyer, *The Genesis Apocryphon*, 28.

[18] Crawford, *Rewriting Scripture*, 106; Daniel K. Falk, *The Parabiblical Texts: Strategies for Extending the Scriptures among the Dead Sea Scrolls* (CQS 8/LSTS 63; London: T&T Clark, 2007), 29; and Fitzmyer, *The Genesis Apocryphon*, 28.

[19] Avigad and Yadin, *A Genesis Apocryphon*, 38; Geza Vermes, *Scripture and Tradition in Judaism* (Leiden: Brill, 1961), 96, n. 2; Cana Werman, "Qumran and the Book of Noah," in *Pseudepigraphic Perspectives: The Apocrypha and Pseudepigrapha in Light of the Dead Sea Scrolls* (ed. Esther G. Chazon and Michael E. Stone; STDJ 31: Leiden: Brill, 1999), 172; Esther Eshel, "The *Imago Mundi* of the Genesis Apocryphon," in *Heavenly Tablets: Interpretation, Identity and Tradition in Ancient Judaism* (ed. Lynn LiDonnici and Andrea Lieber; JSJSup 119; Leiden: Brill, 2007), 111–131, esp. 130–131; Machiela, *The Dead Sea Genesis Apocryphon*, 16–17.

[20] See also Falk, *Parabiblical Texts*, 30.

Not only do the two parts center around different characters; their styles of composition are disparate enough to assume two separate sources, brought together in one scroll by a redactor.[21] The first part, the narratives concerning Noah, are attached to the Genesis text by only slender threads; they are extensively reworked, bringing in elements from other sources, including the books of Enoch and Jubilees.[22] The second part concerning Abraham follows the scriptural narrative much more closely, with more modest reworking. At times it is targum-like, translating the Hebrew into Aramaic word-for-word. I will treat the two parts separately, and then close this section with some remarks concerning the Apocryphon's purpose.

Columns 0–1, which are extremely fragmentary, are concerned with the depraved state of the world prior to the birth of Noah. This depraved state is the result of the descent of the Watchers, divine beings who descended to earth to mate with human women. While this episode is told briefly in Gen 6:1–4, a full-blown, seemingly independent narrative is found in the Book of Watchers, *1 En.* 1–36, as well as a shorter version in *Jub.* 5. The remains of the Apocryphon give hints that the corruption of the earth is the result of the acts of the Watchers. The lines "that in every (way) we shall welcome an adulterer" (col. 0, line 2) and "the mystery of evil" (col. 1, line 2) indicate that evil on earth begins with the Watchers. This accords with Enoch and Jubilees, and situates the Apocryphon squarely in that tradition.

Columns 2–5 contain a narrative concerning the birth of Noah. It is based on the brief notice in Gen 5:28–29: "When Lamech had lived one hundred and eighty-two years, he became the father of a son; he named him Noah, saying, 'Out of the ground that the LORD has cursed this one shall bring us relief from our work and from the toil of our hands.'" However, the Apocryphon's narrative goes far beyond Genesis by emphasizing the miraculous nature of Noah's birth and his connections to Enoch, Methusaleh, and

---

[21] See most recently Moshe J. Bernstein, "The Genre(s) of the Genesis Apocryphon," in *Aramaica Qumranica: Proceedings of the Conference on the Aramaic Texts from Qumran in Aix-en-Provence, 30 June – 2 July 2008* (ed. Katell Berthelot and Daniel Stöckl ben Ezra; STDJ 98; Leiden: Brill, 2010), 318–343, esp. 335. I would like to thank Professor Bernstein for making this article available to me prior to publication. See also his "Genre Just Gets in the Way Anyway: Reading the Genesis Apocryphon Multigenerically," given at the 2010 Society of Biblical Literature meeting in Atlanta, where he states, "the two halves of the Genesis Apocryphon, the Lamech-Noah material in cols. 0–18 that I call Part I, and the Abram material in 19–22 designated Part II, are of fundamentally divergent natures and probably derive, ultimately, from different sources, the former from 1 Enoch, and the latter, perhaps, from Jubilees."

[22] Crawford, *Rewriting Scripture*, 110–116; Machiela, *The Dead Sea Genesis Apocryphon*, 8–17.

the Watchers. Extensive parallels exist with *1 En.* 106–107. According to the Apocryphon Noah is such a special baby that his father Lamech doubts his legitimacy, and accuses his wife Bitenosh (cf. *Jub.* 4:28) of adultery with the Watchers. Although she angrily and passionately denies this,[23] Lamech is not reassured and goes to his father Methusaleh, asking him to ask his father Enoch, now residing with the angels, to verify the child's legitimacy. Enoch does assure Methusaleh that Noah is Lamech's son (col. 5, line 4), and further that Noah has a special role to play on earth.

A new section begins in col. 5, line 29, with the heading "[A copy of] the book of the words of Noah[." Whether or not this is an actual source being cited by the composer of Part 1, or if such a book actually existed, is uncertain.[24] At this point the Apocryphon shifts into first person narration, in the voice of Noah (Lamech speaks in the first person in col. 2, and Enoch speaks in the first person in cols. 3–5). The material that follows (cols. 6–17) is loosely based on Gen 6–9, but much of it is reworked and incorporates other traditions, especially those of Enoch and Jubilees.

Noah begins by describing his own righteousness, clearly a contrast to the depravity of the Watchers and the humans who follow them. Noah then recounts the events of his life, including the marriage of his sons (col. 6, lines 1–11). Like the name of his mother, Bitenosh, the name of his wife, Emzara, is supplied. After this Noah receives a vision of the Flood and its consequences (cols. 6, line 11 – col. 7, line 5). This vision is unique to the Genesis Apocryphon and places Noah on the same level as the übervisionary Enoch. Likewise it adds an apocalyptic flavor to the narrative. Noah's reaction to the vision of the destruction wrought by the Flood is joy, as befits a righteous man: "and I rejoiced at the words of the Lord of Heaven and cried out" (col. 7, line 7).

The actual narrative of the Flood is very fragmentary; our extant text picks up with the ark coming to rest on the mountains of Ararat (col. 10, line 12). Noah, upon exiting the ark, immediately makes a sacrifice, as in Gen 8:20–21. However, the sacrifice is narrated in much more detail, having Noah follow the sacrificial laws of Leviticus, which accords with the portrait

---

[23] George W.E. Nickelsburg, "Patriarchs Who Worry About Their Wives: A Haggadic Tendency in the Genesis Apocryphon," in *Biblical Perspectives: Early Use and Interpretation of the Bible in Light of the Dead Sea Scrolls* (ed. Michael E. Stone and Esther G. Chazon; STDJ 28; Leiden: Brill, 1998), 137–158.

[24] In favor of this is Richard C. Steiner, "The Heading of the *Book of the Words of Noah* on a Fragment of the Genesis Apocryphon: New Light on a 'Lost' Work," *DSD* 2 (1995): 66–71, while against it is Werman, "Qumran and the Book of Noah," 181.

of Noah in *Jub.* 6:2–3 and demonstrates that Noah, like the other righteous ancestors, followed the Sinai regulations long before they were given to Moses.

In col. 11 Noah traverses the land, symbolically taking possession of it. This detail is unique to the Apocryphon, and will be found again in the Abraham cycle (col. 21).

Column 12, lines 10–12, contains the genealogy of Noah (Gen 10:1–32), moving it in front of the episode of the vineyard (Gen 9:18–27), and emphasizing Shem as the firstborn. The episode of the vineyard follows in lines 12–17. The narration differs from the Genesis base text by including Noah's sons, and especially by having Noah observe the injunctions of Lev 19:23–25 and only drinking the wine produced by the vineyard in the fifth year (see also *Jub.* 7:7–13). The incident of Noah's drunkenness appears to be missing, although the bottom of col. 12 is very fragmentary. If the drunkenness was omitted, it fits into a tendency in Second Temple texts to "clean up" the actions of the ancestors, a tendency clearly at work in the Abraham narrative in the second part of the Apocryphon.[25]

Columns 13–15 contain a series of visions by Noah, visions unique to the Apocryphon. The first vision is about the first generations of the created world and the destruction wrought by the Watchers and their descendants. A beautiful olive tree, symbolizing Adam and his descendants, is eventually struck down (line 16–20). In col. 14, line 9, a vision is being explained to Noah by an unidentified divine being. Noah is identified as a cedar tree, from which three shoots (Shem, Ham and Japheth) grow. Column 15's vision is eschatological and apocalyptic, featuring the destruction of the rebellious and evil by God (lines 10–12). These visions take the Apocryphon far from the Genesis base text and move it much closer to apocalyptic words like Enoch and Jubilees.

The land is divided among the sons of Noah in cols. 16 and 17. The division is loosely based on Gen 10:2–32, but has closer ties to the parallel episode in *Jub.* 8:12–9:13. Some of the place names Jubilees and the Apocryphon have in common include the Tina River, the tongue of the sea of Egypt, the Gihon River, and the Euphrates. The relationship between these two narratives remains an open question. Eshel and Machiela in particular have argued for the priority of the Apocryphon's version and Jubilees' dependence on it,

---

[25] But see Moshe J. Bernstein, "Re-Arrangement, Anticipation and Harmonization as Exegetical Features in the Genesis Apocryphon," *DSD* 3 (1996): 37–57, esp. 42.

or alternatively, their dependence on a common source.[26] Fitzmyer simply notes that the two accounts are "related."[27] Whether or not there was direct dependence of one work on the other, it is clear that both are drawing on traditions that are not part of Genesis.

Part 1 of the Apocryphon, the story of Noah, is only loosely tied to Gen 5–10, and shows equal dependence on other sources, two of which appear to be Enoch and Jubilees. Part 1 may be characterized as parabiblical, rather than rewritten scripture.[28] In Part 2, however, the Apocryphon adheres much more closely to its Genesis base text, with much more modest reworkings, although the influence of traditions also found in Jubilees remains strong.

The story of Abram probably began in col. 18, but the extant text opens in col. 19 with Abram already in the land of Canaan. Abram speaks in the first person, a deliberate parallel with the first person speech of Lamech, Enoch and Noah in Part 1. Column 19 places Abram in Bethel, where he builds an altar and worships God (Gen 12:8). Abram departs from Bethel and goes to Hebron, a location not mentioned in Genesis but found in *Jub.* 13:10. At this point we find a major expansion in the Apocryphon, found neither in Genesis nor in Jubilees:

> And I, Abram, had a dream in the night of my entering to the land of Egypt, and I saw in my dream [that there wa]s a cedar tree and a date-palm, [very beauti]ful. Some men came, seeking to cut down and uproot the cedar and leave the date-palm by itself. Now the date-palm cried out and said, "Do not cut down the cedar, for we are both sprung from one stock." So the cedar was spared by the protection of the date-palm, and it <was> not cut [down.]
> (col. 19, lines 14–19)

This dream serves an important function in the Apocryphon's narrative. In Gen 12:10–20, when Abram and Sarai sojourn in Egypt, Abram instructs Sarai to conceal the fact that he is her husband, identifying him instead as her brother. The purpose of this dubious subterfuge is to save Abram's neck; the result is that Sarai is taken into Pharaoh's harem, compromising her virtue. The story reflects poorly on the supposedly righteous Abram; the composer of the Apocryphon (or his source) attempts to remove that blemish by inserting this dream. The symbolism of the dream parallels the tree imagery found earlier in Noah's visions, and the same symbolism of

---

[26] Eshel, "The *Imago Mundi*"; Machiela, *The Dead Sea Genesis Apocryphon*, 105, 128–130.

[27] Fitzmyer, *The Genesis Apocryphon*, 173.

[28] Crawford, *Rewriting Scripture*, 14–15: "[Parabiblical] texts use a passage, event, or character from a scriptural work as a 'jumping off' point to create a new narrative or work." See also Bernstein, "The Genre(s) of the Genesis Apocryphon," 331–332.

cedar and date-palm also occurs in Ps 92:12.[29] Abram interprets the dream for Sarai in col. 19, lines 19–21. Because dreams were known to be divine messages, this dream gives God's sanction to Abram and Sarai's deception, thus clearing Abram of the charges of lying and endangering his wife (note that Jubilees omits the episode entirely).

In this section the chronology of the episodes is emphasized; Abram and Sarai are in Hebron for two years; they stay in Egypt for five years before Sarai is taken away, and she is in Pharaoh's palace for two years. This chronology accords with the chronology found in *Jub.* 13:10–16. At the end of the five years in Egypt, Abram is sought out by Pharaoh's courtiers on account of his wisdom, which is related to Enoch's wisdom (col. 19, lines 24–29). It is at this time that Sarai is discovered by the Egyptians.

The second major expansion in this section is the Egyptian Hyrcanus's praise of Sarai's beauty:

> How spend[did] and beautiful the form of her face, and how [plea]sant [and] soft the hair of her head; how lovely are her eyes, and how graceful is her nose; all the radiance of her face [ ]; how lovely is her breast, and how beautiful is all her whiteness! Her arms, how beautiful! And her hands, how perfect! And (how) attractive all the appearance of her hands! How lovely (are) her palms, and how long and dainty all the fingers of her hands. Her feet, how beautiful! How perfect are her legs! There are no virgins or brides who enter a bridal chamber more beautiful than she. Indeed, she greatly surpasses in beauty all women; and in her beauty she ranks high above all of them. Yet with all this beauty there is much wisdom in her; and whatever she has is lovely.
>
> (col. 20, lines 2–8)

This addition has been compared to the Arabic *wasf* ("description") form, and is certainly poetic.[30] It fits with a trend in late Second Temple literature towards greater interest in female beauty (as opposed to the remarkably laconic notice in Gen 12:15). Compare the description of Judith's toilet in Jdt 10:3–4, the description of Esther in the Septuagint version of Esther, Addition D, or the story of Susanna.

Pharaoh does take Sarai by force and threaten Abram's life, thus confirming Abram's dream as divinely given (col. 20, lines 9–10). Sarai's abduction triggers the third major expansion in the Apocryphon.

---

[29] Marianne Luijken Gevirtz, "Abram's Dream in the Genesis Apocryphon: Its Motifs and Their Function," *Maarav* 8 (1992): 229–243.

[30] Moshe H. Goshen-Gottstein, "Philologische Miszellen zu den Qumrantexten," *RevQ* 2 (1959–1960): 43–51; James C. VanderKam, "The Poetry of 1QApGen XX, 2–8a," *RevQ* 37 (1979): 57–66.

> I was not killed, but I wept bitterly—I, Abram, and Lot, my nephew, along with me—on the night when Sarai was taken from me by force. That night I prayed, I entreated, and I asked for mercy. In sorrow I said, as my tears ran down, "Blessed (are) you, O God Most High, my Lord, for all ages! For you are Lord and Sovereign over all! You have power to mete out justice on all the kings of the earth. Now I lodge my complaint with you, my Lord, against Pharaoh Zoan, the king of Egypt, because my wife has been taken away from me by force. Mete out justice to him for me, and show forth your great hand against him and against all his house. May he not be able to defile my wife tonight—that it may be known about you, my Lord, that you are Lord of all the kings of the earth." I wept and I talked to no one. (col. 20, lines 10–16)

Here we find Abram weeping and praying to God on Sarai's behalf, details noticeably lacking in Genesis. Lot also appears in a favorable light, weeping and praying with Abram. In fact, when, after two years, Pharaoh sends a request that Abram come and heal his household, it is Lot who reveals the source of the problem: "Abram, my uncle, will not be able to pray for the king, while his wife Sarai is with him." The episode ends as it does in Genesis, with Abram considerably richer. The Apocryphon adds the detail that Hagar was given to Sarai at this time (col. 20, line 32).

The narrative resumes with Abram's departure from Egypt and return to Canaan (Gen 13). The separation from Lot in Gen 13:5–13 triggers the last large expansion in the extant Genesis Apocryphon (col. 21, lines 5–20). In it, Abram's generosity toward Lot and his grief at his departure are emphasized. However, in line 8, God appears to Abram in a vision, promising him the land and ordering him to walk around it, in order to take possession of it symbolically, as Noah did in col. 11 (col. 21, lines 8–20).

The following parallels between the stories of Noah and Abram in the Apocryphon should be noted. Both stories have strong female characters (Bitenosh, Sarai) whose sexual purity is question, but who are ultimately justified. Both heroes have visions, are known for their wisdom, and offer appropriate sacrifices. Both traverse the land to possess it. The parallels indicate a shaping hand belonging to a redactor who wished to equate Noah, the father of the (second) humanity, and Abraham, the father of the Jews.

The last extant column of the Apocryphon, col. 22, contains the closest thing in the manuscript to a simple translation. The base text is Gen 14 and the beginning of 15. The narrative switches from first to third person, and introduces only minor changes to the base text for the purposes of modernization or clarification. For example, in Gen 14:1 Shinar is modernized to Babylon, and Ellasar to Cappadocia. In Gen 14:20 it is unclear whether Abram tithes to Melchizedek or vice versa; the Apocryphon makes it clear that Abram tithes to Melchizedek (col. 22, line 17). The reason for this sudden shift in style is uncertain. The manuscript breaks off at Gen 15:4, and we cannot be sure how far into Genesis it continued.

A major question concerning the Genesis Apocryphon is its function and purpose. Unlike the Reworked Pentateuch discussed above, the Apocryphon does not present itself as authoritative scripture. Although the beginning and the end of the manuscript is missing, it does not appear to be written in the name of Enoch, Moses, or other authoritative figure from the past. It does contain first person dialogue, but its function is dramatic rather than hortatory.[31] The fact that it was written in Aramaic indicates that it was not meant as a substitute for the Hebrew Genesis. It was found in only one copy in Cave 1 at Qumran, which implies that it was not a central document of the community that resided there. On the other hand, it does combine traditions found in works that the Qumran community did consider authoritative, Genesis, the books of Enoch, and Jubilees.[32] So if the Genesis Apocryphon was not meant to be and was not accepted as authoritative scripture, what was it?

Moshe Bernstein has recently suggested that at least one of its purposes was as a "literary narrative," that is, a didactic, entertaining work that made no claim to authority at all.[33] This suggestion is very attractive, as it seems to get to the heart of the Genesis Apocryphon's purpose: it wishes to educate its audience about important Jewish traditions with a compelling, memorable story (or stories) about familiar, important figures from their past.

COMMENTARY ON GENESIS A

This single manuscript, as its name implies, contains passages from Genesis with exegetical remarks. Its paleographical date is the last half of the first century BCE, and we possess fragments of all six of its columns.[34]

---

[31] Contrast, as an example, the Testaments of the Twelve Patriarchs.
[32] For one list of such works, see James C. VanderKam and Peter Flint, *The Meaning of the Dead Sea Scrolls: Their Significance For Understanding the Bible, Judaism, Jesus, and Christianity* (New York: HarperCollins, 2002), 178–180.
[33] Bernstein, "Genre Just Gets in the Way Anyway," who adds, "I should furthermore love to know why this narrative was composed out of the pieces that comprise it; was it intended to educate, to edify, to entertain, or some combination of those? And how did its readers receive it? We read it looking for interpretation; the ancient reader/listener may have simply been listening to a good story derived from the Bible" (n.p.).
[34] George J. Brooke, "4QCommentary on Genesis A," in *Qumran Cave 4, XVII, Parabiblical*

Commentary on Genesis A is an important example of changing methods of exegesis in the late Second Temple period, because it combines the implicit exegesis of rewritten scripture compositions such as Reworked Pentateuch or Jubilees, and the explicit, "lemma plus commentary" exegesis found in the Qumran pesharim and later rabbinic literature. The late first century BCE, when this manuscript was copied, was a transition period between the former and latter methods.[35] The first half of the Commentary, cols. 1–4, line 2, contains the implicit exegesis of rewritten scripture, while the second half contains "lemma plus commentary" exegesis. This is signaled by the use of פשרו, "its interpretation is" in col. 4, line 5, a usage unique to the Qumran pesharim.[36] It is possible that the two halves stem from two different sources, brought together by the composer/redactor of the document.

The Genesis passages on which the manuscript comments are 6:3a, 7:10–12, 7:24, 8:3–6, 8:8–14, 8:18, 9:24–25, 9:27, 11:31, 15:9, 15:17, 18:31–32, 22:10–12, 28:3–4, 36:12, 49:3–4, 49:10, and 49:20–21. The passages chosen are not random, but illustrate the themes important to the composer/redactor of the Commentary.

The first of the themes emphasized in the Commentary is chronology and calendar. The Commentary opens with a rewritten quotation of Gen 6:3a (the rewritten text is indicated by italics):

> [In] *the four hundred and eightieth year of Noah's life their end came for Noah*, and God said, "My spirit will not dwell among humanity forever," *and* their days *were determined at* one hundred and twenty years *until the time of the waters of the flood.*[37]

This abrupt beginning indicates that the composer/redactor assumed that his audience knew Genesis, and would recognize that he was only commenting on selected passages. Gen 6:3a contains a chronological ambiguity: does "their days shall be numbered one hundred and twenty years" mean that God is giving humanity 120 years to repent before bringing the flood, or does it limit the human life span to 120 years? Commentaries ancient and

---

Texts, Part 3 (ed. George J. Brooke et al.; DJD 22; Oxford: Clarendon, 1996), 185–208. There are also three smaller manuscripts that appear to be commentaries on passages from Genesis: 4Q253, 4Q254, and 4Q254a. See Brooke, *Qumran Cave 4, XVII*, 209–212, 217–236.

[35] Crawford, *Rewriting Scripture*, 130.

[36] See Timothy H. Lim, *Pesharim* (CQS 3; London: Sheffield Academic Press, 2002), 50.

[37] All translations (with slight modifications) are taken from Brooke, "4QCommentary on Genesis A."

modern have split over this question.³⁸ Commentary on Genesis A understands the passage to refer to the amount of time left before God brings the flood (although it does not mention repentance).

The Commentary continues the theme of chronology in the first two columns, dealing with the Flood. The sometimes vague chronological formulations of Genesis are made explicitly (e.g. col. 1, lines 5–10), and also importantly are made to conform to the solar, rather than the lunar, calendar. The other place where chronology surfaces is col. 2, lines 8–10, the time of Abram's sojourn in Haran.

The second major theme found in the Commentary is the land and its rightful possession.³⁹ This theme begins in the exegesis of Gen 9:24–25, when Noah, waking from his drunken stupor, realizes that his son Ham has dishonored him and so curses Ham's son Canaan. Noah's curse of Canaan explains why the Israelites are commanded to dispossess the Canaanites and take control of their land (e.g. Num 33:50–53). But it does not explain why Noah curses Canaan instead of Ham, who is, after all, the guilty party. Commentary on Genesis A answers that question thusly:

> And Noah awoke from his wine and knew what his youngest son had done to him. And he said, "Cursed be Canaan! A slave of slaves will he be to his brothers." *But he did not curse Ham, but his son, because* God blessed the sons of Noah, and in the tents of Shem may He dwell. (col. 2, lines 5–7)

This theme of the land and its possession continues through the remainder of the Commentary by contrasting those in Genesis who are dispossessed on account of bad behavior with the righteous who are rewarded. The wrongdoers include Sodom and Gomorrah (col. 3, lines 1–6), Amalek (col. 4, lines 1–3), and Reuben (col. 4, lines 3–6), while the righteous include Noah (cols. 1–2, line 7), Abraham (cols. 2, line 8 – 3, line 14), and Judah (col. 5).

The third theme, which is connected to the second, is the theme of sexual wrongdoing. All those who have lost their claim to the land are somehow guilty (even if only by association) with less than honorable sexual conduct. Canaan, as Ham's son, pays the price for Ham's sin. Amalek is the son of a concubine. Reuben violated Bilhah, his father's concubine, as is made

---

³⁸ The latter explanation is favored by Jubilees, Josephus, Pseudo-Philo, and *Gen Rab.* 26:6, while the former is found in the Targums, *Gen. Rab.* 30:7, *b. Sanhedrin*, *Avot de Rabbi Nathan*, and *Mekhilta de Rabbi Ishmael*; Moshe J. Bernstein, "4Q252: From Re-Written Bible to Biblical Commentary," *JJS* 45 (1994): 1–27, esp. 6.

³⁹ George J. Brooke, "The Thematic Content of 4Q252," *JQR* 85 (1994): 33–59, esp. 45.

clear in the exegetical comment in col. 4, lines 5–6: "Its interpretation is that he [Jacob] reproved him [Reuben] for when he slept with Bilhah his concubine."

This theme of sexual wrongdoing also ties Commentary on Genesis A more closely to the interests of the Qumran community than has been the case for either Reworked Pentateuch or the Genesis Apocryphon. Fornication is one of the "three nets of Belial" listed in the Damascus Document (CD col. 4, lines 14–18).[40] Sexual conduct, right and wrong, is a major theme throughout the sectarian documents.[41]

There are also other indications that the Commentary could be a product of the sectarian movement which included the Qumran community. The use of a chronology based on weeks and years signals an adherence to a solar calendar.[42] Another sectarian sign is the exegetical addition of the phrase באחרית הימים, "in the latter days," to a quotation of Deut 25:19 (col. 5, line 2). This phrase refers to the eschatological age and frequently occurs in sectarian texts.[43] Finally, in col. 5, line 5 the phrase אנשי היחד, "the men of the community," is found. The word היחד is one of the self-designations used by the sectarians (see, e.g., 1QS 5:1, 6:21, 7:20, 8:11, and 9:7, 10). All of these indicators lead to the conclusion that 4QCommentary on Genesis A is a product of the sectarian movement of which the Qumran community was a part.

Enoch and Aramaic Levi

These two works are parabiblical texts, that is, they use particular passages in Genesis as starting points for much more complex narratives that make liberal use of other traditions. Both Enoch and Aramaic Levi were composed prior to the foundation of the Qumran community, and appear to be central texts of the wider parent movement of which Qumran was a part.

---

[40] James H. Charlesworth, ed., *The Dead Sea Scrolls: Hebrew, Aramaic, and Greek Texts with English Translations: Damascus Document, War Scroll, and Related Documents* (PTSDSSP 2; Tübingen/Louisville: Mohr Siebeck/Westminster John Knox, 1995), 19.

[41] William Loader, *The Dead Sea Scrolls on Sexuality: Attitudes Towards Sexuality in Sectarian and Related Literature at Qumran* (Grand Rapids: Eerdmans, 2009).

[42] James C. VanderKam, *Calendars in the Dead Sea Scrolls: Measuring Time* (London: Routledge, 1998).

[43] Annette Steudel, "אחרית הימים in the Texts from Qumran," *RevQ* 16 (1993–1995): 225–246.

Enoch

The books of Enoch have come down to us in their entirety only in the form preserved as scripture by the Abyssinian Orthodox Church, 1 Enoch. 1 Enoch consists of five separate booklets: the Book of the Watchers (chs. 1–36), the Book of Parables (chs. 37–71), the Astronomical Book (chs. 72–82), the Dream Visions (chs. 83–90), and the Epistle of Enoch (chs. 91–105, with an appendix on the birth of Noah, chs. 106–107, and a concluding chapter, 108).[44] Four of these five booklets, with the exception of the Parables, were found in fragmentary form in the Qumran caves. A different fifth booklet, the Book of Giants, was discovered at Qumran.[45]

Enoch uses two Genesis passages as its starting point. Gen 5:21–24 gives the antediluvian patriarch Enoch's biographical summary:

> When Enoch had lived sixty-five years, he became the father of Methuselah. Enoch walked with God after the birth of Methuselah three hundred years, and had other sons and daughters. Thus all the days of Enoch were three hundred sixty-five years. Enoch walked with God; then he was no more, because God took him.

This passage differs from the other notices in Gen 5 in two key ways: Enoch lives only 365 years, and he does not actually die, but is mysteriously taken by God. The significance of the number 365 as the length of the solar year is obvious, and gives the composer/redactor of Enoch the basis for extensive astronomical speculation and validation for a luni-solar religious calendar. Enoch's disappearance from human society drives the tradition that places him among the angels, the privileged recipient of esoteric divine revelations that he passes on to his descendants.

The second passage is Gen 6:1–4:

> When people began to multiply on the face of the ground, and daughters were born to them, the sons of God saw that they were fair; and they took wives for themselves of all that they chose. Then the LORD said, "My spirit shall not abide in mortals forever, for they are flesh; their days shall be one hundred twenty years." The Nephilim were on the earth in those days—and

---

[44] George W.E. Nickelsburg and James C. VanderKam, *1 Enoch: A New Translation* (Minneapolis: Fortress, 2004), provide a very readable translation. For commentaries, see George W.E. Nickelsburg, *1 Enoch 1* (Hermeneia; Minneapolis: Fortress, 2001); and Loren T. Stuckenbruck, *1 Enoch 91–108* (CEJL; Berlin: de Gruyter, 2007).

[45] J.T. Milik, *The Books of Enoch: Aramaic Fragments of Qumrân Cave 4* (Oxford: Clarendon, 1976); Loren T. Stuckenbruck, *The Book of Giants from Qumran: Texts, Translation, and Commentary* (TSAJ 63; Tübingen: Mohr Siebeck, 1997).

also afterward—when the sons of God went in to the daughters of men, who bore children to them. These were the heroes that were of old, warriors of renown.

This enigmatic story becomes the basis in Enoch for the introduction of evil to the earth and the corruption of humanity, eventually resulting in the Flood. It is the centerpiece for the Book of the Watchers, in which Enoch is privy to the deed and fate of the fallen angels, and even serves as an envoy for them to God (*1 En.* 13:4–7). Material based on the Book of the Watchers appears in Jubilees, the Genesis Apocryphon, the Damascus Document, and other smaller works found in the Qumran collection.[46]

The books of Enoch were preserved in their original language, Aramaic, at Qumran and seem to have been given a scriptural status by the community. Including the Book of Giants, parts of Enoch are preserved in twenty manuscripts, the earliest dating to the early second century BCE.[47] Enoch traditions are extensively employed in the Qumran literature, as was seen in the discussion of the Genesis Apocryphon above. The luni-solar calendar advocated for in Enoch was evidently used by the community, and was a point of controversy with other Jewish groups in the period. Enoch and its traditions are central to the thought world of the Qumran community and the wider movement to which it belonged.

Aramaic Levi Document (ALD)

ALD, a work newly discovered in the Cairo Genizah and then at Qumran,[48] is, as its name suggests, based on the life of the patriarch Levi in Genesis. In Genesis, Levi is not portrayed as particularly righteous, but rather the opposite. In Gen 49:5–7 Jacob says,

> Simeon and Levi are brothers; weapons of violence are their swords.
>
> May I never come into their council; may I not be joined to their company—for in their anger they killed men, and at their whim they hamstrung oxen.
>
> Cursed be their anger, for it is fierce, and their wrath, for it is cruel! I will divide them in Jacob, and scatter them in Israel.

---

[46] Nickelsburg, *1 Enoch 1*, 77.
[47] Nickelsburg, *1 Enoch 1*, 76.
[48] H.L. Pass and J. Arendzen, "Fragment of an Aramaic Text of the Testament of Levi," *JQR* 12 (1900): 651–661; Michael E. Stone and Jonas C. Greenfield, "Aramaic Levi Document," in *Qumran Cave 4, XVII, Parabiblical Texts, Part 3* (ed. George J. Brooke et al.; DJD 22; Oxford: Clarendon, 1996), 1–72.

Further, the priesthood that is central to the identity of the tribe of Levi in Jewish tradition is never mentioned in Genesis. ALD remedies these deficiencies by stressing the origin of the cultus with Noah, the commandments for which were passed on to Abraham and culminate in Levi. Levi is righteous, and the covenant of the priesthood belongs to him and his descendants. They as priests are given a special teaching role and are credited with particular wisdom. Finally, ALD employs a 364 solar calendar, tying it to Enoch, Jubilees, and Qumran sectarian works.[49]

At Qumran, ALD was found in seven copies, all dating to the first century BCE. Its editors date its composition to the late third or early second century BCE, thus making it part of the literature inherited by the Qumran community.[50]

Miscellaneous Texts

The Qumran collection contains several, small, fragmentary texts that feature characters or events from Genesis in one way or another, further testifying to the importance of Genesis in the thought of the Qumran sect and its parent movement. They are listed here in numerical order.[51]

- 3Q7, Testament of Judah?
- 4Q215, Testament of Naphtali
- 4Q370, Admonition on the Flood
- 4Q422, Paraphrase of Genesis and Exodus
- 4Q464, Exposition on the Patriarchs
- 4Q474, Text Concerning Rachel and Joseph
- 4Q484, Testament of Judah?
- 4Q534–536, Birth of Noah Aramaic
- 4Q538, Testament of Judah Aramaic
- 4Q539, Testament of Joseph
- 4Q573, Testament of Jacob? Aramaic
- 4Q577, Text Mentioning the Flood

Although the fragmentary nature of these manuscripts makes certainty difficult, there appears to be two themes around which these texts cluster. The

---

[49] For commentary, see Jonas C. Greenfield, Michael E. Stone, and Esther Eshel, *The Aramaic Levi Document: Edition, Translation and Commentary* (SVTP 19; Leiden: Brill, 2004). See also Robert A. Kugler, *From Patriarch to Priest: The Levi-Priestly Tradition from Aramaic Levi to Testament of Levi* (SBLEJL 9; Atlanta: Society of Biblical Literature, 1996).

[50] Greenfield, Stone, and Eshel, *The Aramaic Levi Document*, 19.

[51] All bibliographic information for these manuscripts can be found in Tov, *Texts from the Judaean Desert*, 27–114.

first is Noah and the Flood, a prominent theme already in the Genesis Apocryphon and Commentary on Genesis A. The second is the words and actions of the patriarchs, again already encountered in the Genesis Apocryphon, Aramaic Levi, and Commentary on Genesis A.

CONCLUSIONS

This survey has established beyond doubt the importance of the book of Genesis in the thought world of the Qumran community and its forebears. Three themes in particular stand out. The first is the evil introduced into the world by the Watchers, which God is eventually compelled to wipe out in the Flood (thus the emphasis on Enoch and Noah in these texts). The second theme argues that both the prediluvian and postdiluvian ancestors of Israel fulfilled the Law correctly and fully before the revelation at Sinai (as seen in the actions of Noah, Abraham, and Levi), and they did this via a written revelation received from the über-righteous Enoch (who received it from the angels), which was passed down through the generations. The third theme, tied to the second, attempts to remove any suggestion of wrongdoing or bad character from the portraits of the ancestors found in Genesis (cf. Abraham).

The ultimate recipient of this non-Mosaic revelation, the chosen descendants of Noah and Abraham and the true followers of the Law, is the Community (or its parent movement) itself. Thus a direct line is established from the revelation and wisdom of Enoch to the revelation and wisdom of the Community.

SELECT BIBLIOGRAPHY

Avigad, Nahman, and Yigael Yadin. *A Genesis Apocryphon: A Scroll from the Wilderness of Judaea*. Jerusalem: Magnes Press, 1956.
Bernstein, Moshe J. "Re-Arrangement, Anticipation and Harmonization as Exegetical Features in the Genesis Apocryphon." *Dead Sea Discoveries* 3 (1996): 37–57.
Crawford, Sidnie White. *Rewriting Scripture in Second Temple Times*. Grand Rapids: Eerdmans, 2008.
Davila, James R. "Genesis, Book of." Pages 299–300 in vol. 1 of *The Encyclopedia of the Dead Sea Scrolls*. Edited by Lawrence H. Schiffman and James C. VanderKam. 2 vols. New York: Oxford University Press, 2000.
Falk, Daniel K. *The Parabiblical Texts: Strategies for Extending the Scriptures among the Dead Sea Scrolls*. Companion to the Qumran Scrolls 8. Library of Second Temple Studies 63. London: T&T Clark, 2007.

Fitzmyer, Joseph A. *The Genesis Apocryphon of Qumran Cave 1 (1Q20): A Commentary*. 3rd ed. Biblica et orientalia 18B. Rome: Pontifical Biblical Institute, 2004.
Greenfield, Jonas C., Michael E. Stone, and Esther Eshel. *The Aramaic Levi Document: Edition, Translation, and Commentary*. Studia in veteris testamenti pseudepigrapha 19. Leiden: Brill, 2004.
Hendel, Ronald S. *The Text of Genesis 1–11: Textual Studies and Critical Edition*. New York: Oxford University Press, 1998.
Kugler, Robert A. *From Patriarch to Priest: The Levi-Priestly Tradition from Aramaic Levi to Testament of Levi*. Society of Biblical Literature Early Judaism and Its Literature 9. Atlanta: Society of Biblical Literature, 1996.
Machiela, Daniel A. *The Dead Sea Genesis Apocryphon: A New Text and Translation with Introduction and Special Treatment of Columns 13–17*. Studies on the Texts of the Desert of Judah 79. Leiden: Brill, 2009.
Nickelsburg, George W.E., and James C. VanderKam. *1 Enoch: A New Translation*. Minneapolis: Fortress, 2004.
Segal, Michael H. "4QReworked Pentateuch or 4QPentateuch?" Pages 391–399 in *The Dead Sea Scrolls Fifty Years After Their Discovery: Proceedings of the Jerusalem Congress, July 20–25, 1997*. Edited by Lawrence H. Schiffman, Emanuel Tov, and James C. VanderKam. Jerusalem: Israel Exploration Society, 2000.

GENESIS AND ITS RECEPTION IN JUBILEES

C.T.R. Hayward

The Book of Jubilees in its final form comes to us as an extended narrative, the bulk of whose text reports events recorded in the biblical books Genesis and Exodus 1–16, maintaining for the most part the narrative sequence of those same books in language often closely resembling theirs.[1] This narrative incorporates extensive information not relayed by Genesis and Exodus. Most conspicuously, a precise chronological scheme orders the reported events: time is measured in "weeks of years," seven of these weeks making up a "jubilee" of forty-nine years.[2] Almost every incident reported by Genesis which Jubilees also records is dated with reference to this chronology;[3] and the lives of the main characters of Genesis, from Adam up to Joseph, are regularly punctuated with detailed notes about the times and events which involve them. Equally prominent are references to laws regulating observance of Sabbaths and festivals, sacrificial procedures, sexual conduct, and intermarriage. These laws are brought into direct association with

---

[1] This seems to be the case, although due consideration must be granted to the fact that the most complete text of Jubilees is available to us only in an Ethiopic version, itself a translation from a Greek rendering of the text out of an original Semitic language, which, since the manuscript discoveries at Qumran, can be identified as Hebrew. See James C. VanderKam, *The Book of Jubilees* (2 vols.; CSCO 510–511; Louvain: Peeters, 1989), 2:vi–xxxi. This volume contains VanderKam's English translation of Ethiopic Jubilees, from which all quotations in this essay are taken. Jubilees 50:6–12 may refer to aspects of Sabbath law presented in Exod 16, though this is not entirely clear; the account of events at the Passover of Egypt given in Exod 12, however, are certainly utilised by the book. The final form of the book as represented in the Ethiopic witnesses translated by VanderKam will be the subject of this essay.

[2] The laws of the biblical "jubilee" are set out in Lev 25, where the "jubilee" occupies the fiftieth year following a period of seven times seven years. The Book of Jubilees, by contrast, understands a "jubilee" to be a forty-nine year period; but it significantly dates Israel's Exodus from Egypt and her entry into the Land of Israel in the fiftieth jubilee, thus recalling the biblical model. On this, see James C. VanderKam, "Das chronologische Konzept des Jubiläenbuches," *ZAW* 107 (1995): 81–85; and Martha Himmelfarb, *A Kingdom of Priests: Ancestry and Merit in Ancient Judaism* (Philadelphia: University of Pennsylvania Press, 2006), 53–54.

[3] This also applies to incidents not recorded in Genesis and reported by Jubilees, such as Isaac's cursing of the Philistines during the first year of the first week of the 44th jubilee (see 24:21–38), and the Israelites' battle against the Amorite kings (34:1–9) in the sixth year of the sixth week of the 44th jubilee.

characters familiar from the Genesis narrative, Jubilees interpreting or adducing incidents in their lives mentioned by Genesis to tell the reader how the laws came to be known, introduced, and understood. Some of these laws are said to be inscribed on "the heavenly tablets": these celestial writings contain a range of information besides legal rulings, some of which Jubilees evidently reports to its readers.[4] Indeed, Jubilees refers to considerable numbers of documents by name, often in discussion of items which do not feature, or feature only occasionally, in Genesis and Exodus 1–16, such as priesthood, the heavenly world, polemic against idolatry, and evil spirits.[5] Thus, for example, the reader is told about writings of Enoch on a variety of topics (4:17–23); inscriptions of the ancients recording the lore of the Watchers discovered by Kainan (8:2–4); a book in Noah's possession recording the division of the earth's territories among his descendants (8:11–12); a book on medicines which Noah himself composed, and other books belonging to him (10:13–14);[6] books written in Hebrew belonging to Abraham's father Terah (12:27; see also 21:7, 10); and seven tablets presented by an angel to Jacob relating the future for him and his descendants, which he is said to have copied and given to Levi (32:36; 45:16). Jacob

---

[4] Thus, for example, these tablets also record divine judgment of the angels (5:13); the name of Isaac (16:3); the status of Abraham as "friend of God" (19:9); and Isaac's blessing of Levi and Judah (31:32). On their contents, see F. García Martínez, "The Heavenly Tablets in the Book of Jubilees," in *Studies in the Book of Jubilees* (ed. Matthias Albani, Jörg Frey, and Armin Lange; TSAJ 65; Tübingen: Mohr Siebeck, 1997), 243–260. The heavenly tablets may be closely associated, or even identical, with the "tablets of the divisions of the years" (*Jub.* 1:29). For detailed discussion of this matter in relation to CD 16:3–4 and other Qumran texts, see Devorah Dimant, "What is 'The Book of the Divisions of Times'?," in *Connected Vessels: The Dead Sea Scrolls and the Literature of the Second Temple Period*, Asuppot III (Jerusalem: Bialik Institute, 2010 [Hebrew]), 97–109. *Pace* Cara Werman, "'The תורה and the תעודה' engraved on the Tablets," *DSD* 9 (2002): 75–103; Jubilees gives no indication that it is a copy of the heavenly tablets: everything the reader is told about these is merely reported in speeches of the angel of the presence delivered to Moses. It is these words of the angel, not the wording of the heavenly tablets, which the narrator claims to relay to the reader. I am indebted for this observation to Alex Samely (private communication).

[5] The number of books and documents listed in those parts of Jubilees which overlap with the Genesis narrative is truly astonishing, given that Genesis only once mentions a book (Gen 5:1). Documents named by Jubilees are time and again associated with characters whom Jubilees regards as priests: see Himmelfarb, *Kingdom of Priests*, 58–59. There are also references to heavenly documents besides the heavenly tablets: see 30:22–23, where there is mention of "the book of the living" and "the book of those who will be destroyed," and of a "written notice" in heaven that Jacob's sons had rightly destroyed Shechem.

[6] On the vexed question whether a Book of Noah as such existed (see 1QapGen 5.29, and MS Athos Koutloumous 39), see Loren T. Stuckenbruck, *1 Enoch 91–108* (CEJL; Berlin: de Gruyter, 2007), 610–612.

is also said (*Jub.* 39:6) to have read to his son Joseph "the words of Abraham," which contained a law against adultery, for commission of which the death penalty "has been ordained ... in heaven before the most high Lord."[7]

This additional information, which extends to amplified and often idealized portraits of known biblical characters and their lives, is related within a framework recognizable as closely related to Genesis and Exodus 1–16. Likewise, Jubilees almost certainly refers directly to the Hebrew Scriptures at 4:30, when it cites God's words to Adam about the tree of knowledge: "on the day that you eat from it you will die" (Gen 2:17), and again at 33:12, where it cites the wording of the law of Deut 27:20 in its account of Reuben and Bilhah. In this last instance, the narrator states that this law, directed against incest, is written "a second time": this follows the narrator's earlier implicit citation of Lev 20:11, where we learn that the law is written on the heavenly tablets. An implicit quotation of Exod 24:12 is also discernible in the title of Jubilees and in the opening verse of the book. The "book of the first law" (*Jub.* 6:22; see also 2:24), written for Moses by an angel, seems most likely to refer to the Hebrew Scriptures.

The reader is thus presented with a text containing both scriptural and non-scriptural information within a narrative framework provided by the books Genesis and Exodus 1–16. Consequently, Jubilees is not uncommonly presented as a prime example of "re-written Scripture" or "re-written Bible."[8] Whether or not this, or a similar label, may properly be attached to Jubilees, this text undoubtedly offers its readers a very particular understanding of

---

[7] Given the large number of documents cited in its text, it is hard to see how Jubilees could be identical with the heavenly tablets (see above, n. 4); and the explicit referencing of so many documents strongly suggests that Jubilees is taking care not to identify itself as a whole with any one or group of them; again, I owe this observation to Alex Samely in private communication.

[8] The variegated meanings ascribed to these terms and the propriety of their uses as genre labels are subject of intense current discussion; see, for example, James C. VanderKam, "Revealed Literature in the Second Temple Period," in *From Redemption to Canon: Studies in the Hebrew Bible and Second Temple Literature* (JSJSup 62; Leiden: Brill, 2002), 1–30; Moshe J. Bernstein, "'Rewritten Bible': A Generic Category Which Has Outlived its Usefulness?," *Textus* 22 (2005): 169–196; Daniel K. Falk, *The Parabiblical Texts: Strategies for Extending Scriptures among the Dead Sea Scrolls* (London: T&T Clark, 2007); Antti Laato and Jacques Van Ruiten, eds., *Rewritten Bible Reconsidered: Proceedings of the Conference in Karkku, Finland, August 24–26 2006* (SRB 1; Turku: Åbo Akademi, 2008); and Sidnie White Crawford, *Rewriting Scripture in Second Temple Times* (Grand Rapids: Eerdmans, 2008). For critical discussion and a judicious analysis of the views expressed in these and other studies, see Daniel A. Machiela, "Once More, with Feeling: Rewritten Scripture in Ancient Judaism—A Review of Recent Developments," *JJS* 61 (2010): 308–320.

the book of Genesis; and the manner in which it presents itself as a text to those readers will repay some initial investigation.

How Jubilees Presents Itself

All witnesses to Jubilees provide the text with a title or prologue not included in the traditional enumeration of the book's chapters and verses, but which is quite separate from what follows it. It describes the text as "the words regarding the divisions of the times of the law and of the testimony, of the events of the years, of the weeks of their jubilees throughout all the years of eternity." These, we are informed, were told to Moses on Mount Sinai when he went up there to receive the tables of stone, the law and the commandments, at the Lord's request "that he should come up to the summit of the mountain."[9] This title announces the close integration of chronology and legal matters which pervades Jubilees, and is informative in more than one respect. First, Gen 1:14 tells how God created the luminaries on the fourth day of creation to divide between light and darkness and to serve as signs, set feasts, days, and years. It says nothing of weeks and jubilees, which will feature so prominently in the Book of Jubilees itself; rather, the regulations for these are found in Lev 25, which will inform much of what Jubilees has to say about chronology. The narrator of the bulk of the text of Jubilees, from 2:1b to 50:13, is an "angel of the presence" (see *Jub.* 2:1), who as a matter of course will introduce information from other Pentateuchal books into the re-working of the Genesis narrative. A well known example of this procedure is found already at *Jub.* 3:8–14, which directly applies the laws of impurity following childbirth set out in Lev 12:2–5 to the period of time which needed to elapse between the creation of Adam on the one hand and Eve on the other before they could be admitted to the Garden of Eden.[10]

---

[9] This seems to be a citation of Exod 24:12, and it is of interest to note that Targum Pseudo-Jonathan of that verse explains the "tablets of stone" as conveying information not only about the traditional 613 commandments, but also "the rest of the words of the Torah." On the connections between this Targum and information contained in Jubilees, see C.T.R. Hayward, "Jacob's Second Visit to Bethel in Targum Pseudo-Jonathan," in *A Tribute to Geza Vermes: Essays on Jewish and Christian Literature and History* (ed. Philip R. Davies and Richard T. White; JSOTSup 100; Sheffield, JSOT Press, 1990), 185–188.

[10] *Jub.* 8:19 explicitly identifies the Garden of Eden with the Sanctuary, which a woman after childbirth may not enter until she is purified (Lev 12:4). The time required for purification is forty days after the birth of a male child, eighty after the birth of a female (Lev 12:1–5). See further John R. Levison, *Portraits of Adam in Early Judaism from Sirach to 2 Baruch* (JSPSup 1; Sheffield: Sheffield Academic Press, 1988), 93–94, 215.

Second, in mentioning "the events of the years," the title contrives to suggest Jubilees' concern with a broader history, which finds further expression in a number of tacit references to the other books of the Hebrew Scriptures found throughout its narrative. These allusions are common, and sometimes dramatic. Examples include *Jub.* 17:15–17, which recounts how Mastema, the prince of the demons, persuaded the Almighty to order Abraham to sacrifice Isaac his son: the implicit reference to Satan's activity in Job 1:6–12 is unmistakeable, and arises from very close and careful reading of both scriptural texts, which permitted the judicious introduction of extra-scriptural information.[11] Abraham's ridicule of idol-worshippers reported in *Jub.* 22:18 presents the latter addressing idols as gods, in words which clearly recall Jer 2:27. Verses from Ps 90 likewise inform the discourse about the span of human life in *Jub.* 23:9–15, the last verse of which offers an unambiguous reference to Ps 90:10. The description of Abraham as "the friend of God" in *Jub.*19:9 is well known from Isa 41:8. In short, there is abundant evidence to show that Jubilees made use of Hebrew Scriptures outside the Pentateuch and saw no difficulty in blending them into the narrative structure of the work.[12] Thereby the narrator manages to broaden very considerably the scope and remit of the scriptural Genesis.

Finally, the title of Jubilees presents the delivery of this text into the public domain as unambiguously tied to a person, a time, and a place. The place is Mount Sinai, and the first chapter of Jubilees will tell us more about its relationship to the writing of Jubilees, as we shall see presently. The full significance of Sinai for Jubilees, however, can be properly appreciated only when that mountain's intimate link to Mount Zion and the Garden of Eden is taken into account; for according to *Jub.* 4:26, Mounts Sinai and Zion make up two of the "four places on earth that belong to the Lord," the first named

---

[11] See Devorah Dimant, "The Biblical Basis of Non-Biblical Additions: The Binding of Isaac in *Jubilees* in Light of the Story of Job," in *Connected Vessels: The Dead Sea Scrolls and the Literature of the Second Temple Period*, Asuppot III (Jerusalem: Bialik Institute, 2010 [Hebrew]), 348–368.

[12] The designation "angel of the presence" for the narrator of *Jub.* 2:1b–50:13 most probably derives from Isa 63:9, where the MT can be read as speaking of "the angel of his (viz. God's) presence" acting to save Israel; see the Vulgate and Peshitta translations of this verse, and compare with them Targum Jonathan of the verse. For further discussion of this verse in Jewish exegesis, see Peter Kuhn, *Gottes Trauer und Klage in der rabbinischen Überlieferung (Talmud und Midrasch)* (AGJU 13; Leiden: Brill, 1978), 323–327. The "angels of holiness" or angels of sanctification, who also feature prominently in Jubilees, are quite likely to be, or to include in their number, the seraphim mentioned in Isa 6:2–3. See further James C. VanderKam, "The Angels of the Presence in the Book of Jubilees," *DSD* 7 (2000): 378–393.

of which is the Garden of Eden. Furthermore, Sinai is the middle of the desert, and Zion "is in the middle of the navel of the earth":[13] so we learn from *Jub.* 8:19, which also reports that the Garden of Eden is the holy of holies and the Lord's residence, and these three, "the one facing the other— were created as holy (places)." Thus Mounts Sinai and Zion, which play no role in the narrative of Genesis as presented by the Hebrew Bible, can be drawn into Jubilees' representation of the Genesis story precisely because of their direct affinity with the Garden of Eden: they are holy places facing one another, in some mysterious sense corresponding to one another, each the place of the divine presence.[14] While Genesis says nothing of Adam as a priest, Jubilees presents him as offering up incense as he departed from the Garden of Eden, underscoring Eden's status as sanctuary.[15] Jubilees presents Moses as the one human being involved in the delivery of its text, at the time when he ascended Sinai to receive the Torah and the commandments. This person, the place, and the time are named in language strongly redolent of Exod 24:12, with its mention of ascent of the mountain Sinai, the tablets of stone, the Torah and the commandments; and it should be recalled that Exod 24:12 follows immediately the making of a covenant between God and Israel which required the construction of an altar, the appointment of young men to act as sacrificing priests, the oblation of whole burnt offerings, and the sprinkling of blood, and the appearing of God in majesty (Exod 24:4– 11). In short, Sinai operated as the sanctuary of the Lord at that time,[16] just as Zion with its Temple would function later, and as the Garden of Eden operated from the beginning.

---

[13] The notion that Zion (and thus its temple) was in the navel of the earth may be related to another prophetic source, this time Ezek 38:12; 5:5; see also *1 En.* 26:1. For discussion of this topic, see the classic treatment of A.J. Wensinck, *The Idea of the Western Semites concerning the Navel of the Earth* (Amsterdam: Verhandelingen der K. Akademie van Wettenschappen, 1917); Philip S. Alexander, "Jerusalem as the Omphalos," in *Jerusalem: Its Sanctity and Centrality in Judaism, Christianity, and Islam* (ed. Lee I. Levine; New York: Continuum, 1990), 104–119; and Jonathan Klawans, *Purity, Sacrifice, and the Temple: Symbolism and Supersessionism in the Study of Ancient Judaism* (Oxford: Oxford University Press, 2006), 124, 283.

[14] For the significance of the sanctuary and its service in Jubilees, see C.T.R. Hayward, *The Jewish Temple: A Non-biblical Sourcebook* (London: Routledge, 1996), 85–107; see 89–91 for discussion of it relationship to the Garden of Eden.

[15] The "trigger" for this exegesis is most probably Gen 3:24 with its reference to the Cherubim (a feature of the later Temple of Solomon) stationed at the entrance to Eden. On this episode, see James C. VanderKam, "Adam's Incense Offering (Jubilees 3:27)," in *Meghillot: Studies in the Dead Sea Scrolls V–VI—A Festschrift for Devorah Dimant* (ed. Moshe Bar-Asher and Emanuel Tov; Jerusalem: Bialik Institue, 2007), *141–*156.

[16] See further Nahum M. Sarna, *The JPS Torah Commentary: Exodus* (Philadelphia: Jewish Publication Society, 1991/5751), 105–107.

Since the sanctuary provides a link between the heavenly and the earthly realms, it is most suitable for revelation of heavenly instruction and lore. The text of Jubilees, however, remains somewhat reticent about certain details of the revelation it contains. If the title of Jubilees suggests trajectories for the forthcoming re-presentation of Genesis, its first chapter directs its readers towards an ultimate goal beyond the scope of Genesis. From *Jub.* 1:1 up to and including 2:1a, the reader hears the voice of an anonymous narrator, announcing the Lord's command to Moses to ascend Sinai on the sixteenth day of the first month of the first year of the departure from Egypt of the children of Israel.[17] There is no mention of "Israel" in Hebrew Scripture until Gen 32:29; but Jubilees sets forth this name as defining the starting point of its chronology. From the viewpoint of the anonymous narrator, who is talking of events at Sinai, the name "Israel" is evidently already known; but its prime position in *Jub.* 1:1 is not fully accounted for by this observation alone: it is illuminated by that same narrator's implication and involvement of this very name in the actual presentation of the text of Jubilees to the reader. This occurs in *Jub.* 1:28–29, just before the voice of the anonymous narrator is replaced by the voice of the angel of the presence, who will act as narrator of the whole text from 2:1b until 50:13. This angel is told by the Lord to "dictate"[18] for Moses events from the beginning of creation until the temple is built for all eternity, when the Lord will appear in the sight of all, "and all will know that I am the God of *Israel*, the father of Jacob's children, and the king on Mt. Zion for the ages of eternity" (*Jub.* 1:28). The next verse tells how this angel, now further defined as the one "who was going along in front of the *Israelite* camp,"[19] took the tablets which contained the information about the divisions of the years from the beginning "until the time of the new creation" when the Lord's temple will be created in Jerusalem in Zion (*Jub.* 1:29). The status and function of "Israel" as implicated in the beginning

---

[17] This anonymous narrator cannot be identified as an angel, Moses, or the Almighty; and at no point in his/her narrative does s/he claim that the words of the angel of the presence in 2:1b–50:13 represent a quotation from a *document*.

[18] VanderKam, *Jubilees*, 6 notes that the Ethiopic text of *Jub.* 1:27 has God telling the angel to "write" these events: he points out that verses such as *Jub.* 1:27; 30:12, 21; 50:5, 13 present the angel of presence as being responsible for writing the book, while *Jub.* 1:5, 7, 26; 2:1; 23:32; 33:18 ascribe this task to Moses. For his decision to read "dictate" in this verse, see James C. VanderKam, "The Putative Author of the Book of Jubilees," *JSS* 26 (1981): 209–217.

[19] The reference may be to Exod 14:19, which tells how the angel who went in front of Israel as they journeyed through the desert went behind Israel and, along with the pillar of cloud, separated and protected the Israelites from the Egyptian army. On the other hand, this may be the angel of Exod 23:21, of whom the Lord says: "my name is in him," and who leads Israel into the Land to destroy the sanctuaries and cults of the Gentiles.

and end of time could hardly be more emphatically expressed; yet within the following narrative spoken by the angel of the presence Israel's status is, indeed, further enhanced. Properly to understand Jubilees' approach to Genesis, it is crucial that we have a clear idea of how that text envisages Israel.

Israel in the Narrative of the Angel of the Presence

This narrative opens with a bare mention of the six days of creation, and then moves immediately to signal the Sabbath day:[20] after the works made during the six days, God "kept Sabbath on the seventh day. He sanctified it for all ages and set it as a sign for all his works" (*Jub.* 2:1). Israel alone on earth is to keep this Sabbath, just as the angels of the presence and the angels of sanctification alone in heaven observe it; and just as the Sabbath is blessed and sanctified, so are those who keep it. Such is the burden of *Jub.* 2:26–33, which thus effectively writes Israel into the account of creation at the beginning of the angelic narrator's story. This same story also concludes with mention of both Israel and Sabbath together once more: *Jub.* 50:1–13 sets out legislation for this holy day, Israel being explicitly named at 50:5, 9, 10, and 13. There is one final point of exceptional importance: *Jub.* 50:9 declares of the Sabbath that it is "to be the day of the holy kingdom for all Israel throughout all time." This reference to kingship at the end of the text will alert the attentive reader to words of the anonymous narrator of *Jub.* 1:28 predicting the Lord's future presence on Zion as king for all eternity. These references to kingship serve not only to bring together the two narrators in a common enterprise, but also to highlight the royal elements in Jubilees' narrative. Once again, a theme almost entirely absent from Genesis (and from Exod 1–16) is brought to the reader's attention as significant for the meaning of Genesis as Jubilees understands that text.[21]

---

[20] Sabbath, of course, is not named in the narrative of Genesis until Gen 2:2–3 at the end of the first account of creation; by introducing it very early in the narration, Jubilees is able to set it neatly alongside Israel both chronologically and thematically. For Sabbath as a key organizing principle in the Book of Jubilees, see Lutz Doering, "The Concept of the Sabbath in the Book of Jubilees," in *Studies in the Book of Jubilees* (ed. Matthias Albani, Jörg Frey, and Armin Lange; TSAJ 65; Tübingen: Mohr Siebeck, 1997), 179–205, who notes (195) Jubilees' maximalist interpretation of the law forbidding work, and its application of the law of *karet* (Exod 31:14).

[21] Genesis often mentions Gentile kings, but only twice does it speak of kings of Israelite stock. On both occasions, a prophetic type of prediction is in view. Thus at Gen 17:6, God

It will be helpful to record here the further information which Jubilees provides about Israel: the name itself is not at all common in the mouth of the angelic narrator, and appears significantly concentrated in discourses on particular themes. The first of these is the covenant of circumcision, whose institution is recorded without any reference to the name "Israel" in Gen 17:1–14. Following his re-telling of the story set out in Genesis, the angel manages to introduce that name on some six occasions as he expounds the significance of the rite (*Jub.* 15:28–33). At the same time, he reveals a crucial item of information not given by Genesis, that the angels of the presence and the angels of holiness were created circumcised, and that Israel shares this privilege with them (15:27). The angel accordingly commands Moses to instruct the Israelites "to keep this sign of the covenant ... because the command has been ordained as a covenant so that they should keep it for ever on all the Israelites" (*Jub.* 15:28–29). It indicates God's choice of Israel out of all other peoples and their holy status: while spirits rule over the other nations, the Lord alone is Israel's ruler, no angel or spirit having this privilege (*Jub.* 15:31–32).[22] This discourse ends, however, with a warning that Israel will in future abandon circumcision, with calamitous consequences (*Jub.* 15:33–34). In the course of all this, we learn that this ordinance is set on the heavenly tablets, and permits no "circumcising of days" for the performance of the rite, that is, no shortening of the period of eight days after the birth of the child which are set for the observance (*Jub.* 15:25). Gen 17:14, on which this ruling is based, lacks in the Masoretic Hebrew text any reference to the eighth day as the time for the performance of the rite; but such a command is to be found in the Samaritan Pentateuch and the

---

promises to Abraham kings among his descendants, at the very time he accepts the covenant of circumcision. As we see here, circumcision elicits emphatic references to "Israel" on Jubilees' part. The second text, Gen 35:11, presents God informing Jacob that kings shall come forth from him: this prediction is made immediately following Jacob's change of name to Israel (Gen 35:9). The royal aspects of Israel, therefore, Jubilees can further explore, with special reference to Judah as the progenitor or the royal line in additions to the Genesis narrative such as 31:18–20, where Isaac blesses his grandson Judah in words recalling God's blessing of Abraham in Gen 12:3.

[22] A clear distinction is thus drawn between Israel and the other nations, who are not like the two highest orders of angels, and over whom "spirits" have dominion; such a notion is suggested by Deut 32:8–9, where the Lord alone appears as Israel's ruler, the nations by implication being divided among other rulers. The point is made more sharply in the LXX than in the MT. See Cécile Dogniez and Marguerite Harl, *La Bible d'Alexandrie V: Le Deutéronome* (Paris: Cerf, 1992), 325–326.

Septuagint of this verse.[23] Here, once more, chronology and legal ruling are bound together. The narrator also insists that non-circumcision entails non-membership of Abraham's people, and such of his descendants who fail to perform it are destined *for destruction and uprooting* from the earth (*Jub.* 15:26). This is strongly underlined: in 15:28, Moses is told to command Israel to keep this sign of the covenant lest they be uprooted from the earth; and it applies only to "Israel" as defined in this section of the text, namely, those who are not the descendants of Ishmael, his sons, and his brothers, or of Esau (15:30).

The name Israel likewise looms large in Jubilees' re-presentation of the story of Dinah's rape recorded in Gen 34:1–31. In the biblical story, the name Israel occurs but once (Gen 34:7), and the deaths of Hamor, Shechem, and all the men of their city at the hands of Simeon and Levi (Gen 34:25–26), followed by the plunder of that city undertaken by their brothers (Gen 34:27–29), earns the censure of their father Jacob (Gen 34:30). Jubilees brings Israel to the centre of this narrative, using the proper noun and its corresponding adjective no fewer than sixteen times,[24] and praises the conduct of Simeon and Levi for rescuing their sister Dinah from sexual relations with Gentiles. It is one of the best known examples of the sometimes quite radical ways in which Jubilees can make use of information from Genesis: in this instance, the narrator's explicit use of the law forbidding an Israelite to give any of his seed to "cross over" to Molech (Lev 18:21; see also Lev 20:2), interpreted as a prohibition of sexual relations with Gentiles, is both illustrated and reinforced by re-telling of the Genesis account of Dinah and her fate.[25] Indeed, the narrator adds a stark warning at *Jub.* 30:15–16, and points out that those who give women to foreigners, or those who condone such activity, defile the Lord's sanctuary, profane his name, and condemn the whole nation because of "all this impurity and this contamination." As a consequence, God will not accept any of Israel's sacrificial offerings in the sanctuary.[26] It was Levi's decisive action in preventing such a thing befalling Israel in the matter of Dinah that merited his election to the priesthood, a privilege

---

[23] See R.H. Charles, "The Book of Jubilees," in *The Apocrypha and Pseudepigrapha of the Old Testament* (ed. R.H. Charles; 2 vols. Oxford: Clarendon, 1912–1913), 1:36.

[24] See *Jub.* 30:5 (twice), 6 (twice), 7 (three times), 8, 9, 10, 11, 13 (twice), 14, 16, 17.

[25] Jubilees' interpretation of this verse is discussed in relation to Targumic and Midrashic explanations by Geza Vermes, "Leviticus 18:21 in Ancient Jewish Bible Exegesis," in *Studies in Aggadah, Targum and Jewish Liturgy in Memory of Joseph Heinemann* (ed. Jacob J. Petuchowski and Ezra Fleischer; Jerusalem: Magnes, 1981), 108–124.

[26] On this point, see further Himmelfarb, *Kingdom of Priests*, 69–72.

extended to his descendants who will serve before the Lord on earth like the angels in heaven (*Jub.* 30:18–21). At stake in this episode is Israel's genealogical integrity, which Jubilees understood in light of its repeated conviction that Israel is "the holy seed."[27]

Jubilees' frequent use of the name Israel in the context of regulations for Passover is to be expected, given that this name has been well established by the time they are promulgated.[28] There is, however, an important addition to the laws of Passover which directly relates to the text's presentation of the Genesis narrative. This is the note in *Jub.* 49:2, stating that on the night of the Passover in Egypt "all the forces of Mastema" were sent to kill the first-born:[29] it was the blood of the Passover lamb which prevented them from entering the houses of Israel while they were celebrating the Passover. Thus, all the forces of Mastema "passed over all the Israelites. The plague did not come on them to destroy any of them" (*Jub.* 49:4). Mastema, leader of the spirits (*Jub.* 10:8), seems determined to thwart God's plans for Israel:[30] most significantly, it is "Prince Mastema" who persuades God to test Abraham's loyalty by ordering him to sacrifice his son Isaac in the same manner that Satan urged God to test Job (*Jub.* 17:16–18). This event occurred on the twelfth day of the first month (*Jub.* 17:13), and Abraham reached the place of sacrifice three days later (*Jub.*18:3). Although the feast

---

[27] For the "holy seed," see *Jub.* 16:17, 18, 26–27,30; 21:24; 22:11–12, 13, 27; 25:12, 18; and compare 31:14–15. Further discussion of this may be found in Betsy Halpern-Amaru, *The Empowerment of Women in the Book of Jubilees* (JSJSup 60; Leiden: Brill, 1999), 154–159, who regards Jubilees' emphasis on Israel's genealogy as arising from its perception of the nation as a kingdom of *priests* and a holy people (Exod 19:6), priestly office being handed down in families whose genealogies must be secure; and Christine E. Hayes, *Gentile Impurities and Jewish Identities: Intermarriage and Conversion from the Bible to the Talmud* (New York: Oxford University Press, 2002), 27–33, 73–81, who also points to the strong priestly ideology bound up with "the holy seed." See also, on the whole episode, Cara Werman, "Jubilees 30: Building a Paradigm for the Ban on Intermarriage," *HTR* 90 (1997): 1–22.

[28] See *Jub.* 49:4, 6, 8, 10, 13, 14, 15, 16, 18, and 22. By this point in the narrative, the angel is re-presenting information which overlaps with the book of Exodus.

[29] The idea is very close to that expressed in Ps 78:49 with its description of the "angels of evil ones" (so MT) or "evil angels" (LXX) operating in Egypt at that time.

[30] On Mastema, see Devorah Dimant, "New Light from Qumran on the Jewish Pseudepigrapha—4Q390," in *The Madrid Qumran Congress: Proceedings of the International Congress on the Dead Sea Scrolls, Madrid 18–21 March 1991* (ed. Julio Trebolle Barrera and Luis Vegas Montaner; 2 vols.; STDJ 2; Leiden: Brill, 1992), 2:408–448, esp. 437–445; Esther Eshel, "Mastema's Attempt on Moses' Life in the 'Pseudo-Jubilees' Text from Masada," *DSD* 10 (2003): 359–364; and Archie T. Wright, *The Origin of Evil Spirits: The Reception of Genesis 6:1–4 in Early Jewish Literature* (WUNT 2/198; Tübingen: Mohr Siebeck, 2005), 157–160.

of Passover is not directly mentioned in these chapters, it seems clear that Jubilees dated the activity of Mastema, and the loyal response of Abraham and Isaac, to that very time. At the moment that Abraham took up the knife to kill his son, the angelic narrator speaks in the first person: "Then I stood in front of him and in front of the Prince Mastema,"[31] and the Lord ordered Abraham not to slay his son. The prince Mastema, says the narrator, was put to shame (*Jub.* 18:12). The presence of Mastema here, and the integration of this character into the larger narrative of Genesis as given by Jubilees, will require further investigation; for the present, the threat which this spirit represents to Israel until the time of the Passover of Egypt should be noted.

Jubilees' account of the matter of Bilhah, where sexual misconduct is again a central concern, must be considered. Genesis reports in one brief verse (35:22) that Reuben had relations with his father's concubine Bilhah: this is preceded and followed with reference to Israel, who in this verse is Jacob the Patriarch. Jubilees massively expands this report, with graphic details of Reuben's sexual assault on Bilhah (33:3–6), Bilhah's declaration that she is impure as a result of it (33:7), and an account of Jacob's anger (33:8). Jubilees throughout refers to Jacob by this name: he is not called Israel. *Jub.* 33:9 insists that Jacob never approached Bilhah again, "because Reuben had defiled her." So much for the event, which is followed by an extended comment (*Jub.* 33:9b–12) implicitly invoking the law of Lev 20:11, which prescribes the death penalty for one who has intercourse with his father's wife. This is followed by a quotation of Deut 27:20 and its declaration that such a man is cursed. "Israel" features, not as Patriarch, but as nation, in the orders which the angelic narrator now gives to Moses, who is told to emphasise these commandments to the Israelites (*Jub.* 33:13), indicating that anyone in Israel guilty of similar misconduct is to be put to death "because he is despicable and impure" (*Jub.* 33:14). No-one, says the angel, is to undermine these laws by claiming that Reuben was not subjected to the death penalty: the law had only been revealed in part in his lifetime (*Jub.* 33:15–16). Rather, it is an eternal law, and those who break it "are to be uprooted among the people." Moses must warn his people not to break it, so that they shall not be "destroyed or uprooted from the earth" (*Jub.* 33:19). The upshot of all this is given in *Jub.* 33:20, which declares that no sin is

---

[31] The expressions and ideas employed here recall Dan 10:10–14, 20–21, which perhaps supplies Jubilees with an "intertext" at this point.

greater than sexual impurity, "Because Israel is a holy people for the Lord its God. It is the nation which he possesses; it is a priestly nation; it is a priestly kingdom; it is what he owns."[32]

In all these sections of Jubilees where "Israel" is repeatedly named, the language of "destruction" and "uprooting" is encountered. This terminology is not found in Genesis. For Jubilees, however, an Israelite who is not circumcised is destined for "destruction and uprooting" (15:26); an Israelite who marries a Gentile will be recorded "in the book of those who will be destroyed and with those who will be uprooted from the earth" (30:22); and one who fails to offer the Passover sacrifice is to be uprooted (49:9). The supreme importance of these ordinances is underscored by their being written on the heavenly tablets (15:25; 30:9–10; 33:10; 49:8), and by emphatic declarations that these things serve to separate Israel from the other nations, as a people owned and ruled by the Lord.

Mention of destruction leads to what, perhaps, is the most dramatic introduction of the name Israel into Jubilees' re-presentation of the Genesis narrative. Before the story of Noah and the great flood, Gen 6:1–4 tells how the sons of God cohabited with human women, and how giants appeared on the earth. *Jub.* 5:1–7 elaborates this brief narrative. The reader is told that the sons of God were angels of the Lord; that the giants were their children; that the whole natural order had become corrupted; that God's anger was directed against these angels and their offspring; and that the divine judgment against them was inscribed on the heavenly tablets (*Jub.* 5:13).[33] Without warning, the reader is told that it has been written and ordained about the Israelites, that God will forgive them and pardon their sins if they turn to him; and all who turn aside from their sins once each year

---

[32] It is striking that Jubilees speaks of the pollution and impurity of persons who are complicit in sexual misconduct rather than of the defilement of the land, which is in view in the scriptural laws of Lev 18:24–30. See Jacob Milgrom, "The Concept of Impurity in Jubilees and in the Temple Scroll," *RevQ* 16 (1993–1994): 277–284. On the Bilhah story in particular, see Gary A. Anderson, "The Status of the Torah before Sinai: The Retelling of the Bible in the Damascus Covenant and the Book of Jubilees," *DSD* 1 (1994): 19–29.

[33] For the depiction of angels and spirits in other texts of the Second Temple period—notably 1 Enoch, *Aramaic Levi*, 1QapGen and other Qumran texts, and the relationship of these texts to Jubilees—see Todd R. Hanneken, "Angels and Demons in the Book of Jubilees and Contemporary Apocalypses," *Henoch* 28 (2006): 11–25; and Jacques van Ruiten, "Angels and Demons in the Book of Jubilees," in *Deuterocanonical and Cognate Literature Yearbook 2007: Angels: The Concept of Celestial Beings—Origins, Development and Reception* (ed. Friedrich Vinzenz Reiterer, Tobias Nicklas, and Karin Schöpflin; Berlin: de Gruyter, 2007), 585–609.

will receive his mercy (*Jub.* 5:17–18).[34] The story of the flood, which destroys everything, and the rescue of Noah and his family are now related. However, events after the flood are presented so as to accommodate Israel, named on five separate occasions, and a mass of information not included in Genesis is given.[35] Noah's sacrifice on leaving the ark (Gen 8:20–21) is expanded with a wealth of technical detail; but it is the divine command not to eat blood (Gen 9:4–6) which Jubilees reinforces as of special significance for Israel. First, *Jub.* 6:7–8 reiterates the commandment, but incorporates within it the declaration that "the vital force of all animate beings is in the blood" (*Jub.* 6:7). This statement derives from Lev 17:11, with its assertion that the Lord appointed blood upon the altar to make purgation of sins. Consequently, Jubilees makes it abundantly plain that use of blood is entirely restricted to the sphere of the sacred, and presents Noah and his offspring as swearing an oath never to eat blood, and making a covenant which is to have eternal validity (*Jub.* 6:10). At this point, the angelic narrator reminds Moses (*Jub.* 6:11–12) that the covenant at Sinai "with the Israelites" was made with blood; and prohibition of its use outside the sanctuary is again firmly prohibited: "command the Israelites not to eat blood so that their descendants may continue to exist before the Lord" (*Jub.* 6:13). Having already proclaimed that one who eats blood "will be uprooted from the earth" (6:12), the angel sees fit to reinforce this decree by shifting its focus: Israelites are not to eat blood, but to offer supplication with it before the altar every day, morning and evening continually to ask pardon "and not be uprooted" (*Jub.* 6:13–14). Thus Jubilees presents the regulations for the offering of the daily sacrifice of lambs in the Temple, the Tamid, as indissolubly tied to the covenant with Noah, the prohibitions of bloodshed and murder being set alongside the institution of a continual daily sacrifice in which blood effects purgation of sin.[36]

These are not the only references to Israel in the story of Noah as Jubilees re-tells it. Noah's sacrifice and covenant were made on the feast of Shavuʿot,

---

[34] The reference is to Yom Kippur, whose inauguration Jubilees will later connect with Jacob's sorrow and affliction on hearing that his son Joseph had been killed by a wild animal; see *Jub.* 34:18–19.

[35] Non-scriptural texts are discussed by Jack P. Lewis, *A Study of the Interpretation of Noah and the Flood in Jewish and Christian Literature* (Leiden: Brill, 1968).

[36] See further Himmelfarb, *Kingdom of Priests*, 63–66, who notes how Jubilees specifies the laws on bloodshed as applying not only to Israel, but to humanity as a whole. Noah thus declares to all his descendants that the flood was brought about by bloodshed in particular (*Jub.* 7:23–25); and bloodshed, for Jubilees, defiles not simply the land of Israel but the whole earth.

and the angelic narrator tells Moses to command the Israelites to keep this festival for ever on its correct date (*Jub.* 6:20). Indeed, the angel states that Moses has been told about the sacrifices of Noah so that "the Israelites may continue to remember and celebrate it throughout their generations this month—one day each year."[37] The calendar is now explicitly in view, and the two remaining references to Israel in this section of text order the Israelites to keep a calendar of 364 days (*Jub.* 6:32), while predicting that they will, in fact, forget it (*Jub.* 6:34). After Moses' death, the angel says, the Israelites will make mistakes about "the first of the month, the season, the Sabbath, and the festivals" (*Jub.* 6:38). They will also eat blood; but the consequences of this are not rehearsed here.

In fine, in particular sections of narrative where Genesis makes no mention of Israel or Israelites as a people, the Jubilees narrator makes a point of introducing them—in the account of creation, with special reference to observance of the Sabbath; in the story of Noah's sacrifice with its repeated commands not to eat blood, but to reserve it for the altar where sacrifices to purge sin are daily to be offered; in the story of Noah's sacrifice as part of a divine covenant made on one particular day, intimating that Israel must keep a calendar which allows them to renew that covenant annually; in the account of the institution of the covenant of circumcision, with its observation that Israelites are to be circumcised like the two highest orders of angels, and that God alone is their ruler; in the story of Dinah, forbidding intermarriage with Gentiles; in the account of Bilhah, emphasising the centrality of Israel's laws concerning incest; and in the account of the Passover of Egypt. Jubilees evidently considers these items to be fundamental to Israel's identity, and is equally clear that Genesis was concerned with that identity and its preservation. Indeed, the narrator's final comment on the Bilhah story sets out in plain language what has been gradually accumulating throughout the story as Jubilees relates it: Israel is a holy people, a nation which God possesses, a priestly nation, and a priestly kingdom (*Jub.* 33:20).

This tacit reference to Exod 19:6 parallels Jubilees' earlier use of the same scriptural verse at 16:18, where angels of the presence inform Abraham that one of Isaac's sons (namely, Jacob) would have descendants forming a

---

[37] The interpretation of Shavu'ot which Jubilees offers is compared with that represented in other Jewish texts by Werner Eiss, "Das Wochenfest im Jubiläenbuch und im antiken Judentum," in *Studies in the Book of Jubilees* (ed. Matthias Albani, Jörg Frey, and Armin Lange; TSAJ 65; Tübingen: Mohr Siebeck, 1997), 165–178. See also Jean Potin, *La Fête juive de la Pentecote* (LD 65; Paris: Cerf, 1971).

people belonging to the Lord out of all the nations: "they would become a kingdom, a priesthood, and a holy people." The angel does not employ the term "Israel" here; however, in repeating the reference to this verse following the Bilhah story, Israel can be named in direct connection with these words from Exodus, since by that point in the narrative Israel exists as a formally constituted nation upon the earth. Very shortly before the Bilhah episode, Jacob had been granted the name "Israel" (*Jub.* 32:3), since by that time it has become evident that his twelve sons are all present to make up "the children of Israel" (*Jub.* 32:3); that his son Judah will provide royal princes to embody Israel's kingly aspects (*Jub.* 31:18–20); and that his son Levi and his descendants will become Israel's priests (*Jub.* 31:14–17). Provision of the "holy people" has long been in train, as those earlier sections of text where the narrator concentrates references to Israel and the Israelites have shown. In each and every one of those sections is involved some vital aspect of law, whose careful observance is essential if Israel and individual Israelites are not to be "destroyed and uprooted." Almost all those laws have been made known over the larger part of the time covered by the Genesis narrative, that is, up until the moment when Jacob is named as Israel, and Israel as a formally constituted nation of kings, priests, and holy people becomes a reality on earth. We must, then, enquire further how and why Jubilees understood Genesis as providing information on chronology and law.

Genesis as Provider of Chronology and Law

Although Genesis offers a connected narrative, it nonetheless provides the reader with particular highlighted events without giving details about the transition from one episode to the next. The text may suggest that its characters have certain motivations, or display behaviour implying a particular moral or religious position; but Genesis rarely indicates what these motivations or positions may be, or on what criteria they may be based. Jubilees orders the narrative of Genesis so that it becomes more unified: a strong and constantly re-asserted chronological scheme binds one event to the next, and a distinct set of principles, often set out in detail and explicated, is presented as governing right conduct. The reader is left in no doubt that there is one God, the God of Israel; and while it is possible to read Genesis up to ch. 32 without reference to Israel, and as an account of different families and groups, Jubilees sets Israel at the beginning of creation, and at regular intervals traces her growing presence in the history of the universe.

Genesis has sufficient indications that a chronology might underpin its narrative. From the outset, the story of the creation marks out a time scheme, without which the narrative would make no sense. As we have seen, Gen 1:14 sets the heavenly luminaries as chronological markers for seasons, days, and years, and it is literally "after a period of days" (Gen 4:3) that Cain and Abel offered sacrifice. From these brief notices the author of Jubilees, or any other ancient interpreter, could conclude that the association of "days" with sacrifice in this context might imply that Cain and Abel possessed information not made explicit in Genesis. Such a conclusion might appear justified by other parts of this scriptural text as well. Thus when Enoch is said to have "walked with God" for three hundred years (Gen 5:22) it might reasonably be asked what he learned during that time, and the period of time involved might be deemed significant in itself. Noah is said to have built an altar and offered sacrifices (Gen 8:20–21). How did he know the correct procedures for these activities, and which victims to select? Abraham, too, built altars (Gen 12:7, 8; 13:4; 22:9) and sacrificed a lamb instead of Isaac his son (Gen 22:13). He also seems to have known the custom of tithing (Gen 14:20).[38] More noticeably, he is said to have been privy to "the way of the Lord, to perform justice and judgment," and to be prepared to teach these things to his children (Gen 18:19). Given the vocabulary which the Hebrew text of this verse employs, there is more than a suggestion that Abraham knew divine commandments of the kind contained in the Torah of Moses.

Given all this, Jubilees could properly seek to expound Genesis by associating its characters with a particular chronology and with the teaching of particular commandments which close reading of the text, an eye to the other parts of Hebrew scripture, and knowledge of other valued writings might suggest. Unsurprisingly, Jubilees commands the observance of a 364-day calendar to Noah. The origins of this calendar and the question of how widely it was known, and the manner of its use, cannot detain us here.[39] We must, however, take particular notice of the Genesis account of Noah's flood, which fairly bristles with precise chronological information of

---

[38] It is in answer to questions such as these that Jubilees invokes extra-scriptural information: thus Noah delivers the laws of fourth year produce, regulations for the first-fruits of wine and oil, and instructions for the year of release to his children, explicitly informing them that these regulations came ultimately from Enoch, having been handed down the generations to Noah's father Lamech (7:34–39). See further Abraham's instruction to Isaac regarding sacrificial procedures in *Jub.* 21:7–20.

[39] See James C. VanderKam, "The Origin, Character, and Early History of the 364-Day Calendar: A Reassessment of Jaubert's Hypothesis," *CBQ* 41 (1979): 390–411.

a kind conspicuously absent from the rest of Genesis. Not only is the passage of time meticulously recorded (e.g., Gen 7:4, 12, 17, 24; 8:3, 6, 10, 12), exact dates are also given specifying the day and the month (e.g., Gen 7:11, the seventeenth day of the second month; 8:4, the seventeenth day of the seventh month; 8:5, the first day of the tenth month; 8:13, the first day of the first month; and 8:14, the twenty-seventh day of the second month). From the information which Gen 7:14–8:14 supplies, it becomes clear that this chronology is determined entirely by the Almighty. No human being is in any position to alter this time scheme. Noah is utterly dependent on it. If, then, any scriptural verses might be taken to reveal something of God's determination of times and seasons, the story of Noah certainly qualifies.[40] *Jub.* 6:28–29 (see also 6:23–27) implies as much with its institution by Noah of four "memorial festivals" now recorded on the heavenly tablets: they commemorate four key events in the history of the flood, and in the process mark out the four seasons of the year, each consisting, according to *Jub.* 6:29–30, of exactly thirteen weeks.[41] The four "memorial festivals" occupy the first days of the first, fourth, seventh, and tenth months and, like the rest of the festivals and Sabbaths, they occur without disturbance "in harmony with their testimony" (*Jub.* 6:32) year after year.[42]

On leaving the ark, Noah built an altar and offered sacrifice (Gen 8:20–21). We have seen how Jubilees gave a precise date for this event, on the feast of Shavu'ot; by punning on the Hebrew name of the feast, the narrator was able to define it as both a feast of weeks and a feast of oaths.[43]

---

[40] Genesis 8:22, with God's declaration that from Noah's days onwards seed time and harvest, cold and heat, summer and winter, day and night shall not cease might also be understood as a divine decree ordaining how time and season should operate henceforth.

[41] See James C. VanderKam, *Calendars in the Dead Sea Scrolls: Measuring Time* (London: Routledge, 1998), 28–30 for the significance accorded by Jubilees to Noah in matters to do with calendar. Although *Jub.* 4:17, 18, 21 accord to Enoch a knowledge of how time should be measured, significant elements of the calendar(s) attested in Enochic texts are not found in Jubilees; this corresponds to the latter's presentation of Noah as intimately involved with the 364-day calendar.

[42] Although the sun is explicitly stated to have been divinely appointed as "a great sign above the earth for days, Sabbaths, months, festivals, years, Sabbaths of years, jubilees, and all times of the years" (*Jub.* 2:9), it may be slightly misleading to refer to the chronology of Jubilees as witnessing to a "solar calendar." See Klawans, *Purity, Sacrifice, and the Temple*, 157. The calendar consists simply of 364 days, and the moon is to play no part in its calculation, lest festivals and Sabbath be observed on incorrect days, and consequently profaned; see *Jub.* 6:36–37.

[43] These two explanations of the name of the feast are engendered by the slightly different vocalization of the same Hebrew consonants, to yield first *shavu'ot*, "weeks," and then *shevu'ot*, "oaths."

God's covenant with Noah Jubilees understood as an oath: that a covenant might be described in terms of oath is an entirely biblical notion, and is significantly attested by Deut 29:9–12 [29:10–13].[44] Shavu'ot is thus the feast on which oaths or covenants are made, and it falls on the fifteenth day of the third month.[45] Once this has been established, other Patriarchs can be credited with having observed other festivals. Thus Abraham was the first to celebrate the feast of Tabernacles (*Jub.* 16:20–31); he also observed Passover and Unleavened Bread for seven days as "the festival of the Lord" (18:29). Jacob's life provided an occasion for the observance of what would later be the Day of Atonement (*Jub.* 34:18–19), when his sons deceived him into thinking that Joseph was dead and caused him to weep.

The last festival to be instituted according to Jubilees during the times described in Genesis was Shemini 'Atzeret (*Jub.* 32:28), the day following the seventh day of the feast of Tabernacles reckoned as an additional eighth day of the feast. This feast commemorates Jacob's reception of the name "Israel," and the formal inauguration of his descendants as "kings, priests, and a holy nation," which has been described at length in *Jub.* 32:1–26. The scriptural basis for this is provided by Gen 35:9–15. The complex relationship which Jubilees envisages as existing between chronology and law reaches its climax on this day, the twenty-second day of the seventh month. Chronology, the precise passage of time and exact fixing of dates implicates law not only in respect of the Sabbaths, festivals, and jubilees, but also in respect of the other commandments which Jubilees specifies as vital for Israel's well-being and which are revealed at specified times. Circumcision, laws of purity, and rules about intermarriage are all rooted in time, and with the celebration by Jacob-Israel of Shemini 'Atzeret, the presence of Israel on earth to keep Sabbath as the highest angels keep it in heaven is assured.[46]

---

[44] The character of Noah's covenant as an oath, which is to be re-affirmed and renewed each year (indeed, the covenant made at Sinai is one such renewal) is discussed by Annie Jaubert, *La Notion d'Alliance dans le Judaïsme aux abords de l'ère chrétienne* (Paris: Editions de Seuil, 1963), 107–115.

[45] The narrator notes (*Jub.* 14:20) that the covenant with Abraham "between the sacrificial pieces" (see Gen 15) was made on this day, as was the covenant of circumcision (*Jub.* 15:1), and the agreement or treaty between Jacob and Laban (*Jub.* 29:7). Other events which Jubilees dates on this festival are analysed by J. van Goudoever, *Fêtes et Calendriers Bibliques* (ThH 7; Paris: Beauschesne et ses Fils, 1967), 97–100.

[46] See further C.T.R. Hayward, *Interpretations of the Name Israel in Ancient Judaism and Some Early Christian Writings: From Victorious Athlete to Heavenly Champion* (Oxford: Oxford University Press, 2005), 139–152.

It is the Genesis narrative which provides the framework and scaffolding for this fusion of chronology and law in Jubilees: it never disappears from view and, central as Israel undoubtedly is to Jubilees' concerns from the outset, the recognition that the Genesis narrative has a universal dimension and significance is never forgotten.[47] Not only are other nations constantly mentioned and evaluated in relation to Israel; more fundamentally, the narrator makes plain that Israel's observance (or non-observance) of the times, the laws, and the moral precepts set forth in Jubilees have an effect, for good or ill, on the nations of the world and the whole universe. This much is spelled out in Jubilees' account of Noah's sacrifice, the covenant which accompanies it, and the instructions about blood which follow. The exact role which Israel plays in the universal scheme determined by the Almighty, however, can only be comprehended in light of what Jubilees has to say about the heavenly world where, as we have learned, Israel was a reality in the divine plan from the beginning.

Angels and the Heavenly World

Angels play sometimes prominent roles in the Genesis narrative, from the story of Hagar's banishment (Gen 16:7–11; 21:17), through the account of the destruction of Sodom and Gomorrah (Gen 19:1, 15), the binding of Isaac (Gen 22:1, 15), and the search for a wife for Isaac (Gen 24:7, 40). They are dramatically present in the account of Jacob's dream at Bethel (Gen 28:12) and accompany him, it seems, throughout his life (Gen 31:11; 32:2; 48:16). Their relationship to Jacob-Israel is thus particularly noticeable, and is further developed by the narrator of Jubilees.[48] Unlike Genesis, however,

---

[47] In certain respects, it is even enhanced: while Israel is the "holy seed" descended from Isaac and Jacob alone, nonetheless Abraham solemnly requests all his descendants, including the children of Ishmael the son of his slave-girl Hagar, and the family of his second wife Keturah, to keep the way of the Lord, which involves righteousness, love of neighbour, just action, performance of circumcision, and avoidance of sexual misconduct and impurity (*Jub.* 20:1–4). Ishmael's children are held in regard by Jubilees, which makes a point of granting a higher status to Hagar than she is accorded in Genesis; see David Rothstein, "Text and Context: Domestic Harmony and the Depiction of Hagar in *Jubilees*," *JSP* 17 (2008): 243–264.

[48] It should be observed that, as far as concerns the books of Moses, angels are not mentioned in Leviticus and Deuteronomy. In Numbers an angelic being appears, to confront the wicked Balaam (Num 22:22–35). Otherwise, angels from God appear in Genesis and Exodus (and there mostly in the early chapters, e.g., 3:2; 14:9; 23:20, 23; but see also 32:34). In other words, angels appear in those parts of the books of Moses which Jubilees has chosen to re-present.

Jub. 2:2 tells of the creation of the angels: this took place on the first day of creation, when "spirits" were created along with the heavens, earth, the waters, the abysses, darkness, and light. These spirits are designated as seven classes of angels and "the spirits of his creatures." Apart from the angels of the presence and the angels of holiness, the other angels are described as being in charge of various atmospheric and natural phenomena, and such duties prescribed here for angels would be familiar to readers of 1 Enoch and other texts from Second Temple times.[49] Once created, the angels bless and praise God because he had made "seven great works on the first day" of creation (*Jub.* 2:3), a statement calling to mind Job 38:4–7. The angels of the presence and angels of holiness are superior to the other angels, and alone are privileged to keep Sabbath with God in heaven, just as the sons of Jacob will keep it on earth (*Jub.* 2:17–20). This correspondence between the two highest orders of angels in heaven and Israel on earth extends to observation of the feast of Shavuʿot (*Jub.* 6:18), the mark of circumcision (*Jub.* 15:26–27), and priestly activity such that Levi and his descendants are said to function as priests on earth as the angels serve in heaven (*Jub.* 31:13–14). In fine, Israel on earth is to replicate the activities which the two great orders of angels carry out in heaven. There seems to be no other text from Second Temple times which demands this careful correspondence between Israel and these highest angels.

We noted above that readers of 1 Enoch and some other texts would be familiar with duties which Jubilees allocates to particular groups of angels.[50] They would also be aware of disruption in the heavenly and earthly spheres caused by the activity of angels, often called the "Watchers."[51] These celestial beings (see Dan 4:13, 17, 23) play no part in Genesis. They play a prominent role, however, in Enochic writings; and the author of Jubilees conveys information about them and their activities which sometimes overlap with information known to us from those writings and from other texts. The exact relationship between Jubilees and 1 Enoch, the Qumran Genesis Apocryphon, and other texts which mention disruptive angels is by no means clear, and space forbids discussion of it here.[52] But certain observations are

---

[49] See, for example, *1 En.* 60:12–21; 75; 80, and Raija Sollamo, "The Creation of Angels and Natural Phenomena Intertwined in the *Book of Jubilees* (4QJubᵃ)," in *Biblical Traditions in Transmission: Essays in Honour of Michael A. Knibb* (ed. Charlotte Hempel and Judith M. Lieu; JSJSup 11; Leiden: Brill, 2006), 97–124.

[50] See George W.E. Nickelsburg, *1 Enoch 1* (Hermeneia; Minneapolis: Fortress, 2001), 43–45.

[51] For a valuable summary of our knowledge of this designation, and its relationship to the titles "sons of God," "sons of heaven," "holy ones," see Nickelsburg, *1 Enoch 1*, 43–45.

[52] See Loren T. Stuckenbruck, "The Origins of Evil in Jewish Apocalyptic Tradition: Inter-

necessary, beginning with the fact that Jubilees, by adopting the narrative of Genesis as its framework, was to some degree compelled by that same framework to fit extra-scriptural information shared with other texts into an already existing narrative sequence and progression. This necessarily entailed the imposition of a particular order on the accounts of the Watchers and their associates.

According to *Jub.* 4:15, the Watchers, identified as "the angels of the Lord," descended to earth in the days of Jared (Gen 5:15) to teach humanity and to perform justice and judgement.[53] But these Watchers mingled with the daughters of human beings (*Jub.* 4:22). For Jubilees, regardless of what other sources may say or imply about them, the Watchers are identical with the "sons of God" named in Gen 6:2 as having cohabited with human women.[54] Consequently, they became polluted. The children of these unions *Jub.* 5:1 declares to have been giants, the word used by the LXX of Gen 6:4; injustice and corruption flourished, all creatures ate one another (and thus ate blood); and the thought of all humanity was continually evil (*Jub.* 5:2). Their activities bring about the flood. The angels who had been sent to earth were judged, God sending angels of the presence "to tie them up in the depths of the earth" (*Jub.* 5:6), thus inspiring their children to internecine warfare (*Jub.* 5:9). God subsequently condemned them all, and wiped them out (*Jub.* 5:11).

This section fits, and to some extent overlaps, with the Genesis account of the flood as divine punishment and a process for elimination of evil from the world. Further information about the Watchers and their progeny, however, Jubilees derives from Noah, who towards the end of his life is said to have exhorted his children to righteousness. It is he who explains (*Jub.* 7:21–22) that the children of the Watchers, now called Nephilim (a name found in Gen 6:4, without explanation), were killed by giants;[55] the Naphil killed the Elyo, the Elyo killed human beings, and people killed their colleagues (*Jub.* 7:21–23). The cause of this state of affairs is starkly set out:

---

pretation of Genesis 6:1–4 in the Second and Third Centuries BCE," in *The Fall of the Angels* (ed. Christopher Auffarth and Loren T. Stuckenbruck; TBN 6; Leiden: Brill, 2004), 86–118; and Wright, *Origin*, 139–165.

[53] On the "sons of God" of Gen 6:2 as angels or Watchers in the Enochic literature, see Wright, *Origin*, 98–101.

[54] On the similarities and differences between the Enochic portrayal of the Watchers and that reported by Jubilees, see Wright, *Origin*, 105.

[55] The identity of the Nephilim so suddenly introduced in Gen 6:4 along with *gibbôrîm*, "heroes" or "giants," clearly puzzled exegetes, and was widely discussed in antiquity; for a survey and discussion of ancient explanations of the terms, see Wright, *Origin*, 79–90.

it was brought about by nudity, failure to acknowledge the creator, breach of the command to honour father and mother, along with the practice of fornication, uncleanness, and injustice (*Jub.* 7:20). Without preamble, *Jub.* 7:27 announces that *demons* were actively working against the sons of Noah; not until Noah has uttered a prayer against them (*Jub.* 10:5) do we learn that in fact the Watchers were "the fathers of these spirits" who have remained alive.[56] Noah begs God for their complete destruction; but Mastema, their chief, pleads for some to be preserved, because "if none of them is left for me I shall not be able to exercise the authority of my will among mankind." Their purpose is to destroy and mislead, because human evil is very great (*Jub.* 10:8). God agrees to Mastema's request, leaving one tenth of these spirits under his control (*Jub.* 10:9). While the bulk of this material is not represented in Genesis, and has clear affinities with 1 Enoch and other related literature, it is the links which Jubilees has forged between the sons of God, their evil activities, and Noah's Flood, all of which do feature in Genesis, which permit Noah to offer this disquisition on the demons and their forebears as a kind of testament to his children. By utilising basic elements of Genesis information in this way, Jubilees allows for the gradual emergence of Mastema as a serious adversary of Israel who, from *Jub.* 10:8 onwards, will appear at regular intervals in the narrative, seeking to corrupt characters known to us from Genesis, and to disrupt their activities. Receiving a damaging set-back at the binding of Isaac (*Jub.* 17:15–18:12), Mastema and his cohorts appear at the end of Jubilees (48:15–19; 49:2–6) compelled by God to act as his agents on Passover night in the destruction of Egyptian first-born. Viewed with hindsight, the presence of corrupt and virulent beings in the early stages of the narrative gives way to the slow, but utter humiliation of their remnant, Mastema and his depleted minions, in the liberation of Israel from foreign domination.

Israel, in her properly constituted and ordered state, should act on earth in complete harmony with God and the two highest orders of angels. These have as one of their principal duties the keeping of Sabbath; and they are told directly that they will share this privilege with the children of Jacob (*Jub.* 2:17–22). It is at this point that the angelic narrator declares that there

---

[56] See James C. VanderKam, "The Demons in the Book of Jubilees," in *Die Dämonen—Demons: Die Dämonologie der israelitisch-jüdischen und frühchristlichen Literatur im Kontext ihrer Umwelt* (ed. Armin Lange, Hermann Lichtenberger, and K.F. Dietland Römheld; Tübingen: Mohr Siebeck, 2003), 339–364. On the activity of the demons and evil spirits after the flood, see Wright, *Origin*, 157.

were twenty-two "leaders of humanity" from Adam to Jacob,[57] and twenty-two kinds of works were made up to the seventh day of creation (*Jub.* 2:23). It was on the twenty-second day of the seventh month that Jacob received the name Israel, commemorating the occurrence with the feast of Shemini ʿAtzeret (*Jub.* 32:17–29). By these means, Jubilees indicates how Jacob-Israel is to serve as the link between the earthly and the heavenly realms, a notion already suggested by Genesis in its account of Jacob's dream at Bethel (Gen 28:10–22) with its vision of a ladder joining heaven and earth, angels going up and down, while Jacob lies on the earth at the foot of the ladder reaching up to the place where the Lord is stationed. Just as Jacob was delivered by God from all his opponents, so Israel will be victorious over hostile demonic powers and earthly foes if she remains true to her identity, adhering to the commandments which will be fully revealed to Moses on Sinai—the point at which the anonymous narrator of Jubilees begins the story.

Deuteronomy, Speeches, and Testaments

The anonymous narrator, who presents the information conveyed by *Jub.* 1:1–2:1a, is heavily indebted to Deuteronomy, a text which, as Hindy Najman has shown, provided for writers of the Second Temple period a theoretical model permitting the exposition, re-presentation, and re-ordering of the laws revealed at Sinai in such a way that their compositions could be regarded as genuine, detailed expressions of the principles and concerns set out in the Torah first delivered to Moses on Sinai, and subsequently expounded by him before Israel's entry into the promised land.[58] The opening phrases of the *Shemaʿ* (Deut 6:5) feature in *Jub.* 1:15, 23, with their reference to Israel's future return to God "with all their minds" and "with all their souls"; God's prediction that he will "hide his face" from sinful Israel (*Jub.* 1:13) takes up a theme announced in Deut 31:17–18; and Deut 31:19–24, with its complex commands to Moses to write "this song" in a book as a witness for Israel and for himself, and may provide elements of the *raison d'être* for

---

[57] This number depends on the presence of Adam's descendant Kainam, whom LXX Gen 10:24; 11:12 list as the thirteenth Patriarch, but whose name is not found in the Masoretic or Samaritan Hebrew texts of Genesis. See Helen R. Jacobus, "The Curse of Cainan (*Jub.* 8:1–5): Genealogies in Genesis 5 and Genesis 11 and a Mathematical Pattern," *JSP* 18 (2009): 207–232.

[58] See Hindy Najman, *Seconding Sinai: The Development of Mosaic Discourse in Second Temple Judaism* (JSJSup 77; Leiden: Brill, 2003), the second chapter of which deals specifically with Jubilees and the Qumran Temple Scroll.

the enterprise we know as the Book of Jubilees. Deuteronomy itself is in large part an extended speech, often urging right conduct, recalling past events, or suggesting future developments for Israel.

Speeches play an important role also in Jubilees. Prominent among them are *blessings*, which serve to bind together past generations to their successors, urging fidelity to the laws which have been received in the past, and promising good things for the future.[59] Thus Abraham is presented as blessing Jacob (*Jub.* 19:26–29), having first admonished Rebecca to watch over him (*Jub.* 19:17–25). This blessing parallels and reflects the blessed character of Jacob and his children, as Abraham makes plain to Rebecca: "through his descendants may my name and the name of my ancestors Shem, Noah, Enoch, Malaleel, Enos, Seth, and Adam be blessed." Jacob in some manner sums up and recapitulates the generations before him back to Adam; and the fundamental importance of the ancestors, and Jacob's confirmation of them, is apparent from further words of Abraham: "may they serve (the purpose of) laying heaven's foundations, making the earth firm, and renewing all the luminaries which are above the firmament" (*Jub.* 19:25). A more forthright statement of the centrality of Israel and her patriarchs for the stability and ordering of the cosmos could hardly be imagined. Blessing, it will be recalled, is tied also to the keeping of Sabbath, which Israel alone observes on earth (*Jub.* 2:23–25, 31–33).

Notable is Rebecca's blessing of Jacob (*Jub.* 25:15–23), which is bonded to the concern of Jubilees, already noted, that Jacob and his descendants preserve genealogical integrity. Having urged Jacob to avoid marrying a Canaanite (*Jub.* 25:1–3), Rebecca begins her blessing by praising God who has given her a holy seed: she ask God to grant her "a righteous blessing" wherewith to bless Jacob (*Jub.* 25:13), and for this purpose "the spirit of righteousness" descends into her mouth (*Jub.* 25:14). The prophetic inspiration and nature of Rebecca's blessing are unmistakeable. Nothing of this kind is found in Genesis. Rebecca's words of blessing take up the theme of the "holy seed" again (*Jub.* 25:18), bringing to prominence the part played by the Matriarchs in the divine scheme projected by Jubilees.[60]

---

[59] Abraham in particular utters blessing, no doubt since Genesis so insistently associates his name with it (Gen 12:2–3); thus at *Jub.* 22:10–24 he blesses Jacob in a long (poetic?) speech, only to bless him again almost immediately (*Jub.* 22:27–30).

[60] See Halpern-Amaru, *The Empowerment of Women*, 154–159. Rebecca delivers not only speeches of blessing, but of advice and encouragement: her words are recorded at length and include (for example) her advice to Jacob to flee to Haran to protect himself from Esau (*Jub.* 27:1–12); her prediction of her forthcoming death to Jacob (*Jub.* 35:1–6); her persuasion

Patriarchal speeches at the end of their lives are brought into prominence. Thus Abraham addresses "last words" to all his children together (*Jub.* 20:6–10); to Isaac (*Jub.* 21:1–26); and, as we have seen, to Jacob (*Jub.* 22:10–30). Isaac before his death addresses Jacob (*Jub.* 31:26–30); and Noah has final words for his descendants (*Jub.* 7:20–39). In Genesis, Jacob alone makes a formal, solemn speech before his death (Gen 49:1–27), which intriguingly is not represented in the Jubilees narrative. The placing of these speeches is mostly determined by the progression and sequence of the Genesis narrative and, like the chronological scheme which Jubilees adopts, has the effect of making the narrative more cohesive and integrated, episodes from the past being recalled by speaking characters who relate those episodes to the concerns of their own times. Instructive here are the speeches of Noah about the outcome of the Watchers' intervention in human affairs, and his warnings to his descendants that that intervention continues to have repercussions for the future (*Jub.* 7:20–39).[61]

A final word must be said about prayer, to which reference is made but briefly at Gen 20:7, 17; 25:21. Both narrators introduce prayer at key points, reflecting its place in the life of Second Temple Jews: the anonymous narrator includes a beautifully crafted prayer of petition to God (1:19–21), to which God immediately responds (1:22–26); further, the angel who narrates the bulk of the text reports prayers uttered from the time of Noah onwards.[62]

---

of Isaac to enforce an agreement of peace between Jacob and Esau (*Jub.* 35:9–17); and her maternal requests to Esau first, and then to Jacob, that the two men live in peace (*Jub.* 35:18–27).

[61] The abundance of speeches in Jubilees presents an important parallel to the large number of named, written documents which the text claims to know. The possibility that Jubilees in its final form may combine material from a number of different sources is perhaps suggested by the text itself. The most recent modern examination of that possibility has been undertaken by Michael Segal, *The Book of Jubilees: Rewritten Bible, Redaction, Ideology and Theology* (JSJSup 117; Leiden: Brill, 2007), who supports his theory of a layered, literary development of the book by identifying inconsistencies, contradictions, and disparities within the text, and by discerning therein three different theories of the origins of evil. Since this essay has been concerned with the final form of Jubilees, Segal's arguments do not directly concern us. However, it may be worth emphasising that the complete text of Jubilees is known to us only in a translation of a translation, that inconsistencies now apparent in the Ethiopic may not have been present in the original, and that such are the difficulties involved that discussions of the origin and nature of "evil," even when undertaken by modern scholars, may not always be systematic and entirely consistent.

[62] So *Jub.* 10:2–6, noting that Noah's sacrifice on leaving the ark (*Jub.* 6:1–3) did not, apparently, involve prayer; nor did his sacrifice following his observance of the law of fourth year produce (*Jub.* 7:1–6). See John C. Endres, "Prayers in Jubilees," in *Heavenly Tablets: Interpretation, Identity and Tradition in Ancient Judaism* (ed. Lynn LiDonnici and Andrea Lieber; JSJSup 119; Leiden: Brill, 2007), 31–47.

With Abraham, however, prayer assumes a prominent role: a determined opponent of idolatry, Abraham utters a prayer to the creator, petitioning the Most High God to deliver him from evil spirits which rule human thoughts and led people astray from following God. While Gen 14:19 places Abraham in relation to God Most High, creator or possessor of heaven and earth, the portrait of Abraham as a champion against idolatry has been introduced from sources outside Genesis; and it is with this recognition of the God of Israel as the only God that prayer is further recorded in respect of Abraham in passages not represented in Genesis, such as the formula he utters on sacrificing at Bethel (*Jub.* 13:15–16). It is also noted (*Jub.* 16:26–27) that Abraham "blessed his creator," that is, he uttered formal prayer (although on this occasion no record of his words is preserved) following his observance of the feast of Tabernacles.

Concluding Remarks

Jubilees preserves the essential narrative framework and the characters of Genesis. It presents both framework and characters to the reader with reference to other parts of Hebrew scripture, which are implicitly cited or alluded to throughout the text. The remit of Genesis is thus greatly expanded. The words of the anonymous narrator at the start of the text are clearly informed by Deuteronomy, itself a re-presentation of an older corpus of information involving Moses to whom, we are told, Jubilees was also revealed on Mount Sinai. The words of Exod 19:6, God's promise and decree that Israel would be a kingdom, priests, and a holy nation, are twice implicitly quoted (*Jub.* 16:18; 33:20); and by the end of the text, the reader realizes, with hindsight, that Genesis has served the narrator as a resource for describing the gradual emergence, over periods of time meticulously recorded, of the people called Israel. This already constituted nation stands at the head of the anonymous narrator's introduction, just as she stands at the head of the creative process: the gradual process whereby Israel becomes constituted on earth then becomes the major theme of the angelic narrator's discourse. First a holy nation is prepared, laws necessary for the definition and preservation of "holiness" being made known as the narrative proceeds. In this matter, Genesis provided a series of events which could be used to demonstrate this crucial development, and its situation in the legal framework which holds together Israel as a people. Next, priesthood with its sacral responsibilities and its role in the handing on of tradition is gradually revealed, until it is inaugurated in full fashion in the person of Levi. Kingship, with its duties and privileges, is brought into play with the blessings imparted to Judah; however, even a casual reader of Jubilees will note how much less is said about it than about priesthood. These things completed, Jacob receives the name "Israel," that nation to whom the complete Torah would be granted on Mount Sinai at the hands of Moses. Genesis implied that in the time of Abrham, and even earlier, elements of the Torah were already known: Jubilees explicitly tells the reader what they were, and why and in what circumstances they were revealed.

The metaphor of growth, or gradual development, is emphasized by Jubilees' use of the imagery of the holy seed. Genesis had stressed that Abraham's seed would be named through Isaac (Gen 21:12), and genealogical integrity, already recognized by Genesis as a key factor in the divine plan, assumes a crucial role for the Jubilees narrator. Yet this does not exhaust the significance of the metaphor: "seed" implies growth and development. Israel is to be a "righteous plant" (*Jub.* 1:16); but it cannot become such if, for any reason, it is *uprooted*. This last expression is repeatedly mentioned in places where Israel's disobedience to certain key laws is being emphasised. Observance of these laws should ensure the growth of the holy seed into a righteous plant. Even so, this process faces impediments. Running in tandem with this re-presentation of the Genesis narrative is a story of evil forces: Jubilees is able to relate the beginnings of this to events mentioned in Gen 6–9 concerning Noah's flood, its causes, and its aftermath. But the detailed information which Jubilees provides about Watchers, Nephilim, Mastema, and demons comes not from Genesis, but from outside that book, although crucially Jubilees maintains the narrative framework of Genesis to give order and significance to it. The activities of the evil forces are directed particularly against Israel, though they affect the whole world. Indeed, the very process of Israel's coming into being is put in jeopardy by Mastema, with his malicious suggestion that God should test Abraham's character by demanding that he sacrifice the "seed" Isaac. The defeat of Mastema's malignant powers on that occasion prepares the reader for their further humiliation at the end of the text. Mastema has spirits under his control: Jubilees does not explicitly state that it is *these* spirits who rule the nations, though the nations are indeed ruled by spirits according to Jubilees. If the nations are ruled by spirits under Mastema's control, then they, too, are humbled by Israel both at the Exodus from Egypt, and in the victories granted to Israel over Amorites and descendants of Esau described elsewhere in the text.

Genesis reports activities of angels, particularly in relation to Jacob who will be named Israel, a character who has been aware of angelic presence and assistance throughout his life. At Gen 48:15 he speaks of the angel who had redeemed him from all evil, and it is with this angel that the Jubilees narrative may connect with the angel of the presence named (according to one manner of reading) at Isa 63:9 who had saved Israel. His association with the heavenly world is so emphasised by Jubilees that Israel is pervasively treated as a priestly society, to whom the commandments of the Torah specific to the priesthood may be applied. Thus nudity, nowhere in the Torah explicitly prohibited to non-priests, can be forbidden to all Israel on the grounds that priests are strictly prevented from approaching the altar in a state of undress (Exod 20:26). This priestly character of Israel goes hand in hand with Jubilees' focus on Sabbaths, festivals, and the calendar: properly celebrated in due season, these maintain and express the harmony and unity of the earthly and heavenly realms essential for the stability of the cosmos. Such is the message of Jubilees' interpretation of Noah's flood and its succeeding sacrifice and covenant. Here, Genesis places chronology, repeatedly referring to it, and sacrifice and laws regarding moral conduct side by side. The far-reaching implications of this juxtaposition were not lost on the narrator of Jubilees.

The narrative of Genesis involves the whole cosmos, and tells of the emergence on earth of a people called the "children of Israel." Jubilees never loses sight of the universal aspects of the Genesis story. It is precisely as a priestly people that the Israel of Jubilees is entrusted with maintaining the stability and order of the creation following the flood; and others, who are not of the holy seed, are expected to perform justice and right judgment with the same end in view. The final form of Jubilees is commonly dated to a period around the middle of, or in the first half of, the second century BCE, its antipathy towards nudity, the improper use of blood, laxity in respect of the laws of circumcision, and irregular sexual conduct (especially with foreigners) signalling its opposition to those who would embrace non-Jewish ways. Certainly deep anxieties about the extent to which Jews have abandoned ancestral custom in favour of Greek modes of life inform the text; yet that is by no means the whole story. For Jubilees has received Genesis in such a way as to demonstrate to its readers that the negative commandments of the Torah have a positive function, and that relations with other nations can be conducted as they were in the days of the pious ancestors. Obedience to the Torah as expressed by Jubilees will result in a future where all will acknowledge the God of Israel as King on Mount Zion, and a renewal of the created order in perfection.

Select Bibliography

Albani, Matthias, Jörg Frey, and Armin Lange, eds. *Studies in the Book of Jubilees.* Texte und Studien zum Antiken Judentum 65. Tübingen: Mohr Siebeck, 1997.
Davenport, Gene L. *The Eschatology of the Book of Jubilees.* Studia post-biblica 20. Leiden: Brill, 1971.
Endres, John C. *Biblical Interpretation in the Book of Jubilees.* Catholic Biblical Quarterly Monograph Series 18. Washington, D.C.: Catholic Biblical Association of America, 1987.
Halpern-Amaru, Betsy. *The Empowerment of Women in the Book of Jubilees.* Journal for the Study of Judaism in the Persian, Hellenistic and Roman Period Supplement Series 60. Leiden: Brill, 1999.
Hayes, Christine E. *Gentile Impurities and Jewish Identities: Intermarriage and Conversion from the Bible to the Talmud.* Oxford: Oxford University Press, 2007.
Himmelfarb, Martha. *A Kingdom of Priests: Ancestry and Merit in Ancient Judaism.* Philadelphia: University of Pennsylvania Press, 2006.
Najman, Hindy. *Seconding Sinai: The Development of Mosaic Discourse in Second Temple Judaism.* Journal for the Study of Judaism in the Persian, Hellenistic and Roman Period Supplement Series 77. Leiden: Brill, 2003.
Segal, Michael. *The Book of Jubilees: Rewritten Bible, Redaction, Ideology and Theology.* Journal for the Study of Judaism in the Persian, Hellenistic and Roman Period Supplement Series 117. Leiden: Brill, 2007.
Testuz, Michel. *Les Idées religieuses du Livre des Jubilés.* Paris: Librairie Minard, 1960.
VanderKam, James C. *Textual and Historical Studies in the Book of Jubilees.* Harvard Semitic Monographs 14. Missoula, Mont.: Scholars Press, 1997.
———. *The Book of Jubilees.* 2 vols. Corpus scriptorum christianorum orientalium 510–511. Leuven: Peeters, 1989.
———. *The Book of Jubilees.* Guides to Apocrypha and Pseudepigrapha. Sheffield: Sheffield Academic Press, 2001.
Van Ruiten, J.T.A.G.M. *Primaeval History Interpreted: The Rewriting of Genesis 1–11 in the Book of Jubilees.* Journal for the Study of Judaism in the Persian, Hellenistic and Roman Period Supplement Series 66. Leiden: Brill, 2000.

TEXTUAL AND TRANSLATION ISSUES IN GREEK GENESIS

Robert J.V. Hiebert

Septuagint Origins and Significance

In the third century BCE—perhaps shortly before the first of the Dead Sea Scrolls was written, and not long after the cultural tsunami that swept through the Fertile Crescent and significant portions of Asia in the wake of Alexander the Great's conquest—Jewish scholars in Egypt began work on the first translation of the Hebrew Bible into another language. The language was Greek, the *lingua franca* of that time and place. The initial phase of this undertaking involved the Pentateuch, and Genesis may well have been the first of those five books to be translated. The version that those translators produced came to be known as the Septuagint, and it provides us with an important window on the world of Hellenistic Judaism, on the increasingly involved history of the transmission of the Jewish Scriptures, and on the cultural and theological factors that shaped their interpretation of those sacred texts.

The significance of the Septuagint is not, however, limited to its status as a Hellenistic Greek religious text. Because the earliest and greatest number of extant witnesses to the Hebrew Scriptures are in fact Septuagint manuscripts, the Greek translation is also an important resource for the discipline of Hebrew Bible textual criticism, the goal of which is to reconstruct its original text. This Greek version is, furthermore, the "Old Testament" that was studied by the early church as it spread throughout the Graeco-Roman world and became distinguished from Judaism. Proof of this is the fact that the majority of quotations of the Jewish Scriptures in the New Testament are from the Septuagint, and the fact that early patristic exegesis is so dependent on that Greek Old Testament. In one sense, then, the Septuagint functions as something of a bridge between ancient Judaism and early Christianity in regard to the interpretation of the Hebrew Bible / Old Testament and in the formation of the New Testament.

Recent Developments in Septuagint Research

The past twenty years or so have seen a significant upsurge in Septuagint research, one indicator of which has been the inauguration of as many as nine translation projects of the Septuagint into modern languages. These include *A New English Translation of the Septuagint* or NETS,[1] the goal of which is to reflect what the Septuagint text would have meant to the Greek translators at its point of origin; *La Bible d'Alexandrie*,[2] whose focus tends to be on the meaning(s) the text came to have in the course of its subsequent reception history; and *Septuaginta Deutsch*,[3] which aspires to chart something of a middle course between these two *modi operandi*. A collaborative undertaking involving more than thirty scholars from around the world, NETS is the first English translation of the Old Greek version since the nineteenth century editions of Charles Thomson[4] and Lancelot Brenton.[5] While Thomson's and Brenton's translations are still available, they are deficient on two counts. First, they are based on Greek texts that do not incorporate the wealth of textual evidence that has come to light since that time. Second, their English style is understandably antiquated. NETS, on the other hand, is a translation of the best available critically-reconstructed text of the Septuagint for each book, rendered into contemporary English.

Another marker of increased activity in the field of Septuagint research is the launch of several commentary series. These exhibit varying degrees of comprehensiveness and depth. The forthcoming Society of Biblical Literature Commentary on the Septuagint (SBLCS)—jointly sponsored by the Society of Biblical Literature and the International Organization for Septuagint and Cognate Studies (IOSCS)—will focus on explicating the meaning of the whole Septuagint as it was perceived at the point of its inception rather than sometime during its reception history.[6] *La Bible d'Alexandrie*

---

[1] Albert Pietersma and Benjamin G. Wright, eds., *A New English Translation of the Septuagint and the Other Greek Translations Traditionally Included under That Title* (New York: Oxford University Press, 2007).
[2] *La Bible d'Alexandrie* (Paris: Cerf, 1986–).
[3] Wolfgang Kraus and Martin Karrer, eds., *Septuaginta Deutsch: Das griechische Alte Testament in deutscher Übersetzung* (Stuttgart: Deutsche Bibelgesellschaft, 2009).
[4] Charles Thomson, *The Holy Bible, Containing the Old and the New Covenant, Commonly Called the Old and the New Testament* (4 vols.; Philadelphia: Jane Aitken, 1808).
[5] Lancelot C.L. Brenton, *The Septuagint Version of the Old Testament, According to the Vatican Text, Translated into English: With the Principal Various Readings of the Alexandrine Copy* (2 vols.; London: Samuel Bagster and Sons, 1844).
[6] See the commentary prospectus online at http://ccat.sas.upenn.edu/ioscs/commentary/prospectus.html.

integrates the French text and commentary for each book or section of the Septuagint in a single volume, while *Septuaginta Deutsch* features the German text of the entire Septuagint in one volume and all book introductions and annotations in the other. For Genesis, the French version is based on both Alfred Rahlfs' preliminary edition of the Septuagint of Genesis[7] and John Wevers' full-fledged critical edition.[8] The German version and SBLCS, on the other hand, both rely upon Wevers' edition, in accordance with the policy of each of those two series to follow the best available critical edition. The launch of SBLCS represents the fulfillment of a longstanding dream cherished by many Septuagintalists regarding a comprehensive English commentary on the Septuagint based on the critically-reconstructed original Greek text. This represents a different direction than the one taken by the recently begun Septuagint Commentary Series[9] in which each volume is a commentary on a single Septuagint manuscript—one of the great uncial Bible manuscripts of the fourth and fifth centuries CE (Vaticanus, Sinaiticus or Alexandrinus). More in line with the principles that guide SBLCS are the publications by R.R. Ottley on Isaiah[10] and John Wevers on each of the books of the Pentateuch,[11] though these are somewhat limited in scope in comparison to what is intended for the SBLCS series.

Textual History of the Greek Genesis

It goes without saying that an essential requirement for all serious literary research is a reliable text. As a rule, that is understood to be its final form rather than any of the preceding drafts that may have been prepared in the lead-up to the ultimate product. In the case of the Septuagint, that product

---

[7] Alfred Rahlfs, ed., *Septuaginta: Societatis Scientiarum Gottingensis auctoritate—I: Genesis* (Stuttgart: Privilegierte Württembergische Bibelanstalt, 1926).

[8] John William Wevers, ed., *Septuaginta: Vetus Testamentum Graecum Auctoritate Academiae Scientiarum Gottingensis editum—I: Genesis* (Göttingen: Vandenhoeck & Ruprecht, 1974).

[9] Septuagint Commentary Series, currently edited by Stanley E. Porter, Richard S. Hess, and John Jarick (Leiden: Brill, 2005–).

[10] R.R. Ottley, *The Book of Isaiah according to the Septuagint (Codex Alexandrinus)* (2 vols.; London: Cambridge University Press, 1906–1909).

[11] *Notes on the Greek Text of Genesis* (SBLSCS 35; Atlanta: Scholars Press, 1993); *Notes on the Greek Text of Exodus* (SBLSCS 30; Atlanta: Scholars Press, 1990); *Notes on the Greek Text of Leviticus* (SBLSCS 44; Atlanta: Scholars Press, 1997); *Notes on the Greek Text of Numbers* (SBLSCS 46; Atlanta: Scholars Press, 1998); *Notes on the Greek Text of Deuteronomy* (SBLSCS 39; Atlanta: Scholars Press, 1995).

is, of course, a translation. In field of Septuagint research, scholars have debated whether or not all extant textual witnesses of a given book or unit go back to a single original, but it is fair to say that the current consensus is that this is the case. Of the various Septuagint text-critical projects that have been undertaken, the one sponsored by the Septuaginta-Unternehmen der Akademie der Wissenschaften zu Göttingen is the only one that involves the attempt to reconstruct systematically the original form of the Greek text of all the Septuagint books based on the extant evidence. The volume on Genesis in the Göttingen Septuaginta series was prepared by John Wevers, and it is the text of that edition that will be cited in the present study.

Wevers has provided a detailed overview of the textual history of Septuagint Genesis, both in the introduction to his Göttingen edition[12] and in a separate volume entitled *Text History of the Greek Genesis*.[13] He reports that the oldest substantial textual materials still extant are found in codices Alexandrinus (A) and Vaticanus (B)[14]—the latter of which has been preserved from only 46:28 onward—and in the fragmentary papyri 911, 961, and 962. Each of these is dated to sometime between the third and fifth centuries and is a potential witness to a text that was not affected by later recensions.[15]

The kind of text that the Septuagint translator of Genesis produced could, in linguistic parlance, be characterized as one of formal, rather than dynamic, equivalence. In other words, this Greek version typically represents its Hebrew source text isomorphically. This does not mean, however, that the product of this undertaking is not genuine Greek. In fact, it has been demonstrated in various studies of the language of the Septuagint that the translators, including the one who produced the Greek Genesis, normally employed vocabulary and often even grammatical constructions that are attested in antecedent and/or contemporaneous non-translation Greek literature.[16] The Septuagint of Genesis may then be characterized as a

---

[12] Wevers, *Septuaginta: Vetus Testamentum Graecum ... Genesis*, 10–73.

[13] John William Wevers, *Text History of the Greek Genesis* (MSU 11; AAWG.PH 3/81; Göttingen: Vandenhoeck & Ruprecht, 1974).

[14] With regard to the book of Genesis in Codex Sinaiticus (iv CE), another important uncial Greek Bible text, only fragments of chs. 23 and 24 have survived. In order to conserve space, frequently throughout this essay I designate centuries by means of small Roman numerals rather than writing out the numbers as words.

[15] Wevers, *Text History of the Greek Genesis*, 186, 228.

[16] Adolf Deissmann, *Bible Studies* (trans. Alexander Grieve; Edinburgh: T&T Clark, 1901); Deissmann, *Light from the Ancient East: The New Testament Illustrated by Recently Discovered Texts of the Graeco-Roman World* (trans. Lionel R.M. Strachan; London: Hodder and Stoughton, 1910); Albert Thumb, *Die griechische Sprache im Zeitalter des Hellenismus: Beiträge*

translation that both exhibits a dependent linguistic relationship to its Hebrew parent text and shares a lexicon with compositional Koiné Greek literature.[17]

In a famous passage in the prologue to the Latin Vulgate version of Paralipomenon (Chronicles), Jerome states:

> Alexandria et Aegyptus in Septuaginta suis Hesychium laudat auctorem: Constantinopolis usque Anthiochiam, Luciani ... martyris exemplaria probat. Mediae inter has provinciae Palaestinos [*Al.* Palaestinae] codices legunt: quos ab Origene elaboratos Eusebius et Pamphilus vulgaverunt; totusque orbis hac inter se trifaria varietate compugnat.[18]

> Alexandria and Egypt for their Septuagint acclaim Hesychius as author. From Constantinople to Antioch the copies of Lucian the martyr are approved. Between these the intervening provinces of Palestine read the codices over which Origen laboured and which Eusebius and Pamphilus promulgated. And the whole world is in conflict with itself over this threefold variety.

Wevers' conclusion with regard to the textual history of Greek Genesis does not reflect the state of affairs described by Jerome for the Greek Jewish Scriptures in his day: "As far as Jerome's three recensions were concerned, I found no trace of the shadowy Hesychius, nor to my surprise of a Lucianic text."[19] Thus the only such recensional activity for which there is evidence in Genesis is that of Origen in what has come to be known as the hexaplaric recension.

With respect to the non-Septuagintal Greek translations of the second century CE—i.e., those attributed to Aquila, Symmachus, and Theodotion—some readings of all three are attested for Genesis, typically as marginal readings in certain manuscripts.[20] 'The Three' are indicators of the

---

zur Geschichte und Beurteilung der Koiné (Strasbourg: Trübner, 1901; repr., Berlin: de Gruyter, 1974); Henry St. John Thackeray, *A Grammar of the Old Testament in Greek according to the Septuagint* (Cambridge: Cambridge University Press, 1909), 16–31; John A.L. Lee, *A Lexical Study of the Septuagint Version of the Pentateuch* (SBLSCS 14; Chico, Calif.: Scholars Press, 1983), 1–10, 145–149; Natalio Fernández Marcos, *The Septuagint in Context: Introduction to the Greek Version of the Bible* (trans. Wilfred G.E. Watson; Atlanta: Society of Biblical Literature, 2000), 3–17; and Karen H. Jobes and Moisés Silva, *Invitation to the Septuagint* (Grand Rapids: Baker Academic, 2000), 105–107.

[17] Albert Pietersma and Benjamin G. Wright, "To the Reader of NETS," in Pietersma and Wright, *A New English Translation of the Septuagint*, xiv, xvii.

[18] Jerome, *Praefatio Hieronymi in Librum Paralipomenon* (PL 28:1324–1325).

[19] John William Wevers, "Apologia pro Vita Mea: Reflections on a Career in Septuagint Studies," *BIOSCS* 32 (1999): 70–71; and Wevers, *Text History of the Greek Genesis*, 228.

[20] Wevers, *Septuaginta: Vetus Testamentum Graecum ... Genesis*, 59–61.

evident dissatisfaction with the Septuagint that manifested itself soon after that original translation came into being, due, it seems, to its perceived failure to reflect the source text as exactly or clearly as some would have liked.

Translation Strategies

Genesis is, of course, a book of beginnings, chronicling the origins of the cosmos, humankind, and the particular people with whom the creator God establishes a special covenant relationship. The Old Greek Pentateuch is the result of probably the first major translation project involving religious literature in history, and Genesis is, as noted above, also likely to have been the first of these five books to have been translated into Greek. This undertaking constituted a new way of representing the Jewish Scriptures that will have involved the development of innovations and strategies by the Septuagint translator in order to accomplish such a task. In this study, I will discuss two of the phenomena in Greek Genesis that reflect these developments—namely neologisms, or at least terms for which there are no previously attested occurrences in currently existing Greek literature, and Greek counterparts to Hebrew names.

Neologisms in Septuagint Genesis

Neologisms are presumably created and added to an existing lexicon in order to remedy a perceived deficiency. In the following table, Greek terms (listed alphabetically) that are not found in extant literature prior to Septuagint Genesis, along with their Hebrew counterparts, are paralleled by the English equivalents in NETS and the NRSV, respectively.

LXX	NETS	MT	NRSV	Reference
ἀκροβυστία	foreskin	ערלה	foreskin	17:11
ἀνεμόφθοροι	wind-blasted	שדפות קדים *qal* pass. ptcp.	blighted by the east wind	41:23
ἀνταπόδομα	requital	שוב *hipʻil* inf. abs. (+ imperf.)	(pay back) in full	50:15
ἀποδεκατόω	tithe	עשר *piʻel*	give one tenth	28:22
ἀποπεμπτόω	take one-fifth	חמש *piʻel*	take one-fifth	41:34
ἀροτρίασις	plowing	חריש	plowing	45:6

TEXTUAL AND TRANSLATION ISSUES IN GREEK GENESIS 411

LXX	NETS	MT	NRSV	Reference
ἀρχιδεσμοφύλαξ	chief jailer	שר בית הסהר	chief jailer	39:21
ἀρχιδεσμώτης	chief jailer	שר הטבחים	captain of the guard	40:4
ἀρχιμάγειρος	chief butcher	שר הטבחים	captain of the guard	37:36
ἀρχιοινοχοΐα	chief cupbearership	כן	office	40:13
ἀρχιοινοχόος	chief cupbearer	משקה	cupbearer	40:1
ἀρχισιτοποιός	chief baker	אפה	baker	40:1
βαρυωπέω	be heavy-sighted	כבד *qal*	be dim	48:10
γαμβρεύω	act the part of a brother-in-law	יבם *pi'el*	perform the duty of a brother-in-law	38:8
δευτερόω	repeat	שנה *nip'al*	double	41:32
διασάφησις	clarification	פתרון	interpretation	40:8
ἐγκισσάω	come into heat	יחם *qal*	breed	30:38(39)
εἰσσπάομαι	draw	בוא *hip'il*	bring	19:10
ἑκατοστεύω (κριθήν)	bear a hundredfold (barley)	מאה שערים	a hundredfold	26:12
ἐκπορνεύω	play the whore	זנה *qal*	play the whore	38:24
ἐλαττονόω	diminish	חסר *qal*	lack	18:28
ἐνευλογέομαι	bless	ברך *nip'al*	bless	12:3
ἐνταφιάζω	prepare for burial	חנט *qal*	embalm	50:2
ἐνταφιαστής	undertaker	רפא *qal* act. ptcp.	physician	50:2
ἐνυπνιαστής	dreamer	בעל החלמות	dreamer	37:19
ἐπιγαμβρεύω	make marriages	חתן *hitpa'el*	make marriages	34:9
ἐπισκοπή	visitation	פקד *qal* inf. abs. (+ imperf.)	surely (come)	50:24
εὐλογητός	bless	ברוך *qal* pass. ptcp.	bless	9:26
θηριάλωτος	that which is caught by wild beasts	טרפה	that which is torn by wild beasts	31:39
θηριόβρωτος	eaten by wild beasts	טרף *qal* inf. abs. (+ perf. pass.)	(tear) to pieces	44:28
θυσιαστήριον	altar	מזבח	altar	8:20

LXX	NETS	MT	NRSV	Reference
κατάβρωσις	a devouring	אכל qal (pret. +) inf. abs.	(use) up	31:15
κατακενόω	empty	ריק hip'il	empty	42:35
κατακυριεύω	subdue	כבש qal	subdue	1:28
κατανύσσω	be cut to the quick	עצב hitpa'el	be indignant	34:7
κλοποφορέω	rob	גנב qal	deceive	31:26(27)
λέπισμα	stripe	פצלה	streak	30:37
οἰωνισμός	ornithomancy	נחש pi'el inf. abs. (+ imperf.)	indeed (use for divination)	44:5
ὁλοκάρπωσις	whole burnt offering	עלה	burnt offering	8:20
ὀπισθοφανής	looking backward	אחרנית	turned away	9:23
ὀπισθοφανῶς	backward	אחרנית	backward	9:23
ὀρθρίζω	start early	שכם hip'il	go early	19:27
ὁ περάτης	the emigrant	העברי	the Hebrew	14:13
ποτιστήριον	watering trough	שקת	trough	24:20
προσοίγνυμι	shut	סגר qal	shut	19:6
πρωτοτόκια	rights of primogeniture	בכרה	birthright	25:31
ὑπερασπίζω	shield	מגן (noun)	shield	15:1
φαῦσις	illumination	מאורת	lights	1:15
φωστήρ	luminary	מארת	lights	1:14
χήρευσις	widowhood	אלמנות	widow's (garments)	38:14

A number of strategies have been employed to create the terms in the preceding table. It must be acknowledged at the outset, however, that, in some of these cases, the words were quite likely in use at the time of the translation of Genesis, but that through accidents of literary history they have not survived in extant Greek literature. As John Lee has pointed out, terms that would fall into this category include ὀρθρίζω, whose cognate ὀρθρεύω is attested by Euripides (v BCE); διασάφησις, whose cognate διασαφέω is used by Euripides (v BCE) and Plato (v/iv BCE); and ἀρχιδεσμοφύλαξ, whose cognate δεσμοφύλαξ occurs in papyri from the third century BCE onward.[21] It seems

---

[21] Lee, *Lexical Study*, 46–48; LSJ, ὀρθρεύω, διασαφέω; and BDAG, δεσμοφύλαξ.

that compounds with ἀρχι- were rather commonly created in the Hellenistic period,[22] so it is quite possible that the following terms were also current by the time of the Genesis translator:[23]

> ἀρχιδεσμώτης (δεσμώτης: Herodotus v BCE; Thucydides v BCE).
> ἀρχιμάγειρος (μάγειρος: Aristophanes v/iv BCE; Plato v/iv BCE).
> ἀρχιοινοχοΐα and ἀρχιοινοχόος (οἰνοχόος: Homer; Herodotus v BCE; Euripides v BCE).
> ἀρχισιτοποιός (σιτοποιός: Thucydides v BCE).

While the preceding words may have been in use at the time of the translation of Septuagint Genesis, others will have been coined by the translator. One cannot always be certain as to when new word forms entered the Greek vocabulary, particularly in situations in which cognates of various kinds or constituent parts of new compounds are attested in Greek literature that antedates, or is contemporaneous with, the Septuagint of Genesis. Such is the case with the assorted categories of words that are discussed below. Nonetheless, at least some of them are sure to have been creations of the Septuagint translator.

1. *Nominal or Adjectival Cognates of Existing Verbs:*[24]

> ἀνταπόδομα (ἀνταποδίδωμι: Herodotus v BCE; Thucydides v BCE).
> ἀροτρίασις (ἀροτριάω: Theophrastus iv/iii BCE; Callimachus iii BCE).[25]
> ἐνυπνιαστής (ἐνυπνιάζω: Aristotle iv BCE).
> ἐπισκοπή (ἐπισκοπέω: Sophocles v BCE; Xenophon v/iv BCE).
> εὐλογητός (εὐλογέω: Aeschylus vi/v BCE; Sophocles v BCE).
> καταβρῶσις (καταβιβρώσκω: Antiphanes iv BCE).
> λέπισμα (λεπίζω: Antiphanes iv BCE; Aristotle iv BCE).
> ποτιστήριον (ποτίζω: Hippocrates v BCE; Plato v/iv BCE).
> φαῦσις (φαίνω: Homer; Aeschylus vi/v BCE; Pindar v BCE).
> χήρευσις (χηρεύω: Isaeus iv BCE; Demosthenes iv BCE; Aristotle iv BCE).

2. *Verbal Cognates of Existing Nouns or Adjectives:*[26]

> ἀποδεκατόω (δέκατος: Homer).
> ἀποπεμπτόω (πέμπτος: Homer; Thucydides v BCE; Herodotus v BCE).

---

[22] Lee, *Lexical Study*, 48; MM, ἀρχι-; and Robert J.V. Hiebert, "Genesis: To the Reader," in Pietersma and Wright, *A New English Translation of the Septuagint*, 2.
[23] See LSJ, δεσμώτης, μάγειρος, οἰνοχόος, σιτοποιός.
[24] LSJ, ἀνταποδίδωμι, ἀροτριάω, ἐνυπνιάζω, ἐπισκοπέω, εὐλογέω, καταβιβρώσκω, λεπίζω, ποτίζω, φαίνω, χηρεύω.
[25] Lee, *Lexical Study*, 113.
[26] LSJ, δέκατος, ἐντάφιον, πέμπτος, γαμβρός, δεύτερος, ἑκατοστός, ἐλάττων, ἀσπίς.

γαμβρεύω (γαμβρός: Homer; Herodotus v BCE; Sophocles v BCE).
δευτερόω (δεύτερος: Herodotus v BCE; Sophocles v BCE).
ἑκατοστεύω (ἑκατοστός: Herodotus v BCE).
ἐλαττονόω (ἐλάττων: Aristophanes v/iv BCE; Demosthenes iv BCE).
ἐνταφιάζω (ἐντάφιον: Simonides vi/v BCE; Isocrates v/iv BCE)[27] on the basis of which the translator apparently also coined the noun ἐνταφιαστής.
ὑπερασπίζω (ἀσπίς: Homer; Aeschylus vi/v BCE).

3. Substantival Forms Derived from Existing Cognate Nouns or Adjectives:[28]

οἰωνισμός[29] (οἰωνός: Homer; Hesiod; Sophocles v BCE; οἰώνισμα: Euripides v BCE).
πρωτοτόκια (πρωτοτόκος: Homer).
φωστήρ (φῶς: Euripides v BCE; Sophocles v BCE).

4. Compound Verb Forms with Prepositions Based on Simplex Forms:[30]

εἰσσπάομαι (σπάομαι: Homer; Aeschylus vi/v BCE).
ἐκπορνεύω (πορνεύω: Herodotus v BCE; Eupolis v BCE; Lysias v BCE).
ἐνευλογέομαι (εὐλογέομαι: Sophocles v BCE; Isocrates v/iv BCE).
κατακενόω (κενόω: Euripides v BCE; Plato v/iv BCE).
κατακυριεύω (κυριεύω: Xenophon v/iv BCE; Aristotle iv BCE).
κατανύσσω (νύσσω: Homer; Hesiod; Theocritus iii BCE).
προσοίγω / προσοίγνυμι (οἴγω / οἴγνυμι: Homer; Hesiod; Aeschylus vi/v BCE).

5. Other Compound Forms Consisting of Combinations of Verbs, Adverbs, Nouns, or Adjectives:

ἀνεμόφθοροι (ἄνεμος + φθείρω / φθόρος).
βαρυωπέω (βαρύς + ὤψ).[31]

---

[27] Robert J.V. Hiebert, "Lexicography and the Translation of a Translation: The NETS Version and the Septuagint of Genesis," *BIOSCS* 37 (2004): 73–86, here 82.

[28] LSJ, οἰωνός, πρωτοτόκος, φῶς. Note that πρωτότοκος, which is first attested in the Septuagint of Genesis, denotes *"first-born"* and is the semantic cognate of πρωτοτόκια, whereas πρωτοτόκος denotes *"bearing* or *having borne her first-born."*

[29] The term οἰωνισμός is found in version 3 of the fable about the crow and the raven attributed to Aesop (vi BCE; *Fab.* 127.3.7), but in version 1 the term is οἰωνός (*Fab.* 127.1.8). The fact that the latter term is well attested in Greek literature from the time of Homer onward, whereas the former one appears otherwise in Greek literature only from the time of the origins of the Septuagint onward (*TLG*), makes one suspect that οἰωνισμός is a variant that was introduced into the Aesopic material after the term was coined in iii BCE.

[30] LSJ, σπάομαι, πορνεύω, εὐλογέομαι, κενόω, κυριεύω, νύσσω, οἴγω / οἴγνυμι.

[31] Hiebert, "Genesis: To the Reader," 2.

κλοποφορέω (κλοπή + φορέω).³²
ὀπισθοφανής / ὀπισθοφανῶς (ὀπίσω / ὄπισθεν + φαίνω).

6. Technical Terms:

Certain words in Septuagint Genesis that would appear to have been formulated as technical terms and that can be regarded as distinctively biblical vocabulary are θηριάλωτος, θυσιαστήριον, and ὁλοκάρπωσις.³³

7. An Isolate:

In another category is the word περάτης, which occurs in the Septuagint only in Gen 14:13 and is based on the adverb πέρα. This is an isolate rendering of the Hebrew gentilic עברי, created by the Genesis translator presumably to establish a semantic connection between words in both languages with etymological links to verbs meaning 'traverse' and cognate forms with the connotation 'on the other side.'³⁴ Lee calls περάτης a nonce-formation, "unlikely to occur again."³⁵

8. A Lexical Oddity:

The term ἀκροβυστία 'foreskin' is a puzzling composite whose first recorded occurrence is in Septuagint Genesis. It is presumably derived from ἀκροποσθία 'tip of the foreskin,' a word that is attested by Hippocrates (v BCE) and Aristotle (iv BCE). Some have speculated that ἀκροβυστία is the product of the combination of ἄκρος and a Semitic root *bšt* signifying 'pudenda' or 'shame.'³⁶

Alternative Readings in Post-Septuagint Greek Translations of Genesis

In place of some of the items in the preceding table of neologisms, one or more of 'The Three' (Aquila, Symmachus, and Theodotion) have opted

---

³² Marguerite Harl, *La Bible d'Alexandrie: La Genèse* (2nd ed.; Paris: Cerf, 1994), 237; Wevers, *Notes on the Greek Text of Genesis*, 509.
³³ Lee, *Lexical Study*, 52; LSJ, θηριάλωτος, θυσιαστήριον, ὁλοκάρπωσις.
³⁴ LSJ, πέρα, πέραν, περάτης, περάω; BDB, עָבַר, I. עֵבֶר, I. עִבְרִי; HALOT, I עבר, I עֵבֶר, עברי.
³⁵ Lee, *Lexical Study*, 52.
³⁶ LSJ, ἀκροβυστία, ἀκροποσθία; BDAG, ἀκροβυστία; LEH, ἀκροβυστία; Wevers, *Notes on the Greek Text of Genesis*, 234; and Hiebert, "Genesis: To the Reader," 2–3.

for alternative readings. These, along with other non-Septuagintal readings that are either attributed or unattributed in the manuscript sources, are recorded in the second apparatus of Wevers' edition.[37] It is instructive to see what kinds of equivalents these younger Greek versions exhibit in places where the Old Greek features terms that are not attested in extant Greek literature that antedates the Septuagint.

41:23 ἀνεμόφθοροι] α´ ἐφθαρμένοι (φθαρμ. 550; -νους 730) καύσωνι; σ´ πεφρυγμένοι (εφρ. 550; -φυρμ. 79; -φραγμ. 730) ἀνέμῳ 25(ind mend ad λεπτοί)-57´^{cat}(s nom)-79^{cat}-500´^{cat}-550(s nom)-551^{cat}-615´^{cat} 730. In place of the Septuagint translator's newly-minted term ἀνεμόφθοροι "wind-blasted" as the equivalent for שדפות קדים "blighted by the east wind" to describe the ears of grain in Pharaoh's dream, Aquila's rendering of the Hebrew expression is ἐφθαρμένοι καύσωνι 'destroyed/ruined by burning heat,' and Symmachus's is πεφρυγμένοι ἀνέμῳ 'parched by wind.'[38] Both of these latter alternatives involve two separate words arranged in the sequence of verb followed by noun, as is the case in the Hebrew but not in the Septuagint. Quantitatively speaking, therefore, the readings of Aquila and Symmachus are closer to the Hebrew.

40:8 διασάφησις] α´ ἐπίλυσις M 57´(s nom)-550(s nom) 344´ Syh; σ´ διάκρισις M 344 Syh. Eschewing the Septuagint's term διασάφησις "clarification," Aquila has translated פתרון "interpretation" as ἐπίλυσις 'release / explanation,' while Symmachus has chosen διάκρισις 'differentiation / interpretation.'[39] All three terms have somewhat different connotations with respect to meeting the challenge of interpreting the dreams of Pharaoh's cupbearer and baker, though it may be that ἐπίλυσις and διάκρισις were considered by Aquila and Symmachus, respectively, to approximate more closely the idea of a solution to a problem that seems to be inherent in the term פתרון and its cognates than does διασάφησις with its nuance of making something clear.[40]

26:12 ἑκατοστεύουσαν κριθήν] α´ ἑκατὸν εἰκασμούς Hi 32. In this case, the Septuagint translator seems to have associated שערים with שערה 'barley' rather than with the hapax legomenon שער, whose Aramaic cognates have to do with measurement, calculation, or estimation.[41] Thus ἑκατοστεύουσαν κριθήν "barley bearing a hundredfold" as a translation of מאה שערים "a hun-

---

[37] Wevers, *Septuaginta: Vetus Testamentum Graecum ... Genesis*, 59–61.
[38] LSJ, φθείρω, καύσων, φρύγω, ἄνεμος.
[39] LSJ, ἐπίλυσις, διάκρισις.
[40] BDB, פָּתַר, פִּתְרוֹן; *HALOT*, פתר, פִּתְרוֹן; and LSJ, διασαφέω; διασάφησις.
[41] Jastrow, שְׁעַר, שַׁעַר II; *HALOT*, שְׂעֹרָה, II שַׁעַר; and Wevers, *Text History of the Greek Genesis*, 404.

dredfold" represents a plus in relation to the reading of the MT. Aquila's rendering—ἑκατὸν εἰκασμούς 'a hundred conjecturings/guessings' or perhaps 'a hundred likenesses'[42]—is more in line with the intention of the Hebrew author.

1:28 κατακυριεύσατε] α'σ'θ' ὑποτάξατε Philop 283. Wevers maintains that the choice by 'The Three' of ὑποτάξατε 'place under, subject, subdue' as a counterpart to כבש "subdue" constitutes a more literal rendering than does the Septuagint's κατακυριεύσατε "subdue."[43] That is debatable, though perhaps with כבש and ὑποτάσσω the focus is on the situation of the one being subdued, whereas with κατακυριεύω it might be more on that of the one doing the subduing.[44]

34:7 κατενύχθησαν] α' διεπονήθησαν 344' 346; σ' ὠδυνήθησαν 108. The *hitpaʿel* of עצב 'be vexed'[45] occurs only twice in the Hebrew Bible—here, and in Gen 6:6 where the Septuagint has the aorist passive of διανοέομαι 'to think over,' Aquila's text has the aorist passive of διαπονέω 'to be worn out / troubled,' and Symmachus's has the aorist active of ἐπιπίπτω 'to fall upon / over.'[46] In Gen 34:7, Aquila has rendered the Hebrew with the same root and stem as in 6:6, whereas Symmachus has adopted the aorist passive of ὀδυνάω 'to feel / suffer pain.'[47] The equivalents for the *hitpaʿel* of עצב chosen by these latter two translators create different word pictures to convey the vexation or distress experienced by Dinah's brothers after her violation than the one suggested by the Septuagint's κατανύσσω (aorist passive) to be stabbed / pricked'[48] or 'to be cut to the quick.'

44:5 οἰωνισμῷ] τὸ σαμ' ... πειρασμῷ 135 57; μαντείᾳ F[b]. The equivalent for the *piʿel* infinitive absolute of נחש 'practise divination'[49] attributed to the Samariticon, a Greek translation of the Samaritan Pentateuch,[50] is a form of the noun πειρασμός 'test, trial.'[51] It has no explicit connection with the kind of heterodoxy that is associated with a term like the Septuagint's οἰωνισμός

---

[42] Note that the cognate nouns εἰκασία and εἴκασμα denote "likeness" (LSJ).
[43] Wevers, *Notes on the Greek Text of Genesis*, 16, n. 54.
[44] BDAG, ὑποτάσσω: "to cause to be in a submissive relationship"; HALOT, כבש: "to subdue somebody, to subjugate"; BDAG, κατακυριεύω: "to have mastery, be master, lord it over), rule"; and LSJ, κατακυριεύω: "gain dominion over."
[45] BDB, I. עצב.
[46] LSJ, διανοέομαι, διαπονέω, ἐπιπίπτω.
[47] LSJ, ὀδυνάω.
[48] LSJ, κατανύσσω.
[49] BDB, II. נחש.
[50] Sidney Jellicoe, *The Septuagint and Modern Study* (Oxford: Oxford University Press, 1968; repr., Ann Arbor: Eisenbrauns, 1978), 245.
[51] BDAG, πειρασμός.

'ornithomancy,' or with the choice of μαντεία 'divination' by an unidentified translator in a reading recorded by the second corrector of the uncial F.[52] Both of the latter two practices are proscribed in Deut 18:10. They are also mentioned in 4 Reigns (2 Kgs) 17:17 in the description of the offences that the Israelites committed, provoking the Lord to anger and resulting in their exile and the destruction of the Northern Kingdom. The fact that οἰωνισμός typically has to do with reading omens in the flight and cries of birds may also have been regarded as an unusual form of divination to be associated with Joseph's silver cup, and that may have been reason enough for later Greek translators to opt for alternatives to it.

8:20 ὁλοκαρπώσεις] σ' (+ τας 127) ἀναφοράς (-ραν M 739) M 64(nom absc) 57'-128-739(s nom) 130-344'; ὁλοκαυτώσεις 413. Symmachus's equivalent in this verse for עלת "burnt offerings" is ἀναφοράς. This is a cognate of the verb ἀνήνεγκεν (from the root ἀναφέρω 'to offer')[53] that immediately precedes ὁλοκαρπώσεις in the same verse. In the Septuagint, however, only once—in Ps 50(51):21—is ἀναφορά used to designate an offering on an altar. In Gen 8:20, the unattributed reading ὁλοκαυτώσεις in the margin of manuscript 413[54] is the plural accusative form of ὁλοκαύτωσις 'whole burnt offering,' a term first attested in the Septuagint Pentateuch (e.g., as the counterpart to עלה in Exod 29:25), though the cognate verb ὁλοκαυτόω is used by Xenophon (v/iv BCE).[55] The decision by later Greek translators of Gen 8:20 to employ ἀναφοράς and ὁλοκαυτώσεις, respectively, as equivalents for the עלת of animals and birds that Noah offers up is understandable in view of the fact that the etymological meaning of the Septuagint's ὁλοκαρπώσεις is 'whole fruit offerings.'

14:13 τῷ περάτῃ] α' (+ τω 344') περαΐτη 57-413(s nom) s⁻³⁴³ Ish 145 Barh; σ' τῷ Ἑβραίῳ 57-413(s nom) s⁻³⁴³; περάτης ἑρμηνεύεται παρὰ τοῖς περὶ Ἀκύλαν ὁ Ἑβραῖος 135^cat. Wevers remarks that Aquila's reading περαΐτη is synonymous with the Septuagint's περάτη, which denotes 'emigrant,' whereas Symmachus's rendering Ἑβραίῳ is the more usual equivalent for עברי.[56] In the catena of manuscript 135 it is stated that περάτης is interpreted as 'the Hebrew' among those of Aquila's circle, which is in line with the reading attributed to Symmachus. If Aquila himself is to be included in that group, then this would appear to be a case of different sources attributing divergent

---

[52] Wevers, *Septuaginta: Vetus Testamentum Graecum ... Genesis*, 60.
[53] BDAG, ἀναφέρω.
[54] Wevers, *Septuaginta: Vetus Testamentum Graecum ... Genesis*, 17.
[55] LSJ, ὁλοκαυτόω.
[56] Wevers, *Notes on the Greek Text of Genesis*, 193, n. 26.

readings to him. Such anomalies are not uncommon in the extant witnesses to these non-Septuagintal versions.

1:15 φαῦσιν] α' φωστῆρας Field. The equivalent in this verse for the plural noun מארת 'lights'[57] attributed to Aquila in the collection of hexaplaric readings published by Frederick Field is likewise a plural noun, φωστῆρας[58] 'luminaries,' in contrast to the Septuagint's singular form, φαῦσιν 'illumination.' The Aquilanic reading is consistent with the מארת = φωστῆρες equivalence that one finds in the Septuagint of Gen 1:14.

GREEK SUBSTITUTIONS FOR HEBREW NAMES IN SEPTUAGINT GENESIS

A number of different strategies are employed by the Septuagint translator of Genesis in order to render the names of the Hebrew parent text. These involve transcribing the phonemes that comprise the Hebrew form of a name into Greek characters (e.g., אדם – 'Ἀδάμ – Adam)[59] or providing substitutions of various sorts for Hebrew names (e.g., חדקל – Τίγρις – Tigris). In the following discussion, I will focus only on the latter category. The table below contains a complete list of the Greek substitutions for Hebrew names in the book of Genesis.[60]

LXX	NETS	MT	NRSV	Reference
Αἰγυπτία	Egyptian	מצרית	Egyptian	16:1
οἱ Αἰγύπτιοι	the Egyptians	המצרים	the Egyptians	12:12

---

[57] BDB, מָאוֹר.

[58] Frederick Field, *Origenis Hexaplorum quae supersunt sive veterum interpretum graecorum in totum Vetus Testamentum fragmenta* (2 vols.; Oxford: Clarendon, 1875), 1:9. In n. 31 on this page, Field acknowledges that this attribution to Aquila is based on the testimony of Bernard de Montfaucon (*Origenis Hexaplorum quae supersunt, multis partibus auctiora quam a Flaminio Nobilio et Joanne Drusio edita fuerint* [2. vols.; Paris: Apud Ludovicum Guerin ... viduam Joannis Boudot ... et Carolum Robustel, 1713]) and that, in fact, with respect to this reading "non memorato auctore."

[59] The Greek-English letter equivalents for transcriptions are: α = a, β = b, γ = g, δ = d, ε = e, ζ = z, η = e, θ = th, ι = i, κ = k, λ = l, μ = m, ν = n, ξ = x, ο = o, π = p, ρ = r, σ/ς = s, τ = t, υ = y, φ = ph, χ = ch, ψ = ps, ω = o, αυ = au, ευ = eu, ηυ = eu, ου = ou, υι = ui.

[60] This does not include Greek renderings of Hebrew or Aramaic names that are merely the Septuagint translator's ad hoc interpretations of their perceived meaning, such as Ζωή "Life"—חוה "Eve" (3:20), Φρέαρ ὁρκισμοῦ "Well-of-adjuration" (21:31) / Φρέαρ ὅρκου "Well-of-oath" (26:33)—באר שבע "Beer-sheba" (21:31), Βουνὸς τῆς μαρτυρίας "Mound-of-the-witness"—יגר שהדותא "Jegar-sahadutha" (31:47), Βουνὸς μαρτυρεῖ "Mound-bears-witness"—גלעד "Galeed" (31:48), and Βάλανος πένθους "Acorn-tree-of-mourning"—אלון בכות "Allon-bacuth" (35:8).

LXX	NETS	MT	NRSV	Reference
Αἴγυπτος	Egypt	מצרים	Egypt	12:10
Αἰθιοπία	Ethiopia	כוש	Cush	2:13
Ἀμμανῖται	the Ammanites	בני־עמון	the Ammonites	19:38
ὁ Ἀμορραῖος	the Amorrite	האמרי	the Amorites	10:16
ὁ Ἀράδιος	the Aradian	הארודי	the Arvadites	10:18
ὁ Ἀρουκαῖος	the Aroukite	הערקי	the Arkites	10:17
ὁ Ἀσενναῖος	the Hasennite	הסיני	the Sinites	10:17
Ἀσσύριοι	the Assyrians	אשור	Assyria	2:14
Βαβυλών	Babylon	בבל	Babel	10:10
Γάζα	Gaza	עזה	Gaza	10:19
ὁ Γεργεσαῖος	the Gergesite	הגרגשי	the Girgashites	10:16
Δαμασκός	Damascus	דמשק	Damascus	14:15
Ἑβραῖος	Hebrew	עברי	Hebrew	39:14
ὁ Εὐαῖος	the Heuite	החוי	the Hivites	10:17
Εὐφράτης	the Euphrates	פרת	the Euphrates	2:14
Ἡλίου πόλις	Heliopolis	אן	On	41:45
Ἡρώων πόλις	Heroonpolis	גשן	Goshen	46:28
Ἰδουμαία	Idumea	אדום	Edom	36:16
ὁ Ἰεβουσαῖος	the Iebousite	היבוסי	the Jebusites	10:16
ὁ Ἰορδάνης	the Jordan	הירדן	the Jordan	13:10
Ἰσμαηλῖται	Ismaelite(s)	ישמעאלים	Ishmaelites	37:25
οἱ Κεδμωναῖοι	the Kedmonites	הקדמני	the Kadmonites	15:19
οἱ Κεναῖοι	the Kenites	הקיני	the Kenites	15:19
οἱ Κενεζαῖοι	the Kenezites	הקנזי	the Kenizzites	15:19
Κίτιοι	Kitians	כתים	Kittim	10:4
Μαδιηναῖοι	Madienite(s)	מדינים	Midianite(s)	37:28
ἡ Μεσοποταμία	Mesopotamia	ארם נהרים	Aram-naharaim	24:10
ἡ Μεσοποταμία	Mesopotamia	פדן ארם	Paddan-aram	25:20
ἡ Μεσοποταμία Συρίας	Mesopotamia of Syria	פדן ארם	Paddan-aram	28:6
Μεσοποταμία τῆς Συρίας	Mesopotamia of Syria	פדן ארם	Paddan-aram	35:9
Μεσοποταμία τῆς Συρίας	Mesopotamia of Syria	פדן	Paddan	48:7

LXX	NETS	MT	NRSV	Reference
Μωαβῖται	the Moabites	מואב	the Moabites	19:37
Ὀδολλαμίτης	Odollamite	עדלמי	Adullamite	38:1
οἱ Ὀμμαῖοι	the Ommites	האימים	the Emim	14:5
Πετεφρῆς	Petephres	פוטיפר	Potiphar	37:36
Πετεφρῆς	Petephres	פוטי פרע	Potiphera	41:45
Ῥαμεσσή	Ramesses	גשן	Goshen	46:28
Ῥαμεσσή	Ramesses	רעמסס	Rameses	47:11
Ῥόδιοι	Rhodians	דדנים	Rodanim[61]	10:4
ἡ Ῥοωβὼθ πόλις	Rooboth-city	רחבת עיר	Rehoboth-ir	10:11
ὁ Σαμαραῖος	the Samarite	הצמרי	the Zemarites	10:18
ὁ Σιδών	Sidon	צידן	Sidon	10:15
Σίκιμα	Sikima	שכם	Shechem	35:4
οἱ Σοδομῖται	the Sodomites	אנשי סדם	the men of Sodom	19:4
Συρία	Syria	ארם	Aram	28:6
ὁ Σύρος	the Syrian	הארמי	the Aramean	25:20
Τίγρις	Tigris	חדקל	Tigris	2:14
οἱ Φερεζαῖοι	the Pherezites	הפרזי	the Perizzites	13:7
οἱ Χαλδαῖοι	the Chaldeans	כשדים	the Chaldeans	11:28
οἱ Χαναναῖοι	the Chananites	הכנעני	the Canaanites	10:18
ἡ Χανανῖτις	the Chananite woman	הכנענית	a Canaanite woman	46:10
ὁ Χετταῖος	the Chettite	חת	Heth	10:15
οἱ Χετταῖοι	the Chettites	החתי	the Hittites	15:20
οἱ Χορραῖοι	the Chorrites	החרי	the Horites	14:6

Some of the names in the preceding list will be familiar to English speakers because the commonly-used English place names or gentilics are based on the Greek rather than the completely different Hebrew forms. These Greek names are, in fact, attested by authors who predate the Septuagint, some of whom are identified below in parentheses:

---

[61] In Gen 10:4, the NRSV reflects the reading attested in some Hebrew manuscripts, the LXX, and the SamP (cf. 1 Chr 1:7)—i.e., רדנים (BHS).

Αἴγυπτος (Homer; Herodotus [v BCE])[62] Egypt (מצרים Egypt).
Αἰθιοπία (Herodotus [v BCE]; Thucydides [v BCE])[63] Ethiopia (כוש Cush).
Ἡλίου πόλις (Hecataeus of Abdera [iv/iii BCE])[64] Heliopolis (אן On).
Μεσοποταμία (Megasthenes [iv/iii BCE])[65] Mesopotamia (ארם נהרים Aram-naharaim / פדן ארם Paddan-aram).
Σύρος (Antiphanes Comicus [iv BCE])[66] Syrian (ארמי Aramean).

In other cases, the Hebrew and Greek forms of the names are similar to one another, though not identical. The Greek names, which, like the ones immediately above, are attested in Greek sources that antedate the Septuagint, belong in the replacement category because they are, in fact, more than simple transcriptions of the Hebrew ones:

Βαβυλών (Alcaeus Lyricus [vii/vi BCE])[67] Babylon (בבל Babel).
Γάζα (Hecataeus of Abdera [iv/iii BCE]; early Ptolemaic papyri)[68] Gaza (עזה Gaza).
Δαμασκός (Theophrastus [iv/iii BCE])[69] Damascus (דמשק Damascus).
Σιδών (Homer; Herodotus [v BCE])[70] Sidon (צידן Sidon).

---

[62] LSJ, Αἴγυπτος; Herodotus, *Hist.* 2.5.
[63] LSJ, Αἰθιοπία.
[64] Hecataeus of Abdera, *Fragmenta* 3a.264.F, frag. 25, line 679 (*FGH* 264).
[65] Megasthenes, *Fragmenta* 40.15.
[66] Antiphanes Comicus, *Fragmenta* 168.3 (Theodor Kock, ed., *Comicorum Atticorum fragmenta* [3 vols.; Leipzig: Teubner, 1880–1888], 2:79).
[67] LSJ, Βαβυλών. It is declined as a third declension feminine noun: Βαβυλών: nominative (Gen 10:10), Βαβυλῶνος: genitive (4 Reigns [2 Kgs] 17:24), Βαβυλῶνι: dative (4 Reigns [2 Kgs] 25:28), (τὴν) Βαβυλῶνα: accusative (Jer 28[51]:9); Thackeray, *Grammar*, 169.
[68] *P. Cair. Zen.* I.59009b.3,5 (C.C. Edgar, *Zenon Papyri I* [Catalogue général des antiquités égyptiennes du Musée du Caire 79; Cairo: Imprimerie de l'Institut Français d'Archéologie Orientale, 1925]) and *PSI* VI.616.21 (*Papiri greci e latini* [Pubblicazioni della Società italiana per la ricerca dei Papiri greci e latini in Egitto; Firenze: E. Ariani, 1920]); and LSJ, xl, xli. Josephus says that Hecataeus of Abdera mentions a battle near Gaza between the forces of Ptolemy and those of Demetrius (*C. Ap.* 1.183–185; Frederick W. Knobloch, "Hebrew Sounds in Greek Script: Transcriptions and Related Phenomena in the Septuagint, with Special Focus on Genesis" [Ph.D. diss., University of Pennsylvania, 1995], 291; and Menahem Stern, ed., *Greek and Latin Authors on Jews and Judaism* [3 vols.; Jerusalem: The Israel Academy of Sciences and Humanities, 1974–1984], 1:22–25). This place name is declined as a first declension feminine noun: Γάζα: nominative (Josh 14:47), Γάζης: genitive (Deut 2:23), Γάζῃ: dative (Josh 10:22), Γάζαν: accusative (Gen 10:19); Thackeray, *Grammar*, 167.
[69] Theophrastus, *Hist. plant.* 3.15.3. It is declined as a second declension feminine noun: Δαμασκός: nominative (Gen 15:2), Δαμασκοῦ: genitive (2 Reigns [Sam] 8:5), Δαμασκῷ: dative (Amos 3:12), (τὴν) Δαμασκόν: accusative (4 Reigns [2 Kgs] 14:28).
[70] LSJ, Σιδών. It is declined as a third declension masculine/feminine noun: Σιδών: nominative (Zech 9:2), Σιδῶνος: genitive (Gen 10:19), Σιδῶνι: dative (Jdt 2:28), (τὸν) Σιδῶνα: accusative (Gen 10:15), (τὴν) Σιδῶνα: accusative (Jer 29[47]:4).

Greek substitutions for Hebrew names may be formed by adding various derivational suffixes to transcribed Hebrew roots. For example, -αῖος etc. is affixed to such transcriptions to replace the Hebrew gentilic suffix י:[71]

ὁ Ἰεβουσαῖος the Iebousite (היבוסי the Jebusites).
οἱ Κεναῖοι the Kenites (הקיני the Kenites).
οἱ Φερεζαῖοι the Pherezites (הפרזי the Perizzites).
οἱ Χαναναῖοι the Chananites (הכנעני the Canaanites).
οἱ Χετταῖοι the Chettites (החתי the Hittites).

Likewise, -ίτης etc. is added to Greek transcriptions of Hebrew root forms:[72]

Ἀμμανῖται Ammanites (בני־עמון Ammonites).
Ἰσμαηλῖται Ismaelites (ישמעאלים Ishmaelites).
Μωαβῖται Moabites (מואב Moabites).
Σοδομῖται Sodomites (אנשי סדם men of Sodom).

Another derivational suffix is -ιος:[73]

Ἀσσύριοι Assyrians (אשור Assyria).
Κίτιοι Kitians (כתים Kittim).
Ῥόδιοι Rhodians (דדנים Rodanim).

Some names ending in -ης in the nominative singular are declined as first declension forms:

Εὐφράτης the Euphrates (פרת the Euphrates).[74]
ὁ Ἰορδάνης the Jordan (הירדן the Jordan).[75]

Another name ending in -ης displays a mixed declension pattern:

Πετεφρῆς Peterphres (פוטיפר Potiphar / פוטי פרע Potiphera).[76]

Finally, one of the Greek names in the table above involves translation of part of its Hebrew counterpart:

ἡ Ῥοωβὼθ πόλις Rooboth-city (רחבת עיר Rehoboth-ir).

---

[71] Thackeray, *Grammar*, 171; Herbert W. Smyth, *Greek Grammar* (rev. Gordon M. Messing; Cambridge: Harvard University Press, 1956), §§ 824, 833, 858.2a; Eugene Van Ness Goetchius, *The Language of the New Testament* (New York: Charles Scribner's Sons, 1965), § 166.
[72] Thackeray, *Grammar*, 171; Smyth, *Greek Grammar*, §§ 833b, 843a.N, 844.2.
[73] Thackeray, *Grammar*, 171; Smyth, *Greek Grammar*, § 844.3.
[74] Εὐφράτης: nominative (Gen 2:14), Εὐφράτου: genitive (Gen 15:18), Εὐφράτῃ: dative (Jer 13:5), Εὐφράτην: accusative (2 Reigns [Sam] 8:3); Thackeray, *Grammar*, 160.
[75] Ἰορδάνης: nominative (Deut 3:17), Ἰορδάνου: genitive (Gen 13:10, 11; 50:10, 11), Ἰορδάνῃ: dative (Josh 3:8), Ἰορδάνην: accusative (Gen 32:10[11]).
[76] Πετεφρῆς: nominative (Gen 39:1), Πετεφρῆ: genitive (Gen 41:45, 50; 46:20), Πετεφρῇ: dative (Gen 37:36); Thackeray, *Grammar*, 163–164.

Conclusion

The focus of the present study has been on certain strategies employed by the translator of Septuagint Genesis to render the underlying Hebrew parent text. In particular, neologisms—or at least terms that appear for the first time in the extant corpus of Greek literature within the Old Greek version of Genesis—and names have been investigated. Comparisons of some of the lexical choices of subsequent Greek translators—especially Aquila, Symmachus, and Theodotion—with those of the Septuagint translator have also been made. This investigation has provided an indication both of the variety of solutions to the challenges of translation that were devised by the unknown individual responsible for the Old Greek Genesis, and of the ways in which those who produced later Greek versions responded to this initial translation effort with alternatives that were, by and large, more closely aligned with their Hebrew source texts.

Select Bibliography

Deissmann, Adolf. *Bible Studies*. Translated by Alexander Grieve. Edinburgh: T&T Clark, 1901.

———. *Light from the Ancient East: The New Testament Illustrated by Recently Discovered Texts of the Graeco-Roman World*. Translated by Lionel R.M. Strachan. London: Hodder and Stoughton, 1910.

Fernández Marcos, Natalio. *The Septuagint in Context: Introduction to the Greek Version of the Bible*. Translated by Wilfred G.E. Watson. Atlanta: Society of Biblical Literature, 2000.

Field, Frederick. *Origenis Hexaplorum quae supersunt sive veterum interpretum graecorum in totum Vetus Testamentum fragmenta*. 2 vols. Oxford: Clarendon, 1875.

Harl, Marguerite, trans. and ed. *La Bible d'Alexandrie: La Genèse*. 2nd ed. Paris: Cerf, 1994.

Hiebert, Robert J.V. "Lexicography and the Translation of a Translation: The NETS Version and the Septuagint of Genesis." *Bulletin of the International Organization for Septuagint and Cognate Studies* 37 (2004): 73–86.

———. "Ruminations on Translating the Septuagint of Genesis in the Light of the NETS Project." Pages 71–86 in *"Translation Is Required": The Septuagint in Retrospect and Prospect*. Edited by Robert J.V. Hiebert. Society of Biblical Literature Septuagint and Cognate Studies 56. Atlanta: Society of Biblical Literature, 2010.

———. "The Hermeneutics of Translation in the Septuagint of Genesis." Pages 85–103 in *Septuagint Research: Issues and Challenges in the Study of the Greek Jewish Scriptures*. Edited by Wolfgang Kraus and R. Glenn Wooden. Society of Biblical Literature Septuagint and Cognate Studies 53. Atlanta: Society of Biblical Literature, 2006.

———. "Translating a Translation: The Septuagint of Genesis and the New English Translation of the Septuagint Project." Pages 263–284 in *X Congress of the International Organization for Septuagint and Cognate Studies: Oslo, 1998*. Edited by Bernard A. Taylor. Society of Biblical Literature Septuagint and Cognate Studies 51. Atlanta: Society of Biblical Literature, 2001.

———. "Translation Technique in the Septuagint of Genesis and Its Implications for the NETS Version." *Bulletin of the International Organization for Septuagint and Cognate Studies* 33 (2000): 76–93.

Hiebert, Robert J.V., ed. *"Translation Is Required": The Septuagint in Retrospect and Prospect*. Society of Biblical Literature Septuagint and Cognate Studies 56. Atlanta: Society of Biblical Literature, 2010.

Jellicoe, Sidney. *The Septuagint and Modern Study*. Oxford: Oxford University Press, 1968. Repr., Ann Arbor: Eisenbrauns, 1978.

Jobes, Karen H., and Moisés Silva. *Invitation to the Septuagint*. Grand Rapids: Baker Academic, 2000.

Kraus, Wolfgang, and Martin Karrer, eds. *Septuaginta Deutsch: Das griechische Alte Testament in deutscher Übersetzung*. Stuttgart: Deutsche Bibelgesellschaft, 2009.

Lee, John A.L. *A Lexical Study of the Septuagint Version of the Pentateuch*. Society of Biblical Literature Septuagint and Cognate Studies 14. Chico, Calif.: Scholars Press, 1983.

Liddell, Henry G., Robert Scott, and Henry S. Jones. *A Greek-English Lexicon*. 9th ed. with revised supplement. Oxford: Clarendon, 1996.

Pietersma, Albert, and Benjamin G. Wright, eds. *A New English Translation of the Septuagint and the Other Greek Translations Traditionally Included under That Title*. New York: Oxford University Press, 2007.

Smyth, Herbert W. *Greek Grammar*. Revised by Gordon M. Messing. Cambridge: Harvard University Press, 1956.

Swete, Henry Barclay. *An Introduction to the Old Testament in Greek*. New York: Ktav, 1968.

Thackeray, Henry St. John. *A Grammar of the Old Testament in Greek according to the Septuagint*. Cambridge: Cambridge University Press, 1909.

Thumb, Albert. *Die griechische Sprache im Zeitalter der Hellenismus: Beiträge zur Geschichte und Beurteilung der Koiné*. Strasbourg: Trübner, 1901. Repr., Berlin: de Gruyter, 1974.

Wevers, John William. "Apologia pro Vita Mea: Reflections on a Career in Septuagint Studies." *Bulletin of the International Organization for Septuagint and Cognate Studies* 32 (1999): 65–96.

———. *Notes on the Greek Text of Genesis*. Society of Biblical Literature Septuagint and Cognate Studies 35. Atlanta: Scholars Press, 1993.

———. *Text History of the Greek Genesis*. Mitteilungen des Septuaginta-Unternehmens 11. Abhandlungen der Akademie der Wissenschaften in Göttingen. Philologisch-Historische Klasse 3/81. Göttingen: Vandenhoeck & Ruprecht, 1974.

———. "The Göttingen Pentateuch: Some Post-partem Reflections." Pages 51–60 in *VII Congress of the International Organization for Septuagint and Cognate Studies, Leuven, 1989*. Society of Biblical Literature Septuagint and Cognate Studies 31. Edited by Claude E. Cox. Atlanta: Scholars Press, 1991.

———. "The Interpretative Character and Significance of the Septuagint Version."

Pages 84–107 in *Hebrew Bible/Old Testament: The History of Its Interpretation, Volume 1: From the Beginnings to the Middle Ages (Until 1300)*. Edited by Magne Sæbø, in cooperation with Chris Brekelmans and Menahem Haran. Göttingen: Vandenhoeck & Ruprecht, 1996.

Wevers, John William, ed. *Septuaginta: Vetus Testamentum Graecum Auctoritate Academiae Scientiarum Gottingensis editum—I: Genesis*. Göttingen: Vandenhoeck & Ruprecht, 1974.

WHEN THE BEGINNING IS THE END: THE PLACE OF GENESIS IN THE COMMENTARIES OF PHILO[1]

Gregory E. Sterling

The Book of Genesis has played a pivotal role in biblical scholarship. The opening chapters helped to give rise to source criticism specifically and historical critical scholarship more generally.[2] The stories of the ancestors became the basis for form criticism as it was applied to narrative.[3] The Joseph story has been a focal point of interest in literary analyses of the Bible.[4] While these three statements hardly exhaust the role of Genesis in the development of biblical scholarship, they illustrate its centrality and importance. It would be possible to trace a good deal of the history of the methods of biblical scholarship during the last two hundred years by writing a history of the interpretation of Genesis.

The importance of Genesis for biblical interpretation is not new. It was the most significant book for Second Temple Judaism's greatest interpreter of Scripture, Philo of Alexandria (20 BCE – 50 CE). He wrote forty-three treatises on Genesis within his three commentary series. This is in marked contrast to the other large body of commentaries that we have from this period of Judaism, the commentaries among the scrolls found at or near Qumran. The majority and most significant group of these commentaries are known as *pesharim* from the practice of offering an eschatological interpretation (*pesher*) of the biblical text.[5] The Sons of the Covenant left six

---

[1] I gave a draft of this chapter as a public lecture at Amherst College on December 13, 2010. I am grateful to Robert Doran for his kind invitation and for the faculty and students at Amherst and Smith Colleges for their comments.

[2] One of the most important early contributions to the development of the documentary hypothesis was the work of Jean Astruc, *Conjectures sur les memoires originaux, dont il paroit que Moyse s'est servi pour composer le livre de la Genèse* (Bruxelles: Fricx, 1753; repr., Paris: Noesis, 1999).

[3] E.g., Hermann Gunkel, *Genesis: Translated and Interpreted* (trans. Mark E. Biddle; Macon, Ga.: Mercer University Press, 1997); trans. of *Genesis übersetzt und erklärt* (3rd ed.; KAT 1/1; Göttingen: Vandenhoeck & Ruprecht, 1910). The preface has also appeared in a separate English translation: Hermann Gunkel, *The Legends of Genesis: The Biblical Saga and History* (trans. W.H. Carruth; 1901; repr., New York: Schocken, 1964).

[4] E.g., Donald B. Redford, *A Study of the Biblical Story of Joseph (Genesis 37–50)* (VTSup 20; Leiden: Brill, 1970).

[5] On the *pesharim* see Maurya P. Horgan, *Pesharim: Qumran Interpretations of Biblical*

manuscripts of commentaries on Isaiah;[6] three on the Psalter;[7] two each on Hosea,[8] Micah,[9] and Zephaniah;[10] and one each on Nahum[11] and Habbakuk.[12] They left only one manuscript of a *pesher* commentary on Genesis.[13] There are other fragments that appear to share the same format as the *pesharim*, but do not use the term *pesher*. We know of three such works on Genesis[14] and two works on Malachi.[15] If we total both groups of commentaries, we have sixteen manuscripts that preserve commentaries on the prophets, three on the psalms, and four on Genesis. The concentration on prophetic texts and the Psalter is hardly a surprise given the apocalyptic nature of the community: they interpreted texts that they believed pointed to their community and its understanding of the eschaton. Philo offers us a very different point of orientation. In contrast to his forty-three treatises on Genesis, he did not write any commentaries on the prophets or the Psalter. Why did Philo favor Genesis? What was it about Genesis that the Alexandrian found so inviting in contrast to his contemporaries on the Northwest side of the Dead Sea?

THE THREE COMMENTARY SERIES[16]

Before we attempt to answer this question directly, we need to understand the nature of Philo's commentaries. He wrote three independent sets of commentaries on the Pentateuch.[17]

Books (CBQMS 8; Washington, D.C.: The Catholic Biblical Association of America, 1979); and James H. Charlesworth, ed., *The Dead Sea Scrolls: Hebrew, Aramaic, and Greek Texts with English Translations: Pesharim, Other Commentaries, and Related Documents* (PTSDSSP 6B; Tübingen/Louisville: Mohr Siebeck/Westminster John Knox, 2002).

[6] 3QpIsa (3Q4); 4QpIsa^a (4Q161); 4QpIsa^b (4Q162); 4QpIsa^c (4Q163); 4QpIsa^d (4Q164); and 4QpIsa^e (4Q165).

[7] 1QpPs (1Q16); 4QpPs^a (4Q171); and 4QpPs^b (4Q173).

[8] 4QpHos^a (4Q166) and 4QpHos^b (4Q167).

[9] 1QpMic (1Q14) and 4QpMic (4Q168).

[10] 1QpZeph (1Q15) and 4QpZeph (4Q170).

[11] 4QpNah (4Q169).

[12] 1QpHab.

[13] 4Q252.

[14] 4QCommGen B (4Q253); 4QCommGen C (4Q254); and 4QCommGen D (4Q254a).

[15] 4QCommMal (4Q25) and 5Q210.

[16] I have summarized Philo's commentaries in other publications as well. There is, of necessity, some overlap with the summary that follows. E.g., Gregory E. Sterling, "The Interpreter of Moses: Philo of Alexandria and the Biblical Text," in *A Companion to Biblical Interpretation in Early Judaism* (ed. Matthias Henze; Grand Rapids: Eerdmans, 2011), 413–433.

[17] I use the term Pentateuch rather than Torah because Philo worked with a Greek text.

The Questions and Answers on Genesis and Exodus. The first series is *The Questions and Answers on Genesis and Exodus.*[18] Unfortunately, the original Greek text has been lost except for fragments;[19] we are dependent on a partial Armenian translation from the sixth century[20] and an even more partial Latin translation of the fourth century.[21] I say partial because both are incomplete. For example, the longer Armenian preserves four books for Genesis and two for Exodus, although these can not represent the original division of the material. The problem is immediately obvious by considering the proportions of the four books for Genesis: book 1 contains 100 questions and answers, book 2 has 82, book 3 contains 62, while book 4 has 245 or one more than the first three books combined. Further, Codex Vindobonensis theol. Gr. 29 assigned six books to the *Questions and Answers on Genesis.*[22] Ralph Marcus noted that the coverage of some of the books corresponded to the *parashiyyot* or weekly reading cycles of the Babylonian lectionary, and suggested that Philo may have naturally structured the

---

[18] This series has been relatively neglected in Philonic scholarship. The most important treatments are: Charles Mercier, trans., *Quaestiones et solutiones in Genesim I et II: e versione armeniaca* (OPA 34A; Paris: Cerf, 1979), 15–60; David M. Hay, ed., *Both Literal and Allegorical: Studies in Philo of Alexandria's* Questions and Answers on Genesis and Exodus (BJS 232; Atlanta: Scholars Press, 1991); and Sze-Kar Wan, "The *Quaestiones et solutions in Genesim et in Exodum* of Philo Judaeus: A Synoptic Analysis" (Ph.D. diss., Harvard University, 1992), which is summarized in Sze-Kar Wan, "*Quaetiones et Solutiones in Genesim*: A Synoptic Approach," in *Society of Biblical Literature 1993 Seminar Papers* (ed. Eugene H. Lovering, Jr.; SBLSP 32; Atlanta: Scholars Press, 1993), 22–53.

[19] Françoise Petit, trans., *Quaestiones in Genesim et in Exodum: Fragmenta graeca* (CPA 33; Paris: Cerf, 1978). See also James R. Royse, "Further Greek Fragments of Philo's *Quaestiones*," in *Nourished with Peace: Studies in Hellenistic Judaism in Memory of Samuel Sandmel* (ed. Frederick E. Greenspahn, Earle Hilgert, and Burton L. Mack; Chico, Calif.: Scholars Press, 1984), 143–153; and Royse, "Philo's *Quaestiones in Exodum* 1.6," in Hay, *Both Literal and Allegorical*, 17–27.

[20] The only edition of the Armenian is J.B. Aucher, *Judaei paralipomena Armena (Libri videlicet quottuor In Genesin, libri duo In Exodum, sermo unus De Sampsone, alter De Jona, tertius De tribus angelis Abraamo apparentibus): Opera hactenus inedita (Ex Armena versione antiquissima ab ipso originali textu Graeco ad verbum stricte exequuta saeculo v. nunc primum in Latium fideliter translata)* (Venice: L. Lazarus, 1826). Aucher provided a Latin translation. English speakers have access to Philo most easily through Francis Henry Colson, George Herbert Whitaker, and Ralph Marcus, eds., *Philo* (10 vols. and 2 supplementary vols.; LCL; Cambridge: Harvard University Press, 1929–1962). Hereafter abbreviated PLCL. *The Questions and Answers* are translated in the two supplementary volumes.

[21] Françoise Petit, trans., *L'ancienne version latine des Questions sur la Genèse de Philon d'Alexandrie* (2 vols.; TUGAL 113–114; Berlin: Akademie, 1973).

[22] Leopold Cohn, Paul Wendland, Sigofred Reiter, and Ioannes Leisegang, eds., *Philonis Alexandrini opera quae supersunt* (7 vols.; Berlin: Georg Reimer, 1896–1930; 2nd ed.; Berlin: de Gruyter, 1962), 1:xxxvi–xxxvii. Hereafter abbreviated PCW.

books of his *Questions and Answers* along similar lines.[23] The situation is also complicated for Exodus where the Armenian only preserves two books. Eusebius knew five.[24] If we follow Marcus' suggestion, we can identify six books for Genesis and six for Exodus.[25]

The Armenian translation that we have provides a running commentary on Gen 2:4–28:9 and Exod 12:2–28:24, although there are lacunae. While it is possible that Philo provided treatments of other sections of Genesis and Exodus or even other books in the Pentateuch, the evidence for this is problematic.[26] We are on *terra firma* for Genesis and Exodus but no more.

Philo's *modus operandi* was to work sequentially through the biblical text posing questions and then providing answers. The questions typically begin with "why" or "what is" followed by a citation from the biblical text. The occasion for the question varies but often is provoked by a difficulty in the text or a philosophical issue that Philo believed the text elucidates. The answers offer both literal and symbolic options much in the same way that modern commentators provide readers with possible readings for difficulties in the biblical text. Each question and answer is relatively brief, although the length varies.[27]

As a work the *Questions and Answers* belongs to the zetematic literary tradition or what medieval scribes called *erotapokriseis*—a compound word from "question" (ἐρώτησις) and "answer" (ἀπόκρισις). The tradition began with Aristotle's *Homeric Problems* and became commonplace in philosophical circles in the Hellenistic and Roman worlds, e.g., Plutarch's *Platonic Questions*.[28] Previous Jewish authors such as Demetrius (frgs. 2 and 5)[29] and

---

[23] Markus in PLCL Sup. 1:xiii–xv.

[24] Eusebius, *Hist. eccl.* 2.18.5.

[25] For more recent discussions see Enzo Lucchesi, "La division en six livres des *Quaestiones in Genesim* de Philon d'Alexandrie," *Muséon* 89 (1976): 383–395; James R. Royse, "The Original Structure of Philo's *Quaestiones*," *SPhilo* 4 (1976–1977): 41–78; and Royse, "Philo's Division of His Works into Books," *SPhA* 13 (2001): 76–85.

[26] See Royse, "The Original Structure of Philo's *Quaestiones*," 42–43, 52–53, for a sober treatment of the evidence.

[27] For an analysis of *Questions on Genesis* 1 see Gregory E. Sterling, "Philo's *Quaestiones*: Prolegomena or Afterthought?," in Hay, *Both Literal and Allegorical*, 101–105.

[28] The most important treatments of the genre are Wan, "The *Quaetiones et solutions in Genesim et in Exodum* of Philo Judaeus"; and Annelie Volgers and Claudio Zamagni, eds., *Erotapokriseis: Early Christian Question-and-Answer Literature in Context* (CBET 37; Leuven: Peeters, 2004), esp. the essay by Pieter W. van der Horst, "Philo and the Rabbis on Genesis: Similar Questions, Different Answers," 55–70.

[29] Demetrius frg. 2 (= Eusebius, *Praep. ev.* 9.21.14), which discusses why Joseph gave Benjamin a fivefold portion; frg. 5 (= Eusebius, *Praep. ev.* 9.29.16), which discusses how the

Aristobulus (frg. 2)[30] had used the format, but Philo is the first known Jewish author to cast a full-scale commentary as an *eratopokrisis*. He did not need to create all of the questions or all of the answers, but he is the first to put these together in a systematic form.

The important point for our purposes is that Philo devoted half (six out of twelve)—if the divisions of the books followed ancient Jewish lectionary cycles—or two-thirds (four out of six)—if we simply follow the Armenian translation—to Genesis.

The Allegorical Commentary. The second major commentary series is the Allegorical Commentary. The name of the series is not original to Philo but was taken from some of the initial treatises in the commentary. Eusebius was the first to call these treatises by this name when he summarized Philo's library as it existed in Caesarea in his day and the name has endured in the tradition.[31] The series is Philo's largest and most famous commentary series. We have nineteen treatises[32] and a fragment of another;[33] however, we know of at least twelve others that have been lost.[34]

Israelites obtained their weapons. The standard edition of Demetrius is Carl R. Holladay, *Fragments from Hellenistic Jewish Authors, Volume 1: Historians* (SBLTT 20; Atlanta: Scholars Press, 1983), 51–91.

[30] Aristobulus frg. 2 (= Eusebius, *Praep. ev.* 8.9.3–8.10.1), which discusses why the Pentateuch uses anthropomorphisms for God. The standard edition is Carl R. Holladay, *Fragments from Hellenistic Jewish Authors, Volume 3: Aristobulus* (SBLTT39; Atlanta: Scholars Press, 1995).

[31] Eusebius, *Hist. eccl.* 2.18.1; Origen, *Comm. Matt.* 17:17; Origen, *Cels.* 4.51; Photius, *Bibliotheca*, col. 103.

[32] Philo, *Alleg. Interp.* 1 (from *Alleg. Interp.* 1–2), 3; *Cherubim, Sacrifices, Worse, Posterity, Giants* and *Unchangeable* (originally one treatise but now two), *Agriculture, Planting, Drunkenness* 1; *Sobriety, Confusion, Migration, Heir, Prelim. Studies, Flight, Names, Dreams* 2 and 3 (= *Dreams* 1 and 2). The standard critical edition is PCW. An ET is available in PLCL.

[33] *De Deo* is preserved in an Armenian fragment. See Folker Siegert, *Philon von Alexandrien, Über die Gottesbezeichnung "wohltätig verzehrendes Feuer" (De Deo): Rückübersetzung des Fragments aus dem Armenischen, deutsche Übersetzung und Kommentar* (WUNT 46; Tübingen: Mohr Siebeck, 1988); and Siegert, "The Philonian Fragment De Deo: First English Translation," *SPhA* 10 (1998): 1–33.

[34] Some of these can be posited by lacunae, others by references to them: Gen 1:1–31 is missing (see Thomas H. Tobin, "The Beginning of Philo's *Legum Allegoriae*," *SPhA* 12 [2000]: 29–43); Gen 3:1b–8a is missing (= *Leg.* 2); Gen 3:20–23 is missing (= *Leg.* 4; see also *Sacr.* 51); Gen 4:5–7 is missing; Gen 5:32, on Shem is lost (see *Sobr.* 52); *On the covenants*, 2 vols. are lost (see *Mut.* 53 and Eusebius, *Hist. eccl.* 2.18.3); *Drunkenness* vol. 2 (see *Sobr.* 1 and Eusebius, *Hist. eccl.* 2.18.2); Gen 15:1, *On rewards* (see *Heir* 1); *On dreams* vol. 1, 4, 5 (see Eusebius, *Hist. eccl.* 2.18.4).

Like the *Questions and Answers*, the treatises form a running commentary;[35] however, in this case the commentary is on Gen 2:1–18:2, if we include the fragment preserved in Armenian that we know as *De Deo*. There are some notable gaps within this treatment; for example, Philo appears to have skipped a discussion of the flood. We do not know how far the series extended into Genesis. The treatises *On Dreams* interpret later texts in Genesis and do not form a direct continuation, but probably belong to the series. There is no evidence that the series extended beyond Genesis.

Philo's *modus operandi* is both similar to and dissimilar to his pattern in the *Questions and Answers*.[36] It is most similar in the beginning of each exposition. Just as he posed a question and cited the biblical text in the *Questions and Answers*, so he cited the biblical text in Genesis at the outset of his exposition in the Allegorical Commentary. We call these citations the primary lemmata. He also frequently made use of the same questions, although he did not always cast them as interrogatives in the Allegorical Commentary.[37] The most obvious difference lies in the length of his interpretation. So, for example, whereas he treated Gen 9:20 in a single short question in the *Questions and Answers*,[38] he devoted a separate treatise to Gen 9:20a (*On Agriculture*) and a separate treatise to Gen 9:20b (*On Planting*) in the Allegorical Commentary. While this is an extreme example, it provides an idea of the difference in the scope of the treatments. Philo worked through the primary lemma by citing a word or phrase from the lemma and commenting on it before repeating the process with a subsequent word or phrase. He expanded his treatment of each word or phrase by introducing secondary and tertiary biblical lemmata that were linked by word plays or thematic comparisons. The result is an elaborate tapestry of exegetical treatments. While these can—and often do—bewilder a reader, Philo appears to have thought of these as part of a larger unity. The treatises appear to have unifying themes to which Philo returns, no matter how far afield his interpretations of secondary and tertiary lemmata take him.

---

[35] Eusebius, *Hist. eccl.* 2.18.1, noted this when he introduced the works.

[36] For a recent treatment of Philo's allegorical exegesis see Adam Kamesar, "Biblical Interpretation in Philo," in *The Cambridge Companion to Philo* (ed. Adam Kamesar; Cambridge: Cambridge University Press, 2009), 65–91.

[37] So Valentin Nikiprowetzky, "L'Exégèse de Philon d'Alexandrie dans le *De Gigantibus* et le *Quod Deus sit Immutabilis*," in *Two Treatises of Philo of Alexandria* (ed. David Winston and John M. Dillon; BJS 25; Chico, Calif.: Scholars Press, 1983), 8. For specific examples see Sterling, "Philo's *Quaestiones*," 112–115.

[38] Philo, *QG* 2.67.

The form that the commentaries took is most similar to the shape of commentaries in the philosophical tradition, especially the anonymous *Theatetus Commentary*, Plutarch's *On the Generation of the Soul in the Timaeus*, and Porphyry's *On the Cave of Nymphs*.[39] There is, however, a basic difference between these individual commentaries and the thirty-two treatises in the Allegorical Commentary: Philo linked all of his treatises together into a unified whole. He created the unity in two ways: first—as we have suggested—he worked through the text sequentially.[40] Second, he linked his treatments together through secondary prefaces. The practice of writing secondary prefaces goes back to the fourth century BCE historian Ephorus[41] and became a commonplace among some Hellenistic historians such as Diodorus[42] and Josephus.[43] Philo followed the tradition and wrote secondary prefaces for at least six of the treatises in this commentary.[44] For example, he opened *On Flight and Discovery* with a reference to *On the Preliminary Studies*: "Having discussed in the preceding the things that were appropriate to the preliminary studies and evil, we will next record the treatment of fugitives."[45] In these two ways he has created a single commentary out of thirty-two treatises.

---

[39] John M. Dillon, "The Formal Structure of Philo's Allegorical Exegesis," in *Two Treatises of Philo of Alexandria* (ed. David Winston and John M. Dillon; BJS 25; Chico, Calif.: Scholars Press, 1983), 77–87, which also appeared in John Glucker and André Laks, eds., *Jacob Bernays: Un philologue juif* (Cahiers de Philologie 16; Villeneuve d'Ascq: Presses universitaires du Septentrion, 1996), 123–131; David T. Runia, "The Structure of Philo's Allegorical Treatises: A Review of Two Recent Studies and Some Additional Comments," *VC* 38 (1984): 209–256; Runia, "Further Observations on the Structure of Philo's Allegorical Treatises," *VC* 41 (1987): 105–138 (both reprinted in his *Exegesis and Philosophy: Studies on Philo of Alexandria* [CSS 332; London: Variorum, 1990], chs. 4 and 5); and Runia, "The Structure of Philo's Allegorical Treatise *De agricultura*," *SPhA* 22 (2010): 87–109, provide the most helpful discussions of the nature of the commentaries in the Allegorical Commentary series.

[40] There are some exceptions. See the cautions of Runia, "The Structure of Philo's Allegorical Treatise *De agricultura*," 89–91.

[41] Ephorus, *FGrH* 70.

[42] All of the extant books of the *Bibliotheke Historike* have full prefaces except for 2, 3, and 11. Many of the partially preserved books also have secondary prefaces. For Diodorus' practice see Kenneth S. Sacks, "The Lesser Prooemia of Diodorus Siculus," *Hermes* 110 (1982): 434–443, and Sacks, *Diodorus Siculus and the First Century* (Princeton: Princeton University Press, 1990), 9–22.

[43] Josephus, *Ant.* 8.1; 13.1; 14.1; 15.1; 20.1. For an analysis see Gregory E. Sterling, *Historiography and Self-definition: Josephos, Luke-Acts and Apologetic Historiography* (NovTSup 64; Leiden: Brill, 1992), 247–248.

[44] Philo, *Plant.* 1; *Ebr.* 1; *Sobr.* 1; *Heir* 1; *Fug.* 2; *Somn.* 1.1.

[45] Philo, *Fug.* 2. The treatise opens with a citation of Gen 16:6–9, 11–12. These are the first words following the biblical text. All translations are my own.

The most significant aspect of this commentary for our present purposes is that Philo devoted his *magnum opus* exclusively to an exposition of Genesis.

Exposition of the Law. Philo's third commentary series—probably written late in his life—was the Exposition of the Law.[46] The name of the series is a modern construct rather than an ancient heading.[47] Fortunately, we have twelve[48] of the original fifteen treatises.[49]

Unlike the first two series that were devoted either to Genesis and Exodus or exclusively to Genesis, the Exposition attempts to cover the entire Pentateuch. We are fortunate that Philo explained his understanding of the Pentateuch and plan for the series in three different statements.[50] The statements do not agree in all of the specifics, but the general outline is clear. We will consider the statement from the final treatise that reflects his view of the work when he could look back across the entirety of it:[51] "There are three types of oracles (given) through the prophet Moses: the first is the creation of the cosmos, the second is historical, and the third is legislative." In his two other programmatic statements he had envisioned two parts. In this statement he separated creation out as a distinct category and made the ancestors the historical part. Philo continued by explaining the legislative part: "Of the legislative, one part consists of a general subject, the other consists of the commandments of specific laws." He unpacked the distinction between general subject and specific laws based on the medium through which the laws came: "On the one hand there are the ten heads, which are

---

[46] Philo's reference to civil concerns in *Spec.* 3.1–6 probably refers to the pogrom in Alexandria and his role in the embassy to Gaius in 39–40. Since the treatises in the Exposition are linked by secondary prefaces, he may have written them sequentially, a fact that does not require but suggests that they were written in approximately the same time period. There is also some evidence from the cross references in the commentaries. Philo indicated that he planned to write treatises in the Exposition while he was working on the Allegorical Commentary: *Sacr.* 136 (an apparent reference to *Spec.* 1.212–219); *Sobr.* 9 (a reference to *Isaac*); *Somn.* 1.168 (a reference to *Abraham*). He appears to refer back to the lost treatise in the Allegorical Commentary on Gen 1 in *Decal.* 101.

[47] Leopold Cohn, "Einleitung und Chronologie der Schriften Philos," *Philologus: Supplementband* 7 (1899): 405.

[48] Philo, *Mos.* 1 and 2; *Creation; Abraham; Joseph; Decalogue; Spec.* 1, 2, 3, 4; *Virtues; Rewards.* The standard critical edition is PCW. The text with an English translation can be found in PLCL.

[49] The three lost treatises are *Isaac* (see *Joseph* 1); *Jacob* (see Joseph 1); and *Passions* (see *Leg.* 3.139).

[50] Philo, *Abr.* 2–5; *Mos.* 2.45–47; *Praem.* 1–3.

[51] I will treat the other two texts below in the introduction to the second half, "The Importance of Genesis."

said to have been delivered not through an interpreter but—formed in the height of the atmosphere—are rational articulation. On the other hand, the particular laws were delivered through the prophet." He has in mind the distinction between the Ten Words set out in *On the Decalogue* and the use of the ten commandments as headings for specific laws in *On the Special Laws*. He then moved on to standard secondary preface language: "I have gone through all of these as was opportune in the preceding treatises and in addition, the virtues that he allots to peace and war"—a reference to *On the Virtues*—"I now pursue in sequence the rewards set out for the good and the punishments for the evil"—a reference to the present work *On Rewards and Punishments*.[52] The scope of the work thus coincides with the entire Pentateuch: it began with creation in Gen 1 (*Creation*) and extended to the blessings and curses in Moses' final speech in Deuteronomy (*Rewards*). The unity of the treatises as a single work is confirmed by the secondary prefaces that open every treatise except *Creation* for which we would not expect a secondary preface since it is the first treatise.[53]

There is one important piece missing from this description. Philo also wrote a two volume *Life of Moses*. The place of the life has been disputed.[54] Two factors make me think that it belongs to the Exposition of the Law: first—as we have seen—it provides an explanation of the Exposition; and second, Philo referred back to it in the last two treatises of the Exposition.[55] He routinely referred to previous works in the same commentary series and only rarely to works in a different series. But how did it relate to the series? He did not refer to it when he mentioned his treatments of the lives of Abraham, Isaac, and Jacob in the secondary preface that opened

---

[52] Philo, *Praem.* 1–3.

[53] Philo, *Abr.* 1–6; *Ios.* 1; *Decal.* 1; *Spec.* 1.1; 2.1; 3.7; 4.1, 132–135 (for *Virtues*); *Praem.* 1–3. Peder Borgen, "Philo of Alexandria—A Systematic Philosopher or an Eclectic Editor? An Examination of His Exposition of the Laws of Moses" *SO* 71 (1996): 115–134, argued that Philo disclosed his views of the text in these transitional statements.

[54] The most important treatments are Erwin R. Goodenough, "Philo's Exposition of the Law and his *De vita Mosis*," *HTR* 26 (1933): 109–125; Valentin Nikiprowetzky, *Le Commentaire de l'écriture chez Philon d'Alexandrie, son caractère et sa portée: Observations philologiques* (ALGHJ 11; Leiden: Brill, 1977), 194–197; Jenny Morris, "The Jewish Philosopher Philo," in Emil Schürer, *The History of the Jewish People in the Age of Jesus Christ* (rev. and ed. Geza Vermes, Fergus Millar, and Martin Goodman; 3 vols.; Edinburgh: T&T Clark, 1973–1987), 3.2:854–855; Folkert Fendler, *Studien zum Markusevangelium: Zur Gattung, Chronologie, Messiasgeheimnistheorie und Überlieferung des zweiten Evangeliums* (GTA 49; Göttingen, Vandenhoeck & Ruprecht, 1991), 62–68; and Louis H. Feldman, *Philo's Portrayal of Moses in the Context of Ancient Judaism* (CJA 15; Notre Dame, Ind.: University of Notre Dame Press, 2007), 11–33.

[55] Philo, *Virt.* 52; *Praem.* 53.

The Life of Joseph. The best explanation is that it was an introductory life designed to introduce the series in the same way that Porphyry's *Life of Plotinus* introduced the *Enneads*.[56]

The Exposition differs from Philo's other two commentary series in another significant way. Unlike the *Questions and Answers* and the Allegorical Commentary where he worked directly from biblical lemmata, Philo rarely cited the biblical text as a basis for his exegesis in the Exposition. For example, in the treatise *On the Creation of the Universe* he only cited the biblical text verbatim six times.[57] He occasionally paraphrased the text, but preferred to weave words or phrases into his interpretations.[58] This was not unusual in the Exposition. His standard procedure was to summarize the biblical text and to provide a commentary on his summary in much the same way that a contemporary homilist summarizes a biblical text and then comments on her or his summary.

The fact that Philo summarized the biblical narrative led Peder Borgen to call Philo's treatment of the biblical text "rewritten Bible."[59] Borgen argued that the best parallels for Philo's handling of the biblical text in the Exposition of the Law are *Jubilees*, the *Genesis Apocryphon*, Pseudo-Philo's *Biblical Antiquities*, and Josephus' *Jewish Antiquities*. However, there is a significant difference between Philo's handling of the text and that of his compatriots: he added a layer of commentary at the figurative or allegorical level that they did not. For this reason, I think that it would be preferable to say that Philo appropriated the tradition of rewriting the text in the Exposition but used it as a technique within the commentary tradition. If this is correct, the Exposition is not rewritten Scripture, but a commentary that uses the technique of rewritten Scripture to summarize the text rather than to cite it as Philo had done in the other two commentary series.

In this series, Philo's attention extends well beyond Genesis. Still, he devoted five of the fifteen treatises or 33% of the treatises to Genesis.

Summary. We can summarize the evidence of Philo's use of Genesis in two ways. First, if we count the number of treatises in his commentary series

---

[56] Albert C. Geljon, *Philonic Exegesis in Gregory of Nyssa's* De vita Moysis (BJS 333; Providence, R.I.: Brown University Press, 2002), 7–46.

[57] Gen 1:1 in *Opif.* 26; Gen 1:2 in *Opif.* 32; Gen 1:26 in *Opif.* 72; Gen 2:4–5 in *Opif.* 129; Gen 2:6 in *Opif.* 131, 133; and Gen 2:7 in *Opif.* 134–135, 139.

[58] For an analysis see David T. Runia, *Philo of Alexandria,* On the Creation of the Cosmos according to Moses: *Introduction, Translation and Commentary* (PACS 1; Leiden: Brill, 2001), 10–17.

[59] Peder Borgen, *Philo of Alexandria: An Exegete for His Time* (NovTSup 86; Leiden: Brill, 1997), 46–79, esp. 63–79.

that he devoted to Genesis, it runs to forty-three out of fifty-nine or 73%. If we want to be more nuanced in our calculations, we can count the number of times that he cited or alluded to the biblical text throughout the entirety of his corpus. I have counted these based on the tabulations in the *Biblia patristica* Supplement devoted to Philo.[60] Here are the results:

Citations or Echoes of Scripture in Philo

Biblical Text	Number of Citations or Echoes
Genesis	4,303
Exodus	1,755
Leviticus	737
Numbers	586
Deuteronomy	834
Joshua	4
Judges	4
1 Samuel	24
1 Kings	9
2 Kings	2
Isaiah	24
Jeremiah	18
Ezekiel	7
Hosea	7
Zechariah	2
Psalms	50
Job	8
Proverbs	30
Ecclesiastes	2
Esther	1
1 Chronicles	10
2 Chronicles	2
Wisdom	32
Sirach	11

The importance of the Pentateuch is unambiguous; however, so is the importance of Genesis. Philo cited or alluded to Greek texts that eventually became recognized as Scripture 8,462 times. Of these, 8,215 or 97% are from

---

[60] The numbers are based on the references in Jean Allenbach et al., eds., *Biblia patristica, Supplément: Philon d'Alexandrie* (Paris: Centre national de la recherché scientifique, 1982).

the Pentateuch and 4,303 or 51% are from Genesis. No other book comes close. Here are the percentages of the citations and echoes from the books in the Pentateuch:

Biblical Book	Number of Citations and Echoes	Percentage of the Total
Genesis	4,303	51%
Exodus	1,755	21%
Leviticus	737	9%
Numbers	586	7%
Deuteronomy	834	10%

Genesis has more citations and echoes than all of the other books of the Pentateuch combined. If we add up the totals for Exodus through Deuteronomy, they run to 3,912. Their total constitutes 46% of the total. Thus Genesis has 391 more citations and echoes or 5% more than the other four books of the Pentateuch combined. Even if we allow for the fact that the Allegorical Commentary that focuses exclusively on Genesis is Philo's most extensive commentary and that he worked directly from the biblical text in it, the fact that he elected to write his major work exclusively on Genesis is telling.

The Importance of Genesis

Why did Philo devote his life's work to Genesis? What did he find in Genesis that was so attractive that he spent his life commenting on it? We can begin by looking at his summaries of the book itself. He knew and used the book by the name Genesis on at least three occasions. For example, Philo opened his *Life of Abraham* with these words: "The first of the sacred laws that have been written in five books is called and entitled Genesis from the genesis of the universe that it contains in its opening." He added that it "received this appellation even though it contains many other events."[61] He explained the relationship of these other events to creation in his statements on the plan of the Exposition of the Law. In the introductory *Life of Moses*,

---

[61] Philo, *Abr.* 1. Philo mentioned it explicitly on two other occasions: *Post.* 129 and *Aet.* 19. The name Genesis was taken from Gen 2:4 and 5:1, although Philo does not make the connection when he interprets Gen 2:4 (*QG* 1.1; *Leg.* 1.19–20; *Post.* 65; *Opif.* 129). On Philo's knowledge and use of the names of biblical books see Helmut Burkhardt, *Die Inspiration heiliger Schriften bei Philo von Alexandrien* (2nd ed., Giessen: Brunnen, 1992), 73–74.

Philo suggested that the Pentateuch consisted of two parts: the first was historical and the second the commands and prohibitions. He wrote: "The historical consists of two parts: one deals with the creation of the universe, the other is genealogical."[62] By "genealogical" he meant the lives of the family of ancestors. The reference became clear in Philo's *Life of Abraham* where he again divided the Pentateuch into two parts, only this time he suggested that the creation of the universe was the historical part and the laws were the second part. In his final treatise—as we have already noted— he argued that there were three parts: creation, the historical part or lives of the ancestors, and the laws.[63] Philo thus understood Genesis to consist of two major sections: creation and the lives of the ancestors. We will need to keep both in mind as we attempt to answer our question.

His statements about the contents of Genesis do not, however, tell us why he considered it so important. Unfortunately, he never addressed this directly. We are left to deduce his answer based on what he accomplished and in the few comments that he made. There are at least three major reasons that led him to prefer Genesis.

Narrative and Allegory. The first is that Genesis is a narrative while half of Exodus, all of Leviticus, most of Numbers, and almost all of Deuteronomy are legal codes or non-narrative material. Philo inherited a tradition of commenting on a narrative. In particular the Stoics had developed allegorical interpretations of the Homeric epics and Hesiod.[64] The most famous is the first century CE. Cornutus.[65] While some have recently challenged whether the Stoics developed allegories from narratives or only offered etymological interpretations of names,[66] the debates have shown that the Stoics were more than etymologists; the etymologies gave meaning to a

---

[62] Philo, *Mos.* 2.47.
[63] Philo, *Praem.* 1–3.
[64] David Dawson, *Allegorical Readers and Cultural Revision in Ancient Alexandria* (Berkeley: University of California Press, 1992), 23–72, esp. 23–52, has a helpful overview. For a broader survey see Glenn W. Most, "Hellenistic Allegory and Early Imperial Rhetoric," in *The Cambridge Companion to Allegory* (ed. Rita Copeland and Peter T. Struck; Cambridge: Cambridge University Press, 2010), 26–38.
[65] The standard critical text is Carolus Lang, *Cornuti theologiae graecae compendium* (Leipzig: Teubner, 1881). For recent treatments see Glenn W. Most, "Cornutus and Stoic Allegoresis: A Preliminary Report," *ANRW* 2.36.3 (1989): 2014–2065; and Heniz Günther Nesselrath, ed., Cornutus, *Die Griechischen Götter: Ein Überblick über Namen, Bilder und Deutungen* (SAPERE 14; Tübingen: Mohr Siebeck, 2009).
[66] See, in particular, A.A. Long, "Stoic Readings of Homer," in *Homer's Ancient Readers: The Hermeneutics of Greek Epic's Earliest Exegetes* (ed. Robert Lamberton and John J. Keaney; Princeton: Princeton University Press, 1992), 41–66; and Long, "Allegory in Philo and Etymology in Stoicism: A Plea for Drawing Distinctions," *SPhA* 9 (1997): 198–210.

narrative—even if they did not create a grand allegory of the narrative.[67] Philo knew the Stoic interpretations of Homer.[68] It is possible—although not demonstrable—that he knew allegorizing traditions among Platonic or Pythagorean circles.[69] The Stoic etymological allegories at least serve as a precedent. It was quite natural for him to turn to Genesis and give it an allegorical interpretation. His use of etymologies in allegorical interpretation is, in fact, an important piece of evidence in the debates over Stoic allegoresis. It is difficult to believe that Philo invented the connection between etymology and a grand allegory of a narrative; he assumes the connection and does not argue for it.[70]

Precedent is, however, not an adequate motive. There may have been another quality of the Genesis narrative that appealed to Philo. Philo's allegory was an allegory of the soul.[71] He was fundamentally interested in how a human could experience the divine.[72] He read Genesis allegorically because he believed that it taught us how we could cultivate virtue and progress towards the experience of the divine. The narrative permitted him to trace movement or progress in a way that legal codes did not. So, for example, he understood Abraham's migration from Mesopotamia to the promised land to illustrate his progress towards virtue. The command to leave Haran was a command to leave the body, the realm of sense-perception and speech, and move towards the higher realities of the mind.[73] Again, Abraham's relationship with Hagar represents his training in the encylia. He left her for Sarah who represents philosophy.[74] While it was

---

[67] For a summary of one set of debates see L. Michael White, "Special Section: Etymology and Allegory, Introduction," *SPhA* 16 (2004): 96–100, esp. 97–98; and David T. Runia, "Etymology as an Allegorical Technique in Philo of Alexandria," *SPhA* 16 (2004): 101–121.

[68] Philo, *Prov.* 2.40–41. For details see Robert Lamberton, *Homer the Theologian: Neoplatonist Allegorical Reading and the Growth of the Epic Tradition* (TCH 9; Berkeley: University of California Press, 1986), 44–54.

[69] On the Pythagorean material see Ekaterina D. Matusova, "Allegorical Interpretation of the Pentateuch in Alexandria: Inscribing Aristobulus and Philo in a Wider Literary Context," *SPhA* 22 (2010): 1–51.

[70] See Runia, "Etymology as an Allegorical Technique in Philo of Alexandria," 116–119.

[71] The phrase is drawn from Philo, *Praem.* 158, where Philo says that Isa 54:1 "allegorizes about the soul" (ἐπὶ ψυχῇ ἀλληγογεῖται).

[72] Philo's allegory is similar in some striking ways to later Neoplatonic allegoresis. For an overview of the latter see Peter T. Struck, "Allegory and Ascent in Neoplatonism," in *The Cambridge Companion to Allegory* (ed. Rita Copeland and Peter T. Struck; Cambridge: Cambridge University Press, 2010), 57–70.

[73] Philo, *Migration*.

[74] Philo, *Preliminary Studies*.

possible to argue for progress towards virtue by allegorically interpreting the laws, the narratives of the ancestors offered possibilities that the legal codes of the next four books did not.

Biography and Virtue. This leads us to a second factor. There is a natural connection between the cultivation of virtue and biography. The most famous exploitation of this connection in the ancient world was the set of parallel Greek and Roman lives written by Plutarch. The Middle Platonic philosopher paired Greek and Roman lives to illustrate virtues and vices. Forty-four lives have survived in the manuscript tradition; the initial pair of *Epameinondas* and *Scipio* and any opening preface unfortunately did not. Plutarch explained the basic orientation of his lives in some of the prefaces to later works.[75] He wrote: "For it is not histories that I am writing but lives (βίους). The disclosure of virtue or vice is not always in the most glorious deeds, but it is often an insignificant thing, a word, a joke, that makes a person's character more evident than the deadliest battles, the greatest armaments, or the sieges of cities."[76] He did not write, however, merely to illustrate the virtues and vices of famous persons; rather, he believed that readers would find lives of virtue compelling models and want to imitate them. In this way he composed *Lives* to shape *lives*. He wrote in another preface: "Virtue in deeds immediately leads to such a disposition that a person both admires the accomplishments and seeks to imitate those who accomplished them."[77] Nor was this only for the sake of others. He once remarked: "I began to write my *Lives* for the sake of others, but I continue to write and to delight in it for my own sake as well, using history like a mirror to adorn and clothe my life with the virtues of the lives I set out."[78]

Philo shared this biographical orientation. As we have already seen, in the Exposition of the Law he explained Genesis in terms of creation and the lives of the ancestors. He had a particular understanding of the ancestors. They represented types of virtue or the acquisition of virtue.[79] He organized them into two triads. The first triad consisted of Enos, Enoch, and Noah.[80] Philo drew from a careful reading of the text to identify each ancestor with

---

[75] On the use of Plutarch's prefaces for understanding the purpose of the *Lives* see Alan Wardman, *Plutarch's Lives* (Berkeley: University of California Press, 1974), 18–26 and Tim Duff, *Plutarch's Lives: Exploring Virtue and Vice* (Oxford: Clarendon Press, 1999), 13–51.
[76] Plutarch, *Alex.* 1.2. See also *Nic.* 1.5.
[77] Plutarch, *Per.* 1.2. See 1.1–2.4.
[78] Plutarch, *Tim.* 1 (original preface to *Aemilius Paulus*). Cf. *Virt. Prof.* 84B–85B.
[79] For an analysis of the intellectual framework of this identification see Kamesar, 'Biblical Interpretation in Philo," 85–91.
[80] He worked out the details in *Abr.* 7–47 and *Praem.* 7–23.

a particular virtue. He identified Enos with hope (ἐλπίς) on the basis of the Greek translation of Gen 4:26: "he hoped (ἤλπισεν) to call on the name of the LORD God."[81] He thought that Enoch represented repentance on the basis of the Greek translation of Gen 5:24: "Enoch pleased God and was no more because God transferred him."[82] Philo understood "transferred" (μετέθηκεν) to indicate repentance (μετάνοια), since "transferred" implied a change that led to God's approval. It was thus his repentance that led God to take him. Noah illustrated perfection as Gen 6:9 said explicitly: "Noah was a just person and was perfect (τέλειος) in his generation."

Philo developed the second triad much more fully. For the second triad, he based his analysis on the larger narrative about their lives rather than a single statement. Each of the ancestors represented a type of soul and the way in which it can progress toward virtue. Abraham represented virtue through learning since he left his polytheistic home and set out for the monotheism of the promised land. Isaac represented native virtue: he was born virtuous. Jacob, the practiser, acquired virtue through practice.[83]

The biographical nature of Genesis lent itself to this understanding. Like Plutarch, Philo did not write his lives for the sake of history. He said: "These are the lives of men who have lived blamelessly and well; whose virtues have been inscribed in the most sacred Scriptures not for their praise alone, but for the benefit of those who read to encourage them to lead the same life."[84] While it would have been possible to have developed some of the figures in the other books of the Pentateuch—as Philo did in some of his treatments of secondary and tertiary lemmata—Genesis was particularly open to it.

A Universal Perspective. This leads us to the third and final point. In the Exposition of the Law Philo had to address the issue of the place of Genesis in the Pentateuch. Why did Moses begin his laws with an account of creation and with the lives of ancestors who lived prior to the law? He gave the same answer to both.

He addressed the problem directly at the outset of *On the Creation of the Universe*. He opened with a comparison between Moses and other lawgivers who plunged directly into their codes. Moses did not: "The beginning, as I just said, is most marvelous, consisting of the creation of the universe." Philo

---

[81] The MT reads: "then he began (הוחל) to call on the name of the LORD."

[82] The MT reads: "Enoch walked with God and was no more because God took (לקח) him."

[83] Philo made the connection between these three ancestors and the different paths to virtue repeatedly: *Sobr.* 65; *Congr.* 34–38; *Mut.* 12, 88; *Somn.* 1.168; *Abr.*52–54; *Ios.* 1; *Mos.* 1.76; *Praem.* 24–51, 57–66.

[84] Philo, *Abr.* 4.

explained that Moses began in this way to indicate "that the universe is in harmony with the law and the law with the universe and that a law-abiding person is a citizen of the universe, regulating his actions according to the will of nature by which the entire universe is managed."[85] It would be difficult to think of a more straightforward statement of natural law.[86] Philo offered a very similar statement in the *Life of Moses* where he again compared Moses to other authors: "He did not, like any other historian, make it his aim to leave records of ancient events to following generations for the sake of profitless amusement, but went back to the ancient period starting from the genesis of the universe." Moses began with creation "so that he could demonstrate two essential principles: one, that the same Father and Creator of the universe was in reality the Lawgiver; and two, that the person who keeps the laws will gladly follow the lead of nature and will live according to the order of the universe, through the harmony and concord of his words with his actions and his actions with his words."[87]

Philo made the same point in connection with the ancestors. He faced the challenge of explaining how Israel could have ancestors who lived prior to the law of Moses. He argued that they represented embodied law. His fullest statement occurs at the outset of his first life, *The Life of Abraham*: "These men were embodied and rational laws whom he praised for two reasons. First, he wanted to show that the legislated ordinances are not out of harmony with nature"—the same point that Philo made in connection with creation as we have just noted; "second, that it does not require an enormous effort for those who want to live by the stipulated laws, since the ancestors made use of unwritten legislation with perfect ease before any of the individual laws were recorded." He concluded: "Someone could say that the enacted laws are nothing but memorials of the lives of the ancients setting out from antiquity the deeds and words they used."[88]

Philo thus gave the same basic answer to the place of creation and the role of the ancestors: creation demonstrated that the universe was in harmony with the law and the law with the universe. The ancestors lived prior to a written code to demonstrate how law could be embodied in

---

[85] Philo, *Opif.* 2. See 1–3 and *Abr.* 2; *Mos.* 2.45–47.
[86] On the relationship between the law of nature and the Law of Moses see John W. Martens, *One God, One Law: Philo of Alexandria on Mosaic and Greco-Roman Law* (SPAMA 2; Leiden: Brill, 2003); and the essays in David T. Runia, Gregory E. Sterling, and Hindy Najman, eds., *Laws Stamped with the Seals of Nature: Law and Nature in Hellenistic Philosophy and Philo of Alexandria* (SPhA 15; BJS 337; Providence, R.I.: Brown University Press, 2003), 1–99.
[87] Philo, *Mos.* 2.48.
[88] Philo, *Abr.* 2–5.

people without a written code. Both answers moved Philo away from a narrow understanding of Judaism as an ethnic religion to a grasp of Judaism as an understanding of God that is open to all who live a rational life.[89] This does not mean that Philo eschewed the rituals of Judaism; he did not. On one famous occasion he criticized those who wanted to abolish Sabbath observance and circumcision by countering that to do so would undermine the identity of the community. Boundary markers needed to be observed.[90] The tensions between these two forces in Philo has led to a debate about the place of particularism and universalism in this thought.[91] My own view is that the most accurate way to speak of his position would be to think of particular universalism, that is to say that Philo thought universally, but argued that this universalism had been expressed most accurately and fully by Moses.

What role did Genesis play? Philo focused on Genesis because it recounted the period of Israel's history prior to the particular code of law that made the Jewish people distinct. It offered the opportunity to speak of Judaism prior to the specific code that pagans found problematic. He capitalized on the option.

Conclusions

Select books of the Bible have played significant roles in history. One need only think of the role of Paul's letter to the Romans in the life and thought of Augustine, Luther, Wesley, and Karl Barth to realize how individual books can have an enormous impact on history. Philo of Alexandria had a favorite biblical book: Genesis. He devoted his life to an exposition of it. The commentaries that he left easily constitute the largest body of exegesis on a single biblical book written by an individual ancient Jew. I am not aware of any equivalent body of exegesis for another biblical book until later centuries whether written by one person or many.

Genesis is the beginning book of Scripture. Philo understood it to be not only the beginning but the end. It was the point of orientation by which he read the remainder of Scripture. He thought that the goal or end of Scripture

---

[89] See his formulation in *Virt.* 65.
[90] Philo, *Migr.* 89–93.
[91] Ellen Birnbaum, *The Place of Judaism in Philo's Thought: Israel, Jews, and Proselytes* (BJS 290; Atlanta: Scholars Press, 1996), 3–6, 224–228, provides a helpful statement of the problem.

was already embedded within the very first book. It was for this reason that he devoted his life's work to it.

In a world where too many have narrowed religion and made it ethnocentric or sequestered it from the larger world, it is refreshing to find an ancient example of someone who devoted a lifetime of trying to develop a sense of identity in the larger world by reading his ancestral Scriptures through a lens that broadened rather than constricted his reading of sacred texts.

SELECT BIBLIOGRAPHY

Introductions to the Philonic Corpus

Morris, Jenny. "The Jewish Philosopher Philo." Pages 809–889 in vol. 3.2 of Emil Schürer, *The History of the Jewish People in the Age of Jesus Christ*. Revised and edited by Geza Vermes, Fergus Millar, and Martin Goodman. 3 vols. Edinburgh: T&T Clark, 1973–1987.

Royse, James R. "The Works of Philo." Pages 32–64 in *The Cambridge Companion to Philo*. Cambridge Companions to Philosophy. Edited by Adam Kamesar. Cambridge: Cambridge University Press, 2009.

Philo as an Exegete

Borgen, Peder. *Philo of Alexandria: An Exegete for His Time*. Supplements to Novum Testamentum 86. Leiden: Brill, 1997.

Burkhardt, Helmut. *Die Inspiration heiliger Schriften bei Philo von Alexandrien*. 2nd ed. Giessen: Brunnen, 1992.

Kamesar, Adam. "Biblical Interpretation in Philo." Pages 65–91 in *The Cambridge Companion to Philo*. Cambridge Companions to Philosophy. Edited by Adam Kamesar. Cambridge: Cambridge University Press, 2009.

Nikiprowetzky, Valentin. *Le Commentaire de l'écriture chez Philon d'Alexandrie, son caractère et sa portée: Observations philologiques*. Arbeiten zur Literatur und Geschichte des hellenistischen Judentums 11. Leiden: Brill, 1977.

Runia, David T. "The Structure of Philo's Allegorical Treatise De agricultura." Pages 87–109 in *The Studia Philonica Annual: Studies in Hellenistic Judaism Volume, XXII*. Edited by David T. Runia, and Gregory E. Sterling. Brown Judaic Studies. Atlanta: Society of Biblical Literature, 2010.

Siegert, Folker. "Early Jewish Interpretation in a Hellenistic Style." Pages 162–188 in *Hebrew Bible/Old Testament: The History of Its Interpretation, Volume 1: From the Beginnings to the Middle Ages (Until 1300)*. Edited by Magne Sæbø, in cooperation with Chris Brekelmans and Menahem Haran. Göttingen: Vandenhoeck & Ruprecht, 1996.

Sterling, Gregory E. "The Interpreter of Moses: Philo of Alexandria and the Biblical Text." Pages 413–433 in *A Companion to Biblical Interpretation in Early Judaism*. Edited by Matthias Henze. Grand Rapids: Eerdmans, 2011.

The Place of Israel and the Law in Philo's Thought

Birnbaum, Ellen. *The Place of Judaism in Philo's Thought: Israel, Jews, and Proselytes.* Brown Judaic Studies 290. Atlanta: Scholars Press, 1996.

Martens, John W. *One God, One Law: Philo of Alexandria on Mosaic and Greco-Roman Law.* Studies in Philo of Alexandria and Mediterranean Antiquity 2. Leiden: Brill, 2003.

Runia, David T., Gregory E. Sterling, and Hindy Najman, eds. *Laws Stamped with the Seals of Nature: Law and Nature in Hellenistic Philosophy and Philo of Alexandria. The Studia Philonica Annual* 15. Brown Judaic Studies 337. Providence, R.I.: Brown University Press, 2003.

THE RECEPTION OF GENESIS IN PSEUDO-PHILO'S
LIBER ANTIQUITATUM BIBLICARUM

Rhonda J. Burnette-Bletsch

Pseudo-Philo's *Liber Antiquitatum Biblicarum* (*L.A.B.*) is an interesting witness to Jewish interpretation and reception of scripture in the first century CE. Like other examples of the literary corpus sometimes dubbed 'rewritten Bible,' *L.A.B.* evinces great creativity in compressing, embellishing, and interpreting the biblical storyline from the creation of Adam to the death of Saul. It is Pseudo-Philo's imaginative retelling of scripture through the lens of Jewish interpretive traditions that makes *L.A.B.* "one of the most significant links between early haggadah and rabbinic midrash."[1]

The first section of this article will introduce the reader to what have been dominant interpretive issues in the scholarly reception of Pseudo-Philo's *L.A.B.* While not claiming to be exhaustive, this discussion will suffice as a brief survey of academic research on this text over the last half century.[2] The remainder of this article will specifically examine Pseudo-Philo's varied reception of Genesis traditions, making a distinction between the sequential retelling of Genesis offered in *L.A.B.* 1–8 and out-of-sequence citations of Genesis found in later chapters of the work. In particular, the Noahide and Abrahamic covenant traditions will be examined to illustrate the interpretive strategies that Pseudo-Philo brings to bear on Genesis.

L.A.B. IN RECENT SCHOLARSHIP

Pseudo-Philo's work survives in eighteen complete and three fragmentary Latin manuscripts dating from the eleventh to the fifteenth centuries.[3] It is quite possible that an original longer ending of *L.A.B.* has been lost since all

---

[1] Louis H. Feldman, "Prolegomenon," in *The Biblical Antiquities of Philo, Now First Translated from the Old Latin Version* by M.R. James (reissued ed.; New York: Ktav, 1971), ix.
[2] For a summary of Pseudo-Philo research prior to 1970, see Feldman, "Prolegomenon," ix–clxix.
[3] Daniel J. Harrington, "Pseudo-Philo," *OTP* 2:298. For a more in depth discussion of the manuscripts and their relationships see Harrington, *Les antiquités bibliques: Introduction et text critiques* (trans. Jacques Cazeaux; SC 229; Paris: Cerf, 1976), 15–59.

complete manuscripts end abruptly in the middle of Saul's final testament, but it is impossible to determine how much further the text may have once extended. Leopold Cohn reintroduced *L.A.B.* to the academic community in 1898, but the lack of a critical edition hampered scholarly research on this text for most of the twentieth century.[4] Daniel Harrington's publication of a Latin critical text in 1976 laid the necessary foundation for all subsequent work on Pseudo-Philo.[5] Since that date, English translations of *L.A.B.* have been produced by Harrington in 1985 and Howard Jacobson in 1996.[6]

During much of the twentieth century, scholarly research on *L.A.B.* focused on determining the original language, precursor text type, provenance, date, and polemical stance or social location of Pseudo-Philo's work. Following Cohn, most interpreters argue that the text was originally composed in Hebrew before being translated into Greek and then Latin.[7] Perhaps the most compelling evidence for an original Hebrew composition is Pseudo-Philo's apparent reliance upon a Hebrew biblical text. Harrington's contention that the biblical text presupposed in *L.A.B.* was of the Palestinian type (as opposed to Babylonian or Alexandrian) has gained widespread acceptance.[8] However, as Jacobson rightly notes, Pseudo-Philo's tendency to paraphrase scripture and cite it from memory might reasonably call into question any attempt to draw secure conclusions about *L.A.B.*'s precursor text.[9]

If Pseudo-Philo did use a Palestinian-type text and if *L.A.B.* was indeed composed in Hebrew, then a Palestinian provenance for the work would be all but certain. The likelihood of this provenance is also supported by Pseudo-Philo's apparent familiarity with Palestinian geography and *L.A.B.*'s strong literary parallels with *4 Ezra* and *2 Baruch* (both of Palestinian ori-

---

[4] Leopold Cohn, "An Apocryphal Work Ascribed to Philo of Alexandria," *JQR* 10 (1898): 277–332. On earlier strides toward establishing a critical text, see the comments of Feldman, "Prolegomenon," xviii–xix, lxxviii.

[5] Harrington, *Les antiquités bibliques*, 60–386.

[6] Harrington, "Pseudo-Philo," 297–377; and Howard Jacobson, *A Commentary on Pseudo-Philo's* Liber Antiquitatum Biblicarum *with Latin Text and English Translation* (2 vols.; AGJU 31; Leiden: Brill, 1996), 89–194. Unless otherwise stated, quotations of *L.A.B.* in this article will be drawn from Jacobson's translation.

[7] Cohn, "An Apocryphal Work," 277–332. See the repetition and expansion of these arguments in Harrington, "Pseudo-Philo," 298–299; Harrington, "The Original Language of Pseudo-Philo's *Liber Antiquitatum Biblicarum*," *HTR* 63 (1970): 503–514; James, *Biblical Antiquities of Philo*, 27–29; Jacobson, *Commentary*, 215–224.

[8] Daniel J. Harrington, "The Biblical Text of Pseudo-Philo's *Liber Antiquitatum Biblicarum*," *CBQ* 33 (1971): 1–17.

[9] Jacobson, *Commentary*, 254–256.

gin).¹⁰ There is, however, insufficient evidence to justify greater specificity in determining *L.A.B.*'s place of origin. Jacobson overreaches the available evidence when he tries to locate Pseudo-Philo near an urban area of the Galilee based on affinities with Greek culture, in particular the text's interest in magic and demons.¹¹ There is no compelling evidence supporting Cheryl Brown's attempt to place Pseudo-Philo in Syria.¹²

L.A.B. clearly cannot be attributed to Philo, even though it circulated alongside Latin translations of his authentic works. The Alexandrian philosopher's exegetical approach to the biblical text differs sharply from that taken by Pseudo-Philo. Moreover, *L.A.B.* explicitly contradicts Philo's authentic works on a number of details.¹³ While it is unlikely that the specific author(s) of *L.A.B.* can ever be identified, some scholars have offered theories regarding the social location and purpose of this text. Such attempts to pin down Pseudo-Philo's ideological commitments based upon literary themes or polemics allegedly found within the work have rendered mixed and sometimes even contradictory results. For example, Samuel Olyan reads *L.A.B.* as an attempt to drum up support for the Jewish rebellion against Rome, whereas D. Mendels reaches the opposite conclusion that Pseudo-Philo represents a moderate voice over and against radical Zealot

---

¹⁰ Harrington, "Pseudo-Philo," 299–300; Jacobson, *Commentary*, 210–211; Bruce Norman Fisk, *Do You Not Remember? Scripture, Story and Exegesis in the Rewritten Bible of Pseudo-Philo* (JSPSup 37; Sheffield: Sheffield Academic Press, 2001), 40–41.

¹¹ He does not explain why Hellenistic influence would be more likely in the Galilee. Jacobson, *Commentary*, 211. Others have attempted to locate Pseudo-Philo in the Galilee as an anti-Samaritan polemic. See J. Hadot, "Le milieu d'origine du 'Liber Antiquitatum Biblicarum,'" in *La littérature intertestamentaire* (ed. A. Caquot; Paris: Presses Universitaires de France, 1985), 153–171.

¹² Cheryl Anne Brown, *No Longer Silent: First Century Portraits of Biblical Women* (Louisville: Westminster John Knox, 1992), 23–27. Brown rejects a Palestinian provenance based upon *L.A.B.*'s polemic against mixed marriages, which she does not believe would be an issue in Palestine, and what she sees as its overwhelmingly positive portrayal of women. She argues that Syria is a more likely setting for *L.A.B.* due to the concentration of goddess worship in this area in the first century. The brunt of her argument rests on the problematic assumption that goddess worship is a necessary precondition for the positive valuation of women. Moreover, the attribution of 'feminist sensibilities' to Pseudo-Philo may be overstated as discussed later in this article.

¹³ *L.A.B.* specifies 1,652 years between the creation of Adam and the great flood against Philo's 2,242; *L.A.B.*'s depiction of Balaam is less negative than Philo's; in *L.A.B.* spies are sent into Canaan on the initiative of God rather than Moses; and in *L.A.B.* Moses is buried by God rather than by angels. On *L.A.B.*'s pseudonymity see James, *Biblical Antiquities of Philo*, 46–58; Feldman, "Prolegomenon," xxiii–xxiv; Harrington, "Pseudo-Philo," 299–300; Jacobson, *Commentary*, 195–196; and Frederick J. Murphy, *Pseudo-Philo: Rewriting the Bible* (New York: Oxford University Press, 1993), 3.

and Sicarri sects.¹⁴ Neither proposal has won widespread support, nor have alternative interpretations of *L.A.B.* as an Essene text or an anti-Samaritan polemic.¹⁵ The work simply is not marked by any clearly identifiable political or sectarian bias, making it difficult to link *L.A.B.* to a particular group in first century Palestine. For this reason, several recent interpreters have proposed that Pseudo-Philo should be viewed as representative of mainstream (nonsectarian) Palestinian Judaism.¹⁶

A given scholar's understanding of *L.A.B.*'s social location often determines the date that he or she assigns to this text. While most interpreters place Pseudo-Philo's work in the first century CE, an ongoing point of dispute is whether it was penned before or after Titus's capture of Jerusalem and destruction of the Temple in 70 CE.¹⁷ Unfortunately, there is little conclusive evidence with which to settle this question.

Many scholars follow Cohn in assigning a post-war date, but none of the standard arguments for this position are beyond dispute. The most common argument for a post-70 date involves what might be a veiled reference to the Second Temple's destruction in *L.A.B.* 19:7.¹⁸ However, dissenting

---

¹⁴ Samuel M. Olyan, "The Israelites Debate their Options at the Sea of Reeds: L.A.B. 10:3. Its Parallels, and Pseudo-Philo's Ideology and Background," *JBL* 110 (1991): 87–91; Doron Mendels, "Pseudo-Philo's *Biblical Antiquities*, the 'Fourth Philosophy,' and the Political Messianism of the First Century CE," in *The Messiah: Developments in Earliest Judaism and Christianity* (ed. James H. Charlesworth; Minneapolis: Fortress, 1992), 261–275.

¹⁵ These and other proposals have been reviewed and found wanting by Feldman, "Prolegomenon," xxxiii–xlvii.

¹⁶ Murphy, *Pseudo-Philo*, 6–7; Harrington, "Pseudo-Philo," 300; Fisk, *Do You Not Remember*, 41–42; and Charles Perrot and Pierre-Maurice Bogaert, *Les antiquités bibliques: Introduction littéraire, commentaire et index* (SC 230; Paris: Cerf, 1976), 31–34.

¹⁷ A *terminus a quo* of 135 BCE is established by the identification of the Ammonite king, Getal, mentioned in 39:8–9 and Kotylas, a ruler of Philadelphia (Ammon) mentioned by Josephus. If Pseudo-Philo used a 'Palestinian' biblical text, then the *terminus ad quem* is around 100 CE after which such texts were suppressed. See Murphy, *Pseudo-Philo*, 6; Harrington, "Pseudo-Philo," 299; and Perrot and Bogaert, *Les antiquités bibliques*, 73. A few scholars have proposed earlier or later dates for *L.A.B.* that have not garnered consensus. One interpreter proposes a very late date (3rd or 4th century CE) based on alleged aggadic similarities to the school of Rabbi Yohanan. See A. Zeron, "Erwägungen zu Pseudo-Philos Quellen und Zeit," *JSJ* 11 (1980): 38–52. Another advocates a date in the first century BCE based on alleged affinities with Essene thought. See Hadot, "Le milieu d' origine," 153–171.

¹⁸ *L.A.B.* 19:7 alludes to a destruction of the Temple on the 17th day of the 4th month, a date that later rabbinic tradition associated with the destruction of the Second Temple (e.g., *m. Ta'an.* 4:6). James, *Biblical Antiquities of Philo*, 29–33; Michael Wadsworth, "A New Pseudo-Philo," *JJS* 29 (1978): 186–191; Eckart Reinmuth, *Pseudo-Philo und Lukas: Studien zum Liber Antiquitatum Biblicarum und seiner Bedeutung für die Interpretation des lukanischen Doppelwerks* (WUNT 74; Tübingen: Mohr Siebeck, 1994), 18–26. Jacobson adds a similar

scholars counter that this verse could just as easily allude to desecrations of the Temple by Nebuchadnezzar, Antiochus IV, or Pompey.[19] Jacobson emphasizes *L.A.B.*'s similarities to *4 Ezra* and *2 Baruch* (both late first century texts) and argues that all three of these works must, therefore, reflect the same historical, social, and cultural context.[20] Yet significant differences also exist among these works, which have been used to justify a pre-70 date.[21] Elsewhere, Jacobson suggests the presence of an anti-Christian polemic in *L.A.B.* that would indicate a late first century date, but he marshals little evidence to support this claim.[22] Finally, several scholars argue that particular literary themes might be more suited to circumstances of the post-war period.[23] Unsurprisingly, these arguments have also been criticized and countered by scholars preferring an earlier date for the text.

Yet the evidence for a pre-70 date is no more persuasive, especially since the main rationale for placing the text earlier is an argument *ex silentio*. Namely, *L.A.B.* lacks clear references to the Jewish War or the Temple's destruction, rather momentous events which do tend to preoccupy late first century texts.[24] In a similar vein, Perrot and Bogaert contend that Pseudo-Philo's attitude toward the Temple and sacrifice, which continues "unto

---

argument based on *L.A.B.* 26:13. He contends that only an author writing after 70 CE would claim that God had taken possession of stones from the priestly breastplate, which was presumably kept in the temple before 70 CE. See Jacobson, *Commentary*, 202–206.

[19] Harrington, "Pseudo-Philo," 299; Perrot and Bogaert, *Les antiquités bibliques*, 67–70; and Murphy, *Pseudo-Philo*, 6.

[20] Jacobson, *Commentary*, 201. See also James, *Biblical Antiquities of Philo*, 46–59.

[21] The theological emphases of *4 Erza* and *2 Baruch* are very different from those of *L.A.B.* Harrington, "Pseudo-Philo," 299.

[22] His argument rests primarily on the phrase *quia non erit aliud*, "because there will be no other [sacrifice like Isaac]," in *L.A.B.* 32:3. See Jacobson, *Commentary*, 866–867. This would be a very weak and indirect polemic if that were Pseudo-Philo's intention and a very thin thread on which to hang an argument for dating the larger text.

[23] Wadsworth suggests affinities between *L.A.B.* and the concerns of post-70 sages like R. Yohanan ben Zakkai especially in allusions to suffering and dislocation. See Wadsworth, "A New Pseudo-Philo," 188–189. Similarly, Nickelsburg notes that *L.A.B.*'s message of hope would be appropriate in the grim post-war context, but he also fairly acknowledges that this message would also fit the chaotic pre-70 years. See George W.E. Nickelsburg, "Good and Bad Leaders in Pseudo-Philo's *Liber Antiquitatum Biblicarum*," in *Ideal Figures in Ancient Judaism: Profiles and Paradigms* (ed. John J. Collins and George W.E. Nickelsburg; SBLSCS 12; Chico, Calif.: Scholars Press, 1980), 49–65.

[24] Here *L.A.B.* is contrasted with *2 Ezra* and *4 Baruch*, both of which frequently refer to the events of 70 CE. See Harrington, "Pseudo-Philo," 299; Murphy, *Pseudo-Philo*, 6; and Pierre-Maurice Bogaert, *L'apocalypse de Baruch: Introduction, traduction du syriaque et commentaire* (SC 144; Paris: Cerf, 1969), 246–252. The argument from silence has been roundly criticized by Jacobson, *Commentary*, 200; and Wadsworth, "A New Pseudo-Philo," 186–191.

this day" according to *L.A.B.* 22:8, suggests a date prior to the destruction.[25] Jacobson, however, rightly points out that these details reveal nothing about the 'real author' of *L.A.B.*; they prove only that Pseudo-Philo intended for the text's audience to believe that its 'implied author' lived during the First Temple period.[26] Additional arguments for a pre-war date depend on particular assumptions regarding the text's social location and thematic emphases, none of which are beyond dispute.[27] Nor does Pseudo-Philo's free use of scripture necessarily place its composition before 70 CE as Perrot and Bogaert have argued.[28] While this style of biblical interpretation does eventually give way to a different type of rabbinic exegesis by the end of the first century, the choice of 70 CE as the pivotal date of this transition seems rather arbitrary. For the moment, evidence does not allow Pseudo-Philo's work to be assigned a more certain date within the first century.

Although *L.A.B.*'s use of scripture cannot resolve the problems involved in dating this text, it is relevant to the genre discussions that have occupied much of late twentieth and early twenty-first century Pseudo-Philo research. While some interpreters are still wont to describe *L.A.B.* as 'midrash,' it is clear that this descriptor can be retained only in its broadest, and ultimately least useful, sense.[29] Rabbinic midrash formally distinguishes

---

[25] Perrot and Bogaert, *Les antiquités bibliques*, 71–72.

[26] Jacobson, *Commentary*, 200, 709. See also Feldman, "Prolegomenon," xxviii. This point is disputed by Murphy who argues that this distinction is a modern one with no counterpart in ancient literature (Murphy, *Pseudo-Philo*, 262–263).

[27] Harrington suggests the presence of an anti-Herodian polemic in Pseudo-Philo's "negative attitude toward Jewish rulers not chosen by God," which would have been a dead issue after the defeat of Jerusalem (Harrington, "Pseudo-Philo," 299). Jacobson, however, disputes the importance of this theme to Pseudo-Philo since not all of *L.A.B.*'s good leaders are explicitly chosen by God (Jacobson, *Commentary*, 201). Olyan and Mendels both assign a pre-70 date because they see Pseudo-Philo respectively as a supporter of the revolt or a pre-war voice of moderation. See Olyan, "The Israelites Debate," 87–91; Mendels, "Pseudo-Philo's," 261–275. Perrot and Bogaert suggest that Pseudo-Philo's use of the verb "act zealously" (*L.A.B.* 45:6) presupposes a pre-70 date since its association with the Zealots might preclude its use after that date. Unfortunately, they offer no evidence to support this conclusion. See Perrot and Bogaert, *Les antiquités bibliques*, 204–205. Halpern-Amaru assigns a pre-war date based on Pseudo-Philo's tendency to define the covenant in terms of 'peoplehood' rather than land. See Betsy Halpern-Amaru, *Rewriting the Bible: Land and Covenant in Postbiblical Jewish Literature* (Valley Forge, Pa.: Trinity Press International, 1994), 94.

[28] Perrot and Bogaert describe this style of biblical interpretation as *texte continué*, as opposed to *texte expliqué*, which maintains a distinction between text and commentary (e.g., midrash). See Perrot and Bogaert, *Les antiquités bibliques*, 71–72.

[29] Fisk, for example, uses the term to refer to any early composition that cites, alludes to, or comments on an authoritative biblical text and stand in some (undefined) methodological continuity with later midrash (*Do You Not Remember*, 25). See also Feldman, "Prole-

between the biblical text and its explication in a manner that is foreign to Pseudo-Philo. In *L.A.B.* citations of scripture are intertwined with commentary to produce a new narrative account of Israel's sacred history. In this sense, Pseudo-Philo's work is more closely related to Chronicles than to rabbinic midrash. This approach to biblical interpretation also characterizes other early Jewish texts including *Jubilees*, the *Genesis Apocryphon*, Josephus's *Jewish Antiquities*, and the *Testament of Moses*. Geza Vermes coined the term 'rewritten Bible' to categorize this small literary corpus, which was later defined by Harrington as "those products of Palestinian Judaism at the turn of the era that take as their literary framework the flow of the biblical narrative itself and apparently have as their major purpose the clarification and actualization of the biblical story."[30]

A healthy debate has been waged over whether these texts have sufficient commonalities to constitute a cohesive literary genre. Some scholars argue that they bear little in common aside from a narrative framework that is heavily dependent on antecedent scripture.[31] Others have worked to establish a more precise definition of the genre by delineating its formal literary characteristics.[32] In brief, most of these scholars agree that *L.A.B.* and its literary cousins selectively retell in their own words a substantial portion of the biblical narrative, which is used as the base text into which legendary materials are incorporated as secondary elements. The end result is a new freestanding composition that presupposes audience familiarity with a biblical text, rather than attempting to replace or supersede it. When

---

gomenon," lxviii–lxx; and Richard Bauckham, "The *Liber Antiquitatum Biblicarum* of Pseudo-Philo and the Gospels as 'Midrash'," in *Studies in Midrash and Historiography* (ed. R.T. France and David Wenham; GP 3; Sheffield: JSOT Press, 1983): 33–76.

[30] Geza Vermes, *Scripture and Tradition in Judaism: Haggadic Studies* (Leiden: Brill, 1961), 95, 124–126; and Daniel J. Harrington, "Palestinian Adaptations of Biblical Narratives and Prophecies. I. The Bible Rewritten," in *Early Judaism and its Modern Interpreters* (ed. Robert A. Kraft and George E.W. Nickelsburg; SBLBMI 2; Philadelphia: Fortress, 1986), 239.

[31] Fisk contends that these works are remarkably diverse in terms of their purpose, modes of embellishment, and the demands they place on readers (*Do You Not Remember*, 13–15).

[32] Philip Alexander concludes that the differences among 'rewritten Bible' texts are much less important than their similarities, and he is able to list nine principle characteristics of the genre. See Philip S. Alexander, "Retelling the Old Testament," in *It Is Written: Scripture Citing Scripture, Essays in Honor of Barnabas Lindars* (ed. D.A. Carson and H.G.M. Williamson; Cambridge: Cambridge University Press, 1988), 99–121. See also Halpern-Amaru, *Rewriting the Bible*, 4–7; Sidnie White Crawford, *Rewriting Scripture in Second Temple Times* (Grand Rapids: Eerdmans, 2008), 1–18; and Moshe J. Bernstein, "'Rewritten Bible': A Generic Category Which Has Outlived Its Usefulness?" *Textus* 22 (2005): 169–196.

read alongside scripture, rewritten Bible texts provide an indirect interpretive commentary whose full significance can only be grasped by those who bear in mind the original story.

Two caveats are in order. First, because the process of rewriting inherited traditions clearly begins within the Bible itself and the biblical canon remained fluid throughout the first century, the line between Bible and rewritten Bible can be rather fuzzy. Moshe Bernstein warns that one group's rewritten Bible may be another's canonical text.[33] Second, Sidnie White Crawford has pointed out that the nomenclature 'rewritten Bible' erroneously implies the existence of a fixed and universally accepted biblical text available for rewriting in the first century. She helpfully suggests using the term 'rewritten scripture' to avoid this implication.[34] While acknowledging these two legitimate caveats, it remains useful to consider *L.A.B.* as one of many examples of rewritten scripture that flourished in early Judaism.

Scholars who deal with *L.A.B.* and other rewritten scripture texts tend to follow one of two interpretive approaches. Some emphasize the exegetical nature of this literature by asking how Pseudo-Philo explicates scripture by resolving difficulties, answering questions, and filling lacunae perceived in the antecedent text.[35] Others emphasize its ideological nature by asking how the authors of rewritten scripture attempted to make inherited traditions more relevant to their own audiences. Louis Feldman, in particular, insists that each retelling of scripture follows discernable patterns that likely reflect the social and historical circumstances of its author.[36] Similarly, Frederick Murphy describes Pseudo-Philo's primary concern as the 'actualization' of Israel's sacred stories in the context of new situations and new problems faced by a first century audience.[37] This idea has been taken up by several interpreters, most recently White Crawford who sees works like *L.A.B.* as a continuation of that two-fold scribal task evident in scripture itself, namely, preserving and actualizing inherited traditions.[38]

---

[33] Bernstein, "'Rewritten Bible'," 175.

[34] White Crawford, *Rewriting Scripture*, 3–9.

[35] Fisk argues that Pseudo-Philo's interpretation of scripture is almost always exegetically motivated, and he offers only minimal discussions of social and historical context (*Do You Not Remember*, 22–24, 126–135).

[36] See, for example, Louis H. Feldman, "Philo, Pseudo-Philo, Josephus, and Theodotus on the Rape of Dinah," *JQR* 94 (2004): 253–277.

[37] Murphy, *Pseudo-Philo*, 12–13, 262–270.

[38] White Crawford, *Rewriting Scripture*, 3–4.

It is reasonable to suppose that both exegetical and ideological factors were operative in the retelling of scripture.[39] Clearly ancient interpreters like Pseudo-Philo adopted scripture as the formal starting point for their own compositions, and the changes or additions that they introduce are often anchored in some tantalizing detail found within the precursor text. Yet, there is no such thing as 'pure' or disinterested exegesis divorced from the interpreter's own historical situation. This recognition, of course, does not grant scholars free rein to read specific first-century issues and events into *L.A.B.*; nor can it be assumed that every deviation from scripture is an ideologically motivated attempt to insert the concerns of the author's day into inherited traditions. Caution is warranted most especially when dealing with a text as difficult to date with precision as Pseudo-Philo's *L.A.B.* Any observations about the significance of this text for a nonsectarian Jewish audience in first-century Palestine must be recognized as provisional.

Many interpreters have addressed the major themes of Pseudo-Philo's work, the most prominent of which is the utter indestructibility of God's covenant with Israel no matter how unfaithful the Jewish people might be or how bleak their circumstances.[40] While this idea is already present in scripture, it becomes much more pronounced and intentional in *L.A.B.* As Bruce Fisk rightly points out, this theme receives a polemical edge when Pseudo-Philo allows various characters to call into question God's fidelity. Other characters answer this challenge by insisting that the covenant was not established 'in vain' and God's faithfulness will ultimately be vindicated.[41] No event in *L.A.B.*, no matter how seemingly inconsequential, is beyond God's control. This point is demonstrated at length by Jacobson who concludes that Pseudo-Philo goes far beyond the biblical precursor in presenting God as the prime mover of history.[42] God's control expresses itself through the principle of moral causality, which is often made more absolute through alterations to the biblical story.[43]

---

[39] Such a mediating position is found in James L. Kugel, *Traditions of the Bible: A Guide to the Bible as It Was at the Start of the Common Era* (Cambridge: Harvard University Press, 1998), 20–22.

[40] Cohn, "An Apocryphal Work," 322; Murphy, *Pseudo-Philo*, 244–246; Jacobson, *Commentary*, 241–242; and Fisk, *Do You Not Remember*, 45–50.

[41] Fisk, *Do You Not Remember*, 47–48.

[42] Jacobson, *Commentary*, 241–245. See also Frederick J. Murphy, "God in Pseudo-Philo," *JSJ* (1988): 1–18.

[43] For example, Pseudo-Philo depicts the Levite's concubine as promiscuous to account for her terrible fate (*L.A.B.* 45:3), and he adds moral judgments to the biblical tales of Gideon and Samson (*L.A.B.* 36:4; 43:5). Murphy, *Pseudo-Philo*, 247–248.

All of the great disasters that have befallen Israel are viewed as God's righteous punishment for their sin. Pseudo-Philo repeatedly illustrates the devastating evils that result from anything less than absolute devotion to Israel's God. The closely related dangers of idolatry and sexual relations with Gentiles are especially emphasized by Pseudo-Philo often in places where those concerns are absent in the biblical precursor.[44] Nevertheless, because Israel's ultimate salvation is assured, in the end divine mercy always triumphs over divine justice. So irrevocable are God's promises in *L.A.B.* that Israel's deliverance is not even dependent upon repentance.[45]

According to Pseudo-Philo sins that are not punished in this life will be dealt with appropriately in the afterlife or at a final eschatological judgment. Although such statements are frequent in *L.A.B.*, Jacobson warns that any attempt to construct from them a coherent and consistent eschatology is doomed to failure.[46] While Pseudo-Philo clearly breathed the eschatological air of first century Palestine, *L.A.B.* haphazardly combines a number of inconsistent and sometimes even incompatible eschatological concepts. Jacobson is likely correct in concluding that Pseudo-Philo adopts whatever view suits his purpose at a given moment. Similarly, Perrot and Bogaert contend that Pseudo-Philo is little concerned with eschatology for its own sake, but merely uses these ideas to engender obedience.[47] Nor is there credible evidence that Pseudo-Philo thought in terms of an eschatological Messiah since only two or three ambiguous allusions to messianism may by found in *L.A.B.*[48]

Finally, many recent studies have been devoted to the role of women in *L.A.B.*[49] It has become commonplace to note that, in comparison to Jose-

---

[44] Frederick J. Murphy, "Retelling the Bible: Idolatry in Pseudo-Philo," *JBL* 107 (1988): 275–287; Feldman, "Prolegomenon," xlvi; Harrington, "Pseudo-Philo," 301; Jacobson, *Commentary*, 246–247; and Fisk, *Do You Not Remember*, 50–52.

[45] Murphy, *Pseudo-Philo*, 246.

[46] Jacobson, *Commentary*, 247–250.

[47] Perrot and Bogaert, *Les antiquités bibliques*, 53–57. See also, Murphy, *Pseudo-Philo*, 256–257.

[48] Perrot and Bogaert, *Les antiquités bibliques*, 57–59; Murphy, *Pseudo-Philo*, 260–261; and Jacobson, *Commentary*, 250. Mendels reads *L.A.B.* as an attempt to counter the extreme messianism of some Zealot sects. See Mendels, "Pseudo-Philo's," 261–275.

[49] Perrot and Bogaert, *Les antiquités bibliques*, 52–53; Murphy, *Pseudo-Philo*, 258–259; Brown, *No Longer Silent*, 12; Mary Therese DesCamp, "Why Are These Women Here? An Examination of the Sociological Setting of Pseudo-Philo through Comparative Reading," *JSP* 16 (1997): 53–80; Pieter W. van der Horst, "Portraits of Biblical Women in Pseudo-Philo's *Liber Antiquitatum Biblicarum*," *JPS* 5 (1989): 29–46; and Rhonda Burnette-Bletsch, "At the Hands of a Woman: Rewriting Jael in Pseudo-Philo," *JSP* 17 (1998): 53–64.

phus and other early Jewish writers, Pseudo-Philo seems particularly well disposed toward women. Clearly, *L.A.B.* gives a lot of attention to its female characters most of whom are portrayed positively. Some interpreters go so far as to comment upon the 'feminism' of Pseudo-Philo and to suggest the possibility of a female author for *L.A.B.* For instance, Mary Therese DesCamp suggests that *L.A.B.* may have been written by a Palestinian Jewish woman as a polemic against intermarriage and a persuasive argument extolling the virtues of endogamy.[50] While this is an intriguing possibility, it is difficult to imagine how one might establish a satisfactory set of criteria to determine the gender of an ancient author.

Moreover, other studies have called into question the extent and function of Pseudo-Philo's so-called feminist sensibilities. Jacobson points out that *L.A.B.* virtually ignores the matriarchs and its genealogies are invariably populated with more sons than daughters.[51] Betsy Halpern-Amaru notes that, while female characters do occupy a prominent place in *L.A.B.*'s narrative, they do so in association with motherhood and are often masculinized.[52] Eileen Schuller, likewise, argues that women's stories are muted in *L.A.B.* though to a lesser extent than is the case elsewhere in early Jewish literature.[53] Any claims pertaining to the 'feminism' of Pseudo-Philo must be qualified in light of these thoughtful studies.

Pseudo-Philo's Use of Genesis

The remainder of this article will survey the various uses that Pseudo-Philo makes of Genesis traditions. The book of Genesis provides the main storyline of *L.A.B.* 1–8 which selectively summarizes and interprets material from Israel's primeval and ancestral traditions. These chapters offer a very

---

[50] DesCamp recognizes the difficulty (impossibility?) of establishing criteria to determine the gender of an author. She suggests the best criterion is not the presence of some identifiable ideological stance, but the occurrence of details reflecting the particularities of the social location women occupy in the originating society. See DesCamp, "Why Are These Women Here," 53–80.

[51] Jacobson, *Commentary*, 250–251.

[52] Halpern-Amaru, "Portraits of Women in Pseudo-Philo's *Biblical Antiquities*," in *'Women Like This': New Perspectives on Jewish Women in the Greco-Roman World* (ed. Amy-Jill Levine; SBLEJL 1; Atlanta: Scholars Press, 1991), 106. See also, Donald C. Polaski, "On Taming Tamar: Amram's Rhetoric and Women's Roles in Pseudo-Philo's *Liber Antiquitatum Biblicarum* 9," *JSP* 13 (1995): 98–99.

[53] Eileen M. Schuller, "Women of the Exodus in Biblical Retellings of the Second Temple Period," in *Gender and Difference in Ancient Israel* (ed. Peggy L. Day; Minneapolis: Fortress, 1989), 178–194.

compressed retelling of Genesis that relies extensively on genealogical material and census lists with only a few chapters of narrative. On the surface, *L.A.B.* appears to hurry through the subject matter of Genesis to arrive at later biblical material, especially the Exodus and the Judges traditions, which receive more extensive treatment in the work. However, Pseudo-Philo's reception of Genesis is also evident in later chapters of *L.A.B.*, which are steeped in out-of-sequence biblical quotations, allusions, and echoes. Much of the Genesis material that is omitted or skimmed over briefly in *L.A.B.* 1–8 is revisited in later chapters. These narrative analepses have been widely recognized as one of Pseudo-Philo's preferred exegetical techniques, one that permits this author to draw connections between disparate biblical episodes and render them mutually interpretive.[54] Frequent use of this technique demonstrates that *L.A.B.* presupposes a general familiarity with the biblical storyline on the part of its readers to the point that they are expected to recognize and understand allusions to biblical episodes that have not been narrated in their expected sequence. It also suggests that Pseudo-Philo's thought world was more significantly formed by Genesis traditions than the scant space that they are allotted in chapters 1–8 would initially seem to indicate.

L.A.B.'s retelling of scripture begins abruptly with two genealogies tracing the lines of Seth and Cain. Creation narratives, the garden story, and the Cain and Abel story are not narrated in sequence within *L.A.B.* although all receive attention elsewhere in the work. Only slight traces of the narrative material in Gen 1:1–4:15 are preserved in the text's opening words (*Initio mundi*), the name Adam (1:1), and an allusion to Cain's murder of Abel (2:1). Readers are apparently expected to understand these references without further explanation.

L.A.B. 1–2 reverses the order in which these genealogies appear in Gen 4–5 suggesting that God had prepared a preemptive response to human immorality in Seth's descendant Noah before that immorality was even manifest through the line of Cain. This also eliminates a theological difficulty of the precursor text in which God seems surprised by the emergence of human wickedness and subsequently repents of creating humanity (Gen 6:6). In *L.A.B.* the inevitability of destruction is present from the very beginning of the story and part of God's design in providing Noah.

---

[54] Jacobson, *Commentary*, 224–241; Fisk, *Do You Not Remember*, 13–33; and Reinmuth, *Pseudo-Philo und Lukas*, 93–111. Also see Jacobson, "Biblical Quotation and Editorial Function in Pseudo-Philo's *Liber Antiquitatum Biblicarum*," *JSP* 5 (1989): 47–64.

Pseudo-Philo modifies the biblical precursor in at least two ways in these chapters to heighten the contrast between Seth and Cain's families. First, *L.A.B.* 1:20 (the good Lamech's naming of Noah) is rewritten to contrast more sharply with its parallel in *L.A.B.* 2:10 (the evil Lamech's speech).[55] Genesis associates Noah's naming with relief from the hard labor that characterizes human existence (Gen 5:29). Pseudo-Philo transforms this speech into a moral statement contrasting Noah's righteous family with their unrighteous contemporaries (presumably the yet-to-be-described line of Cain). Second, *L.A.B.* goes beyond its biblical precursor in disparaging the line of Cain. Whereas Genesis credits Cain's descendants with the introduction of music and metallurgy, Pseudo-Philo associates these respective innovations with the beginning of sexual immorality and idolatry. Whereas human civilization as introduced by Cain remains morally ambiguous in Genesis, for Pseudo-Philo it leads only to moral degeneration. *L.A.B.*, therefore, provides a more thoroughgoing justification for the flood than does Genesis.[56]

Although it has been noted that *L.A.B.* 3 follows Gen 6:1–9:17 relatively closely, Pseudo-Philo's more abbreviated flood account still eliminates several ambiguities, inconsistencies, and theological difficulties found in its biblical precursor.[57] First, the 120 years in Gen 6:3 might be taken as a limitation of the individual human lifespan or of human existence in general. Pseudo-Philo expands the text to clarify his own interpretation of Gen 6:3—that the pre-flood generation was given 120 years to repent and so avert the flood.[58] Second, like many Jewish interpreters, Pseudo-Philo addresses the question of why Noah's family was spared from destruction, a circumstance explained only by general assertions of Noah's righteousness in Gen 6:8–10. While retaining the language of Genesis, Pseudo-Philo adds that this is the first of many instances in *L.A.B.* in which divine mercy tempers divine justice. Third, Pseudo-Philo eliminates unnecessary repetition and

---

[55] Murphy, *Pseudo-Philo*, 30; Jacobson, *Commentary*, 291–292.

[56] Pseudo-Philo also retains the sons-of-god/daughters-of-man tradition (Gen 6:1–4) in *L.A.B.* 3:1–2 to provide a secondary rationale for the flood. Jacobson has noted Pseudo-Philo's tendency to preserve distinct traditions that serve similar purposes (*Commentary*, 307, 373).

[57] Murphy uses the flood account as an example of a passage where Pseudo-Philo depends heavily on biblical quotations while making only small-scale changes to the biblical precursor. See Murphy, *Pseudo-Philo*, 20, 33–35; and Jacobson, *Commentary*, 307–331.

[58] Giving the pre-flood generation time to repent is a common motif in Jewish tradition and not unexpected in a narrative theodicy like *L.A.B.* See Jacobson, *Commentary*, 309–310; and Louis H. Feldman, "Questions about the Great Flood, as Viewed by Philo, Pseudo-Philo, Josephus, and the Rabbis," *ZAW* 115 (2003): 408–412. Other interpreters attempt to render *terminos seculi* "the limits of [a person's] life" rather than the more obvious "limit of the age." See Harrington, "Pseudo-Philo," 307; and Perrot and Bogaert, *Les antiquités bibliques*, 68–69.

inconsistencies found within the Genesis account by selectively conflating biblical passages. For instance, the conflicting instructions Noah receives from God in the precursor text (Gen 6:13–21 and 7:1–4) are combined into one consistent and much shorter speech in *L.A.B.* 3:4. Fourth, Pseudo-Philo modifies the depiction of God to downplay the anthropomorphisms of the precursor text in which God 'smells' the order of Noah's sacrifice and appears to require memory aids (Gen 8:21; 9:12–17).[59] In *L.A.B.*, God merely 'accepts' the sacrifice and the rainbow serves as a memorial of the covenant and a reminder for humanity (*L.A.B.* 3:8, 12; 4:5). Finally, some ambiguity exists in the biblical precursor regarding the divine oath never again to destroy the earth by flood (Gen 8:21–22; 9:9–17). Pseudo-Philo chooses to read these passages in Genesis as leaving open the possibility that the earth may still be destroyed by some other means.[60] This leads to an eschatological digression involving a final judgment followed by a new creation (*L.A.B.* 3:10).

Omitting the embarrassing tradition of Noah's drunkenness, Pseudo-Philo combines the genealogical material in Gen 10–11 into a single genealogy for Noah (*L.A.B.* 4) and provides a census of Noah's descendents (*L.A.B.* 5) that is not paralleled in Genesis. Repeating the pattern established in *L.A.B.* 1–2, Pseudo-Philo again rewrites his precursor text so that the birth of a hero is reported and his significance explained (*L.A.B.* 4:11) before the advancement of human civilization leads inexorably to moral degeneration (*L.A.B.* 4:16).[61] This establishes a strong narrative association between Abram and Noah. Both characters are presented in *L.A.B.* as God's preemptive response to human immorality. Both also belong to righteous lineages that are distinguished from the rest of sinful humanity.[62] In addition, Abram and Noah are linked linguistically by the adjective *inmaculatus* ("blame-

---

[59] This would include Pseudo-Philo's skillful elimination of the problematic notion that God repented of creating humanity (Jacobson, *Commentary*, 320, 330–331).

[60] This interpretation is widely found in midrashic texts, as is the opposing interpretation that God has promised never to destroy the earth again by any means. See. Jacobson, *Commentary*, 322–327; and Feldman, "Questions about the Great Flood," 409.

[61] Either Pseudo-Philo has preserved two distinct traditions explaining the origin and spread of sin (*L.A.B.* 2:7–9 and 4:16), or he intends to demonstrate that earlier mistakes of humanity are replicated by the post-flood generation. See Jacobson, *Commentary*, 337–338; and Eckart Reinmuth, "Beobachtungen zur Rezeption der Genesis bei Pseudo-Philo (LAB 1–8) und Lukas (APG 7.2–17)," *NTS* 43 (1997): 552–569, esp. 555.

[62] *L.A.B.* is unique in excluding both Abram and his family from idol worship. Cf. *Jub.* 11:6–7 which depicts Abram's family as idolators; Josh 24:2 which suggests that Abram was himself an idolator; and *Gen. Rab.* 11:28 which connects Abram to astrology and divination.

less"), which Pseudo-Philo applies only to these two characters.[63] Similarly, Melcha's assertion that the seed of Abram will be multiplied forever echoes the language of God's command to Noah upon exiting the ark (*L.A.B.* 3:8, 11).

Abram/Abraham receives more attention than any other ancestor in *L.A.B.* even though Pseudo-Philo preserves little material from the Abraham cycle (Gen 12–25) in its expected narrative sequence. Instead *L.A.B.* exploits Genesis's juxtaposition of the Tower of Babel story and the call of Abraham to introduce a tradition that links these two otherwise unrelated accounts.[64] In Pseudo-Philo's rewritten narrative, Abram's life is threatened when he and eleven other righteous men refuse to participate in tower building. While the other eleven protestors agree to be hidden away by well-meaning tribal elder Joktan, Abram stubbornly insists upon remaining behind to face the consequences of his stance. He is condemned to death in the fiery furnace that is being used to cast bricks for the tower, but God rescues Abram by causing the fire to consume his accusers instead.

Some interpreters understand Abram's initial protest in *L.A.B.* 6:4 as a monotheistic proclamation.[65] However, Pseudo-Philo does not associate the tower not with idolatry, but rather with humanity's desire to achieve security, maintain peace, and make a name and glory for themselves (*L.A.B.* 6:1).[66] Other than hubris, there is nothing particularly sinful about the tower project. Likewise, Joktan's intention to save the twelve protestors seems admirable in itself, but *L.A.B.* clearly uses both Joktan and the tower builders as foils for righteous Abram. Murphy may be correct that Pseudo-Philo is deliberately contrasting the schemes of humans (tower builders and Joktan) with the plans of God.[67] Abram not only refuses to participate in tower building, a scheme that has not been endorsed by God, he also rejects Joktan's scheme for avoiding the consequences of this decision. Citing the

---

[63] Jacobson, *Commentary*, 313; Murphy, *Pseudo-Philo*, 38; and Perrot and Bogaert, *Les antiquités bibliques*, 87, 92.

[64] Bauckham, "*Liber Antiquitatum Biblicarum*," 41–43; Michael Wadsworth, "Making and Interpreting Scripture," in *Ways of Reading the Bible* (ed. Michael Wadsworth; Sussex: Harvester, 1981), 11–14.

[65] Perrot and Bogaert, *Les antiquités bibliques*, 94–95. Cf. Murphy, *Pseudo-Philo*, 41–42, who recognizes that the tower is not explicitly connected to idolatry but continues to refer to the tower builders as idolators.

[66] Jacobson notes that in most midrashic elaborations of the tower story the builders intend the tower to be used in idol-worship or to wage war against heaven. Neither of these goals is present in either the Genesis or *L.A.B.* (*Commentary*, 354–358).

[67] Frederick J. Murphy, "Divine Plan, Human Plan: A Structuring Theme in Pseudo-Philo," *JQR* 77 (1986): 5–14.

principle of moral causality, Abram declares that those guilty of sin cannot escape judgment by fleeing into the mountains, but those who are innocent will be saved by God (*L.A.B.* 6:11). This is, of course, precisely what happens when an earthquake causes the tower builders, rather than Abram, to be consumed by fire.

L.A.B. 7 preserves a separate version of the tower story, which Pseudo-Philo explains as a second attempt by the tower builders to complete their project. This tower account, which follows Gen 11:1–9 more closely, results in God both confusing the language and altering the appearance of the builders. Pseudo-Philo stitches together the two stories by basing God's selection of Abram as covenant recipient in *L.A.B.* 7:4 on his actions in the previous chapter. In so doing, *L.A.B.* provides a rationale for God's choice of Abram, which is left unexplained in Genesis. Like Noah, Abram and his seed are set in stark relief against the backdrop of sinful humanity. As a reward, God grants to Abram's descendants a special land that remained untouched by the waters of the flood allowing Pseudo-Philo to highlight once again what appears to be a significant link between Noah and Abram.

Genesis 12–50 is quickly paraphrased in a single chapter constituted almost entirely by wide-ranging biblical quotations (*L.A.B.* 8). Much is passed over here that appears out of sequence later in the work. Again Pseudo-Philo presupposes that his readers' familiarity with the biblical story will allow them to follow his condensed tale and fill in the missing pieces. It is possible that the omissions in this chapter are governed in part by Pseudo-Philo's desire to present Israel's ancestors in the most positive light possible. Much potentially embarrassing material is missing including the Melchizedek tradition, the Sarah/Hagar rivalry, the expulsion of Hagar, Lot's incestuous relationship with his daughters, Jacob's trickery, the Rachel/Leah rivalry, Joseph's imprisonment in Egypt, and Joseph's manipulation of his brothers.[68] Strangely, given all of these omissions, the rape of Dinah is retained in *L.A.B.*'s stripped down ancestral tradition.[69] The Sodom tradition receives only a brief mention that serves to highlight the

---

[68] Several scholars have noticed the diminished role of the biblical matriarchs in this chapter, which seems to run counter to Pseudo-Philo's tendency elsewhere to expand the roles of female characters. This point is perhaps overstated given the highly condensed nature of this material. See Jacobson, *Commentary*, 251; and Murphy, *Pseudo-Philo*, 50–51.

[69] Feldman notes that *L.A.B.* omits from this episode any details that might create sympathy for the Shechemites and the Hivvites or that might indict Simeon and Levi of cruelty. He also suggests that moral causality temporarily upset by the rape of Dinah is reaffirmed when she marries Job (Feldman, "Rape of Dinah," 266).

contrast between Lot and Abram. Pseudo-Philo does take the time to articulate Israel's ancestral covenant (*L.A.B.* 8:3). This verse quotes heavily from Gen 12 and 17, but it adds the significant phrase *semen sempiternum* ("eternal seed") with no biblical precedent, highlighting once again Pseudo-Philo's concern for the indestructibility of Israel's covenant.[70] Thus ends Pseudo-Philo's sequential retelling of Genesis.

In the remaining chapters of *L.A.B.*, the prominent place of Genesis traditions in Pseudo-Philo's imagination remains evident through the presence of citations, allusions, flashbacks, intertextual connections, and scriptural echoes. *L.A.B.* repeatedly calls upon material from Genesis to illuminate and interpret later, ostensibly unrelated episodes. Much work has been published over the last two decades pertaining to Pseudo-Philo's use of out-of-sequence or secondary biblical citations. Jacobson has focused on identifying and categorizing forms of biblical citation in *L.A.B.*[71] Eckart Reinmuth has also examined the functions of discursive analepses in Pseudo-Philo's work.[72] Moving beyond a strictly taxonomic approach, Fisk has considered the compositional strategies and hermeneutical significance of secondary scripture in *L.A.B.*[73]

The limited scope of the present article does not permit analysis of every Genesis citation or allusion in *L.A.B.* 9–65. Nor is there space for a critical evaluation of the criteria that may be used to identify more elusive intertextual references.[74] Clearly, Pseudo-Philo's reception of Genesis is more readily apparent where *L.A.B.* provides explicit references to its biblical precursor. While Pseudo-Philo's use of Genesis clearly spans the spectrum of intertextuality, attempts to identify fainter echoes of the precursor text eventually become speculative especially in a work like *L.A.B.* that, in its extant form, is two translations removed from its original language. Therefore, this article will attempt only a brief overview of some of the more

---

[70] *L.A.B.* usually makes the promise of descendents, rather than land, the focal point of the ancestral covenant (Halpern-Amaru, *Rewriting the Bible*, 78).

[71] Jacobson's earlier work classified Pseudo-Philo's varied uses of scripture. See his "Biblical Quotation and Editorial Function," 47–64. In his later commentary, he addresses Pseudo-Philo's combination of distinct biblical passages in his discussion of narrative and exegetical techniques in *L.A.B.* (Jacobson, *Commentary*, 224–241).

[72] Reinmuth is primarily interested in identifying parallels between *L.A.B.* and Luke-Acts to demonstrate the Jewish character of the latter work (*Pseudo-Philo und Lukas*, 126).

[73] Fisk has published extensively on Pseudo-Philo's use of secondary scripture, but his most comprehensive treatment of this topic appears in his 2001 monograph, *Do You Not Remember* (see esp. 109–126).

[74] For a full discussion of this topic, see Fisk, *Do You Not Remember*, 54–108.

clearly marked references to Genesis in *L.A.B.* 9–65 and then comment on two out-of-sequence citations that illuminate Pseudo-Philo's reception of the covenant traditions in Genesis.

Genesis traditions feature prominently in three extended historical recitations occasioned by Balaam's nighttime epiphany (*L.A.B.* 18:5–6), Joshua's covenant renewal ceremony (23:4–9), and the hymn of Deborah (32:1–10). In addition, Pseudo-Philo often deploys isolated episodes or verses from Genesis in foreign contexts within the latter chapters of *L.A.B.* The most prominent out-of-sequence references to the creation myths of Genesis are found in the twelve spies tradition (15:5–6) and in the account of Saul's exorcism (60:2–3). References to the Garden of Eden story appear in relation to the festival calendar (13:7–9), Cenaz (26:6), Jotham's fable (37:3), and Jephthah (39:5).

Most of the Genesis traditions that appeared in the sequential account of *L.A.B.* 1–8 also reappear in later chapters of the work. The Cain and Abel tradition, which received a brief mention in *L.A.B.* 2:1, reappears later in the account of Korah's Rebellion (16:2) and in a Davidic psalm (59:4). Although the flood tradition received extensive treatment in *L.A.B.* 1–8, it also reappears in later chapters, most especially in conjunction with the festival calendar (13:7–8) and near the death of Moses (19:11). The sons of God and daughters of man tradition reappears in God's response to Amram (16:2) and at the death of Phineas (59:4). Likewise, the Tower of Babel, which played such an important role in the presentation of Abraham in *L.A.B.* 6–7, reappears in the golden calf story (12:3). An out-of-sequence allusion to the destruction of Sodom also reappears in the story of the Levite's concubine (42:2–5).

Finally, much of what Pseudo-Philo omits from its brief summary of the ancestral traditions in *L.A.B.* 8 appears out-of-sequence in later chapters. The *aqedah* tradition, in particular, appears to be a pivotal story for Pseudo-Philo since it appears on three occasions in *L.A.B.*, twice in historical recitations (18:5; 32:2–4) and again in the story of Jephthah's daughter (40:2–3). Episodes from the Jacob cycle in Genesis appear several times in the later chapters of *L.A.B.* (17:2–4; 21:5; 24:5–6; 50:1–3). Pseudo-Philo uses the story of Joseph to comment upon the radiant visage of Moses (12:1) and the sexual misadventures of Samson (43:5). The Tamar story of Gen 38 appears in the speech of Amram in *L.A.B.* 9:5–6.

Two out-of-sequence uses of Genesis in *L.A.B.* 9–65 particularly illuminate Pseudo-Philo's understanding of the relationship among Israel's various covenant traditions. The first of these passages is the golden calf story (*L.A.B.* 12), in which the Mosaic covenant is almost compromised by Israel's unfaithfulness. Pseudo-Philo draws the main storyline for this episode from Exod 32 but also makes use of citations from Genesis and elsewhere. Freely rewriting scripture, Pseudo-Philo has God declare that Israel's apostasy at Sinai fulfills the words that God had spoken earlier at Babel (Gen 11:6; *L.A.B.* 7:2).[75] This exegetical move assures Pseudo-Philo's audience that God had foreseen Israel's apostasy long ago at the time of Abram and the tower builders. It also transforms an indictment that was originally inveighed against all of humanity (excluding Abram) into an indictment of Israel (excluding Moses). Through their apostasy at Sinai, Israel risks repudiating the Abrahamic covenant by placing themselves on the side of the tower builders rather than their ancestor.[76]

This risk is averted, not by repentance or by Mosaic intercession (as in Exod 32), but by God's own unprompted recollection of the ancestral promises.[77] In *L.A.B.* 12:4, God ruminates with Moses over the nation's sinfulness and how much worse it might become when Israel eventually gains the Promised Land. Nevertheless, the deity resolves to be reconciled with Israel because the ancestral promises are irrevocable. Embedded in this speech is yet another reference to the ancestral covenant (Gen 12:7). The Genesis citations in this passage underwrite the Mosaic covenant with ancestral promises and clarify what Pseudo-Philo understands to be the relationship between these two traditions. The conditional Mosaic covenant is undergirded, if not subsumed, by the unconditional Abrahamic covenant.

The second passage that sheds light on Pseudo-Philo's reception of covenant traditions is *L.A.B.* 19:10–11, which details God's response to the final prayer of Moses. This passage is drawn loosely from Deut 34 but includes a clearly marked citation of Gen 9:13, 17.[78] After showing Moses the Promised

---

[75] Treating God's statement at Babel as a prediction of the Sinai apostasy appears to be unique to *L.A.B.* (Jacobson, *Commentary*, 485; see also Fisk, *Do You Not Remember*, 145–152).

[76] Reinmuth claims that this text establishes a typology between the tower builders and unfaithful Israel (*Pseudo-Philo und Lukas*, 53). The connection is reinforced by the allusion to Isa 40:15 that Pseudo-Philo has inserted into both episodes. In *L.A.B.* 7:3 sinful humanity (excluding Abram) is likened to a drop of water or spittle in God's sight. *L.A.B.* 12:4 applies these expressions to Abraham's sinful descendants.

[77] This is one of many ways in which Pseudo-Philo rewrites the golden calf episode to mitigate the threat of Israel's annihilation. Aaron is all but exonerated in *L.A.B.*, and the resultant plague is omitted. Consult Jacobson, *Commentary*, 11; and Christopher T. Begg, "The Golden Calf Episode According to Pseudo-Philo," in *Studies in the Book of Exodus: Redaction, Reception, Interpretation* (ed. Marc Vervenne; BETL 126; Leuven: Leuven University Press, 1996), 577–594.

[78] This verse may also reflect the influence of Gen 6:17. Jacobson, *Commentary*, 640.

Land and revealing to him cosmological secrets, God contrasts Moses with the rest of sinful humanity. This recalls previous occasions in *L.A.B.* where both Noah and Abraham are set apart from the rest of the human race on account of their righteousness (*L.A.B.* 1:20; 3:4; 4:11; 7:4).

Once again the deity recalls words spoken on an earlier occasion and redeploys them in a new context, this time to draw a correlation between the Mosaic and Noahide covenants. Just as the post-diluvium rainbow serves as a memorial of God's unconditional promise never again to flood the earth, the staff of Moses will remind the deity to bestow mercy upon Israel even when they deserve divine wrath. Pseudo-Philo simply appropriates the symbolic significance that the flood account attaches to the rainbow and transfers it to the staff of Moses.[79] In so doing, the Mosaic covenant is made eternal and unconditional like God's covenant with Noah.

At the same time, the Noahide tradition is also modified by Pseudo-Philo in at least two ways. First, the hermeneutical implications of *L.A.B.* 19:11 flow in both directions. Not only are features of the Noahide covenant (eternal, unconditional) appropriated and reapplied to the Mosaic tradition, but the nationalistic focus of the Mosiac covenant is transferred to the Noahide tradition.[80] Second, the repeated thematic and linguistic connections between Noah and Abraham in *L.A.B.* 1–8 suggest that the former in some sense prefigures the latter. Pseudo-Philo understands Noah, like Abraham, as an early ancestor of Israel whose 'blameless' character sets him apart from the rest of sinful humanity. To a much greater extent than Genesis, *L.A.B.* depicts God's promises to Noah as the first of several covenants intended to preserve and protect Israel.[81]

Overall, Pseudo-Philo's tendency is to collapse Israel's various covenant traditions into one another so that they all take on similar characteristics

---

[79] For the sake of the parallel, Pseudo-Philo here lapses into the anthropomorphism of God requiring a memory aid, which was downplayed in *L.A.B.* 3:12 and 4:5. Correlating the rainbow with Moses' staff appears to be unique to Pseudo-Philo, although Isa 54:9–10 also compares the covenants God made with Noah and Israel. See Jacobson, *Commentary*, 638; and Fisk, *Do You Not Remember*, 277–279.

[80] An out-of-sequence citation not only illuminates the primary passage, but it may also be transformed as new meaning is created by intertextual juxtaposition (Fisk, *Do You Not Remember*, 115).

[81] Newman points out that *L.A.B.*'s linkage of God's covenants with Noah and Israel is unexpected given the universal character of the former; see Judith H. Newman, "The Staff of Moses and the Mercy of God: Moses' Final Intercession in Pseudo-Philo 19," in *Israel in the Wilderness: Interpretations of the Biblical Narratives in Jewish and Christian Traditions* (ed. Kenneth E. Pomykala; TBN 10; Leiden: Brill, 2008), 154–155.

and become mutually interpretive.[82] It is the unconditional and irrevocable ancestral covenant, however, that plays the central role in Pseudo-Philo's imagination. References to the promises that God made to Israel's ancestors are nearly ubiquitous in L.A.B. (e.g., 9:3; 10:2; 12:4; 14:2; 19:3; 20:4; 21:9; 22:3–7; 23:11–13; 35:2; 49:6; 61:5). Yet those foundational promises are prefigured by God's covenant with Noah and fulfilled in Israel's covenant at Sinai.

SELECT BIBLIOGRAPHY

Bauckham, Richard. "The *Liber Antiquitatum Biblicarum* of Pseudo-Philo and the Gospels as 'Midrash.'" Pages 33–76 in *Studies in Midrash and Historiography*. Edited by R.T. France and David Wenham. Gospel Perspectives 3. Sheffield: JSOT Press, 1983.

Burnette-Bletsch, Rhonda. "At the Hands of a Woman: Rewriting Jael in Pseudo-Philo." *Journal for the Study of the Pseudepigrapha* 17 (1998): 53–64.

Cohn, Leopold. "An Apocryphal Work Ascribed to Philo of Alexandria." *Jewish Quarterly Review* 10 (1898): 277–332.

DesCamp, Mary Therese. "Why Are These Women Here? An Examination of the Sociological Setting of Pseudo-Philo through Comparative Reading." *Journal for the Study of the Pseudepigrapha* 16 (1997): 53–80.

Feldman, Louis H. Prolegomenon to *The Biblical Antiquities of Philo, Now First Translated from the Old Latin Version*. Reissued ed. Edited by M.R. James New York: Ktav Publishing House, 1971. Orig. ed. London: SPCK, 1917.

Fisk, Bruce Norman. *Do You Not Remember? Scripture, Story and Exegesis in the Rewritten Bible of Pseudo-Philo*. Journal for the Study of the Pseudepigrapha Supplement Series 37. Sheffield: Sheffield Academic Press, 2001.

Halpern-Amaru, Betsy. *Rewriting the Bible: Land and Covenant in Postbiblical Jewish Literature*. Valley Forge, Pa.: Trinity Press International, 1994.

Harrington, Daniel J. *Les antiquités bibliques: Introduction et text critiques*. Translated by Jacques Cazeaux. Sources chrétiennes 229. Paris: Cerf, 1976.

———. "Pseudo-Philo." Pages 296–377 in vol. 2 of *Old Testament Pseudepigrapha*. Edited by J.H. Charlesworth. 2 vols. New York: Doubleday, 1983–1985.

Jacobson, Howard. "Biblical Quotation and Editorial Function in Pseudo-Philo's Liber Antiquitatum Biblicarum." *Journal for the Study of the Pseudepigrapha* 5 (1989): 47–64.

———. *A Commentary on Pseudo-Philo's* Liber Antiquitatum Biblicarum *with Latin Text and English Translation*. 2 vols. Arbeiten zur Geschichte des antiken Judentums und des Urchristentums 31. Leiden: Brill, 1996.

Murphy, Frederick J. *Pseudo-Philo: Rewriting the Bible*. New York: Oxford University Press, 1993.

---

[82] Newman describes the Sinai covenant in *L.A.B.* as an amalgamated covenant, not entirely distinct from the prior covenants with Noah and the ancestors. See Newman, "Staff of Moses," 140.

Newman, Judith H. "The Staff of Moses and the Mercy of God: Moses' Final Intercession in Pseudo-Philo 19." Pages 137–156 in *Israel in the Wilderness: Interpretations of the Biblical Narratives in Jewish and Christian Traditions*. Edited by Kenneth E. Pomykala. Themes in Biblical Narrative 10. Leiden: Brill, 2008.

Perrot, Charles, and Pierre-Maurice Bogaert. *Les antiquités bibliques: Introduction littéraire, commentaire et index*. Sources chrétiennes 230. Paris: Cerf, 1976.

Reinmuth, Eckart. "Beobachtungen zur Rezeption der Genesis bei Pseudo-Philo (LAB 1–8) und Lakas (APG 7.2–17)." *New Testament Studies* 43 (1997): 552–569.

———. *Pseudo-Philo und Lukas: Studien zum Liber Antiquitatum Biblicarum und seiner Bedeutung für die Interpretation des lukanischen Doppelwerks*. Wissenschaftliche Untersuchungen zum Neuen Testament 74. Tübingen: Mohr Siebeck, 1994.

GENESIS IN THE NEW TESTAMENT

Craig A. Evans

The writings that make up the New Testament quote or allude to dozens of Genesis passages, from creation (chs. 1 and 2) to Jacob's blessing of his son Judah (ch. 49). Almost every chapter of Genesis is accounted for, with 18 or 19 of the 27 books of the New Testament appealing to or in some way making use of the well known book.[1]

The function of Genesis in the New Testament is not incidental or of minor importance. On the contrary, Genesis is foundational to several major New Testament doctrines, including creation, the fall of humankind, and the covenant with Abraham and his descendants. One thinks of the opening words of the Gospel of John, "In the beginning was the Word, and the Word was with God, and the Word was God ... all things through him became, and apart from him not one thing became ..." (1:1, 3). These words allude to the creation narrative of Gen 1: "In the beginning God created the heavens and the earth," as interpreted in the light of wisdom and targumic traditions.[2]

The late Paul Minear has shown how themes in Gen 1–4 echo at key points in the literature of the New Testament, drawing the old and new covenants together.[3] The patriarchs serve as paradigms in the book of Hebrews (esp. ch. 11). The experience of Noah serves as a warning of future judgment (cf. Matt 24:37; Luke 17:26–27; 1 Pet 3:20; 2 Pet 2:5). Melchizedek serves as a type of Christ (Heb 5:6–10; 6:20; 7:10–17). In Adam's fall Paul is able to explain the saving work of Christ (Rom 5:12–21). Balaam (Num 22–24) serves as a type of villain and arch-heretic (2 Pet 2:15; Rev 2:14). Jezebel,

---

[1] Some 230 quotations and allusions are tabulated in the "Index of Quotations," in *The Greek New Testament* (ed. Kurt Aland et al.; 2nd ed., Stuttgart: Deutsche Bibelgesellschaft, 1968), 897–898. The book of Genesis was known in the Gentile world (as seen, e.g., in quotations and allusions in Longinus, *De sublimitate* 9.9; Alexander of Lycopolis, *Contra Manichaei* 24 and 25; Porphyry, *Ad Gaurum* 11). We should assume that some Gentiles read Philo's allegorical and philosophical treatises, in which Genesis and its stories are often mentioned.

[2] On this, see Craig A. Evans, *Word and Glory: On the Exegetical and Theological Background of John's Prologue* (JSNTSup 89; Sheffield: JSOT Press, 1993).

[3] See Paul Sevier Minear, *Christians and the New Creation: Genesis Motifs in the New Testament* (Louisville: Westminster John Knox, 1994).

Ahab's idolatrous and evil wife (1 Kgs 16–21), also serves as a type of false prophet and seductress (Rev 2:20). Pharaoh is the arch-enemy of the people of God (Exod 1–14), but his rise and fall illustrate the sovereignty of God (Rom 9:17).

Our survey could go on and on, but in the confines of the present chapter I shall limit myself to two examples: (1) Genesis and Jesus on monogamy, and (2) Genesis and Paul on Abraham's faith. The first topic is usually debated in reference to divorce and remarriage. In my discussion the focus will be different. The question of monogamy will, of course, have implications for marriage, divorce, and remarriage. The second topic is much debated by theologians and Pauline scholars. My goal in this study is to throw some light on how the faith and obedience of Abraham were understood in Jewish sources roughly contemporaneous with Paul. In my view, some of the theological debate is not as familiar with some of this extra-biblical literature as it should be. Once Jewish views of Abraham are understood better, we may find that the gap between Paul and James, concerning faith and works, is not so very wide.

Genesis and Jesus on Monogamy

The Synoptic Gospels tell us that Herod Antipas, tetrarch of Galilee, arrested John the Baptist for, among other things, saying to the would-be king: "It is not lawful for you to have your brother's wife" (Mark 6:17–18; cf. Matt 14:3–4; Luke 3:19–20). John has referred to Herodias, who had divorced Philip, Antipas's half-brother. In his account of the execution of John Josephus expands on the political dangers that the Baptist presented to Antipas. Nevertheless, he too speaks critically of Herod's marriage to Herodias: "... Herodias, taking it into her head to flout the way of our fathers, married Herod, her husband's brother by the same father, who was tetrarch of Galilee; to do this she parted from a living husband" (*Ant.* 18.136).

Josephus seems to have objected to this marriage on the grounds that Herodias had been married to the brother (or at least half-brother, i.e., "brother by the same father") of Herod Antipas and that this brother was still "living." Because Philip still lived and because Herodias had given birth to at least one child we know of, the law of levirate marriage did not apply (Lev 18:16; 20:21).

At some point subsequent to the death of John Jesus was himself asked about divorce. We cannot be certain, but it is probable that Jesus was questioned about divorce and remarriage because of his association with

John. It may well be that his opponents knew this and raised the question, in order to place Jesus in a politically dangerous position. In any event, here is how the story is told in the oldest Gospel:

> ² And Pharisees, approaching to test him, were asking him if it is lawful for a man to divorce his wife. ³ But answering he said to them, "What did Moses command you?" ⁴ And they said, "Moses permitted *a man* to write a bill divorce and to release *his wife*." ⁵ But Jesus said to them, "On account of your hardness of heart he wrote this commandment for you. ⁶ From the beginning of creation 'male and female he made them'; ⁷ on account of this 'a man shall leave his father and mother [and shall be united to his wife], ⁸ and the two shall be one flesh.' So that they are no longer two but one flesh. ⁹ Therefore, what God has joined together let no man divide."
>
> ¹⁰ And in the house the disciples were again asking him about this. ¹¹ And he says to them, "Whoever should divorce his wife and marry another woman commits adultery against her. ¹² And if she, divorcing her husband, marry another man she commits adultery." (Mark 10:2–12)

The Pharisees[4] appeal to Deut 24:1–4, in which the procedure for obtaining a divorce is spelled out. Their point is that Moses *permitted* (ἐπέτρεψεν) a man to divorce his wife. He needed grounds, of course, and he was required to take specified steps. But what Moses permitted was not necessarily what God desired. To make his point Jesus appealed to two passages from Genesis: πρὸς τὴν σκληροκαρδίαν ὑμῶν ἔγραψεν ὑμῖν τὴν ἐντολὴν ταύτην. ⁶ ἀπὸ δὲ ἀρχῆς κτίσεως ἄρσεν καὶ θῆλυ ἐποίησεν αὐτούς· ⁷ ἕνεκεν τούτου καταλείψει ἄνθρωπος τὸν πατέρα αὐτοῦ καὶ τὴν μητέρα [καὶ προσκολληθήσεται πρὸς τὴν γυναῖκα αὐτοῦ], ⁸ καὶ ἔσονται οἱ δύο εἰς σάρκα μίαν· ὥστε οὐκέτι εἰσὶν δύο ἀλλὰ μία σάρξ. ⁹ ὃ οὖν ὁ θεὸς συνέζευξεν ἄνθρωπος μὴ χωριζέτω. Moses provided the law of divorce, not because God approved of divorce but because such a law was necessary "for the hardness of heart." What God intended is seen in the creation of the first man and woman. Here Jesus appeals to two passages from Genesis: (1) 1:27 "male and female he made them"; and (2) 2:24 "a man shall leave his father and mother [and shall be united to his wife], ⁸and the two shall be one flesh."

---

[4] D and several old Italic authorities omit "Pharisees." Despite the impressive external attestation of "Pharisees" (read by ℵ A B C L Δ Ψ and many other authorities), an early scribe may have introduced the Pharisees as the interlocutors, perhaps under the influence of the parallel passage in Matthew (cf. Matt 19:3). On other occasions the evangelist Mark introduces speakers without identifying them (cf. Mark 2:3, 18; 3:2; 5:35; 10:13). In any event, the nature of the question leads us to assume the presence of either Pharisees or scribes with Pharisaic leanings, as the Matthean evangelist evidently assumed. On this, see R.T. France, *The Gospel of Mark* (NIGTC; Grand Rapids: Eerdmans, 2002), 387, 390.

The quotation of Gen 1:27, ἄρσεν καὶπαρ θῆλυ ἐποίησεν αὐτούς, follows the LXX verbatim, which in turn is a literal rendering of the Hebrew זָכָר וּנְקֵבָה בָּרָא אֹתָם.[5] There is some variation in the targums. Whereas Onqelos renders this part of the verse literally, Neofiti reads "male and his partner he created them." What is rendered "partner" (זוּג) is a Greek loanword (representing either ζεῦγος or ζυγόν) found elsewhere in the Palestinian midrashim and targums.[6] Interestingly, the verbal form of this word appears in Jesus' conclusion, "what God has joined together [συνέζευξεν] ...." This could be no more than a coincidence, but it could also indicate that Jesus' language, if not interpretation, reflects one stream of Jewish interpretation known in his time.[7] Another reading is found in Pseudo-Jonathan: "male and female in their appearance he created them." Pseudo-Jonathan's rendering probably reflects a late rabbinic tradition that Adam was initially created with two faces, one male and one female. The female face was given to Eve when she was created (*b. Ber.* 61a; *'Erub.* 18a; *Gen. Rab.* 8.1 [on 1:27]).

The quotation of Gen 2:24 presents a number of features of interest. The text reads: καταλείψει ἄνθρωπος τὸν πατέρα αὐτοῦ καὶ τὴν μητέρα [καὶ προσκολληθήσεται πρὸς τὴν γυναῖκα αὐτοῦ],[8] καὶ ἔσονται οἱ δύο εἰς σάρκα μίαν. The bracketed material ("and he shall be united to his wife") is read by several important authorities, including D W Θ *f*[13] (and, in a somewhat different form, by A C L N Δ Σ *f*[1]). The material is omitted in ℵ B Ψ and a few other mss and versions. The material may well have been carried over from the parallel at Matt 19:5. Nevertheless, its presence in the text clarifies the antecedent of οἱ δύο ("the two"), which of course refers to the man and his wife, not the man's mother and father.[8] The quotation in Mark 10:7–8 follows the LXX verbatim. The LXX offers a literal rendering of the Hebrew, with one important exception. The Hebrew only says "they shall be one flesh" (הָיוּ לְבָשָׂר אֶחָד); there is no equivalent of "the two" (οἱ δύο). At this point Onqelos follows the Hebrew, but Neofiti's reading agrees with the LXX: "and the two of them [תריהו] will become one flesh." Other authorities agree with

---

[5] So also the Latin: *masculum et feminam creavit eos.*

[6] For a summation of the Palestinian tradition, see Martin McNamara, *Targum Neofiti 1: Genesis* (ArBib 1a; Collegeville, Minn.: Liturgical Press, 1992), 18, 55 n. 16.

[7] On this point, see David Daube, *The New Testament and Rabbinic Judaism* (JLCRS 2; London: Athlone, 1956), 73–74.

[8] On the ms evidence, see Bruce M. Metzger, *A Textual Commentary on the Greek New Testament* (corr. ed.; New York: United Bible Societies, 1975), 104–105.

the LXX. "Two of them" also appears in Pseudo-Jonathan, the Samaritan Pentateuch, the Peshitta, the Vulgate, and the Arabic.[9] It is possible that "two of them" came from Gen 2:25 (Hebrew: שְׁנֵיהֶם; LXX: οἱ δύο),[10] but it may also reflect an attempt to qualify the text in support of monogamy, that is, marriage made up of only *two* persons, one man and one woman. This possibility raises a complicated question, which needs to be addressed at this point: How monogamous were the Jewish people in the time of Jesus?

It must be acknowledged that in the Hebrew text of Gen 2:24 ("they become one flesh"), there is "no recognition of monogamy."[11] In light of whole of the book of Genesis, this seems obvious. After all, the great patriarchs (e.g., Abraham, Isaac, and Jacob) were polygamists. Israel's famous kings, David and Solomon, were polygamists. Polygamy is presupposed in the literary world of the Old Testament narratives and in many cases seems to have been understood as a sign of wealth and power.[12]

From a legal point of view, polygamy was presupposed in the world of the Hebrew Bible. The legislation of Exod 21:10–11, Lev 18:18, and Deut 21:15–17 not only assumes polygamy but provides laws designed to protect wives and their interests. In the first passage, the husband is warned against treating poorly the first wife when he takes a second wife ("he shall not diminish her food, her clothing, or her marital rights"). In the second, taking the wife's sister as a second wife is forbidden. In the third, the husband is prohibited from showing favoritism to the son of a second wife—whatever his feelings for her—in matters of inheritance: the first-born son (i.e., the son of the first wife) is to be favored with a double-portion of his father's estate. Polygamy, of course, accommodates the practice of the levirate marriage, by which a

---

[9] For discussion of the LXX in relation to other authorities, see John William Wevers, *Notes on the Greek Text of Genesis* (SBLSCS 35; Atlanta: Scholars Press, 1993), 35. The last part of Gen 2:24 reads oddly in the SamP: "And there became one flesh out of the two of them [משניהם]."

[10] So Gordon J. Wenham, *Genesis 1–15* (WBC 1; Dallas: Word, 1987), 47 n. 24b.

[11] As rightly stated by Gerhard von Rad, *Genesis: A Commentary* (rev. ed.; OTL; Philadelphia: Westminster, 1972), 85. But see S.R. Driver, *The Book of Genesis, with Introduction and Notes* (6th ed.; WC; London: Methuen, 1907 [1st ed. 1904]), 43, who seems to think monogamic marriage is hinted at. But this is to read later monogamic strictures into the text. In the survey that follows I am indebted to David Instone Brewer, "Jesus' Old Testament Basis for Monogamy," in *The Old Testament in the New Testament: Essays in Honour of J.L. North* (ed. Steve Moyise; JSNTSup 189; Sheffield: Sheffield Academic Press, 2000), 75–105.

[12] For a brief overview, see M. Stephen Davis, "Polygamy in the Ancient World," *BI* 14 (1987): 34–36.

man (or close relative), even if already married, is obligated to take as wife the childless widow of his brother (cf. Gen 38:1–11; Deut 25:5–10; Ruth 4:1–12).[13]

Polygamy may have been allowed in Jewish society, but it does not seem to have been widespread. Moreover, polygamous marriages in the Old Testament narratives often provide the setting and occasion for strife and negative experiences (e.g., the rivalry between Sarah and Hagar, or the rivalry between Leah and Rachel). One could say that in Old Testament law and narrative polygamy was viewed with ambivalence.[14] Polygamy does not seem to have been encouraged. Later traditions, including wisdom, seem to assume monogamy as normative (Prov 12:4; 18:22; 19:14; 31:10–31; Ps 128:3; Sir 25:1, 8, 22; 26:1–3 [though see 26:6 "when a wife is envious of a rival"]; Tob 1:20; 7:8; 4 Macc 2:11).

Nevertheless, in the approximate time of Jesus there is evidence of some polygamy among the Jewish people. Josephus explains to his Roman readers (who were themselves monogamous) that "it is an ancestral custom of ours to have several wives at the same time" (*Ant.* 17.14). Of Herod the Great Josephus says: "His wives were numerous, since polygamy [γαμεῖν πλείους] was permitted by Jewish custom and the king gladly availed himself of the privilege" (*J.W.* 1.477). Because Greek and Roman culture viewed polygamy with distaste (and forbade it by law),[15] Josephus may well have downplayed the extent of polygamy among the Jewish people, especially among the elite, of which Josephus himself was part.

Early rabbinic tradition speaks of polygamy in certain first-century families. In a discussion of the children of "co-wives" (צרות) of ruling priests the

---

[13] For an overview of the practice, see Dale W. Manor, "A Brief History of Levirate Marriage as it Relates to the Bible," *RestQ* 27 (1984): 129–142. For critical discussion, see Eryl W. Davies, "Inheritance Rights and the Hebrew Levirate Marriage: Part 1," *VT* 31 (1981): 138–144; and Davies, "Inheritance Rights and the Hebrew Levirate Marriage: Part 2," *VT* 31 (1981): 257–268. One should also consult Ron du Preez, "Does Levirate Law Promote Polygamy?" in *To Understand the Scriptures: Essays in Honor of William H. Shea* (ed. David Merling; Berrien Springs, Mich.: Siegfried H. Horn Archaeological Museum of Andrews University, 1997), 273–289. Du Preez argues that levirate marriage did not "promote" polygamy. Perhaps not, but it did nothing to discourage it.

[14] For more on the biblical views of marriage, see Gordon P. Hugenberger, *Marriage as a Covenant: A Study of Biblical Law and Ethics Governing Marriage, Developed from the Perspective of Malachi* (VTSup 52; Leiden: Brill, 1994); and Craig S. Keener, "Marriage," in *Dictionary of New Testament Background* (ed. Craig A. Evans and Stanley E. Porter; Downers Grove, Ill.: InterVarsity, 2000), 680–693. For an older work that includes rabbinic law, see Louis M. Epstein, *Marriage Laws in the Bible and the Talmud* (HSS 12; Cambridge: Harvard University Press, 1942).

[15] For a succinct summary of the pertinent primary literature, see Keener, "Marriage," 683.

Rabbis agree that these children should not be given the status of *mamzer*, that is, a person of dubious birth (cf. *t. Yebam.* 1.1–10, esp. 1.10). Interestingly enough, one of the examples cited is from the "house of Qayapha" [בית קיפאי], possibly related to the family of Caiaphas, the well known high priest who condemned Jesus (cf. Matt 26:3), whose ornate ossuary some scholars think was discovered in 1990.[16] In an imaginative conversation with the Rabbis the chief administrator of Agrippa II (ca. 27–93 CE), great grandson of Herod the Great, alludes to his two wives, one who lives in Tiberias and one who lives in Sepphoris (*b. Sukkah* 27a). The historicity of this story is impossible to ascertain. The Rabbis also relate a story about Abba, the brother of Gamaliel (early first century), who had two wives (*b. Yebam.* 15a). But again, the historical worth of this tradition is doubtful.

We have data from the second century that is much firmer. Justin Martyr (ca. 150 CE) refers to Jewish polygamy as though it was still practiced by some: "If it were allowable to take any wife, or as many wives as one chooses, and how he chooses, which the men of your nation do over all the earth, wherever they sojourn, or wherever they have been sent, taking women under the name of marriage ..." (cf. *Dial.* 141). As the next example will show, Justin's description, even if hyperbolic, is factual.

A specific case of early second-century Jewish polygamy is attested in the Babatha archive recovered in the 1960s by Yigael Yadin and his team at Nahal Hever (near the Dead Sea), not far from En Gedi. In all, some three dozen letters, depositions, summons, replies, and petitions were found.[17] We infer from this correspondence that by 124 CE the woman Babatha had a

---

[16] On this possible identification, see William Horbury, "The 'Caiaphas' Ossuaries and Joseph Caiaphas," *PEQ* 126 (1994): 32–48. Horbury discusses both the Caiaphas ossuaries and the various rabbinic traditions that may refer to this priestly family. The matter will now have to be revisited in light of the recent announcement (29 June 2011) that another ornate ossuary has surfaced, bearing the inscription "Miriam, daughter of Yeshua, son of Qayapha [or Caiaphas], priest of Ma'aziah, of Beth 'Imri." The details of this surprising discovery are now available in B. Zissu and Y. Goren, "The Ossuary of 'Miriam Daughter of Yeshua Son of Caiaphas, Priests of Ma'aziah from Beth 'Imri'," *IEJ* 61 (2011): 74–95.

[17] See Naphtali Lewis, ed., *The Documents from the Bar Kokhba Period in the Cave of Letters: Greek Papyri; with Aramaic and Nabatean Signatures and Subscriptions*, edited by Yigael Yadin, and Jonas C. Greenfield (Jerusalem: Israel Exploration Society, 1989); and Yigael Yadin et al., eds, *The Documents from the Bar-Kokhba Period in the Cave of Letters: Hebrew, Aramaic and Nabatean-Aramaic Papyri* (Jerusalem: Israel Exploration Society, 2002), 118–141 (P.Yadin 10, the only Babatha document in this volume). See the helpful review of the first volume in Martin Goodman, "Babatha's Story," *JRS* 81 (1991): 169–175. The Babatha documents are also edited, translated, and annotated in H.M. Cotton and A. Yardeni, *Aramaic, Hebrew and Greek Documentary Texts from Nahal Hever and Other Sites: With an Appendix Containing Alleged Qumran Texts* (DJD 27; Oxford: Clarendon, 1997).

son and was widowed (cf. P.Yadin 12, where Babatha works out support for her "orphan" son). It is assumed that she was 18 to 20 years old at the time. It is also surmised that Babatha died in 132 CE, along with others whose skeletal remains were discovered in one of the caves of Nahal Hever. Much of the correspondence concerned her marriages, her son's support, and disputes over property.

Babatha was twice married and twice widowed. Admittedly, there is nothing Jewish about her name, but the names of her son and husbands,[18] as well as the names of a number of other officials and witnesses mentioned in her correspondence and legal papers, and the circumstances and context of her death (in the company of Jewish revolutionaries and supporters of Simon bar Kosiba) strongly suggest that Babatha was herself Jewish.[19]

For the purposes at hand, two documents are of especial importance. In the first, a summons and reply, dating to 9 July 131, we read: "Mariame replied, saying: 'Before this I summoned you [Babatha] not to go near the possessions of my and your late husband [μου καὶ σου ἀνδρὸς ἀπογενομένου]'" (P.Yadin 26, lines 11–14). The late husband is Judah. Mariame's language, "my and your late husband," is understood to mean that Mariame and Babatha were both married to Judah (Babatha's second marriage) *at the same time*.[20] Babatha was Judah's second wife; Mariame his first (so far as we know). In a petition, dating to about the same time as the summons and reply, we read: "Babatha, (daughter) of Simon the Moazene ... 'I entreat you, lord, against Mariame, (daughter) of Beianos the Engedene, wife of Judah ... late husband of her and of me [ἀνδρὸς αὐτῆς καὶ ἐμοῦ ἀπογενομένου]'" (P.Yadin 34, lines 2–5).[21] Again, the language implies that Mariame and Babatha had been married to Judah as "co-wives" and now with the man's death they were "co-widows."[22]

---

[18] Persons of interest: Babatha of the village Moaza, daughter of Shimon (son of Menahem) and wife of Jesus, son of Jesus (and mother of his son Jesus), and (later) wife of Judah, son of Eleazar. See the family tree(s) in Lewis, *The Documents from the Bar Kokhba Period in the Cave of Letters*, 25.

[19] As succinctly argued in Goodman, "Babatha's Story," 174.

[20] Lewis, *The Documents from the Bar Kokhba Period*, 113–115 + pls. 34 and 35; Goodman, "Babatha's Story," 171–174.

[21] Lewis, *The Documents from the Bar Kokhba Period*, 127–128.

[22] This interpretation has been challenged by Ranon Katzoff, "Polygamy in P.Yadin?" *ZPE* 109 (1995): 128–132. Katzoff argues that P.Yadin 26 and 34 may be referring to serial monogamy. In this case, we should think that Judah was married first to Miriam and then, after divorcing her, he married Babatha. Katzoff's argument is rebutted by Naphtali Lewis, "Judah's Bigamy," *ZPE* 116 (1997): 152. Lewis, rightly in my opinion, appeals to the words "my and your late husband," which clearly implies that Miriam and Babatha had been co-

The nature of Babatha's legal correspondence (including references to various endowments and properties), the quality of her clothing, jewelry, and other possessions found by Yadin and his colleagues, and her association with families close to Simon ben Kosiba, the leader of the rebellion who was called "Prince of Israel" (*nasi yisrael*) suggest that Babatha was from an affluent and (probably) influential family. All of this is consistent with the kind of Jewish families that sometimes practiced polygamy in late antiquity.

However, we should not assume that all Jewish men with two or more wives were wealthy. In an early rabbinic tradition the Sages discuss the case of a man "who was married to four wives and who died" (*m. Ketub.* 10:5). The discussion assumes that all four wives survive the husband and debates who has priority in the division of his modest estate. (The first wife has priority over the second, the second over the third, etc.) Later rabbinic tradition states that a man is limited to four wives (*b. Yebam.* 44a).

In the eleventh century polygamy among Jews was officially banned,[23] probably due in part to Christian influence, thus bringing to completion a move toward monogamy that got under way in the post-exilic setting and was encouraged under Greek and Roman influence. Well before the official ban, Rabbis were speaking against polygamy. Says one: "If it had been appropriate for ten wives to be given to Adam, God would have given them to him. But it was not appropriate for him to be given more than one wife. One wife alone was appropriate for him; and for me too my wife is sufficient" (*'Abot R. Nat.* [version B] §2).[24] In short, Judaism in the Medieval period had become more Western and more European than Middle Eastern. In the Middle East polygamy was now the practice of Islam.

Now let us return to Jesus' response to the question about divorce. That Jesus is opposed to divorce is quite clear, not so much from his appeal to Genesis, but from his concluding pronouncement: "Therefore, what God has joined together let no man divide" (Mark 10:9).

Neither Philo nor Josephus, or any rabbinic authority, bans divorce and remarriage; yet the Markan Jesus does. For this reason, one New Testament

---

wives of Judah and after his death co-widows. Lewis also reminds readers of local (Nabatean) acceptance of polygamy. I might add that the nature of the litigation we find in the Babatha archive is easier to understand in reference to a widowed Mariame rather than a divorced Mariame.

[23] For references, see Instone Brewer, "Jesus' Old Testament Basis for Monogamy," 78 n. 17.

[24] Translation from Anthony J. Saldarini, *The Fathers According to Rabbi Nathan* (*Abot de Rabbi Nathan Version B*): *A Translation and Commentary* (SJLA 11; Leiden: Brill, 1975), 39. See also Saldarini's commentary on p. 39 in nn. 5 and 6.

scholar has argued that "Mark's version of the question is inconceivable in a Palestinian Pharisaic milieu ...."[25] This scholar goes on to argue for Matthean priority, since the Markan version reflects, he believes, a non-Palestinian, non-Jewish setting.[26] Qumran, however, does provide an important parallel to Jesus' thought. Expanding on Deut 17:17 ("he shall not multiply wives for himself, lest his heart turn away") the Temple Scroll enjoins:

> (The king) may not take a wife from any of the nations. Rather, he must take himself a wife from his father's house—that is, from his father's family. He is not to take another wife in addition to her; no, she alone will be with him all the days of her life. If she dies, then he may take himself another wife from his father's house, that is, his family.[27]   (11QTemple 57:15b–19)

The phrase "all the days of her life [חַיֶּיהָ]" (line 18) alludes to Lev 18:18 ("And you shall not take a woman as a rival wife to her sister ... while her sister is yet alive [חַיֶּיהָ]"). Indeed, Yadin thinks Lev 18:18 had been in the text of 11QTemple, at the top of col. 57, which is no longer extant.[28]

One might object to the relevance of the Temple Scroll passage, since it is referring to Israel's king. But the next text shows that the Essenes evidently did apply this teaching universally:

> They [Qumran's opponents] are caught in two traps: fornication, by taking two wives in their lifetimes, although the principle of creation is 'male and female he created them' [Gen 1:27] and those who went into the ark 'went into the ark two by two' [Gen 7:9]. Concerning the Leader it is written 'he shall not multiply wives to himself' [Deut 17:17]; but David had not read the sealed book of the Law, which was in the ark (of the covenant), for it was not opened in Israel since the day of the death of Eleazar and Joshua and the elders. For (their successors) worshiped the Ashotoreth, and that which had been revealed was hidden until Zadok arose, so David's works were accepted, with the exception of Uriah's blood, and God forgave him for them.[29]
>
> (CD 4:20–5:6)

Again we have an allusion to Lev 18:18. The opponents of the Qumran community commit fornication, says the author of the Damascus Covenant, "by taking two wives in their lifetimes" (בחייהם). Polygamy was forbidden; so

---

[25] David L. Dungan, *The Sayings of Jesus in the Churches of Paul: The Use of Synoptic Tradition in the Regulation of Early Church Life* (Oxford: Blackwell, 1971), 233.
[26] Dungan, *Sayings of Jesus*, 102–124.
[27] Translation based on Michael O. Wise, Martin G. Abegg Jr., and Edward M. Cook, *The Dead Sea Scrolls: A New Translation* (San Francisco: HarperCollins, 1996), 485.
[28] Yigael Yadin, *The Temple Scroll* (3 vols., Jerusalem: Israel Exploration Society, 1977–1983), 1.355; 2.300; 3.72 (= pl. 72). Plate 72 makes clear loss of text at the top of the column.
[29] Translation based on Wise, Abegg, and Cook, *Dead Sea Scrolls*, 55.

were divorce and remarriage.[30] The author makes his argument by appeal to Gen 1:27 ("male and female he created them") and Gen 7:9 ("two by two into the ark"). The author does not appeal to Gen 2:24, because "the two of them" does not appear in the Hebrew text, at least not in the text widely acknowledged. A legal argument of this nature cannot rest on a disputed reading. So the author of the Damascus Covenant finds his "two" in another passage in Genesis. The author then applies his ruling to the king, who is not to "multiply wives for himself" (Deut 17:17). Of course, the author knows that David—a model king and father of the Messiah to come—did have more than one wife. But David is excused, because he had not had opportunity to read the "book of the Torah" (Deuteronomy?), where the proscription against multiplying wives is found.

Nevertheless, Gen 2:24 is appealed to elsewhere in the Scrolls. In one of the wisdom texts that instruct the disciple in the way he should live, marital advice is given:

> When you are united, live together with your fleshly helper [... For as the verse says, "A man should leave] ¹ his father and his mother [and adhere to his wife and they will become one flesh" (Gen 2:24).] ² He has made you ruler over her, so [...] ³ he did not give [her father] authority over her, he has separated her from her mother, and to you [he has given authority ... He has made your wife] ⁴ and you into one flesh. He will take your daughter away and give her to another, and your sons [...] ⁵ But you, live together with the wife of your bosom, for she is the kin of [...] ⁶ Whosoever governs her besides you has "shifted the boundary" of his life [...] ⁷ He has made you ruler over her, for her to live the way you want her to, not adding any vows or offerings [...] ⁸ Turn her spirit to your will, and every binding oath, every vow [...] ⁹ annulling the utterance of your mouth, and forbidding the doing of your will [...] ¹⁰ your lips, forgive her, for your sake do not [...] ¹¹ your honor in your inheritance [...] ¹² in your inheritance lest [...] ¹³ the wife of your bosom and shame ....[31]
>
> (4Q416 frag. 2, 3:21b–4:13a)

The text is fragmentary and much of the quotation of Gen 2:24 has to be restored. But the gist of the advice is pretty clear. 4Q416 is one of seven fragmentary copies of a work scholars call 4QInstruction (i.e., 1Q26, 4Q415, 416, 417, 418a, 418b, 423), a work thought to have originated in the second or third century BCE. The scholarly literature devoted to 4QInstruction has

---

[30] On this interpretation, see Joseph A. Fitzmyer, "The Matthean Divorce Texts and Some New Palestinian Evidence," *TS* 37 (1976): 197–226; and Instone Brewer, "Jesus' Old Testament Basis for Monogamy," 81–83.

[31] Translation based on Wise, Abegg, and Cook, *Dead Sea Scrolls*, 385.

grown considerably in the last dozen years or so, in part because of a number of interesting and helpful parallels with Philo and New Testament literature.

Probably not produced by the Essenes (on account of the early date and vocabulary distinctives), 4QInstruction nonetheless coheres with Essenic teaching at many important points. We should assume that many copies of this text were found at Qumran because the sectarians approved of it and studied it. Much of its wisdom draws upon the early chapters of Genesis. While it is not certain, the discussion of marriage in the passage quoted above, a discussion that includes a quotation of Gen 2:24, almost certainly presupposes monogamy as the norm. The point of the passage is that the faithful disciple will not allow his wife to distract him or lead him away from righteousness. The disciple is to guide his wife, to "turn her spirit" to his will, so that she will not annul the word of the disciple.[32]

Although Qumran's teaching regarding marriage is sparse and fragmentary, what little of it we have seems to cohere with Jesus' teaching, including appeals to Gen 1:27 and 2:24. It seems, then, that the question the Pharisees (or whoever) put to Jesus was very much an item of debate in Jewish Palestine of the early first century. Accordingly, the Pharisees wonder if Jesus allows for divorce, as do the Rabbis, or forbids it, as do the Essenes. It is quite possible that the Pharisees' question may very well have been occasioned by Jesus' known association with John and the assumption that he held to his views, views which seem to have been the same as those held by the Essenes. Thus, the question may not have been so innocent, but a question designed to draw Jesus out and show that his view is the same as John's and therefore just as politically dangerous as John's had been.[33] If their question had an ulterior motive of this sort lying behind it, this could explain why the story appears where it does, in that part of Mark where Jesus and his opponents engage in an escalating polemic.[34]

---

[32] For critical analysis of 4Q416 frag. 2, 3:21b–4:13a, see Daryl F. Jefferies, *Wisdom at Qumran: A Form-Critical Analysis of the Admonitions of the Admonitions in 4QInstruction* (GDNES 3; Piscataway, N.J.: Gorgias, 2002), 248–264.

[33] As has been expressed by older commentators: H.B. Swete, *The Gospel According to St Mark* (3rd ed.; London: Macmillan, 1909 [orig. 1898]), 215: "to excite the anger of Antipas"; and Vincent Taylor, *The Gospel According to St. Mark* (London: Macmillan, 1952), 417: "compromising him in the eyes of Herod."

[34] Most commentators, e.g., Ernest Best, *Following Jesus: Discipleship in the Gospel of Mark* (JSNTSup 4; Sheffield: JSOT Press, 1981), 101, assume that the pericope has relevance for Mark's Greco-Roman audience, but have difficulty explaining why it appears at this point in the Gospel.

In any event, lying behind the rejection of divorce is a rejection of polygamy.[35] Commitment to monogamy, informed by the texts from Genesis, militates against the easy divorce some of Jesus' contemporaries advocated (so long as the law of Deut 24:1–4 is followed!). But monogamy is not merely informed by the Genesis texts; it is the true expression of marriage, as can be inferred from the Genesis texts. It is not surprising that monogamy is presupposed by Paul in his instructions regarding marriage (as in 1 Cor 7:1–40). Nor is it surprising that monogamous marriage is not only viewed as normative in the Christian church but is required of church leaders. After all, the man who aspires to be an overseer (or bishop) should be "the husband of one wife" (1 Tim 3:2; Titus 1:6).

Genesis and Paul on Abraham's Faith

The great patriarch Abraham was celebrated in early Judaism and Christianity. In paraphrases of Genesis and examples of "rewritten Bible," including targumic and midrashic traditions, the patriarch's virtues are exaggerated and his failings are either mitigated or omitted altogether. Abraham rejects idolatry, refuses to assist in building the tower of Babel, and is willing to suffer martyrdom for his monotheistic faith.[36]

Abraham's life and example are of great importance for Paul. The apostle refers to the patriarch by name some eighteen times in three of his letters, including two of his most important theological letters, Galatians and Romans.[37] Abraham's example of believing God's promise and then having this faith "reckoned to him as righteousness" (Gen 15:6) is foundational for Paul's understanding of faith and justification before God. Abraham's faith makes it possible for Paul to reject the idea that "works of the Law" can establish one's righteousness.

---

[35] As is rightly and ably argued by Instone Brewer, "Jesus' Old Testament Basis for Monogamy," 92–105.

[36] For an overview of Abraham in these diverse post-biblical materials, see Craig A. Evans, "Abraham in the Dead Sea Scrolls: A Man of Faith and Failure," in *The Bible at Qumran: Text, Shape, and Interpretation* (ed. Peter W. Flint; SDSSRL 5; Grand Rapids: Eerdmans, 2001), 149–158; and Jacqueline C.R. de Roo, *'Works of the Law' at Qumran and in Paul* (NTM 13; Sheffield: Sheffield Phoenix, 2007), 99–128.

[37] Abraham appears in Rom 4:1, 9, 12, 13, 16; 9:7; 11:1; 2 Cor 11:22; Gal 3:6, 14, 16, 18; 4:22. The occurrences in Paul's writings account for one quarter of occurrences of Abraham in the writings of the New Testament.

Pauline scholars debate a number of points related to Paul's understanding of works and Abraham's faith. Aspects of this debate have implications for the long-standing problem of the tension between Paul's apparent *rejection* of works as a means of salvation and James's apparent *requirement* of works as a means of salvation. Study of Abraham's faith in the context of a lively Jewish exegesis of late antiquity may help us find a solution, and if not a solution, then at least a way that could lead to one. I shall begin with one of the much-talked about texts found at Qumran.

The discovery and eventual publication of 4QMMT,[38] in which appear the phrases "works of the law" and "it will be reckoned to you as righteousness," have thrown the debate over Paul's meaning of this language into a whole new light. The purpose of the present section is to make a modest contribution to this discussion, focusing on the figure of Phinehas. I make no claim to resolve any important aspect of the debate concerning Paul, but I do contend that proper understanding of works of law and being declared righteous, either for what one does or what one believes, whether or not in reference to Abraham, must take into account the way Phinehas the zealous priest was appreciated among Jews and Christians in late antiquity.

Phinehas appears in Exod 6:25, where he is identified as Aaron's grandson (cf. 1 Chr 6:4, 50; 9:20; Ezra 7:5). He makes his next appearance in Num 25, in the episode in which many Israelites joined Moabites and Midianites in worshipping the god (or "Baal," presumably Chemosh; cf. Num 21:29) in Mount Peor (cf. Num 23:28; 31:16; Deut 4:3; Ps 106:28). These activities included sexual promiscuity and feasting in honor of the god of Peor and resulted in a plague.[39] While Moses and others are weeping before the entrance of the tent of meeting an Israelite man brings a foreign woman into the camp. He does this in the very sight of the grieving Moses. The reader should infer that this man has no regard whatsoever for Moses or for Israel's sacred covenant with God.

When Phinehas sees this outrage, he takes a spear, kills both the man and the woman, and so brings the plague to an end. The reader learns why, when God tells Moses:

---

[38] 4QMMT is a composite text made up of six fragmentary copies (4Q394–399).

[39] For discussion of setting and background, see George Buchanan Gray, *A Critical and Exegetical Commentary on the Book of Numbers* (ICC; Edinburgh: T&T Clark, 1903), 381–383; John Sturdy, *Numbers* (CBC; Cambridge: Cambridge University Press, 1976), 183–185; Philip J. Budd, *Numbers* (WBC 5; Dallas: Word, 1984), 281–283; and Timothy R. Ashley, *The Book of Numbers* (NICOT; Grand Rapids: Eerdmans, 1993), 516–519.

> [11] Phinehas the son of Eleazar, son of Aaron the priest, has turned back my wrath from the people of Israel, in that he was jealous with my jealousy among them, so that I did not consume the people of Israel in my jealousy. [12] Therefore say, "Behold, I give to him my covenant of peace; [13] and it shall be to him, and to his descendants after him, the covenant of a perpetual priesthood, because he was jealous for his God, and made atonement for the people of Israel." (Num 25:11–13)

What is translated "he was jealous with my jealousy" (בְּקַנְאוֹ אֶת־קִנְאָתִי / ἐν τῷ ζηλῶσαί μου τὸν ζῆλον) could also be translated "he was zealous with my zeal." So also, "jealous for his God" (קִנֵּא לֵאלֹהָיו / ἐζήλωσεν τῷ θεῷ αὐτοῦ) in v. 13 could be translated "zealous for his God."

On account of this episode Phinehas was remembered for his zeal. God gave this priest a "covenant of peace" (בְּרִיתִי שָׁלוֹם / διαθήκην εἰρήνης) and his descendants a "covenant of a perpetual priesthood" (בְּרִית כְּהֻנַּת עוֹלָם / διαθήκη ἱερατείας αἰωνία).

Phinehas reappears in the war with Midian (Num 31:1–12). He joins the army and is entrusted with the holy vessels and the trumpets (v. 6). Israel routes the kings of Midian, taking spoils and captives (vv. 7–12). Phinehas reappears again in Josh 22, in which he is sent as an emissary of sorts, to rebuke the tribes of Reuben, Gad, and Manasseh (vv. 13–20). When the leaders of these tribes convince the priest of their fidelity, Phinehas is pleased and is able to give the rest of Israel a favorable report (vv. 30–34). Phinehas is mentioned later in Judg 20, when readers are reminded that he used to stand before the ark of the covenant and minister (vv. 27–28). In his recounting of the principal priests in Israel's early history the Chronicler mentions Phinehas, saying "Phinehas the son of Eleazar was the ruler over them in time past; the Lord was with him" (1 Chr 9:20).

Phinehas makes his final appearance in Hebrew Scripture in Ps 106, a psalm of repentance that recalls and confesses the many instances of Israel's sin and rebellion, including the aforementioned apostasy at Peor:

> [28] Then they attached themselves to the Baal of Peor, and ate sacrifices offered to the dead; [29] they provoked the Lord to anger with their doings, and a plague broke out among them. [30] Then Phinehas stood up and interposed, and the plague was stayed. [31] And that has been reckoned to him as righteousness from generation to generation for ever.

The importance of the phrase "reckoned to him as righteousness" will be considered shortly.

The zeal of Phinehas, dramatically witnessed in the incident at Peor, resulted in an almost iconic status for this priest. One of the oldest testimonies is found in Sirach, who lauds Phinehas in his Praise for Famous

Men (Sir 44–51). In his praise of Phinehas one hears echoes of Num 25 and Ps 106:

> [23] Phinehas the son of Eleazar is the third in glory, for he was zealous in the fear of the Lord [ἐν τῷ ζηλῶσαι αὐτὸν ἐν φόβῳ κυρίου], and stood fast, when the people turned away, in the ready goodness of his soul, and made atonement for Israel.
>
> [24] Therefore a covenant of peace [διαθήκη εἰρήνης] was established with him, that he should be leader of the sanctuary and of his people, that he and his descendants should have the dignity of the priesthood for ever.
>
> (Sir 45:23–24)

Joshua ben Sira (or, in Greek, "Jesus the son of Sirach") composed his work in Hebrew sometime around 180 BCE. About fifty years later his grandson prefaced and translated it into Greek. Phinehas appears in exalted company indeed, preceded by Moses (vv. 1–5) and Aaron (vv. 6–22) and followed by David (vv. 25–26). The appearance of David is chronologically out of sequence, for Joshua the son of Nun, successor to Moses, will make his appearance in Sir 46:1–12. Mention of David is brought forward, because he too was honored with a covenant. A covenant of peace and priesthood was established with Phinehas and a covenant of kingship was established with David. The coupling of Phinehas with David, each blessed with a covenant, one priestly and the other royal, is highly significant, testifying to the diarchic nature of Israel's ordained leadership.

In 1 Maccabees the zealous actions of Mattathias, father of Judas Maccabeus and his brothers, are compared to the zeal and violence of Phinehas:

> [24] When Mattathias saw it, be burned with zeal [ἐζήλωσεν] and his heart was stirred.[40] He gave vent to righteous anger; he ran and killed him upon the altar. [25] At the same time he killed the king's officer who was forcing them to sacrifice, and he tore down the altar. [26] Thus he burned with zeal for the law [ἐζήλωσεν τῷ νόμῳ], as Phinehas did against Zimri the son of Salu. [27] Then Mattathias cried out in the city with a loud voice, saying: "Let every one who is zealous for the law and supports the covenant [ὁ ζηλῶν τῷ νόμῳ καὶ παριστῶν διαθήκην] come out with me!"   (1 Macc 2:24–27)

Phinehas is again mentioned by name in Matthathias' farewell to his sons, a farewell modeled after Jacob's farewell to his sons in Gen 49, which gave rise to a genre that became very popular in late antiquity. Here is part of Mattathias' farewell:

---

[40] Literally, the text reads "his kidneys trembled" (ἐτρόμησαν οἱ νεφροὶ αὐτοῦ).

⁵⁰ Now, my children, show zeal for the law [ζηλώσατε τῷ νόμῳ], and give your lives for the covenant of our fathers. ⁵¹ Remember the deeds of the fathers [τὰ ἔργα τῶν πατέρων], which they did in their generations; and receive great honor and an everlasting name. ⁵² Was not Abraham found faithful when tested [ἐν πειρασμῷ εὑρέθη πιστός], and it was reckoned to him as righteousness [ἐλογίσθη αὐτῷ εἰς δικαιοσύνην]? ⁵³ Joseph in the time of his distress kept the commandment, and became lord of Egypt. ⁵⁴ Phinehas our father, because he was deeply zealous [ἐν τῷ ζηλῶσαι ζῆλον], received the covenant of everlasting priesthood [διαθήκην ἱερωσύνης αἰωνίας] .... ⁵⁸ Elijah because of great zeal for the law [ἐν τῷ ζηλῶσαι ζῆλον νόμου] was taken up into heaven .... (1 Macc 2:50–54, 58)

Zeal for the law is the theme that runs throughout this farewell testament. Once again we find Phinehas in illustrious company. The author of 1 Maccabees, a book that was composed some time around 100 BCE, cites the examples of Abraham, Joseph, Joshua, Caleb, David, Elijah, Daniel and the three young men (cf. 1 Macc 2:55–60). Mattathias, of course, is a priest and can find no better example of priestly zeal than that of Phinehas, grandson of Aaron. The allusion to the testing of Abraham and his faith being reckoned as righteousness will be taken up below.

Phinehas is mentioned in two writings from the first century CE. In the retelling of the martyrdom of the mother and her seven sons (4 Macc 18:6–19; cf. 2 Macc 7:22–29) the mother reminds her sons that their father "told you of the zeal of Phineas [τὸν ζηλωτὴν Φινεες], and he taught you about Hananiah, Azariah, and Mishael in the fire" (4 Macc 18:12, alluding to 1 Macc 2). Writing some time later the author of *Liber antiquitatum biblicarum* describes Phinehas as the priest who "guards the commands of the Lord" (*L.A.B.* 28:1). We are told, moreover, that "truth goes forth from his mouth and a shining light from his heart" (28:3). Later in *Liber antiquitatum biblicarum* Phinehas, who lived beyond 120 years, is exalted in terms reminiscent of Elijah (48:1–3). Phinehas is also mentioned in a pseudepigraphal synagogue prayer, perhaps dating to the second century CE. Here the zealous priest is cited in a list of heroes of the faith (*Hel. Syn. Pr.* 8.4). The phrase that appears in the next line, "from iniquity into righteousness" (v. 5), may refer to Phinehas' achievement.

Finally, Phinehas appears by name in three fragmentary scrolls from Qumran. In one we find "Phinehas (father) of Abishua" (4Q243 frag. 28, line 2; cf. 1 Chr 6:4). In another we read (with some reconstruction): "and Zadok shall serve as priest there, first from the sons of Phinehas and of Aaron and with him he will be pleased in all the days of his life" (4Q522 frag. 9 2:6–7). In the third we find the phrase "from the sons of Phinehas" (6Q13 frag. 1, line 4).

Mention should also be made of *Jubilees*, another intertestamental writing, in which the law prohibiting marriage with foreigners (cf. Gen 34:7, 14) is emphasized. *Jubilees* retells the story of the Shechemites, who out of vengeance were slaughtered by Jacob's sons Simeon and Levi (Gen 34:25–26). In the Genesis narrative Jacob expresses displeasure over his sons' treachery (Gen 34:30) and finds it necessary to relocate (Gen 35:1–3). But in *Jubilees* Simeon and Levi are praised for their violent action: "And it was a righteousness for them and it was written down for them for righteousness" (*Jub*. 30:17). The author of *Jubilees* goes on to say that those who violate the law that prohibits intermarriage will be "blotted out of the book of life and will be written in the book of those who will be destroyed" (*Jub*. 30:22). At the conclusion of the section the action of Simeon and Levi is again praised, with the author noting that when the sons of Jacob killed the Shechemites God "wrote for them a book in heaven that they did righteousness and uprightness and vengeance against the sinners and it was written down for a blessing" (*Jub*. 30:23). There is little doubt that this remarkable revision of the Genesis story has been inspired by Scripture's praise for the zeal of Phinehas.

In sum, we have four major texts in which the zeal of Phinehas is underscored. In Num 25 we hear of the priest's zeal, a promised covenant of peace, and an eternal priesthood. In Ps 106 we hear of zeal, his action being reckoned to him as righteousness, and "from generation to generation," which may allude to the promise of perpetual priesthood. In Sir 45 we hear of zeal, the covenant of peace, and an eternal priesthood. And in 1 Macc 2 we hear of zeal and everlasting priesthood. In 1 Macc 2 we also hear of Abraham's faith being reckoned as righteousness.

This brings us to one more text, in which the name Phinehas does not appear, a text which, however, probably does allude to the zealous action of the famous priest. As his halakic letter draws to a close, the author of 4QMMT exhorts his readers to embrace his teaching regarding "some of the works of the Law" (מקצת מעשי התורה), about which he had written. If they follow his teaching, "it will be reckoned to (them) as righteousness." The relevant portion of the text reads as follows:

> Now, we have written to you [3] (C27) some of the works of the Law, those which we determined would be beneficial for you and your people, because we have seen that [4] (C28) you possess insight and knowledge of the Law. Understand all these things and beseech Him to set [5] (C29) your counsel straight and so keep you away from evil thoughts and the counsel of Belial. [6] (C30) Then you shall rejoice at the end time when you find the essence of our words to be true. [7] (C31) And it will be reckoned to you as righteousness, in that you have

done what is right and good before Him, to your own benefit ⁸ (C32) and to that of Israel (4Q398 frags. 14–17, col. ii, lines 2b–8 = 4Q399 1:10–2:5 [= C26b–C32]).⁴¹

Only two passages in the Hebrew Bible link the verb "reckon" (חשב) and the noun "righteousness" (צדקה). They are Gen 15:6 and Ps 106:31:

Gen 15:6—And he believed the Lord; and he reckoned it to him as righteousness [וַיַּחְשְׁבֶהָ לּוֹ צְדָקָה].

Ps 106:31—And that has been reckoned to him as righteousness [וַתֵּחָשֶׁב לוֹ לִצְדָקָה] from generation to generation for ever.

The verb "he reckoned" (וַיַּחְשְׁבֶהָ) in Gen 15:6 is a qal, while in Ps 106:31, "has been reckoned" (וַתֵּחָשֶׁב) is a nifal, the same form that appears in 4QMMT.⁴² There is more than simply the grammar that suggests the author of 4QMMT has in mind Ps 106 and the zealous priest Phinehas. The priestly orientation of 4QMMT and the Qumran sect itself also encourages us to think that we have an allusion to Ps 106 and not Gen 15. Perhaps even more important is the observation that the author of 4QMMT is sharply opposed to intermarriage with non-Jews. Recall that this was part of Israel's apostasy at Peor that prompted Phinehas to take violent action.⁴³ For these reasons I think it is probable that 4QMMT has alluded to the famous zealous priest, not to the great patriarch Abraham.

The point that the author of 4QMMT is making seems clear enough. He has enumerated some two dozen legal rulings, about half of which are bans on various foods and practices, including prohibition of mixing the holy with the profane. These are the "works of the law" mentioned near the end of his letter. In doing these works readers of the letter will benefit and "will rejoice at the end time," which probably refers to future judgment.

Martin Abegg Jr., James Dunn, and others believe that in 4QMMT we finally have a true parallel to the position that Paul opposes with such

---

⁴¹ Translation is based on Wise, Abegg, and Cook, *Dead Sea Scrolls*, 364. The translation in E. Qimron and J. Strugnell, *Qumran Cave 4. V: Miqsat Ma'ase Ha-Torah* (DJD 10; Oxford: Clarendon, 1994), 63, fails to sound the scriptural echo.

⁴² See Abegg's comment in Wise, Abegg, and Cook, *Dead Sea Scrolls*, 359. See also de Roo, 'Works of the Law' at Qumran and in Paul, 81. De Roo believes 4QMMT alludes to Gen 15:6, as well as to Ps 106:31. She rightly argues (82–98) that the "works of the law" refer to deeds and not halakhic rulings. More will be said on this theme below.

⁴³ On this important point, see Carolyn J. Sharp, "Phinehan Zeal and Rhetorical Strategy in 4QMMT," *RevQ* 18 (1997): 207–222.

heat in Gal 2 and 3.[44] I think there is little doubt they are correct. It will be sufficient to cite one verse:

> We ourselves ... who know that a human is not justified [δικαιοῦται] by works of the law [ἔργων νόμου] but through faith in Jesus Christ, even we have believed in Christ Jesus, in order to be justified [δικαιωθῶμεν] by faith in Christ, and not by works of the law [ἔργων νόμου], because by works of the law [ἔργων νόμου] shall no one be justified [δικαιωθήσεται]. (Gal 2:16)

The phrase "works of law" occurs in Paul several times (cf. Rom 3:20, 28; Gal 3:2, 5, 10). Moreover, his "works of law" (ἔργα νόμου) and "justified" (δικαιόω) language echoes the language we find in the two passages of Old Testament Scripture already mentioned. However, whereas Paul explicitly draws on Gen 15:6, the author of 4QMMT draws on Ps 106:31. The difference is that Paul focuses on faith, the faith of Abraham (cf. Rom 4:3, 9, 22; Gal 3:6), while the author of 4QMMT focuses on obedience to the law, as exemplified by the zealous Phinehas.

What Paul is challenging so passionately in Galatians and then again with somewhat reduced emotions in Romans is an understanding of the law that requires the performance of certain "works of the law" in order to maintain one's place in the covenant. Paul is especially opposed to works of law that encourage holding Gentiles at arm's length. Some of the works of the law articulated in 4QMMT do just that. One example states: "No one should eat from the Gentile grain nor bring it into the sanctuary" (4Q394 frags. 3–7, 1:6–8). Other examples articulate bans against Gentile offerings and Jews with blemishes. Attempts to establish righteousness such as these are what Paul so vigorously opposes. Recall the apostle's anger at Peter for withdrawing

---

[44] Martin G. Abegg Jr., "Paul, 'Works of the Law' and MMT," *BAR* 20.6 (1994): 52–55, 82; Abegg, "4QMMT C 27,31 and 'Works Righteousness'," *DSD* 6 (1999): 139–147; Abegg, "4QMMT, Paul, and 'Works of the Law'," in *The Bible at Qumran: Text, Shape, and Interpretation* (ed. Peter W. Flint; SDSSRL 5; Grand Rapids: Eerdmans, 2001), 203–216; Michael Bachmann, "4QMMT und Galaterbrief, מעשי התורה und ΕΡΓΑ ΝΟΜΟΥ," *ZNW* 89 (1998): 91–113; Bachmann, "Was für Praktiken? Zur jüngsten Diskussion um die ἔργα νόμου," *NTS* 55 (2009): 35–54; Martinus C. de Boer, "Paul's Use and Interpretation of a Justification Tradition in Galatians 2.15–21," *JSNT* 28 (2005): 189–216; de Roo, 'Works of the Law' at Qumran and in Paul, 72–98; James D.G. Dunn, "4QMMT and Galatians," *NTS* 43 (1997): 147–153; Pierre Grelot, "Les oeuvres de la Loi (A propos de 4Q394–398)," *RevQ* 16 (1994): 441–448; Otfried Hofius, "'Werke des Gesetzes': Untersuchungen zu der paulinischen Rede von den ἔργα νόμου," in *Paulus und Johannes: Exegetische Studien zur paulinischen und johanneischen Theologie und Literatur* (ed. Dieter Sänger and Ulrich Mell; WUNT 198; Tübingen: Mohr Siebeck, 2006), 271–310; Hofius, "'Werke des Gesetzes'—Zwei Nachträge," in *Exegetische Studien* (WUNT 223; Tübingen: Mohr Siebeck, 2008), 89–94; and John Kampen, "4QMMT and New Testament Studies," in *Reading 4QMMT: New Perspectives on Qumran Law and History* (ed. John Kampen and Moshe J. Bernstein; SBLSymS 2; Atlanta: Scholars Press, 1996), 129–144, esp. 138–143.

from Gentile Christians when "certain people came from James" (Gal 2:11–13). Peter and Barnabas, Paul charges, "were not acting consistently with the truth of the gospel" (Gal 2:14).

The difficulty interpreters have in relating Paul's application of Gen 15 to the application we find in Jas 2 is that the debate itself, of which both Paul and James reflect but small parts, is not appreciated in its entirety. I have examined the Phinehan tradition because I think it provides the thread that ties together most of the elements that make up this larger discussion. We need to pull as many of these elements together as we can, if we are to make sense of the smaller parts we find in Paul and James. It may be that what we will discover is that James and Paul can be reconciled after all.

Several of these key components appear in 1 Macc 2. The narrator asserts that the violent action of Mattathias, in which he killed both a foreigner and an Israelite, who were engaged in pagan sacrifice, is comparable to the action of Phinehas. Indeed it is, for Phinehas killed an Israelite and a Midianite, who were engaged in foreign worship. Accordingly, the narrator can say that Mattathias "burned with zeal for the law, as Phinehas did" (1 Macc 2:26). On his deathbed Mattathias once again refers to the zeal of Phinehas (vv. 50, 54), but he also refers to Abraham, who was "found faithful when tested," and "it was reckoned to him as righteousness" (v. 52). The testing to which the author of 1 Maccabees refers is the binding of Isaac (Gen 22:15–18). The reference to having it reckoned as righteousness refers, of course, to Gen 15:6, but understood in the light of Gen 22. In other words, Abraham's faithfulness, as seen in his willingness to sacrifice his son Isaac, is what was "reckoned as righteousness." The faith, or faithfulness, of which Gen 15:6 speaks is qualified by the act of obedience narrated in Gen 22. True faith results in righteous deeds.[45]

James makes a similar point. He begins the discussion by asking if faith that does not result in works can save (v. 14). He illustrates the point by showing that greetings and platitudes, but no actions, do not fulfill the commandment to love one's neighbor as one's self (vv. 15–16). Accordingly, a faith that has no works is dead (v. 17). James then mounts a scriptural argument that is very similar to the thinking underlying 1 Macc 2. Abraham was "justified by works, when he offered his son upon the altar" (v. 21). His offering Isaac meant that his faith was more than a mere belief, more than pious words, but a readiness to obey God, to put one's faith into action, as it were. Because Abraham's "faith was active along with his works, and

---

[45] On this important point, see de Roo, *'Works of the Law' at Qumran and in Paul*, 217–222.

(his) faith was completed by works" (v. 22), the earlier Scripture, "Abraham believed God, and it was reckoned to him as righteousness" (Gen 15:6), was fulfilled. Accordingly, James can say that a human "is justified by works and not by faith alone" (v. 24). For James and the author of 1 Maccabees deeds demonstrate real faith. Accordingly, deeds must accompany faith.[46]

It is also important to recognize the allusions to dominical teaching in the letter of James. I have in mind primarily the treatment of the Double Commandment in the second chapter, to which I shall turn shortly, but there are some important antecedents. James exhorts his readers to accept trials and testing with joy and to let it have its "perfect work [ἔργον τέλειον]" (1:3–4). He urges his readers to become "doers of the word" (ποιηταὶ λόγου) and not hearers only (1:22). He speaks of the "perfect law [νόμον τέλειον]" (1:25a). He urges his readers not to be forgetful hearers but be one who is "a doer of work" (ποιητὴς ἔργου), who will be blessed (1:25b).

The spirit of this teaching, as well as some of the vocabulary, brings to mind the teaching of Jesus, especially as we find it assembled in the Sermon on the Mount. According to Jesus, the person who "does and teaches [ποιήσῃ καὶ διδάξῃ] (the commandments) shall be called great in the kingdom of heaven" (Matt 5:19). The righteousness (δικαιοσύνη) of the disciples must exceed that of the scribes and Pharisees. How this can be accomplished is spelled out in the five antitheses that follow (Matt 5:21–47). At the conclusion of the antitheses Jesus sums up his teaching: "You, therefore, must be perfect [τέλειοι], as your heavenly Father is perfect [τέλειος]" (Matt 5:48).[47] Perfection cannot be achieved without doing the commandments, as Jesus has taught. The conclusion of the Sermon on the Mount drives home this point:

---

[46] We see a similar combination of faith and works in *4 Ezra*, composed ca. 100 CE: "He who brings the peril at that time will himself protect those who fall into peril, who have works and have faith [*qui habent operas et fidem*] in the Almighty" (*4 Ezra* 13:23). See also *4 Ezra* 9:7–8 "And it shall be that everyone who will be saved and will be able to escape on account of his works [*per opera sua*], or on account of the faith by which he has believed [*per fidem in qua credidit*], will survive the dangers that have been predicted ..." For further discussion of texts such as these, see Craig A. Evans, "Paul and 'Works of Law' Language in Late Antiquity," in *Paul and His Opponents* (ed. Stanley E. Porter; Pauline Studies 2; Leiden: Brill, 2005), 201–226.

[47] Jesus' "you must be perfect, as your heavenly father is perfect," is analogous to the logic expressed in the Holiness Code: "And the Lord said to Moses, 'Say to all the congregation of the people of Israel, You shall be holy; for I the Lord your God am holy'" (Lev 19:1–2). It is in this context that the command to love one's neighbor as one's self appears (i.e., Lev 19:18).

> Matt 7:21 "Not every one who says to me, 'Lord, Lord,' shall enter the kingdom of heaven, but he who *does* the will of my Father who is in heaven."
>
> Matt 7:24 "Every one then who hears these words [τοὺς λόγους] of mine and *does* them will be like a wise man who built his house upon the rock."
>
> Matt 7:26 "And every one who hears these words of mine and *does not do* them will be like a foolish man who built his house upon the sand." (italics added)

Elsewhere in dominical material we find similar teaching:

> Matt 12:50 "For whoever *does* the will of my Father in heaven is my brother, and sister, and mother."
>
> Matt 21:31 "Which of the two *did* the will of his father?"
>
> Matt 23:3 "*Do and observe* whatever they tell you, but not what they do; for they preach, but do not do."
>
> Matt 23:5 "They *do* all their works to be seen by people ...." (italics added)

We may well hear echoes of this teaching in James's exhortations to be "doers of the word" and a "doer of work," works that exemplify the "perfect work," "perfect law," and the "royal law."

Verse 27 sums up the point of the first chapter of James: "Religion that is pure and undefiled before God and the Father is this: to visit orphans and widows in their affliction, and to keep oneself unstained from the world."

This brings us to Jas 2. The second chapter is chiefly concerned to explicate the second commandment of the famous Great (or Double) Commandment (Mark 12:28–34; Luke 10:25–29), whereby one is to love God with all that one is and all that one has (Deut 6:4–5) and to love one's neighbor as one's self (Lev 19:18). The partiality described in Jas 2:1–13 fails to fulfill the second commandment, which is quoted in Jas 2:8. Although the remainder of the chapter (vv. 14–26) defines genuine faith, the focus remains on what it means to fulfill the second commandment. To fulfill the "royal law" (Jas 2:8) is to fulfill Lev 19:18, a commandment that lay behind much of what Jesus taught, either explicitly or implicitly.[48]

Failure to fulfill the second commandment has implications for the first commandment, to which allusion is made in v. 19: "You believe God is one; you do well. Even the demons believe—and shudder." The mere belief, or faith, that God is "one" hardly fulfills the obligations to love one's neighbor,

---

[48] See Scot McKnight, *The Letter of James* (NICNT; Grand Rapids: Eerdmans, 2011), 206–207. See also Wiard Popkes, *Der Brief des Jakobus* (THKNT 14; Leipzig: Evangelische Verlags-Anstalt, 2001), 171–175.

or, harking back to Jas 1:27, hardly fulfills the command to "visit orphans and widows in their afflictions."

To support his argument James appeals to the example of Abraham, who was "justified by his works [ἐξ ἔργων ἐδικαιώθη], when he offered his son Isaac upon the altar" (2:21). His willingness to obey God demonstrated that his faith was genuine. His "work" in Gen 22 fulfilled the statement of scripture in Gen 15:6 (Jas 2:23). I suspect James had in mind Abraham's example of faith early on. We may hear an allusion to it in Jas 1:3, when James declares that "the testing of your faith produces steadfastness," which in turn will lead to perfection (1:4).

The argument of James at this point parallels the argument in 1 Macc 2 very closely. In both books the claim is made that Abraham's faith in God was witnessed in his willingness to offer up his son. It was this faith that was reckoned to him as righteousness. The overlap in the scriptural appeal of 1 Maccabees and James helps us understand more clearly the differences in the respective arguments of James and Paul.

Paul is not countering James or 1 Maccabees, where Abraham's faith is defined in terms of obedience. Paul is countering a theology similar to what we see in 4QMMT, which assumes that works of law save. What Paul faced in the churches of Galatia was the teaching that "works of law," such as circumcision, *kashruth*, and Sabbath observance, were necessary if converts (especially Gentile converts) were to mature and grow in righteousness. This parallels the thinking in 4QMMT, in which one's righteous standing in the covenant would be assured if one practiced certain works of the law. Paul and the author of 4QMMT are squarely at odds.

However, the works of 4QMMT are not the "works" to which James makes reference. The "works" that demonstrate the reality of faith are not circumcision, *kashruth*, and Sabbath observance, but fulfillment of the "royal law" (Jas 2:8), as he dubs it, that is, the law of loving one's neighbor as one's self, the very commandment that Jesus enjoined and his early movement attempted to fulfill in its care for widows and orphans and the poor (cf. Acts 2:44–45; 4:32–37; 6:1; Rom 15:26; Gal 2:10; 1 Tim 5:3, 16). James does not have in mind the zealous works of Phinehas, which are appealed to explicitly in 1 Macc 2 and alluded to in 4QMMT. He has in mind genuine faith that proves itself in righteous works, especially with regard to love for one's neighbor.

Paul and his disciples know this well, as we see in Eph 2:8–10:

> For by grace you have been saved through faith; and this is not your own doing, it is the gift of God—[9] not because of works, lest any man should boast. [10] For we are his workmanship, created in Christ Jesus for good works, which God prepared beforehand, that we should walk in them.

Whatever one's view of the authorship of Ephesians, this passage sums up the Pauline perspective. By God's grace human beings are saved through faith and not through their works. Salvation is God's gift; it is not something earned by righteous deeds. But genuine faith demonstrates itself in good works, such as love for one another (Rom 12:10; 13:8; Gal 5:13; 1 Thess 3:12; 4:9). Christians are "created in Messiah Jesus for good works, which God prepared beforehand, that we should walk in them" (2:10). With this assertion James would be in hearty agreement.

The example of Phinehan zeal and the interpretive tradition that grew up alongside it clarify an important facet of the discussion of faith, works of law, and having one's faith or deeds accounted as righteousness, a discussion that developed at least two centuries before the emergence of the Christian movement. James, Paul, and other writers presuppose this larger discussion, each embracing and/or qualifying or denying parts of it. James and Paul both appeal to the faith of Abraham and to God's reckoning of the patriarch's faith as righteousness, but the point each is trying to make is very different.

Paul's declaration that "a human is not justified by works of the law [οὐ δικαιοῦται ἄνθρωπος ἐξ ἔργων νόμου] but through faith" (Gal 2:16; cf. Rom 3:20; 4:2) squarely opposes the thinking expressed in 4QMMT. James' conclusion that "a human is justified by works [ἐξ ἔργων δικαιοῦται ἄνθρωπος] and not by faith alone" (Jas 2:24; cf. 2:21, 25) is not a rebuttal of Pauline teaching or even in reference to Paul. It is instead a challenge directed against those whose faith fails to take practical form, especially in reference to the neighbor in need. In other words, a faith that fails to comply with Jesus' teaching to love God and love neighbor as one's self is no faith at all. With this assertion Paul would be in hearty agreement.

Summing Up

It is difficult to overestimate the importance of Genesis for Jesus and the early church. For Jesus the ancient book provided insight into the true nature of the marriage union, a permanent, unbreakable union that reflected the will of the Creator. On this foundation rested Jesus' views of marriage and divorce. For Paul the book of Genesis was also of immense importance, providing an explanation for human sin and need of redemption and providing an explanation for God's sovereignty in election. The story of Abraham speaks to both of these great themes. In the life of the patriarch God's redemptive plan begins to unfold. In the faith and obedience of Abraham the pattern has been established for all to follow.

The book of Genesis may be rightly described as a book of "origins" or "beginnings," but in reference to early Christian theology it was a book that helped the new movement come to some very important conclusions. For early Christians to understand the eschatological and redemptive import of God's work in Messiah Jesus and his apostles it was necessary to go back to the very beginning and rethink what God had done long ago.

SELECT BIBLIOGRAPHY

Epstein, Louis M. *Marriage Laws in the Bible and the Talmud.* Harvard Semitic Studies 12. Cambridge: Harvard University Press, 1942.

Fitzmyer, Joseph A. "The Matthean Divorce Texts and Some New Palestinian Evidence." *Theological Studies* 37 (1976): 197–226

Hugenberger, Gordon P. *Marriage as a Covenant: A Study of Biblical Law and Ethics Governing Marriage, Developed from the Perspective of Malachi.* Vetus Testamentum Supplements 52. Leiden: Brill, 1994.

Instone Brewer, David. "Jesus' Old Testament Basis for Monogamy." Pages 75–105 in *The Old Testament in the New Testament: Essays in Honour of J.L. North.* Edited by Steve Moyise. Journal for the Study of the New Testament Supplement Series 189. Sheffield: Sheffield Academic Press, 2000.

McKnight, Scot. *The Letter of James.* New International Commentary on the New Testament. Grand Rapids: Eerdmans, 2011.

McNamara, Martin. *Targum Neofiti 1: Genesis.* The Aramaic Bible 1a. Collegeville, Minn.: Liturgical Press, 1992.

Minear, Paul Sevier. *Christians and the New Creation: Genesis Motifs in the New Testament.* Louisville: Westminster John Knox, 1994.

Popkes, Wiard. *Der Brief des Jakobus.* Theologischer Handkommentar zum Neuen Testament 14. Leipzig: Evangelische Verlags-Anstalt, 2001.

Wevers, John William. *Notes on the Greek Text of Genesis.* Society of Biblical Literature Septuagint and Cognate Studies 35. Atlanta: Scholars Press, 1993.

GENESIS IN ARAMAIC: THE EXAMPLE OF CHAPTER 22

Bruce Chilton

INTRODUCTION

The Aramaic word *targum* by itself denotes "translation" in Aramaic, yet the purpose of the rendering involved in Judaism means the term also refers to a type of literature. We need to appreciate the phenomenon of targum, and the specific documents called Targumim, before we can approach Genesis in Aramaic on a critical basis.

Aramaic survived the demise of the Persian Empire as a *lingua franca* in the Near East. Jews and other peoples, such as Nabateans and Palmyrenes, embraced the language, and the Aramaic portions of the Hebrew Bible attest a significant change in the linguistic constitution of Judaism. The linguistic situation in Judea and Galilee demanded translation of the Hebrew Bible into Aramaic, for purposes of popular use and worship among the majority of Jews. Although fragments of Leviticus and Job in Aramaic, which have been discovered at Qumran, are technically *targumim*, in that they are translations, they are unrepresentative of the genre targum in literary terms. They are reasonably "literal" renderings; that is, there is a formal correspondence between the Hebrew rendered and the Aramaic that is presented, and a programmatic commitment to interpretation does not appear. The *Targumim* that Rabbinic Judaism produced are of a different character.

The aim of targumic production was to give the sense of the Hebrew Scriptures, not just their wording, so paraphrase is characteristic of the Targumim and interpretations are typically embedded in their renderings. Theoretically, a passage of Scripture was to be rendered orally and from memory in the synagogue by an interpreter (a *meturgeman*) after the reading in Hebrew from a scroll; the *meturgeman* was not to be confused with the reader, lest the congregation mistake the Aramaic interpretation with the original text (see Mishnah *Meg.* 4:4–10 and Talmud *Meg.* 23b–25b). Regulations that specify the precise number of verses that may be read prior to the delivery of a targum probably date from the third century CE and later. The same may be said of cycles of specified lectionary readings. Although the renderings so delivered were oral in principle, over the course of time, traditions in important centers of learning became fixed, and coalescence became possible.

The emergence of the Rabbis as the shapers of Judaism after 70 CE provided a centralizing tendency without which literary Targumim could never have been produced. Yet it is quite clear that the Rabbis never exerted complete control over Targumic production. The Targums preserved by the rabbis are paraphrases, yet the theological ideas conveyed are not always consistent, even within a given Targum. Although the Rabbis attempted to regulate targumic activity, the extant Targumim sometimes even contradict rabbinic rules directly. For example, *m. Meg.* 4:9 insists that Lev 18:21 ("You must not give of your seed, to deliver it to Moloch") should not be interpreted in respect of sexual intercourse with Gentiles; the Targum Pseudo-Jonathan—a late work, produced well after rabbinic authority had been established—takes just that line.

The Targumim evince such oddities because they are the products of a dialectical interaction between folk practice and rabbinic supervision—sometimes mediated through a love of dramatic and inventive speculation, and this dynamic tension continued over centuries. Each of the extant Targumim crystallizes that complex relationship synagogue and academy at a given moment, focalizing that encounter within the biblical text. The Aqedah—the story of Abraham's near or actual sacrifice of Isaac in Gen 22—is an especially interesting moment in interpretation, because popular practice, rabbinic teaching, and biblical tradition met and influenced one another.[1] The result was a sometimes stunning transformation of a familiar text.

The Targumim divide themselves up among those of the Torah (the Pentateuch), those of the Prophets (both "Former Prophets," or the so-called historical works in the English Bible, and the "Latter Prophets," or the Prophets as commonly designated in English), and those of the Writings (or Hagiographa), following the conventional designations of the Hebrew Bible in Judaism. The Targumim are irreducibly complex in dates, origins, purposes, and dialects of Aramaic. They cannot be assigned to a single epoch of Rabbinic Judaism, although we shall encounter clear evidence of their composition under the influence of Tannaitic and Amoraic interpretation.

---

[1] Among recent treatments, see Lukas Kundert, *Die Opferung/Bindung Isaaks: Gen 22,1–19 im Alten Testament, im Frühjudentum, und im Neuen Testament* (WMANT 78; Neukirchen-Vluyn: Neukirchener, 1998); Edward Kessler, *Bound by the Bible: Jews, Christians and the Sacrifice of Isaac* (Cambridge: Cambridge University Press, 2004); and Bruce Chilton, *Abraham's Curse: Child Sacrifice in the Legacies of the West* (New York: Doubleday, 2008).

Among the Targumim to the Pentateuch, Targum Onqelos corresponds best of all the Targumim to Rabbinic ideals of translation. Although paraphrase is evident, especially in order to describe God and his revelation in suitably reverent terms, the high degree of correspondence with the Hebrew of the MT (and evidently with the Hebrew text current in antiquity) is striking. The dialect of Onqelos is commonly called "Middle Aramaic," which would place the Targum between the first century BCE and 200 CE. A better designation, however, would be "Transitional Aramaic" (200 BCE – 200 CE) embracing the various dialects (Hasmonaean, Nabataean, Palmyrene, Arsacid, Essene, as well as Targumic) that came to be used during the period. Since what followed was a strong regionalization in dialects of Aramaic, which we can logically refer to as Regional Aramaic (200 CE – 700 CE). Because the dialect of 200 BCE – 200 CE was transitional between earlier Persian forms and later regionalization, various Targumim were produced in Transitional Aramaic even after its demise as a common language. For that reason, the year 200 CE is not a firm date, after which a Targum in Transitional Aramaic cannot have been composed. Onqelos should probably be dated towards the end of the third century, in the wake of similar efforts to produce a literal Greek rendering, and well after any strict construal of the principle that targumim were to be oral. By contrast with the later Rabbinic ethos, which permitted the creation and preservation of Onqelos in writing, one might recall the story of Rabbi Gamaliel, who is said during the first century to have immured a Targum of Job in a wall of the Temple (Talmud Šabb. 115a), scarcely a gesture of approval.

The Targum Neophyti I was discovered in 1949 by Alejandro Díez Macho in the Library of the Neophytes in Rome. Neophyti paraphrases more substantially than Onqelos. Entire paragraphs are added, as when Cain and Abel argue in the field prior to the first case of murder (Gen 4:8):

> Cain answered and said to Abel,
>
> I know the world is not created with mercies,
> and it is not led in respect of fruits of good deeds,
> and there is accepting of persons in judgment:
> for what reason
> was your offering received with favor
> and my offering was not received from me with favor?
> Abel answered and said to Cain,
> I know the world is created with mercies,
> and in respect of fruits of good deeds it is led:
> and because my good deeds surpassed yours
> my offering was received from me with favor
> while your offering was not received from you with favor.

> Cain answered and said to Abel,
> there is no judgment and there is no judge,
> and there is no other world,
> there is no giving good reward to the righteous
> and there is no repaying from the wicked.
> Abel answered and said to Cain,
> there is judgment and there is a judge,
> and there is another world,
> and there is giving good reward to the righteous
> and there is repaying from the wicked in the world to come.

This is no mere "rendering" as we usually understand translation, but a substantial theodicy.[2] Abel is right according to the Targum: in this world, God's favor is a matter of justice and mercy, because it hangs on good deeds. In the world to come, all wrongs are to be righted. When the remarkable freedom to introduce a theology of this kind prevails over the text, it is impossible to predict in purely literary terms what meanings will emerge.

The dialect of Neophyti has been known as "Palestinian Aramaic," although "Tiberian" (or Galilean) is a better designation, because the Rabbis did not establish permanent academies in Jerusalem or Judea after 70 CE. In any case, the dialect is a form of Regional Aramaic (200 CE – 700 CE), distinct from what used to be called the "Babylonian Aramaic" of Onqelos. The distinction between "Tiberian" and "Babylonian" manifests the nascent regionalization in the Aramaic language to which we have already referred. But Neophyti is produced in a frankly Regional Aramaic, while Onqelos appears in a Transitional Aramaic that is on the way to becoming Regional. Still, the chronology of the two Targums is about the same, although Neophyti appears somewhat later; the differences between them more are a function of interpretative program than of dating. The Rabbis of Babylonia, who called Onqelos "our Targum," exerted greater influence over the Rabbinic movement as a whole than did their colleagues in the west, as the normative status of the Talmud of Babylonia (the *Bavli*) attests.

The latest representative of the type of expansive rendering found in Neophyti is Targum Pseudo-Jonathan. Its reference to the names of Mohammed's wife and daughter in Gen 21:21 put its final composition sometime after the seventh century CE. This oddly designated Targum is so called

---

[2] See Bruce Chilton, "Theodicy in the Targumim," in *Theodicy in the World of the Bible* (ed. Antii Laato and Johannes C. de Moor; Leiden: Brill, 2003), 728–752.

because the name "Jonathan" was attributed to it during the Middle Ages, when reference to the document was abbreviated with the letter *yod*. The letter probably had stood for "Jerusalem," although that designation is also not provably original. The title "Pseudo-Jonathan" is therefore an admission of uncertainty. Neophyti and Pseudo-Jonathan are together known as "Palestinian Targums," to distinguish their dialects and their style of interpretation from those of Onqelos. In fact, however, Pseudo-Jonathan was produced at the dawn of the period of Academic Aramaic (700 CE – 1500 CE), during which Rabbinic usage continued to develop the language in a literary idiom after it has been supplanted by Arabic as a *lingua franca* in the Near East.

Neophyti and Pseudo-Jonathan are associated with two other Targums, or to be more precise, Targumic groups. The first group, in chronological order, consists of the fragments from the Cairo Geniza. They were originally part of more complete works, dating between the seventh and the eleventh centuries, which were deposited in the Geniza of the Old Synagogue in Cairo. In the type and substance of its interpretation, these fragments are comparable to Neophyti and Pseudo-Jonathan. The same may be said of the Fragments Targum, which was collected as a miscellany of targumic readings during the Middle Ages. An interesting feature of the Targumim of this type is that their relationship might be described as a synoptic one, in some ways comparable to the relationship among the Gospels. All four of the paraphrastic Targumim, for example, convey a debate between Cain and Abel comparable to what has been cited from Neophyti, and they do so with those variations of order and wording, which are well known, to students of the Synoptic Gospels.[3]

In what follows I first survey how Gen 22 has functioned within early Jewish and rabbinic texts, before exploring how the passage as has been presented and transformed in the Targums. In doing so, we will see that the Targums possess an allusive quality in which fresh versions of the Hebrew text are brought out, rendered in idioms of rabbinic interpretation.

---

[3] See Bruce Chilton, "A Comparative Study of Synoptic Development: The Dispute between Cain and Abel in the Palestinian Targums and the Beelzebul Controversy in the Gospels," *JBL* 101 (1982): 553–562; and Chilton, "Sennacherib: A Synoptic Relationship among Targumim of Isaiah," in *Society of Biblical Literature 1986 Seminar Papers* (ed. Kent H. Richards; SBLSP 25; Atlanta: Scholars Press, 1986), 544–554.

The Aqedah in Early Jewish and Rabbinic Literature

The narrative of Gen 22 undergoes significant changes from the time of the Maccabees in the second century BCE, to the late Rabbinic period about 600 CE, from a story about a young passive Isaac being sacrificed by Abraham to one in which Isaac becomes a willing, adult participant in his own slaughter. As part of a developing understanding of the role of martyrdom in early Judaism, in some accounts Isaac even appears to die and to be restored to life. Because the Targumim were composed over centuries, as the Rabbis evolved their understanding of Gen 22, we need to become familiar with pre-Rabbinic and Rabbinic tellings of the story in order to understand what the Targums say.

The transformed story of Genesis is known as the *Aqedah*, the "Binding of Isaac." The term "binding" relates to the use of the verb *'qd* in Gen 22:9 to say that Abraham "bound" Isaac on the altar, but the noun *'qdh* (*Aqedah*) itself appears in the Mishnah to refer in particular to the binding of the lamb for daily sacrifice (*m. Tamid* 4:1). To speak of the "binding" of Isaac therefore implied that his intended death was sacrificial, and over time this story came progressively to be associated with the daily sacrifice (the *tamid*), with the celebration of the New Year when the ram's horn—the *shofar*—was blown, and finally with Passover. These interpretations also find echoes and reactions in Christian writings and exegesis.

In the Hebrew text of Genesis, God and his angel interact only with Abraham. Not only does God give Abraham the command, but also at the story's end, God's angel gives Abraham the blessing. Isaac is subsidiary throughout: Abraham does not even tell him the truth about the sacrificial victim when Isaac asks him directly. Isaac is passive; he neither protests nor complains when put upon the altar—much as a sacrificial animal should behave.

That is one of two puzzling elements in the story. The other is that, while God directly commands Abraham to offer his son in sacrifice, an angel—rather than God himself—prevents Abraham from following through on his action. That change was the consequence of ancient editorial adaptation in the story, but it opened the possibility that God had really wanted the sacrifice. That possibility, together with the thought that Isaac was a willing participant, lead to radical re-readings of Gen 22.

In the biblical story, God "tests" Abraham, much as God allowed the Accusing Angel (*hasatan*) to test Job. In *Jub.* 7:16, as we shall see, this connection was actually made; Mastemah (an alternative name for Satan) challenges God to test Abraham.[4] Apparently God never had any intention of having Isaac killed. Despite this, the story raises the disturbing question of why Isaac was so passive. If he were a young boy, as the biblical story implies but does not state, that might explain his behavior. But if he were an adult, as later Judaic tradition maintained, we would expect him to have a categorical opinion about what was being done to him. He should either protest or give his consent. As will become clear, the Palestinian Targums and Pseudo-Jonathan address this question through their additional material, but the earliest Pentateuch Targum, Targum Onqelos, does not.

Post-biblical interpretations of Gen 22 begin with an association with martyrdom. The second-century BCE, non-canonical Book of Jubilees—which derives from a group that had been allied with the Maccabees, separating from them later in the second century BCE—provides a case in point. According to Jubilees' version of the story, the Aqedah was the seventh, climactic test of faith that Abraham faced, so that his heroism is marked (*Jub.* 7:17–18).[5] Yet Jubilees also makes the example of Abraham pertinent to Israelites as a whole, individually and collectively, by comparing his test at the time of the Aqedah to what Job, the Judaic equivalent of Everyman, had to endure. In Jubilees, Mastemah challenges God to test Abraham, claiming that the patriarch loves his son more than God (*Jub.* 17:16). One cannot miss hearing here a precise echo of the opening of Job. By introducing Satan into the Aqedah, Jubilees protects God from the charge that he commanded human sacrifice, and at the same time equates the Seleucid persecutor with this Prince of Darkness that all the faithful are to resist.

Deepening political divisions set those who opposed the Seleucids into differing camps over time, yet they agreed that the story of the Aqedah served as the symbol of the faithfulness demanded of all Jews. In 1 Macc 2:52 Mattathias himself poses the question, "Was not Abraham found faithful in trial, and it was reckoned to him as righteousness?" This link between Abraham's test and the faith demanded of Israelites, as if the allusion to Abraham's righteousness were to Gen 22 rather than to Gen 15, generally proved durable.

The author of 2 Maccabees, who was more pro-Hasmonean than Jubilees' writer, nonetheless praises the victorious leader Judas Maccabeus only with

---

[4] This interpretation also appears in 4Q225; see Moshe J. Bernstein, "Angels at the Aqedah: A Study in the Development of a Midrashic Motif," *DSD* 7 (2000): 263–291, at 267–269.

[5] As counted in Joseph A. Fitzmyer, "The Sacrifice of Isaac in Qumran Literature," *Bib* 83 (2002): 211–229, at 214.

restraint (as compared to 1 Maccabees) and ignores the brothers who were his lieutenants, all the while attributing the defeat of Antiochus IV and the salvation of Israel to the fortitude of the Jewish martyrs and to divine intervention. With different concerns from those of 1 Maccabees, 2 Maccabees places the responsibility for the sufferings of the Jewish people and the desecration of the Temple on *both* the Jewish people and the Seleucid ruler, arguing that, because many of the people—and especially the leaders—deserted Jewish law in favor of Greek ways, God brought punishment to Jerusalem. It is the martyrs' fidelity that brings about the community's reconciliation with God according to 2 Maccabees, in a theology which is less activist yet more radical than 1 Maccabees.

Second Maccabees shows how it values martyrdom over military resistance through the stories of the Eleazar, an aged scribe (2 Macc 6:18–31), and a woman with her seven sons (2 Macc 7). The narrative praises their martyr's sacrifice and encourages all who hear their stories to be equally faithful. The martyrs give speeches expressing their fidelity to God's law, desiring to set a good example for those who come after them, and display confidence that in the resurrection from the dead their mutilated bodies will be replaced and restored.

Eleazar, aged ninety, refused to eat pork forced into his mouth, and even to eat kosher meat disguised as if it were pork (at the suggestion of a sympathetic executioner). He summarizes both his personal sense of responsibility and the author's perspective when he says, "By manfully giving up my life now, I will show myself worthy of my old age and bequeath to the young a noble example of how to die a good death willingly and nobly for the revered and holy laws" (2 Macc 6:27–28). Viewed from the angle of the community's commitment to the Torah, death was preferable, not only to apostasy, but even to the appearance of apostasy.

The mother of seven sons shows herself even more radical than Eleazar in her commitment; her ordeal is set in a surreal encounter with Antiochus Epiphanes himself. After seeing six of her sons being tortured to death—by whips, cords, cutting of flesh, amputation, and fire—for their refusal to eat pork, the mother refuses Antiochus's advice that she encourage her last remaining child to transgress his ancestral traditions. "In derision of the cruel tyrant, she leaned over close to her son and said in Aramaic, their native language, Son, have mercy on me, who carried you in my belly for nine months, nursed you for three years, nurtured and brought you up, to your present productive age .... Do not be afraid of this executioner, but become worthy of your brothers and accept death, so that in mercy I may receive you again with them" (2 Macc 7:27, 29). After the death of her youngest child by the cruelest tortures of all, the mother also suffers execution. But she has already endured worse than death, strengthened by having—as the text says (2 Macc 7:21)—"aroused female thought with male resolution." In the conception of this Maccabean theology, women achieved a greater motherhood even than giving birth by providing their children as martyrs in the resolute manner of Abraham.

The Second Book of Maccabees pioneered a style of presentation later repeated and intensified in Jewish (as well as Christian and Muslim) stories of martyrdom, portraying physical suffering in exquisite detail. This violence, however, was by no means gratuitous; rather, blood and pain sealed the accomplishment of sacrifice, and encouraged further sacrifice by arousing admiration, awe, and the desire to follow noble examples of the triumph of devotion over fear. In this way, 2 Maccabees put into action the praise of Abraham that links his pivotal role specifically to his willingness to offer his son. The second century BCE, the Maccabean century, made Abraham's willingness to sacrifice his son (cited in 1 Macc 2:52 by Mattathias, the founder of the Maccabean dynasty), together with the willingness of Israelites to give their children to the cause of the Torah, into the model of what Jews should do as Jews.

The Seleucid threat to Judaism came and went, only to be replaced by Roman hegemony, which was formally established over Jerusalem in 63 BCE when Pompey entered the city. During Judaism's long and sporadically violent struggle with the Romans, a shift occurred in the depiction of Abraham's offering of Isaac. Because previous studies of the Aqedah have often been purely literary in their orientation, many readings have not taken account of the direct correspondence between the portrayal of events on Moriah and historical conditions in Judea. Just as Maccabean literature remains inexplicable unless its emergence is seen within the context of Seleucid policy, so Roman hegemony proves key to the understanding the development of the Aqedah.

During the Roman period, Abraham's obedience as the proof of his virtue remained, but Isaac's willing complicity with his father—reflecting the determination necessary for a martyr—emerged as a principal theme. Philo of Alexandria, Hellenistic Judaism's preeminent intellectual during the first half of the first century CE, pictures Abraham as a priest with his son as a victim (*Abr.* 197–198), making explicit the connection between sacrifice and noble warfare that the Maccabean literature had already forged. Philo retains the biblical text's focus on Abraham as the primary actor, even though he refers to the passive, uninformed Isaac as being God's "son," because divine intervention had made his birth possible, *and* because Isaac was perfectly obedient (*Somn.* 1.195). In a clear departure from the biblical text, Abraham did not even have to bind Isaac in Philo's description (*Abr.* 176), but—articulating an image frequently portrayed by Western artists during the centuries after Philo—simply placed Isaac on the altar.

Another first-century Jewish intellectual, Josephus, had been a Jewish general in the disastrous revolt that resulted in the destruction of the Temple by fire in 70 CE. He defected to the Romans when his campaign in Galilee failed; in addition to changing his allegiance, his name changed from Yosef bar Matthiyah to Josephus. In libraries in the West, he is still called Flavius Josephus, because the Flavian dynasty of Rome protected him. When he came to produce his *Antiquities of the Jews* in Greek (ca. 93 CE) from the comfort of his property in Italy, a gift from his Roman protectors, Josephus nonetheless let slip some of the Maccabean theology that had motivated him as a young man—and spurred many Jews to embrace death rather than capitulate to the Romans.

Josephus takes up the interpretive challenge posed by the Bible's passive Isaac and transforms him into a warrior-martyr. Perfectly obedient to his father and to God, Isaac knew exactly what he was doing when he enthusiastically agreed to be a sacrifice because he was *twenty-five years old* (*Ant.* 1.227), no longer the youth of the Hebrew Bible, but the same age as the soldiers Josephus commanded in the field. Josephus takes pride in relating how, in the midst of an array of adventures, he organized the young men under his command at Jotapata in Galilee to commit mass suicide rather than surrender to the Romans. Drawing lots, each offered his naked throat to a brother-in-arms turned executioner. Once the executioner had struck, he in turned offered his own neck to another colleague.

Josephus escaped his own order as general, convinced by a revelation, he said, that power was passing from Jerusalem to Rome by divine will (*J.W.* 3.141–408). Instead, the defeated general who had seen his own troops embrace an honorable death in the manner of Isaac gave himself up to Vespasian. Becoming a propagandist for Vespasian and his son Titus, Josephus accepted Flavian protection for the rest of his life. In depicting the scene on Moriah, Josephus may allude to Agamemnon and Iphigenia[6] in Euripides, signaling his desire to bring together Judaic and Hellenistic culture. Although allusions are notoriously difficult to pin down, the motif of the willing victim features among various cultures in Antiquity that have long

---

[6] See Kessler, *Bound by the Bible*, 101. Kessler also helpfully refers to other classical portrayals, namely, Homer's depiction of Hector and Priam (59).

been appreciated. The links that bind together Isaac's offering, sacrifice, and martyrdom by military means are not merely theoretical possibilities, but have been openly acknowledged for the better part of two thousand years.

So Josephus makes Isaac into a willing and knowledgeable martyr (*Ant.* 1.232), who rushes to his sacrifice and his fate. Defeat at the hands of the Romans made Jewish interpreters emphasize the noble sacrifice of Isaac to the point that new elements—his adult maturity and enthusiasm to be offered, for example—supplemented or even supplanted what was written in Gen 22. The famous case of mass suicide at Masada in 73 CE was not an isolated incident, but represents a pattern of suicide-martyrdom that had been promoted by generals such as Josephus, who conducted the failed revolt against Rome.[7] The Maccabean martyrs had been glorified both by divine approval and by eventual victory for their nation: under Rome, the Jewish martyr's only reward was divine approval, and he embraced his fate to the point of joining in mass suicide.

The final reward of the martyrs, immortality, is laid out during the Roman period in terms drawn from Hellenistic thought. When 4 Maccabees, written at the turn of the first and second centuries CE, comes to describe the young men who embraced death rather than desert the Torah, the description is a mix of the image of Isaac that Josephus had presented, along with the Hellenistic term "immortality" (*athanasia*): "all of them, as though running a race for immortality, hastened to death by torture" (4 Macc 14:5). The author believes that the martyrs atone for Israel's sins, like animal sacrifices, by their blood: Eleazar prays for his people: "Make my blood their purification, and take my life in exchange for theirs" (4 Macc 6:29). The death of martyrs is portrayed as redemptive for the sins of Israel (4 Macc 17:20–22), so that sacrifice, the imagery of Isaac, and the promise of afterlife all combine to move the martyr to his ultimate offering. In a single, striking image, the author portrays Isaac as unafraid, even when he sees his father's hand coming upon him with a *sword*, depicting the sacrificial scene in Gen 22 in terms of the threat of martyrdom under Roman arms (4 Macc 16:20).

In a work from early in the second century CE that rewrites the primordial stories of Israel, the *Book of Biblical Antiquities* (or *Liber Antiquitatum Biblicarum*—written by an anonymous author referred to as Pseudo-Philo), a fully mature Isaac calmly informs his father that he had been born into the

---

[7] Josephus reports (*J.W.* 7.320–401) that in 73, after a lengthy siege, when it appeared the Romans would soon break through the final defenses, the 960 Jewish men, women, and children determined that suicide was preferable to either slavery or execution.

world to be offered as a sacrifice to God (*L.A.B.* 32:2–3). He perfectly reflects the ideal of martyrdom, the prototypical witness to the value of the Torah in the face of danger, pain, and death.

The *Book of Biblical Antiquities* represents a transitional moment, fueled by the reality and the remembrance of martyrs who really did die, when Isaac was seen as an actual sacrifice, and had been intended as such by God. This is the moment, very early in the second century CE, when the term "Aqedah" came into its own, because it was a reference to the way the sheep of the daily offering (the Tamid) was tied up for slaughter, foreleg to hind leg. Isaac became a ritual offering and his death appeased God for the sins of Israel.[8]

This human sacrifice emerged as the paradigm of all sacrifice at a crucial moment in Israelite history. The Romans had burned the Temple when they occupied Jerusalem in 70 CE, preventing the public practice of the sacrificial ritual that had until that time been the principal seal of the covenant. How could God have allowed this place, the intersection of heaven and earth, to be defiled by Gentiles? The fundamental challenge of the Romans to Israelite identity made a second great revolt, during 132–135 CE, as inevitable as it was inevitably disastrous. The *Book of Biblical Antiquities*, written either between these two wars or after them both, has Isaac say that his willingness to die at Abraham's hand proves that God has made human life a worthy sacrifice (*L.A.B.* 32:3): only the prototype of offering remained after the Temple's destruction, and it becomes understandable that within Judaism Isaac's offering should be seen as complete and perfect. That interpretative move permitted Jews to conceive of the covenant as continuing even after the most visible sign of the covenant, sacrifice in the Temple, had been wiped off the face of the earth by the Romans.

When Abraham placed Isaac on the altar as a burnt offering, both father and son were rejoicing as well as ready to act (*L.A.B.* 40:2–3). Here the older theology of the Maccabees finds its capstone. Although the *Book of Biblical Antiquities* stops short of saying that Isaac died on Moriah, it stands as the earliest reference to Isaac's "blood" (*L.A.B.* 18:5): "on account of his blood I chose them." The intention of father and son was so perfect, their

---

[8] See *m. Tamid* 4:1 and the comments of Shalom Spiegel his landmark book, the single most useful work ever written on the Aqedah, *The Last Trial: On the Legends and Lore of the Command to Abraham to Offer Isaac as a Sacrifice: The Akedah* (trans. Judah Goldin. Philadelphia: Jewish Publication Society, 1967), xix–xx. See also Aharon R.E. Agus, *The Binding of Isaac and Messiah: Law, Martyrdom, and Deliverance in Early Rabbinic Religiosity* (Albany: SUNY Press, 1988).

offering was accepted as if it had been completed, and that "blood" seals the election of their progeny. In the interpretation of Gen 22, the turn toward the primordial reflex of child-sacrifice is the consequence of violent external forces—the Roman demolition of the Temple—combined with a theology designed to enable the community to survive in desperate circumstances—Maccabean martyrdom.

Isaac's "blood" in the Aqedah stood for sacrifice, and—because the Romans had burned the Temple down in 70 CE and then razed the remaining masonry in 135 CE—Isaac came to embody the only sacrifice that God would or could accept. During the second century (*m. Ta'an.* 2:5), some Rabbis taught that the sound of the ram's horn with prayer and fasting would cause God to answer the community as he had once answered Abraham on Moriah. The Aqedah eventually took the place offering of the daily sacrifice required in the Temple, the Tamid lamb. Centuries later, around 450 CE, the Rabbinic midrash of the Book of Leviticus explained that, when any Israelite reads about the Tamid, God remembers the Aqedah (*Lev. Rab.* 2:11). Because the Aqedah is presented as the true ideal that the offering of the daily lamb recollects, Isaac and the martyrs took the place of the discontinued ritual in the Temple.

Once the connection between Isaac's Aqedah and ritual sacrifice had been made, it was possible for it to be articulated in other sacrificial contexts. A second-century midrash called the *Mekhilta*, for example, has God explain in Exod 12:13 why he will pass over houses where he sees blood at the threshold of Israel's houses during the first Passover: "when I see the blood, I see the blood of Isaac's Aqedah." In this creative reading, typical of the ancient genre of midrash and quite unlike a commentary in the modern sense, the association of the Aqedah extends into a new paschal connection without breaking the earlier connections with the Tamid sacrifice.

Some of the reasons for this innovative association with Passover only become plain when Christian claims during the second century, which presented Jesus' death at Passover as the true sacrifice foreshadowed by Isaac, are taken into account. But Isaac's status as the prototype of martyrdom and sacrifice made that Christian theology possible, and enabled Rabbinic Judaism to reply to the association between Christ and Isaac on the part of those whom the Rabbis considered heretics.

In his role of the prototypical martyr offering his life, Isaac crossed the line from readiness for sacrifice into sacrifice itself. When sacrificial blood is at issue, what God sees might be considered metaphorical or literal, and there is good evidence that Rabbinic interpretation took the image both ways. Perhaps, some interpreters said, Abraham went so far as to nick Isaac's carotid artery, so that he lost a quarter of his blood before his father was stopped in the course of his sacrificial routine.[9]

As this trajectory of interpretation developed, Isaac's awareness about all the events around him also sharpened. Now he was no longer twenty-five years old, but thirty-seven, and he approached the sacrifice, no longer as a zealous martyr, but in mournful humility. Tears fall from his eyes as—contradicting Philo's picture—he asks his father to bind him fast, so that he will not struggle and blemish his body, which had to be perfect to be acceptable as a sacrifice. When the midrash Genesis Rabbah came to completion during the fifth century, Isaac's determination became quieter and deeper than in earlier interpretations, and for good reason. By then Constantine's recognition of Christianity put Judaism as a religion in a more perilous position than ever before within the Roman Empire.

The sacrifice that Abraham made of his son by this stage meant to some interpreters, not only that Isaac's blood was shed, but also—in the later presentation of the Babylonian Talmud (*Ta'an.* 16a)—that he had been reduced to ashes. No more extreme statement of the completion of the ritual could be imagined. By the same token, means could be imagined by which Isaac would appear again in the biblical narrative: God must have raised Abraham's son, the child of promise, not merely from death, but from the ashes of a sacrifice by fire. Isaac symbolized a human offering that pleased God, but at the same time the will of God for Israel's survival by any means necessary, including physical resurrection from the dead. Isaac was redeemed from Moriah, no matter how far the sacrifice had gone, just as the people Israel had returned from what seemed certain extinction in Babylon.

The treatment of Gen 22 in the midrash Genesis Rabbah, found in chapters 55–56, apparently took several centuries to evolve into its present, essentially fifth-century, form. It interleaves a number of different interpretations of these verses, focusing on different questions and topics, sometimes compatible, some contradictory. Read as a whole, Isaac is now fur-

---

[9] See Jacob Mann, *The Bible as Read and Preached in the Old Synagogue: A Study in the Cycles of the Readings from Torah and Prophets, as well as from Psalms, and in the Structure of the Midrashic Homilies* (2 vols.; Cincinnati: Union of American Hebrew Congregations, 1940–1966), 1:67; Hans Joachim Schoeps, "The Sacrifice of Isaac in Paul's Theology," *JBL* 65 (1946): 385–392; and Eduard Lohse, *Märtyrer und Gottesknecht: Untersuchungen zur urchristlichen Verkündigung vom Sühntod Jesu Christi* (2nd ed.; FRLANT 46; Göttingen: Vandenhoeck & Ruprecht).

nished with a temperament, character, and spiritual experience commensurate with his resurrection. By that stage, *Isaac's* Aqedah had taken on a literary fullness such that Isaac nearly eclipsed Abraham within the narrative of events on Mount Moriah.

No longer, for example, did God simply test Abraham, as in the Hebrew text, nor did Mastemah push God to act in the way he does in Jubilees out of jealousy of Abraham. Instead, the impetus for the test comes from a dispute between Isaac and Ishmael (*Gen. Rab.* 55:4), in which Ishmael brags that, since he was circumcised at the age of thirteen, his devotion was greater than Isaac's, who—circumcised as an eight-day old infant—had neither choice nor consciousness in the matter. Isaac replied that, were God to ask all his members in sacrifice, he would not deny them. The Aqedah then transpired.

After the events in Gen 22, *Gen. Rab.* 56:11 indicates that Isaac went to study with Shem, the son of Noah. Targum Pseudo-Jonathan of Gen 22:19 even indicates that he was taken to Shem's study house by angels.[10] Shem is identified with Melchizedek, the mysterious figure that once gave Abraham a priestly blessing (Gen 14:18–20).

Just by looking at two key elements in Genesis Rabbah—the dispute between Ishmael and Isaac and Isaac's studying in the academy of Shem—the allusive quality of the interpretations is obvious, and all the more so, when read in the context of the many other interpretations also presented in Genesis Rabbah. Are we to understand these statements literally? Today scholars still debate that question, just as they have argued over whether the Aqedah as a whole should be seen as post-Christian or pre-Christian. Yet it seems wise not to insist on a categorical reading when Genesis Rabbah so carefully constructs a series of possibilities—rather than a linear set of events—for virtually every turning point in the story, reflecting the compositional care of generations of sages.

Side by side with these creative and often surreal developments in the story of the Aqedah, the laconic power of the original text of Genesis remained. Many Jews saw their experience of persecution by Romans, whether under a pagan or a later Christian aegis, as impossibly cruel compared to Abraham's trial. In Lamentations Rabbah, we find a midrash on the Maccabean story of the woman who saw her seven sons die. The mother

---

[10] See Martin McNamara, "Melchizedek: Gen 14,17–20 in the Targums, in Rabbinic and Early Christian Literature," *Bib* 81 (2000): 1–31. As McNamara shows, the Targumim belong within a more generally Rabbinic pattern.

embraces her last child before his death and says, "My son, go tell Abraham, our father, My mother says to you, Do not take pride, claiming, I built an altar and offered up my son, Isaac. Now see, my mother built seven altars and offered up seven sons in one day. And yours was only a test, but I really had to do it."[11] Yet even as she gives her message to her son, the woman articulates the Maccabean belief that her child will live again to speak with Abraham, and she takes up the Maccabean imperative to sacrifice life, limb, and children for the sake of faith.

The Aqedah put these convictions in narrative form, in Isaac's resurrection and in his competition with Ishmael, and gave Christianity and Islam opportunities to develop interpretations that suited their characteristic teachings on sacrifice and martyrdom. From the Maccabean period on, martyrdom was no longer merely an extreme response to social crisis by means of human sacrifice, such as occurs sporadically in most religious cultures; instead, Mount Moriah occupied a permanent place at the center of ethics, and self-sacrifice had become a standard virtue. Not only in the specialist literature represented by the Talmud, but as we shall now see, in the Targumic versions of Scripture that were designed to be recited in synagogues for all who attended, Isaac offered his neck willingly for sacrifice, was praised by the angels, and gave his blood so that it would be remembered at the time of the Passover. The historical conditions that brought about this new theology were unique, but the persistence of the confrontation between loyal Jews and imperial oppression—whether by Seleucids or Romans—at a time of relatively high educational levels within Judaism ensured that the image of the glorious martyr would be embedded within Jewish literature. Judaism has made Isaac into the image of the necessary readiness for martyrdom, a requirement of all true Israelites.

Targumic Transformations of Genesis 22

The Targumic renderings of Gen 22 present interpretations that intersect with a whole range of the pre-Rabbinic and Rabbinic interpretations already discussed. Although no tannaitic midrashic work to Genesis has survived, even pre-Tannaitic elements are evident in the Targums as they can be read to day. For example (as we shall see), the Targumic motif that the

---

[11] See Jacob Neusner, *Lamentations Rabbah: An Analytical Translation* (BJS 193; Atlanta: Scholars Press, 1989), § 50.1. The midrash names the woman as Miriam, daughter of Tanhum, and also has her suckle her two and a half year old son before his death.

Aqedah was the tenth test of Abraham is related to Jubilees' enumeration of his tests; the mention of Isaac being reduced to dust and ashes echoes Amoraic theology (Talmud Bavli, *Taʿan.* 16a); Pseudo-Jonathan's narrative of the quarrel between Isaac and Ishmael and of Isaac's angelic vision reveals a connection with late and rich midrashic developments. How these influences combine with a strategic rendering of the Hebrew text in the Targumim reveals the particular intent and talent of the interpreters.

Targum Onqelos is not particularly interested in Isaac's willingness to be a sacrifice; the vital point is rather God's choice of a site for the altar. Onqelos identifies the choice of a worship location for Abraham with God's later choice of a worship location for the Israelites—i.e., the Jerusalem Temple—who will take possession of the Land long after Abraham's death. Already in the Hebrew Bible (2 Chron 3:1), these two locations are identified as the same, and *Jub.* 18:13 takes up this connection.

Targum Onqelos wants to make it clear that genuine worship took place and will take place in the same location. In order to do so, it relies not on the name of the place, but on its function. Abraham is directed and goes to the "land of *worship*" (in v. 2); there is only one place where worship can take place. (Here, as elsewhere, Targumic deviations from the underlying Hebrew are italicized.[12]) This rendering sets up Onqelos' version of Gen 22:14. Rather than naming the place where God's angel appeared, Onqelos has Abraham pray to God in a way that makes it clear that the location of his sacrifice will become the location of his descendants' sacrifices: "Then Abraham *worshipped and prayed* there *in* that place *and said, Here*

---

[12] This has become a standard practice since the publication of the series, "The Aramaic Bible" (Collegeville, Minn.: Liturgical Press), which provides the most widely cited translations into English. This method, and certain conventions pioneered or taken up in "The Aramaic Bible," are followed in an introduction I have written with Paul V.M. Flesher; see our *The Targums: A Critical Introduction* (Waco, Tex.: Baylor University Press, 2011). My collaboration with Professor Flesher has enabled me to develop work first articulated in other publications, including: "The Aqedah: A Revised Tradition History," *CBQ* 40 (1978): 514–546 (written jointly with Phillip R. Davies); "Isaac and the Second Night: A Consideration," *Bib* 61 (1980): 78–88; "Irenaeus on Isaac," in *Studia Patristica XVII: Papers Presented to the Eighth International Conference on Patristic Studies, Oxford 1979* (ed. Elizabeth A. Livingstone; Oxford: Pergamon, 1982), 643–647; *Targumic Approaches to the Gospels: Essays in the Mutual Definition of Judaism and Christianity* (Studies in Judaism; Lanham, Md.: University Press of America, 1986); and "Prophecy in the Targumim," in *Mediators of the Divine: Horizons of Prophecy, Divination, Dreams and Theurgy in Mediterranean Antiquity* (ed. Robert M. Berchman; SFSHJ 163; Atlanta: Scholars Press, 1998), 185–201. The *Introduction* gives the most detailed treatment of targumic issues; I have here extracted data from our collaboration and set it within the concerns of the present volume. Unless otherwise noted, translations of targumic texts are my own.

generations will be worshipping before the Lord. *Then* it will be said *as on* this day, On this mountain *Abraham worshipped before* the Lord."

Abraham in his prayer envisions his future descendants praying and sacrificing in the place where he has just offered the ram. They will remind themselves that in this same spot Abraham worshiped God by offering his son Isaac. In this way, Onqelos ties the Temple site to the place where Abraham followed God's command by attempting to sacrifice his son.

As given in the MT, the crucial verb in v. 14 is a *niphal* imperfect third-person masculine singular. Assuming that God is the subject, it should be interpreted as "God will be seen" or "God will appear." The Targum by contrast understands the subject to be the worshipper rather than God. That translational logic lies behind the targumic rendering provided here, that people *"will be worshipping before* the Lord." And, since the phrase appears twice, the meturgeman applies it once to future generations and once to Abraham, altering its grammatical character to make the sentence work.

The verb for "worship" does not require the preposition "before" to indicate the recipient of worship. The preposition's addition comes from the Targum's tendency to avoid wording that seems to anthropomorphize God. Worshipping God directly might cause some people to infer his physical presence. To avoid that outcome, the meturgeman regularly adds "before" to imply that the worshipper is not speaking directly to God. This notion also applies to how one treats exalted royalty; a person having an audience with a king does not speak directly to them, but "before" them. This avoidance of anthropomorphisms of God is common to targumim generally.[13] Despite the additional material in these two phrases, the Hebrew text finds literal representation in this Targum. Every word of the Hebrew has a corresponding term in the translation, and in the same order as the original. To be sure, those corresponding terms are interwoven with added words, but the requirements of formal correspondence met.

In contrast to Targum Onqelos, other Targums—especially Neophyti and certain manuscripts of the Fragments Targum—respond to the central question raised by Abraham's attempt to sacrifice his son. Through key additions in Gen 22:8, 10, and 14, these Targums aim to remove the impropriety and questionable circumstances Scripture's version of the story seems to imply. The question focuses on the role of Isaac: Why is he so passive? Does he agree with his own slaughter or not, and what truly was God's intent?

---

[13] Another example of an anti-anthropomorphic rendering in this story appears in the last word of Gen 22:18, where the term "my memra" is substituted.

Targum Neophyti refocuses the story by elevating Isaac's role, because he knows that he will be the sacrificial animal (v. 8):

> Then Abraham said, The lamb for the burnt offering has been prepared *before the Lord. But if not, you are the lamb of the burnt offering.* So the two of them walked on together *with a peaceful heart.*

The first phrase has Abraham tell Isaac directly that if God provides no lamb, Isaac becomes the sacrifice. Just as important are the two added words in the last sentence, they "walked on together *with a peaceful heart.*" This indicates that Isaac accepted Abraham's statement and his own designation as the sacrifice. They walk not just together, as in the MT, but with peaceful acceptance and surety of what is to come. The two manuscripts of Fragment Targums contain this verse, and their version of the translation with its additional material is quite close to that found in Neophyti, including both the added phrase indicating that Isaac may be the sacrificial victim and the remark about the "peaceful heart" of father and son.

At Gen 22:10, these Palestinian Targums begin with a literal translation of the Hebrew verse, and then they add a sizeable, self-contained addition, involving three confirmations of Isaac's intentional self-sacrifice. (In this case, the statements are so innovative that we forego usage of italics.) First, he says, "Father, bind me well, so that I do not kick you and your offering become unfit for you, and I be thrust into the pit of destruction in the world to come." Isaac indicates that he protects his father's cultic integrity in addition to his own status as an offering.

In his purity he is contrasted favorably with Abraham:

> The eyes of Abraham were gazing at the eyes of Isaac, but the eyes of Isaac were gazing at the angels of the height. Abraham was not seeing them.

The *meturgeman* here elevates Isaac above Abraham. Abraham's gaze is earthbound while Isaac is blessed with a vision of the heavenly angels—which Abraham specifically does not see. But in the third addition, the two are joined in their sacrificial intent, and praised in heaven, "At that moment a *bat qol* came out from heaven and said, Come, see two unique ones in my world. One sacrifices and one is being sacrificed; the one who sacrifices does not hold back, and the one who is being sacrificed stretches out his neck." This addition brings the two men into parity in their roles of sacrificer and victim. The *bat qol*—a heavenly voice—lauds both of them for their selflessness and obedience to God.

The emphasis on Isaac in these transformations is so strong that he begins to eclipse Abraham in importance. Not only does Isaac agree to be sacrificed, but he also tells his father to take extra precautions to prevent any accidental blemishing of the sacrifice. This is Isaac the willing martyr, which appears outside the Targums in Josephus, Pseudo-Philo, and later rabbinic materials. The heavenly voice echoes Isaac's importance as parallel to Abraham's by praising both men equally. Even more than this, however, Isaac receives a heavenly vision of angels denied to Abraham. By the end of v. 10, it seems that Isaac has become more important to the story than Abraham.

To help redress the focus on Abraham, the meturgeman specifies that this was *"the tenth test"* of Abraham (v. 1) This addition reminds the hearers that God has been giving Abraham tests throughout this period, a situation that does not apply to Isaac. Furthermore, the notion of Abraham receiving ten tests is well established in rabbinic literature, appearing as early as *m. 'Abot* 5:3.[14] This represents an extension of the tradition found in Jubilees (17:17–18), according to which the events of Gen 22 represented the climactic *seventh* test that Abraham confronted.

Abraham's importance in this tale is reasserted in Gen 22:14, when Abraham asks God to remember his faithfulness and help Isaac's descendants when they are in need. Yet the wording of Neophyti echoes one of the most emphatic Rabbinic indications that Isaac's offering had been completed, because Abraham here says, "my heart was not divided the first time when you said to me to offer Isaac my son, to make him dust and ashes before you." The binding of Isaac as a completed sacrifice[15] now should cause God to deliver the Israelites from future distress.

Targum Pseudo-Jonathan accepts the enhanced role of Isaac, the willing martyr; indeed it views Isaac as the central figure of Gen 22, not Abraham. The Amoraic conception of the quarrel between Isaac and Ishmael is added to the first verse:

> Then it came about after these things, *after Isaac and Ishmael had quarreled, Ishmael was saying, It is fitting for me to inherit my father because I am his firstborn son. Then Isaac was saying, It is fitting for me to inherit my father, because I am the son of Sarah his wife, but you are the son of Hagar, my mother's maidservant. Ishmael answered and said, I am more righteous than you because I was circumcised at thirteen years old, but if it had been my will to refuse, I*

---

[14] Bernard Grossfeld and Lawrence H. Schiffman, *Targum Neofiti 1: An Exegetical Commentary to Genesis including Full Rabbinic Parallels* (New York: Sepher-Hermon, 2000), 173–174.

[15] The wording in the Fragment Targum refers to sacrifice, rather than using the metaphor of "dust and ashes." Fragments Targum (manuscript P) at some points gives a different rendering of the material from Neophyti, but there are few significant differences in the overall point of the event and its interpretation.

would not have handed over myself to be circumcised, but you were circumcised at eight days old. If the knowledge had been in you, perhaps you would not have handed yourself over to be circumcised. Isaac answered and said, Behold, I am today thirty seven years old, and if the Holy One, blessed is He, would require it, I would not hold back all *of my members. Immediately these words were heard before the Master of the Universe, and immediately the Word of* the Lord tested Abraham and said to him, Abraham, and he said to him, Here I am.

Isaac and Ishmael debate who should be Abraham's heir. Ishmael opens his case by citing his position as first-born son. When Isaac counters by comparing the status of their mothers, Ishmael one-ups Isaac in his adherence to God's command: Ishmael as an adult had chosen to allow himself to be circumcised, but Isaac had been circumcised as a baby and hence had made no choice. Isaac's response—that God could have all his members—sounds exaggerated, as one might expect in a fraternal argument and occurs also in the debate between Cain and Abel. God, however, decides to take Isaac at his word and gives him the opportunity to live up to his statement. He immediately calls to Abraham in order to put the test in motion.

This addition in Pseudo-Jonathan constitutes a dramatic version of the dispute between Isaac and Ishmael that appeared in *Gen. Rab.* 55:4, discussed above. But in Genesis Rabbah, the debate stands alone, without any literary or thematic connection to the other interpretations of Gen 22; in Pseudo-Jonathan the event launches the reader into the rest of the story.

Since Abraham here does not tell Isaac directly that he was to be the sacrifice, Isaac's prior resolve, expressed in v. 1, becomes the context of Pseudo-Jonathan's addition to v. 10, already familiar from Neophyti:

> Then Abraham stretched out his hand and took the knife to slaughter his son. *Isaac answered and said to his father, "Bind me well, so that I do not jerk convulsively from pain of my soul, and I be thrust into the pit of destruction, and there be found a blemish in your offering." The eyes of Abraham were looking on the eyes of Isaac, but the eyes of Isaac were looking on the angels of the height. Isaac was seeing them, but Abraham was not seeing them. The angels of the height were answering, Come and see two unique ones who are in the world. One sacrifices and one is being sacrificed; the one who sacrifices does not hold back, and the one who is being sacrificed stretches out his neck.*

Although the material overlap with Neophyti is evident, the narrative innovation consequent on the introduction is even more striking.

Instead of linking Abraham's mountain with the future Temple, as in Onqelos, Pseudo-Jonathan uses an addition in v. 9 to identify the Aqedah with past sacrifices:

> Then they came to the place that the Lord had told him, and Abraham built there the altar *that Adam had built, though it had come apart in the waters of*

the deluge. But again Noah had built it, and it had come apart in the generation of the division. Then he arranged the wood on it, and he bound Isaac his son, and put him on the altar over the wood.

In this way, the Aqedah in Pseudo-Jonathan becomes identified with an eternal offering that endures even beyond the time of the Temple, just it reaches back to time immemorial.

Conclusion

The Pentateuchal Targums pursue different goals for their recasting of Gen 22, even as they use related and sometimes identical exegetical materials. Onqelos leaves the story pretty much as it is in the Hebrew text, making changes to bring out its point about the identification of the mountain on which Abraham attempts to sacrifice Isaac with the Temple Mount. Neophyti and related Targums use additional material to address the question raised about Isaac's passive role in the biblical version of the tale and reshape it in the process. They emphasize Isaac's willing agreement with Abraham carrying out God's command, even though it means his own death. They do not want Isaac's new role to overshadow that of Abraham, so they add material at the beginning and end to ensure Abraham's prominence, although in doing so they refer to Isaac's sacrifice as completed. Pseudo-Jonathan largely agrees in heightening Isaac's participation, and takes that motif further. Its recasting of the story makes Isaac even more central to the tale and removes some aspects of Abraham's role. It works to prevent Abraham's actions from detracting from Isaac's role as martyr.

Just by looking at a few key elements in Targumic presentation—the dispute between Ishmael and Isaac, Isaac's being reduced to ashes, and his return to life from the academy of Shem, for example—the allusive quality of the interpretations is obvious. When such motifs stand alone in Midrash Rabbah or in the Talmud, they may convey a surreal or theoretical impression. All the more so, when they are read in the context of the many other interpretations also presented in that literature. Are we to believe that the brothers really fought prior to the Aqedah, and that Isaac came back from the dead after a sojourn in the heavenly academy, when so many other readings are possible? Those points remain debatable, and it seems wise not to insist on a categorical reading when Genesis Rabbah and the Talmud offer a series of possibilities for virtually every turning point in the story.

The Pentateuchal Targumim join in this allusive investigation of possibilities, while following the demands of both text and narrative. The result are renderings that operate with levels of meaning on parallel planes, with Isaac's offering conveyed as both obviated by God and completed by the intention of Isaac himself as well as Abraham. Conceived in the crucible of popular usage, the Targumim to Gen 22 crystallized the ethos of martyrdom in fresh versions of the Hebrew text rendered in idioms of rabbinic interpretation. Gen 22 in Aramaic connects what might have been with what might be, confronts the hearer or reader with a martyr's identity, and opens intriguing perspectives on the tasks and pleasures of interpretation.

SELECT BIBLIOGRAPHY

Agus, Aharon R.E. *The Binding of Isaac and Messiah: Law, Martyrdom, and Deliverance in Early Rabbinic Religiosity*. Albany: State University of New York Press, 1988.
Bernstein, Moshe J. "Angels at the Aqedah: A Study in the Development of a Midrashic Motif." *Dead Sea Discoveries* 7 (2000): 263–291.
Chilton, Bruce. *Abraham's Curse: Child Sacrifice in the Legacies of the West*. New York: Doubleday, 2008.
———. "A Comparative Study of Synoptic Development: The Dispute between Cain and Abel in the Palestinian Targums and the Beelzebul Controversy in the Gospels." *Journal of Biblical Literature* 101 (1982): 553–562.
———. "Sennacherib: A Synoptic Relationship among Targumim of Isaiah." Pages 544–554 in *Society of Biblical Literature 1986 Seminar Papers*. Edited by Kent H. Richards. Society of Biblical Literature Seminar Papers 25. Atlanta: Scholars Press, 1986.
———. "Theodicy in the Targumim." Pages 728–752 in *Theodicy in the World of the Bible*. Edited by Antii Laato and Johannes C. de Moor. Leiden: Brill, 2003.
Davies, Philip R., and Bruce Chilton. "The Aqedah: A Revised Tradition History." *Catholic Biblical Quarterly* 40 (1978): 514–546.
Fitzmyer, Joseph A. "The Sacrifice of Isaac in Qumran Literature." *Biblica* 83 (2002): 211–229.
Flesher, Paul V.M., and Bruce Chilton. *The Targums: A Critical Introduction*. Waco, Tex.: Baylor University Press, 2011.
Kessler, Edward. *Bound by the Bible: Jews, Christians and the Sacrifice of Isaac*. Cambridge: Cambridge University Press, 2004.
Kundert, Lukas. *Die Opferung/Bindung Isaaks: Gen 22,1–19 im Alten Testament, im Frühjudentum und im Neuen Testament*. Wissenschaftliche Monographien zum Alten und Neuen Testament 78. Neukirchen-Vluyn: Neukirchener, 1998.
Lohse, Eduard. *Märtyrer und Gottesknecht: Untersuchungen zur urchristlichen Verkündigung vom Sühntod Jesu Christi*. 2nd ed. Forschungen zur Religion und Literatur des Alten und Neuen Testaments 46. Göttingen: Vandenhoeck & Ruprecht, 1963.
McNamara, Martin. "Melchizedek: Gen 14,17–20 in the Targums, in Rabbinic and Early Christian Literature." *Biblica* 81 (2000): 1–31.

Schoeps, Hans Joachim. "The Sacrifice of Isaac in Paul's Theology." *Journal of Biblical Literature* 65 (1946): 385–392.

Spiegel, Shalom. *The Last Trial: On the Legends and Lore of the Command to Abraham to Offer Isaac as a Sacrifice: The Akedah*. Translated by Judah Goldin. Philadelphia: Jewish Publication Society, 1967.

THE *VETUS LATINA* AND THE VULGATE OF THE BOOK OF GENESIS

David L. Everson

The Origin and Nature of the *Vetus Latina*

The term *Vetus Latina* or 'Old Latin' (hereafter OL) is a term used to identify the Latin versions of the Bible, which were translated from the Greek and do not correspond to the Vulgate of Jerome.[1] As Latin became ever more prominent as an imperial and commercial language in the Mediterranean world, the language of the early church became increasingly Latinate. The earliest evidence for a Latin version of the Bible appears in the second century CE and following. According to the *Passion of the Scillitan Martyrs*, a certain Speratus, who was beheaded in CE 180, is said to have possessed "the books and letters of Paul, a just man" (*Libri et epistulae Pauli, viri iusti*).[2] Further testimony from the second century for a Latin Bible is Tertullian (ca. CE 130–220), who states that Latin was the exclusive language of the African church. Additionally, the quotations of scripture found within his works have led some to believe that Tertullian may have had access to two separate Latin versions. In the third century, for the first time, Cyprian provides lengthy citations of a Latin Bible.[3]

The OL is well-known for its lack of textual uniformity. In his *Preface to the Four Gospels*, Jerome laments that there are as many forms (*exemplaria*) of the text as there are copies.[4] This complaint is reiterated by Augustine

---

[1] The Greek origin of the OL may be proven by observing Greek neologisms, loan words, septuagintal syntax, and the preservation of Greek errors.

[2] The Latin of this text appears in J.A. Robinson, ed., *The Passion of S. Perpetua* (TS 1/2; Cambridge: Cambridge University Press, 1891; repr., Piscataway, N.J.: Gorgias, 2004), 114. See also *ANF* 9:280–282.

[3] Benjamin Kedar-Kopfstein, "The Latin Translations," in *Mikra: Text, Translation, Reading and Interpretation of the Hebrew Bible in Ancient Judaism and Early Christianity* (ed. Martin Jan Mulder; CRINT 2/1; Assen: Van Gorcum, 1988), 299–338, esp. 299.

[4] "For if our faith should be applied to the Latin texts, they should tell us which ones; for there are nearly as many (forms) as there are copies" (*Si enim latinis exemplaribus fides est adhibenda, respondeant quibus; tot sunt paene quot codices*). All of the biblical prefaces

who writes, "Those who have translated the scriptures from the Hebrew language into Greek can be numbered, but the Latin translators are in no way numerable. For in the early days of the faith, when a Greek book fell into someone's hand and he believed himself to have some ability in both languages, he dared to translate."[5]

This testimony of textual diversity is supported by the manuscript evidence for the OL of Genesis. Considering the number of extant manuscripts and the scriptural citations of approximately fifty church fathers, the number of variant readings is consistently overwhelming. For the Book of Genesis, the number of extant manuscripts is relatively small.[6] There are three Vulgate manuscripts which contain OL marginalia (91, 94 and 95), two palimpsests (101 and 103), and four OL manuscripts (100, 103, 105 and 111). All of these materials are fragmentary and range in date from the fifth century (e.g. 103, 105) to the sixteenth century (e.g. 94). There are nearly fifty church fathers frequently cited within Bonifatius Fischer's edition of the OL of Genesis, which provide an enormous amount of textual evidence for the OL and the Vulgate. Such a large number of sources, many of which are considerably late, is due to the fact that the Vulgate did not effectively replace the OL until the seventh century.[7] Based on these manuscripts, Fischer has suggested the following Latin text-types for the Book of Genesis:

L: A general form of the OL
  K: An African text
  C: A revised African text
  E: A European text
    A: A revised text from Augustine
    M: A revised text from Ambrose
    O: A Hexaplaric text aligned with Jerome
    P: A text aligned with Quodvultdeus, deacon of Carthage
  X: Dubious texts
  H: The Vulgate of Jerome

---

have been taken from *Biblia Sacra: Iuxta Vulgatam Versionem* (4th ed.; ed. Robert Weber and Roger Gryson; Stuttgart: Deutsche Bibelgesellschaft, 1994). Translations are my own.

[5] *Doctr. chr.* 2.16; *Qui enim scripturas ex Hebraea lingua in Graecam verterunt, numerari possunt, Latini autem interpretes nullo modo. Ut enim cuique primis fidei temporibus in manus venit codex Graecus, et aliquantulum facultatis sibi utriusque linguae habere videbatur, ausus est interpretari.*

[6] All manuscript citations are according to the Institut Vetus Latina of the St. Martin's Abbey at Beuron. See Bonifatius Fischer, ed., *Vetus Latina: Die Reste der altlateinischen Bibel nach Petrus Sabatier neu gesammelt und herausgegeben von der Erzabtei Beuron, 2. Genesis* (Freiburg: Herder, 1949–1954), 1–21.

[7] Natalio Fernández Marcos, *The Septuagint in Context: Introduction to the Greek Version of the Bible* (trans. Wilfred G.E. Watson; Leiden: Brill, 2000), 356.

In light of this categorization of manuscripts, one wonders if it is possible to determine a potential schema for the OL manuscripts of Genesis and/or if there might be a single OL *Vorlage*. There are a number of factors which make such a determination difficult. First, unlike the origin of the Vulgate, there is no clear ancient testimony pinpointing the number of translators, the location or the timeframe for the origin of the OL of Genesis. Second, considering the late date of the manuscripts, the OL may have been influenced or corrupted by Hexaplaric or Jeromian manuscripts. As Matthew Kraus has shown, it is likely that OL manuscripts with Hebraizing tendencies have been influenced by Hexaplaric LXX manuscripts.[8] Though he never endeavored to assemble a thorough analysis of the data to prove his opinion, Fischer believed that there was a single OL *Vorlage* for the Book of Genesis and probably for Samuel and Kings as well.[9] Others are inclined to share the opinion of A.V. Billen who, regarding this difficult matter, writes, "The whole question of the Latin and LXX texts of Genesis however is likely to prove one of exceptional difficulty."[10]

The Origin and Nature of the Vulgate

According to Jerome's preface to the Gospels, in the year 382, at the invitation of Pope Damasus, he began revising the Gospels. This was followed by two revisions of the Psalter (one according to the LXX and another according to Hexaplaric revisions). He also revised a number of OT books according to the LXX of Origen's Hexapla, namely, Chronicles, Job, and 'Solomon's Books.' One should keep in mind that these initial efforts were not translations but revisions. Catherine Brown Tkacz suggests that Jerome alludes to this distinction in his own writing, referring to the Gospels as a *novum opus* and his OT translations as *interpretationem novam* and *nostra translatio*.[11]

---

[8] Matthew A. Kraus, "Hebraisms in the Old Latin Version of the Bible," *VT* 53 (2003): 487–513.

[9] Eugene Ulrich, "Characteristics and Limitations of the Old Latin Translation of the Septuagint," in *La Septuaginta en la investigación contemporánea: (V Congreso de la IOSCS)* (ed. Natalio Fernández Marcos; Textos y estudios "Cardenal Cisneros" 34; Madrid: Instituto Arias Montano, 1985), 67–80, esp. 69. This article has been reprinted in Eugene Ulrich, *The Dead Sea Scrolls and the Origins of the Bible* (SDSSRL 2; Grand Rapids: Eerdmans, 1999), 275–289.

[10] A.V. Billen, *The Old Latin Texts of the Heptateuch* (Cambridge: Cambridge University Press, 1927), 105.

[11] Catherine Brown Tkacz, "Labor Tam Utilis: The Creation of the Vulgate," *VC* 50 (1996): 42–72, esp. 50.

In light of the *Prologus Galeatus* (i.e. Jerome's 'Helmeted Preface' to Samuel and Kings), Samuel and Kings are often believed to have been the first books translated by Jerome. Therein Jerome writes, "This preface of the Scriptures can be understood as a helmeted beginning to all of the books, which we turn from Hebrew into Latin."[12] According to H.J. White, this preface "is really an introduction to the whole OT, and shows that even thus early he must have conceived some idea of translating all the books."[13] Similarly, J.N.D. Kelly maintains that the *Prologus Galeatus* makes it "practically certain" that Samuel and Kings were translated first.[14] A different position is held by Benjamin Kedar-Kopfstein who, in light of the theological importance of the respective books and the development of Jerome's technique, believes that the translations of the Prophets and Psalms preceded those of Samuel and Kings. He also notes that information found in the prefaces to Isaiah and Daniel would be redundant if Samuel/Kings had been translated first.[15] In any case, Jerome translated Samuel, Kings, the Psalms, the Prophets, and Job between 390 and 394; Ezra and Nehemiah between 394 and 395; Chronicles in 395; Proverbs, Canticles, and Ecclesiastes in 398; the Octateuch between 398 and 404/5; and Tobit and Judith in 407.[16] For our purposes, it is important to note that Jerome is translating the Book of Genesis after nearly ten years of translating and more than two dozen translations under his belt.

In terms of method, the Hebrew text was the primary source for Jerome (*fons veritatis*).[17] In his preface to Ecclesiastes, he describes his method of

---

[12] *Hic prologus Scripturarum quasi galeatum principium omnibus libris, quos de hebraeo vertimus in latinum, convenire potest.* For the translation of *convenio*, see Alexander Souter, *A Glossary of Later Latin to 600 A.D.* (Oxford: Oxford University Press, 1949), 78.

[13] H.J. White, "Vulgate," in *A Dictionary of the Bible* (ed. James Hastings; 5 vols.; New York: Charles Scribner's Sons, 1898–1904), 4:873–890, esp. 875.

[14] J.N.D. Kelly, *Jerome: His Life, Writings, and Controversies* (London: Duckworth, 1975), 161. Tkacz maintains the same position. See her "Labor Tam Utilis," 50–53, and *"Quid Facit Cum Psalterio Horatius?*: Seeking the Classical Allusions in the Vulgate," in *Nova Doctrina Vetusque: Essays on Early Christianity in Honor of Fredric W. Schlatter, S.J.* (ed. Douglas Kries and Catherine Brown Tkacz; Bern: Peter Lang, 1999), 93–104.

[15] Kedar-Kopfstein, "The Latin Translations," 321. Elsewhere, he maintains that Jerome's reference to having translated the OT from Hebrew into Latin in *Vir. ill.* 135 (*vetus* [*testamentum*] *iuxta hebraicum transtulit*) refers to the Psalms and the Prophets, which are mentioned as having been translated in the previous chapter. See Benjamin Kedar-Kopfstein, "The Vulgate as a Translation: Some Semantic and Syntactical Aspects of Jerome's Version of the Hebrew Bible" (Ph.D. diss., The University of Jerusalem, 1968), 53.

[16] For a discussion of these dates, see Kelly, *Jerome*, 156–162; and Tkacz, "Labor Tam Utilis," 50–51.

[17] *Epist.* 20.2; 34.4.; cf. Adam Kamesar, *Jerome, Greek Scholarship, and the Hebrew Bible: A Study of the* Quaestiones Hebraicae in Genesim (OCM; Oxford: Clarendon, 1993), 45.

translation.[18] First, he examines the Hebrew and determines its meaning. Second, he compares the meaning of the Hebrew with Rabbinic interpretation. Third, he considers the LXX when it is in agreement with the Hebrew. Fourth, he considers the other Greek sources, especially Symmachus. Kedar-Kopfstein has pointed out that despite Jerome's testimony of consultation, his translations remain largely independent. He writes, "The moment we survey the overall picture, his relative independence becomes apparent: He never agrees with one of his informants for more than a short clause."[19] Similarly, H.F.D. Sparks notes that "Jerome in practice translated very much as he happened himself to feel at any particular moment."[20] This may be due to the fact that Jerome intended on creating a coherent text. In his *Preface to Job*, he writes, "Moreover, this translation follows no translator of old but comes from the Hebrew and Arabic speech and sometimes from the Syriac: here it reflects the word, here the sense and now both together."[21]

RELATIONSHIP BETWEEN THE VERSIONS

In order to demonstrate the relationship between the LXX, the OL, the Vulgate, and the MT, and to gain a sense for the quality of each translation, I have conducted four analyses. Two of these concern proper nouns while the other two concern Hebraisms which do not lend themselves to Greek and Latin.

Proper Nouns as Hapax Legomena. All of the proper nouns which appear as *hapax legomena* within the Book of Genesis (according to the MT) have been listed below. Examining this list is a particularly useful inquiry in that, as *hapax legomena*, deviation from the LXX for a more Hebraic

---

[18] ... *hoc breviter admonens, quod nullius auctoritatem secutus sum; sed de hebraeo transferens, magis me septuaginta interpretum consuetudini coaptavi, in his dumtaxat, quae non multum ab Hebraicis discrepabant. Interdum Aquilae quoque et Symmachi et Theodotionis recordatus sum, ut nec novitate nimia lectoris studium deterrerem, nec rursum contra conscientiam meam, fonte veritatis omisso, opinionum rivulos consectarer* (CCSL 72.249).

[19] Kedar-Kopfstein, "The Latin Translations," 323. Adler comes to a similar conclusion; see William Adler, "*Ad Verbum* or *Ad Sensum*: The Christianization of a Latin Translation Formula in the Fourth Century," in *Pursuing the Text: Studies in Honor of Ben Zion Wacholder on the Occasion of his Seventieth Birthday* (JSOTSup 184; ed. John C. Reeves and John Kampen; Sheffield: Sheffield Academic Press, 1994), 321–348, esp. 334.

[20] H.F.D. Sparks, "Jerome as Biblical Scholar," in *The Cambridge History of the Bible, Volume 1: From the Beginnings to Jerome* (ed. P.R. Ackroyd and C.F. Evans. Cambridge: Cambridge University Press, 1970), 510–541, esp. 526.

[21] *Haec autem translatio nullum de veteribus sequitur interpretem, sed ex ipso hebraico arabicoque sermone et interdum syro, nunc verba, nunc sensus, nunc simul utrumque resonabit.*

transliteration (in both the Vulgate and the OL) is more likely to be seen. That is, the respective translators are less likely to reject a Hebraic rendering of the noun due to the influence of a standardized spelling.[22] At the same time, because the following nouns are so rare, they are prime candidates for corruption. Hence, textual dependence will more clearly be seen and textual deviation is more likely to occur.

	LXX	Old Latin	Vulgate	MT
1. Gen 50:11	Πένθος Αἰγύπτου	Luctus Aegypti	Planctus Aegypti	אבל מצרים
2. Gen 10:27	Αιζηλ	Ezel	Uzal	אוזל
3. Gen 26:26	Οχοζαθ	Ochozath	Ochozath	אחזת
4. Gen 36:24	Αιε	Aep	Ahaia	איה
5. Gen 10:10	Αρχαδ	Archad	Archad	אכד
6. Gen 10:10	Ορεχ	Orech	Arach	ארך
7. Gen 36:28	Αραμ	Arran	Aran	ארן
8. Gen 25:3	Ασσουριιμ	Assyrin	Assurim	אשורם
9. Gen 22:21	Βαυξ	Bauz	Buz	בוז
10. Gen 35:18	Υἱὸς ὀδύνης	Filius doloris	Benoni id est filius doloris	בן־אוני
11. Gen 19:38	Αμμαν	Ammon	Ammon	בן־עמי
12. Gen 22:24	τὸν Γααμ	Guam	Gaom	גחם
13. Gen 10:4	Ῥόδιοι	Rodi	Dodanim	דדנים
14. Gen 36:39	Αραδ	Arad	Adad	הדר
15. Gen 36:22	Αιμαν	Enam (I); Omman (O)	Heman	הימם
16. Gen 14:5	ἅμα αὐτοῖς	simul cum eis	cum eis	(בהם) הם
17. Gen 14:5	ἔθνη ἰσχυρὰ	gentes fortes	Zuzim	זוזים
18. Gen 14:15	Χωβα	Choba	Hoba	חובה
19. Gen 22:22	τὸν Αζαυ	Azan	Azau	חזו
20. Gen 36:26	Αμαδα	Emadan	Amdan	חמדן
21. Gen 22:24	Ταβεκ (var. Ταβελ)	Taber	Tabee	טבח
22. Gen 4:20	Ιωβελ	Iobel	Iabel	יבל

---

[22] Here and elsewhere, I refer to the OL rendering the Hebrew but only for the simplicity of expression. Of course, the OL can only render the Hebrew as it is received through a Greek text or another Latin text.

THE *VETUS LATINA* & THE VULGATE OF THE BOOK OF GENESIS 525

	LXX	Old Latin	Vulgate	MT
23. Gen 22:22	Ιεδλαφ	Iudul	Iedlaph	ידלף
24. Gen 26:34	Ιουδιν	Iudin	Iudith	יהודית
25. Gen 46:13	Ιασουβ	Iasup	Iob	יוב
26. Gen 4:21	Ιουβαλ	Iobal	Iubal	יובל
27. Gen 11:29	Ιεσχα	Iescae	Ieschae	יסכה
28. Gen 46:17	Ιεσουα	Iessua	Iesui/Iesua	ישוי
29. Gen 36:40	Ιεθερ	Ierthe(t)	Ietheth	יתת
30. Gen 38:5	Χασβι	Chasbin	cessavit	כזיב
31. Gen 36:26	Χαρραν	Chorram	Charan	כרן
32. Gen 22:22	Χασαδ (var. χαζαναθ)	Canazat	Chased	כשד
33. Gen 25:3	Λοωμιμ	Lomomin	Loommim	לאמים
34. Gen 10:13	Λουδιιμ	Ludim	Ludim	לודים
35. Gen 25:3	Λατουσιιμ	Latisin	Lathusim	לטושים
36. Gen 10:19	Λασα	Laban (X); Lecem (O)	Lesa	לשע
37. Gen 10:2	Μαδαι	Madae	Madai	מדי
38. Gen 46:21	Μαμφιν	Mamfim	Mophim	מפים
39. Gen 10:23	Μοσοχ	Mosoch	Mes	מש
40. Gen 10:30	Μασση	Masse	Messa	משא
41. Gen 4:16	Ναιδ	Naid	profugus	נוד
42. Gen 4:22	Νοεμα	Noemma	Noemma	נעמה
43. Gen 10:30	Σωφηρα	Gophera	Sephar	ספר
44. Gen 36:35	Γεθθαιμ	Cetthem	Ahuith	עוית
45. Gen 14:7	τὴν πηγὴν τῆς κρίσεως	fontem iudicii	fontem Mesfat	עין משפט
46. Gen 36:40	Γωλα	Golla	Alva	עלוה
47. Gen 36:27	Ουκαν	Uschan	Acham	עקן
48. Gen 26:20	Ἀδικία	Iniquitas	Calumniam	עשק
49. Gen 14:5	Ασταρωθ Καρναιν	Astaroth Carnaim	Astharothcarnaim	עשתרת קרנים
50. Gen 48:7	Μεσοποταμίας τῆς Συρίας	Meopotamia[m] Syriae	Mesopotamiam	פדן
51. Gen 2:11	Φισων	Fison	Phison	פישון
52. Gen 22:22	Φαλδας	Faldas	Pheldas	פלדש
53. Gen 32:32	τὸ Εἶδος τοῦ θεοῦ	Faciem dei	Phanuhel	פנואל

	LXX	Old Latin	Vulgate	MT
54. Gen 32:31	Εἶδος θεοῦ	Faciem dei	Phanuhel	פניאל
55. Gen 10:14	Πατροσωνιιμ	Patrosin	Phetrusim	פתרסים
56. Gen 46:16	Σαφων	Safon	Sephion	צפיון
57. Gen 41:45	Ψονθομφανηχ	Psompthomfanech	Salvatorem mundi	צפנת פענח
58. Gen 15:19	Κεδμωναίους	Celmonaeos	Cedmoneos	קדמני
59. Gen 22:24	Ρεημα	Regma	Roma	ראומה
60. Gen 46:21	Ρως	Ros	Ros	ראש
61. Gen 10:11	τὴν Ροωβωθ πόλιν	Roboth civitatem	plateas civitatis	רחבת עיר
62. Gen 10:3	Ριφαθ	Rifan	Rifath	ריפת
63. Gen 10:12	Δασεμ	Dasem	Resen	רסן
64. Gen 26:21	Ἐχθρία	Inimicitia	Inimicitias	שטנה
65. Gen 14:5	Σαυη τῇ πόλει	Sauhe civitate	Savecariathaim	שוה קריתים
66. Gen 46:16	Σαυνις	Saunis	Suni	שוני
67. Gen 36:23	Σωφ	Sofa	Sephi	שפו
68. Gen 22:24	Τοχος	Tocus	Thaas	תחש

In light of the data listed above, there are seven possible alignment scenarios.

1. MT = Vulgate; LXX = OL: 33 instances (numbers 2, 6, 9–10, 13–15, 17, 20, 22, 24, 25, 29, 32, 38–42, 44–46, 50, 53–54, 56–57, 61, 63, 65–68).
2. LXX = OL = Vulgate = MT: 19 instances (numbers 1, 3, 8, 12, 18, 26–28, 31, 33, 34, 37, 48, 49, 51–52, 55, 60, 64).
3. OL unique; LXX = Vulgate = MT: 10 instances (numbers 4, 19, 21, 23, 35–36, 43, 47, 58, 62).
4. MT unique; LXX = OL = Vulgate: 3 instances (numbers 5, 11, 16).
5. LXX unique; OL = Vulgate = MT: 1 instance (numbers 7).
6. Vulgate = MT; LXX = OL = MT: 1 instance (number 30).[23]
7. MT = Vulgate; LXX & OL = unique: 1 instance (number 59).

Among the possible alignment scenarios, it is most common for the Vulgate and MT to be aligned on the one hand, while the LXX and the OL are aligned on the other. It is significant that nearly half of the above instances have the Vulgate deviating from the OL in favor of a more Hebraic reading, thus

---

[23] In Gen 38:5 (§30), Jerome appears to read בכזיב as an infinitive construct of כזב. Accordingly, he may understand כזב as 'to fail' instead of 'to lie,' hence *cessare*.

demonstrating Jerome's independence from the LXX and the OL during this period of translation. This also demonstrates the relative infrequency of the OL deviating from the LXX because of the Hexaplaric or Jeromian influence. It should be noted that there are a number of instances where Jerome contradicts the LXX and the OL by choosing to translate the meaning of the Hebrew, instead of transliterating (e.g. numbers 30, 41, 57 and 61). There are also instances where just the opposite is the case (e.g. numbers 17, 45, 53–54 and 65). There are nine instances where the OL is unaligned with any of the other traditions. Some of these unique reading might be explained by corruption due to graphic similarity (e.g. § 58) or a similarity of sound (e.g. § 21), while others are more difficult to explain.

Rendering יסף. Another useful inquiry in determining the relationship between the LXX, the OL, the Vulgate, and the MT would be to examine standard Hebrew syntagms, which, having no syntactic corollary in the target language, lend themselves to awkward Greek and Latin translations. A good example of this would be the adverbial use of the infinitive as a complement to יסף.[24] There are eleven instances within the Book of Genesis where יסף is awkwardly rendered in the LXX with the use of προστίθημι.

	LXX	OL	Vulgate	MT
Gen 4:2	καὶ προσέθηκεν τεκεῖν	adiecit parere	rursusque peperit	ותסף ללדת
Gen 4:12	οὐ προσθήσει ... δοῦναί	et non adiciet ... dare	non dabit	לא־תסף תת
Gen 8:12	οὐ προσέθετο τοῦ ἐπιστρέψαι	et non adposuit reverti	non est reversa	ולא־יספה שוב
Gen 8:21	οὐ προσθήσω ἔτι τοῦ καταράσασθαι	non adiciam ultra maledicere	nequaquam ultra maledicam	לא־אסף לקלל
Gen 8:21	οὐ προσθήσω οὖν ἔτι πατάξαι	(M) non ergo adhuc adiciam percutere (A) non adiciam ergo adhuc percutere	non igitur ultra percutiam	לא אסף עוד להכות
Gen 18:29	καὶ προσέθηκεν ἔτι λαλῆσαι	vacat	rursumque locutus est	ויסף עוד לדבר

---

[24] See Bruce K. Waltke and M. O'Connor, *An Introduction to Biblical Hebrew Syntax* (Winona Lake, Ind.: Eisenbrauns, 1990), §§ 36.2.1d, and 39.3.1b. For a list of additional awkward Hebraisms within the LXX, see Henry St. John Thackeray, *A Grammar of the Old Testament in Greek According to the Septuagint, Volume 1: Introduction, Orthography and Accidence* (Cambridge: Cambridge University Press, 1909), § 4.

	LXX	OL	Vulgate	MT
Gen 25:1	προσθέμενος δὲ Ἀβρααμ ἔλαβεν	adiciens autem Abraham accepit	Abraham vero aliam duxit uxorem	ויסף אברהם ויקח
Gen 37:8	καὶ προσέθεντο ἔτι μισεῖν αὐτὸν	et adiecerunt magis odisse eum	invidiae et odii fomitem ministravit	ויוספו עוד שנא אתו
Gen 38:5	καὶ προσθεῖσα ἔτι ἔτεκεν	et iterum concipiens et peperit	tertium quoque peperit	ותסף עוד ותלד
Gen 38:26	καὶ οὐ προσέθετο ἔτι τοῦ γνῶναι αὐτήν	(I) et non fuit amplius ausus contigere (S) et non est ausus amplius cognoscere (A) et non adposuit amplius scire	attamen ultra non cognovit illam	ולא־יסף עוד לדעתה
Gen 44:23	οὐ προσθήσεσθε ἔτι ἰδεῖν	non adponetis videre	non videbitis amplius	לא תספון לראות

In nine of these instances, the aforementioned syntagm (i.e. προστίθημι + infinitive complement) is rendered literally by the LXX. The OL consistently repeats this awkward language. In the remaining two instances (Gen 25:1 and 38:5), the LXX literally renders יסף with a participial form of προστίθημι, while the second verb is rendered as an aorist. This awkward language is again repeated within the OL. It should be noted that this language is awkward only in its use of προστίθημι/adicio/adpono to convey repetition. There are no rules of grammar being broken (i.e. infinitive complements commonly appear in both languages). Perhaps it is for this reason that the OL so consistently repeats the awkward language of the LXX (cf. the rendering of בין ב ... בין below).

In contrast, Jerome consistently avoids the use of *adicio* or *adpono*, and uses an adverb (i.e. *rursus* or *ultra*), an adjective (*alius*) or nothing at all to render יסף. Such an *ad sensum* rendering of יסף can be seen throughout the Octateuch.[25] It is likely that such sensitivity to the Hebrew demonstrates Jerome's increasing proficiency and/or freedom in the language. This seems especially true when one considers that the awkward language of the LXX and OL is precisely the language used by Jerome to render יסף in his earlier translations.[26] Kedar-Kopfstein writes, "There is a noticeable direction

---

[25] See also Exod 5:7; 8:25; 9:28; 10:28; 14:13; Num 22:15, 19; Deut 3:26; 5:25; 13:11; 18:16; Josh 7:12; 8:28; Judg 9:37; 11:14; 13:1, 21; 20:22–23, and 28.

[26] See 1 Sam 3:6, 8; 3:21; 27:4; 2 Sam 5:22; 7:10, 20; 14:10; 24:1; and 1 Kgs 16:33. By the time

in Jerome's technique from the earliest stages to the final one: it proceeds away from the use of stock equivalents towards the introduction of transformative rendition."[27]

Rendering בין ... בין. Among the various Hebrew prepositions, בין is unique in that it is usually paired with another preposition, namely בין or ל. If a Greek or Latin translator prefers to translate *ad verbum*, the resulting translation will include redundant elements (e.g. *inter* X *inter* Y). In a word, this creates bad Greek and Latin. Take for example Gen 3:15, where the LORD God tells the serpent that he will place enmity between him and the woman and between his seed and her seed. Accordingly, בין appears four times. The LXX faithfully imitates this by using the phrase ἀνὰ μέσον four times. In contrast, Jerome uses the preposition *inter* a single time in his translation. Within the Book of Genesis, the pairing of בין occurs 31 times.[28] Of these instances, there are only four occasions when Jerome chooses to translate the pairing of בין with a double use of the preposition *inter* (Gen 9:13, 16–17; and 17:7).[29] Thus a literal rendering appears only thirteen percent of the time.

Among the OL manuscripts, the overall rendering of this phrase is mixed. There are three instances where the passage is partially or entirely missing from the OL.[30] There are twelve instances where the OL manuscripts vary in their rendering of בין ... בין (i.e. both literal and non-literal readings appear).[31] There are twelve instances where the OL manuscripts unanimously avoid a literal rendering of the Hebrew phrase[32] and there are four instances where the OL manuscripts unanimously employ a literal rendering of the phrase.[33] Though the OL manuscripts are not entirely consistent, it is significant that the OL often deviates from the LXX by refusing a literal

---

Jerome reached 2 Kings, he appears to have stopped such redundancy (cf. 2 Kgs 6:23; 21:8; and 28:7).

[27] Kedar-Kopfstein, "The Vulgate as a Translation," 281–284. A similar notion is expressed by Kelly, *Jerome*, 162, who asserts that Jerome "tended to take greater liberties with the books he translated latest, so that while he justly scorned any suggestion that his Samuel and Kings could be described as a paraphrase, his version of Judges (404/5) comes pretty near to being one."

[28] Gen 1:4, 14, 18; 3:15 (×2); 9:12–13, 15–17; 10:12; 13:3, 7, 8 (×2); 16:5, 14; 17:2, 7, 10–11; 20:1; 23:15; 26:28; 30:36; 31:44, 48–51; and 32:17.

[29] Among these, Gen 9:13 is particularly interesting in that the Vulgate is the only version to include redundant elements.

[30] Gen 9:17; 23:15; and 31:51.

[31] Gen 1:4, 14, 18; 3:15 (×2); 9:12; 13:8 (×2); 17:2, 7, 10; and 26:28.

[32] Gen 9:13, 15; 10:12; 13:7; 16:5; 17:11; 20:1; 31:44, 48–50; and 32:17.

[33] Gen 9:16; 13:3; 16:14; and 30:36.

or redundant rendering. However, the OL never deviates from the rendering of the LXX when it is less literal or non-redundant. Thus it appears that, in this instance, the OL has a preference for non-awkward language. This may be due to influence of another tradition (Hexaplaric or Jeromian) or simply due to the awkwardness of the language.

Outside of the Vulgate of the Book of Genesis, we once again find that Jerome becomes increasingly periphrastic with the passage of time.[34] Within the prophets, a literal rendering appears for eight of the twenty occurrences (40%). Within Samuel and Kings, a literal rendering appears for eight of the twenty-eight occurrences (29%). Within Chronicles, a literal rendering is never used for the eight occurrences (0%). Within the Pentateuch, a literal rendering appears for six of the forty-six occurrences (13%). Finally, within Joshua, Judges, and Ruth, a literal rendering appears for only one of the sixteen occurrences (6%).[35]

Omission of Redundant Nouns. The development of Jerome's technique and/or ability within the Vulgate may be seen in his steady reduction of seemingly unnecessary proper nouns. Take the following verse for example:

Gen 16:2 (MT) וישמע אברם לקול שרי ... ותאמר שרי אל־אברם

Gen 16:2 (Vg.) *dixit marito suo ... cumque ille adquiesceret deprecanti ...*

Gen 16:2 (LXX) εἶπεν δὲ Σαρα πρὸς Αβραμ ὑπήκουσεν ... δὲ Αβραμ τῆς φωνῆς Σαρας

Gen 16:2 (OL) *dixit autem Sara ad Abram ...* [vacat]

By rendering 'Abram' once as 'husband' (*maritus*) and a second time as 'he' (*ille*), the identification of both Abram and Sarai becomes clear in each instance and Jerome is able to remove four of the five proper nouns found within this verse. This reduction of proper nouns can be seen throughout

---

[34] Our data is somewhat limited in that this phrase never appears in the Psalms, Job, Ezra, Nehemiah, Proverbs, Ecclesiastes, Canticles or Esther. Nevertheless, it should be noted that this steady decline in literal rendering supports the order of translation suggested by Kedar-Kopfstein (see above). In addition to the Genesis passages mentioned above, the relevant passages are Exod 8:19; 9:4; 11:7; 14:2, 20; 16:1; 18:16; 26:33; 30:18; 31:13, 31:17; 40:7, 30; Lev 10:10 (×2); 11:47 (×2); 26:46; 27:12, 14; Num 17:13; 21:13; 30:17; 35:24; Deut 1:1, 16 (×2); 5:5; 17:8; Josh 3:4; 8:9, 11–12; 18:11; 22:25, 27–28; 24:7; Judg 4:5, 17; 9:23; 11:27; 13:25; 16:31; Ruth 1:17; 1 Sam 7:12, 14; 14:42; 17:1; 20:3, 23, 42 (×2); 24:13, 16; 2 Sam 3:1, 6; 18:9; 21:7; 1 Kgs 5:26; 7:46; 14:30; 15:6–7, 16, 19 (×2), 32; 22:1, 34; 2 Kgs 11:17 (×2); 16:14; 1 Chr 21:16; 2 Chr 4:17; 13:2; 16:3 (×2); 18:33; 19:10; 23:16; Isa 5:3; 59:2; Jer 7:5; Ezek 4:3; 8:3, 16; 10:6; 20:12, 20; 34:20; 43:8; 44:23; 47:16, 18 (×2); 48:22; Zech 5:9; 11:14; Mal 2:14; and 3:18.

[35] The LXX consistently prefers a more literal rendering of the phrase: 16/20 (80%) for the Prophets; 21/28 (75%) for Samuel and Kings; 6/8 (75%) for Chronicles; 38/46 (83%) for the Pentateuch; and 11/16 (69%) for Joshua, Judges, and Ruth.

the Book of Genesis. By doing comparative searches on twenty of the most frequently appearing proper nouns within Genesis (which accounts for 45% of all proper nouns),[36] it can be demonstrated that, in these cases, Jerome has decreased the number of seemingly unnecessary proper nouns by 26%. That is, these same twenty nouns appear only 1041 times within the Vulgate, while they appear 1413 times within the MT (a ratio of 74 to 100). Compared to the LXX, this reduction is quite striking, considering that these twenty nouns appear a total of 1570 times within the LXX (a ratio of 111 to 100).[37]

Using Kedar-Kopfstein's classification and ordering of the books, I have conducted a similar comparative search of proper nouns for the remaining biblical books. A separate set of frequent proper nouns was determined for each group.[38]

	Vulgate	MT	LXX	Vg./MT	LXX/MT
(1) Psalms, Prophets	6954	6402	6376	108.62%	99.59%
(2) Samuel, Kings, Job	4479	3972	4622	112.76%	116.36%
(3) Ezra, Neh, Chron	2700	2753	2817	98.07%	102.32%
(4) Prov, Eccl, Song, Pent	5073	6046	6411	83.91%	106.04%
(5) Josh, Judg, Ruth, Esth	1487	1862	1967	79.86%	105.64%

The first three columns contain the number of proper nouns appearing from each frequency-set. The last two columns contain the percentage of proper

---

[36] These are: Lord, God, Moses, Israel, Egypt, Aaron, Pharaoh, Jacob, Joseph, Abraham, Isaac, Canaan, Esau, Levi, Levite, Jordan, Abram, Reuben, Balaam, and Noah. The proper nouns were searched in morphologically tagged databases in their respective languages (e.g. מֹשֶׁה, Μωυσῆς, and *Moses*). Searching on the twenty most common proper nouns yields a high percentage (usually a majority) of the total number of appearances of all proper nouns within any given biblical book.

[37] These comparisons are somewhat problematic in that they assume the texts created by and available to Jerome are the same as those of the digital versions. This is less problematic in the case of the MT, which, according to Emanuel Tov (*Textual Criticism of the Hebrew Bible* [Minneapolis: Fortress, 1992], 153), is "almost identical" with the source of the Vulgate. Regarding the Greek texts that were available to Jerome, in light of his numerous references to the LXX, his numerous references to various Hexaplaric readings, and his knowledge of the Hexapla in Caesarea, one may assume that Jerome would have had access to a broad range of readings. See Dennis Brown, *Vir Trilinguis, A Study in the Biblical Exegesis of Saint Jerome* (Kampen: Kok Pharos, 1992), 55–62.

[38] Kedar-Kopfstein has classified the various books into separate groups according to chronology and quality. Accordingly, with the passage of time, each group becomes less literal. According to his terminology: (1) Psalms, Prophets = rigid, detached; (2) Samuel, Kings, Job = imitative, detached; (3) Ezra, Nehemiah, Chronicles = detached, (4) Solomon's books, Pentateuch = detached, transformative, (5) Joshua, Judges, Ruth, Esther = transformative. See Kedar-Kopfstein, "Vulgate as a Translation," 284.

nouns in the Vulgate and the LXX as compared to those of the MT. Notice that in the books translated earlier (i.e. groups one and two), Jerome has actually increased the number of proper nouns when compared to the MT. In the case of group two, Jerome may have done so under the influence of the LXX, which also has a ratio of proper nouns in excess of 100% when compared to the MT.[39] A sharp decline to 98% is seen when proceeding down to group three. Similarly groups four and five see an even further decrease in seemingly redundant proper nouns.

Narrowing our focus to individual books and limiting our analysis to books containing substantial amounts of narrative, like Genesis, here is a further breakdown of the numbers.

	Vg.	MT	LXX	Vg./MT	LXX/MT
(2) Samuel	2429	2034	2395	119.42%	117.75%
(2) Kings	1900	1888	2089	100.64%	110.65%
(3) Ezra	280	197	270	142.13%	137.06%
(3) Nehemiah	268	260	259	103.08%	99.62%
(3) Chronicles	2152	2296	2288	93.73%	99.65%
(4) Genesis	1041	1413	1570	73.67%	111.11%
(4) Exodus	1264	1459	1455	86.63%	99.73%
(4) Leviticus	545	616	673	88.47%	109.25%
(4) Numbers	1037	1232	1276	84.17%	103.57%
(4) Deuteronomy	1045	1189	1276 *sic!*	87.89%	107.32%
(5) Joshua	745	899	920	82.87%	102.34%
(5) Judges	600	764	792	78.53%	103.66%
(5) Esther	113	168	216	67.26%	128.57%

Overall, the ratio of proper nouns in the Vulgate as compared to the MT sees a steady decrease from one book to the next. Two unusual ratios are those of Ezra and Genesis. Though Ezra was translated after both Samuel and Kings, it contains a much higher ration of proper nouns. Considering the LXX's similarly high ratio, it may be that Jerome was influenced by his Greek copy of Ezra. Though Jerome translated Genesis at an earlier period, its ratio of

---

[39] The increased percentage of the Vg./MT score might be problematic for Kedar-Kopfstein's position that the Prophets were translated prior to Samuel and Kings. However, the *genre* of the literature may be an influential factor in this regard (i.e. prose literature might lend itself to such emendations more so than poetry). For data which supports Kedar-Kopfstein's position, see the distribution of בין ... בין (above) and David L. Everson, "An Examination of Synoptic Portions within the Vulgate," *VT* 58 (2008): 178–190.

proper nouns is considerably lower than the ratio for the remainder of the Pentateuch and for Joshua and Judges. Among all the books of the Vulgate, in this instance, Genesis provides one of the least literal translations.

Conclusion

In light of the four analyses above, the following observations may be offered. We have observed that the OL tends to follow the LXX more so than reflect the influence of Jeromian or Hexaplaric traditions. In examining all of the proper nouns that appear as *hapax legomena* within the book of Genesis, we observed that the OL usually does not deviate from the LXX. Significantly, when the OL does deviate from the LXX, it does not appear to be under the influence of the Vulgate or another tradition (i.e. the OL reading is unique). In the rendering of יסף, the OL again does not deviate from the LXX, despite the awkwardness of the resulting translation. In the rendering of בין ... בין, we observed that it is common for the OL manuscripts to deviate from the LXX by refusing a literal or redundant rendering of בין ... בין. At the same time, the OL manuscripts *never* deviate from the LXX when the reverse is true. Thus it appears that, in this instance, the OL has a preference for non-awkward language. To put it briefly, the OL consistently follows the LXX and, in doing so, is happy to bend the rules of grammar, though it occasionally prefers not to break them.

In all of the analyses above, Jerome consistently follows the MT vis-à-vis the LXX but does so with ever increasing freedom in his translation. Of the sixty-eight *hapax legomena* listed above, there are only three occasions where the Vulgate agrees with the LXX and OL against the MT. Moreover, of the sixty-five instances of agreement between the Vulgate and the MT, thirty-two of those disagree with the LXX. Thus not only does Jerome prefer the reading of the MT, he often does so in disagreement with the LXX. In the three remaining analyses, Jerome's increasing freedom in translating Hebrew is clearly demonstrated. In rendering יסף, the Vulgate consistently avoids the awkward use of *adicio* or *adpono* but, rather, uses an adverb, an adjective or nothing at all to render the verb. Likewise, of the thirty-one occurrences of בין ... בין in the Book of Genesis, there are only four instances with the awkward redundancy of prepositions. Such freedom once again appears to be a characteristic of this later period of translation, since his earlier translations regularly included redundant prepositions in rendering this phrase (i.e. in Samuel in Kings). Finally, in examining more than 20,000 occurrences of frequently appearing common proper nouns within the MT, we observed a steady reduction of seemingly redundant proper nouns within the Vulgate.

What might account for Jerome's increasing freedom in translating the MT? One possibility is that, since the books translated at a later period were of lesser theological importance to him, Jerome may have felt freer to take liberties. However, as Kedar-Kopfstein has pointed out, the free renderings of important theological passages within the Pentateuch make this option seem less likely. He writes, "it seems that changes in the translation technique follow a chronological pattern rather than an ideological motivation."[40] Thus it seems most likely that as the years went by, having translated an ever-increasing number of Hebrew books, Jerome's confidence and proficiency with the Hebrew language would have allowed him greater freedom, which resulted in freer translations.

SELECT BIBLIOGRAPHY

Barr, Jane. "The Vulgate Genesis and St. Jerome's Attitude to Women." Pages 268–273 in *Papers Presented to the Eighth International Conference on Patristic Studies Held in Oxford, 1979*. Edited by E.A. Livingstone. Studia patristica 18. Oxford: Pergamon, 1982.

Brown, Dennis. *Vir Trilinguis: A Study in the Biblical Exegesis of Saint Jerome*. Kampen: Kok Pharos, 1992.

Cummings, J.T. "St. Jerome as Translator and as Exegete." Pages 279–282 in *Papers Presented to the Sixth International Conference on Patristic Studies Held in Oxford, 1971*. Edited by E.A. Livingstone. Studia patristica 12. Berlin: Akademie-Verlag, 1975.

Evans, Craig A. "Jerome's Translation of Isaiah 6:9–10." *Vigiliae Christianae* 38 (1984): 202–204.

Fischer, Bonifatius. *Vetus Latina: Die Reste der altlateinischen Bibel nach Petrus Sabatier neu gesammelt und herausgegeben von der Erzabtei Beuron, 2. Genesis*. Freiburg: Herder, 1949–1954.

Ginzberg, Louis. "Die Haggada bei den Kirchenvätern, VI: Der Kommentar des Hieronymus zu Jesaja." Pages 279–314 in *Jewish Studies in Memory of George A. Kohut*. Edited by Salo W. Baron and Alexander Marx. New York: The Alexander Kohut Memorial Foundation, 1935.

Graves, Michael. *Jerome's Hebrew Philology: A Study Based on his Commentary on*

---

[40] Kedar-Kopfstein, "The Vulgate as a Translation," 285. Also, the seemingly incremental developments in technique from one book to the next (or even within the same book) occurring steadily over long periods of time, would suggest that these resulted from natural developments in Jerome's Hebrew proficiency and not theologically determined decisions.

Jeremiah. Supplements to Vigiliae Christianae: Texts and Studies of Early Christian Life and Language 90. Leiden: Brill, 2007.

Hagendahl, Harald. "Jerome and the Latin Classics." *Vigiliae Christianae* 28 (1974): 216–227.

Hayward, C.T.R. *Saint Jerome's Hebrew Questions on Genesis: Translated with an Introduction and Commentary.* Oxford Early Christian Studies. Oxford: Clarendon, 1995.

Hennings, Ralph. "Rabbinisches und Antijüdisches bei Hieronymus Ep. 121,10." Pages 49–71 in *Christliche Exegese zwischen Nicaea und Chalcedon.* Edited by J. van Oort and U. Wickert. Kampen: Kok Pharos, 1992.

Kamesar, Adam. *Jerome, Greek Scholarship, and the Hebrew Bible: A Study of the 'Quaestiones Hebraicae in Genesim'.* Oxford Classical Monographs. Oxford: Clarendon, 1993.

Kamin, Sarah. "The Theological Significance of the Hebraica Veritas in Jerome's Thought." Pages 243–253 in *'Sha'arei Talmon': Studies in the Bible, Qumran, and the Ancient Near East Presented to Shemaryahu Talmon.* Edited by Michael A. Fishbane and Emanuel Tov. Winona Lake, Ind.: Eisenbrauns, 1991.

Kedar-Kopfstein, Benjamin. "Textual Gleanings from the Vulgate to Hosea." *The Jewish Quarterly Review* 65 (1974): 73–97.

———. "The Latin Translations." Pages 299–338 in *Mikra: Text, Translation, Reading and Interpretation of the Hebrew Bible in Ancient Judaism and Early Christianity* Edited by Martin Jan Mulder. Compendia Rerum Iudaicarum ad Novum Testamentum 2/1. Assen: Van Gorcum, 1988.

———. "The Vulgate as a Translation: Some Semantic and Syntactical Aspects of Jerome's Version of the Hebrew Bible." Ph.D. diss., The University of Jerusalem, 1968.

Kelly, J.N.D. *Jerome: His Life, Writings, and Controversies.* London: Duckworth, 1975.

Klein, Samuel. "Targumische Elemente in der Deutung biblischer Ortsnamen bei Hieronymus." *Monatsschrift für Geschichte und Wissenschaft des Judentums* 83 (1939): 132–141.

Kraus, Matthew A. "Hebraisms in the Old Latin Version of the Bible." *Vetus Testamentum* 53 (2003): 487–513.

Kreuzer, Siegfried. "Towards the Old Greek: New Criteria for the Analysis of the Recensions of the Septuagint (Especially the Antiochene/Lucianic Text and Kaige Recension)." Pages 239–253 in *XIII Congress of the International Organization for Septuagint and Cognate Studies, Ljubljana, 2007.* Edited by Melvin K.H. Peters. Society of Biblical Literature Septuagint and Cognate Studies 55. Atlanta: Scholars Press, 2008.

Marcos, Natalio Fernández. "The Old Latin of Chronicles Between the Greek and the Hebrew." Page 123–136 in *IX Congress of the International Organization for Septuagint and Cognate Studies, Cambridge, 1995.* Edited by Bernard A. Taylor. Society of Biblical Literature Septuagint and Cognate Studies 45. Atlanta: Scholars Press, 1997.

Meerschoek, G.Q.A. *Le latin biblique d'après saint Jérôme.* Latinitas Christianorum Primaeva 20. Nijmegen: Dekker & Van de Vegt, 1966.

Plater, W.E., and H.J. White. *A Grammar of the Vulgate: Being an Introduction to the Study of the Latinity of the Vulgate Bible.* Oxford: Clarendon, 1926.

Rebenich, Stefan. *Jerome*. The Early Church Fathers. London: Routledge, 2002.
Sparks, H.F.D. "Jerome as Biblical Scholar." Pages 510–541 in *The Cambridge History of the Bible, Volume 1: From the Beginnings to Jerome*. Edited by P.R. Ackroyd and C.F. Evans. Cambridge: Cambridge University Press, 1970.
Tkacz, Catherine Brown. "Labor tam Utilis: The Creation of the Vulgate." *Vigiliae Christianae* 50 (1996): 42–72.
Ulrich, Eugene. "Characteristics and Limitations of the Old Latin Translations of the Septuagint." Pages 67–80 in *La Septuaginta en la Investigacion contemporanea (V Congreso de la IOSCS)*. Edited by Natalio Fernández Marcos. Textos y estudios "Cardenal Cisneros" de la Biblia Políglota Matritense 34. Madrid: Instituto "Arias Montano," 1985.

GENESIS IN SYRIAC

Jerome A. Lund

Three translations of the Book of Genesis into Syriac exist, namely the Peshitta,[1] the translation made by Paul of Tella that we call the Syrohexapla,[2] and the translation made by Jacob of Edessa.[3] The Peshitta renders a Hebrew

---

[1] The Leiden scientific edition of the Peshitta version of Genesis was prepared by members of the Peshitta Institute in Leiden based on material collected and studied by Taeke Jansma. The resultant volume (co-edited with Marinus D. Koester), *The Old Testament in Syriac According to the Peshitta Version—Part I, 1. Preface, Genesis – Exodus* (Leiden: Brill, 1977), forms the basis of this essay. I will hereafter refer to this as "Leiden Genesis." The term "Peshitta" (ܦܫܺܝܛܬܳܐ; "simple," "straightforward"), first attested in the writings of the ninth century theologian Moshe bar Kepha, was introduced to distinguish the earlier translations of the Old and New Testaments from the seventh century translations (Sebastian P. Brock, *The Bible in the Syriac Tradition* [GH 7; rev. ed.; Piscataway, N.J.; Gorgias, 2006], 23; for other views see Piet B. Dirksen, "The Old Testament Peshitta," in *Mikra: Text, Translation, Reading and Interpretation of the Hebrew Bible in Ancient Judaism and Early Christianity* [ed. Martin Jan Mulder; CRINT 2/1; Assen: Van Gorcum, 1988], 255–256). Further, one should be aware of the fact that the history of the Old Testament Peshitta has nothing to do with the history of the New Testament Peshitta which begins some 300 years after that of the Old Testament.

[2] Two MSS of the Syrohexapla to Genesis are known: British Library Add 14442, described by William Wright as a document written in a seventh century Estrangela script in his *Catalogue of Syriac Manuscripts in the British Museum, acquired since the year 1838*, Part I, entry XLVIII (London: Trustees of the British Museum, 1870; repr., Piscataway, N.J.: Gorgias, 2002) and published by Paul de Lagarde in his *Bibliothecae Syriacae* (Göttingen: Dietrich Lueder Horstmann, 1892), and a Midyat MS published by Arthur Vööbus in his *The Pentateuch in the Version of the Syro-Hexapla: A Facsimile Edition of a Midyat MS Discovered 1964* (CSCO 369, Subsidia 45; Leuven: Peeters, 1975). The British Library MS contains Gen 4:8b–9:24a; 16:2b–12a; 20:1b–12; 31:53b–32:12; 36:2b–40:17; 43:1b–47:16a; and 50:17a–26. The Midyat MS preserves Gen 32:9–50:26. At the time of the Renaissance in the sixteenth century, the European scholar Andreas Masius had access to the entire text of Genesis in a volume containing the first half of the Old Testament, but his text vanished without a trace (Brock, *The Bible in the Syriac Tradition*, 47; and Brock, *An Introduction to Syriac Studies* [GH 4; Piscataway, N.J.: Gorgias, 2006], 36).

[3] His text of Genesis has not yet been published, preserved in large part in MS Paris, Bibliothèque Nationale Syr. 26. According to Alison Salvesen, Gen 1:16–3:20, 32:13–33:10, and 43:33–44:28 are missing from the MS (Alison Salvesen, "The Genesis Texts of Jacob of Edessa: A Study in Variety," in *Text, Translation, and Tradition: Studies on the Peshitta and Its Use in the Syriac Tradition, Presented to Konrad D. Jenner on the Occasion of his Sixty-Fifth Birthday* [ed. W.Th. van Peusen and R.B. ter Haar Romeny; MPIL 14; Leiden: Brill, 2006], 178). Based on several citations of Genesis found in Philoxenus' commentary on Matthew and Luke, R.G. Jenkins has suggested that Philoxenus had a fourth translation of Genesis at his

text that stands in the proto-Masoretic tradition. Paul of Tella translated the Greek text into Syriac to give Syrian church pastors and scholars access to the Greek for comparative purposes.[4] He incorporated hexaplaric annotations in the text and notes in the margins, so that this text constitutes a valuable witness not only to the Old Greek translation, but also to those of Aquila, Symmachos, and Theodotion. Jacob of Edessa used the Peshitta as his base text, while utilizing the Greek Bible, apparently directly, rather than utilizing the Syrohexapla.[5] His purpose was to update the language, producing a contemporary translation.[6]

Jews translated the Book of Genesis from Hebrew into Syriac about CE 150 in the environs of Edessa,[7] though Christians preserved the text as their translation. Michael Weitzman has suggested that the same community that translated the text preserved the text, moving from being adherents to a form of Judaism to being Christians.[8] Since Tatian cites the Peshitta Old Testament in his Diatessaron, the text had been in use by CE 170.[9]

Paul of Tella did his work in Alexandria, Egypt, in 615–617.[10] One could guess that he translated Genesis first. He rendered the Old Greek translation of Origen into Syriac, preserving references to Aquila, Symmachos, and Theodotion in the margins using signs utilized by Origen. Paul of Tella represented as much of the Greek as possible in his translation. Thus, he rendered "your name" by two words, ܫܡܐ ܕܝܠܟ, as in Greek in contrast

---

disposal from CE 508, possibly produced under his auspices (R.G. Jenkins, *The Old Testament Quotations of Philoxenus of Mabbug* [CSCO 514; Subsidia 84; Louvain: Peeters, 1989], 130–156, 203–204). So far, this meagre evidence drawn from a commentary on the New Testament has failed to convince anyone else of such a revised version of Genesis termed "Philoxenian."

[4] Vööbus, *Pentateuch*, 18. See also Jerome A. Lund, "Syntactic Features of the Syrohexapla of Ezekiel," *AS* 4 (2006): 67–81, at 81.

[5] R.B. ter Haar Romeny, "Jacob of Edessa on Genesis: His Quotations of the Peshitta and his Revision of the Text," in *Jacob of Edessa and the Syriac Culture of His Day* (ed. R.B. ter Haar Romeny; MPIL 18; Leiden: Brill, 2008) 149–150. See also Salvesen, "Genesis Texts of Jacob of Edessa," 177–188.

[6] Ter Haar Romeny, "Jacob of Edessa," 145.

[7] Michael P. Weitzman, *The Syriac Version of the Old Testament: An Introduction* (UCOP 56; Cambridge: Cambridge University Press, 1999), 258.

[8] Weitzman, *The Syriac Version*, 259, states: "The reason why a Jewish translation came to be transmitted by the eastern churches is simple: a Jewish community converted to Christianity, bringing with it a version of the Hebrew Bible."

[9] Jan Joosten, *The Syriac Language of the Peshitta and Old Syriac Versions of Matthew: Syntactic Structure, Inner-Syriac Developments and Translation Technique* (SSL 22; Leiden: Brill, 1996), 25–27; and Joosten, "The Old Testament Quotations in the Old Syriac and Peshitta Gospels," *Textus* 15 (1990): 55–76, esp. 75–76.

[10] Brock, *The Bible in the Syriac Tradition*, 28.

to the Peshitta ܫܡܟ (Gen 35:10). Moreover, he distinguished the Greek imperfect from the aorist by rendering it as a compound, denoting duration: he rendered the Greek imperfect κατῴκει as ܗܘܐ ܝܬܒ ("and he was dwelling"; Gen 37:1).[11] Yet, while retaining a one to one correspondence in number of words, Paul of Tella retained the infinitive absolute of the Peshitta against the Greek: ܡܐܬܐ ܢܐܬܐ ܐܢܐ ܘܐܡܟ ܘܐܚܝܟ ܠܡܣܓܕ ܠܟ ܥܠ ܐܪܥܐ ("Should I and your mother and your brothers in fact come to bow down to you on the ground?"; Gen 37:10).[12]

The polymath Jacob of Edessa produced his "rectified" (ܡܬܩܢ)[13] translation using both the version found among the Greeks and the version found among the Syrians,[14] finishing his version of Genesis in 704.[15] Jacob seems to have used the Peshitta as his base text, while using a text of the Greek Bible directly, as he was fluent in Greek. He did not need to use Paul of Tella's version as a crutch for accessing the Greek. His updating of language appears in Genesis.[16] Whereas the Peshitta could use the suffix conjugation of the verb ܗܘܐ as a past tense, Jacob could not do so. Jacob substituted current language by using the compound ܐܝܬ ܗܘܐ to indicate past tense. Contrast his rendering ܐܝܬܝܗ ܗܘܬ ܥܩܪܬܐ "Sarai was barren" with the rendering of the Peshitta ܗܘܬ ܥܩܪܬܐ having the same meaning (Gen 11:30). Further, with regard to vocabulary, Jacob uses the noun ܡܕܝܢܬܐ to connote "city" as over against ܩܪܝܬܐ used by the Peshitta (Gen 11:4). By the time of Jacob of Edessa, the lexeme ܩܪܝܬܐ had taken on the meaning "field, village" in contrast to "city."

---

[11] Paul rendered the aorist παρῴκησεν later in the verse by ܐܬܬܘܬܒ ("he sojourned").

[12] Greek: ἀρά γε ἐλθόντες ἐλευσόμεθα ἐγώ τε καὶ ἡ μήτηρ σου καὶ οἱ ἀδελφοί σου προσκυνῆσαί σοι ἐπὶ τὴν γῆν. It would be interesting to compare the translation technique of Genesis with a book translated later to see whether Paul of Tella changed the way he handled this problem. The Old Greek rarely used an infinitive to represent the Hebrew infinitive absolute; here it uses the participle. On the Old Greek, see Emanuel Tov, "Renderings of Combinations of the Infinitive Absolute and Finite Verbs in the Septuagint—Their Nature and Distribution," in *The Greek and Hebrew Bible: Collected Essays on the Septuagint* (VTSup 72; Leiden: Brill, 1999), 247–256, esp. 247–248.

[13] By "rectified," Jacob meant the amplification of the text of the Peshitta with secondary readings from the Greek or the replacing of difficult readings in the Peshitta with less ambiguous phraseology from the Greek (Salvesen, "Genesis Texts of Jacob of Edessa,' 188). Salvesen suggests that Jacob held the view that the differences between the Syriac and Greek traditions arose providentially "and that one tradition could be used to explain the obscurities in the text of the other" (Salvesen, "Genesis Texts of Jacob of Edessa," 188).

[14] Ter Haar Romeny, "Jacob of Edessa," 147.
[15] Ter Haar Romeny, "Jacob of Edessa," 146.
[16] Ter Haar Romeny, "Jacob of Edessa," 152–153.

This essay will treat the Peshitta version of Genesis since it is a primary version of the Hebrew text. Issues discussed will include the Syriac text of the Peshitta, techniques of translation utilized by the Peshitta, Palestinian Jewish influence on the Peshitta, Hebrew variants indicated by the Peshitta, and interpretations of the Hebrew offered by the Peshitta.

THE TEXT OF THE PESHITTA OF GENESIS: THE ISSUE OF MS 5B1

The first issue facing the researcher focuses on the question of what is the text of the Peshitta of Genesis? The Peshitta Institute of Leiden has published the first scientific edition of the Peshitta text of Genesis. The editor used MS 7a1 as the base text since it is the earliest complete MS of the entire Old Testament. The early MS 5b1 provides some interesting Syriac variants and there seems to be a consensus that it generally represents a more primitive text than 7a1.[17] Some pages in the MS,[18] in which 5b1 appears, are apparently replacement pages representing the fifth century text, some copied in the eighth century and, hence, labeled 8/5b1 and some from the tenth century and, hence, labeled 10/5b1.[19] For the most part, the Syriac text of Genesis is homogenous. Sebastian Brock articulates the theory of textual development widely held, dividing the text history of the Peshitta into three periods: 1) the oldest text, which lies closest to the Hebrew preserved by the MT; 2) the middle stage represented by MSS from the sixth to eighth centuries, in which scribes made slight improvements "in the interest of good Syriac idiom"; and 3) the Received Text witnessed from the ninth century on, during which time further improvements were made.[20]

---

[17] M.D. Koster, *The Peshitta of Exodus: The Development of its Text in the Course of Fifteen Centuries* (SSN 19; Assen: Van Gorcum, 1977), advocates this view. See also his studies "Which Came First: the Chicken or the Egg? The Development of the Peshitta of Genesis and Exodus in the Light of Recent Studies," in *The Peshitta: Its Early Text and History. Papers Read at the Peshitta Symposium held at Leiden 30–31 August 1985* (ed. Piet B. Dirksen and Martin Jan Mulder; MPIL 4; Leiden: Brill, 1988), 99–126; and "Peshitta Revisited: A Reassessment of its Value as a Version," *JSS* 38 (1993): 235–268. Koster confirmed the view propounded by John Pinkerton, "The Origin and Early History of the Syriac Pentateuch," *JTS* 15 (1914): 14–41, as against that put forth by W.E. Barnes, "A New Edition of the Pentateuch in Syriac," *JTS* 15 (1914): 41–44.
[18] London, British Museum, Add. Ms 14.425. Folios 1b-115b contain Genesis.
[19] Leiden Genesis, vi.
[20] Brock, *The Bible in the Syriac Tradition*, 46.

When it comes to Genesis, one can not determine the best text without examining each case individually. For example, 5b1 reads ܘܠܚܘܝܐ "and the Hivites" instead of ܘܠܚܘܪܝܐ "and the Horites" (7a1 = MT; Gen 14:6), an obvious transmission error in 5b1. Moreover, 5b1 reads ܡܢ ܐܪܥܐ ܕܡܨܪܝܢ "from the land of Egypt" against ܡܢ ܢܗܪܐ ܕܡܨܪܝܢ "from the river of Egypt" (7a1 = MT; Gen 15:18). Again, the reading of 5b1 is secondary in light of the MT. By contrast, 8/5b1 preserves the better reading in Gen 5:4 where, like the MT, it reads ܘܗܘܘ ܝܘܡܬܗ ܕܐܕܡ "and the days of Adam were" against 7a1 which reads ܘܚܝܐ ܐܕܡ "and Adam lived." In Gen 19:16, 5b1 reads ܓܒܪܐ "men" (MT: הָאֲנָשִׁים) in agreement with the MT, while 7a1 renders ܡܠܐܟܐ "messengers, angels" conforming the text to the previous verse where these same beings are identified as ܡܠܐܟܐ. In short, the Syriac text form that stands closest to the MT represents the earliest text form for Genesis.

In Genesis, 5b1 often preserves the more primitive Syriac reading as over against 7a1. In Gen 30:30, 5b1 contains the preferred primitive reading ܒܪ ܪܓܠܝ in the clause ܘܒܪܟܟ ܡܪܝܐ ܒܪ ܪܓܠܝ ("and the Lord blessed you at my foot"), mirroring the Hebrew of the MT וַיְבָרֶךְ יְהוָה אֹתְךָ לְרַגְלִי ("and the LORD blessed you at my foot"). 7a1 contains the inner Syriac variant ܡܛܠܬܝ ("on account of me") for ܒܪ ܪܓܠܝ, which reading clarifies the meaning of the text. In Gen 21:30, 7a1 adds the expressed subject "Abraham" to the earlier text form represented by 5b1 = MT, making clear the shift in subject from Abimelech of the previous verse. 7a1 also adds the expressed subject "Jacob" in Gen 28:19, 29:25, 30:29, and 32:9, where 5b1 = MT do not have an expressed subject. Further, the text attested by 7a1 also adds the indirect object in a number of cases, where 5b1 (= MT) has none: 7a1 reads ܘܐܡܪ ܐܠܗܐ ܠܐܒܪܗܡ ("and God said to Abraham") against 5b1 (= MT) which reads ܘܐܡܪ ܐܠܗܐ ("and God said"); 7a1 reads ܘܐܡܪ ܐܒܝܡܠܟ ܠܐܒܪܗܡ ("and Abimelech said to Abraham") against 5b1 (= MT) which reads ܘܐܡܪ ܐܒܝܡܠܟ ("and Abimelech said"). In Gen 26:3, 5b1 reads ܟܠܗܝܢ ܐܪܥܬܐ ܗܠܝܢ ("all these lands"; = MT) against ܟܠܗܝܢ ܡܠܟܘܬܐ ܗܠܝܢ ("all these kingdoms") of 7a1. In Gen 39:20, 5b1 reads ܘܢܣܒܗ ܡܪܗ ܠܝܘܣܦ ("and his master took Joseph"; = MT) against 7a1 which reads only ܘܢܣܒܗ ܡܪܗ ("and his master took him"). In Gen 7:13, 8/5b1 reads ܥܡܗܘܢ ("with them") in conformity to the MT, while 7a1 reads ܥܡܗ ("with him"), which appears to be an "improvement" of the text. When using the Leiden scientific edition of the Peshitta, then, one must always look at the apparatuses for variants represented by 5b1 in determining the earliest Syriac text form.

In cases where both Syriac readings conform to the Hebrew preserved by the MT, it is difficult to determine the more primitive reading. The most interesting variant has to do with the rendering of the "sons of God" in

Gen 6. MS 7a1 transliterates the word "God," rendering ܒܢܝ̈ ܐܠܘܗܝܡ "sons of Alohim" (Gen 6:2, 4). By contrast, 8/5b1 preserves an early Jewish exegesis of the "sons of God" as ܒܢܝ̈ ܕܝܢܐ "sons of judges." Arie van der Kooij has discussed these readings at length and believes that the reading of 7a1 was original in this instance.[21] In Gen 6:6–7, 7a1 reads the verb ܐܬܬܘܝ as over against 8/5b1 which reads ܐܬܬܘ, both meaning "to regret." Where there is no difference in meaning one can not argue convincingly for one reading over against the other.[22]

Throughout Genesis, 5b1 renders Hebrew כֶּסֶף as ܟܣܦܐ. 7a1 exhibits an inner Syiac development in expression, according to M.D. Koster, where it retains ܟܣܦܐ to indicate "silver" as money, but uses Greek ܐܣܐܡܐ to indicate "silver" as metal (Gen 13:2; 24:35, 53; 44:2, 8).[23] This, in his opinion, demonstrates an inner Syriac development for clearer expression in the text. Gen 44:8, according to 7a1, serves as the parade example because it contains both meanings, silver as money and silver as metal: ܗܐ ܟܣܦܐ ܕܐܫܟܚܢ ܒܦܘܡ ܛܥܢܝ̈. ܐܗܦܟܢܝܗܝ، ܡܢ ܐܪܥܐ ܕܟܢܥܢ. ܐܝܟܢܐ ܓܢܒܝܢ ܗܘܝܢ ܡܢ ܒܝܬ ܡܪܟ ܕܗܒܐ ܐܘ ܐܣܐܡܐ. (NRSV: "Look, the money that we found at the top of our sacks, we brought back to you from the land of Canaan; why then would we steal silver or gold from your lord's house?"). According to Koster, then, the 7a1 tradition changed the reading preserved by 5b1, namely, the second ܟܣܦܐ, into ܐܣܐܡܐ. Arie van der Kooij disagrees with this assessment, viewing the differentiation between the usages as original, bringing other cases of two Syriac words translating the same Hebrew word for a purpose.[24]

In Gen 24:55, the Hebrew preserved by the MT reads תֵּשֵׁב הַנַּעַר[25] אִתָּנוּ יָמִים אוֹ עָשׂוֹר ("let the young woman stay with us days or ten"), while the

[21] Arie van der Kooij, "Peshitta Genesis 6: 'Sons of God'—Angels or Judges?," *JNSL* 23 (1997): 43–51, esp. 48–49. Cf. Jerome A. Lund, "Observations on Some Biblical Citations in Ephrem's Commentary on Genesis," *AS* 4 (2006): 205–218, esp. 211–212.

[22] Outside of this context, there is very meagre evidence for the existence of the root ܬܘܝ in Syriac. See Robert Payne Smith, ed., *Thesaurus Syriacus* (Oxford: Clarendon, 1879–1901), col. 4406. See also Lund, "Observations on Some Biblical Citations in Ephrem's Commentary," 209–210.

[23] Koster, *The Peshitta of Exodus*, 70–72 and Jan Joosten, "Greek and Latin Words in the Peshitta Pentateuch: First Soundings," in *Symposium Syriacum VII* (ed. René Lavenant; OrChrAn 256; Roma: Pontificio Istituto Orientale, 1998), 41.

[24] Arie van der Kooij, "On the Significance of MS 5b1 for the Peshitta Genesis," in Piet B. Dirksen and Martin Jan Mulder (eds.), *The Peshitta: Its Early Text and History. Papers Read at the Peshitta Symposium held at Leiden 30–31 August 1985* (MPIL 4; Leiden: Brill, 1988) 183–199, esp. 192–193 and 197.

[25] Perhaps read with the qere הַנַּעֲרָה—see also v. 14.

Samaritan Hebrew reads תשב הנערה אתנו ימים או חדש ("let the young woman stay with us for days or a month"). The Peshitta according to 7a1 reads ܬܬܒ ܥܠܝܡܬܐ ܥܡܢ ܝܪܚ ܝܘܡܝܢ ("let the young woman stay with us a month of days"), as though it has read חדש ימים (Gen 29:14; Num 11:20–21). But 5b1 reads ܬܬܒ ܥܠܝܡܬܐ ܥܡܢ ܙܒܢ ܚܕ ܐܘ ܥܣܪܐ ܝܪܚܝܢ ("let the young woman stay with us some time or ten months"), which is precisely the reading of Targum Onqelos: תתיב עולימתא עימנא עידן בעידן או עסרה ירחין. Due to its identity with the reading of Targum Onqelos, 5b1 probably reflects the earlier Peshitta text, while 7a1 contains an updating of the language.

Translation Technique
(From Hebrew Source Text to Syriac)

Idiomatic Syriac characterizes the Peshitta of Gen 4:9, which reads ܕܠܡܐ ܐܢܐ ܢܛܪ ܐܚܝ ("Am I my brother's keeper?"). The translator added the Semitic particle ܕܠܡܐ to mark this sentence as a rhetorical question.[26] Further, the translator added the Semitic particle ܕܝܢ in the apodosis to express a condition incapable of being fulfilled: ܘܐܪܐ ܐܠܘ ܠܐ ܐܫܬܘܚܪܢ ܕܝܢ ܟܒܪ ܗܦܟܢ ܬܪܬܝܢ ܙܒܢܝܢ ("And if we had not delayed, we would have already returned twice"; Gen 43:10).[27] The following case also belongs here, where the protasis is understood: ܫܕܪܬܟ ܕܝܢ ܒܚܕܘܬܐ ܘܒܙܡܝܪܬܐ ([Had you not done so,] "then I would have sent you away with mirth and with song"; Gen 31:27).

Constructions using syndeton and asyndeton vary from Hebrew to Syriac. Consequently, the translator rendered the Hebrew syndetic construction of the type לְכוּ וְנַהַרְגֵהוּ ("come and let us kill him"; Gen 37:20) and לְכוּ וְנִמְכְּרֶנּוּ ("come and let us sell him"; Gen 37:27)[28] asyndetically as ܬܘ ܢܩܛܠܝܘܗܝ, ("come, let us kill him") and ܬܘ ܢܙܒܢܝܘܗܝ, ("come, let us sell him") respectively in conformity with the rules of Syriac grammar. Furthermore, where Hebrew has the asyndetic construction כִּתְמוֹל שִׁלְשׁוֹם ("as yesterday, the day before"), the Syriac has a syndetic construction ܐܝܟ ܕܐܬܡܠܝ ܘܐܝܟ ܕܡܢܬܡܠܝ ("as yesterday and as the day before"; Gen 31:2, 5).

---

[26] Jan Joosten, "The Use of Some Particles in the Old Testament Peshitta," *Textus* 14 (1988): 178–179. This Semitic ܕܠܡܐ has been joined by the Greek intruder ܕܠܡܐ in Syriac.

[27] Joosten, "The Use of Some Particles," 179–180. Semitic ܕܝܢ means "then" if translated.

[28] That is, imperative + *waw* + cohortative.

In introducing main clauses after subordinate time clauses and conditional clauses, the Peshitta omits the *waw* found in the Hebrew in keeping with Syriac grammar. Thus, it renders Hebrew וַיְהִי כִשְׁמֹעַ לָבָן ... וַיָּרָץ לִקְרָאתוֹ as ܘܟܕ ܫܡܥ ܠܒܢ ... ܪܗܛ ܠܐܘܪܥܗ ("and it was when Laban heard ... he ran toward him"; Gen 29:13), omitting the *waw* of Hebrew וַיָּרָץ after the temporal clause. Moreover, it renders the Hebrew אִם־אֶמְצָא בִסְדֹם חֲמִשִּׁים צַדִּיקִם בְּתוֹךְ הָעִיר וְנָשָׂאתִי לְכָל־הַמָּקוֹם בַּעֲבוּרָם ("If I find at Sodom fifty righteous in the midst of the city, I will forgive the whole place because of them") as ܐܢ ܐܫܟܚ ܒܣܕܘܡ ܚܡܫܝܢ ܙܕܝܩܝܢ ܒܓܘܗ ܕܡܕܝܢܬܐ ܐܫܒܘܩ ܠܟܠܗ ܐܬܪܐ ܡܛܠܬܗܘܢ ("If I find at Sodom fifty righteous in the city, I will forgive the whole place because of them"; Gen 18:26), omitting the *waw* of Hebrew וְנָשָׂאתִי after the conditional clause.

While Hebrew employs the infinitive absolute in the construction infinitive absolute + *waw* + infinitive absolute or adjective to express duration, Syriac does not. The Syriac translator found different solutions to this dilemma. In Gen 8:3, for the Hebrew וַיָּשֻׁבוּ הַמַּיִם מֵעַל הָאָרֶץ הָלוֹךְ וָשׁוֹב ("and the waters receded from the earth continually"), he rendered ܘܗܦܟܘ ܡܝܐ ܡܢ ܐܪܥܐ ܐܙܠܝܢ ܘܗܦܟܝܢ ("and the waters receded from the earth continually"), using participles as formal equivalents to the Hebrew infinitive absolutes. He also used participles in place of the Hebrew infinitive absolute in Gen 8:5, rendering וְהַמַּיִם הָיוּ הָלוֹךְ וְחָסוֹר ("and the waters continued abating") by ܘܡܝܐ ܐܙܠܝܢ ܗܘܘ ܘܚܣܪܝܢ ("and the waters were continually abating"). In Gen 12:9, however, he reformulated the sentence, giving the same general sense, rendering ܘܫܩܠ ܐܒܪܡ ܘܐܙܠ. ܘܡܫܩܠܢܘܗܝ ܠܬܝܡܢܐ ("and Abram journeyed and went and his journey was to the south") for Hebrew וַיִּסַּע אַבְרָם הָלוֹךְ וְנָסוֹעַ הַנֶּגְבָּה ("and Abram journeyed continually journeying to the south"). In Gen 26:13, the translator renders וַיִּגְדַּל הָאִישׁ וַיֵּלֶךְ הָלוֹךְ וְגָדֵל עַד כִּי־גָדַל מְאֹד ("and the man became great and he continued becoming great until he became very great") by ܘܪܒܝ ܓܒܪܐ.ܘܐܙܠ ܗܘܐ ܘܪܒܐ ܥܕܡܐ ܕܪܒ ܛܒ ("and the man became great and he went on until he became very great"). The translator omits the adjective וְגָדֵל.

The Syriac translator treats the Hebrew verbal constructions with טֶרֶם and with בְּטֶרֶם differently. Where the Hebrew has טֶרֶם + prefix conjugation, the Syriac renders it with ܥܕ ܠܐ followed by the suffix conjugation. For example, the Syriac translator rendered the Hebrew טֶרֶם אֲכַלֶּה לְדַבֵּר ("before I had finished speaking"; Gen 24:45) as ܥܕ ܠܐ ܫܠܡܬ ܠܡܡܠܠܘ ("while I had not yet finished speaking").[29] But, where the Hebrew has בְּטֶרֶם

---

[29] See also Gen 2:5 and 19:4.

+ prefix conjugation, the Syriac renders it with ܥܕ followed by the prefix conjugation. For example, the translator rendered the Hebrew וּבְטֶרֶם יִקְרַב אֲלֵיהֶם ("and before he came near to them" Gen 37:18) as ܘܥܕ ܠܐ ܩܪܒ ܠܘܬܗܘܢ ("and while he had not come near to them"; Gen 37:18).[30]

With regard to the syntax of the numeral ܚܕ ("one"), the translator placed it before its nominal head in Gen 2:24 to stress "the concept of oneness," that is, to stress "one flesh" (ܚܕ ܒܣܪ) as over against "the two of them" (ܬܪܝܗܘܢ), the Hebrew reading בָּשָׂר אֶחָד ("one flesh").[31]

In Gen 39:9 the Peshitta reads ܒܝܫܬܐ ܗܕܐ ܪܒܬܐ ("this great evil") in keeping with Syriac word order in tripartite nominal phrases with a demonstrative pronoun and adjective, namely nominal head + demonstrative pronoun + adjective.[32] In Hebrew, the word order of such phrase differs, that is, nominal head + adjective + demonstrative pronoun, as demonstrated by the source text הָרָעָה הַגְּדֹלָה הַזֹּאת ("this great evil").

Interestingly, the translator follows the Hebrew *qĕrê* in rendering the Hebrew אֲדֹנָי יהוה by ܡܪܝܐ ܐܠܗܐ ("Lord God"; Gen 15:2, 8).[33] This translation also corresponds to that of יהוה אֱלֹהִים in Genesis 2–3.

On the fourth day of creation, the Hebrew text reads as follows: God said, Let there be lights (מְאֹרֹת) in the expanse of the heavens ... and let them become lights (וְהָיוּ לִמְאוֹרֹת) in the expanse of the heavens ... And God made the two great lights (הַמְּאֹרֹת), the greater light (הַמָּאוֹר) ... and the lesser light (הַמָּאוֹר) ... (Gen 1:14–16). Repetition of the same words does not make for a clear translation. How can the lights become lights? The Syriac translator clarified the meaning for his audience by rendering the Hebrew as follows: ... ܘܐܡܪ ܐܠܗܐ ܢܗܘܘܢ ܢܗܝܪܐ ܒܪܩܝܥܐ ܕܫܡܝܐ ... ܘܢܗܘܘܢ ܡܢܗܪܝܢ ܒܪܩܝܥܐ ܕܫܡܝܐ ... ܘܥܒܕ ܐܠܗܐ ܬܪܝܢ ܢܗܝܪܐ ܪܘܪܒܐ ... ܢܗܝܪܐ ܪܒܐ ... ܘܢܗܝܪܐ ܙܥܘܪܐ ... ("And God said, Let there be lights in the expanse of the heavens ... and let them shine in the expanse of the heavens ... and God made the two great lights, the greater light ... and the lesser light ..."). The Palestinian Targum (Targum Neofiti) handles the problem of the Hebrew in the same fashion by reading "Let there be lights (נהורין) in the expanse of the heavens ... and let them shine (ויהוון מנהרין) in the expanse of the heavens ... and the Word of the LORD created the two great lights

---

[30] See also Gen 27:4, 33; 41:50; 45:28.
[31] Takamitsu Muraoka, "Remarks on the Syntax of Some Types of Noun Modifier in Syriac," *JNES* 31 (1972): 192.
[32] Muraoka, "Remarks on the Syntax of Some Types of Noun Modifier," 194.
[33] Targum Onqelos reads יוי אלהים ("LORD God") in both verses. On this problem, see Weitzman, *The Syriac Version*, 53.

(נהוריא), the greater light (נהורא) ... and the lesser light (נהורא) ...." This case, then, demonstrates that the translator of the Peshitta of Genesis aimed at clarity in his translation, even if it meant modifying the Hebrew a bit.

In his pronouncement of judgment on the snake, the Lord says הוּא יְשׁוּפְךָ רֹאשׁ וְאַתָּה תְּשׁוּפֶנּוּ עָקֵב ("he [the seed of the woman] will bruise you on the head and you will bruise him on the heel"; Gen 3:15). The Hebrew employs the same verb twice, the precise meaning of which is unclear. The Peshitta renders it with clarity as ܗܘ ܢܕܘܫ ܪܝܫܟ. ܘܐܢܬ ܬܡܚܘܝܗܝ, ܒܥܩܒܗ ("he [the seed of the woman] will trample your head and you will strike him on his heel"). In addition to altering the verb, the Peshitta also adds an appropriate preposition and appropriate pronominal suffixes. These slight changes bring clarity to the translation.

The translator of the Peshitta of Genesis made a deliberate change for theological reasons in his rendering of the words of Abraham to Abimelech in Gen 20:13.[34] The Hebrew reads הִתְעוּ אֹתִי אֱלֹהִים מִבֵּית אָבִי ("the gods made me go astray from my father's house"), the verb presenting two problems to the translator: the meaning of the verb ("make go astray") and the number of the verb (plural). Ostensibly, the Syriac translator wanted to avoid rendering "the gods made me go astray." Consequently, he used the verb "bring out" and changed the number to singular, thus rendering ܐܦܩܢܝ ܐܠܗܐ ܡܢ ܒܝܬ ܐܒܝ ("God brought me out from my father's house"). This is a clear case of translation *ad sensum*.

Israel had expressed his dying wish to his son Joseph that he might be buried in the land of Canaan as follows: ܒܩܒܪܝ. ܕܙܒܢܬ ܠܝ ܒܐܪܥܐ ܕܟܢܥܢ ܬܡܢ ܬܩܒܪܢܝ ("in my grave which I purchased for myself in the land of Canaan there bury me"; Gen 50:5). The Peshitta seemingly deviates slightly from the Hebrew preserved by the MT: בְּקִבְרִי אֲשֶׁר כָּרִיתִי לִי בְּאֶרֶץ כְּנַעַן שָׁמָּה תִּקְבְּרֵנִי ("in my grave which I have X-ed for myself in the land of Canaan there bury me"). On the surface, one might claim that the Peshitta read a Hebrew variant קָנִיתִי ("I purchased"), if one assumes that כָּרִיתִי must mean "I dug out."[35] Yeshayahu Maori has pointed out, however, that this case demonstrates good knowledge of Hebrew on the part of the translator, choosing an appropriate definition for the context.[36]

---

[34] Yeshayahu Maori, *The Peshitta Version of the Pentateuch and Early Jewish Exegesis* [תרגום הפשיטתא לתורה והפרשנות היהודית הקדומה] (Jerusalem: Magnes, 1995), 89–91.

[35] So BHK, 3rd ed. BHS has eliminated this erroneous evaluation.

[36] Yeshayahu Maori ("Methodological Criteria for Distinguishing between Variant *Vorlage* and Exegesis in the Peshitta Pentateuch," in *The Peshitta as a Translation: Papers Read at the II Peshitta Symposium Held at Leiden 19–21 August 1993* [ed. Piet B. Dirksen and Arie van

Another type of translation technique is deconstructing a metaphor. In Gen 15:1, the Peshitta deconstructs the metaphor of God as shield. The Peshitta here renders the metaphoric language of the Hebrew אָנֹכִי מָגֵן לָךְ ("I am your shield") in plain language as ܐܢܐ ܡܥܕܪܢܟ ("I will help you"). Further examples of demetaphorization appear in the words of dying Jacob to his sons. The Hebrew text calls Issachar "a strong donkey" (חֲמֹר גָּרֶם), which the Peshitta renders as ܓܒܪܐ ܓܢܒܪܐ ("a mighty man"; Gen 49:14); and Naphtali "a hind let loose" (אַיָּלָה שְׁלֻחָה), which the Peshitta deconstructs as ܐܓܪ ܓܠܝܠܐ ܩܠܝܠܐ ("a swift messenger"; Gen 49:21). In reference to Asher, the Hebrew states שְׁמֵנָה לַחְמוֹ ("his bread is fat"), which the Peshitta deconstructs as ܛܒܐ ܐܪܥܗ ("his land is good"; Gen 49:20).

The Peshitta of Genesis transliterates a number of Hebrew words: ܬܗܘ ܘܒܗܘ (Gen 1:2), ܐܠܗܝܡ (Gen 6:2, 4), ܐܠܫܕܝ = ܐܠܫܕܝ (Gen 17:1; 28:3; 35:11; 43:14; 48:3; 49:25),[37] and ܐܠ (Gen 33:20; 35:1; 46:3). Ephrem interprets ܬܗܘ ܘܒܗܘ (Gen 1:2) as meaning the earth was "deserted and empty" (ܨܕܝܐ ܗܘܐ ܘܣܪܝܩܐ).[38] Ephrem interprets the phrase ܒܢܝ ܐܠܗܐ ("the sons of God"—note the *syame* with the word God, alluding to the Hebrew transliteration ܐܠܗܝܡ) as the sons of Seth.[39] The average person must have known that ܐܠܗܝܡ was equivalent to ܐܠܗܐ and plural in form. It also transliterates the Aramaic of the source text יְגַר שָׂהֲדוּתָא as ܝܓܪ ܣܗܕܘܬܐ ("heap of witness"; Gen 31:47) with slight linguistic modifications.

Deliberately, the Syriac translator uncharacteristically rendered the marker of the direct object אֵת in Gen 1:1 twice as ܝܬ, a matter that greatly concerned subsequent Syriac exegetes.[40]

---

der Kooij; MPIL 8; Leiden: Brill, 1995], 109) points out that Hebrew כרי can mean "to buy," citing Deut 2:6 as evidence: וְגַם מַיִם תִּכְרוּ מֵאִתָּם בַּכָּסֶף ("and water, too, shall you buy from them for silver"). The Peshitta correctly translates Deut 2:6 as ܘܐܦ ܡܝܐ ܒܟܣܦܐ ܬܙܒܢܘܢ ܡܢܗܘܢ.

[37] Ephrem takes it for granted that his readers understood ܐܠ ܫܕܝ (spelled as two words) to be a name of God that needed no explanation (R.M. Tonneau, ed., *Sancti Ephraem Syri in Genesim et in Exodum Commentarii* [2 vols.; CSCO 152–153; Scriptores Syri 71–72; Louvain: Durbecq, 1955], Sectio XLI.3, 110, l. 6).

[38] Tonneau, *Ephraem Syri in Genesim*, Sectio I.3, 9, l. 15.

[39] Tonneau, *Ephraem Syri in Genesim*, Sectio VI.3, 56, l. 1.

[40] Ephrem (Tonneau, *Ephraem Syri in Genesim*, Sectio I.1, 8, l. 17), for example, interprets the ܝܬ substantively as God creating "the substance of the heavens and the substance of the earth" (ܩܢܘܡܗ ܕܐܪܥܐ ܘܩܢܘܡܗ ܕܫܡܝܐ). Bar Hebraeus points out that the ܝܬ marks the direct object as in Palestinian Aramaic, whereas Syriac marks it with *lamadh* (Martin Sprengling and William Creighton Graham, eds., *Barhebraeus' Scholia on the Old Testament, Part I: Genesis – II Samuel* [Chicago: Chicago University Press, 1931], 4): ܝܬ ܫܡܝܐ ܘܝܬ ܐܪܥܐ ... ܘܗܘܐ ܠܗܕܐ ܡܠܬܐ ܒܦܠܣܛܝܢܐ ܐܝܟ ܕܠܠܡܕ ܒܣܘܪܝܝܐ ... "ܝܬ ܫܡܝܐ ܘܝܬ ܐܪܥܐ ... and it [ܝܬ] takes the place of *lamad* in Palestinian usage as if it were ܠܫܡܝܐ ܘܠܐܪܥܐ."

Palestinian Jewish Influence on the Peshitta of Genesis

Palestinian Jewish translation circles left their stamp on the Peshitta of Genesis through oral communication and oral tradition, but not through the written Targums that they produced.[41] Brock has argued convincingly that the use of the idiom ܐܬܚܙܝ ܠ "to be revealed to" (Gen 12:7; 17:1; 18:1; 35:1, 9; 48:3) derives from Palestinian Jewish translation circles, where one should expect ܐܬܓܠܝ ܠ- as in Gen 26:2.[42] Further, the translator of Peshitta of Genesis updated the toponyms "Ararat" as "Qardu" (ܩܪܕܘ; Gen 8:4) and "Hazazon-tamar" as "En Geddi" (ܥܝܢ ܓܕܝ; Gen 14:7) in accord with the Palestinian Targumic tradition as well.[43]

In Gen 30:8, the problem of rendering נַפְתּוּלֵי אֱלֹהִים confronts the translator. What possibly can this mean? Should one understand אֱלֹהִים as "God"? The Syriac translator believed that God was in focus and so rendered the phrase according to the context as ܒܥܝܬ ܡܢ ܡܪܝܐ ("I asked from the Lord"). This interpretation reveals the influence of Palestinian Jewish translation circles, for the Palestinian Targum (Targum Neofiti) reads בצלותא די צלית קדם ייי דיתן לי בנין היך מה דיהב לאחתי לחוד אשתמעת ("in the prayer which I prayed before the Lord that he would give me children as he had given my sister I was indeed heard"). The Syriac translator followed the Palestinian Jewish translation tradition in rendering נַפְתּוּלֵי אֱלֹהִים but then returned to the Hebrew text to render נִפְתַּלְתִּי עִם־אֲחֹתִי גַּם־יָכֹלְתִּי as ܐܬܟܬܫܬ ܥܡ ܚܬܝ ܘܐܦ ܐܙܕܟܝܬ ("and I wrestled with my sister and I also prevailed").[44] This rendering points to an oral, not a written, source for Palestinian Jewish influence.

In the past, researchers have regarded the Syriac reading ܡܢ ܛܠܝܘܬܝ, ("from my youth") of Gen 48:15 as pointing to a Hebrew variant מִנְּעוּרַי ("from my youth") for the MT מֵעוֹדִי.[45] The Palestinian Targum here reads the same

---

[41] The writing down of the Palestinian Targums (Targum Neophyti, the Fragmentary Targums, the Genizah fragments) that we possess post dates the translation of the Peshitta. Targum Onqelos, not strictly a Palestinian targum, took written shape about the time of the translation of the Peshitta.

[42] Sebastian P. Brock, "A Palestinian Targum Feature in Syriac," *JJS* 46 (1995): 271–282, esp. 276.

[43] Sebastian P. Brock, "Jewish Traditions in Syriac Sources," *JJS* 30 (1979): 212–232, esp. 213-214.

[44] It is possible that the source text of the Peshitta read ונפתלתי עם אחתי וגם יכלתי, that is, had a connective *waw* in two places.

[45] So BHK, 3rd ed. BHS has eliminated this pseudo variant.

as the Peshitta מִן טליותי ("from my youth"). This is a further example of Palestinian Jewish translation circles influencing the Peshitta translation of Genesis.

Hebrew Prototext of the Peshitta
(Variant Hebrew Readings)

The Peshitta is an idiomatic translation, concerned about conveying the proper sense of its Hebrew source text without slavish adherence to it. Quantitative literalism (a one-to-one correspondence) and fidelity to the plain sense of the Hebrew text generally characterize the Peshitta of Genesis. For the Book of Genesis, the Hebrew prototext of the Peshitta corresponds by in large to that preserved by the MT. However, it did contain some variant Hebrew readings.

There are some cases of contextual harmonization in the Hebrew prototext of the Peshitta. For example, the Peshitta reads ܥܡܣܒܐ ܕܡܙܕܪܥ ܙܪܥܐ ܠܓܢܣܗ ("vegetation that bears seed according to its kind"; Gen 1:11), reflecting the Hebrew plus לְמִינֵהוּ ("according to its kind") in its source text, the reading of which derives from harmonization with v. 12. Moreover, the Peshitta reads ܘܠܐ ܚܣܟܬ ܠܒܪܟ ܠܝܚܝܕܟ ܡܢܝ ("and you have not withheld your son, your unique one, from me"; Gen 22:16), reflecting a Hebrew plus מִמֶּנִּי that derives from an earlier verse (Gen 22:12).

The MT of Gen 2:2 presents a problem. How can the text of the MT say that God finished his work on *the seventh* day, when he did so on the sixth day? Another Hebrew reading arose, which "corrected" this problem by changing "the seventh" to "the sixth." The Peshitta, along with the Samaritan Hebrew text and the Old Greek, witness to this alternate Hebrew reading, declaring that God finished his work on *the sixth* day.

In response to the Lord God's question "Where are you?," Adam replies "I heard your voice in the garden *and I saw* (וָאֵרֶא) that I was naked and I hid myself" (Gen 3:10) according to the Peshitta.[46] The Hebrew variant preserved by the MT reads "and I feared" (וָאִירָא) in place of "and I saw." These Hebrew readings differ in the plus or minus of *yodh* and subsequently in vocalization. Given the context, both readings are reasonable.

In Gen 4:15, the Peshitta (ܠܐ ܗܟܢܐ) shares the Hebrew variant לֹא כֵן ("not so") with the Old Greek (οὐξ οὗτως) over against the Hebrew of the MT לָכֵן ("therefore").

---

[46] ܩܠܟ ܫܡܥܬ ܒܦܪܕܝܣܐ ܘܚܙܝܬ ܕܥܪܛܠܝ ܐܢܐ ܘܐܬܛܫܝܬ

In Gen 7:1, the Peshitta reads ܘܐܡܪ ܐܠܗܐ ܠܢܘܚ ("and God said to Noah") against the Hebrew of the MT which reads וַיֹּאמֶר יהוה לְנֹחַ ("and the LORD said to Noah"). The Samaritan Hebrew shares the variant of the divine name with the Peshitta, reading ויאמר אלהים אל נח ("and God said to Noah"). The Old Greek conflates the two readings: καὶ εἶπεν κύριος ὁ θεὸς πρὸς Νεω ("and the Lord God said to Noah").

In Gen 14:4, the Peshitta reads "Twelve years they served Chedorlaomer,[47] but *in* the thirteenth year they rebelled." In comparison with the MT, which reads ושלש עשרה שנה ("and thirteen years"), the Peshitta reads ובשלש עשרה שנה ("and in the thirteenth year"), having the plus of the preposition *beth* before the phrase "thirteen years." Both the Samaritan Hebrew and the Old Greek agree with the Peshitta in reading this plus, which is the preferred reading.[48]

A Hebrew variant to the MT appears in Gen 14:7, where the Peshitta's prototext read "all the *princes* (שָׂרֵי) of the Amalekites" instead of "all the *field* (שְׂדֵה) of the Amalekite." The primary difference between the readings is the difference between two letters that closely resemble each other, namely between *resh* and *daleth*. The letters *yodh* and *he* could have been confused in a worn Hebrew manuscript, especially one using the ancient script. Since the Old Greek shares this variant with the Peshitta, the secondary reading, whether preserved by the Peshitta and the Old Greek or by the MT, must have entered the textual tradition early.

In the story of the testing of Abraham's faith, as the angel stops Abraham from sacrificing his son Isaac, Abraham sees "a ram behind (אַיִל אַחַר) caught in a thicket by its horns" according to the MT (Gen 22:13). The prototext of the Peshitta read the Hebrew variant אֶחָד ("a"[49]) instead of the MT אַחַר ("behind"), a difference between the similarly looking letters *daleth* and *resh*. The Peshitta, then, reads "a ram caught in a thicket by its horns" (ܕܟܪܐ ܚܕ ܐܚܝܕ ܒܣܘܟܬܐ ܒܩܪܢܬܗ).

In Gen 30:11, when Leah joyfully declares the birth of a son through her surrogate Zilpah, the Peshitta reads ܐܬܐ ܓܕܝ ("my fortune has come"), similar to the *qĕrê* of the MT בָּא גָד ("fortune has come"). This may be a case of exegesis of a Hebrew reading בְּגָד (the *kĕtîb* of the MT), rather than a prototext בא גדי.

---

[47] I am emending the text of the Peshitta to read accordingly. The Peshitta reads the personal name as ܟܕܪܠܥܘܡܪ, which I correct to ܟܕܪܠܥܘܡܪ, the inner Syriac corruption being caused by the metathesis of *resh* and *daleth*.

[48] So BHS.

[49] As in Hebrew, so in Syriac: the numeral "one" can function as an indefinite article.

In Gen 36:2, the Peshitta reads "Oholibamah the daughter of Anah the *son* (בֶּן) of Zibeon the Hivite" against the MT, which reads "Oholibamah the daughter of Anah the *daughter* (בַּת) of Zibeon the Hivite." While Maori regards this as translation technique on the part of the translator of the Peshitta in light of v. 24 where Anah is listed as a son of Zibeon,[50] the Samaritan Pentateuch preserves the Hebrew reading בן. In this case, the Old Greek also reads בן. The matter is further complicated by v. 25, where the MT, the Old Greek, and the Samaritan Hebrew read "These are the children of Anah: Dishon and Oholibamah the daughter of Anah." The Peshitta reads only "These are the children of Anah: Dishon and Oholibamah" in v. 25, not attesting the reading "the daughter of Anah." It seems that only the MT and the Peshitta offer real alternatives, either Oholibamah had a father named Anah (the Peshitta) or both of her parents had the same name (MT).

In Gen 36:6, the Peshitta reads "and he (Esau) went to the land of Seir," its prototext reading וילך אל ארץ שעיר, against the MT which reads "and he (Esau) went to a land" (וַיֵּלֶךְ אֶל־אֶרֶץ). The formal plus of "Seir" attested by the Peshitta is the preferred reading.[51]

In Gen 41:54, the Peshitta reads "and there was a famine in all the lands and in the entire land of Egypt there was not bread," against the MT which reads "and there was a famine in all the lands and in the entire land of Egypt there was bread." The Hebrew prototext of the Peshitta read the negative לֹא before the verb הָיָה, whereas the MT has only הָיָה. The tension in the text was whether Egypt was included in "all the lands."

In Gen 45:23, Joseph sends his father ten female donkeys, loaded with provisions, to sustain him on his journey from Canaan to Egypt. The Peshitta reads that these female donkeys carried ܥܒܘܪܐ ܘܚܡܪܐ ܘܙܘܕܐ ("grain and wine and provisions") in contrast to the Hebrew represented by the MT בָּר וָלֶחֶם וּמָזוֹן ("grain and bread and provision"). The formal equivalent of ܚܡܪܐ to לֶחֶם leads one to believe that the prototext of the Peshitta read יַיִן ("wine").[52]

In Gen 47:31, the Hebrew prototext of the Peshitta reads that aged Israel bowed upon the head of the *staff* (הַמַּטֶּה), corresponding to that of the Old Greek, as over against that of the MT which reads that he bowed on the head of the *bed* (הַמִּטָּה). A difference in vocalization marks these Hebrew variants.

---

[50] So Maori, *Peshitta Version*, 63, n. 69.
[51] So BHS.
[52] Maori ("Methodological Criteria," 111) believes that the reading of the Peshitta came from a rabbinic story, not from a variant Hebrew text.

With regard to pluses, the Peshitta reads expressed subjects often. P.B. Dirksen attributed most of these cases to translation technique, by which the translator added the express subject understood in the text rather than attesting to a variant Hebrew reading.[53] In Gen 2:24, for example, the Peshitta reads ܘܢܗܘܘܢ ܬܪܝܗܘܢ ܐܝܟ ܚܕ ܒܣܪ ("and the two of them will become one flesh") over against the MT which reads וְהָיוּ לְבָשָׂר אֶחָד ("and they will become one flesh"). In this case, the Old Greek adds an expressed subject, too, reading καὶ ἔσονται οἱ δύο εἰς σάρκα μίαν ("and the two will become one flesh"). One could argue that the Old Greek attests the Hebrew variant שניהם ("the two of them"—see v. 25), but it could also have read השנים ("the two"). What is more interesting is that the Palestinian Targum also reads the plus ויהוון תריהון לבסר חד ("and the two of them will become one flesh"). This fact leads one to ponder the issue of text versus translation technique. This could be a case where the Palestinian *meturgeman* added an expressed subject and that this Palestinian Jewish gloss influenced the translator of the Peshitta, adding clarity to his target text.

The Peshitta also adds an expressed subject in Gen 3:1, reading ܘܐܡܪ ܚܘܝܐ ܠܐܢܬܬܐ ("and the serpent said to the woman"), where the Hebrew preserved by the MT reads וַיֹּאמֶר אֶל־הָאִשָּׁה ("and it said unto the woman"). The Old Greek also attest this same expressed subject, reading καὶ εἶπεν ὁ ὄφις τῇ γυναικί ("and the serpent said to the woman"). Of course, the problem for the translator or for the transmitter of the Hebrew text was that snakes do not speak. So to make it clear that this snake speaks someone added the expressed subject "snake." In this case, the Palestinian Targums saw no reason to add an expressed subject. Probably, the reading of the Peshitta points to an actual Hebrew variant in this case.

Again, in Gen 15:6, the Peshitta adds an expressed subject, reading ܘܗܝܡܢ ܐܒܪܡ ܒܐܠܗܐ ("and Abram believed in God") against the Hebrew of the MT וְהֶאֱמִן בַּיהוָה ("and he believed in the LORD"). In addition, the Peshitta reads the variant באלהים ("in God") for the MT ביהוה ("in the LORD"). The Old Greek shares both variants with the Peshitta, reading καὶπαρ ἐπίστευσεν Αβραμ τῷ θεῷ ("and Abram believed in God"). The Palestinian Targum (Targum Neofiti) adds the expressed subject "Abram": והיימן אברם בשם ממרא דייי ("and Abram believed in the name of the Word of the LORD"). The addition of the expressed subject in Targum Neofiti points to an exegetical plus by the *meturgeman*, not to an actual Hebrew text.

---

[53] Piet B. Dirksen, "The Peshitta and the Textual Criticism of the Old Testament," VT 42 (1992): 382–383.

The Peshitta as an Interpreter of the Hebrew Bible

The Peshitta constitutes an early source for the exegesis of the Hebrew Bible, being the first translation of the Hebrew Bible into another Semitic language. Issues with which its translators wrestled also confront the modern translator and interpreter. I will highlight some interesting examples, but in no way will I exhaust the material for Genesis. The interested scholar will have to do that for him or herself.

In Gen 2:2, the Peshitta, conditioned by a Hebrew variant "sixth day" versus "seventh day" preserved by the MT as the day on which God completed his work, renders Hebrew וַיִּשְׁבֹּת as ܘܐܬܬܢܝܚ ("and he rested"): ܘܫܠܡ ܐܠܗܐ ܒܝܘܡܐ ܫܬܝܬܝܐ ܥܒܕܘܗܝ ܕܥܒܕ, ܘܐܬܬܢܝܚ ܒܝܘܡܐ ܫܒܝܥܝܐ ܡܢ ܟܠܗܘܢ ܥܒܕܘܗܝ ܕܥܒܕ ("and God completed on the sixth day his works that he did and rested on the seventh day from all his works that he did"). This choice of lexeme corresponds with Targumic tradition.[54]

In Gen 3:6, the Hebrew reads וְנֶחְמָד הָעֵץ לְהַשְׂכִּיל, which the Peshitta interprets as ܘܪܓܝܓ ܗܘ ܐܝܠܢܐ ܠܡܚܙܐ ܒܗ ("and the tree was desirable to look at"). The interpretation of the Peshitta corresponds to that found in Targum Onqelos and Targum Neofiti, which read ומרגג אילנא לאסתכלא ביה and ויאי אילנא למסתכלא ביה respectively. Twice in the Book of Psalms, the Peshitta renders Hebrew השכיל by ܚܙܐ: ܛܘܒܘܗܝ ܠܡܢ ܕܚܐܪ ܒܡܣܟܢܐ ("blessed is he who looks upon the poor") renders אַשְׁרֵי מַשְׂכִּיל אֶל־דָּל (Ps 41:2) and ܘܚܙܘ ܒܥܒܕܐ ܕܐܝܕܘܗܝ ("and they will look at the work of his hands") renders וּמַעֲשֵׂהוּ הִשְׂכִּילוּ (Ps 64:10). The verb ܚܙܐ governs the preposition ܒ.

The Hebrew preserved by the MT in Gen 3:16 reads וְאֶל־אִישֵׁךְ תְּשׁוּקָתֵךְ ("and unto your husband shall be your תְּשׁוּקָה"), while the Peshitta renders ܘܠܘܬ ܒܥܠܟܝ ܬܬܦܢܝܢ ("and unto your husband shall you turn"). In the past, it has been suggested that the Peshitta read the postulated Hebrew variant תשובתך, derived by retroverting the Old Greek reading ἡ ἀποστροφή σου to Hebrew, where the MT reads תְּשׁוּקָתֵךְ.[55] However, the Peshitta reads a finite verb form ("you shall turn"), not a noun. Further, the Targums interpret the Hebrew noun on the basis of the root תוב[56] so what might be construed as a Hebrew variant attested by the Old Greek at first

---

[54] Targum Onqelos and the text of Neofiti read the *peal* ונח, while the margin of Neofiti and Fragment Targum P read ואתניח and ואתניה.
[55] So BHK, 3rd ed. BHS has removed this pseudo variant.
[56] Targum Onqelos reads ולות בעליך תהי תיובתיך ("and to your husband shall be your turning"), while Targum Neofiti reads ולוות בעליך יהוי מתביך ("and to your husband shall be your returning").

may in fact not be so. It appears, then, that the translator of the Peshitta interprets this rare Hebrew word.⁵⁷

In Gen 4:8 of the Hebrew preserved by the MT, the direct speech of Cain to Abel appears to be missing. The MT reads: וַיֹּאמֶר קַיִן אֶל־הֶבֶל אָחִיו וַיְהִי בִּהְיוֹתָם בַּשָּׂדֶה ("And Cain said to Abel his brother and when they were in the field"). Targum Onqelos conforms to the MT. By contrast, the Samaritan Hebrew adds the words נכלה השדה ("Let us go to the field") after the introductory statement "And Cain said to Abel his brother," which reading makes good sense. The Old Greek reads the same as the Samaritan Hebrew διέλθωμεν εἰς τὸ πεδίον ("Let us pass through into the field"). So, there was a Hebrew variant text that supplied the words of Cain. Now, the Palestinian Targums also add the words of Cain, which raises the question of whether or not they added these words because the text demands it of an interpreter or whether they actually had a Hebrew variant text. Targum Neofiti reads איתה ונפק תרין לאפי ברא ("Come and let the two of us go out into the field") followed by Cain's complaint and Abel's reply. The Geniza fragment B preserves a similar reading to that found in Targum Neofiti. By contrast, the Geniza fragments I and FF of the Palestinian Targum start with the complaint by Cain about injustice, omitting speech about going out into the field. Both traditions of the Fragmentary Targum follow Targum Neofiti. Retroverting the Aramaic of Neofiti to Hebrew would yield לך ונצא שנינו לשדה. The fact that this is a far cry from the reading of the Samaritan Hebrew and the Old Greek cast doubts on its genuineness as an actual Hebrew reading, indicating rather that a midrash added these words to the text of the MT. Now, the Peshitta adds the words of direct speech as ܢܚܘܬ ܠܦܩܥܬܐ ("Let us descend to the valley"), far different from the readings of the Samaritan Hebrew and Old Greek on the one hand and the Palestinian Targums on the other hand. In fact, the wording with "valley" stands opposed to the later "field" (ܚܩܠܐ)⁵⁸ of the verse within the Peshitta itself. Consequently, it appears that the translator of the Peshitta added these words from an oral tradition that located the place of the murder in the valley.⁵⁹ Brock

---

⁵⁷ The Peshitta renders the expression וְאֵלֶיךָ תְּשׁוּקָתוֹ of Gen 4:7 similarly as ܐܢܬ ܬܬܦܢܐ ܠܘܬܗ ("you will turn toward it [sin]"). While it modifies the subject and the object of the preposition, it retains the same exegesis of תְּשׁוּקָה.

⁵⁸ Aware of this problem, a twelfth century text witness corrected the Peshitta to read "valley" throughout the verse.

⁵⁹ B.O.G. Kvam correctly labels this "an exegetically motivated supplement" (B.O.G. Kvam, "'Come, Let the Two of Us Go Out into the Field': The Targum Supplement to Genesis 4:8a—A Text-Immanent Reading?" in *Targum and Scripture: Studies in Aramaic Translation and Interpretation in Memory of Ernest G. Clarke* [ed. Paul V.M. Flesher; SAIS 2; Leiden: Brill, 2002], 98, n. 4).

has astutely called attention to the tradition that Paradise was located on the top of a mountain and that Adam and Eve, when expelled, lived in the foothills.[60] In short, the translator of the Peshitta of Genesis added these words to clarify the text from a tradition known to him.

The translator explains the meaning of "walking with God" as "pleasing God," rendering the Hebrew וַיִּתְהַלֵּךְ חֲנוֹךְ אֶת־הָאֱלֹהִים ("and Enoch walked with God"; Gen 5:22) as ܘܫܦܪ ܚܢܘܟ ܠܐܠܗܐ ("and Enoch pleased God") and הִתְהַלֵּךְ לְפָנַי ("walk before me") as ܫܦܪ ܩܕܡܝ ("be pleasing before me"; Gen 17:1). This is the regular interpretation of the Hebrew התהלך in reference to God throughout Genesis (Gen 5:24; 6:9; 48:15). However, in Gen 24:40, the translator renders יהוה אֲשֶׁר־הִתְהַלַּכְתִּי לְפָנָיו ("the LORD before whom I have walked") as ܡܪܝܐ ܕܦܠܚܬ ܩܕܡܘܗܝ ("the Lord before whom I have worshiped"). By contrast with these exegetical translations, a non exegetical translation appears in Gen 13:17, where the translator rendered הִתְהַלֵּךְ בָּאָרֶץ ("walk about in the land") by ܗܠܟ ܒܐܪܥܐ ("walk about in the land").

In Gen 6:3 the Peshitta reads ܠܐ ܬܥܡܪ ܪܘܚܝ ܒܐܢܫܐ ܠܥܠܡ ("my Spirit will not live with/in man forever"), where the MT reads לֹא־יָדוֹן רוּחִי בָאָדָם לְעֹלָם ("my Spirit will not יָדוֹן with/in man forever"). The question is what is the meaning of the form יָדוֹן? The Old Greek comes close to the Peshitta by rendering οὐ μὴ καταμείνῃ τὸ πνεῦμά μου ἐν τοῖς ἀνθρώποις τούτοις εἰς τὸν αἰῶνα ("my Spirit will not remain with these men forever"). Although somewhat different, Targum Onqelos follows a similar understanding of the verb: לא יתקיים דרא בישא הדין קדמי לעלם ("this evil generation will not be endure before me forever"). Thus, the Peshitta, Old Greek, and Targum Onqelos more or less agree that the verb has the meaning "to remain" or the like. By contrast, Targum Neofiti exegetes the form as from דין "to judge," rendering: לא יתדנון כל דריה דעתידין למקום כסדר דינא דדריה דמבולא ("none of the generations which will arise will be judged according to the order of judgment of the generation of the flood").

---

[60] Brock, "Jewish Tradition," 217. Ephrem states in his commentary on Genesis that "paradise is situated on a great height" (ܒܪܘܡܐ ܪܒܐ ܣܝܡ ܦܪܕܝܣܐ; Tonneau, *Ephraem Syri in Genesim*, Sectio II.6, 29, ll. 6–7). Ephrem comments on the phrase "Let us descend to the valley" as follows: ܐܘ ܒܛܘܪܐ ܕܥܩܒܝ ܦܪܕܝܣܐ ܥܡܪܝܢ ܗܘܘ ܘܕܒܪܗ ܘܢܚܬ ܠܦܩܥܬܐ. ܐܘ ܒܛܘܪܐ ܪܥܐ ܗܘܐ ܗܒܝܠ ܥܢܐ. ܘܣܠܩ ܐܚܬܗ ܠܦܩܥܬܐ ܕܡܥܕܪܐ ܗܘܬ ܠܗ. ܡܛܠ ܫܒܠܝܗ ܘܡܕܪܗ. ("either they were dwelling on a mountain on the foothills of paradise and he [Cain] led him [Abel] and descended to the valley or Abel was shepherding the flock on the mountain and he [Cain] ascended [and] brought him [Abel] down to the valley which was useful for him because of its ears of grain and its soil"; Tonneau, *Ephraem Syri in Genesim*, Sectio III.5, 49, ll. 9–12).

The MT of Gen 8:7 reads וַיְשַׁלַּח אֶת־הָעֹרֵב וַיֵּצֵא יָצוֹא וָשׁוֹב עַד־יְבֹשֶׁת הַמַּיִם מֵעַל הָאָרֶץ ("and he [Noah] sent the raven away and it went back and forth until the waters dried up from upon the earth"). By contrast, the Peshitta reads ܘܫܕܪ ܠܚܘܪܒܐ ܢܘܦܩ ܡܦܩ ܘܠܐ ܗܦܟ ܥܕܡܐ ܕܝܒܫܬ ܡܝܐ ܡܢ ܐܪܥܐ ("and he [Noah] sent away the raven and it went forth but did not return until the waters dried up from the earth"). The problem facing the translator of the Peshitta was the Hebrew reading וָשׁוֹב which could mean "return." Now, the dove sent out in v. 8 does return in v. 9, where the Hebrew uses the same verb שׁוּב ("to return"), which the Peshitta renders properly with the verb ܗܦܟ. The dove stands in sharp contrast to the scavenger raven.[61] So, in order not to confuse matters, the translator of the Peshitta cleverly added the negative and rendered the Hebrew infinitive absolute as a finite verb, making Hebrew וָשׁוֹב into ܘܠܐ ܗܦܟ ("but it did not return").

Contextual guessing can be detected in translation of the verb וַיֶּאֱהַל twice in the same context (Gen 13:12, 18). The Peshitta renders ܘܝܪܬ ("and he inherited") and ܘܐܬܐ ("and he came") respectively. At first, one might think this unproblematic because we know that the noun אֹהֶל means "tent" and so one should deduce that the verb would mean "move a tent."[62] However, Chaim Rabin has pointed out that, assuming this etymology for the verb, one would have to give the verb two opposite meanings, "to pitch a tent" (v. 12) and "to strike a tent" (v. 18).[63] On the basis of an Arabic cognate, Rabin suggests the meaning "to get grazing rights to an area," which fits the context well.[64] Thus, the contextual guesses offered by the Peshitta are reasonable.

In Gen 25:22, Rebekah ponders her pregnant condition as the boys struggled within her and speaks. The Peshitta interprets the difficult Hebrew of her words אִם־כֵּן לָמָּה זֶּה אָנֹכִי as ܐܢ ܗܟܢܐ ܗܘ ܠܡܢܐ ܚܝܐ ܐܢܐ ("If it is so, why am I living?"), adding the participle ܚܝܐ for clarification of the meaning.

In Gen 29:7, the Peshitta translator clarifies the meaning of "the day is still great" (עוֹד הַיּוֹם גָּדוֹל) by rendering "the day still continues" (ܥܕܟܝܠ ܝܘܡܐ ܩܐܡ).

---

[61] Ishodad (J.-M. Vosté and C. Van den Eynde, eds., *Commentaire d'Išo'dad de Merv sur l'ancien Testament—I. Genèse* [CSCO 126; Scriptores Syri 67; Louvain: Durbecq, 1950], 121, l. 18) explains that the raven did not return because it was resting on the corpses (ܠܐ ܗܦܟ ܥܠ ܫܠܕܐ ܕܒ).
[62] So NRSV and ESV, for example.
[63] Chaim Rabin, "Etymological Miscellanea," *ScrHier* 8 (1961): 384–400, at 384.
[64] Rabin, "Etymological Miscellanea," 385.

The following case, where the Peshitta diverges slightly from the Hebrew, could be due either to the translator or to a Hebrew variant text. In Gen 35:12, the Peshitta reads ܘܐܪܥܐ ܗܕܐ ܕܝܡܝܬ ܕܐܒܪܗܡ ܘܠܐܝܣܚܩ ܠܟ ܐܬܠܝܗ ("and the land that *I swore* to Abraham and to Isaac I will give to you"), where the Hebrew reads וְאֶת־הָאָרֶץ אֲשֶׁר נָתַתִּי לְאַבְרָהָם וּלְיִצְחָק לְךָ אֶתְּנֶנָּה ("and the land that *I gave* to Abraham and to Isaac I will give to you"). Certainly, the translator of Genesis could have had a problem accepting the literal translation of the Hebrew since the Lord had not yet given Abraham and Isaac the land and so substituted the verb "I swore" for "I gave."[65] Yet, in other books of the Pentateuch, in the expression "the land that I gave" (Num 20:12, 24; Deut 9:23), the Peshitta uses "the land that I gave" (ܐܪܥܐ ܕܝܗܒܬ). However, different translators could have translated the different books of the Pentateuch and this may be a case of divergence between translators.

As Joseph rides in honor in Pharaoh's chariot, Gen 41:43 records וַיִּקְרְאוּ לְפָנָיו אַבְרֵךְ ("and they called before him אַבְרֵךְ"). While the third person plural verb expresses an indefinite subject, one should note that some Hebrew MSS and the Samaritan Hebrew text read the singular form ויקרא with the same meaning. The key question is what does אַבְרֵךְ mean? The Peshitta renders the phrase ܘܩܪܘ ܩܕܡܘܗܝ, ܐܒܐ ܘܫܠܝܛܐ ("and he called before him 'father and ruler'"). It appears that the Peshitta follows an interpretation of this *hapax legomenon* put forth in the targums, although in a different manner, by dividing the Hebrew word אַבְרֵךְ into two constituents, אב ("father") and רך ("king" < Latin *rex*).[66] One might wish for a reading ܐܒܐ ܕܫܠܝܛܐ ("father of the ruler") in the Peshitta to bring it closer to the Palestinian Targums, but such is not the case.

The Peshitta clarifies the meaning of the Hebrew וְאֶת־הָעָם הֶעֱבִיר אֹתוֹ לֶעָרִים in Gen 47:21 by rendering ܘܠܥܡܐ ܐܥܒܪ ܡܢ ܡܕܝܢܐ ܠܡܕܝܢܐ ("and the people he moved from city to city"), that is, Hebrew לֶעָרִים in this context means "from city to city."[67]

The Hebrew text of Gen 48:10 presents a problem. It states that Jacob was not able not see (לֹא יוּכַל לִרְאוֹת). But how can this be since the text has already informed the reader that Jacob *saw* the sons of Joseph (Gen 48:8)? The translator of the Peshitta added the adverb "well" (ܫܦܝܪ) to

---

[65] Maori, "Methodological Criteria," 106.
[66] The Targums use the words אבא ("father") and מלכא ("king"), interpreting the Hebrew אַבְרֵךְ as "father of the king."
[67] Modern versions follow the Samaritan Hebrew variant text ואת העם העביד אתו לעבדים ("and the people he made slaves") in rendering this verse. The Old Greek more or less follows the Samaritan reading.

clarify the situation, reading ܘܠܐ ܡܨܚܒ ܗܘܐ ܕܢܚܙܐ ܫܦܝܪ ("and he was not able to see well"). The text really means, according to the translator of the Peshitta, that Jacob could not see well, not that he was totally blind.

In the famous prophecy about Judah in Gen 49:10, the Peshitta interprets the Hebrew עַד כִּי־יָבֹא שִׁילֹה ("until Shiloh comes") as ܕܢܐܬܐ ܗܘ ܕܕܝܠܗ ܗܝ ("until he to whom it belongs comes"), understanding the word שִׁילֹה as a compound of the relative שֶׁ and the preposition *lamadh* plus attached personal pronoun. Exegesis identifies this as a Messianic prophecy and the feminine noun which belongs to the coming King is the kingdom.[68] From the ninth century on, the reading ܕܢܐܬܐ ܗܘ ܕܕܝܠܗ ܗܝ ܡܠܟܘܬܐ ("until he to whom the kingdom belongs comes") enters the Biblical textual stream.[69]

Conclusion

Study of the Peshitta of Genesis draws one into a serious examination of the text and meaning of the Hebrew Bible, the source from which it derived. While skillfully representing its parent text, the Peshitta of Genesis offers interesting textual, translational, and exegetical insights. Far too long has this version been marginalized in study of the Old Testament to the detriment of textual and exegetical understanding of Genesis. Further, study of the Peshitta of Genesis reveals the dynamics of Palestinian Jewish influence on its translation, an often-overlooked and misunderstood dimension.

---

[68] See *St. Ephrem the Syrian, Selected Prose Works, Commentary on Genesis* (trans. Edward G. Matthews, Jr., and Joseph P. Amar; ed. Kathleen McVey; The Fathers of the Church 91; Washington, D.C.: Catholic University Press of America, 1994), 203. Summarizing his exegesis, Ephrem states as though quoting: ܠܐ ܢܥܢܕ ܡܠܟܐ ܘܠܐ ܢܒܝܐ ܡܢ ܒܝܬ ܝܗܘܕܐ ܥܕܡܐ ܕܢܐܬܐ ܗܘ ܕܕܝܠܗ ܗܝ ܡܠܟܘܬܐ ("neither the king nor the prophet will depart from the house of Judah until he to whom the kingdom belongs comes"; Tonneau, *Ephraem Syri in Genesim*, Sectio XLII.5, 113, ll. 19–20). While this points to the homiletical addition of the word "kingdom" to the text, that is to say, oral tradition, it does not necessarily point to a variant Syriac biblical text which contained the word.

[69] A ninth century Melkite lectionary (Vat. sir. Ms 278) contains the word ܡܠܟܘܬܐ in the margin. Subsequently, the word enters the text itself as attested by two eleventh century Melkite lectionaries and a twelfth century Biblical manuscript.

Select Bibliography

Borbone, P.G., J. Cook, K.D. Jenner, and D.M. Walter, in collaboration with J.A. Lund and M.P. Weitzman. *The Old Testament in Syriac According to the Peshitta Version—Part V, Concordance I: The Pentateuch.* Brill: Leiden, 1997.

Brock, Sebastian P. *The Bible in the Syriac Tradition.* Gorgias Handbooks 7. Rev. ed. Piscataway, N.J.: Gorgias, 2006.

———. *An Introduction to Syriac Studies.* Gorgias Handbooks 4. Piscataway, N.J.: Gorgias, 2006.

———. "A Palestinian Targum Feature in Syriac." *Journal of Jewish Studies* 46 (1995): 271–282.

———. "Jewish Traditions in Syriac Sources." *Journal of Jewish Studies* 30 (1979): 212–232.

Comprehensive Aramaic Lexicon. Online: http://cal1.cn.huc.edu/.

Dirksen, P.B. "The Peshitta and Textual Criticism of the OT." *Vetus Testamentum* 42 (1992): 376–390.

Jansma, Taeke, and Marinus D. Koester, eds. *The Old Testament in Syriac According to the Peshitta Version—Part I, 1. Preface, Genesis – Exodus.* Leiden: Brill, 1977.

Joosten, Jan. "Greek and Latin Words in the Peshitta Pentateuch: First Soundings." Pages 37–47 in *Symposium Syriacum VII.* Edited by René Lavenant, S.J. Orientalia Christiana Analecta 256. Roma: Pontificio Istituto Orientale, 1998.

———. "The Old Testament Quotations in the Old Syriac and Peshitta Gospels." *Textus* 15 (1990): 55–76.

———. "The Use of Some Particles in the Old Testament Peshitta." *Textus* 14 (1988): 175–183.

Kooij, Arie van der. "On the Significance of MS 5b1 for the Peshitta Genesis." Pages 183–199 in *The Peshitta: Its Early Text and History. Papers Read at the Peshitta Symposium held at Leiden 30–31 August 1985.* Edited by Piet B. Dirksen and Martin Jan Mulder. Monographs of the Peshitta Institute, Leiden 4. Leiden: Brill, 1988.

———. "Peshitta Genesis 6: 'Sons of God'—Angels or Judges?" *Journal of Northwest Semitic Languages* 23 (1997): 43–51.

Koster, M.D. *The Peshitta of Exodus: The Development of its Text in the Course of Fifteen Centuries.* Studia semitica neerlandica 19. Assen: Van Gorcum, 1977.

———. "Which Came First: The Chicken of the Egg? The Development of the Text of the Peshitta of Genesis and Exodus in Light of Recent Studies." Pages 99–126 in *The Peshitta: Its Early Text and History. Papers Read at the Peshitta Symposium held at Leiden 30–31 August 1985.* Edited by Piet B. Dirksen and Martin Jan Mulder. Monographs of the Peshitta Institute, Leiden 4. Leiden: Brill, 1988.

Lund, Jerome A. "The Influence of the Septuagint on the Peshitta: A Re-evaluation of Criteria in Light of Comparative Study of the Versions in Genesis and Psalms." Ph.D. diss., The Hebrew University of Jerusalem, 1989.

———. "Observations on Some Biblical Citations in Ephrem's Commentary on Genesis." *Aramaic Studies* 4 (2006): 205–218.

Maori, Yeshayahu. "Methodological Criteria for Distinguishing Between Variant *Vorlage* and Exegesis in the Peshitta Pentateuch." Pages 103–120 in *The Peshitta as a Translation: Papers Read at the II Peshitta Symposium Held at Leiden 19–21*

August 1993. Edited by Piet B. Dirksen and Arie van der Kooij. Monographs of the Peshitta Institute, Leiden 8. Leiden: Brill, 1995.

———. "The Relationship between the Peshitta Pentateuch and the Pentateuchal Targums." Pages 57–73 in *Targum Studies, Volume Two: Targum and Peshitta*. Edited by Paul V.M. Flesher. South Florida Studies in the History of Judaism 165. Atlanta: Scholars Press, 1998.

———. *The Peshitta Version of the Pentateuch and Early Jewish Exegesis* (תרגום הפשיטתא לתורה והפרשנות היהודית הקדומה). Jerusalem: Magnes, 1995.

Owens, Robert J. *The Genesis and Exodus Citations of Aphrahat the Persian Sage*. Monographs of the Peshitta Institute, Leiden 3. Leiden: Brill, 1984.

Romeny, R.B. ter Haar. "Techniques of Translation and Transmission of the Earliest Text Forms of the Syriac Version of Genesis." Pages 177–185 in *The Peshitta as a Translation: Papers Read at the II Peshitta Symposium Held at Leiden 19–21 August 1993*. Edited by Piet B. Dirksen and Arie van der Kooij. Monographs of the Peshitta Institute, Leiden 8. Leiden: Brill, 1995.

———. *A Syrian in Greek Dress: The Use of Greek, Hebrew and Syriac Biblical Texts in Eusebius of Emesa's Commentary on Genesis*. Traditio Exegetica Graeca 6. Leuven: Peeters, 1997.

Tonneau, R.M., ed. *Sancti Ephraem Syri in Genesim et in Exodum Commentarii*. 2 vols. Corpus scriptorum christianorum orientalium 152–153. Scriptores Syri 71–72. Louvain: Durbecq, 1955.

Weitzman, Michael P. *The Syriac Version of the Old Testament: An Introduction*. University of Cambridge Oriental Publications 56. Cambridge: Cambridge University Press, 1999.

THE FATHERS ON GENESIS

Andrew Louth

It might be thought that to think about the Fathers on Genesis is one of a series of quite similar topics: the Fathers on Exodus, or Deuteronomy, or one of the prophets, or any other book of the Bible. It is simply focusing, for one reason or another, on one of the books of the Bible. That might be true for other periods of church history (though I am not claiming that it is, and indeed, rather doubt it). But in the case of the patristic period, interest in Genesis is quite extraordinary. It is mainly a matter of interest in the account of creation in Gen 1 (often spilling over into the immediately subsequent chapters), for it is striking how frequently Christians in the early centuries reflected on the Six Days of Creation—the *Hexaemeron* as it appears in Greek.[1] It was a tradition inherited from the Jews: Philo's treatise *On the Creation of the World* had a great influence on subsequent Christian exegesis. The fourth-century writer, Eusebius, refers in his *Ecclesiastical History* to eight accounts of commentary on the creation narrative in Genesis, mostly now lost, mainly from the end of the second century of the Christian era. Origen, the great third-century theologian, perhaps the greatest of all Christian exegetes, wrote both a commentary and homilies on Genesis; of the commentary only fragments survive, and in his homilies he moves through Genesis quite quickly, only in the first homily discussing the Six Days. The later Greek tradition is dominated by Basil's *Homilies on the Hexaemeron*; Gregory of Nyssa's *On the Making of Humankind* is explicitly supplementary, but there are many discussions of the Genesis account of creation by other Greek thinkers, though Basil's tends to cast a shadow over his successors. This reflection on the Genesis creation account is not at all confined to

---

[1] There is relatively little secondary literature on the subject. Apart from the article by Yves M.-J. Congar cited in n. 2 below, see: *In Principio: Interprétations des premiers versets de la Genèse* (École pratique des Hautes Études—Section des Sciences Religieuses: Centre d'Études des Religions du Livre, Laboratoire associé au C.N.R.S. 152; Paris: Études Augustiniennes, 1973); Johannes Zahlten, *Creatio mundi: Darstellungen des sechs Schöpfungstage und naturwissenschaftliches Welt im Mittelalter* (SBGP 13; Stuttgart: Klett-Cotta, 1979); and D.S. Wallace-Hadrill, *The Greek Patristic View of Nature* (Manchester: Manchester University Press, 1968). As well, see recently, Peter C. Bouteneff, *Beginnings: Ancient Christian Readings of the Biblical Creation Narratives* (Grand Rapids: Baker Academic, 2008).

the Greek tradition. One of the longest and most comprehensive commentaries on Genesis, including the Hexaemeron, was composed by St. Ephrem, Basil's contemporary, who wrote in Syriac, the form of Aramaic spoken in Syria, and there are several later Syriac theologians who discuss the Six Days. The fifth-century Armenian writer, Eznik of Kolb, has a good deal of discussion of the creation account in his treatise, *On God*. Exposition of Genesis was especially rich in the Latin tradition. The fourth-century Ambrose of Milan was not the first, and Augustine, on whom Ambrose made such an impression while he was still a rhetor, five times made an attempt at exposition of the Genesis creation account. Whereas Basil's single account seems to have hampered later Greek reflection, Augustine's five different accounts only stimulated further reflection; in an article surveying the tradition of Hexaemeral commentary, the late Père Yves Congar listed nearly forty Latin commentators between Augustine and the end of the Middle Ages (including the Venerable Bede and the twelfth-century Laurence of Durham), and that list is certainly not exhaustive.[2]

Early Christian interest in the book of Genesis was not, however, confined to the creation account. The account of Adam and Eve in the Garden of Eden was also of intense interest, as were the succeeding chapters up to the account of the Tower of Babel. After that there come the accounts of the patriarchs, from Abraham, through Isaac and Jacob, to Joseph. All of these attracted immense interest, though not, perhaps, as much as the creation account. In this essay, we shall look at each of these parts of the Genesis narrative, one by one.

THEOPHILUS OF ANTIOCH

It is perhaps worth beginning with the earliest Christian discussion of the early chapters of Genesis to survive: that contained in the second book of the apology, *To Autolycus*, by Theophilus of Antioch. The discussion of Genesis is in many ways the heart of the work, and presents the account of creation in Genesis in the context of a refutation of the notions of the Greeks, both those found in the philosophers and the poets. But we need to go back

---

[2] See Yves M.-J. Congar, "Le thème de *Dieu-créateur* et les explications de l'Hexaméron dans la tradition chrétienne," in *L'Homme devant Dieu: Mélanges offerts au père Henri de Lubac* (3 vols.; Théologie Series 56–58; Paris: Aubier, 1963–1964), 1:189–222 ("inventaire littéraire" on 1:215–222).

to the beginning of the treatise, to the very beginning of the discussion, if we are to understand Theophilus properly. He begins with a challenge: "if you should say, 'Show me your God,' I may reply to you, 'Show me your man and I will show you my God.' You must show me that the eyes of your soul can see and that the ears of your heart can hear" (*Autol.* 1.2). But most humans cannot see or hear God, for they live lives that blind the soul and stop up the ears of the heart. The soul and heart must be restored to their original pristine state, if they are to behold God, and quickly Theophilus unfolds the idea of God as transcendent, as creator of the universe out of nothing. This can be understood only by a soul that is pure. An impure soul, entangled in the world through selfishness, and all that goes with it— theft, anger, envy, unbridled sexual passion—cannot see God, but rather projects on to the world the kind of divinity revealed in the mythology of the Greeks. This makes clear that knowledge of God is not a matter of acquiring some kind of information, but the fruit of a struggle for purity and wisdom. It also paves the way for Theophilus' attack on the notions of the Greeks, as a preparation for his presentation of the truth found in the Scriptures.

Theophilus' God is utterly different from the universe; he is, indeed, its creator—he has created the universe out of nothing. "God made everything out of what did not exist, bringing it into existence so that his greatness might be known and apprehended through his works" (1.4). In asserting this, he cites the verse from Maccabees (2 Macc 7:28), the first explicit assertion of the doctrine of creation out of nothing. For Theophilus, God created the universe out of nothing, and for this reason he is apprehended "through his providence and his works" (1.5). As he expounds this, Theophilus introduces something else: belief in the Resurrection, which he justifies by reference to his belief in God's creative power. Because of that, we can entrust ourselves to God, confident that he can raise from the dead what he has created out of nothing, trusting in the "first pledge ... that he created you, bringing you from non-existence to existence" (1.8). It is worth noting, in passing, that this is precisely the argument of Salomina, the mother of the seven brothers, whose martyrdom is recorded in Maccabees, and whose words Theophilus has already quoted: it is faith in the Resurrection, entailed by the doctrine of creation out of nothing, that justifies the martyr's faith. Theophilus goes on to attack idolatry and worship of the divine Emperor (1.9–11), before turning in Book II to attack Greek mythology and then the theology of the philosophers and the poets (2.2–8). This is the context in which Theophilus presents his interpretation of Genesis. He first asserts that this is the unanimous teaching of the prophets; they all say the same thing, unlike the Greek philosophers and poets, who disagree amongst themselves—even the Sibyl agrees with them. He then embarks on his presentation of the teaching of Genesis:

> In the first place, in complete harmony they taught us that he made everything out of the non-existent (ὅτι ἐξ οὐκ ὄντων τὰ πάντα ἐποίησεν). For there was nothing coeval with God; he was his own place; he lacked nothing; he existed before the ages [Ps 54:20]. He wishes to make man so that he might be known by him; for him then, he prepared the world. For he who is created has needs, but he who is uncreated lacks nothing. (2.10)

This creation takes place through God's *Logos* and *Sophia*, through his Word and his Wisdom. Theophilus then remarks that "Light is the beginning of the creation, since light reveals the things being set in order"; this light is pronounced by God "good"—"good, that is to say, for men" (1.11). And he proceeds to quote the rest of the account of the six days of creation from Genesis.

Theophilus prefaces his interpretation by asserting that "no man can adequately set forth the whole exegesis and plan of the Hexaemeron, even if he were to have ten thousand mouths and ten thousand tongues" (2.12). Although Theophilus has spoken disparagingly of the poets and philosophers, he cannot refrain from alluding here to Homer's account of the massed Achaean army, which he says he could not recount, "had he even ten tongues, or ten mouths."[3] It worth noticing, too, how much Theophilus draws on the Stoics in seeing the order and harmony of the cosmos as demonstrating the existence of God, and in seeing the cosmos as created for the sake of the human. He then goes on to interpret the account of the creation in Genesis. He interprets the sea of Gen 1:10 as an image of the world we live in (not the natural world, but the world of human relationships and society), a place of danger in which we need God's guidance. He continues this way of interpreting the creation narrative as containing δεῖγμα καὶ τύπον ... μεγάλου μυστηρίου, "a pattern and type of a great mystery" (2.15). The sun is a type of God, and the moon of humankind:

> as the sun greatly surpasses the moon in power and brightness, so God greatly surpasses humankind; and just as the sun always remains full and does not wane, so God always remains perfect and is full of all power, intelligence, wisdom, immortality, and all good things. But the moon wanes every month and virtually dies, for it exists as a type of the human; then it is reborn and waxes as a pattern of the future resurrection. (2.15)

---

[3] Homer, *Il.* 2.489.

The three days prior to the luminaries are types of God, his Word and Wisdom. Humans, who need light, stand in the fourth place, which is why the luminaries come into being on the fourth day. Stars, clearly visible and radiant, symbolize the prophets; the wandering planets changeable humankind (2.15). The animal kingdom manifests virtues and vices (2.16–17), but there is something retrospective about this, for in themselves they are good; it was only with the fall of man, that the animals experienced a fall into mutual preying on each other. Theophilus underlines the deliberation that lies behind the creation of humans, in contrast to the rest of creation, with God's saying, "Let us make man after our image and likeness," addressing his Word and his Wisdom. The human is presented as the pinnacle of God's creative work, created more intimately, as it were, by God's breathing "the breath of life into his face," so that man became a "living soul" (Gen 2:6–7). And he comments: "This is why the soul is called immortal by most people. After forming man, God chose a place for him in the eastern regions, excellent for its light, brilliant with brighter air, most beautiful with its plants. In this he placed man" (2.19).

Theophilus goes on to quote Gen 2:8–3:19—the description of Paradise, the creation of Eve, and the account of the Fall—and after commenting on aspects of this continues his discussion of Genesis up to the account of the Flood, and beyond that, the Tower of Babel (Gen 11). Then, after a long quotation from the Sibyl (2.36), he returns to discussing the poets, this time finding in them support for the biblical narrative.

We cannot follow Theophilus in detail any further, but it is worth pondering what kind of significance he invests in Genesis and its account of the creation of the world and the early history of humankind. What is most fundamental to Theophilus is the fact that the cosmos was created out of nothing by God who, uncreated, possesses an utterly different form of reality. From this flows a second fundamental point, namely, that the cosmos, the created order, contains a "pattern and type of a great mystery," that mystery being God, and his dealings with his creation. For Theophilus, the cosmos is a great symbolic structure, which, when read properly, speaks to us of God and his dealings with humankind. The Hexaemeron contains the key to this symbolic system. In *To Autolycus*, an apology, Theophilus is mostly concerned with expounding Christianity in the context of the persecution of Christians by the Roman authorities because of their refusal to worship the traditional gods. The doctrine of creation, which he finds in the Hexaemeron, fulfils a number of critical roles. First, creation out of nothing disposes of the traditional gods, and thus of the reason (or occasion) for the persecution of Christians. Secondly—and perhaps more importantly—creation out of nothing justifies Christian belief in the Resurrection (as it justifies Jewish belief in the Resurrection in Maccabees), for the one who created out of nothing can surely raise the dead. Thirdly—and most importantly—creation out of nothing by God makes it clear that it is in the one God, recognized as creator, witnessed in the Scriptures and the Gospel, that we find our only recourse for the problem of human existence.

To Autolycus presents us with Theophilus the apologist, the defender of persecuted Christianity against the Roman society of his day. Eusebius' brief account of Theophilus, in his *Ecclesiastical History*, introduces a more diverse figure. He mentions *To Autolycus* ("three rudimentary treatises"), but he mentions other works: an *Against Hermogenes*, which draws on the book of the Apocalypse and is concerned with the doctrine of creation out of nothing (to judge from Tertullian's treatise of the same name, which acknowledged Theophilus' work), as well as his constant struggle against "heretics," both by word of mouth and written treatise, including a treatise against Marcion. This suggests a further dimension of Theophilus' theological concern: his involvement in what scholars nowadays call "gnosticism." It is, indeed, in the context of the struggle against Gnosticism that many scholars locate the emergence of the Christian doctrine of *creatio ex nihilo*. Certainly, the way Theophilus interprets Genesis would have served him well in his struggle against Gnosticism, and it may well be that struggle that led him to see the significance of creation *ex nihilo*. For the critical role of creation *ex nihilo* in the thought of Theophilus (and Tertullian) needs some explanation: the older apologist Justin seems much close to traditional Platonism with his assertion that God created the cosmos out of "unformed matter" (*1 Apol.* 10, cf. 59).[4]

However, although this solves one problem, it raises another. It may well be that for Theophilus the heart of the message of Gen 1 was creation out of nothing, but the Gnostics were interested in Genesis, too, and found there rather a different picture, much more congenial to their own views. A glance at the index to Werner Foerster's *Gnosis: A Selection of Gnostic Texts* reveals that out of two and a half pages of references to the Old Testament, one whole page is devoted to Genesis.[5] It is no surprise to learn

---

[4] In *Autol.* 4, Theophilus specifically rejects the view of "Plato and his followers" that God created the world out of pre-existent matter. In *1 Apol.* 59, Justin is concerned to demonstrate that Plato is dependent on Moses and uses the term "pre-existent" of that from which the whole cosmos was created according to Moses.

[5] Werner Foerster, ed., *Gnosis: A Selection of Gnostic Texts* (2 vols.; Oxford: Clarendon,

what they found there: much dualistic language (light/darkness, and so on), a narrative which offered many passages that demanded interpretation, and a good deal of mystery, a narrative that could easily be read "slant." So the question about the interpretation of Genesis in the second century, at least, needs to be rephrased. It is not just, Why was there so much interest in Genesis among those writers Eusebius tells us about in the second and third centuries, an interest that continued in the Church of the fourth century and thereafter? But the broader question: Why is it that anyone interested in interpreting the Christian message in the first centuries seems to be drawn irresistibly to Genesis, and especially its early chapters? I have no answer, but rather want to insist that we need to address this question. The answer cannot be that Genesis provided an answer to the Gnostics, though it may be that Genesis was so important to the Gnostics that any answer to them needed to show that this answer could be derived from Genesis. (I am conscious of the difficulties involved in talking about "Gnostics," and would rather not use the term, but for the purposes of this discussion it provides a convenient shorthand.) Several recent scholars—Stroumsa, Pétrement, Williams—have emphasized that "Gnosticism" grew out of traditions of exegesis;[6] but why exegesis of Genesis? In his *Excerpts from Theodotus*, Clement of Alexandria included the haunting summary of *gnosis* as "who we were, what we have become, where we were or where we have been placed, whither we hasten, whence we have been redeemed, what is birth, what rebirth" (*Exc.* 78.2). Concern with the beginning and the end might lead one to Genesis, but leaves one with a desire to know more. But here we must leave this riddle, and pursue further the question of the Fathers and Genesis.

The *Hexaemeron* in the Fathers

Theophilus of Antioch introduces us to many of the themes we shall find in the later Fathers, notably the assertion of the doctrine of *creatio ex nihilo*, and the idea of the created order as a symbolic structure. But in other

---

1972–1974), index on 2:350–352 (first column), of which virtually the whole of p. 350 is devoted to references to Genesis.

[6] See Simone Pétrement, *Le Dieu séparé: Les origines du gnosticisme* (Paris: Cerf, 1984); Guy G. Stroumsa, *Hidden Wisdom: Esoteric Traditions and the Roots of Christian Mysticism* (2nd ed.; SHR 70; Leiden: Brill, 2005); and Michael Allen Williams, *Rethinking 'Gnosticism': An Argument for Dismantling a Dubious Category* (Princeton: Princeton University Press, 1996).

respects, Theophilus is less typical. For instance, he, for the most part, draws a fairly sharp line between what he finds in Genesis and the views of the philosophers, not least Plato. There is not much trace of the conviction that Plato derived his ideas from Moses, such as we find in Justin Martyr (cf. *1 Apol.* 59–60) and generally in the Fathers, which leads to a way of reading Genesis in the light of Plato's *Timaeus*. Indeed, in many of the Fathers Genesis is read as if it told the same story as the myth in Plato's *Timaeus*. There are differences, certainly—the idea of the cosmos as a living being is fairly uniformly rejected—but the similarities are more striking. An illustration of this can be found in St. Gregory of Nyssa's *On the Making of Humankind*: at the very beginning, after the introduction, he quotes Gen 2:4—"This is the book of the coming into being of heaven and earth"—and then proceeds to give an account of the cosmos in accordance with the Ptolemaic model, with the earth at the centre surrounded by the planetary spheres and the sphere of the fixed stars, whirling round the earth at fearsome speeds.[7] There is no trace of any sense that there is any difference between the biblical account and the generally accepted scientific account of the origin of the universe. Christian accounts of the cosmos—in commentary on the Six Days of Creation, and elsewhere—draw readily on the accepted scientific knowledge of the day. St. John Damascene's account of creation in his *On the Orthodox Faith*—though not a commentary, based on the Genesis account, supplemented by the Psalms—proceeds by dealing with eternity and time, heaven and the angels, the four elements (the section on fire including a good deal of calendrical and astronomical information, the signs of the zodiac and so forth), before proceeding to the creation of humankind and an analysis of the human, seen as in the image of God, consisting of soul and body, the former analysed according to its various faculties, the latter in accordance with the senses, leading to a discussion of human activity and willing, and then finally leading to a discussion of Paradise and the fall, and human redemption through the Incarnation. This sequence is more reminiscent of Plato's *Timaeus* than Genesis, although it is the latter that is cited.

This presents a rather different picture from what we find in Theophilus, much more at home in the world of Greek culture, as was indeed the case with the Fathers of the fourth century and thereafter. Because of his desire to put a distance between the biblical account and the accounts of the Greeks, he tends towards a rather literalist interpretation of Genesis. He dismisses the idea that the earth is a sphere or a cube, and seems rather to speak of the

---

[7] Gregory of Nyssa, *De hominis opificio* 2.

earth as a flat surface,⁸ whereas most of the Fathers envisage the earth as a sphere, in accordance with the Ptolemaic model, the believers in a flat earth being in a minority (which, however, includes Cosmas Indicopleustes, the author of the influential *Christian Topography*).

To survey all the accounts of the Hexaemeron in the Fathers would demand a volume to itself. Here we must be more modest. It might, however, be useful to say a little more about the most influential of the Greek commentaries on the Hexaemeron, that of St. Basil the Great, and compare that with the work of the most influential of the Latins, St. Augustine of Hippo.

Basil the Great

Basil's lectures on the Hexaemeron were sermons delivered during Lent. There are nine of them, and they appear to be incomplete as a set, partly because Basil promises that he is going to deal with the creation of humankind towards the end of the ninth homily, and partly because his brother Gregory of Nyssa clearly thought the series incomplete, and wrote is *On the Making of Humankind* to bring the series to completion. There are two other homilies, dealing precisely with the creation of humankind, that are in some manuscripts appended to the set of nine. It is generally thought by scholars that these are genuine, but were never edited by Basil and thus not included in the published set of nine; Gregory clearly knew nothing of them. Basil draws from the text of Genesis an account of the formation of the visible universe. This does not include an account of the angels, though he clearly believes that there are angelic beings who were created by God, but the account of their creation belongs elsewhere—it is ἀνιστόρητον, it does not belong to history. For history is concerned with time, and the question of time and eternity is one of the topics he discusses in his homilies. Basil devotes a good deal of the first homily to discussing the beginning of creation, the moment of creation. The words "in the beginning" mean "in this temporal beginning" or "in the beginning of time." But Basil faces a philosophical puzzle here, which others wrestled with—St. Augustine, John Philoponos, St. Thomas Aquinas. How does the eternal God, who is beyond time, create in time? Or, to quote a poet, where is "The point of intersection of the timeless / with time"? T.S. Eliot was concerned in *Four Quartets*

---

⁸ Theophilus, *Autol.* 2.32. At least, I think that is what he means, though he says κόσμος, not γῆ.

with how timebound beings discern this point. Basil is rather looking at it from the other side. He is clearly anxious to avoid the kind of anthropomorphism that would effectively make God a temporal being, intervening in the temporal sequence from alongside, as it were. To solve this Basil draws on contemporary mathematical thought, the kind of speculation that goes back to Pythagoras, but which had experienced a revival among the Neoplatonists such as Plotinos. He suggests that "the beginning" refers to "something momentary and timeless belonging to creation";[9] it is worth noting that Basil's phrase includes no noun—it is something that escapes ostensive definition—and he goes on to suggest that this beginning is "indivisible and without extension," initiating what follows, but not part of it. "For, just as the beginning of a road is not yet a road, nor the beginning of a house a house, so the beginning of time is not yet time, not even the smallest part of it."[10] The analogy that lies behind his illustrations is the idea of a mathematical series, the same analogy the Neoplatonists used to illustrate procession from the One. This beginning, not itself part of the series, is, in this context, "the point of intersection of the timeless / with time." Basil treats this question very briefly, but his thoughts are significant.

In his account of the creation of the earth and the world of animals, birds and creatures of the sea, Basil draws extensively on some works of natural history, now lost (though parallels can be found in those that survive, notably Pliny's). He also discusses the four elements, the sequence of seasons, and the constellations of the heavens. However, he rejects astrology, on the grounds that it overrides human free choice. There are two overriding concerns in his account of the creation of the cosmos: first, that it is created by God, and that it therefore has a beginning; secondly, that the cosmos is a source of wonder, both as a whole and in its parts, and that this wonder leads us to God Himself. All through his homilies, Basil conveys his sense of the majesty and glory of God, revealed in the wonder and beauty of the cosmos. When, at the beginning of his discussion of the fourth day of creation, he considers the two great luminaries created on that day, he exclaims:

> If sometimes on a clear night you look up at the inexpressible beauties of the stars, you get an idea of the maker of the universe, of who it is who has adorned the heavens with the variety of these flowers, and how in these visible bodies the serene necessity of their movements surpasses what is merely

---

[9] Basil, *Hom. in Hex.* 1.6 (Stanislas Giet, ed., *Basile de Césarée: Homélies sur l'Hexaéméron* [Paris: Cerf, 1968], 110).

[10] Basil, *Hom. in Hex.* 1.6 (Giet, *Basile de Césarée*, 112).

pleasant. And again if in the day you consider with sober thought the wonders of the day, and through what is seen make an analogy with what is unseen, you will be ready as a hearer, fit to join the august and blessed assembly.[11]

A further concern of Basil's is to avoid any notion that created beings are helpless creatures of fate. The darkness mentioned in Genesis is certainly opposite to the light of God, but it is not a spirit of evil, rather an absence of light; nor is the abyss a multitude of evil powers (*Hom. in Hex.* 2.4). Basil rules out any ontological dualism. Neither, however, is God the source of evil, rather evil is a disposition of the soul, contrary to nature. "Do not then search for evil outside, nor imagine that any nature can be the cause of wickedness, but recognize that each of us is the author of the evil that is in us" (*Hom. in Hex.* 2.5).

AUGUSTINE OF HIPPO

The interpretation of the early chapters of Genesis was a recurring theme in Augustine's writings. His first attempt at interpreting Genesis is found in his *On Genesis against the Manichees*, which he composed in 389, while still living in Thagaste. In this short work, he endeavoured to rebut the arguments the Manichees used to discredit Genesis. In the course of it he found himself having recourse to allegorical interpretation in order to undermine the Manichees. It is worth noting how his concern with Genesis parallels one of the major preoccupations of Basil, who also was concerned to demonstrate from Genesis that error of the Manichees (in his case, not just their dualism, but also their belief that the earth has a soul: *Hom. in Hex.* 8.1). Augustine, however, was unhappy about his ready recourse to allegory, and about four years later, he began a literal commentary on Genesis, which he soon abandoned, reaching only Gen 1:26. His next attempt to wrestle with Genesis came in his famous work, his *Confessions*; the last two books, books XI and XII, take the form of reflections inspired by verses from the account of the creation in Genesis. The *Confessions* was composed in the last three years of the fourth century; very shortly after completing that Augustine embarked on his major commentary on Genesis, his *Literal Commentary on Genesis*, which occupied him from 401 until 415, though much of it was composed towards the beginning of this period. Then, finally, shortly after completing his *Literal Commentary*, Augustine turned again

---

[11] Basil, *Hom. in Hex.* 6.1 (Giet, *Basile de Césarée*, 326).

to Genesis in book XI of his *City of God*, in which he begins to trace in scripture the story of the two cities, the *civitas Dei* and the *civitas terrena*, and continues to follow Genesis, with frequent digressions until the end of book XVI (thereafter, until the end of book XVIII, he is following, in a similarly digressive way, the later history of Israel). Although three of these works are commentaries (which, however, do not advance very far: none of them get beyond Gen 3), Genesis does not really engage Augustine as a commentator. Augustine remarks in his account of the *Incomplete Literal Commentary on Genesis* in his *Retractations*, that he was merely a novice in exegesis when he attempted it, and quickly found the burden too great (*Retract.* 1.18[17]). Even in his later *Literal Commentary on Genesis*, exegesis only really engages him in the first three books; thereafter we have a series of treatises on the nature of human corporality, on the relation between soul and body, the nature of Paradise, on woman and marriage, on the Fall—all of these can be related without too much difficulty to the biblical text, though there are considerable digressions—as well as treatises on creation and the seminal reasons, on the origin of the human soul, and on different kinds of vision. The engagement with Genesis in the *Confessions* takes the biblical text as a *point de départ*: for his famous discussion of time and eternity in book XI, and on ideas of creation, and the nature of exegesis itself, in book XII. In the *City of God*, the narrative of Genesis provides a thread, that he keeps on abandoning and then returning to, on which he hangs his account of the two cities, and the various problems—philosophical, literary, historical and textual—he raises along the way. What we find in Augustine is not the exegete that we find, for example, in his *Enarrationes on the Psalms* or his *Tractates on the Gospel of John*, but rather someone who has been living with Genesis all his life, finding their ample material to feed his restless intellect.

The Image of God

If Genesis attracted the special attention of the Fathers, and within Genesis the account of the Six Days of Creation, within that chapter or so, one verse, or rather half a verse, assumed immense significance in the thought of the Fathers. That passage is the opening words of Gen 1:26: "And God said, 'Let us make man in accordance with our image and our likeness.'" It has often been noticed that the notion of the human as created in God's image is hardly taken up elsewhere in the Old Testament (outside Genesis itself, Ps 8:6 and Wis 2:23), and even in the New Testament, there is not much more than allusion to it, and what allusion there is is scarce. In the Fathers, however, it became absolutely central to their understanding of human nature. The Dominican theologian, père Th. Camelot once remarked: "This theme of the image is, in the theology of the Fathers, above all the Greek Fathers, central: in that doctrine there converge at once their Christology and theology of the Trinity, their anthropology and psychology, their theology of creation and that of grace, the problem of nature and the supernatural, the mystery of deification, the theology of the spiritual life and the laws of its development and of its progress."[12] Most of the Fathers interpret the notion of the human as being in the image of God from the premiss that *the* image of God is Christ, as the New Testament affirms (2 Cor 4:4; Col 1:15). The human is created *in accordance with*, κατά, the image of God: Christ, the incarnate Logos or Word of God, is the archetype of humanity. What is distinctively human can then, for the Greek Fathers, be summed up in the adjective rational, λογικός, which makes contact with the Greek philosophical tradition, but imparts to it a new fullness and amplitude. Furthermore, the text of Genesis suggests a contrast of some kind between image and likeness. The Greek word used in Genesis for likeness is ὁμοίωσις, which suggests not simply likeness, but a process of likening, assimilation. Plato had said, in a much quoted phrase, φυγὴ δὲ ὁμοίωσις θεῷ κατὰ τὸ δυνατόν—"flight [from the world] is assimilation to God as much as is possible" (*Theaet.* 176A). The verse from Genesis, to a Greek philosophical ear, suggested that the human was made in the image of God and that human destiny was assimilation to God, what the Greek Fathers, especially, came to call deification. It is doubtless because of the way this verse resonated with philosophical, especially Platonic, notions that the notion of the image became so central to the theology of the Fathers.

THE FALL—THE FIRST MURDER— THE FLOOD—THE TOWER OF BABEL

I have put all these together, because though the account of the fall of Adam and Eve, understood as the fall of humanity, is unquestionably important in patristic reflection on the human condition, it is possible to exaggerate its significance, at least for the Greek Fathers (the Greek term, ancestral sin, προπατερικὸν ἁμάρτημα, has a broader reference than the Latin term,

---

[12] Père Th. Camelot, "La théologie de l'image de Dieu," *RSPT* 40 (1956): 443–471, esp. 443–444.

original sin, *peccatum originale*, probably coined by Augustine). It is often remarked that Rabbinic interpretation of Genesis sees the Fall of Adam as one act of human rebellion against God, not *the* act of rebellion; the Fathers do not altogether abandon that perception. Indeed, the way modern theology tends to objectify the sin of Adam as the "Fall" is foreign to the theology of the Fathers; the Greek word for fall (so used in modern Greek theology), πτῶσις, is not commonly used to refer to the "Fall of Adam."[13] There is a further factor that marks a difference between a patristic reading of the Old Testament and how it tends to be read today. We have a much stronger sense of the linearity of history than either the Hebrews or the Greeks. Adam's fall is the beginning of all that follows in a simply historical sense. Both Hebrews and Greeks tend more to collapse history and read past events as present. Reading the events of Genesis is not reading about a remote past, but about events that are in some sense still present, events in which we participate in some way. The sin of Adam and the expulsion from Paradise is certainly an event of immense significance. And that significance is enhanced by the notion of Christ as the Second Adam, who restores what Adam damaged or destroyed. As is well known, the parallel between Adam and Christ spills over into a range of other correspondences: the tree of life in the Garden of Eden and the tree of the cross; Eve, the "mother of the living," but in reality the mother of the living dead, and the Virgin Mary, who is truly the mother of the living; Eve's disobedience and Mary's obedience, and so on. But this parallelism links the events connected with Adam with the events connected with Christ; "as in Adam all died, so in Christ shall all be made alive" (1 Cor 15:22). Without any suggestion that the events of Gen 3 are unhistorical, the Fathers readily read them as events that tell of the human condition. When Athanasius remarks in his account of the "first of human to come into being," that "he was named Adam in the Hebrew tongue," betraying his awareness of the meaning of the word in Hebrew, he seems to be revealing that this is a story about humanity, who turned from contemplation of God to contemplation of them and the nothingness from which they had been drawn—a nothingness which now consumes them (*C. Gent.* 2–3). This sense of a typical story—revealing the human condition, and also God's great mercy—is manifest in patristic comments on the murder of Abel, the Flood and the Tower of Babel. Bede, for instance, remarks that "Some understand ... the killing of Abel as the passion of the Lord and Saviour, and the earth that opened its mouth and received Abel's

---

[13] Lampe's *PGL*, 1205, records no examples of the word used in this way.

blood from Cain's hand as the church (which received, in the mystery of its renewal, the blood of Christ ...)" (*Homilies on the Gospels* 1.14). Noah's ark is, according to Augustine, "undoubtedly a symbol of the city of God on its pilgrimage in history" (*Civ.* 15.26).

Patristic exegesis of the sin of Adam and the expulsion from Paradise has no one explanation of the events. Augustine, addressing the question as to why God allowed Adam to be tempted when he foresaw that Adam would fall, prefaces his explanation with the words: "I cannot sound the depths of divine wisdom, and I confess that the solution is far beyond my powers. There may be a hidden reason, made known only to those who are better and holier than I ..." (*Gen. litt.* 2.4.6). Adam may have fallen through pride (one reason Augustine advances); but it may be that Adam advanced towards self-knowledge too quickly and could not cope with it (St. John Damascene). Eve may have been attracted by the fairness of the fruit (Diadochos of Photike); it may have been that she was easily misled by the guile of the serpent because she had only learnt of the prohibition from Adam, not directly from God (Ambrose). The account of the Fall is seen as a key to the frailty of humanity, a story patient of repeated pondering.

THE PATRIARCHS

The rest of Genesis consists of the stories of the patriarchs, Abraham, Isaac, Jacob and his sons, especially Joseph. This interest in the stories of the patriarchs can be traced back to the Hebrew tradition. Early examples of Christian interest in the patriarchs (more specifically, Jewish-Christian interest) can be found in the *Testaments of the Twelve Patriarchs* (the sons of Jacob) and of individual Patriarchs, Abraham, Isaac and Jacob, as well as Job, Moses, Solomon, and Adam.[14] They often use the form of the testament to give apocalyptic visions of the future. More important, however, for patristic interest in the patriarchs are the treatises of the first-century Jew, Philo of Alexandria. He has treatises on Abraham and Joseph, and it is likely that treatises on other patriarchs have been lost; some of his treatises that survive (all on the books of the Pentateuch) have discussion of the patriarchs.[15] Of the Fathers, Ambrose is most explicit in his attention to the patriarchs, with works on the patriarchs as a whole, as well as works

---

[14] *OTP* 2:773–995.

[15] For more on Philo, and his preoccupation with Genesis, see Sterling's article in this volume.

on Isaac (subtitled, "The Soul"), "Jacob and the Happy Life," and Joseph.[16] Ambrose was inspired by Philo, to such an extent that Jerome accused him of plagiarism. For Ambrose the patriarchs are ethical models, and he uses their lives as ways of commending the Christian moral life. In this he is following the way the patriarchs are appealed to in the New Testament, Abraham in particular being regarded as an example of faith (see Romans, Galatians, and Hebrews). The patriarchs, or events from their lives, are often treated as foreshadowing the Christian dispensation. The account of Abraham greeting three guests at the Oak of Mamre in Gen 18 is seen as disclosing the doctrine of the Trinity: *tres vidit, et unum adoravit*, "he saw three, and worshipped one," as Augustine put it (*Maxim.* 2.26.7). The account of the sacrifice of Isaac in Gen 22 is interpreted in relation to Christ's sacrifice and the Eucharist. John Chrysostom says of the sacrifice of Isaac that "all this, however, happened as a type of the cross. Hence Christ too said to the Jews, 'Your father Abraham rejoiced to see my day, he saw it and was glad.' How did he see it if he lived so long before? In type, in shadow. Just as in our text the sheep was offered in place of Isaac, so here the rational Lamb was offered for the world ... Notice, I ask you, dearly beloved, how everything was prefigured in shadow: an only-begotten son in that case, an only-begotten in this; dearly loved in that case, dearly loved in this ..." (*Hom.Gen.* 47.14). The story of Joseph is mostly treated by the Fathers as an example of virtue and God's protection of the virtuous, though his being sold into slavery provokes several of the Fathers to find here a figurative account of Christ's betrayal. Caesarius of Arles offers an elaborate parallel with the passion of Christ: his being stripped, thrown into a pit, his being brought out of the pit for a price and the price itself foreshadowing Christ's being stripped of his tunic, his descent into hell, his being bought by the nations at the price of faith, and the thirty pieces of silver (Caesarius even makes something of the way the different translations have sometime twenty, sometimes, thirty, pieces of silver as the price exacted for Joseph).

Conclusion

I have tried to show some of the variety of ways in which the book of Genesis provided material for the Fathers to explore the ramifications of the Christian faith. Some are rather obvious (in particular finding moral

---

[16] For Ambrose's treatment of the patriarchs, see Marcia L. Colish, *Ambrose's Patriarchs: Ethics for the Common Man* (Notre Dame, Ind.: University of Notre Dame Press, 2005).

examples, though some of the Fathers were conscious of the problems of finding moral examples in the polygamous patriarchs: see Augustine's discussion in *Doctr. chr.* 3.18.60–21.31), others are more elaborate not least some of the attempts to find everything that Christians believed about creation (for instance, the creation of the angels) in Gen 1. But I think all we have seen illustrates something about patristic exegesis that it is easy to forget. They take the text of Scripture extremely seriously; indeed, they regard it as inspired, but they do not approach Scripture in any "fundamentalist" way. There is none of the anxiety one finds in fundamentalist readings of Scripture today. They are not afraid of reason, nor are they afraid to say that there are things that Scripture does not tell us about. Basil, at one point, does not hesitate to say that the Bible is not a treatise on cosmology,[17] nor, as we have seen, is he unwilling to draw on the scientific wisdom of his day—it is easy to detect parallels with Galen or Pliny. Yet, at the same time, the Fathers take the text of the Bible very seriously: it bears any amount of careful pondering. We find what one can only call a sustained engagement with the text, tracing its allusions, exploring its symbolism, delighting in its imagery. Inspiration does not guarantee an infallible text, as exponents of scriptural inspiration have claimed from the Enlightenment onwards: it does ensure a reliable text, if approached in the right spirit, but what we find in the Fathers is rather a conviction that reading the text of Scripture is itself an inspired activity—the Spirit moving in us to enable an engagement with the Spirit present in the Scriptures. That is something worth recovering.

SELECT BIBLIOGRAPHY

In Principio: Interprétations des premiers versets de la Genèse. École pratique des Hautes Études—Section des Sciences Religieuses: Centre d'Études des Religions du Livre, Laboratoire associé au C.N.R.S. 152. Paris: Études Augustiniennes, 1973.
Bouteneff, Peter C. *Beginnings: Ancient Christian Readings of the Biblical Creation Narratives.* Grand Rapids: Baker Academic, 2008.
Camelot, père Th. "La théologie de l'image de Dieu." *Revue des sciences philosophiques et théologiques* 40 (1956): 443–471.
Colish, Marcia L. *Ambrose's Patriarchs: Ethics for the Common Man.* Notre Dame, Ind.: University of Notre Dame Press, 2005.
Congar, Yves M.-J. "Le thème de *Dieu-créateur* et les explications de l'Hexaméron dans la tradition chrétienne." Pages 189–222 in vol. 1 of *L'Homme devant Dieu:*

---

[17] Basil, *Hom. in Hex.* 9.1 (80D–81A).

Mélanges offerts au père Henri de Lubac. 3 vols. Théologie 56–58. Paris: Aubier, 1963–1964.

Foerster, Werner, ed. *Gnosis: A Selection of Gnostic Texts.* 2 vols. Oxford: Clarendon, 1972–1974.

Hall, Christopher A. *Reading Scripture with the Church Fathers.* Ancient Christian Commentary on Scripture. Downers Grove, Ill.: InterVarsity, 1998.

Kannengiesser, Charles. *Handbook of Patristic Exegesis: The Bible in Ancient Christianity.* 2 vols. Leiden: Brill, 2004.

Louth, Andrew, ed. *Genesis 1–11.* Ancient Christian Commentary on Scripture: Old Testament 1. Downers Grove, Ill.: InterVarsity, 2001.

Sheridan, Mark, ed. *Genesis 12–50.* Ancient Christian Commentary on Scripture: Old Testament 2. Downers Grove, Ill.: InterVarsity, 2002.

Simonetti, Manlio. *Biblical Interpretation in the Early Church: An Historical Introduction to Patristic Exegesis.* Translated by John A. Hughes. Edinburgh: T&T Clark, 1994.

Wallace-Hadrill, D.S. *The Greek Patristic View of Nature.* Manchester: Manchester University Press, 1968.

Zahlten, Johannes. *Creatio mundi: Darstellungen des sechs Schöpfungstage und naturwissenschaftliches Welt im Mittelalter.* Stuttgarter Beiträge zur Geschichte und Politik 13. Stuttgart: Klett-Cotta, 1979.

GENESIS IN RABBINIC INTERPRETATION

Burton L. Visotzky

Nobel laureate in literature Isaac Bashevis Singer famously quipped, "I am still learning the art of writing from the book of Genesis."[1] Although Singer was writing with a twinkle in his aging eye, his comment captures a truth about the rabbinic reception of the first book of Moses. The rabbis turned to Genesis for inspiration and revelation, and in doing so, followed Ben Bag Bag's advice about the Torah, "turn it, turn it, round and round; in it all things can be found."[2] Genesis was an anomaly for the rabbis, who were masters of Jewish law. While Genesis certainly had important, even essential laws woven into the weft and warp of its narrative—viz. the command to be fruitful and multiply[3] and the command of circumcision[4]—the vast majority of the book is devoted to story: precisely what recommended it to Singer. The lack of law probably dictated there would be no extant early (Tannaitic) compilation of rabbinic interpretations of Genesis. It was not until the heyday of the rabbinic era, the first half of the fifth century, that a major collection of rabbinic commentary on the book, Genesis Rabbah (*Gen. Rab.*), was redacted.[5] While this expansive reading of Genesis quotes the early rabbis, the reliability of those attributions is somewhat suspect.[6] Because

---

[1] David Rosenberg, ed., *Congregation: Contemporary Writers Read the Jewish Bible* (New York: Harcourt Brace Jovanovich, 1987), 7.

[2] *'Abot* 5:26 (end).

[3] Gen 1:28; Jeremy Cohen, *'Be Fertile and Increase, Fill the Earth and Master It': The Ancient and Medieval Career of a Biblical Text* (Ithaca: Cornell University Press, 1989).

[4] Gen 17:10–14; Lawrence Hoffman, *Covenant of Blood: Circumcision and Gender in Rabbinic Judaism* (CSJH; Chicago: University of Chicago Press, 1996); and Shaye J.D. Cohen, *Why Aren't Jewish Women Circumcised?: Gender and Covenant in Judaism* (Berkeley: University of California, 2005).

[5] Julius Theodor and Chanoch Albeck, eds., *Midrash Bereshit Rabbah: Critical Edition with Notes and Commentary* (2nd ed.; 3 vols.; Jerusalem: Wahrmann, 1965). This critical edition is based on the British Museum MS. See Michael Sokoloff, ed., *Midrash Bereshit Rabba: Ms. Vat. Ebr. 30* (Jerusalem: Makor, 1971); and Sokoloff, *The Geniza Fragments of Bereshit Rabba: Edited on the Basis of Twelve Manuscripts and Palimpsests with an Introduction and Notes* (Jerusalem: Israel Academy of Sciences and Humanities, 1982).

[6] E.g., on the debate between R. Aqiba and Rabbi Ishmael in *Gen. Rab.* 1:14, with the discussion of spurious attributions and invented dialogues in *Gen. Rab.*, see Burton L. Visotzky,

rabbinic Jews read Genesis publicly,[7] this seminal midrash spawned subsequent collections of rabbinic commentary on and exegeses of Genesis. These latter works were also studied in rabbinic academies and by preachers, in an attempt to garner traditional and novel insights into the sacred text.

Rabbinic interpretations of Scripture varied in hermeneutic methods, intentions, and audiences over time and place. In some instances the goal of the rabbinic exegete was to capture what they imagined to be the simple meaning of the biblical text.[8] Other rabbis used the interpretation of the Bible as a place to engage with ideologies they found alien, be they Roman paganism, Christianity, Gnosticism, or Islam.[9] The rabbis also were masters of retelling the Torah in synagogue settings, which are collected in the late Aramaic Targums and medieval Hebrew midrashim.[10] Further, the rabbis were not shy about using hermeneutic methods of their surrounding culture among their interpretive strategies.[11]

"Trinitarian Testimonies," in *Fathers of the World: Essays in Rabbinic and Patristic Literatures* (WUNT 80; Tübingen: Mohr Siebeck, 1995), 67, at n. 13.

[7] In the land of Israel, public reading of the Torah was spread over three to three and one-half years. In Babylonia the Pentateuch was read on an annual cycle. See Charles Perrot, "The Reading of the Bible in the Ancient Synagogue," in *Mikra: Text, Translation, Reading and Interpretation of the Hebrew Bible in Ancient Judaism and Early Christianity* (ed. Martin Jan Mulder; CRINT 2/1; Assen: Van Gorcum, 1988), 137–159; cf. Shlomo Naeh, "The Torah Reading Cycle in Early Palestine: A Re-examination," *Tarbiz* 67 (1998): 167–187, with the response by Ezra Fleischer, "Remarks Concerning the Triennial Cycle of the Torah Reading in Eretz Israel," *Tarbiz* 73 (2004): 83–124 [Hebrew with English abstracts].

[8] Azzan Yadin, *Scripture as Logos: Rabbi Ishmael and the Origins of Midrash* (Philadelphia: University of Pennsylvania, 2004); and Yadin, "Resistance to Midrash? Midrash and Halakhah in the Halakhic Midrashim," in *Current Trends in the Study of Midrash* (ed. Carol Bakhos; JSJSup 106; Leiden: Brill, 2006), 35–58.

[9] Hermann L. Strack and Günter Stemberger, *Introduction to the Talmud and Midrash* (trans. and ed. Markus Bockmuehl; Philadelphia: Fortress, 1992); Burton L. Visotzky, "The Literature of the Rabbis," in *From Mesopotamia to Modernity: Ten Introductions to Jewish History and Literature* (ed. Burton L. Visotzky and David E. Fishman; Boulder: Westview, 1999), 71–102; Visotzky, *Reading the Book: Making the Bible a Timeless Text* (3rd ed.; Philadelphia: Jewish Publication Society, 2005); for anti-Christian polemic, Marc Hirshman, *A Rivalry of Genius: Jewish and Christian Biblical Interpretation* (Albany: SUNY Press, 1996); and Visotzky, *Fathers of the World*. For images of Islam, see Carol Bakhos, *Ishmael on the Border: Rabbinic Portrayals of the First Arab* (Albany: SUNY Press, 2006).

[10] Geza Vermes, *Scripture and Tradition in Judaism: Haggadic Studies* (2nd ed.; StPB 4; Leiden: Brill, 1973); and Avigdor Shinan, *The Embroidered Targum: The Aggadah in Targum Pseudo-Jonathan of the Pentateuch* (Jerusalem: Magnes, 1992 [Hebrew]).

[11] Saul Lieberman, "Rabbinic Interpretation of Scripture," and "The Hermeneutic Rules of the Aggadah," in *Hellenism in Jewish Palestine: Studies in the Literary Transmission, Beliefs and Manners of Palestine in the I Century BCE – IV Century CE* (2nd ed.; New York: Jewish

This essay examines representative interpretations of Genesis in rabbinic literature. Its scope precludes an exhaustive survey, as rabbinic literature on Genesis begins in the early third century and extends to this very day. Where possible, highlights from the varieties of rabbinic exegeses and commentaries will be considered within their historic milieux. In general the survey will consider selections from significant rabbinic texts and commentaries on Genesis, including: Sifre on Deuteronomy (early third century), *Gen. Rab.* (fifth century), the Babylonian Talmud (sixth century), Tanḥuma Genesis (seventh to ninth century), Pirqe Rabbi Eliezer (ninth century), ʾAbot de Rabbi Nathan (ninth century), and the commentary of Rabbi Solomon ben Isaac (also known as Rashi, France, eleventh century). This broad swath of rabbinic interpretation covers texts from an eight hundred year period, ranging geographically from Troyes to the Tigris. The texts are composed in rabbinic Hebrew, western and eastern Aramaic.

Among the representative topics and characters surveyed will be rabbinic cosmologies (Gen 1:1–2:4), Adam and Eve (Gen 1:26–3:24), Abraham, Ishmael, and Isaac (Gen 21–22), Jacob/Israel (Gen 25:19–50), and Joseph (Gen 37–50). The order of Genesis will be followed and each selection will examine texts from the rabbinic corpus.

We begin "In the beginning" (Gen 1:1). Of course the Hebrew text of Genesis says no such thing. Rather, the Hebrew preserves a solecism much remarked upon by commentators and translators alike.[12] *Gen. Rab.* takes up the problem in its very first section, interpreting the letter *Bet*, with which the Torah begins, as instrumental.

> (Gen 1:1) The Torah said, "I was the artisan's instrument of the Blessed Holy One." In the way of the world, when a human king builds a palace he does not build it through his own knowledge, but rather employs the knowledge of an artisan. And the artisan does not build it from his knowledge, but rather uses blue-prints and site-drawings[13] so he knows how to build the rooms and doorways.

Theological Seminary, 1962), 47–82; Visotzky, "Jots and Tittles: On Scriptural Interpretation in Rabbinic and Patristic Literatures," in *Fathers of the World*, 28–40; and Visotzky, "Midrash, Christian Exegesis, and Hellenistic Hermeneutic," in *Current Trends in the Study of Midrash* (ed. Carol Bakhos; JSJSup 106; Leiden: Brill, 2006), 111–131.

[12] "In the beginning" follows the LXX (ἐν ἀρχῃ); the Hebrew is better reflected in the NJPS: "When God began to create ..."; see Harry M. Orlinsky, *Notes on the New Translation of the Torah* (Philadelphia: Jewish Publication Society, 1969), 49–52; apud Rashi.

[13] The Hebrew transliterates two loan-words from Greek architecture, *diphthera* and *pinax*. See Lieberman, *Hellenism*, 203–208; and, for the interpretation that follows, Visotzky, "The Architecture of the Universe," in *Reading the Book*, 204–224.

Thus the Blessed Holy One looked into the Torah and created the world. And the Torah said, "By means of The First (*be-Reisheet*) God created." The word 'The First,' (*Reisheet*) means Torah, as you say, "God created me The First (*Reisheet*) of His ways" (Prov 8:22).[14]

Now, Gen 1:1 is to be understood, "By means of Torah God created the heaven and the earth." This reading solves the problem of biblical grammar by inserting a reified Torah into the Genesis text. Torah (*reisheet*) is simply equated with the Wisdom (*reisheet*) of the biblical quotation from Prov 8:22. It is neither "in the beginning," nor "when God began to create;" instead the midrash imagines the Torah as the very instrument of creation. Further, God does not create by fiat, but rather consults a pre-existent plan, a sort of platonic ideal, which becomes the very blue-print of creation.[15] This reading maintains the *creatio ex nihilo* of the LXX's reading, while giving it a rabbinic spin.[16] It takes a trope from Greco-Roman architecture familiar to the literati of the Hellenistic *oikoumene*,[17] and transforms it into an instrument of rabbinic propaganda.

In *Gen. Rab.*, God is likened to the architect who consults blue-prints and site-drawings. In the building trades, these are very different types of documents. The former, on parchment, are deposited in the archives as the official written records. The site-drawings, however, are subject to change and are incised with a stylus on an easily altered wax tablet, a *pinax*. When the midrashist turns to God, God looks in the Torah. But if the architect has two sets of plans to consult, what is the corresponding Torah that God views? It, too, is a two-part document. The first is the Written Torah, inscribed on parchment.[18] The second is the rabbinic law and interpretation of Scripture, the Oral Torah. These rabbinic texts were meant to remain oral, and not written.[19] Nevertheless, unofficial, easily

---

[14] Excerpt taken from the end of *Gen. Rab.* 1:1 (Theodor and Albeck, *Midrash Bereshit Rabbah*, 2). All translations are by the author of this essay.

[15] Cf. Plato, *Tim.*, in *Plato VII: Timaeus, Critias, Cleitophon, Menexenus, Epistles* (trans. R.G. Bury; LCL 234; Cambridge: Harvard University Press, 1929); apud Philo, *Opif.*, in *Philo I: On the Creation. Allegorical Interpretation of Genesis 2 and 3* (trans. F.H. Colson and G.F. Whitaker; LCL 226; Cambridge: Harvard University Press, 1929).

[16] Marien Niehoff, "Creatio Ex Nihilo Theology in 'Genesis Rabbah' in Light of Christian Exegesis," *HTR* 99 (2006): 37–64; cf. Menahem Kister, "*Tohu wa-Bohu*, Primordial Elements and *Creatio ex Nihilo*," *JSQ* 14 (2007): 229–256.

[17] See Vitruvius, *On Architecture* (trans. Frank Granger; 2 vols.; LCL 251, 280; Cambridge: Harvard University Press, 1931, 1934).

[18] See *m. Yad.* 4:5, which requires a Torah scroll to be written on skin = parchment. See the discussion in Lieberman, *Hellenism*, 203–208.

[19] "The Publication of the Mishnah," in Lieberman, *Hellenism*, 84–92.

erased, wax-tablet notes on the Oral Torah were recorded on pinaces by earnest students. So the analogy between the architect-builder and God-Creator is precise. When God created the world, God looked in a two-part Torah, on parchment scrolls and on wax-tablets, just like the architect in the midrash. God consults the Written Torah and the rabbinic Oral Torah, so that "By means of Torah, God created the heaven and the earth." As it were, God consults rabbinic interpretation of Genesis in order to create the universe!

The rabbis believed that Scripture was divinely inspired and, so, packed with meaning. What was called for was the appropriate key to unlock that meaning.[20] They were equally keen to read their own hellenistic *Weltanschauung* into the record of Genesis. We have just seen that these fifth century sages displayed some awareness of the cosmologies of their contemporaries. By reading the first letter of the Torah as instrumental, they were able to imagine the Torah as the platonic ideal (*nous*) from which God created the world. They were equally capable of reading the Platonic creation-followed-by-ordering of the universe[21] into that first verse of Genesis by means of the biblical Hebrew word *et*, which functions as an indicator of the object in a verse. For the rabbis, this grammatical particle, too, is packed with both meaning and the physical stuff of the universe.

> (Gen 1:1) "*et* The heaven and *et* the earth" (Gen 1:1). Rabbi Ishmael asked Rabbi Aqiba, "Since you served [as a disciple to] Nahum of Gimzo for twenty-two years [and studied the principle that the Hebrew particles] *akh* and *rak* limit the sense of Scripture whilst *et* and *gam* expand the sense of Scripture, these *et*s written here, what do you make of them?"
>
> [Aqiba rejoined, "And what do you make of them?"][22]
>
> He said, "If the Bible had said, 'In the beginning created God[s]: Heaven and Earth,' we might have said that Heaven and Earth are also gods."
>
> He said, "'For it is no empty thing for you,' (Deut 32:47)—and if it is empty, you are to blame, for you do not know how to interpret! '*Et* the heaven' includes the sun, moon, stars, and constellations. 'And *et* the earth' includes trees, grasses and the Garden of Eden."[23]

---

[20] Visotzky, "Jots and Tittles."
[21] Plato, *Tim.*; apud Philo, *Opif.*
[22] See Visotzky, "Jots and Tittles," 31, at n. 16. Note that this dialogue may be pseudonymous in its entirety.
[23] *Gen. Rab.* 1:14 (Theodor and Albeck, *Midrash Bereshit Rabbah*, 12, following the emendation of H. Graetz cited therein).

This commentary reads into the verse on Day One the creation of those elements listed in Genesis as being created on later days. God's role has changed in this understanding in a significant way. No longer is God creating *ex nihilo* day after day, but on Day One creates everything and spends the next five days putting everything in its proper place. As Rashi says, "Scripture has not come to explicate the order of creation, for were that Scripture's intent, it would have said, 'At first, God created heaven and earth' instead of 'When God began to create ...'"[24] Further, *Gen. Rab.* refutes a possible polytheist or dualist reading of the verse, rejecting reading "heaven" and "earth" as subjects rather than objects. The discarded reading, which admits of multiplicity in the Godhead, may also be Gnostic.[25]

The negative valence which Gnostic systems placed upon the substance of the universe[26] was roundly rejected by the rabbis of *Gen. Rab.*

> (Gen 1:2) Rav said, ... "In the way of the world, a human king may build a palace near a sewer or a trash-heap or rot; and anyone who comments that the palace is, in fact, built near a sewer or a trash-heap or rot, does he not give offense?! So too, anyone who comments that this world has been created from 'chaos and confusion and darkness,' (Gen 1:2), does he not give offense?!"[27]

The rabbis reject any negative assessment of matter even as they refute that there was any demiurge involved in the creation. This anti-Gnostic reading is explicitly addressed:

> (Gen 1:1) Rabbi Yohanan said, "[Angels] were created on the second day [of creation]" ... Rabbi Hanina said, "[Angels] were created on the fifth day [of creation]" ... Rabbi Julian son of Tiberius quoted Rabbi Yitzhak, "Whether according to Rabbi Hanina or according to Rabbi Yohanan, all agree that [angels] were not created at all on Day One of creation," so no one could say

---

[24] Rashi at Gen 1:1. See Niehoff, "*Creatio*," n. 19.

[25] See Ephraim E. Urbach, *The Sages: Their Concepts and Beliefs* (Jerusalem: Magnes, 1969 [Hebrew]), 161–162.

[26] See Hans Jonas, *The Gnostic Religion: The Message of the Alien God and the Beginnings of Christianity* (Boston: Beacon, 1958), 212–215. This work is out of date since the publication of James M. Robinson, ed., *The Nag Hammadi Library* (San Francisco: Harper and Row, 1977) and the stream of Gnosticism studies which have followed; e.g., Charles W. Hedrick and Robert Hodgson, Jr., eds., *Nag Hammadi, Gnosticism, and Earliest Christianity* (Peabody, Mass.: Hendrickson, 1986); Karen L. King, *What is Gnosticism?* (Cambridge: Harvard University Press, 2003); as well as the publications of A. Henrichs and L. Koenen, "Der Kölner Mani-Kodex," in *ZPE* 19 (1975): 1–85; *ZPE* 32 (1978): 87–199; *ZPE* 44 (1981): 201–318; and *ZPE* 48 (1982): 1–59. See also Ron Cameron and Arthur J. Dewey, eds., *The Cologne Mani Codex (P. Colon. inv. nr. 4780): 'Concerning the Origin of His Body'* (SBLTT 15; Missoula, Mont.: Scholars Press, 1979). Jonas still accurately portrays the Gnostics' dark view of matter.

[27] *Gen. Rab.* 1:5, end (Theodor and Albeck, *Midrash Bereshit Rabbah*, 3). Cf. Niehoff, "*Creatio*," 55–60; and Kister, "*Tohu wa-Bohu*."

that [the angel] Michael was stretching out [heaven] from the south, while [the angel] Gabriel was [stretching out heaven from the] north, while the Blessed Holy One was measuring it all in the middle. Rather "I, YHWH, create everything, I stretch forth the heavens alone, I flatten the earth, on my own (*mayiti*)" (Isa 44:24). It is written *mi iti*,[28] "who is with Me?" Who [possibly could have been] associated with Me in the creation of the world?!"[29]

Rabbis Yohanan and Hanina each offer proof-texts from Scripture (omitted here) to buttress their claims as to when angels were created. But all agree on essentially two points: the first is that God and God alone created the universe on Day One without associates. The second is that angels are created beings, creatures and not creators.[30]

Yet the rabbis could tolerate the potentially dangerous idea of pre-mundane creation. They employ the hermeneutic device of *notarikon*,[31] which presumes that a given word of Scripture is, in fact, short-hand, to parse the opening word of Genesis. Thus the word *beresheet* (בראשית) is rendered as two words *bara sheet* (ברא שית); the first, *bara*, Hebrew for "created," while the second, *sheet*, is read as Aramaic for "six." *Gen. Rab.* then asserts:

> (Gen 1:1) Six things preceded the creation of the universe. Some were created, while others arose in [God's] mind to be created. The Torah and [God's] Throne of Glory were created ... while the Fathers ..., Israel ..., the Holy Temple ..., and the Name of the Messiah ... arose in [God's] mind. Rabbi Ahava berebbi Zeira said, "Also Repentance" ... but I do not know which had precedence, Torah before the Throne of Glory or the Throne of Glory before Torah. Rabbi Abba bar Kahana said, "The Torah preceded the Throne of Glory ..." Rabbi Huna quoted Rabbi Yirmiah in the name of Rabbi Shmu'el bar Yitzhak, "The idea of Israel preceded everything!"[32]

Here again, rabbinic ideology is stressed through the primacy of Torah and Israel (= rabbinic Judaism). It is not clear what the distinction is between that which was "created" and that which "arose in [God's] mind." Perhaps the difference is God speaking (*logos*) something into being, as opposed to thinking (*nous*) it. Be that as it may, the emphasis is on Torah in the

---

[28] In the Masoretic text the consonantal letters are written as two words, מי אתי, yet the Masoretes determined that they should be read and pointed as one word, מֵאִתִּי "on My own."
[29] Excerpted from *Gen. Rab.* 1:3 (Theodor and Albeck, *Midrash Bereshit Rabbah*, 5). However, cf. Peter Schäfer, *Rivalität zwischen Engeln und Menschen: Untersuchungen zur rabbinischen Engelvorstellung* (SJ 8; Berlin: de Gruyter, 1976).
[30] This may have anti-Christian dualist or anti-Trinitarian overtones, or be directed at Christian Gnosticism. For more on anti-Trinitarian polemic, see below.
[31] See Lieberman, "The Hermeneutic Rules of the Aggadah," in *Hellenism*, 69–70.
[32] Excerpted from *Gen. Rab.* 1:4 (Theodor and Albeck, *Midrash Bereshit Rabbah*, 6). Proof-texts have been omitted.

original list of six and on repentance as the extra added ingredient, for a rabbinic conception of a viable universe.[33]

The rabbis read Scripture carefully and slowly, again and again. They not only imbued every word with deep meaning, but noted every quiddity of the sacred text. God's creation of light on Day One (Gen 1:3) posed a conundrum for the rabbinic reader, for the sun was only created on the fourth day (Gen 1:14–19). The puzzle gave rise to mystical speculation.

> (Gen 1:3) Rabbi Shime'on b. Yehotzadaq asked Rabbi Shmu'el b. Nahman, "I have heard about you that you are a master of Aggadah,[34] [can you answer this question:] Where does the light [created on Day One] come from?"
>
> He said, "The Blessed Holy One wrapped Himself in it like a garment, and the splendor of His beauty shone forth from one end of the universe to the other."
>
> He said this in a whisper.[35]
>
> He replied, "It is a clear verse of Scripture, 'He wears light like a garment, etc.' (Ps 104:2); and you tell me in a whisper?!"
>
> He said, "Just as I heard it in a whisper, so I told you in a whisper."[36]

We witness here a beautiful method of rabbinic mystical exegesis. Psalms employs a poetic trope, meant to be read allegorically. Yet the mystic takes the phrase literally so that God wears light like a garment. According to this reading, the light must be physical matter, capable of being wrapped around God's body. And God, it should be noted, has a body upon which to drape the garment. Of course, biblical readers will not be surprised to read of God's body,[37] but later rabbis (notably Maimonides in the twelfth century) vigorously eschewed any notion of an incarnate God. So despite the protestation that 'it is a clear verse of Scripture,' it is appropriately whispered as esoteric. This supernal light stymies rabbinic interpreters, for it disappears from the Genesis account with the creation of the sun. Where did it go?

---

[33] In *Pirqe R. El.* ch. 3, this text is retold so that the universe will not "stand" until the creation of repentance.

[34] While the term most often refers to rabbinic narrative, in the cosmological contexts of *Gen. Rab.* it refers to mystical speculation.

[35] A technical term for the transmission of esoteric lore. See Gershom G. Scholem, *Jewish Gnosticism, Merkabah Mysticism, and Talmudic Tradition* (New York: Jewish Theological Seminary of America, 1960) 58, n. 10. For Scholem's discussion of the passage, see 56–64.

[36] *Gen. Rab.* 3:4 (Theodor and Albeck, *Midrash Bereshit Rabbah*, 20).

[37] Benjamin D. Sommer, *The Bodies of God and the World of Ancient Israel* (Cambridge: Cambridge University Press, 2009).

(Gen 1:3) It is taught, the light that was created during the six days of creation could not illuminate during the day, for it would have eclipsed the orb of the sun, nor at night, for it was not created to illuminate the night, but the day. So where is it? It was hidden away for the righteous for the Coming [messianic] Future.[38]

Let us turn from the creation of the elements of the first five days to the creation of humanity on Day Six. A sublime verse of Genesis has God proclaim, "Let us make humanity in our image" (Gen 1:26). It appears from the grammatical construction, which uses the noun *elohim* (pl) for God's name and the verb *na'aseh* (also a plural), as though God could be speaking in the royal "We." Yet the Genesis account of creation is replete with singular verbs, as well as singular nouns (e.g. YHWH) for God's name. But the plural for God also is reflected by the creation of Adam and Eve, for Gen 1:27 reads, "in the image (singular) of God he created him (singular); male and female God created them (plural)." This gender dualism requires the rabbis to harmonize the Gen 1 account of humanity created male and female in God's image, with the Gen 2 creation story, where God creates Adam first, alone, and only subsequently creates woman from the man's rib (Gen 2:21–22).

> (Gen 1:26) Rabbi Yirmiah b. Lazar said, "When God created Adam, God created him *androgynous*."[39] Rabbi Shmu'el b. Nahman said, "When God created Adam, God created him two-faced (*di-prosopon*),[40] then sawed him apart, one back this way and one back that way."
>
> They objected to him, "It is written, 'And God took one of his ribs [מצלעותיו]' (Gen 2:21)."
>
> He said to them, "[It means]: from his side, as you say, 'And for the side [ולצלע] of the Tabernacle' (Exod 26:20)."[41]

Taking the problematic noun for "rib" in the Genesis account as it is used in Exodus, the rabbis of *Gen. Rab.* harmonize two contradictory texts. Adam is created androgynous, with both a male and female side (like a Roman Hermes), and is subsequently sawed in two. Now both Genesis chapters tell the same story, and again, the rabbis have explicated the text through their own hellenistic lens. Further, they have likened the representation of God

---

[38] *Gen. Rab* 3:6 (Theodor and Albeck, *Midrash Bereshit Rabbah*, 21).

[39] A Greek loan-word in the Hebrew text. The ideas found here are also in Plato and Philo. See the notes in Theodor and Albeck, *Midrash Bereshit Rabbah*, 55, line 2.

[40] A Greek loan-word in the Hebrew text. Literally: "two-faced" or "two-personed." Compare J.N.D. Kelly, *Early Christian Doctrines* (2nd ed.; New York: Harper and Row, 1960), 110–115. For the anti-Christian anxieties that Gen 1:26 provokes in the rabbis, see below.

[41] *Gen. Rab.* 8:1 (Theodor and Albeck, *Midrash Bereshit Rabbah*, 55).

in humanity as a dual, similar to representations of the gods of the Roman world. Yet this is a disturbing move as it opens the doors to pagan, Gnostic and, of course, Christian readings of Scripture; or as the rabbis would have it, heresy!

> (Gen 1:26) The heretics[42] asked Rabbi Simlai, "How many gods created the world?"
>
> He replied, "Let's you and me ask the days of yore, thus it is written, 'You have but to inquire of bygone ages that came before you' (Deut 4:32). 'Ever since gods created (plural) humanity' is NOT written, but rather 'ever since God created (sing) humanity' (ibid)."
>
> They returned and asked him, "What of this which is written, 'In the beginning God (pl) created' (Gen 1:1)."
>
> He replied, "God created (pl) is not written, but 'God created (sing) Heaven and Earth.'"
>
> Rabbi Simlai said, "In each place that you find a refutation for the heretics, you will find its cure at its side."[43]
>
> They returned and asked, "What of this which is written, 'Let us make (pl) man in our image' (Gen 1:26)."
>
> He said, "Read on to what follows, and God created (pl) is not written but 'God created (sing)' (Gen 1:27)."
>
> When they went out his disciples said, "You pushed them off with a mere straw, but what will you reply to us?"
>
> He explained, "In the past, Adam was created from the earth and Eve was created from Adam. From this point onward, 'In our likeness, after our image,' no man without woman, nor woman without man, nor the two of them without God's Presence (*shekinah*)."[44]

In *Gen. Rab.*'s representation of this discussion there are three parties: the rabbi, the heretics, and the rabbi's students. The rabbi replies to the persistent heretics each time by pointing to a singular verb in the verse in question. This is a sufficient sop to those heretics, who now have an answer to the seeming plurality of the godhead in Genesis. Yet his students want

---

[42] Hebrew: *minim*; see Martin Goodman, "The Function of Minim in Early Rabbinic Judaism," in *Geschichte—Tradition—Reflexion: Festschrift für Martin Hengel zum 70. Geburtstag* (ed. Hubert Cancik, Hermann Lichtenberger, and Peter Schäfer; 3 vols.; Tübingen: Mohr Siebeck, 1996) 1:501–510; and Visotzky, "Prolegomenon to the Study of Jewish-Christianities in Rabbinic Literature," in *Fathers of the World*, 129–149, esp. 144.

[43] Parallels read: "in every place the heretics rend a verse from its context, the reply is nearby"; see Visotzky, "Trinitarian Testimonies," 61–74.

[44] *Gen. Rab.* 8:9 (Theodor and Albeck, *Midrash Bereshit Rabbah*, 62–63).

a better reply. The rabbi offers one, indicating the difference between the two Genesis accounts of Scripture, so that the royal "We" of the "Let us make," now refers to God, man, and woman. That this is also a reference to a trinity is lost on his students, as is the fact that the rabbi's explanation is a close paraphrase of 1 Cor 11:11–12, especially as it was used in third to fifth century Christological controversies.[45] We may identify the "heretics" of this passage with Trinitarian Christians, busily seeking to prove their theology by testimonies from the OT.[46]

Although anti-Christian polemic and rabbinic-Christian dialogue take only a very small portion of *Gen. Rab.*'s agenda,[47] where they do appear is of interest today. When Genesis recalls God's blessings of the Sabbath, the midrash finds an opportunity to address Christianity.

> (Gen 2:3) Tineius Rufus asked Rabbi Aqiva,[48] "What is today [Shabbat] of all days?"
>
> He said to him, "And what is this man of all men?"
>
> He said, "What did I say to you and what did you say to me?"
>
> He said, "You asked me how Shabbat differs from other days, while I asked you how Rufus differs from other men."
>
> Rufus replied, "Well, the king wishes to honor him!"
>
> "So, too, God wishes to honor the Sabbath!"
>
> "How can you prove it to me?"
>
> He said, "The Sabatayon River will prove it, for its [current] drags stones all week long, but on Shabbat it rests."

---

[45] For discussion of the passage and its place within the context of Trinitarian controversies, see Visotzky, "Trinitarian Testimonies," 61–74.

[46] A longer version of the exchange is recorded in the Talmud Yerushalmi. Burton L. Visotzky, "Goys 'Я'n't Us: Rabbinic Anti-Gentile Polemic in Yerushalmi Berachot 9a," in *Heresy and Identity in Late Antiquity* (ed. Eduard Iricinschi and Holger M. Zellentin; TSAJ 119; Tübingen: Mohr Siebeck, 2008), 299–313.

[47] About twenty sections of *Gen. Rab.* relate to Christianity (and whether these address Christianity remains subject to debate). There are about 100 chapters of *Gen. Rab.*, each with approximately ten subsections; so, the total attention to Christianity is about 2% of *Gen. Rab.* This is among the *largest* percentage of materials attending to Christianity within rabbinic literature. The early rabbis essentially ignored Christianity and later rabbis (post-325) rarely addressed it.

[48] I read this and the following story about Rabbi Hoshaya as pseudonymous; *pace* Moshe D. Herr, "The Historical Significance of the Dialogues Between Jewish Sages and Roman Dignitaries," *ScrHier* 22 (1971): 123–150. For these stories in the context of Jewish-Christian debate, see Hirshman, *Rivalry*, 43–54, who reads the fifth-century narrative in dialogue with Justin Martyr. Hirshman relies on Herr, "Historical," 133–135.

He said, "You are being a drag!"

So Aqiva said, "Let a necromancer prove it, for he can bring up the dead all week, but not on the Sabbath."

Rufus went and checked [by raising the shade of] his father, who rose all week, but on Shabbat did not rise. After Shabbat he raised him and said, "Dad, you've become Jewish since you died?! Why did you rise all week but not rise on Shabbat?"

His father said, "All those who do not willingly observe the Sabbath among you [the living], observe it here against their will."

Rufus asked, "What labor do you have [that you need Sabbath rest]?"

He explained, "All week long we are tortured, but on Shabbat we rest."

Rufus returned to Rabbi Aqiva and said, "If it is as you say, that the Blessed Holy One honors the Sabbath, then wind should not blow and rain should not fall!"

Aqiva retorted, "Drop dead![49] [God's involvement in Nature on Shabbat] is like one who carries within [the permitted] four cubits."[50]

This bitter exchange about the applicability of Sabbath law represents challenges to the rabbis similar to Tertullian's *Adversus Judaeos*.[51] Since this is rabbinic literature, the rabbi has the upper hand. However, the argument here is not with a Christian, but a pagan.[52] In it, the rabbinic character can tell him to "drop dead" and belittle his religious beliefs as being nothing more than necromancy.[53] Further, the rabbi 'proves' that the dead father suffers torture in the after-life. Finally, it is proven that Sabbath law is natural law, observed by those who wish to and those who do not. Even God, as it were, observes the Sabbath.

This midrash, within its redactional context in *Gen. Rab.*, engages Christianity. This is evident in the very next text, which abandons Gen 2:3 in favor of debating circumcision, another commonplace of Jewish-Christian debate.

---

[49] Literally: "may the breath of that man blow [away]."

[50] *Gen. Rab.* 11:5 (Theodor and Albeck, *Midrash Bereshit Rabbah*, 93–94). God observes Sabbath law according to rabbinic prescription.

[51] Chapter 3. Hirshman compares the passage with Justin, who was born in Nablus and was a contemporary of Rabbi Aqiva. Tertullian's argument more closely mirrors the one here.

[52] Pagans also critiqued Jewish Sabbath practices; see Henry Chadwick, ed., *Origen: Contra Celsum* (Cambridge: Cambridge University Press, 1953). Celsus lived in the right time-period for R. Aqiva, if not *Gen. Rab.*

[53] This might be a slur on Christian resurrection theology.

(Gen 2:3) A philosopher[54] asked Rabbi Hoshaya, "If circumcision is so beloved, why was it not given to Adam?"[55]

He replied, "If so, why does that man[56] shave the corners of his head, yet leaves his beard unshorn?"

He said, "Because [the hair on my head] grew with me since my [days of youthful] ignorance."

The rabbi replied, "If so, that man should blind his eyes and chop off his hand!"

He [the monk] said, "Have we come to such words?!"

The rabbi replied, "I cannot let you off free, but you should know that all that was created in the six days of creation requires repair [human involvement]: mustard needs to be sweetened, lupines need to be sweetened, and wheat needs to be ground. So too, man needs repair."[57]

We have surveyed *Gen. Rab.*, a collection of rabbinic interpretations of Genesis redacted in fifth century Galilee. A century later, the rabbis of Iraq began the process of editing the Babylonian Talmud, a thirty-seven volume commentary on the Mishnah.[58] The second chapter of the Mishnah tractate Hagigah states, "One may not expound upon the 'Works of Creation' with two [or more] ... unless they are sages, who understand of their own accord."[59] Despite this stricture, the Talmudic commentary on that Mishnah dilates on rabbinic cosmology:

(Gen 1–3) Rav Judah quoted Rav, "Adam [extended] from one end of the world to the other, as it is said: 'Since the day that God created Adam upon the earth, and from one end of heaven to the other' (Deut 4:32). And when he sinned, the Blessed Holy One set His hand upon him and diminished him, as it is said: 'And laid Your hand upon me' (Ps. 139:4)" ...

Rav Judah quoted Rav: "Ten things were created on Day One, and these are: heaven, earth, chaos (*tohu*), confusion (*bohu*), light, darkness, wind, water, the measure of day and of night. Heaven and earth, as it is written: 'In the beginning God created heaven and earth' (Gen 1:1)" ...[60]

---

[54] A common term for Christian monks; see Visotzky, "Goys," 307, n. 22.
[55] I.e. why are not all males born circumcised.
[56] Speaking of his interlocutor in the third person; who seems to be a tonsured monk.
[57] *Gen. Rab.* 11:6 (Theodor and Albeck, *Midrash Bereshit Rabbah*, 94–95). MS Oxford adds, "as it is written 'God ceased from all the work which He did' (Gen 2:3) is not written here, but 'which He had done' meaning that everything needs [human] repair."
[58] See Visotzky, "Literature of the Rabbis"; on the Babylonian Talmud, see Visotzky, "Talmud," in *The New Interpreter's Dictionary of the Bible* (ed. Katharine Doob Sakenfeld; 5 vols.; Nashville: Abingdon, 2006–2009), 5:463–468.
[59] *m. Ḥag.* 2:1. The Mishnah limits public exposition of certain mystical speculation.
[60] I here omit remaining proof-texts.

But was the light created on the first day? It is written: "And God set them in the firmament of the heaven" (Gen 1:17) and it is written: "And there was evening and there was morning a fourth day" (Gen 1:19) This is according to the view of R. Elazar who said, "The light which the Blessed Holy One created on Day One, one could see with it from one end of the world to the other. But when the Blessed Holy One saw the corrupt deeds of the generation of the Flood and the generation of the Dispersion,[61] God rose and hid it from them, as it is said, 'But from the wicked their light is withheld' (Job 38:15). And for whom did God hide it away? For the righteous in the Coming Future, as it is said: 'And God saw the light, that it was good' (Gen 1:4). 'Good' refers to the righteous, as it is said, 'Say of the righteous that he is good' (Isa 3:10)" ...

R. Zutra b. Tuviah quoted Rav, "With ten things the world was created: wisdom, understanding, knowledge, strength, rebuke, might, righteousness, judgment, love, and mercy" ...

Rav Yehudah said, "When the Blessed Holy One created the world, it went on expanding like two spools of thread until the Blessed Holy One rebuked it and stopped it, as it is said: 'The pillars of heaven were trembling, but they became astonished at His rebuke' (Job 26:11)" ...

Our Rabbis taught: Bet Shammai say, "Heaven was created first and afterwards earth, as it is said, 'In the beginning God created the heaven and the earth' (Gen 1:1)."

Bet Hillel say, "Earth was created first and afterwards heaven, as it is said, 'On the day that the Lord God made earth and heaven' (Gen 2:4)."

Bet Hillel said to Bet Shammai, "According to you, a man builds the upper story and afterwards builds the house!" ...

Bet Shammai said to Bet Hillel, "According to you, a man makes the footstool, and afterwards he makes the chair!" ...

But the Sages say, "Both were created at the same time."

What does 'heaven' (*shamayim*) mean? R. Jose b. Hanina said, "It means, There (*sham*) is water (*mayim*)." In a Tannaitic source it is taught, fire (*eish*) and water (*mayim*); this teaches that the Blessed Holy One brought them and mixed them and made them into the firmament ...

What does the earth stand upon? On the pillars ... and the pillars upon the waters ... The waters upon the mountains ... The mountains upon the wind ... The wind upon the storm ... The storm is suspended upon the arm of the Blessed Holy One ... But the Sages say, "[The world] rests on twelve pillars." And some say seven pillars ... R. Elazar b. Shammua' says, "On one pillar, and its name is 'Righteous', for it is said: '"Righteous' is the foundation of the world' (Prov 10:25)."

---

[61] That is, in the story of the tower of Babel.

R. Judah said, "There are two firmaments, as it is said, 'Behold, unto the Lord thy God heaven and the heaven of heavens' (Deut 10:14)." Resh Lakish said, "Seven" ...

R. Aha b. Jacob said, "There is another Heaven above the heads of the living creatures, as it is written, 'Over the heads of the living creatures there was a likeness of a firmament, like the color of the terrible ice, stretched forth over their heads above' (Ezek 1:22)."

Thus far you have permission to speak, from this point onward you do not have permission to speak, for it is written in the Book of Ben Sira, "Seek not things that are too hard for you, and search not things that are hidden from you. That which has been permitted, think about; but you have no business with things that are hidden." (Sir 3:21) ...

The distance from the earth to the firmament is a journey of five hundred years, and the thickness of the firmament is a journey of five hundred years, and so between one firmament and the other. Above the firmament are the holy creatures: the feet of the living creatures are equal to [the distance of] all of them, the ankles of the living creatures are equal to all of them; their calves ... their knees ... their thighs ... their torsos ... their necks ... their heads .. the horns of the living creatures are equal to all of them. Above them is the throne of glory; the legs of the throne of glory are equal to all of them; the throne of glory is equal to all of them. And the King, the Living and Eternal God, High and Exalted, dwells above them all.[62]

In this excerpt, the Babylonian Talmud has reworked cosmological traditions largely from Palestinian sources[63] under the rubric of "Works of Creation." The passage flirts with mysticism, speculating on angelology, the geography of heaven, and even the size of the angelic members of God's retinue. Ironically, the distances of the heavens and the angels are so vast that one has no greater apprehension of the ineffable than at the outset.

Why do the rabbis study the creation account, especially given the stern warning they quote from Ben Sira? Some time following the editing of the Babylonian Talmud it was famously remarked:

(Gen. 1:1) Rabbi Yitzhak said, "The Torah need not have begun until the verse 'This month shall be for you the beginning of the months' (Exod 12:2).[64] So why was it written from 'In the beginning' (Gen 1:1)? To make known God's

---

[62] Excerpted from *b. Ḥag.* 12a–13a. Peter Schäfer, "From Cosmology to Theology: The Rabbinic Appropriation of Apocalyptic Cosmology," in *Creation and Re-creation in Jewish Thought: Festschrift in Honor of Joseph Dan on the Occasion of His Seventieth Birthday* (ed. Rachel Elior and Peter Schäfer; Tübingen: Mohr Siebeck, 2005), 39–58; Ben Ammi Sarfatti, "Talmudic Cosmography," *Tarbiz* 35 (1966): 137–148 [Hebrew].

[63] Primarily *Gen. Rab.* and *y. Ber.*

[64] The start of the legal materials of the Torah (Rashi).

might, as it is said, 'God recounted the power of His works to His people, so that He give them the heritage of the nations' (Ps 111:6)."[65]

As Rashi comments, following his quotation of this midrash in the very beginning of his Genesis commentary,

> (Gen 1:1) If the nations of the world were to say to the Jews, "You are thieves for you have stolen the lands of the seven nations;" the Jews can reply, "All of the earth belongs to the Blessed Holy One. He created it. He gave it to whoever seemed right in His eyes. By His will He gave it to them, and by His will he took it from them and gave it to us."[66]

This comment shows the attitude of a French rabbi writing on the cusp of the First Crusade. But this display of a medieval Jew's loyalty to the Land of Israel removes us somewhat from the Genesis account. Let us return to Adam and Eve.[67] Rather than explicate the text out of context and piecemeal, as in *Gen. Rab.*, let us read a medieval retelling replete with talking trees who reply to the serpent in the Garden of Eden.

We turn not to a commentary on Genesis, but to an expansion of the Mishnaic tractate *'Abot*. The work, *'Abot de Rabbi Nathan*, was redacted post-Talmud, in the eighth or ninth century. *'Abot* reads, "Put a fence around the Torah." *'Abot R. Nat.* interprets:

> (Gen 2:17) What is the fence that Adam made for his words? It says, "The Lord God commanded Adam, You may eat from all trees in the Garden, but you may not eat from the Tree of Knowledge of Good and Evil, for the day you eat from it you shall surely die" (Gen 2:17). Now Adam did not wish to say to Eve what the Blessed Holy One had told him. Rather he said to her, "The Lord

---

[65] *Tanḥ.* 1:11, on Gen 1:1 (Solomon Buber, ed., *Midrash Tanhuma* [2 vols.; Vilna: Romm, 1885; repr., Jerusalem: Ortsel, 1963–1964], 1:7). *Tanḥ.* dates generally between the seventh and ninth centuries, but represents a genre that stretches into the tenth century. It quotes extensively from Palestinian literature, but may have been redacted in Babylonia. See Visotzky, "Literature of the Rabbis," 91.

[66] Rashi to Gen 1:1.

[67] No survey could do justice to the Garden narrative, as should be obvious by the poverty of the treatment of the hexhaemeral materials above. Among the texts that inform my treatment of Adam and Eve are: Elaine Pagels, *Adam, Eve, and the Serpent* (New York: Random House, 1988); Gregory A. Robbins, ed., *Genesis 1–3 in the History of Exegesis: Intrigue in the Garden* (SWR 27; Lewiston, N.Y.: Edwin Mellen, 1988); Peter Brown, *The Body and Society: Men, Women and Sexual Renunciation in Early Christianity* (New York: Columbia University Press, 1988); Hanneke Reuling, *After Eden: Church Fathers and Rabbis on Genesis 3:16–21* (JCP 10; Leiden: Brill, 2006); and Burton L. Visotzky, "Will and Grace: Aspects of Judaising in Pelagianism in Light of Rabbinic and Patristic Exegeses of Genesis," in *The Exegetical Encounter Between Jews and Christians in Late Antiquity* (ed. Emmanouela Grypeou and Helen Spurling; JCP 18; Leiden: Brill, 2009), 43–62.

said that from the tree which is in the midst of the Garden we may not eat, nor may we touch it, lest we die" (Gen 3:3).

At that moment the evil serpent took heart, thinking, "Since I cannot trip up Adam, I will go and cause Eve to stumble." The serpent went, sat near her, and chatted with her. It said, "If you're telling me that the Blessed Holy One commanded us about touching, look: I'll touch it and I will not die."

What did the evil serpent do? At that moment it stood up and grabbed the tree with its hands and feet and shook it until its fruit fell to the ground. But there are those who say it did not touch the tree at all; for when the tree saw the serpent coming it shrieked, "Evil One! Evil One! Do not touch me!" As it is said, "May the foot of pride not approach me, nor the hand of the wicked drive me out" (Ps 36:12) ...

It then said to her, "If you claim that the Blessed Holy One commanded us about eating, look: I'll eat from it and I will not die. So you too may eat from it and not die."

What did Eve think? "All the things my master"—for Eve referred to Adam as her master from the outset—"commanded me were lies from the outset!"

She immediately took it, ate, gave it to Adam, and he ate, as it is said, "The woman saw that the tree was good for eating and a delight to the eyes, etc." (Gen 3:6).

Eve was cursed with ten curses at that hour, as it is said, "God said to the woman, I will greatly multiple your pain and anguish, you will birth children in sorrow, yet you will desire your husband and so he shall rule you" (Gen 3:16). "[I will greatly multiple your pain]" refers to the two bloody discharges: menstruation and at the loss of virginity. "And anguish" refers to the pain of pregnancy. "You will birth children in sorrow" means what it sounds like. "Yet you will desire your husband" means that a wife yearns for her husband when he is away on a journey. "And so he shall rule you" for a man asks his desires aloud, while the woman but desires in her heart. Her head is wrapped up like a mourner, and she is imprisoned as though in jail, banned from all men.

What caused Eve to touch the Tree? It was the fence that Adam placed around his words. Thus they said, "If a man fences in his words, he will not be able to abide by them." Thus they said, "One should not add to what one has heard." Rabbi Yosi said, "Better ten handbreadths that stand than one hundred cubits that fall."

What did the evil serpent think at that time? "I will go kill Adam and marry his wife, and I will be ruler of the entire world, walking erect and eating all the delicacies in the world!"

The Blessed Holy One said to the serpent, "You wished to kill Adam and marry Eve, therefore 'I will put enmity between you and the woman' (Gen 3:15) You wanted to rule the entire world, therefore 'you are cursed among all the beasts' (Gen 3:14). You wished to walk erect, therefore 'on your belly you shall crawl' (ibid.). You wished to eat all the delicacies in the world, therefore 'dust you shall eat all the days of your life' (ibid.)."

Rabbi Shime'on ben Menasia said, "Alas that a great servant was lost to the world; for had the serpent not transgressed, each and every Jew might have had two serpents in his home: one to send east and one to send west. They would have brought back sardonyx and precious stones and pearls and every desirable thing in the world and no creature could have harmed them. Furthermore, one could have put them beneath camels, donkeys, and mules and they would have taken the manure out to gardens and orchards!"

Rabbi Yehuda ben Beteira said, "Adam was reclining in the Garden of Eden and the ministering angels were at his beck and call, grilling meats and cooling wines. The serpent came, saw him, peeked at all that glory, and grew jealous."

How was Adam created? In the first hour of the day [Day Six of Creation] the dust from which he was created was collected. In the second hour his form was made. In the third hour he was made a lifeless lump.[68] In the fourth hour his limbs were tied on. In the fifth hour his orifices were opened. In the sixth hour he was given a soul. In the seventh hour he stood on his feet. In the eighth hour he was given Eve as a mate. In the ninth hour he was brought into the Garden of Eden. In the tenth hour God commanded him. In the eleventh hour he sinned. In the twelfth hour he was driven out and left, to fulfill that which was said, "Adam will not lodge the night in glory" (Ps 49:13).[69]

The midrash here carries forward many earlier rabbinic traditions[70] and adds its own local touches, such as the grilled meats and cooling wine of the Garden, a vision often associated with the afterlife in the Islamic world. The twelve hours of Adam's creation is a common motif in earlier Jewish and Christian interpretations, and the ordering of sex, sin, and expulsion from the Garden is a locus for Jewish-Christian polemic about original sin and free will.[71] Much of the commentary imagines a sequence by which God's punishments of Adam, Eve, and the serpent fit their sins. Yet it is also strikingly sympathetic to the seemingly cursed nature of women in the broader Muslim society. The assignment of motive for the serpent is startlingly Freudian, even Oedipal.

---

[68] *Golem.*
[69] Solomon Schechter, ed., *Aboth De Rabbi Nathan* (Vienna: Lippe, 1887; repr. with corrections, New York: Feldheim, 1967), 4–5 (version A, ch. 1); and Menahem Kister, *Studies in Avot de-Rabbi Nathan: Text, Redaction and Interpretation* (Jerusalem: Yad Izhak Ben-Zvi, 1998 [Hebrew]).
[70] See Schechter's notes.
[71] See Pagels, *Adam, Eve, and the Serpent*; Reuling, *After Eden*; and Visotzky, "Will and Grace."

Two other tendencies should be noted in this rabbinic reading. The first is comic: the rabbis cannot read a biblical narrative about talking snakes[72] without adding their own cartoonish details of squawking trees and housekeeping serpents who undertake the despised task of spreading manure. The second is the acknowledgement of the rabbinic tendency to stringency in legal matters. The rabbis lament that Adam's very desire to 'put a fence around' his Torah, as it were, led to sin. This is an unusual form of the slippery-slope argument, in which leniency is preferred to mindless severity in the application of law.[73]

Rabbinic interpretation of Genesis became appreciably more complex after the advent of Islam. If earlier interpretations engaged paganism or polemicized against Christianity or Gnosticism, now the rabbinic exegete must add Islamic understandings of the biblical narratives to the mix. When debating Christianity, the rabbis occasionally had to endure complaints about faithful transmission of the biblical text. The Quran, however, constituted an entirely new revelation with differing narratives. Further, Muslims transmitted Hadith traditions about the prophet and his circle which occasionally touched on biblical characters. Tafsir, or Quranic commentary, offered Islamic readings of the characters from Genesis (e.g. Noah, Abraham, Ishmael, and Joseph) mentioned in the Quran. Islamic histories, as well as Tales of the Prophets, added to the record.[74]

The ninth century rabbinic retelling of the Torah, Pirqe Rabbi Eliezer, considered the Abraham story in this historic context. While it expansively narrated Abraham's life in Genesis, it interspersed episodes and details

---

[72] Note the clever question of the Gaon Samuel ibn Hofni (d. 1034), who asked why was it that serpents no longer spoke if they did so in biblical times (quoted by Wilhelm Bacher, s.v. "Samuel ben Hofni" in *Jewish Encyclopedia* [12 vols.; New York: Funk and Wagnalls, 1901–1906], 11:17–19, here 19). For talking trees, see Burton L. Visotzky, "The Conversation of Palm Trees," in *Tracing the Threads: Studies in the Vitality of Jewish Pseudepigrapha* (ed. John C. Reeves; SBLEJL 6; Atlanta: Scholars Press, 1994), 205–214.

[73] Usually the argument is in favor of severity, suggesting that any leniency ultimately leads to total abrogation of the law. Cf. *Gen. Rab.* 19:3 (Theodor and Albeck, *Midrash Bereshit Rabbah*, 172). Another argument against mindless stringency is in *y. Pesaḥ.* 6:1 (Venice edition; D. Bomberg [1523–1524], 33a).

[74] On Genesis and Islamic interpretation, see Carol Bakhos in this volume, as well as her *Ishmael on the Border*. For English translations of Muslim sources, see Muhammad ibn 'Abd Allah al-Kisa'i, *Tales of the Prophets* (*Qisas al-anbiya'*) (trans. Wheeler M. Thackston, Jr.; Chicago: Kazi, 1997); *The History of al-Tabari, Volume II: Prophets and Patriarchs* (trans. William M. Brinner; Albany: SUNY Press, 1987); and *Sahih al-Bukhari* (trans. Muhammad M. Khan; Medina: Islamic University, 1980). See also Reuven Firestone, *Journeys in Holy Lands: The Evolution of the Abraham-Ishmael Legends in Islamic Exegesis* (Albany: SUNY Press, 1990).

formulated in response to Islam and perhaps Christianity. Pirqe Rabbi Eliezer recounts Gen 21–22, which according to the rabbis report the penultimate and final of the ten trials by which God tried Abraham.[75]

> (Gen 21) The ninth Trial ... Sarah said to Abraham, "Write a divorce document and send that maid and her son away from me and my son, in this world and in the world to come."
>
> And of all the ills that befell Abraham, this was the most difficult and grievous, as it is said, "The matter was most grievous in Abraham's eyes, out of concern for his son" (Gen 21:11) ...
>
> So he sent Hagar forth with a divorce document. She yoked a water barrel to her hips so that it would sweep the ground behind her and make known that she was a servant. Not only that, but [a path would be there] when Abraham sought Ishmael and the way he went ...
>
> "God heard the cry of the boy, where he was" (Gen 21:17). God opened for them the well that had been created during twilight [of the Sixth Day of Creation].[76]
>
> Ishmael took a wife from the wilderness of Moab named Ayesha.[77] After three years, Abraham went to visit his son Ishmael, swearing to Sarah that he would not descend from his camel in Ishmaelite territory.[78] He arrived at midday and found Ayesha, Ishmael's wife. He asked her, "Where is Ishmael?"
>
> She said, "He and his mother have gone to collect fruit and dates from the desert."
>
> He asked, "Give me a bit of water and bread, for my soul is weary from the desert journey."
>
> She replied, "There is no bread and no water."
>
> He replied, "When Ishmael comes tell him that an elder came from the land of Canaan to see him and said, 'The threshold of your house is not sound.'"
>
> When Ishmael returned his wife told him this, so he divorced her.[79]
>
> His mother sent and took him a wife from her father's household, named Fatima ...[80]

---

[75] See 'Abot ch. 5 for the ten trials. *Pirqe R. El.* enumerates and identifies each.

[76] 'Abot 5, where the well is among the ten things that were created in the primordial twilight-zone. In most midrashic traditions, the well follows the Israelites through the wilderness by merit of Miriam. For Hagar and the well of Zamzam, see al-Tabari § 280.

[77] A wife of the prophet Muhammad.

[78] See al-Tabari § 283.

[79] See al-Tabari § 281, *Tales of the Prophets* § 52.

[80] *Pirqe R. El.*, ch. 30 (Jerusalem: Eshkol, 1973). Cf. the edition by Michael Higger, *Horev* 8–10 (1944–1948). Fatima was Muhammad's daughter and wife of Ali. In the continuation of *Pirqe R. El.*, Abraham visits again. Fatima feeds him and Abraham prays for God's blessings

Our midrash reads Genesis through the lens of Islamic tradition. The expulsion of Ishmael is virtually on a par with the final trial of the binding of Isaac.[81] The story of the barrel scraping a path is lacking in earlier rabbinic texts, but found in Muslim traditions. The well is taken in Muslim tradition to be Zamzam, the well of Mecca. The wives of Ishmael are named for the women of Mohammad's household. Many of the details of this narrative have close parallels in al-Tabari and other contemporary Muslim sources.[82] At the end of this chapter of Pirqe Rabbi Eliezer, we read the following aside:

> The Ishmaelites will do fifteen things in the Holy Land at the end of days: they will measure the land with ropes, they will make the cemeteries into trash heaps for grazing sheep ... the use of paper and quill will diminish, royal coinage will be debased, ... the breaches in Jerusalem's walls will be repaired, and a building will be erected on the Temple Mount. Two brothers will arise as princes in the end, and in their day the sprout of the Davidic dynasty shall arise ... three wars of devastation shall be fought by the Ishmaelites ... one in the forest in the West ... one upon the sea ... and one in the mighty city Rome ...[83]

This passage anticipates the messianic advent as a result of the Islamic conquest. The geographic survey of the Holy Land took place during the land reforms of Caliph Muʾawiya, the two princes are presumably the sons of Caliph Haroun al-Rashid, the building on the Temple Mount would be the Dome of the Rock, while the war in Rome might refer to the Arab sack of the city in 846 CE.[84] In this Islamic setting Pirke Rabbi Eliezer turns to Gen 22.

> (Gen. 22) The tenth Trial. "And it came to pass after these things that God tried Abraham" (Gen 22:1). God tried Abraham each time to know if in his heart he was prepared to follow and observe all of the commandments of the Torah, as it is said, "Because Abraham hearkened to My voice, and observed My observances, commandments, laws, and teachings" (Gen 26:5).[85]

---

upon his son, which he receives. According to *Pirqe R. El.* (relying on older rabbinic traditions), when Sarah died Abraham remarried Hagar.

[81] This may be a close reading of Genesis, in which God promises the same benefits to Hagar and Ishmael (twelve tribes, numerous offspring) as to Sarah and Isaac.

[82] See Firestone, *Journeys*; and Bakhos, *Ishmael on the Border*, for more detail and bibliography.

[83] *Pirqe R. El.*, ch. 30, end. N.B. this passage is lacking in some printed editions and manuscripts.

[84] Burton L. Visotzky, "Jerusalem in Geonic Era Aggadah," in *Jerusalem: Its Sanctity and Centrality in Judaism, Christianity, and Islam* (ed. Lee I. Levine; New York: Continuum, 1999), 438–446, esp. 442–446.

[85] Cf. Rom 4:1–3; Gal 3:6–9; and Heb 11:17–19.

Ishmael had come from the wilderness to visit his father Abraham. Rabbi Yehudah said, "On that very night the Blessed Holy One was revealed to Abraham and said, 'Take your son' (Gen 22:2)."

Abraham had mercy on Isaac and said, "Master of all worlds, which son; the son of uncircumcision or the son of circumcision?"[86]

God said, "Your only one" (ibid).

Abraham replied, "This one is an only child to his mother and this one is an only child to his mother!"[87]

God said, "Whom you love" (ibid.).

Abraham replied, "I love this one and I love that one!"

God said, "Isaac" (ibid.) ...

Abraham rose early in the morning and took Ishmael, Eliezer, and his son Isaac ...

An argument broke out between Eliezer and Ishmael. Ishmael said to Eliezer, "Abraham is now offering his son Isaac as a burnt offering, bound upon the altar; and I, his first-born, will inherit Abraham."

Eliezer replied, "He sent you away like a woman divorced from her husband and exiled you to the wilderness. But I, his household servant day and night, I shall inherit Abraham!"

The Holy Spirit replied to them saying, "Neither this one shall inherit, nor this one shall inherit" ...[88]

Our rabbi attends closely to the text of Genesis. In an otherwise laconic narrative,[89] the author imagines a dialogue between God and Abraham, interpreting a wordy verse of Scripture. It would have been enough to say take Isaac. Why does Genesis add: "your son, your only one, whom you love?" Each clause elicits a response from Abraham in the midrash.[90] The opening of the chapter seems to reply to Christian claims that Abraham's

---

[86] Cf. Gal 5:3–6.

[87] Ishmael's thirteen year, only-child status is adduced by modern Muslims as proof that he was the son for sacrifice. See, e.g., the commentary to Quran Sura 37 in Mushaf al-Madinah An-Nabawiyah, ed., *The Holy Quran* (Medinah: King Fahd Holy Qur-an Printing Complex, 1410 H [1990]), 1357, n. 4101. On the son intended for sacrifice in Quranic tradition, see al-Tabari § 290–301. Firestone, *Journeys, passim*.

[88] *Pirqe R. El.*, ch. 31 (Jerusalem: Eshkol, 1973).

[89] Erich Auerbach, "Odysseus' Scar," in *Mimesis: The Representation of Reality in Western Literature* (trans. Willard R. Trask; Princeton: Princeton University Press, 1953), 3–23.

[90] Burton L. Visotzky, "Binding Isaac," in *Reading the Book*, 76–99.

response to God is a display of faith. Our midrash sees the test regarding whether Abraham will perform the commandments God lays upon him. The "son of the circumcision" is Isaac, a type for rabbinic Judaism.

When Ishmael and Eliezer appear on the scene, our text engages in what Isaac Heinemann called midrashic "flight from anonymity."[91] Rather than having two nameless servants accompany Abraham on this seminal journey, the midrash names the two other known males of Abraham's household. The son of Hagar and the faithful servant also serve as types for Islam and Christianity. When they argue over who will inherit Abraham, the rabbi's audience imagines Islam and Christianity vying for Abraham's patrimony. The Holy Spirit reassures the Jews: neither will inherit in Isaac/Judaism's stead.[92]

Pirqe Rabbi Eliezer returns to Abraham and Isaac in a spectacular (mis)reading of Gen 22, in which Isaac is not only a willing participant in the event, but dies and is resurrected![93]

> (Gen 22) Isaac said to his father Abraham, "Father, tie my hands and feet because I might lash-out and transgress the commandment to honor my father."[94] So he tied him hand and foot and bound him upon the altar, arranging the fire and wood with Isaac upon them. Then Abraham put his foot upon Isaac, as one would when slaughtering an animal, so that he might not kick. Abraham flexed his arms and thighs and picked up the cleaver ... The Blessed Holy One sat and watched a father bind and a son be bound with all their heart, and reach out his hand to the cleaver, as though he were a High Priest offering a grain and wine offering! The ministering angels were wailing and crying ... saying, "Master of the Universe, you are called Merciful and Compassionate, with mercy upon all your creations, have mercy upon Isaac, who is a human bound before you like an animal, 'deliver man and beast, God' (Ps 36:7)."

---

[91] Isaac Heinemann, *The Methods of Aggadah* (3rd ed.; Jerusalem: Magnes, 1970 [Hebrew]), 28.

[92] Following Bernhard Heller, "Muhammendanische und Anti-Muhammedanische in den Pirke Rabbi Eliezer," *MGWJ* 69 (1925): 47–54; Heller, "The Relationship of the Aggadah to Islamic Legends," *JQR* 24 (1934:) 393–340; as well as Josef Heinemann, *The Aggadah and Its Development* (Jerusalem: Keter, 1974 [Hebrew]), 181–199.

[93] Shalom Spiegel, *The Last Trial: On the Legends and Lore of the Command to Abraham to Offer Isaac as a Sacrifice: The Akedah* (trans. Judah Goldin; Philadelphia: Jewish Publication Society, 1967). See Edward Kessler, *Bound by the Bible: Jews, Christians and the Sacrifice of Isaac* (Cambridge: Cambridge University Press, 2004).

[94] Some texts read: "tremble" in place of "lash-out," in which case the sacrifice would go awry and Isaac dishonor his father. For Isaac asking to be well bound, see al-Tabari § 302; *Tales of the Prophets* § 54; and Firestone, *Journeys*, ch. 14.

> Rabbi Yehudah said, "When the sword touched his throat, Isaac's soul flew from him. And when God's voice was heard between the two cherubs saying, 'Do not touch the lad' (Gen 22:12), the soul returned to his body."
>
> He untied himself and stood. Thus Isaac witnessed resurrection of the dead from the Torah, as all the dead will resurrect in the Future. At that moment Isaac said, "Praised are you God, Who resurrects the dead."[95]

Such pathos! Isaac is a willing partner in the submission to God's command. Elsewhere in the chapter Pirqe Rabbi Eliezer reckons Isaac to be thirty-seven years old. He asks to be bound well, lest he spoil the sacrifice.[96] The angels protest that God could be so lacking in mercy. The critique is harsh, and reflects the midrashist's own situation; God watches impassively as Jews are led to slaughter, as though they were no more than a pancake and a splash of wine on the altar!

Despite Isaac's willingness, when the sword (sic!) touches his throat, he dies (of fright?). When the angelic command is issued, it is anachronised as spoken through the cherubim on the ark of the tabernacle, centuries hence. At the divine command, Isaac's soul returns to his body. Because the rabbis insist that the doctrine of bodily resurrection is in the Torah,[97] readers, along with Isaac, indeed learn resurrection of the dead from the Torah by this forced reading. In a midrash chapter that might be engaged with Christian and Muslim thought, Isaac serves as a counter-text to the typological readings of those religious traditions. For Pirqe Rabbi Eliezer, Isaac is portrayed as Abraham's authentic inheritor. The first benediction in the 'Amidah, the traditional rabbinic liturgy, reads, "Praised are You God, shield of Abraham." It is mete that the second benediction is now imagined as Isaac's, "Praised are you God, Who resurrects the dead."

Our survey of rabbinic interpretation of Genesis has taken us through the first half of the biblical book, offering close readings and retellings, rabbinic cosmology, theology, and ideology, as well as polemics and interactions with other communities of Scripture. We have sampled representative texts from the universal narratives of Gen 1–11, and from the patriarchal saga of Gen 12–22. We turn now to the second half of Genesis, to Jacob/Israel and his favored son, Joseph.

---

[95] *Pirqe R. El.*, ch. 31. See Bakhos, *Ishmael on the Border*.

[96] The midrash reckons Isaac's age by assuming a causal nexus with Gen 23, where Sarah's death is reported at age 127. She was 90 at Isaac's birth. Cf. Quran, Sura 37. For Isaac urging Abraham to bind him, see al-Tabari § 302–303; and *Tales of the Prophets* § 54.

[97] *m. Sanh.* 10:1.

In Gen 37:2–3, Joseph is introduced:

> Joseph was seventeen years old and herded sheep with his brothers. He served as a helper to the sons of Bilhah and Zilpah, his father's wives. Joseph brought bad reports about them to their father. And Israel loved Joseph more than any other of his sons for he was a child of his old age. He made for him a striped garment.[98]

Despite his tale bearing, Joseph succeeds in life, even in the face of adversity. Part of his success (and adversity) is his attractiveness to admirers of either gender. The rabbis note:

> (Gen 37:2) "Joseph was seventeen years old … He served as a helper to the sons of Bilhah and Zilpah." He was seventeen and yet you say he was but a helper?[99] Rather he did youthful/feminine things: he used eye-shadow, fixed his hair, and wore high-heels.[100]

The rabbis also recognize Joseph's sexual appeal to women, made clear by the Genesis narrative about Potiphar's wife. One midrash frames the question:

> (Gen 37:2) A matron asked Rabbi Yossi, "Isn't it possible that Joseph, seventeen years old, with all that heat, actually did the deed?"[101]

Other rabbis reply by debating what happened, apropos the verse, "One day when he came into the house to do his work; there was no man at home …" (Gen 39:11).

> (Gen 49:24) Rabbi Shmu'el b. Nahman said, "'To do his work,' quite so, but 'there was no man!' He tried but was unmanned." As Rabbi Shum'el said, "The bow was taut, but then unstrung, thus it is written, 'The tautness of his bow receded' (Gen 9:24)."[102] Rabbi Yitzhak said, "His sperm shot out through

---

[98] "Striped garment" is translated in NJPS as 'ornamented tunic.' *Gen. Rab.* offers many interpretations of the clothing. The term appears in only one other place in Scripture, where it is described as a *women's* garment: "She was wearing a striped garment/ornamented tunic, for virgin princesses wore such garments" (2 Sam 13:18).

[99] "Helper" (נער) connotes youth, like the French *garçon*.

[100] *Gen. Rab.* 84:7 (Theodor and Albeck, *Midrash Bereshit Rabbah*, 1008). 'Youthful/feminine' in Hebrew: נערות, which depending on vowel pointing can be translated either way. The activities are associated with femininity, but in the Greek world are also associated with young men or catamites. 'Wore high heels' (מתלה בעקבו) also might be translated, 'took mincing steps,' lit. 'raised up his heels.' Maren Niehoff, *The Figure of Joseph in Post-Biblical Jewish Literature* (AGJU 16; Leiden: Brill, 1997).

[101] *Gen. Rab.* 87:6 (Theodor and Albeck, *Midrash Bereshit Rabbah*, 1070–1071).

[102] This is a midrashic rendering of Gen. 49:24. NJPS reads, "Yet his bow stayed taut/and his arms were made firm/by the hand of the Mighty One of Jacob." The passage is from Jacob's blessing of Joseph.

his finger-nails, 'the sperm of his hands was dispersed' (ibid.)." Rabbi Huna quoted R. Matna, "He saw the image of his father and his blood cooled, 'By the hands of the Mighty One of Jacob' (ibid.)."[103]

The rabbis at least offered Joseph some dignity by invoking his too loving, but otherwise absent father. Jacob, the eponymous ancestor of Israel, was a difficult character for the rabbis to evaluate. As Israel, the rabbis wished to see him as flawless, even saintly, particularly when juxtaposed with his brother Esau.[104] Yet they expected Jacob would be punished measure for measure for his earlier failings. An early (Tannaitic) rabbinic commentary internalizes the retribution as Jacob reflects on his family. Jacob is presented not only as forbear of Israel, but as the original neurotic Jewish parent!

> (Gen 28:20) "Hear O Israel, the Lord our God, the Lord is One" (Deut 6:4). Why is it said, "Speak to the children of Israel" (e.g. Ex 25:2); yet not written, Speak to the children of Abraham or speak to the children of Isaac?
>
> Jacob merited that the divine word would be spoken to *his* offspring for he worried his entire life. He would say, "Oy, what if my offspring are disreputable like my forefathers ... Abraham brought forth Ishmael and Isaac brought forth Esau! But I do not want to bring forth disreputable offspring like my forefathers did."
>
> Thus it says, "And Jacob took a vow, saying 'If God remains with me'" (Gen 28:20). Now would it occur to you that our father Jacob could say, "*if* God protects me ... and gives me bread to eat and clothing to wear ... *then* the Lord shall be my God" (ibid). And if not, what, God will not be my God?! So what does it mean when he says, "the Lord shall be my God?" That God will join His name to me, so that I will not bring forth disreputable offspring from beginning to end![105]

The rabbis imagine a neurotic Jacob worrying about his offspring, lest he, like his immediate ancestors, have bad seed. Given the antics of Jacob's offspring, his worry is not unfounded.

> (Gen 47:31) Thus it says, "It came to pass while Israel dwelled in that land that Reuven went and bedded Bilha, his father's concubine; and Israel heard" (Gen 35:22). When Jacob heard he trembled and exclaimed, "Oy, maybe one of my sons really is disreputable!"

---

[103] *Gen. Rab.* 87:7 (Theodor and Albeck, *Midrash Bereshit Rabbah*, 1072–1073).

[104] The classic study remains Gerson D. Cohen, "Esau as Symbol in Early Medieval Thought," in *Jewish Medieval and Renaissance Studies* (ed. Alexander Altmann; STLI 4; Cambridge: Harvard University Press, 1967). See too, Bakhos, *Ishmael on the Border*.

[105] Indeed, God changes Jacob's name, adding El to his new name Israel. *Sipre Deut* § 31 (*Siphre ad Deuteronomium* [ed. Louis Finkelstein; Corpus Tannaiticum 3/3; Berlin: Jüdischer Kulturbund, 1939], 49–52).

Until he was informed by the mouth of the Holy One that Reuven had repented ...

And so you find that when our father Jacob was departing the world he called his sons together ... He asked them, "Do you have any dispute in your hearts with the One-Who-Spoke-and-So-the-World-Was?"

They said to him, "'Hear O Israel,' our father, just as you have no dispute in your heart, so we have no dispute with the One-Who-Spoke-and-So-the-World-Was; 'the Lord our God, the Lord is One' (Deut 6:4)" ...

Thus it says, "Then Israel bowed at the head of the bed" (Gen 47:31) ... he gave thanks and praise that he had not brought forth disreputable offspring ... and the Blessed Holy One said to him, "Jacob, this is what you have yearned for all your life, that your sons every morning and evening will recite the *Shema!*"[106]

In this creative re-reading of the story, Jacob frets like every other Jewish parent. The rabbis use their midrashic wiles to solve the truncated verse in Gen 35:22, "and Jacob heard." Heard what? Did what? Worried, that's what! They also interpret the apparently conditional verse in Gen 28:20 ("If ... then ...") and contextualize it within the narrative of the rabbis' neurotic Jacob. They offer a lovely explanation for Jacob's new name, Israel, in noting it is theophoric. The addition of God's name is the very assurance of continuity that every Jewish parent craves: your children will turn out okay. And so, the Jewish credo of the *Shema* henceforth will be heard not only invoking corporate Israel; but also as Jacob's children's reassurance to their father: "Us, too."

As the midrash points out, this is what Jewish parents yearn for: that their children will turn out okay and there will be Jewish continuity. This is the consistent message of all rabbinic interpretation of Genesis throughout the ages: "Us, too."

Select Bibliography

Anderson, Gary A. *The Genesis of Perfection: Adam and Eve in Jewish and Christian Imagination*. Louisville: Westminster John Knox, 2001.

Bakhos, Carol. *Ishmael on the Border: Rabbinic Portrayals of the First Arab*. Albany: State University of New York Press, 2006.

Cohen, Gerson D. "Esau as Symbol in Early Medieval Thought." Pages 19–48 in *Jewish Medieval and Renaissance Studies*. Edited by Alexander Altmann. Studies and Texts. Philip W. Lown Institute of Advanced Judaic Studies 4. Cambridge: Harvard University Press, 1967.

---

[106] *Sipre Deut* § 31 (Finkelstein, *Siphre ad Deuteronomium*, 52–53).

Cohen, Jeremy. *'Be Fertile and Increase, Fill the Earth and Master It': The Ancient and Medieval Careel of a Biblical Text.* Ithaca: Cornell University Press, 1989.

Kessler, Edward. *Bound by the Bible: Jews, Christians and the Sacrifice of Isaac.* Cambridge: Cambridge University Press, 2004.

Mulder, Martin Jan, ed. *Mikra: Translation, Reading, and Interpretation of the Hebrew Bible in Ancient Judaism and Early Christianity.* Compendia rerum iudaicarum ad novum testamentum 2/1. Assen: Van Gorcum, 1988.

Niehoff, Maren. *The Figure of Joseph in Post-Biblical Jewish Literature.* Arbeiten zur Geschichte des antiken Judentums und des Urchristentums 16. Leiden: Brill, 1997.

Reuling, Hanneke. *After Eden: Church Fathers and Rabbis on Genesis 3:16–21.* Jewish and Christian Perspectives 10. Leiden: Brill, 2006.

Robbins, Gregory A., ed. *Genesis 1–3 in the History of Exegesis: Intrigue in the Garden.* Studies in Women and Religion 27. Lewiston, NY: Edwin Mellen, 1988.

Spiegel, Shalom. *The Last Trial: On the Legends and Lore of the Command to Abraham to Offer Isaac as a Sacrifice: The Akedah.* Translated by Judah Goldin. Philadelphia: Jewish Publication Society, 1967.

Teugels, Lieve M. *Bible and Midrash: The Story of 'The Wooing of Rebekah' (Gen. 24).* Contributions to Biblical Exegesis and Theology to 35. Leuven: Peeters, 2004.

Visotzky, Burton L. *Reading the Book: Making the Bible a Timeless Text.* 3rd ed. Philadelphia: Jewish Publication Society, 2005.

GENESIS, THE QUR'ĀN AND ISLAMIC INTERPRETATION

Carol Bakhos

Three of the world's major monotheisms—Judaism, Christianity, and Islam—share a rich scriptural heritage. Similar stories are recounted and many of the same figures populate their holy texts. Noah, Abraham, Pharaoh, Moses, David, Solomon, Jesus, and Mary, to name just a few, are discussed in the Qur'ān. Moreover, they are also found in all types of literature of the Islamic tradition such as the Ḥadīth (the sayings of the Prophet Muḥammad), tafsīr (Qur'ān commentary), and historical writings.

Before interrogating the ways in which stories and personages in the Book of Genesis are treated in the Qur'ān and in the Islamic classical exegetical tradition, several observations are in order. To begin with, Genesis qua book does not exist in the Qur'ān. The Jewish and Christian reception of Genesis assumes its canonical status, however, the Islamic tradition does not, to the extent that it is believed to have been falsified by Jews and Christians who distorted (taḥrīf), and altered (tabdīl) the divine message.[1] Taḥrīf is the notion that the Jews and Christians who indeed received divine revelation over time corrupted God's word.[2] The Old Testament/Hebrew Bible and New Testament as they are preserved today are not the authentically revealed word of God, but rather the Qur'ān is the true word of God, sent from above to the Prophet Muḥammad, the seal of prophecy.

It is therefore important that we avoid approaching Islamic sources as interpretations of the Book of Genesis, or that we assume the Qur'ān contains versions of stories found in the Bible.[3] Stories about Adam and

---

[1] See Q. 2:42, 59, 75–79; 3:71, 78; 4:46; 5:13, 41; 6:91; 7:162. This assertion explains, inter alia, why Muḥammad's mission is not explicitly mentioned in Jewish and Christian scriptures.

[2] Both Jews and Christians are given a special status as ahl al-Kitāb, "People of the Book," a term applied to pre-Islamic religious groups possessing sacred texts. Zoroastrians, Samaritans, and Mandeans are also included in this category. As Islam expanded east, the term also came to encompass Buddhists and Hindus who lived under Muslim rule.

[3] Marilyn R. Waldman, "New Approaches to 'Biblical' Materials in the Qur'an," *Muslim World* 75 (1985): 1–13, (repr. in William M. Brinner and Stephen D. Ricks, eds., *Studies in Islamic and Judaic Traditions* [2 vols. Atlanta: Scholars Press, 1986], 1:47–64), discusses problematic approaches to the study of scriptural material as "versions" of a story. She

Eve, Noah, Abraham, Joseph and other scriptural figures circulated widely in Arabia well before the seventh century CE by Jews and Christians, who spread not only biblical stories, but also legends about the biblical patriarchs, rabbis, monks and martyrs.[4] And, although we possess no extent Arabic translation of parts of the Bible from pre-Islamic Arabia, in all likelihood such translations circulated among the Christians of pre-Islamic Arabia for liturgical and missionary purposes. According to Sydney Griffith, "It seems not improbable that Arabic-speaking, Christian priests, preachers, and teachers in pre-Islamic times may have had private notes or texts, even in Arabic, which would have served them as *aides de memoire*."[5] Moreover, much like the Aramaic-speaking Jews who read the Bible in Hebrew, and explained it to listeners in Aramaic, it is reasonable to assume that the Arabian Jews read the Bible in Hebrew and explained it in Arabic.[6] Apart from Jewish and Christian stories, however, different types of narratives were also widespread and popular among the inhabitants of Arabia,[7] and are no less part of the qurʾānic literary contexts.

To be sure, anyone somewhat acquainted with rabbinic scriptural interpretation, midrash, will observe a striking similarity and overlap between Jewish and Islamic exegesis of the medieval period in terms of style and content. The striking similarities found in Jewish and Muslim narratives and exegetical writing has led scholars of previous generations to assume erroneously that late medieval rabbinic stories are earlier than Islamic parallels. Scholars took for granted that parallels between the two traditions are de facto indicative of Islam's reliance on Judaism, that what we find in the Islamic tradition is derivative. A new generation of scholars, however, has challenged reductionist assumptions and has presented a more nuanced

---

illustrates this point by demonstrating how the Joseph story is not a version of the biblical account but rather a vision of the relationship between humans and God that the Qurʾān espouses.

[4] M.J. Kister, "Ādam: A Study of Some Legends in Tafsīr and Ḥadīth Literature," in *Israel Oriental Studies XIII* (ed. Joel L. Kraemer; Leiden: Brill, 1993), 113–174, here 113; and Camilla Adang, *Muslim Writers on Judaism and the Hebrew Bible: From Ibn Rabban to Ibn Hazm* (IPTS 22; Leiden: Brill, 1996), 1.

[5] Sidney H. Griffith, *The Church in the Shadow of the Mosque: Christians and Muslims in the World of Islam* (Princeton: Princeton University Press, 2008), 50.

[6] Adang, *Muslim Writers*, 2. According to Griffith, *Church in the Shadow*, 50, the earliest translations of the Bible into Arabic for which there is any clear documentary evidence come from the late seventh century.

[7] H.T. Norris, "Fables and Legends in Pre-Islamic and Early Islamic Times," in *Arabic Literature to the End of the Umayyad Period* (ed. A.F.L. Beeston et al; Cambridge: Cambridge University Press, 1983), 374–384.

understanding of the synergistic,[8] multi-directional way in which Medieval traditions developed such that we can detect an interchange of motifs and images that are part and parcel of a literary matrix comprising that which we locate as Jewish, Christian, and Muslim.[9] On occasion, I will note parallels between rabbinic and Islamic traditions for those who are interested in making carefully circumscribed comparative assessments. One should, however, eschew creating a textual "dialogue" between these texts in order to discern the direction of influence for the reasons discussed above.

What follows is an exploration of how scriptural figures also in the Book of Genesis are rendered in the Qurʾān, as well as interpreted, embellished, and expanded upon in extra-scriptural Islamic traditions. Attention will be paid to how that rendering is reflective of several of the Qurʾān's fundamental themes. Each of the following stories, Adam and Eve, Noah, Abraham, and Joseph, illustrates recurring qurʾānic themes, such as humanity's dependence on an omniscient, forgiving God who reveals the path of salvation through his prophets, Satan's machinations to lead humans astray, and the rewards and punishments awaiting humanity on the Day of Judgment.

Background

The Qurʾān recounts many of the same stories as those in Genesis, and on numerous occasions makes reference to other stories elliptically. According to the Islamic tradition, several of the major characters of the OT/Hebrew Scriptures and the NT are referred to as prophets and messengers. The most common term, rasūl, used over 300 times in the Qurʾān, generally means "messenger," "apostle," or "someone who was sent." It also has a more

---

[8] Steven M. Wasserstrom, in his *Between Muslim and Jew: The Problem of Symbiosis under Early Islam* (Princeton: Princeton University Press, 1995), describes the bi-directionality between Judaism and Islam as a "synergy." With respect to Judaism, he avers, "we know that it was altered, root and branch, in its growth in the soil of Islamicate civilizations" (181). See also Shari L. Lowin, *The Making of a Forefather: Abraham in Islamic and Jewish Exegetical Narratives* (IHC 65; Leiden: Brill, 2006); and Marc S. Bernstein, *Stories of Joseph: Narrative Migrations between Judaism and Islam* (Detroit: Wayne State University Press, 2006).

[9] For a discussion of previous and current scholarly approaches to the relationship between Jewish and Muslim sources, and the notion of "borrowing," see Brannon M. Wheeler, "The Jewish Origins of Qurʾān 18:65–82? Reexamining Arent Jan Wensinck's Theory," *JAOS* 118 (1998): 153–171; Lowin, *Making of a Forefather*, 27–38; and Michael E. Pregill, "The Hebrew Bible and the Quran: The Problem of the Jewish 'Influence' on Islam," *Religion Compass* 1 (2007): 643–659.

specific meaning of one who has been appointed by God to communicate a specific message. Biblical prophets who are explicitly referred to as messengers are Noah, Ishmael, Moses, Lot, and Jesus. Included in this list are also non-biblical prophets: Hūd, Ṣāliḥ and Shu'ayb.[10]

Another term used is nabī ("prophet"). Occurring less often in the Qur'ān than rasūl yet inclusive of a greater number of biblical figures, the term is used in connection with many more biblical characters: Lot, Abraham, Isaac, Jacob, Joseph, Aaron, David, Solomon, Job, Idrīs (Enoch), Jonah, Zechariah, John the Baptist, Elisha, and Elijah. There are qur'ānic passages that refer to unnamed prophets that the Muslim exegetes such as al-Ṭabarī (d. 923 CE)[11] and al-Tha'labī (d. 1035)[12] identify by name: Ezekiel, Samuel, and Daniel.

These messengers and prophets were sent to their people to spread the same belief that would be preached by Muḥammad in the seventh century CE. As the Qur'ān explicitly states in 6:87–90, it is to these men (Idrīs is not listed) that the Book, wisdom, and prophethood were given. They were entrusted to guide the people, to exhort them to follow the straight path. Other passages likewise express the notion that these biblical figures were recipients of revelation. Thus we read in Q. 3:84, "Say: We believe in God and that which is revealed to us and that which was revealed to Abraham, Ishmael, Jacob and the tribes, and that which was given to Moses and Jesus, and the prophets from their Lord. We make no distinction between any of them, and to Him have we surrendered."[13] The prophets preached monotheism and the need to accept and live by God's revelation. In this sense the message of the Qur'ān is not a radically new message from that of the OT/HB and the NT, but rather it conceives of itself as a continuation of the message of the revelation sent to Jews and Christians.

---

[10] See Roberto Tottoli, *Biblical Prophets in the Qur'ān and Muslim Literature* (trans. Michael Robertson; Richmond: Curzon, 2002).

[11] A prolific exegete and renowned Persian historian, al-Ṭabarī is considered one of the greatest scholars of his century. In both his classical history, *Ta'arīkh al-rusul wal-l-mulūk*, which traces the history of the world from its inception to his own era (including non-Muslim societies), and his monumental Qur'ān commentary, *Jami' al-bayān 'an ta'wīl ay al-Qur'ān*, his objective is to report traditions, than to offer his position.

[12] al-Tha'labī al-Naysabūrī's *al-Kashf wa-al-bayān 'an tafsīr al-Qur'ān* is considered the first major medieval commentary that ushered in the high classical style of qur'ānic interpretation, and his '*Arā'is al-Majalis fī Qiṣaṣ al-anbiyā*' (Cairo, n.d.), is one of the most well-known collections of stories of the prophets. For an examination of his exegetical work and its role in the history of qur'ānic exegesis, see Walid A. Saleh, *The Formation of the Classical Tafsīr Tradition: The Qur'ān Commentary of al-Tha'labī* (TSQ 1; Leiden: Brill, 2004).

[13] See also Q. 4:163.

God's revelation in the Qurʾān is for all humankind. All are relentlessly called to follow the path set out by God through the prophets. Those who follow it will be rewarded; those who reject or stray from it will be held accountable for their actions on the Day of Judgment.

Randomly referring to episodes in no sequential order, the Qurʾān is a series of revelations given to Muḥammad, divided into 114 sūras ("chapters," sūra, sg.), and ordered from the longest to shortest sūra.[14] These chapters recount inter alia the attempts by generations of prophets to call people to the worship of the one true God. Whereas the Qurʾān often mentions prophetic figures in passing, events surrounding their lives are recounted in greater detail by exegetes and storytellers (quṣṣāṣ).

These stories, which share details found in Jewish and Christian sources, fill in the gaps of the qurʾānic narrative with homiletical and historical flourishes and flesh out these characters with engaging detail. This is most evidenced in the Qiṣaṣ al-Anbiyāʾ ("The Stories of the Prophets").[15] They are also known as the isrāʾīliyyāt,[16] a term applied to narratives about the "Children of Israel" (Banū Isrāʾīl),[17] that is, the ancient children of Israel. A precise definition of the term has eluded scholars; however, perhaps it is best defined as Muslim renditions of narratives also found in the Jewish tradition.

Qiṣaṣ al-Anbiyāʾ (or isrāʾīliyyāt),[18] unlike the Qurʾān, are ordered for the most part chronologically. In the early Islamic period, those gathering traditions looked favorably on these stories, considered early testimonies of

---

[14] The one exception is the opening sūra, the Fātiḥa.

[15] For an introduction, see William M. Brinner, trans., *Lives of the Prophets: As Recounted by Abū Ishāq Ahmad Ibn Muḥammad Ibn Ibrāhīm al-Thaʿlabī* (SAL 24; Leiden: Brill, 2002), xi–xxxiii; and Tottoli, *Biblical Prophets*. For a flawed, yet useful compendium of legends associated with biblical and qurʾānic personages, see Haim Schwartzbaum, *Biblical and Extra-Biblical Legends in Islamic Folk-Literature* (Beiträge zur Sprach- und Kulturgeschichte des Orients 30; Walldorf-Hessen: Verlag für Orientkunde Dr. H. Vorndran, 1982).

[16] While I refer to the terms interchangeably, some scholars argue that the generic terms qiṣaṣ al-anbiyāʾ covers three different categories: legends about creation, legends about prophets and stories specifically dealing with the Israelites (isrāʾīliyyāt) and their rulers beginning with the death of Moses and their entry into the promised land. Others, however, hold the opinion that the qiṣaṣ al-anbiyāʾ are a subdivision of the isrāʾīliyyāt. See discussion in Adang, *Muslim Writers, supra*.

[17] On isrāʾīliyyāt, see Roberto Tottoli, "Origin and Use of the Term Isrāʾīliyyāt in Muslim Literature," *Arabica 46* (1999): 193–210; and Adang, *Muslim Writers*, 8–10.

[18] Wahb ibn Munnabih (654-55–728 or 732), of Persian or Yemeni descent, is inextricably linked with the qiṣaṣ al-anbiyāʾ genre. Because his writings appear to have drawn heavily from Jewish and Christian sources, later Muslim sources look down upon his writings. See Adang, *Muslim Writers*, 10–12, for a brief discussion of his role in disseminating Jewish and Christian traditions, and Tottoli, *Biblical Prophets*, 139–141.

the true religion, Islam. In fact, in the Qur'ān God instructs Muḥammad to consult those who have read the Book if he doubts what God reveals to him (10:94). Keep in mind, however, that consulting these traditions for legal advice was prohibited and, despite its favorable acceptance early on, by the fourteenth century the term isrā'īliyyāt officially came to designate dubious traditions, the content of which was deemed objectionable.[19] Be that as it may, the orthodox attitude toward the isrā'īliyyāt did not prevent their wide readership and preservation in various literary corpora throughout the centuries.

In the introduction to his Stories of the Prophets, *Tales of the Prophets* (*'Arāis al-Majalis fī Qiṣaṣ al-Anbiyā'*), the eleventh century Qur'ān commentator al-Thaʿlabī enumerates several reasons for transmitting stories about the prophets. Not only did they serve as a model for the Prophet Muḥammad, but they offer moral instruction; through the prophets' exemplary behavior, they guide all who are subject to transgressions. Accounts of the moral depravity of generations long gone and the fate they faced as a consequence of their wretchedness assured Muḥammad and his followers of God's bestowed favor to those who live righteously. They also secure the prophetic legacy for posterity. Far from being dry didactic disquisitions, these fanciful, colorful tales entertain and edify. They convey Muslim beliefs and mores in the same way that Jewish aggadah, non-legal narrative, not only fills in scriptural and theological lacunae, but also transmits rabbinic teachings and religious, social, and cultural values.

In addition to collections of Tales of the Prophets (*Qiṣaṣ al-Anbiyā'*), compilations of extra-qur'ānic traditions abound. Volumes of qur'ānic exegesis play an important role in the Islamic tradition and the production of different collections over the centuries reflects heterogeneity often overlooked when discussing "the" Islamic tradition. Some of the major collections of tafsīr are those of Muqātil ibn Sulaymān (d. 767 CE),[20] al-Ṭabarī (d. 923 CE), al-Thaʿlabī (d. 1035 CE),[21] and Ibn Kathīr (d. 1373 CE).[22] In what follows I will

---

[19] See Norman Calder, "Tafsīr from Ṭabarī to Ibn Kathīr: Problems in the Description of a Genre, Illustrated with Reference to the Story of Abraham," in *Approaches to the Qur'an* (ed. G.R. Hawting and Abdul-Kader A. Shareef; New York: Routledge, 1993), 101–140.

[20] His tafsīr is one of the earliest and thus features less of an interest in grammar and more on narrative expansion. See Fred Leemhuis, "Origins and Early Development of the Tafsir Tradition," in *Approaches to the History of the Interpretation of the Qur'an* (ed. Andrew Rippin; New York: Oxford University Press, 1988), 1–30.

[21] See nn. 3 and 4.

[22] In addition to his qiṣaṣ and tafsīr, Ibn Kathīr's *al-Bidāya wa-l-nihāya* is a major historical work of the Mamluk period.

rely most heavily on the *Qiṣaṣ al-Anbiyā'* because some of the most popular collections have been translated into English and are therefore accessible to a wider audience. I will also draw on non-translated works. All translations are mine unless stated otherwise. With this brief background in mind, let us now turn to an examination of several qur'ānic narratives.

ADAM (ĀDAM) AND EVE (ḤAWWĀ')

As noted above, the Qur'ān is not ordered chronologically. Nor does it recount primeval history beginning with the creation of the world. While the Qur'ān does not open with the creation of the world, the notion that God created the heavens and earth and placed humans as his vicegerent echoes throughout its 114 sūras. In Q. 6:1 we read: "Praise be to God, who created the heavens and earth and made the darkness and light." As in the biblical account, creation takes place over a period of six days (Q. 7:54), although the Qur'ān does not detail what is created on each day.[23] Moreover, in the Qur'ān all of creation is to serve humankind: "And He has subjected to you all that is in the heavens and on earth" (Q. 45:13). Q. 22:65 similarly states: "Have you not seen how Allah has made all that is in the earth?"[24] The Qur'ān

---

[23] As John Kaltner, *Ishmael Instructs Isaac: An Introduction to the Qur'an for Bible Readers* (Collegeville, Minn.: Liturgical Press, 1999), 27, observes, the Qur'ān does, however, identify "a clear division within the six-day period." This is evidenced in Q 41:9–10: "Say, 'Do you really disbelieve in the one who created the earth in two days? Do you set up equals (other gods) for Him?' That is the Lord of the worlds. He placed mountains above the earth. He then blessed it and in four days provided sustenance within it indiscriminately for those who seek.' "

[24] To quote a lengthy, yet illustrative passage: "It is He who sends down water from the sky for you to drink and from whence are trees on which you feed your cattle. He causes crops to grow for you, and the olive and the date-palm and grapes and all kinds of fruit. Truly in that there is a sign for thoughtful people. He has subjected night and day to you; the sun and the moon, and the stars are in subservience by His command. Surely there are signs in this for people who ponder. And the things on this earth which He has multiplied of varied hues most surely in this is a sign for people who are mindful. It is He who subjected the sea to you, that you might eat moist flesh from it and bring forth from it ornaments to wear, and you see the ships cleaving through it, and that you might seek of His bounty and that you may give thanks" (Q 16:10–16). As these verses indicate, animals are discussed in relation to humans, who according to the Qur'ān received "the best of all constitutions" (Q 95.4). Humans benefit from creation yet at the same time must be its caretakers. Humans' privileged status obligates them to behave responsibly toward all creatures. Other verses to consider: "He has bestowed on you cattle and sons," (Q. 26:133); "And he has created cattle for you: you derive warmth from them, and other uses; and from them you obtain food; and you find beauty in them when you drive them home in the evenings and when you take them out to pasture in the mornings. And they carry your loads to a place which you would be unable to reach without great hardship to

incessantly reminds readers that it is God who is the creator and provider of all. It is God, the supreme authority, who subjects all of creation to humanity and who created the first human, Adam.

Almost all commentators are of the opinion that Adam was sent as a messenger, to whom God revealed the letters of the alphabet which were written on twenty-one pages. According to another tradition, God revealed to him forty books. It is said that Adam was the first person to have prayed in the morning, and that the angel Gabriel instructed him in the practices of the pilgrimage to Mecca.[25] When he was created, God commanded the angels accompanying Iblīs[26] to prostrate themselves before him: "When I have fashioned him, and breathed my spirit into him, kneel down and prostrate yourselves before him" (Q. 15:29); however, Iblīs refuses to do so.

Told in several chapters (Q. 2:28–39; 7:10–25; 15:19–48; 20:115–122), the story of Adam and Eve resonates with the biblical narrative, yet at the same time is strikingly, though not surprisingly, different. The fullest account is found in Q. 7:10–25:

> We have set you firmly on the earth and provided you with a livelihood, but you give little thanks. We created you and gave you shape. Then We said to the angels, "Prostrate yourselves before Adam," and they all prostrated themselves except Iblis, who was not among those who prostrated. "What prevented you from prostrating when I commanded you?" He asked. "I am better than he," he replied. "You created me of fire, but You created him of clay." God said, "Go down from here! You are not to be proud here. Leave! You are now among the despised." Iblis replied, "Grant to me a delay until the day they are raised up." He said, "You are among those who are reprieved." "Because You have caused me to err," he declared, "I will surely lie in wait for them on Your straight path. Then I will come upon them from the front and from behind, upon their right side and upon their left side. Then You will not

---

yourselves. And He created for you horses and mules and asses to ride, as well as for their beauty; and He will yet create things of which you have no knowledge" (Q 16:5–8). These verses demonstrate God's concern for humans. We learn that animals were created for their benefit, to provide warmth and nourishment, to carry their burdens and to provide them with transportation. See, too, Q. 2:22, 13:17, 14:32–33; 16:80–81; 17:70; 21:31–32; 22:36; 23:18–22; 43:10–12; 55:1–78; 78:6–16. In translating the Qurʾān, I have consulted several English translations.

[25] See Kister, "Ādam," 117 ff.

[26] Many scholars contend that the word is not Arabic, but rather is a distortion of the Greek word *diabolos*. The fallen angel, or jinn, is known by two names in the Qurʾān—Iblīs and Shayṭān (Satan)—and qurʾānic exegetes identify them as one and the same figure. Whereas the word shayṭān is used 70 times in the Qurʾān, iblīs, on the other hand is used less often, only 11 times, and always as a proper name. See Franz Rosenthal, trans., *The History of al-Ṭabarī, Volume 1: General Introduction and From the Creation to the Flood* (Albany: SUNY Press, 1989), 249–257.

find the majority of them thankful." He said, "Be gone, banished and driven away! As for those that follow you, I will surely fill Hell with you all. Oh Adam, you and your wife dwell in the garden, and eat from where you wish; but do not approach this tree or you shall be among those who do wrong." But Satan whispered to them, so that he might reveal to them what was hidden from them of their shame. He said, "Your Lord has forbidden you to approach this tree only to prevent you from becoming angels or being among those who are immortal." Then he swore to them, "I am truly among those who give honest counsel to you." Thus did he guide them by deceit. And when they had tasted of the tree, their shame became apparent to them, and they began to cover themselves with the leaves of the garden. Their Lord called out to them, saying, "Did I not forbid you to approach the tree, and did I not warn you that Satan is a clear enemy to you?" They said, "Our Lord, we have harmed ourselves. If You do not forgive us and have mercy on us we shall surely be among the lost." He said, "Go! Some of you will be enemies of each other. For a while, the earth will provide a dwelling and life's necessities. There you shall live and there you shall die, and from there you shall be brought out."

The qur'ānic account does not depict God walking in the cool of the day, nor does God ask Adam, "Where are you?" (Gen 3:9). Anthropomorphic telltales are absent. Furthermore, both Adam and his wife Eve disobey God and express remorse for their wrongdoing (Q. 7:5). They act in tandem, quite unlike the biblical account which raises the issue of whether Adam is more culpable than Eve, or vice versa. Satan is the seducer, not the snake, nor Eve who gave her husband of the fruit. In the biblical account Adam and Eve blame others for their downfall as evidenced in Adam's response to God's inquiry: "The woman whom you gave to be with me, she gave me of the tree and I did eat" (Gen 3:12). Not only is Eve the culprit, but God is implicated ("the woman whom *you* gave me ..."). Eve, too, avoids responsibility: "The serpent beguiled me and I did eat" (Gen 3:13). In the Qur'ān, however, they immediately confess their wrongdoing, ask for forgiveness, and acknowledge their utter dependency on God: "for if you do not forgive us and show mercy on us, we will surely be among the lost."

Furthermore, in the biblical narrative both Adam and Eve are punished. Eve is given a list of hardships. She will suffer through childbirth and be subject to her husband. Man will have to toil for subsistence, and humans will experience death. As Kaltner observes: "Although the Qur'ān considers the couple's transgression to be a serious mistake that has important consequences, it does not present such a bleak picture of its aftermath. In general, they are the same people at the end of the text that they were at the beginning. They do not undergo the transformation that Adam and Eve experience in Genesis, where they leave the garden cursed, rejected and mortal."[27] In the Qurʾān they are neither cursed nor made mortal, for it seems as if their mortality was understood as part of the human condition prior to the incident. There is no sense of the fall of humanity, nor of original sin. Although they are banished from the Garden, God forgives them and assures them that as long as they continue to accept His guidance, they will not fall into misery (Q. 20:122–123).

The biblical story explains the broken condition of humanity, the fact that we suffer, toil, and eventually face death, whereas the qurʾānic narrative emphasizes God's mercy upon the repentant. To be sure, although the Qurʾān does not include the litany of punishments humanity endures as a result of Adam and Eve's disobedience, it makes clear before they even encounter Satan that in Paradise, "you shall not hunger or be naked; you shall not thirst, or feel the scorching heat."[28] If they succumb to Satan's seduction, they will be expelled out of the Garden and plunged into affliction. Yet, even though Adam and Eve are cast down from the Garden, they are comforted by knowledge that if they embrace God's guidance, they will avoid misery (v. 123).

Described as the comrade to unbelievers, the enemy of the righteous, Satan whispers, slinks and sneaks around, makes promises, and provokes strife. When God informs the angels of his decision to create a vicegerent on earth, they inquire: "Will you place therein one who will make mischief and shed blood?" (Q. 2:30).[29] After demonstrating to the angels Adam's superior knowledge, that is, God taught Adam the names of all things, the angels recognize their own limitations and extol the glory of God, the All Knowing, the Wise. Then God commands Adam to dwell freely with his wife in the Garden, but prohibits them to eat from "this tree," lest they become evildoers. The passage continues: "But Satan caused them to slip from the (garden), and get them expelled from the felicitous state in which they had been."

The qurʾānic story of Adam and Eve illustrates several themes that reverberate throughout the Qurʾān. Humankind must be ever so vigilant against

---

[27] Kaltner, *Ishmael Instructs Isaac*, 35.

[28] Al-Thalʿabī's *Lives of the Prophets* mentions ten afflictions Adam suffered on account of his disobedience, and "Eve and her daughters were afflicted with these traits, and with fifteen other traits besides" (Brinner, *Lives of the Prophets*, 55).

[29] Cf. *Gen. Rab.* 8:5 (Julius Theodor and Chanoch Albeck, eds., *Midrash Bereshit Rabbah: Critical Edition with Notes and Commentary* [2nd ed.; 3 vols.; Jerusalem: Wahrmann, 1965], 1:60). Genesis Rabbah is a rabbinic collection of interpretation on verses from the Book of Genesis, compiled at the end of the fourth, or early fifth century CE. For more, see the essay by Visotzky in this volume.

temptation that lurks in every corner. An ever merciful God reminds humans to remain on constant guard and to follow the way God has set before us. Humans must rely on God for guidance and protection. The story also introduces the reader to the concept of the resurrection: "For a while, the earth will provide a dwelling and life's necessities. There you shall live and there you shall die, and from there you shall be brought out." Life on earth is temporary and at some point humans will be resurrected and will be relegated to the appropriate eternal dwelling. Although the story does not explicitly mention heaven and hell, readers of the Qurʾān are well aware of the Day of Judgment and its consequences.

Noah (Nūḥ)

Generally speaking, the prophets are commissioned to warn the people of the consequences of their sinful behavior, but the people invariably ignore the call. This is a recurring motif, exemplified in the case of Noah, who tirelessly exhorts his people to turn from their wicked ways. In Sūra 71, "Noah," (Nūḥ) God sends Noah to his people in order to warn them before a woeful scourge overtakes them. The chapter opens as follows: "Lo! We sent Noah unto his people, saying: 'Warn your people before there comes upon them a grievous chastisement.'" Whereas readers of the biblical account are left wondering why God did not warn the people of the impending destruction, the deluge is anything but a sneak attack in the Qurʾān where Noah confronts his people.[30]

Unlike his voiceless biblical counterpart, the Noah of the Qurʾān is vocal; he pleads with them "night and day" to turn from their sinful path, and

---

[30] Cf. the story of Jonah and the Ninevites. In this well-known story, God sends the reluctant prophet, Jonah ben Amittai to warn the people of Nineveh of the city's impending destruction unless the inhabitants repent. Not only is the contrast between the Genesis flood narrative in which humans are not offered an opportunity to repent of interest, but the treatment of the animals in the Book of Jonah demonstrates God's comprehensive concern for Jews, non-Jews, humans and animals. An illustration of the important role animals play in the biblical worldview, the story ends with a question God poses to Jonah, "And should I not care about Nineveh, that great city, in which there are more than a hundred and twenty thousand persons who do not yet know their right hand from their left, and many beasts as well?" The question reiterates God's concern for all, including animals. For a different take on the Book of Jonah as parody, see John A. Miles, "Laughing at the Bible: Jonah as Parody," *JQR* 65.3 (1975): 168–181. David Marcus' *From Balaam to Jonah: Anti-prophetic Satire in the Hebrew Bible* (BJS 301; Atlanta: Scholars Press, 1995) is a comprehensive study of previous scholarship on the subject, and analysis of the satirical aspects of the narrative.

to fear and obey God. He implores the people to seek forgiveness, but to no avail, for they willfully continue to follow those who will lead to their destruction. His unrelenting, strident exhortations fall on deliberately deaf ears (71:7). Alas, Noah makes no headway with his people.

In both Genesis and the Qurʾān, no reason is given for why Noah is signaled out as righteous.[31] Even though in Gen 7:1 God tells Noah: "... for you alone have I found righteous before Me in this generation," it remains unclear why this is so. The Qurʾān assumes Noah's unalloyed righteousness by the sheer fact that he is a messenger of God.[32] The Qurʾān underscores Noah's attempts to warn the people. It highlights humanity's evil, Noah's steadfast commitment to his mission, and at the same time explicitly reaffirms God's justice. Several qurʾānic verses (7:60–65; 11:25–49) recall the haughtiness of the people of Noah's generation, and his unrelenting admonishments, urging the obstinate to turn from their evil ways. Their unequivocal rejection of Noah's message is vividly captured in Sura 71:7, "And lo! Whenever I call to them that you may pardon them, they thrust their fingers in their ears and cover themselves with their garments and persist in their refusal and magnify themselves in pride."

The extra-qurʾānic narratives amplify the portrayal of the abuse Noah endured. We learn that Noah would be beaten, wrapped in felt, thrown into his house, and taken for dead. According to al-Kisāʾī:

> The people would come out of their houses and beat him until he swooned. Then they would drag him by the feet and throw him on the refuse heaps. When he came to, he would go back and be treated the same way. This continued for three centuries (reckoning one hundred years to the century), with Noah constantly struggling against them and calling them to worship God. Woman and children would gather around him and beat him until he

---

[31] The rabbis (*Gen. Rab.* 30:9) discuss Noah's relative righteousness, that is, relative to his generation. Cf. *Sanh.* 108a. Similarly, on Noah Jerome comments: "*Scripture says distinctly in his generation, to indicate that he was righteous not in respect of the highest degree of righteousness, but relative to the righteousness of his own generation. And this is what is expressed in the Hebrew: Noah, a righteous man, was perfect in his generations*" (*Saint Jerome's Hebrew Questions on Genesis: Translated with Introduction and Commentary* [trans. C.T.R. Hayward; Oxford: Clarendon, 1995], 37). Cf. Louis H. Feldman, "Josephus' Portrait of Noah and its Parallels in Philo, Pseudo-Philo's *Biblical Antiquities*, and Rabbinic Midrashim," *PAAJR* 55 (1988): 31–57.

[32] The qurʾānic prophets are portrayed in the best light as possible. When they err, they plead for forgiveness. The Qurʾān does not explicitly refer to the concept of impeccability, ʿiṣma, but according to theologians the term is crucial in order to maintain the prophets' impeccability and ensure the authenticity of their message. For a discussion of ʿiṣma, see Wilfred Madelung, "ʿIṣma," *EI* 4:182–184. I am not offering ʿiṣma as an explanation for the absence of the scene between Noah and Ham in the Qurʾān, but rather raise it suggestively.

fainted. When he awoke he would wipe his face, pray two *rak'as*[33] and say, 'By the Glory and Splendor, may my patience be increased that I may endure that with which they afflict me!'[34]

al-Tha'lbī reports an incident of a boy accompanying his father who is leaning on a staff. The father points to Noah and says, "My son, see that old man; beware lest he deceive you." "My father," the boy replies, "place the staff in my hand." The father gives his son the staff and then the boy instructs his father to lay him on the ground, at which point he went up to Noah and beat him with the staff.[35]

Did Noah's family heed his warnings? Was Noah's family righteous? In Q. 66:10 we are told that God gave the wives of Lot and Noah as examples to unbelievers: "They were under two of Our righteous servants but they betrayed them (their husbands) so they availed them naught against Allah. They were told: 'Enter the fire along with those who enter.'" Although the Qur'ān does not indicate how Noah's wife died, most exegetes claim that she died in the deluge, along with Lot's wife. In their tales of the prophets, however, both Ibn Kathīr[36] and al-Kisā'ī[37] follow the biblical tradition and report that Noah's wife was on board the ark.[38]

It is important to note that in the Qur'ān, not all members of Noah's family are saved but rather those who were believers. In fact, if we compare the biblical and qur'ānic stories of Noah, we discover an important, fundamental Islamic understanding of family, namely it is a lineage of believers. In Genesis, Noah's family is understood in biological terms. Whereas, too, the immediate members of Noah's family are saved in the biblical account, in the Qur'ān one of Noah's sons is not saved. When Noah pleads with God

---

[33] A *ra'ka* is a single complete prayer unit.
[34] Wheeler M. Thackston Jr., trans. *Tales of the Prophets (Qiṣaṣ al-Anbiyā')* (Chicago: Great Books of the Islamic World, 1997), 95.
[35] Al-Tha'labī, Qiṣaṣ, chapter on Noah. For English translation, see Brinner, *Lives of the Prophets*, 93.
[36] Born in Basra in 1300 and died in Damascus in 1373 CE, Ibn Kathīr was a famous exegete and historian of Mamluk Syria. He is noted for his historical work, *al-Bidāya wa-l-nihāya*, as well as his qur'ānic exegetical work, *Tafsīr al-Qur'ān al-'aẓīm*, and the oft-cited qiṣaṣ collection. On Ibn Kathīr in the history of tafsīr, see Calder, "Tafsīr from Ṭabarī to Ibn Kathīr."
[37] Intended for a more popular than scholarly audience, his *Qiṣaṣ al-anbiyā'*, dating to the eleventh century, is one of the most fanciful. As Lowin, *Making of a Forefather*, 267, writes: "In many cases, he adopted stories of Jewish origin which other authors did not know of or accept. Because of his rampant use of Jewish or *isrā'īlī* sources, normative Muslim scholars often look askance at al-Kisā'ī's work."
[38] Cf. Barbara Freyer Stowasser, *Women in the Qur'an, Traditions, and Interpretation* (Oxford: Oxford University Press, 1994), 41.

to save his son, God responds that the son is guilty and thus not part of Noah's family (Q. 11:46). Instead members of Noah's family are not those who share his blood, but rather his righteousness. This is illustrative of the qurʾānic meaning of "family," which is confessional, not biological, a distinction that sketches the contours of the Islamic tradition with its emphasis on the *umma*, community of believers.

Noah and the flood narrative occur more than once in the Qurʾān, but in all instances no significant attention is given to the actual building of the Ark and its dimensions.[39] Nor is special attention paid to the events surrounding Noah's family before and after the flood. The Qurʾān devotes more attention to Noah's role as a messenger, thus emphasizing both human depravity and God's concern for all creatures. The extra-scriptural sources, however, furnish details with respect to the Ark's dimensions, and indicate that God sent Gabriel to teach Noah how to build it.

Of the prophets depicted in the Qurʾān, Noah (Nūḥ) stands out as one who tirelessly preached to his people, and none suffered the blows of ridicule as much as he. Noah is a model prophet—long suffering and steadfast in his faithfulness. According to al-Thalʿbī he lived the longest among the prophets and was called "the greatest of the prophets and the elder of the Messengers." Noah was made second to Muḥammad regarding covenant and inspiration. "And in resurrection—for he will be the first for whom the earth will open up on the Day of Resurrection, after Muḥammad."[40]

Abraham (Ibrāhīm)

The prophets are evoked as exemplars of proper behavior and their strife is a harbinger of what Muḥammad will confront when he brings his message to his people. One of the most prominent figures in the Qurʾān is Abraham. He is the quintessential hanīf, pure monotheist, and "a friend of God" (4:125). In many respects, Abraham models the Prophet Muḥammad. As has been noted by several scholars even as early as the nineteenth century, Abraham is typologically connected to Muḥammad, who is depicted as attempting to restore the religion of Abraham, which is neither Judaism nor Christianity. Parallels between their lives are numerous. Both completely reject idolatry

---

[39] Q. 11:38 reads: "So he was building the ark, and whenever a council of his people passed by him, they scoffed at him."

[40] Brinner, *Lives of the Prophets*, 103.

and are forced to leave their homeland. Both suffer the verbal slings of their contemporaries and establish alternative religious beliefs and practices.

The Qurʾān (6:76–80) recounts Abraham's revelation of the one true God who is not a celestial body (e.g., a star, the moon, or the sun). The mufassirūn, that is, the qurʾānic exegetes, reiterate this story adding, as usual, details such as where the event took place, and in some instances a conversation with his mother or with both parents as to the nature of their god.

Pre-Islamic Arabia was a tribal society where idol worship reigned supreme; however, according to Islam this was not always the case. Centuries before Muḥammad, Abraham travelled with his son, Ishmael, to build a house of worship to God, the Kaʿba. Over time the people lost their way and strayed from the worship of the one true God, and turned to idolatry. Muḥammad was sent to the people of the Arabian peninsula in order to restore the faith of Abraham, *millat Ibrāhīm*.

Although the Qurʾān relates precious little about Abraham's early years, tafsīr and Qiṣaṣ al-Anbiyāʾ fill in the lucanae.[41] The extra-scriptural sources share a basic motif. A tyrannical king, Nimrod (Namrūd), sees a star, in some versions in a dream, a prophecy according to Nimrod's priest that a boy will be born who will overturn the idolatrous ways of the people and destroy his kingdom. Taking precautionary steps, Nimrod orders the slaughter of every boy born that year, and also he decrees the segregation of men and women, except for when the women are ritually impure when sexual relations are prohibited. But Nimrod's plans are thwarted for Āzar when Abraham's father impregnates his wife, and Abraham is born.[42]

Of the several stories revolving around Abraham, the story of his battle against his father's idolatry is taken up in numerous qurʾānic passages (Q. 6:74, 79–83; 19:41–50; 21:51–71; 26:69–104; 29:16–25; 37:83–98; 43:26–28; 60:4). Abraham's entreatments to turn from Satan to the true God serve only to fuel his father's anger against his son (Qurʾān 19:40). Abraham faces

---

[41] The sources I have consulted include: Muqātil ibn Sulaymān, *Tafsīr Muqātil* (ed. ʿAbdullāh Maḥmūd Shiḥāta; 5 vols.; Cairo: al-Hayʾa al-Miṣriyya al-ʿamma lil-kitāb, 1979–1989); Isḥāq ibn Bishr, *Mubtadaʾ al-dunya wa-qiṣaṣ al-anbiyāʾ* (Bodleian Library, Oxford: MS Huntington 388); al-Masʿūdī, *Murūj al-dhahab wa-maʿādhin al-jawhār* (ed. Charles Pellat; Beirut: Publications de L'Université Libanaise, 1966–1974); Muḥammad ibn Jarīr al-Ṭabarī, *Taʾrīkh al-rusul wa-al-Mulūk* (Leiden: Brill, 1879–1901); Isaac Eisenberg, ed., *Vita Prophetarum auctore Muḥammad ben Abdallah al-Kisāʾī* (Leiden: Brill, 1922); Mujāhid ibn Jabr, *Tafsīr al-imām Mujāhid ibn Jabr* (ed. Muḥammad ʿAbd al-Salām Abū al-Nīl; Cairo: Dār al-fikr, 1989); and Aḥmad ibn Muḥammad al-Thaʿlabī, *Qiṣaṣ al-anbiyāʾ* al-mussama *ʿArāʾis al-Majalis* (Cairo: Matbaʾat al-anwār al-Muḥammadiyya, n.d.).

[42] Brinner, *Lives of the Prophets*, 126.

the same adverse reaction when he exhorts his father's people to abandon their gods (Q. 26:70–71).

Abraham smashes their idols except for the supreme god (21:51–71). When in horror they ask him who destroyed their idols, Abraham tells them that it was their chief who smote them. Riled up, they attempt to burn him at the stake, but God keeps him safe (21:69) by turning the fire cold. According to Muslim interpreters, Abraham was saved from the fire because he spoke the words: "God is sufficient for me. Most Excellent is He in whom I trust."[43] Another tradition tells of God sending down and angel to keep Abraham company within the fire.

As in the Book of Jubilees (12:1–8), and the Apocalypse of Abraham (1–8), in the Stories of the Prophets we read that Abraham's father was an idol maker. In one of the most respected collections of Qiṣaṣ al-Anbiyāʾ, that of Thaʿlabī, his father gives Abraham the idols to obey. Abraham runs out with the idols and announces: "Who wants to buy that which does not cause harm or benefit?" No one would buy. He took them to the river and crushed their heads and said to them: "Drink." The other major episodes are Abraham and his son Ishmael building the House of God, the Kaʿba in Mecca, the establishment of the pilgrimage to Mecca (the Hajj, one of the Five Pillars of Islam) and its environs during the month of Dhū l-Ḥijja, and Abraham's near sacrifice of Ishmael. The Qurʾān (Q. 2:127) refers to Abraham and Ishmael in Mecca but does not provide a context for why and how they traveled there. Qurʾānic exegetes, however, narrate the story of the expulsion of Ishmael and Hagar from Abraham's household, which takes them to Mecca.[44] In all versions, Abraham personally brings them to Mecca of his own volition, and then returns to Syria to be with Sarah. After some time, he goes to visit Ishmael. He asks Sarah for her permission to do so and she agrees to let him journey on the condition that he does not remain there, or dismount from his steed. When Abraham arrives in Mecca he is greeted by Ishmael's inhospitable wife who tells him that he is out hunting, or in some versions seeking food. Abraham asks her to convey a message to Ishmael: "Change the threshold of your door." Upon Ishmael's return, Ishmael smells his father's scent, his wife gives him the message, and he knows that he must divorce his wife. After some time, Abraham visits again and Ishmael's second wife is everything the first was not. She offers him

---

[43] Brinner, *Lives of the Prophets*, 132–133.
[44] See Reuven Firestone, *Journeys in Holy Lands: The Evolution of the Abraham-Ishmael Legends in Islamic Exegesis* (Albany: SUNY Press, 1990).

something to eat and washes his head. This time the message conveyed to Ishmael is that his threshold is sound.⁴⁵

In Mecca, Abraham and Ishmael build the Kaʿba, a cube-shaped structure in Mecca, the spiritual and geographic focal point of Islam. Muslims circumambulate the Kaʿba seven times counterclockwise. Moreover, Muslims are required to face its direction when fulfilling the daily requirement to prayer five times throughout the day. We read: "And when Abraham, and Ishmael with him, raised up the foundations of the House, (Abraham prayed) 'Our Lord accept this from us; You are the All-Hearing, the All-Knowing, and our Lord. Make us submissive to you and our descendants submissive to you, and show us our holy rites and turn to us with mercy. You are the merciful and all-compassionate'" (Q. 2:127–128).

Abraham's role in Islam cannot be underestimated. In fact, Abraham asks God to send a prophet to the Arabs, a prophet of their own race who could lead them to faith. Abraham, therefore, is not only the author of one of the fundamental rites of Islam, and the precursor to Muḥammad who comes to call people to the one true God, but also the one who presages Muḥammad's mission in Arabia.

Joseph (Yūsuf)

Joseph is another biblical figure who plays an important role in the Islamic tradition. As in the case of prophets previously discussed, the trials of Joseph were precursors for the challenges the Prophet would face. Unlike other figures, the Joseph narrative is found complete in Sūra 12 of the Qurʾān, aptly titled "The Sūra of Joseph."⁴⁶ Most sūras are named after a key word in the opening verses, and not usually after individuals.⁴⁷ The special nature of the tale is clear from the beginning (Qurʾān 12:3): the qurʾānic story emphasizes

---

⁴⁵ This story is also preserved in *Pirqe Rabbi Eliezer* (chapter 30), a ninth century CE Jewish retelling of biblical stories, as well as in Midrash Ha-Gadol, a thirteenth century Yemenite midrash on the Torah, which to a great extent preserves earlier rabbinic texts. Scholars have debated whether the story of Abraham's visit to Ishmael originated in Islamic or Jewish sources. For a discussion of the debate and an analysis of the narratives, see Carol Bakhos, *Ishmael on the Border: Rabbinic Portrayals of the First Arab* (Albany: SUNY Press, 2006), 104–128.

⁴⁶ With the exception of chapter twelve, Joseph is mentioned only twice: in Q. 7:84, where he is listed among other biblical prophets, and in 40:34, where we read: "Joseph came before to you with clear signs, but you never ceased to doubt the message he brought you. When he expired, you said, 'God will not send another messenger.'"

⁴⁷ Sūras named after biblical individuals include Noah, Abraham, and Mary.

the protagonist's moral virtue. Joseph is an exemplar of one who is steadfast in times of tribulation, of one who withstands temptation and overcomes the "guile of women," and of one who speaks the truth and yet endures suffering at the hands of those who deceive.[48]

The purpose of the story of Joseph in the Qurʾān is didactic, warning of temptations that befall us at every turn, be it jealousy as in the case of Joseph's brother, or seduction, and at the same time exemplifying righteousness and its rewards. The tale is also a reminder of God's providence, which is reiterated throughout the sūra. It is God who gives Joseph wisdom and knowledge (v. 22), who teaches Joseph how to interpret dreams (vv. 21, 101), who shields him from the wiles of women (v. 33), and who reveals this tale as an admonition to all humankind (v. 104).

The story refers to itself in v. 3 as "the finest of all tales." According to the interpretive tradition, opinions vary as to the meaning of the phrase. It is taken literally, to mean that it is the most beautiful of stories, while others are of the opinion that it is the most beautiful in that "no other story in the Qurʾān is as rich in good counsel, wisdom, subtleties, and miraculous events."[49] According to Zamakhsharī (d. 538), a Muʾtazilite Qurʾān commentator, it is set apart from all others because of the manner in which the story is told, and not necessarily because of its content.[50] Yet others maintain it was called as such because "it speaks of many things: prophets and pious folk, angels and devils, jinn and men, livestock and birds, the lives of kings and slaves, scholars and merchants, wise men and fools, the behavior of men, and of women, with their plots and stratagems. It deals with matters such as chastity, belief in the unity of God, lives of the great, dream

---

[48] The story exhibits an intertextual relationship with the HB and Jewish and Christian exegetical narrative traditions, but with respect to the episode between Joseph and his master's wife, we find parallels with the ancient Egyptian "Story of Two Brothers," and the tale of Bellerophon of the *Iliad*. For an exploration of these parallels, see Shalom Goldman, *The Wiles of Women/The Wiles of Men: Joseph and Potiphar's Wife in Ancient Near Eastern, Jewish and Islamic Folktale* (Albany: SUNY Press, 1995). On the "Tale of Two Brothers," see Susan Tower Hollis, *The Ancient Egyptian 'Tale of Two Brothers': A Mythological, Religious, Literary, and Historico-Political Study* (2nd ed.; Oakville, Conn.: Bannerstone, 2008). See, too, Bernstein, *Stories of Joseph*.

[49] Brinner, *Lives of the Prophets*, 182.

[50] Also, according to al-Rāzī, "It may be safely assumed that the adjective 'best' refers not to the contents of 'that which is set forth'—i.e., the particular story narrated as such—but rather to the manner in which the Qurʾān (or this particular surah) is set forth." Muhammad Asad, *The Meaning of the Quran* (Gibralter: Dar al Andalus, 1980), 357, quoted in Goldman, *Wiles*, 10.

interpretation, the proper way to govern and behave towards others, and planning a people's subsistence."[51] Yet others say that it is because Joseph forgives his brothers and remains ever steadfast even in the face of adversity. When he meets his brothers, he never mentions their wrong and he repays their evil with generosity. And, finally, it is deemed the most beautiful of stories because it is a treasure trove of hidden meanings about life and belief, about the rewards of this world and the world to come.

A Synopsis of the Qurʾānic Joseph Story

The tale of Joseph commences with his relating to his father, Jacob, his vision of eleven stars, the sun and the moon prostrating before him. To this his father replies: "O my dear son! Do not tell your brothers of your vision, lest they plot against you. Lo, Satan is an avowed enemy of man." Although in the Qurʾān he heeds his father's advice and does not fan his brothers' jealousy, they nonetheless plot against him: "Surely Joseph and his brother are dearer to our father than we though we are many. Surely, our father is in grave error" (v. 8). They scheme against him and cast him into a dark pit with the expectation that a caravan will draw him out. When they approach their father with the news that a wolf devoured him, Jacob cries, "No! Your souls have tempted you to evil. I need good patience. God alone can help me endure the loss you speak of" (v. 18).

An Egyptian, al-ʿAzīz,[52] buys Joseph and as in the biblical account, his wife attempts to seduce him. Despite his protestations, had God not intervened Joseph would have succumbed to her advancements (v. 24). They both rush to the door, at which point she tears his shirt and they encounter her husband. The master's wife says: "Shall not the man who wished to violate your wife be put in prison or severely punished?" Joseph defends himself: "She was the one who tried to seduce me." A witness from her family testifies: "If the shirt is torn from the front, she is telling the truth. If it is torn from the back, then he is speaking the truth and she is lying." When her husband sees that it is rent from behind, he acknowledges her wrongdoing: "Your cunning is great indeed!" He then commands her to ask for pardon for her sin.

---

[51] Brinner, *Lives of the Prophets*, 182.
[52] al-ʿAzīz is a title, in Arabic literally meaning "mighty," "cherished." For a discussion of his name in the Qurʾān and in the commentary tradition, see Bernstein, *Stories of Joseph*, 208–209.

What follows is a fascinating episode that dramatizes the extraordinary effect the qur'ānic Joseph has on women:

> Certain women in the city said, "The Chief's wife is seeking to seduce her page. He smote her heart with love; we see her in manifest error." When she heard of their malicious talk, she sent for them and prepared a banquet for them. She gave each of them a knife and she said (to Joseph), "Come out before them." When they saw him, they did extol him, and (in their amazement) cut their hands. They said, "God preserve us! No mortal is this! This is none other than a noble angel!" She said, "This is he on whose account you blamed me. I asked of him an evil act, but he proved continent, but if he does not yield to my request, he shall surely be imprisoned, and shall surely be of the humbled."[53]
> (Q. 12:30–34)

Yet, despite this evidence, he is sent to jail where he meets two men. One of them says, "I dreamt that I was pressing grapes," and the other reports, "I saw in a dream that I was carrying a loaf upon my head and the birds came and ate it." When asked for its interpretation, Joseph responds: "Before the food that is provided for you comes to you, I shall interpret these dreams for you. This is knowledge that my Lord has given me, for I forsake the religion of those who disbelieve in God and deny the life to come. I follow the religion of my forefathers, Abraham, Isaac and Jacob. We attribute no partners to God. Such is the grace which God has bestowed on us and on all humankind, yet most do not give thanks." Joseph continues: "Fellow prisoners! Are sundry gods better than God, the One who conquers all? Those you serve besides him are nothing but names which you and your fathers have devised and for which God has revealed no sanction. Judgment rests only with God. He has commanded you to worship none but him. That is the right religion but most people do not know it" (v. 39). After this proclamation of the oneness of God, he interprets the dreams: one will serve his lord with wine, and the other will be crucified, and the birds will peck at his head. He then asked the one who would survive to

---

[53] Scholars have debated whether the Qur'ān serves as a source for Sefer ha-Yashar and Midrash ha-Gadol, or vice versa. See James L. Kugel, "The Assembly of Ladies," in *In Potiphar's House: The Interpretive Life of Biblical Texts* (Cambridge: Harvard University Press, 1994), 28–65, where he discusses the relationship between the qur'ānic women of the city incident and other versions. As the folklorist Stith Thompson, *Motif Index of Folk Literature* (Bloomington: University of Indiana Press, 1955), V, Motif K 2111, has demonstrated, the motif of a woman who makes vain overtures to a man and then accuses him of attempting to force her, has universal appeal. For narratives on the same motif, see John D. Yohannan, *Joseph and Potiphar's Wife in World Literature: An Anthology of the Story of the Chaste Youth and the Lustful Stepmother* (New York: New Directions Books, 1968).

mention him in the presence of his lord. Satan, however, made him forget and thus Joseph remained imprisoned for several years.

When the king asks for an interpretation of his dream (seven fatted cows devoured by seven leans ones, and seven ears of corn and seven other ears that are dry), the servant remembers Joseph and goes to him for an interpretation. Joseph obliges and the king asks that Joseph be sent to him, but when the envoy comes to him, Joseph says, "Go back to your master and ask him about the women who cut their hands. My master knows their cunning." When the king interrogates the women, they reply, "God forbid! We know of no evil on his part," but al-ʿAzīz's wife admits the truth that she was the one who seduced him and that Joseph is absolutely truthful (v. 51). Joseph asked for this inquiry so that his master might know for certain that Joseph did not betray him in his absence, and that God does not guide the snares of the false ones. "I do not claim to be free of sin, for humans are prone to evil, except to the one on whom God shows mercy. My Lord is surely forgiving and merciful" (v. 52).

The king commands that he see Joseph and claims him for himself. Joseph requests charge of the granaries and the king consents. The Qurʾān at this point reiterates the mercy and rewards to the righteous: "Thus we gave Joseph power in the land, and he dwelt there as he pleased. We bestow our mercy on whom We will, and shall never deny the righteous their reward. Most assuredly, better is the recompense of the life to come for those who believe in God and keep from evil" (vv. 56–57).

The story plot continues with the arrival of Joseph's brothers, except the youngest,[54] to the court. As in the biblical account, they do not realize they are in the presence of their brother, but Joseph recognizes them, commands them to bring the youngest brother back with them, and although initially Jacob is reluctant to do so, he permits him to go on the condition that the brothers swear an oath. As in Genesis, Jacob travels to Egypt; however, in the Qurʾān Joseph orders that the brothers return with all their people, including his parents. Thus we read: "He raised his parents on a throne, and they fell on their knees and prostrated themselves before him. Joseph said to his father, 'This is the meaning of my vision of old. My Lord has fulfilled it. He was indeed good to me when he released me from imprisonment, and brought you out of the desert after Satan had sown enmity between me and my brothers. Truly my Lord is gracious to whom he will. Indeed my Lord is all Knowing and Wise'" (Q. 12:100).

---

[54] Benjamin, the youngest of Jacob's sons in Genesis, is not named in the Qurʾān.

The story of Joseph ends with an affirmation of the revelatory nature of the story of Joseph, and its role as a guide to true believers. Declarations of God's patience, forgiveness, beneficence, and omniscience punctuate the narrative flow, and underscore the didactic quality of this most entertaining tale: "Until when the messengers despaired and thought that they were denied, then came unto them Our help, and whom We would was saved. And Our wrath cannot be averted from the guilty. In their history there is certainly a lesson for men of understanding. It is no invented story but a confirmation of the existing (Scripture) and a detailed explanation of everything, and a guidance and a mercy for those who believe" (Q. 12:110–111).

Unlike the biblical account, God is omnipresent in the qur'ānic narrative, protecting Joseph at every turn. So, too, Satan is on the scene, causing Joseph's tribulations, whether by inciting his brothers' jealousy toward him, or making the fellow prisoner forget to mention Joseph to his lord. Between them rests Joseph, an ordinary man who struggles against temptation, and remains steadfast in his belief in the one God (v. 40).

Joseph in Qur'ānic Exegesis

Indeed much is made of Joseph's beauty. In Gen 39:6 we read that he is "comely of form and comely of appearance," but the qur'ānic episode with the women from the city dramatically captures the effect his beauty had on women. The mufassirūn provide greater detail. According to a report related in al-Tha'labī, when Joseph would walk in the alleys of Cairo, "the glimmer of his face would reflect from the walls just as the light of the Sun or the Moon."[55] It is also related that God apportioned two-thirds of all beauty to Joseph and divided the remaining third among humanity.[56] The beauty of Joseph is compared to the light of day and "his skin was fair, his face comely, his hair curly, eyes large, he stood upright, had strong legs, upper arms and forearms, a flat belly with a small navel, he was hook-nosed, and had a dark mole on his right cheek which beautified his face." The description continues:

---

[55] Brinner, *Lives of the Prophets*, 183.

[56] The distribution of beauty is reminiscent of a passage in the Babylonian Talmud, tractate Qiddushin 49b, that discusses the apportioning of qualities among peoples. Ten kabs (an ancient Hebrew measure) of beauty, for example, descended to the world and nine were taken by Jerusalem, and one by the rest of the world.

A white birthmark between his eyes resembling the Moon when it is full, and eyelashes like the fore-feathers of eagle wings. His teeth sparkled when he smiled, and light emanated from his mouth between his incisors when he spoke. No human would be able to describe Joseph, no one. ... He gave Joseph unblemished skin, and so much beauty as He had not given to any other human. When he swallowed, greens and fruits which he ate could be seen in his throat and chest until they reached his stomach.[57]

Moreover, Muḥammad marvels at Joseph's beauty which he encounters in heaven as he goes on his Night Journey.[58]

Qurʾānic commentators preserve traditions that flesh out the Qurʾān, that is, they furnish details, such as the names of personages. We are told, for example, the name of the one who bought Joseph—Potiphar[59] b. Rahib, who was a ruler of Egypt in charge of the grain storehouses of the Great King, al-Rayyan b. al-Walid b. Tharwan b. Arashah b. Qaran b. ʿAmr b. ʿImlaq b. Lawudh b. Shem, son of Noah, and also Qiṭfir.[60] His wife is named Raʿil or Zulayka (also Zuleika).[61] The women of the city are also identified as follows: the wife of the cupbearer, the wife of the baker, the wife of the master of the inkwell, the wife of the prison-master and the wife of the chamberlain.

---

[57] Brinner, *Lives of the Prophets*, 184. Another interpretation: "Wahb said, 'Beauty is in ten parts; nine belong to Joseph and one to the rest of mankind.'" See n. 56 above on the talmudic passage. Wahb ibn Munnabih was known for his familiarity with Jewish sources, including the Talmud.

[58] Some illustrated manuscripts of the Night Journey (mirʿaj) depict Muḥammad meeting Joseph. See Marie-Rose Séguy, ed., *The Miraculous Journey of Mohamet: Mirâj Nâmeh* (Paris: Bibliothèque Nationale), Manuscript Supplément Turc 190 (trans. Richard Pevear; New York: George Braziller, 1977), Plate XVI. In al-Thaʿlabī he also comments that Joseph inherited his looks from Isaac, who in turn inherited his looks from his mother, Sarah. In Genesis Rabbah, the rabbis make a connection between Gen 39:6, "comely of form and comely of appearance," a reference to Joseph, and Gen 29:17, "comely of form and comely of appearance," a reference to Rachel: "Said R. Isaac, 'Toss a stick into the air and it will fall to the same spot.'" Whereas the tafsīrist (mufassir) traces Joseph's beauty back to Sarah and ultimately to Eve, the midrashmakes the philological connection between the two verses and traces Joseph's beauty immediately to his mother, Rachel. At the same time, there is another midrash (*Gen. Rab.* 84:8) that asserts "Joseph's face was similar to Jacob's." See *Gen. Rab.* 84:6 for a litany of similarities between Jacob and Joseph.

[59] See Bernstein, *Stories of Joseph*, 208–209.

[60] Other variations deriving from the biblical Potiphar include Qiṭfīr, Iṭfīr, Qūṭifar, Qiṭṭin. See A.F.L. Beeston, *Baidawi's Commentary on Surah 12 of the Qur'an: Text, Accompanied by an Interpretative Rendering and Notes* (Oxford: Clarendon, 1963), 13, n. 51.

[61] In later medieval Jewish works, such as Sefer Hayashar, and in Persian Islamic folklore, Potiphar's wife is consistently named Zuleika. See Goldman, *Wiles*, 162, n. 27. Beeston, *Baidawi's Commentary on Surah 12*, 13. See Louis Ginzberg, *The Legends of the Jews* (7 vols.; Philadelphia: Jewish Publication Society, 1909–1938), 5:339 n. 113; and also John MacDonald, "Joseph in the Qur'an and Muslim Commentary: A Comparative Study," *Muslim World* 46 (1956): 113–131, 207–224 (esp. 124).

Joseph's attractiveness was not lost on his master, Potiphar (Qiṭfīr). According to several Islamic interpretive traditions, he desired Joseph sexually. According to al-Ṭabarī, Qiṭfīr was a man who did not have intercourse with women, despite the fact his wife Raʿil was beautiful, tender and endowed with property and possessions.[62] The master's desire for Joseph is also mentioned in the Talmud, as well as in Jerome's translation of Genesis.[63] Furthermore, even the other prisoners who saw Joseph, fell in love with him.[64]

Muslim exegetes go into detail with respect to the exchanges between Potiphar's wife and Joseph. She tries to seduce him with flattery, with jewels, and not least with her burning desire. Then, according to Ibn ʿAbbas, the devil rushed into the space between the two and, putting one hand around Joseph and the other around the woman, he drew them together. Ibn ʿAbbas said, "Now Joseph's desire grew so strong that he undid his waistband, and lay down next to her, in the manner of a man about to commit adultery." As in Jewish sources, Joseph is indeed tempted. At every turn, Joseph refuses, yet Joseph would have surrendered to his desires had not God intervened, as the Qurʾān states: "But for the clear sign from his Lord" (12:24). The qurʾānic commentators expand the narrative in a variety of ways and differ as to the details of the sign he received. Some maintain that he saw the Angel Gabriel disguised as his father, Jacob, biting his fingertips, whereas others relate that it was indeed his father, beating his breast. His father's apparition immediately tempered his sexual desire.[65] Thus we read in al-Thaʿlabī:

> ... Abū l-Ḥasan ʿAbd al-Raḥman b. Muḥammad b. ʿAbdullah al-Ṭabarānī—Ḥasan b. ʿAṭiyah—Isrāʾīl b. Abī Ḥusayn—Abū Saʿīd—Ibn Abbās who, commenting on the Qurʾān words, "But for the clear sign from his Lord," (12:24) said, "Jacob appeared to him and hit him on the chest with his hand, and

---

[62] Brinner, *The History of al-Ṭabarī*, Volume 3 (Albany: SUNY Press, 1991), 148–186. Also, Brinner, *Lives of the Prophets*, 197.

[63] Goldman, *Wiles*, 162, n. 25.

[64] Brinner, *Lives of the Prophets*, 204.

[65] A passage from the Babylonian Talmud, Sotah 36b: "'And she seized his garment'—At that moment the image of his father [Jacob] entered and appeared to him in the window. He said to him, 'Joseph, your brothers are destined to have their names written on the priestly breastplate, and yours is amongst theirs. Do you want it to be erased, and yourself be called a shepherd of harlots,' as it says in scripture, 'A shepherd of harlots loses his wealth' (Prov 29:3). Immediately, his bow remained strong [that is, he overcame his desires]." See also, *Gen. Rab.* 87:7: "R. Samuel said, 'The bow was drawn but it relaxed,' as it was written, 'And his bow returned in strength' (Gen 49:24). ... R. Huna said in R. Mattena's name, 'He saw his father's face, at which his blood cooled,' thus: [Gen 49:24–25 continues], 'By the hands of the mighty one of Jacob, there, the Shepherd, the rock of Israel—the God of your father who helps you.'" For a detailed discussion of Joseph's innocence, and questionable virtue on that "fateful day in Potiphar's house," see Kugel, "The Assembly of Ladies," 94–124.

Joseph's desire left through his fingertips." According to al-Ḥasan, Mujāhid, ʿIkrimah, and al-Ḍaḥḥāk, the roof of the house split open for him and he saw Jacob biting his fingers. ... God said to Gabriel, "Gabriel! Take hold of my servant before he commits a sin." Gabriel went down, biting his fingers (or hand), and said, "Joseph, are you doing what fools do, you whom God destined to be one of the Prophets?"[66]

Here again, however amusing the image may be, we are met with God's providence. Joseph is not reprimanded for his desires, for he is only human, but he is guarded from straying. This is a recurring motif throughout the Qurʾān—humans must be wary of the temptations that Satan puts before them. Be it the qurʾānic narrative or the exegetical tradition, the story of Joseph, exhorts, edifies, and entertains such that it is indeed the finest of tales.

Conclusion

It must be emphasized that the above survey of how the Qurʾān and the classical interpretive tradition treat various figures and narratives found also in the Book of Genesis is exceedingly limited. One cannot possibly do justice to the vast corpora of exegetical material. Be that as it may, this examination gives readers a sense of how the Islamic interpretative tradition, especially the qiṣaṣ al-anbiyʾā, fills the gaps of the qurʾānic story by adding detail. In some cases, the literary flourishes give a story greater depth, or make it more entertaining. In other cases, they amplify its didactic quality.

As I stated at the outset the stories of Genesis resonate within the Islamic tradition, yet at the same time the qurʾānic narratives create their own distinct rhythms. The affinities between several stories in Genesis and in the Qurʾān abound, but formal similarities do not make them the same story, certainly not, as Waldman notes, in "a thematic, moral, or theological sense,"[67] even though at times they share a theological worldview, or attempt to teach the same moral lesson. The challenge of comparative studies is to detect the common treads while at the same time to appreciate the purpose and manner in which they are distinctly woven into each tradition, and woven again and again through the interpretive traditions.

---

[66] Brinner, *Lives of the Prophets*, 199.
[67] Waldman, "'Biblical' Materials in the Qurʾān," 13.

Select Bibliography

Adang, Camilla. *Muslim Writers on Judaism and the Hebrew Bible: From Ibn Rabban to Ibn Hazm*. Islamic Philosophy, Theology, and Science 22. Leiden: Brill, 1996.

Beeston, A.F.L. *Baidawi's Commentary on Surah 12 of the Qur'an: Text, Accompanied by an Interpretative Rendering and Notes*. Oxford: Clarendon Press, 1963.

Bernstein, Marc S. *Stories of Joseph: Narrative Migrations between Judaism and Islam*. Detroit: Wayne State University Press, 2006.

Brinner, William M., trans. *Lives of the Prophets: As Recounted by Abū Isḥāq Aḥmad Ibn Muḥammad Ibn Ibrāhīm al-Thaʿlabī*. Studies in Arabic Literature 24. Leiden: Brill, 2002.

Calder, Norman. "Tafsīr from Ṭabarī to Ibn Kathīr: Problems in the Description of a Genre, Illustrated with Reference to the Story of Abraham." Pages 101–140 in *Approaches to the Qur'an*. Edited by G.R. Hawting and Abdul-Kader A. Shareef. Routledge/SOAS Series on Contemporary Politics and Culture in the Middle East. New York: Routledge, 1993.

Firestone, Reuven. *Journeys in Holy Lands: The Evolution of the Abraham-Ishmael Legends in Islamic Exegesis*. Albany: State University of New York Press, 1990.

———. "YŪSUF b. Yaʿḳūb." Pages 352–354 in vol. 11 of *Encyclopaedia of Islam*. 2nd ed. Edited by P.J. Bearman, Th. Bianquis, C.E. Bosworth, E. van Donzel, and W.P. Heinrichs. 12 vols. Leiden: Brill, 2002.

Goldman, Shalom. *The Wiles of Women/The Wiles of Men: Joseph and Potiphar's Wife in Near Eastern, Jewish and Islamic Folklore*. Albany: State University of New York Press, 1995.

Hauglid, Brian M. "On the Early Life of Abraham: Biblical and Qur'anic Intertextuality and the Anticipation of Muhammad." Pages 87–106 in *The Bible and the Qurʾān: Essays in Scriptural Intertextuality*. Edited by John C. Reeves. Society of Biblical Literature Symposium Series 24. Atlanta: Scholars Press, 2003.

Kaltner, John. *Ishmael Instructs Isaac: An Introduction to the Qur'an for Bible Readers*. Collegeville, Minn.: The Liturgical Press, 1999.

Kugel, James L. *In Potiphar's House: The Interpretive Life of Biblical Texts*. Cambridge: Harvard University Press, 1994.

Lassner, Jacob. *Demonizing the Queen of Sheba: Boundaries of Gender and Culture in Postbiblical Judaism and Medieval Islam*. Chicago: University of Chicago Press, 1993.

Lowin, Shari L. *The Making of a Forefather: Abraham in Islamic and Jewish Exegetical Narratives*. Islamic History and Civilization: Studies and Texts 65. Leiden: Brill, 2006.

Saleh, Walid A. *The Formation of the Classical Tafsīr Tradition: The Qurʾān Commentary of al-Thaʿlabī (D. 427/1035)*. Texts and Studies on the Qur'an 1. Leiden: Brill, 2004.

Thackston, Wheeler M., trans. *Tales of the Prophets (Qiṣaṣ al-Anbiyāʾ)*. Chicago: Great Books of the Islamic World, 1997.

Tottoli, Roberto. *Biblical Prophets in the Qurʾān and Muslim Literature*. Translated by Michael Robertson. Richmond: Curzon, 2002.

PART FOUR

GENESIS AND THEOLOGY

THE THEOLOGY OF GENESIS*

Joel S. Kaminsky

Perhaps the way to begin an essay reflecting on the theology of Genesis is to note that at least some of the theological significance of this book can be gleaned from probing its connection to the other four books of the Torah. Exodus-Deuteronomy narrate the seminal events surrounding the birth of the Israelite people and these events all are framed within the 120 year lifetime of Moses, by far the most important character in the Pentateuch. Some have even called the Torah a biography of Moses, a description that highlights the distinctness of Genesis. This distinctness becomes clearer yet when one examines the contents of this unusual book. Chapters 1–11 have little direct relevance to the specific history of Israel. And while major parts of Gen 12–50 are about the lives of Israel's earliest ancestors, many stories focus on non-Israelite characters like Hagar, Ishmael, Lot and Esau. Furthermore, sometimes the behaviors of revered characters like the patriarchs and matriarchs stand at odds with or even directly violate legal and ethical norms found elsewhere in the Torah. Walter Moberly tries to capture the theological import of Genesis by calling it the Old Testament of the Old Testament.[1] By this he means that the theological distinctness of Genesis in relation to the rest of the Torah in particular, and the Tanakh more broadly, raises theological issues analogous to those that occur as Christians seek to understand the relationship between the Hebrew Bible and the New Testament.

Already in antiquity Jewish interpreters commented upon the oddity that the Torah, a book centered upon and preoccupied with the laws given at Sinai, contains such an extended prologue. The *Mekhilta of Rabbi Ishmael*, an anthology of legal midrashim from 2nd century Palestine, has an opening reflection on the Ten Commandments that asks why this passage is not

---

* This essay was improved by the helpful feedback from a number of readers including Joel Lohr, Anne Stewart, Nathan Macdonald, Walter Moberly, and members of the St. Andrews University Old Testament Seminar located at St. Mary's College. I am indebted to Bill Tooman for inviting me to present this essay at St. Andrews.

[1] R.W.L. Moberly, *The Old Testament of the Old Testament: Patriarchal Narratives and Mosaic Yahwism* (OBT; Minneapolis: Fortress, 1992).

placed at the beginning of the Torah. The *Mekhilta* answers its own rhetorical question with a wonderful parable about how a king who wishes to rule over people must first do things to earn the respect of his subjects; likewise God first redeemed Israel from Egypt and also provided them with manna and quails before asking for the fealty of the Israelites. Similarly, Rashi, the great medieval Jewish exegete, initiates his running commentary on Genesis by asking why the Torah does not begin with the first commandment given to the whole people of Israel, a command that occurs in Exod 12:2. Rashi sees Genesis as necessary so that other nations cannot claim that Israel simply stole the Holy Land. Here God's ownership over creation is stressed. While the *Mekhilta* and Rashi generate slightly different answers, each is an attempt to explain why we have this extended prologue in the Pentateuch.

Contemporary interpreters continue to recognize the theological uniqueness and richness of the first book of the Bible as demonstrated by the vast secondary literature surrounding Genesis. The modest task of this essay is to provide the reader with a survey of some of the most important theological currents raised within recent scholarly discussions of Genesis.

CREATION

Genesis begins with two creation stories, attributed by critical scholarship to two distinct theological schools, Gen 1:1–2:4a stemming from the Priestly or P source and Gen 2:4b–2:25 authored by the Yahwist or J source. These two stories shed a tremendous amount of light on the theological underpinnings of the Hebrew Bible and one could easily devote a full monograph to each story's theology and its history of interpretation. P's theocentric creation story represents Israel's God as a transcendent creator who stands apart from the created order. Scholars have long noted that this account challenges aspects of the cosmogonic myth found in much of the ancient Near East, which sees creation occurring in the aftermath of a cosmic battle between various gods such as that described in the Enuma Elish, the Babylonian Creation Epic. Elements of the creation through combat mythology are indeed preserved elsewhere in the Bible, especially in certain hymnic material, but in Gen 1 God faces no resistance when creating the world.[2]

---

[2] For a thoughtful set of theological meditations on the Bible's preservation of these ancient myths about creation through combat, see Jon D. Levenson, *Creation and the Persistence of Evil: The Jewish Drama of Divine Omnipotence* (San Francisco: Harper & Row, 1985).

While important aspects of P's account are quite unique, other elements of P's creation story reveal great continuity with the larger Near Eastern cultural context in which ancient Israel flourished. For example, unlike later Jewish and Christian readings of this text that assume that Gen 1 endorses the notion of creation from nothing, here God neither creates the waters nor the dry land, but rather he puts each in its proper place. Furthermore, most contemporary scholars believe that the plural language used by Gen 1:26, "let us make humankind in our image, according to our likeness," indicates that even in P, often viewed as a late source, and all the more so in much of the rest of the Hebrew Bible, one finds a religious outlook better described as a type of monolatry (worship of one God while acknowledging the existence of other deities), rather than as monotheism, which is posited to be a very late biblical development.[3]

One of the most theologically innovative moves made in the P creation account is the high place accorded human beings. In the Enuma Elish humans are created from the blood of the rebel deity Kingu to alleviate the workload of the lower gods. In this view, human life is an endless task of low-level servitude. In effect humans function as a type of guest workers created to help the lowest status inhabitants of the divine realm avoid chores they find demeaning. In contrast, within Gen 1, the first ancestors of human beings, both male and female, are created in God's own image and given dominion over the world. While some environmentally oriented critics have attempted to blame this passage for supposedly permitting humans to abuse the environment and other critics of religion at times blame the Bible for disempowering humans by its emphasis on their creaturely status, each of these polar readings overlooks the place humans are given in P's creation account. Far from infantilizing humans this passage comes close to deifying them.[4] But it does not in fact give humans full divinity, reserving

---

[3] Standard treatments of this issue can be found in Mark S. Smith, *The Early History of God: YHWH and the Other Deities in Ancient Israel* (New York: Harper & Row, 1990), or Robert Karl Gnuse, *No Other Gods: Emergent Monotheism in Israel* (JSOTSup 241; Sheffield: Sheffield Academic Press, 1997).

[4] Thus J. Richard Middleton, *The Liberating Image: The* Imago Dei *in Genesis 1* (Grand Rapids: Brazos, 2005), argues that the notion that all humans are created in God's image is a democratization of ancient Near Eastern royal ideology. In short all humans are functionally kings in relation to the non-human created world. I reject the notion advocated by some scholars that negative human behavior in Gen 3–11 leads to the removal of the image of God from humanity at large, leaving it present within Israel alone. See, for example, John T. Strong, "Israel as a Testimony to YHWH's Power: The Priests' Definition of Israel," in *Constituting the Community: Studies on the Polity of Ancient Israel in Honor of S. Dean McBride Jr.* (ed.

for God alone the right to create and to destroy creation. And the theological import of the story does not end here. This creation account is capped with a notice that God saw that everything he created was very good (Gen 1:31), immediately followed by a passage linking the Sabbath as a day of rest to God's own rest on the seventh day after creating the world over the previous six days. As often noted by Jewish thinkers, one of the central points of the commandment to rest on the Sabbath is to recognize that God, not human beings, created and controls the universe.

Alternatively, J's creation story is notable for its earthy language and anthropocentric viewpoint. In this account, God is portrayed as not only much less transcendent, but even as somewhat fallible, as he learns through experimentation. The creation of animals is attributed to God's attempt to find a suitable partner for the first human being, or to use the text's own language, the earth creature (the text puns on the word Adam by relating it to the Hebrew word for 'ground' אדמה). Discovering that none of the animals would serve as a helper to Adam, God removes a piece of Adam and builds a woman whom the earth creature recognizes as his partner.[5] This wonderful tale provides an aetiological explanation of the attraction to the opposite sex, and suggests that this author sees heterosexuality as normative in that it is grounded in the very way in which gendered human beings were created. This passage, even more so than, for example, the Sodom story or the few laws in Leviticus, presents a much more serious challenge to those in church and synagogue who argue that Judaism and Christianity can fully embrace those maintaining a homosexual lifestyle. This is so because, unlike Aristophanes' speech in Plato's *Symposium* in which male and female homosexuality is seen as part and parcel of the original creation of human beings, such is not the case in the biblical text. Or to use academic jargon, the Bible's worldview is hetero-normative.

As one can see, these first two chapters of Genesis provide a veritable theological feast of ideas. Yet one should not overlook two foundational theological ideas not yet mentioned but clearly exhibited within Gen 1–2. The first is that the Hebrew Bible rarely engages in extended abstract analysis

---

John T. Strong and Steven S. Tuell; Winona Lake, Ind.: Eisenbrauns, 2005), 89–106. God's covenant with Noah and the many non-Israelite righteous characters in Genesis such as Abimelech in Gen 20 or Pharaoh in the Joseph story indicate otherwise.

[5] The Hebrew text is not completely clear if it is Adam or God who discovers that none of the animals is a proper companion for Adam. Even if my assumption that the subject of this verb is God proves wrong, the thrust of this narrative is that God adapts to humans who regularly surprise him.

such as one finds in Greek philosophic speculation or in much postbiblical Christian theology. Rather, the Hebrew Bible's theology tends to be communicated through narratives, and these stories call for interpretation and are often open to many different readings. The narrative forms of the Bible may in fact make them ideal to transmit certain key ancient Israelite theological ideas such as the notion that God is transcendent but also interacts with humans in a personal and relational fashion.[6] Narratives also allow one to see the development of characters over time. And this is true not only of human characters such as Judah and Joseph who both evolve over the course of Gen 37–50, but of God's character as well. Furthermore, the complex set of interrelated narratives in Genesis, or more broadly in the Torah as a whole, inevitably prod the reader to compare and contrast the morality and motives of various characters to each other. The result is that all readers are forced to become interpreters and even in a sense, theologians.

The second general theological insight is connected to the juxtaposition of these two different, and at times even contradictory, creation stories. One of the most interesting features of the theology of the Hebrew Bible is the willingness of the final redactors to incorporate diverse and even seemingly contradictory theological ideas within a single text, often in close proximity to each other. The theology of the Bible is in many ways a raucous argument spanning centuries, which in turn has inspired later readers, perhaps more so in Jewish tradition than in Christianity, to continue to argue with the text and each other.[7]

Corruption

For centuries, Christians have read Gen 3 as the story of the "Fall of Man" in which God punishes all humans on account of Adam's disobedience by taking away the immortality God had initially bestowed upon them. This interpretation gave rise to the widespread theological doctrine of original

---

[6] Robert Alter, *The Art of Biblical Narrative* (New York: Basic Books, 1981), argues that the narrative forms utilized within the Hebrew Bible are particularly well suited for expressing ancient Israel's monotheistic theology.

[7] Two recent books that examine the theological significance of the Bible's tendency to include and often juxtapose differing theologies are Walter Brueggemann, *Theology of the Old Testament: Testimony, Dispute, Advocacy* (Minneapolis: Augsburg Fortress, 1997) and Israel Knohl, *The Divine Symphony: The Bible's Many Voices* (Philadelphia: Jewish Publications Society, 2003).

sin.⁸ In such a reading, humans fell from a perfect state to a sinful one on the basis of a single human error. However, an examination of Gen 3–11 indicates that it contains a series of linked narratives that describe the ongoing corruption of human beings and God's attempts to remedy this situation. There is little evidence to suggest that Gen 3 marks a complete change in the divine-human relationship. Furthermore, it is far from clear that Gen 3 describes a loss of human immortality because such a reading presumes that humans were created immortal, a widespread ancient Jewish and Christian belief, but an idea never explicitly stated in Gen 3.⁹ One of the primary reasons to study a book like Genesis is to learn that the theological assumptions that later believers read back into the Bible are often quite different from those held by the authors of the biblical text. Genesis 3 is more properly described as a story about the missed opportunity to obtain immortality than about the loss of immortality that humans had originally been granted.¹⁰ One can see that this is the case by noting that the curses God puts on humanity in 3:16–19 presume that they are mortal. It is only later that God decides he must prevent humans from obtaining immortality and consequently he must drive them from Eden (3:22–24).

None of this is to argue that Gen 3 is not a theologically significant story, because clearly it is. It reveals psychologically sophisticated and mythically compelling insights about how humans are led to sin and the ways in which sin distorts human relationships as well as fractures the tripartite relationship between humanity, nature, and God. An often-missed aspect of this text is that it appears to contain a subtle two-pronged critique of the Deity, less surprising once one remembers that J portrays God as developing alongside his human creation. The first element of this implicit divine critique is that God seemed not to have anticipated how quickly humans would push beyond the limits God set or that the snake, having been created by God (possibly representing the natural world and its temptations), would be the

---

⁸ For extensive background on the rich set of theological interpretations that ancient Jews and Christians derived from this story, see Gary A. Anderson, *The Genesis of Perfection: Adam and Eve in the Jewish and Christian Imagination* (Louisville: Westminster John Knox, 2001).

⁹ For more on the background of this interpretation, see Joel S. Kaminsky, "Paradise Regained: Rabbinic Reflections on Israel at Sinai," in *Jews, Christians, and the Theology of the Hebrew Scriptures* (ed. Alice Ogden Bellis and Joel S. Kaminsky; SBLSymS 8; Atlanta: SBL, 2000), 15–43.

¹⁰ For a probing theological discussion of this Genesis passage and its connections to other biblical reflections on immortality, see James Barr, *The Garden of Eden and the Hope of Immortality* (Minneapolis: Fortresss, 1992).

catalyst of human corruption. The second element is that the punishment might be judged disproportionately harsh (even though it is not as severe as the penalty of immediate death announced earlier in 2:17), in that all humans from this point forward suffer the consequences of this one act of disobedience.

Genesis 4 deepens the Bible's probing of human corruption by narrating the first murder, a fratricide inspired by jealousy over God's preference for Abel's over Cain's sacrifice. This short episode is the first of a host of stories in Genesis in which God's favor toward a specific person sets off the jealousy of those not chosen. Since this theme will receive further attention below, here I will draw out just a few basic points. While critics have suggested various reasons why God prefers Abel's offering to Cain's, the text remains enigmatic. Equally important is that God's favor toward Abel does not indicate that Cain is hated or cut off from God. Thus it is Cain with whom God discourses, not Abel. It is only after Cain commits murder that he is driven from God's presence. Perhaps most importantly, the story seems to present Cain as the archetype for any human who in a fit of jealousy might lash out and kill another. This is what enables modern authors like Herman Melville in *Billy Budd* and John Steinbeck in *East of Eden* to use this text so productively.

After this incident the text goes on to describe a number of technological innovations, which it places between Cain's murder of Abel and Lamech's vengeful taunt (Gen 4:20–22). Here two particular trends stand out. Firstly, the growing ability of humans to manipulate and master the natural world is a mixed blessing in that such technical knowledge is paired with the growing corruption of human beings. In short, the evolving technical mastery exhibited by humans is tainted by a lack of human moral development. This insight seems particularly prescient in the contemporary world in which scientific achievement frequently runs well ahead of the human community's ethical track record. The second related trend concerns the linkage between the deterioration of God's creation and the failure of human beings to occupy their proper place in the cosmos. This can occur when humans seek to become godlike as Eve and Adam attempt to do in Gen 3, or when humans devolve into animals who engage in unrestrained violence, as witnessed in Lamech's taunt and in the limits God places on the shedding of innocent human blood (Gen 9:5–6).[11] At other times the threat comes from

---

[11] For an insightful investigation of this theme, see Patrick D. Miller, *Genesis 1–11: Studies in Structure & Theme* (JSOTSup 8; Sheffield: JSOT Press, 1978).

the heavenly realm, as occurs in Gen 6:1–4, when divine beings lust after and procreate with human women, an incident that immediately precedes God's plan to destroy his creation by flood. The idea that humans who violate their place in the cosmic order threaten the stability of God's creation recurs in the Tower of Babel incident and again in the Exodus account when Pharaoh arrogates to himself divine privileges and in turn brings a series of ecological disasters upon Egypt.[12]

Turning to the flood narrative, once again one encounters the juxtaposition of substantially differing theologies. The P strand of the narrative views the flood as God's righteous judgment on a wicked humanity (Gen 6:11). In contrast, J appears to show a more ambivalent deity who first exhibits regret at having created humankind and in the end regrets having destroyed the world by the flood (Gen 6:5–8; 8:21). Walter Moberly notes that contrary to the somewhat widespread view that the flood reveals an unmerciful God, in actuality the story suggests that the world only exists due to God's continuing mercy toward a humanity that remains corrupt.[13] Moberly's point receives further support from an astonishing facet of this narrative that occurs immediately after the flood. In 9:1–6 God adjusts the human diet, now granting humans permission to eat animal meat as long as they drain the blood. This is an implicit recognition that God's original standard which (at least according to P) limited human and animal consumption to a vegetarian diet (Gen 1:29–30) was unrealistic and so strict that rather than reducing violence it led to an escalation in violence.[14] God appears to permit the use of controlled violence in hopes of reducing the most problematic form of human violence, murder. This theological shift suggests that God is becoming ever more willing to work with humans as they are rather than as he had hoped they might be.

This passage is immediately followed by the Bible's first covenant in which God promises all humanity and all animals that he will not again flood the world. In spite of God's move to ameliorate human violence and set the divine-human relationship on a new footing, events in the

---

[12] For more on the creation imagery evoked in the plagues of Exodus, see Terence E. Fretheim, "The Plagues as Ecological Signs of Historical Disaster," *JBL* 110 (1991): 385–396.

[13] R.W.L. Moberly, *The Theology of the Book of Genesis* (OTT; Cambridge: Cambridge University Press, 2009), 110–120.

[14] Abel's meat offering in Gen 4 likely indicates that J thought humans were always permitted to eat meat. In private correspondence, Nathan Macdonald noted that this change in God's plan shows that even P's more transcendent image of God has some of the flexibility often associated exclusively with the J source.

immediate aftermath of the flood indicate that God is still failing to obtain the response he hoped to elicit from humans. Thus Ham's behavior toward Noah, while enigmatic, indicates a breach or more likely an inversion in what the biblical text sees as the natural order, and the Tower of Babel incident in Gen 11 describes yet another human attempt to violate the barrier separating the divine from the human realm.

THE THEOLOGICAL SIGNIFICANCE OF GOD'S CALL TO ABRAHAM

Chapters 3–11 in Genesis reveal the full extent to which the three-way relationship between humans, nature, and God has been fractured. In the wake of this disappointing situation, God moves from a plan in which he demands equal obedience from all humans to a two-tiered plan. While most people are held to a minimal religio-moral standard (which later Judaism came to conceive of as the seven Noahide commandments that all Gentiles must observe), one man's extended family is given a special place in the divine economy requiring that they maintain a higher religio-moral standard.[15] As Gen 12:2–3 makes clear, Abraham's and thus Israel's election is closely bound-up with God's larger plan to bring blessing to the whole world, even while God's purposes in choosing Abraham and his descendants are not exhausted by this linkage.[16]

---

[15] The ancient rabbis developed the idea that Israel is bound by 613 commandments, while the rest of humanity is bound by only a few. The exact number varies in different texts, but commonly one finds references to seven commandments Gentiles must observe including such basic ideas as setting up proper courts, *not* murdering, stealing, committing idolatry, committing adultery, et al.

[16] For recent attempts to unpack the complicated syntax of Gen 12:1–3, see William Yarchin, "Imperative and Promise in Genesis 12:1–3," *Studia Biblica et Theologica* 10 (1980): 164–178; Patrick D. Miller "Syntax and Theology in Genesis xii 3a," *VT* 34 (1984): 472–476; or the just published, Joel S. Baden, "The Morpho-Syntax of Genesis 12:1–3: Translation and Interpretation," *CBQ* 72 (2010): 223–237. For a sensitive theological reading of the placement of these verses and their relationship to the larger structure of the Patriarchal (perhaps better labeled the Ancestral) Narratives in Genesis, see Hans Walter Wolff, "The Kerygma of the Yahwist," in *The Vitality of Old Testament Tradition* (ed. Walter Brueggemann and Han Walter Wolff; Atlanta: John Knox, 1975), 41–66. For a close analysis of these verses in relation to larger canonical themes, see R.W.L. Moberly, *The Bible, Theology and Faith: A Study of Abraham and Jesus* (CSCD 5; Cambridge University Press, 2000), 120–127 and Jo Bailey Wells, "Blessing to all the Families of the Earth: Abram as Prototype of Israel," ch. 6 in her *God's Holy People: A Theme in Biblical Theology* (JSOTSup 305; Sheffield: Sheffield Academic Press, 2000) 185–207.

I will make of you a great nation, and I will bless you, and make your name great, so that you will be a blessing. I will bless those who bless you, and the one who curses you I will curse; and in you all the families of the earth shall be blessed.

It seems quite likely, based on the heavy use of the root for "bless" ברך, employed five times in vv. 2–3, that Abraham and his descendants are the ones who will undo the earlier divine curses connected to human evil doing (Gen 3:17; 4:11; 5:29; 8:21; and 9:25). The use of the word אדמה "earth" at the end of Gen 12:3 calls to mind the curses that both Adam and Cain brought upon the earth (Gen 3:17; 4:11). That v. 2 promises Abraham a great name may suggest that Abraham's obedience to God will succeed where those who sought to make a name for themselves by building a tower (as an assault on heaven) failed (Gen 11:1–9). While Noah is invoked as one who will provide comfort from the curse (Gen 5:29), the fact is that after the flood God merely promises not to curse the ground again due to human misbehavior (Gen 8:21). Yet Ham's behavior (Gen 9:22) along with the Tower of Babel incident indicate that the divine-human rift remains unhealed.

It is clear that Abraham is part of a larger divine plan which will bring blessing to the whole world, even though the exact meaning of the *niphal* of ברך "bless" used in the all important final clause of Gen 12:3 remains hotly debated.[17] Is this rare verbal form best translated as a passive and rendered as "all the families of the earth will be blessed" by or through Abraham, his name, or his descendants? Or should one look to the alternate places in which this similar blessing is rendered by the *hithpael* (Gen 22:18; 26:4), opting for the reflexive, "all the families of the earth will bless themselves" by/through Abraham.[18] The two renderings imply two differing scenarios. If one reads this verb as a reflexive, the sense communicated may be something akin to members of the Gentile nations saying, "may you be blessed like God blessed Abraham" (see similarly Gen 48:20). If one opts for the passive meaning this seems to imply the stronger notion that Abraham's family will be a conduit through which blessing will pass to the other nations of the

---

[17] For a full discussion of all the possible options, see Paul R. Williamson, *Abraham, Israel and the Nations: The Patriarchal Promise and its Covenantal Development in Genesis* (JSOTSup 315; Sheffield: Sheffield Academic Press, 2000), 220–234, or more recent yet, Keith N. Grüneberg, *Abraham, Blessing and the Nations: A Philological and Exegetical Study of Genesis 12:3 in its Narrative Context* (BZAW 332; Berlin: de Gruyter, 2003).

[18] As Williamson and Grüneberg note, it is possible that the authors of the text wished to communicate two distinct but related ideas through the use of these two different verbal forms. If so, then the *niphal* and the *hithpael* should be translated in differing ways rather than assimilated to each other.

world, or possibly that the other families of the earth will receive blessing in direct proportion to how these nations treat Abraham and his chosen descendants. Interestingly enough, the text seems to envision most others responding positively in that the plural participle is used for those who bless in contrast to the singular for the few who curse, or perhaps better lightly esteem, Abraham and his chosen descendants.[19]

Although neither translation of Gen 12:3 makes it absolutely clear how all the families of the earth might be blessed or bless themselves through Abraham and his descendants, passages later in Genesis suggest that part of this blessing comes about through mediatorial services rendered by Abraham and Israel. This is made rather explicit in a divine speech that reveals God's motivation for telling Abraham that he is about to destroy Sodom and Gomorrah:

> The LORD said, "Shall I hide from Abraham what I am about to do, seeing that Abraham shall become a great and mighty nation, and all the nations of the earth shall be blessed in him? No, for I have chosen him, that he may charge his children and his household after him to keep the way of the LORD by doing righteousness and justice; so that the LORD may bring about for Abraham what he has promised him" (Gen 18:17–19).

In this passage, God, either having an internal dialogue with himself, or possibly talking to the other divine beings who go on to Sodom in v. 22, initially suggests that he was going to destroy Sodom and Gomorrah without notifying Abraham. However, he convinces himself that this is a wrong course of action because to do so would impede the mission of Abraham and his future descendants to do righteousness and justice. This speech evokes Gen 12:3 when it links God's decision to tell Abraham about the coming destruction of Sodom to the fact that through Abraham and the nation that will grow from his progeny, blessing will extend to all the nations of the world (Gen 18:18). The fact that Abraham proceeds to question God's justice as the story unfolds strongly implies that at least one duty of Abraham and his descendants is to call God to account if he is acting unjustly.[20] Further proof that Abraham's election entails an intercessory role can be gleaned

---

[19] The Hebrew of 12:3a uses a singular participle from the root קלל to describe the few who lightly esteem Abraham but employs the root ארר of God's cursing response to such behavior.

[20] For a theologically oriented reflection on Gen 18 see, Joseph Blenkinsopp, 'Abraham and the Righteous of Sodom," *JJS* 33 (1982): 119–132, and for a very different theological counter-reading, see Nathan MacDonald, "Listening to Abraham—Listening to YHWH: Divine Justice and Mercy in Genesis 18:16–33," *CBQ* 66 (2004): 25–43.

from Gen 20:7, 17 in which he intercedes for Abimelech and his larger household. Thus at least one part of Abraham's and later Israel's elective service involves functioning as a mediator pleading for God's mercy, even for those who may not deserve it on the basis of their own behavior, as Abraham does on behalf of the residents of Sodom.[21]

Having highlighted the universal implications of Abraham's and thus of the people of Israel's election by suggesting that Israel serves a mediatorial role between the Gentile nations and God, it is important to add a cautionary note. In particular, I am concerned about a Christian tendency to reduce Israel's election to its service to the larger world. A number of Christian critics have, in my opinion, placed a disproportionate emphasis on what I call the "instrumental" aspects of Israel's election. They do so because they wish to argue that God's special relationship to Abraham, and thus to the people of Israel as a whole, is primarily for the sake of the eventual universal salvation of all the Gentiles. For example, in his influential essay "The Kerygma of the Yahwist," Hans Walter Wolff, puts tremendous weight on Gen 12:1–3, particularly on the final phrase in 3b.[22] The attempt to read this text in missional and instrumental terms recurs regularly among Christian exegetes, as demonstrated by the following statement from Terence Fretheim's recent book on Abraham: "God's choice of Abraham is an initially exclusive move for the sake of a maximally inclusive end. Election is for mission (in the broadest sense of the term)."[23]

The most serious difficulty with this reading of Gen 12:1–3, as pointed out by Walter Moberly, is that this passage is directed to Abraham as a message of assurance rather than addressed to those others with whom Abraham and his children will later interact. Note Moberly's words concerning Abraham in Gen 12:1–3:

> He is a solitary figure, who in response to God is leaving behind the usual securities of territory and family. As such, he may fear rapid extinction and oblivion. ... Because of God's blessing the solitary and vulnerable Abraham will become a nation to be reckoned with, and the object of extensive respect and prayer for emulation.[24]

---

[21] The intercessory role played by Abraham/Israel on behalf of the nations of the world is emphasized in Wolff, "Kerygma," 56.

[22] See n. 16 above for full reference.

[23] Terence E. Fretheim, *Abraham: Trials of Family and Faith* (Columbia, S.C.: University of South Carolina, 2007), 34.

[24] Moberly, *The Bible, Theology, and Faith*, 123–124.

This is not to deny the theological importance of the idea that all the families of the earth will somehow obtain blessing through their relationship to Abraham and his descendants. But the blessing that the other nations of the world experience is a consequence that flows from God's special election of Abraham and his select descendants, (an interpretation supported by Gen 18:18), rather than something that explains the purpose of Israel's election.

Even if one reads Gen 12:3 a la Wolff as an explanation for Abraham's election, how this would work is never clearly articulated within the Hebrew Bible. In any case, much of the Hebrew Bible speaks against the idea that this passage authorizes the conversion of the nations to Israel's religion or a total dissolution of all distinctions between Abraham's family and the other nations of the world. In fact, the word mission seems to obscure rather than illuminate many of the texts that do emphasize the instrumental dimensions of election. It is useful to keep in mind that these more instrumental passages reflect the people of Israel's attempts to understand the fuller meaning of their chosen status. Yet, within the Bible, God never discloses the total meaning of his unique relationship to Israel and several seminal passages ground this relationship in the mystery of God's special love for the patriarchs and their later descendants, the nation of Israel (e.g., Deut 7:7–8). Paul uses this insight to explain how, in spite of what he sees as Israel's rebellion from God, Abraham's physical descendants remain beloved by God. While to human eyes it seems that God's plan has gone awry, even these detours may be fulfilling God's purposes, purposes that remain somewhat inscrutable to the human mind (Rom 9–11). The God of the Hebrew Bible has an ongoing relationship with his people Israel, and thus, one needs to be cautious in employing the metaphor of service in a heavy-handed fashion that ignores the relational elements at the root of Israel's election theology. God's special favor toward Israel involves a mysterious act of divine love that precedes any call to service and persists even when Israel fails to respond to God properly. Most importantly, in all of these texts Abraham and his chosen descendants, the people of Israel, remain God's elect, affirming an enduring distinction between God's chosen people and the other nations of the world.

An additional point of note is that Genesis regularly refers to God's solemn oath to give the land of Canaan to Abraham and his descendants through Isaac and Jacob (Gen 12:7; 15:17–21; 26:2–5; 28:13–15; 35:9–12). Many scholars think that the current compound form of these promises is due to an extended process of coagulation in which older elements like the promise of progeny may have been linked together with younger ones such as the promise of land, but in the current canon these ideas are now inseparably fused into a coherent whole.[25] The promise of the land receives tremendous emphasis within the biblical text and rightly remains a central theme in postbiblical Jewish theological reflection. While some contemporary Christians remain uncomfortable with this emphasis, one needs to recognize that incarnational ideas so prevalent in Christianity grew out of and only make sense in relation to the theology of the land and other location oriented theological streams like those that surround the temple.

Although the topic of covenant was briefly mentioned in the discussion of the Noah story, its central place in the Abraham narrative makes this an appropriate place to give a wider overview of this important theological trope. Genesis includes several texts that refer to the making of covenants. A covenant is a way to formalize an agreement between two parties, and it sometimes involves a ritual element or a type of sacrifice. Scholars have long noted that there are two broad categories of covenants in the Hebrew Bible, those between human individuals and/or nations (e.g., Gen 21:27; 31:44–54), and covenants that occur between God and human individuals, nations, and/or the whole human community. For the purposes of this theological discussion it makes sense to focus on the latter type in which God is a partner. Divine/human covenants also fall into two distinct patterns. Scholars describe some of these covenants as conditional, indicating that much of the burden falls on the humans involved, while others are frequently labeled unconditional, meaning most if not all of the obligations fall upon God.[26]

The divine-human covenants found within Genesis include the Noahic (Gen 9:8–17) and Abrahamic covenants (Gen 15 and 17), which are usually identified as examples of unconditional covenants in which the obligations fall primarily, if not exclusively, upon the deity. Thus they tend to

---

[25] For a fuller scholarly portrait of this issue, see Claus Westermann, *The Promises to the Fathers: Studies on the Patriarchal Narratives* (Philadelphia: Fortress, 1980). Westermann actually speaks of six distinct forms of promise texts as well as numerous combined forms. He sees the promise of a son and its separate but close ally, the promise of numerous progeny, as being earlier. Westermann believes that the promise of land in its current form is a later development that might have had an ancient analogue that became irrelevant once the Patriarchal cycle included the notion that Abraham arrived in Canaan.

[26] The literature on covenant is extensive; what follows are some of the most important works on this topic: Delbert R. Hillers, *Covenant: The History of a Biblical Idea* (Baltimore: Johns Hopkins, 1969); Jon D. Levenson, *Sinai and Zion: An Entry into the Jewish Bible* (Minneapolis: Winston Press, 1985); Dennis J. McCarthy, *Treaty and Covenant* (AnBib 21A; Rome: Pontifical Biblical Institute, 1978); George E. Mendenhall, "Covenant Forms in Ancient Israel," *BA* 17 (1954): 50–76; Ernest W. Nicholson, *God and his People: Covenant and Theology in the Old Testament* (Oxford: Clarendon Press, 1986).

utilize the language of divine promise or oath. However, even in the Abrahamic covenant (and perhaps in the Noahic one as well), human behavior energizes and seals the covenant that previously was only an incomplete promise. Abraham's fulfillment of God's command to circumcise all the males in his household in Gen 17 along with Abraham's obedience to God's command to sacrifice his son Isaac in Gen 22 bring the Abrahamic promises to fruition.[27] Such a reading is strongly supported by Gen 22:15–18 as well as Gen 26:2–5.[28] While the Noahic covenant contains no explicit human behavioral conditions, evidence from elsewhere in the Bible suggests that ancient Israel understood it to contain an implicit demand for a proper human response, without which it became null and void (Zeph 1:2–3).

One final point concerning the Hebrew Bible's view of God's various covenants is that all humans stand in some covenantal relationship to God because all humans are descendants of Noah who received a covenantal promise from God. Thus the people of Israel envision God's covenant with Abraham and some of his select descendants as a specialized covenant that nests within a more universal covenant put into place after the flood. In analogous fashion, God's later covenants with David and his descendants or with a certain line of Aaron's descendants (2 Sam 7; Num 25:10–13) are more specialized covenants that nest within the broader covenantal oaths made to Abraham. While Israel's relationship to God is uniquely close, it is a further intensification of a relationship that God has with all of humanity. Furthermore, as will be explored in greater detail below, biblical evidence suggests that God's more specialized covenants may have benefits for those who stand outside of their framework.

Chosenness and Family Strife

Genesis is in many ways a sustained meditation on the problems that arise when someone is mysteriously favored by God. This theme first appears in the Cain and Abel narrative in rather terse form and is given greater complexity in the following sibling stories, those of Isaac and Ishmael, and Jacob

---

[27] Contemporary Christian interpreters with a strong Calvinist streak have argued that it is a mistake to call the covenant with Abraham unconditional. See Ronald Youngblood, "The Abrahamic Covenant: Conditional or Unconditional?," in *The Living and Active Word of God: Essays in Honor of Samuel J. Schultz* (ed. Morris Inch and Ronald Youngblood; Winona Lake, Ind.: Eisenbrauns, 1983), 31–46.

[28] R.W.L. Moberly, "The Earliest Commentary on the Akedah," *VT* 38 (1988): 302–323.

and Esau (which contains the Rachel and Leah rivalry as well), reaching its zenith in the Joseph story. In all four of these stories, a younger sibling is divinely favored over the elder sibling(s), a motif that recurs throughout the Hebrew Bible (e.g., Ephraim, Moses, Samuel, David, and Solomon are all younger favored siblings). These texts provide little justification for God's choice, with the possible exception of the Cain and Abel story where interpreters have long argued over whether Cain's offering was inferior to Abel's (Gen 4:3–4). But even in this story, God's enigmatic speech to Cain focuses upon Cain's reaction to God's favoritism of Abel, not upon the quality of Cain's offering (Gen 4:6–7), thus highlighting the mysterious and seemingly arbitrary nature of God's choice.

This divine preference for the younger sibling suggests that God favors individuals not favored by human convention. But why does a tradition-bound culture like ancient Israel's preserve images of a deity who does not abide by the community's norms enshrined within its divinely ordained laws (Deut 21:15–17)? One explanation for this unusual state of affairs is that the Hebrew Bible time and again reveals God's power by showing how human attempts to control outcomes are subverted by God. This recurring literary pattern might be labeled the Bible's "underdog motif." God's plan always prevails, frequently even by means of resistance to it or through those who seem to be marginal and powerless.[29]

Another likely factor contributing to this motif's prominence is Israel's self-perception in relation to its older and more dominant neighbors, Egypt and Mesopotamia. Various biblical thinkers appear to polemicize against Mesopotamian and Egyptian religious ideas (e.g., P in Gen 1). Thus, it seems that at least part of the stress on the underdog motif, particularly the way in which younger brothers supersede their elders by divine choice, is connected to Israel's own sense of her late-born status.

Within these narratives of sibling rivalry, the non-favored brother(s) is not necessarily hated by God or excluded from God's blessing. When one looks at the language in Gen 17 and 21 describing Ishmael's status, it is clear that even though he is outside of the covenant (17:19, 21), he is just barely outside of it. Not only is he circumcised, thereby receiving the bodily mark of the very covenant from which he is excluded, but furthermore he receives a special divine blessing (Gen 17:18–26; 21:12–13). Much the same can be said of Esau who prospers in life and fathers a host of progeny (Gen 36). Cain

---

[29] I explore a number of these ideas in greater depth in my essay "Humor and the Theology of Hope in Genesis: Isaac as a Humorous Figure," *Interpretation* 54 (2000): 363–375.

was not driven from God's presence because he was not chosen, but rather because his jealousy drove him to kill his more favored brother. Chosenness is not to be equated with a guarantee of salvation, and non-chosenness is not a sign of damnation.

Nor is being chosen a purely positive experience. Chosenness often brings mortal danger in its wake. Thus Abel is killed (Gen 4); Abraham who is selected to be the father of the chosen people is immediately driven by famine to Egypt where his life is in potential danger (Gen 12:10–20); Isaac is nearly sacrificed to God by Abraham (Gen 22); Esau had at one time planned to murder Jacob (Gen 27:41–45); and Joseph is nearly killed by his brothers (Gen 37). This pattern of the endangerment of the chosen, which usually precedes his eventual exaltation, is central to both the Hebrew Bible and New Testament, as indicated by the Exodus and Gospel narratives. It is likely that this recurring trope aims to reinforce the special divine claim made upon those who are divinely favored. The favored one who has his life returned to him by God, now owes his new existence to God alone. This trope is closely entwined with, and perhaps is a further extension of the allied motif of the barren wife who bears the chosen child. This is most clearly seen in the case of Sarah, whose ability to bear Isaac so late in life is proof of a direct divine intervention, a divine intervention which suggests that Isaac is not a natural child but a miracle child upon whom God has a special claim. God exercises his claim on Isaac in the *akedah* narrative and upon the whole people of Israel in the Exodus account.[30]

Turning to the Joseph story, one encounters the idea that even within the group favored by God, some are more favored than others. While not often noticed, this idea recurs a number of times in the Bible and likely explains why the tribe of Judah and the family of David are viewed as being specially designated as the royal tribe and family, as well as why the Levites and the family of Aaron become the specially chosen groups designated for temple service. Thus distinctions exist even among God's one chosen people. It is also in this narrative that one most clearly glimpses the notion that chosenness may directly benefit those not favored. The favor shown toward Joseph benefits Potiphar's household, Pharaoh's kingdom and the wider famine-starved world, and most especially Joseph's brothers and father (Gen 39:5; 41:57; 45:5).

---

[30] This theme is explored with great theological sensitivity in Jon D. Levenson, *The Death and Resurrection of the Beloved Son: The Transformation of Child Sacrifice in Judaism and Christianity* (New Haven: Yale University Press, 1993).

In these stories there is a complex interplay between divine initiative and human action. Certain of these narratives imply that human actions can help secure a person's election. For example, Jacob obtains Esau's primogeniture under duress (Gen 25:29–34), and Rebekah helps manipulate Isaac to bless Jacob rather than Esau (Gen 27). It seems clear that being a morally upright person is not a prerequisite for being favored by God. Even when elect individuals act inappropriately, such as when Abraham twice attempts to pawn Sarah off as his sister (Gen 12 and 20), or when Joseph lords his chosen status over his brothers (Gen 37), they remain mysteriously favored by God regardless of their behavior (Gen 39:2–4, 21–23).[31] One also sees this pattern in relation to the Israelites as a whole in Exodus. Even when Israel fails to respond properly to God's gracious actions (Exod 14:11–12), God continues to favor them. This is not to suggest that Israelites are not morally accountable for their ethical lapses, or that ethics are irrelevant to God's larger creative purposes. A number of narratives in Genesis show specific moral failings of various Israelite characters, sometimes in clear contrast to a non-Israelite who acts more ethically (e.g., Abimelech in Gen 20 and possibly Esau in Gen 33). Election may not be grounded in a character's ethical disposition, but the text regularly points to an ethical ideal that all should embody, most especially the elect.[32]

One further nuance concerning the theological tension between divine initiative and human action is the occasional tendency in the Bible to attribute the same result to both a divine and a human cause.[33] While God gifts the land of Canaan to Abraham in Gen 12, in Gen 13 Lot, on his own volition, chooses to settle in the then lush area of Sodom, leaving Abraham in uncontested control of what will later turn out to be the more fertile part of Canaan. In such instances, a single result comes about through a human and a divine action that mirror and reinforce each other.

A few additional insights about divine favor and the blessing that often accompanies it are worth highlighting. Many of these narratives describe not only sibling rivalry, but more broadly, family strife or even strife between various groups or nations. While contemporary sociological theory fre-

---

[31] On this point, see the theological treatment of the Wife-Sister stories in Mark E. Biddle, "The 'Endangered Ancestress' and Blessing for the Nations," *JBL* 109 (1990): 599–611.

[32] For a thoughtful discussion of this idea, see J.G. McConville, *God and Earthly Power: An Old Testament Political Theology, Genesis-Kings* (LHBOTS 454; London: T&T Clark, 2006), 30–49.

[33] For some reflections on this phenomenon, see Yairah Amit, "The Dual Causality Principle and its Effects on Biblical Literature," *VT* 37 (1987): 385–400.

quently attributes strife to infighting over limited resources, Genesis provides an insightful corrective by noting that the proliferation of wealth can lead to strife just as easily. Thus Lot and Abraham must separate not because each is impoverished but because they each own too much (Gen 13). The blessing that Jacob brings to Laban's household does not bring family peace, but rather sets almost every family member against each other (Gen 30–31).

Although the possibility of reconciliation does indeed occur within several of these texts, quite frequently the fractured relationships are only partially healed. Thus Laban and Jacob agree to separate, which is exactly what happens in the wake of the partial reconciliation between Jacob and Esau (Gen 33). The Joseph story contains one of the most powerful scenes of brotherly reconciliation within Western literature. Yet, even here, family tensions continue to recur in the future (Gen 50:15–21). George Coats nicely sums up the theology implied within these narratives:

> God's chosen appears consistently as a figure embroiled in strife. And, moreover, the strife leads to separation that is not healed by reconciliation. ... But perhaps the affirmation in all this strife and its corresponding lack of reconciliation is that God's blessing appears in spite of strife, as an alternative to reconciliation. If reconciliation occurs, so much the better (Gen 45:4–15). But blessing can emerge from relationships that cannot be reconciled.[34]

Gender and Theology in Genesis

Genesis has rightly been receiving ever greater attention by scholars interested in the nexus between theology and constructions of gender. It is important to emphasize that there are many different types of "feminist" stances found among contemporary interpreters of Genesis. Views range from those who argue that the characterization of women in Genesis is demeaning and beyond redemption, to those who read the text suspiciously yet think the picture is mixed, to those who argue that Genesis has a model view of women and in fact contains the rudiments of modern feminism. The seminal study in this area was Phyllis Trible's probing analysis of Gen 2–3 in her book *God and the Rhetoric of Sexuality*.[35] One might contest

---

[34] George W. Coats, "Strife Without Reconciliation: A Narrative Theme in the Jacob Traditions," in *Werden and Wirken des Alten Testaments: Festschrift für Claus Westermann zum 70. Geburtstag* (ed. Rainer Albertz et al.; Göttingen: Vandenhoeck & Ruprecht, 1980), 82–106, here 106.

[35] Phyllis Trible, *God and the Rhetoric of Sexuality* (OBT; Philadelphia: Fortress, 1978), 72–143.

elements of Trible's argument (e.g., her contention that Adam was originally an androgyne seems open to question), but her basic point, that later more patriarchal interpretive traditions have distorted our ability to read what the text actually says, is an insight of enduring value. In particular, Trible showed how a careful reading of the Hebrew text of Gen 2 reveals a much greater balance between Adam and Eve than many previous interpreters had recognized.

It is difficult to deny the strongly patriarchal character of biblical religion, but it is equally foolish to deny that the Hebrew Bible in general and the book of Genesis in particular contain complex portraits of a number of female characters including: Eve, Sarah, Hagar, Rebekah, Rachel, Leah, Dinah, Tamar, and Potiphar's wife. Within Genesis Adam, Abraham, Isaac, Jacob, and Judah all at times find their lives shaped by powerful women. From a theological standpoint, it is certainly significant that one of the central themes of Genesis, that of God's unique favor toward specific individuals and groups, is often directly tied to certain female characters. Thus in at least two instances, those concerning Isaac and Joseph, it is not enough for the child to be the progeny of a favored father. Rather, the special favor shown to each of these two children is itself bound up with the initial infertility of Sarah and Rachel, as well with the fact that Rachel is Laban's youngest daughter and Jacob's favorite wife.

Additionally, it must be pointed out that at least a few of the female characters in Genesis are set in stories that one could reasonably call protofeminist. By this I mean that certain narratives in Genesis critique various patriarchal ideas. One thinks particularly of the story of Tamar in Gen 38. In this text, the narrator skillfully conveys how the patriarchal presumption that Tamar is responsible for the death of Judah's first two sons is completely mistaken. In contrast to Judah's view of the matter, the reader is permitted to see that Er and Onan each died on account of their own sinful behavior. At the end of this story, Judah pronounces Tamar to be more righteous than he is, despite her actions, which might appear (to a modern audience at least) deceptive and even licentious. In a similar fashion, one senses that the wife-sister stories in Gen 12, 20, and 26, along with the Dinah story in Gen 34, provide a critique of how the patriarchal treatment of women distorts social relationships more generally, often leading to unnecessary social conflicts that sometimes result in bloodshed. While critics will continue to argue over precisely how patriarchal Genesis is, or how one might assess the morality of certain specific characters like Sarah, Hagar, or, Rebekah, there is no doubt that theological reflection on Genesis has been greatly deepened by recent attention to gender issues raised by the text.

Concluding Reflections

This survey of the theology of Genesis may not have produced a clear answer to why the Torah begins with this unusual extended prologue. But hopefully it has highlighted some of the major theological themes first found in Genesis but of great relevance for understanding the larger Torah. In fact, when one begins reading Exodus one immediately sees reference back not only to the just concluded Joseph story, but to important themes drawn from the creation account in Gen 1. In short, it is doubtful that one can make sense of the Torah or even more broadly the Bible, whether that be the Jewish or Christian Bible, without Genesis.

This unusual book has exerted extraordinary influence over Western culture and society for over two thousand years, and it continues to do so today. Attempts to reshape aspects of our socio-political culture have time and again involved arguments that invoked the Bible more generally, with certain passages from Genesis often receiving a good deal of attention. One could argue that the ongoing movement toward greater inclusion of once marginalized voices is in an attempt to realize P's insight that all humans are worthy of fundamental dignity because we are all created in God's image. Thus one should not be surprised that Genesis played an important part in the debates over slavery and women's rights and that it continues to be a touchstone in current discussions surrounding the treatment of the environment, the acceptance or rejection of homosexuality, and more broadly on issues surrounding family values.[36] In short, studying the theology of Genesis is far from an exercise relevant only to historians interested in ancient Israelite culture or to theologians seeking biblical grounding for various doctrines. Genesis is not only the first biblical book in literary sequence, it is as well the book that contains the foundational teachings for a host of theological topics such as the character of God, the root causes of human sin, and the meaning and purpose of divine election. It also contains the fullest biblical treatment of certain seminal issues such as those surrounding creation and it lays the foundations for exploring the unusual theological status of human beings, creatures who dwell on earth but are created in God's own image.

---

[36] Thus the growing literature on Genesis and family values, including: Burton L. Visotzky, *The Genesis of Ethics: How the Tormented Family of Genesis Leads Us to Moral Development* (New York: Crown, 1996) and the 2005 SBL Presidential address by David L. Petersen, "Genesis and Family Values," *JBL* 124 (2005): 5–23.

Select Bibliography

Alter, Robert. *The Art of Biblical Narrative*. New York: Basic Books, 1981.
Anderson, Gary A. *The Genesis of Perfection: Adam and Eve in the Jewish and Christian Imagination*. Louisville: Westminster John Knox, 2001.
Barr, James. *The Garden of Eden and the Hope of Immortality*. Minneapolis: Fortress, 1992.
Brett, Mark G. *Genesis: Procreation and the Politics of Identity*. Old Testament Readings. London: Routledge, 2000.
Coats, George W. *From Canaan to Egypt: Structural and Theological Context for the Joseph Story*. Catholic Biblical Quarterly Monograph Series 4. Washington, D.C.: Catholic Biblical Association, 1976.
Fretheim, Terence E. *Abraham: Trials of Family and Faith*. Columbia, S.C.: University of South Carolina, 2007.
Kaminsky, Joel S. *Yet I Loved Jacob: Reclaiming the Biblical Concept of Election*. Nashville: Abingdon, 2007.
Levenson, Jon D. *Creation and the Persistence of Evil: The Jewish Drama of Divine Omnipotence*. San Francisco: Harper & Row, 1985.
———. *The Death and Resurrection of the Beloved Son: The Transformation of Child Sacrifice in Judaism and Christianity*. New Haven: Yale University Press, 1993.
Carol Myers, *Discovering Eve: Ancient Israelite Women in Context*. Oxford: Oxford University Press, 1988.
Miller, Patrick D. *Genesis 1–11: Studies in Structure & Theme*. Journal for the Study of the Old Testament Supplement Series 8. Sheffield: JSOT Press, 1978.
Moberly, R.W.L. *The Theology of the Book of Genesis*. Old Testament Theology. Cambridge: Cambridge University Press, 2009.
———. *The Old Testament of the Old Testament: Patriarchal Narratives and Mosaic Yahwism*. Overtures to Biblical Theology. Minneapolis: Fortress, 1992.
Turner, Laurence A. *Announcements of Plot in Genesis*. Journal for the Study of the Old Testament Supplement Series 96. Sheffield: Sheffield Academic Press, 1990.
Westermann, Claus. *Genesis 1–11: A Commentary*. Translated by John J. Scullion. Continental Commentaries. Minneapolis: Augsburg, 1984.
———. *Genesis 12–36: A Commentary*. Translated by John J. Scullion. Continental Commentaries. Minneapolis: Augsburg, 1985.
———. *Genesis 37–50: A Commentary*. Translated by John J. Scullion. Continental Commentaries. Minneapolis: Augsburg, 1986.
Wolff, Hans Walter. "The Kerygma of the Yahwist." Pages 41–66 in *The Vitality of Old Testament Tradition*. Edited by Walter Brueggemann and Han Walter Wolff. Atlanta: John Knox, 1975.

GENESIS IN THE CONTEXT OF JEWISH THOUGHT

Marvin A. Sweeney

Introduction

Genesis, or *Běrē'šît*, "in (the) beginning of," as it is known in Hebrew, is the foundational text of the Torah ("Instruction"), the Bible, and Jewish tradition as a whole.[1] Although Genesis does not encompass the entirety of Jewish thought, its preoccupation with G-d, creation, human beings, Israel's ancestors, and the covenant between G-d and Israel makes Genesis a quintessentially important text that informs much of Jewish life, tradition, and thinking. Genesis is not presented as a systematic account of Jewish philosophy or theology. Instead, it appears as a narrative account of Judaism's understanding of creation and the origins of the Jewish people.

Genesis takes up G-d's creation of the world at large (Gen 1:1–2:3); the origins and early history of human beings (Gen 2:4–11:9); and the history of the ancestors of Israel (Gen 11:10–50:26), including Abraham and Sarah (Gen 11:27–25:11); Isaac and Rebekah (Gen 21–22; 24; 26; 27); Jacob, his wives, Leah and Rachel, and their handmaidens, Bilhah and Zilpah (Gen 25:19–35:29); and the twelve sons of Jacob whose descendants formed the twelve tribes of Israel (Gen 37:2–50:26). Genesis also takes up figures such as Ishmael (Gen 25:12–18) and Esau (Gen 36:1–37:1), but these figures receive only minimal notice as their descendants branch off from the people of Israel to form foreign nations. Genesis thereby stands as the introduction to the Torah narrative which continues in Exodus, Leviticus, Numbers, and Deuteronomy with Israel's exodus from Egyptian slavery (Exod 1–15), the revelation of YHWH's Torah at Mt. Sinai (Exod 19–Num 10), the years of

---

[1] For Jewish commentary on Genesis, see esp. Tamara Cohn Eskenazi and Andrea L. Weiss, eds., *The Torah: A Women's Commentary* (New York: Union of Reform Judaism Press, 2008); Jon D. Levenson, "Genesis," in *The Jewish Study Bible* (ed. Adele Berlin and Marc Zvi Brettler; Oxford: Oxford University Press, 2003), 8–101; W. Gunther Plaut and David E.S. Stein, *The Torah: A Modern Commentary* (New York: Union of Reform Judaism Press, 2005); Nahum M. Sarna, *The JPS Torah Commentary: Genesis* (Philadelphia: Jewish Publication Society, 1989/5749); Nossom Scherman, *The Chumash: The Stone Edition* (Brooklyn: Mesorah, 1993); and Meir Zlotowitz, *Bereishis* (2 vols.; Brooklyn: Mesorah, 1986).

wandering through the wilderness on the way to the promised land of Israel (Exod 16–18; Num 11–36), and Moses' last speeches to the people as they prepare to take possession of the land (Deuteronomy).

Because of the central role that the Torah plays in Jewish life and thought, portions of the Torah are read as the central feature of Shabbat, weekday, and holiday worship service.[2] The current annual cycle for reading the Torah originated in the Babylonia Diaspora at some point following the composition of the Mishnah, and it has been in use for well over a millennium and a half. As the first book of the Torah, Genesis is divided into twelve Parashiyot or weekly Shabbat portions of roughly equal length. Each Parashah is accompanied by a Prophetic or Haftarah ("Completion") portion that aids in interpreting the Torah text. The liturgical reading of the Torah thereby serves as a means of divine revelation insofar as every Jew has the opportunity to encounter and study the text of the Torah in the context of Jewish worship. As an expression of the revelation of divine instruction to Judaism, the liturgical reading of the Torah becomes the basis for applying the divine teachings to daily Jewish life.

The discussion that follows proceeds first with consideration of the literary structure of Genesis within the context of the Torah as a whole, and then continues with consideration of creation, human origins, Abraham and Sarah, Jacob, Rachel, and Leah, and Joseph and his brothers. Each segment indicates important concerns that become the subjects of reflection in Jewish thought.

The Literary Structure and Worldview of Genesis

Modern literary critical research has identified the formula, *'ēlleh tôlĕdōt*, "these are the generations of," as a key organizing feature that points to the literary structure and theological worldview of Genesis in particular and the Torah at large.[3] The term, *tôlĕdâ*, "generation," plural, *tôlĕdōt*, "generations," is derived from the Hebrew verb root, *yld*, "to give birth," and therefore refers to the successive generations of human beings that were born during the course of early human history.

---

[2] Ismar Elbogen, *Jewish Liturgy: A Comprehensive History* (trans. Raymond P. Scheindlin; Philadelphia: Jewish Publication Society, 1993).

[3] Frank M. Cross, Jr., "The Priestly Work," in *Canaanite Myth and Hebrew Epic* (Cambridge: Harvard University Press, 1973), 293–325; cf. Marvin A. Sweeney, *Tanak: A Theological and Critical Introduction to the Jewish Bible* (Minneapolis: Fortress, forthcoming).

The first instance of the formula appears in Gen 2:4, "these are the generations of the heavens and the earth when they were created," which introduces the following account of human origins with the creation of Adam and Eve in Gen 2:4–4:26. The formula appears subsequently in Gen 5:1; 6:9; 10:1; 11:10; 11:27; 25:12; 25:19; 36:1; and 37:2 where in each instance it signals progressive stages in the history of humanity and Israel, from "the generations of Adam" in Gen 5:1 through "the generations of Jacob" in Gen 37:2.

Scholars initially identified this pattern as a feature of Genesis alone, but subsequent research points to the significance of the formula in Num 3:1, "and these are the generations of Aaron and Moses on the day that YHWH spoke to Moses at Mt. Sinai," as a text that deliberately continues the pattern initiated in Genesis.[4] Although the narratives concerning the Exodus from Egypt, the revelation of Torah at Mt. Sinai, the Wilderness period, and Moses' last speeches to Israel in Exodus, Leviticus, Numbers, and Deuteronomy are structurally organized according to a sequence of itinerary formulas that trace Israel's journey from Egyptian bondage to the borders of the promised land of Israel, the formula, *'ēlleh tôlĕdōt*, in Num 3:1 serves as a redactional device that ties these narratives together with those of Genesis. The sequence of history in the final form of the Torah narrative therefore culminates with Moses and Aaron, the two Levitical or priestly leaders of Israel at the time of the revelation of Torah at Mt. Sinai. Moses is the leader of Israel in the Exodus and Wilderness period through whom G-d's Torah was revealed to Israel at Mt. Sinai. His older brother Aaron is the founder of the priestly line of Israel through which Torah continued to be revealed and taught to the people in the monarchic and Second Temple periods. Because the *'ēlleh tôlĕdōt* formula plays the dominant role in the literary structure of the Torah, the accounts of the Exodus and Sinai revelation in Exod 1:1-Num 2:34 are thereby subsumed under the account of twelve tribes of Israel in Gen 37:2–50:29 so that the entirety of Gen 37:2-Num 2:34 becomes the account of the history of the Twelve Tribes of Israel. The *'ēlleh tôlĕdōt* formula in Num 3:1 then introduces the account of the history of Israel under the guidance of the Levites, Moses and Aaron, then follows in Num 3:1-Deut 34:12.

---

[4] Matthew Thomas, "These are the Generations: Identity, Promise, and the Toledoth Formulae" (Ph.D. diss.; Claremont Graduate University, 2006), to be published in revised form by T&T Clark.

The following diagram of the formal literary structure of the Torah indicates the key role played by the *'ēlleh tôlĕdōt* formula in presenting the synchronic literary structure of the Genesis narratives within the larger context of the Torah as well as the secondary role played by the itinerary formula in Exodus-Deuteronomy:

Synchronic Literary Structure of the Torah: History of Creation/Formation of People Israel

I.	Creation of Heaven and Earth	Gen 1:1–2:3
II.	Human Origins	Gen 2:4–4:26
III.	Human Development/Problems	Gen 5:1–6:8
IV.	Noah and the Flood	Gen 6:9–9:29
V.	Spread of Humans over the Earth	Gen 10:1–11:9
VI.	History of the Semites	Gen 11:10–26
VII.	History of Abraham (Isaac)	Gen 11:27–25:11
VIII.	History of Ishmael	Gen 25:12–18
IX.	History of Jacob (Isaac)	Gen 25:19–35:29
X.	History of Esau	Gen 36:1–37:1
XI.	History of the Twelve Tribes of Israel	Gen 37:2–Num 2:34
	A. Joseph and His Brothers in Egypt	Gen 37:2–50:26
	B. Deliverance from Egyptian Bondage: Rameses	Exod 1:1–12:36
	C. From Rameses to Sukkot: Consecration of First Born	Exod 12:37–13:19
	D. From Sukkot to Etam: Pillar of Fire and Cloud	Exod 13:20–22
	E. From Etam to the Sea (Pihahirot/Baal Zephon): Deliverance at Sea	Exod 14:1–15:21
	F. From Reed Sea to Wilderness of Shur/Elim: Water in Wilderness	Exod 15:22–27
	G. From Elim to Wilderness of Sin: Quails and Manna	Exod 16:1–36
	H. From Sin to Rephidim: Amalek and Jethro	Exod 17:1–18:27
	I. From Rephidim to Sinai: Revelation of Torah	Exod 19:1–Num 10:10
	1. Arrival at Sinai	Exod 19:1–2
	2. Revelation from mountain: 10 commandments; covenant code; building of the tabernacle	Exod 19:3–40:38
	3. Revelation from tabernacle: laws of sacrifice and holiness code	Lev 1–27
	4. Census and organization of people around tabernacle	Num 1:1–2:34
XII.	History of Israel under the Guidance of the Levites	Num 3:1-Deut 34:12
	A. Sanctification of the people led by the Levites	Num 3:1–10:10
	B. From Sinai to Wilderness of Paran/Kibroth Hattaavah: rebellion in the wilderness	Num 10:11–11:35a
	C. From Kibroth Hattaavah to Hazeroth	Num 11:35a–12:15
	D. From Hazeroth to the Wilderness of Paran	Num 12:16–19:22
	E. From Paran to Wilderness of Zin/Kadesh: water from rock	Num 20:1–21
	F. From Zin/Kadesh to Mount Hor: death of Aaron	Num 20:22–21:3
	G. From Mt. Hor to Edom/Moab: defeat of Sihon and Og	Num 21:4–35

H. Arrival at Moab: Balaam; Census and Organization of People	Num 22:1–36:13
I. Moses' Final Address to Israel: Repetition of the Torah	Deut 1:1–34:12

This diagram indicates that the Genesis narratives serve as a prelude to those concerned with the Exodus from Egypt, the revelation of Torah at Sinai, the Wilderness period, and Moses' repetition of the Torah in Deuteronomy immediately prior to Israel's entry into the promised land. Genesis thereby serves as a means to establish Jewish identity. As the descendants of Abraham and Sarah, who first established the covenant with YHWH, Israel emerges as a distinct and holy people among the nations of the world to whom YHWH's Torah is revealed. YHWH's Torah is designed to provide the basis for a just and holy national life in the land of Israel in which Israel may serve as partners with G-d in sanctifying and completing creation and by which Israel might serve as a model to the nations of the world. By the same token, Israel or Judaism has obligations to G-d and to the world at large to live in accordance with divine Torah to further the task of sanctifying and completing creation by establishing a just and holy human society. Such a conceptualization forms the basis of the system of Jewish Halakhah, Jewish law and practice, which comes to expression in the Talmudic and subsequent Rabbinic tradition to develop the teachings of the Torah so that they might be applied to the entirety of Jewish life.

CREATION

The initial narrative concerning creation in Gen 1:1–2:3 points to a number of important issues in Jewish thought, including the fundamental concept of creation as an act of overcoming chaos and establishing order in the world, the sanctity of all creation, the role of speech as creative act, and the interrelationship between G-d and human beings.

Interpreters are accustomed to read the first statement of the creation account in Gen 1:1 as a statement of *creatio ex nihilo*, or "creation out of nothing," which presupposes that nothing existed prior to G-d's creation of the world.[5] In English, Gen 1:1–2 would then read, "in the beginning, G-d created the heavens and the earth, and the earth was formless and void ..." But such a statement conflicts with other depictions of creation in the

---

[5] See Jon D. Levenson, *Creation and the Presence of Evil: The Jewish Drama of Divine Impotence* (New York: Harper & Row, 1988).

Bible, e.g., Job 38; Ps 74; and Isa 51, which indicate that G-d overcame a chaos monster as part of the process of creation in which a pre-existing world of chaos was brought into order. Close analysis by the medieval biblical commentator Rashi (Rabbi Solomon ben Isaac, 1040–1105) of the initial words of Gen 1:1, *bĕrē'šît bārā' 'lhym*, indicate that they cannot be read as "in the beginning G-d created," because the term *bĕrē'šît* is a construct form that lacks a definite article. The verb, *bārā'*, cannot be read as a perfect verb, but it must be rendered as an infinitive that forms a construct chain with the terms that precede and follow. Consequently, the verse must be read as, "in (the) beginning of G-d's creating the heavens and the earth, the earth was formless and void ..." The result is a statement in which the earth pre-existed creation in a state of chaos that was put into order by G-d. G-d's act of creation then becomes a model for human action in the world, viz., the task of human beings modeled on G-d becomes one of overcoming chaos in the world and placing the world into order. This emerges as a fundamental foundation for halakhah or Jewish law and practice in which the task of the Jew is to act as a partner with G-d in the world to sanctify and complete creation by observing G-d's mitzvot (*miṣwôt*) or commandments. Although the former reading is known in Judaism, its model of divine power presents G-d as an absolute figure who appears to be less amenable to interaction with human beings or the world at large. Nevertheless, these two understandings of the initial statement of Genesis indicate both the transcendent character of G-d as an absolute power distant from creation and as an imminent power who is intimately engaged in the world of creation. In fact, both models of G-d are operative in Jewish thought.[6]

The model for overcoming chaos in the world of creation appears to influence the seven day sequence of creation, which plays a significant role in indicating the sacred character of creation. G-d creates by calling into being the various aspects of creation over a six day period and then rests on the seventh day. Creation thus emerges as a progressive revelation of elements of order and holiness in our world, i.e., light, the heavens, earth and sea, day and night, living creatures and birds, and finally human beings. The culmination of this six-day sequence of creation in the Shabbat is a fundamental feature of the world of creation in which Saturday, the seventh

---

[6] E.g., Franz Rosenzweig, *The Star of Redemption* (trans. William W. Hallo; Notre Dame, Ind.: Notre Dame University Press, 1985); Martin Buber, *I and Thou* (trans. Walter Kaufmann; New York: Charles Scribner's Sons, 1970).

day, is sanctified as the holy day of rest. The Shabbat thereby serves as a means by which human beings become partners with G-d in completing and sanctifying creation. The seventh day might otherwise appear as any other, but observance of the Shabbat recognizes and establishes the holiness of the day—and thus of time in general—and serves as a means by which order, sanctity, and the recognition of the role of G-d in the world are then made known to and encountered by all.[7] Interpreters have noted the correlation between the language of Gen 2:1-3 concerning the completion of work on the Shabbat and that of Exod 40 concerning the completion of the wilderness tabernacle, which of course functions as a model for the Holy Temple in Judaism. In this respect, the creation narrative in Gen 1:1-2:3 anticipates the institution of the Temple as the holy center of creation and the holy center of Israel in Jewish thought.[8] Indeed, the observance of halakhah in Judaism is conceived as creating the Temple within each individual as corollary to the institution of the holy Temple in Jerusalem.

Although creation is portrayed as a seven day sequence of work and sanctification, G-d's acts of creation actually comprise ten speech acts in which G-d speaks and elements of creation come into being (see Gen 1:3, 6, 9, 11, 14, 20, 24, 26, 28, and 29). Speech functions as the fundamental act of creation in Genesis. Insofar as speech is to a certain degree intangible, i.e., words cannot be seen or defined in three-dimensional terms, and yet they are perceived and clearly have an impact on the world of creation, the power of speech motivates human beings to act and to create in the world. These ten "words" in Gen 1:1-2:3 point to divine speech as an epistemological factor in creation in which YHWH's instruction or Torah constitutes the epistemological foundation of creation. Even within the Bible, Prov 8 points to the notion of divine wisdom, here portrayed as an abstract principle personified as a woman and the first of G-d's creations, as the epistemological foundation of the world. Jewish mystical works, such as *Sefer Yetzirah* or the *Book of Creation*, then examine the phenomenon of divine speech and the characteristics of the Hebrew letters by which G-d's words are formed in order to articulate an understanding of G-d's interrelationship with the

---

[7] Abraham Joshua Heschel, *The Sabbath: Its Meaning for Modern Man* (New York: Farrar, Straus, and Giroux, 1951).

[8] See Michael Fishbane, "Genesis 1:1-2:4a: The Creation," in *Text and Texture: Selected Readings of Biblical Texts* (New York: Schocken, 1979), 1-16; and Jon D. Levenson, "The Temple and the World," *JR* 64 (1984): 275-298.

world.⁹ G-d's ten speech acts thereby become the basis by which G-d's ten fundamental qualities or emanations then inform or infuse all of creation. Human beings share the capacity of speech with G-d, and they therefore have an obligation to recognize that they serve as a crucial means by which the ten divine emanations are manifested in the world.

The above understandings of divine and human speech point to a fundamental aspect of the account of creation in Gen 1:1–2:3, viz., human beings are created in the image of G-d. Genesis 1:27 indicates that there is already some gender ambiguity in the creation of human beings, insofar as it first states that G-d created "the human being," Hebrew, *hā'ādām*, as a single entity, but then immediately follows with a statement that G-d created "them" as "male and female." Such a statement is traditionally understood as an indication that human beings are incomplete until they recreate the union of the primal human being, i.e., through human union and procreation, human beings act like G-d in creating human life. Such an act is sacred, however, insofar as it entails not only the sexual act of reproduction but also the educational act of raising a child with proper instruction and guidance to become a full human being, ready to accept one's own responsibilities for completing and sanctifying the world of creation. Consequently, G-d's statement in Gen 1:28, "Be fruitful and multiply and fill the earth," becomes the first commandment of Jewish tradition that is incumbent upon all Jewish men. Furthermore, the following command that humans should "master" the earth and "exercise dominion over the fish of the sea, the birds of the heavens, and all the living things that creep on earth" entails a human responsibility to sustain creation as well.

But the construction of the human being as both male and female in Gen 1:26–29 has another dimension, viz., that the "image," Hebrew, *ṣelem*, of G-d in which the primal human being is created is in fact a combination of both male and female (Gen R 8:1; Zohar 134b). In other words, just as the primal human being is a combination of male and female, so is G-d. Such a construction of the divine is apparent in the Kabbalistic literature which defines G-d's ten qualities to balance the male and female aspects of G-d. It is on the basis of these considerations that Gen 1:31 emphasizes that the creation of human beings was "very good." In other words, human beings are conceived as partners with G-d in creation who are tasked with the sustenance, completion, and sanctification of creation at large.

---

⁹ A. Peter Hayman, *Sefer Yesira: Edition, Translation, and Text-critical Commentary* (TSAJ 104; Tübingen: Mohr Siebeck, 2004).

Human Beings

The next four segments of Genesis, Gen 2:4–4:26; 5:1–6:8; 6:9–9:29; and 10:1–11:9, each take up different aspects of the conceptualization of human beings.

Genesis 2:4–4:26 takes up the issue of human origins. This passage is well known in modern critical scholarship as the second account of the creation of human beings, Eve's interaction with the snake in the Garden of Eden leading to the expulsion of Adam and Eve, and Cain's murder of Abel. Each of these passages raises issues addressed in subsequent Jewish thought.

The account of human creation in Gen 2:4–24 provides important foundations for the conceptualization of human beings in Judaism. At the most fundamental level, G-d's creation of the human being is accomplished when G-d blows "the soul of life," Hebrew, *nišmat ḥayyîm*, into the human's nostrils. The Hebrew term, *nĕšāmâ*, then becomes the term for "soul" in Rabbinic discourse. Furthermore, the use of the term, *hā'ādām*, is often translated as "Adam," but the use of the definite article indicates that it is not a proper name. The term should be understood as, "the human," and once again we see a figure that has not yet been differentiated into two gendered beings. Interpreters have noted that the process of creating Eve calls for imposing a deep sleep on the human and then removing a *ṣela'* from him. Although this term is often understood to be a "rib," the term *ṣela'* actually means, "side," which has been understood in Rabbinic and Kabbalistic circles to indicate that the creation of Eve was in fact a gender differentiation of the primal human being into a male, Adam, and a female, Eve, which builds upon the above noted statement in Gen 1:26 that G-d had created a human being, identified concurrently as a single androgynous human being and as two gendered figures.

The two references to the creation of male and female also provides the basis for the Rabbinic legends concerning Adam's first wife, Lilith, who was linked to Gen 1:26.[10] Because the wording of this verse indicates a simultaneously produced male and female figure, Lilith is said to have demanded equality with Adam, which Adam and G-d found intolerable. As a result, Lilith was expelled from the presence of Adam and G-d to become a demon figure known for giving birth to the myriads of demon figures in Jewish folklore and for causing the deaths of infants. Lilith, however, has

---

[10] For discussion of Lilith, see esp. Raphael Patai, *The Hebrew Goddess* (Detroit: Wayne State University Press, 1990).

been rehabilitated in Jewish feminism as the model woman who refused to submit to Adam's authority.[11] The second creation of a female in Gen 2:21-24 then produced Eve, who was considered subordinate to Adam because he was created first. Our observations concerning the non-gendered character of the primal human in this passage undermines such an interpretation, however, and modern interpreters have noticed that the phrase employed to describe her in Gen 2:18, 'ēzer kĕnegdô, does not mean, "a helper fit for him," as it is so frequently translated. Instead, the term 'ēzer is frequently employed to describe G-d, and the term kĕnegdô means, "over against him," indicated her status as a power figure equal to Adam.[12]

Our passage also serves as an important basis for the field of Jewish ethics. The Rabbinic sage, Akiba ben Joseph, employed a system of hermeneutics which viewed every feature of the text of the Torah, no matter how seemingly insignificant, as a source for understanding deeper meaning within the Torah text. One of his parade examples was the development of the Rabbinic notion of human free will, expressed through the concepts, yeṣer haṭṭôb, "the inclination for good," and yeṣer hārā', "the inclination for evil," that is found within every human being, prompting humans to choose between them in making moral decisions.[13] Akiba's development of these concepts depends upon the subtle differences in rendering the verb, wayyîṣer, indicating the creation of the human being in Gen 2:7 and the verb, wayyiṣer, indicating the creation of animals in Gen 2:19 (see b. Berakot 61a). The difference between the two verbs is simply orthographic, i.e., the rendition in v. 7 is written with a long i-class vowel, hireq, which requires an extra consonant, yod, whereas the rendition in v. 19 is written with a short hireq, which requires no extra yod. Akiba interpreted the extra yod in the verbal form of v. 7 to indicate that human beings were created with something extra, deriving the terms, yeṣer haṭṭôb and yeṣer hārā', from the verb root, yṣr, "to create, form," which appears in two verbal forms of vv. 7 and 19. The notion of human free will is an essential feature of Jewish moral philosophy or ethics, and it is developed further in the works of Saadia Gaon, Moses Maimonides, and others.[14]

---

[11] E.g., Judith Plaskow, *Standing Again at Sinai: Judaism from a Feminist Perspective* (New York: Harper & Row, 1990).

[12] See Carol Meyers, *Discovering Eve: Ancient Israelite Women in Context* (Oxford: Oxford University Press, 1988), 78-86, esp. 84-85.

[13] Ephraim E. Urbach, *The Sages: Their Concepts and Beliefs* (2 vols.; Jerusalem: Magnes, 1979), 1:471-483.

[14] Saadia Gaon, Sefer Emunot ve-Deot, Treatise 4 (*Book of Beliefs and Opinions* [trans. Samuel Rosenblatt; YJS 1; New Haven; Yale University Press, 1948], 180-204); Moses ben

The dual references to human creation also provide the basis for R. Joseph B. Soloveitchik's discussion of the dual nature of the human being in modern Jewish thought.[15] Soloveitchik argues that the first instance in Gen 1:26 indicates the creation of Adam I, "the majestic man," who employs his mind and efforts to master or utilize his environment, whereas the second instance in Gen 2:4–24 indicates Adam II, "the covenantal man," who submits to G-d as his master and works to "till" or "sustain" the universe as holy in keeping with the human mandate from G-d. This differentiation in human types becomes the basis for understanding the interrelationship between secular life and thought on the one hand and halakhic life and thought on the other.

Eve's encounter with the snake in the Garden of Eden in Gen 3:1–24 also raises important issues concerning the nature of human beings. Many follow the Genesis account in accusing Eve of sin for eating the forbidden fruit and feeding it to her "husband with her" (v. 6). Such accusations are based on the clear divine instruction in Gen 2:16–17 in which G-d forbade the human to eat from the tree of knowledge of good and evil lest the human die. One may note that Eve was not yet created, and so there is a question as to whether she even knew of the prohibition, but the fact that Adam and Eve were both created from the primal human being indicates that she should have known and not been persuaded by the snake's arguments. One may also ask about the role of Adam. If he was present "with her" as indicated in v. 6, why did he not take the responsibility to prevent the eating of the fruit? A further question pertains to the claim that Adam and Eve will die as a result of eating the fruit. The denial of this claim was part of the snake's argument, although the text indicates that Adam and Eve would become mortal when they were expelled from the Garden of Eden. Nevertheless, the text never makes it clear that they had been immortal in the Garden. In any case, the text serves as an illustration of human free will among the earliest human beings, i.e., they made their choices to disobey G-d's instruction and they were punished for it. There is a question of theodicy in G-d's concern that the human might become like G-d in learning to distinguish good and evil. Why did G-d attempt to prevent humans from gaining knowledge of good and evil? In fact, Eve gives human beings this fundamental capacity which likewise provides foundations for human moral thought and action.

Maimon, Guide for the Perplexed, 3:17 (*The Guide for the Perplexed* [2nd ed.; ed. and trans. M. Friedländer; London: Routledge & Kegan Paul, 1951], 282–288).

[15] Joseph B. Soloveitchik, "The Lonely Man of Faith," *Tradition* 7 (1965): 56.

Finally, the narrative in Gen 4:1–26 concerning Cain's murder of his brother Abel raises further issues. The introduction of murder raises a fundamental problem in human life. The narrative makes it clear that the shedding of human blood is an unacceptable disruption of the sanctity and order of creation, but it also points to a question of human responsibility. When G-d asks Cain where his brother Abel might be following the murder, Cain's response, "Am I my brother's keeper?" in v. 9 functions as a rhetorical question that answers itself. Of course he is responsible for his brother, and his punishment underscores that responsibility.

The narrative in Gen 5:1–6:8 concerning human development focuses on the spread of humans throughout the earth. We may note the issue created when divine beings, "the sons of G-d", here understood as angels, mated with the daughters of human beings to produce the Nephilim or giants in the world. The issue here is the blurring of boundaries between the heavenly and the earthly realms, or the sacred and profane. Such mixing of the divine and human realms is strictly prohibited in Judaism insofar as it points to a scenario in which human beings seek to become divine or in which G-d is conceived in human terms, thereby compromising G-d's holy and eternal character.

The portrayal of Noah and the flood in Gen 6:9–9:29 presents the flood as divine punishment for the moral issues of violence that arose among human beings in prior narratives. Noah, identified as a righteous man, is instructed by G-d to build an ark, gather his family and pairs of all the animals of the earth, and place them in the ark so that they survive G-d's flood. The narrative is a fundamental depiction of the reversal of creation in Gen 1:1–2:3 insofar as the water that inundates the earth reverses the separation of dry land and water that was the basis of creation. To a certain degree, the construction of the ark anticipates the construction of the Jerusalem Temple in that both have upper windows for light, both are compartmentalized, both employ bitumen to seal the wood construction, both are constructed with three levels, and both play roles in saving humanity from destruction before the holy presence of G-d. Once the flood is over, the drying of the waters and the release of animals to populate the earth once again functions as a new creation narrative as the earth is put back into order.

A key element in the narrative is the establishment of the divine covenant with humanity in Gen 9:1–17 never again to destroy the earth with a flood. The issue here is the human capacity to shed blood. In order to assuage the human capacity for violence, G-d grants human beings the right to eat animals for food, with the provision that the flesh of animals may not be eaten with its blood in it. Blood is the locus of life in Jewish thought, and it thereby conveys a degree of sanctity that must be respected. Consequently, animal offerings made at the altar of the Temple must have the blood drained from the body in the sacrificial service. The prohibition of the eating of blood thereby becomes the first and fundamental element of the system of Kashrut, the Jewish dietary laws that govern the eating of meat, beginning with the treatment of blood as the sacred locus of life.[16] By limiting the means by which human beings may eat meat, Genesis limits the means by which blood can be shed to satisfy the human capacity for violence. The illicit shedding of blood, whether human or animal, remains prohibited and will require a reckoning by G-d, i.e., humans are held accountable for the shedding of blood as shed blood compromises the sanctity and integrity of creation.

Genesis 10:1–11:9 again takes up the spread of human beings throughout the world in the aftermath of the flood as Noah's sons become the ancestors of the world's major population, viz., Shem becomes the ancestor of the Semites in the Near East, Japhet becomes the ancestor of humans in Europe, and Ham becomes the ancestor of humans in Africa. At this point, all humans speak the same language and the nations cooperate to build the tower of Babel so that they might ascend the heavens to prevent themselves from being scattered all over the world. What the people mean by such a statement is unclear; perhaps they intend to challenge G-d, but this is never stated. It is clear, however that G-d objects to this action, and confounds their languages to prevent their further cooperation and completion of the project. The basic issue appears to be the challenge of divine authority. Babel after all is the Hebrew name for the city of Babylon, which is built on the plain of Shinar. One the one hand, Babel thereby represents human authority and empire that in biblical tradition are considered as contrary to G-d. At the same time, it is difficult to understand why G-d objects to peaceful human cooperation, particularly when such ideals are articulated in texts such as Isaiah 2:2–4 and Micah 4:1–5 in which humans stream to Zion to learn G-d's Torah. The difference lies in the purpose of the cooperation, suggesting that the intent to challenge G-d—much as the Babylonian empire challenged divine order in the world by destroying Jerusalem and the Temple—rather than to learn from divine instruction is the basic concern of this narrative.

---

[16] J. Feliks and H. Rabinowicz, "Dietary Laws," *EncJud* 6:26–45.

Abraham and Sarah

The next two segments of the Genesis narrative include the History of the Semites in Gen 11:10–26 and the History of Abraham in Gen 11:27–25:11. Genesis 11:10–26 focuses specifically on the descendants of Shem as a means to narrow the focus to Abraham within the larger context of humanity. Genesis 11:27–25:11, titled "and these are the generations of Terah," concentrates on Abraham (Abram) ben Terah who, together with his wife, Sarah (Sarai), becomes the ancestor of Israel.

Two major issues for Jewish thought emerge in the Abraham narratives. The first is Abraham's covenant with YHWH which defines the terms by which the people of Israel and G-d are bound together. The second is the question of YHWH's fidelity to that covenant, which in the aftermath of the Shoah or Holocaust has become an increasingly problematic question in modern Jewish thought.

The major texts which take up the question of covenant appear in Gen 12:1–9; 15:1–21; and 17:1–27, each of which states divine promises to Abraham, including the promise that his descendants will become a great nation, that G-d will grant them the land of Israel, and that Abraham's descendants will be obligated to adhere to YHWH and YHWH's expectations. Genesis 12:1–9 lays out the general parameters of YHWH's promises to Abraham, and Gen 15:1–21 and 17:1–27 take up the sealing of the covenant between the two parties.

Unfortunately, modern critical scholarship has often functioned as an impediment in reading these chapters as scholars have sought to identify the J, E, and P strata that have formed these narratives. Although identification of the compositional history of Genesis is a legitimate and important task, source-critical work often neglects the literary coherence and theological significance of the final form of these texts. Two fundamental issues stand out.

First, full understanding of the ratification of the covenant requires that these texts be read in relation to each other, not as separate elements of discrete historical sources.[17] Gen 12:1–9 introduces the theme of YHWH's promise to Abraham. Genesis 15:1–21 portrays a covenant ceremony in which YHWH, symbolically represented by a flaming torch and smoking fire

---

[17] For discussion, see Marvin A. Sweeney, "Form Criticism," in *To Each its Own Meaning: An Introduction to Biblical Criticisms and Their Application* (ed. Steven L. McKenzie and Stephen R. Haynes; Louisville: Westminster John Knox, 1999), 58–89.

pot, passes between the pieces of sacrificial animals to ratify the covenant just as kings subject to Assyria would ratify their covenants or treaties with the Assyrian king.[18] In other words, YHWH signs the covenant in Gen 15. Genesis 17:1–27 portrays Abraham's ratification of the covenant through the ceremony of circumcision, known from ancient Egyptian practice as a means by which young priests were dedicated to holy service, which symbolizes the oath to adhere to YHWH and to observe YHWH's expectations. In other words, Abraham signs the covenant in Gen 17.[19] With both YHWH and Abraham as signatories, the covenant is ratified. Adherence to YHWH and the observance of YHWH's will provides important religious foundations for Jewish monotheism and the observance of halakhah as a function of that adherence.

Second, YHWH's promise to Abraham includes not only a son and descendants, but the land of Israel as a central element as well. YHWH explicitly states in Gen 12:7; 15:18; and 17:8 variations of the formula, "I will grant this land to your offspring." Gen 17:15–22 makes sure to specify that YHWH's covenant with Abraham and the promise of the land of Israel includes his son by Sarah, Isaac and his descendants, but it does not include his son by Hagar, Ishmael and his descendants. Ishmael and his descendants will receive their own covenant with YHWH to become the ancestor of the Arab peoples and Islam in general so that Judaism and Islam have a relationship with each other due to their common ancestry from Abraham. But the promise of land to Isaac and his descendants marks an important distinction in Jewish thought that provides the religious foundations for modern Zionism as the political dimension of Judaism.[20]

But the question of YHWH's fidelity to the covenant also comes into play when one recognizes that Israel's loss of land is a factor in the composition of Genesis, insofar as much of this material is written in the aftermath of the fall of the northern kingdom of Israel to Assyria in 722–721 BCE and the fall of Jerusalem and Judah to Babylon in 587–586 BCE.[21] To a large extent, the present form of the Abraham narratives is designed to examine critically YHWH's fidelity to the covenant in light of the question as to whether or

---

[18] Sarna, *Genesis*, 114–115.
[19] Sarna, *Genesis*, 125–126.
[20] Harry M. Orlinsky, "The Biblical Concept of the Land of Israel: Cornerstone of the Covenant between G-d and Israel," in *The Land of Israel: Jewish Perspectives* (ed. Lawrence A. Hoffman; Notre Dame, Ind.: University of Notre Dame Press, 1986), 27–64.
[21] Marvin A. Sweeney, *Reading the Hebrew Bible after the Shoah: Engaging Holocaust Theology* (Minneapolis: Fortress, 2008), 23–41.

not Abraham and Sarah will have a son to carry on the promises of many descendants, a land in which they will live, and an ongoing relationship with YHWH.

The Abraham narrative raises this question at the very outset. In identifying the line of Terah in Gen 11:27–32, the narrative makes sure to focus on Abram/Abraham as the primary character but it also includes his wife, Sarai/Sarah, noting that she is barren in v. 30. The motif of Sarah's barrenness then becomes the Leitmotif of the Abraham/Sarah narratives. Although the question of Sarah's barrenness is ultimately resolved, the narrative is constructed to highlight the tensions inherent in this question throughout.

The first four episodes in the Abraham/Sarah narrative are designed to portray Abraham as a righteous servant of G-d whereas G-d's character comes into question. Genesis 12:1–9 portrays YHWH's grandiose promises to Abraham just as YHWH commands Abraham to travel to the land of Canaan so that these promises may be realized. Abraham obeys YHWH without question, but when he settles in Canaan, Abraham is faced with drought and starvation. Genesis 12:10–20 is the first example of the wife-sister motif in which the patriarch claims that his wife is in fact his sister while dwelling in a foreign land to avoid the threats of death to the patriarch posed by foreigners who would take the wife by force.[22] Many interpreters condemn Abraham for claiming that Sarah is his sister and allowing her to be taken into Pharaoh's harem, but such condemnations ignore the mortal threats to both of them. In a patriarchal society, Abraham takes action that constitutes the ultimate humiliation for a man precisely because of his desperation at the situation in which G-d placed him. Abraham's actions nevertheless insure that he and Sarah will live. Ultimately, G-d intervenes to inform Pharaoh of the truth concerning Sarah's identity, but readers must recall that this threat is entirely of YHWH's making. Genesis 13 shows Abraham's magnanimity. When Abraham's shepherds quarrel with those of his nephew Lot over pasturage rights, Abraham settles the issue by telling Lot to choose his pasturage and Abraham will pasture his flocks elsewhere. As the senior male in the extended family, Abraham has every right to take the choice pasturage, but he does not do so. Finally in Gen 14, Abraham does not hesitate to rescue Lot when he is abducted by

---

[22] Marvin A. Sweeney, "Form Criticism: The Question of the Endangered Matriarchs in Genesis," in *Method Matters: Essays on the Interpretation of the Hebrew Bible in Honor of David L. Petersen* (ed. Joel M. LeMon and Kent Harold Richards; SBLRBS 56; Atlanta: Society of Biblical Literature, 2009), 17–38.

Mesopotamian raiders. Upon the successful release of the hostages, Abraham pays his tithe to El Elyon, G-d on High, at the sanctuary at Salem, later known as Jerusalem. But he nevertheless refuses to accept reward from the King of Sodom, thereby ensuring that he has no relationship with this evil city. Altogether, Abraham's character is upheld, but YHWH's is questionable.

The covenant texts in Gen 15; 16; and 17 highlight the question of YHWH's character. When YHWH promises Abraham that he will become a great nation in Gen 15, Abraham astutely points out that he has no son to continue his heritage and inherit his land and property, prompting YHWH to show him the future of his nation and to define its land. The birth of Ishmael to the Egyptian handmaiden, Hagar, in Gen 16 seems like a cruel joke, especially since Sarah was earlier taken into the harem of the Egyptian Pharaoh and Egypt would later become the oppressor of Israel in the Exodus narratives. The circumcision of Ishmael as part of the eternal covenant in Gen 17 highlights this tension, prompting YHWH's promises that the covenant will go to Isaac, who remains unborn.

Resolution comes in Gen 18–19; 20; and 21, only to be resumed in Gen 22 and 23. When YHWH, in the form of one of three visitors, informs Sarah that she will have a son at age ninety, she laughs, prompting the name Isaac for her son, which in Hebrew means, "he laughs." YHWH's promises are many, but fulfillment remains wanting. The issue of credibility is heightened once again when Abraham becomes the moral voice of the narrative demanding that YHWH not kill the righteous with the wicked in the impending destruction of Sodom and Gomorrah. The wife-sister motif emerges once again in Gen 20 while Abraham and Sarah reside in Philistia, and Abraham must once again take desperate means of protection until YHWH finally intervenes. When Isaac is finally born in Gen 21, all seems well, until YHWH demands that Abraham sacrifice Isaac as a test of his faith. Abraham does not hesitate to fulfill YHWH's command as the reader is left aghast at the thought that the sacrifice might actually go through, until YHWH intervenes at the very last moment to affirm Abraham's righteousness. The irony is not lost on the reader who has seen a righteous Abraham throughout, but has questions about YHWH's own fidelity. The issue continues in Gen 23 when Sarah dies. Rabbinic commentators note that Sarah died without ever seeing her son Isaac again and speculate that this was a punishment for her own treatment of Hagar following the birth of Ishmael (*b. Roš Haš.* 16b; *Gen. Rab.* 45:5; 58:5).

Although the human characters, Abraham, Sarah, and Isaac, suffer tremendously in these narratives, YHWH's fidelity is finally affirmed as

Abraham marries Isaac to Rebekah, ensuring that there will be a future for the line and the covenant that G-d has made.

The question of the reality or continuity of the covenant has been a key issue in modern Jewish thought. Richard Rubenstein denied the covenant altogether and argued that modern Judaism must abandon its theological myths concerning a righteous G-d to pursue a cultural expression of Jewish life in the land of Israel and the world at large.[23] Emil Fackenheim called for affirmation of G-d as the 614th commandment of Jewish tradition to ensure the continuity of Judaism, thereby denying Hitler a posthumous victory.[24] Eleazer Berkowitz argued that the hidden face of G-d in the Shoah affirmed the Jewish principle of human free will in allowing human beings the freedom of divine control so that they might learn to choose righteousness.[25] Abraham Joshua Heschel argued that G-d suffers as a result of human wrongdoing.[26] Elie Wiesel points to the absurdity of G-d in the Shoah,[27] and David Blumenthal likens G-d to an abusive parent who must be forgiven so that the victim of abuse may heal.[28] Despite the trauma suffered by Jews in the Shoah, the relationship with G-d, no matter how difficult it may be, must be affirmed as humans take on their roles as partners with G-d in the sanctification of creation.

Jacob, Rachel, and Leah

The next components of Genesis include the History of Ishmael in Gen 25:12–18 and the History of Jacob in Gen 25:19–35:29. The History of Ishmael accounts for Ishmael and his descendants so that the narrative might narrow its focus to Isaac and his descendants in the History of Jacob. The History of Jacob, titled, "and these are the generations of Isaac ben Abraham," then focuses on Jacob as the ancestor of the twelve tribes of Israel.

---

[23] Richard L. Rubenstein, *After Auschwitz: Radical Theology and Contemporary Judaism* (Indianapolis: Bobbs-Merrill, 1966).

[24] Emil Fackenheim, *G-d's Presence in History: Jewish Affirmations and Philosophical Reflections* (New York: New York University Press, 1970).

[25] Eliezer Berkovits, *Faith after the Holocaust* (New York: KTAV, 1973).

[26] Abraham Joshua Heschel, *G-d in Search of Man: A Philosophy of Judaism* (New York: Meridian and Jewish Publication Society, 1955).

[27] Elie Wiesel, *Night* (New York: Random House, 1973).

[28] David R. Blumenthal, *Facing the Abusing G-d: A Theology of Protest* (Louisville: Westminster John Knox, 1993).

The Jacob narrative is characterized by its focus on characters who represent the eponymous ancestors of Israel, each of the twelve tribes of Israel, and Israel's neighbors, Edom and Aram. Although source-critical scholarship frequently divides the Jacob narrative into J, E, and P components, the source critical approach has proved to be particularly unhelpful in reading the Jacob narratives insofar as it fragments the plot and character development of the narrative as a whole. Overall, the narrative depicts Jacob, the ancestor of Israel, in relation to his fraternal twin brother, Esau, the ancestor of Edom, and his uncle, Laban, the ancestor of Aram. The narrative also portrays the births of Jacob's twelve sons, each of whom is the ancestor of one of the tribes of Israel.

Insofar as the narrative portrays tension in the relationships between Jacob/Israel and Esau/Edom and Laban/Aram, it appears to presuppose the historical and political events of the late-ninth and early-eighth centuries BCE when Edom broke free of Israelite/Judean control and Israel ultimately broke free of Aramean vassalage.[29] Throughout this period, which extends from the reign of Ahab ben Omri through the reign of Jeroboam ben Joash, Israel was a vassal first of Aram and later of Assyria.

Throughout the narrative, Jacob overcomes obstacles that appear before him, such as his rivalry with his brother, Esau, for the affections of his parents; his repeated entrapment into servitude for the hands of his wives, Rachel and Leah, as well as the means to support them by his uncle, Laban; and the antagonism between his wives as they compete with each other for his affection. The narrative makes it clear that sometimes these obstacles are the result of his own shortcomings, such as his attempts to outdo the dimwitted Esau or his clear preference for Rachel over Leah. In the end, Jacob is crippled by his encounter with the unnamed man at the River Jabbok, who names him Israel, and he suffers the death of his beloved Rachel, ironically because of his own statement that whoever possesses the household gods of Laban should die (Gen 31:32).

The Jacob narrative is designed to reflect upon the character of the nation Israel during a difficult period in its history when it was oppressed and subjugated by the Arameans, lost control of Edom, and undoubtedly suffered from internal tensions as its political fortunes waned. Such critical self-reflection is also characteristic of the modern state of Israel throughout its own history.

---

[29] Marvin A. Sweeney, "Puns, Politics, and Perushim in the Jacob Cycle: A Case Study in Teaching the English Hebrew Bible," *Shofar* 9 (1991): 103–118.

Many are well aware of the role that Theodor Herzl played as perhaps the best-known of the leading figures in the foundation of modern Zionism.[30] Following his encounter with anti-Semitism in France during the trial of Captain Alfred Dreyfus, Herzl concluded that Jews had no place in the modern nation-state and that they must therefore found their own. In his view, all Jews must move to the proposed Jewish homeland or be forever lost to Judaism. Although he was a consummate politician and fundraiser, Herzl was a highly assimilated Austrian Jew who had little understanding of Jewish identity and history. Consequently, he was willing to accept the British offer of Uganda to serve as the new Jewish homeland. Even when he was compelled to accept Ottoman-ruled Palestine as the only viable home for Jews, he had little conception of the interrelationship that modern Jews might have with the Palestinian population of the land of Israel or with the larger Arab and Muslim world.

Ahad Ha-Am (Hebrew, "One of the People"), the pen name of Asher Ginsberg, was less well-known in the western world, but was far more effective and self-reflective than Herzl in conceptualizing the modern Jewish state.[31] Ha-Am first of all recognized the importance of the land of Israel, the historic homeland of the Jews, as the necessary location for a modern Jewish state, and compelled Herzl to accept only Ottoman Palestine as the homeland for modern Jews. Ha-Am called for a culturally-defined Zionism, which recognized Jews as a distinctive culture that had existed throughout its history both in the land of Israel and in the Diaspora. Ha-Am envisioned a continuing relationship between the modern state of Israel and Diaspora Jewish culture in which Israel would serve as the foundation for continuing Jewish identity and the Diaspora would function as the source for new ideas that would enable the modern Jewish state to progress. Because of his focus on cultural identity, Ha-Am recognized that the modern Jewish state would have to forge a constructive relationship with its Palestinian Arab population as well as with its neighbors in the larger Arab and Muslim world.

The debate on the character of modern Israel continues today. Modern religious Zionism, evolved from the thought of ultra-Orthodox scholars, such as R. Abraham Isaac Kook and his son Tzvi Judah Kook, as well as political and labor parties, such as the Mizrachi labor movement and Gush Emu-

---

[30] Walter Laquer, *A History of Zionism* (New York: Schocken, 1976), 84–135.
[31] Laquer, *History*, 162–171.

nim.³² Religious Zionism views G-d's commandment that Jews should settle the entire land of Israel and live in accordance with Torah as imperatives for modern Jewish life. Indeed, the religious and political right in Israel is especially influenced by Sephardi Jews whose ancestors suffered under Arab rule and were expelled when modern Israel was created. Many on the Jewish left question the character of Israel as a modern Jewish state and instead envision a secular democratic state that would encompass both its Jewish and Arab populations.³³ But Yasser Arafat's refusal to accept a peace agreement in 2000, the Hamas seizure of Gaza following the Israeli withdrawal in 2005, and the rise of Iranian-backed Hizbullah in Lebanon have convinced the majority of the Israeli public that a viable peace agreement may not be possible. Indeed, Natan Sharansky, a former leader of the Soviet Refusenik movement and former Israeli Cabinet Minister, argues that modern Israel must simultaneously affirm both its democratic and Jewish identity while defending itself from threats and pursuing peace with its neighbors.³⁴

JOSEPH

The final components of the Genesis narrative include the History of Esau in Gen 36:1–37:1 and the History of the Twelve Tribes of Israel in Gen 37:2–50:26. The History of Esau accounts for the descendants of Jacob's fraternal twin brother, Esau, who is the eponymous ancestor of Edom. Genesis 37:2–50:26 is introduced by the formula, "these are the generations of Jacob," and it focuses on Joseph ben Jacob, the first son of Jacob's beloved wife Rachel, and his turbulent relations with his brothers. Despite the focus on Joseph, the narrative is ultimately concerned with the eponymous ancestors of the Twelve Tribes of Israel who will continue the covenant initiated with Abraham and Sarah. The narrative therefore introduces the lengthy segment in Gen 37:2-Num 2:34 that takes up the early history of the nation Israel during the times of the Exodus from Egypt and the revelation at Mt. Sinai.

---

³² Aviezer Ravitzky, *Messianism, Zionism, and Jewish Religious Radicalism* (trans. Michael Swirsky and Jonathan Chipman; Chicago: University of Chicago Press, 1996).
³³ Yoram Hazony, *The Jewish State: The Struggle for Israel's Soul* (New York: Basic Books, 2000).
³⁴ Natan Sharansky, *The Case for Democracy: The Power of Freedom to Overcome Tyranny and Terror* (New York: Public Affairs, 2004); and Sharansky, *Defending Identity: Its Indispensible Role in Protecting Democracy* (New York: Public Affairs, 2008).

The Joseph narrative is especially concerned with the figure of Joseph, his conflicts with his brothers who sell him into Egyptian slavery, and his rise to power and maturity in Egypt that ultimately enables him to reconcile with his brothers and save their lives.

The narrative raises two key issues in subsequent Jewish thought. The first is the question of Jewish assimilation into a Gentile culture, and the second is the question of conflict and difference within the people of Israel.

With regard to the issue of assimilation, Joseph is ultimately a successful figure in Egyptian society who, despite various obstacles that he must overcome, rises to a position of power in Egypt second only to Pharaoh. As a member of the royal court, he is given an Egyptian name, Zaphenath Paneah, and married to an Egyptian woman, Asenath the daughter of the priest Potiphera, who bears his sons, Manasseh and Ephraim. The narrative subtly indicates the problematic nature of Joseph's situation. The first instance is by the inclusion of a side narrative in Gen 38 concerning Tamar and Judah in which Tamar takes action that ultimately ensures that Judah's descendants are Jewish.[35] The second is by Jacob's adoption of Manasseh and Ephraim as his own sons in Gen 48. Although the adoption ensures the status of Manasseh and Ephraim as eponymous ancestors of tribes in Israel, their identity as the key tribes of northern Israel and the Judean character of the Tamar narrative suggests some polemic by southern Judah against the north.

Rabbinic Judaism defines a Jew as one who is born of a Jewish mother or one who has converted to Judaism.[36] The Jewish identities of Manasseh and Ephraim are resolved in Rabbinic tradition by assertions that Asenath is the daughter of Dinah adopted by Poti-phera (*Pirqe R. El.* 38; *Tg. Ps.-J.* Gen 41:45; 46:20) or that her father must have converted to Judaism as Joseph only gave grain to Egyptians who were circumcised (*Gen. Rab.* 85:2; 90:6; 91:5). Nevertheless, Joseph's sojourn in Egypt points to the question of Jewish assimilation. Throughout the history of the Jewish Diaspora, Jews have been under tremendous pressure to assimilate into Gentile societies, either by converting to Christianity or Islam or by intermarrying with non-Jewish spouses.[37] Modern experience with intermarriage indicates that

---

[35] Gen 38 is part of a sequence of narratives that take up the motif of the endangered matriarch and tie it into the question of assimilation in the Joseph narrative (see Sweeney, "The Question of the Endangered Matriarch").

[36] Lawrence H. Schiffman, *Who was a Jew? Rabbinic and Halakhic Perspectives on the Jewish-Christian Schism* (Hoboken, N.J.: KTAV, 1985).

[37] E.g., Arthur Hertzberg, *The Jews in America: Four Centuries of an Uneasy Encounter* (New York: Simon & Schuster, 1989).

without the conversion to Judaism of the non-Jewish spouse, the children born to such a marriage are unlikely to maintain a Jewish identity. Indeed, with intermarriage rates of approximately fifty percent in the United States, assimilation into the larger secular society emerges as a major threat to the continuity of Judaism in the Diaspora. Consequently, the various Jewish movements have had to rethink traditional attitudes to intermarriage, which is strictly forbidden in halakhah but is nevertheless a reality in Jewish life. The Reform Jewish movement accepts children born to Jewish men as Jewish, although the other movements flatly reject this option. The Conservative movement is becoming more and more open to Gentile spouses, although it does not authorize intermarriage and envisions the conversion of the Gentile spouse to Judaism. All forms of Orthodoxy require the halakhic conversion of the Gentile spouse before a marriage can take place.

The second issue raised by the Joseph narrative is conflict and competition within the Jewish community, particularly with regard to the different understandings of Judaism that have developed through history. Indeed, this phenomenon is evident in the condemnation of the northern kingdom of Israel for idolatry throughout the books of Kings, but modern research indicates that King Jeroboam's use of the golden calves was not a deliberate attempt at idolatry, but emblematic of a very different construction of Israelite religion or Judaism in his day in which the calves functioned as mounts or thrones for the invisible YHWH much as the Ark of the Covenant functioned in the Jerusalem Temple.[38]

Every major period in Jewish history saw any number of movements that were frequently in competition with each other.[39] The later Second Temple period saw a variety of parties that held to different constructions of Judaism. The Sadducees were a Zadokite priestly group who maintained that the Jerusalem Temple constitutes the foundation of Jewish identity and religious practice, whereas the Pharisees or early Rabbis focused on Torah observance. The Essenes viewed the Temple as corrupt and envisioned a holy war in which non-observant Jews and Gentiles would be defeated by the army of the Sons of Light, and the Zealots envisioned a very real war in which the Romans and their supporters would be defeated. Even when Rabbinic Judaism emerged as the dominant form of Judaism following the destruction of the Second Temple, the Karaite movement, originating in

---

[38] Sweeney, *Reading*, 67–72.
[39] For an overview of Jewish history, see Robert M. Seltzer, *Jewish People, Jewish Thought: The Jewish Experience in History* (New York: MacMillan, 1980).

Babylonia during the mid-eighth century CE, rejected the oral Torah or Talmudic tradition of the Rabbis in favor of a system of written Torah interpretation that ensured the role of the Bible as the foundation for Jewish thought and practice. The controversy between Rabbinic and Karaite Judaism ultimately led to the inauguration of Jewish rationalist philosophy in the work of Saadia Gaon, who sought to defend Rabbinic Judaism against the Karaite, Muslim, and Christian polemics. He was in turn challenged by Judah ha-Levi, who argued in favor of Judaism based in the experience of the divine in his celebrated work, the Kuzari. In the late-eighteenth century, the rationalist understanding of Judaism promoted by Moses Mendelssohn, who argued that Judaism must be accepted as a religion of reason alongside Christianity, contrasted markedly with the understanding of the Baal Shem Tov (Israel ben Eliezer), whose spiritualistic form of Hasidic Judaism was rooted in earlier Kabbalistic thought.

Contemporary Judaism sees a number of Jewish denominations, each with a differing view of Judaism.[40] Reform maintains that Judaism is rooted in the revelation at Sinai, but the need to change and adapt to modernity is an essential element of that revelation. Conservative Judaism maintains that revelation takes place throughout history as Jews in each generation define Judaism in their own times. Modern orthodoxy has a multitude of movements, such as modern Orthodoxy, Haredi Judaism (ultra-Orthodox), and Habad Judaism, but all hold to traditional halakhah based on the view that all of Jewish tradition was revealed at Sinai and Jews are still in the process of learning its entirety.

Jewish history is replete with examples of different constructions of Judaism. The issue points to the richness of Judaism throughout history, but it also points to divisive conflict with potentially dangerous consequences like those suffered by Joseph, such as the efforts to disenfranchise Ethiopian Jews, Jews born of mixed parentage, or those converted to Judaism by non-halakhic movements.

Conclusion

Although the book of Genesis is written as a narrative history of the origins of the world and the nation Israel, it functions as a foundation for a multitude of issues in subsequent Jewish tradition and thought. The exam-

---

[40] Mark Lee Raphael, *Profiles in American Judaism: The Reform, Conservative, Orthodox, and Reconstructionist Traditions* (San Francisco: Harper & Row, 1984).

ples given here regarding the character of creation, the nature of human beings, the often challenging relationship between G-d and human beings, the character of the nation Israel and its relations with its neighbors, and conflicts and competition among rival movements in Judaism throughout its history point to the importance of Genesis as an ancient book that also addresses Jewish issues of later times.

SELECT BIBLIOGRAPHY

Berkovits, Eliezer. *Faith after the Holocaust*. New York: KTAV, 1973.
Blumenthal, David R. *Facing the Abusing G-d: A Theology of Protest*. Louisville: Westminster John Knox, 1993.
Buber, Martin. *I and Thou*. Translated by Walter Kaufmann. New York: Charles Scribner's Sons, 1970.
Eskenazi, Tamara Cohn, and Andrea L. Weiss, eds. *The Torah: A Women's Commentary*. New York: Union of Reform Judaism Press, 2008.
Elbogen, Ismar. *Jewish Liturgy: A Comprehensive History*. Translated by Raymond P. Scheindlin. Philadelphia: Jewish Publication Society, 1993.
Fackenheim, Emil. *G-d's Presence in History: Jewish Affirmations and Philosophical Reflections*. New York: New York University Press, 1970.
Hayman, A. Peter. *Sefer Yesira: Edition, Translation, and Text-critical Commentary*. Texte und Studien zum antiken Judentum 104. Tübingen: Mohr Siebeck, 2004.
Hazony, Yoram. *The Jewish State: The Struggle for Israel's Soul*. New York: Basic Books, 2000.
Hertzberg, Arthur. *The Jews in America: Four Centuries of an Uneasy Encounter*. New York: Simon & Schuster, 1989.
Heschel, Abraham Joshua. *The Sabbath: Its Meaning for Modern Man*. New York: Farrar, Straus, and Giroux, 1951.
———. *G-d in Search of Man: A Philosophy of Judaism*. New York: Meridian and Jewish Publication Society, 1955.
Laquer, Walter. *A History of Zionism*. New York: Schocken, 1976.
Levenson, Jon D. *Creation and the Presence of Evil: The Jewish Drama of Divine Impotence*. New York: Harper & Row, 1988.
———. "Genesis." Pages 8–101 in *The Jewish Study Bible*. Edited by Adele Berlin and Marc Zvi Brettler. Oxford: Oxford University Press, 2003.
Meyers, Carol. *Discovering Eve: Ancient Israelite Women in Context*. Oxford: Oxford University Press, 1988.
Maimon, Moses ben. *The Guide for the Perplexed*. 2nd ed. Edited and translated by M. Friedländer. London: Routledge & Kegan Paul, 1951.
Orlinsky, Harry M. "The Biblical Concept of the Land of Israel: Cornerstone of the Covenant between G-d and Israel," Pages 27–64 in *The Land of Israel: Jewish Perspectives*. Edited by Lawrence A. Hoffman. Notre Dame, Ind.: University of Notre Dame Press, 1986.
Plaskow, Judith. *Standing Again at Sinai: Judaism from a Feminist Perspective*. New York: Harper & Row, 1990.

Raphael, Mark Lee. *Profiles in American Judaism: The Reform, Conservative, Orthodox, and Reconstructionist Traditions*. San Francisco: Harper & Row, 1984.

Ravitzky, Aviezer. *Messianism, Zionism, and Jewish Religious Radicalism*. Translated by Michael Swirsky and Jonathan Chipman. Chicago: The University of Chicago Press 1996.

Rosenzweig, Franz. *The Star of Redemption*. Translated by William W. Hallo. Notre Dame, Ind.: Notre Dame University Press, 1985.

Rubenstein, Richard L. *After Auschwitz: Radical Theology and Contemporary Judaism*. Indianapolis: Bobbs-Merrill, 1966.

Gaon, Saadia. *Book of Beliefs and Opinions*. Translated by Samuel Rosenblatt. Yale Judaica Series 1. New Haven: Yale University Press, 1948.

Sarna, Nahum M. *The JPS Torah Commentary: Genesis*. Philadelphia: Jewish Publication Society, 1989/5749.

Scherman, Nossom. *The Chumash: The Stone Edition*. Brooklyn: Mesorah, 1993.

Schiffman, Lawrence H. *Who was a Jew? Rabbinic and Halakhic Perspectives on the Jewish Christian Schism*. Hoboken, N.J.: KTAV, 1985.

Seltzer, Robert M. *Jewish People, Jewish Thought: The Jewish Experience in History*. New York: MacMillan, 1980.

Sharansky, Natan. *Defending Identity: Its Indispensible Role in Protecting Democracy*. New York: Public Affairs, 2008.

Soloveitchik, Joseph B. "The Lonely Man of Faith." *Tradition* 7 (1965): 5–67.

Sweeney, Marvin A. *Reading the Hebrew Bible after the Shoah: Engaging Holocaust Theology*. Minneapolis: Fortress, 2008.

———. *Tanak: A Theological and Critical Introduction to the Jewish Bible*. Minneapolis: Fortress, forthcoming.

Urbach, Ephraim E. *The Sages: Their Concepts and Beliefs*. 2 vols. Jerusalem: Magnes, 1979.

Wiesel, Elie. *Night*. New York: Random House, 1973.

Zlotowitz, Meir. *Bereishis*. 2 vols. Brooklyn: Mesorah, 1986.

GENESIS AND ECOLOGY

Terence E. Fretheim

Human beings are a part of an increasingly interconnected "community in relationship" that includes all of God's creatures. Each member of this community touches the 'life' of all others, whether for good or for ill. All live in a spider web like world, within which creaturely words and deeds risk damaging that web. The words and deeds of human beings in particular affect the web of relationships, both positively and negatively. Reality is relational; everyone and everything is in relationship. This includes God. The God of the cosmos has to do with every creature and every creature has to do with God, recognized or not. Even more, God's action in response to creaturely activity will have rippling effects across the environment. Such a relational perspective is basic to thinking about matters ecological in Genesis (and elsewhere), though readers should be cautious about reading these ancient texts through a modern environmental lens.

A negative aspect of this relational world in which we live is that any damage to the communities to which creatures belong diminishes us all. Indeed, this earthly home has been damaged, especially by the actions of human beings, and all have been diminished. Both academic and religious communities bear some responsibility for these developments, not least by their slowness in recognizing the need, their relatively tepid response (even silence), and, all too often, their theological perspective. For example, it is remarkably common among Christians that a 'theology of demolition' is in place: the world is going to end soon anyway, so there is little need to be concerned about the environment. Or, God is portrayed as one who is "in control." Humankind can thus relax regarding care of the environment, for God will do whatever God is going to do.

At the same time, readings of the Bible through an ecological lens have been on the increase in recent years. This salutary development is due in large part not to religious communities or to theological disciplines, but to the emergence of an environmental consciousness in society more generally.[1] In any case, more interpreters are finding helpful resources in

---

[1] It is ironic that the impetus for the concern for matters creational has come largely

the Bible, including Genesis, for this environmentally sensitive age. Still, this conversation is in its infancy—not least because of the secondary status that creation has often played in biblical reflection.[2] A sharper sense that creation is a primary biblical vision is needed and how we think about this matter will have a considerable impact on environmental reflections and practices.

Accompanying this increased interest in relating Bible and environment is another perspective: not all of the Bible's understandings of these issues are "green." Such a negative reading is often traced back to Lynn White's 1967 article in *Science*.[3] He focused on the "dominating" role given to the human in Gen. 1:26–28 ("have dominion"; "subdue"), especially as interpreted by religious communities in recent centuries, and marked its destructive effect upon environmental reflection and practice.

The initial response to White's article was largely negative, at least within Bible-based communities, as many interpreters came to the defense of the Bible and its perspective on matters ecological. The texts were often interpreted in terms of a "stewardship" model; though still anthropocentric in its basic orientation, a call to care for the creation was claimed as a basic biblical perspective. Even less anthropocentric readings of the key biblical texts have emerged over the years and images of partnership, citizenship, and servanthood have been suggested.[4]

At the same time, more recent interpretive efforts have "returned" to White's perspective, insisting that there is more truth in a "domination" reading of Gen 1:26–28 than is first apparent. A recent example is Norman Habel's *Inconvenient Text: Is a Green Reading of the Bible Possible?*[5] While Habel recognizes the presence of "green" texts in the Bible, "grey" texts are

---

from secular sources. That in itself is a considerable witness to the importance of creation theology: God the Creator is pervasively at work in the larger culture, often independent of religious communities.

[2] For a list of eleven factors that have contributed to this neglect, see Terence E. Fretheim, *God and World in the Old Testament: A Relational Theology of Creation* (Nashville: Abingdon, 2005), ix–x.

[3] Lynn White, Jr., "The Historical Roots of Our Ecologic Crisis," *Science* 155 (1967): 1203–1207.

[4] See, e.g., H. Paul Santmire, "Partnership with Nature according to the Scriptures: Beyond the Theology of Stewardship," *CSR* 32 (2003): 381–412; Ellen F. Davis, *Getting Involved with God: Rediscovering the Old Testament* (Cambridge: Cowley, 2001); and J. Baird Callicott, "Genesis and John Muir," in *Beyond the Land Ethic: More Essays in Environmental Philosophy* (ed. J. Baird Callicott; Albany: SUNY Press, 1999), 187–219.

[5] Norman C. Habel, *An Inconvenient Text: Is a Green Theology of the Bible Possible?* (Adelaide: ATL Press, 2009).

not uncommon and must be recognized for what they are (not unlike the Bible's patriarchal perspective). A sharp engagement over these perspectives is taking place in biblical studies, including interpretations of Genesis.

My purpose in this article is to examine three sections of Genesis and the implications they may have for our reflections on environmental matters. They are: the creation accounts (Gen 1–2), the flood narrative (Gen 6:5–9:17), and the story of Sodom and Gomorrah (Gen 13:10–13; 14:10; 18:16–19:29).

The Ecology of Creation: Genesis 1–2

I work with the two creation accounts as a single witness to creation.[6] Whatever the history of tradition may have been, Gen 1 and 2 together constitute Israel's primary witness to the Creator God (and the only non-speculative one). A growing literature of these chapters is available wherein an environmental lens is at work.[7]

The Creator God

How we think about the God of Gen 1–2 and the creational moves God makes will sharply affect how we carry on this conversation.[8] The God of the creation accounts is not explicitly "defined," however; we are left to infer the identity of this God from various clues in the text. Many readers claim that the God of this text creates the world alone, works independently and unilaterally, and is in absolute control of the developing creation.[9] But, is this theological understanding appropriate to the creation passages? Further, what have been the effects of such a perspective on environmental considerations?

---

[6] I assume literary and historical studies of these chapters. It is likely that the Priestly account (Gen 1:1–2:4a) incorporated the second account (2:4a–25) from the beginning and was never intended to stand alone.

[7] An important study with environmental reflections in view is William P. Brown, *The Seven Pillars of Creation: the Bible, Science, and an Ecology of Wonder* (Oxford: Oxford University Press, 2010). He treats the creation accounts as separate "pillars," with strong theological emphases in the discussion. Canonically, it could be argued that this combined account is a "pillar" of creation or at least a third one.

[8] These next paragraphs build on Fretheim, *God and World*, 48–49.

[9] Some formulations of creation by means of "the word" suggest this understanding, as if God's only means of creating is through speaking or speech-events. For ten, perhaps eleven, modes of creation that are described in the creation accounts, see Fretheim, *God and World*, 34–35.

If the above, common understanding of God in creation is correct, then humans created in God's image (so Gen 1:26–28) could *properly* understand their role regarding the rest of creation in comparable terms, that is, in terms of power over, absolute control, and independence. By definition, the natural world thus becomes available for human manipulation and exploitation. That is, if all the creatures of Gen 1 are understood to be but passive putty in the hands of God, that invites a comparable treatment of them by those who are created in the image of that God. In other words, how one images the God of the creation accounts will have a significant impact on our environmental sensitivities and the urgency of our practices.

In what follows, I suggest that the God of the creation accounts is imaged more as one who chooses to share creative activity. Hence, the way in which the human as image of God is to exercise dominion is to be shaped by that relational model, with significant implications for further reflection regarding creatures, their interrelationships, and their environmental responsibilities.

Two perspectives in Gen 1–2 are of special help. (1) God decides to create in community rather than alone; the creatures play an active role in God's creating work. In other words, in creating God chooses to act interdependently in and through creaturely agents, both human and nonhuman. (2) This interdependent action on God's part, as well as other textual realities, reveals that God highly values all creatures. That God so values each creature is the basic theological grounding for biblical reflections on environmental matters. Those created in God's image should seek to care for such creatures *for God's sake* and not simply for their own sake or for the sake of the creatures.

God Decides to Create the World in Community Rather Than Alone

While all creatures are deeply dependent upon God for their creation and continuing life, God has chosen to establish an *interdependent* relationship with them with respect to both originating creation and continuing creation. God's word in creation is often a communicating with others rather than a top-down word. God's approach to creation is communal and relational; in the wake of God's initiating activity, God creates with the world from within rather than working on the world from without. God works with creatures as genuine agents in the creative process. Given the nature of the agents with which God works, the process is imprecise and open-ended. The creation continues to live with the messy effects of that divine decision. The practical implications of such an understanding, not least with respect to environmental matters, are great. The actions of human beings and other creatures matter with respect to the future of creation; indeed, their actions make a difference to *God's* future with creation.

Three modes of creating in Gen 1–2 may be suggested:[10]

1. God creates in and through the use of already existing materials. Male and female are created, not "out of nothing," but out of already existent creatures, both human and nonhuman (Gen 2:7, 22). The Creator "gets down in the dirt" and creates the man in direct contact with the earth; God's creation of the woman out of the side of the man must have been a "bloody mess." And, of course, the matter with which God chooses to work in the creative process has an inevitable and significant effect on what is created.

   Also to be noted is the role of the spirit/wind of God with respect to the "formless void" (Gen 1:2). The image of God's spirit/wind that "moves, sweeps over" the face of the waters suggests creative action that has an ever-changing velocity and direction.[11] Even more, the spirit/wind works with already existing matter such as earth and water; in fact, much of what is created in the rest of Gen 1 is created out of material already present in Gen 1:2.[12] Out of the "mess" of Gen 1:2 (understood as chaos/disorder, not evil)[13] comes the orderliness of 1:3–31—though not without continuing disorder, evident in the omission of certain words and phrases in its normally regular structure.[14]

2. God invites already existent nonhuman creatures to participate in further creating activity: "Let the earth bring forth" and "the *earth* brought forth" (Gen 1:11–13; see also 1:20, 24).[15] By inviting the participation of

---

[10] These items have been developed further in Terence E. Fretheim, *Creation Untamed: The Bible, God, and Natural Disasters* (Grand Rapids: Baker Academic, 2010).

[11] This language is used for a drunken walk in Jer 23:9. See also John 3:8: "the wind blows where it wills."

[12] See Wis 11:17: God "created the world out of formless *matter*."

[13] For detail, see Fretheim, *God and World*, 43–46.

[14] For example, J. Richard Middleton, *The Liberating Image: The Imago Dei in Genesis 1* (Grand Rapids: Brazos, 2005), has shown that considerable variation exists within the seven-day structure of Gen 1 (among others: eight creative acts in six days). Middleton says, "Whereas the world rhetorically depicted in Genesis 1 is certainly ordered, patterned, and purposive, the God who is artisan and maker does not over-determine the order of the cosmos" (306, n. 25). In other words, the work of the Spirit issues in a creation that, for all of its orderliness, is characterized by openness and freedom, and continuing disorder.

[15] Grammatically, the use of the jussive, "let ...," means that God's speaking does not function as command; it leaves room for creaturely response, not unlike the cohortative, "let

that which is not God in the creative process, God thereby *necessarily* limits the divine role. God's creating is accomplished in and through the involvement of creaturely agents. God's creating is not presented as a unilateral act; it is mediated rather than immediate. The nonhuman creatures have a genuine vocational role in enabling the creation to develop into something ever new.

Moreover, it is not only human beings who are blessed and invited to be fruitful, multiply, and fill the earth; animals are also called to do that (1:22). God shares creative powers with that which is not human, enabling a significant point of commonality between human and nonhuman. God thereby chooses to exercise an ongoing restraint and constraint in relation to the future of these creatures. God will not, for instance, suspend the created orders and relieve creatures of these procreational "responsibilities." God will allow these creatures to be what they were created to be—regardless. God has thus not created a ready-made world, but a world in which creatures can make themselves. But for creatures to so participate in creation means that the process will inevitably be "messy."

By creating in this way, God opens up creaturely space for chance and freedom. In textual terms, God keeps the Sabbath day (Gen 2:1–3).[16] The Sabbath is a move to a different sort of creating (God "finished" on that day, Gen 2:2). Resting on God's part means giving time and space over to the creatures to be what they were created to be, from the movement of tectonic plates to volcanic activity to the spread of viruses to the procreation of animals. God commits the divine self to the structures of creation and the freedom of the creatures. God rests so that the creatures can thrive. As a result, creaturely actions make a difference for the future. God's actions will be shaped in part by what creatures do. The world's future is thus to some extent unsettled.

In sum, God takes the ongoing creational process into account in shaping new directions for the world, one dimension of which is using and engaging creatures in creative acts. Divine decisions interact with creaturely activity in the becoming of the world. Creation is process

---

us make" (1:26), leaves room for consultation and the "let them have dominion" (1:28) entails a sharing of power (see also 1:14–15). God's speaking is of such a nature that the receptor of the word is important in shaping the created order.

[16] See the discussion of the Sabbath text in view of other studies in Fretheim, *God and World*, 61–64.

as well as punctiliar act; creation is creaturely as well as divine. God's approach to creation is communal and relational.

The environmental implications of this divine move are significant. This story has been repeated over the millennia as ever-new creatures come into being, mediated by the activity of existing creatures, from glaciers to earthquakes to tsunamis. Some of the most spectacular vistas of the natural order are due to the activity of such nonhuman creatures (e.g., mountains and valleys carved out by glacial movement). These two points demonstrate the immense *value* of nonhuman creatures *for God*. Without these nonhuman creatures God's creation would not live up to its potential of becoming.

3. As God shares creative power in the divine realm (through the council, "let us," 1:26), so also God shares creative power with those created in God's image. God's *first* words to the human constitute a creation-sharing movement, an interdependent divine way of working in the world. Human beings are invited, indeed commanded, to play a key role in the becoming of their world in and through the exercise of creative power: be fruitful, multiply, fill the earth, subdue it, and have dominion.

God thereby chooses not to do everything in the developing world "all by himself." God certainly takes the initiative in distributing this power to the human. But, having done so, God is *committed* to this way of relating; suspending this status is not a divine option. Given the imaging of God as one who creates relationally, these words of commission should be interpreted fundamentally in *creative and communal* terms. Humans are invited to play a key role in the becoming of their world, indeed, bringing into being that which is genuinely new. Note that these charges are made a matter of (pre-sin) *law*. Such a way of stating human responsibilities stresses the importance of human activity *for God*. God's words to the human in Gen 1:26–28 have proved to be controversial.[17] A few comments on each must suffice.

Be fruitful, multiply, fill the earth. If creative power is an essential element in the imaging of God, then likeness to God in one respect consists in procreative capacity (also true of animals; Gen 1:22). By being what they

---

[17] Habel, *An Inconvenient Text*, identifies Gen 1:26–28 as a "grey" text, with a "mandate to *dominate*." He suggests that this text is "ecologically destructive, devaluing Earth" (2); indeed, it is a "horrible intrusion in the plot of the narrative" (67). In what follows, I will suggest that a greater recognition of interpretive issues is in order.

were created to be, they can be productive of new life. God is present in the process (see Ps 139:13), but not in a managerial way, so that human decisions and actions do not count or random events cannot wreak havoc (the gene pool). Humans will do the procreating, not God.

Subdue the earth. I have suggested that the best sense for this verb is "bring order out of continuing disorder."[18] While the verb may involve coercion in interhuman relationships (Num 32:22, 29), no enemies are in view here. The verb is used in a pre-sin context, prior to any effects that sin has had. Moreover, only here does the verb refer to nonhuman creatures.[19] So, later usages of the verb for post-sin and human activities should not be simply transferred to this context.

This command assumes that the earth is not fully developed; no once-for-all givenness to the creation exists at the end of the seventh day. God creates a *dynamic* world; development and change are in view, and God enlists human beings to that end (see below on Gen 2:5, 15, 18–20). God's creation is moving forward and God has entrusted human beings with God-like responsibility relating thereto. God's creation is a long-term project, ever in the process of becoming (as the history of nature shows).[20] Certain constants are in place (Gen 8:22), but beyond that, the future of the world is understood to be open-ended.

Have dominion. This verb refers only to living creatures, not to the larger "environment." Inasmuch as "force" and "harshness" are needed to qualify the basic meaning of the verb in Ezek 34:1–4 and Lev 25:43, 46, the verb itself is positive in its reference: care for, not exploitation or domination (killing animals is a post-sin reality; 9:2–3). The idea was apparently drawn from ideal conceptions of royal responsibility.[21] At the same time, to maintain the democratization theme inherent in the image of God, every human

---

[18] See Fretheim, *God and World*, 52–53.

[19] The "land" is "subdued" in several texts (Num 32:22, 29; Josh 18:1; 1 Chron 22:18), but that has reference to people who occupy the land.

[20] The command may have in view God's own pattern of acting relative to the already existent "earth" in, say, Gen 1:9–10, "let the waters be gathered together and let the dry land appear," which God called Earth.

[21] Brown, *Seven Pillars*, states: "Nowhere does God dominate or conquer" (44). God is presented as "thoroughly interactive" (46) with already existing creatures in the act of creation, though his statement that "God creates by verbal decree" (44) takes the edge off that point. Gen 1 presents "a skewed symmetry," providing one of many links to scientific understandings: "perfect symmetry makes for a lifeless universe. Variation, by contrast, constitutes the story of cosmic evolution as it does the Genesis story of creation" (53). Or, chaos theory "finds an ancient precedent in Genesis as an essential, constructive part of creation's evolving order" (55).

being, without distinction of gender or societal status, is to relate to nonhuman creatures as God would. And so, it is what *God* (not the human king) does that is the model for this human calling. As God chooses to share power in relationship, so the way in which the human as image of God exercises "dominion" is to be shaped by that creative and relational model.

God here exercises a sovereignty that gives genuine power to the creatures for the sake of a relationship of integrity. God does not control their activity, intervening to make sure every detail goes right. This way of relating to creatures reveals a divine vulnerability, for God opens the divine self up to hurt should things not go according to plan (Gen 6:6–7); God's will can be successfully resisted, at least in the near term.

The involvement of the human in the creative process is evident at several other points. For instance, *Gen 2:5* states: "in the day that the Lord God made the earth … there was no one to till the ground."[22] Humans are given a key role in the initial stages of the creation; God does not retain all creative power. Human activity is deemed *essential* if the creation is to be what God intends. Humans are created for the sake of the future of the earth. *Genesis 2:15* speaks more specifically of humans created to till and keep Eden (extended in 3:23), or, as some have suggested, to "serve and preserve" it—a highly positive understanding of the human relationship to the earth. In *Gen 2:18–21*, God lets the *human being* determine whether the animals are adequate to move the evaluation of creation from "not good" to "good" (see below). The human naming of the animals is directly parallel to God's naming of *nonliving* creatures in Gen 1; God gives this assignment in the creative process to the human. *Genesis 4:1* is also indicative: Eve testifies theologically to both human *and* divine involvement in the "creation" of the human firstborn (Eve is the subject of the creating verb [*qānāh*], as God is in Gen 14:19–22).[23] Again, God chooses to act through creatures in matters of new creations. In *Gen 5:1–3*, as God created humankind in the divine image and likeness, so Adam creates ("became the father of") Seth in his "likeness" and "image."[24] Notably, God's creation of humans in the image

---

[22] The responsibility in 2:5 to "till the ground" has creation-wide reference; in 2:15 it has more particular reference to the "garden of Eden."

[23] The woman was created out of man (*'îš*) in 2:23; in 4:1, man (*'îš*) is created out of woman.

[24] From the genealogical reference in Gen 2:4, it could be claimed that the earth and its creatures are understood to be an integral aspect of the human ancestral heritage, with all the implications that these creatures have for continuing human life.

of God is placed as the first generation within an extensive genealogy. So, human procreation, creating ever-new images of God, finds its true parallel in God's creative activity.

This idea of God's interdependent way of creating may also be conveyed by the presentation of the creation in terms of actual days, with evening and morning repeatedly stated. However literally one interprets the seven days, they are emblematic of any period of time that it takes for the creation to come into being and develop. Such language suggests that the creation of the universe takes time, even for God. Claims that God created the universe instantaneously have long been made (e.g., Augustine). Certainly the all-powerful God would not need to take any time to bring the world into being! The text, however, presents God's creative work as coming into being over time. The result is that creation is presented by the text as a dynamic process rather than a finished product. God, who involves the creatures in creational developments, takes the time necessary for creation to come to be.

Once again, the environmental implications are significant. Responsibilities for the future of creation are placed directly on the plates of the creatures, especially human beings. Inasmuch as God acts relationally as Creator, creativity and relationality become fundamental descriptors of those created in the image of God. This understanding of the human gives significant shape to the tasks to which they have been called relative to the environment. They cannot simply rest back and assume that God will take care of everything or that the creation's future is solely in God's hands. Ultimately it is, but in the meantime, they are called to genuine engagement, and the decisions made will have significant implications for the future of the environment and the nature of the future of God.[25]

God Highly Values All Creatures

The most basic statement regarding created beings is that they are "good" and "very good."[26] *Every creature* is evaluated in these terms; the human being is not given a special evaluative word; indeed, human beings are not even given their own creation day.

What does it mean to be evaluated as "good"? The word has the sense of being correspondent to the divine intention, including elements of beauty,

---

[25] See Jer 22:1–5 and the "if, if not" formulation. A number of such texts could be cited.

[26] The only use of "very good" is in Gen 1:31. Some interpreters think "everything" refers only to the sixth day creations (human beings and animals), but it is more likely a reference to all of God's creatures.

purposefulness, and praiseworthiness. God observes a decisive continuity between God's intention and the creational result. At the same time, "good" does not mean static or perfect (in the sense of having no need of improvement or development to be what it truly is). Several textual clues demonstrate this point.[27] If the creation were perfect, how could anything go wrong (see Gen 3–6)? The "not good" of 2:18 suggests that creation is a process, not a finished product, moving *toward* "good." The command to "subdue" the earth (1:28) is the clearest evidence for the claim (see above).

What does it mean to be *evaluated by God*? This evaluation is reported, not as the narrator's assessment, but as *divine*: *God saw that it was good. God* experiences what has been created and the divine reaction shapes the next divine move. This divine way is illumined by God's negative evaluation in 2:18. The creature thereby has an effect on God's ongoing creative actions, making its own contribution to the developing creation. God's creative activity is thus shown not only to be active, but also reactive. Such a divine response to the creation assumes that evaluating the created order is an ongoing process within which adjustments, and even improvements, can be made.

Even more, God involves the *'ādām* in the evaluative process, giving him the task of determining whether the animals will resolve the issue of aloneness. This happens in Gen 2:19–22, with 2:23 constituting an evaluation by the *human*! In that creative and evaluative process, the human is given the power to determine whether the animals will advance the creational situation from "not good" to "good" and then, in view of that decision, the rightness of the woman in meeting the issue of aloneness. These processes show that God values human beings, places confidence in them, and honors what they do and say with respect to matters relating to creation.[28]

That God's first move to address the issue of human aloneness is the creation of animals has long raised questions for interpreters. Does God think the animals will meet the identified problem in some way? Is this a "trial and error" move for God? Though this divine initiative proves not to be a final decision, God's action must at least mean that the *animals are understood by God to constitute a community that could address the issue of human aloneness*. In other words, God here gives to the animals a *very*

---

[27] For further development of these issues, see Fretheim, *Creation Untamed*, 9–37.
[28] This naming task anticipates scientific enterprises through the centuries, especially taxonomy. Naming is part of the task of dominion (1:28). To name the animals is to bear some responsibility for them. Naming does not entail authority over them (shown by Gen 16:13).

high value, indeed a *vocation* in the shaping of *human* community. The environmental implications of such a divine move are extensive.

God's role in this text is to place various creative possibilities before the human being, giving freedom to the human to decide. The human being, not God, deems what is "fit for him." This human decision corresponds to the divine evaluative rhythm of Gen 1. God takes seriously the creative human response in shaping the future of creation. The future is genuinely open here. Will the human being decide for the animals? In some basic sense, God places the very future of the human race in human hands (not the last such divine gesture, we might add), which will in turn shape the future of the world. In the language of Phyllis Trible: God is now present, "not as the authoritarian controller of events, but as the generous delegator of power who even forfeits the right to reverse human decisions."[29] *Whatever* the human being called each animal, that was its name (Gen 2:19). The creation (and its future) is characterized by a remarkable open-endedness, in which more than divine evaluation is involved.

God may be said to "learn" from what the human being actually does with the task that has been assigned.[30] God accepts the human decision, and then goes "back to the drawing boards." Divine decisions interact with human decisions in the creation of the world. It is not that human beings have the capacity to hinder God's movement into the future. But God's relationship with them is such that their decisions about developments in creation truly "count."[31] God recognizes the creational import of the human decision, for no additional divine word or act is forthcoming. God lets the man's exultation over the woman fill the scene; the *human word* (the first uttered in Genesis) carries weight within the evaluation that this creation is now "good."

The environmental implications of this evaluation of goodness are many. God deeply values human and nonhuman life and understands that such creatures are indispensable for creation to develop into a more complex reality. The value of one of the creatures is not dependent on the value

---

[29] Phyllis Trible, *God and the Rhetoric of Sexuality* (OBT; Philadelphia: Fortress, 1978), 93.

[30] See Bruce C. Birch, "Creation and the Moral Development of God in Genesis 1–11," in *'And God Saw That It Was Good': Essays on Creation and God in Honor of Terence E. Fretheim* (eds. Frederick J. Gaiser and Mark A. Throntveit; WWSup 5; Saint Paul, Minn.: Luther Seminary, 2006), 12–22.

[31] One may ask if this is really much different from the contemporary situation, where, say, human environmental (in)sensitivity may have a comparable import for the future of the world. Indeed, such decisions could put an end to the human race as decisively as Adam's choice of the animals would have.

of any other creature. Indeed, the concluding evaluation in Gen 1:31 claims that the entirety of creation has a value that is more than the value of any single creature. Inasmuch as such creatures are of high value to God, certainly they should be of value to human beings. Such a biblical-theological grounding could be stated even more strongly: God has established a special relationship with every creature. This relationship should serve as the primary ground for the care of creation. That is, if God is so closely related to each creature, then those who are created in the image of God must reflect that relationship in all that they do.

This evaluation of "good" is not taken away when sin enters the life of the world. In fact, many texts reinforce that evaluation. With respect to human beings, God says: "you are precious in my sight, and honored" (Isa 43:4). God continues to regard them as "crowned ... with glory and honor" (Ps 8:5). Sin negatively affects the life of human beings, certainly, and through them the life of other creatures. But nowhere does Scripture take away the evaluation "good" from any creature.

The Emergence of Sin and the Environmental Effects (Gen 3–9; 13; 18–19)

When human sin enters the picture in Gen 3, it has negative effects upon the natural order: thorns and thistles complicate the farmer's vocation and the pain of childbirth is *increased* (Gen 3:16–19; see also 4:12). This new reality is a witness to the negative pole of the interconnectedness of life: what human beings do can have a negative effect upon other creatures, including the environment. A question arises: *How* is human sin related to such effects? Is the relationship intrinsic, with environmental effects growing out of the deed itself? If this is the case, as seems likely, how is God related to this movement from sin to consequence? Theoretically, responses to the God question could range from deism to micromanagement. Biblical texts seem not to have a single answer to the question, but they do stay away from both extremes. In any case, in the flood story both human (and animal) behaviors and God's judgment are at work in this chain of events (Gen 6:11–13).

One other introductory matter must be kept in mind as we explore these texts: God created a world in which environmental disasters would occur as a natural part of the world's becoming, quite apart from human sin (e.g., earthquakes).[32] God is involved with such disasters at two levels: (1)

---

[32] For further discussion, see Fretheim, *Creation Untamed*, 9–37.

God created a world in which they would occur naturally; (2) God created the moral order wherein human sin can have consequences, including a negative effect on the environment, and God "sees to" that order. So, *that* natural disasters occur is not necessarily linked to the effects of sin, but the presence of human sin may occasion a negative effect of some sort (e.g., worsen the effects).[33]

Keeping these two dimensions of the issue in mind, we take a closer look at two Genesis texts that speak of natural disasters and link them to human sin in some way: the flood narrative (Gen 6–9) and the story of Sodom and Gomorrah (Gen 18:16–19:29). How to speak of that link is difficult.

The Flood and the Judgment of God

Literarily, one could track the relationship between the biblical flood story and other flood stories, such as the Atrahasis Epic or the Epic of Gilgamesh. One could also delineate the more proximate literary sources of the biblical story, including Yahwistic and Priestly versions and their redactional history. But for these purposes I simply recognize that the present story is a composite text with a complex literary history and I work with the final form of the text.

The discussion of flood geology is remarkably complex.[34] One study argues that the current shoreline of the Black Sea was created about 5600 BCE when a flood from the Mediterranean Sea poured through the Bosporus to inundate an originally small, freshwater, inland sea.[35] The flood refugees carried various stories of their experience throughout the region, one or more of which provided the literary inspiration for the biblical flood story. This hypothesis remains highly speculative, of course, but it may contribute some insight into the text in a way that the common river flooding scenario does not. In any case, it is commonly agreed that some ecological event occurred in that part of the world that prompted various stories of a major flood.

Tensions exist in the flood story regarding matters environmental. Worldwide destruction overwhelms the created order and God is said to be active in its occurrence. Indeed, God is said to plan to "blot out" all living

---

[33] One thinks, for example, of Hurricane Katrina in Southeastern USA (2005), and the effects of inadequate human preparations and response.

[34] For a review, see J. David Pleins, *When the Great Abyss Opened: Classic and Contemporary Readings of Noah's Flood* (Oxford: Oxford University Press, 2003).

[35] William Ryan and Walter Pitman, *Noah's Flood: The New Scientific Discoveries about the Event that Changed History* (New York: Simon & Schuster, 2000).

things "from the earth" (Gen 6:7, 17). The earth remains in some sense, as a place to begin again, but in 6:13 the earth is included in the planned destruction. Then God apparently changes the divine mind and takes special care to see that some human beings and animals are saved from destruction. Even more, at the height of the flood, God "remembers" the ark's occupants, including domestic animals and wild animals (Gen 8:1). And then, at the end of the story, God makes a repeated promise with "every living creature" (Gen 9:10, 15–17). What does it mean for ecological reflection that God both sees to the destruction of many creatures and makes promises never to do this again?

The text specifically links the flood to creaturely behaviors (Gen 6:11–13): human and animal violence ("all flesh," see 9:15–16) has negative effects on the environment. Such "corrupting" violence had the effect of "corrupting" the *earth*. The text does not claim that there would have been no flood had there been no sin. Rather, it is the range and intensity of the flood that seems to be related to the moral order.

Genesis 6:11–13 also relates the flood to divine activity; God will destroy "all flesh … along with the earth." Key questions arise here: *how* is God related to this environmental disaster? Is the flood occasioned by divine action only? Or, is the moral order the key factor and, if so, how is God related to that reality? Before exploring these queries, it is wise to remember that this flood is a one-time event, never-to-be-repeated according to God's own promise (Gen 8:20–22). Hence, the world (or God for that matter) will not "work" in just this way again. Judgment there will be, but not of this range and severity again. Sodom and Gomorrah become an illustration of a local disaster, not a global event (see below).

What does the divine judgment entail?[36] The use of this language for God commonly suggests to readers that God, like a human judge, sits behind a divine bench and hands out punishments for crimes committed. But is the judge metaphor to be understood in such a way? The use of any metaphor for God carries many instances of "No," that is, ways in which this language is *unlike* God. I suggest three ways: (1) God's judgment is never simply justice. In juridical terms, God is much too lenient, "slow to anger," and open to changing the divine mind (see Jonah 4:2). (2) Judgment is understood in relational terms; a relationship is at stake, not an agreement. This dimen-

---

[36] Generally, judgment in the Bible refers to God's ruling in an equitable way. As such, judgment may involve a good or bad outcome: e.g., judgment against the wicked (Ps 94:4) or deliverance of the needy from such people (Ps 76:9).

sion of judgment qualifies juridical understandings. (3) God is not an objective representative of an independent court of justice. God is more like a parent, anguished over what to do about a wayward child. The flood story bears strong witness to such divine anguish (Gen 6:6–7; see Hos 6:4). We might say that this is *not* your typical courtroom. Notably, God's anguish is accompanied by strong references to God as the Creator. Such a portrayal of divine vulnerability assumes that human beings have successfully resisted the Creator's will for creation.[37] While the more objective picture in this story is disastrous judgment, the subjective image is one of divine grief.

Biblical judgment has this sense: it is the *effects* of sin, not a punishment that God "sends." Such effects witness to the way God made the world. This reality is often called the moral order, a complex, loose causal weave of act and consequence. Its basic purpose is that sin and evil not go unchecked and that God's good order of creation be sustained. *That* human sins have consequences, including violence (Gen 6:11–13), witnesses to the functioning of the moral order; this reality is named the judgment of God.

Just how God relates to the movement from sin to consequence is difficult to resolve, not least because the OT does not speak with one voice about the matter.[38] But, generally speaking, the relationship between sin and consequence is conceived more in intrinsic terms than forensic terms; that is, consequences grow out of the deed itself rather than being a penalty imposed from without. The evidence for this point of view is that several key Hebrew words for wickedness (e.g., *rā'āh*) are the same as those used for its effects (e.g., disaster). And so, such disastrous effects are "the fruit of their schemes" (Jer 6:19; 17:10). Like fruit, the consequence grows out of (is intrinsic to) the deed. Ezek 7:27 puts it this way: "according to their own judgments I [God] will judge them." Many everyday expressions make a comparable point: "you reap what you sow" (Prov 22:8); "you stew in your own juices"; and "your sins will find you out" (Num 32:23).

Interpreters have used different formulations to state how God is involved: God 'midwifes,' 'facilitates,' 'sees to,' 'puts in force,' 'mediates' or 'completes' the connection between sin and consequence. Ezek 22:31 says it well: "I (God) have consumed them with the fire of my wrath." What that

---

[37] The juxtaposition of divine wrath and divine grief is common in the prophets, especially Jeremiah.

[38] See Gene M. Tucker, "Sin and 'Judgment' in the Prophets," in *Problems in Biblical Theology: Essays in Honor of Rolf Knierim* (ed. Henry T.C. Sun and Keith L. Eades; Grand Rapids: Eerdmans, 1997), 373–388.

entails is then stated: "I have returned (*natan*) their conduct upon their heads."[39] In some contexts God is more active in this process (e.g., Jer 19:7–9); in other texts, God takes a more passive role (e.g., Ps 81:11–12). But, again, this divine "giving up" is a giving the people over to the consequences of their own choices, a reality that God has built into the very structures of creation.[40] In the flood story, creaturely violence leads to an experience of cosmic violence.

This issue is made more complex in that the moral order does not function in a precise way; it is not a tight causal weave; it is more like burlap than silk. And so it may be that the wicked will prosper (Jer 12:1), the innocent will suffer because of the sins of others (Exod 34:7), or "Time and chance happen to them all" (Eccl 9:11; cf. Matt 5:45).

The issue is made even more complex in that judgment is commonly understood in communal terms. The fall of Jerusalem to Babylon is not unlike, say, the judgment passed on Hitler's Germany by the Allied armies; no clean distinction between the righteous and the wicked is made. This may not be fair (see Gen 18:25 below), but communal judgment works this way in an interconnected world.[41] As we have noted, nonhuman creatures will also be caught up in such effects. One might wish for a world in which such effects on the environment would not occur, but can we be certain that such a world would be better than the one we currently have?

While the flood is understood to be the judgment of God, that reality is not presented as capricious.[42] Genesis 6:11–13 states clearly that violence, the violence of "all flesh," is the reason for the disaster.[43] The words in 6:5 specify the depth and breadth of the sinful *human* condition. "There is nothing hasty, ill-considered or vengeful about God's decision."[44] The divine

---

[39] Over fifty texts in the OT link wrath with such formulations (e.g., Ps 7:12–16; Isa 59:17–18; 64:5–9; Jer 6:11, 19; 7:18–20; 21:12–14; 44:7–8; 50:24–25; Lam 3:64–66).

[40] See the formulation of Gerhard von Rad regarding Israel's "synthetic view of life" and the lack of punishment language in his *Old Testament Theology* (2 vols.; New York: Harper & Row, 1962) 1:265, 385.

[41] For a thorough discussion of this issue in Gen 18–19, see Terence E. Fretheim, *Abraham: Trials of Family and Faith* (Columbia: University of South Carolina Press, 2007), 80–89.

[42] For an earlier expression of these matters, see Fretheim, *God and World*, 163–165.

[43] The phrase "all flesh" includes animals (6:19; 7:15–16; 8:17), not least in view of 9:5, where animals are held accountable for taking the life of another. This text is testimony not only to moral evil but to "natural evil." That is, the violent activity of the nonhuman world has ill effects on the earth's population.

[44] David J.A. Clines, "Theology of the Flood Narrative," in *On the Way to the Postmodern: Old Testament Essays, 1967–1998* (2 vols.; JSOTSup 292–293; Sheffield: Sheffield Academic Press, 1998), 2:508–523, here 512. (Originally published in *Faith and Thought: Journal of the Transactions of the Victoria Institute* 100 [1973]: 128–142.)

motivation is made clear: it has to do with socio-moral evil, inhumanity to others (see Cain and Lamech), not idolatry or divine irritation.

The looseness of the causal weave allows God to be at work in the "system" without violating or suspending it. In these terms, God is a genuine agent. At the same time, in judgment God always works through agents. We learn from the prophets that God and God's agents (e.g., Babylon) are often the subject of the same destructive verbs.[45] God's portrayal is conformed to the agents God uses. To read the flood story in comparable ways, God acts in and through the agents of storm and flood that actually do the destruction. Creaturely violence has had a significant level of "negative fallout," given the interrelatedness of all creatures; God mediates those consequences.

In sum, people's sin generates snowballing effects. At the same time, God is active in the interplay of human sinful actions and their effects, and "third parties" are used by God as agents for that judgment (e.g., flood waters; Babylon). Both divine and creaturely factors are interwoven to produce the judgmental result.

How does the flood story fall into this pattern? The words for "corruption" and "destruction" (Gen 6:11–13) have the same root (*šḥt*). To put it one way, *šḥt* leads to *šḥt*. This verbal linkage shows that the judgment flows out of human wickedness, referencing the appropriate functioning of the created moral order. Destruction is *intrinsically* related to corruption; violence issues in violence. All flesh has "corrupted," indeed "destroyed," its way on the earth. Such violence has disastrous ecological effects, a major flood (see Hos 4:1–3, without referring to God). As with *rā'āh* (see Gen 6:5), noted above, the language refers to both the wicked deed and, at any point along a continuum, the consequences. Certainly God states that destruction is forthcoming, indeed that God will bring a flood, but God is not said to put things on that path. Rather, "the flood of waters came on the earth" (7:6; see 7:11; 9:11, 15). Water and flood are the subjects of the verbs and God mediates those consequences. God is the author of a specific natural event only in Gen 8:1, where God makes a salvific move, making a wind blow over the face of the waters.[46]

---

[45] For a listing, see Terence E. Fretheim, *Jeremiah* (SHBC 15; Macon, Ga.: Smyth & Helwys, 2002), 36.

[46] The reference to "seedtime and harvest" in 8:22 suggests that the divine promise is more extensive than a simple reference to "no more floods."

It is important to look more closely at Gen 8:21. This verse addresses two related matters. The first has reference to *a change in the functioning of the moral order* to which God now stands committed. That is, God "will never again curse the ground [better, regard the ground as cursed] because of humankind."[47] That human wickedness continues in a post-flood world (so Gen 8:21) would threaten another such disaster—*if the basic cause and effect structures of the natural order were to continue unchanged*. In effect, God puts in place a new boundary for the way in which the causal weave functions, providing a constant natural order within which life can develop without concern about human sin "triggering" another disaster of the flood's magnitude. In effect, a flood-like move *will no longer be available to God* in view of God's own edict about the natural order.

This change in the way the created order functions is necessary if the second divine commitment is to be fulfilled, namely, God's promise regarding the future of the creation, formalized with a covenant with "every living creature" in 9:8–17. The effect of that new boundary *for God* is first stated negatively (not destroy "every living creature," 8:21) and then positively ("seedtime and harvest, cold and heat, summer and winter, day and night shall not cease," 8:22). God's promises mean that world annihilation has been set aside as a (divine) possibility. Judgment there will be (e.g., Gen 18–19), but it will be limited in scope. Sin and evil, and their now limited effects, will be allowed to have their day and God will work from *within* such a world, but not overpower it from without. God remains committed to the existence and freedom of "every living creature" and the newly established causal order; even though the effects may be horrendous, they will never again be flood-like.

Sodom and Gomorrah as Environmental Catastrophe

The location of Sodom and Gomorrah is not certainly known, but the cities are usually situated to the southeast of the Dead Sea. They lie in a major geological rift, extending from eastern Turkey to Mozambique. The Dead Sea, with its high levels of salinity, is the lowest point in the rift, some 1,300 feet below sea level; earthquakes and volcanic eruptions have occurred in the region. The text lifts up the geological character of the area (14:3, 10; 19:24, 26), with its extensive deposits of bitumen and sulfur (or

---

[47] This phrase has been thought to refer to (a) no more floods; (b) no additional curses on the ground (see 3:17); (c) the abandonment of the existing curse; or (d) more generally, the end of the reign of the curse. It seems best to regard the phrase as some combination thereof.

"brimstone," which ignites at relatively low temperatures) and petrochemical springs. It may be that an earthquake or volcano with associated fires ignited these deposits, producing a major explosion that "overthrew" these cities. Lot's wife being engulfed in the fallout is probably not a far-fetched image (19:26).

The text claims that the area around the Dead Sea had not always been desolate (see Gen 13:10). When Lot chose to settle in the area, it was a veritable paradise, "like the garden of the Lord" and like "the land of Egypt." In contrast, Deut 29:23 speaks of the area in terms of "soil burned out by sulfur and salt, nothing planted, nothing sprouting, unable to support any vegetation." In modern terms, the area suffered an environmental catastrophe. That ecological event is described in Gen 19:1–29.

What occasioned this natural disaster? According to Gen 13:13, the residents of the city were "wicked, great sinners against the Lord." Readers of Gen 13:10, 13 are thus invited to think about the relationship between the Eden-like character of that environment and the moral character of its population. Will the ecology of the area be adversely affected by the people's wickedness *over time* (see Gen 15:16)?

When readers get to the story of Sodom and Gomorrah itself (18:16–19:29), they are informed again of the cities' wickedness and God's consultation with Abraham regarding "whether they have done altogether according to the outcry that has come to me" (18:20–21; note God's "if"). Upon divine investigation (18:20–33), it is determined that Sodom's time has come. The conclusion for readers regarding the area's present state of environmental degradation is clear: it is due to *human* wickedness.

At the same time, the creational form of the disaster is not fortuitous or the effect of a specific divine decision. It is correspondent to the anti-life, anti-creational form of their wickedness. Like begets like. More specifically, the word "outcry" is also used in Exod 3:7–9 for enslaved *Israel* in Egypt (see 13:10). This link correlates with Ezekiel's view that the sins of Sodom were "pride, excess of food, prosperous ease," and they "did not aid the poor and needy" (16:49). The issue is justice, and the effect of such anti-creational conduct is similar for Sodom and Egypt: the devastation of the environment.

Scholars typically claim that this story is an etiology that seeks to explain how that region came to have its moonscape character. This may be accurate, but we must seek to come to terms with the theological interpretation that the text gives. Genesis 19:24–29 places God in the center of the action, repeatedly: "The LORD rained on Sodom and Gomorrah sulfur and fire from the LORD out of heaven; and he overthrew those cities ... when

God destroyed the cities of the Plain ... when he overthrew the cities." How one unpacks that relationship is important.[48] Keeping our discussion of the flood in mind, we might speak of God's involvement from four perspectives:

1. God created the world in such a way that deeds have consequences (viz., the moral order). The word for Sodom's wickedness in 13:13 is *rāʿāh*; the environmental "disaster" itself is described with the same word in 19:19. Wickedness (*rāʿāh*) has led to disaster (*rāʿāh*).[49] As with the flood,[50] this continuity in language shows that the consequence is *intrinsic* to the deed. Sin and its consequences are on a continuum; the effects of sin flow out of the sin itself and are named with the same word. Such effects are not introduced by God, but are already at work in the situation.
2. A close relationship exists between moral order and natural order; human behaviors can have cosmic effects. Given the interrelationship of all creatures, human wickedness can trigger environmental disruption. So, the environmental devastation in the text is not an arbitrarily chosen divine move, as if foreign armies could have completed the task without having disrupted the environment. As noted, the *creational* form of the disaster is correspondent to the *anticreational* form of the wickedness.
3. But, unlike a deistic understanding, God is not absent in the movement from act to consequence. God midwifes or "completes" the moral order, working through already existing human or nonhuman agents, from Babylonian armies to natural disasters.[51] From the sparse details given regarding this catastrophe, such natural events do take place in God's good creation or have the potential to do so. However one speaks of divine agency, the region was of such a character geologically that the requisite raw materials were available for this type of judgmental

---

[48] On the "cosmological consequences" and the link between moral order and cosmic order, see James K. Bruckner, *Implied Law in the Abraham Narrative: A Literary and Theological Analysis* (JSOTSup 335; Sheffield: Sheffield Academic Press, 2001), 158–169.

[49] The word *ʿawōn*, also used for both iniquity and its effects, occurs in 19:15 (NRSV, "punishment").

[50] Parallels with the flood have been noted, from lack of sexual restraint (6:1–4), to natural disaster, to the remnant (and God's "remembering," 8:1; 19:29), to the drunken aftermath (cf. 9:20–27 with 19:30–38).

[51] See Klaus Koch, "Is There a Doctrine of Retribution in the Old Testament?," in *Theodicy in the Old Testament* (ed. James L. Crenshaw; IRT 4; Philadelphia: Fortress, 1983), 57–87. Note the wind and waves in Exodus 14–15, where the nonhuman also is the vehicle for the *salvation* of the human.

event. One might complain that God could have chosen an agent that would not have devastated the environment in the way described. But God uses means that are available; God does not create the combustible mix of geological realities in this region just for this occasion. Given this creaturely reality with which God works, one could say that God's action is restrained by the nature of the agent available (not unlike, say, Babylon).

4. God *uses* such consequences for God's own purposes, e.g., for discipline or testing or deliverance. This story shows that God is not eager that judgment fall. God consults with Abraham about the possibility of another future; God is open to alternatives. This cuts against the grain of any notion that Israel's God is focused on judgment for its own sake; the issue is life in the midst of unchecked evil (see Ezek 18:32).

When Abraham responds to God's overture regarding the future of these cities, he is concerned that "the Judge of all the earth do what is just" (18:25). If God expects Israel to "do justice" (18:17), then certainly the reverse is true as well: *God* should do the same. Abraham is particularly concerned that the righteous in the city will be destroyed along with the wicked. In effect, he argues that a strict retribution system should be set aside for the sake of the righteous; in the process he discovers that God does not work within any such system.

Abraham's argument proceeds by asking how many righteous persons must be in the city for it to be saved. As Abraham continues to lower the numbers, God responds in a consistently positive way. God's concern matches Abraham's, point for point, marking the ends to which God will go to save the city. These numbers—which should not be pressed—speak to the issue of critical mass relative to the moral order. It is well known that, like the proverbial apple in the barrel, the wickedness of a few can adversely affect the larger group of which they are a part. Here the point is reversed: the righteousness of a few can so permeate a wicked society that they may be able to ameliorate the destructive effects of its ways. However, a build-up of wickedness can become so deep and broad that the effect of the righteous—particularly in small numbers—is too diminished to prevent those destructive effects from snowballing out of control (see Gen 15:16). For Sodom this is fewer than ten persons (cf. Jer 5:1).

By not pursuing the conversation below ten persons, Abraham tacitly admits that there comes a point when even the righteous are too few to turn a situation around and they may "fare as the wicked." At the same time, God has been shown to be more than just (and non-retributive in approach) by the willingness to recognize the potentially positive effect of a comparatively small number of righteous persons on a recognizably wicked city. And God is gracious (so 19:16, 19) in giving an alarm to those who are righteous, but they may not escape because they treat it with jest or delay (19:14, 26).

And so this text witnesses to the importance of the presence of the righteous in any situation: they may be able to subvert the effects of wickedness *from within the community* so that it can be reclaimed for life rather than death. And, the more righteous there are, the more positive difference they can make—for the world and for God. In effect, this is an argument against any defeatism or fatalism that downplays the potential impact of human activity for the good of a community. This is an argument against those who claim that nothing can be done about the environment or other societal ills. Through human activity, communal or cosmic disaster may be averted and even the wicked may participate in the resultant good. The activity of the righteous can in fact make a difference.

Even more, while the righteous *within* the city may ameliorate the effects of sin, the advocacy of those *outside the community* (in this case, Abraham) may have a comparable effect. This applies even to the most wicked of communities. In view of their relationship, God does not hide the concern from Abraham (18:17–18); so, what he has to say counts with God. God takes his energy and insights into account in shaping the divine action. Finally, because of prayers offered, one city (Zoar, even with its wicked inhabitants) and Lot's family were not destroyed (19:21, 29). In other terms, intercessory advocacy may turn a seemingly certain judgment into a new lease on life.

The text focuses on communal responsibility, on what happens when sin and its effects become systemic, so pervasive that entire communities are caught up in them. More specifically, the text links corporate responsibility and the future of the natural environment. Human behavior is understood to affect the entire ecology of an area (though the link may be difficult to discern). Many such events are just part of the normal workings of the natural order. Yet, such texts show that human behaviors can lead to environmental havoc. Sodom and Gomorrah offers a major instance; the depletion of the ozone layer in our day may be another.

In sum, this text calls for righteous action within the communities of which people are a part and intercessory advocacy for those of which they are not. What they do and say may make a difference to God and to the future of the environment. In a given situation, it may be too late. But, as with Abraham, the people of God are called to act and pray as if it were not.

Select Bibliography

Bauckham, Richard. *The Bible and Ecology: Rediscovering the Community of Creation*. Waco, Tex.: Baylor University Press, 2010.

Brown, William P. *The Seven Pillars of Creation: The Bible, Science, and the Ecology of Wonder*. Oxford: Oxford University Press, 2010.

Davis, Ellen F. *Scripture, Culture, and Agriculture: An Agrarian Reading of the Bible*. New York: Cambridge University Press, 2009.

Edwards, Denis. *Ecology at the Heart of Faith: The Change of Heart that Leads to a New Way of Living on Earth*. Maryknoll, N.Y.: Orbis, 2006.

Fretheim, Terence E. *Creation Untamed: The Bible, God, and Natural Disasters*. Grand Rapids: Baker Academic, 2010.

———. *God and World in the Old Testament: A Relational Theology of Creation*. Nashville: Abingdon, 2005.

Habel, Norman C. *An Inconvenient Text: Is a Green Theology of the Bible Possible?* Adelaide: ATL Press, 2009.

Habel, Norman C., and Peter Trudinger, eds. *Exploring Ecological Hermeneutics*. Society of Biblical Literature Symposium Series 46. Atlanta: Society of Biblical Literature, 2008.

Habel, Norman C., and Shirley Wurst, eds. *The Earth Story in Genesis*. The Earth Bible 2. Sheffield: Sheffield Academic Press, 2000.

Hiebert, Theodore. *The Yahwist's Landscape: Nature and Religion in Early Israel*. New York: Oxford University Press, 1996.

Middleton, J. Richard. *The Liberating Image: The Imago Dei in Genesis 1*. Grand Rapids: Brazos, 2005.

Santmire, H. Paul. *The Travail of Nature: The Ambiguous Ecological Promise of Christian Theology*. Theology and the Sciences Series. Philadelphia: Fortress, 1985.

Simkins, Ronald A. *Creator and Creation: Nature in the Worldview of Ancient Israel*. Peabody, Mass.: Hendrickson, 1994.

Westermann, Claus. *Genesis 1–11: A Commentary*. Translated by John J. Scullion. Continental Commentaries. Minneapolis: Augsburg, 1984.

INDICES

SCRIPTURE AND OTHER ANCIENT WRITINGS

Hebrew Bible / Old Testament

Genesis			
1–50	299	1:17	118, 592
1–11	29, 102, 112, 129, 201, 284, 303, 602	1:18	529
		1:19	592
1–9	109	1:20	118, 663, 687
1:1–4:15	458	1:22	320, 688
1–3	118, 281, 591	1:24	663, 687
1–2	685	1:26–3:24	581
1:1–2:4	35	1:26–29	664
1:1–2:3	107, 110, 112, 122, 657, 660–661, 663–664, 668	1:26–28	684, 686
		1:26–27	116, 320
		1:26	118, 313, 436, 587–588, 637, 665, 667, 689
1	20, 132, 435, 469, 577, 636, 655		
		1:27–28	119
1:1–28	353	1:27	470, 472, 478–480, 587, 664
1:1–24	581		
1:1–2	661	1:28–31	108
1:1	55, 113–115, 118, 436, 458, 547, 581, 583–585, 588, 591–592, 594	1:28	44, 118, 119, 282, 320, 412, 417, 579, 663–664, 693
		1:29–30	642
1:2	340, 436, 547, 584, 687	1:29	137, 663
		1:30	118
1:3–31	687	1:31	30, 115, 122, 638, 664, 692, 695
1:3	62, 587, 663		
1:4	529, 592	2:1–18:2	432
1:5	310	2–11	73
1:6	663	2–4	112, 138–140, 156
1:9–10	690	2–3	112, 137, 146, 149, 150, 200, 299, 545
1:9	663		
1:10	564	2	116, 137, 469, 654
1:11	549, 663	2:1–3	20, 30, 663, 688
1:12	549	2:1	110, 118, 458
1:14–19	586	2:2–3	382
1:14–16	545	2:2	549, 553, 688
1:14	378, 391, 412, 419, 529, 663	2:3	114, 590
		2:4–28:9	430
1:15	118, 412, 419	2:4–11:9	657

Genesis (cont.)		3:1–24	667
2:4–8:22	133	3:1–8	431
2:4–4:26	659, 660, 665	3:1	7, 552
2:4–3:24	107, 110, 112–113, 118, 127, 131	3:3	595
		3:6	149, 553, 595
2:4–3:19	19–20	3:7	108
2:4–2:25	636	3:8	150
2:4–24	665–667	3:9	615
2:4–5	436	3:10	549
2:4	73, 76, 77, 113–119, 127, 215, 438, 568, 592, 659	3:12	615
		3:13	615
2:5–7	137	3:14–19	317
2:5	144–145, 148–149, 151, 154, 544, 690–691	3:14	115, 595
		3:15	108, 304, 529, 546
2:6–7	564	3:16–19	640
2:6	145, 436	3:16	108, 128, 553, 595
2:7	108, 115–116, 145, 436, 666, 687	3:17–19	108, 127–128, 151
		3:17	123, 131, 644
2:8–3:19	564	3:18–19	145
2:8	151, 313	3:20–23	431
2:10	148	3:20–21	127
2:11	525	3:20	128, 317, 419
2:13	420	3:21	108
2:14	420–421, 423	3:22–24	640
2:15	148, 690	3:22	108
2:16–17	667	3:23	149, 151
2:17	377, 594	3:24	108, 146, 238, 380
2:18–21	691	4–5	458
2:18–20	690	4	77, 119, 124, 137, 154, 311, 331, 334, 338–339, 342, 344–345, 348–349, 641, 651
2:18–19	108		
2:18	666, 693		
2:19–22	693		
2:19	666, 694	4:1–26	113, 119, 668
2:20	115, 313	4:1–17	157
2:21–22	587	4:1	119, 342
2:22	128, 687	4:1–16	107, 108, 130–131
2:23	128, 317, 693	4:1–2	118, 331
2:24–25	282	4:2–16	299
2:24	282, 470, 472–473, 479, 480, 545, 552	4:2	151, 310, 331, 339, 344, 527
2:25	473	4:3–5	152
3–11	637, 643	4:3–4	285, 650
3:1–11:26	281	4:3	391
3–9	696	4:4–5	311
3–6	693	4:4	120
3	6–7, 92, 116, 127, 317, 572, 637, 640–641	4:5–7	431
		4:6–7	650

4:7	157	5:22	391, 555
4:8	108, 285, 554	5:24	555
4:9	542	5:28–29	113, 118, 359
4:10–11	131	5:28	113
4:10	342–344, 348–349	5:29	93, 123–124, 459, 644
4:11	108, 123, 644	5:30–32	113, 118
4:12	153, 527	5:32	431
4:13–15	318	6–9	19, 74, 81, 112, 360, 402, 696
4:14–15	108		
4:14	108, 153, 304	6:1–9:17	459
4:15	549	6:1–4	38, 39, 40, 75, 108, 113, 132, 133, 359, 369, 387, 396, 459, 642
4:16	139, 525		
4:17–26	118		
4:17–24	120	6:1–2	75
4:17–22	123	6:1	57, 75
4:17	108	6:2	396, 541, 547
4:18	57	6:3	38, 39, 40, 366, 459, 555
4:20–22	108, 641		
4:20	524	6:4	396, 541, 547
4:21	525, 527	6:5–9:17	108, 124, 685
4:22	525	6:5–8:22	112–113
4:23–24	108, 123	6:5–8	40, 123, 126, 131, 642
4:25–26	120, 123	6:5–7	108
4:25	119, 120, 154, 314	6:5	30, 75
4:26	57, 120, 201, 442	6:6–7	541, 691–698
4:48	497	6:6	417, 458
5–10	362	6:7	697
5:1–6:8	660, 665, 668	6:8–10	459
5	119, 120, 123–124, 138, 154	6:9–9:29	660, 665, 668
		6:9–9:17	113
5:1–32	120, 122	6:9–22	125, 126
5:1–27	113	6:9–12	200
5:1	71, 73, 77, 109, 114–115, 117, 215, 281, 320, 358, 369, 376, 438, 659	6:9	77, 109, 114, 121, 215, 220, 282, 555, 659
		6:11	642
		6:11–12	122
5:1–3	35, 119, 691	6:11–13	108, 695, 697–700
5:1–2	119	6:12	122
5:3–28	118	6:13–21	460
5:3–4	304	6:16	125
5:3	119, 314	6:17	465, 697
5:4	539	6:18	282
5:6	120, 313	7:1–4	460
5:9–11	122	7:1	220, 550, 618
5:11	139	7:3	73
5:15	396	7:4	392
5:21–24	369	7:7	113

Genesis (cont.)

7:8–9	73
7:9	478–479
7:10–12	366
7:11	392
7:12	392
7:13	541
7:14–8:14	392
7:17	113, 392
7:22	113
7:23	73, 113
7:24	366, 392
8:1	697, 700
8:3–6	366
8:3	113, 392, 544
8:4	392, 548
8:5	392, 544
8:6	125, 392
8:7	556
8:8–14	366
8:10	392
8:12	392, 527
8:13	125, 392
8:14	392
8:18	366
8:20	285, 313, 411–412, 418
8:20–21	360, 388, 391–392
8:20–22	126, 697
8:21	30, 108, 460, 642, 644, 701
8:21–22	108, 123, 126, 131, 460
8:22	392, 690, 701
9:1–17	97, 126, 668
9:1–7	108
9:1–6	642
9:4–6	388
9:4	343
9:5–6	641
9:6	320
9:7	44
9:8–17	648, 701
9:9–17	108, 460
9:10	697
9:12–17	460
9:12–13	529
9:13	465, 529
9:15–17	529, 697
9:15–16	697
9:16–17	529
9:17	465
9:18–29	112, 127, 132
9:18–27	361
9:18–19	113
9:18	113, 132
9:19	109, 113, 132
9:20–27	113, 299
9:20–21	93
9:20	154, 432
9:22	644
9:23	412
9:24–25	366, 367
9:24	311, 603
9:25–27	285
9:25	644
9:26	411
9:27	366
9:28–29	132
9:28	113
9:29	109
10–11	109, 460
10:1–11:9	660, 665, 669
10	112
10:1–32	109, 317, 361
10:1–7	113
10:1	57, 77, 109, 114, 215, 282, 659
10:2–32	361
10:2	525
10:3	526
10:4	420–421, 524
10:8–19	113
10:10–12	61, 80
10:10	420, 422
10:11	421, 526
10:12	526, 529
10:13	525
10:14	526
10:15–19	78
10:15	421–422
10:16	420
10:17	420
10:18	420–421
10:19	420, 422, 525
10:20	113

SCRIPTURE AND OTHER ANCIENT WRITINGS

10:21	57, 113	12–50	29, 31, 42, 137, 138, 284, 287, 299, 327, 462, 635
10:22–23	113		
10:23	525		
10:24–30	113	12–36	89, 90, 102, 159, 160
10:24	398	12–35	177, 303
10:25	57	12–25	167, 289, 461
10:27	524	12–22	602
10:30	525	12–21	292
10:31–32	113	12–13	38
10:32	109	12	100, 112, 129, 463, 652, 654
11	564, 643		
11–12	36	12:1–9	670, 672
11:1–10	284	12:1–4	173
11:1–9	108, 112–113, 127, 130, 317, 462, 644	12:1–3	30, 128, 130, 170, 288, 295, 643, 646
11:1	42	12:1–2	42
11:4	539	12:2–3	99, 399, 643
11:5	313	12:2	43, 44, 165
11:6	465	12:3	71, 195, 288, 383, 411, 644, 645, 647
11:7	313		
11:9	130, 131	12:4–5	289
11:10–50:26	657	12:4	7
11:10–35:29	298	12:5	191
11:10–32	109	12:6	11–12, 36
11:10–26	113, 122, 660, 670	12:7–8	285
11:10	77, 216, 109, 114, 282, 659	12:7	31, 37, 391, 463, 465, 548, 647, 671
11:11	304	12:8	362, 391
11:12	398	12:9	544
11:18–32	317	12:10–20	42, 77, 290, 362, 651, 672
11:20–27	66		
11:26	7, 137	12:10	99, 175, 420
11:26–27	289	12:12	419
11:27–50:26	281	12:15	99, 363
11:27–25:11	657, 660, 670	12:16	99
11:27–12:5	173	12:17	42, 99
11:27–32	91, 167, 672	12:19	99
11:27	77, 109, 114, 216, 282, 287, 317, 659	12:20	42, 99, 290
		12:26	168
11:28	62, 421	13	285, 293, 364, 652, 672, 696
11:29	317, 525		
11:30	289, 539	13:2–18	289
11:31–32	66	13:2	541
11:31	7, 61–62, 66, 293, 366	13:3	529
		13:4	391
11:32–12:1	7	13:5–13	364
11:32	7	13:7	421, 529

Genesis (cont.)

13:8–12	91
13:8	285, 529
13:10–17	37
13:10–15	37
13:10–13	685
13:10	92, 150, 167, 420, 423, 702
13:11	423
13:12	556
13:13–15	30
13:13	43, 702–703
13:14–17	195, 316
13:15	37
13:17–24	286
13:17	555
13:18	556
14	17, 20, 63, 65, 74, 310, 364, 672
14:1	364
14:4	549
14:5	421, 524–526
14:6	421, 541
14:7	525, 548, 550
14:10	685
14:13	412, 415, 418
14:15	420, 524
14:17–21	291
14:18–20	509
14:19–22	691
14:19–20	201
14:19	55, 401, 526
14:20	364, 391
14:22–24	101
15	42, 63, 74, 174, 312, 364, 393, 489, 501, 648, 673
15:1–21	670
15:1–4	358
15:1–3	318
15:1	412, 431
15:2–3	289, 291
15:2	422, 545
15:4–5	318
15:4	365
15:6	56, 174, 481, 487, 489, 490, 492, 552
15:7	170, 173
15:8	545
15:9–21	285
15:9	366
15:13–16	41, 315
15:14	41
15:16	702–703
15:17–21	647
15:17	366
15:18	423, 541, 671
15:18–21	31, 315
15:19	420
15:20	421
16	167, 280, 284, 289, 292, 673
16:1	93, 419
16:2	280
16:5	529
16:7–11	394
16:11–12	94
16:12	530
16:13	693
16:14	529
17	35, 37, 167, 174, 312, 463, 648–650, 673
17:1	547, 548
17:1–27	670–671
17:1–14	97, 383
17:2	44, 529
17:5	316
17:6	165, 382
17:7	529
17:8	31, 175, 671
17:10–14	579
17:10–11	529
17:11	410
17:12–13	295
17:14	383
17:15–22	671
17:15	316
17:17	57, 292, 313
17:18–26	650
17:19	650
17:20	165
17:21	650
18	92, 171, 327, 576, 645
18–19	673, 696, 701
18:1	548

18:1–8	286	20:7	8, 400, 646
18:6–8	286	20:8	321
18:7–8	144	20:9	102, 103, 298
18:8	316	20:11	250
18:10	93	20:12	290, 291, 298, 402
18:16–19:29	685, 696	20:13–16	298
18:16–33	315	20:13	546
18:17–19	645	20:14–16	100
18:18	645, 647	20:17	400, 394, 646
18:19	391	20:18	100
18:20–33	702	20:22	100
18:20–21	702	20:23	100
18:25	313, 699	21	284, 291–292, 650, 673
18:26	544		
18:28	411	21–22	77, 581, 598, 657
18:29	527	21:1–3	283
18:30–38	283	21:1–2	93
18:31–32	366	21:1	93
19	92, 324	21:3	55
19:1–29	702	21:4	97, 319
19:1–11	296	21:5	9, 55
19:1	394	21:8–21	296, 312
19:4	421, 544	21:8–14	285
19:6	412	21:9–10	93
19:8	321	21:8	286
19:10	411	21:9	296
19:11	321	21:10	296
19:14	321	21:11	598
19:15	394	21:12–13	650
19:16	541	21:12	296
19:19	703	21:14	94
19:24–29	702	21:17	598
19:24	322	21:18	78
19:26	702	21:20	94
19:27	412	21:21	498
19:29–38	18	21:22–34	317
19:30–38	312	21:23	175
19:37	421	21:27	648
19:38	420, 524	21:30	541
20	65, 100, 652, 654, 673	21:31	419
20–21	94	21:34	175
20:1–18	317	22	11, 100, 171, 189, 201, 296, 306, 311, 324, 326, 489, 492, 496, 500, 505, 507, 508–510, 515, 517, 599, 601, 649, 651
20:1	175, 529		
20:2	99		
20:3	100		
20:4–5	100		
20:6	100		

Genesis (cont.)

22:1–19	11	24:22	291, 293
22:1–2	10	24:30	291, 293
22:1	200, 394, 599	24:35	291, 293, 541
22:2	11, 321, 600	24:40	394, 555
22:8	200, 512	24:45	544
22:9–14	285	24:47	291, 293
22:9	200, 312, 391, 500	24:53	291, 293, 296, 541
22:10–12	366	24:55	541
22:10	512, 513	24:58	297, 299
22:11–12	315, 321	24:67	293
22:11	167	25	181–182, 189–190, 196, 207, 210, 356
22:12	11, 250, 602	25–35	181, 190
22:13–14	315	25–33	181
22:13	391, 550	25:1–11	284
22:14	11–12, 512, 514	25:1–6	283
22:15–18	40, 315, 321, 489, 649	25:1	528
		25:2	273
22:15	40, 167, 394	25:3	524, 525
22:17	319, 326	25:5	284
22:18	40, 512, 644	25:6	284
22:19	11	25:7	9
22:20–24	292	25:12–18	298, 657, 674
22:20–23	317	25:12	77, 114, 216, 282, 659
22:21	524	25:19–35:29	657, 660, 674
22:22	524, 525	25:19–50	581
22:23	292	25:19–34	181, 317
22:24	524, 526	25:19–20	190, 191
23	101, 291, 312, 324, 408	25:19	77, 114, 181, 216, 282, 659
23–33	181		
23:2	293	25:20	420–421
23:3–15	315	25:21–23	201
23:4	56	25:21	283, 293, 400
23:6	101	25:22–23	94
23:15	206, 529	25:22	183, 321, 556
23:16	315	25:23	8, 183–185, 294
23:17	206	25:25–26	183
24	54, 63, 66, 74, 291, 293, 296, 312, 408, 657	25:25	95, 188
		25:26	9, 188, 190
		25:27	95
24:2–3	55	25:28	95, 183
24:2	55	25:29–34	183, 285, 286, 294, 652
24:3	55		
24:3	55	25:29–33	317
24:7	55, 394, 412	25:30	95, 188
24:10	291, 293, 420	25:31	412
24:20	412	25:34	95

26	100, 181–182, 190, 654, 657	27:30–36	183
		27:31	286
26:1–6	100	27:33	99, 545
26:2–5	647, 649	27:36	102, 103, 183, 188
26:2–3	42	27:38	223
26:2	548	27:39–40	96
26:3	100, 541	27:39	195
26:4	644	27:40	59, 80, 183
26:3–5	40	27:41–45	651
26:5	40, 599	27:42–45	183
26:7–11	181, 313	27:43	210
26:10	101	27:44	187
26:12–14	101	27:46–28:9	101, 190–192
26:12	411	27:46–28:2	96
26:13	544	28	183, 189–191, 195, 197, 203, 204, 207, 210
26:16	101		
26:17–22	101	28:1–9	192
26:20	525	28:3–4	366
26:21	526	28:3	165, 547
26:24	322	28:6–9	323
26:26	524	28:6	356, 420, 421
26:28	529	28:9	298, 322
26:29	101	28:10–22	12, 181, 197, 314, 398
26:33	419	28:10–19	202
26:34–35	96, 190	28:10	12, 183, 199, 208, 210
26:34	294, 525	28:11–22	191, 208
27–33	181, 196	28:11–19	185, 192
27–30	66	28:11–12	199
27	77, 96, 181–183, 189–191, 201, 207, 209–210, 285, 294, 299, 313, 652, 657	28:11	198, 199
		28:12–15	196
		28:12–13	198, 199
		28:12	203, 394
27:1–4	181	28:13–16	199
27:1	38	28:13–15	30, 194, 647
27:4	545	28:13–14	196
27:5–17	286, 294	28:13	31, 178, 191, 194, 196, 199–200, 203, 209
27:5	181		
27:7	201	28:14	191, 192, 195–196
27:11	95	28:15	191, 195–196
27:18	181, 313	28:16	198–200
27:20	96, 201	28:17–19	199
27:24–27	181	28:17–18	199
27:24	313	28:18	199
27:27–29	322	28:19	199, 541
27:27	201	28:20	199, 202, 604
27:28	96, 181, 195, 201	28:21	183, 199, 202
27:29	183, 185	28:22	199, 202, 410

Genesis (cont.)		31:1	103, 196–197, 202–204, 207
29–31	181, 207, 210		
29–30	197, 218	31:1–16	203
29:1–11	315	31:2	203, 543
29:1	206, 210	31:3	30, 196–197, 204
29:5	194, 210, 294	31:4–12	189, 203
29:7	556	31:4–16	204
29:9	297	31:5	202, 543
29:11	316	31:5–16	204
29:13	543	31:5–53	202
29:14	543	31:7–13	203
29:17	12, 198–199, 628	31:7	203, 285
29:18	293	31:9–12	184
29:24	207	31:10–13	203
29:25	541	31:11–13	356
29:26	103–104	31:11	42, 394
29:29	207	31:13	184, 193, 202, 204, 208
29:30–31	184		
29:31–35	202	31:15	412
29:31–30:24	208	31:17–18	191
29:35	202	31:17	204
30–31	203, 653	31:18–20	383
30	93, 203	31:18	191, 204
30:1–24	284	31:19–23	204
30:1–2	216	31:19	184, 204, 311
30:2	202	31:20	58, 194–195, 204
30:8	548	31:21	194, 204
30:11	550	31:22–23	204, 210
30:21–31:16	312	31:23–53	195
30:21	294	31:23–24	58
30:22–25	184	31:23	204
30:22–24	207	31:24–25	204
30:22	283	31:24	58, 103, 184, 195
30:23	202	31:25	204
30:24	186, 202	31:26–28	204
30:25–43	184, 203	31:26	204, 412
30:25–36	320	31:27	204, 543
30:26–36	356	31:29	184, 204
30:27	196, 202	31:30–40	204
30:28–43	189	31:30	194, 204
30:29	541	31:31	204
30:30	202, 541	31:32–42	318
30:36	529	31:32	194, 675
30:37	412	31:33–35	184
30:38	411	31:33	207
30:41–43	202	31:36–44	187
31	58–59, 62, 80, 285	31:36	204

31:38–42	320	32:10–14	196
31:38–40	204	32:10–13	196, 205
31:38	204	32:10	196, 423
31:39	411	32:13	196
31:40	205	32:14–22	189–190, 205, 206
31:41–44	204	32:14–21	185, 189
31:41–42	189, 204	32:14	185, 197, 205
31:41	419	32:17	189, 529
31:42	204, 209	32:18	205
31:44–54	648	32:19	189
31:44–53	103	32:21–22	206
31:44	529	32:21	189
31:45–54	187	32:22–32	314
31:45–46	205	32:22	185, 205
31:45	205	32:23–33	185, 205–206
31:46	204–205	32:23–25	206
31:47	52, 58, 204–205	32:23	205–206
31:48–51	529	32:24–30	185
31:48–50	205	32:24–25	206
31:48	204–205, 419	32:24	206
31:49–50	205	32:25–32	206, 355
31:49	202, 204	32:25	206, 355
31:50	12	32:27	355
31:51–54	205	32:28	316, 319
31:51–53	210	32:29	322, 381
31:51–52	58, 204–205	32:30	319, 355
31:51	205	32:31	185–186, 202, 206, 356, 526
31:52	205		
31:53–54	184	32:32	525
31:53	204, 209	32:36	355
31:54	285	33	63, 78, 207, 209, 216, 652, 653
32–33	181, 189, 197, 202, 204–205, 216		
		33:1–17	205
32	210, 285, 390	33:1–9	194
32:1–9	189	33:1–7	189
32:1–3	205	33:1	189
32:1	181, 186	33:2	217
32:2–3	181, 185, 189, 206	33:3	189
32:2	185–186, 394	33:4	185–186
32:3	206	33:5	189
32:4–9	205	33:7	207–208
32:4	190, 195, 206	33:8–11	189
32:6	190	33:8	190
32:7	185	33:9	186
32:8–9	185, 189	33:10	186, 202, 206
32:8	189	33:11	189, 193
32:9	197, 541	33:14–16	206

Genesis (*cont.*)		35:19	181
33:14	195, 206	35:21–22	193
33:16–17	186	35:22–29	191
33:16	206	35:22	215, 217–218, 312, 386, 604, 605
33:17	186		
33:18–34:31	20	35:26	57
33:18–20	216	35:27–29	191
33:18	186, 191	35:27	191, 267
33:19	194	35:28	9, 304
33:20	186, 193–194, 547	36–50	294, 303
34–50	215	36:1–37:1	657, 660, 677
34–35	214, 218	36	17, 217, 317, 650
34	181, 190, 192–194, 215–218, 294, 314	36:1–43	20
		36:1	77, 114, 181, 216–217, 282, 659
34:1–31	384		
34:7	104, 384, 417, 486	36:2	322, 551
34:9	411	36:5	57
34:13–25	314	36:6	191, 551
34:14	486	36:9	77, 144, 216
34:25–36	384	36:12	366
34:25–26	486	36:15–42	316
34:27–29	296, 384	36:16	420
34:30–31	193, 217	36:22	524
34:30	384, 486	36:23	526
35	104, 181, 191–192, 312	36:24	524
35:1–7	193	36:26	524–525
35:1–5	192, 194, 202	36:27	525
35:1–3	486	36:28	524
35:1	547–548	36:31	13
35:4	421	36:35	525
35:5	193	36:39	524
35:6–7	186, 192	36:40	525
35:6	192–193	37–50	103, 213, 215, 217, 231, 581, 639
35:7	193, 202, 208		
35:8	419	37	9–10, 65, 77, 214–219, 221, 237, 263–264, 274–275, 651–652
35:9–15	191–192, 314, 393		
35:9–12	647		
35:9–10	192	37:1–2	264, 269
35:9	383, 420, 548	37:1	539
35:10	185, 539	37:2–50:26	657, 660, 677
35:11–15	192	37:2–17	218
35:11–12	104	37:2–11	269
35:11	383, 547	37:2	9, 65, 77, 114, 181, 214–218, 263, 265, 266, 268, 269, 282, 314, 603, 659
35:12	31, 557		
35:14	191		
35:16–20	186		
35:18	66, 324, 524	37:2–4	265

37:2–3	603	37:29–31	265
37:3–11	264, 265–266	37:29–30	264, 265, 267, 272
37:3–6	265	37:29	263
37:3–4	265, 269	37:30	265
37:3	9, 263, 265	37:31–36	273
37:4–5	265	37:31–35	264–266, 273
37:4	224, 265, 270	37:31–33	219
37:5–11	265, 269	37:31	265
37:5–7	237	37:32–36	265
37:5	270	37:32–33	219
37:6–21	265	37:32	265
37:8	238, 270, 528	37:33	265
37:9	237, 311	37:34	265
37:10	238, 539	37:35–36	265
37:11–18	264, 266–267	37:35	9, 265
37:11–17	270	37:36	265, 267, 273, 314, 411, 421, 423
37:11	263, 270		
37:12–28	285	38	9–10, 77, 213–215, 219–221, 224, 296, 304, 312, 677
37:12–18	265		
37:12–17	269		
37:13	265	38:1–34	219
37:14	218, 265	38:1–11	220, 474
37:15–17	218, 265	38:1	9, 55, 219, 421
37:18–36	218	38:2	219
37:18–20	270	38:5	525–528
37:18	263, 265, 270, 545	38:6	55
37:19–20	263–266, 270	38:8	411
37:19	263, 411	38:11	220, 296
37:20	543	38:12–30	219, 283
37:21–24	271	38:14	412
37:21–22	264–265, 267, 271, 312	38:15	219
37:21	218, 265	38:24	411
37:22–24	265	38:25–26	219
37:22	218, 265	38:26	214, 220–221, 224, 249, 528
37:23	265–266, 271		
37:24–25	267	38:27–30	219, 221
37:24	265, 271	39–41	219, 222, 254
37:25–28	272, 314	39	21, 231, 250, 256
37:25–27	217, 264–266	39:1–20	217
37:25	263, 265, 271, 420	39:1	219, 264, 273, 314, 423
37:26–28	219	39:2–4	652
37:26–27	221, 271	39:2	256
37:26	218–219	39:5	256, 651
37:27	263, 271, 543	39:6	628
37:28–30	272	39:7–12	312
37:28	263, 265–267, 271–272, 420	39:8–9	250, 256
		39:9	545

Genesis (cont.)

Reference	Page
39:11	603
39:14	420
39:20	541
39:21–40:23	217
39:21–23	652
39:21	411
40–41	234, 243
40	239
40:1	411
40:4	411
40:8	235, 239, 244–245, 251, 411
40:13	411
40:15	246
40:19	322
40:22	322
41	65, 241, 244, 252, 312, 313, 320
41:1–57	217
41:1–46	241
41:1	241
41:2	320
41:4	241
41:8	320
41:9–19	320
41:15	241, 311
41:16	235, 244–245, 313
41:17	241
41:22	241
41:23	410
41:25	242, 313
41:29	9
41:32	313, 411
41:33–36	259
41:33	245, 247
41:34	410
41:38–39	244
41:38	242, 257, 313
41:39	242, 244, 246
41:40	247
41:43	557
41:45	219, 420, 421, 423, 526, 677
41:45–57	244
41:45–49	247
41:45–46	264
41:46	9–10
41:47	9
41:48	234
41:49	313
41:50	57, 423
41:51–52	222
41:51	313
41:52	313
41:53–57	247
41:54	264, 551
41:57	651
42–45	248
42	217, 222, 314
42:1–4	216
42:6	315
42:7–8	221
42:7	314
42:8–9	248
42:9–14	223
42:9	239
42:16–17	223
42:16	249, 314
42:18–26	223
42:18	250
42:21–22	249
42:21	223, 319
42:24	223
42:28	314
42:30	314
42:35–38	216
42:35	314, 412
42:37–42	218
42:37–38	219
43–45	217
43:1–14	216
43:8–10	221
43:8–9	220
43:10	543
43:14	547
43:16	314
43:23	251
43:26	315
43:27	249
43:28	315
43:29–34	222
43:31	222
43:34	249

44	214	46:17	525
44:1–17	224	46:20	423, 677
44:2	541	46:21	525–526
44:5	412, 417	46:22	57
44:6	307	46:27	57, 304
44:6–13	312	46:28	408, 420–421
44:8	541	47:11	421
44:14–34	221	47:13–26	244, 247–248, 253, 256
44:15	235, 312	47:21	557
44:18–34	219, 220, 224, 249	47:22	247
44:21	249	47:25	247
44:23	528	47:26	247
44:28	411	47:27	43, 103–104
45	214, 228	46:28	221
45:1–15	224	47:29	55
45:1–13	214, 222, 224–225	47:31	551, 604–605
45:3	222, 315	47–50	312
45:4–15	653	47	10
45:4–13	315	47:8–27	318
45:4–11	221	47:9	9
45:5–8	225, 239, 250, 257	47:20–26	323, 326
45:5	251, 272, 651	48–50	213
45:6	9–10, 410	48	226, 356
45:9–13	251	48:3	547–548
45:14–15	321	48:4	165
45:15	224	48:5	57
45:19	225	48:7	420, 525
45:23	551	48:8–20	316
45:24	241	48:8	557
45:26–28	226	48:10	411, 557
46–50	43, 214	48:15	403, 548, 555
46–47	217	48:16	394
46	295	48:17–21	219
46:1–5	42, 43	48:20	644
46:2–4	30	49–50	228
46:3	547	49	20, 213–215, 226, 295, 469, 484
46:4	42–43	49:1–27	20, 319, 400
46:5–7	43	49:3–7	226
46:5–6	191	49:3–4	193, 366
46:6–27	264	49:5–7	193, 370
46:8–27	103, 316	49:8–12	193, 221, 226
46:8–10	310	49:8–10	227
46:10	421	49:9	227
46:12	10	49:10	226, 366, 558
46:13	525	49:11	52–53
46:15	294		
46:16	526		

Genesis (*cont.*)		2	29, 31
49:14	227, 547	2:1	32
49:17	227	2:24–25	45
49:20–21	366	2:24	161, 176–177
49:20	547	3–4	45
49:21	227, 547	3:1–4:17	45
49:22–26	221, 226–228	3	45, 201
49:22	227	3:6	44, 70, 161
49:23–24	227	3:7–9	702
49:24–25	630	3:7	45, 222
49:24	603	3:13–16	201
49:25–26	227	3:15	70, 161
49:25	547	3:16	161
49:27	227	4:1	45
50	31, 43	4:2–9	45
50:1–14	225	4:5	161
50:2	411	4:24–26	355
50:3–4	43	4:27–28	355
50:3	316	4:27	355
50:5	546	5:7	528
50:7–13	43	6	201
50:10	423	6:2–8	45, 97
50:11	423, 524	6:2–3	46, 70
50:12–13	181	6:3	34, 161, 177
50:14	31	6:8	161, 163, 177
50:15–21	214, 215, 225, 653	6:9	45
50:15	223, 410	6:25	482
50:17	225	7–11	34
50:20	246, 250, 257	7:11–12	233
50:23	57	7:12	233
50:24	31, 37–38, 40, 411	7:22	233
50:25–36	194	8:3	233
50:25	20, 36–37, 316	8:14	233
50:26	36, 353	8:15	233
		8:19	530
Exodus		8:25	528
1–16	375–377, 382	9:4	530
1–15	32, 657	9:11	233
1–14	470	9:28	528
1:1–12:36	660	9:30	200
1–2	17, 110	10:28	528
1:1	659	11:7	530
1:6	305	12	375
1:7–9	103	12:2–28:24	430
1:7	30, 165	12:2	593
1:9	44	12:12	34
1:17	250	12:13	507

12:37–13:19	660	32:12	31, 37
12:40	32	32:13	161
13:2	153	33:1	31, 37, 161
13:19	20, 36, 194	34:7	702, 699
13:20–22	660	34:12	48
14:1–15:21	660	34:14	48
14:2	530	34:19	153
14:3	528	35:31	232
14:11–12	652	36:4	232
14:19	381	39:32	30
14:20	530	40	663
15	163	40:7	530
15:6	52–53	40:30	530
15:22–27	660	40:33	30
16–18	658	40:38	32
16	375	41	305
16:1–36	660		
16:1	530	Leviticus	
16:18	389	1–27	660
17:1–18:27	660	10:10	530
18:12	250	11:47	530
18:16	530	12:1–5	378
19:1–2	660	12:2–5	378
19:3–40:38	660	12:4	378
19:6	385, 389, 401	17:11	388
20:3–5	48	18:16	470
20:11	20	18:18	473, 478
20:26	403	18:21	384, 496
21:10–11	473	18:24–30	387
23:32–33	48	19:1–2	490
23:19	153	19:18	250, 490–491
23:21	381	19:23–25	361
24:4–11	380	20:2	384
24:12	377–378, 380	20:11	377
25–40	30, 125	20:21	470
25:2	604	25	375, 378
26:20	587	25:43	690
26:33	530	25:46	690
28:3	245	26:3–4	156
29:25	418	26:9	165
30:18	530	26:42	161
31:6	245	26:46	530
31:12–17	97	27	65
31:13	530	27:12	530
31:17	530	27:14	530
32–34	312	27:26	153
32	465	27:34	32

Numbers				
1:1–2:34	660		2	98
1:1	8		2:6	547
3:1–10:10	660		2:23	422
3:1	114, 117, 659		3:11	12
9:1	8		3:17	423
10:11–11:35	660		3:25–27	39
11–36	658		3:26	528
11:20–21	543		4:3	482
17:13	530		4:27–28	174
18:13	153		4:32	588, 491
20:8	39		5:5	530
20:12	39, 557		5:7–9	48
21:13	530		5:25	528
20:24	557		6	333
22:1–36:13	661		6:4–5	491
22–24	469		6:4	604–605
22:2	53		6:5	398
22:4	53		6:10	37, 161
22:15	528		7:7–8	647
22:19	528		7:13	37
22:22–35	394		8:1	37
23:18	53		8:8	143
23:28	482		9:5	37, 161
24	6		9:23	547
24:6	147		9:27	161
25	482, 484, 486		10:11	37
25:10–13	649		10:14	593
25:11–13	483		11:9	37
30:17	530		11:10–17	92
31:1–12	483		12:10	253
31:16	482		12:29–31	48
32	31		13:11	528
32:11	31, 161		16:21	48
32:22	690		17:8	530
32:23	698		17:17	478–479
32:29	690		18:10	418
33:50–53	367		18:16	528
35:24	530		19:8	37
36:13	32		20:16–25:19	48
			21:15–17	215, 473, 650
Deuteronomy			22:17	163
1:1–34:12	661		24:1–4	470, 481
1:1	12, 530		24:60	163
1:8	37, 161		25:5–10	474
1:16	530		25:18	250
1:34–37	39		25:19	368
			26:3	37

27:20	377, 386	22:27–28	483, 530
28:4	157	22:30–34	483
28:11	37	24	36, 175, 179, 194, 202
28:12	157		
28:36	174	24:1	36
29:9–12	393	24:2–5	161, 173
29:10–13	393	24:2–4	36
29:12	161	24:2–3	177
29:23	702	24:2	66, 194
30:6	30	24:7	530
30:20	37, 161	24:26	36, 194
31:1–2	38	24:32	194
31:7	37		
31:17–18	398	**Judges**	
31:19–24	398	4:5	530
31:22	12	4:17	530
32:8–9	383	5:4–5	209
32:8	71	7	238
32:14	54	7:13–14	235, 238
32:18	168	7:15	238
33	20	9:23	530
33:4	163	9:37	528
33:16	52	11:14	528
33:28	253	11:27	530
34	29, 38, 465	11:37–40	295
34:1–12	12	13:1	528
34:1–4	37–38	13:15	144
34:4	31, 37, 161	13:21	528
34:7	38–40	13:25	530
34:10–12	172	16:31	530
34:12	32, 659	17–18	312
34:27	583	20:22–23	528
		20:28	528
Joshua			
3:4	530	**Ruth**	
3:8	423	1:17	530
7:12	528	4:1–12	474
8:9	530	4:18	114
8:11–12	530		
8:28	528	**1 Samuel**	
10:22	422	3:3	200
14:47	422	3:6	528
18:1	690	3:8	528
18:11	530	3:21	528
21:43–45	30	7:12	530
22:13–20	483	7:14	530
22:25	530	11:6–7	200

1 Samuel (cont.)
14:42	530
17:1	530
20:3	530
20:42	530
24:13	530
24:16	530
24:17	223
27:4	528

2 Samuel
3:1	530
3:6	530
3:9	200
5:22	528
6:7–9	200
7	649
7:10	528
7:20	528
7:25	200
7:26	200
8:3	423
8:5	422
10:16	66
13:13	232
13:36	223
14	201
14:2	232
14:10	232, 528
14:16–17	200
15:31–32	200
18:9	530
20:16	232
21:7	530
24:1	528

1 Kings
4:22–23	144
5:2–3	144
5:5	253
5:9	232
5:26	530
7:46	530
12:25–33	209
12:25	208
14:15	153
14:30	530
15:6–7	530
15:16	530
15:19	530
15:32	530
16–21	469
16:33	528
18:36	161, 177
19:3	209
19:8	209
20:34	58
22	58
22:1	530
22:4	530

2 Kings
6:23	529
8:20–22	60
8:28–29	58
8:28	59
11:17	530
13:23	161, 177
14:28	422
16:14	530
17:17	418
17:24	422
20:6	146
21:8	529
23	161
25:11–12	30
25:28	422
28:7	529

1 Chronicles
1	138
1:7	421
1:18	161
1:27–34	161
1:29	114
3:1	511
6:4	482, 485
6:50	482
9:20	482–483
16:16–17	161
21	201
21:16	530
21:30–22:1	200
22:18	690

SCRIPTURE AND OTHER ANCIENT WRITINGS

2 Chronicles
4:17	530
13:2	530
16:3	530
18:31	200
18:33	530
19:10	530
20:7	164, 170
23:16	530
30:6	161
36:23	55

Ezra
1:2	55
5:12	55
6:9	55
6:10	55
7:5	482
7:12	55
7:21	55

Nehemiah
1:4	55
1:5	55
2:4	55
2:8	149
2:20	55
8:14	55
8:15	55
9	175, 179
9:7–8	164, 173–174
10:31	55
13:1	55
13:16	55

Esther
1:5	150
2:10	55
6:2	55
6:13	238
7:8	150
8:2	247
8:8	247
10:1	248

Job
1:6–12	379
5:13	232
8:16	148
26:11	592
31:39	154
32:8	244
34:14–15	116
34:34	232
38	662
38:4–7	395
39:5–8	227
38:15	592
39:7	232

Psalms
7:12–16	699
8:5	695
8:6	572
34:20	333
36:7	601
36:12	595
37:14	346
41:2	553
47:10	161, 176
49:13	596
50:21	418
56:8	153
63:5	153
64:10	553
68:30	226
74	662
76:9	697
76:12	226
78:49	385
81:11–12	699
90	379
90:10	379
92:12	363
94:4	697
104:2	586
104:29–30	116
105	164, 173, 175–176, 179
105:5	259
105:6	161
105:9–10	161, 164
105:17	260

Psalms (*cont.*)
105:17–22	164
105:17–24	259
105:18–19	259
105:19	259
105:20	260
105:22	260
105:23	260
105:42	164, 176
107:43	232
105:44	164, 176
106	483–484, 486
106:28	482
106:31	487
111:6	594
115:13	250
118:22	244
136:26	55
139:4	591
139:13	690
148:13	117

Proverbs
1:7	232, 250, 255
1:11	347
1:24–27	248
1:33	253
2	244
2:5	250
2:16–22	256
3:23	253
4:6	232
4:9	253
4:11	232
4:26	252
5:1–23	256
6:20–35	256
7	255
7:1–27	256
8	663
8:14	245, 252
8:22	582
9:10	250, 255
10:14	232
10:19	255
10:25	592
10:31	232
11:14	252
11:15	253
11:26	256
11:30	232
12:4	474
12:16	255
12:23	255
13:14	232
14:17	255
14:27	250
14:29	255
14:30	255
15:22	252
15:30	255
15:33	255
16:1–9	251–252
16:9	252, 257
16:14	260
17:28	255
18:12	255
18:22	474
19:12	249
19:14	474
19:21	246, 257
20:22	250
20:24	251, 257
20:27	251
20:26	249
21:3	251
22:4	255
22:14	256
22:29	256
23:27	256
24:6	252
22:8	698
24:21	250
24:22	250
24:29	255
28:3	346
28:26	251
29:3	630
30:21–23	290
31:10–31	474

Ecclesiastes/Qohelet
1:9	23
1:16	232

2:3	232	41:8–9	167
2:5	147–149	41:8	161, 169, 379
2:14–23	260	41:9	167
2:24–25	260	42:6	62, 167
4:1–4	347	42:14	172
4:13	232	43:4	695
5:2	257	43:6–7	172
6:3	346	43:6	170
7:10	232	43:7	167
7:13–14	260	44:24	585
8:1	232	45:1–3	167
8:9–14	260	45:11	172
9:11	261, 699	48:12–15	167
		49:1	167
Song of Songs		49:6	170
4:12	147	49:15	172
4:15	147	51	662
4:16	149	51:1–8	166
		51:1–3	165–169
Isaiah		51:1	168
1:29	147	51:2–3	167, 172
1:30	147	51:2	62, 161, 167–169, 196
2:3–5	177	51:3	150, 166
3:3	232	51:4–5	166
3:10	592	51:9–11	166
5:3	530	51:9–10	166
5:5	146	51:11	165, 167
6	199	52:2	171, 174
6:2–3	379	52:3	171
7:2	153	54:1	168, 440
7:4	253	54:9–10	466
7:9	253	54:11–12	146
11:2	245	55:8	257
11:13	226	58:11	147, 155
18:17	226	58:13–14	170
19:11	232	59:2	530
22:2–4	669	59:17–18	699
22:22–23	169	61:11	148
29:14	232	63:7–64:11	170, 172
29:22	161, 169	63:9	379, 403
31:5	146	63:10–16	172
40:15	465	63:16	161, 169, 179
40:20	232	64:7	172
40:28	170		
41:1–8	170	Jeremiah	
41:5	170	2:27	379
41:8–13	169	4:17	149

Jeremiah (cont.)		20:20	530
4:22	232	28	233
5:1	704	28:5	232
6:11	699	28:13	146, 150
6:19	698–699	28:14	146
7:5	530	28:16	146
8:8	232	31	244
9:11	232	31:8	147, 150
9:22	232	31:9	147, 150
10:23	257	33:23–29	161, 166, 167
12:1	699	33:23–24	162, 166
13:5	423	33:24–29	166
16:13	174	33:24	46, 161, 164, 168, 178, 196
17:10	698		
19:7	699	33:27–29	162
21:12–14	699	34:1–4	690
22:1–5	692	34:20	530
28:9	422	35:10	162
29:4	422	36:2–3	162
29:5	148–149	36:5	162
29:28	148–149	36:35	155–156
30:10	253	38:12	380
31:12	147, 155	38:13	232
33:26	161, 177	43:8	530
39:12	249	44:23	530
41:5–6	208	47:16	530
44:7–8	699	47:18	530
46:2	200	48:22	530
50:24–25	699		

Lamentations		Daniel	
3:64–66	699	1:4	232
		1:8	55
		1:17	234
Ezekiel		1:20	234
1:22	593	2	235, 239, 242–243
4:3	530	2:1	305
5:5	380	2:7	244
7:27	698	2:18	55
8:3	530	2:19	55
8:16	530	2:37	55
10:6	530	2:44	55
11:14–18	162	3	258
17	244	4	235, 243
18:17	703	4:13	395
18:25	703	4:17	395
18:32	703	4:23	395
20:12	530	5	243

5:8	243	7:16	209
6	258	8:14	209
7–10	239	9:14	148, 155
7	235, 243		
8	243	Jonah	
9	243	1:2	61
10–11	243	1:9	55
10:10–14	386	4:2	697
10:20–21	386		
		Micah	
Hosea		4:1–5	669
4:1–3	700	7:20	161, 172
6:4	698		
6:6	215	Habakkuk	
10:10	260	2:4	337
12	209		
12:7	196	Zephaniah	
14:10	232	1:2–3	649
Joel		Zechariah	
2:3	156	5:9	530
		7:2	208
Amos		8:20–23	177
1:11–12	209	9:2	422
3:12	422	11:14	530
5:1	226	12:8	146
5:5	209		
7:7	199	Malachi	
7:9	209	2:14	530
7:10–17	187	3:18	530

Apocrypha

Judith		2 Maccabees	
10:3–4	363	6:18–31	502
		6:27–28	502
1 Maccabees		7	502
2	485–486, 489, 492	7:21	503
2:24–27	484	7:22–29	485
2:26	489	7:27	502
2:50–54	485	7:28	563
2:50	489	7:29	502
2:52	489, 501, 503	8:2–4	344
2:54	489		
2:55–60	485		
2:58	485		

4 Maccabees

2:11	474
6:29	505
14:5	505
16:6–25	333
16:20	505
17:1	333
17:20–22	505
18	333, 338
18:6–19	485
18:10–10	333
18:11–13	333–334
18:11	335
18:12	485
18:15	333

Sirach

1:11–2:18	250
2:18–20	347
3:29	232
8:8	256
11:1	232
14:20	232
21:5	347
21:8	347
25:1	474
25:8	474
25:22	474
26:1–3	474
26:6	474
34:1–7	257
34:6	257
34:19–22	346
44–51	484
45	486
45:1–5	484
45:6–22	484
45:23–24	484
45:25–26	484
46:1–12	484
51:15	232

Tobit

1:20	474
7:8	474

Wisdom of Solomon

2:23	572
10	335
10:1–3	338
10:1–2	332
10:1	332
10:3	332, 339–340
10:4	332, 339
10:5	332
10:3	332–333
10:6	332
10:13	332
10:20	332
11:17	687

New Testament

Matthew

5:19	490
5:21–47	490
5:21–24	341
5:48	490
7:21	491
7:24	491
7:26	491
12:50	491
14:3–4	470
19:3	471
21:31	491
23:3	491
23:5	491
23:35	336, 338
24:37	469
26:3	475

Mark

2:3	471
2:18	471
3:2	471
5:35	471
6:17–18	470
10:2–12	471
10:7–8	472

10:9	477	Galatians	
10:13	471	2	488
12:28–34	491	2:10	492
		2:11–13	489
Luke		2:14	489
3:19–20	470	2:16	488, 493
10:25–29	491	3	488
11:51	336	3:2	488
17:26–27	469	3:5	488
		3:6–9	599
John		3:6	481, 488
1:1	469	3:10	488
1:3	469	3:14	481
8:44	341	3:16	481
		3:18	481
Acts		4:22	481
2:44–45	492	5:3–6	600
4:32–37	492	5:13	493
6:1	492		
		Ephesians	
Romans		2:8–10	492
3:20	488, 493	2:10	493
3:28	488		
4:1–3	599	Colossians	
4:1	481	1:15	573
4:2	493		
4:3	488	1 Thessalonians	
4:9	481, 488	3:12	493
4:12	481	4:9	493
4:13	481		
4:16	481	1 Timothy	
4:22	488	3:2	481
5:12–21	469	5:3	492
9:7	481	5:16	492
9:17	470		
11:1	481	Titus	
12:10	493	1:6	481
13:8	493		
15:26	492	Hebrews	
		4	338
1 Corinthians		5:6–10	469
7:1–40	481	6:20	469
15:22	574	7:10–17	469
		10:38	337
2 Corinthians		11	337, 469
4:4	573	11:1–3	337
11:22	481	11:4	337, 343

Hebrews (cont.)		5:1–6	347–348
11:17–19	599	5:4	348
12:24	343	5:7	348

James		1 Peter	
1:3–4	490	3:20	469
1:3	492		
1:4	492	2 Peter	
1:22	490	2:5	469
1:25	490	2:15	469
1:27	491–492		
2	491	1 John	
2:1–13	491	3	341
2:8	491–492	3:12	336, 340–341
2:14–26	491	3:13	337
2:14	489	3:15	340–341
2:15–16	489		
2:17	489	Jude	
2:19	491	11	340
2:21	489, 492–493		
2:22	490	Revelation	
2:23	492	2:14	469
2:24	490, 493	2:20	470
2:25	493	6:9–11	344

Jewish and Christian Writers and Sources

'Abot deRabbi Natan (A)		Athanasius	
§ 1	596	*Contra Gentes*	
		2–3	574
'Abot deRabbi Natan (B)			
§ 2	477	Augustine	
		De civitate Dei	
Ahiqar		11	572
1.1C.169–170	251	15.26	575
1.1C.170	251	16	572
		18	572
Apocalypse of Abraham		*Confessionum*	
1–8	622	11	571–572
		12	571–572
Apocalypse of Sederach		*Contra duas epistulas Pelagianorum*	
1:18	338	*ad Bonifatium*	
		3.24	338
Apocryphon of John		*Contra Maximinum Arianum*	
NHC II 24.16–25	340	2.26.7	576

Augustine (*cont.*)
De doctrina christiana
| 2.16 | 520 |
| 3.18.60–21.31 | 577 |

De Genesi ad litteram
| 2.4.6 | 575 |

Homilies on Genesis
| 47.14 | 576 |

Retractationum
| 1.18 | 572 |

Babylonian Talmud
Baba Batra
| 121b | 8 |

Berakot
| 61a | 472, 666 |

ʿErubin
| 18a | 472 |

Hagiga
| 12a–13a | 593 |

Megillah
| 23b–25b | 495 |

Pesahim
| 6b | 7–8 |

Qiddushin
| 49b | 628 |

Rosh HaShanah
| 16b | 673 |

Sanhedrin
| 108a | 618 |

Shabbat
| 63a | 13 |
| 115a | 497 |

Sukkah
| 27a | 475 |

Taʿanit
| 16a | 508, 511 |

Yevamot
11b	13
15a	475
24a	13
44a	477

Basil the Great
Homilies on the Hexaemeron
| 1.6 | 570 |

2.4	571
2.5	571
6.1	571
8.1	571

Bede
Homilies on the Gospels
| 1.14 | 575 |

Cairo Damascus Document (CD)
4:14–18	368
4:20–5:6	478
16:3–4	376

1 Clement
| 4:7 | 340 |

Clement of Alexandria
Excerpts from Theodotus
| 78.2 | 567 |

Clementine Homilies
| 2.16 | 337 |

Cyprian
Epistles
| 55.5 | 337 |
| 80.2 | 337 |

Derek Eretz Rabbah
| 11.13 (57b) | 341 |

Ecclesiastes Rabbah
| 1:12 §1 | 7 |
| 6:2 §1 | 346 |

1 Enoch
1–36	359, 369
9:2	343
13:4–7	370
22:5–7	343, 348
22:7	343
26:1	380
37–71	369
60:12–21	395
72–82	369
75	395

1 Enoch (cont.)

80	395
83–90	369
91–105	369
94 ff.	347
99:11–16	347
106–107	360, 369
108	369

Eusebius
Historia ecclesiastica

2.18.1	431–432
2.18.2	431
2.18.4	431
2.18.5	430

Praeparatio evangelica

8.9.3–8.10.1	431
9.17–18	306
9.21.14	430
9.29.16	430

Exodus Rabbah

31.17	347

4 Ezra

9:7–8	490
13:23	490

Genesis Rabbah

1.1	581–582
1.3	585
1.4	585
1.5	584
1.14	579, 583
2.3	340
3.4	586
3.6	587
8.1	472, 587
8.5	616
8.9	588
11.5	590
11.6	591
11.28	460
19.11	340
22.9	346
30.9	618

45.5	673
55–56	508
55.4	509
56.11	509
58.5	673
68.9	12
80.55	10
84	273
84.7	603
84.8	629
84.13	267
85.2	678
87.6	603
87.7	604, 630
90.6	678
91.5	678

George Synkellos
Chronographia

9	337

Gospel of Ps.-Matthew

7	337

Hellenistic Synagogal Prayers

6:4	337
8:4	485
8:5	485
12:53	337
12:54	340

Jerome
Preface to the Four Gospels

	519
Preface to Job	523

Epistulae

20.2	522
34.4	522

Jerusalem Talmud
Pesahim

6.1	597

Josephus
Against Apion

1.50	306
1.183–185	422

SCRIPTURE AND OTHER ANCIENT WRITINGS

Antiquities

1.1–26	303	1.149	304
1.26	310	1.153	317
1.27–2.220	314, 316	1.154–2.200	327
1.27–2.200	303, 305–307, 309, 311, 317–318, 321, 323, 325	1.154–155	326
		1.158–160	305, 309
		1.158	335
		1.161–346	303
1.27–2.20	320	1.161	326
1.27–160	303	1.166–168	326
1.29	310	1.176	304
1.33	310	1.178	310
1.34	310	1.183	318
1.36	317	1.185	315
1.49–50	317	1.193	310
1.50	304	1.199–200	315
1.52–53	345	1.202	321
1.52	311, 344	1.203	310, 311, 322
1.53–54	345	1.204–206	312
1.53	310, 335–336, 339	1.207–212	317
1.54	311	1.208	321
1.55–56	342	1.212	311
1.55	311	1.214	310, 319
1.58	304	1.219	312
1.59	318	1.223–225	321
1.60–61	310	1.227	311, 504
1.60	345	1.228–232	312
1.61	339, 345	1.232	505
1.65	340	1.233–235	315, 321
1.66	339	1.235	319, 326
1.68	314	1.236	311, 315
1.75–103	313	1.237	315
1.80	310	1.240	305–306, 309
1.92	311	1.256	310
1.93–94	305, 309	1.257	321
1.93	311	1.265	322
1.99	335	1.267	322
1.107–108	305, 309	1.272	322
1.110–147	317	1.277	323
1.113–115	310	1.285–293	315
1.114–119	313	1.278–284	314
1.118–119	305, 309	1.317–321	317
1.129	310, 319	1.320–321	320
1.135	310	1.331–334	314
1.136	310	1.332	317, 319
1.142	311	1.333	316, 319, 322
1.148–152	317	1.334	319

Antiquities (cont.)

1.337–340	314
1.343	324
1.346	304, 310
2.1–200	303
2.1–4	317
2.3	310
2.4	322
2.5–6	317
2.10	310
2.13	311
2.21–31	312
2.32–33	314
2.42–53	312
2.63–73	320
2.69	311
2.73	322
2.74	313
2.75–94	313
2.75	305
2.107	319
2.108	306
2.113	314
2.120	314
2.126–136	312
2.126	307
2.140–158	312
2.149	335
2.152	38
2.159	315
2.161–165	315
2.166	315, 321
2.176–177	310, 316, 323
2.177–183	316, 318
2.186	324
2.188	324
2.190–193	323
2.193	326
2.194–195	316
2.194	319
2.196	310
2.198	310
2.199	305
2.338–353	310
3.95	38
4.176–193	38
6.294	335
6.308	335
7.110	335
8.1	433
8.21	335
8.394	335
10.195	305
13.1	433
14.1	433
15.1	433
17.14	474
18.136	470
18.259–260	308
20.1	433

Jewish Wars

1.477	474
3.141–408	504
4.483–485	310
7.320–401	505

Life

424–425	308
429	308

Jubilees

1:1	381
1:5	381
1:7	381
1:13	398
1:15	398
1:16	402
1:19–21	400
1:22–26	400
1:23	398
1:26	381
1:27	381
1:28–29	381
1:28	381
1:29	376
2:1–50:13	379, 381
2:1	378, 381–382
2:2	395
2:3	395
2:9	392
2:17–22	397
2:17–20	395
2:23–25	399
2:23	398

2:24	377	7:21–22	396
2:26–33	382	7:23–25	388
2:31–33	399	7:34–39	391
3:8–14	378	8:2–4	376
4:1	331	8:11–12	376
4:15	340, 396	8:12–9:13	361
4:17–23	376	8:19	378, 380
4:22	396	10:2–6	400
4:26	379	10:5	397
4:28	360	10:8	385, 397
4:30	377	10:9	397
5	359	10:13–14	376
5:1–7	387	11–12	174
5:1	396	11:6–7	460
5:2	396	12:1–8	622
5:6	396	12:27	376
5:9	396	13:10–16	363
5:11	396	13:10	362
5:13	387	13:15–16	401
5:17–18	388	14:20	393
6:1–3	400	15:25	383, 387
6:2–3	361	15:26–27	395
6:7–8	388	15:26	384, 387
6:10	388	15:27	383
6:11–12	388	15:28–33	383
6:12	388	15:28–29	383
6:13–14	388	15:28	384
6:13	388	15:30	384
6:18	395	15:31–32	383
6:20	389	16:17	385
6:22	377	16:18	385, 389, 401
6:23–27	392	16:20–31	393
6:28–29	392	16:26–27	385, 401
6:29–30	392	16:30	385
6:32	389, 392	17:13	385
6:34	389	17:15–18:12	397
6:36–37	392	17:15–17	379
6:38	389	17:16–18	385
7:1–6	400	17:17–18	514
7:7–13	361	18:3	385
7:16	500–501	18:12	386
7:17–18	501	18:13	513
7:20–39	400	19:9	379
7:20	397	19:17–25	399
7:27	397	19:25	399
7:21–23	396	19:26–29	399

Jubilees (cont.)

20:1–4	394	31:14–17	390
20:6–10	400	31:18–20	383, 390
21:1–26	400	31:26–30	400
21:7–20	391	32:1–26	393
21:7	376	32:3	390
21:10	376	32:17–29	398
21:24	385	32:28	393
22:10–30	400	32:36	376
22:10–24	399	33:3–6	386
22:11–12	385	33:7	386
22:13	385	33:8	386
22:18	379	33:9–12	386
22:27–30	399	33:9	386
22:27	385	33:9–10	387
23:9–15	379	33:12	377
23:32	381	33:13	386
24:21–38	375	33:14	386
25:1–3	399	33:15–16	386
25:12	385	33:18	381
25:13	399	33:19	386
25:14	399	33:20	386, 389, 401
25:15–23	399	34:1–9	375
25:18	385, 399	34:18–19	388, 393
27:1–12	399	35:1–6	399
29:7	393	35:9–17	400
30:5	384	35:18–27	400
30:6	384	35:22	386
30:7	384	37–39	327
30:8	384	39:6	377
30:9–10	387	45:16	376
30:9	384	48:15–19	397
30:10	384	49:2–6	397
30:11	384	49:2	385
30:12	381, 384	49:4	385
30:13	384	49:6	385
30:14	384	49:8	385, 387
30:15–16	384	49:9	387
30:16	384	49:10	385
30:17	384, 486	49:13	385
30:18–21	385	49:14	385
30:21	381	49:15	385
30:22–23	376	49:16	385
30:22	387, 486	49:18	385
30:23	486	49:22	385
31:13–14	395	50:1–13	382

50:5	381–382	8:3	463
50:6–12	375	9–65	463–464
50:9	382	9:3	467
50:10	382	9:5–6	464
50:13	381–382	10:2	467
		12	464
Justin Martyr		12:1	464
1 Apology		12:3	464
10	566	12:4	465, 467
59–60	568	13:7–9	464
59	566	13:7–8	464
Dialogue with Trypho		14:2	467
141	475	15:5–6	464
		16:2	464
Leviticus Rabbah		17:2–4	464
2.11	507	18:5–6	464
		18:5	464, 506
Liber antiquitatum biblicarum		19:3	467
1–8	447, 457–458, 464, 466	19:7	450
		19:10–11	465
1–2	458, 460	19:11	464, 466
1:20	459, 466	20:4	467
2:1	458, 464	21:5	464
2:7–9	460	21:9	467
2:10	459	22:3–7	467
3	459	22:8	452
3:1–2	459	23:4–9	464
3:4	460, 466	23:11–13	467
3:8	460–461	24:5–6	464
3:10	460	26:6	464
3:11	461	26:13	451
3:12	460, 466	28:1	485
4	460	28:3	485
4:5	460, 466	32:1–10	464
4:11	460, 466	32:2–4	464
4:16	460	32:2–3	506
5	460	32:3	451, 506
6–7	464	35:2	467
6:1	461	36:4	455
6:4	461	37:3	464
6:11	462	39:5	464
7	462	39:8–9	450
7:2	465	40:2–3	464, 506
7:3	465	42:2–5	464
7:4	462, 466	43:5	455, 464
8	327, 462, 464	45:3	455

Liber antiquitatum biblicarum (cont.)
45:6	452
48:1–3	485
49:6	467
50:1–3	464
59:4	464
60:2–3	464
61:5	467

Martyrdom and Ascension of Isaiah
9:7–10	337
9:28	337

Mekilta deRabbi Yishmael
Beshallah § 7   7

Mishnah
'Abot
5	598
5:3	514
5:26	579

Hagiga
2:1	591

Ketubot
10:5	477

Megillah
4:4–10	495
4:9	496

Sanhedrin
4:40	343
10:1	602

Ta'anit
2:5	507
4:6	450

Tamid
4:1	500

Numbers Rabbah
20.6	340

Origen
Commentarium in evangelium Matthaei
17:17	431

Contra Celsum
4.51	431

Philo
De Abrahamo
1–6	435
1	438
2–5	434, 443
2	443
4	442
7–47	441
52–54	442
176	504
197–198	503

De aeternitate
19	438

De agricultura
21	340

De cherubim
52	340, 345
65	345

De confusione linguarum
122	346

De congressu eruditionis gratia
34–38	442

De decalogo
1	435
101	434

De ebrietate
1	433

De fuga et inventione
2	433
60	340, 346
64	340, 346

De Ioseph
1	434–435, 442
22.125–26.156	327
36.211	307

Legum allegoriae
1	431
1.19–20	438
2	431
3.139	434
4	431

De migratione Abrahami
13.74	344
89–93	444

De mutatione nominum		*De somniis*	
12	442	1.1	433
88	442	1.168	434, 442
De opificio mundi		1.195	504
1–3	443	*De specialibus legibus*	
2	443	1	434
26	436	1.1	435
32	436	1.212–219	434
72	436	2	434
129	436, 438	2.1	435
131	436	3	434
133	436	3.1–6	434
134–135	436	3.7	435
139	436	4	434
De plantatione		4.1	435
1	433	4.132–135	435
De posteritate Caini		*De virtutibus*	
42	339	52	435
49	340	65	444
65	438	199	340
129	438	*De vita Mosis*	
De praemiis et poenis		1	434
1–3	434–435, 439	1.76	442
		2	434
7–23	441	2.45–47	434, 443
24–51	442	2.47	439
53	435	2.48	443
57–66	442	*Quaestiones et solutiones in Genesin*	
72	340	1.1	438
74	340	1.59	334, 336, 340
158	440	1.68	342
De providentia		1.70	343
2.40–41	440	2.67	432
De sacrificiis Abelis et Caini		*Quis rerum divinarum heres sit*	
1.5	340	1	431, 433
10	334	*Quod deterius potiori insidari soleat*	
14	334	32–34	346
51	431	32	334
52–56	345	78	346
136	434	96	340
De sobrietate		103	339
1	431, 433	119	339
9	434		
52	431	Photius	
65	442	*Bibliotheca*	
		col. 103	431

Pirqe Rabbi Eliezer

3	586
30	598–599, 623
31	602
38	678

Ps.-Ignatius
Hero

5	340

Qumran
1QS

5:1	368
6:21	368
7:20	368
8:11	368
9:7	368
9:10	368

1QapGenesis

0–17	358
0:2	359
1:2	359
2–5	359
2	357, 360
3–5	360
5:4	360
5:29	360, 376
6–17	360
6	360
6:11–7:5	360
7:7	360
11	361, 364
12:10–12	361
13–15	361
13:16–20	361
14:9	361
15	361
15:10–12	361
16–17	361
18	358, 362
19–22	357–358
19	362
19:14–19	362
19:19–21	363
19:24–29	363
20:2–8	363
20:9–10	363
20:10–16	364
20:32	364
21	361
21:5–20	364
21:8–20	364
21:8	364
22	364
22:17	365

4QCommentary on Genesis A

1–4	366
1:5–10	367
1:7	367
2:5–7	367
2:8–10	367
2:8	367
3:1–6	367
3:14	367
4:1–3	367
4:2	366
4:5–6	368
4:3–6	367
4:5	366
5:5	368

4Q158
    frags. 1–2   355, 357
4Q243
    frag. 28, line 2   485
4Q364
    frag. 3, col. ii   356–357
    frag. 4b–e, col. ii   356–357
    frag. 5b, col. ii   357
    frag. 10   357
4Q394
    frags. 3–7, 1:6–8   488
4Q398
    frags. 14–17, 2:2–8   486
4Q399
    1:10–2:5   486
4Q416
    frag. 2, 3:21–4:13   479
4Q522
    frag. 9, 2:6–7   485

6Q13
  frag. 1, line 4   485
11QTemple
  57   478
  57:15–19   478
Rashi
  at Gen 1:1   584, 594

Sibylline Oracles
  3.97–104   306
  3:307–313   344
  36:13   313
  36:19   313

Sifre Deuteronomy
  § 31   604–605

Sifre Numbers
  § 64   7
  § 112   7

Tanhuma
  1.11 (on Gen 1:1)   594

Targums
Neofiti
  Gen 4:8   337
  Gen 22:8   513

Onqelos
  Gen 4:14   304
  Gen 22:14   511–512

Ps.-Jonathan
  Gen 3:15   304
  Gen 4:14   304
  Gen 22:1   514–515
  Gen 22:9   515–516

Gen 22:10   515
Gen 41:45   678
Gen 46:20   678

Tertullian
Adversus Judaeos
  3   590
De patientia
  5   340

Testament of Issachar
  5:4   338

Testament of Moses
  9:6–7   344

Theophilus of Antioch
To Autolycus
  1.2   563
  1.4   563
  1.5   563
  1.8   563
  1.9–11   563
  1.11   564
  2.2–8   563
  2.10   564
  2.12   564
  2.15   564–565
  2.16–17   565
  2.19   565
  2.32   569
  2.36   565
  4   566

Tosefta
Yevamot
  1.1–10   475
  1.10   475

EGYPTIAN, GREEK, MESOPOTAMIAN, AND ROMAN WRITERS AND SOURCES

Aesop
Fabulae
  127.1.8   414
  127.3.7   414

Antiphanes
Fragmenta
  168.3   422

Aristobulus			Macrobius	
frag. 2	431		*Saturnalia*	
			5.15	22
Book of the Dead				
30B	240		Megasthenes	
			Fragmenta	
Demetrius			40.15	422
frag. 2	430			
frag. 5	430		Plato	
			Leges	
Egyptian Wisdom			3.679B3–C2	345
Amenemope			*Theaetetus*	
Prol. 1.1–2	253		176A	573
§4	253			
§5	253		Plutarch	
§7	253		*Alexander*	
§15	253		1.2	441
§18	251, 253, 257		*Nicias*	
§30	256		1.5	441
Ptahhotep			*Pericles*	
§6	251, 253, 257		1.1–2.4	441
§10	253		1.2	441
§36	249		*Timoleon*	
			1	441
Epic of Gilgamesh			*Quomodo quis suos in virtute sentiat*	
XI 145–154	126		*profectus*	
			84B–85B	441
Hecataeus of Abdera				
Fragmenta			Theophrastus	
3a.264.F, frag. 25, l. 679			*Historia plantarum*	
	422		3.15.3	422
Homer			Thucydides	
Odyssey			7.55	306
book 9	92			
book 19	189			

Islamic Writings

al-Tabari			Quran	
§280	598		2:22	614
§281	598		2:28–39	614
§283	598		2:30	616
§290–301	600		2:42	607
§302–304	602		2:59	607
§302	601		2:75–79	607

2:127–128	623	12:104	624
2:127	622	12:110–111	628
3:71	607	13:17	614
3:78	607	14:32–33	614
3:84	610	15:19–48	614
4:46	607	15:29	614
4:125	620	16:10–16	613
4:163	610	16:80–81	614
5:13	607	17:70	614
5:41	607	19:40	621
6:1	613	19:41–50	621
6:74	621	20:115–122	614
6:76–80	621	20:122–123	616
6:79–83	621	20:123	616
6:87–90	610	21:31–32	614
6:91	607	21:51–71	621–622
7:1	617	21:69	622
7:5	615	22:36	614
7:10–25	614	22:65	613
7:54	613	23:18–22	614
7:60–65	618	26:69–104	621
7:84	623	26:70–71	622
7:162	607	26:133	613
10:94	612	29:16–25	621
11:25–49	618	37	602
11:38	620	37:83–98	621
11:46	620	40:34	623
12:3	623–624	41:9–10	613
12:8	625	43:10–12	614
12:18	625	43:26–28	621
12:21	624	45:13	613
12:22	624	55:1–78	614
12:24	625, 630	60:4	621
12:30–34	626	66:10	619
12:33	624	71:7	618
12:39	626	78:6–16	614
12:40	628	95:4	613
12:51	627		
12:52	627	*Tales of the Prophets*	
12:56–57	627	§ 52	598
12:100	627	§ 54	601–602
12:101	624		

Papyri

Berlin		Insinger	
15683	236	32.13	234
Cairo Zenophon		*Publicazioni della Società italiana*	
I.59009b.3	422	VI.616.21	422
I.59009b.5	422		
		Tebtunis	
Carlsberg		16	236
XIVa, 2	236	17	236
XIVf, 1	236x		
		Yadin	
Chester Beatty		12	476
III	241	26	476
III.9.26	236	26.11–14	476
III.3.4	236	34	476
III.4.5	236	34.2–5	476
IV.v.2.5–6	235		
IV.v.3.7–8	235		

MODERN AUTHORS

Abegg, Jr., M.G., 478–479, 487–488
Achenbach, R., 36, 132
Ackroyd, P.R., 523, 536
Adang, C., 608, 611, 632
Addis, W.E., 264, 277
Adler, W., 523
Agus, A.R.E., 506, 517
Ahituv, S., 59, 209
Aland, K., 469
Albani, M., 40, 376, 382, 389, 404
Albeck, C., 579, 582–588, 590–591, 597, 603–604
Albertz, R., 62, 107, 195, 210, 653
Alexander, P.S., 380, 453
Alexander, T.D., 4
Allegro, J.M., 354
Allenbach, J., 437
Allison, D.C., 336, 341, 350
Alter, R., 54, 74, 84–89, 92, 94, 98, 104, 137, 228, 249, 276, 639, 656
Altmann, A., 604–605
Amar, J.P., 558
Amit, Y., 652
Anbar, M., 173–174
Anderson, B.W., 27, 49, 265
Anderson, G.A., 226, 351, 387, 605, 640, 656
Anderson, G.W., 28
Andriolo, K.R., 291
Aptowitzer, V., 350
Ariès, P., 279.
Arneth, M., 112, 115, 119, 128, 132–133
Arnold, B.T., 4, 25, 145, 149, 154
Asad, M., 624
Astruc, J., 16–19, 22, 25, 110–111, 113, 427
Attridge, H.W., 321, 328, 335, 337, 339, 347, 354
Aucher, J.B., 429
Auerbach, E., 87, 90, 104, 189, 600
Auffarth, C., 396

Avemarie, F., 40
Avigad, N., 357–358, 372

Bacher, W., 597
Bachmann, M., 488
Baden, J.S., 29, 63, 73, 81, 160, 267, 277, 643
Baillet, M., 353
Bar-Asher, M., 380
Bardtke, H., 110
Barnes, W.E., 54
Baron, S.W., 534
Barr, J(ames), 640, 656
Barr, J(ane), 534
Barrera, J.T., 385
Barstad, H.M., 159
Barthélemy, D., 353
Bakhos, C., 580–581, 597, 599, 602, 604–605, 623
Barton, J., 63, 72
Baker, D.W., 4
Bassler, J.M., 350
Bauckham, R.J., 340, 453, 461, 467, 706
Baumgart, N.C., 109, 112, 125, 131, 133
Bautch, R.J., 179
Bearman, P.J., 632
Becker, J., 250
Beeston, A.F.L., 608, 629, 632
Berchman, R.M., 511
Berkovits, E., 674, 681
Begg, C.T., 318–321, 328, 335, 465
Bellis, A.O., 640
Ben-David, A., 95
Ben Ezra, D.S., 359
Berges, U., 170
Bergman, J., 144
Berlin, A., 86, 88, 104, 657, 681
Bernstein, M.J., 359, 361–362, 365, 367, 372, 377, 453–454, 488, 501, 517
Bernstein, M.S., 609, 624–625, 629

Berthelot, K., 359
Best, E., 480
Beuken, W.A., 169, 171
Bianquis, Th., 632
Biberger, B., 179
Biddle, M.E., 3, 27, 43, 98, 213, 265, 277, 427, 652
Billen, A.V., 521
Birnbaum, E., 444, 446
Blenkinsopp, J., 112, 115, 127, 133, 179, 299, 645
Bloch, H., 328
Blum, E., 4, 29, 30, 34, 36–37, 40–43, 45–46, 49, 55, 108, 111–112, 119, 127–128, 130, 134, 160, 166, 173, 179, 181, 188, 191–196, 198–202, 204, 206–207, 209–210
Blumenthal, D., 674, 681
Bockmuehl, M., 580
Bogaert, P-M., 450–452, 456, 459, 461, 468
Bonfrère, J., 13, 25
Borbone, P.G., 559
Borgen, P., 435–436, 445
Borowski, O., 142–143, 149, 157
Bosshard-Nepustil, E., 112
Bosworth, C.E., 632
Bouteneff, P.C., 561
Bowley, J.E., 305, 328
Bradley, C., 152
Braudel, F., 64–65, 79
Brenton, L.C.L., 406
Brettler, M.Z., 36, 39, 174, 657, 681
Brewer, D.I., 473, 477, 479, 481, 494
Brinner, W.M., 597, 607, 611, 616, 619, 620–622, 624–625, 628–632
Brock, S.P., 350, 537–538, 540, 548, 554–555, 559
Brooke, A.E., 341
Brooke, G.J., 248, 354, 365–367, 370
Brooks, R., 343, 351
Brown, C.A., 449, 456
Brown, D., 531, 534
Brown, P., 594
Brown, R.E., 337, 341
Brown, W.P., 685, 690

Bruckner, J.K., 703
Brueggemann, W., 639, 643, 656
Buber, M., 187–188, 662, 681
Buber, S., 594
Budde, K., 113, 120, 122, 127, 129, 134
Bührer, W., 116, 128
Bultmann, C., 110
Burkhardt, H., 438, 445
Burnette-Bletsch, R., 456
Bury, R.G., 582
Buttmann, P.C., 118
Byron, J., 341, 350

Calder, N., 612, 619, 632
Callicott, J.B., 684
Camelot, P.-T., 573, 577
Cameron, R., 584
Cancik, H., 588
Caquot, A., 449
Carr, D.M., 28, 31, 34–35, 42, 49, 77, 81, 112, 114, 119, 123, 127, 130, 134, 160, 199, 210
Carruth, W.H., 427
Carstens, P., 164
Carson, D.A., 453
Chares, R.H., 383
Chadwick, H., 590
Charlesworth, J., 354, 368, 428, 450, 467
Chavel, C.B., 8, 26
Chazon, E.G., 358, 360
Chilton, B., 350, 496, 498–499, 511, 517
Chipman, J., 677, 682
Choi, J.H., 149
Clifford, R.J., 138
Clines, D.J.A., 37, 39, 49, 699
Coats, G.W., 11, 195, 210, 214, 224, 228, 254, 261, 653, 656
Cogan, M., 60
Cohen, G.D, 604–605
Cohen, J., 579, 606
Cohen, M., 280
Cohen, S.J.D., 579
Cohn, L., 429, 434, 448, 455, 467
Cohn, R.L., 91
Colenso, J.W., 24

Colish, M.L., 576, 577
Collins, J.J., 32, 299, 343, 351, 451
Colson, F.H., 429, 582
Congar, Y.M.-J., 561, 562, 577
Connelly, B., 69
Cook, E.M., 478–479, 487
Cook, J., 559
Cotton, H.M., 475
Cox, C.E., 425
Cox, D., 250
Craven, T., 146
Crawford, S.W., 354, 356, 358–359, 362, 366, 372, 377, 453, 454
Crenshaw, J.L., 254, 703
Cross, F.M., 52, 69–70, 77, 84, 97, 116, 658
Crouzel, H., 5
Crüsemann, F., 63, 112, 129–130
Cummings, J.T., 534

Dahl, N.A., 341
Dalferth, I.U., 200
Damrosch, D., 88, 104
Daube, D., 472
Davenport, G.L., 404
Davies, E.W., 474
Davies, G.I., 45, 49
Davies, J., 132
Davies, P.R., 378, 511, 517
Davila, J.R., 353–354, 372
Davis, E.F., 142, 684, 706
Davis, M.S., 473
Day, P.L., 457
de Boer, M.C., 488
de Hoop, R., 52, 226
de Lange, N., 5
de Lagarde, P., 537
de Lubac, H., 5
de Montfaucon, B., 419
de Moor, J.C., 4, 25
de Pury, A., 34, 50, 180, 192
de Roo, J.C.R., 481, 487
de Vaux, R., 353, 354
de Wette, W.M.L., 23, 25
Demos, J., 280
DesCamp, M.T., 456–457, 467

deSilva, D.A., 333, 337, 343
Denis, A-M., 331, 340
Delitzsch, F.J., 5, 25
Dell, K.J., 45, 49
Dever, W.G., 287
Dewey, A.J., 584
Dibelius, M., 348
Dickens, E.W.T., 28
Diedrich, F., 205
Diesel, A.A., 112, 134
Deissmann, A., 408, 424
Dietrich, W., 4, 46, 134
Dillmann, A., 169, 193, 205, 222
Dillon, J.M., 432, 433
Dimant, D., 376, 379, 385
Dimen, M., 155
Dirksen, P.B., 537, 540, 542, 546, 552, 559–560
Diver, S., 148
Dochhorn, J., 341, 350
Doering, L., 382
Dogniez, C., 383
Dolansky, S., 60, 73
Donaldson, M.E., 288, 299
Dommershausen, W., 142
Douglas, M., 87
Dozeman, T.B., 28, 31, 42, 45, 49, 63, 111, 160, 173, 179, 192, 194
Drechsler, M., 3, 25
Driver, S.R., 56, 264–265, 277, 473
du Boulay, J., 142
du Preez, R., 474
Dungan, D.L., 478
Dunn, J.D.G, 488
Durand, J-M., 67–68
Dutcher-Walls, P., 280, 299
Dyma, O., 206

Eades, K.L., 698
Edelman, D.V., 159
Edgar, C.C., 422
Edgar, D.H., 348
Edwards, D., 706
Edwards, R.B., 341
Ego, B., 40
Ehrlich, A.B., 270

Eichhorn, J.G., 18–19, 25, 111
Eisenberg, I., 621
Eiss, W., 389
Elbogen, I., 658, 681
Elior, R., 593
Elliger, K., 33, 166
Ellingworth, P., 332, 337
Eltester, W., 341
Elwolde, J., 52
Emerton, J.A., 12, 29, 33, 46, 50, 57–59, 62–63, 81, 177, 195
Endres, J.C., 400, 404
Epstein, L.M., 474, 494
Eskenazi, T.C., 657, 681
Evans, C.A., 469, 474, 481, 490, 534
Evans, C.F., 523
Everson, D.L., 532
Eshel, E., 358, 362, 371, 373, 385

Fabry, H-J., 152
Fackenheim, E., 674, 681
Falk, D.K., 358, 372, 377
Feldman, L.H., 303, 305–309, 313, 315–316, 320–323, 325–326, 328, 334, 339, 342, 345, 435, 447–450, 452, 454, 456, 459–460, 462, 467, 618
Fernández Marcos, N., 409, 424, 520–521, 535, 536
Field, F., 419, 424
Finkelstein, I., 159, 208
Finkelstein, L., 604, 605
Firestone, R., 597, 599–600, 622, 632
Fischer, B., 520, 534
Fischer, G., 28
Fischer, I., 171, 179
Fishbane, M.A., 181, 210, 235, 535, 663
Fishman, D.E, 580
Fisk, B.N., 449–450, 452, 454–456, 458, 463, 465–467
Fitzmyer, J.A., 358, 362, 373, 479, 494, 501, 517
Fleischer, E., 384, 580
Fleming, D.E., 66–68, 81
Flesher, P.V.M., 511, 517, 554, 560
Flint, P.W., 365, 481, 488
Flüchter, S., 175

Foerster, W., 566, 578
Fohrer, G., 165, 168, 170
Fokkelman, J.P., 86–87, 104, 181, 187, 211
Fox, M.V., 213, 231, 237, 240, 254, 256–257, 261
France, R.T., 453, 467, 471
Franxman, T.W., 303, 328
Freedman, D.N., 52, 277
Freedman, H., 346
Frei, H.W., 83–84
Feliks, J., 669
Fretheim, T.E., 642, 646, 656, 684–685, 687–688, 690, 693–695, 699–700, 706
Frevel, C., 33, 39
Frey, J., 40, 376, 382, 389, 404
Friedl, E., 155
Friedländer, M., 667, 681
Friedman, R.E, 265, 277
Frye, N., 84
Frymer-Kensky.T., 98

Gaiser, F.J., 694
Galling, K., 27, 46
Gardiner, A.H., 236
Garnsey, P., 141, 143, 156
Garr, W.R., 34, 68
Garscha, J., 162, 179
Garsiel, M., 188
Gaston. L., 175
Geljon, A.C., 436
Gertz, J.C., 31, 36–37, 41, 44, 46, 49, 111–112, 116–117, 123–124, 128–129, 131–134, 160, 176
George, A.R., 74
Gese, H., 33
Gevirtz, M.L., 363
Gibert, P., 14, 16, 25
Ginzberg, L., 534, 629
Gitin, S., 69
Gittin, S., 287
Glenthøj, J.B., 350
Glucker, J., 433
Goldin, J., 506, 518, 601, 606
Goldingay, J., 165
Goldstein, J., 171, 179

Golka, F.M., 213, 228
Good, R.M., 170
Goodenough, E.R., 435
Goodman, M., 435, 445, 475–476
Goren, Y., 475
Goshen-Gottstein, M., 170, 363
Gosse, B., 163
Gottwald, N.K., 155, 157
Grabbe, L.L., 159
Graetz, H., 584
Graf, K.H., 24
Graham, W.C., 547
Granger, F., 582
Graupner, A., 193, 204, 206
Graves, M., 534
Grayson, A.K., 61
Green, W.H., 3, 25
Greenberg, M., 146, 151
Greene-McCreight, K., 201
Greenfield, J.C., 151, 357, 370–371, 475
Greenspahn, F.E., 228, 429
Gregg, J.A.F., 332
Grelot, P., 488
Gnuse, R.K., 637
Gryson, R., 520
Grieve, A., 408, 424
Grigg, D., 142–143
Groenewald, A., 4
Groß, W., 117
Grossfeld, B., 514
Grüneberg, K.N., 195, 644
Grypeou, E., 350, 594
Gunkel, H., 3, 6, 24–25, 27–28, 38, 43, 46, 113, 119, 182, 187, 195–196, 199, 205, 211, 213, 222, 225, 264–265, 267, 277, 427
Gunneweg, A.H.J., 175

Ha, J., 49, 163
Haacker, K., 38
Habel, N.C., 148, 157, 684, 689, 706
Hackett, P., 188
Hagedorn, A.C., 34, 45–46, 50, 107, 112, 134, 179, 209
Hagen, F., 87
Hagendahl, H., 535

Halberstam, C., 86
Hall, C.A., 578
Halpern, B., 69, 154
Halpern-Amaru, B., 307, 328, 385, 399, 404, 452–453, 457, 463, 467
Hanneken, T.R., 387
Haran, M., 267, 426, 445
Hardmeier, C., 180
Hadot, J., 449, 450
Hareven, T.K., 280, 293
Harl, M., 5, 383, 415
Harrington, D.J., 447–453, 456, 459, 467
Hastings, J., 522
Haupt, P., 265
Hartenstein, F., 47
Hawting, G.R., 612, 632
Hay, D.M., 429–430
Hayes, C.E., 385, 404
Hayman, A.P., 664, 681
Haynes, S.R., 670
Harvey, G., 132
Hayward, C.T.R., 350, 378, 380, 393, 535, 618
Hazony, Y., 677, 681
Hedrick, C.W., 584
Heller, B., 601
Heinemann, I., 601
Heinrichs, W.P., 632
Hempel, C., 395
Hendel, R.S., 27, 39, 57, 63–64, 70, 73–76, 78, 81, 84–85, 94, 211, 373
Hengstenberg, E.W., 5, 25
Henke, H.P.C., 114
Hennings, R., 535
Henrichs, A., 584
Henze, M., 428, 445
Herczeg, Y.I.Z., 8, 26
Hermisson, H-J., 165–166
Herr, M.D., 589
Hertzberg, A., 678, 681
Heschel, A.J., 663, 674, 681
Hess, R.S., 154, 407
Hiebert, R.J.V., 413–415, 424–425
Hiebert, T., 144–145, 152, 157, 706
Hieke, T., 119

Higger, M., 598
Hilgert, E., 429
Hirshman, M., 580, 589–590
Hilhorst, T., 343
Hillers, D.R., 648
Himmelfarb, M., 375–376, 384, 388, 404
Hodgson, Jr., R., 584
Höffken, P., 171
Hoffman, P., 336
Hoffman, L., 579
Hofius, O., 488
Hoftijzer, J., 195–196, 211
Hogan, K.M., 332, 339
Holladay, C.R., 431
Hollenberg, J., 174
Hollis, S.T., 624
Holmgren, F., 165
Hölscher, G., 328
Hopkins, D.C., 141, 143, 157
Horbury, W., 475
Horgan, M.P., 427
Hossfeld, F-L., 176–177
Houtman, C., 24–25, 111
Huehnergard, J., 52
Hugenberger, G.P., 474, 494
Hughes, J., 29, 121
Hughes, J.A., 578
Humphreys, W.L., 247, 249, 251, 254, 261
Hupfeld, H., 18, 22, 24–25, 113
Hurowitz, V., 247
Hutton, J.M., 205–206

Ilgen, K.D., 18, 21–23, 25
Iricinschi, E., 589
Ishida, T., 164
Izre'el, S., 52

Jackson, J.R., 139, 149, 156
Jacob, B., 125, 201
Jacobs-Hornig, B., 150, 157
Jacobson, H., 448–452, 455–463, 465–467
Jacobus, H.R., 398
James, M.R, 447–451, 467

Janssen, J.M.A., 242–243
Janzen, J.G., 168
Jarick, J., 16, 22, 26, 110–111, 407
Jaubert, A., 393
Jastrow, M., 416
Jay, N., 299
Jefferies, D.F., 480
Jellicoe, S., 417, 425
Jenkins, R.G., 537–538
Jenner, K.D., 559
Jepsen, A., 120–121
Jeremias, J., 112, 172
Jobes, K.H., 409, 425
Johnston, J., 87
Jonas, H., 584
Jones, H.S., 425
Joosten, J., 56, 81, 538, 542–543, 559
Josipovici, G., 104

Kaestli, J-D., 248
Kaiser, O., 22, 33
Kannengiesser, C., 578
Karenberg, A., 237
Karrer, M., 406, 425
Kaltner, J., 613, 616, 632
Kamesar, A., 432, 441, 445, 522, 535
Kamin, S., 535
Kaminsky, J.S., 91, 98, 217, 640, 650, 656
Kampen, J., 305, 328, 488, 523
Katzoff, R., 476
Kaufmann, W., 662
Kawashima, R.S., 84, 86–87, 89, 92, 94, 97–98, 104
Keaney, J.J., 439
Kedar-Kopfstein, B., 150–152, 155, 157, 519, 522–523, 528–532, 535–534
Keener, C.S., 474
Kelly, J.N.D., 522, 529, 535, 587
Kermode, F., 84
Kessler, E., 496, 504, 517, 601, 606
Kessler, R., 43
Kettler, F.H., 341
Kim, A.Y., 350
Kister, M., 582, 584, 596, 608, 614
Kitchen, K.A., 51, 65
King, K.L., 584

Kittel, R., 169
Klawans, J., 380, 392
Klein, S., 535
Klopfenstein, M.A., 46
Kloppenborg, J.S., 336
Knauf, E.A., 48, 159, 174, 208, 273
Knight, D.A., 84
Knobloch, F.W., 422
Knohl, I., 639
Knoppers, G.N., 36, 48, 278
Koch, K., 121, 703
Köckert, M., 31, 34, 37, 46, 160, 163, 167, 175, 180
Koenen, K., 12
Koenen, L., 584
Koster, H.A., 155
Koster, J.B., 155
Koster, M.D., 540, 542, 559
Kraemer, J.L., 608
Kraft, R.A., 453
Kratz, R.G., 31, 36, 46, 49, 127, 129, 182, 199
Kraus, H-J., 164, 175
Kraus, M.A., 521, 535
Kraus, W., 406, 424–425
Kresuzer, S., 535
Kries, D., 522
Krüger, T., 30
Kuenen, A., 24
Kuhn, P., 379
Kugel, J.L., 211, 228, 341, 343, 350, 455, 626, 630, 632
Kugler, R.A., 371, 373
Kühlewein, J., 180
Kundert, L., 496, 517
Kurtz, J.H., 3, 4, 26
Kutscher, E.Y., 165, 358
Kvam, B.O.G., 554
Kvanvig, H., 38

Laato, A., 377, 498, 517
LaCocque, A., 113
Laks, A., 433
Lamberton, R., 439–440
Lanckau, J., 239
Lane, W.L., 337, 343

Lang, B., 144
Lang, C., 439
Lange, A., 40, 376, 382, 389, 397, 404
Lampe, G.W.H., 574
Laquer, W., 677, 681
Lavenant, R., 542, 559
Layton, S.C., 53
Le Roux, J., 4, 254
Lee, J.A.L., 409, 412–413, 415, 425
Leemhuis, F., 612
Leisegang, I., 429
Leitz, C., 237
Lenski, G., 140
Lemaire, A., 32, 50, 69, 160, 180
Lemche, N.P., 164
LeMon, J.M., 300, 672
Levenson, J.D., 219, 228, 636, 648, 651, 656–657, 661, 663, 681
Levin, C., 30, 35, 113, 119, 123, 127, 134, 159, 173
Levine, A-J., 457
Levine, B.A., 63, 71
Levine, L.I., 380, 599
Levinson, B.M., 36, 48, 73
Levison, J.R., 332, 339, 378
Levy, T.E., 60
Lewis, J.P., 388
Lewis, N., 475–477
Lichtenberger, H., 40, 397, 588
Liddell, H.G., 425
LiDonnici, L., 358, 400
Lieber, A., 358, 400
Lieberman, S., 580–582, 585
Lieu, J.M., 336, 341, 343, 395
Lim, T.H., 366
Limet, H., 144
Lipschitz, O., 173
Livingstone, E.A., 511, 534
Loader, J.A., 254
Loader, W., 368
Lohfink, N., 15, 33
Lohr, J.N., 91, 98, 107, 154, 635
Lohse, E., 508, 517
Long, A.A., 439
Long, V.P., 51

Louth, A., 578
Lovering, Jr., E.H., 429
Lowenthal, E.I., 277
Lowe-Porter, H.T., 242, 262
Lowin, S.L., 609, 619, 632
Lucchesi, E., 430
Lund, J.A., 538, 542, 559
Lust, J., 36
Luttikhuizen, P., 343, 345, 351
Luzzatto, S.D., 245

Macchi, J-D., 28, 52, 159, 176, 211
MacDonald, J., 629
MacDonald, N., 142, 144, 157, 642, 645
Machiela, D.A., 358, 359, 362, 373, 377
Macholz, C., 41, 55, 166
Mack, B.L, 429
Mann, J., 508
Mann, T., 242
Manor, D.W., 474
Maori, Y., 546, 551, 557, 559
Marcus, D., 617
Marcus, R., 334, 429–430
Marks, J.H., 170, 211, 213
Martens, J.W., 443, 446
Martínez, F.G., 40, 376
Marx, A., 534
Mason, S., 303, 321, 328
Matthews, Jr., E.G., 558
Matthews, S., 64
Matusova, E.D., 440
McCarter, P.K., 64
McCarthy, D.J., 648
McConville, J.G., 652
McEvenue, S., 198, 199, 201
McKenzie, S.L., 180, 196, 670
McKnight, S., 491, 494
McNamara, M., 472, 494, 509, 517
McVey, K., 558
Meerschoek, G.Q.A., 535
Meinhold, A., 248
Mell, U., 488
Mendels, D., 450, 452, 456
Mendenhall, G.E., 648

Mercier, C., 429
Merling, D., 474
Mettinger, T.N.D., 115, 134, 138–139, 146, 157
Metzger, B.M., 472
Meyers, C., 143, 146, 157, 287, 299, 666, 681
Michel, A., 206
Middleton, J.R., 637, 687, 706
Miles, J.A., 617
Milgrom, J., 387
Milik, J.T., 353–354, 357, 369
Millar, F., 435, 445
Millard, A.R., 151, 157
Millard, M., 29, 49
Miller, P.D., 641, 643, 656
Minear, P.S., 470, 494
Moberly, R.W.L., 635, 642–643, 646, 649, 656
Mofatt, J., 337
Monkhouse, W., 87
Montaner, L.V., 385
Moran, W.L., 52–53, 75
Morgenstern, M., 357
Morris, J., 435, 445
Most, G.W., 439
Moyise, S., 473, 494
Mulder, M.J., 519, 535, 537, 540, 542, 559, 580, 606
Müller, H-P., 210, 254
Muraoka, T., 545
Murphy, C., 354
Murphy, F.J., 449–452, 454–456, 459, 461–462, 467
Murphy-Judy, K., 76
Murtonen, A.E., 121

Naaman, N., 59
Naeh, S., 580
Najman, H., 345, 398, 404, 443, 446
Nemet-Nejat, K.R., 144
Nentel, J., 205
Neufeld, E., 277
Neusner, J., 510
Newman, J.H., 466–468
Newsom, C.A., 148, 157

Nicholson, E.W, 59, 63, 78, 81, 648
Nickelsburg, G.W.E., 343–344, 360, 369–370, 373, 395, 451, 453
Nicklas, T., 321, 328, 387
Niehoff, M., 582, 584, 604
Niehr, H., 55
Nihan, C., 28, 36
Nikiprowetzky, V., 432, 435, 445
Nodet, E., 303, 305, 328
Noegel, S.B., 239, 243
Nogalski, J.D., 50, 277
Nöldeke, T., 34, 190, 191
Norris, H.T., 608
Noth, M., 27, 46, 49, 111, 191, 197, 204–205, 265
Novak, D., 91

O'Connor, M., 215, 527
Oden, R.A., 288, 299
Oeming, M., 39, 175–176, 208
Olyan, S.M., 143, 157, 450, 452
Oppenheim, A.L., 238, 241
Orlinsky, H.M., 581, 671, 681
Oswald, W., 42, 128, 134, 188
Ottley, R.R., 407
Otto, E., 4, 29, 31, 33, 35–36, 38–39, 44, 46, 49, 112, 115–117, 132, 134
Otto, S., 177

Qimron, E., 357, 487
Quinones, R.J., 351
Owens, R.J., 560

Pagels, E., 594, 596
Painter, J., 341
Pardes, I., 90, 104, 138
Parker, S.B., 94
Pass, H.L., 370
Patai, R., 665
Paul, S.M., 188
Payne, D.F., 165
Pevear, R., 629
Perdue, L.G., 287, 299
Perlitt, L., 107, 112
Pellat, C., 621
Perrot, C., 450–452, 456, 459, 461, 468, 580

Peters, M.K.H., 535
Petersen, D.L., 32–33, 46, 50, 98, 235, 299, 655
Petit, F., 429
Pétrement, S., 567
Petuchowski, J.J., 384
Pfeiffer, H., 34, 45–46, 50, 116, 134
Pietersma, A., 406, 409, 413, 425
Pinkerton, J., 540
Pitman, W., 696
Piquette, K., 87
Plaskow, J., 666, 681
Plater, W.E., 535
Plaut, W.G., 657
Pleins, J.D., 696
Pohlmann, K-F., 162
Popkes, W., 491
Pola, T., 33, 125
Polaski, D.C., 457
Pollack, L., 279
Polzin, R., 56, 57
Pomykala, K.E., 466, 468
Porter, S.E., 407, 474, 490
Potin, J., 389
Pregill, M.E., 609
Prewitt, T.J., 288, 299
Procksch, O., 206
Puech, E., 353–354

Qimhi, D., 240

Rabin, C., 556
Rabinowicz, H., 669
Rahlfs, A., 407
Raphael, M.L., 680, 682
Rappaport, S., 303, 328
Ravitzky, A., 677, 682
Rebenich, S., 536
Reeves, J.C., 305, 328, 523, 597, 656
Redford, D.B., 214, 229, 233, 237, 242–244, 248, 254, 257–258, 262, 267, 277, 427
Rehm, M., 177
Reicke, B., 348
Reinmuth, E., 450, 458, 460, 463, 465, 468

Reiter, S., 429
Reiterer, F.V., 321, 328, 387
Rendsburg, G.A., 55, 277
Rendtorff, R., 28, 30, 134, 169, 195
Reuling, H., 594, 596, 606
Revell, E.J., 198
Richards, K.H., 300, 499, 527, 672
Ricks, S.D., 607
Riedweg, C., 115
Ringgren, H., 144
Rippin, A., 612
Ritner, R.K., 236, 237
Robbins, G.A., 594, 606
Robertson, M., 610, 632
Robinson, J.A., 519
Robinson, J.M., 337, 584
Rofé, A., 54, 56, 63, 81
Rogerson, J.W., 16
Römer, T., 28, 34, 36–37, 39, 41, 45–46, 50, 163–164, 173–177, 180, 196, 211, 248
Römheld, K.F.D., 397
Rooker, M.F., 56–57
Ropes, J.H., 348
Rösel, M., 120–122
Rosenberg, D., 579
Rosenblatt, J.P., 73
Rosenblatt, S., 666
Rosenthal, L.A., 235
Rosenzweig, F., 187–188, 662, 682
Roth, M.T., 292
Royse, J.R., 429–430, 445
Rothstein, D., 294
Rubenstein, R.L., 674, 682
Ruess, E., 24
Runia, D.T., 433, 436, 440, 443, 445–446
Ruppert, L., 213–214, 254
Ruzer, S., 343, 351
Ryan, W., 696

Sæbø, M., 14, 26, 426, 445
Sáenz-Badillos, A., 52
Sacks, K.S., 433
Sakenfeld, K.D., 591
Saldarini, A.J., 477

Saleh, W.A., 610, 632
Salvesen, A., 537–539
Sanders, S.L., 56
Sanderson, J.E., 353
Sänger, D., 488
Santmire, P., 684
Sarfatti, B.A., 593
Sarfatti, G.B., 56
Sarna, N.M., 154, 380, 657, 671, 682
Sasson, A., 140
Schäfer, P., 38, 585, 588, 593
Schalit, A., 329
Schechter, S., 5, 26, 596
Scherman, N., 657, 682
Schiffman, L.H., 354, 358, 372, 514
Schloen, J.D., 287, 299
Schmid, K., 28–32, 34–37, 40–42, 44–46, 48–50, 63, 111–112, 115, 127–128, 134–135, 160, 163, 173, 176–177, 179–180, 192, 194, 277
Schmidt, L., 160, 173
Schmidt, W.H., 32, 135
Schmitt, H-C., 45–46, 50, 159, 205, 278
Schnor, L., 175
Schoeps, H.J., 508, 518
Scholem, G.G., 586
Schöpflin, K., 321, 328, 387
Schrader, E., 113
Schüle, A., 38–39, 112, 115–116, 128, 135
Schuller, E.M., 457
Schürer, E., 435, 445
Schwartz, B.J., 28, 63, 176, 263–265, 270, 278
Schwartz, R.M., 92
Schwartzbaum, H., 611
Scott, R., 425
Scullion, J.J., 3, 138, 214, 229, 254, 264, 278, 656, 706
Seebaß, H., 113, 160, 205, 213
Seeligmann, I.L., 186, 188, 204
Segal, M.H., 354, 355–356, 373, 400, 404
Séguy, M.-R., 629
Seidel, B., 22
Seltzer, R.M., 679, 682

Siegert, F., 431, 445
Seitz, C.R., 201
Sharansky, N., 677, 682
Shareef, A.-K.A., 612, 632
Shanks, H., 64, 84
Sharp, C.J., 487
Sheridan, M., 578
Shinan, A., 580
Shupak, N., 234–235, 239, 262
Silberman, N.A., 159
Silva, M., 409, 425
Silver, A.M., 6
Simon, R., 13–17, 26
Simonetti, M., 5, 578
Simons, M., 346
Singer-Avitz, L., 208
Sitterson, J.C., 73
Sivan, D., 357
Ska, J.L., 12, 22, 46, 50, 81, 111–112, 115, 135
Skehan, P.W., 353
Skinner, J., 196, 264, 278
Smalley, S.S., 341
Smend, R., 33, 111
Smith, A.D., 69
Smith, B., 213–214, 229
Smith, H.S., 240
Smith, M.S., 69, 85, 637
Smith, R.P., 542
Smyth, H..W., 423, 425
Sneed, M., 254
Sohn, S-T., 91
Sokoloff, M., 579
Sollamo, R., 395
Soloveitchik, J.B., 667, 682
Sommer, B.D., 586
Souter, A., 522
Sparks, H.F.D., 523, 536
Speiser, E.A., 264, 278, 290
Spieckermann, H., 185, 211
Spiegel, S., 506, 518, 601, 606
Spiegelberg, W., 259
Spinoza, B., 10, 26
Sprengling, M., 547
Springer, A.J., 351
Spurling, H., 350, 594

Stager, L.E., 287, 299
Steck, O.H., 129, 135, 166–168, 171, 180
Stegemann, E.W., 41, 55, 166
Stein, D.E.S, 145, 657
Steinberg, M., 226
Steinberg, N., 281, 286, 288, 299
Steiner, R.C., 360
Steinmetz, D., 300
Stemberger, G., 580
Sterling, G.E., 428, 430, 432–433, 443, 445–446, 575
Stern, M., 329, 422
Sternberg, M., 86, 104
Steudel, A., 368
Stoellger, P., 200
Stone, M.E., 351, 358, 360, 370–371, 373
Stordalen, T., 116–117, 138, 139, 150, 155, 157
Strachan, L.R.M., 408, 424
Strack, H.L., 580
Strauss, H., 254
Strecker, G., 334, 336
Strickman, H.N., 6, 25
Stroumsa, G.G., 567
Stowasser, B.F., 619
Strong, J.T., 637–638
Struck, P.T., 440
Strugnell, J., 354, 487
Stuckenbruck, L.T., 344, 369, 376, 395–396
Sun, H.T.C., 698
Sweeney, M.A., 658, 670–672, 675, 678–679, 682
Swete, H.B., 425, 480
Swirsky, M., 678, 682
Szpakowska, K., 236

Tadmor, H., 60
Tait, J., 87
Tait, W.J., 236
Talmon, S., 41, 354
Taylor, B.A., 425, 535
Taylor, V., 480
Taschner, J., 187

ter Haar Romeny, B., 537–539, 560
Testuz, M., 404
Teugels, L.M., 606
Thackeray, H. St. J., 303–304, 306, 322, 329, 409, 422–423, 425, 527
Thackston, W.M., 597, 619, 632
Theodor, J., 579, 582–588, 590–591, 597, 603–604, 616
Thiel, W., 177
Throntveit, M.A., 694
Thomas, M., 659
Thompson, S., 626
Thompson, T.L., 4, 26, 51, 64, 159
Thomson, C., 406
Thumb, A., 408, 425
Tiemeyer, L-S., 180
Tigay, J.H., 74
Tilly, L.A., 280
Tkacz, C.B., 521–522, 536
Tobin, T.H., 431
Tonneau, R.M., 547, 555, 558, 560
Tottoli, R., 610–611, 632
Tournay, R.J., 178, 180
Tov, E., 353–354, 356, 371, 373, 380, 531, 535, 539
Trible, P., 148–149, 653–654
Tromp, J., 351
Tsevat, M., 153
Tucker, G.M., 84, 698
Tuell, S.S., 638
Turner, L.A., 656

Uehlinger, C., 60, 128, 135, 176
Ulrich, E., 353, 521, 536
Urbach, E.E., 584, 666, 682
Utzschneider, H., 172

Van Goudoever, J., 393
Van Henten, J.W., 333
Van den Eynde, C., 556
Van der Horst, P.W., 61, 430, 456
Van der Kooij, A., 542, 560
Van der Merwe, B.J., 180
Van der Toorn, K., 61, 73, 84, 286
Van Donzel, E., 632
Van Oorschot, J., 166–168, 170, 180
Van Peusen, W.Th., 537
Van Ruiten, J., 377, 387, 404
Van Seters, J., 26, 29, 45, 50, 64, 159, 180, 196, 199, 211, 278
VanderKam, J.C., 354, 358, 363, 365, 368–369, 372–373, 375, 377, 379–381, 391, 392, 397, 404
Veijola, T., 207
Vermes, G., 343, 351, 358, 384, 435, 445, 453, 580
Vermeylen, J., 135, 171
Vette, J., 176
Vervenne, M., 36, 44, 132, 465
Visotzky, B.L., 580–581, 583, 588, 589, 591, 594, 596–597, 599, 600, 606
Volgers, A., 430
Volten, A., 236, 240
Von Koh, Y., 45, 49
Von Rad, G., 28, 43, 128–129, 187, 211, 213, 231, 238, 245, 253, 255, 257, 260, 473, 699
Vööbus, A., 537, 538
Vorländer, H., 168, 180
Vosté, J.-M., 556.

Wadsworth, M., 450–451, 461
Wahl, H.M., 248
Waldman, M.R., 607, 631
Wallace-Hadrill, D.S., 561, 578
Walsh, J.T., 87
Walter, D.M., 559
Waltke, B.K., 215, 527
Wan, S-K., 429, 430
Wardman, A., 441
Waschke, G., 151
Wasserstrom, S.M., 609
Watson, W.G.E, 132, 409, 424, 520
Watts, J.D.W., 171
Watts, J.W., 48
Weber, R., 520
Webster, B., 353–354
Weeks, S., 246, 254, 368
Weill, J., 303, 329
Weimar, P., 30, 163
Weimar, S.P., 264, 278
Weiss, A.L., 657, 681

Weitzman, M.P., 538, 545, 559, 560
Wellhausen, J., 24, 27, 56, 57, 59–60, 62, 81, 87–88, 127, 129, 160, 191, 193, 199–200, 205
Wells, J.B., 643
Wendland, P., 429
Wenham, D., 453, 467, 473
Wenham, G.J., 65, 117, 213, 216–217, 223, 229, 247, 270, 278
Wénin, A., 31, 49, 81
Wensinck, A.J., 380
Werman, C., 358, 360, 376, 385
Wessels, J.P.H., 254
Westermann, C., 35, 43, 129, 138, 149, 170–171, 214, 219, 229, 254, 264, 278–280, 648, 656, 706
Wevers, J.W., 344, 407–410, 415–418, 425–426, 473, 494
Wheeler, B.M., 609
Whitaker, G.H., 429, 582
White, H., 91
White, H.J., 522, 535
White, L., 684
White, L.M., 440
White, R.T., 378
Whybray, R.N., 253, 278
Wickert, U., 535
Wiesel, E., 674, 682
Wildberger, H., 169
Wilkinson, T.J., 68
Williams, H.G.M., 453
Williams, M.A., 348, 567
Williamson, H.G.M., 453
Williamson, P.R., 644
Willmes, B., 205
Wilson, L., 233, 239, 254, 262
Wilson, R., 300

Winston, D., 332, 432–433
Wise, M.O., 478–479, 487
Witte, M., 31, 36–37, 40–41, 49, 111–112, 115–117, 119, 123, 127, 130–131, 134–135, 160, 173, 176
Witter, H.B., 110, 113
Wolff, H.W., 210, 643
Wooden, R.G., 424
Worthington, M., 87
Wright, A.T., 385, 396–397
Wright, B.G., 406, 409, 413, 425
Wright, W., 537
Wurst, S., 148, 157, 706

Yadin, A., 580
Yadin, Y., 354, 357–358, 372, 475, 478
Yarchin, W., 643
Yardeni, A., 475
Yohannan, J.D, 626
Yoreh, T., 185, 205
Youngblood, R., 649

Zahlten, J., 561, 578
Zakovitch, Y., 188, 195
Zamagni, C., 430
Zauzich, K-T., 236
Zellentin, H.M., 589
Zenger, E., 176–177
Zeron, A., 450
Ziegler, W.C.L., 114
Zimmerli, W., 34, 161–162, 210
Zimmermann, M., 38
Zimmermann, R., 38
Zissu, B., 475
Zlotowitz, M., 657, 682
Zumthor, P., 76
Zvi, E.B., 30, 32